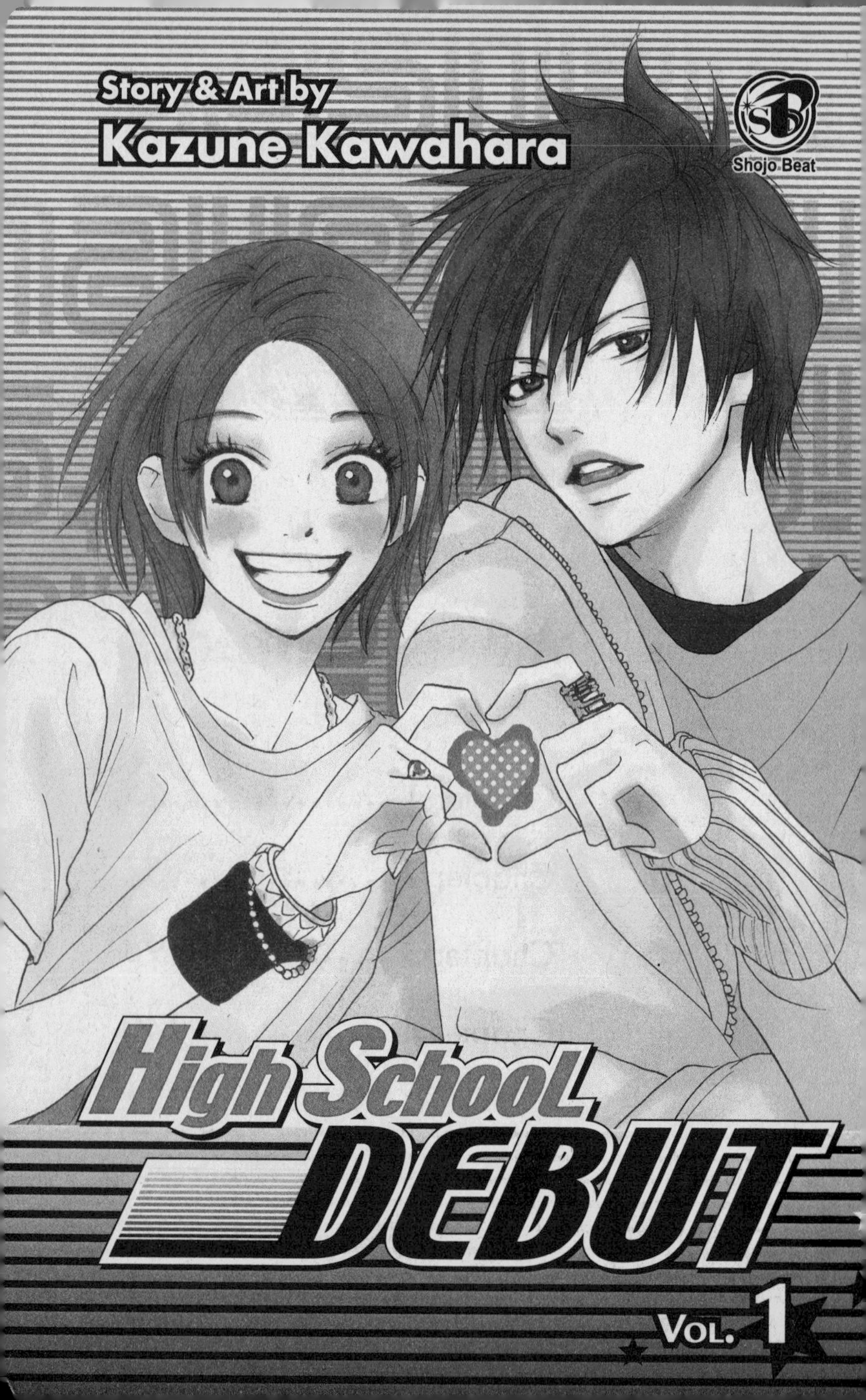
Story & Art by
Kazune Kawahara
Shojo Beat
High School
DEBUT
VOL. 1

High School DEBUT

 Contents

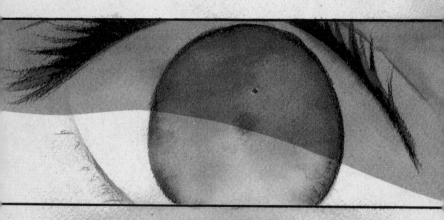

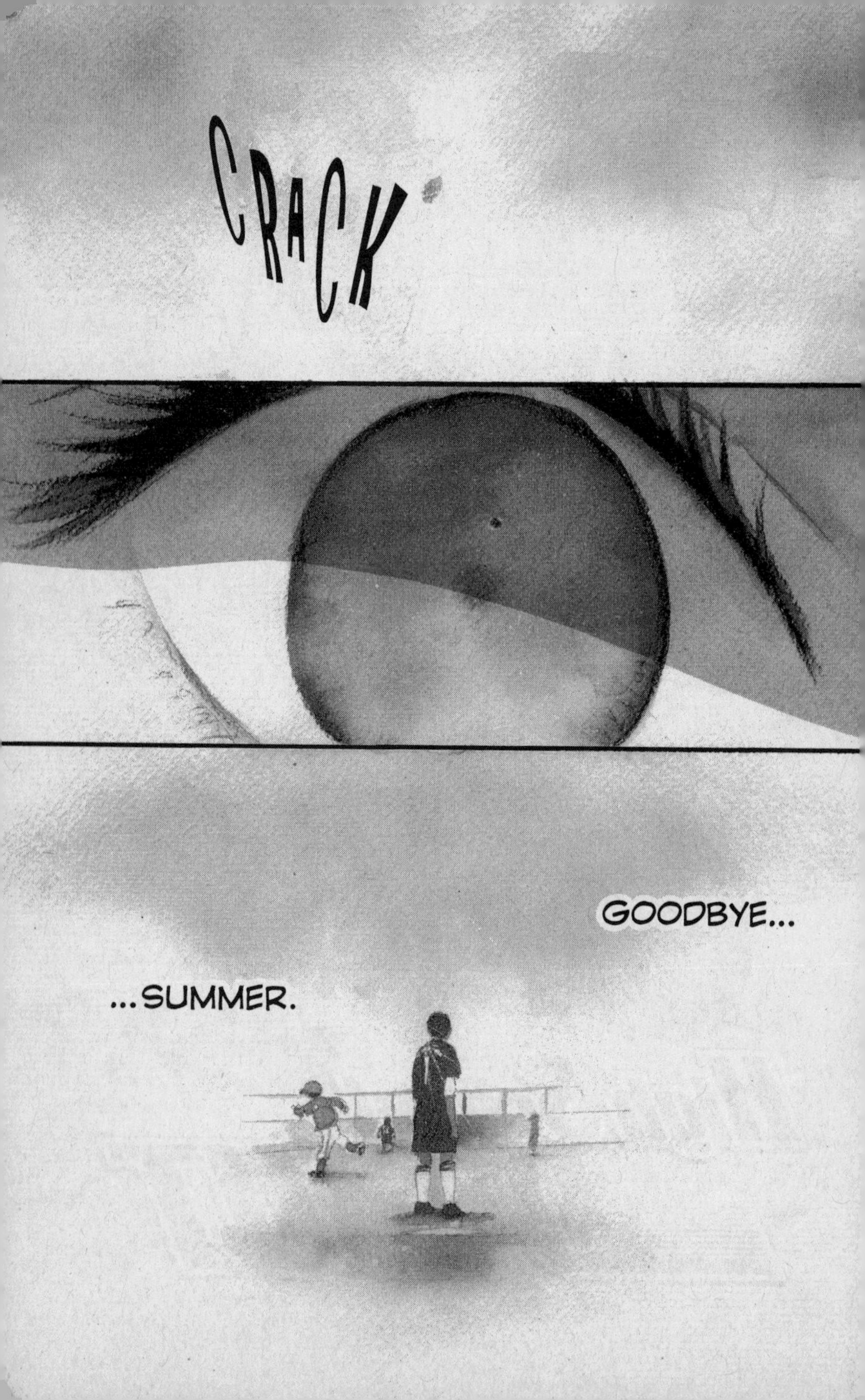

CRACK

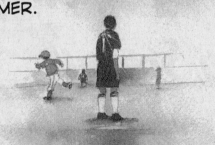

GOODBYE...

...SUMMER.

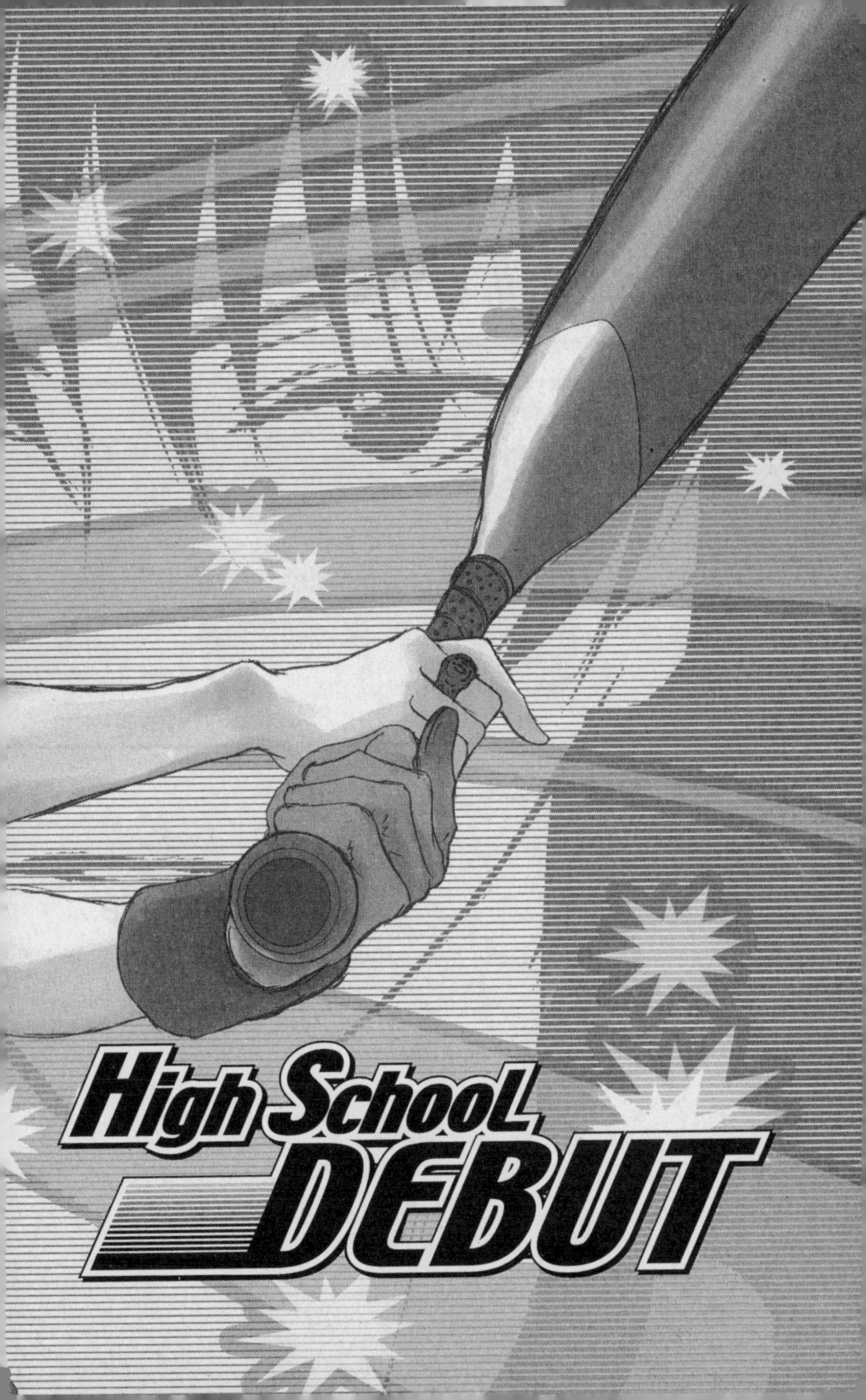
High School
DEBUT

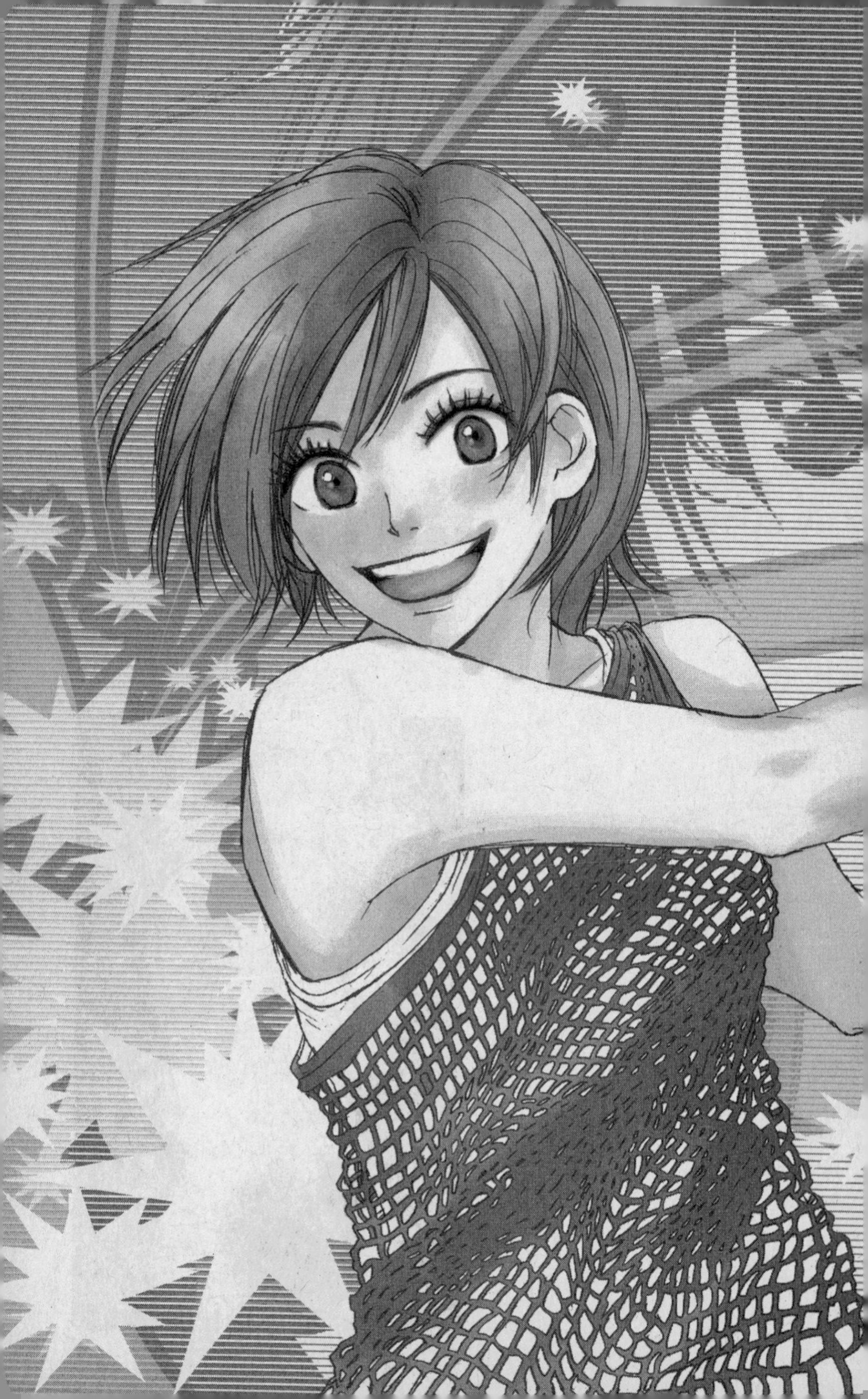

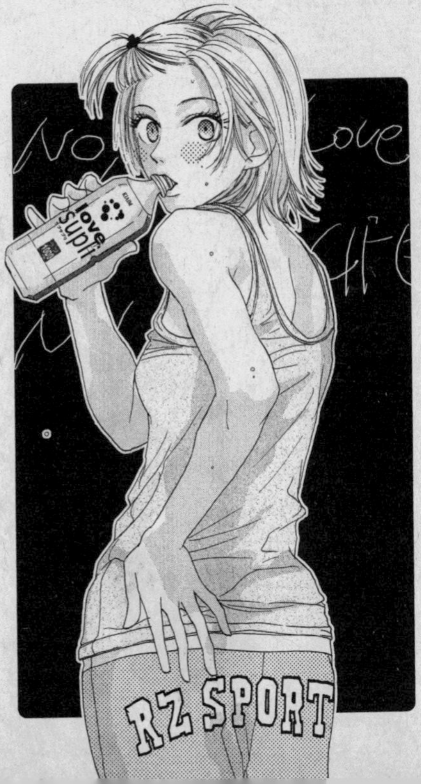
love supli
RZ SPORT

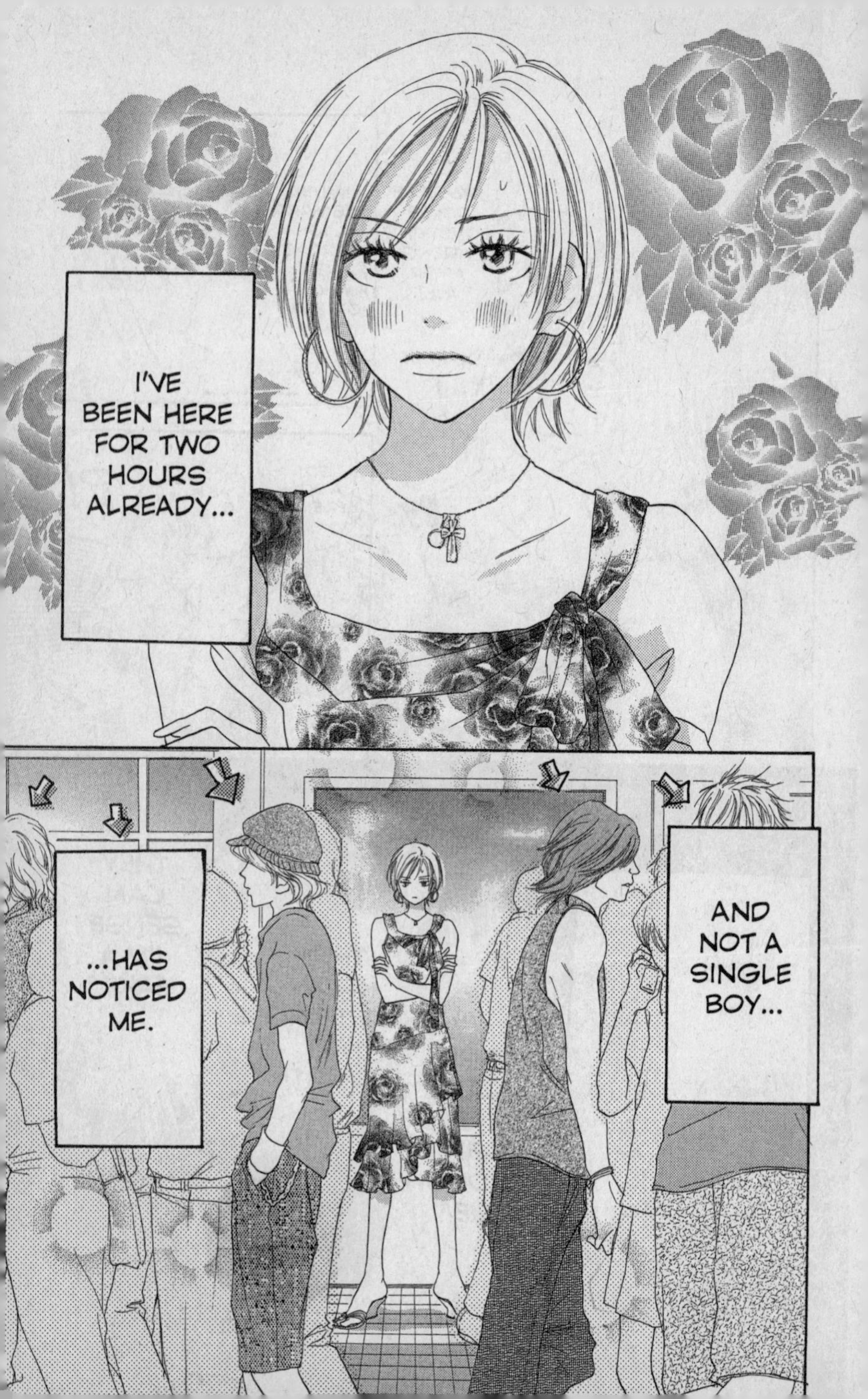
I'VE BEEN HERE FOR TWO HOURS ALREADY...
AND NOT A SINGLE BOY...
...HAS NOTICED ME.

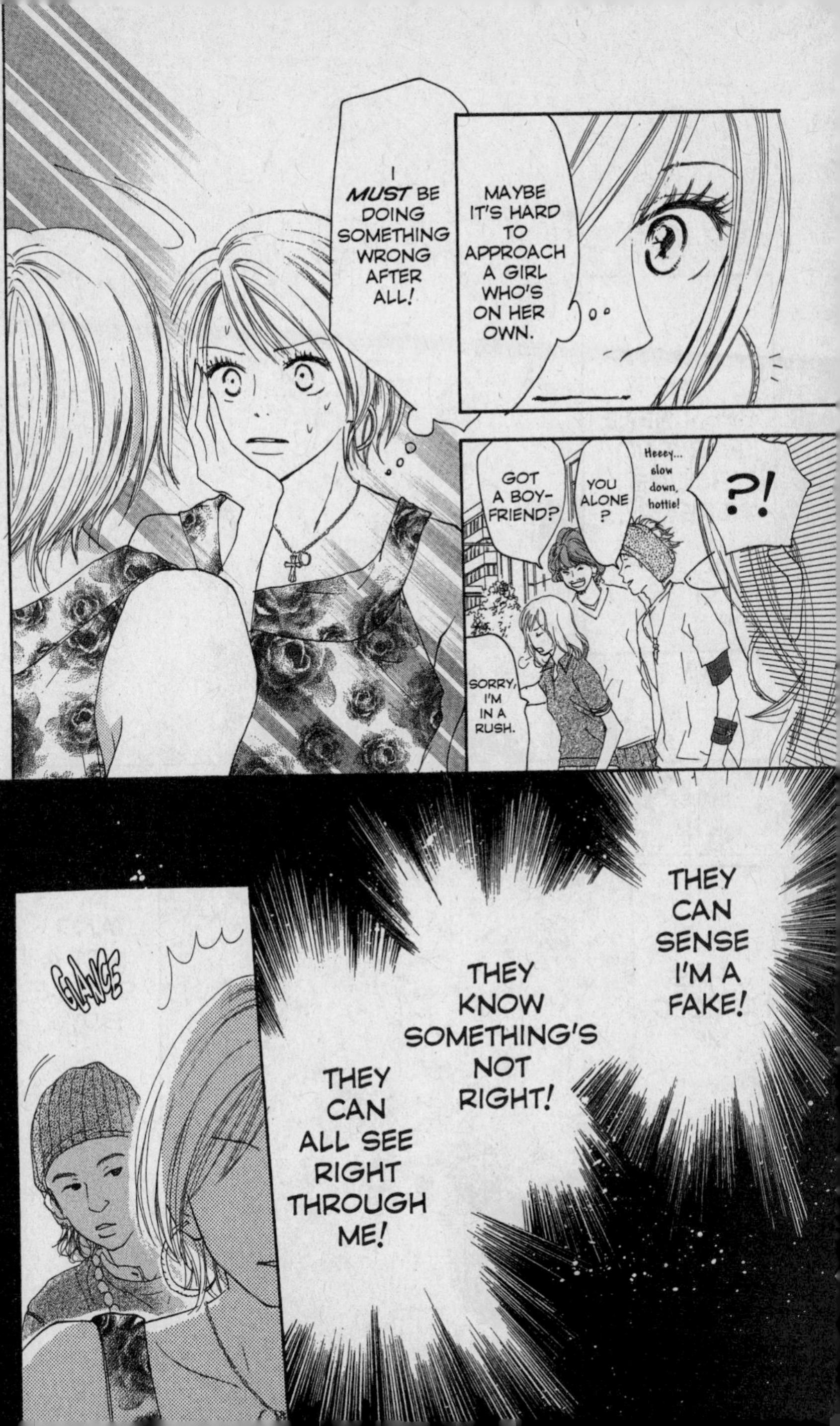
MAYBE IT'S HARD TO APPROACH A GIRL WHO'S ON HER OWN.
?!
Heeey... slow down, hottie!
YOU ALONE?
GOT A BOY-FRIEND?
SORRY, I'M IN A RUSH.
I MUST BE DOING SOMETHING WRONG AFTER ALL!
THEY CAN SENSE I'M A FAKE!
THEY KNOW SOMETHING'S NOT RIGHT!
THEY CAN ALL SEE RIGHT THROUGH ME!
GLANCE

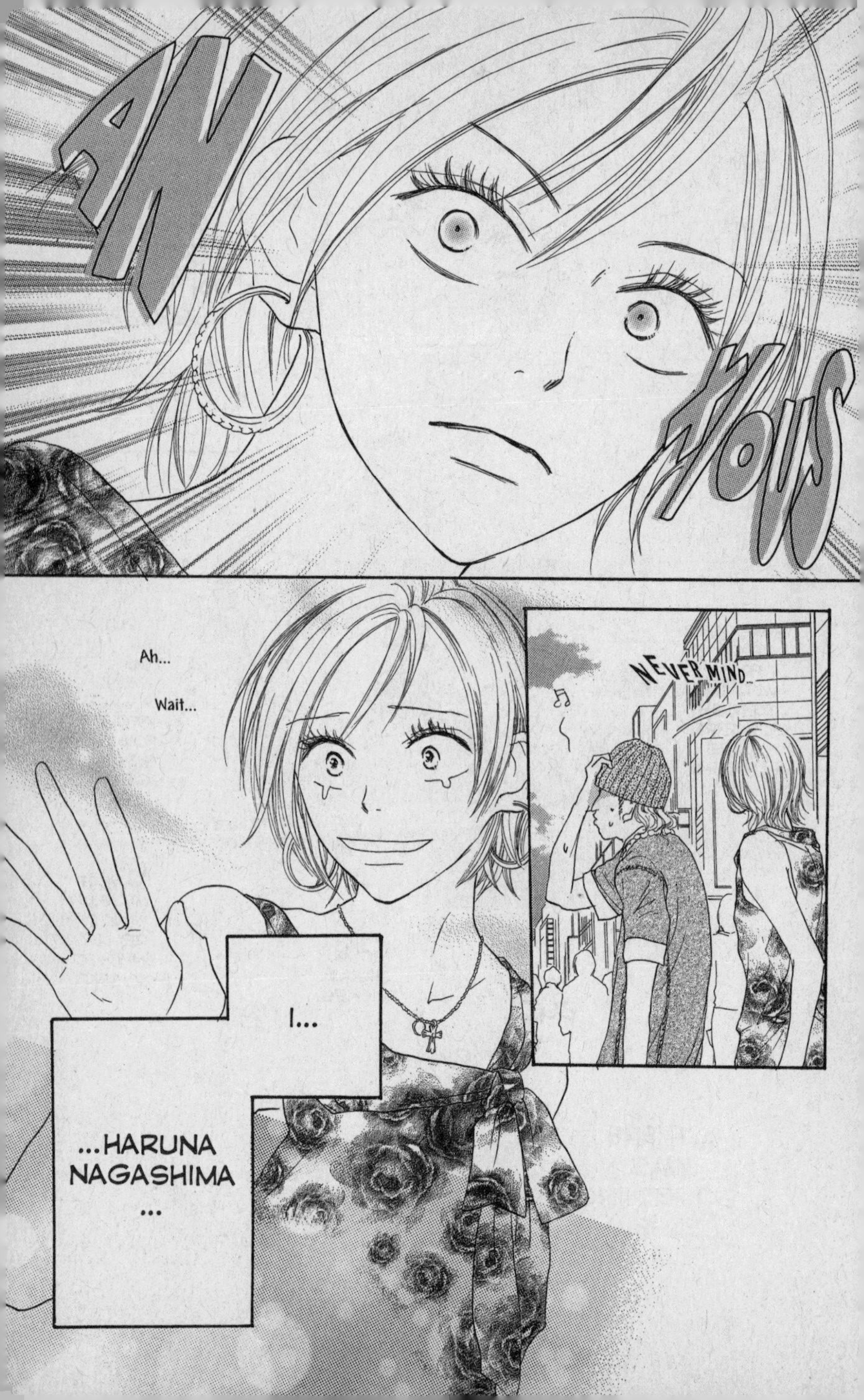
AH
NEVER MIND...
Ah...
Wait...
I...
...HARUNA NAGASHIMA ...

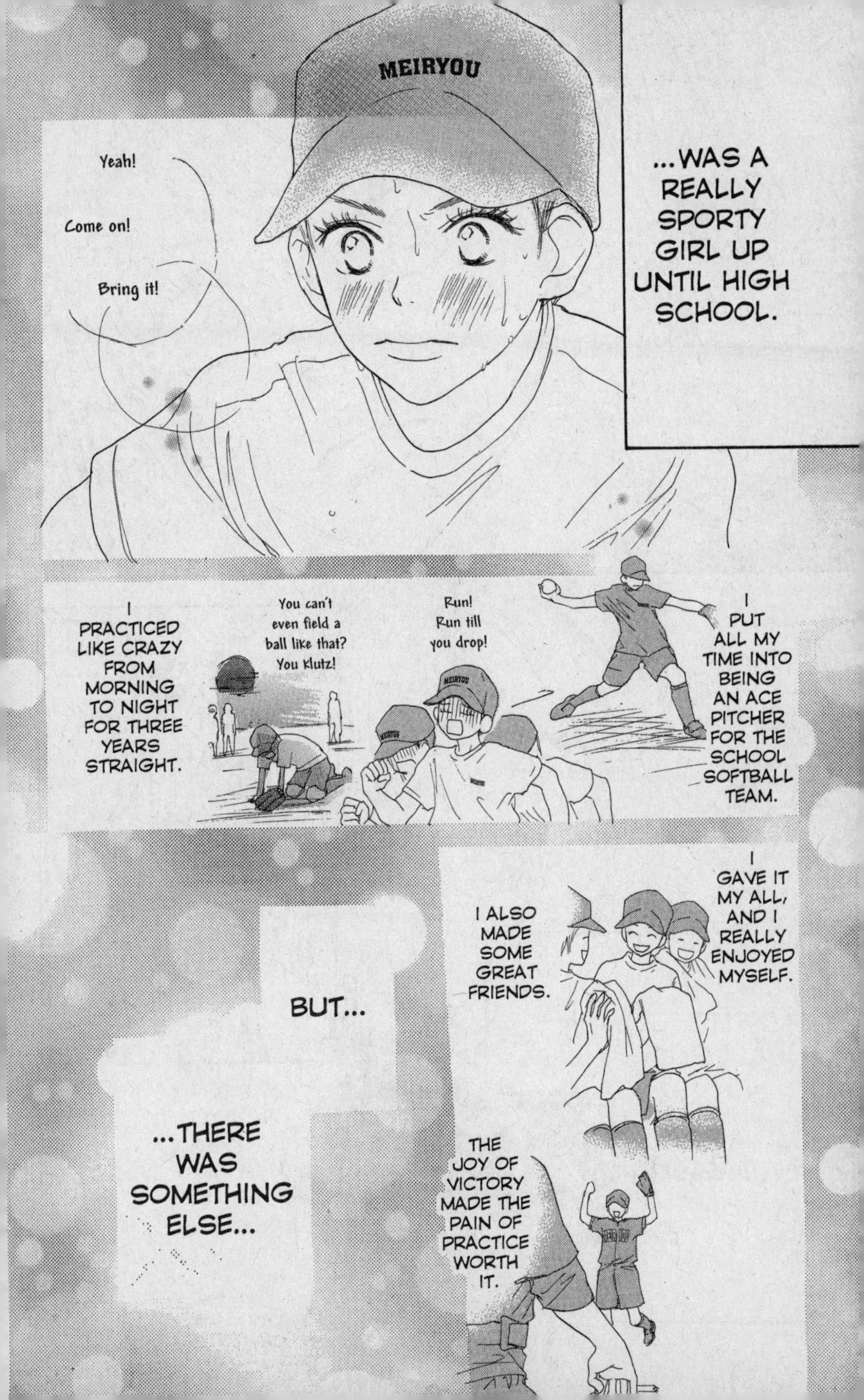

...WAS A REALLY SPORTY GIRL UP UNTIL HIGH SCHOOL.
MEIRYOU
Yeah!
Come on!
Bring it!
I PUT ALL MY TIME INTO BEING AN ACE PITCHER FOR THE SCHOOL SOFTBALL TEAM.
Run! Run till you drop!
You can't even field a ball like that? You klutz!
I PRACTICED LIKE CRAZY FROM MORNING TO NIGHT FOR THREE YEARS STRAIGHT.
I GAVE IT MY ALL, AND I REALLY ENJOYED MYSELF.
I ALSO MADE SOME GREAT FRIENDS.
THE JOY OF VICTORY MADE THE PAIN OF PRACTICE WORTH IT.
BUT...
...THERE WAS SOMETHING ELSE...

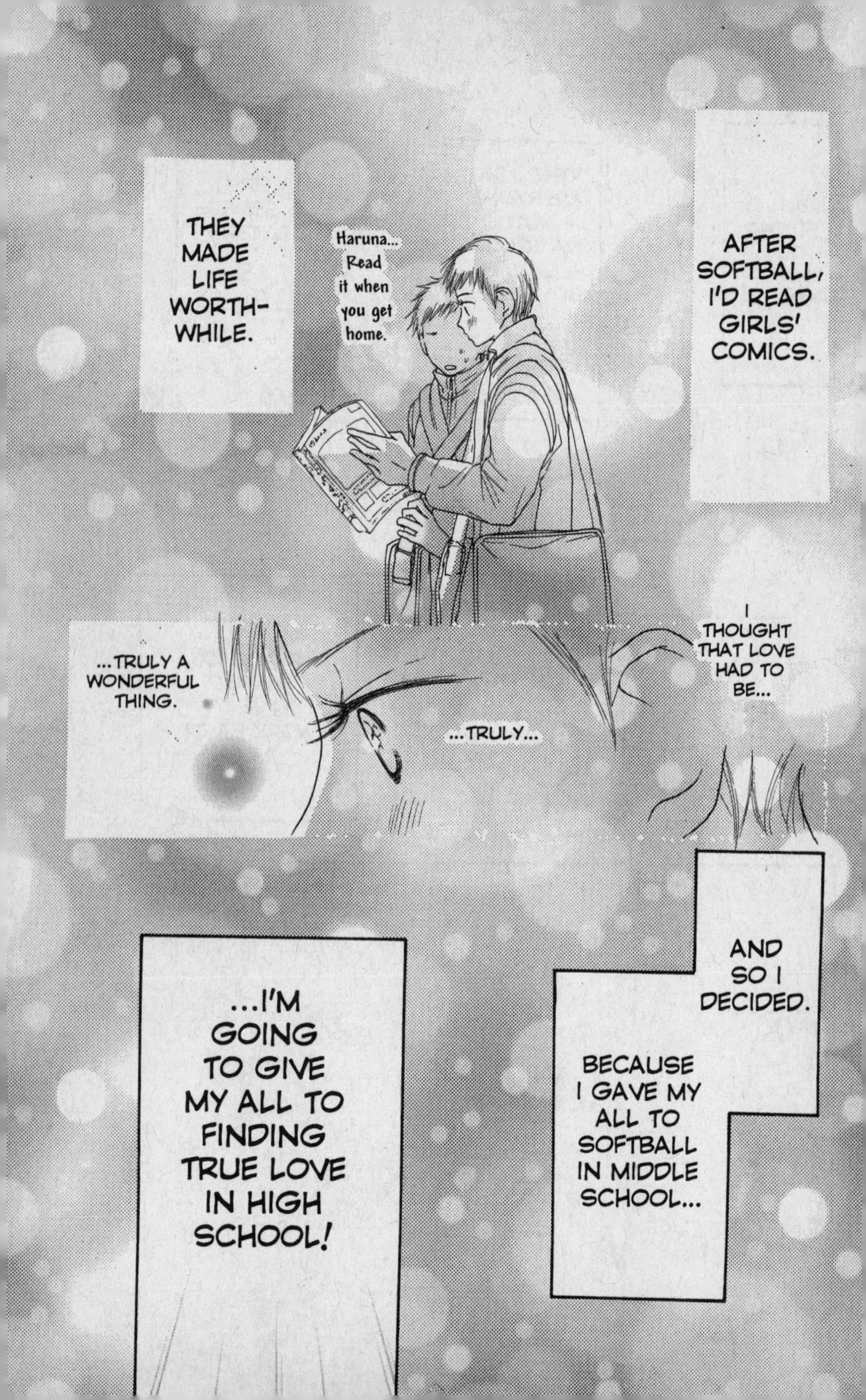
AFTER SOFTBALL, I'D READ GIRLS' COMICS.
Haruna... Read it when you get home.
THEY MADE LIFE WORTH-WHILE.
I THOUGHT THAT LOVE HAD TO BE...
...TRULY...
...TRULY A WONDERFUL THING.
AND SO I DECIDED.
BECAUSE I GAVE MY ALL TO SOFTBALL IN MIDDLE SCHOOL...
...I'M GOING TO GIVE MY ALL TO FINDING TRUE LOVE IN HIGH SCHOOL!

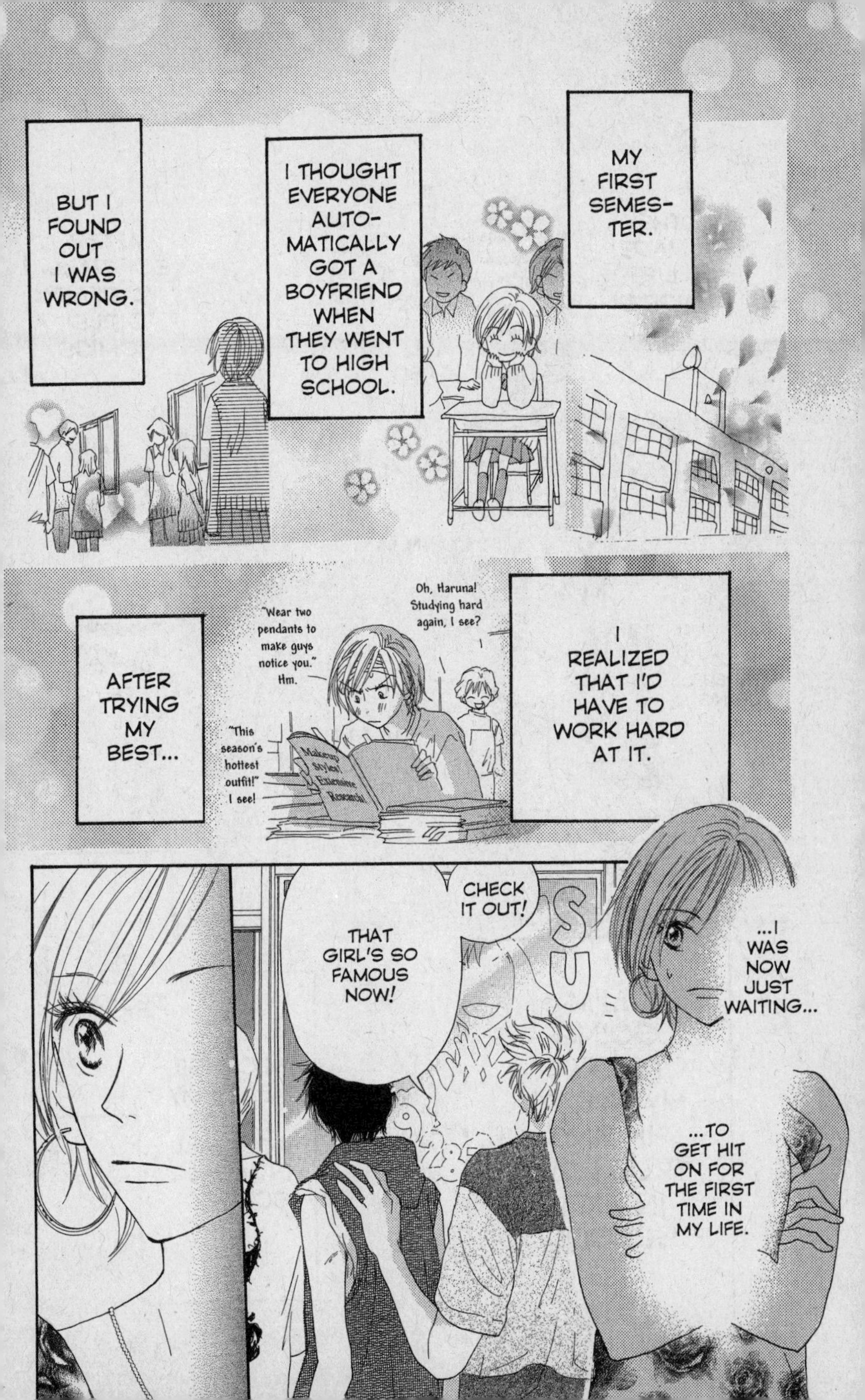
MY FIRST SEMESTER.
I THOUGHT EVERYONE AUTOMATICALLY GOT A BOYFRIEND WHEN THEY WENT TO HIGH SCHOOL.
BUT I FOUND OUT I WAS WRONG.
I REALIZED THAT I'D HAVE TO WORK HARD AT IT.
Oh, Haruna! Studying hard again, I see?
"Wear two pendants to make guys notice you." Hm.
"This season's hottest outfit!" I see!
AFTER TRYING MY BEST...
...I WAS NOW JUST WAITING...
SU
CHECK IT OUT!
THAT GIRL'S SO FAMOUS NOW!
...TO GET HIT ON FOR THE FIRST TIME IN MY LIFE.

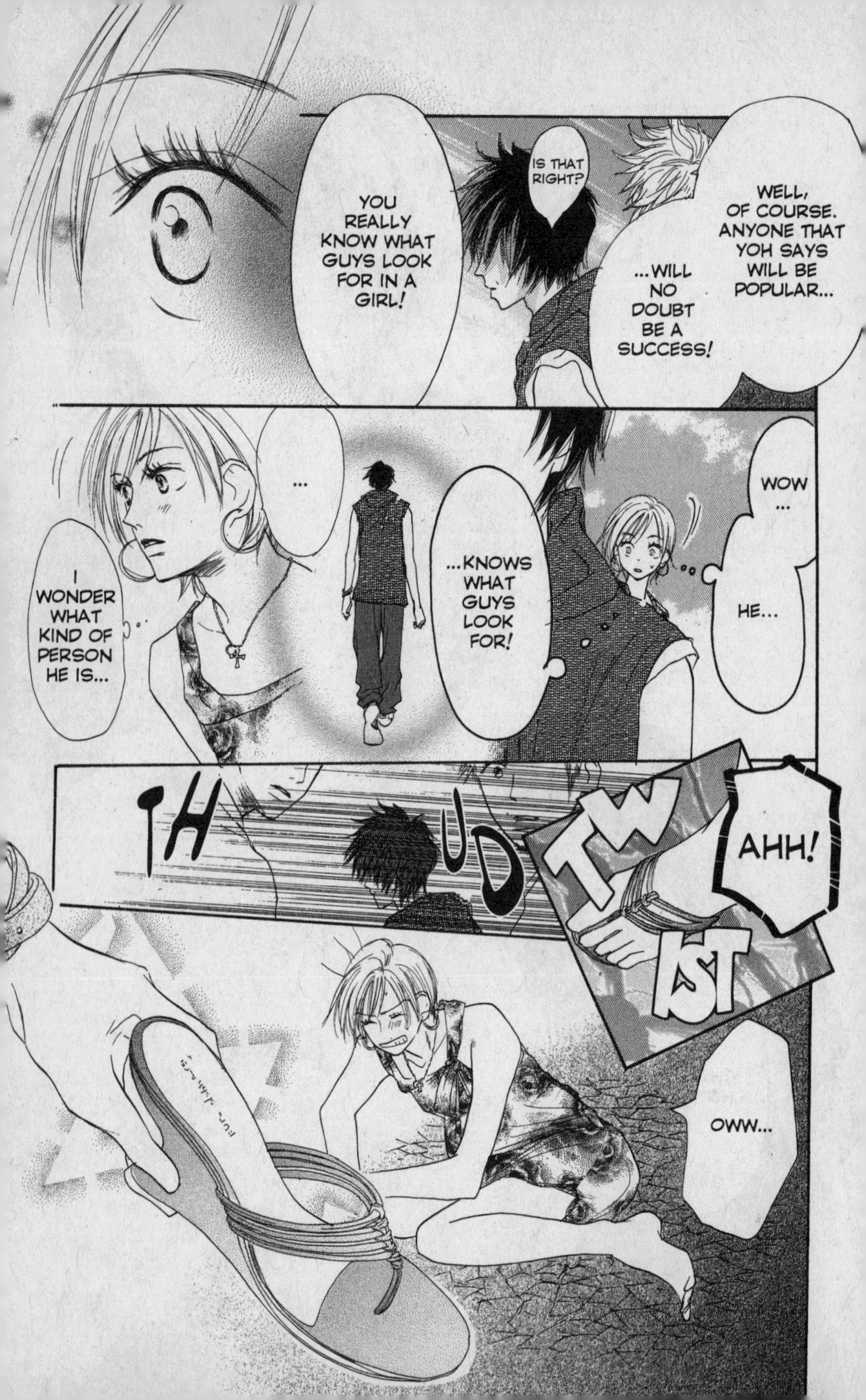
WELL, OF COURSE. ANYONE THAT YOH SAYS WILL BE POPULAR...
...WILL NO DOUBT BE A SUCCESS!
IS THAT RIGHT?
YOU REALLY KNOW WHAT GUYS LOOK FOR IN A GIRL!
WOW... HE...
...KNOWS WHAT GUYS LOOK FOR!
...
I WONDER WHAT KIND OF PERSON HE IS...
AHH!
TWIST
THUD
OWW...

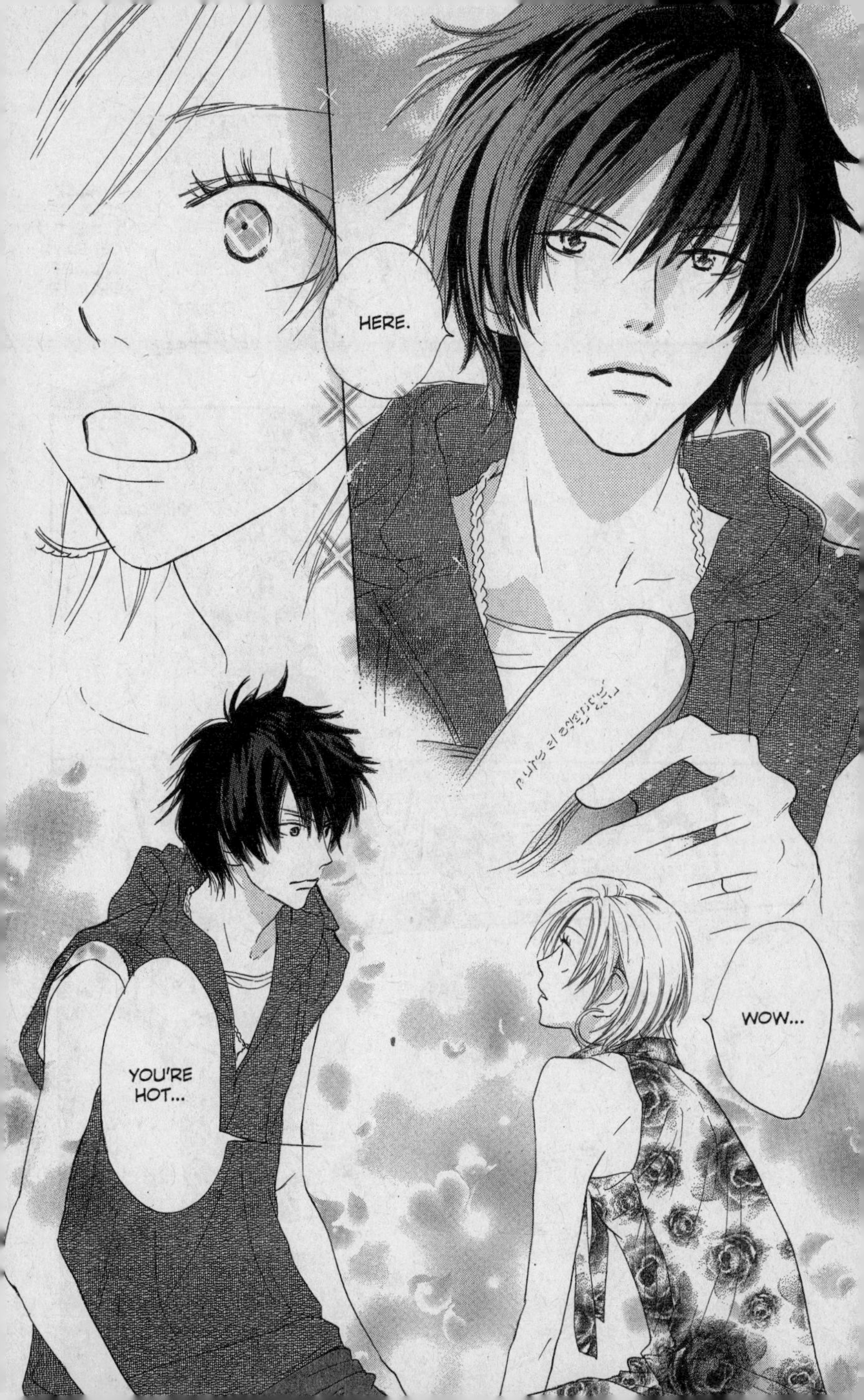
HERE.
WOW...
YOU'RE
HOT...

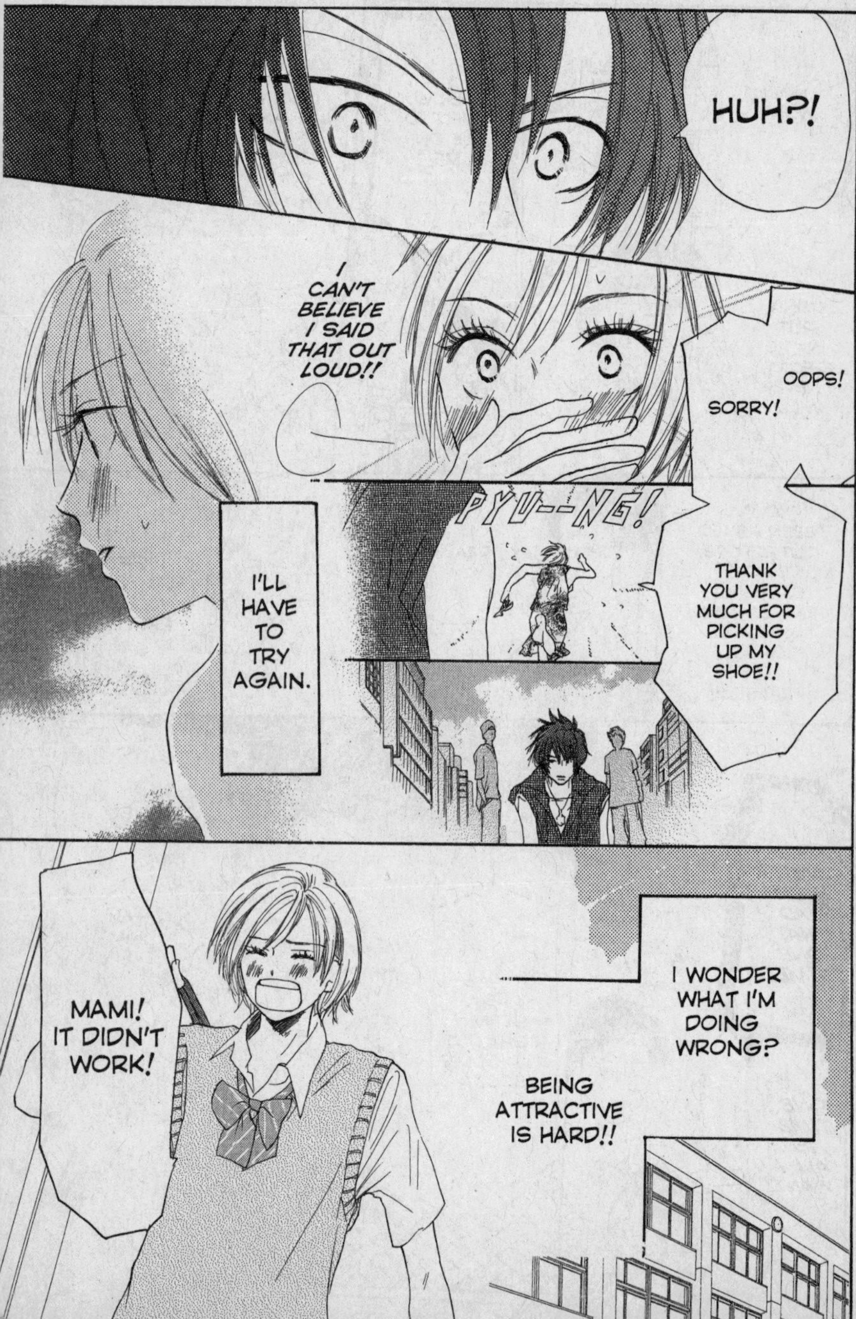
HUH?!
OOPS!
SORRY!
I CAN'T BELIEVE I SAID THAT OUT LOUD!!
PYU--NG!
THANK YOU VERY MUCH FOR PICKING UP MY SHOE!!
I'LL HAVE TO TRY AGAIN.
I WONDER WHAT I'M DOING WRONG?
BEING ATTRACTIVE IS HARD!!
MAMI! IT DIDN'T WORK!

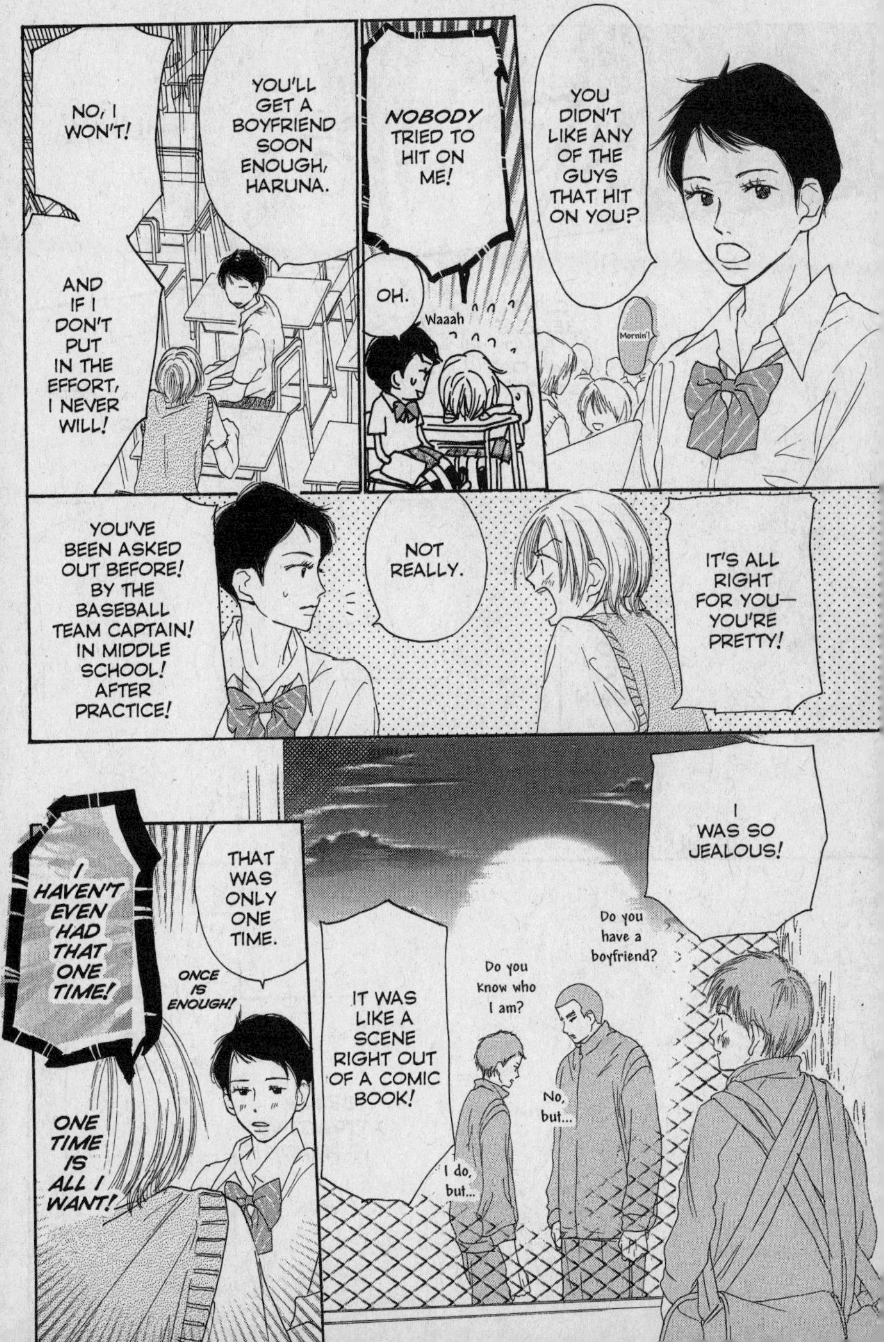
YOU DIDN'T LIKE ANY OF THE GUYS THAT HIT ON YOU?
Mornin'!
NOBODY TRIED TO HIT ON ME!
OH.
Waaah
YOU'LL GET A BOYFRIEND SOON ENOUGH, HARUNA.
NO, I WON'T!
AND IF I DON'T PUT IN THE EFFORT, I NEVER WILL!
IT'S ALL RIGHT FOR YOU—YOU'RE PRETTY!
NOT REALLY.
YOU'VE BEEN ASKED OUT BEFORE! BY THE BASEBALL TEAM CAPTAIN! IN MIDDLE SCHOOL! AFTER PRACTICE!
I WAS SO JEALOUS!
Do you have a boyfriend?
Do you know who I am?
No, but...
I do, but...
IT WAS LIKE A SCENE RIGHT OUT OF A COMIC BOOK!
THAT WAS ONLY ONE TIME.
I HAVEN'T EVEN HAD THAT ONE TIME!
ONCE IS ENOUGH!
ONE TIME IS ALL I WANT!

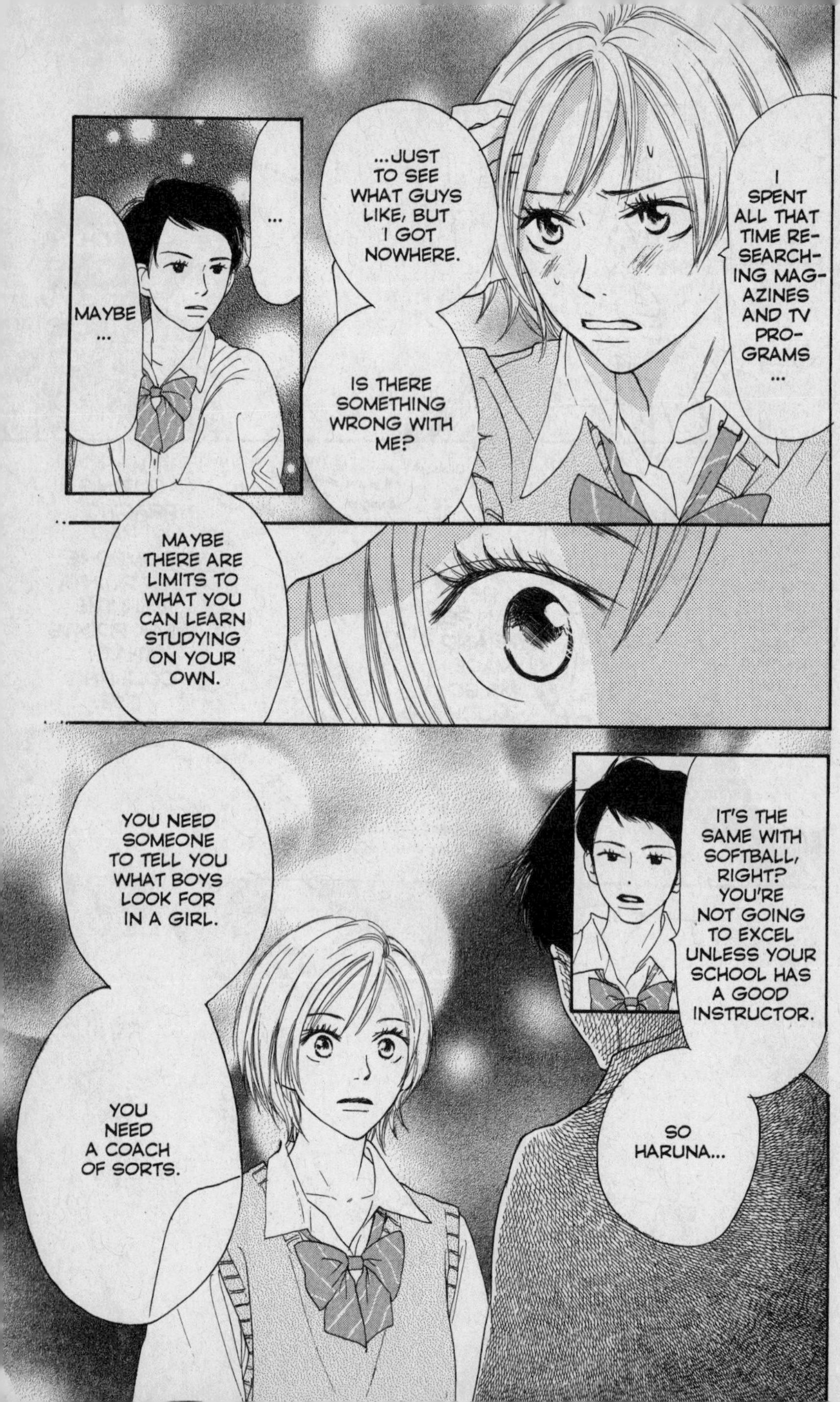
I SPENT ALL THAT TIME RESEARCHING MAGAZINES AND TV PROGRAMS...
...JUST TO SEE WHAT GUYS LIKE, BUT I GOT NOWHERE.
IS THERE SOMETHING WRONG WITH ME?
...
MAYBE...
MAYBE THERE ARE LIMITS TO WHAT YOU CAN LEARN STUDYING ON YOUR OWN.
IT'S THE SAME WITH SOFTBALL, RIGHT? YOU'RE NOT GOING TO EXCEL UNLESS YOUR SCHOOL HAS A GOOD INSTRUCTOR.
SO HARUNA...
YOU NEED SOMEONE TO TELL YOU WHAT BOYS LOOK FOR IN A GIRL.
YOU NEED A COACH OF SORTS.

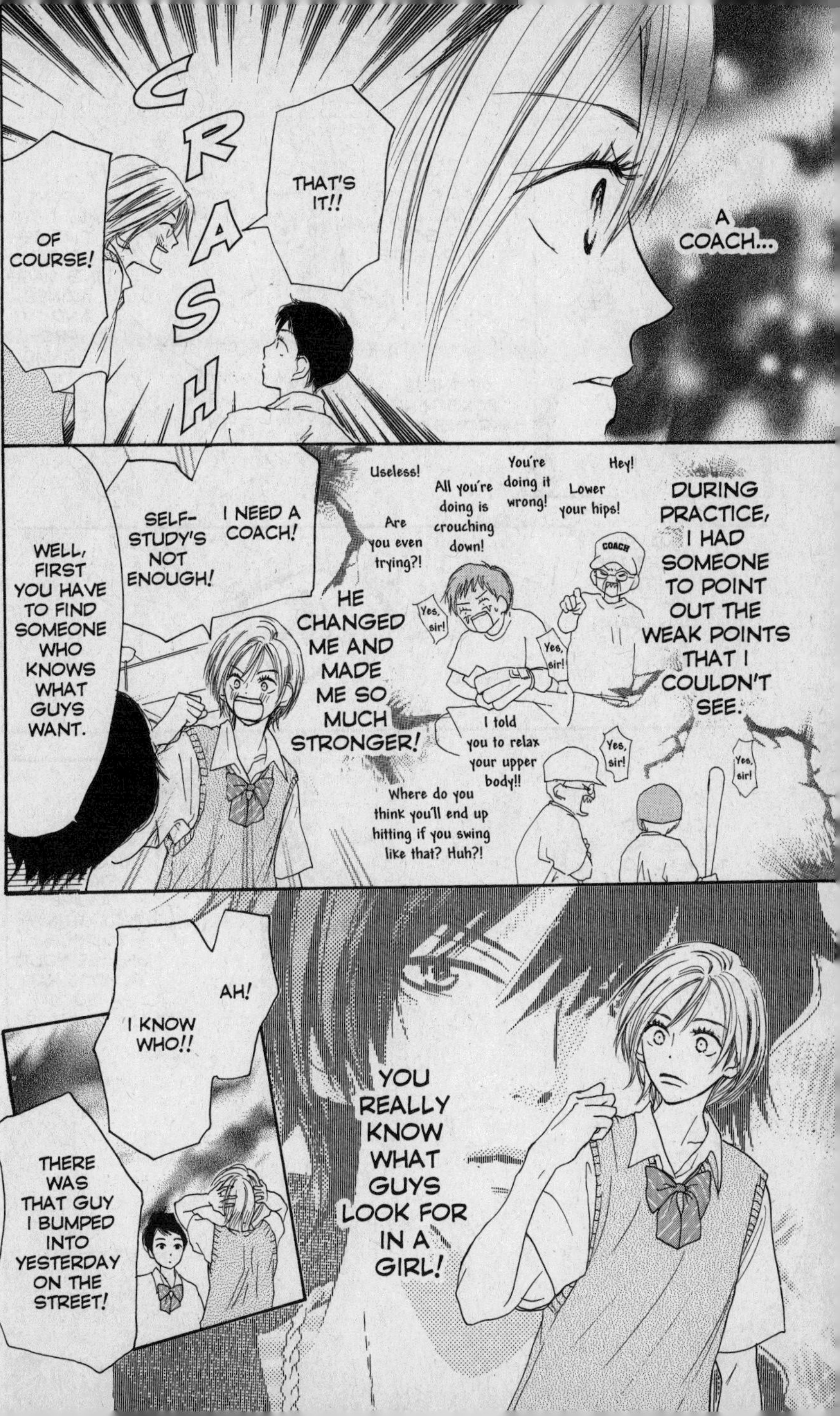
A COACH...
THAT'S IT!!
CRASH
OF COURSE!
DURING PRACTICE, I HAD SOMEONE TO POINT OUT THE WEAK POINTS THAT I COULDN'T SEE.
Hey!
Lower your hips!
You're doing it wrong!
All you're doing is crouching down!
Useless!
Are you even trying?!
Yes, sir!
Yes, sir!
Yes, sir!
Yes, sir!
I told you to relax your upper body!!
Where do you think you'll end up hitting if you swing like that? Huh?!
HE CHANGED ME AND MADE ME SO MUCH STRONGER!
I NEED A COACH!
SELF-STUDY'S NOT ENOUGH!
WELL, FIRST YOU HAVE TO FIND SOMEONE WHO KNOWS WHAT GUYS WANT.
YOU REALLY KNOW WHAT GUYS LOOK FOR IN A GIRL!
AH!
I KNOW WHO!!
THERE WAS THAT GUY I BUMPED INTO YESTERDAY ON THE STREET!

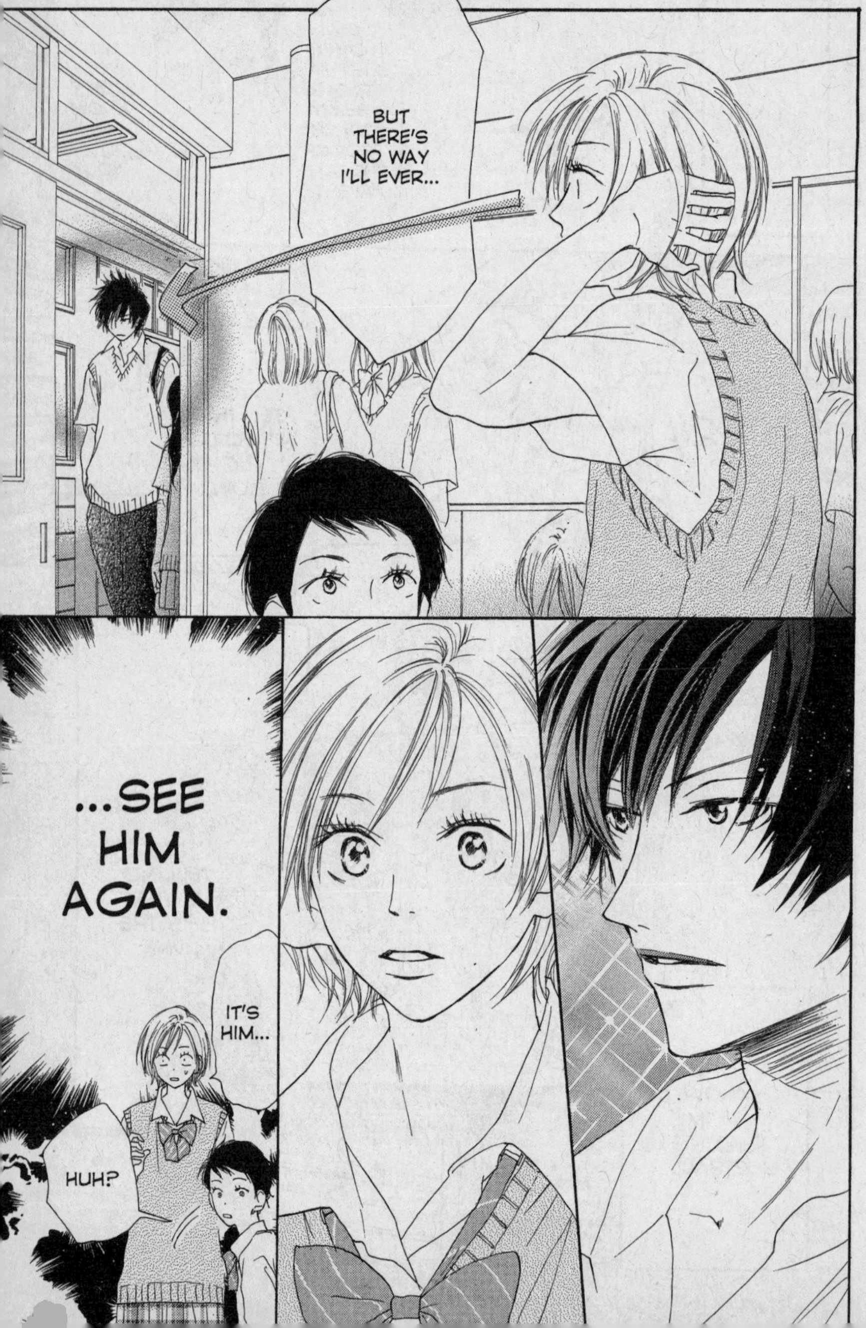
BUT THERE'S NO WAY I'LL EVER...
...SEE HIM AGAIN.
IT'S HIM...
HUH?

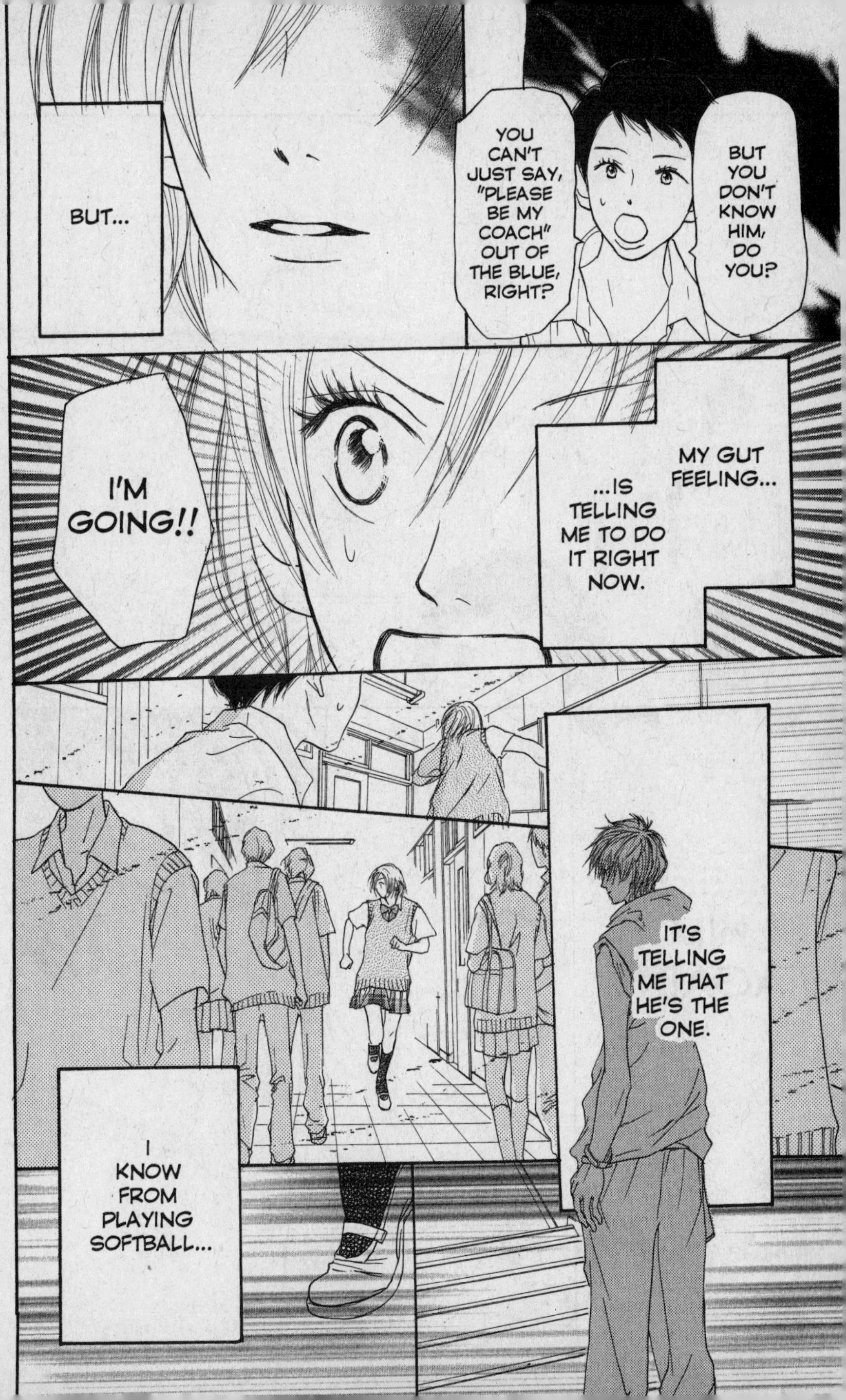
BUT YOU DON'T KNOW HIM, DO YOU?
YOU CAN'T JUST SAY, "PLEASE BE MY COACH" OUT OF THE BLUE, RIGHT?
BUT...
MY GUT FEELING...
...IS TELLING ME TO DO IT RIGHT NOW.
I'M GOING!!
IT'S TELLING ME THAT HE'S THE ONE.
I KNOW FROM PLAYING SOFTBALL...

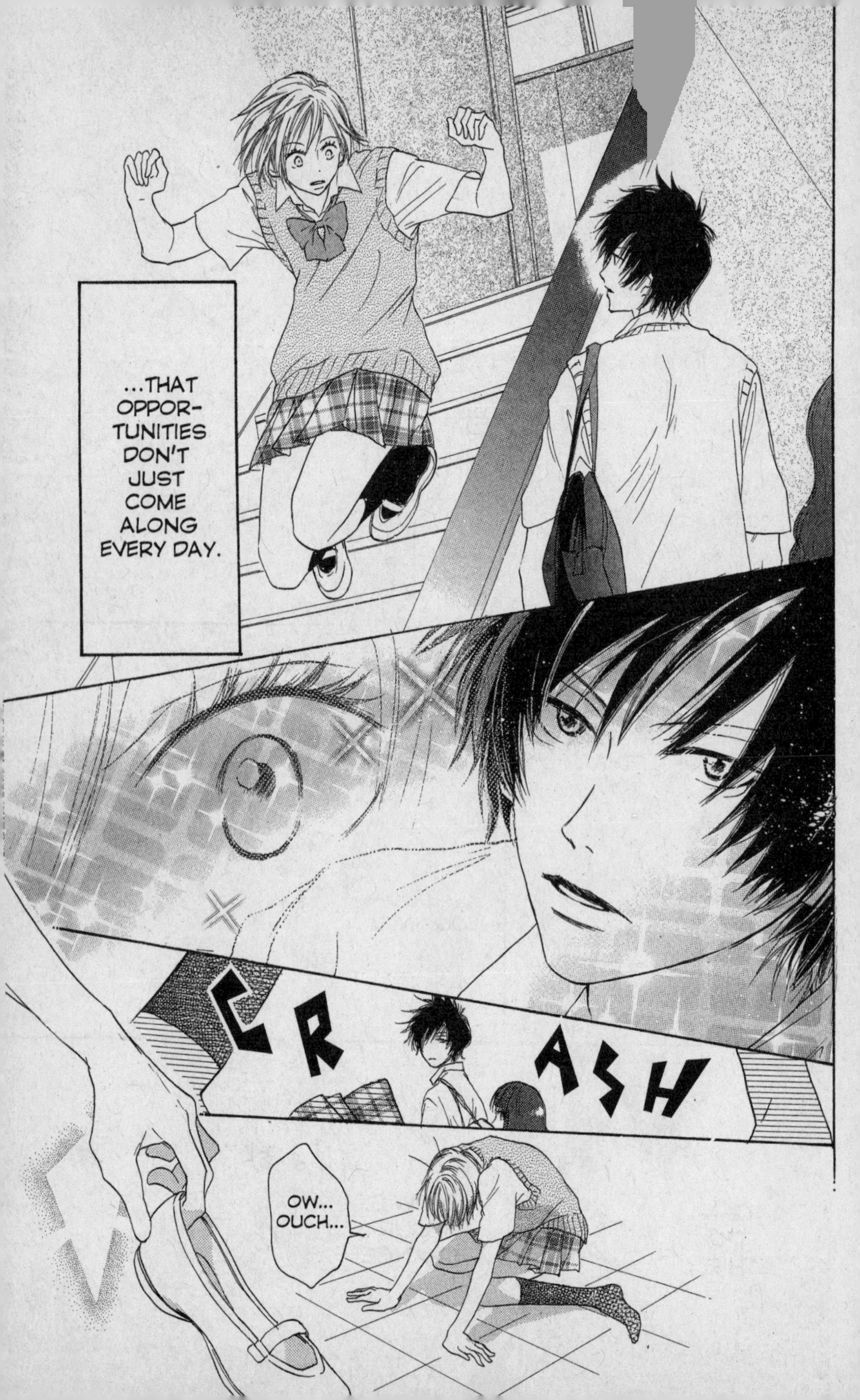
...THAT OPPORTUNITIES DON'T JUST COME ALONG EVERY DAY.
CRASH
OW... OUCH...

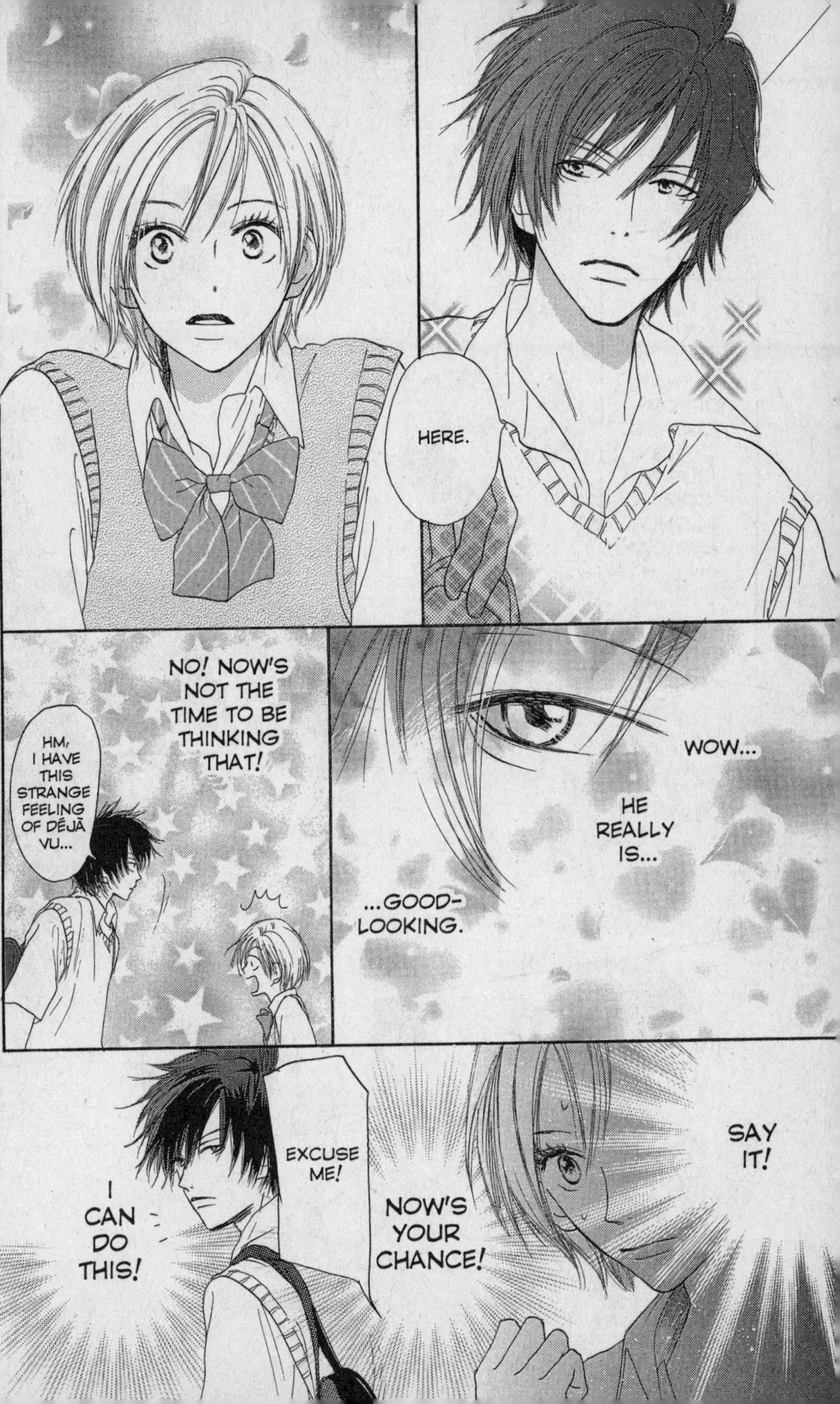
HERE.
WOW...
HE REALLY IS...
...GOOD-LOOKING.
NO! NOW'S NOT THE TIME TO BE THINKING THAT!
HM, I HAVE THIS STRANGE FEELING OF DÉJÀ VU...
SAY IT!
NOW'S YOUR CHANCE!
EXCUSE ME!
I CAN DO THIS!

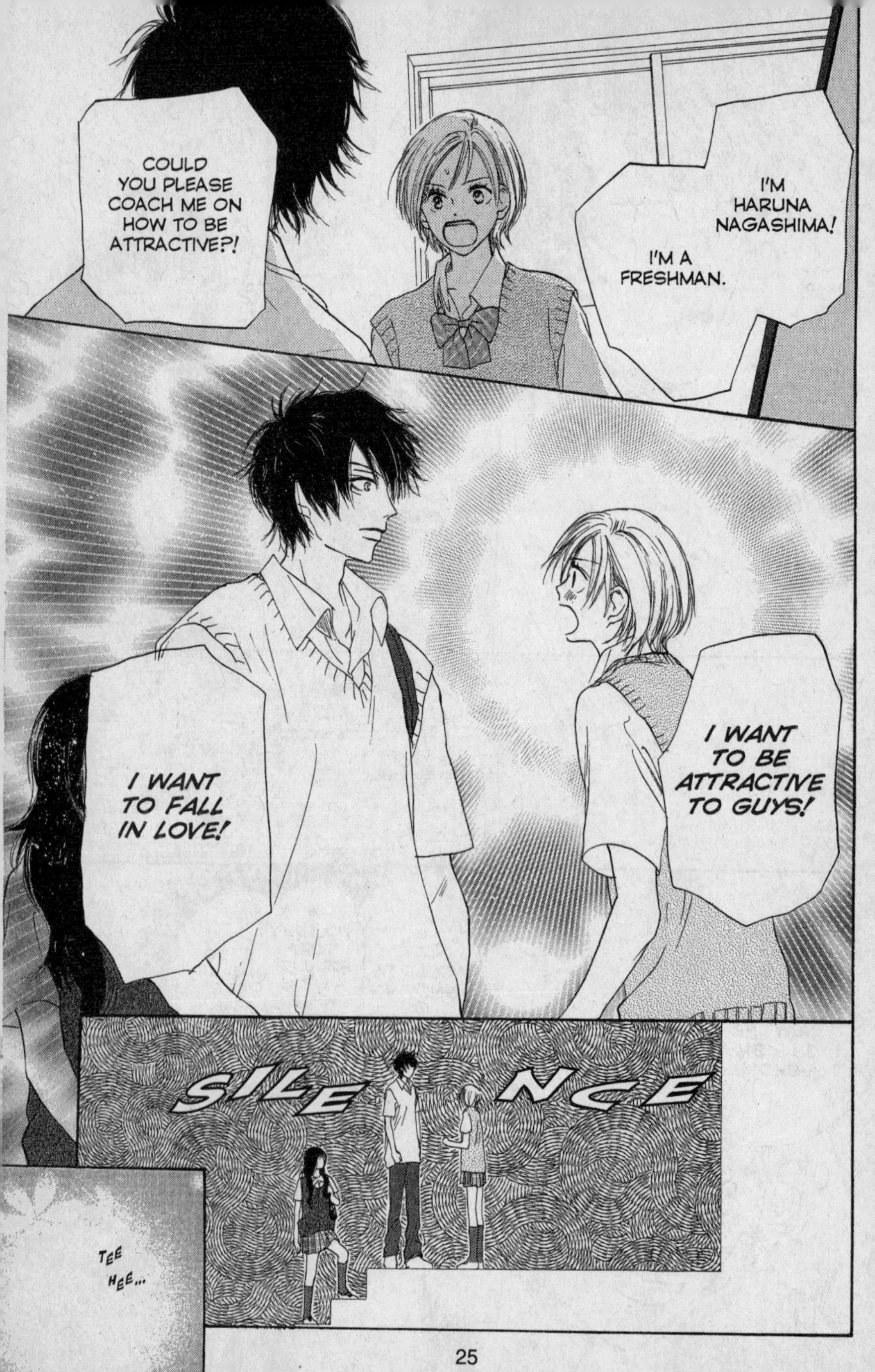
I'M HARUNA NAGASHIMA!
I'M A FRESHMAN.
COULD YOU PLEASE COACH ME ON HOW TO BE ATTRACTIVE?!
I WANT TO BE ATTRACTIVE TO GUYS!
I WANT TO FALL IN LOVE!
SILENCE
TEE HEE...

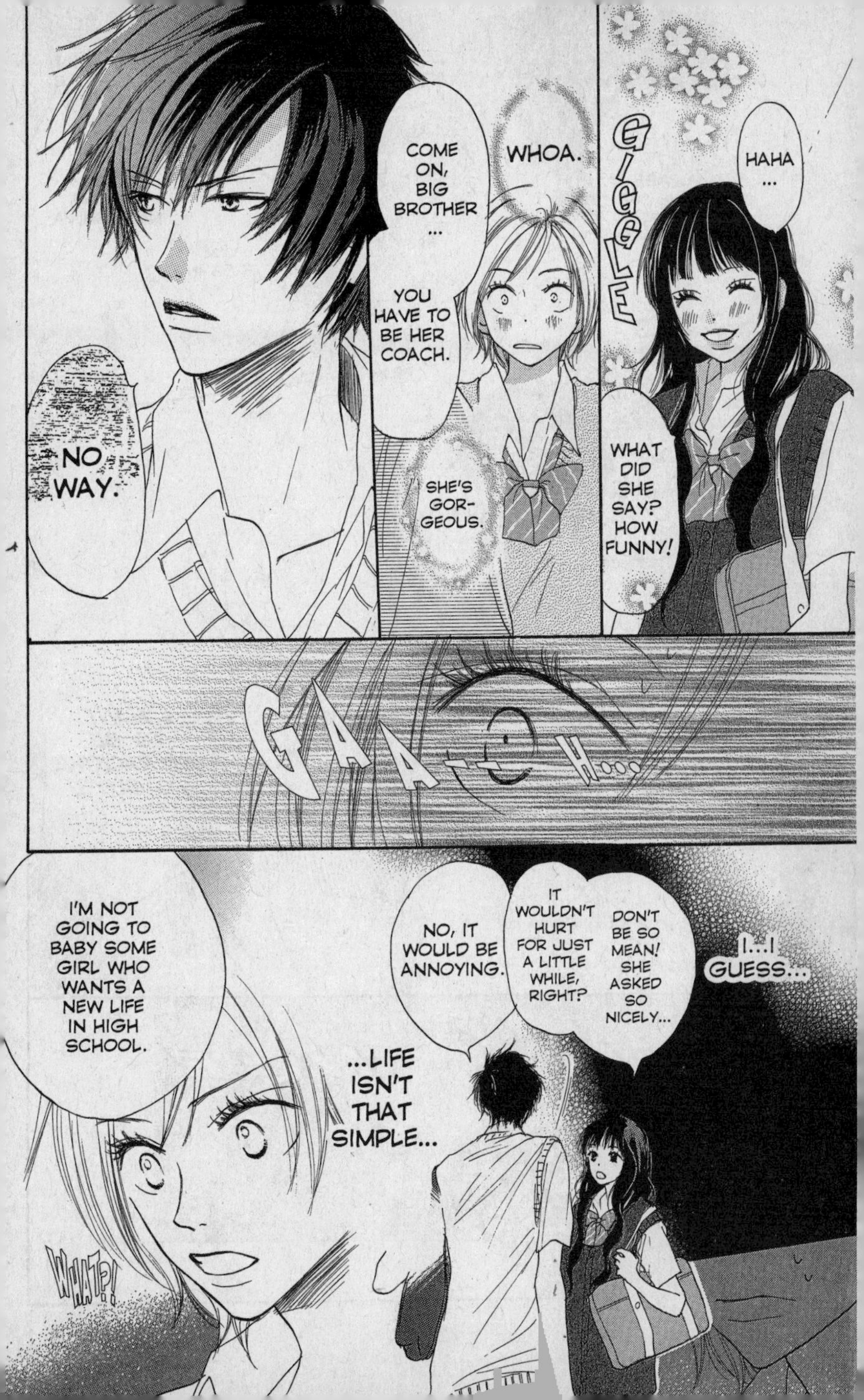
GIGGLE
HAHA ...
WHAT DID SHE SAY? HOW FUNNY!
WHOA.
COME ON, BIG BROTHER ...
YOU HAVE TO BE HER COACH.
SHE'S GORGEOUS.
NO WAY.
GAA-H...
I...I GUESS...
DON'T BE SO MEAN! SHE ASKED SO NICELY...
IT WOULDN'T HURT FOR JUST A LITTLE WHILE, RIGHT?
NO, IT WOULD BE ANNOYING.
...LIFE ISN'T THAT SIMPLE...
I'M NOT GOING TO BABY SOME GIRL WHO WANTS A NEW LIFE IN HIGH SCHOOL.
WHAT?!

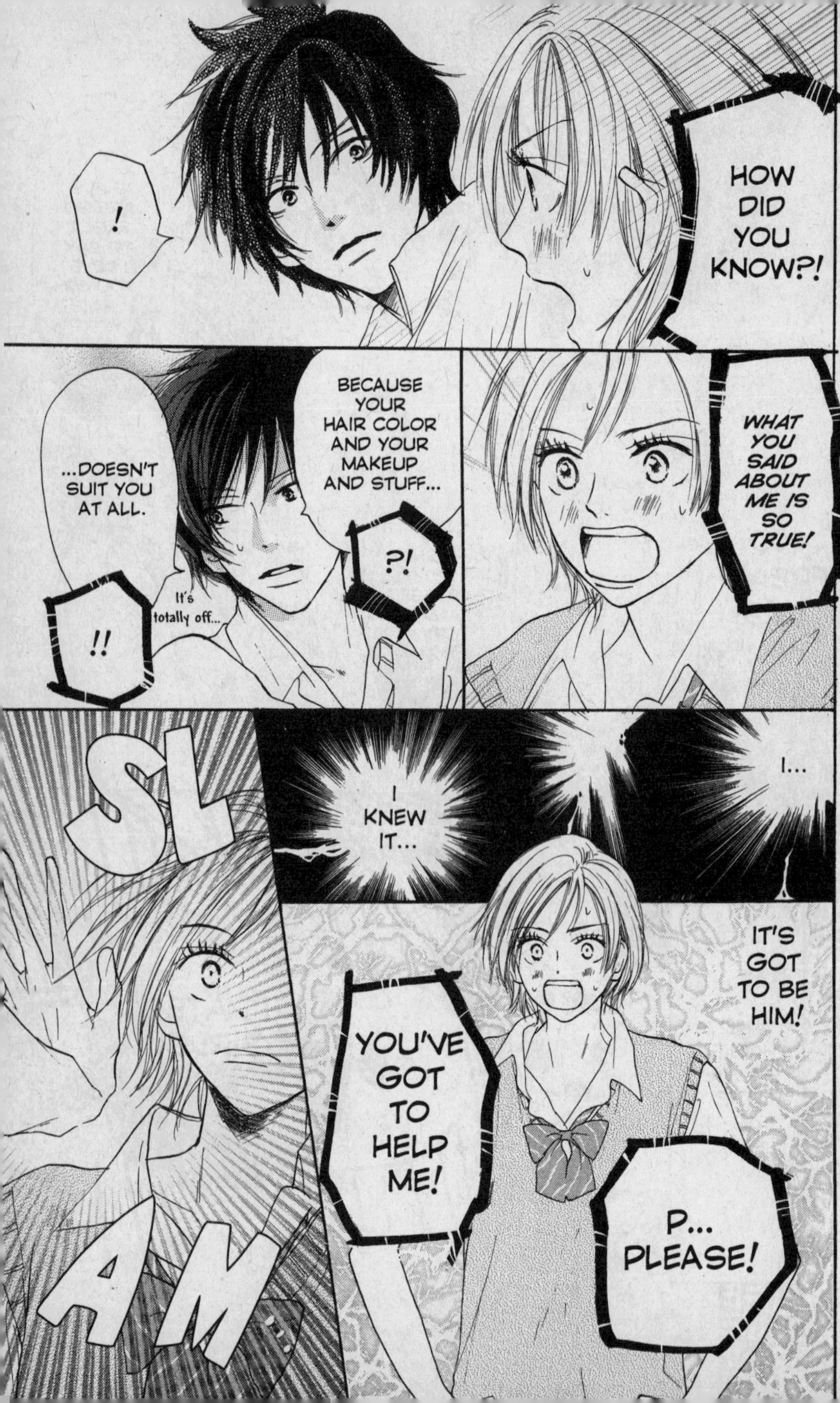
HOW DID YOU KNOW?!
!
WHAT YOU SAID ABOUT ME IS SO TRUE!
BECAUSE YOUR HAIR COLOR AND YOUR MAKEUP AND STUFF...
?!
...DOESN'T SUIT YOU AT ALL.
It's totally off...
!!
I...
I KNEW IT...
IT'S GOT TO BE HIM!
YOU'VE GOT TO HELP ME!
P... PLEASE!
SLAM

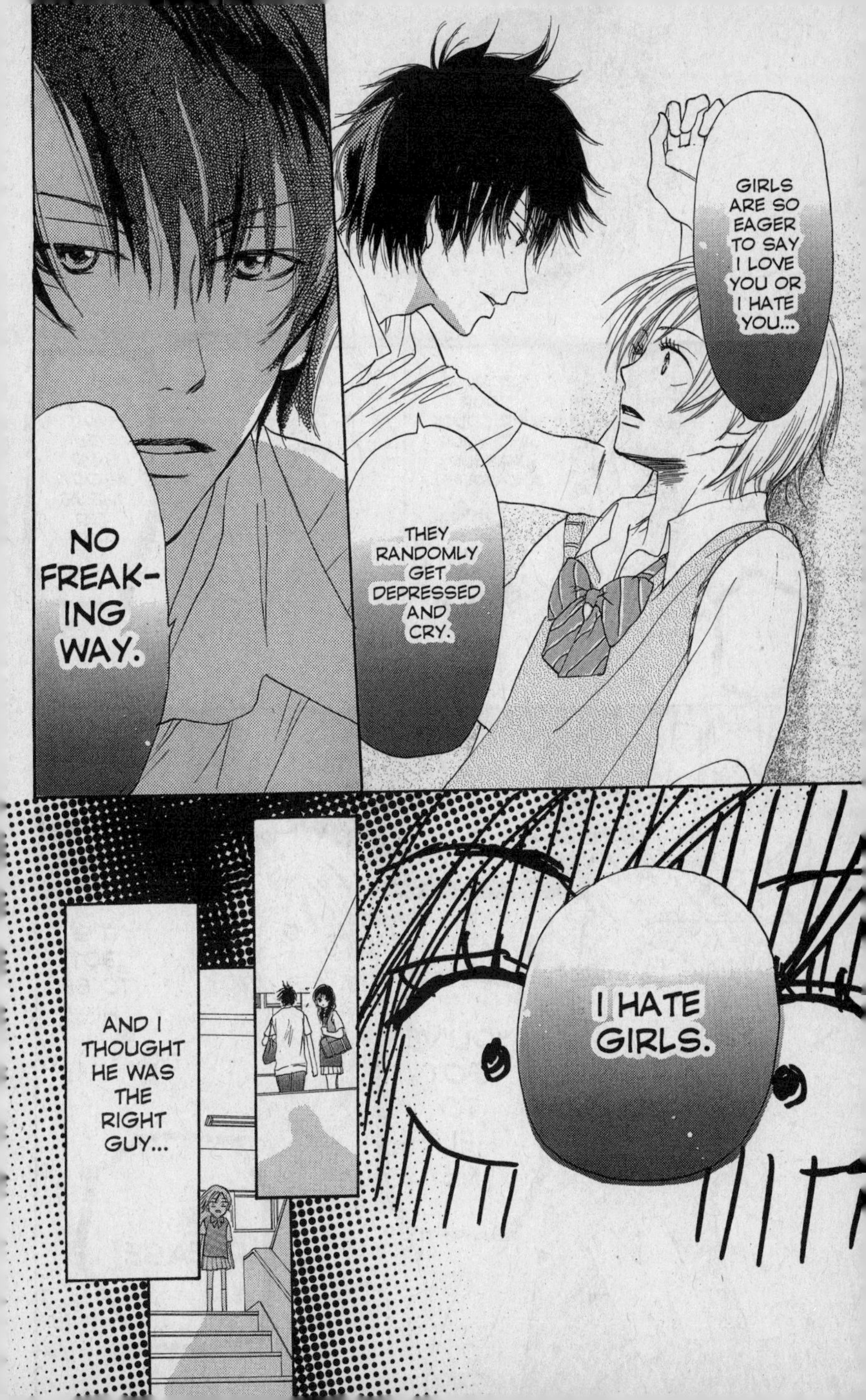
GIRLS ARE SO EAGER TO SAY I LOVE YOU OR I HATE YOU...
THEY RANDOMLY GET DEPRESSED AND CRY.
NO FREAKING WAY.
I HATE GIRLS.
AND I THOUGHT HE WAS THE RIGHT GUY...

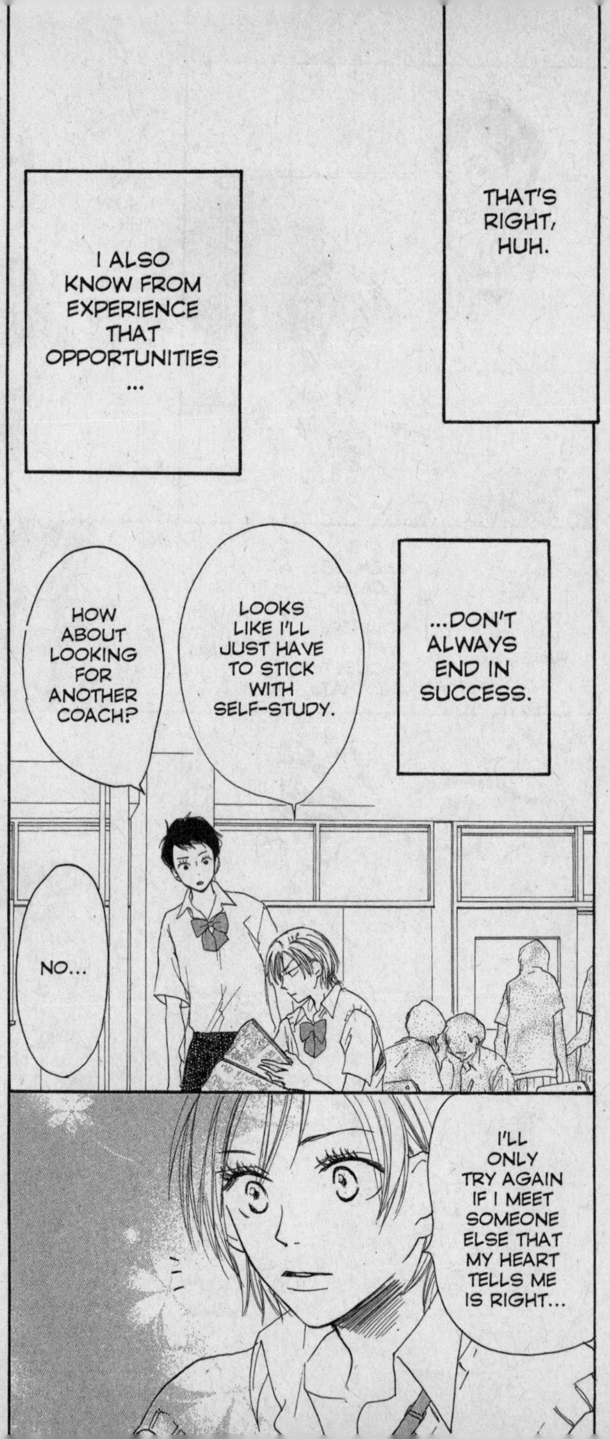
THAT'S RIGHT, HUH.
I ALSO KNOW FROM EXPERIENCE THAT OPPORTUNITIES ...
...DON'T ALWAYS END IN SUCCESS.
LOOKS LIKE I'LL JUST HAVE TO STICK WITH SELF-STUDY.
HOW ABOUT LOOKING FOR ANOTHER COACH?
NO...
I'LL ONLY TRY AGAIN IF I MEET SOMEONE ELSE THAT MY HEART TELLS ME IS RIGHT...

1

Hello! Kawahara here.

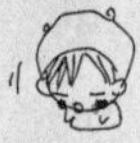

Thank you for picking up my comic!

I'd be delighted if you enjoy it a little. If you enjoy it lots, then I'd be even more delighted.

Thanks to so many people, I've been able to release another title of my own. At any rate, the people who've helped me out have grown in number over the years. I wonder why that is? Tee hee.

↑ Can't take for granted!

↑ Can't act cutesy!

I've caught a cold.

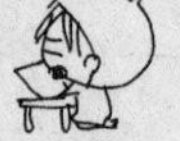
My throat hurts.

2004.
Kazune Kawahara.

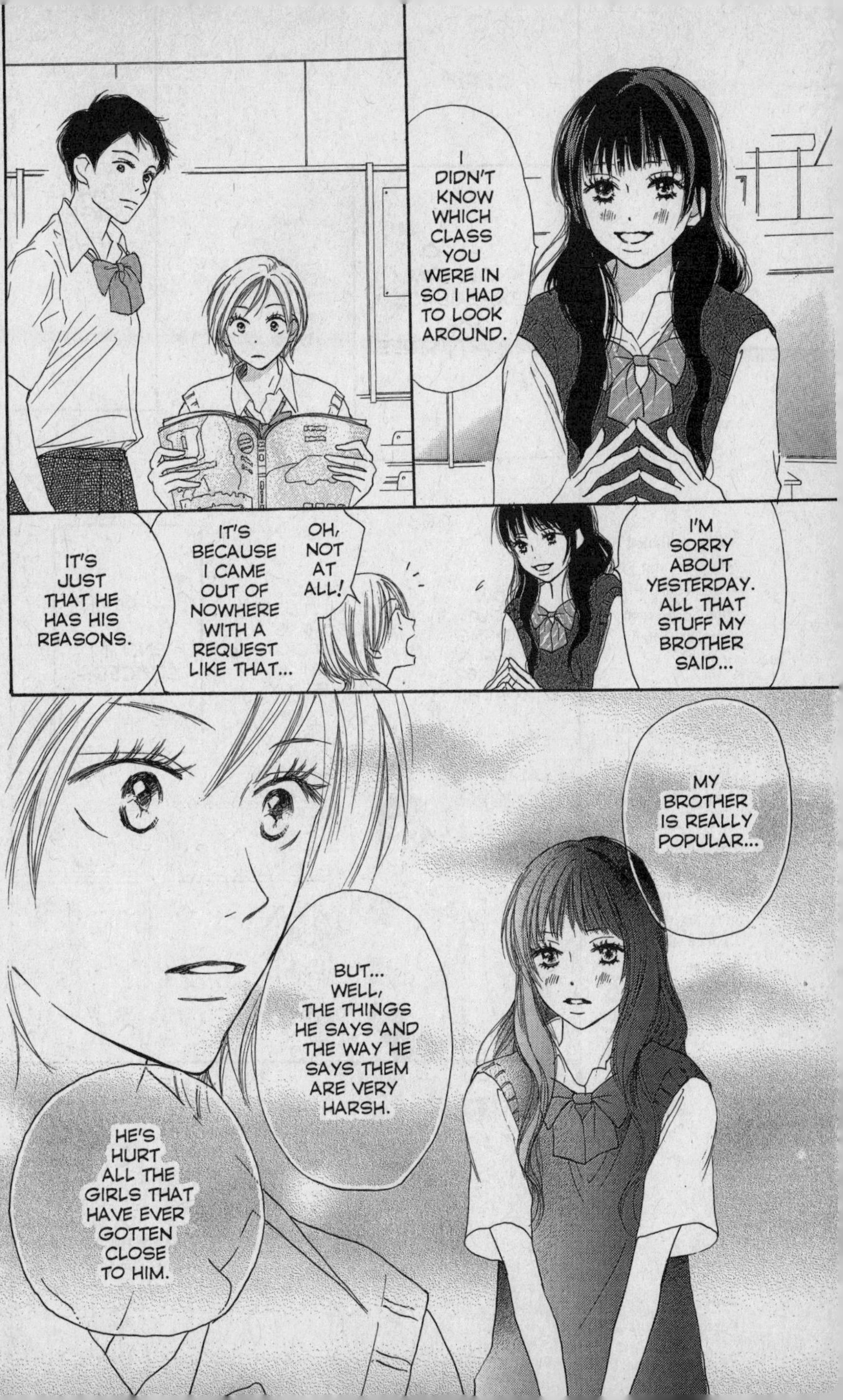
I DIDN'T KNOW WHICH CLASS YOU WERE IN SO I HAD TO LOOK AROUND.
I'M SORRY ABOUT YESTERDAY. ALL THAT STUFF MY BROTHER SAID...
OH, NOT AT ALL!
IT'S BECAUSE I CAME OUT OF NOWHERE WITH A REQUEST LIKE THAT...
IT'S JUST THAT HE HAS HIS REASONS.
MY BROTHER IS REALLY POPULAR...
BUT... WELL, THE THINGS HE SAYS AND THE WAY HE SAYS THEM ARE VERY HARSH.
HE'S HURT ALL THE GIRLS THAT HAVE EVER GOTTEN CLOSE TO HIM.

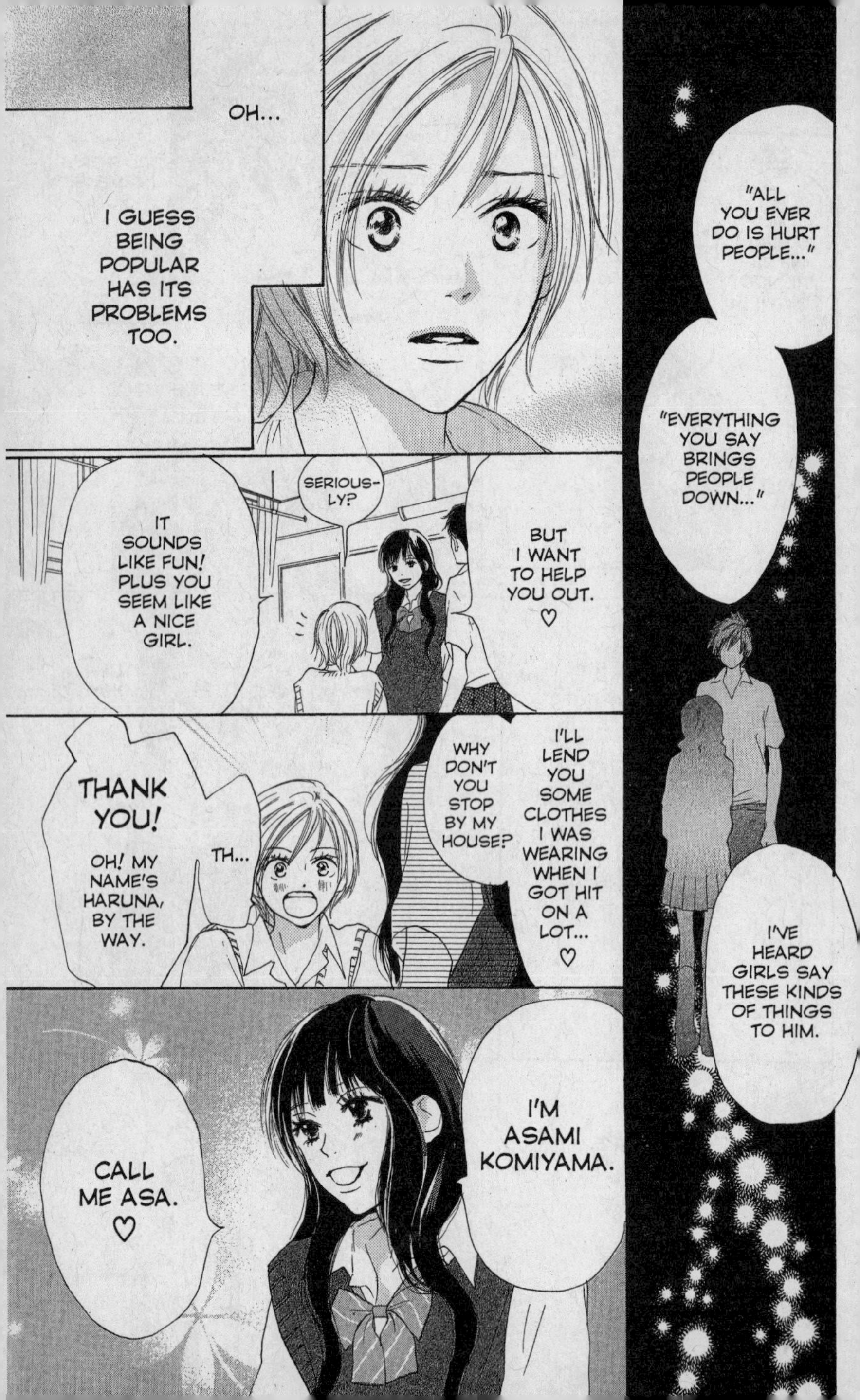
"ALL YOU EVER DO IS HURT PEOPLE..."
"EVERYTHING YOU SAY BRINGS PEOPLE DOWN..."
I'VE HEARD GIRLS SAY THESE KINDS OF THINGS TO HIM.
OH...
I GUESS BEING POPULAR HAS ITS PROBLEMS TOO.
BUT I WANT TO HELP YOU OUT. ♡
SERIOUS-LY?
IT SOUNDS LIKE FUN! PLUS YOU SEEM LIKE A NICE GIRL.
I'LL LEND YOU SOME CLOTHES I WAS WEARING WHEN I GOT HIT ON A LOT... ♡
WHY DON'T YOU STOP BY MY HOUSE?
TH...
THANK YOU!
OH! MY NAME'S HARUNA, BY THE WAY.
I'M ASAMI KOMIYAMA.
CALL ME ASA. ♡

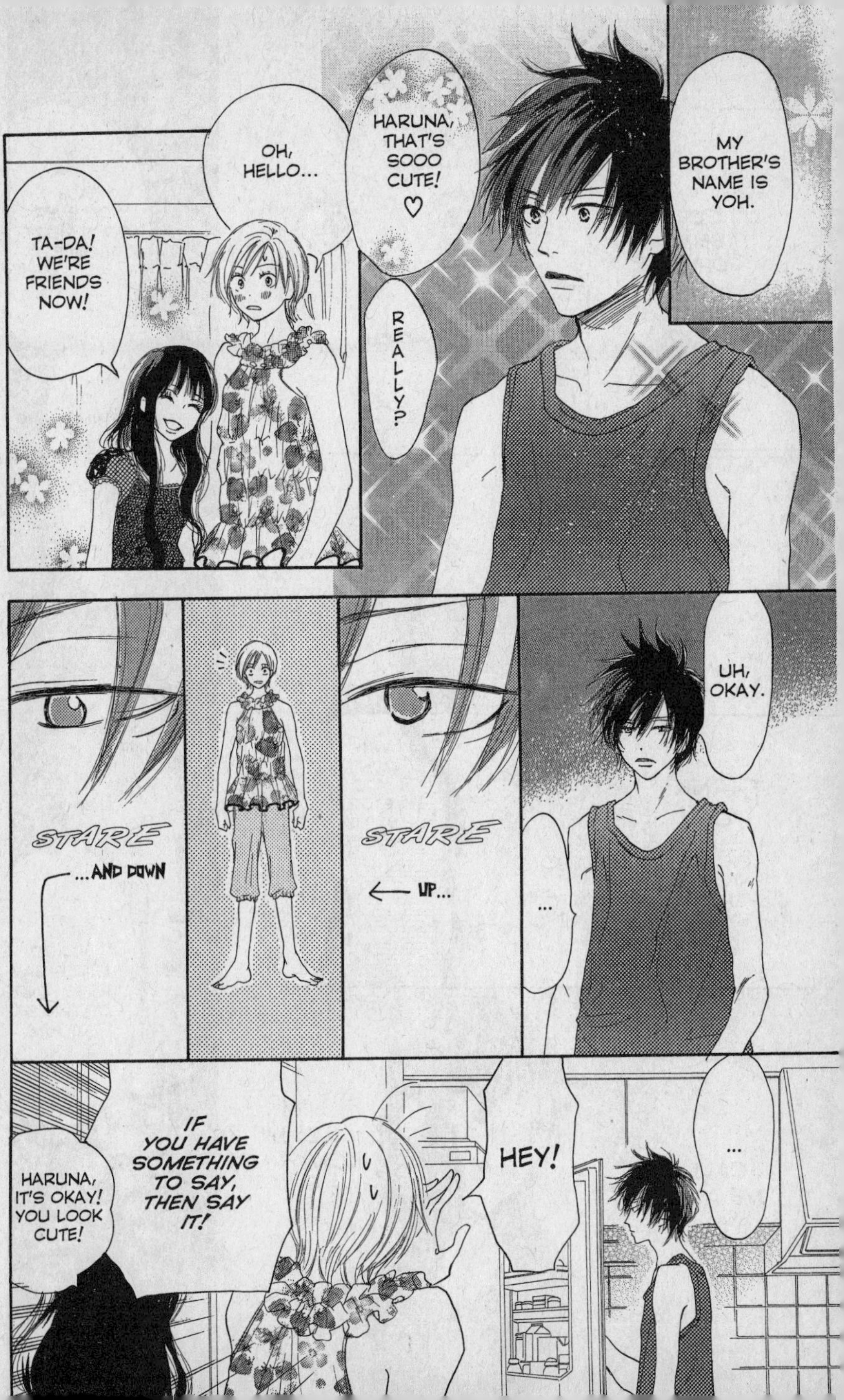

MY BROTHER'S NAME IS YOH.
HARUNA, THAT'S SOOO CUTE! ♡
REALLY?
OH, HELLO...
TA-DA! WE'RE FRIENDS NOW!
UH, OKAY.
...
STARE
← UP...
STARE
...AND DOWN
...
HEY!
IF YOU HAVE SOMETHING TO SAY, THEN SAY IT!
HARUNA, IT'S OKAY! YOU LOOK CUTE!

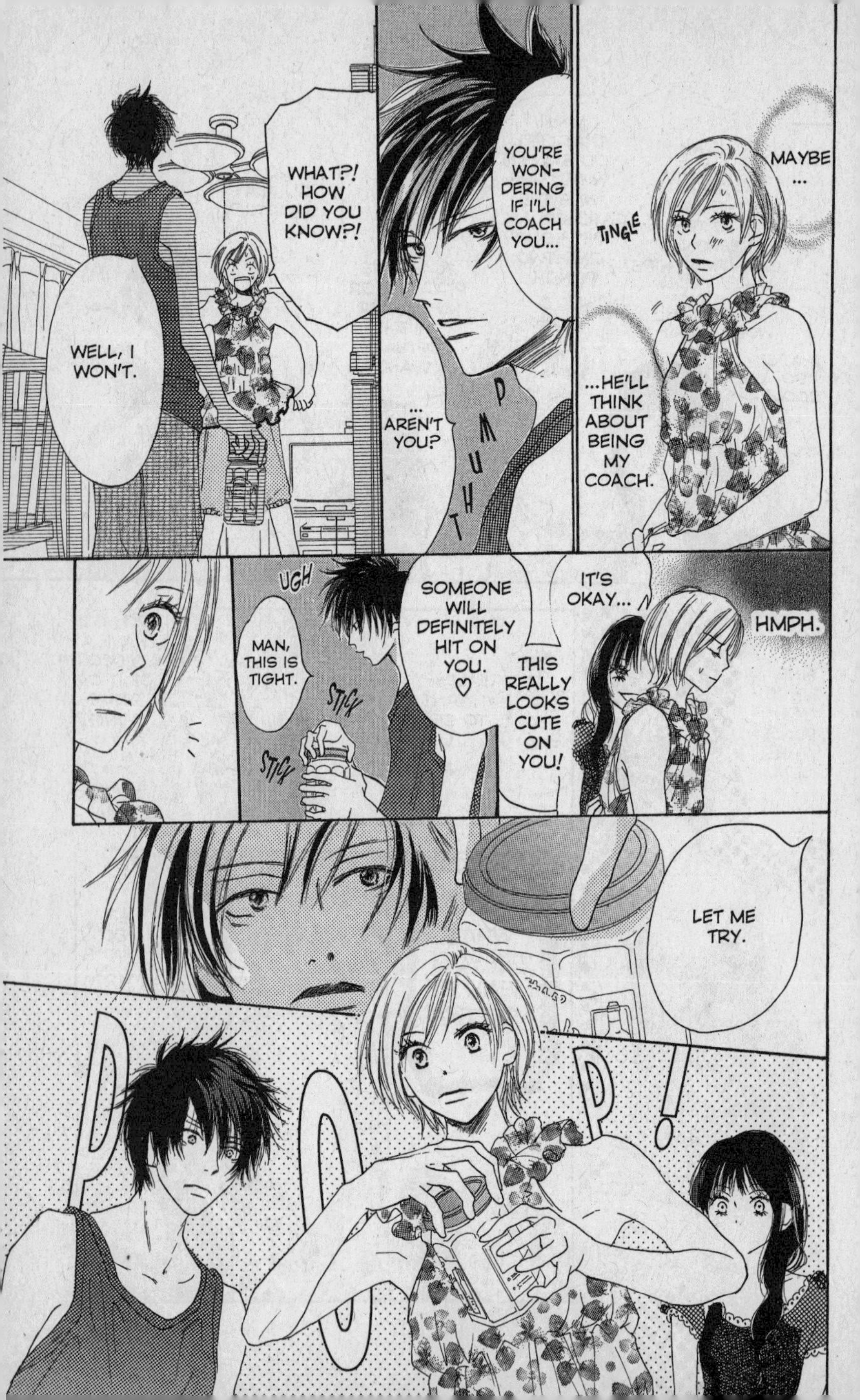
MAYBE...
TINGLE
...HE'LL THINK ABOUT BEING MY COACH.
YOU'RE WONDERING IF I'LL COACH YOU...
...AREN'T YOU?
THUMP
WHAT?! HOW DID YOU KNOW?!
WELL, I WON'T.
IT'S OKAY...
HMPH.
THIS REALLY LOOKS CUTE ON YOU!
SOMEONE WILL DEFINITELY HIT ON YOU. ♡
UGH
MAN, THIS IS TIGHT.
STICK
STICK
LET ME TRY.
POP!

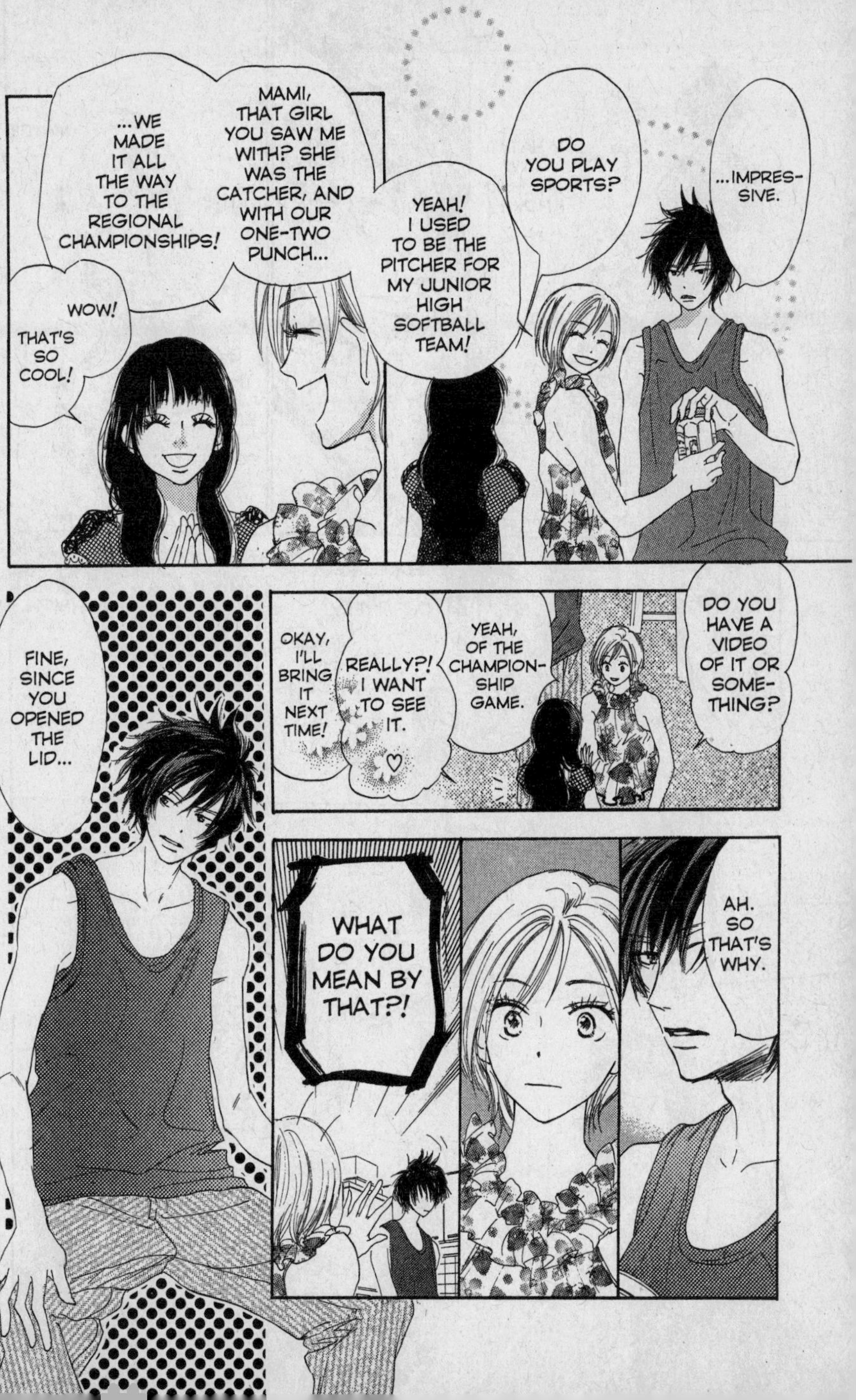
DO YOU PLAY SPORTS?
YEAH! I USED TO BE THE PITCHER FOR MY JUNIOR HIGH SOFTBALL TEAM!
...IMPRES-SIVE.
MAMI, THAT GIRL YOU SAW ME WITH? SHE WAS THE CATCHER, AND WITH OUR ONE-TWO PUNCH...
...WE MADE IT ALL THE WAY TO THE REGIONAL CHAMPIONSHIPS!
WOW! THAT'S SO COOL!
DO YOU HAVE A VIDEO OF IT OR SOME-THING?
YEAH, OF THE CHAMPION-SHIP GAME.
REALLY?! I WANT TO SEE IT. ♡
OKAY, I'LL BRING IT NEXT TIME!
AH. SO THAT'S WHY.
WHAT DO YOU MEAN BY THAT?!
FINE, SINCE YOU OPENED THE LID...

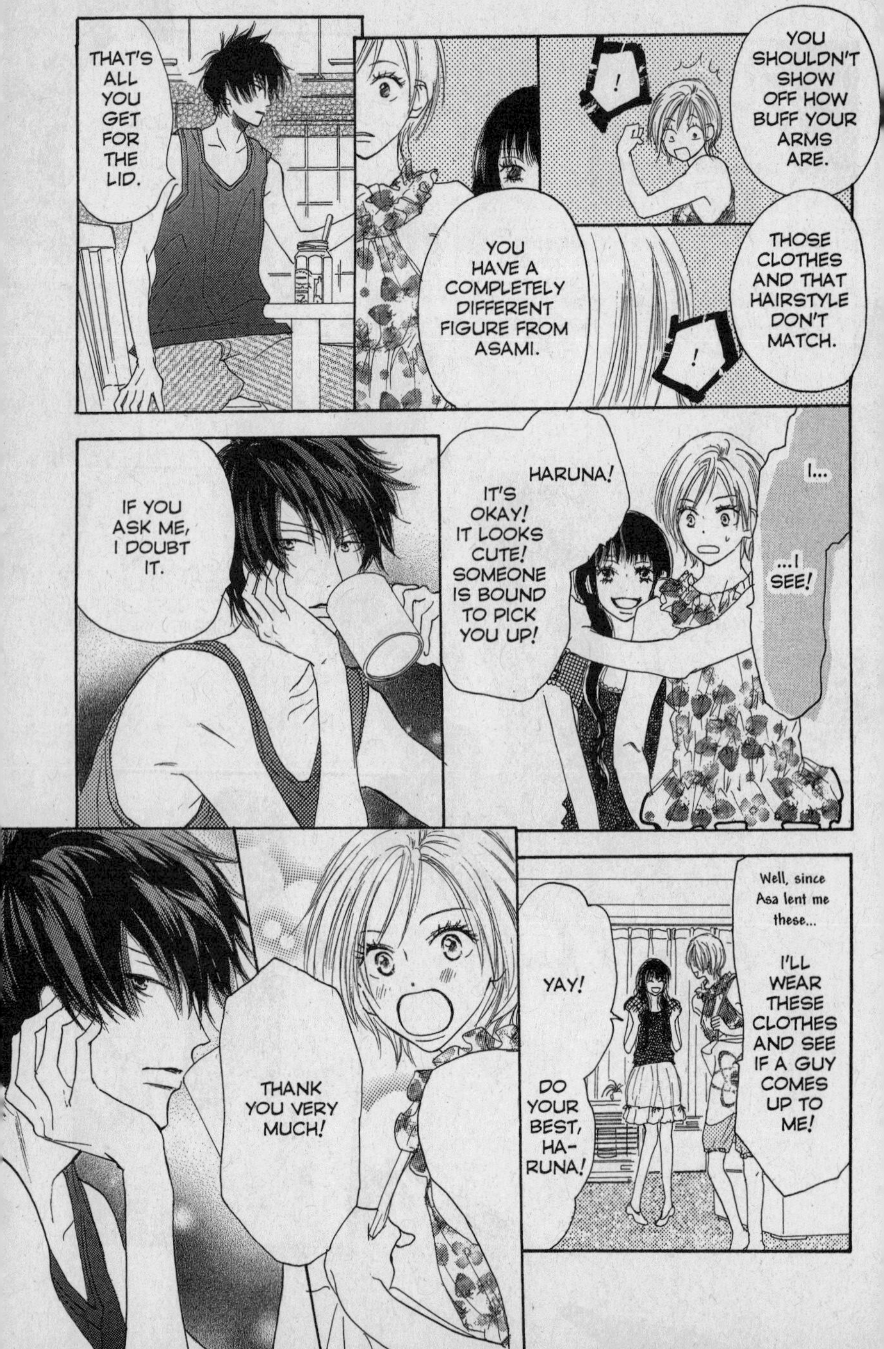
!
YOU SHOULDN'T SHOW OFF HOW BUFF YOUR ARMS ARE.
THOSE CLOTHES AND THAT HAIRSTYLE DON'T MATCH.
!
YOU HAVE A COMPLETELY DIFFERENT FIGURE FROM ASAMI.
THAT'S ALL YOU GET FOR THE LID.
I...
...I SEE!
HARUNA!
IT'S OKAY! IT LOOKS CUTE! SOMEONE IS BOUND TO PICK YOU UP!
IF YOU ASK ME, I DOUBT IT.
Well, since Asa lent me these...
I'LL WEAR THESE CLOTHES AND SEE IF A GUY COMES UP TO ME!
YAY!
DO YOUR BEST, HA-RUNA!
THANK YOU VERY MUCH!

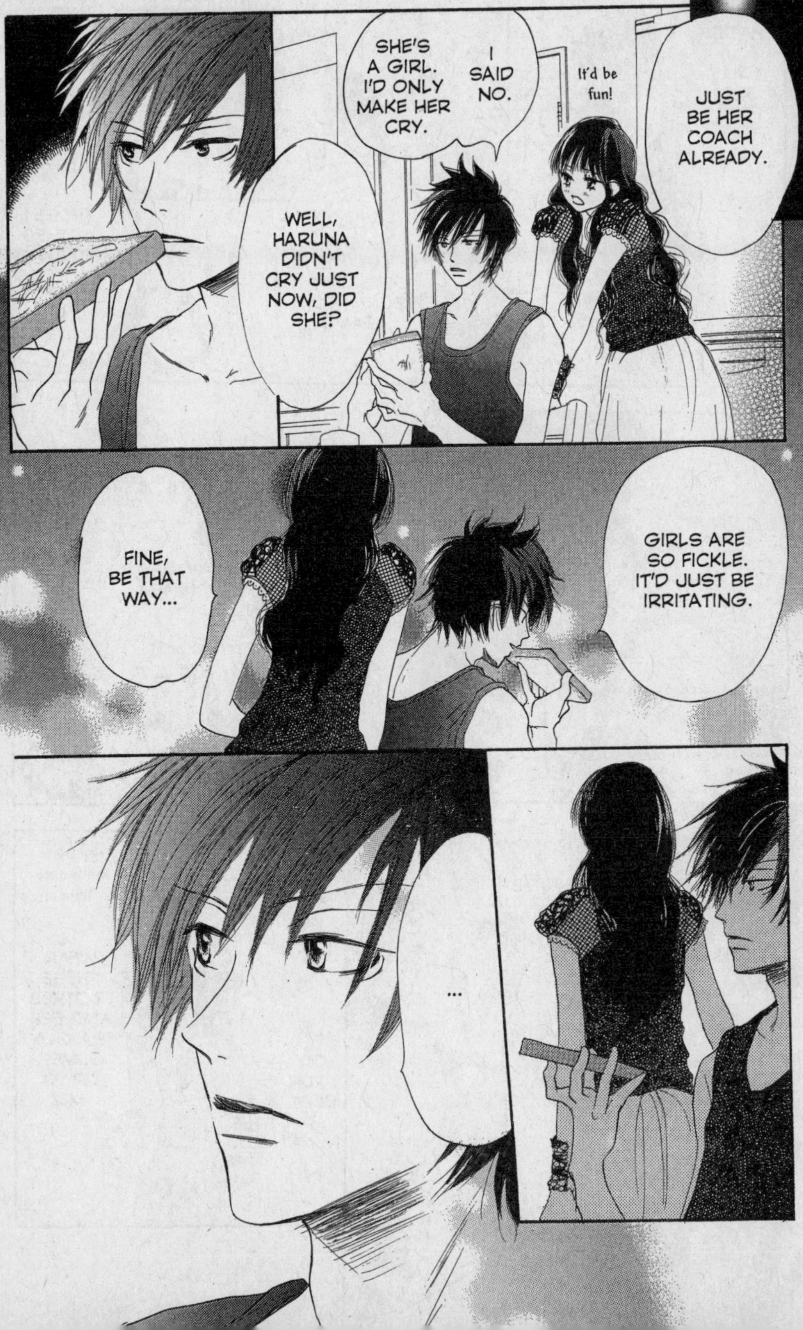
JUST BE HER COACH ALREADY.
It'd be fun!
I SAID NO.
SHE'S A GIRL. I'D ONLY MAKE HER CRY.
WELL, HARUNA DIDN'T CRY JUST NOW, DID SHE?
GIRLS ARE SO FICKLE. IT'D JUST BE IRRITATING.
FINE, BE THAT WAY...
...

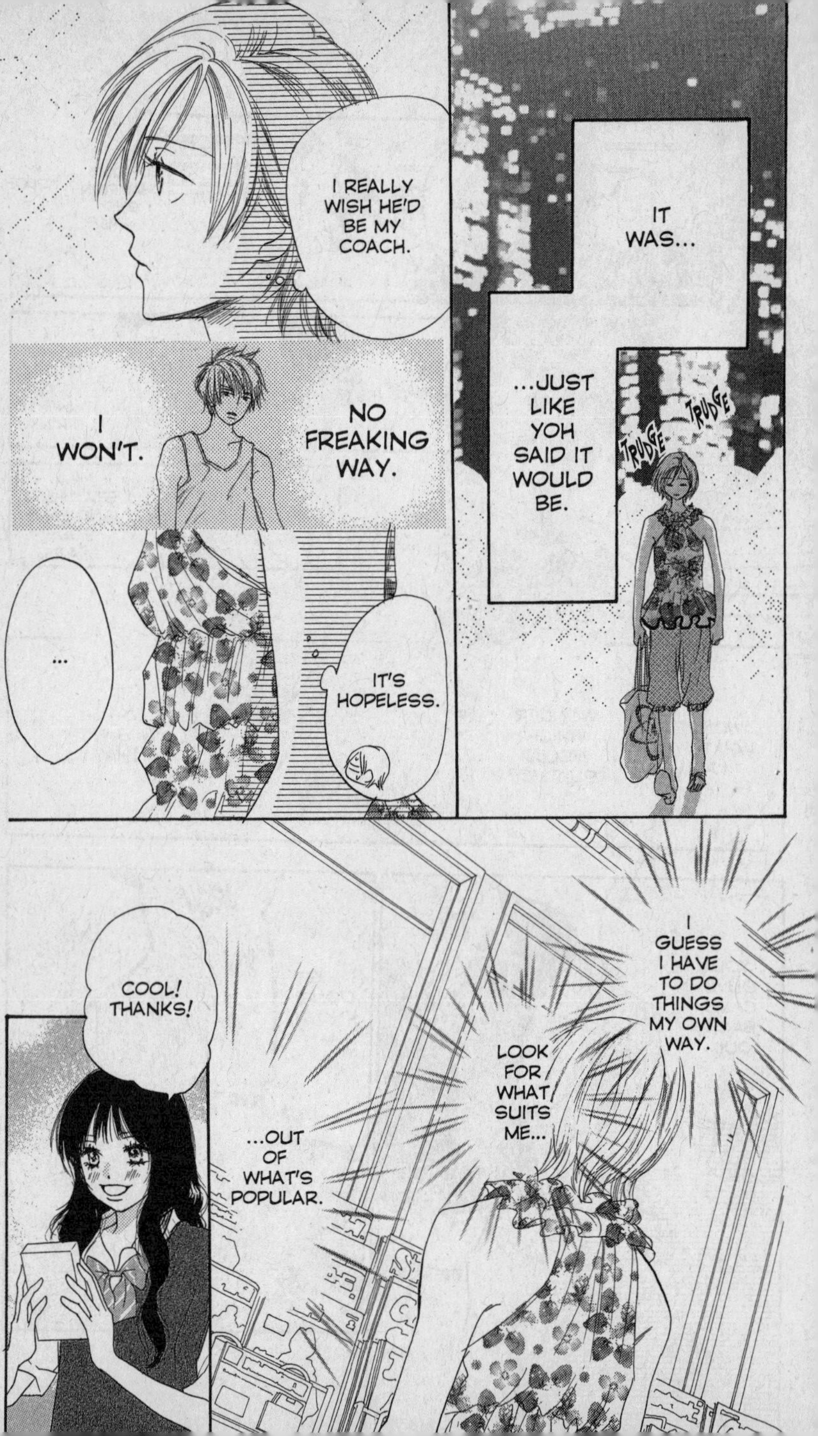
IT WAS...
...JUST LIKE YOH SAID IT WOULD BE.
TRUDGE
TRUDGE
I REALLY WISH HE'D BE MY COACH.
NO FREAKING WAY.
I WON'T.
IT'S HOPELESS.
...
I GUESS I HAVE TO DO THINGS MY OWN WAY.
LOOK FOR WHAT SUITS ME...
...OUT OF WHAT'S POPULAR.
COOL! THANKS!

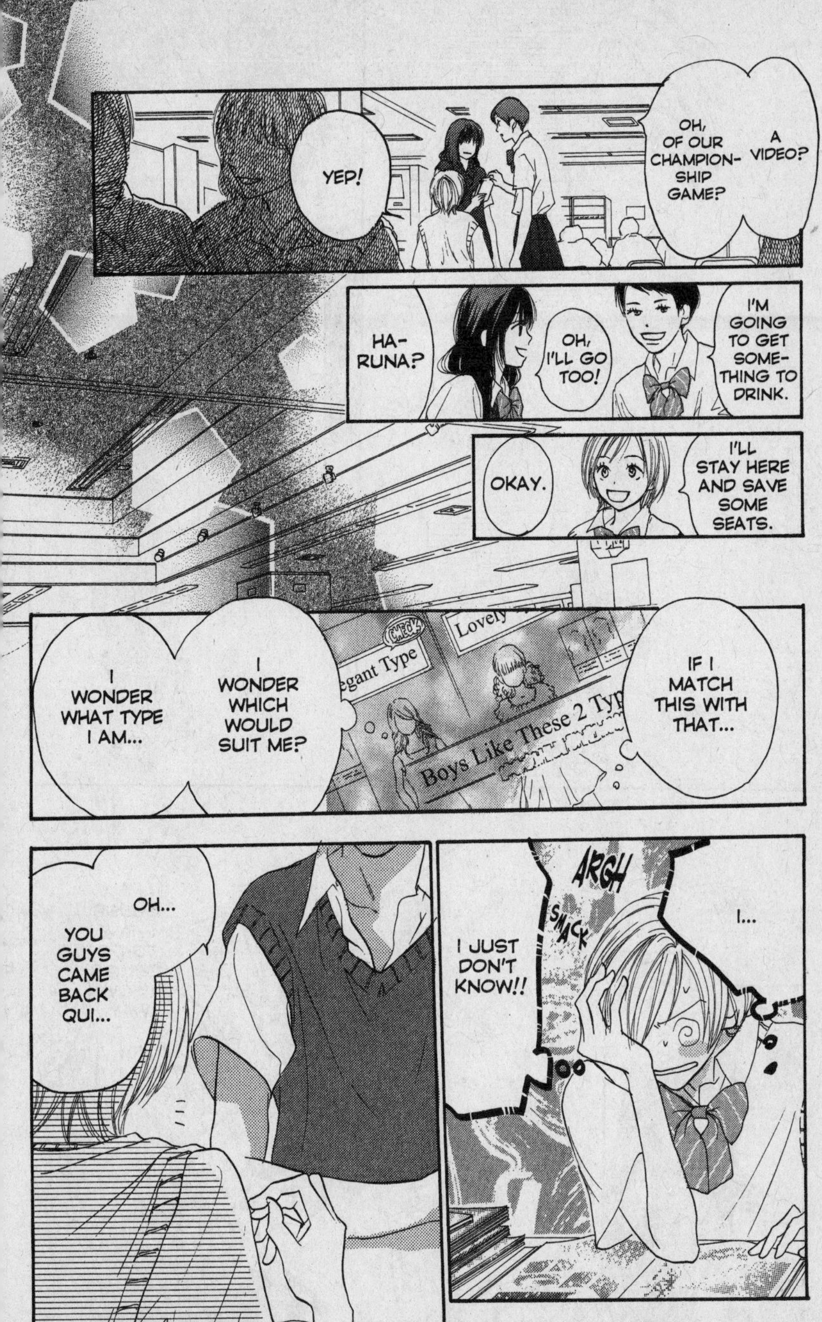
A VIDEO?
OH, OF OUR CHAMPIONSHIP GAME?
YEP!
I'M GOING TO GET SOMETHING TO DRINK.
OH, I'LL GO TOO!
HA-RUNA?
I'LL STAY HERE AND SAVE SOME SEATS.
OKAY.
IF I MATCH THIS WITH THAT...
Lovely
CHECK
egant Type
Boys Like These 2 Typ
I WONDER WHICH WOULD SUIT ME?
I WONDER WHAT TYPE I AM...
I...
ARGH
SMACK
I JUST DON'T KNOW!!
OH...
YOU GUYS CAME BACK QUI...

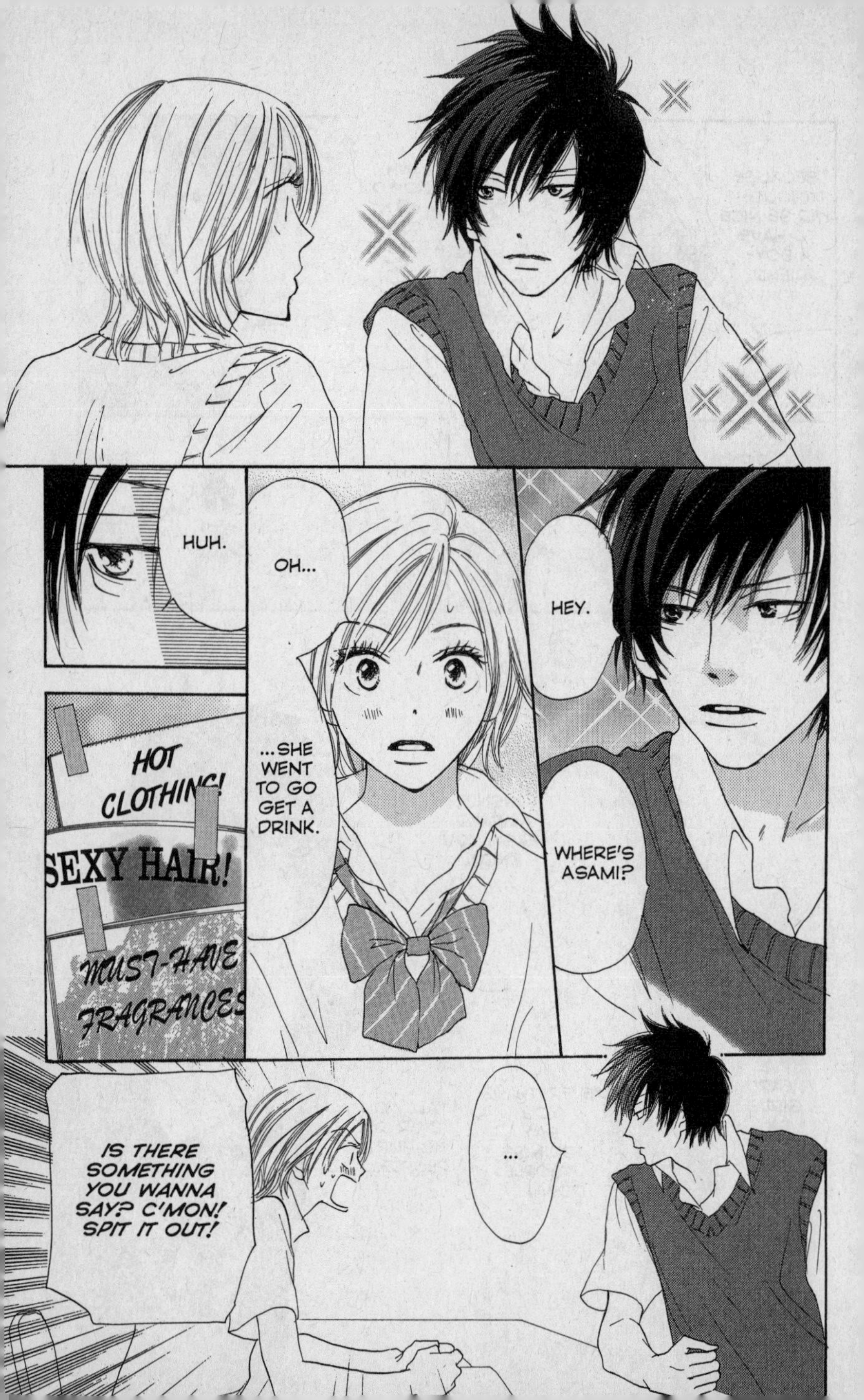
HEY.
WHERE'S ASAMI?
OH...
...SHE WENT TO GO GET A DRINK.
HUH.
HOT CLOTHIN
SEXY HAIR!
MUST-HAVE FRAGRANCES
...
IS THERE SOMETHING YOU WANNA SAY? C'MON! SPIT IT OUT!

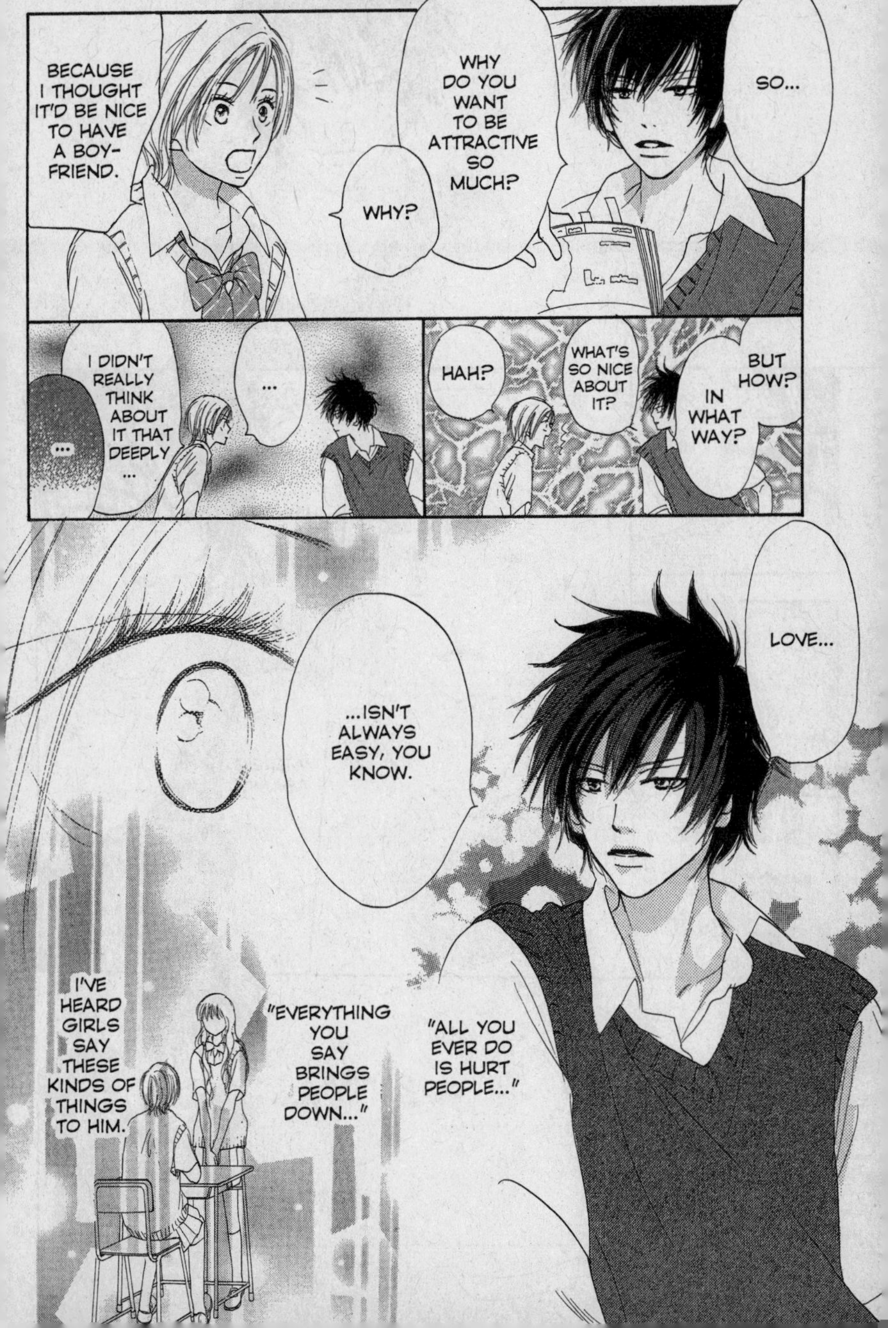
SO...
WHY DO YOU WANT TO BE ATTRACTIVE SO MUCH?
WHY?
BECAUSE I THOUGHT IT'D BE NICE TO HAVE A BOY-FRIEND.
BUT HOW?
IN WHAT WAY?
WHAT'S SO NICE ABOUT IT?
HAH?
...
I DIDN'T REALLY THINK ABOUT IT THAT DEEPLY...
...
LOVE...
...ISN'T ALWAYS EASY, YOU KNOW.
"ALL YOU EVER DO IS HURT PEOPLE..."
"EVERYTHING YOU SAY BRINGS PEOPLE DOWN..."
I'VE HEARD GIRLS SAY THESE KINDS OF THINGS TO HIM.

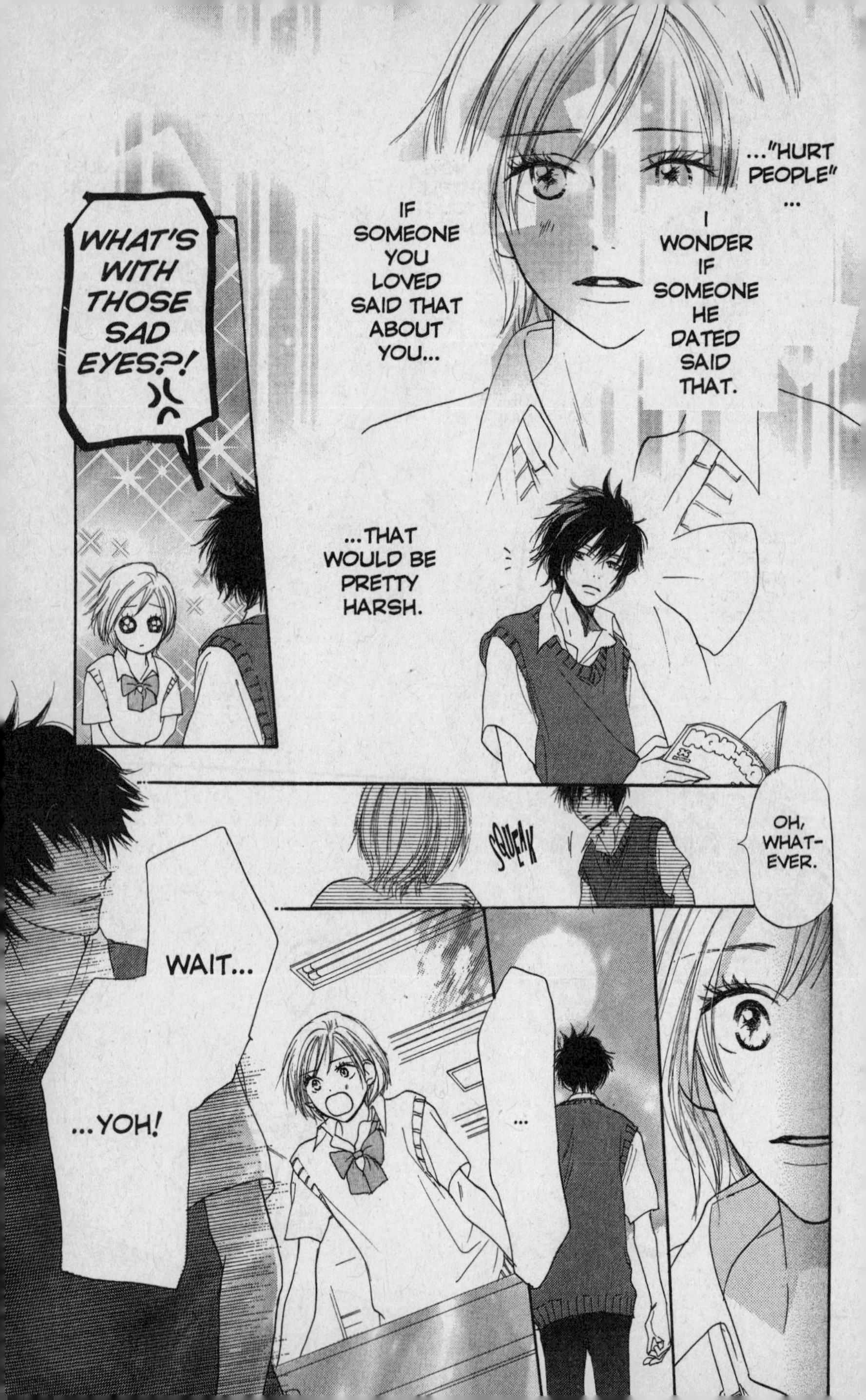
..."HURT PEOPLE"...
I WONDER IF SOMEONE HE DATED SAID THAT.
IF SOMEONE YOU LOVED SAID THAT ABOUT YOU...
...THAT WOULD BE PRETTY HARSH.
WHAT'S WITH THOSE SAD EYES?!
OH, WHAT-EVER.
SQUEAK
...
WAIT...
...YOH!

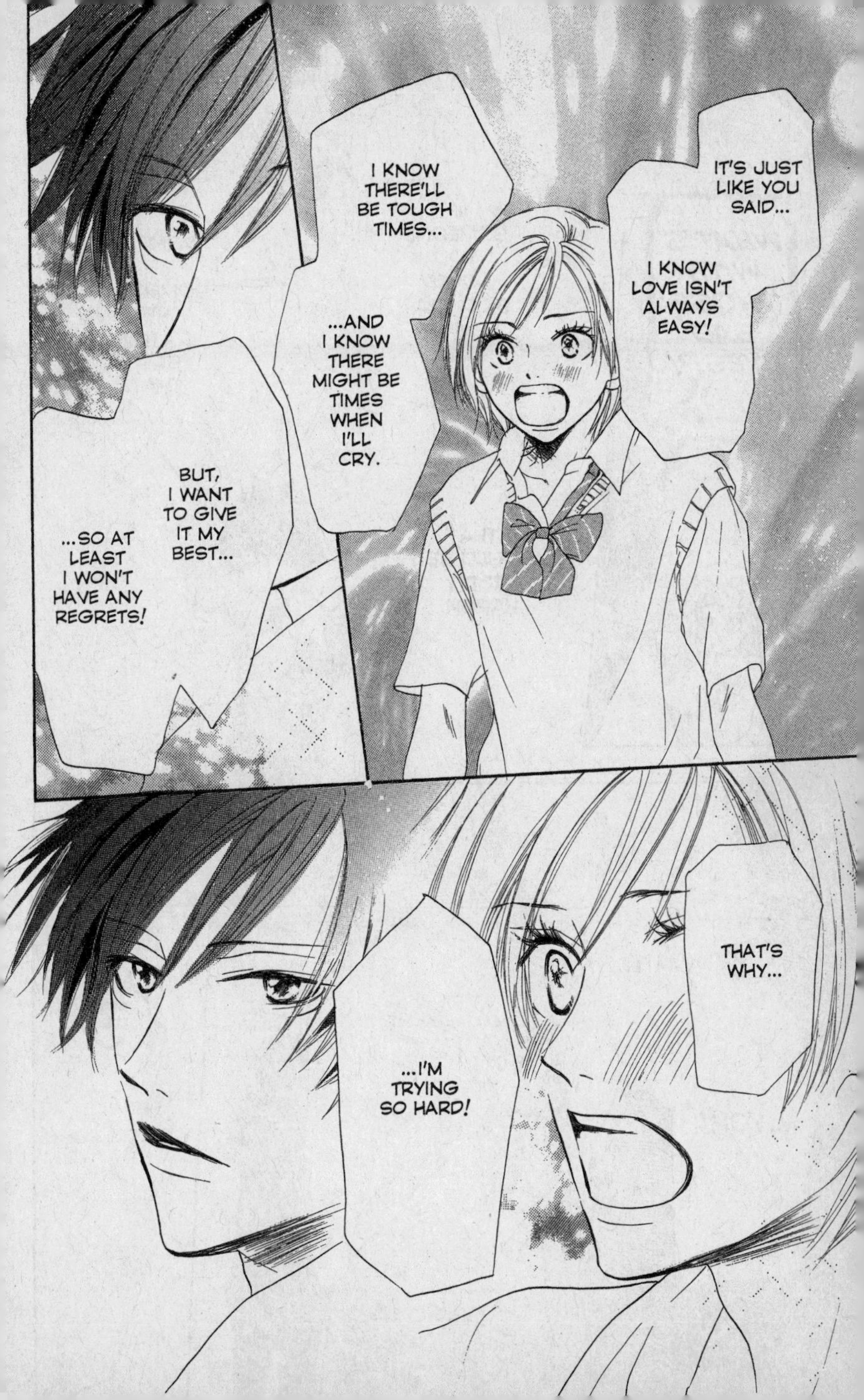
IT'S JUST LIKE YOU SAID...
I KNOW LOVE ISN'T ALWAYS EASY!
I KNOW THERE'LL BE TOUGH TIMES...
...AND I KNOW THERE MIGHT BE TIMES WHEN I'LL CRY.
BUT, I WANT TO GIVE IT MY BEST...
...SO AT LEAST I WON'T HAVE ANY REGRETS!
THAT'S WHY...
...I'M TRYING SO HARD!

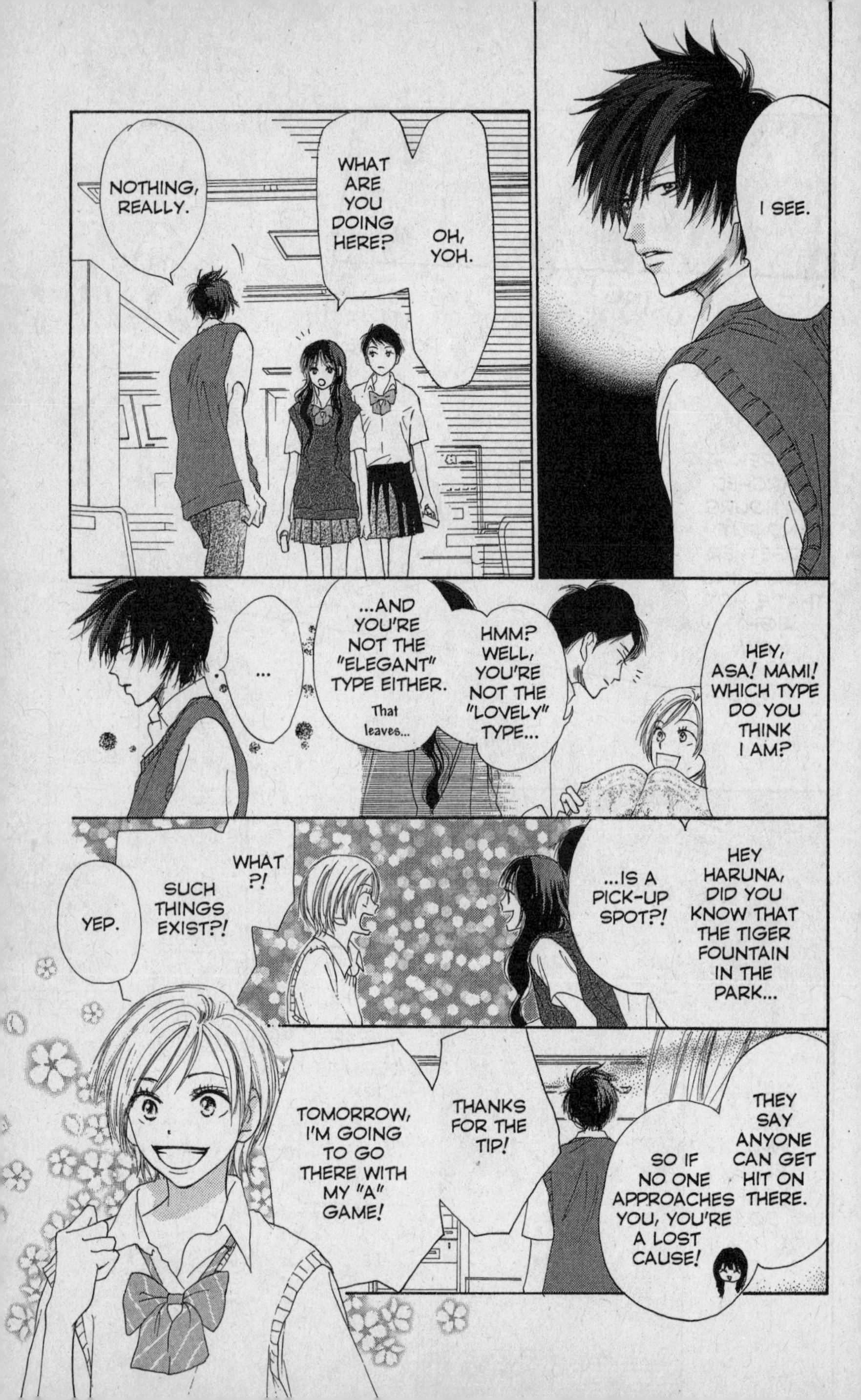
I SEE.
OH, YOH.
WHAT ARE YOU DOING HERE?
NOTHING, REALLY.
HEY, ASA! MAMI! WHICH TYPE DO YOU THINK I AM?
HMM? WELL, YOU'RE NOT THE "LOVELY" TYPE...
...AND YOU'RE NOT THE "ELEGANT" TYPE EITHER.
That leaves...
...
HEY HARUNA, DID YOU KNOW THAT THE TIGER FOUNTAIN IN THE PARK...
...IS A PICK-UP SPOT?!
WHAT?!
SUCH THINGS EXIST?!
YEP.
THEY SAY ANYONE CAN GET HIT ON THERE.
SO IF NO ONE APPROACHES YOU, YOU'RE A LOST CAUSE!
THANKS FOR THE TIP!
TOMORROW, I'M GOING TO GO THERE WITH MY "A" GAME!

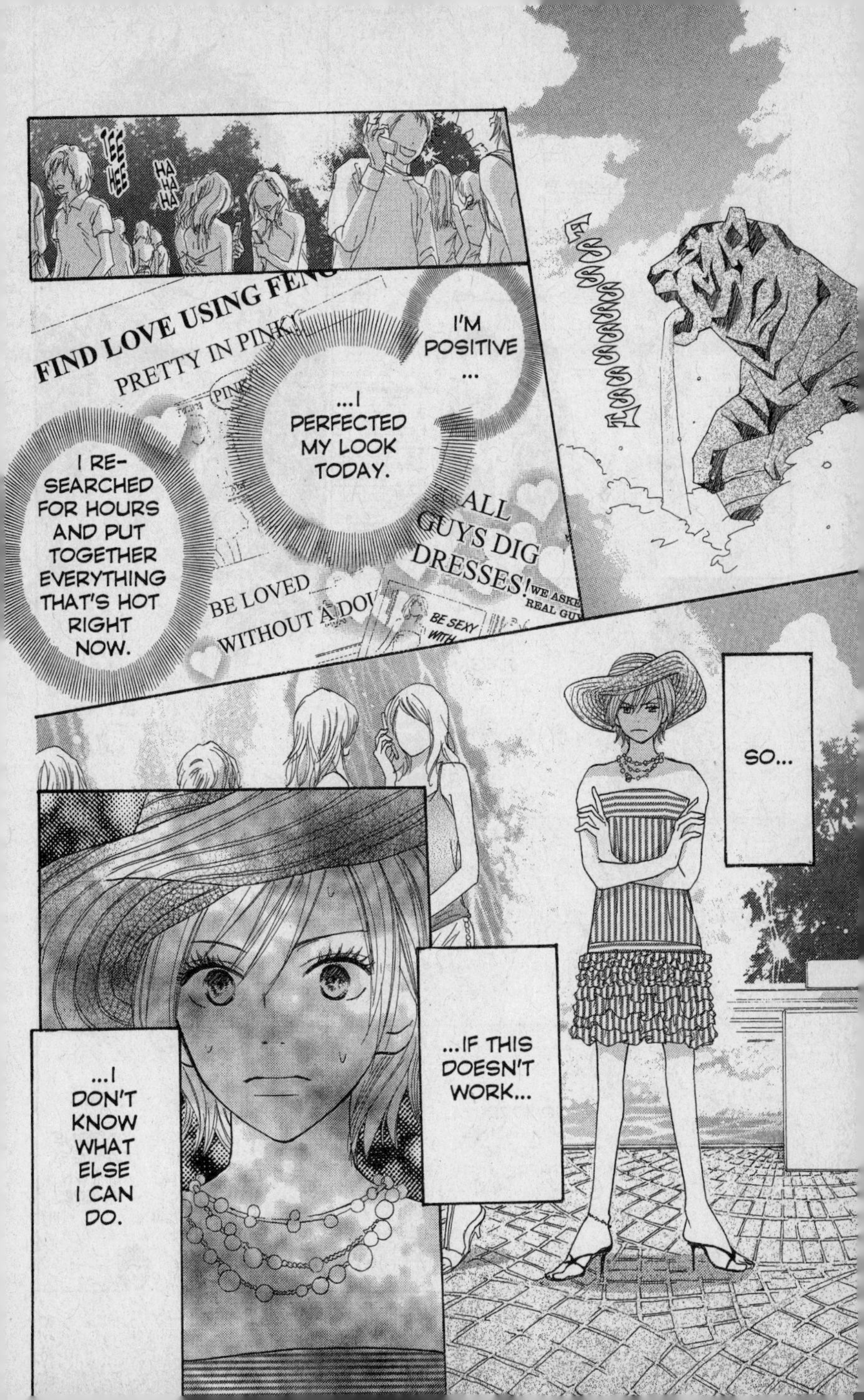
TEE HEE
HA HA HA
ALL GUYS DIG DRESSES!
WE ASKE
REAL GU
I'M POSITIVE...
...I PERFECTED MY LOOK TODAY.
FIND LOVE USING FEN
PRETTY IN PINK!
PINK
I RE-SEARCHED FOR HOURS AND PUT TOGETHER EVERYTHING THAT'S HOT RIGHT NOW.
BE LOVED
WITHOUT A DOU
BE SEXY WITH
SO...
...IF THIS DOESN'T WORK...
...I DON'T KNOW WHAT ELSE I CAN DO.

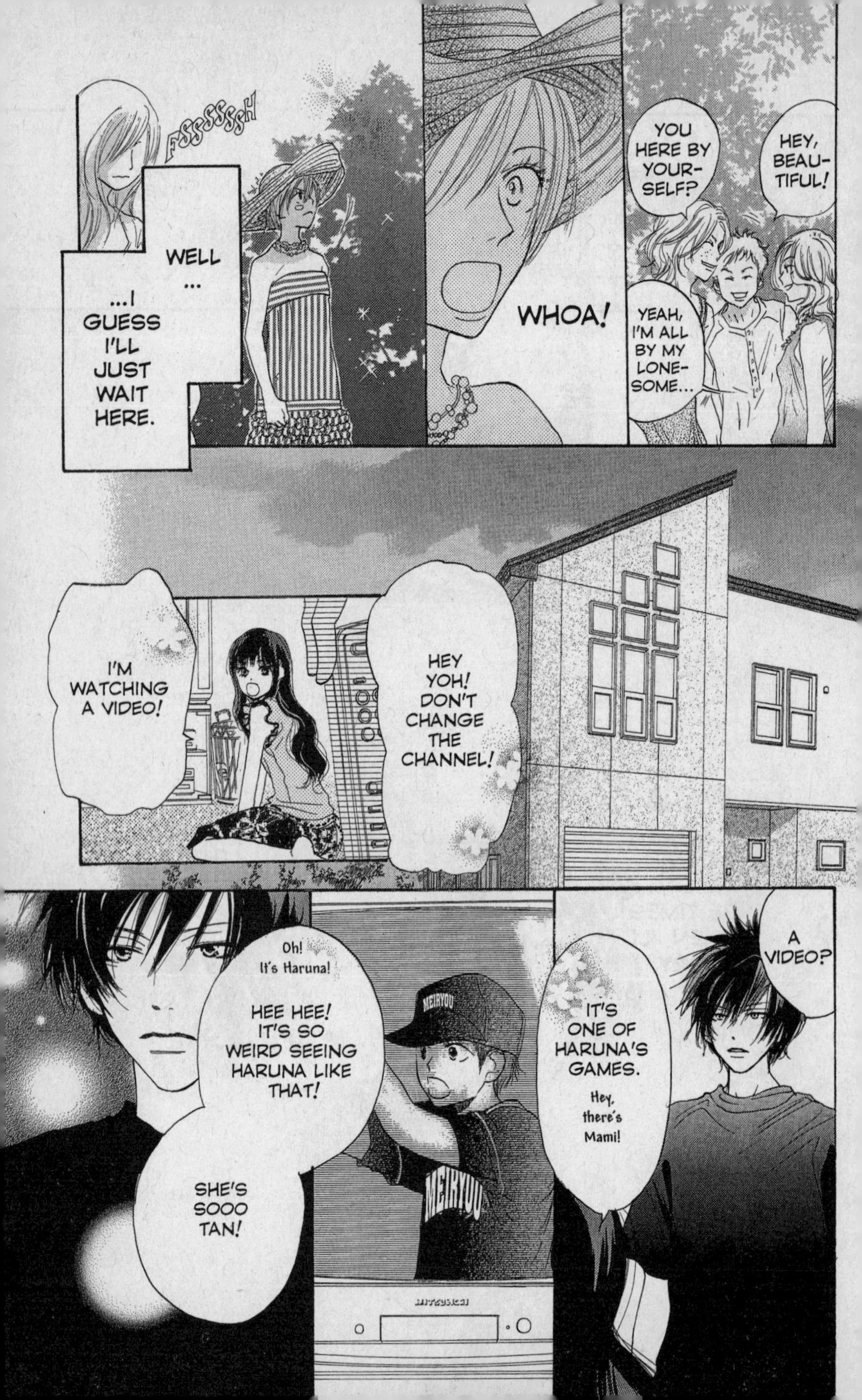
HEY, BEAUTIFUL!
YOU HERE BY YOURSELF?
YEAH, I'M ALL BY MY LONESOME...
WHOA!
FSSSSSSH
WELL ...
...I GUESS I'LL JUST WAIT HERE.
HEY YOH! DON'T CHANGE THE CHANNEL!
I'M WATCHING A VIDEO!
A VIDEO?
IT'S ONE OF HARUNA'S GAMES.
Hey, there's Mami!
Oh! It's Haruna!
HEE HEE! IT'S SO WEIRD SEEING HARUNA LIKE THAT!
SHE'S SOOO TAN!

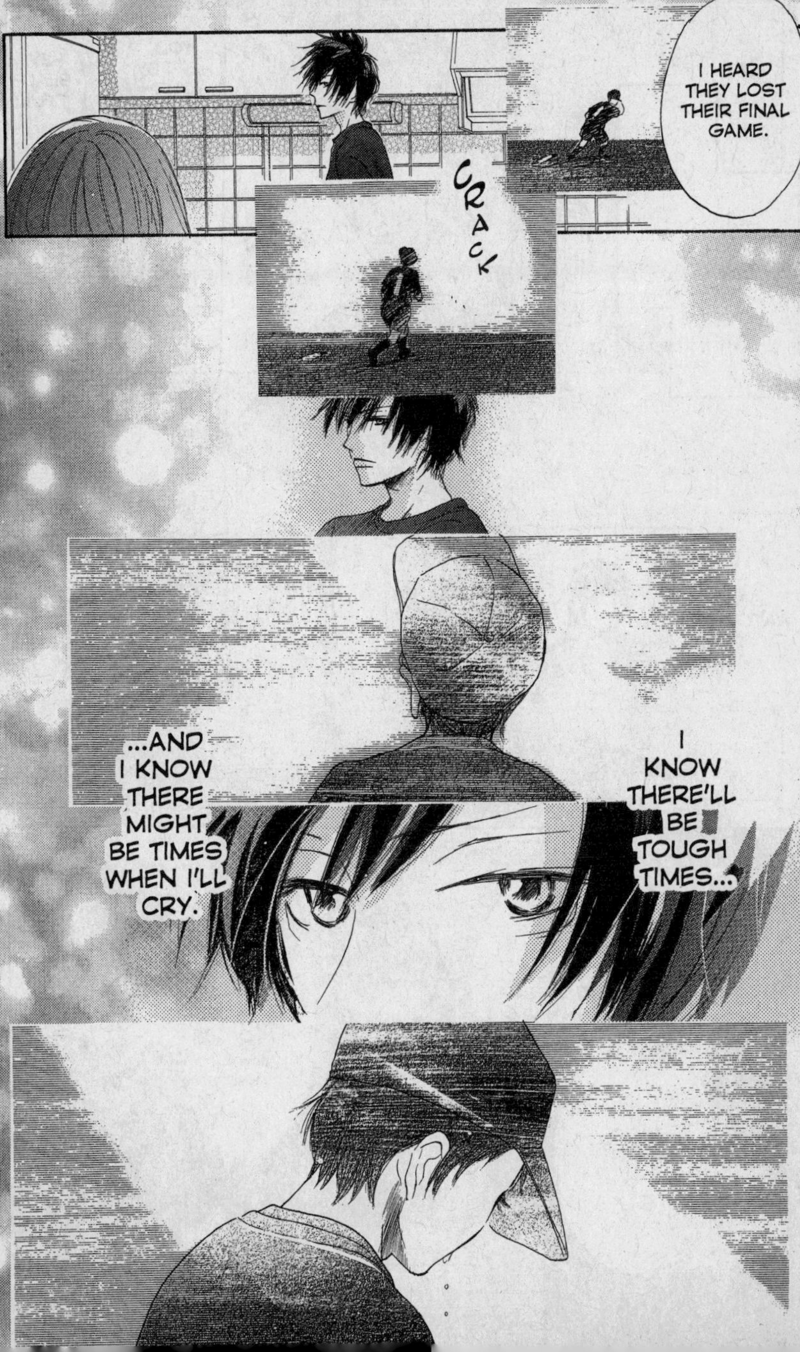
I HEARD THEY LOST THEIR FINAL GAME.
CRACK
I KNOW THERE'LL BE TOUGH TIMES...
...AND I KNOW THERE MIGHT BE TIMES WHEN I'LL CRY.

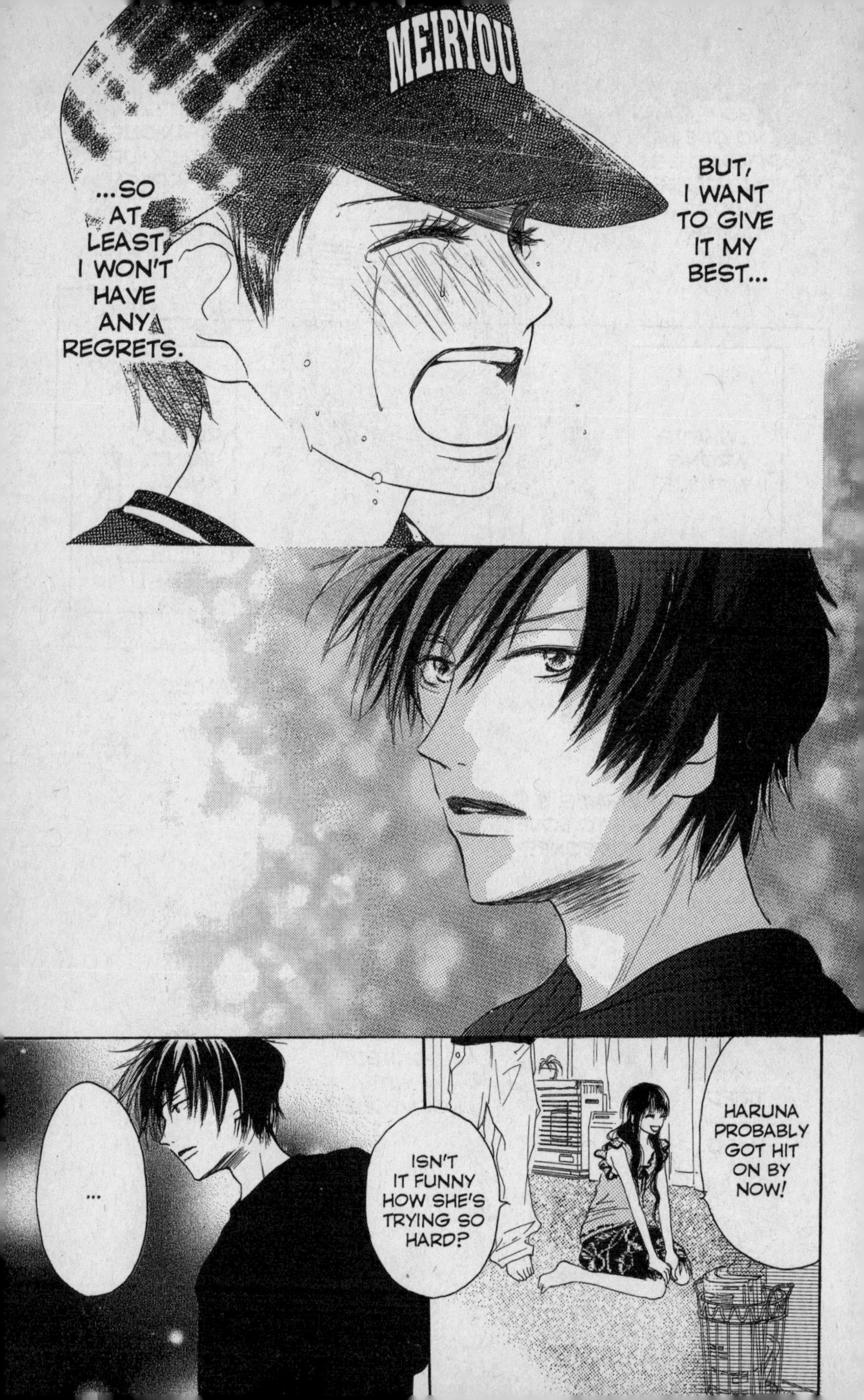
BUT, I WANT TO GIVE IT MY BEST...
...SO AT LEAST I WON'T HAVE ANY REGRETS.
HARUNA PROBABLY GOT HIT ON BY NOW!
ISN'T IT FUNNY HOW SHE'S TRYING SO HARD?
...

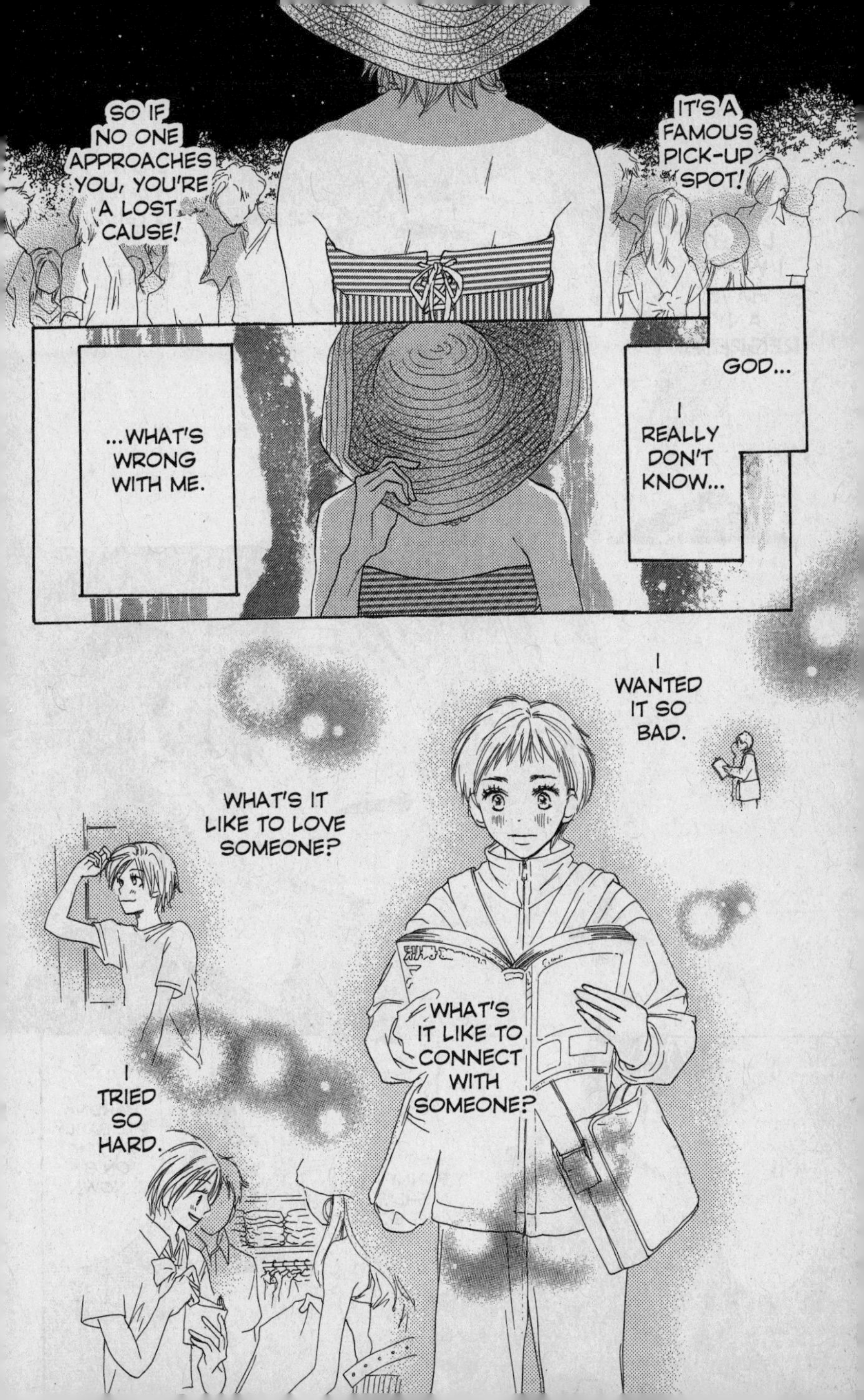
IT'S A FAMOUS PICK-UP SPOT!
SO IF NO ONE APPROACHES YOU, YOU'RE A LOST CAUSE!
GOD...
I REALLY DON'T KNOW...
...WHAT'S WRONG WITH ME.
I WANTED IT SO BAD.
WHAT'S IT LIKE TO LOVE SOMEONE?
WHAT'S IT LIKE TO CONNECT WITH SOMEONE?
I TRIED SO HARD.

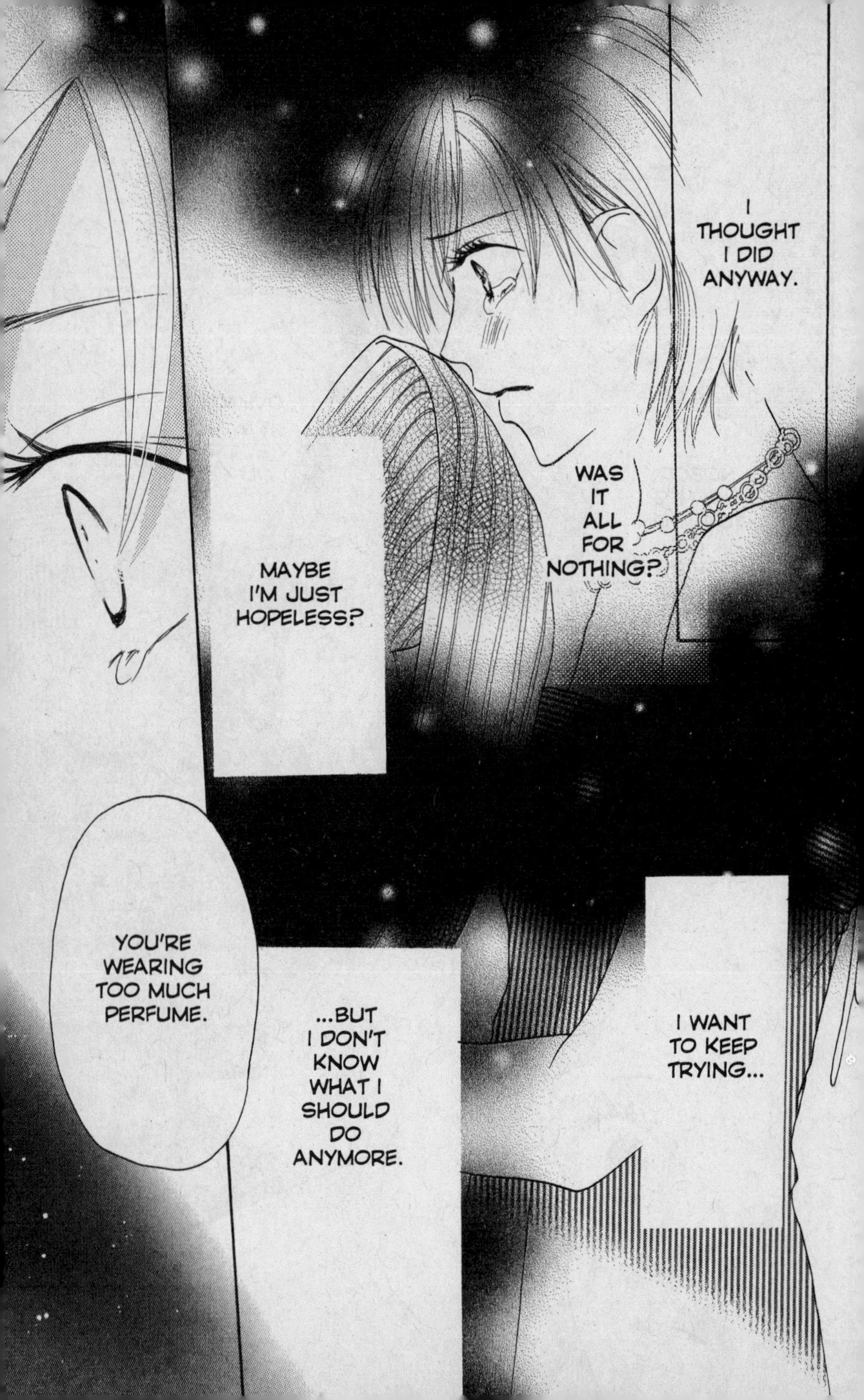
I THOUGHT I DID ANYWAY.
WAS IT ALL FOR NOTHING?
MAYBE I'M JUST HOPELESS?
I WANT TO KEEP TRYING...
...BUT I DON'T KNOW WHAT I SHOULD DO ANYMORE.
YOU'RE WEARING TOO MUCH PERFUME.

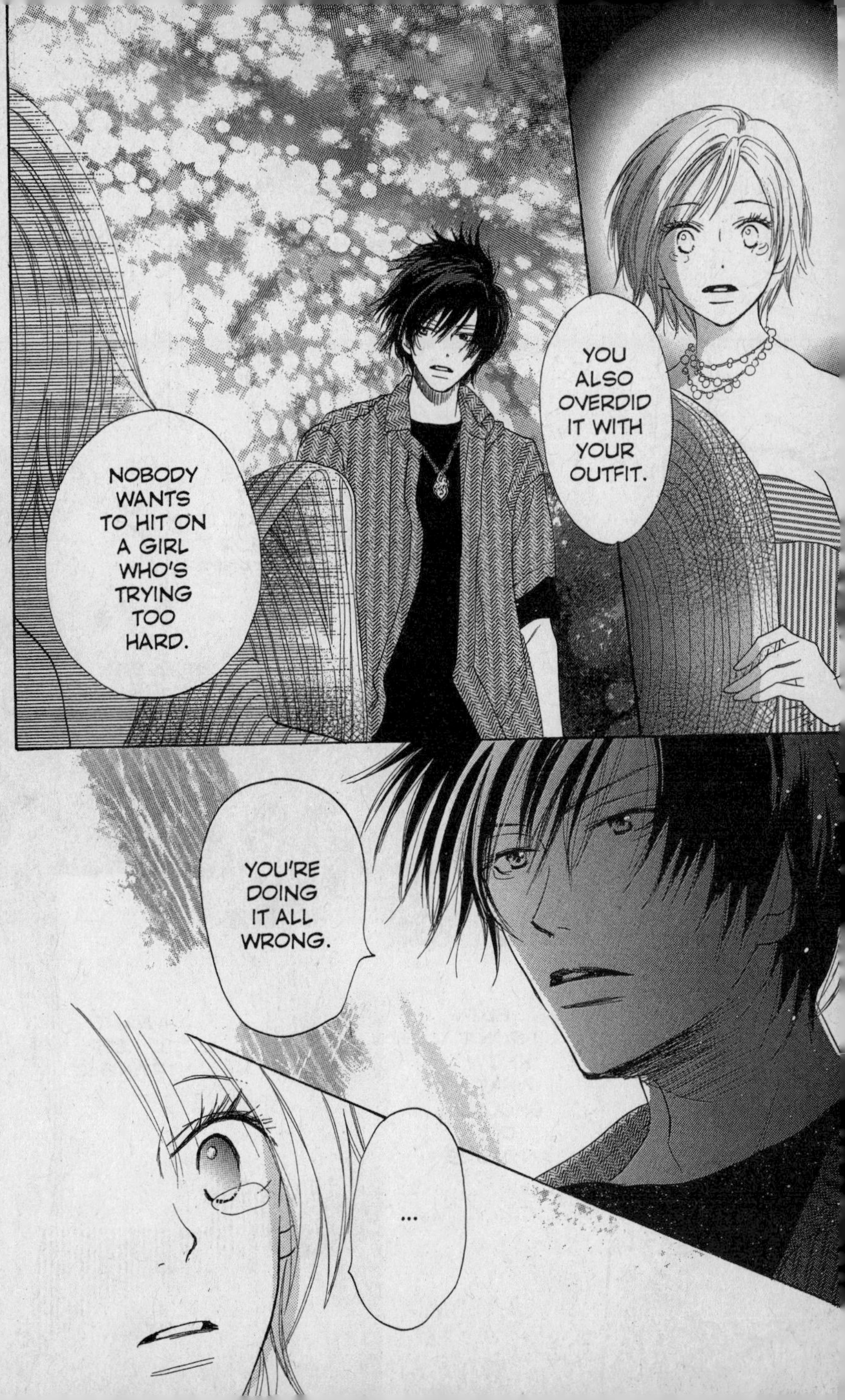
YOU ALSO OVERDID IT WITH YOUR OUTFIT.
NOBODY WANTS TO HIT ON A GIRL WHO'S TRYING TOO HARD.
YOU'RE DOING IT ALL WRONG.
...

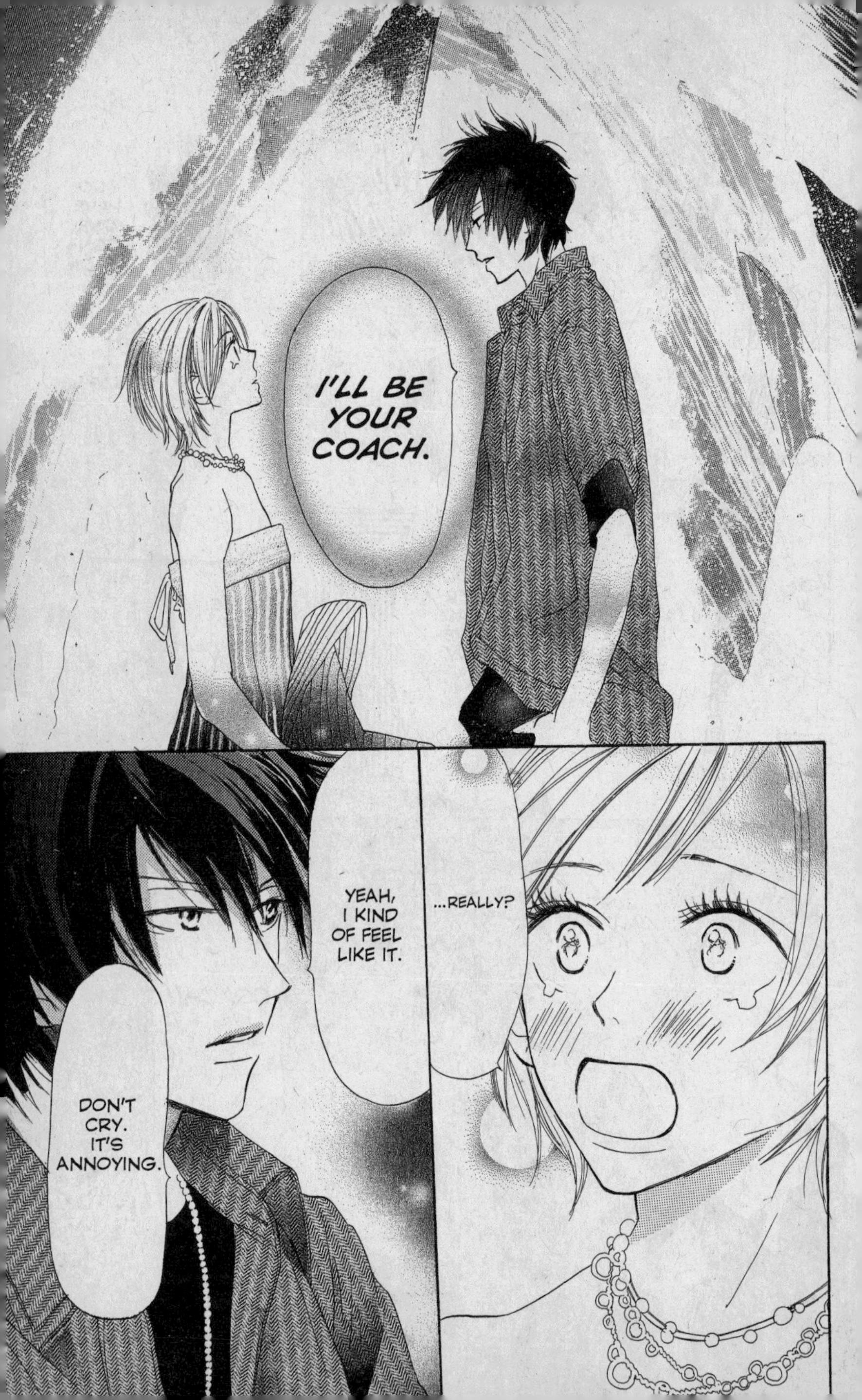
I'LL BE YOUR COACH.
...REALLY?
YEAH, I KIND OF FEEL LIKE IT.
DON'T CRY. IT'S ANNOYING.

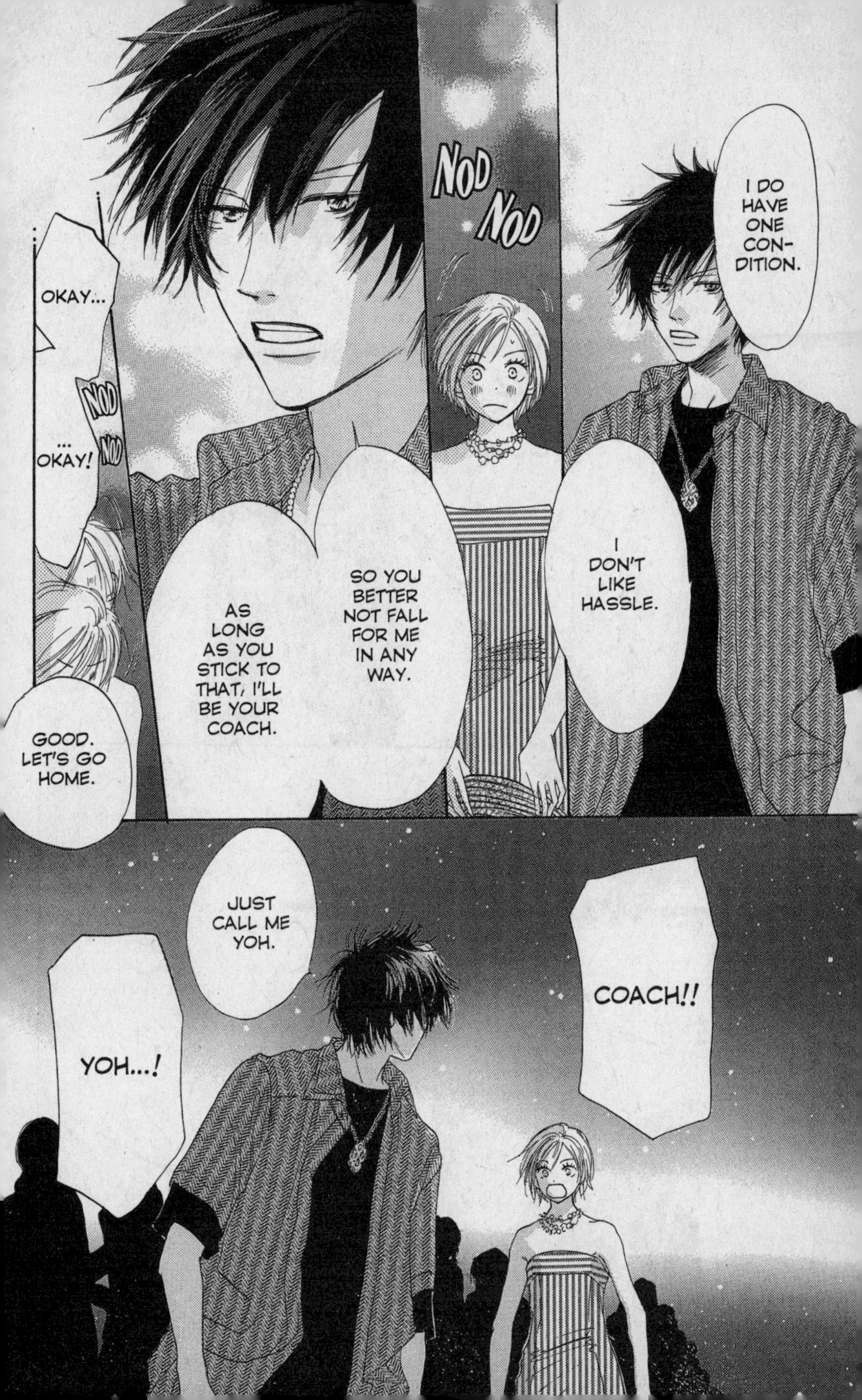
I DO HAVE ONE CON-DITION.
I DON'T LIKE HASSLE.
NOD NOD
SO YOU BETTER NOT FALL FOR ME IN ANY WAY.
AS LONG AS YOU STICK TO THAT, I'LL BE YOUR COACH.
OKAY...
NOD NOD
...OKAY!
GOOD. LET'S GO HOME.
COACH!!
JUST CALL ME YOH.
YOH...!

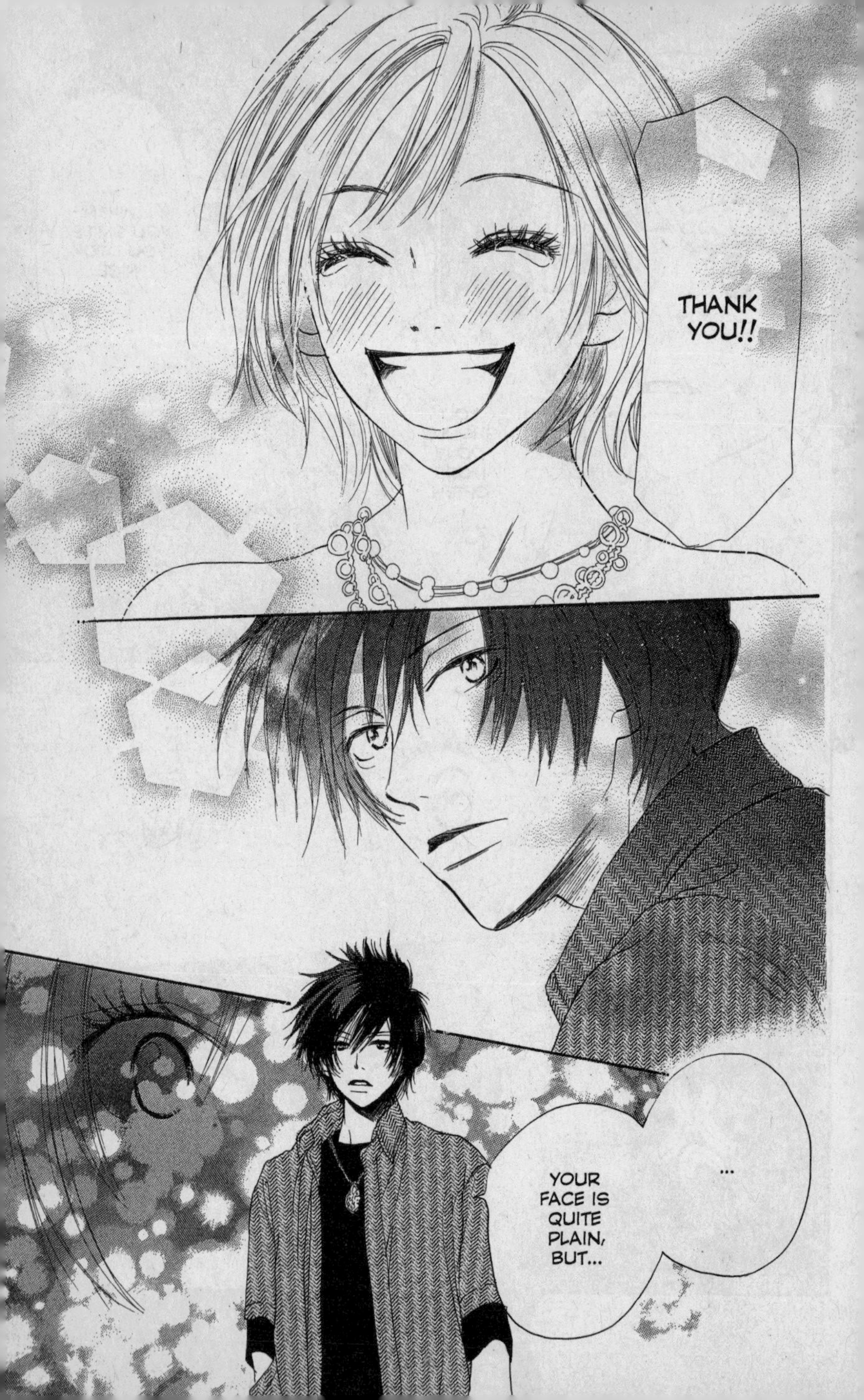
THANK YOU!!
...
YOUR FACE IS QUITE PLAIN, BUT...

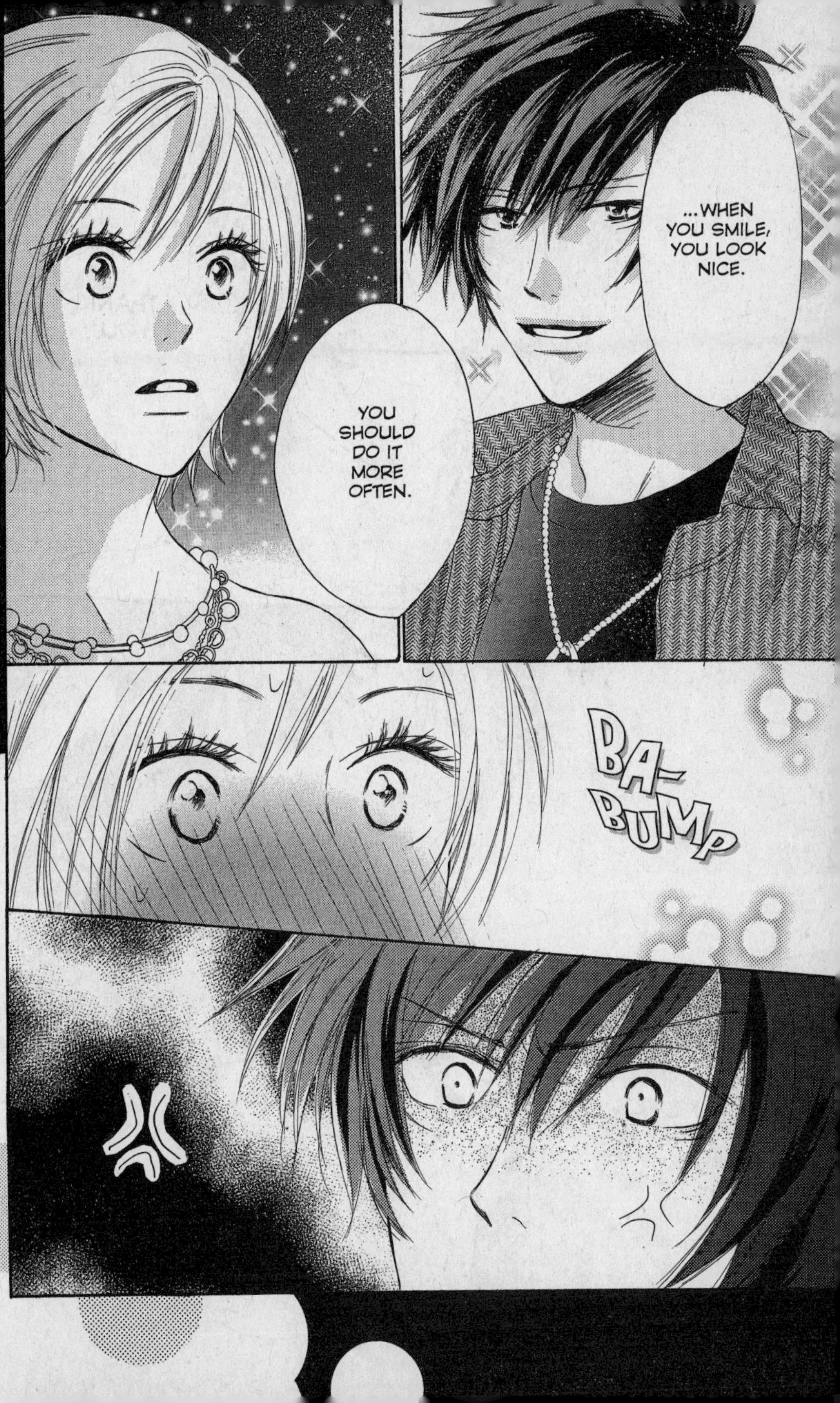
...WHEN YOU SMILE, YOU LOOK NICE.
YOU SHOULD DO IT MORE OFTEN.
BA-BUMP

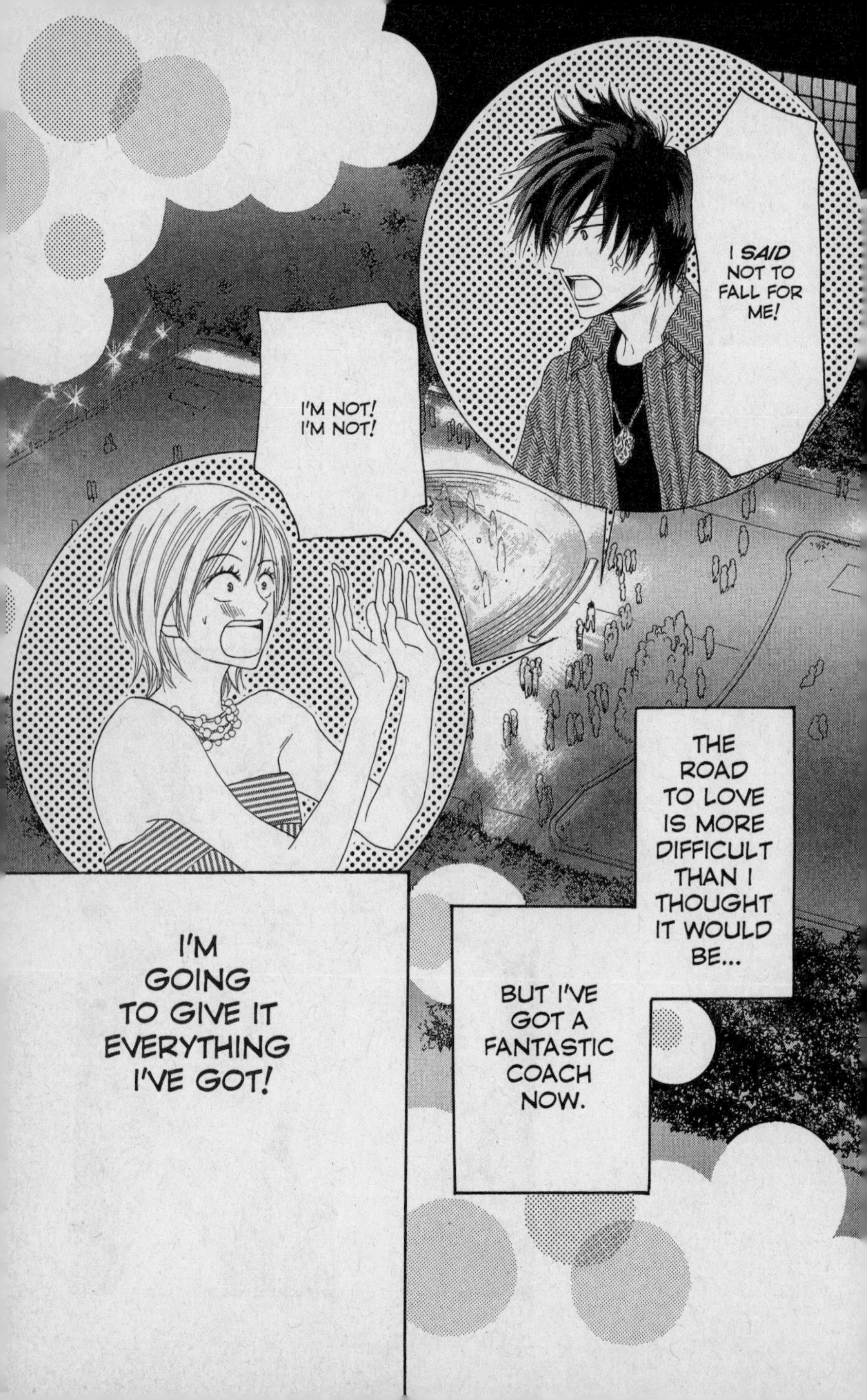
I SAID NOT TO FALL FOR ME!
I'M NOT! I'M NOT!
THE ROAD TO LOVE IS MORE DIFFICULT THAN I THOUGHT IT WOULD BE...
BUT I'VE GOT A FANTASTIC COACH NOW.
I'M GOING TO GIVE IT EVERYTHING I'VE GOT!

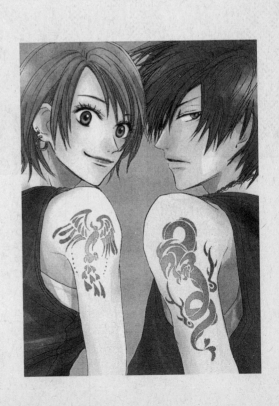

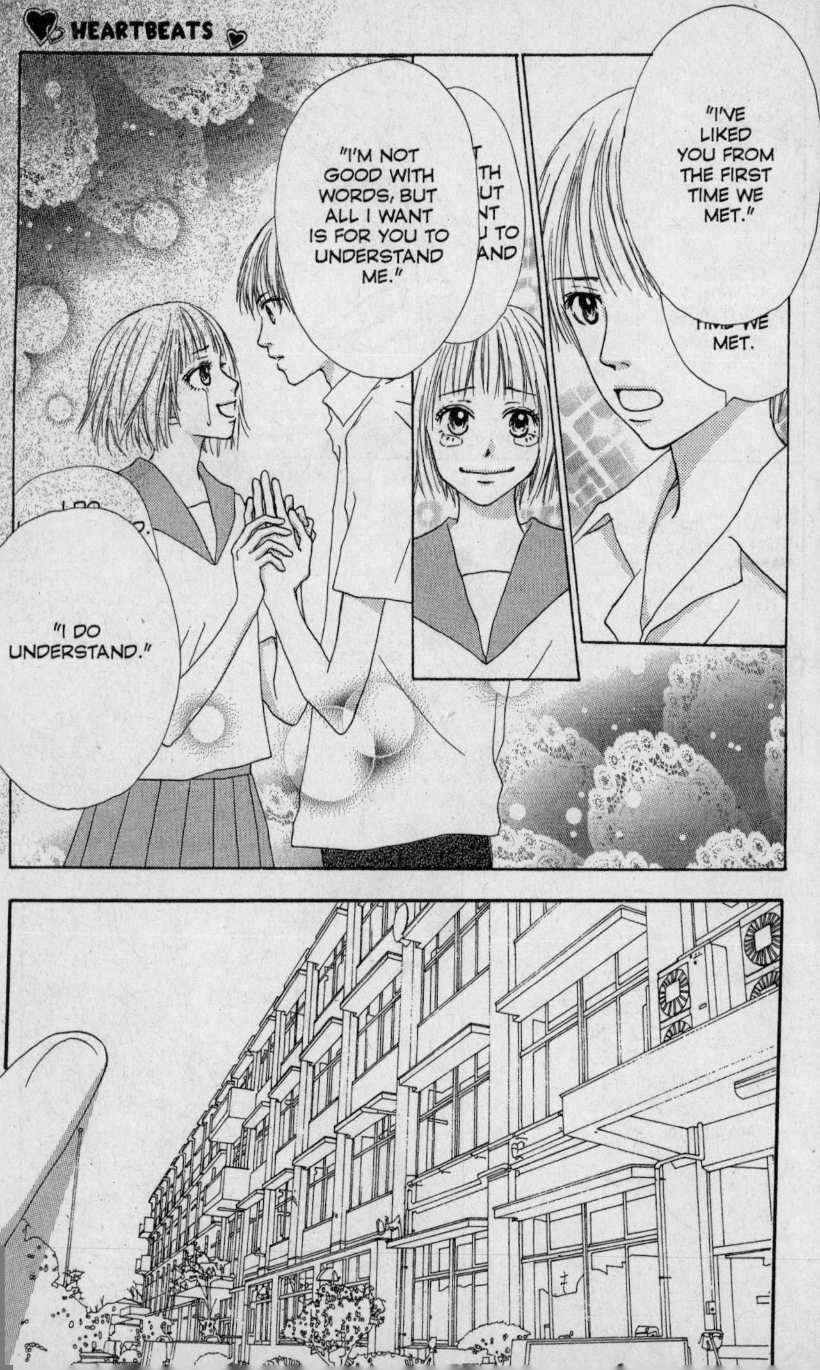
"I'VE LIKED YOU FROM THE FIRST TIME WE MET."
"I'M NOT GOOD WITH WORDS, BUT ALL I WANT IS FOR YOU TO UNDERSTAND ME."
"I DO UNDERSTAND."

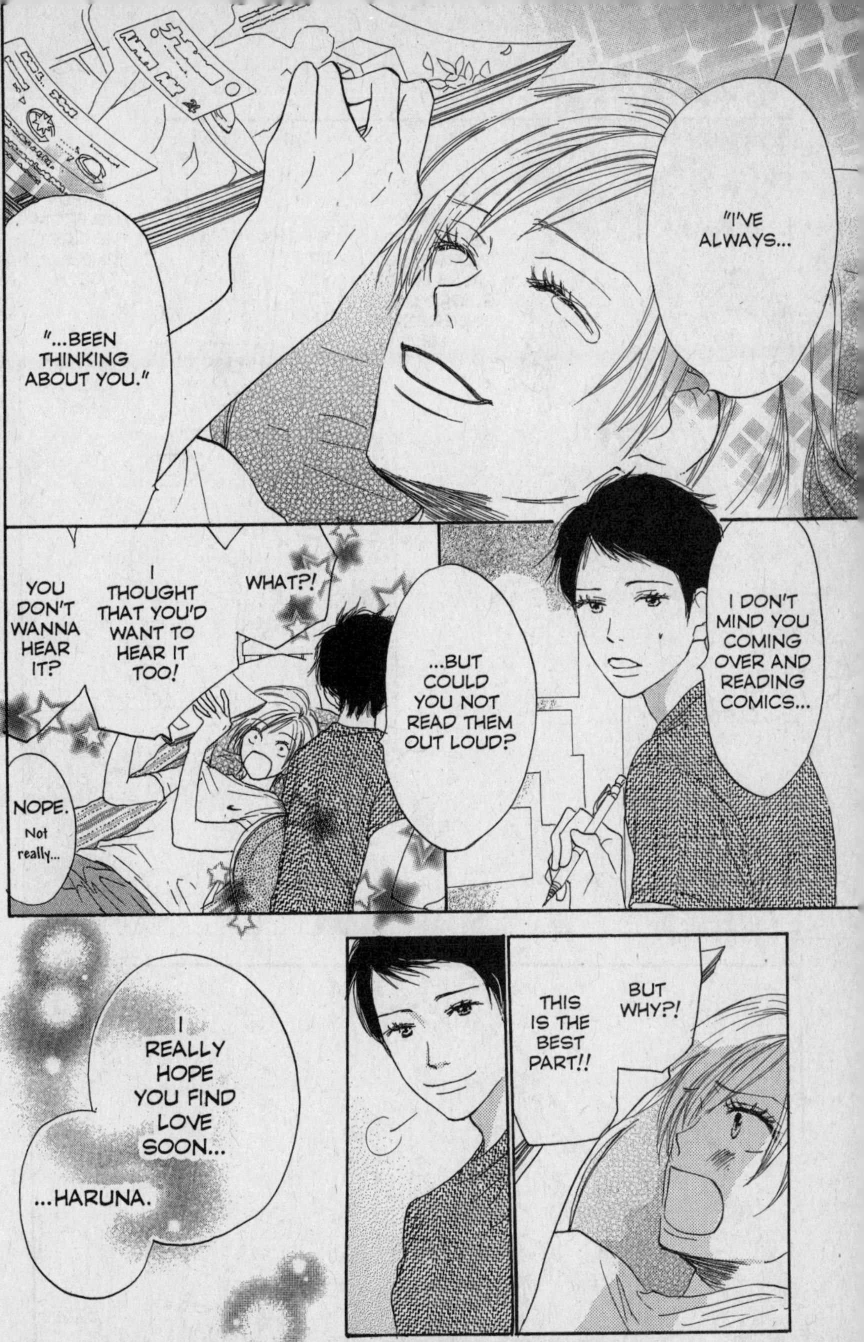
"I'VE ALWAYS...
"...BEEN THINKING ABOUT YOU."
I DON'T MIND YOU COMING OVER AND READING COMICS...
...BUT COULD YOU NOT READ THEM OUT LOUD?
WHAT?!
I THOUGHT THAT YOU'D WANT TO HEAR IT TOO!
YOU DON'T WANNA HEAR IT?
NOPE.
Not really...
BUT WHY?!
THIS IS THE BEST PART!!
I REALLY HOPE YOU FIND LOVE SOON...
...HARUNA.

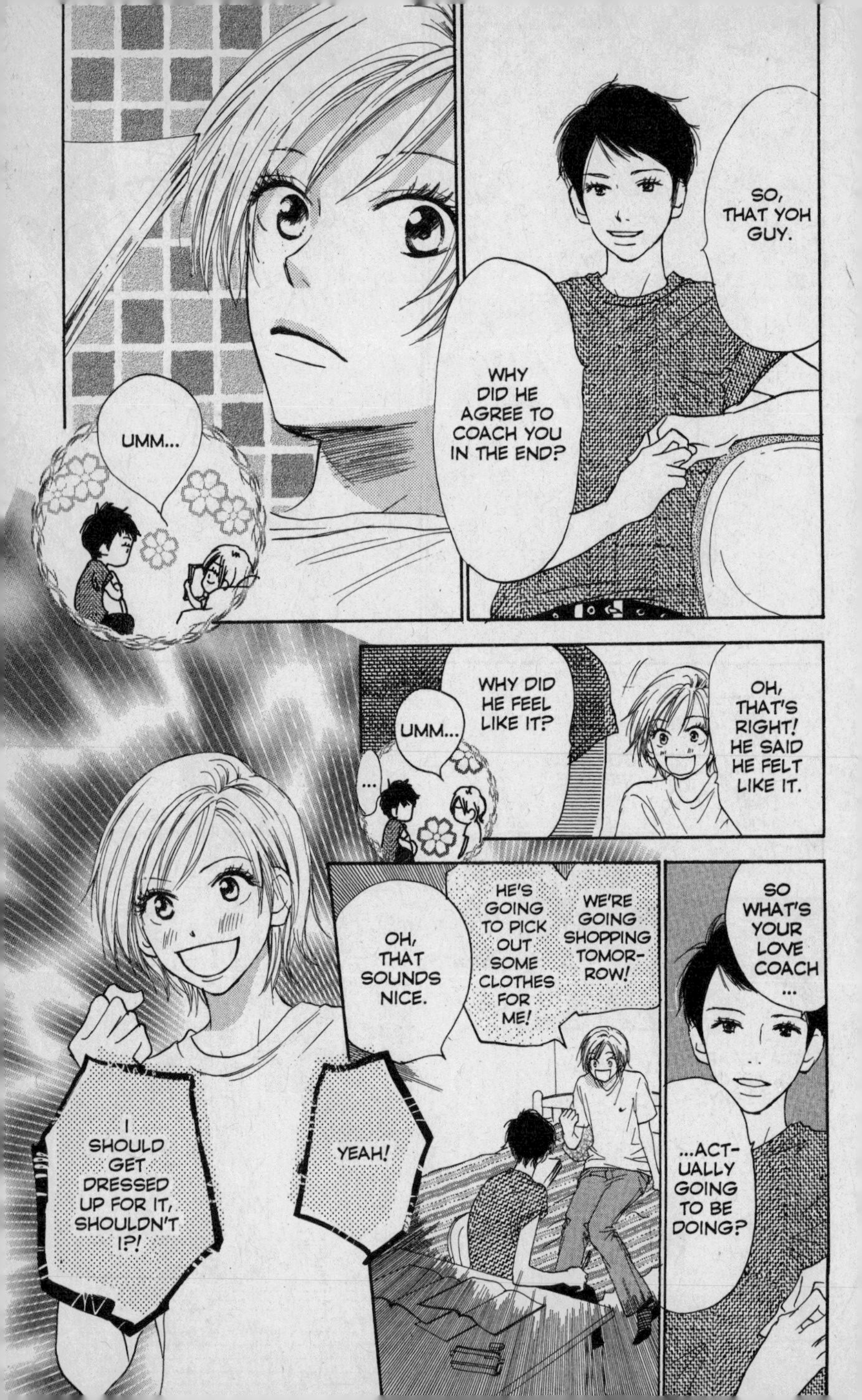
SO, THAT YOH GUY.
WHY DID HE AGREE TO COACH YOU IN THE END?
UMM...
OH, THAT'S RIGHT! HE SAID HE FELT LIKE IT.
WHY DID HE FEEL LIKE IT?
UMM...
...
SO WHAT'S YOUR LOVE COACH ...
...ACTUALLY GOING TO BE DOING?
WE'RE GOING SHOPPING TOMORROW!
HE'S GOING TO PICK OUT SOME CLOTHES FOR ME!
OH, THAT SOUNDS NICE.
YEAH!
I SHOULD GET DRESSED UP FOR IT, SHOULDN'T I?!

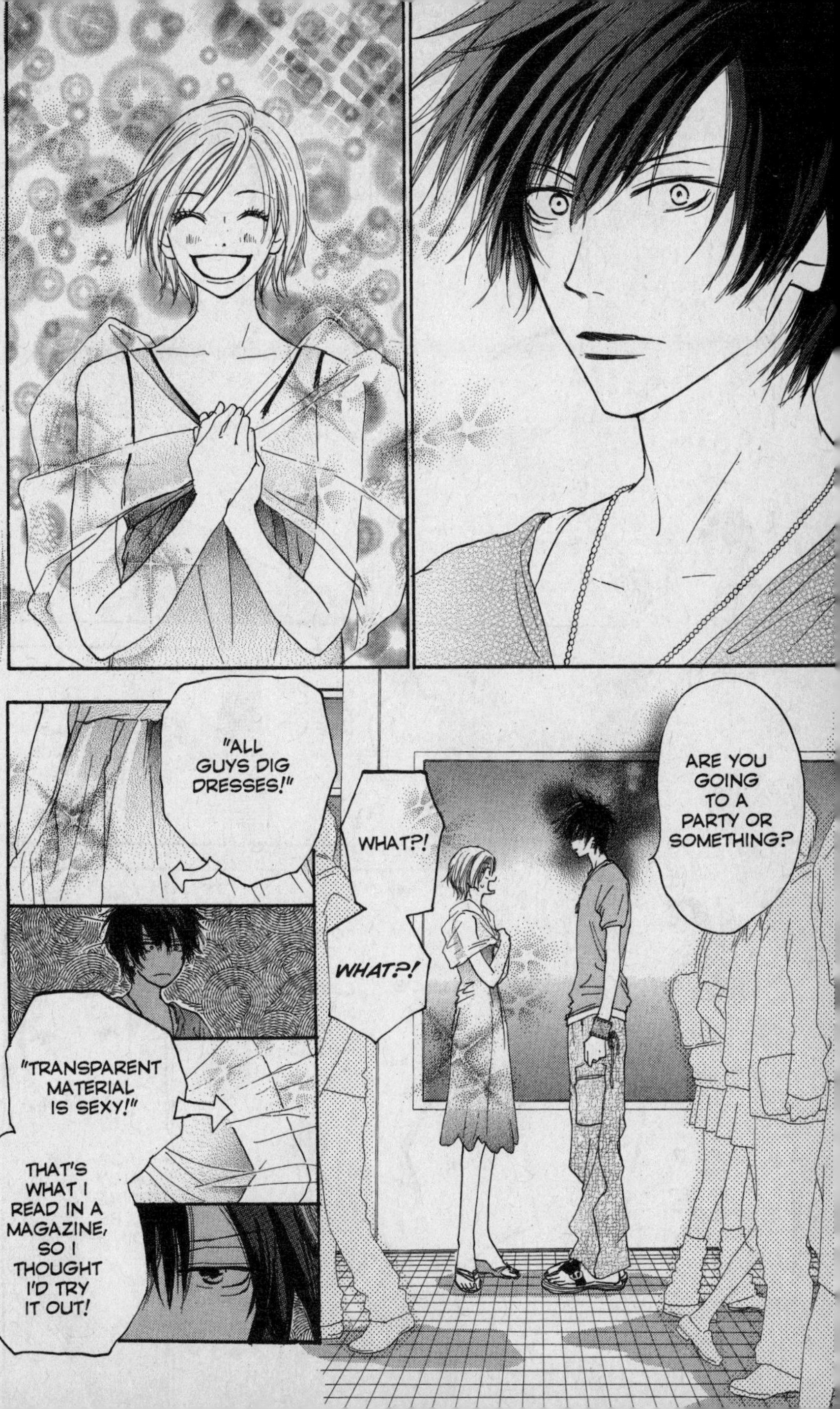
ARE YOU GOING TO A PARTY OR SOMETHING?
WHAT?!
WHAT?!
"ALL GUYS DIG DRESSES!"
"TRANSPARENT MATERIAL IS SEXY!"
THAT'S WHAT I READ IN A MAGAZINE, SO I THOUGHT I'D TRY IT OUT!

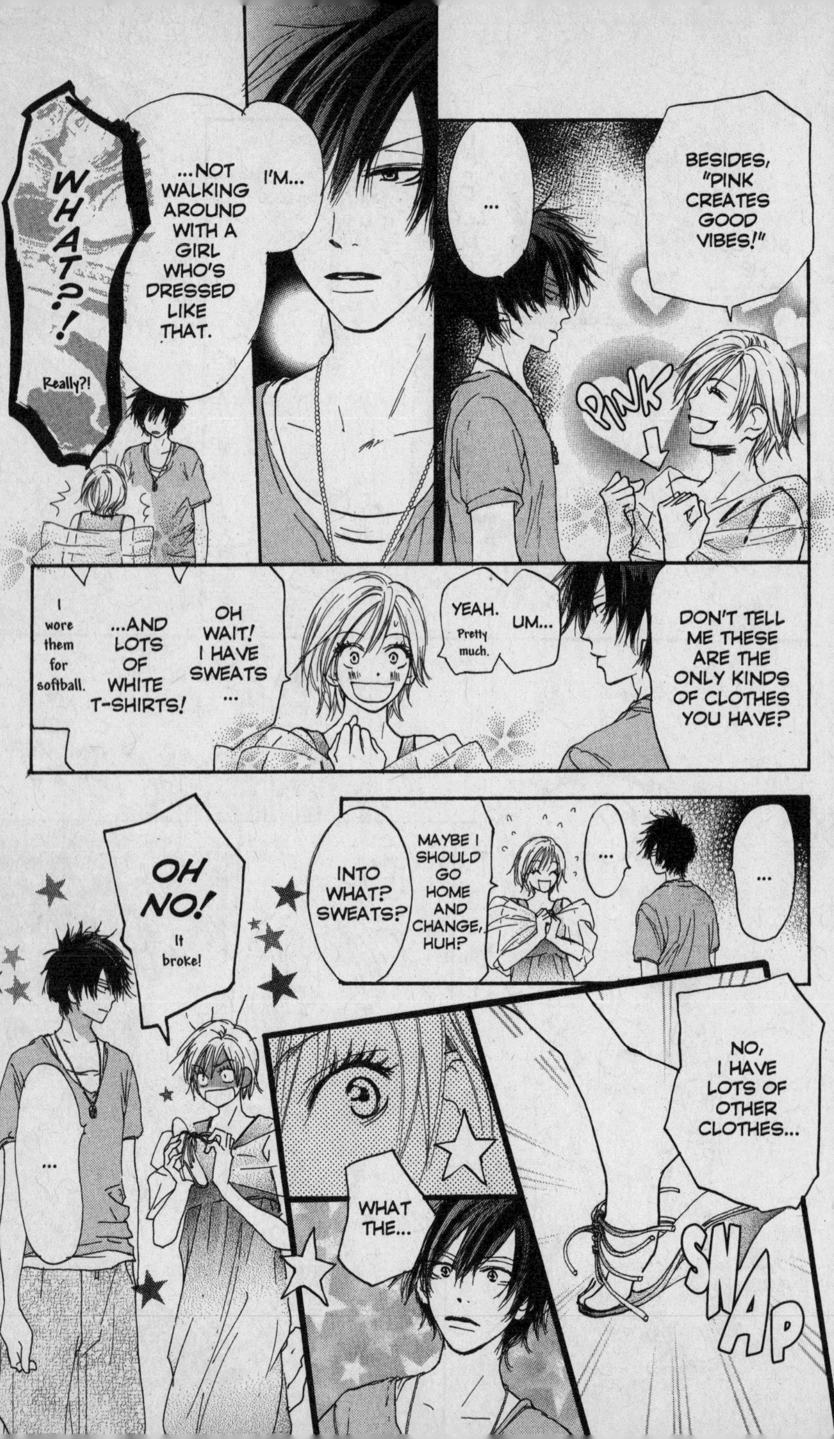
BESIDES, "PINK CREATES GOOD VIBES!"
...
PINK
I'M...
...NOT WALKING AROUND WITH A GIRL WHO'S DRESSED LIKE THAT.
WHAT?!
Really?!
DON'T TELL ME THESE ARE THE ONLY KINDS OF CLOTHES YOU HAVE?
UM...
YEAH.
Pretty much.
OH WAIT! I HAVE SWEATS ...
...AND LOTS OF WHITE T-SHIRTS!
I wore them for softball.
...
...
MAYBE I SHOULD GO HOME AND CHANGE, HUH?
INTO WHAT? SWEATS?
NO, I HAVE LOTS OF OTHER CLOTHES...
SNAP
WHAT THE...
OH NO!
It broke!
...

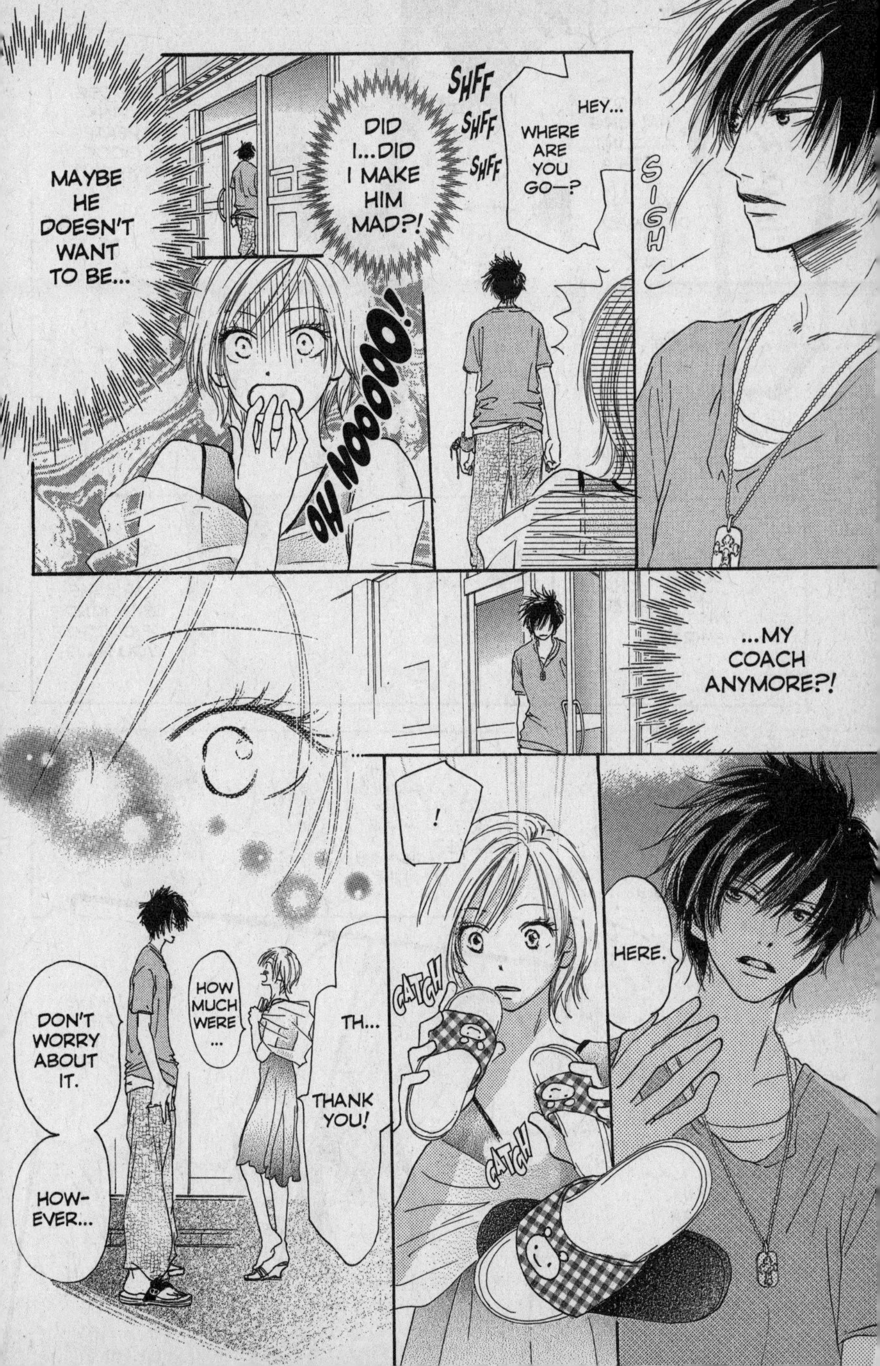
HEY... WHERE ARE YOU GO—?
SIGH
SHFF
SHFF
SHFF
DID I...DID I MAKE HIM MAD?!
OH NOOOOO!
MAYBE HE DOESN'T WANT TO BE...
...MY COACH ANYMORE?!
HERE.
!
CATCH
CATCH
TH...
THANK YOU!
HOW MUCH WERE ...
DON'T WORRY ABOUT IT.
HOW-EVER...

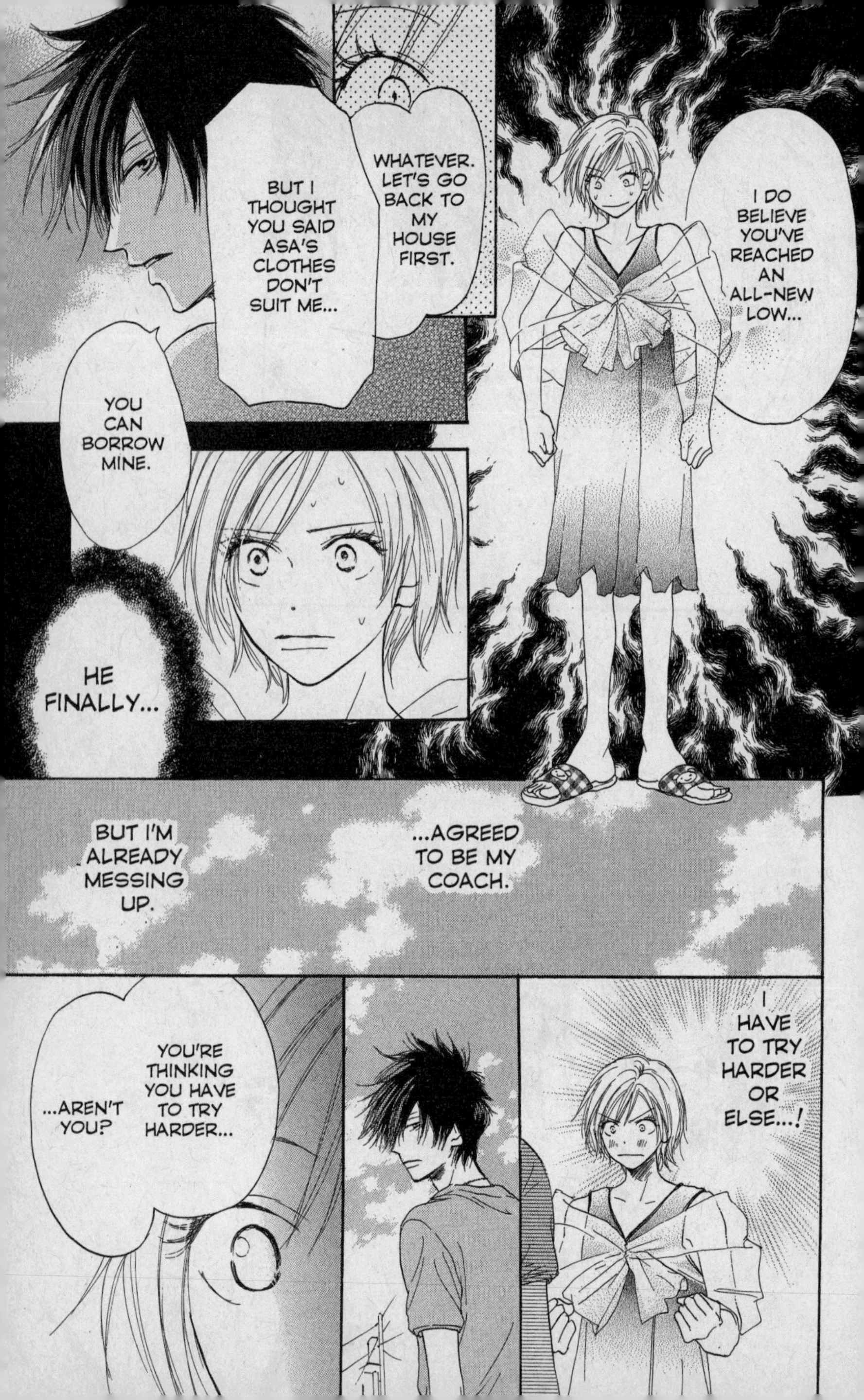
I DO BELIEVE YOU'VE REACHED AN ALL-NEW LOW...
WHATEVER. LET'S GO BACK TO MY HOUSE FIRST.
BUT I THOUGHT YOU SAID ASA'S CLOTHES DON'T SUIT ME...
YOU CAN BORROW MINE.
HE FINALLY...
...AGREED TO BE MY COACH.
BUT I'M ALREADY MESSING UP.
I HAVE TO TRY HARDER OR ELSE...!
YOU'RE THINKING YOU HAVE TO TRY HARDER...
...AREN'T YOU?

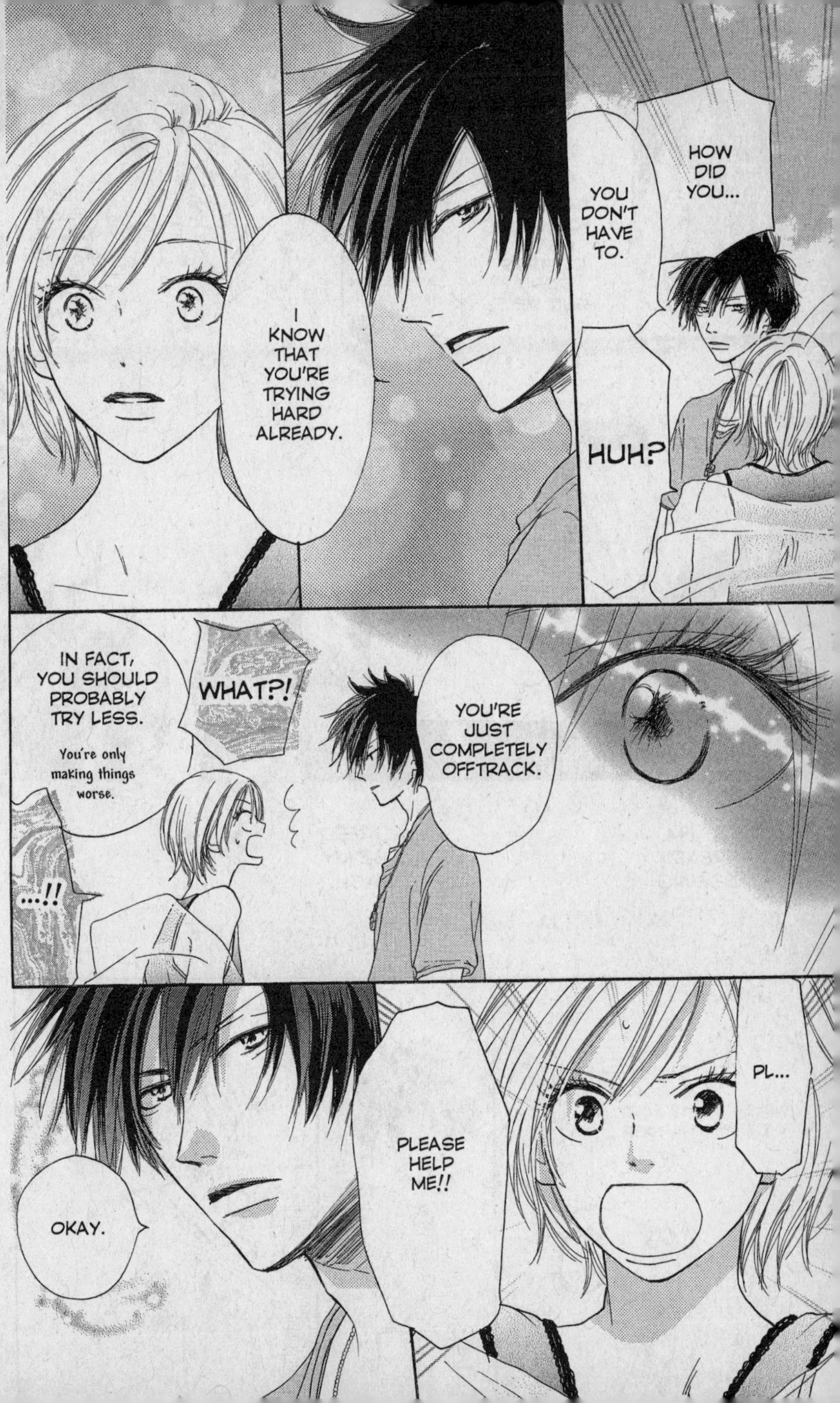
HOW DID YOU...
YOU DON'T HAVE TO.
HUH?
I KNOW THAT YOU'RE TRYING HARD ALREADY.
YOU'RE JUST COMPLETELY OFFTRACK.
WHAT?!
IN FACT, YOU SHOULD PROBABLY TRY LESS.
You're only making things worse.
...!!
PL...
PLEASE HELP ME!!
OKAY.

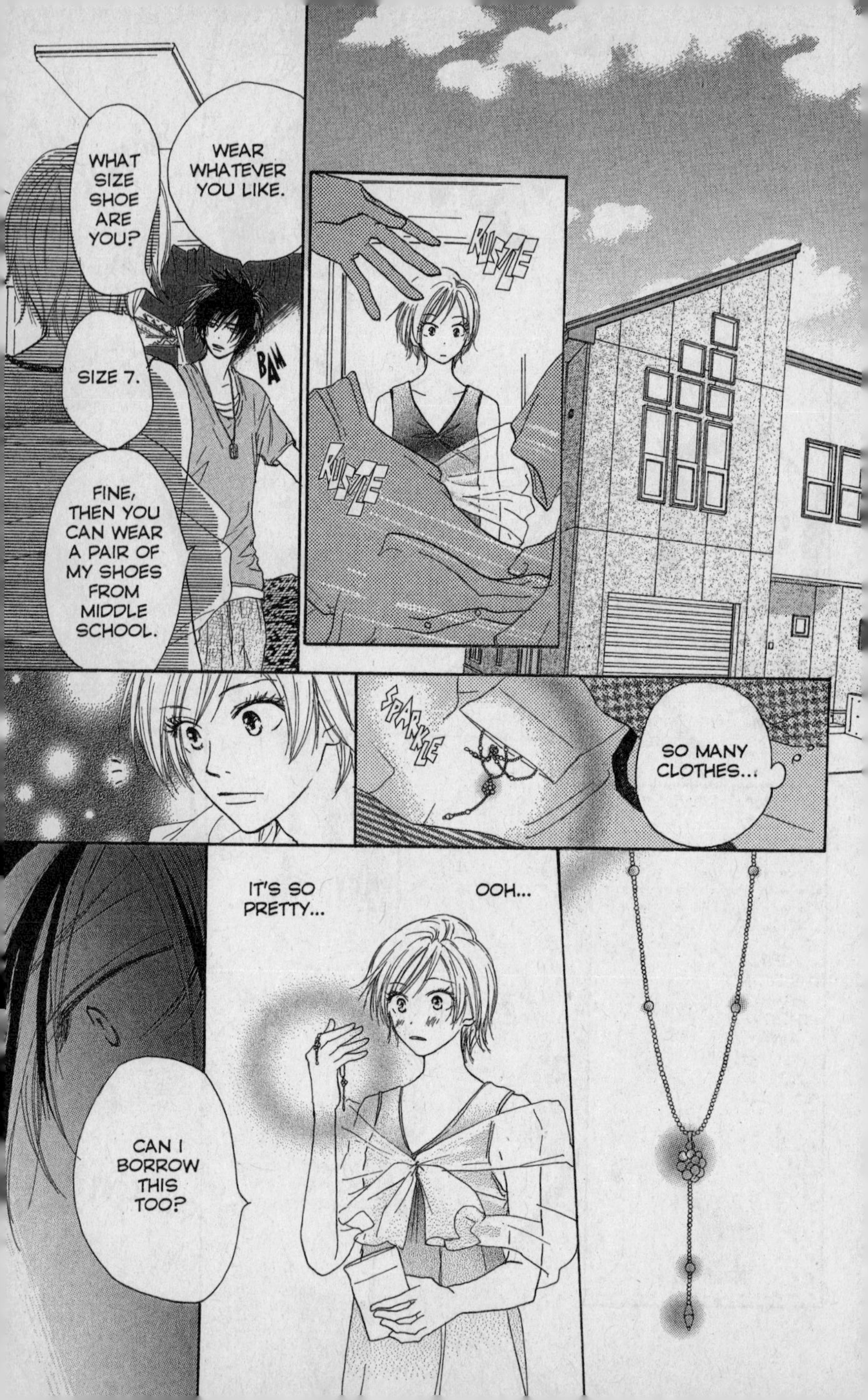
RUSTLE
RUSTLE
WEAR WHATEVER YOU LIKE.
WHAT SIZE SHOE ARE YOU?
BAM
SIZE 7.
FINE, THEN YOU CAN WEAR A PAIR OF MY SHOES FROM MIDDLE SCHOOL.
SO MANY CLOTHES...
SPARKLE
OOH...
IT'S SO PRETTY...
CAN I BORROW THIS TOO?

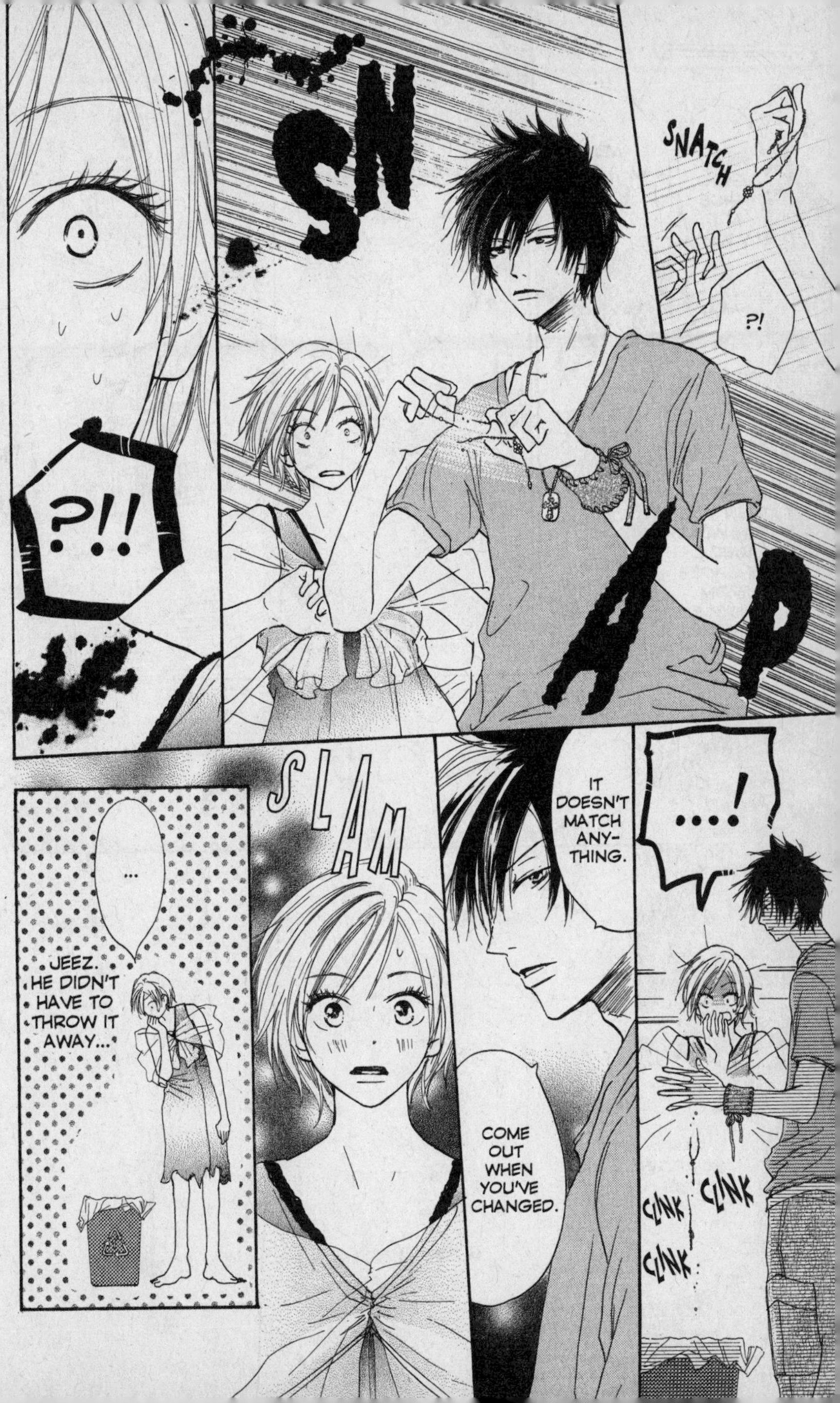
SNATCH
?!
SNAP
?!!
...!
CLINK
CLINK
CLINK
IT DOESN'T MATCH ANY-THING.
COME OUT WHEN YOU'VE CHANGED.
SLAM
...
JEEZ. HE DIDN'T HAVE TO THROW IT AWAY...

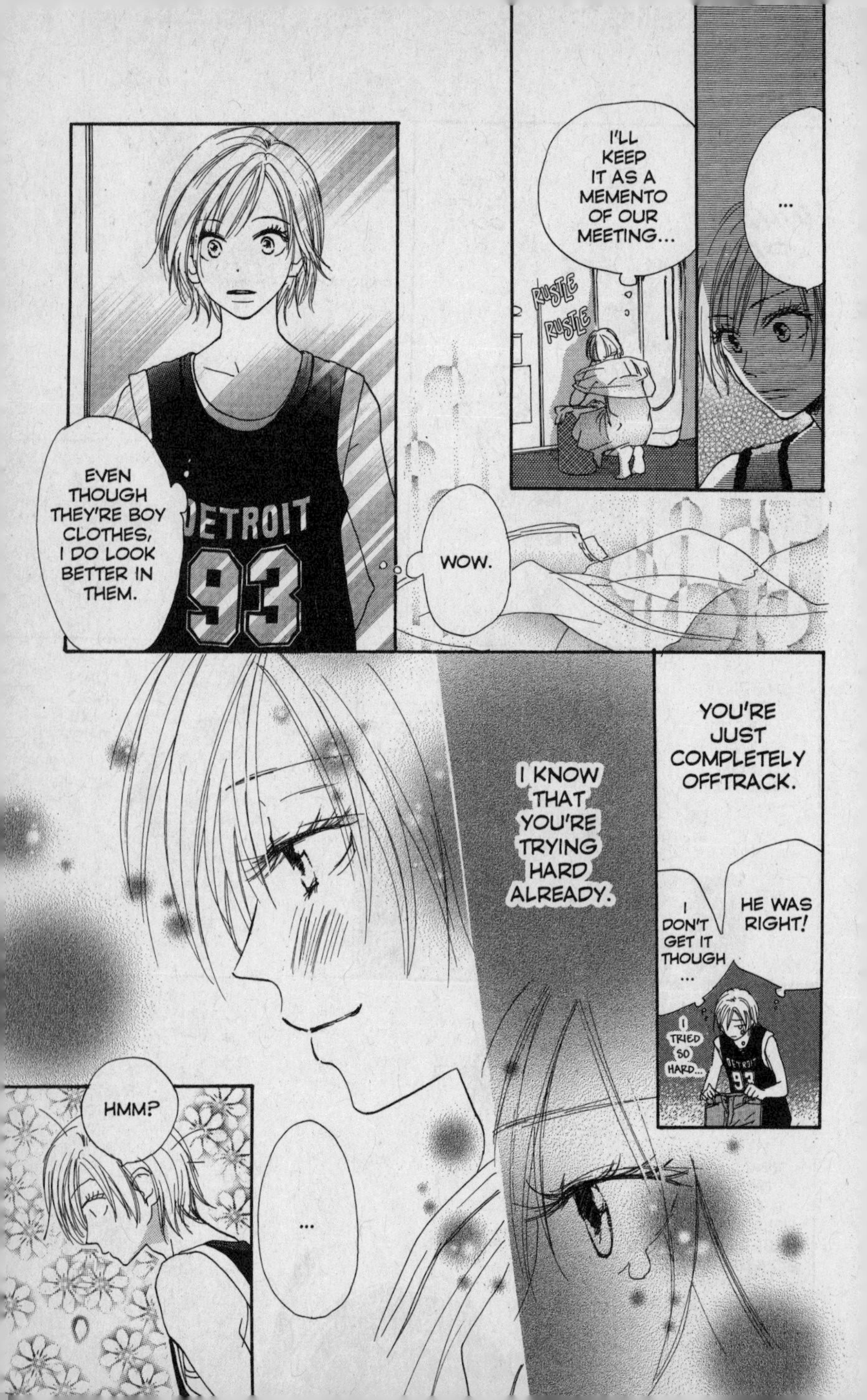
...
I'LL KEEP IT AS A MEMENTO OF OUR MEETING...
RUSTLE
RUSTLE
WOW.
EVEN THOUGH THEY'RE BOY CLOTHES, I DO LOOK BETTER IN THEM.
DETROIT 93
YOU'RE JUST COMPLETELY OFFTRACK.
HE WAS RIGHT!
I DON'T GET IT THOUGH...
I TRIED SO HARD...
I KNOW THAT YOU'RE TRYING HARD ALREADY.
...
HMM?

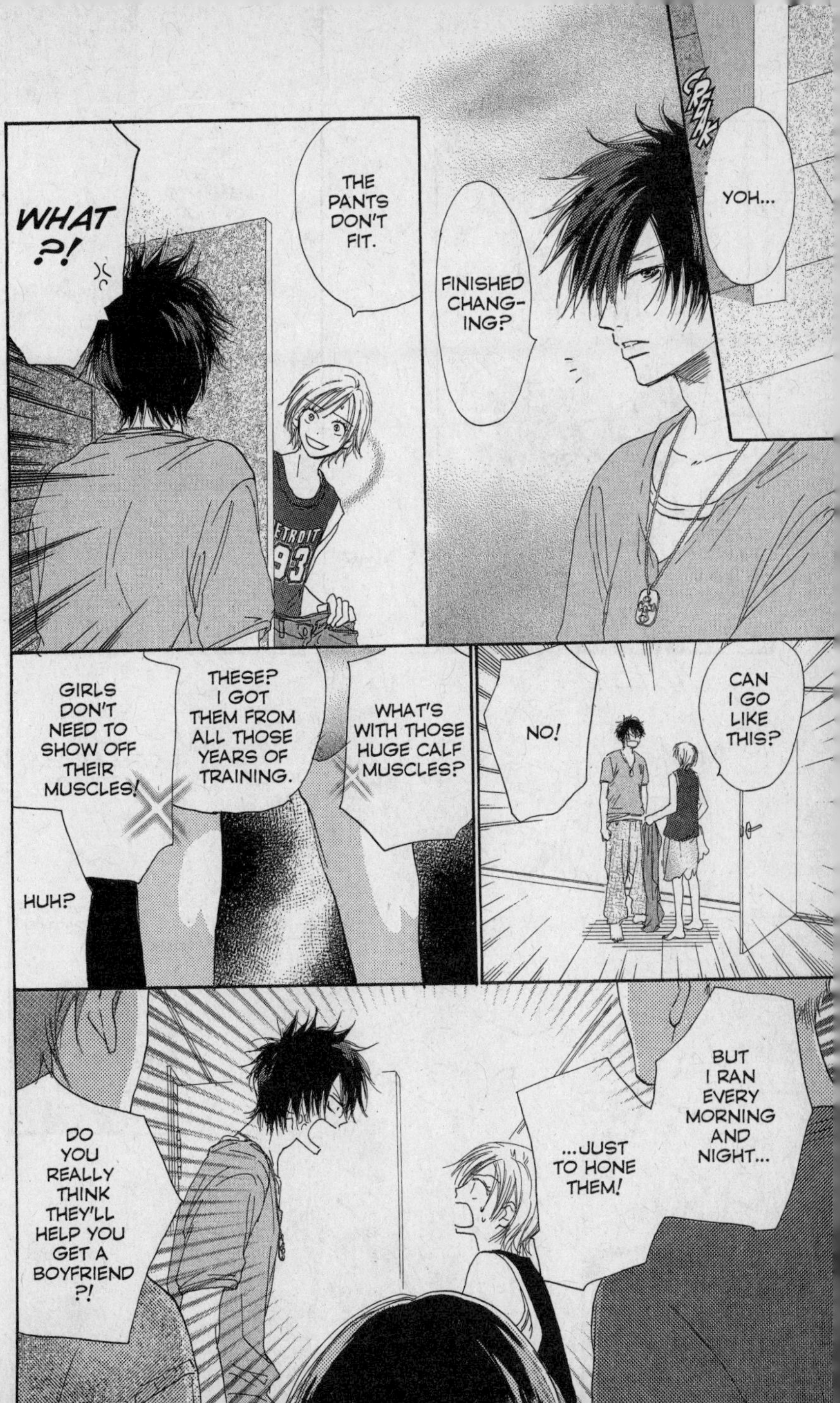
CREAK
YOH...
FINISHED CHANGING?
THE PANTS DON'T FIT.
WHAT?!
CAN I GO LIKE THIS?
NO!
WHAT'S WITH THOSE HUGE CALF MUSCLES?
THESE? I GOT THEM FROM ALL THOSE YEARS OF TRAINING.
GIRLS DON'T NEED TO SHOW OFF THEIR MUSCLES!
HUH?
BUT I RAN EVERY MORNING AND NIGHT...
...JUST TO HONE THEM!
DO YOU REALLY THINK THEY'LL HELP YOU GET A BOYFRIEND?!

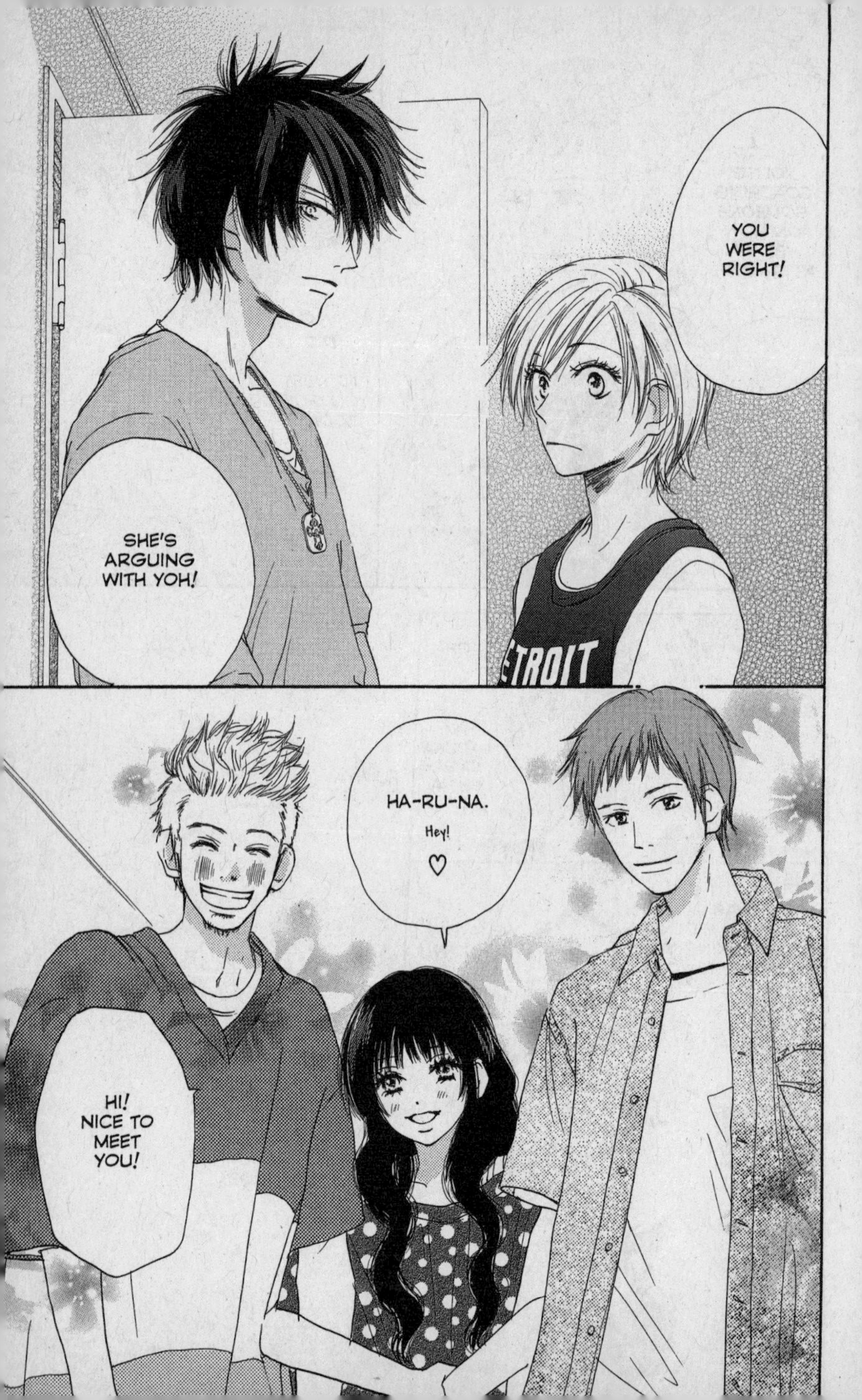
YOU WERE RIGHT!
SHE'S ARGUING WITH YOH!
HA-RU-NA.
Hey!
♡
HI! NICE TO MEET YOU!

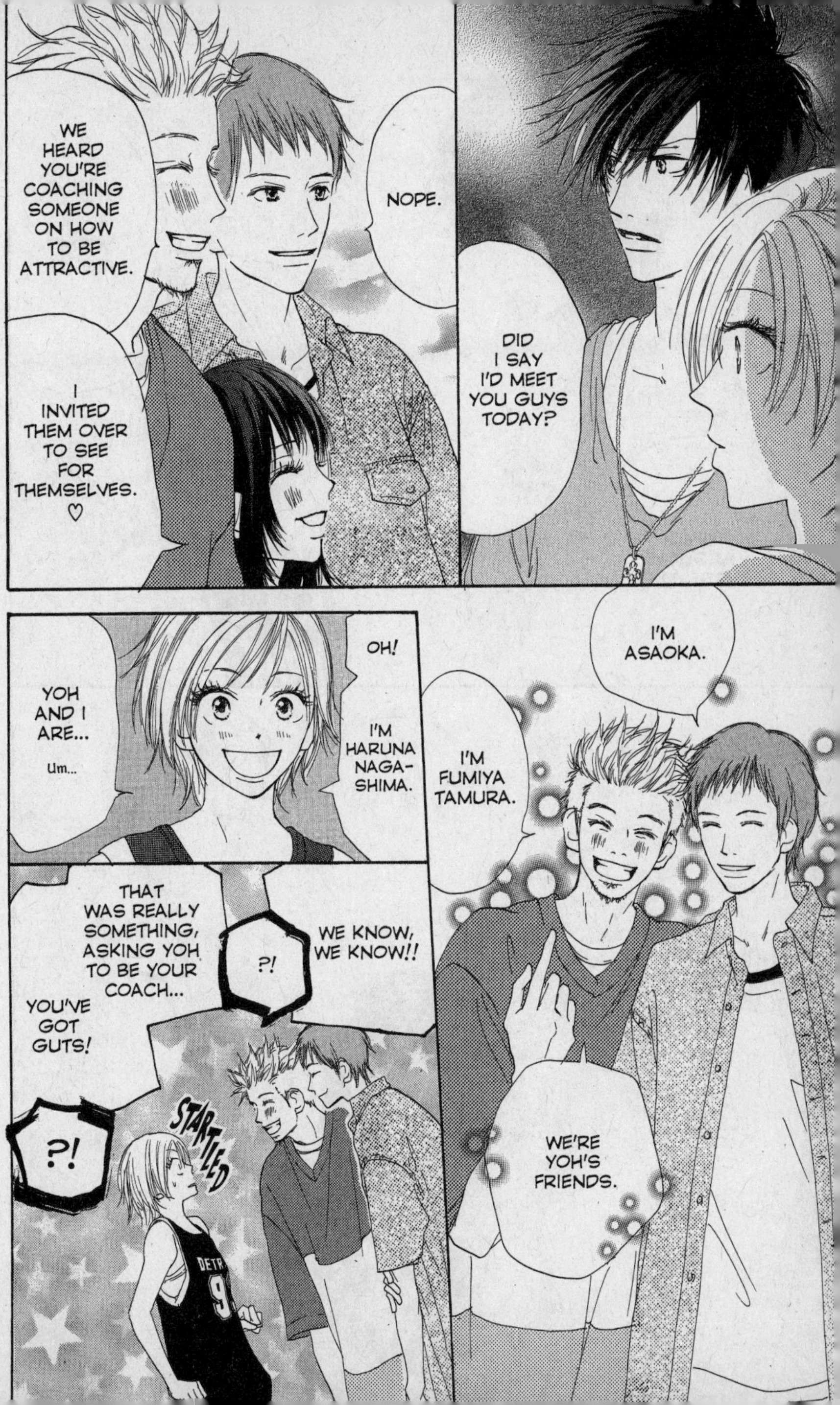
DID I SAY I'D MEET YOU GUYS TODAY?
NOPE.
WE HEARD YOU'RE COACHING SOMEONE ON HOW TO BE ATTRACTIVE.
I INVITED THEM OVER TO SEE FOR THEMSELVES. ♡
I'M ASAOKA.
I'M FUMIYA TAMURA.
WE'RE YOH'S FRIENDS.
OH!
I'M HARUNA NAGA-SHIMA.
YOH AND I ARE...
Um...
WE KNOW, WE KNOW!!
?!
THAT WAS REALLY SOMETHING, ASKING YOH TO BE YOUR COACH...
YOU'VE GOT GUTS!
?!
STARTLED

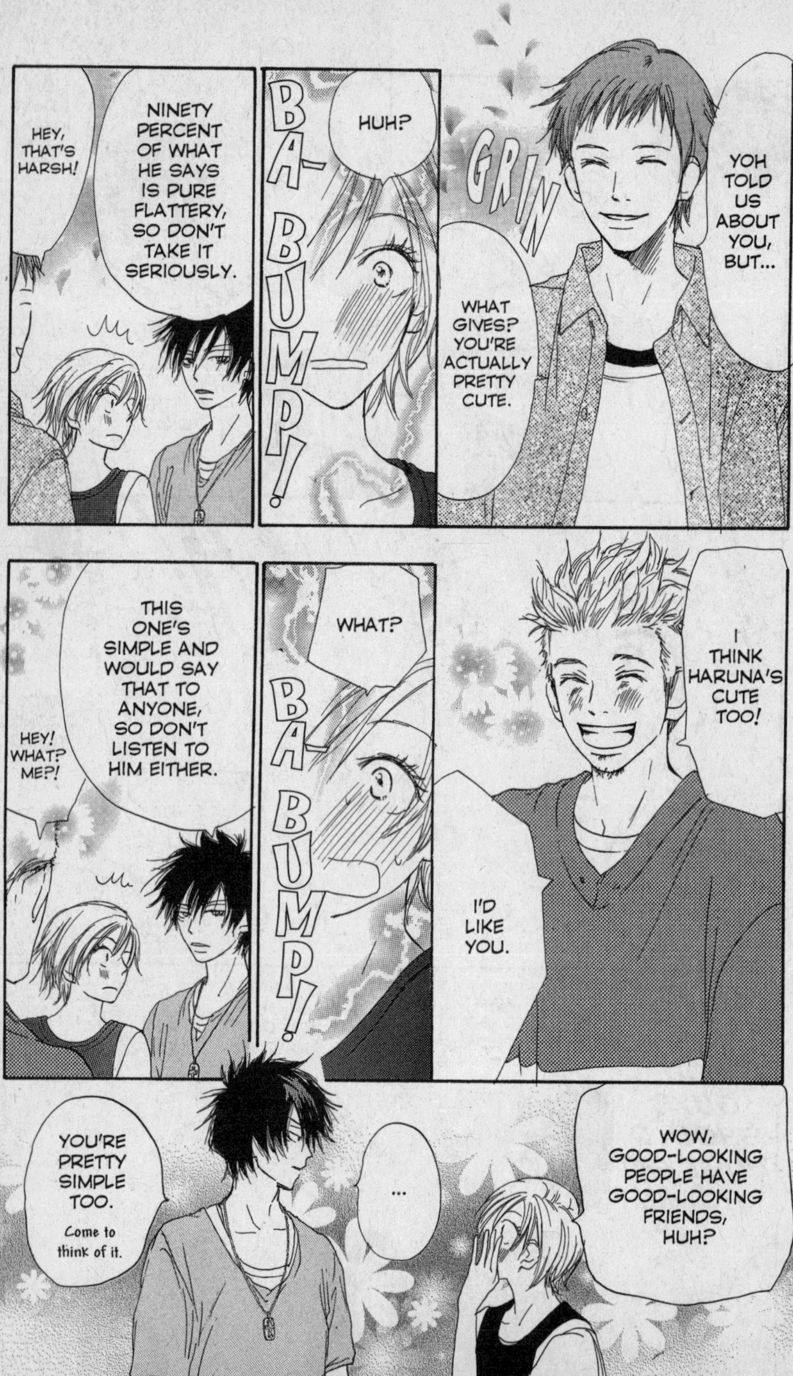
YOH TOLD US ABOUT YOU, BUT...
GRIN
WHAT GIVES? YOU'RE ACTUALLY PRETTY CUTE.
BA-BUMP!
HUH?
NINETY PERCENT OF WHAT HE SAYS IS PURE FLATTERY, SO DON'T TAKE IT SERIOUSLY.
HEY, THAT'S HARSH!
I THINK HARUNA'S CUTE TOO!
I'D LIKE YOU.
WHAT?
BA-BUMP!
THIS ONE'S SIMPLE AND WOULD SAY THAT TO ANYONE, SO DON'T LISTEN TO HIM EITHER.
HEY! WHAT? ME?!
WOW, GOOD-LOOKING PEOPLE HAVE GOOD-LOOKING FRIENDS, HUH?
...
YOU'RE PRETTY SIMPLE TOO.
Come to think of it.

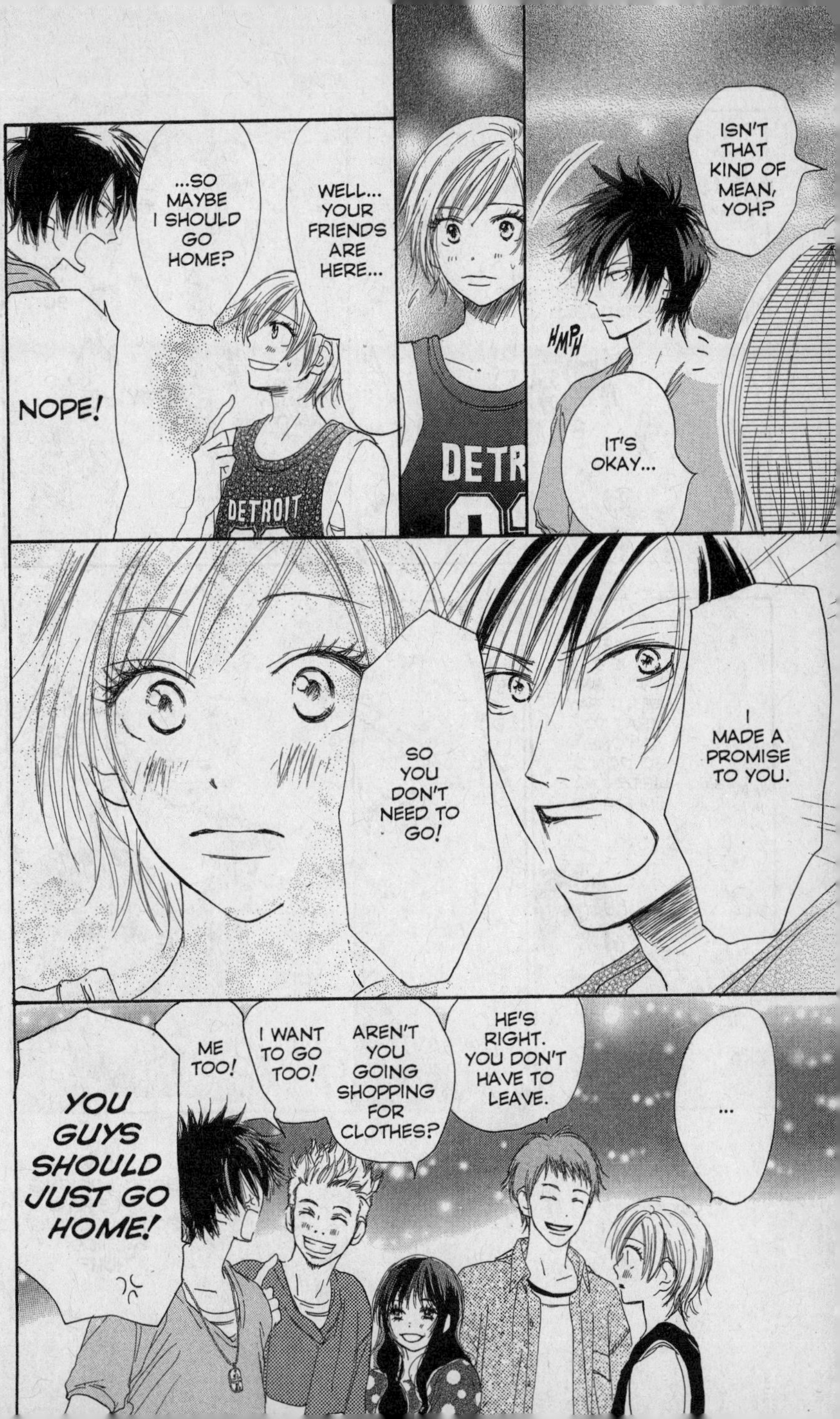
ISN'T THAT KIND OF MEAN, YOH?
HMPH
IT'S OKAY...
WELL... YOUR FRIENDS ARE HERE...
...SO MAYBE I SHOULD GO HOME?
NOPE!
I MADE A PROMISE TO YOU.
SO YOU DON'T NEED TO GO!
...
HE'S RIGHT. YOU DON'T HAVE TO LEAVE.
AREN'T YOU GOING SHOPPING FOR CLOTHES?
I WANT TO GO TOO!
ME TOO!
YOU GUYS SHOULD JUST GO HOME!

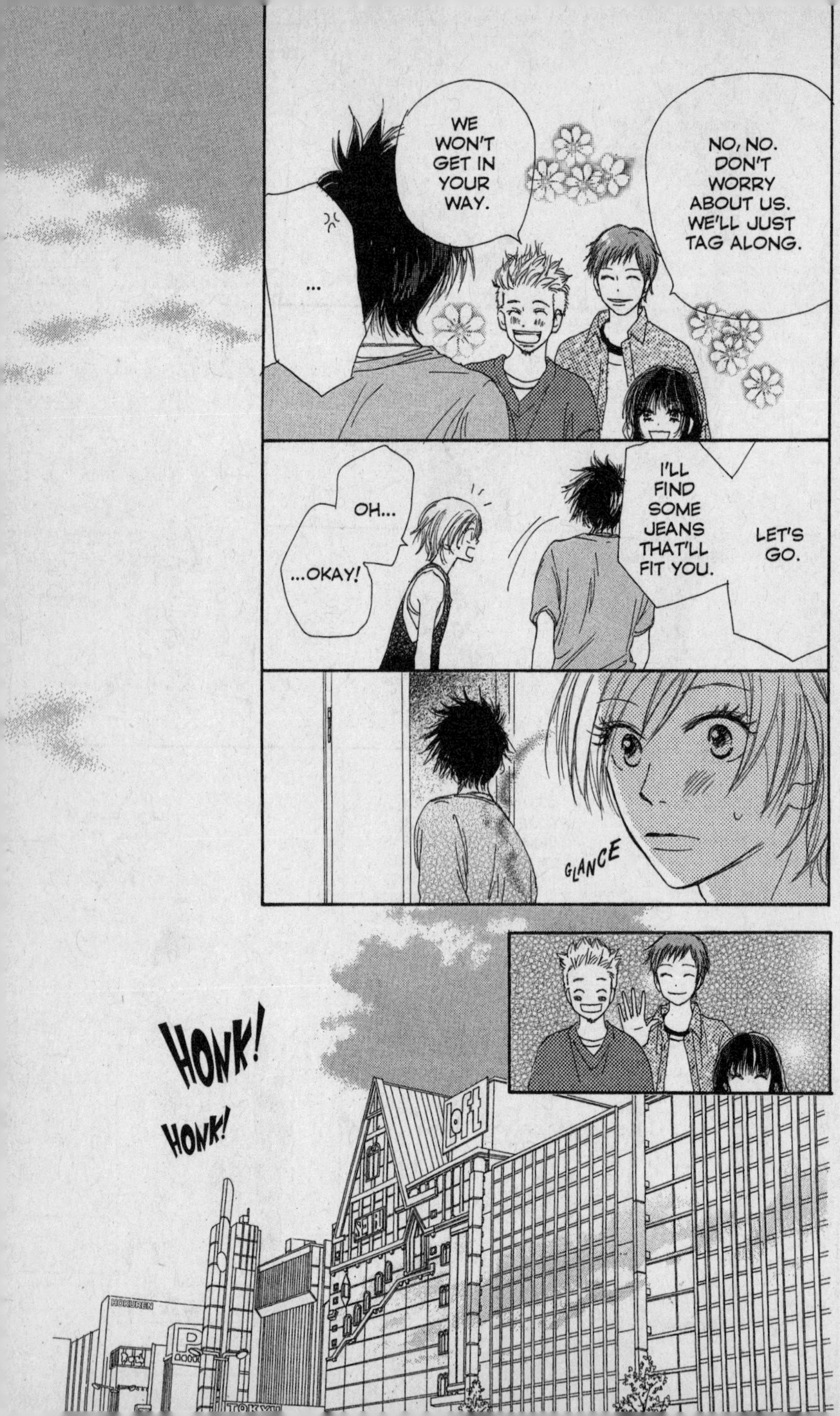
NO, NO. DON'T WORRY ABOUT US. WE'LL JUST TAG ALONG.
WE WON'T GET IN YOUR WAY.
...
LET'S GO.
I'LL FIND SOME JEANS THAT'LL FIT YOU.
OH... ...OKAY!
GLANCE
HONK!
HONK!
loft
HOKUREN

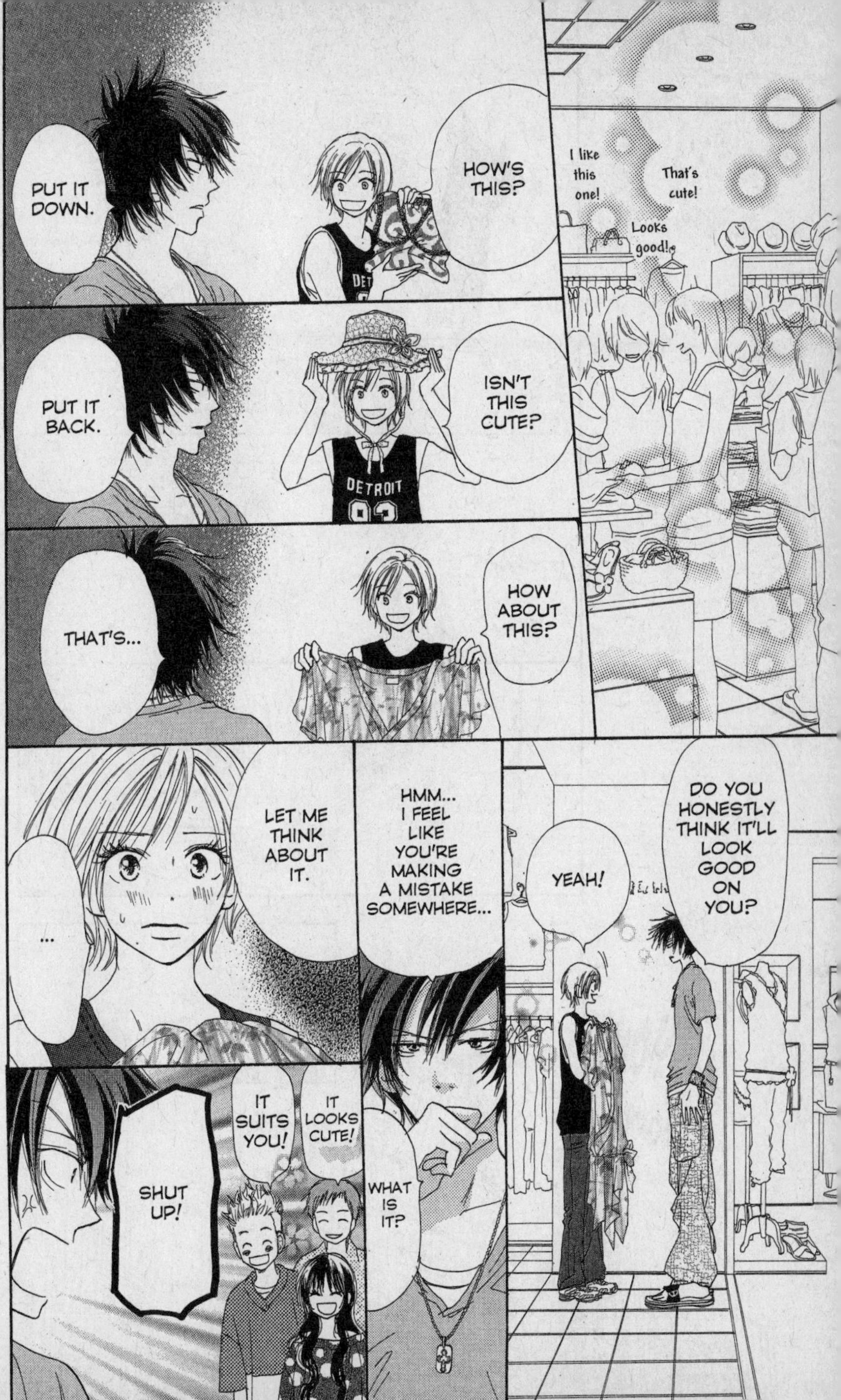
I like this one!
That's cute!
Looks good!
HOW'S THIS?
PUT IT DOWN.
ISN'T THIS CUTE?
PUT IT BACK.
HOW ABOUT THIS?
THAT'S...
DO YOU HONESTLY THINK IT'LL LOOK GOOD ON YOU?
YEAH!
HMM... I FEEL LIKE YOU'RE MAKING A MISTAKE SOMEWHERE...
WHAT IS IT?
LET ME THINK ABOUT IT.
...
IT LOOKS CUTE!
IT SUITS YOU!
SHUT UP!

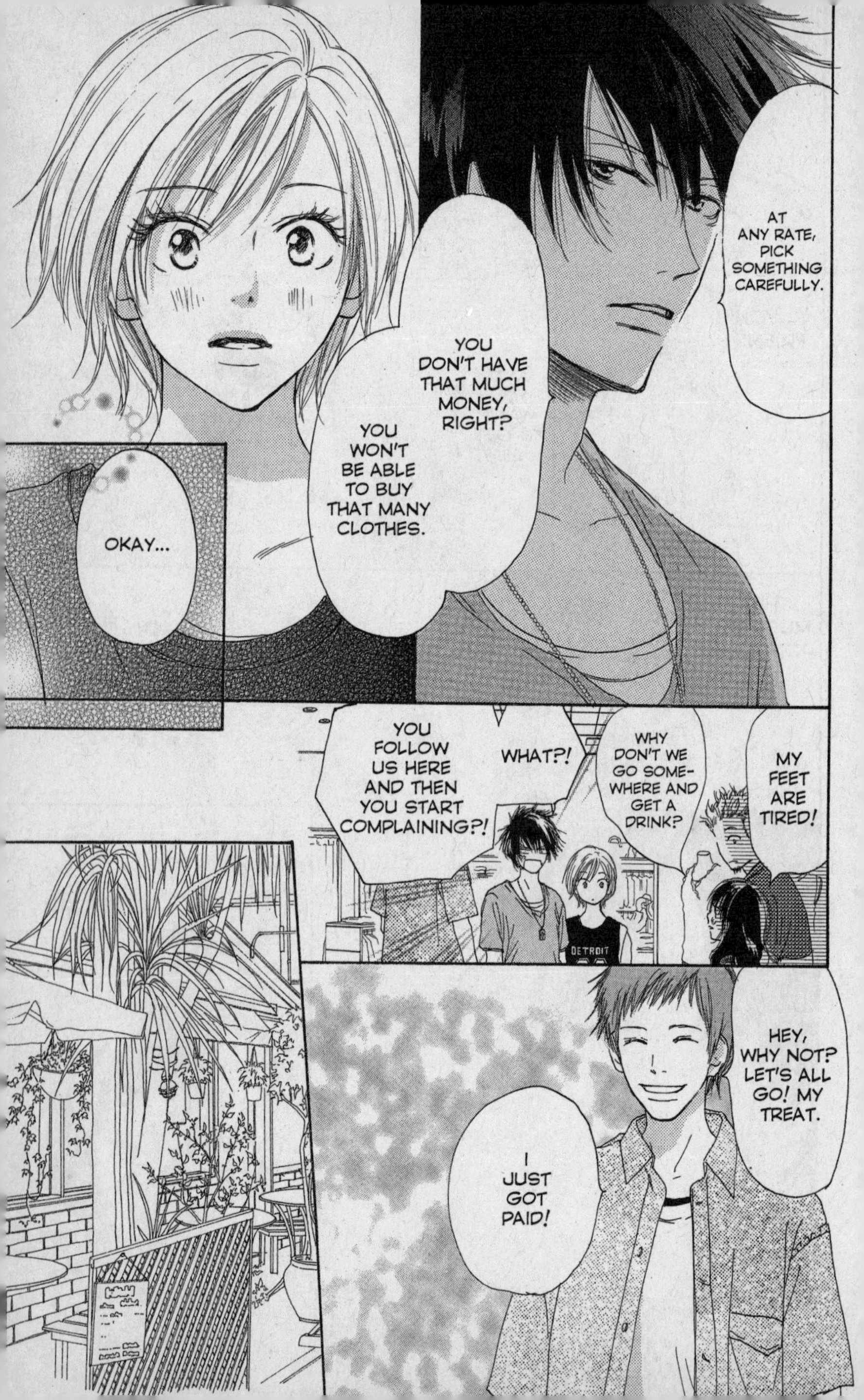
AT ANY RATE, PICK SOMETHING CAREFULLY.
YOU DON'T HAVE THAT MUCH MONEY, RIGHT?
YOU WON'T BE ABLE TO BUY THAT MANY CLOTHES.
OKAY...
MY FEET ARE TIRED!
WHY DON'T WE GO SOME-WHERE AND GET A DRINK?
WHAT?!
YOU FOLLOW US HERE AND THEN YOU START COMPLAINING?!
DETROIT
HEY, WHY NOT? LET'S ALL GO! MY TREAT.
I JUST GOT PAID!

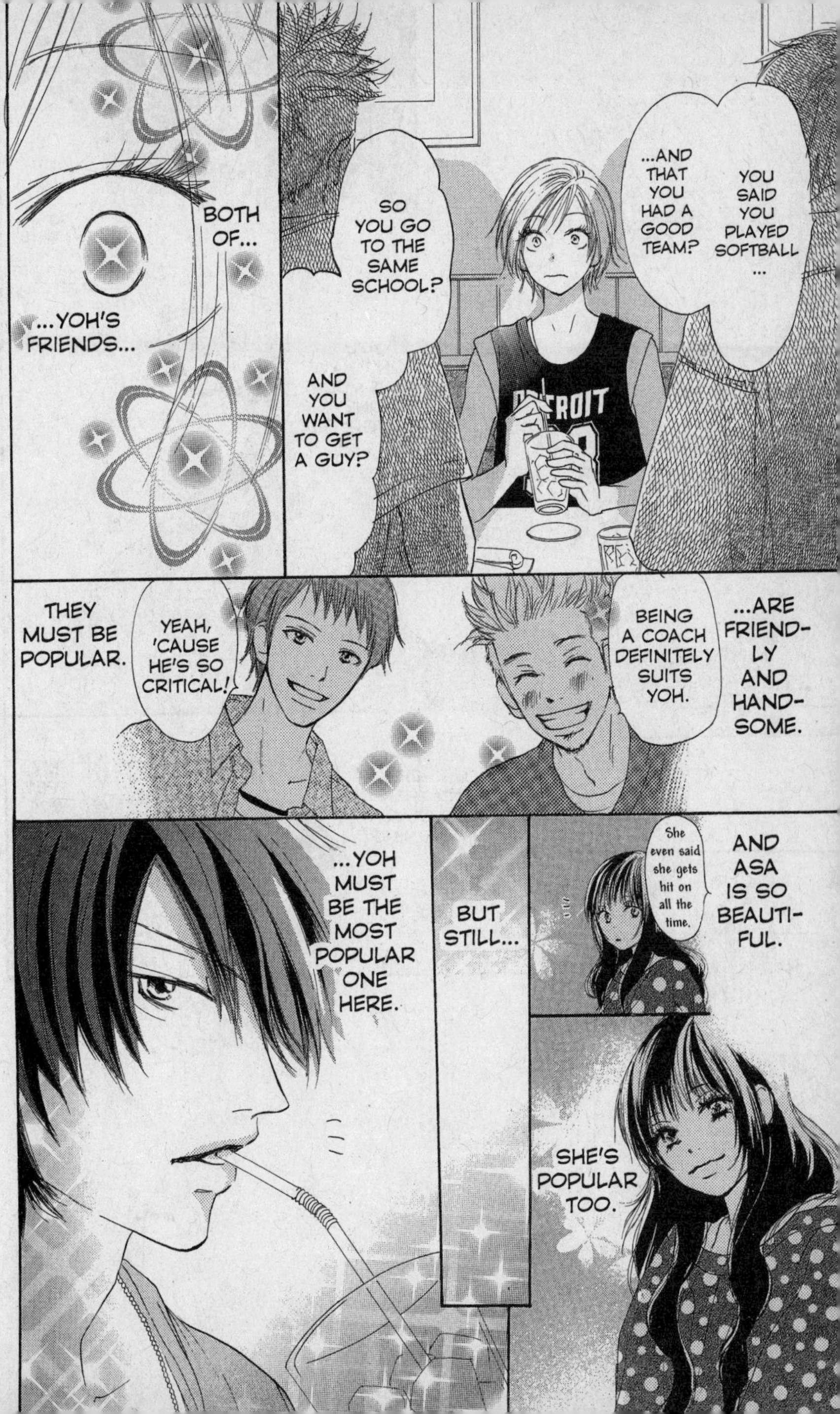
YOU SAID YOU PLAYED SOFTBALL ...
...AND THAT YOU HAD A GOOD TEAM?
SO YOU GO TO THE SAME SCHOOL?
AND YOU WANT TO GET A GUY?
BOTH OF...
...YOH'S FRIENDS...
...ARE FRIEND-LY AND HAND-SOME.
BEING A COACH DEFINITELY SUITS YOH.
YEAH, 'CAUSE HE'S SO CRITICAL!
THEY MUST BE POPULAR.
AND ASA IS SO BEAUTI-FUL.
She even said she gets hit on all the time.
SHE'S POPULAR TOO.
BUT STILL...
...YOH MUST BE THE MOST POPULAR ONE HERE.

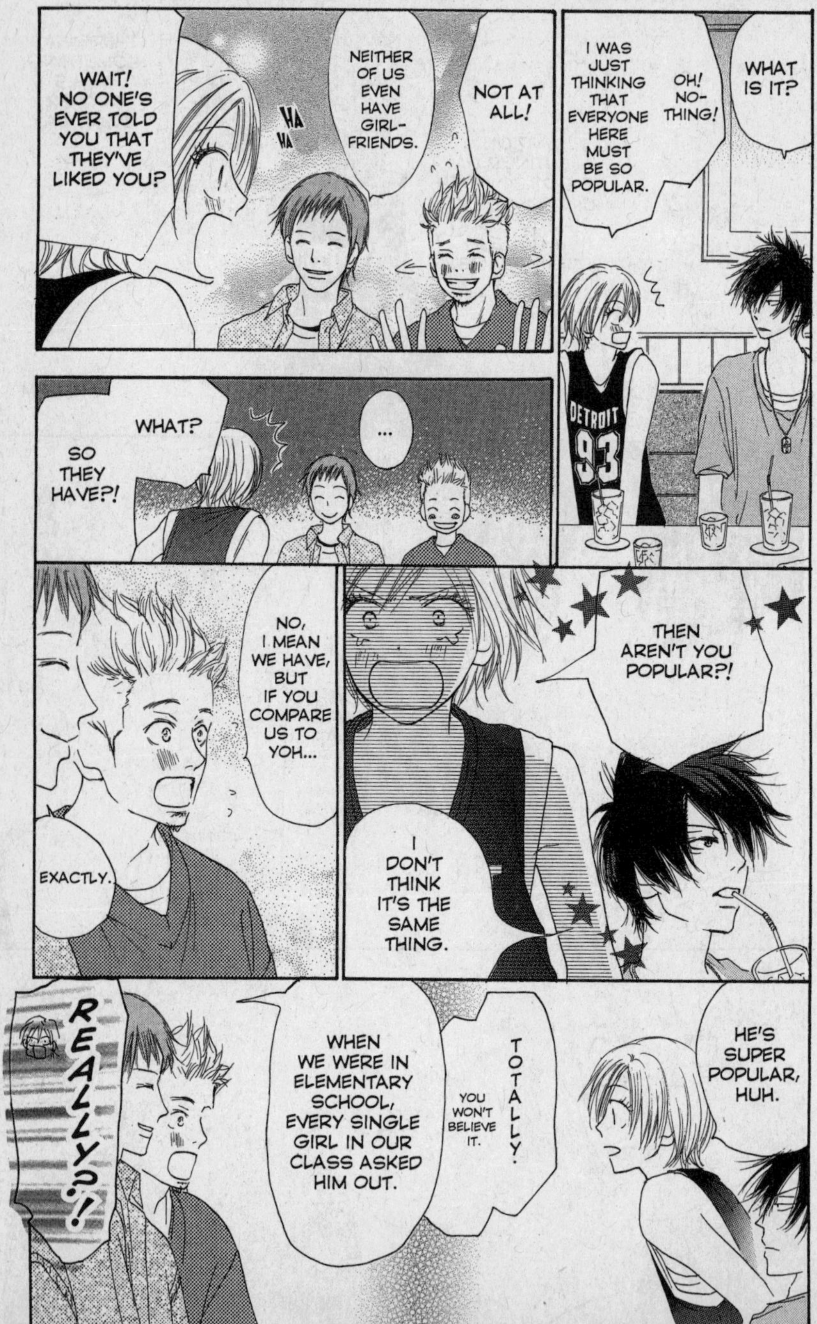
WHAT IS IT?
OH! NOTHING!
I WAS JUST THINKING THAT EVERYONE HERE MUST BE SO POPULAR.
NOT AT ALL!
NEITHER OF US EVEN HAVE GIRLFRIENDS.
HA HA
WAIT! NO ONE'S EVER TOLD YOU THAT THEY'VE LIKED YOU?
...
WHAT?
SO THEY HAVE?!
THEN AREN'T YOU POPULAR?!
I DON'T THINK IT'S THE SAME THING.
NO, I MEAN WE HAVE, BUT IF YOU COMPARE US TO YOH...
EXACTLY.
HE'S SUPER POPULAR, HUH.
TOTALLY.
YOU WON'T BELIEVE IT.
WHEN WE WERE IN ELEMENTARY SCHOOL, EVERY SINGLE GIRL IN OUR CLASS ASKED HIM OUT.
REALLY?!

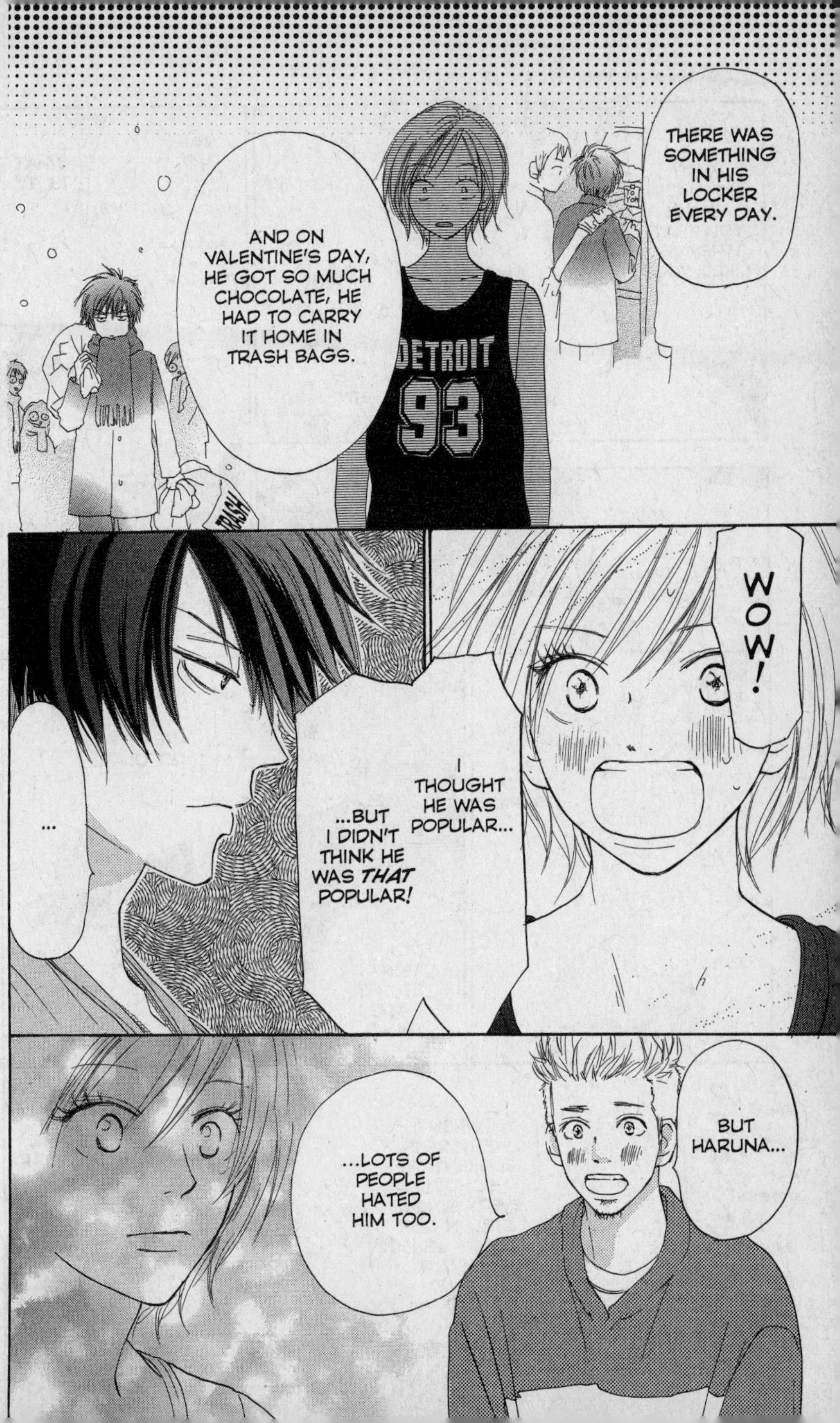
THERE WAS SOMETHING IN HIS LOCKER EVERY DAY.
TO YOU
AND ON VALENTINE'S DAY, HE GOT SO MUCH CHOCOLATE, HE HAD TO CARRY IT HOME IN TRASH BAGS.
DETROIT 93
TRASH
WOW!
I THOUGHT HE WAS POPULAR...
...BUT I DIDN'T THINK HE WAS *THAT* POPULAR!
...
BUT HARUNA...
...LOTS OF PEOPLE HATED HIM TOO.

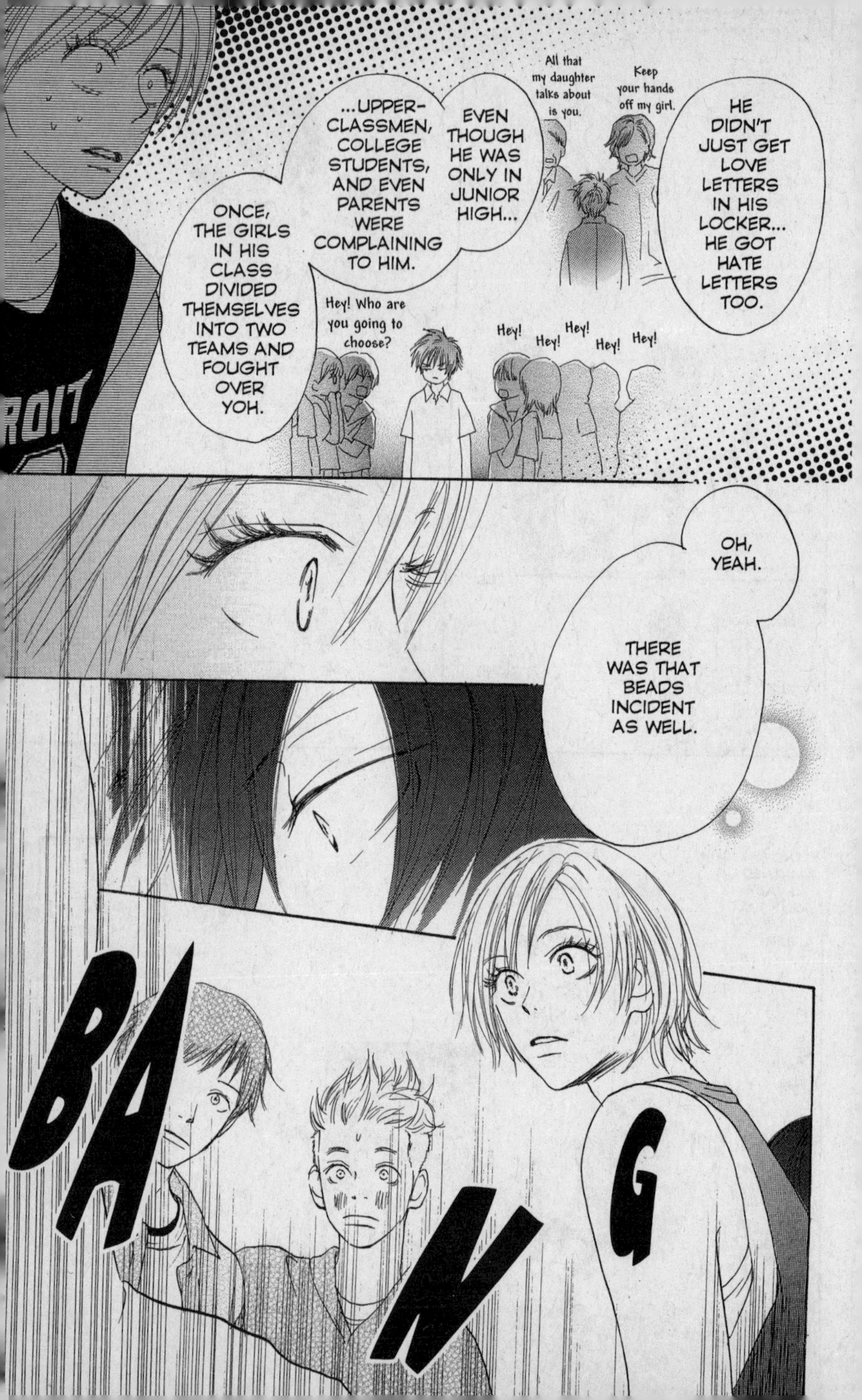
HE DIDN'T JUST GET LOVE LETTERS IN HIS LOCKER... HE GOT HATE LETTERS TOO.
Keep your hands off my girl.
All that my daughter talks about is you.
EVEN THOUGH HE WAS ONLY IN JUNIOR HIGH...
...UPPER-CLASSMEN, COLLEGE STUDENTS, AND EVEN PARENTS WERE COMPLAINING TO HIM.
ONCE, THE GIRLS IN HIS CLASS DIVIDED THEMSELVES INTO TWO TEAMS AND FOUGHT OVER YOH.
Hey!
Hey!
Hey!
Hey!
Hey!
Hey! Who are you going to choose?
OH, YEAH.
THERE WAS THAT BEADS INCIDENT AS WELL.
BANG

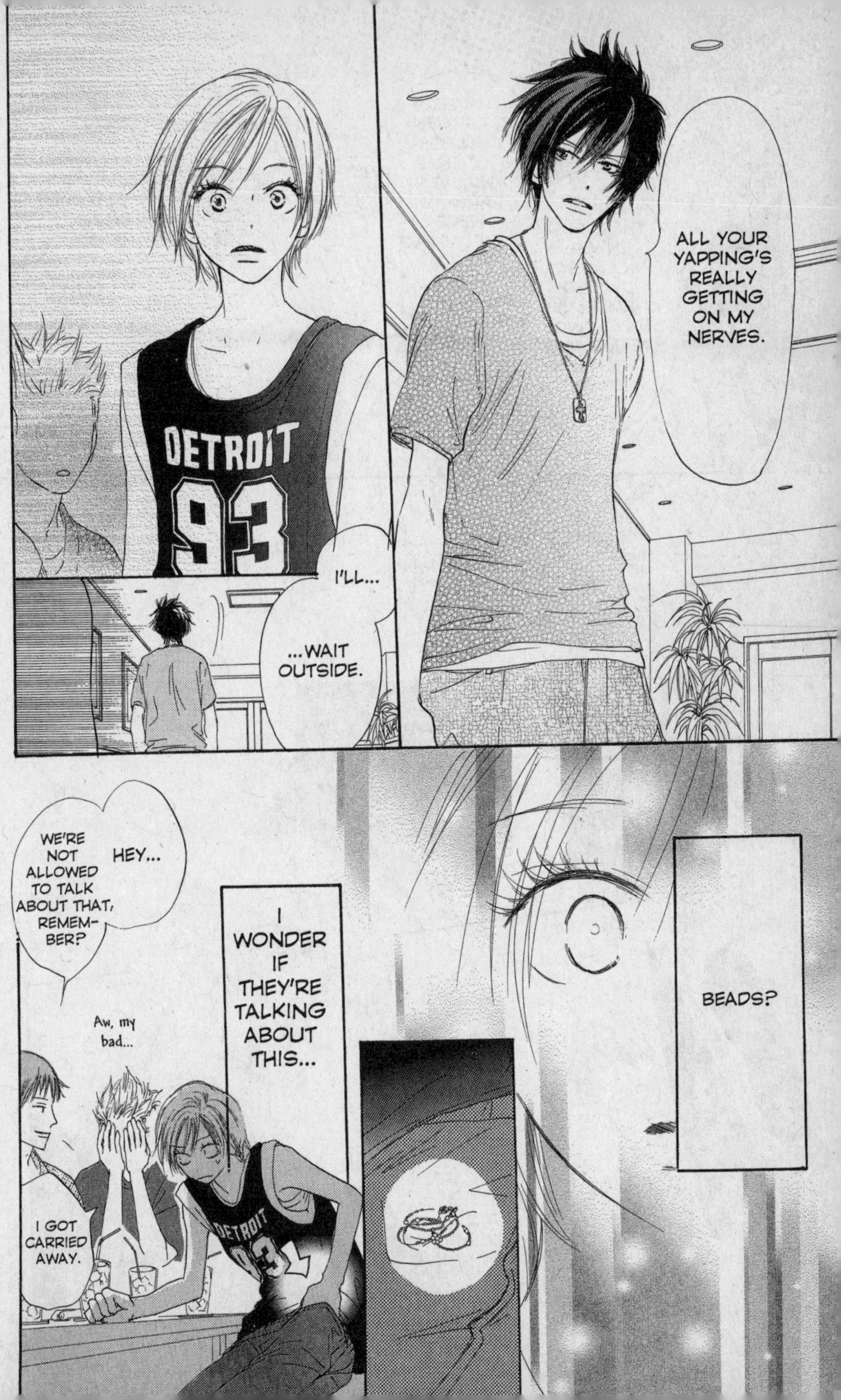
ALL YOUR YAPPING'S REALLY GETTING ON MY NERVES.
I'LL...
...WAIT OUTSIDE.
BEADS?
I WONDER IF THEY'RE TALKING ABOUT THIS...
HEY...
WE'RE NOT ALLOWED TO TALK ABOUT THAT, REMEMBER?
Aw, my bad...
I GOT CARRIED AWAY.

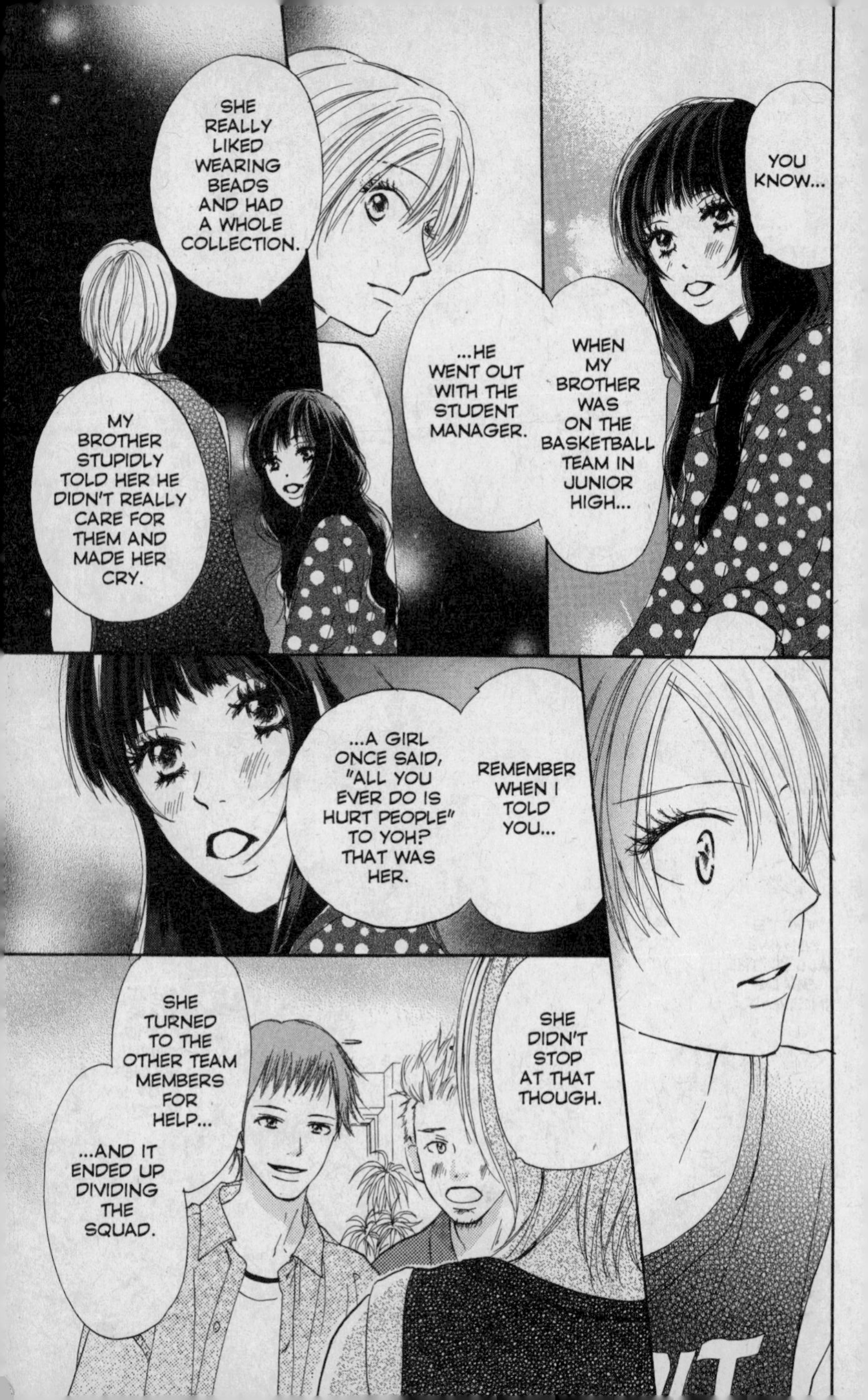
YOU KNOW...
WHEN MY BROTHER WAS ON THE BASKETBALL TEAM IN JUNIOR HIGH...
...HE WENT OUT WITH THE STUDENT MANAGER.
SHE REALLY LIKED WEARING BEADS AND HAD A WHOLE COLLECTION.
MY BROTHER STUPIDLY TOLD HER HE DIDN'T REALLY CARE FOR THEM AND MADE HER CRY.
REMEMBER WHEN I TOLD YOU...
...A GIRL ONCE SAID, "ALL YOU EVER DO IS HURT PEOPLE" TO YOH? THAT WAS HER.
SHE DIDN'T STOP AT THAT THOUGH.
SHE TURNED TO THE OTHER TEAM MEMBERS FOR HELP...
...AND IT ENDED UP DIVIDING THE SQUAD.

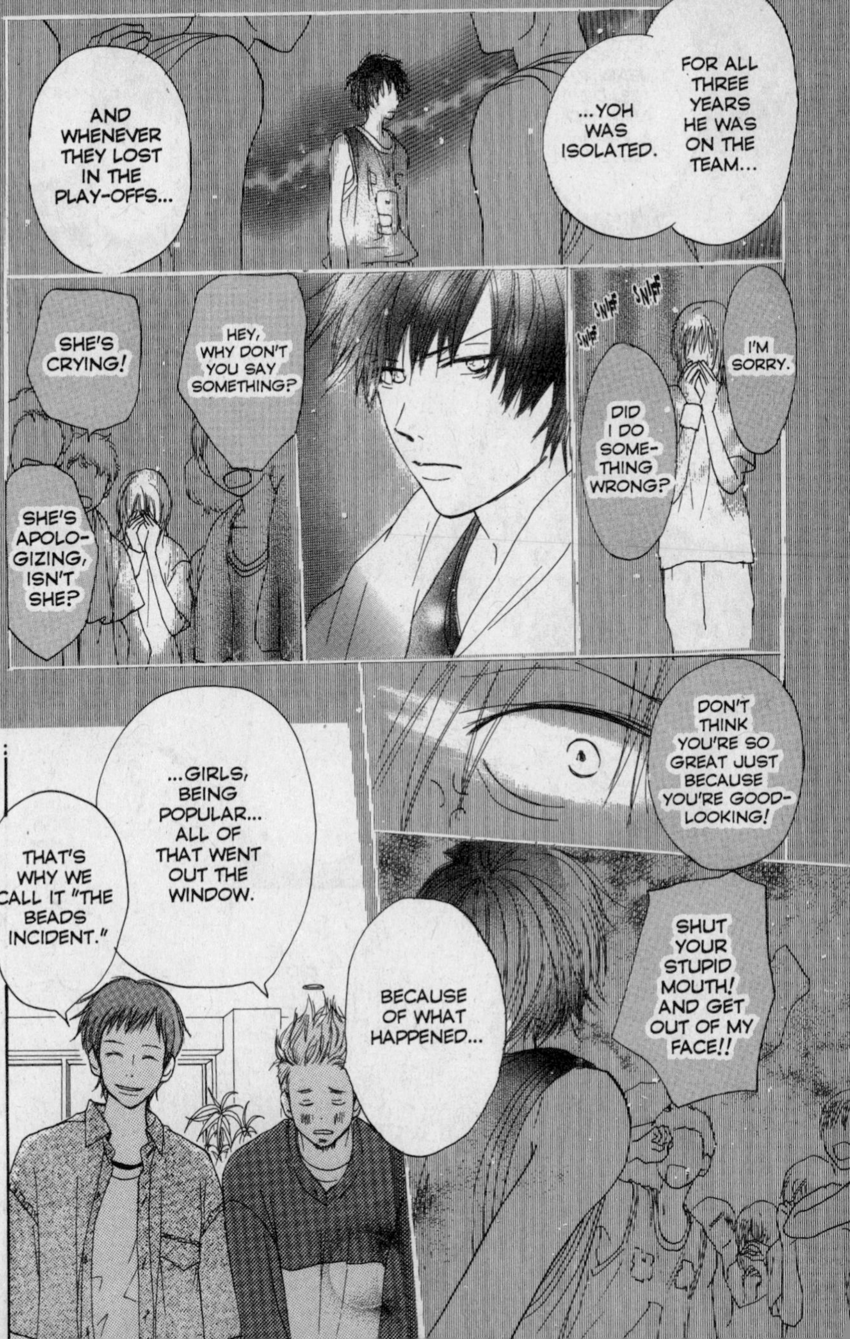
FOR ALL THREE YEARS HE WAS ON THE TEAM...
...YOH WAS ISOLATED.
AND WHENEVER THEY LOST IN THE PLAY-OFFS...
SNIFF
SNIFF
SNIFF
I'M SORRY.
DID I DO SOME-THING WRONG?
HEY, WHY DON'T YOU SAY SOMETHING?
SHE'S CRYING!
SHE'S APOLO-GIZING, ISN'T SHE?
DON'T THINK YOU'RE SO GREAT JUST BECAUSE YOU'RE GOOD-LOOKING!
SHUT YOUR STUPID MOUTH! AND GET OUT OF MY FACE!!
BECAUSE OF WHAT HAPPENED...
...GIRLS, BEING POPULAR... ALL OF THAT WENT OUT THE WINDOW.
THAT'S WHY WE CALL IT "THE BEADS INCIDENT."

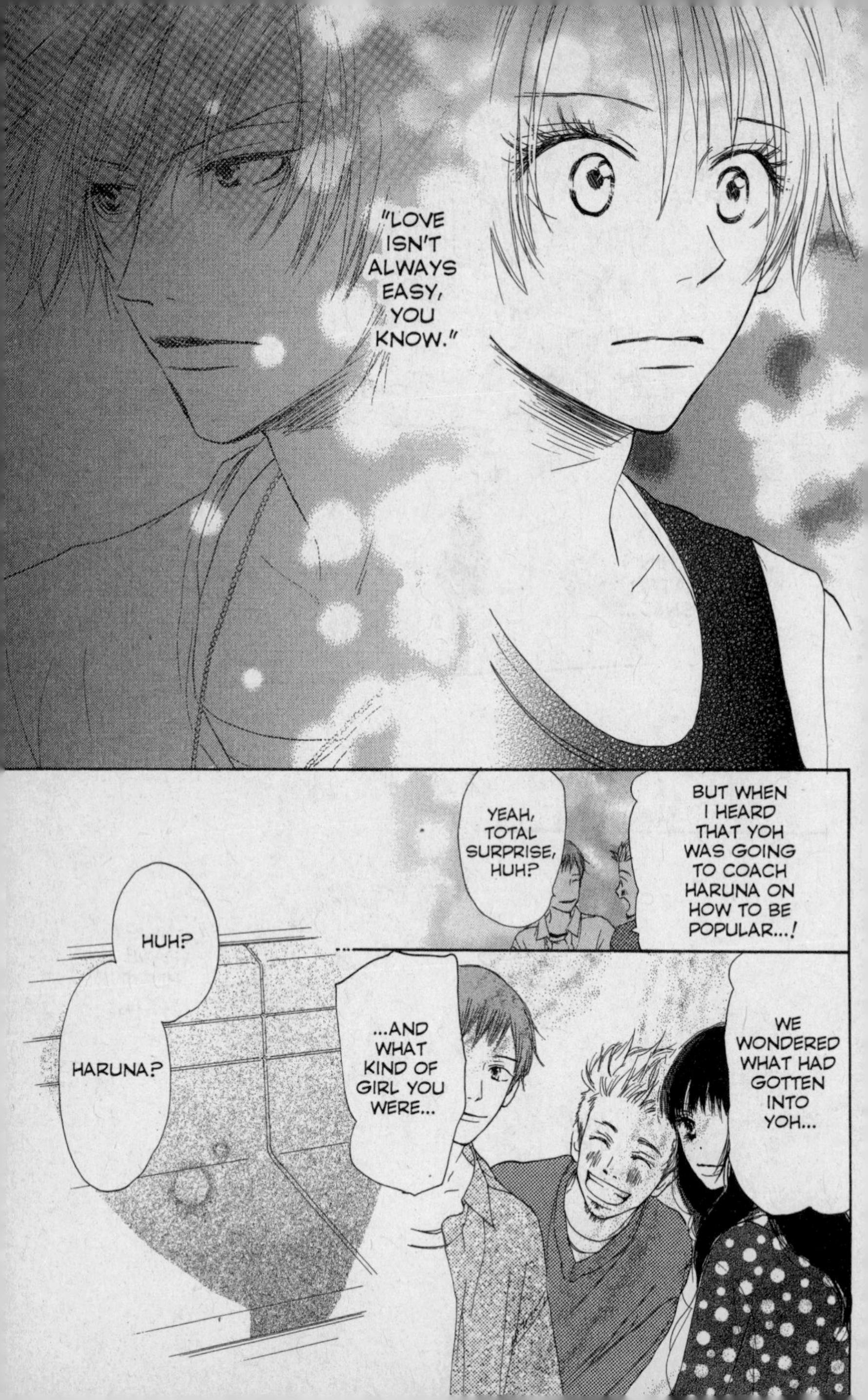
"LOVE ISN'T ALWAYS EASY, YOU KNOW."
BUT WHEN I HEARD THAT YOH WAS GOING TO COACH HARUNA ON HOW TO BE POPULAR...!
YEAH, TOTAL SURPRISE, HUH?
WE WONDERED WHAT HAD GOTTEN INTO YOH...
...AND WHAT KIND OF GIRL YOU WERE...
HUH?
HARUNA?

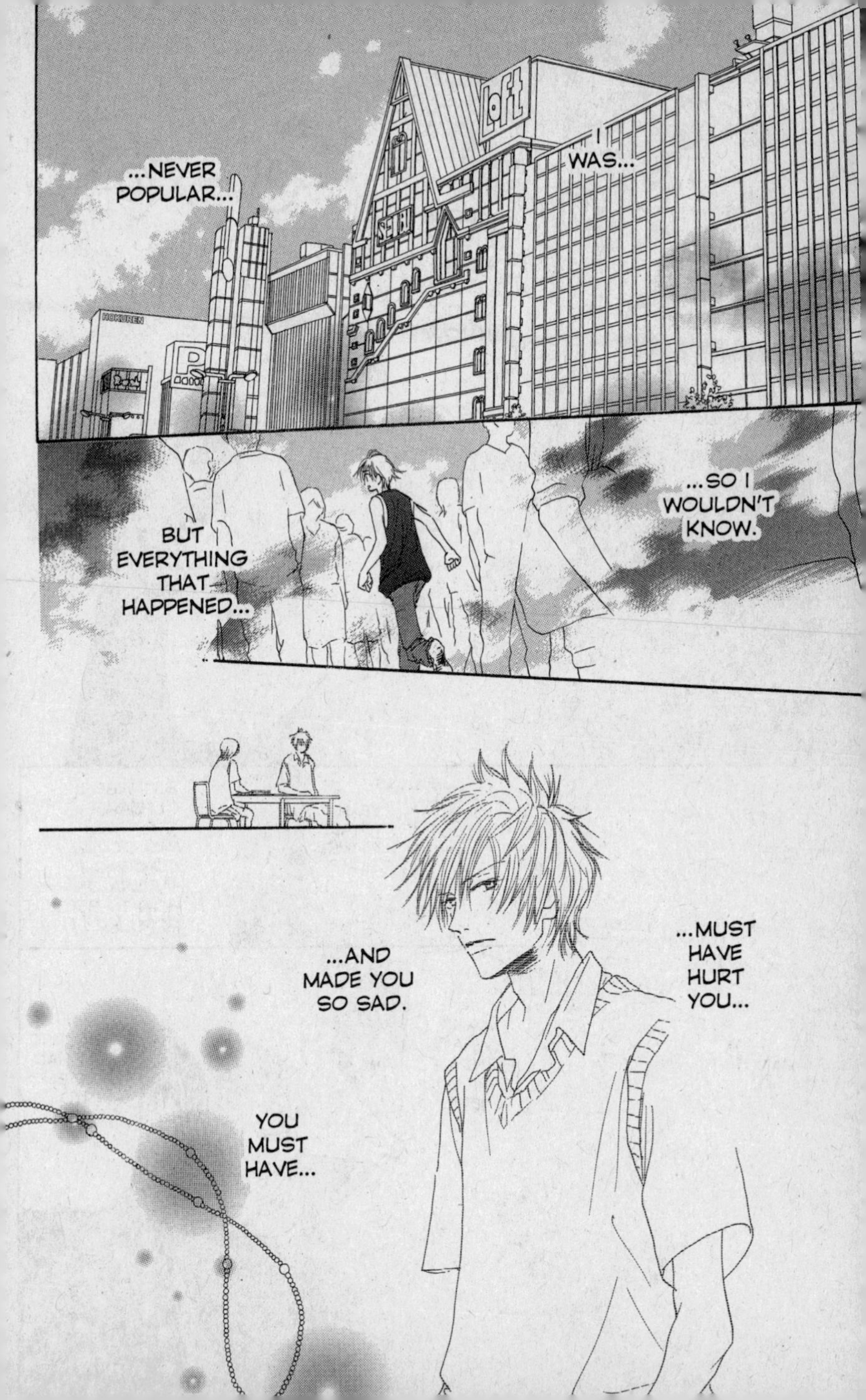
I WAS...
...NEVER POPULAR...
...SO I WOULDN'T KNOW.
BUT EVERYTHING THAT HAPPENED...
...MUST HAVE HURT YOU...
...AND MADE YOU SO SAD.
YOU MUST HAVE...

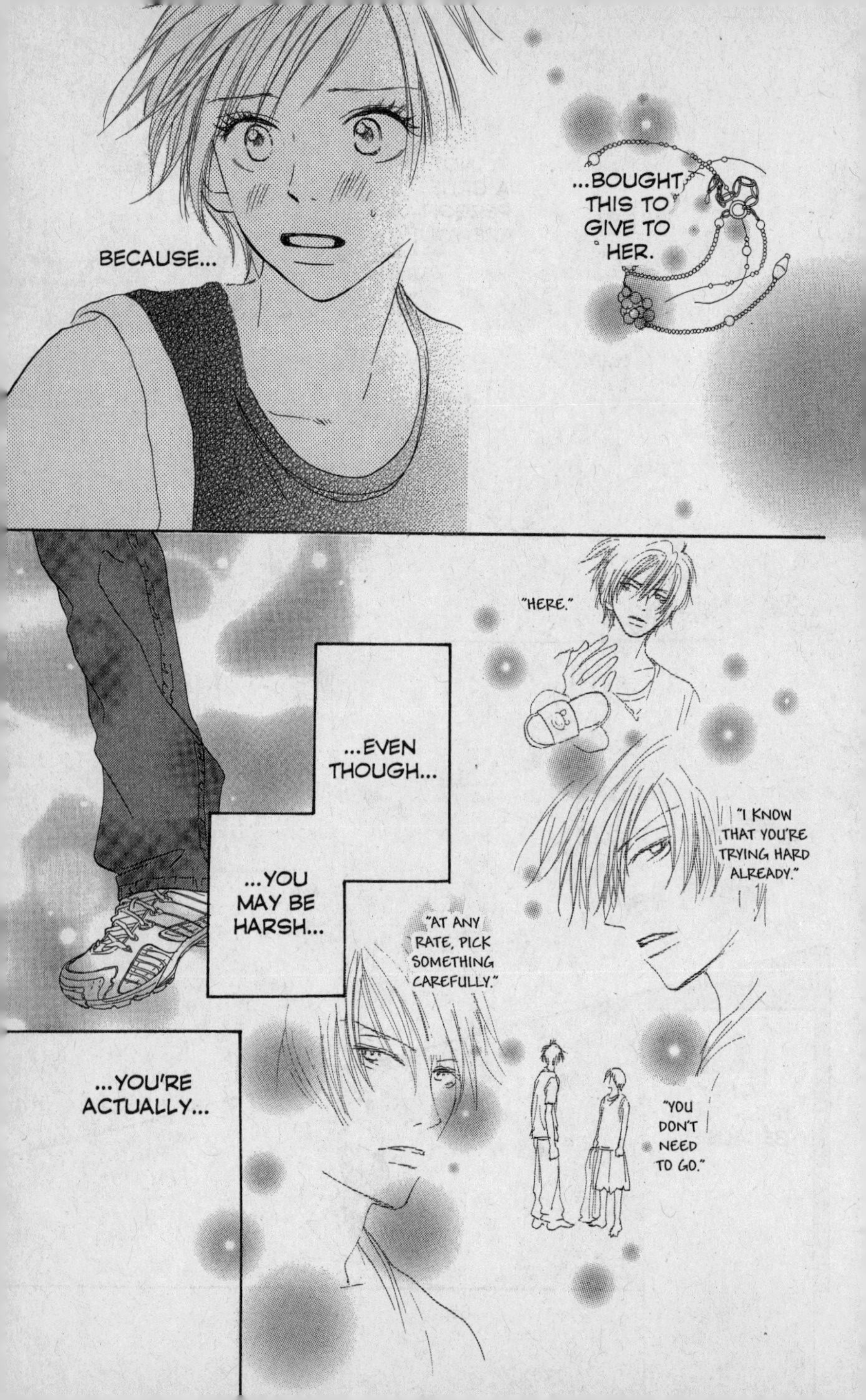
...BOUGHT THIS TO GIVE TO HER.
BECAUSE...
"HERE."
"I KNOW THAT YOU'RE TRYING HARD ALREADY."
...EVEN THOUGH...
...YOU MAY BE HARSH...
"AT ANY RATE, PICK SOMETHING CAREFULLY."
"YOU DON'T NEED TO GO."
...YOU'RE ACTUALLY...

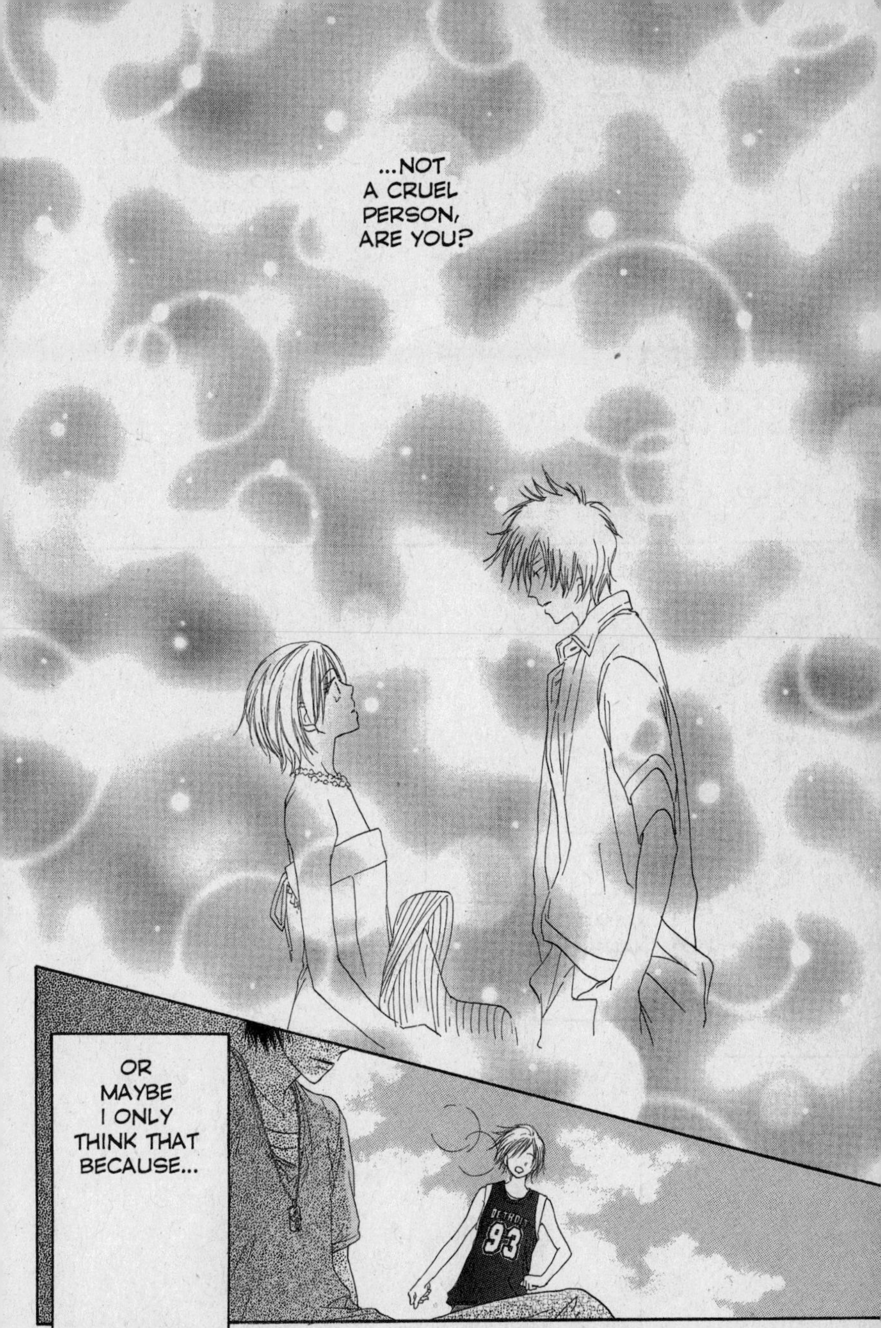
...NOT A CRUEL PERSON, ARE YOU?
OR MAYBE I ONLY THINK THAT BECAUSE...
DETROIT 93

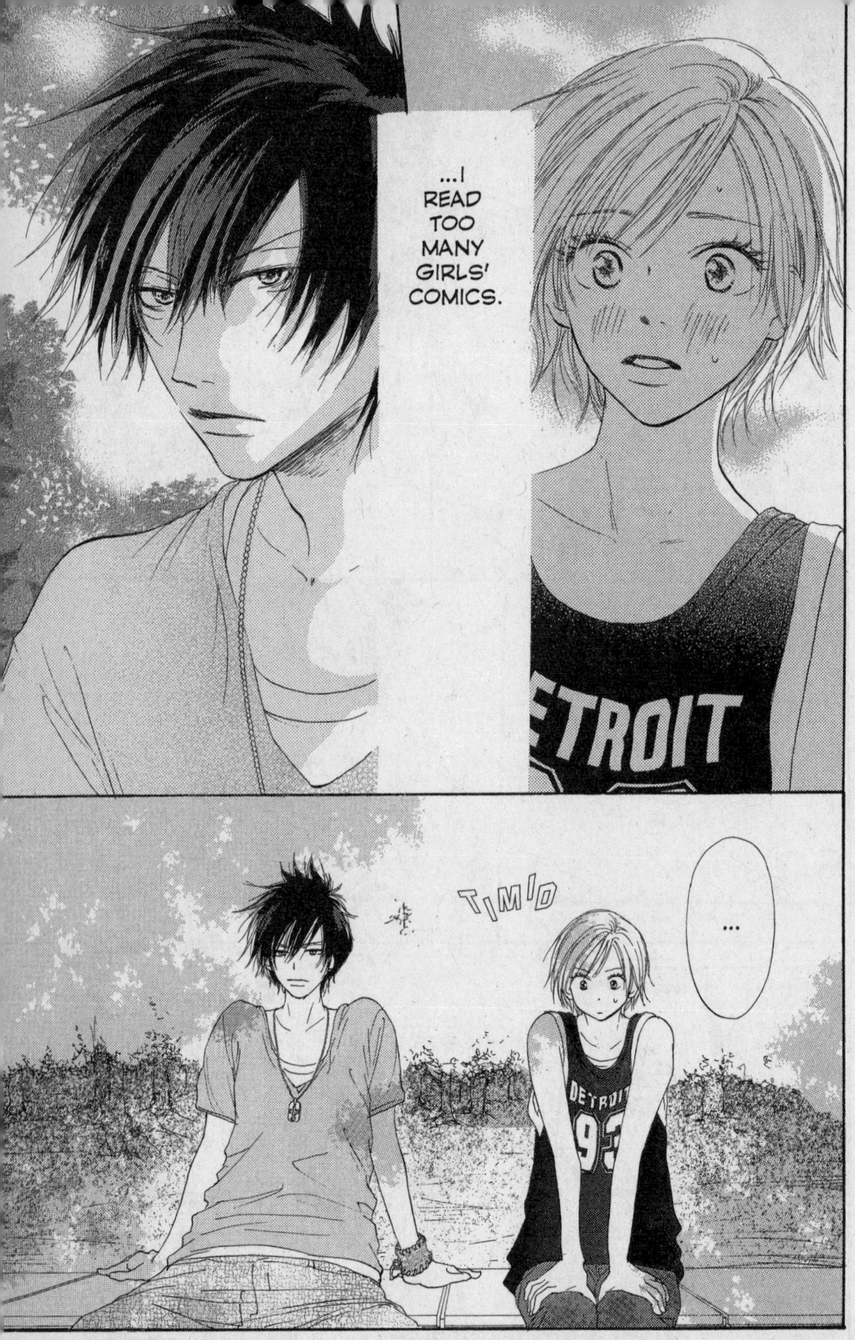
...I READ TOO MANY GIRLS' COMICS.
ETROIT
...
TIMID
DETROIT
93

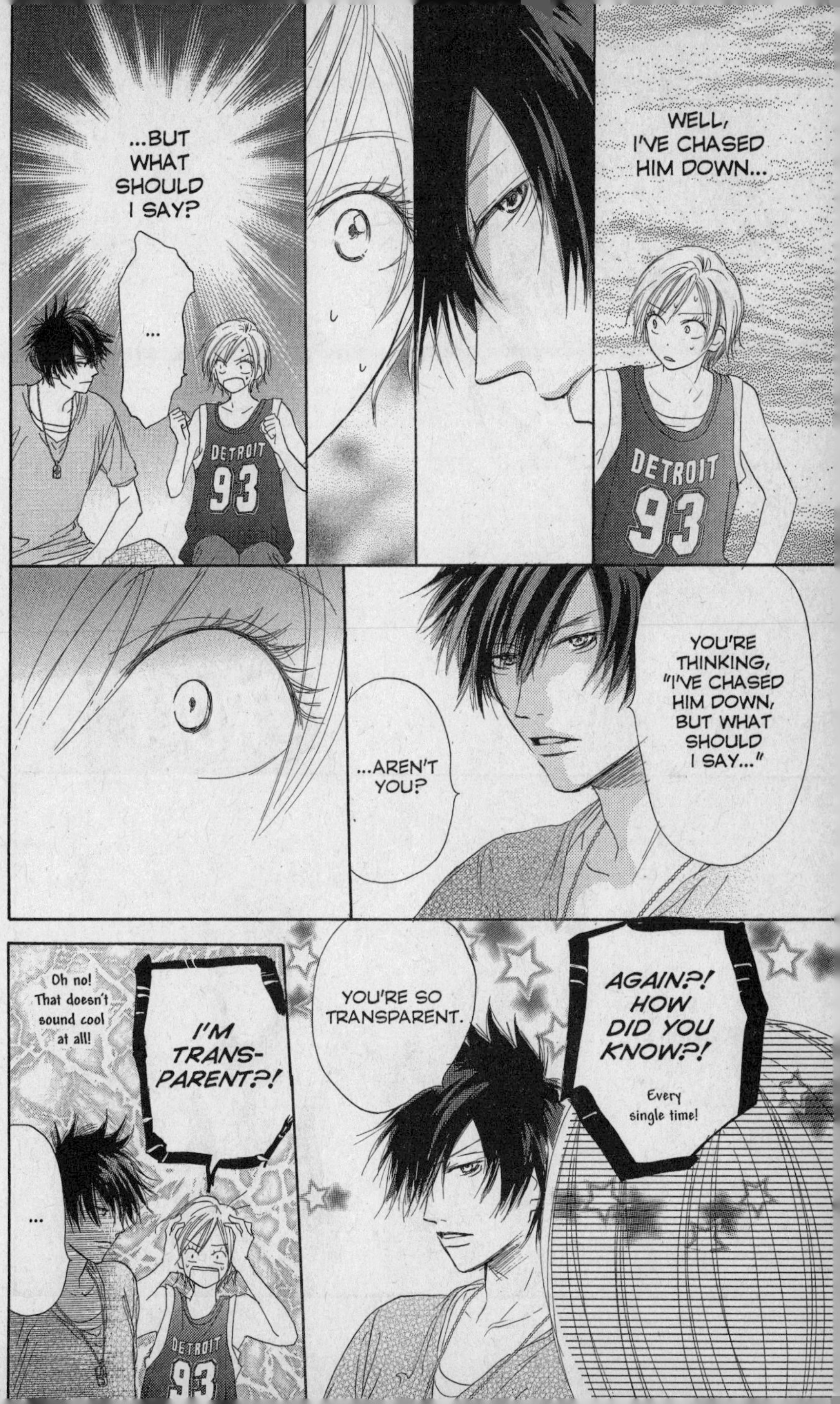
WELL, I'VE CHASED HIM DOWN...
...BUT WHAT SHOULD I SAY?
...
YOU'RE THINKING, "I'VE CHASED HIM DOWN, BUT WHAT SHOULD I SAY..."
...AREN'T YOU?
YOU'RE SO TRANSPARENT.
AGAIN?! HOW DID YOU KNOW?!
Every single time!
I'M TRANS-PARENT?!
Oh no! That doesn't sound cool at all!
...

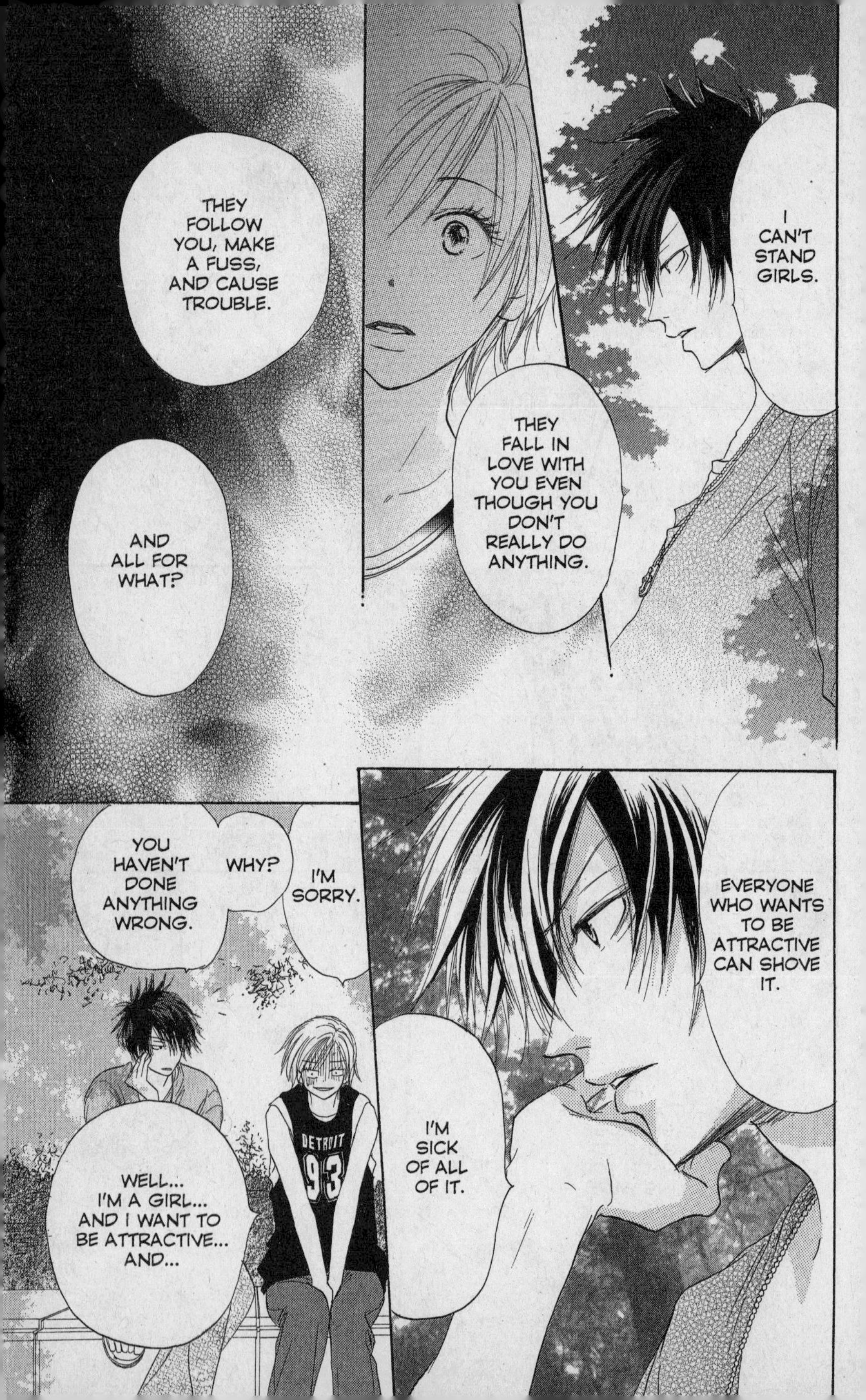
I CAN'T STAND GIRLS.
THEY FALL IN LOVE WITH YOU EVEN THOUGH YOU DON'T REALLY DO ANYTHING.
THEY FOLLOW YOU, MAKE A FUSS, AND CAUSE TROUBLE.
AND ALL FOR WHAT?
EVERYONE WHO WANTS TO BE ATTRACTIVE CAN SHOVE IT.
I'M SICK OF ALL OF IT.
I'M SORRY.
WHY?
YOU HAVEN'T DONE ANYTHING WRONG.
DETROIT 93
WELL... I'M A GIRL... AND I WANT TO BE ATTRACTIVE... AND...

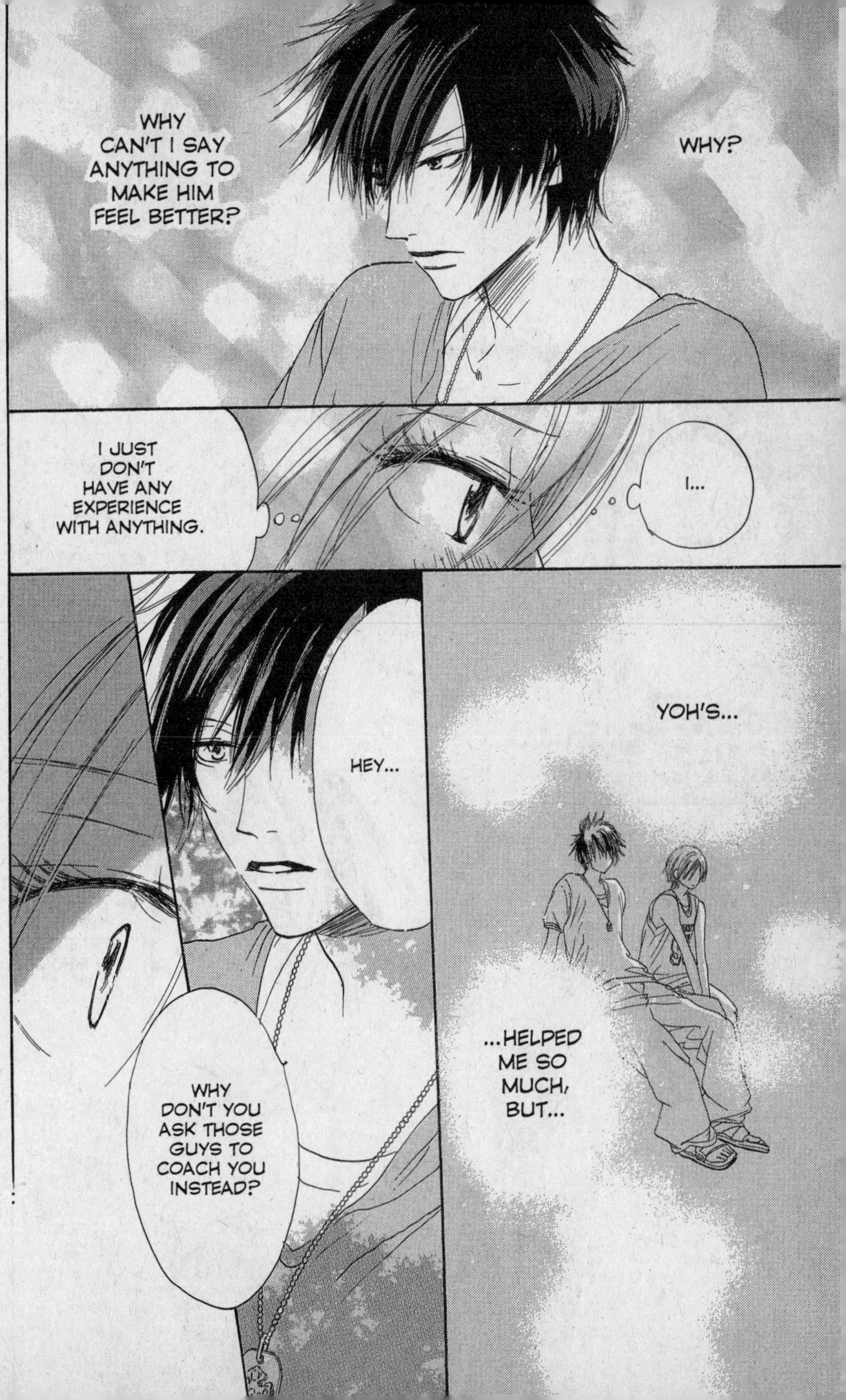
WHY?
WHY CAN'T I SAY ANYTHING TO MAKE HIM FEEL BETTER?
I...
I JUST DON'T HAVE ANY EXPERIENCE WITH ANYTHING.
YOH'S...
...HELPED ME SO MUCH, BUT...
HEY...
WHY DON'T YOU ASK THOSE GUYS TO COACH YOU INSTEAD?

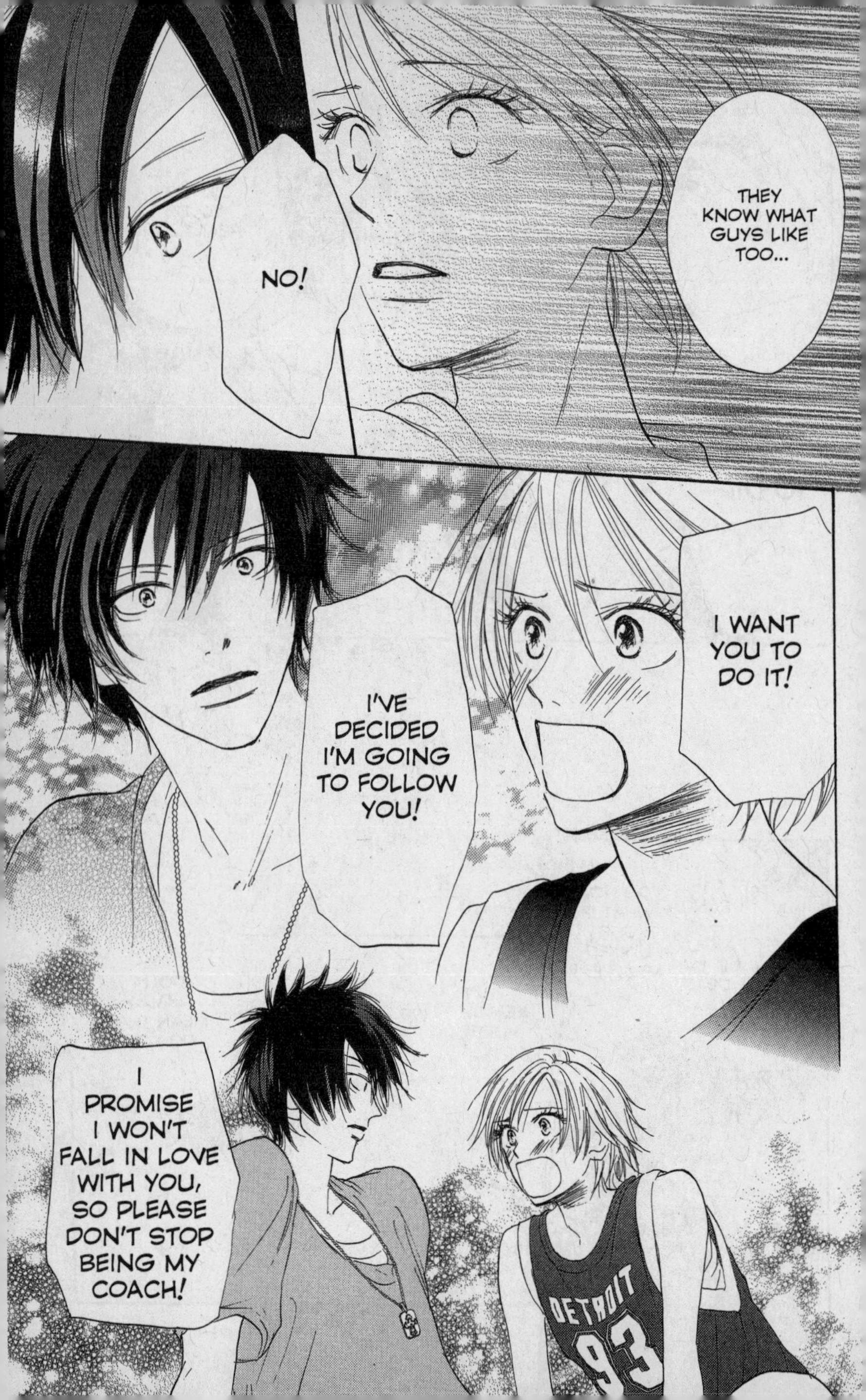
THEY KNOW WHAT GUYS LIKE TOO...
NO!
I WANT YOU TO DO IT!
I'VE DECIDED I'M GOING TO FOLLOW YOU!
I PROMISE I WON'T FALL IN LOVE WITH YOU, SO PLEASE DON'T STOP BEING MY COACH!
DETROIT
93

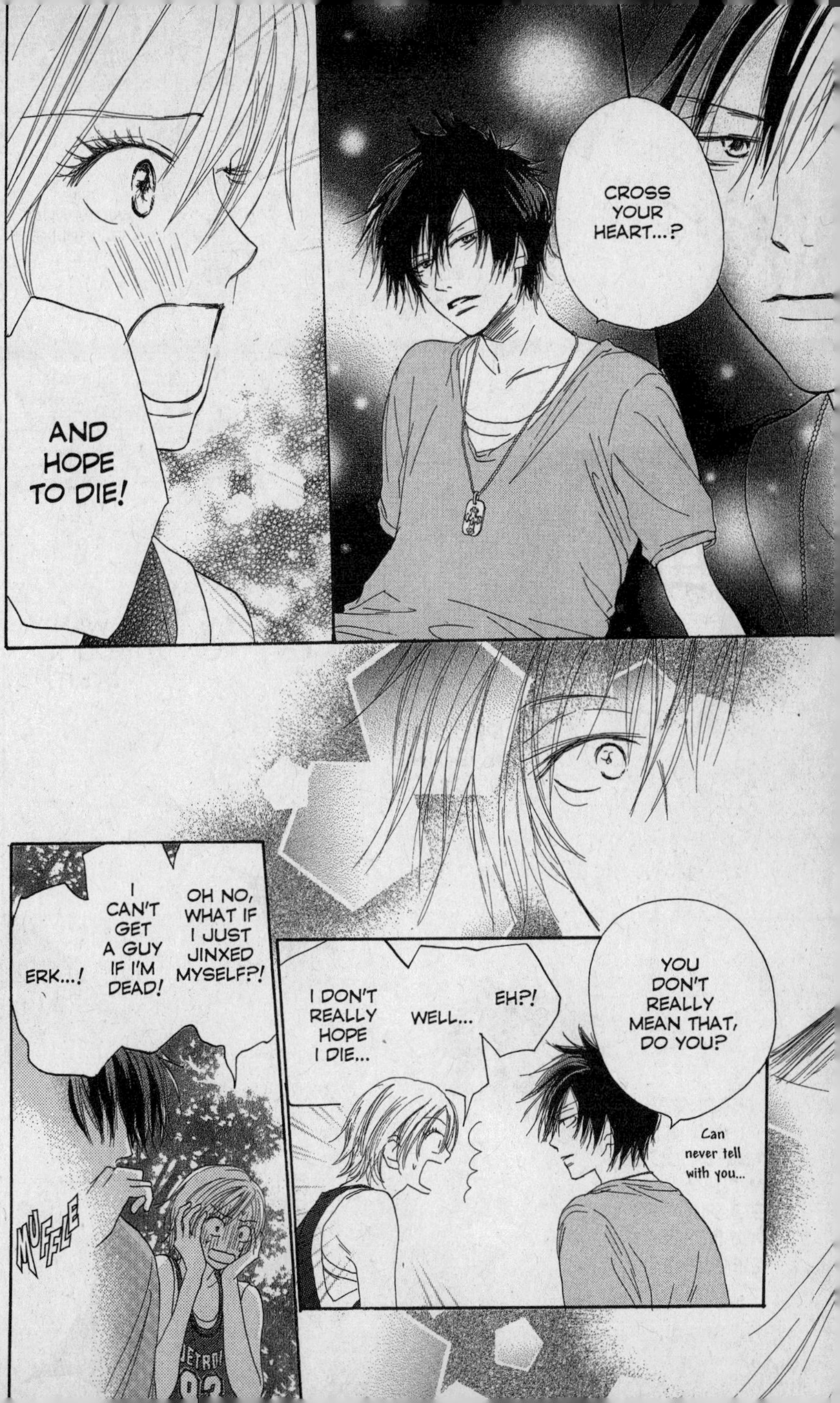
CROSS YOUR HEART...?
AND HOPE TO DIE!
YOU DON'T REALLY MEAN THAT, DO YOU?
Can never tell with you...
EH?!
WELL...
I DON'T REALLY HOPE I DIE...
OH NO, WHAT IF I JUST JINXED MYSELF?!
I CAN'T GET A GUY IF I'M DEAD!
ERK...!
MUFFLE

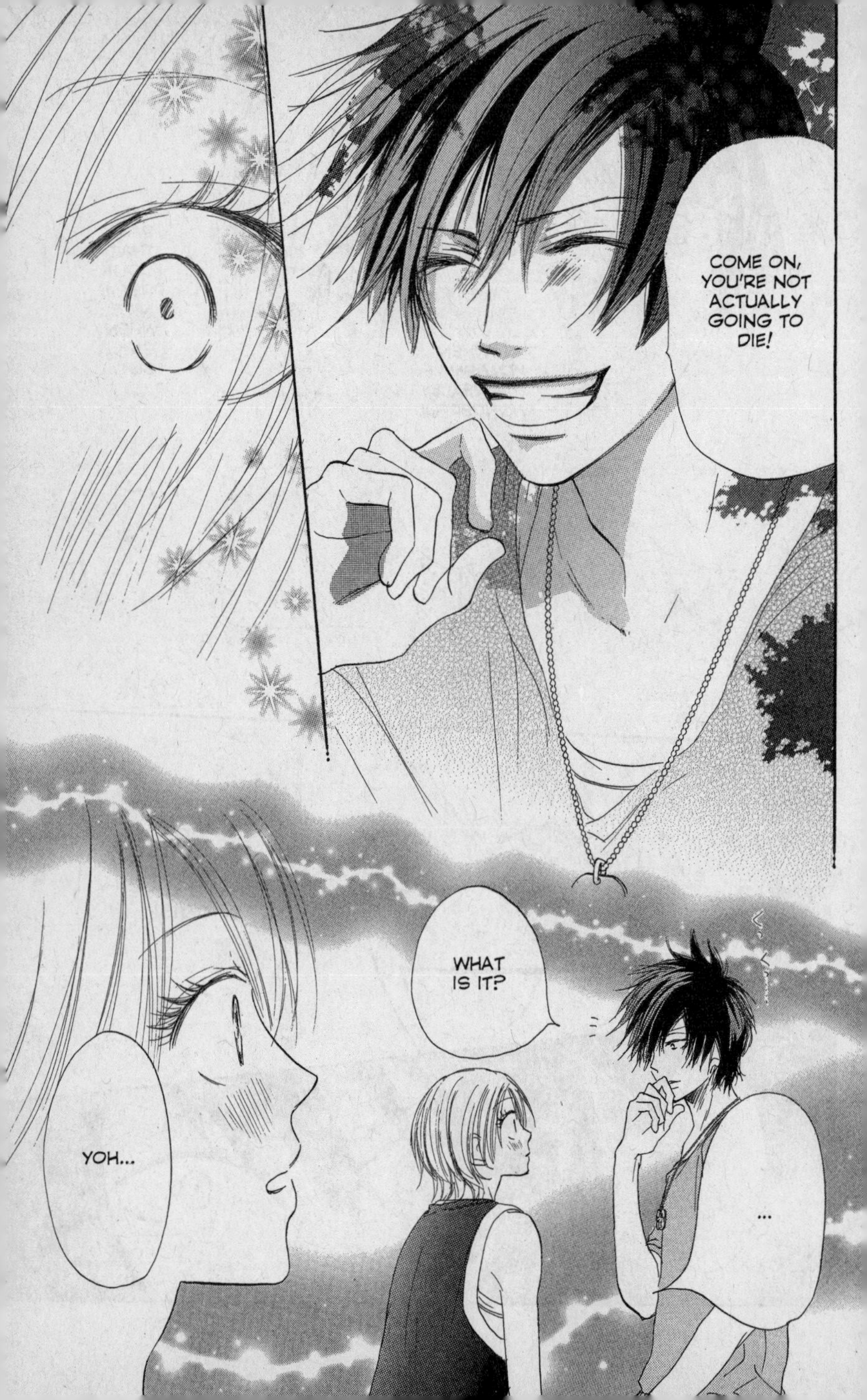
COME ON, YOU'RE NOT ACTUALLY GOING TO DIE!
WHAT IS IT?
...
YOH...

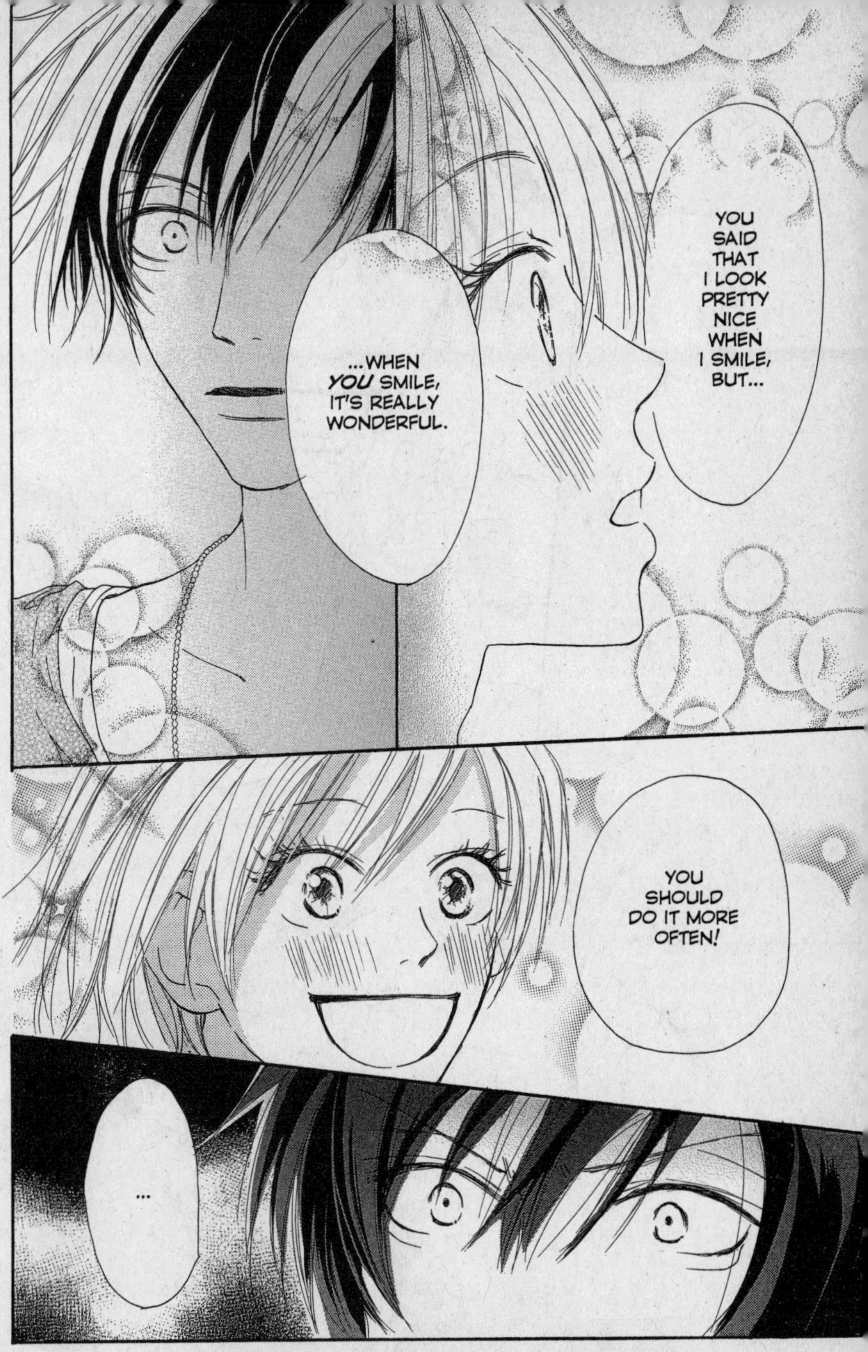
YOU SAID THAT I LOOK PRETTY NICE WHEN I SMILE, BUT...
...WHEN *YOU* SMILE, IT'S REALLY WONDERFUL.
YOU SHOULD DO IT MORE OFTEN!
...

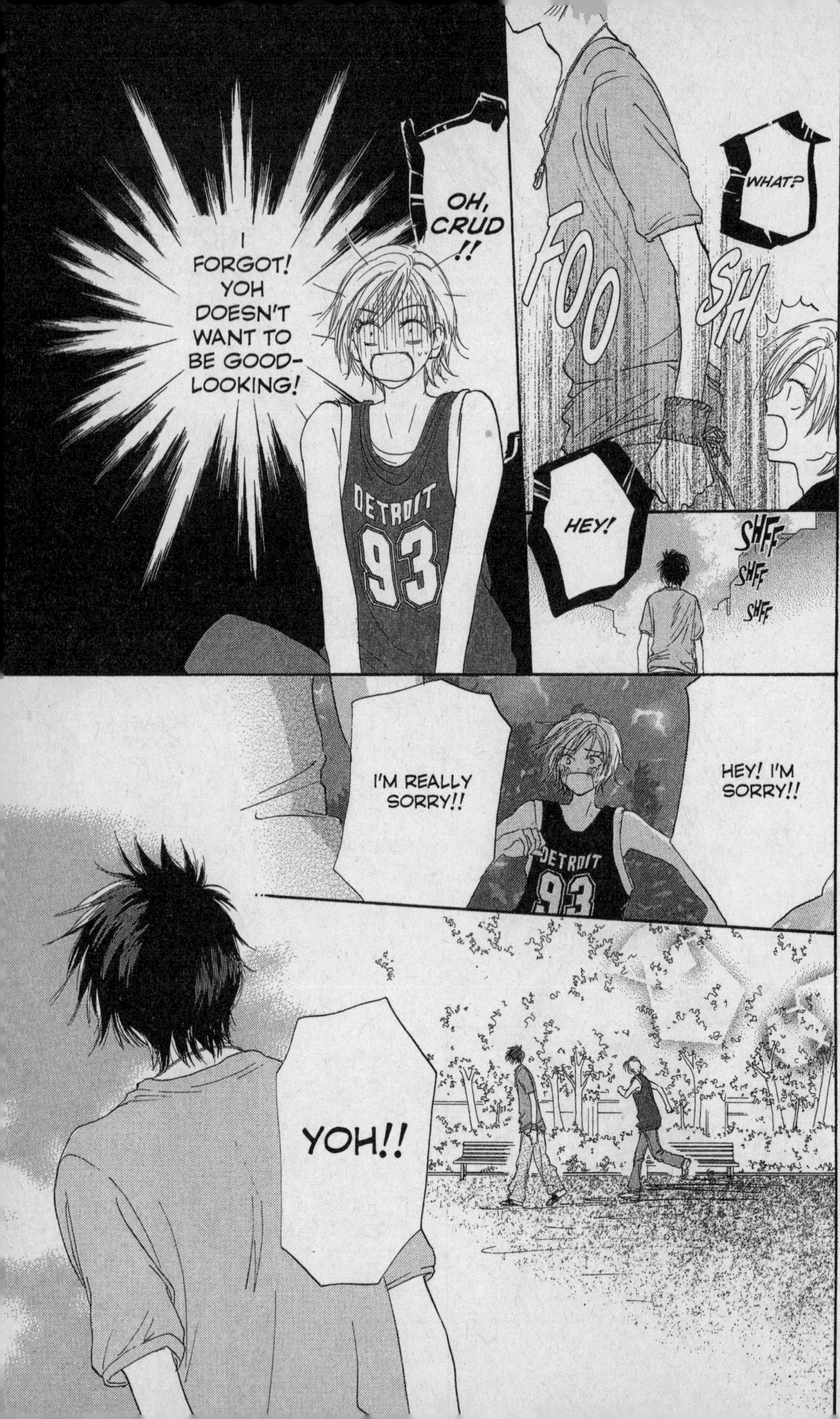
WHAT?
FOOSH
HEY!
SHFF SHFF SHFF
OH, CRUD!!
I FORGOT! YOH DOESN'T WANT TO BE GOOD-LOOKING!
HEY! I'M SORRY!!
I'M REALLY SORRY!!
YOH!!

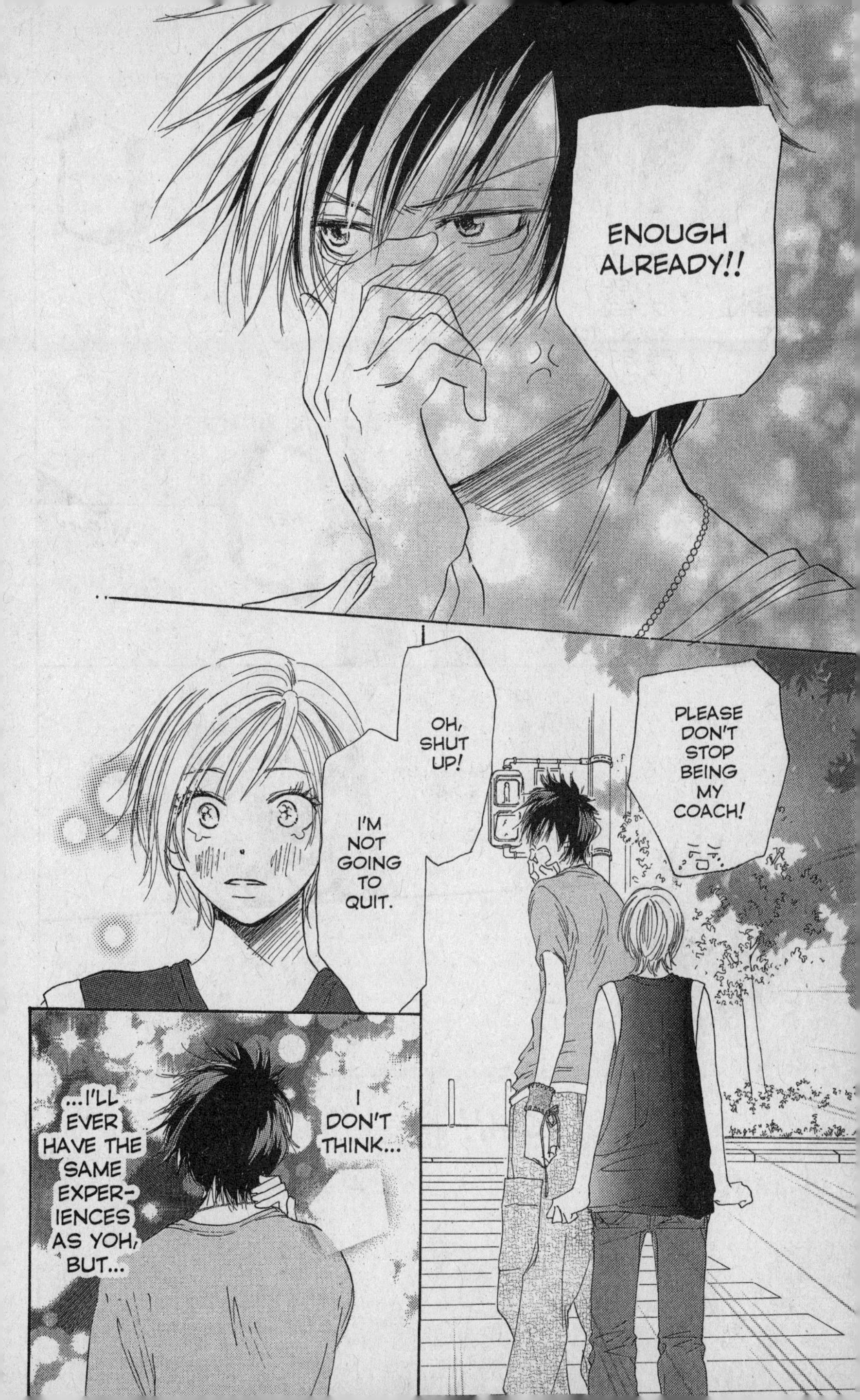
ENOUGH ALREADY!!
PLEASE DON'T STOP BEING MY COACH!
OH, SHUT UP!
I'M NOT GOING TO QUIT.
I DON'T THINK...
...I'LL EVER HAVE THE SAME EXPERIENCES AS YOH, BUT...

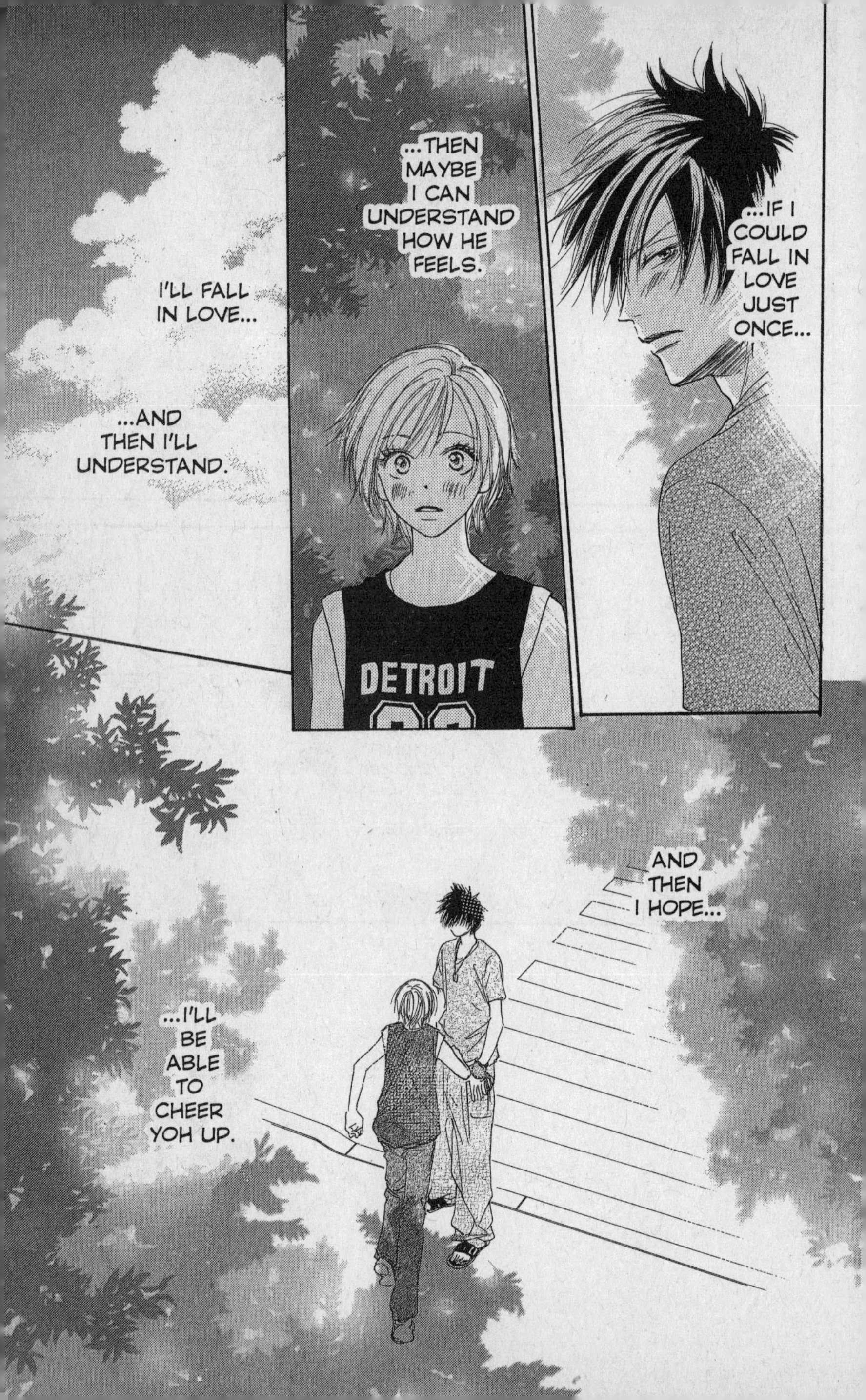
...IF I COULD FALL IN LOVE JUST ONCE...
...THEN MAYBE I CAN UNDERSTAND HOW HE FEELS.
I'LL FALL IN LOVE...
...AND THEN I'LL UNDERSTAND.
AND THEN I HOPE...
...I'LL BE ABLE TO CHEER YOH UP.

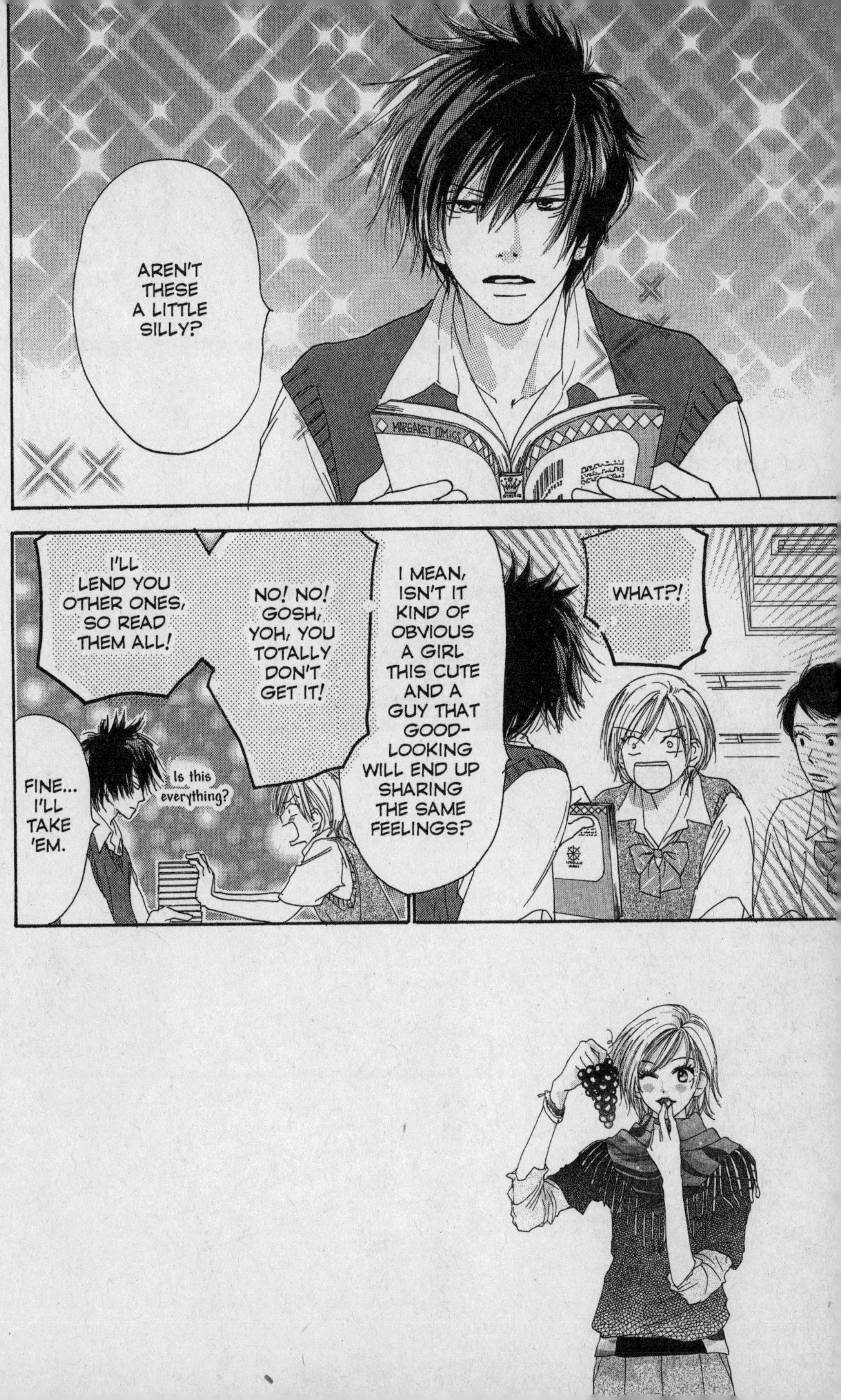
AREN'T THESE A LITTLE SILLY?
WHAT?!
I MEAN, ISN'T IT KIND OF OBVIOUS A GIRL THIS CUTE AND A GUY THAT GOOD-LOOKING WILL END UP SHARING THE SAME FEELINGS?
NO! NO! GOSH, YOH, YOU TOTALLY DON'T GET IT!
I'LL LEND YOU OTHER ONES, SO READ THEM ALL!
Is this everything?
FINE... I'LL TAKE 'EM.

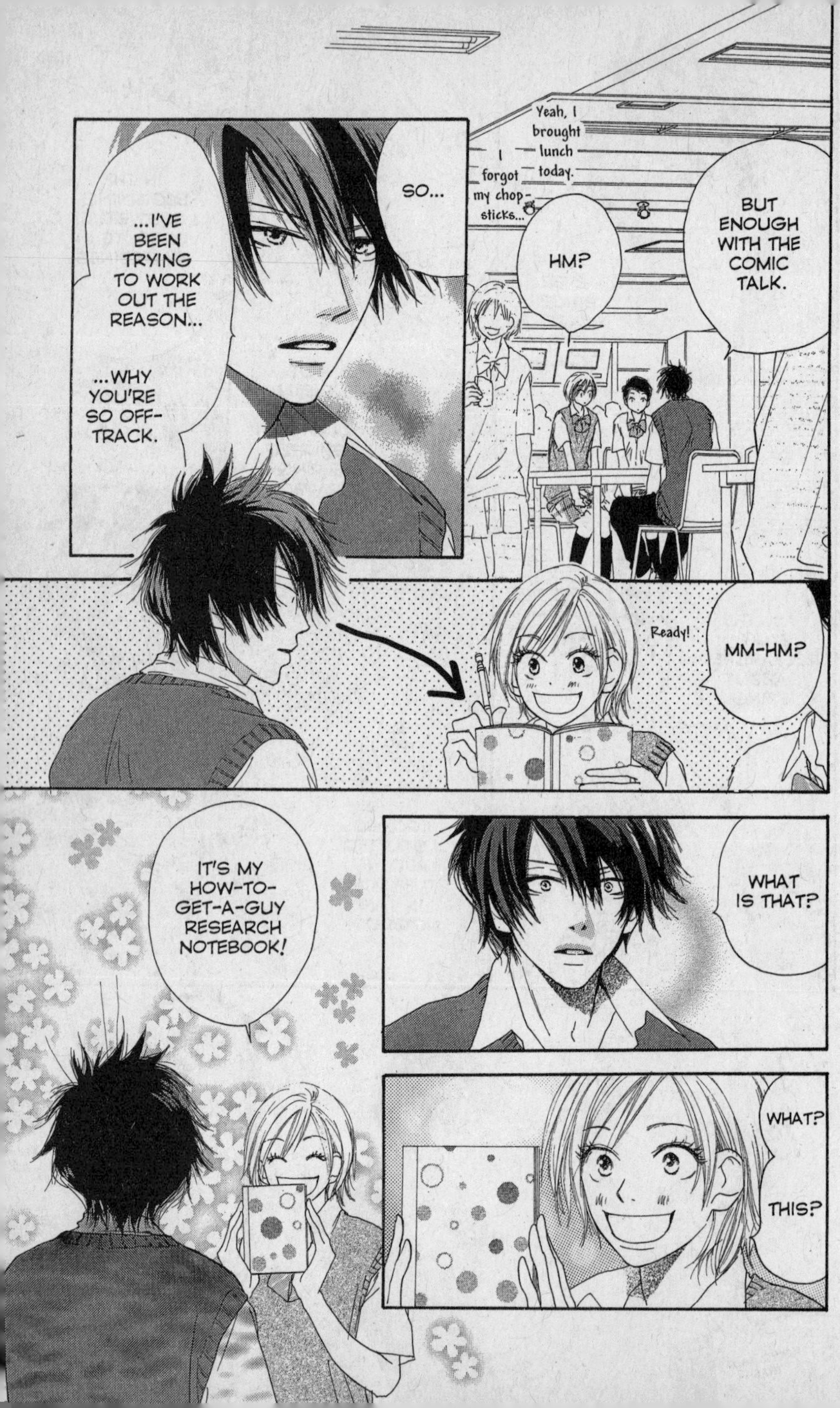
BUT ENOUGH WITH THE COMIC TALK.
Yeah, I brought lunch today.
I forgot my chopsticks...
HM?
SO...
...I'VE BEEN TRYING TO WORK OUT THE REASON...
...WHY YOU'RE SO OFF-TRACK.
MM-HM?
Ready!
WHAT IS THAT?
WHAT?
THIS?
IT'S MY HOW-TO-GET-A-GUY RESEARCH NOTEBOOK!

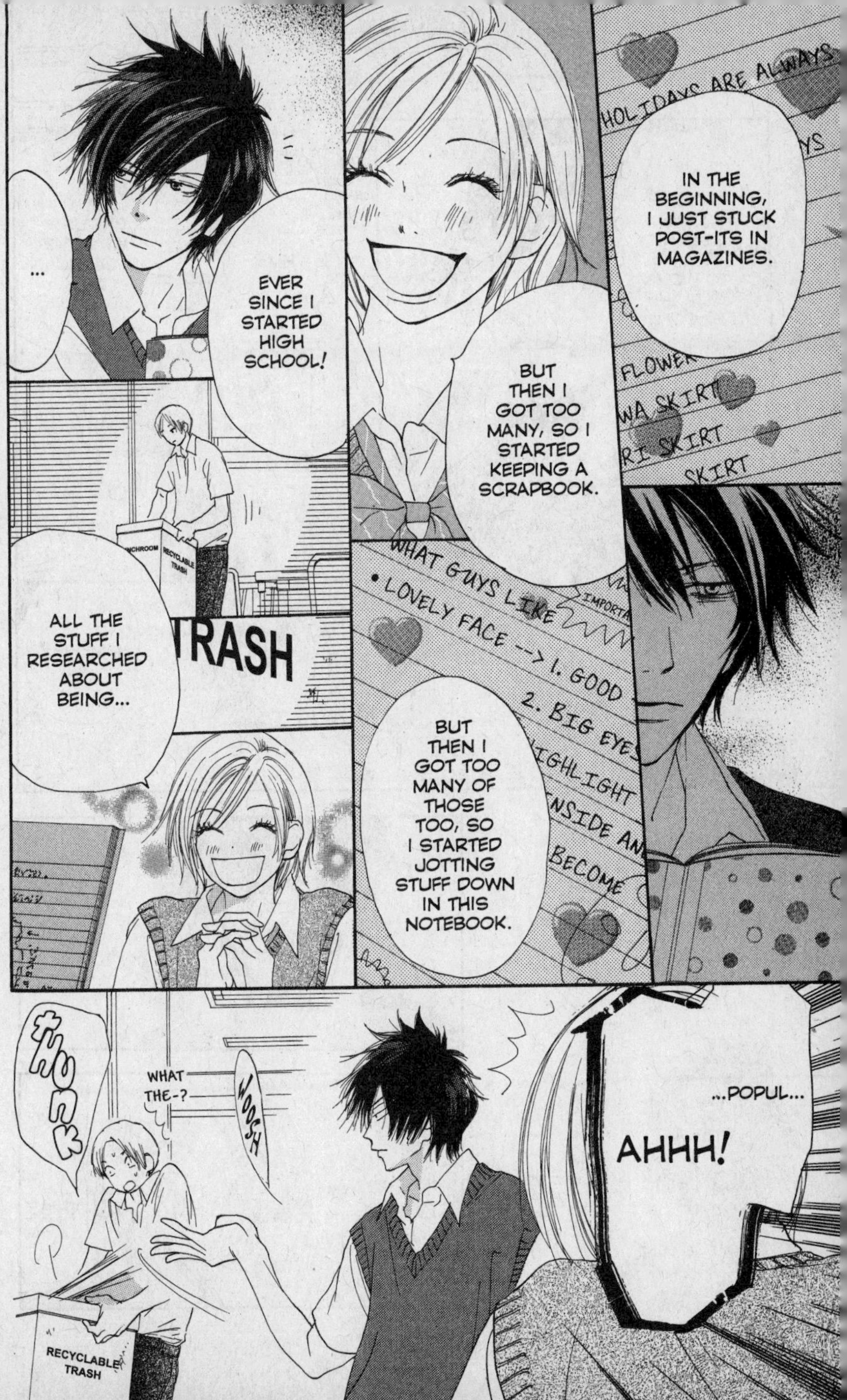
HOLIDAYS ARE ALWAYS
IN THE BEGINNING, I JUST STUCK POST-ITS IN MAGAZINES.
FLOWER
WA SKIRT
RI SKIRT
SKIRT
EVER SINCE I STARTED HIGH SCHOOL!
BUT THEN I GOT TOO MANY, SO I STARTED KEEPING A SCRAPBOOK.
...
WHAT GUYS LIKE
IMPORTA
• LOVELY FACE --> 1. GOOD
2. BIG EYES
IGHLIGHT
NSIDE AN
BECOME
BUT THEN I GOT TOO MANY OF THOSE TOO, SO I STARTED JOTTING STUFF DOWN IN THIS NOTEBOOK.
NCHROOM
RECYCLABLE TRASH
TRASH
ALL THE STUFF I RESEARCHED ABOUT BEING...
...POPUL...
AHHH!
WOOSH
WHAT THE-?
thunk
RECYCLABLE TRASH

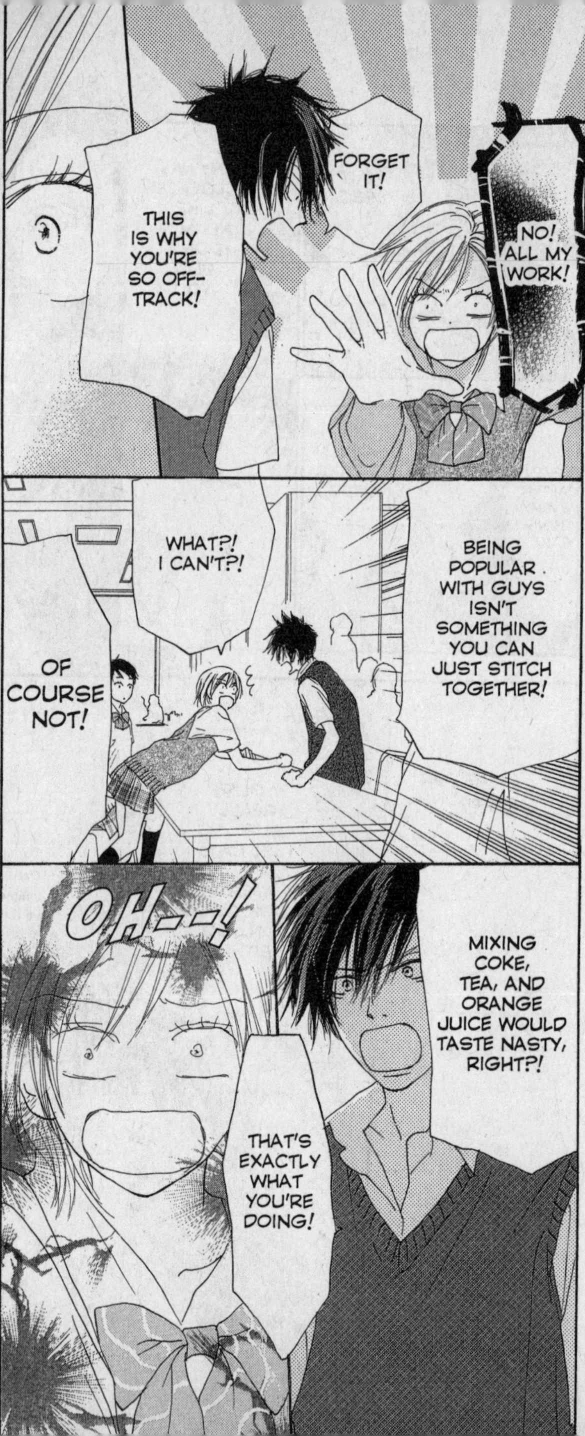
FORGET IT!
NO! ALL MY WORK!
THIS IS WHY YOU'RE SO OFF-TRACK!
BEING POPULAR WITH GUYS ISN'T SOMETHING YOU CAN JUST STITCH TOGETHER!
WHAT?! I CAN'T?!
OF COURSE NOT!
MIXING COKE, TEA, AND ORANGE JUICE WOULD TASTE NASTY, RIGHT?!
OH--!
THAT'S EXACTLY WHAT YOU'RE DOING!

2

Because I wrote about my older niece in the one-shot stories, my little sister told me, "Hey, write about the youngest niece too!" So that's what I'm doing. Sorry I keep talking about my family...

My youngest niece isn't even one yet, but she doesn't get anywhere near the kind of attention her sister got at that age.

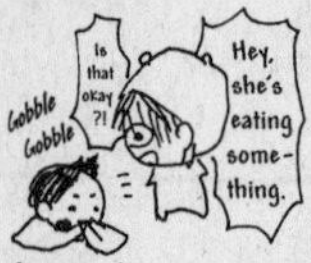
Gobble Gobble
Is that okay?!
Hey, she's eating something.

People aren't overprotective of her. In fact, I think it's quite the opposite.

When the older sister was her age, I'd be told to wash my hands before playing with her, but with this little one, no one even bothers.

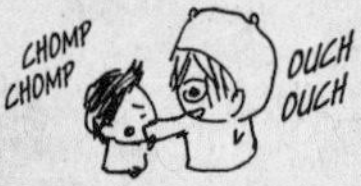
CHOMP CHOMP
OUCH OUCH

Do your teeth feel itchy?

That really hurts! OW!

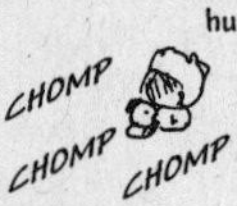
CHOMP
CHOMP
CHOMP

But she's cute! ♡

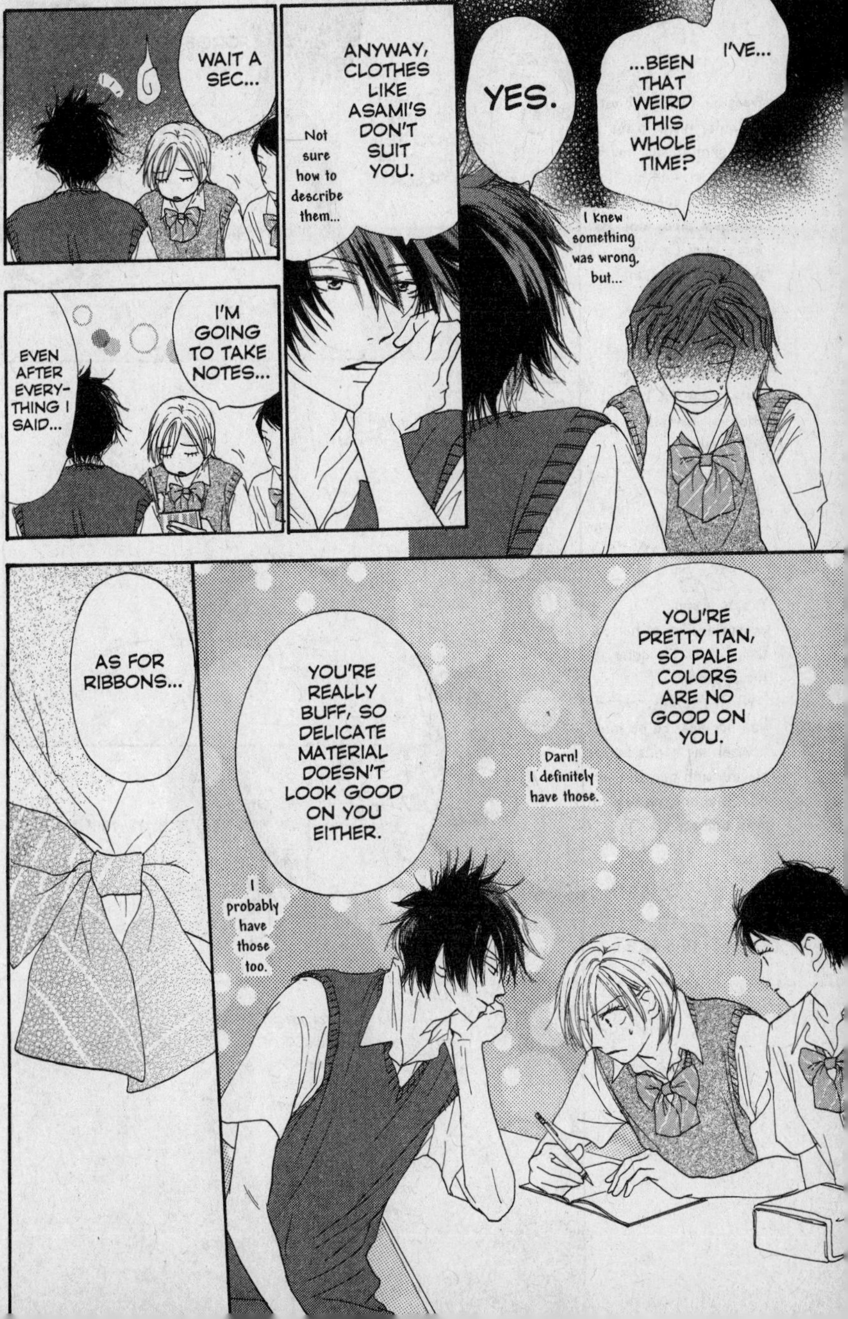
I'VE...
...BEEN THAT WEIRD THIS WHOLE TIME?
I knew something was wrong, but...
YES.
ANYWAY, CLOTHES LIKE ASAMI'S DON'T SUIT YOU.
Not sure how to describe them...
WAIT A SEC...
I'M GOING TO TAKE NOTES...
EVEN AFTER EVERYTHING I SAID...
YOU'RE PRETTY TAN, SO PALE COLORS ARE NO GOOD ON YOU.
Darn! I definitely have those.
YOU'RE REALLY BUFF, SO DELICATE MATERIAL DOESN'T LOOK GOOD ON YOU EITHER.
I probably have those too.
AS FOR RIBBONS...

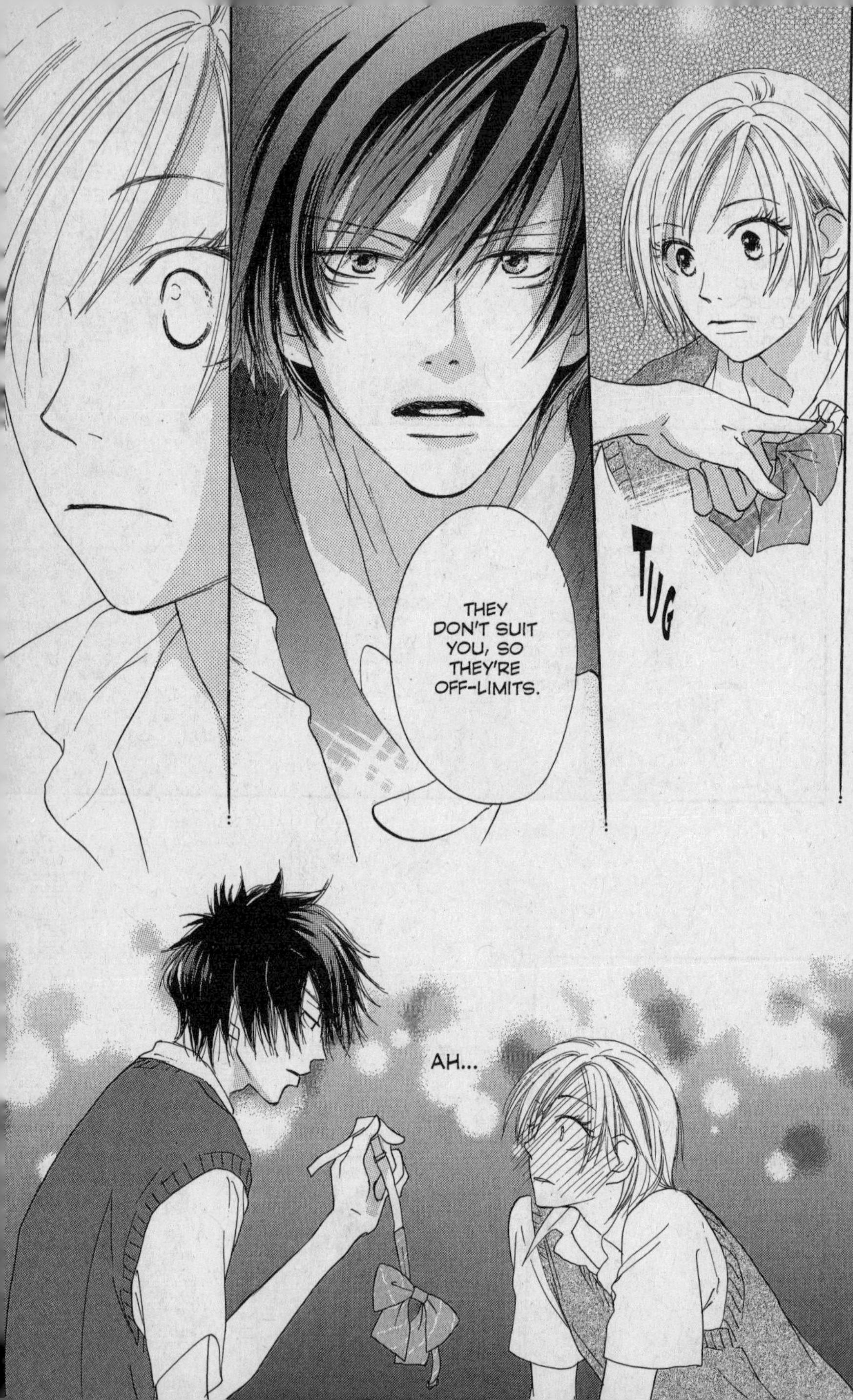
TUG
THEY DON'T SUIT YOU, SO THEY'RE OFF-LIMITS.
AH...

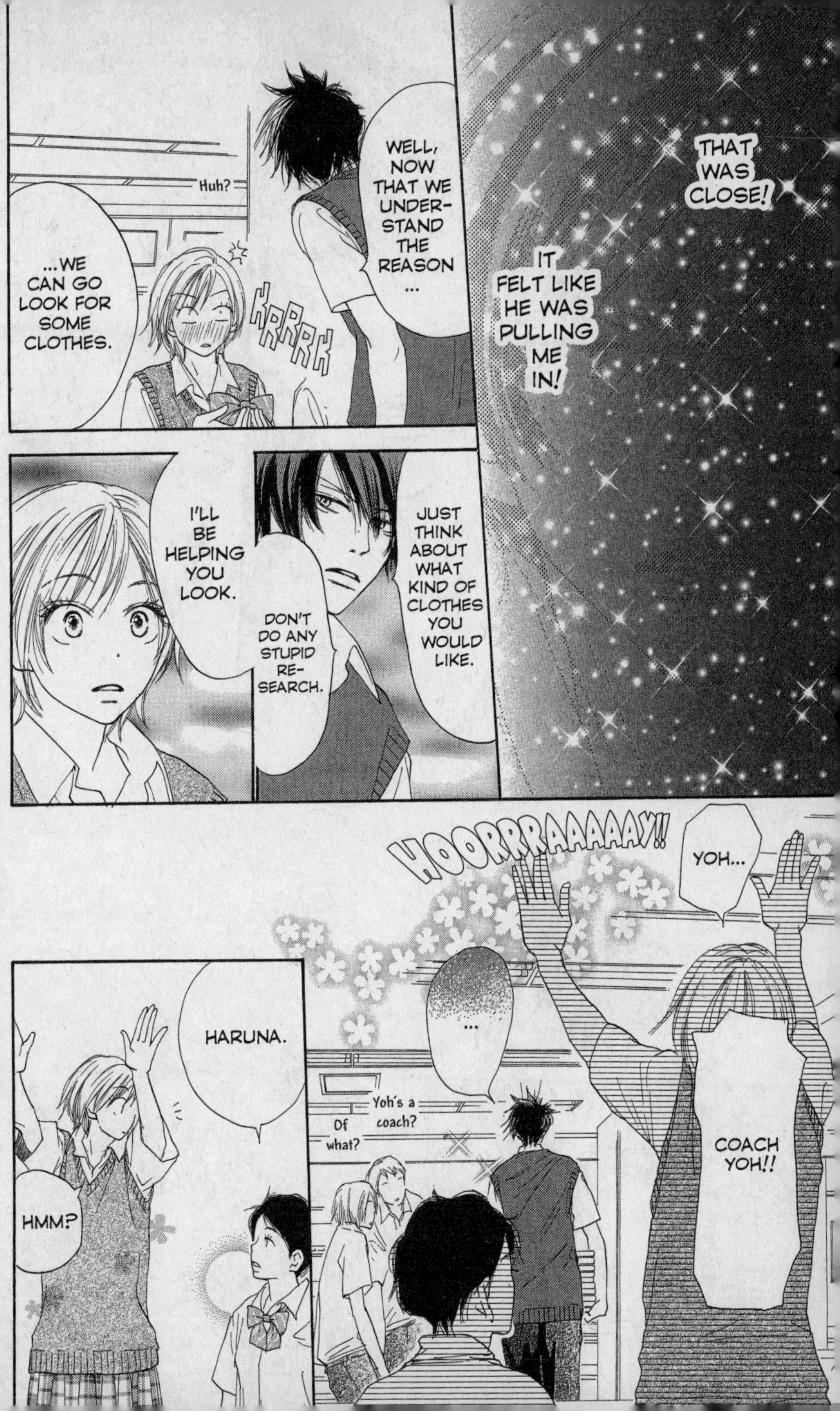

THAT WAS CLOSE!
IT FELT LIKE HE WAS PULLING ME IN!
WELL, NOW THAT WE UNDER-STAND THE REASON...
Huh?
KRRRK
...WE CAN GO LOOK FOR SOME CLOTHES.
JUST THINK ABOUT WHAT KIND OF CLOTHES YOU WOULD LIKE.
DON'T DO ANY STUPID RE-SEARCH.
I'LL BE HELPING YOU LOOK.
HOORRRAAAAAY!!
YOH...
COACH YOH!!
...
Yoh's a coach?
Of what?
HARUNA.
HMM?

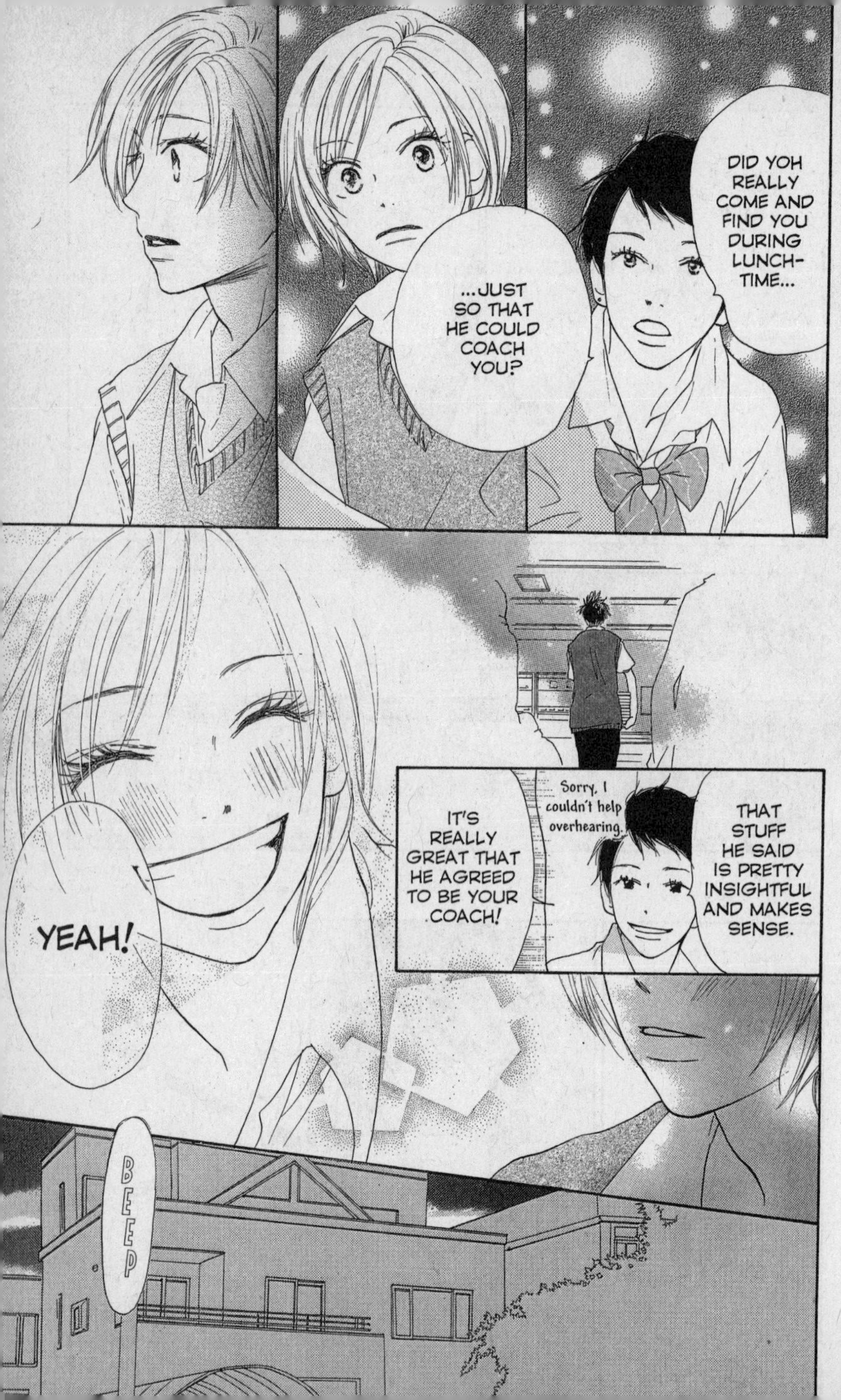
DID YOH REALLY COME AND FIND YOU DURING LUNCH-TIME...
...JUST SO THAT HE COULD COACH YOU?
THAT STUFF HE SAID IS PRETTY INSIGHTFUL AND MAKES SENSE.
Sorry, I couldn't help overhearing.
IT'S REALLY GREAT THAT HE AGREED TO BE YOUR COACH!
YEAH!
BEEP

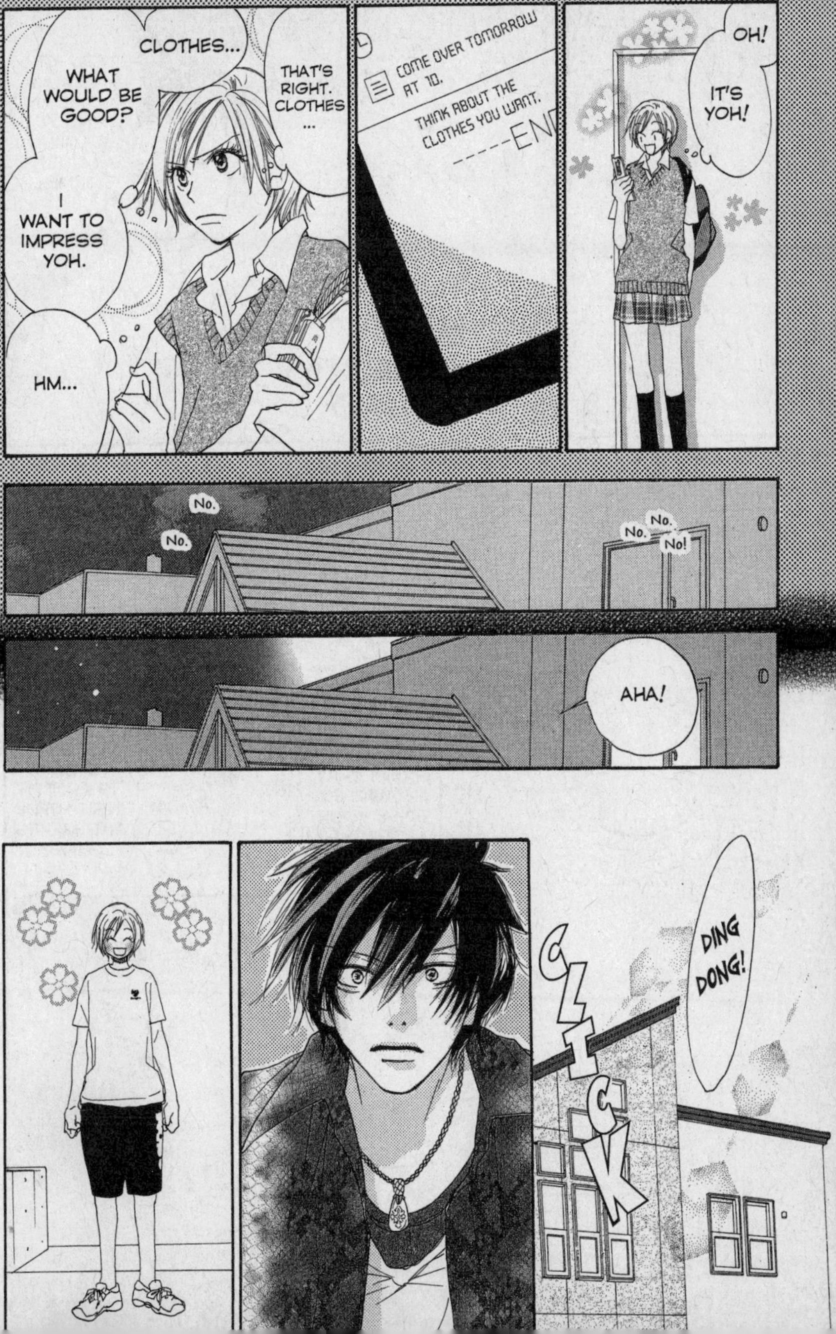
OH!
IT'S YOH!
COME OVER TOMORROW AT 10.
THINK ABOUT THE CLOTHES YOU WANT.
-----END
THAT'S RIGHT. CLOTHES...
CLOTHES...
WHAT WOULD BE GOOD?
I WANT TO IMPRESS YOH.
HM...
No.
No.
No!
No.
No.
AHA!
DING DONG!
CLICK

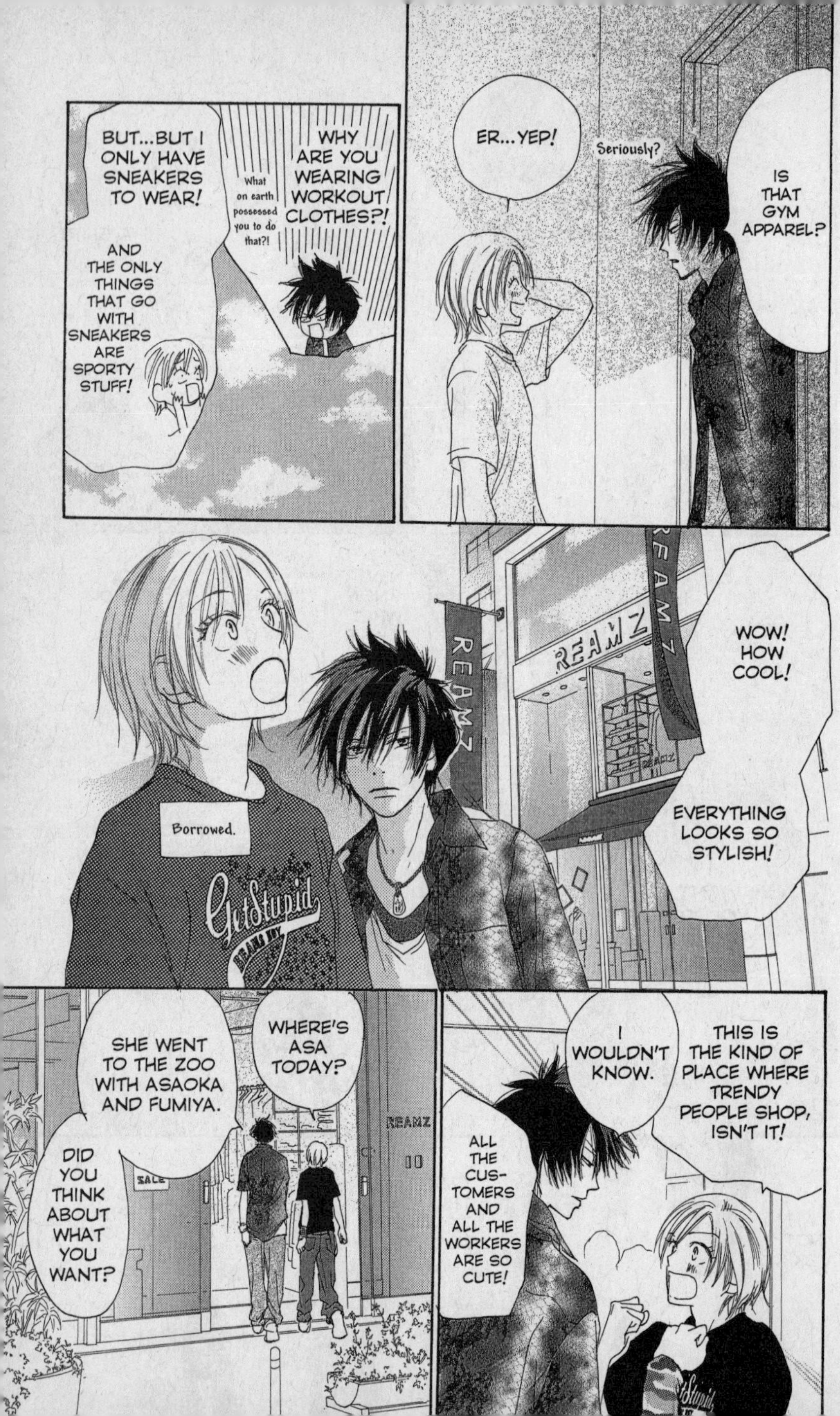
IS THAT GYM APPAREL?
Seriously?
ER...YEP!
WHY ARE YOU WEARING WORKOUT CLOTHES?!
What on earth possessed you to do that?!
BUT...BUT I ONLY HAVE SNEAKERS TO WEAR!
AND THE ONLY THINGS THAT GO WITH SNEAKERS ARE SPORTY STUFF!
WOW! HOW COOL!
EVERYTHING LOOKS SO STYLISH!
REAMZ
Borrowed.
GetStupid
THIS IS THE KIND OF PLACE WHERE TRENDY PEOPLE SHOP, ISN'T IT!
I WOULDN'T KNOW.
ALL THE CUSTOMERS AND ALL THE WORKERS ARE SO CUTE!
WHERE'S ASA TODAY?
SHE WENT TO THE ZOO WITH ASAOKA AND FUMIYA.
REAMZ
SALE
DID YOU THINK ABOUT WHAT YOU WANT?

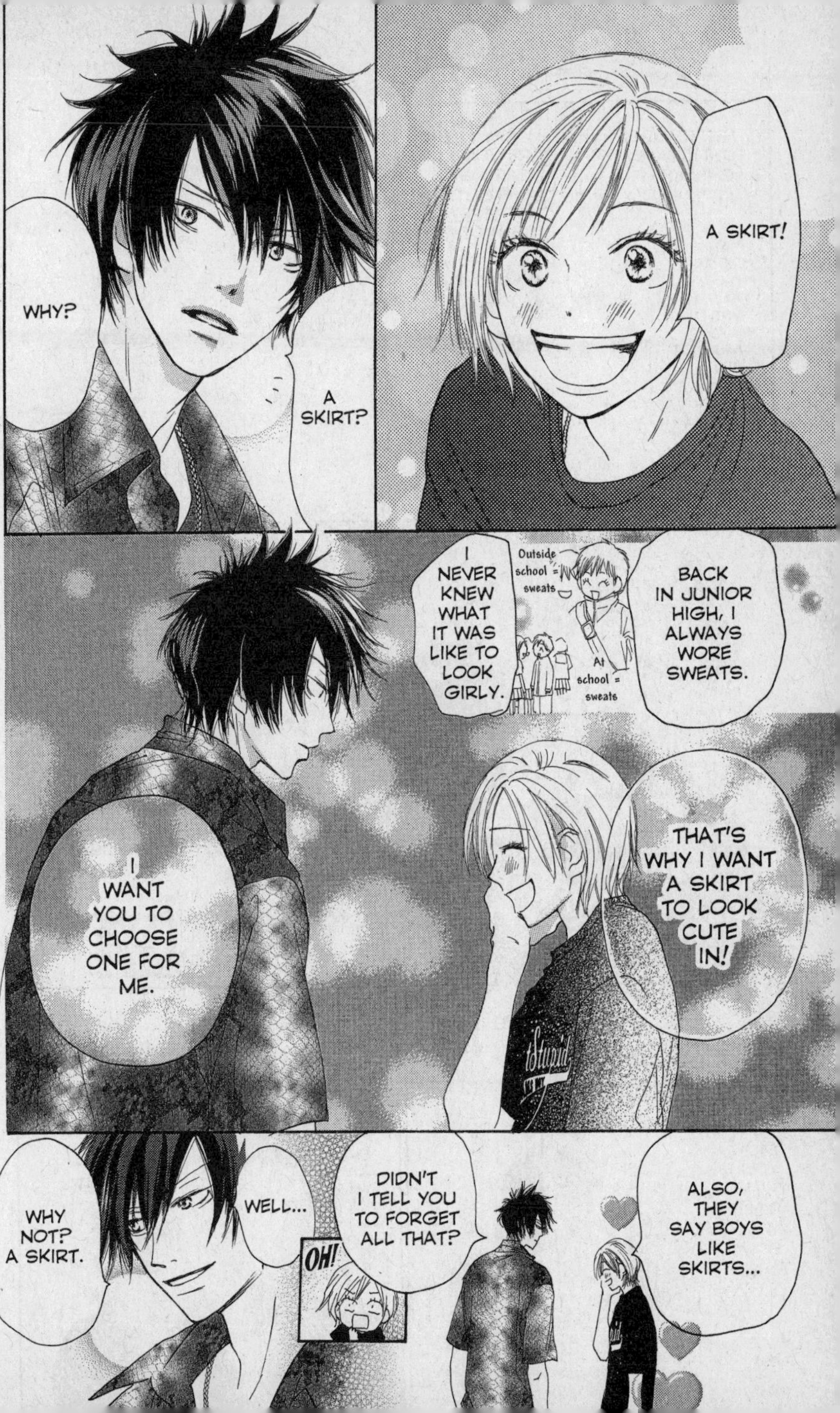
A SKIRT!
A SKIRT?
WHY?
BACK IN JUNIOR HIGH, I ALWAYS WORE SWEATS.
Outside school = sweats
At school = sweats
I NEVER KNEW WHAT IT WAS LIKE TO LOOK GIRLY.
THAT'S WHY I WANT A SKIRT TO LOOK CUTE IN!
I WANT YOU TO CHOOSE ONE FOR ME.
ALSO, THEY SAY BOYS LIKE SKIRTS...
DIDN'T I TELL YOU TO FORGET ALL THAT?
OH!
WELL...
WHY NOT? A SKIRT.

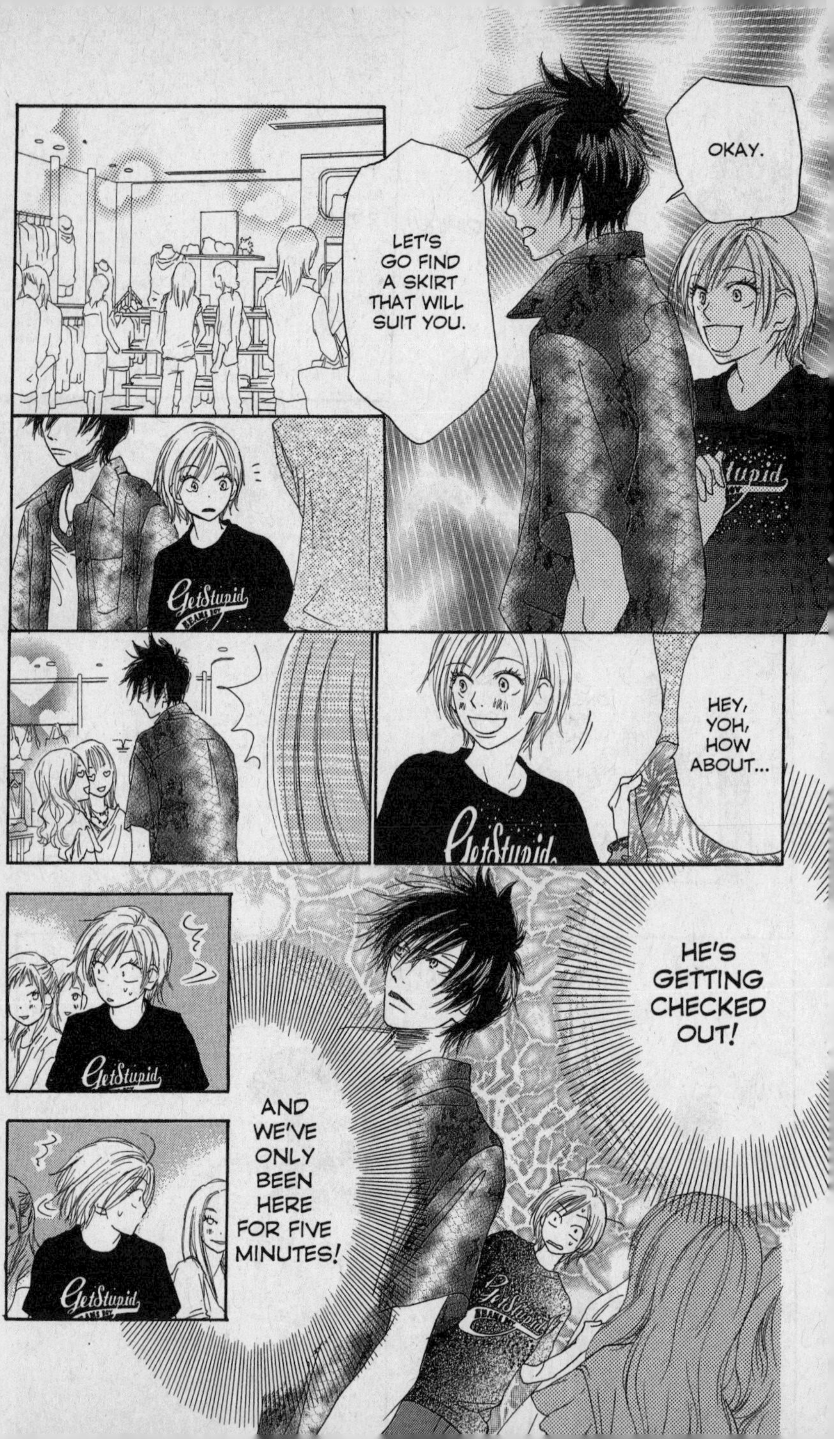
LET'S GO FIND A SKIRT THAT WILL SUIT YOU.
OKAY.
HEY, YOH, HOW ABOUT...
HE'S GETTING CHECKED OUT!
AND WE'VE ONLY BEEN HERE FOR FIVE MINUTES!

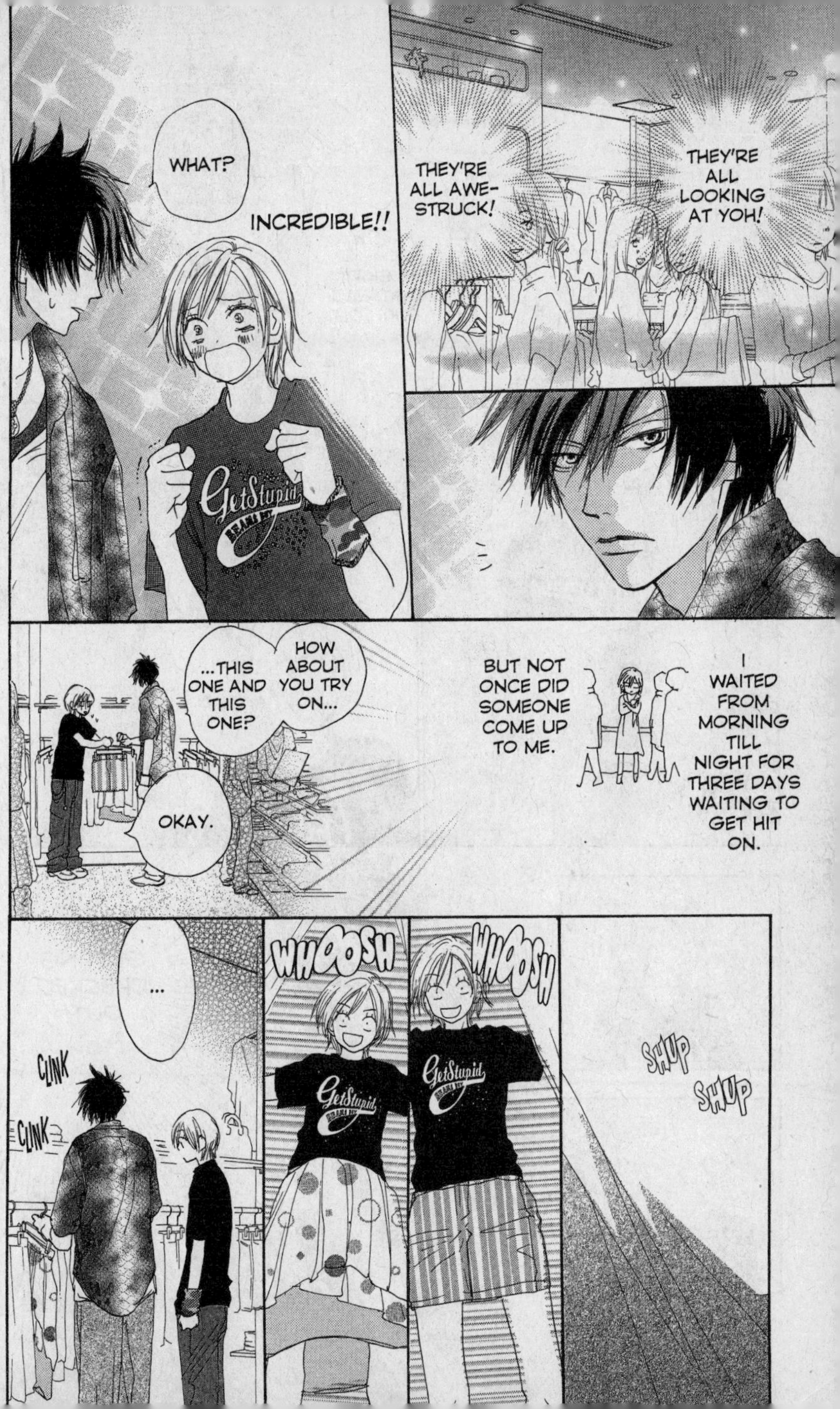
THEY'RE ALL LOOKING AT YOH!
THEY'RE ALL AWE-STRUCK!
INCREDIBLE!!
WHAT?
I WAITED FROM MORNING TILL NIGHT FOR THREE DAYS WAITING TO GET HIT ON.
BUT NOT ONCE DID SOMEONE COME UP TO ME.
HOW ABOUT YOU TRY ON...
...THIS ONE AND THIS ONE?
OKAY.
SHUP
SHUP
WHOOSH
WHOOSH
...
CLINK
CLINK

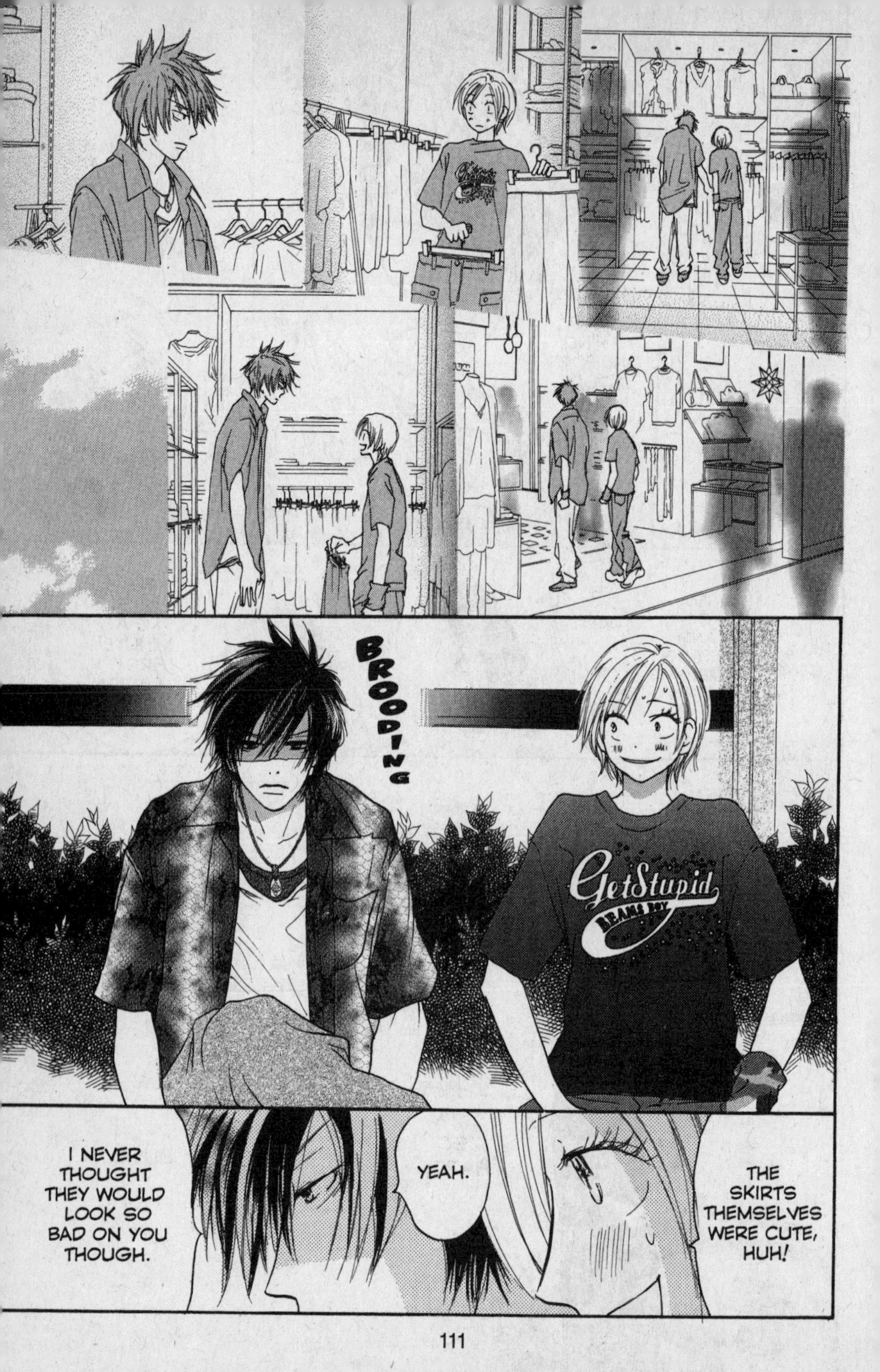
BROODING
GetStupid
BEAMS BOY
THE SKIRTS THEMSELVES WERE CUTE, HUH!
YEAH.
I NEVER THOUGHT THEY WOULD LOOK SO BAD ON YOU THOUGH.

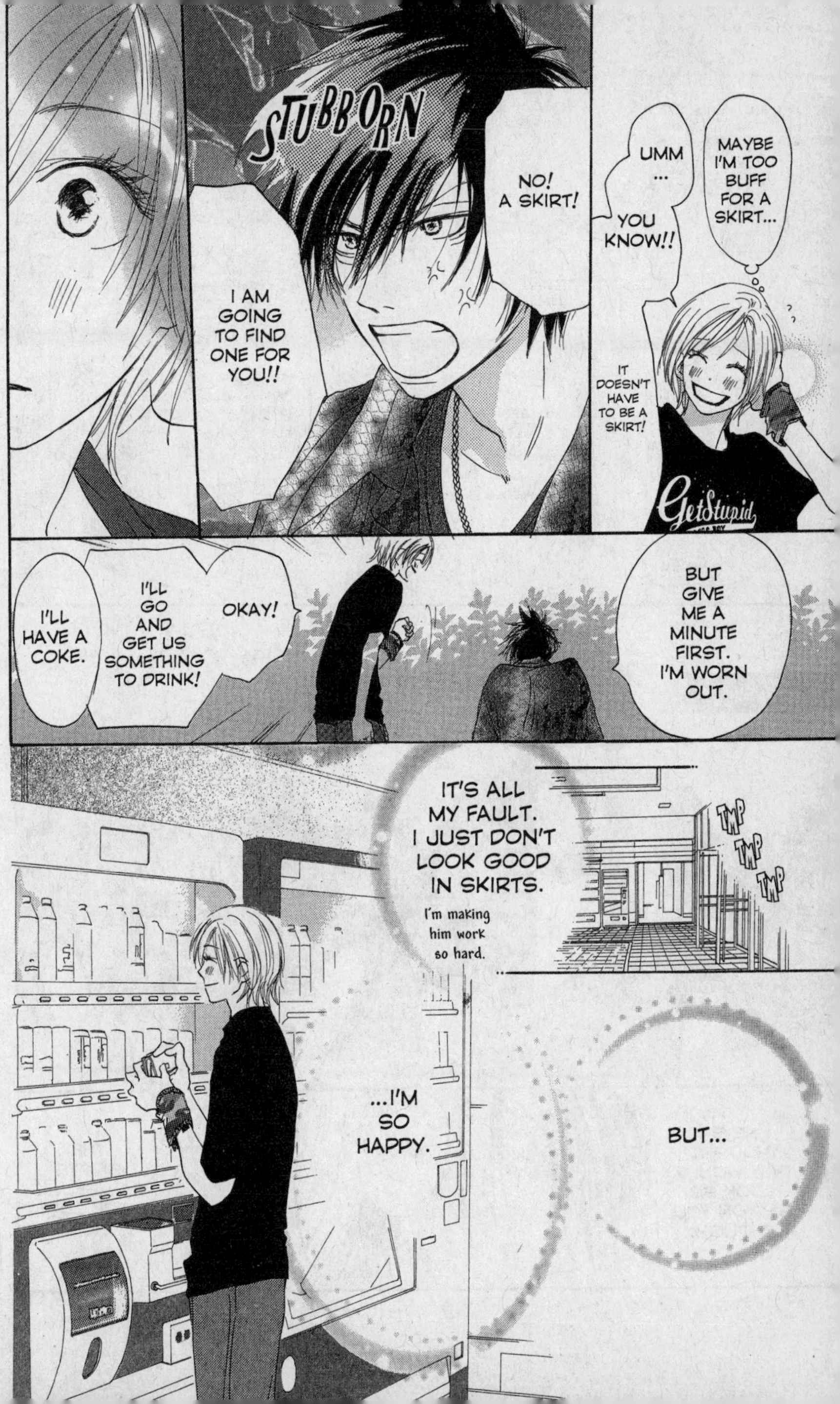
MAYBE I'M TOO BUFF FOR A SKIRT...
UMM ... YOU KNOW!!
IT DOESN'T HAVE TO BE A SKIRT!
GetStupid
STUBBORN
NO! A SKIRT!
I AM GOING TO FIND ONE FOR YOU!!
BUT GIVE ME A MINUTE FIRST. I'M WORN OUT.
OKAY!
I'LL GO AND GET US SOMETHING TO DRINK!
I'LL HAVE A COKE.
TMP
TMP
TMP
IT'S ALL MY FAULT. I JUST DON'T LOOK GOOD IN SKIRTS.
I'm making him work so hard.
BUT...
...I'M SO HAPPY.

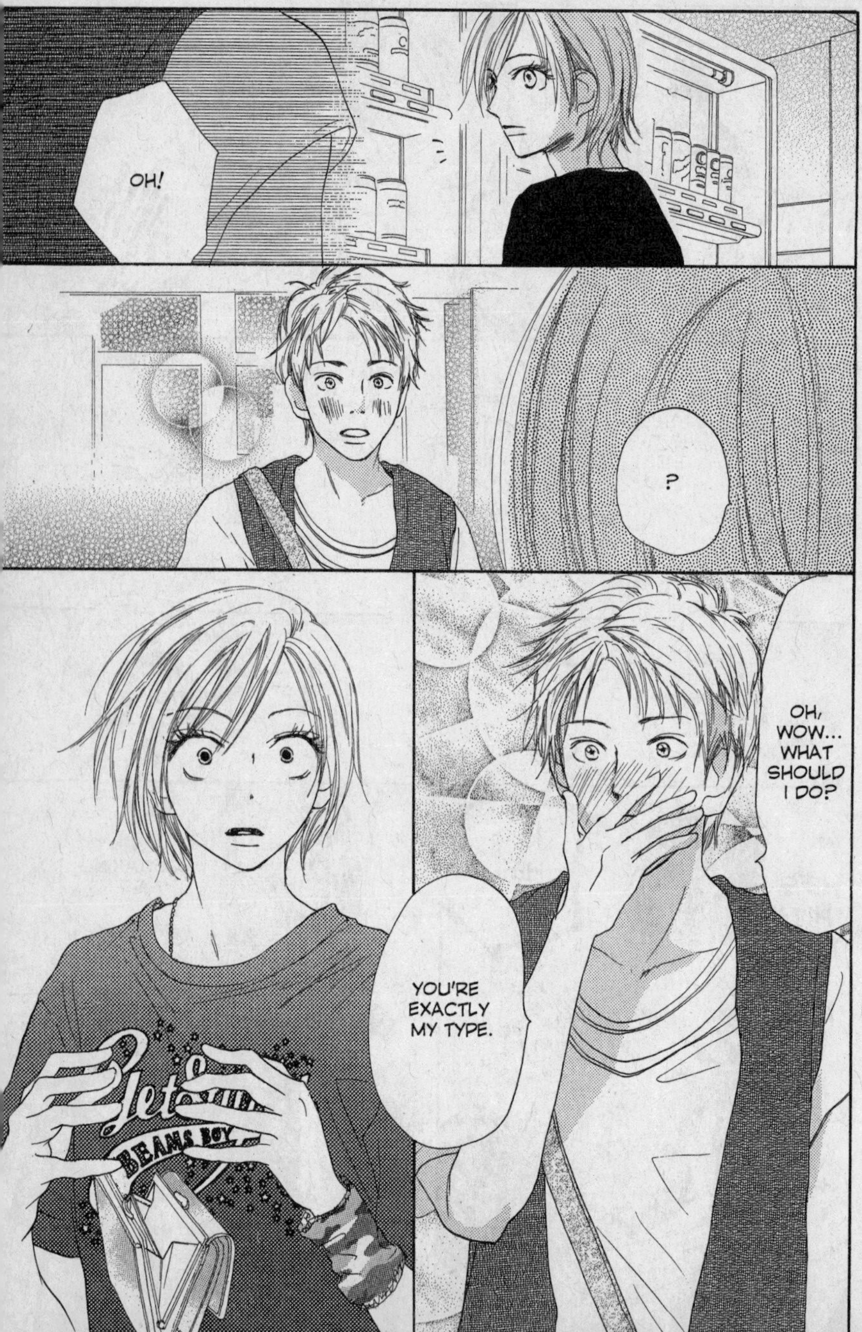
OH!
?
OH, WOW... WHAT SHOULD I DO?
YOU'RE EXACTLY MY TYPE.
BEAMS BOY

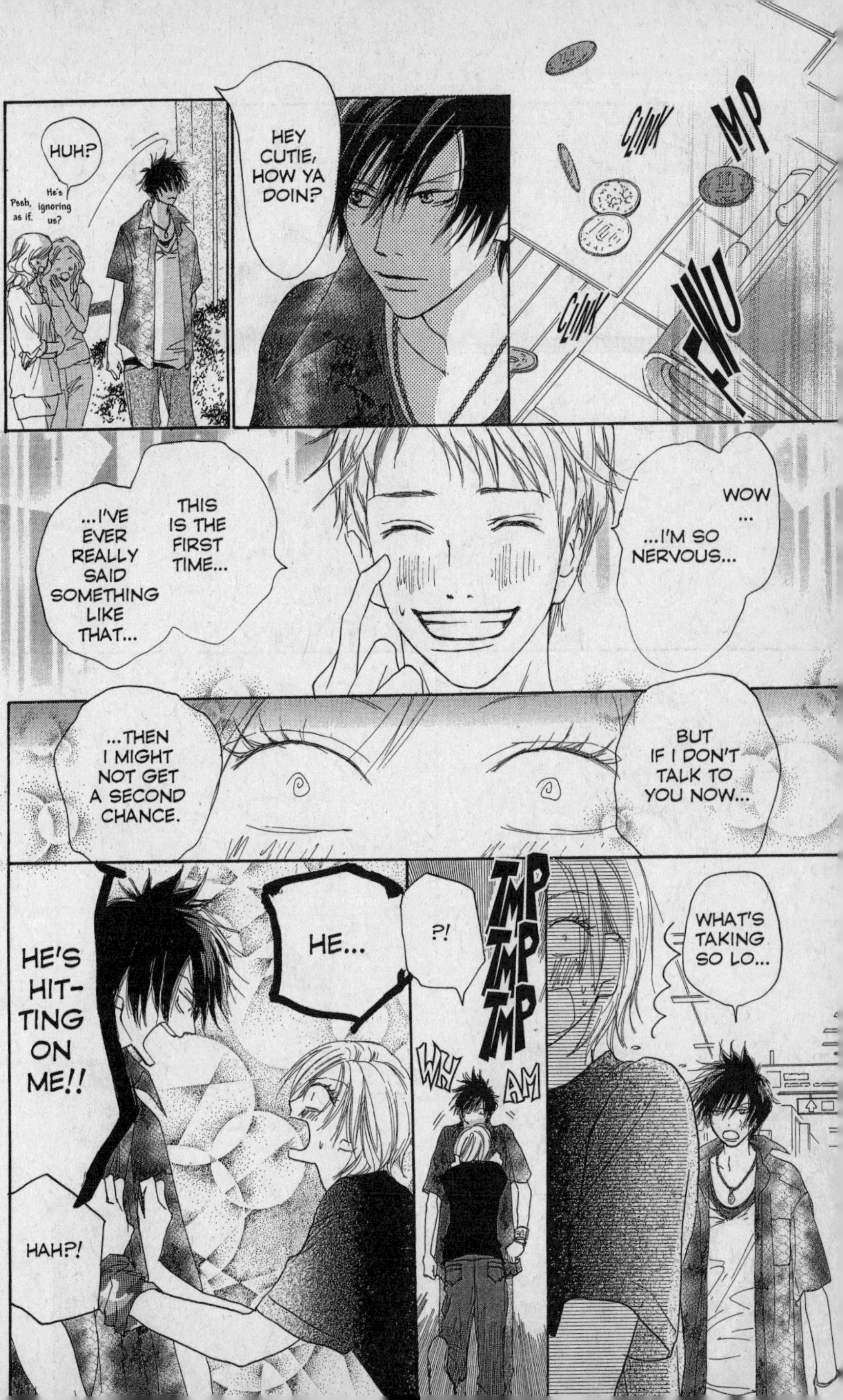
CLINK
CLINK
HEY CUTIE, HOW YA DOIN?
HUH?
He's ignoring us?
Pssh, as if.
WOW ...
...I'M SO NERVOUS...
THIS IS THE FIRST TIME...
...I'VE EVER REALLY SAID SOMETHING LIKE THAT...
BUT IF I DON'T TALK TO YOU NOW...
...THEN I MIGHT NOT GET A SECOND CHANCE.
WHAT'S TAKING SO LO...
TMP TMP TMP
WH AM
?!
HE...
HE'S HIT-TING ON ME!!
HAH?!

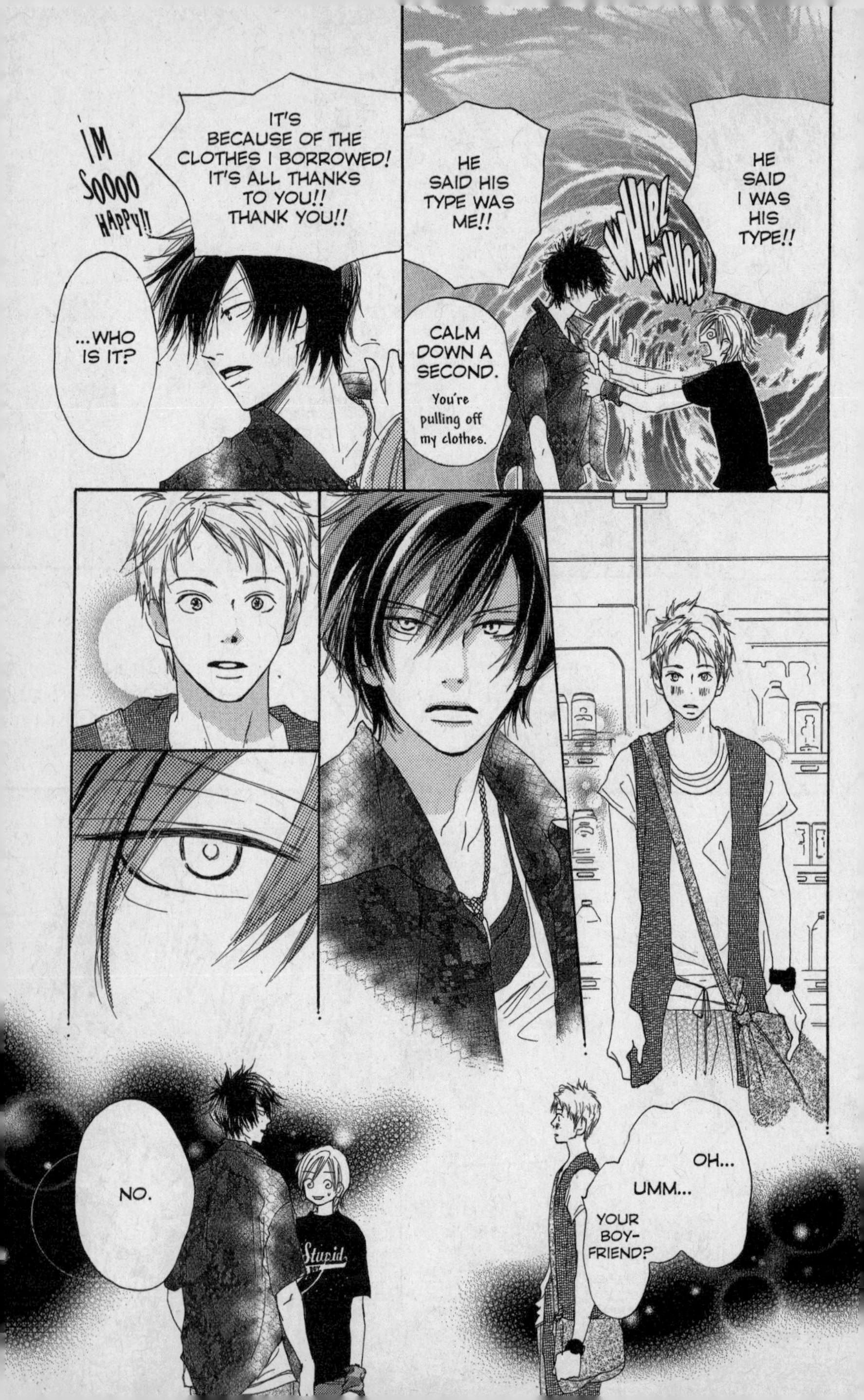
HE SAID I WAS HIS TYPE!!
HE SAID HIS TYPE WAS ME!!
WHIRL WHIRL
CALM DOWN A SECOND.
You're pulling off my clothes.
IT'S BECAUSE OF THE CLOTHES I BORROWED! IT'S ALL THANKS TO YOU!! THANK YOU!!
I'M SOOOO HAPPY!!
...WHO IS IT?
OH...
UMM...
YOUR BOY-FRIEND?
NO.

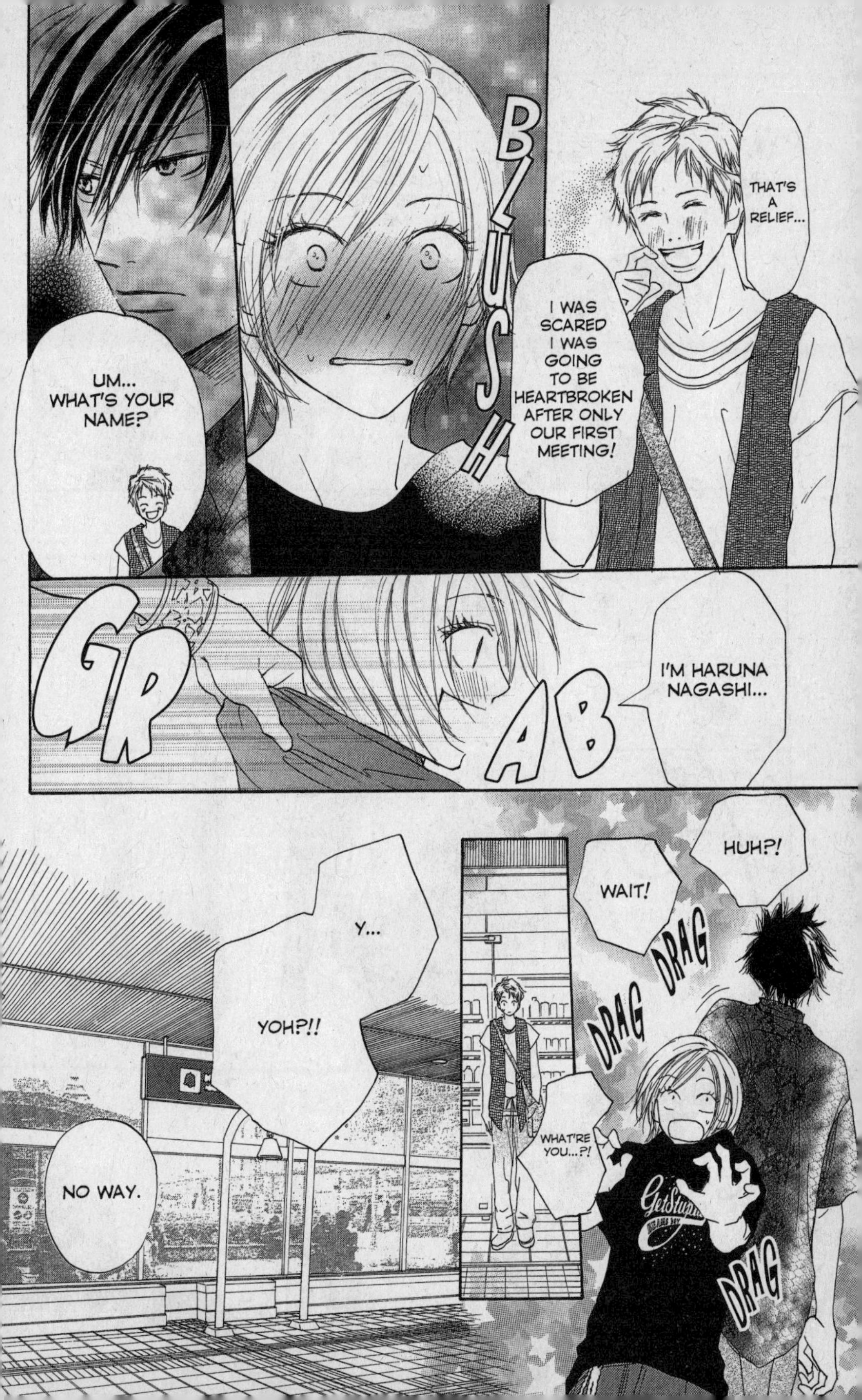
THAT'S A RELIEF...
I WAS SCARED I WAS GOING TO BE HEARTBROKEN AFTER ONLY OUR FIRST MEETING!
BLUSH
UM... WHAT'S YOUR NAME?
I'M HARUNA NAGASHI...
GRAB
HUH?!
WAIT!
DRAG
DRAG
DRAG
WHAT'RE YOU...?!
DRAG
Y...
YOH?!!
NO WAY.

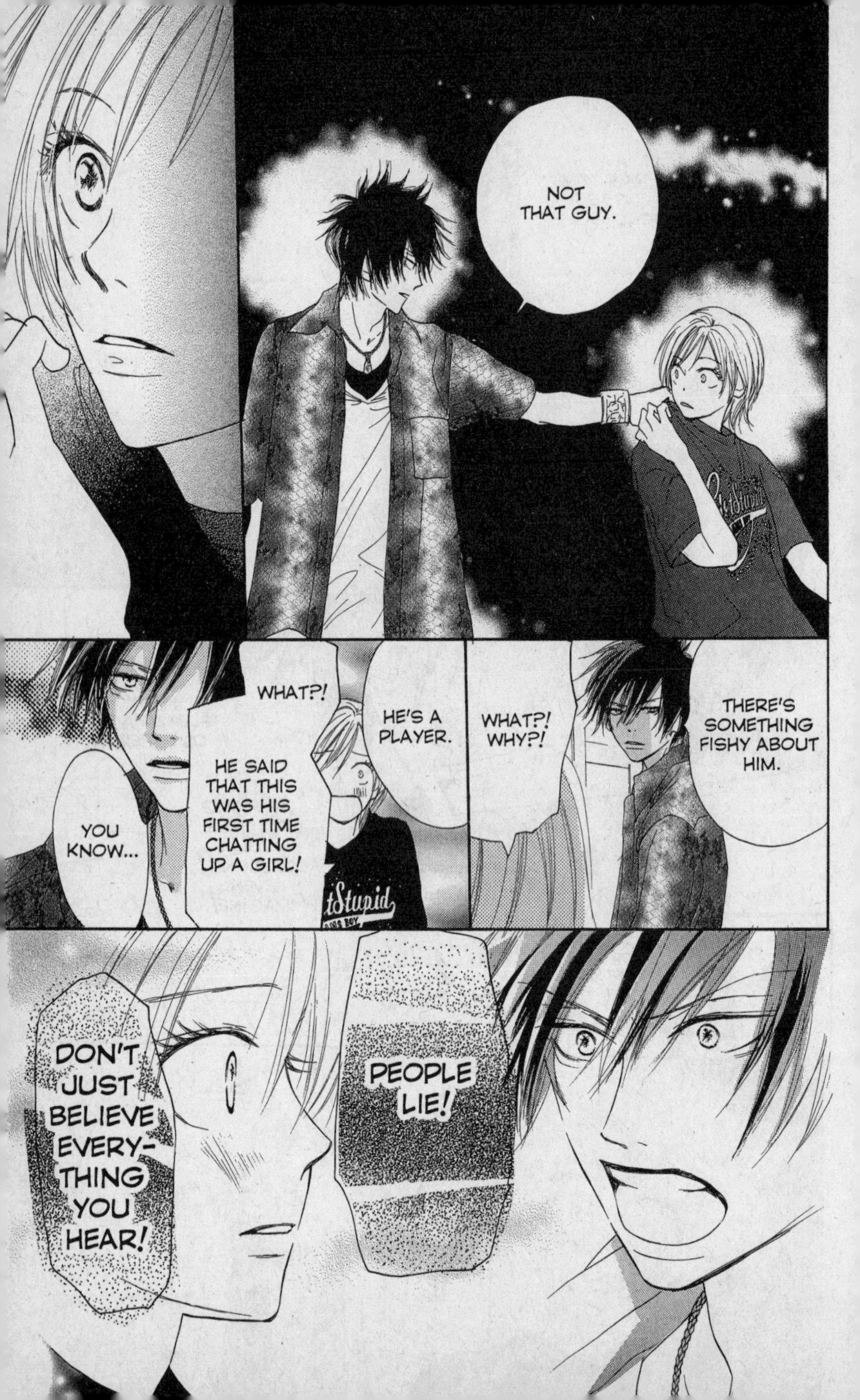
NOT THAT GUY.
THERE'S SOMETHING FISHY ABOUT HIM.
WHAT?! WHY?!
HE'S A PLAYER.
WHAT?!
HE SAID THAT THIS WAS HIS FIRST TIME CHATTING UP A GIRL!
YOU KNOW...
PEOPLE LIE!
DON'T JUST BELIEVE EVERY-THING YOU HEAR!

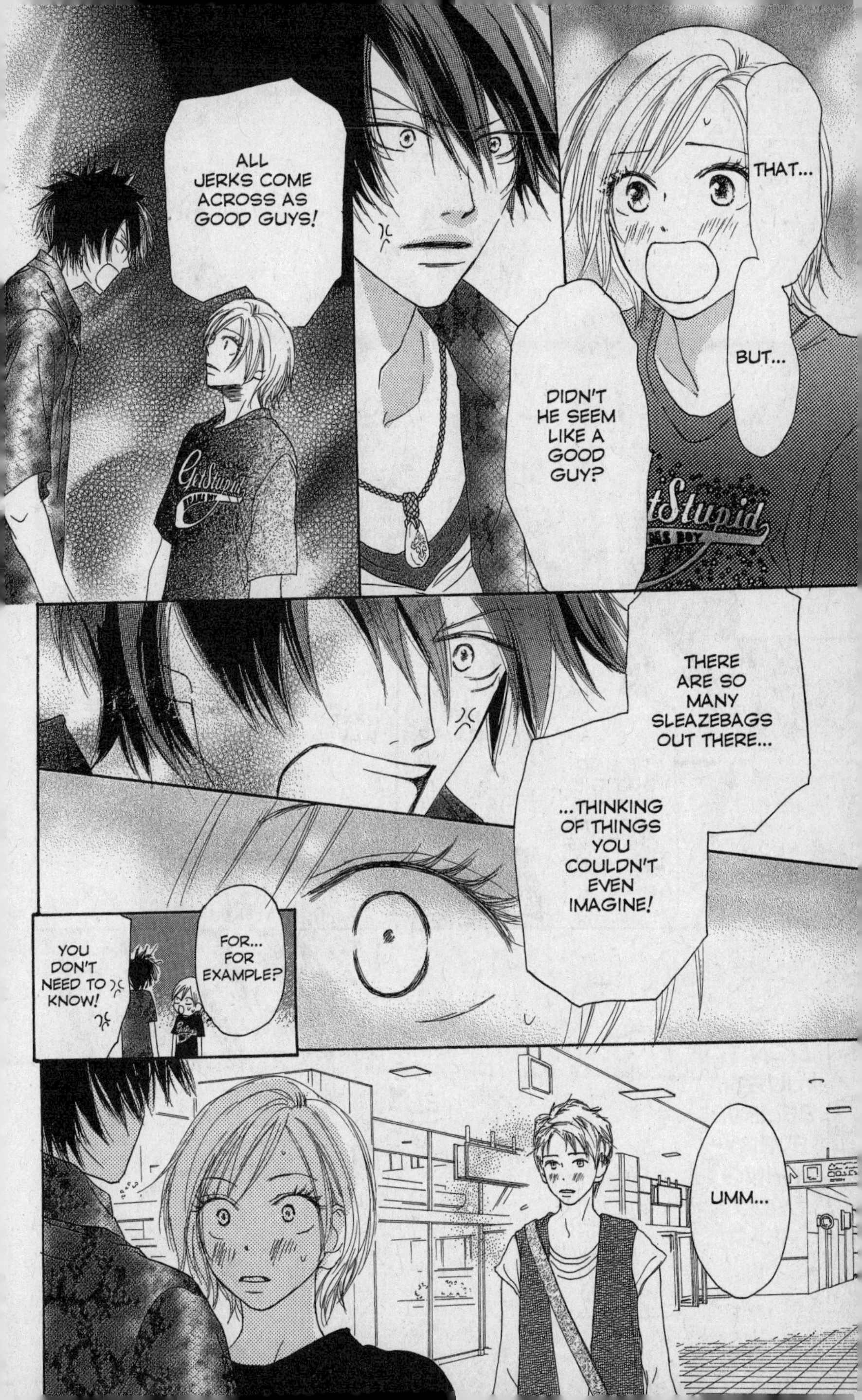
THAT...
BUT...
DIDN'T HE SEEM LIKE A GOOD GUY?
ALL JERKS COME ACROSS AS GOOD GUYS!
THERE ARE SO MANY SLEAZEBAGS OUT THERE...
...THINKING OF THINGS YOU COULDN'T EVEN IMAGINE!
FOR... FOR EXAMPLE?
YOU DON'T NEED TO KNOW!
UMM...

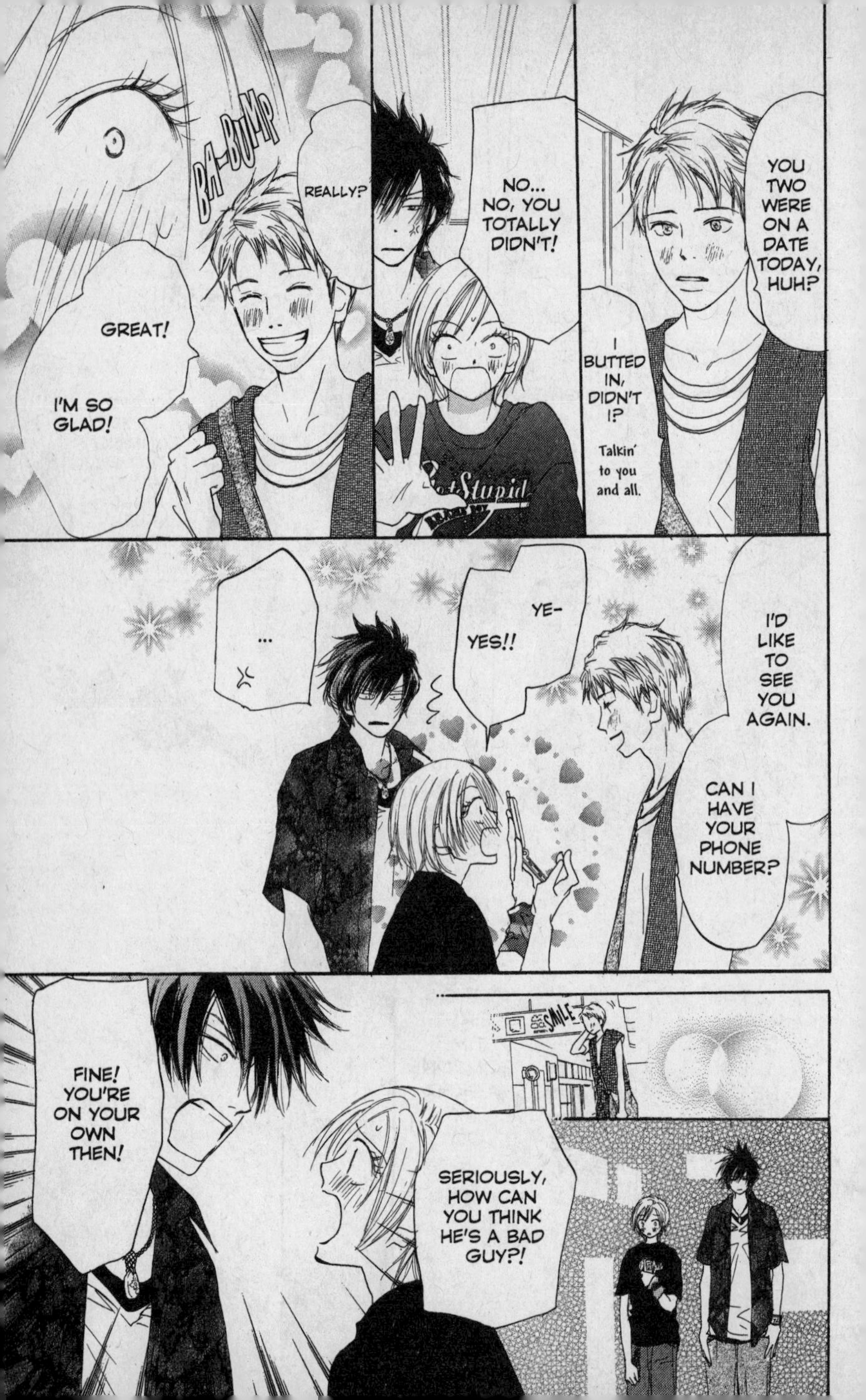
YOU TWO WERE ON A DATE TODAY, HUH?
I BUTTED IN, DIDN'T I?
Talkin' to you and all.
NO... NO, YOU TOTALLY DIDN'T!
REALLY?
BA-BUMP
GREAT!
I'M SO GLAD!
I'D LIKE TO SEE YOU AGAIN.
CAN I HAVE YOUR PHONE NUMBER?
YE- YES!!
...
SMILE
SERIOUSLY, HOW CAN YOU THINK HE'S A BAD GUY?!
FINE! YOU'RE ON YOUR OWN THEN!

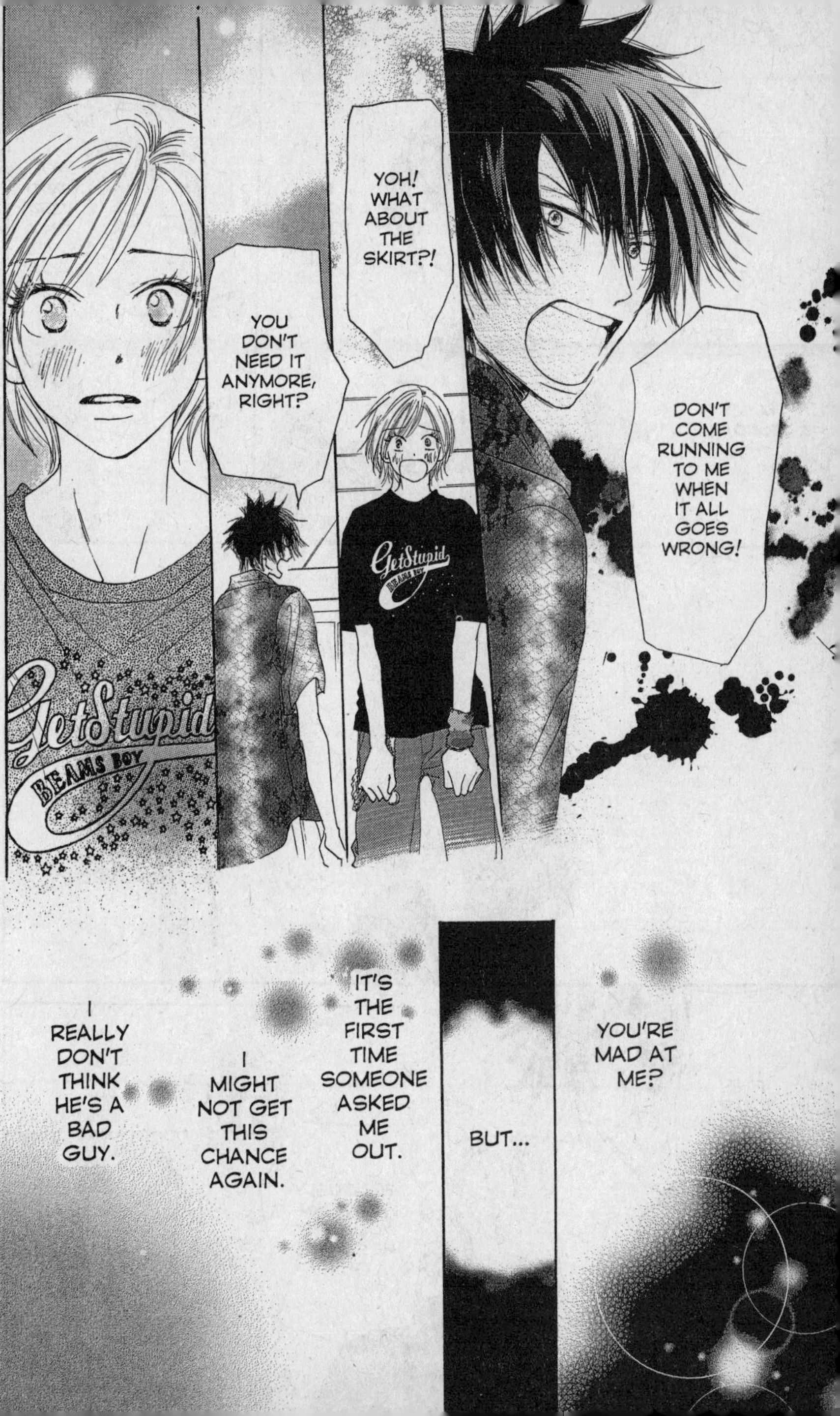
DON'T COME RUNNING TO ME WHEN IT ALL GOES WRONG!
YOH! WHAT ABOUT THE SKIRT?!
YOU DON'T NEED IT ANYMORE, RIGHT?
GetStupid
BEAMS BOY
GetStupid
BEAMS BOY
YOU'RE MAD AT ME?
BUT...
IT'S THE FIRST TIME SOMEONE ASKED ME OUT.
I MIGHT NOT GET THIS CHANCE AGAIN.
I REALLY DON'T THINK HE'S A BAD GUY.

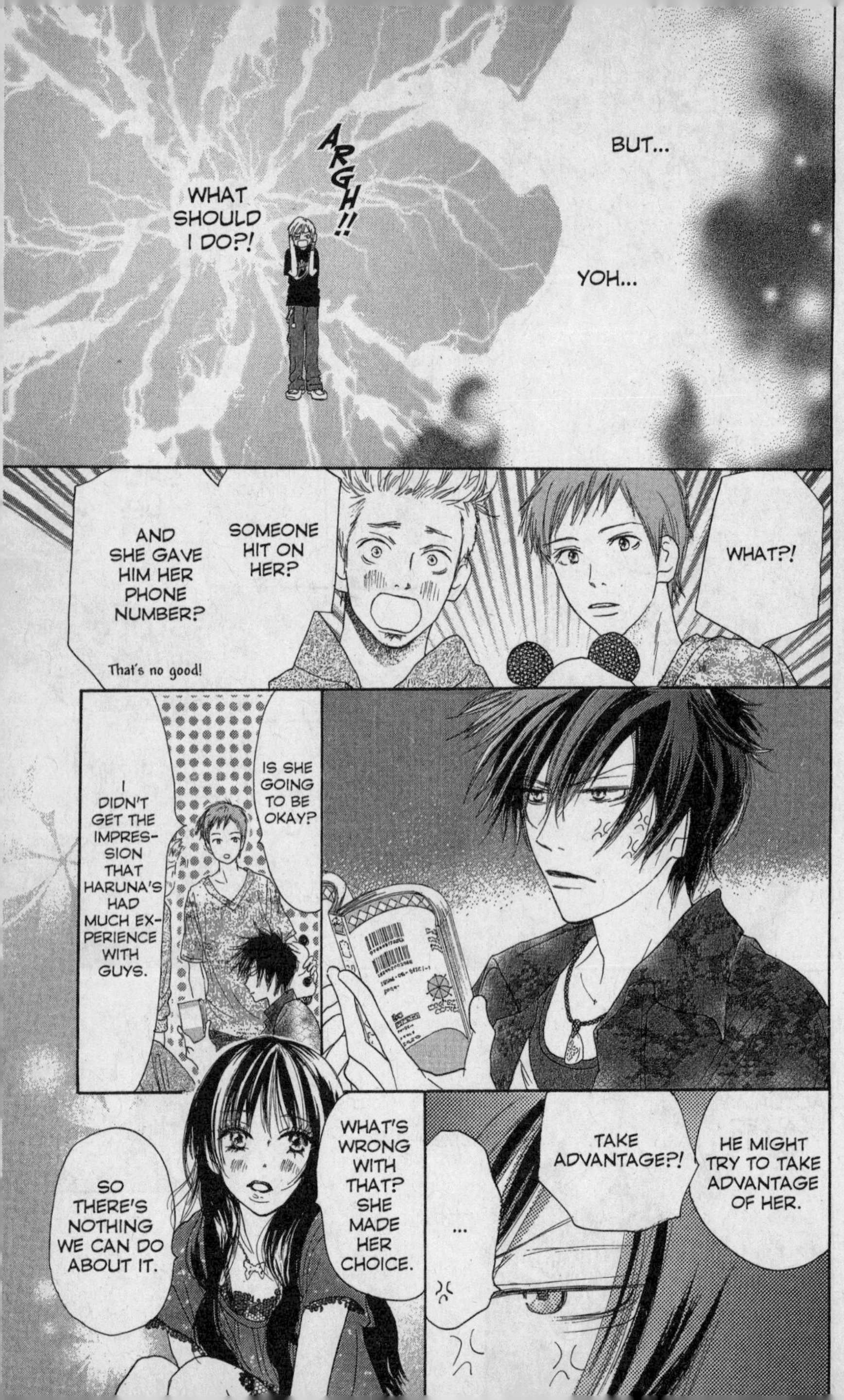
BUT...
YOH...
ARGH!!
WHAT SHOULD I DO?!
WHAT?!
SOMEONE HIT ON HER?
AND SHE GAVE HIM HER PHONE NUMBER?
That's no good!
IS SHE GOING TO BE OKAY?
I DIDN'T GET THE IMPRESSION THAT HARUNA'S HAD MUCH EXPERIENCE WITH GUYS.
HE MIGHT TRY TO TAKE ADVANTAGE OF HER.
TAKE ADVANTAGE?!
...
WHAT'S WRONG WITH THAT? SHE MADE HER CHOICE.
SO THERE'S NOTHING WE CAN DO ABOUT IT.

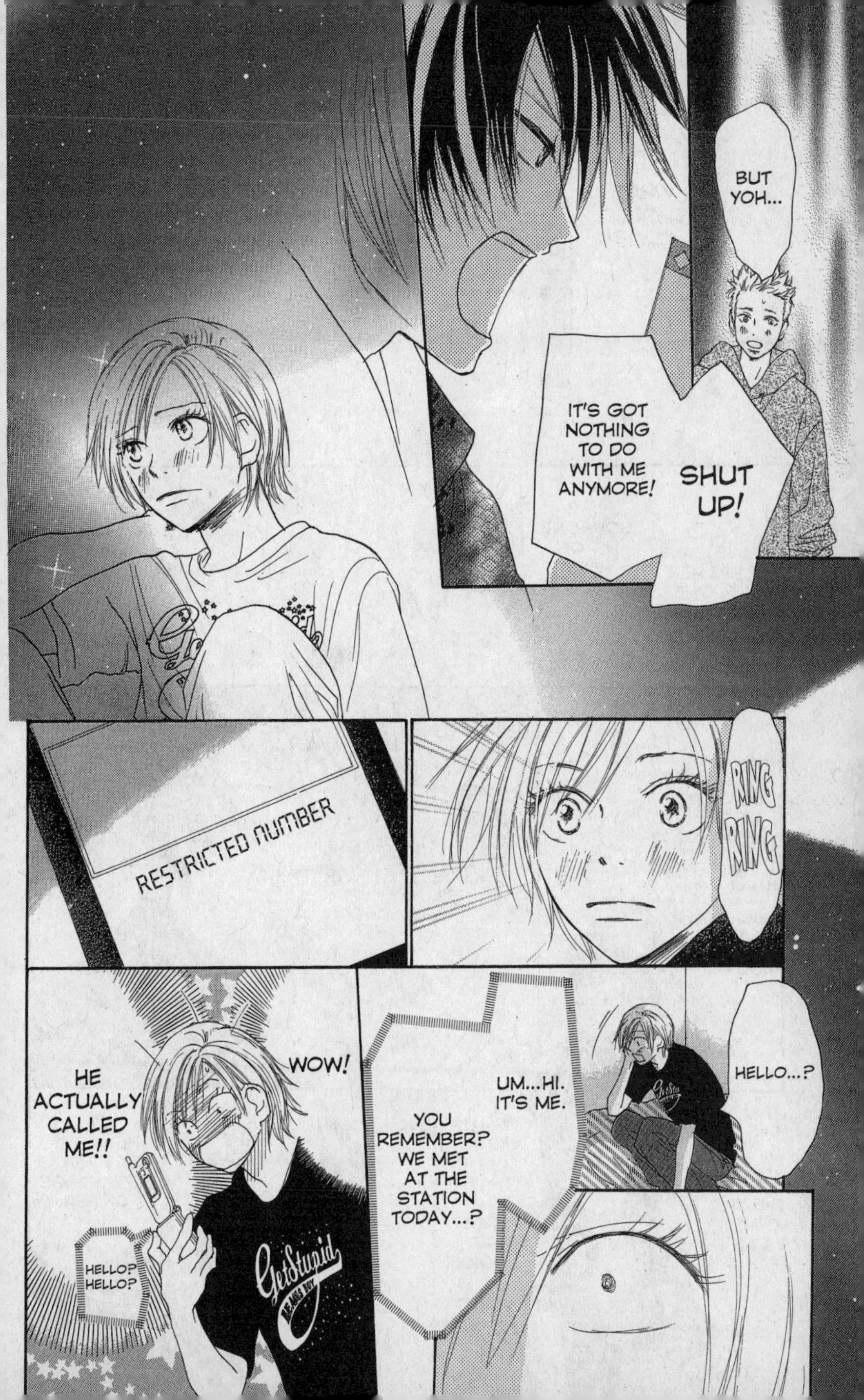
BUT YOH...
SHUT UP!
IT'S GOT NOTHING TO DO WITH ME ANYMORE!
RING RING
RESTRICTED NUMBER
HELLO...?
UM...HI. IT'S ME.
YOU REMEMBER? WE MET AT THE STATION TODAY...?
WOW!
HE ACTUALLY CALLED ME!!
HELLO? HELLO?
GetStupid

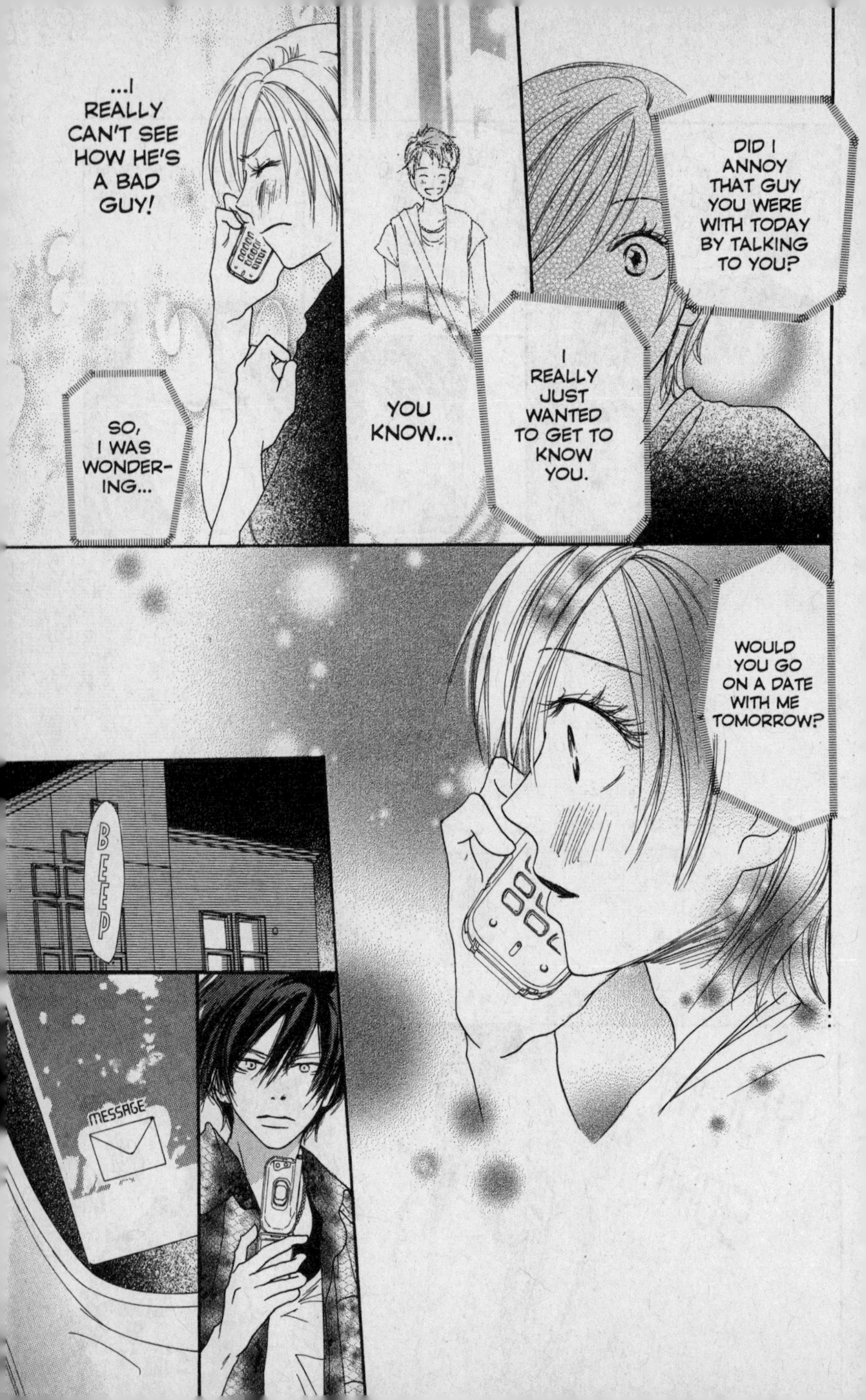
DID I ANNOY THAT GUY YOU WERE WITH TODAY BY TALKING TO YOU?
I REALLY JUST WANTED TO GET TO KNOW YOU.
YOU KNOW...
...I REALLY CAN'T SEE HOW HE'S A BAD GUY!
SO, I WAS WONDERING...
WOULD YOU GO ON A DATE WITH ME TOMORROW?
BEEP
MESSAGE

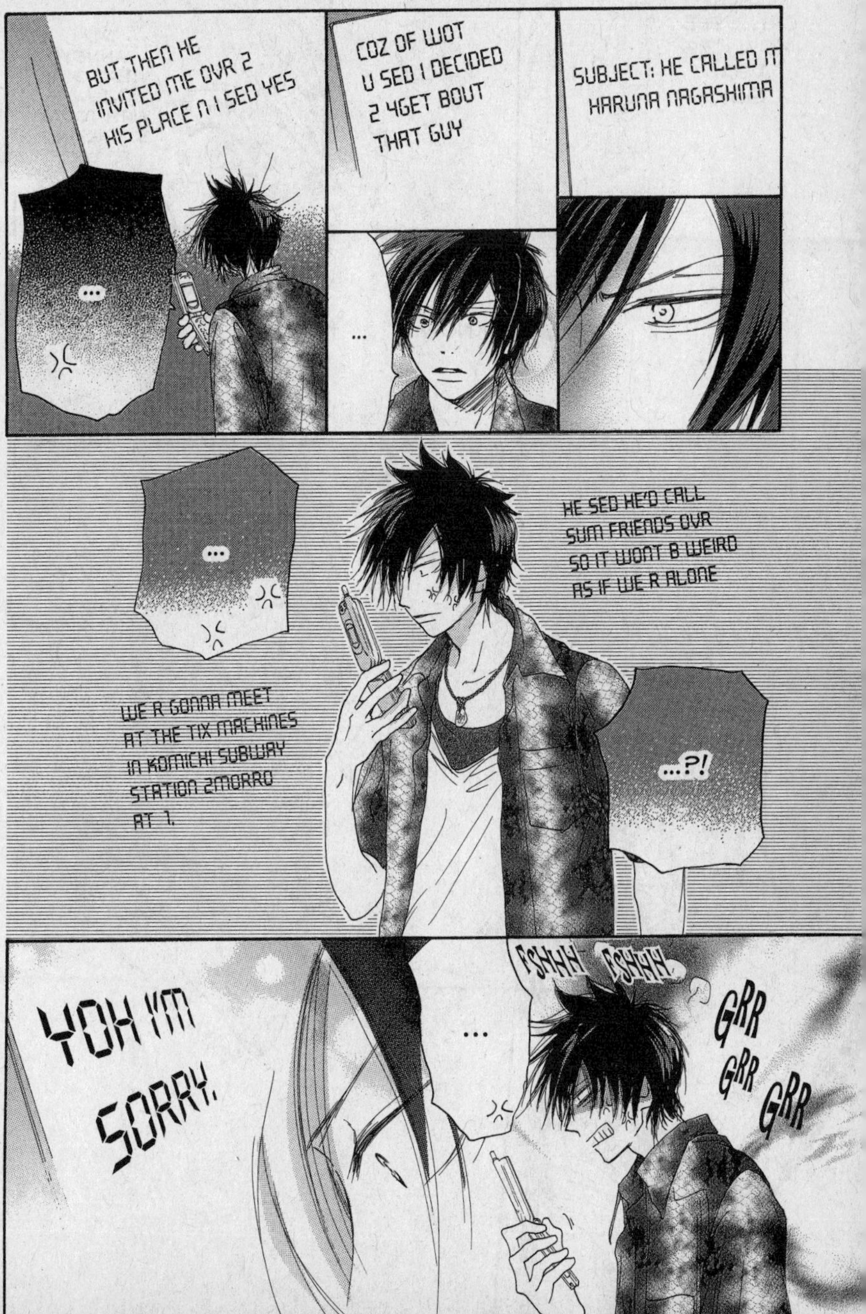
SUBJECT: HE CALLED M
HARUNA NAGASHIMA
COZ OF WOT U SED I DECIDED 2 4GET BOUT THAT GUY
...
BUT THEN HE INVITED ME OVR 2 HIS PLACE N I SED YES
...
HE SED HE'D CALL SUM FRIENDS OVR SO IT WONT B WEIRD AS IF WE R ALONE
...
...?!
WE R GONNA MEET AT THE TIX MACHINES IN KOMICHI SUBWAY STATION 2MORRO AT 1.
GRR GRR GRR
FSHHH FSHHH
...
YOH I'M SORRY.

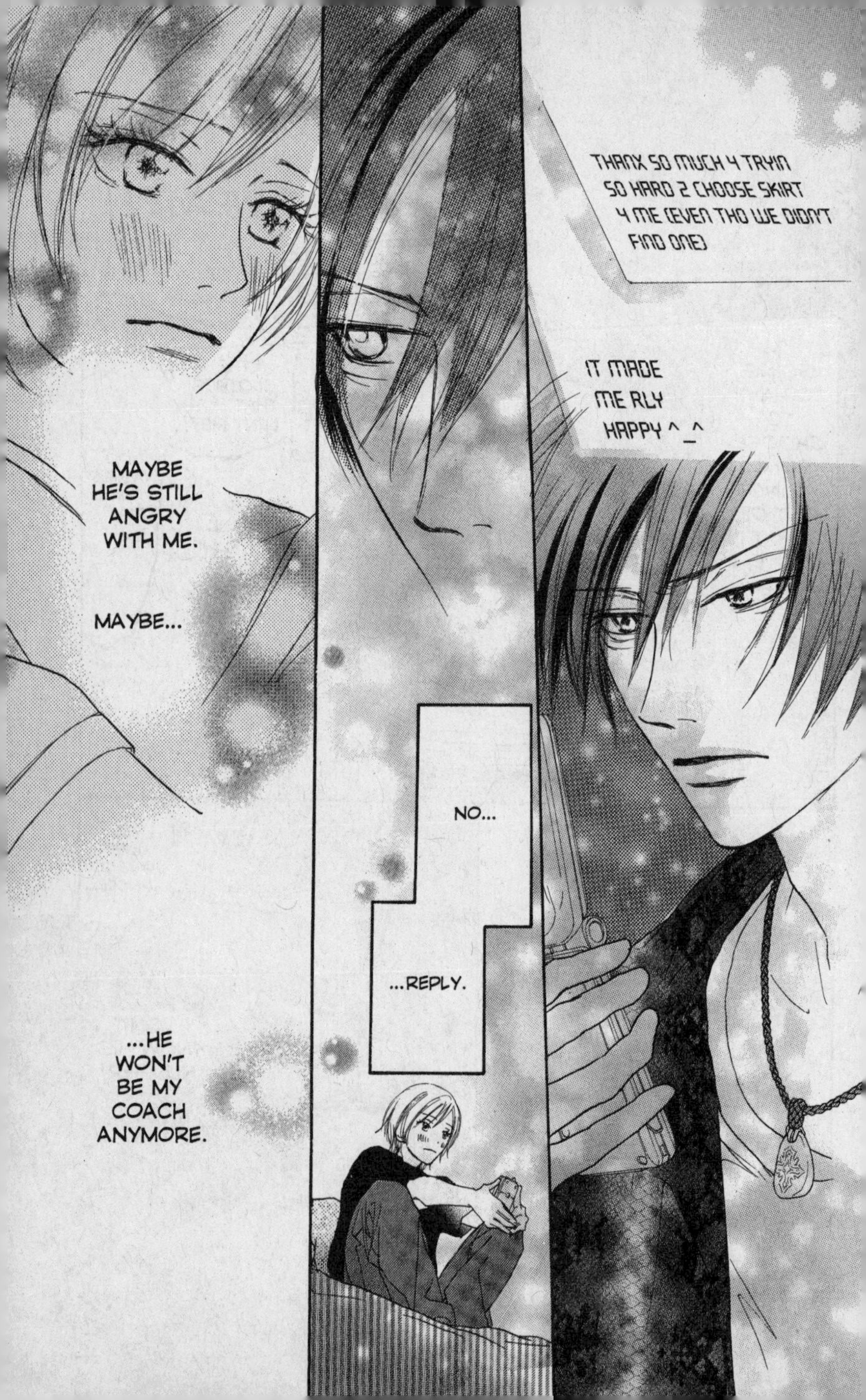
THANX SO MUCH 4 TRYIN SO HARD 2 CHOOSE SKIRT 4 ME (EVEN THO WE DIDN'T FIND ONE)
IT MADE ME RLY HAPPY ^_^
NO...
...REPLY.
MAYBE HE'S STILL ANGRY WITH ME.
MAYBE...
...HE WON'T BE MY COACH ANYMORE.

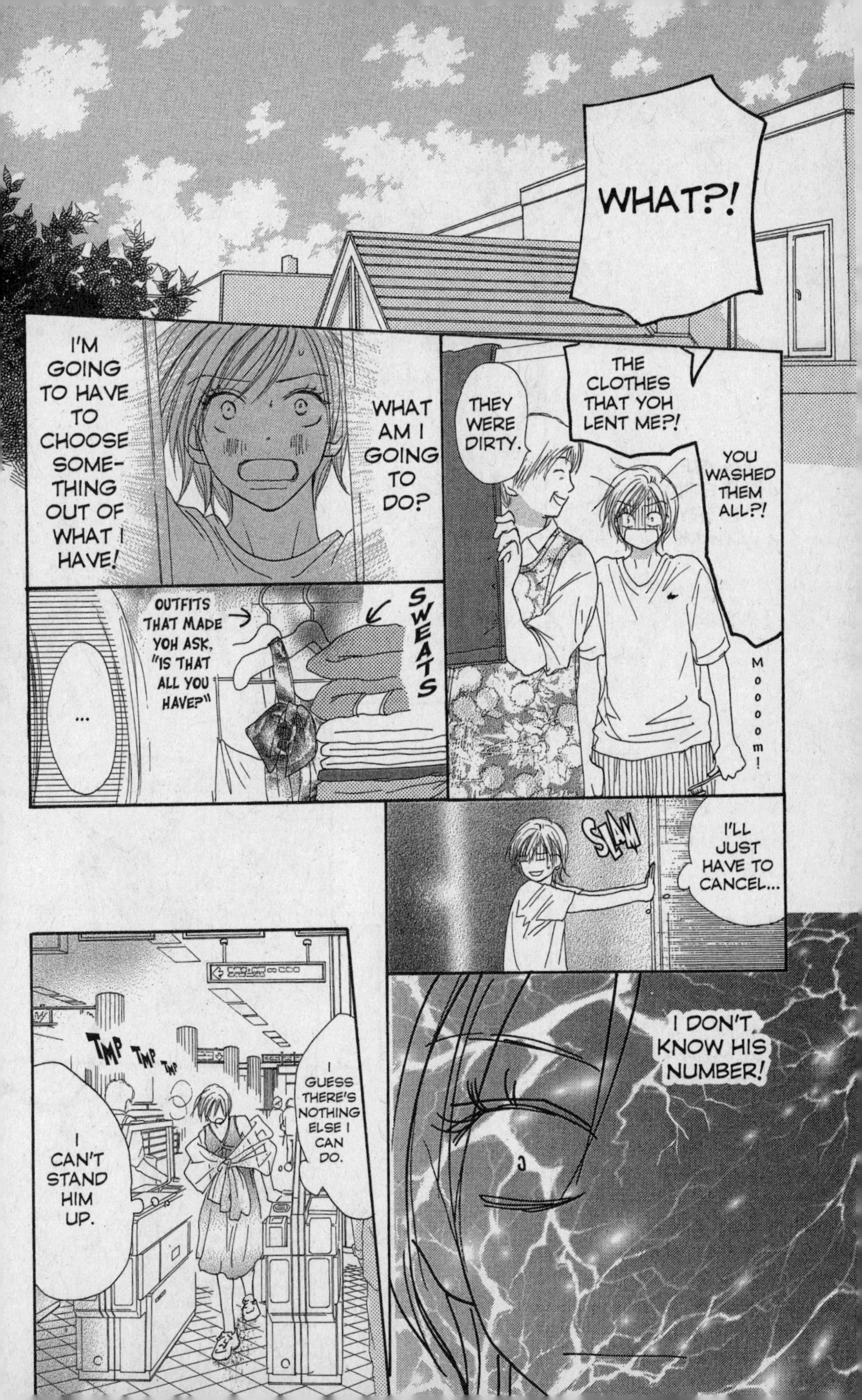
WHAT?!
THE CLOTHES THAT YOH LENT ME?!
THEY WERE DIRTY.
YOU WASHED THEM ALL?!
Mooooom!
WHAT AM I GOING TO DO?
I'M GOING TO HAVE TO CHOOSE SOMETHING OUT OF WHAT I HAVE!
SWEATS
OUTFITS THAT MADE YOH ASK, "IS THAT ALL YOU HAVE?"
...
I'LL JUST HAVE TO CANCEL...
SLAM
I DON'T KNOW HIS NUMBER!
I GUESS THERE'S NOTHING ELSE I CAN DO.
I CAN'T STAND HIM UP.
TMP TMP TMP

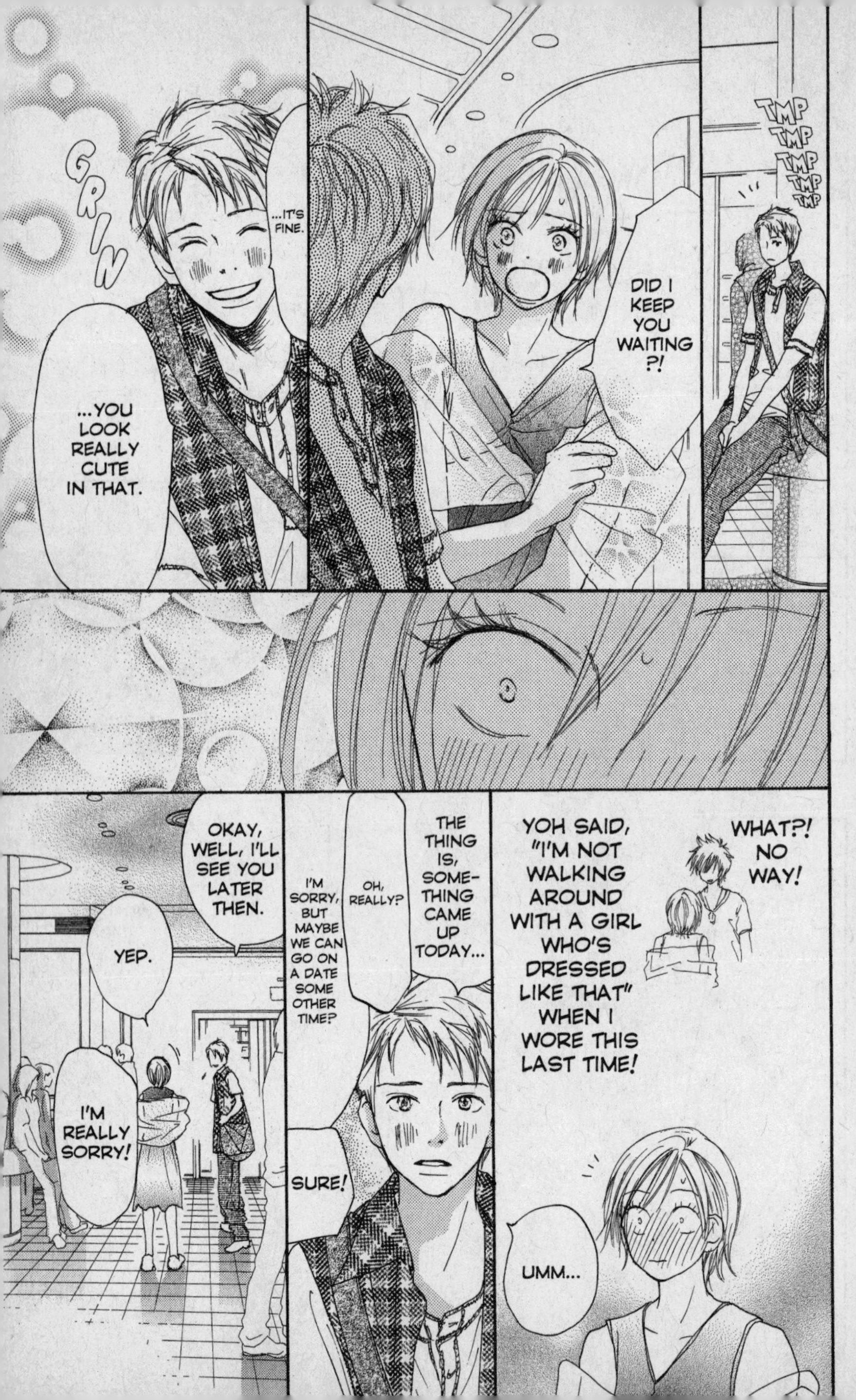
TMP TMP TMP TMP TMP
DID I KEEP YOU WAITING?!
...IT'S FINE.
GRIN
...YOU LOOK REALLY CUTE IN THAT.
WHAT?! NO WAY!
YOH SAID, "I'M NOT WALKING AROUND WITH A GIRL WHO'S DRESSED LIKE THAT" WHEN I WORE THIS LAST TIME!
UMM...
THE THING IS, SOMETHING CAME UP TODAY...
OH, REALLY?
I'M SORRY, BUT MAYBE WE CAN GO ON A DATE SOME OTHER TIME?
SURE!
OKAY, WELL, I'LL SEE YOU LATER THEN.
YEP.
I'M REALLY SORRY!

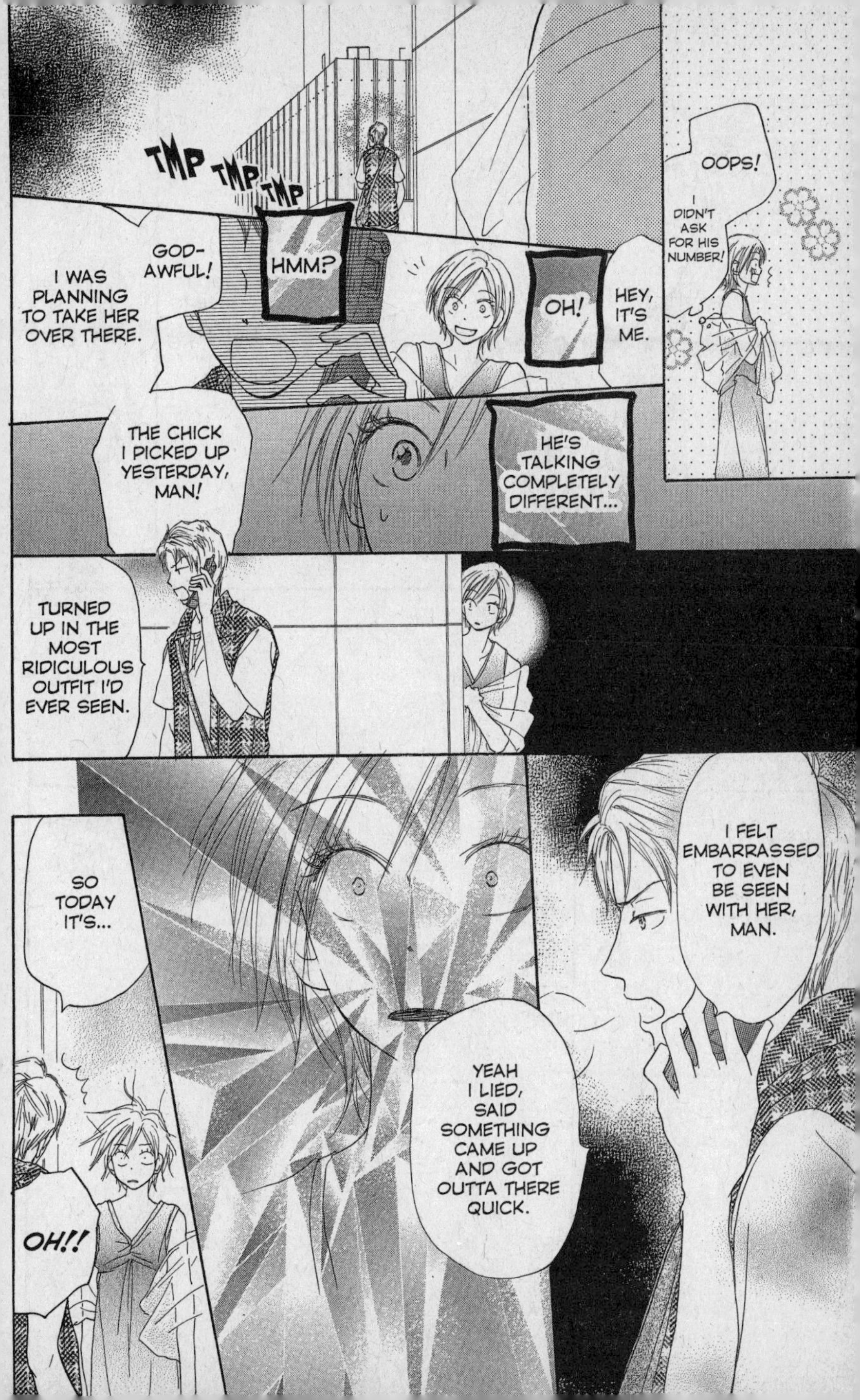
OOPS!
I DIDN'T ASK FOR HIS NUMBER!
TMP TMP TMP
HEY, IT'S ME.
OH!
HMM?
GOD-AWFUL!
I WAS PLANNING TO TAKE HER OVER THERE.
HE'S TALKING COMPLETELY DIFFERENT...
THE CHICK I PICKED UP YESTERDAY, MAN!
TURNED UP IN THE MOST RIDICULOUS OUTFIT I'D EVER SEEN.
I FELT EMBARRASSED TO EVEN BE SEEN WITH HER, MAN.
YEAH I LIED, SAID SOMETHING CAME UP AND GOT OUTTA THERE QUICK.
SO TODAY IT'S...
OH!!

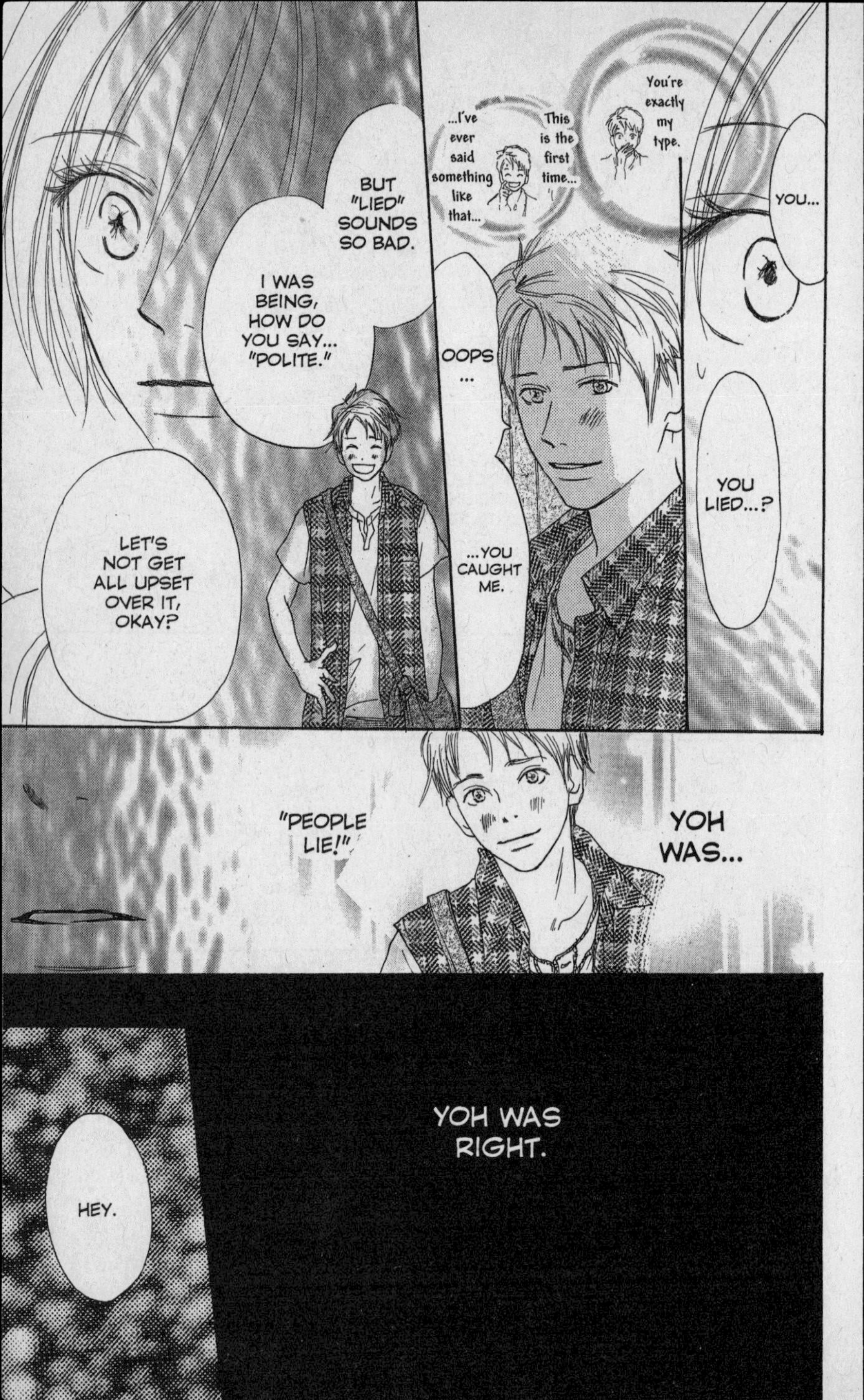
YOU...
YOU LIED...?
You're exactly my type.
This is the first time...
...I've ever said something like that...
OOPS...
...YOU CAUGHT ME.
BUT "LIED" SOUNDS SO BAD.
I WAS BEING, HOW DO YOU SAY... "POLITE."
LET'S NOT GET ALL UPSET OVER IT, OKAY?
YOH WAS...
"PEOPLE LIE!"
YOH WAS RIGHT.
HEY.

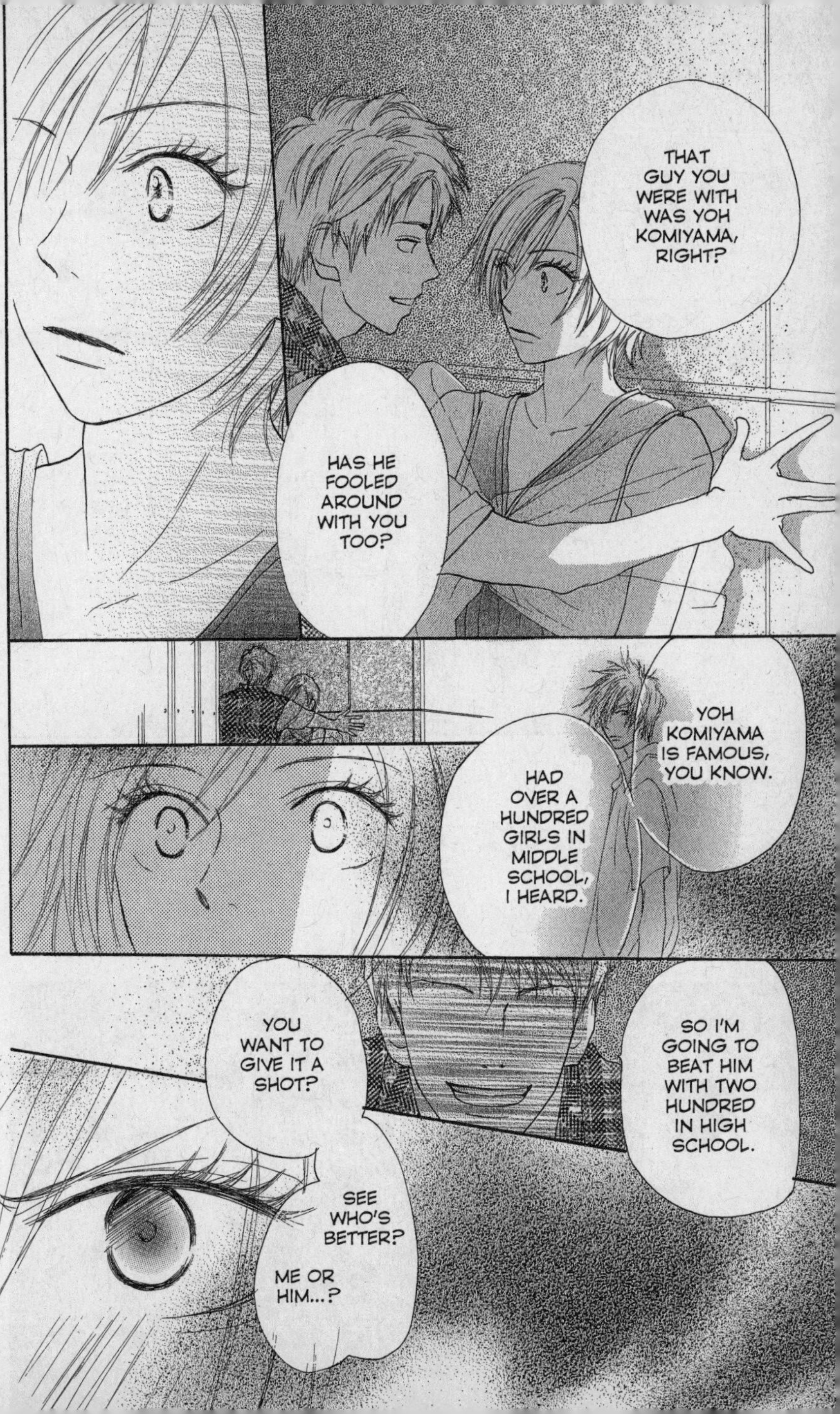
THAT GUY YOU WERE WITH WAS YOH KOMIYAMA, RIGHT?
HAS HE FOOLED AROUND WITH YOU TOO?
YOH KOMIYAMA IS FAMOUS, YOU KNOW.
HAD OVER A HUNDRED GIRLS IN MIDDLE SCHOOL, I HEARD.
SO I'M GOING TO BEAT HIM WITH TWO HUNDRED IN HIGH SCHOOL.
YOU WANT TO GIVE IT A SHOT?
SEE WHO'S BETTER?
ME OR HIM...?

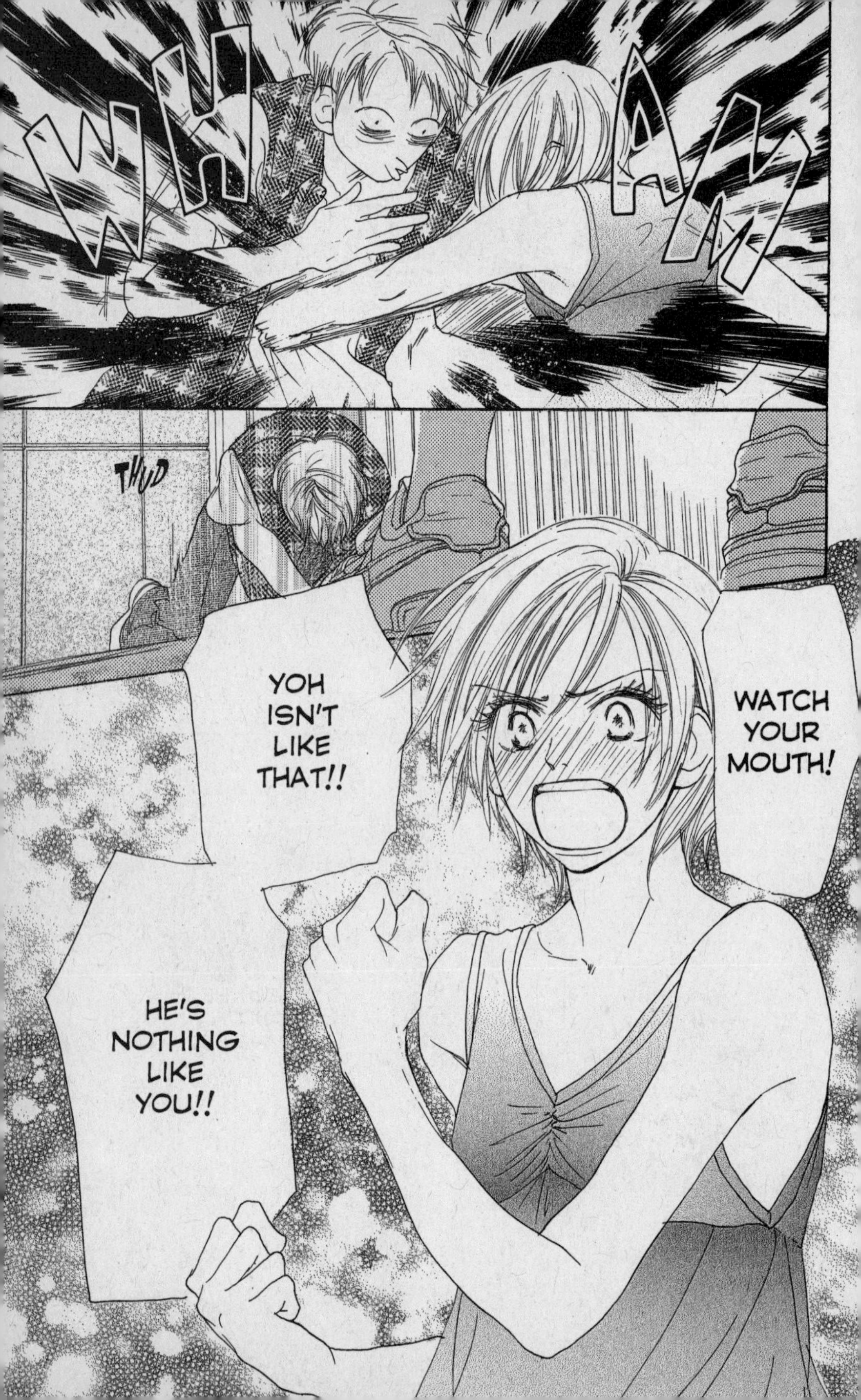
WHAM
THUD
WATCH YOUR MOUTH!
YOH ISN'T LIKE THAT!!
HE'S NOTHING LIKE YOU!!

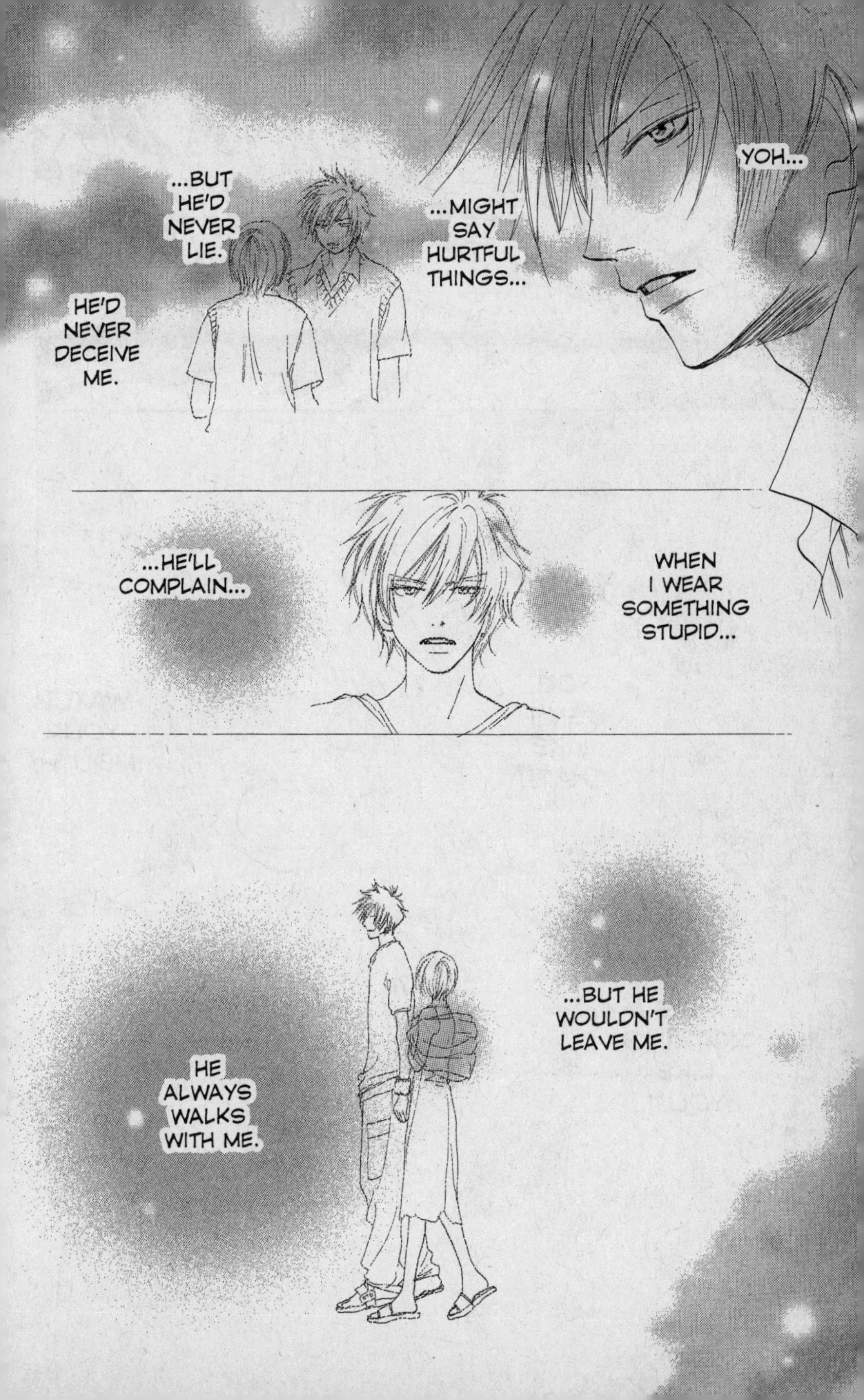
YOH...
...MIGHT SAY HURTFUL THINGS...
...BUT HE'D NEVER LIE.
HE'D NEVER DECEIVE ME.
WHEN I WEAR SOMETHING STUPID...
...HE'LL COMPLAIN...
...BUT HE WOULDN'T LEAVE ME.
HE ALWAYS WALKS WITH ME.

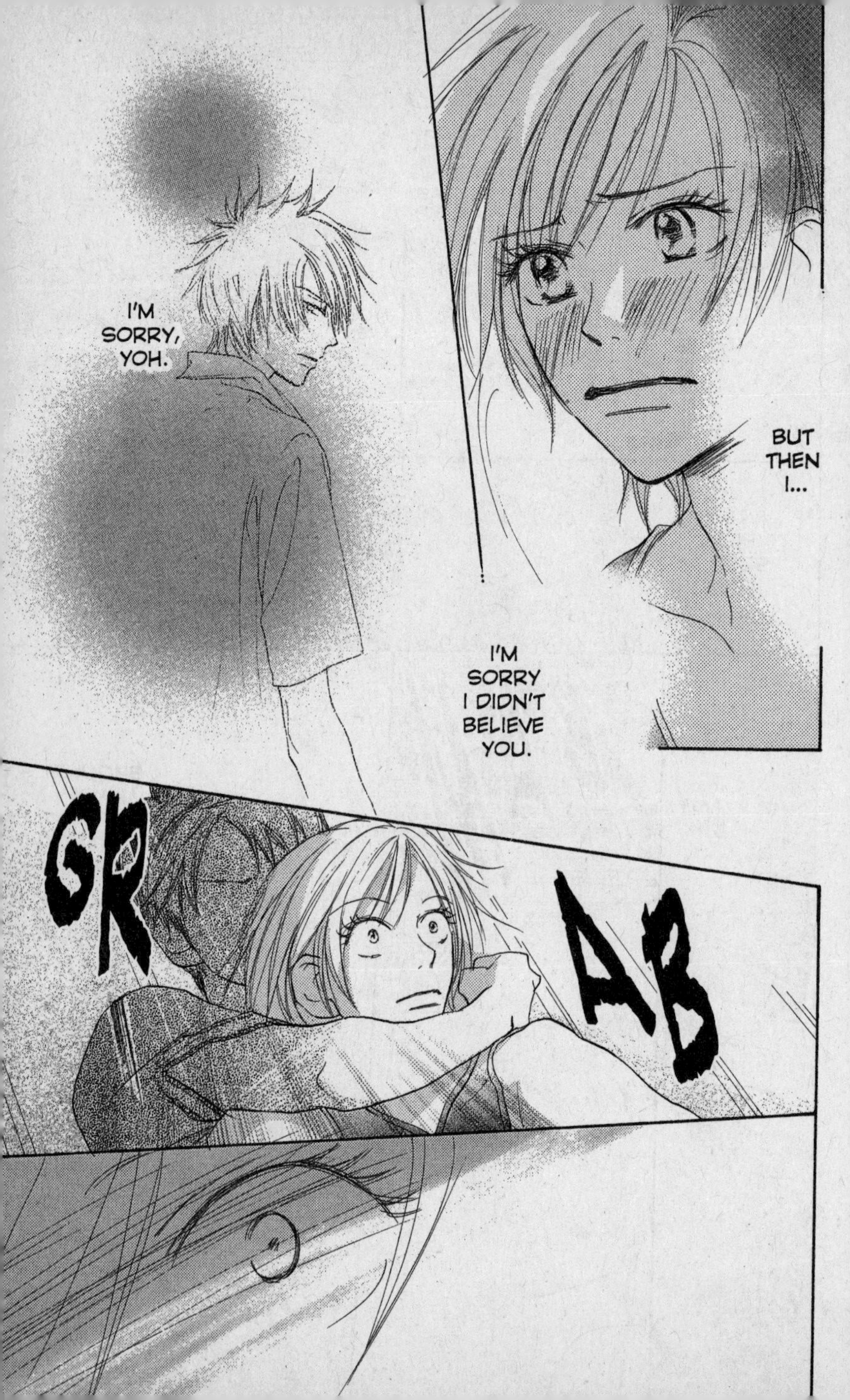
BUT THEN I...
I'M SORRY, YOH.
I'M SORRY I DIDN'T BELIEVE YOU.
GR
AB

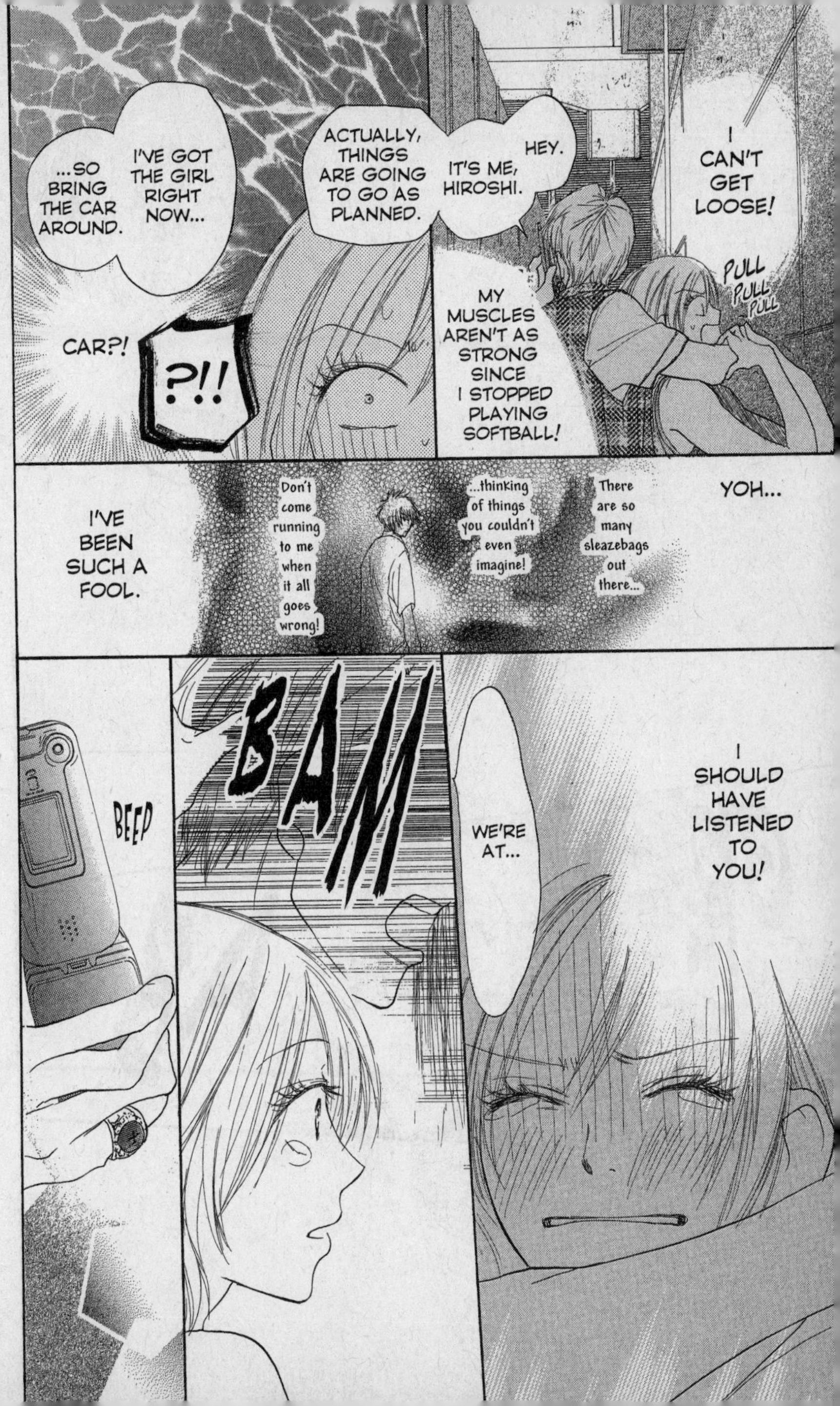
I CAN'T GET LOOSE!
PULL PULL PULL
HEY.
IT'S ME, HIROSHI.
MY MUSCLES AREN'T AS STRONG SINCE I STOPPED PLAYING SOFTBALL!
ACTUALLY, THINGS ARE GOING TO GO AS PLANNED.
I'VE GOT THE GIRL RIGHT NOW...
...SO BRING THE CAR AROUND.
?!!
CAR?!
YOH...
There are so many sleazebags out there...
...thinking of things you couldn't even imagine!
Don't come running to me when it all goes wrong!
I'VE BEEN SUCH A FOOL.
I SHOULD HAVE LISTENED TO YOU!
WE'RE AT...
BAM
BEEP

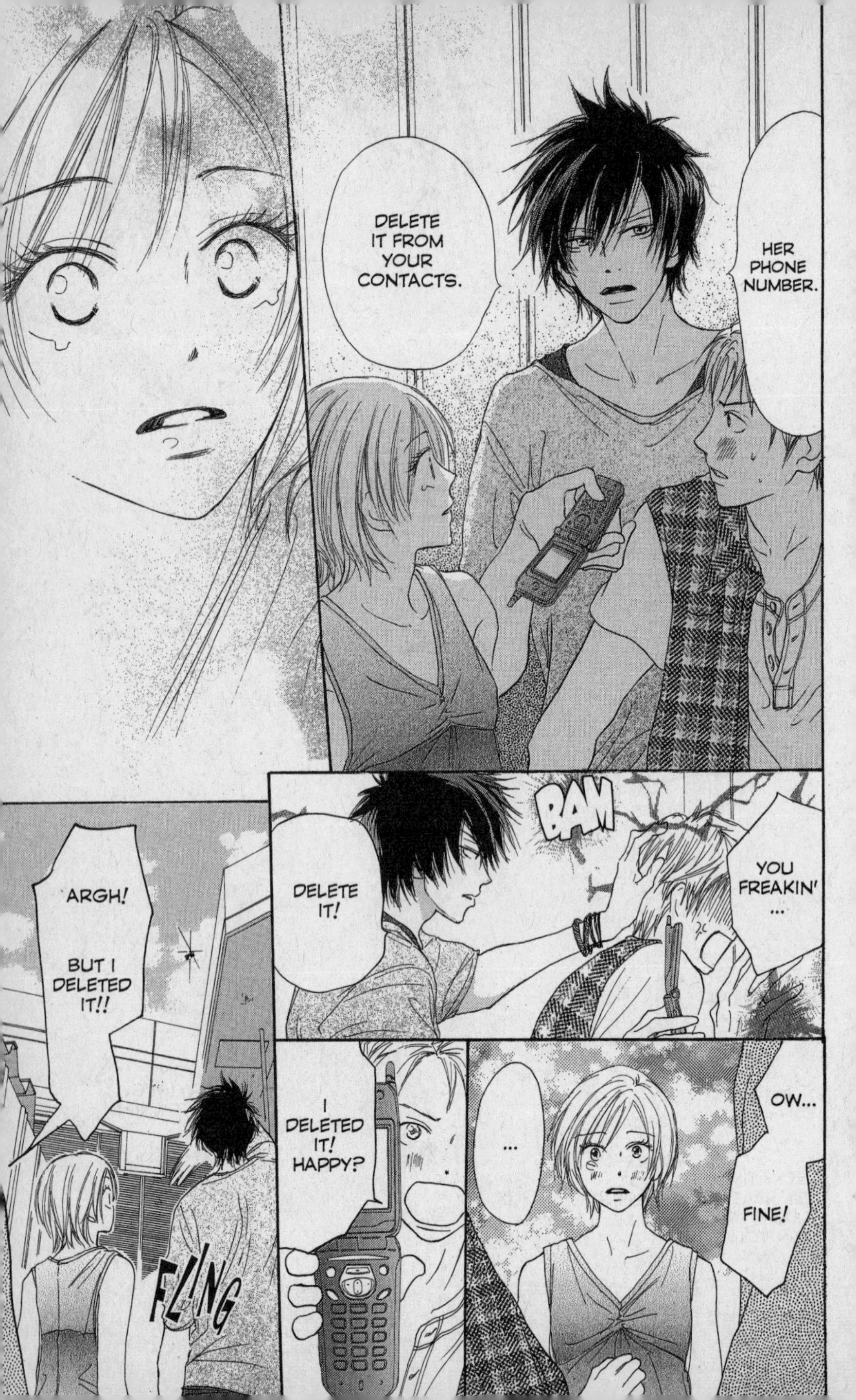
HER PHONE NUMBER.
DELETE IT FROM YOUR CONTACTS.
YOU FREAKIN' ...
BAM
DELETE IT!
OW...
FINE!
...
I DELETED IT! HAPPY?
ARGH!
BUT I DELETED IT!!
FLING

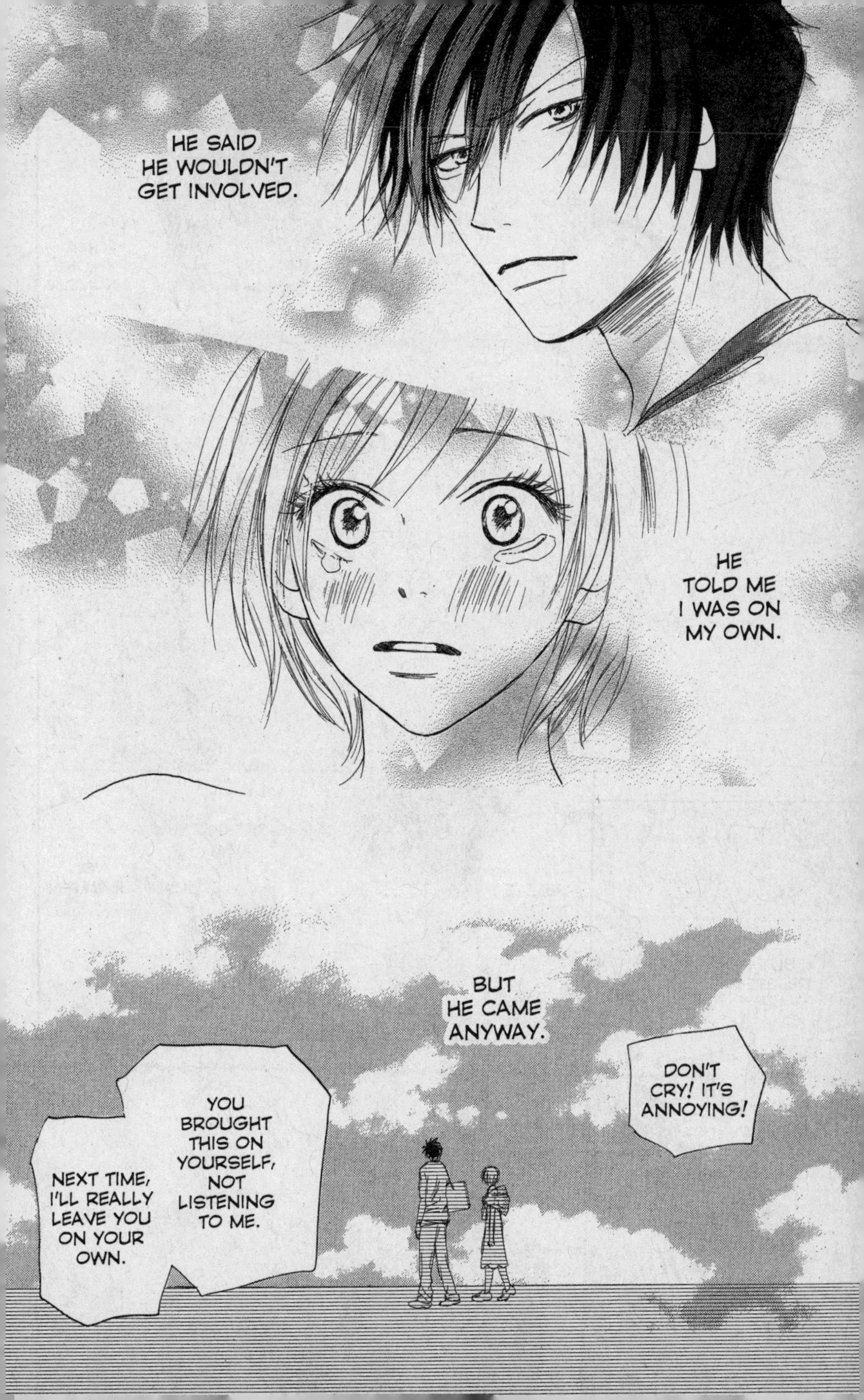
HE SAID HE WOULDN'T GET INVOLVED.
HE TOLD ME I WAS ON MY OWN.
BUT HE CAME ANYWAY.
DON'T CRY! IT'S ANNOYING!
YOU BROUGHT THIS ON YOURSELF, NOT LISTENING TO ME.
NEXT TIME, I'LL REALLY LEAVE YOU ON YOUR OWN.

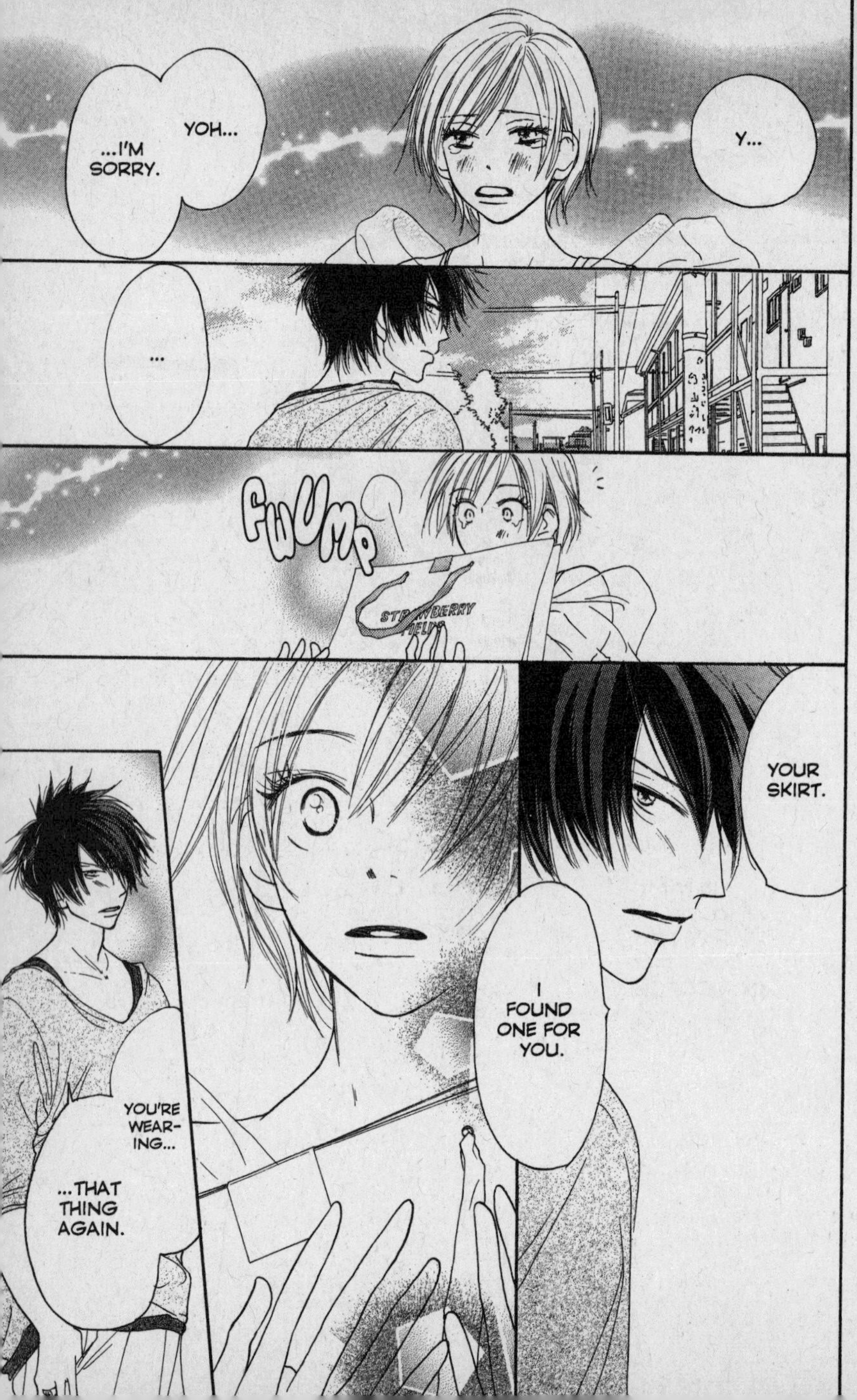
Y...
YOH...
...I'M SORRY.
...
FWUMP
YOUR SKIRT.
I FOUND ONE FOR YOU.
YOU'RE WEARING...
...THAT THING AGAIN.

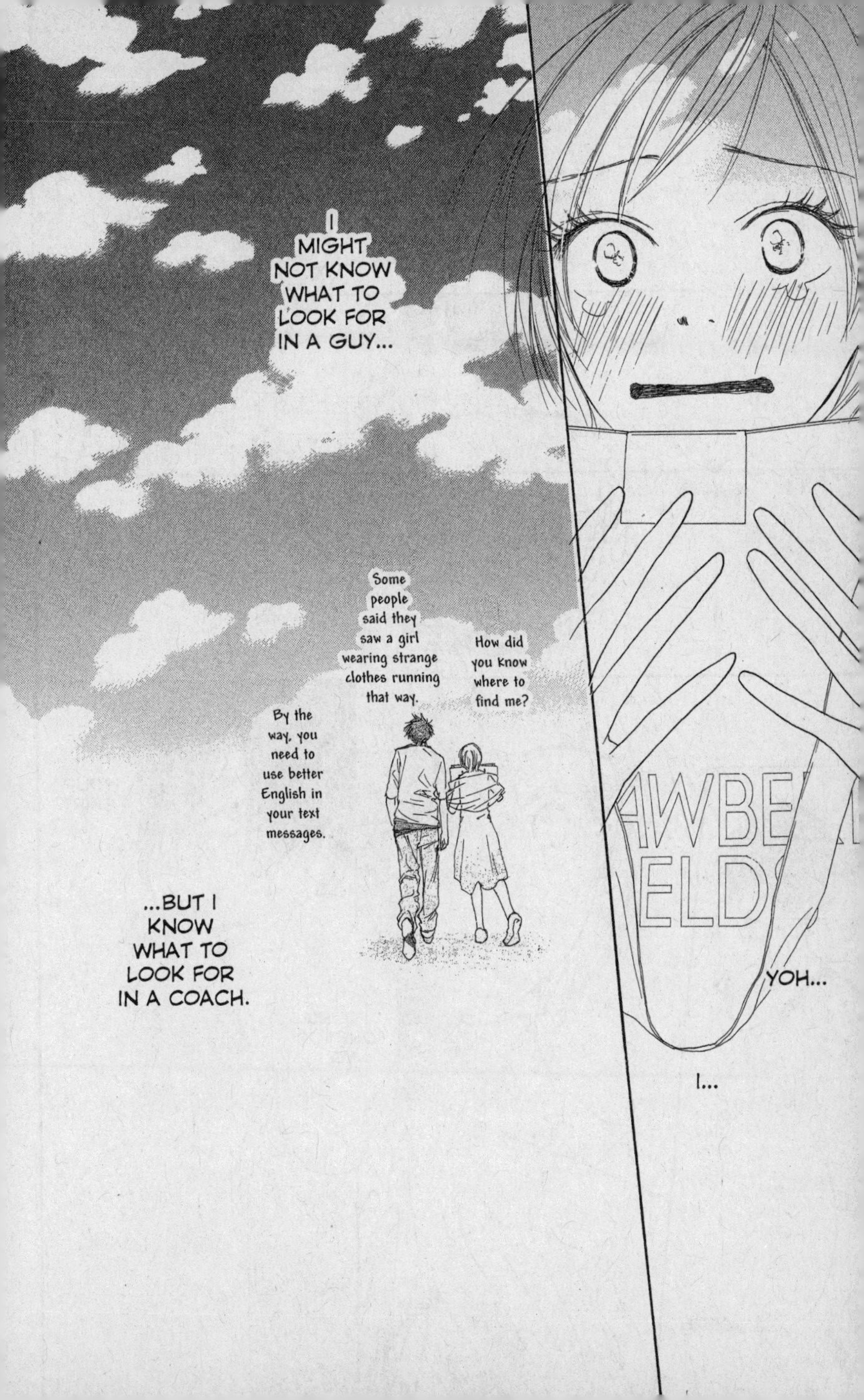
YOH...
I...
I MIGHT NOT KNOW WHAT TO LOOK FOR IN A GUY...
How did you know where to find me?
Some people said they saw a girl wearing strange clothes running that way.
By the way, you need to use better English in your text messages.
...BUT I KNOW WHAT TO LOOK FOR IN A COACH.

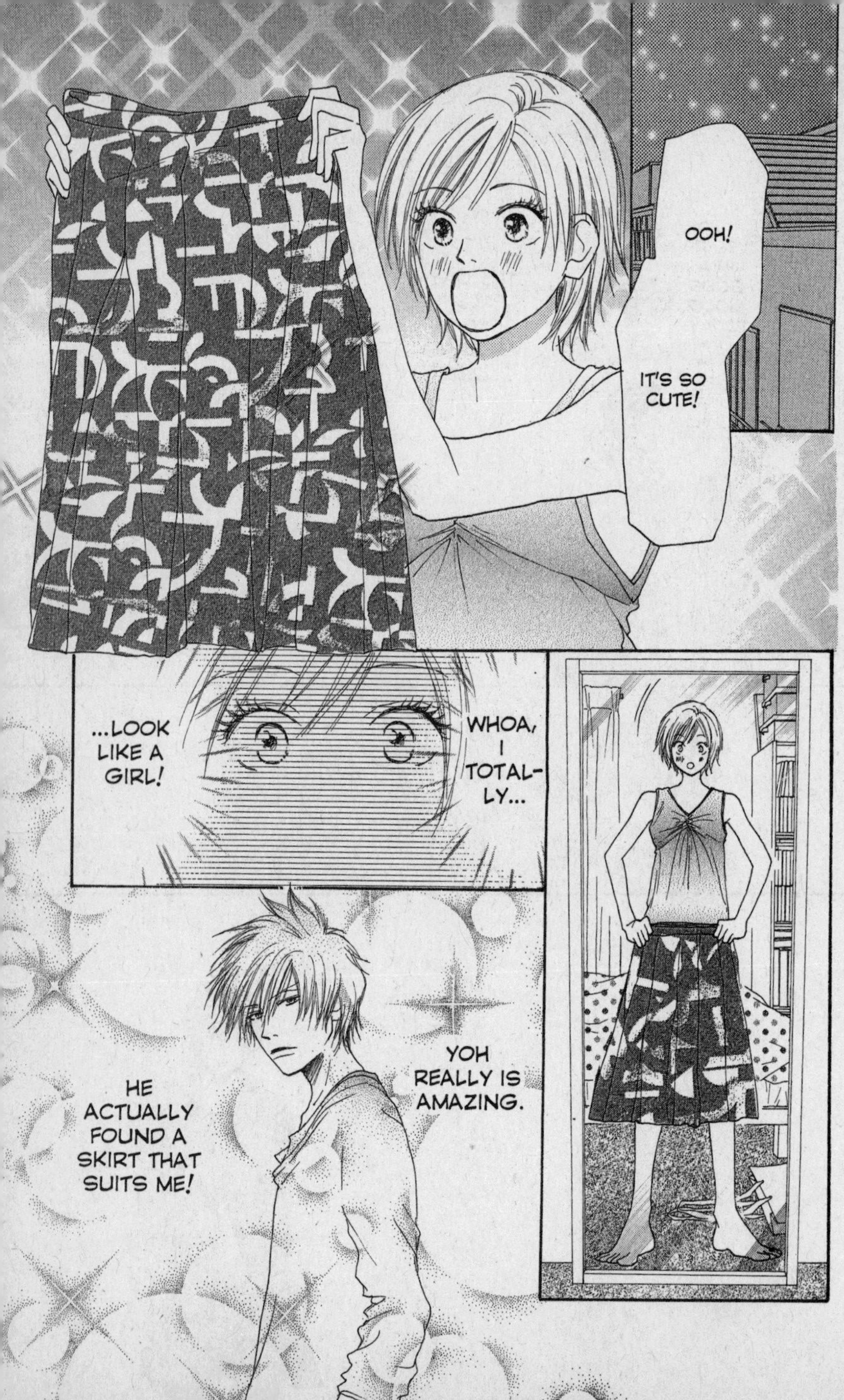
OOH!
IT'S SO CUTE!
WHOA, I TOTALLY...
...LOOK LIKE A GIRL!
YOH REALLY IS AMAZING.
HE ACTUALLY FOUND A SKIRT THAT SUITS ME!

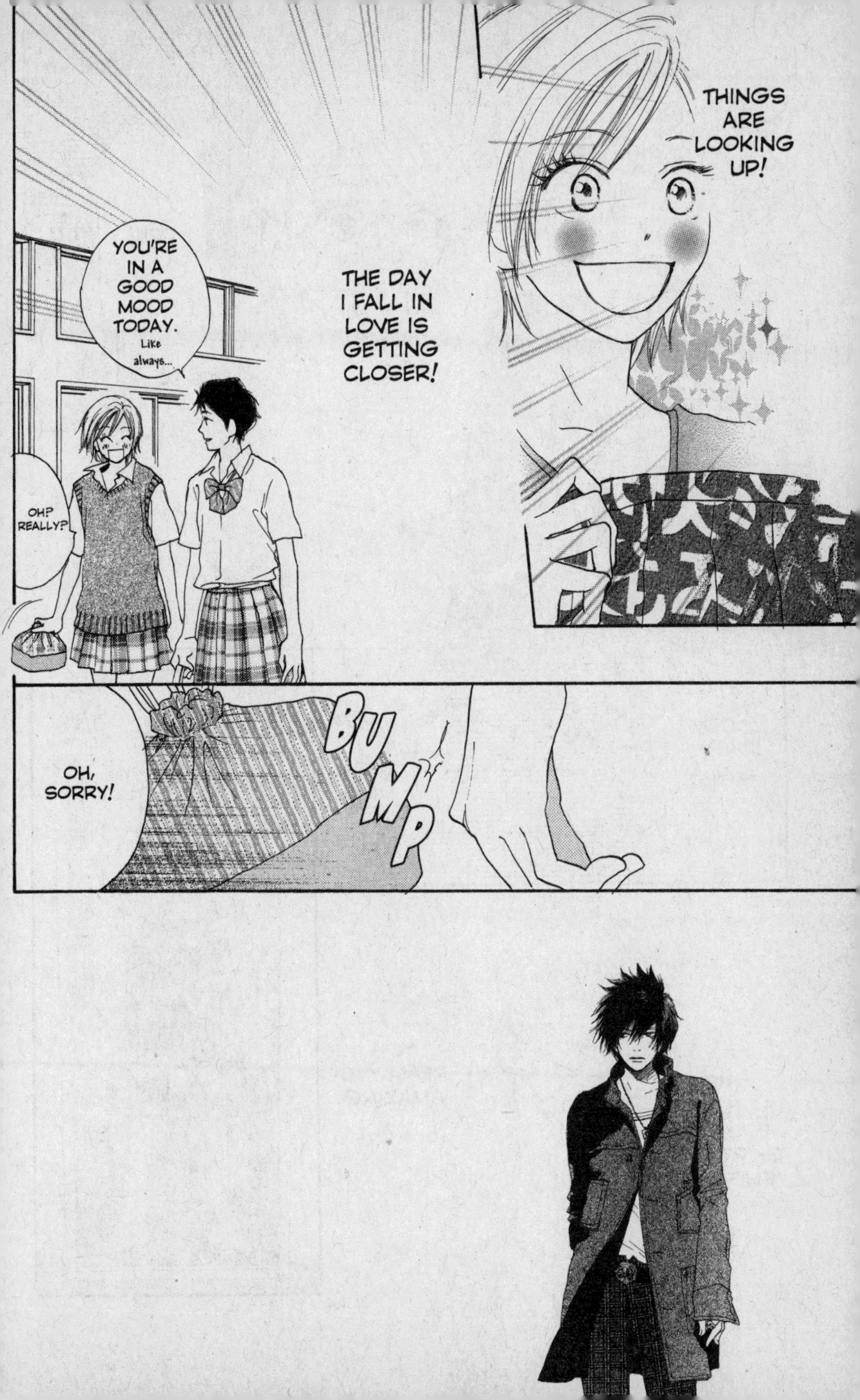
THINGS ARE LOOKING UP!
THE DAY I FALL IN LOVE IS GETTING CLOSER!
YOU'RE IN A GOOD MOOD TODAY.
Like always...
OH? REALLY?
BUMP
OH, SORRY!

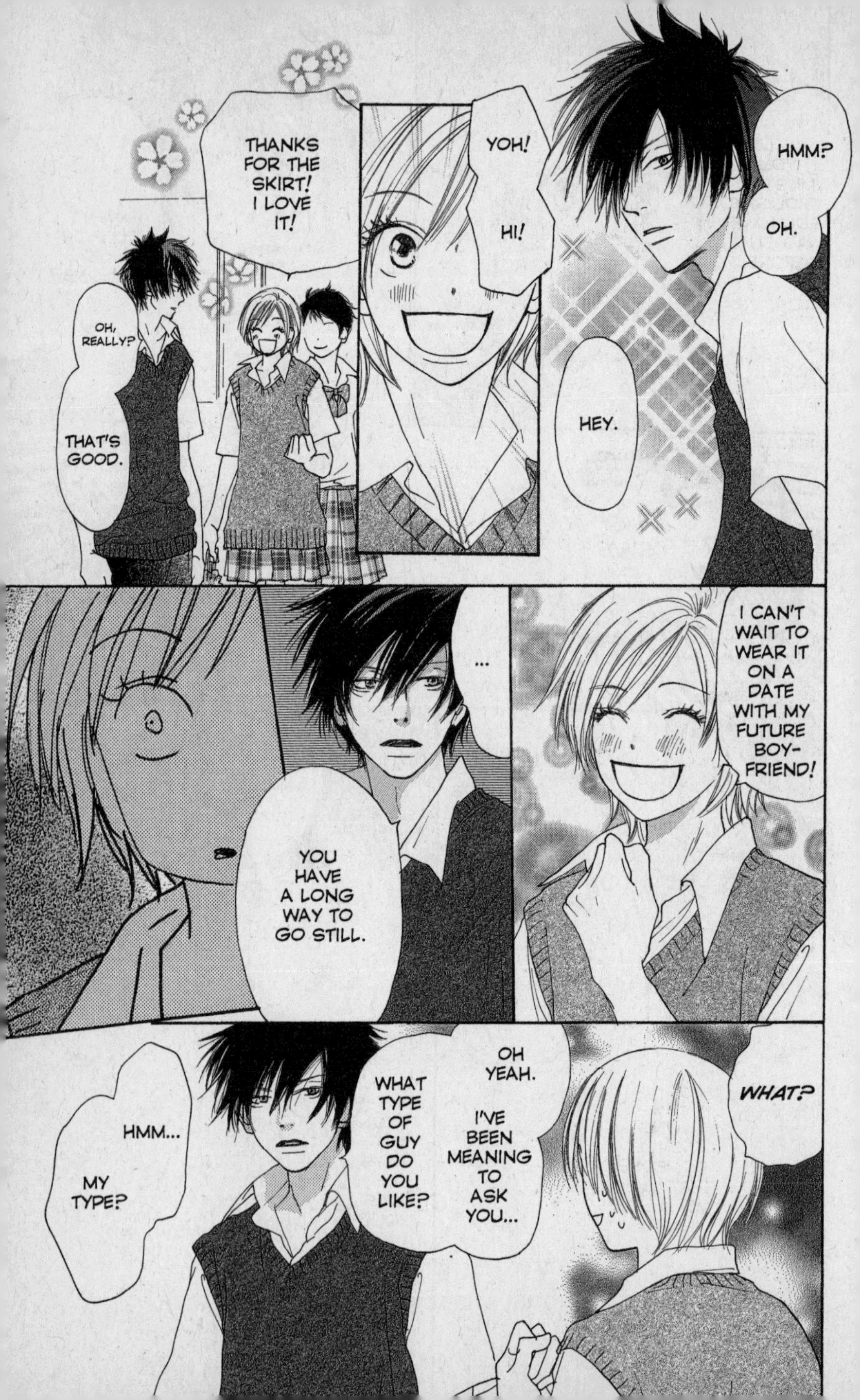
HMM?
OH.
HEY.
YOH!
HI!
THANKS FOR THE SKIRT! I LOVE IT!
OH, REALLY?
THAT'S GOOD.
I CAN'T WAIT TO WEAR IT ON A DATE WITH MY FUTURE BOY-FRIEND!
...
YOU HAVE A LONG WAY TO GO STILL.
WHAT?
OH YEAH.
I'VE BEEN MEANING TO ASK YOU...
WHAT TYPE OF GUY DO YOU LIKE?
HMM...
MY TYPE?

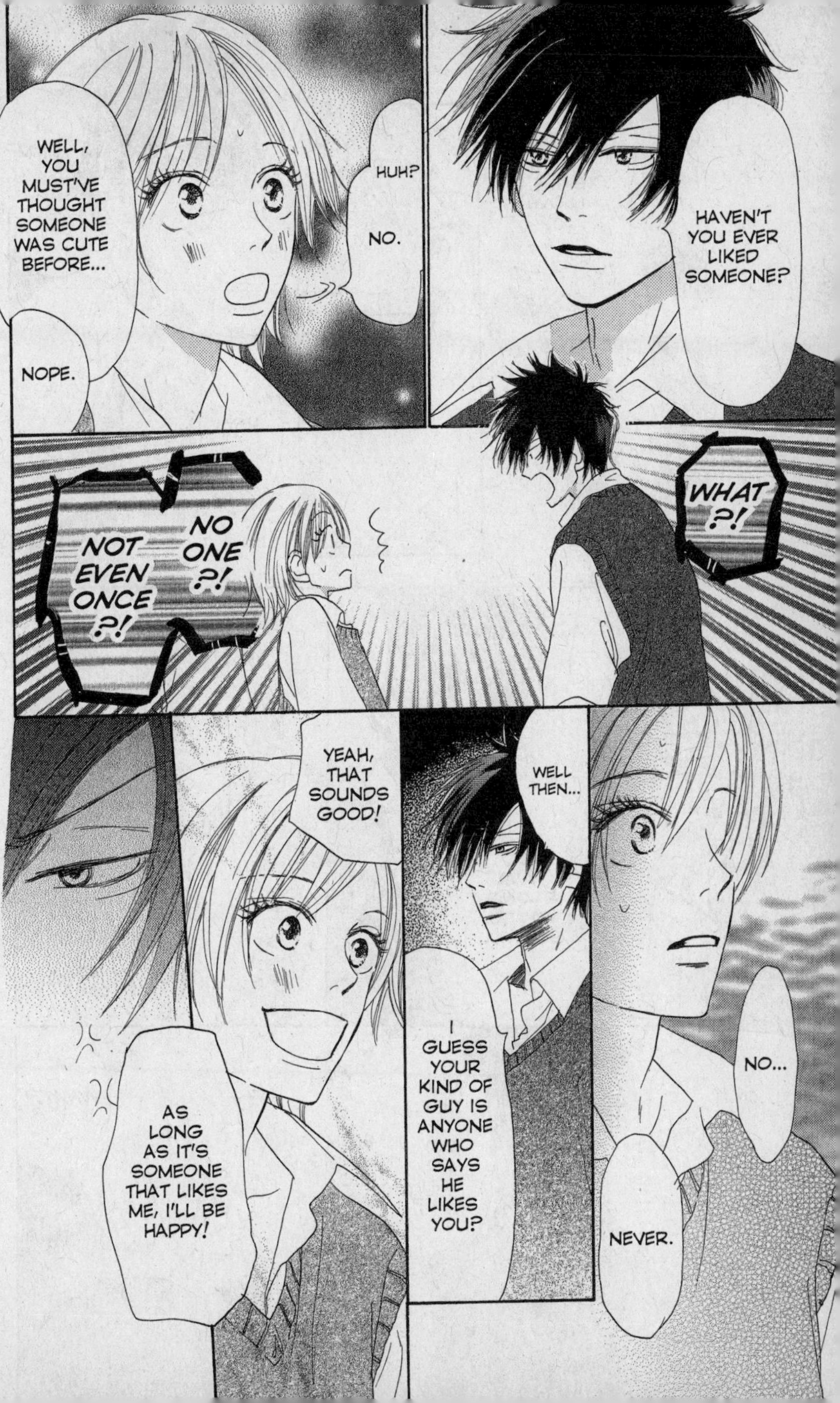
HAVEN'T YOU EVER LIKED SOMEONE?
HUH?
NO.
WELL, YOU MUST'VE THOUGHT SOMEONE WAS CUTE BEFORE...
NOPE.
WHAT ?!
NO ONE ?!
NOT EVEN ONCE ?!
NO...
NEVER.
WELL THEN...
I GUESS YOUR KIND OF GUY IS ANYONE WHO SAYS HE LIKES YOU?
YEAH, THAT SOUNDS GOOD!
AS LONG AS IT'S SOMEONE THAT LIKES ME, I'LL BE HAPPY!

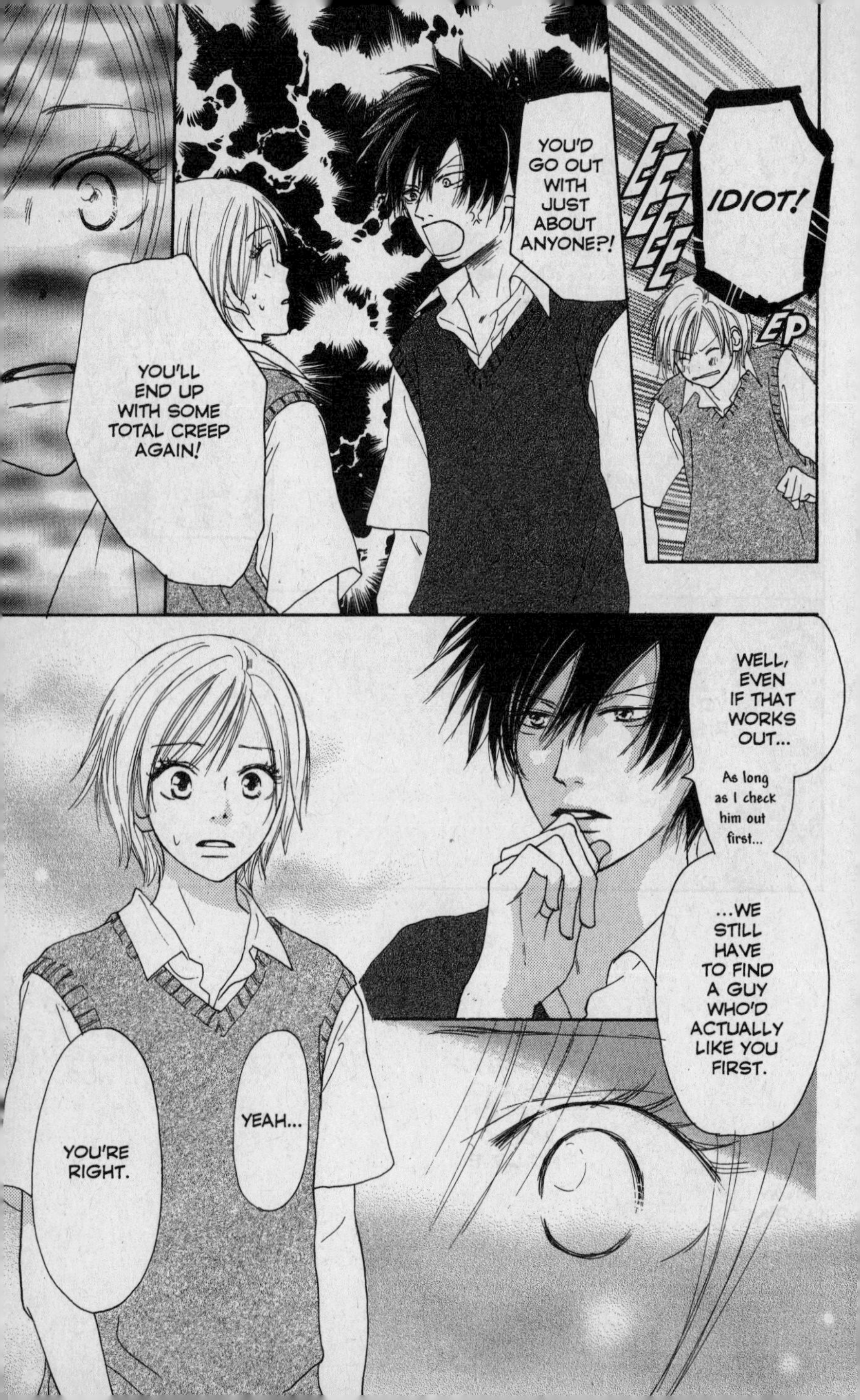
EEEE
IDIOT!
EP
YOU'D GO OUT WITH JUST ABOUT ANYONE?!
YOU'LL END UP WITH SOME TOTAL CREEP AGAIN!
WELL, EVEN IF THAT WORKS OUT...
As long as I check him out first...
...WE STILL HAVE TO FIND A GUY WHO'D ACTUALLY LIKE YOU FIRST.
YEAH...
YOU'RE RIGHT.

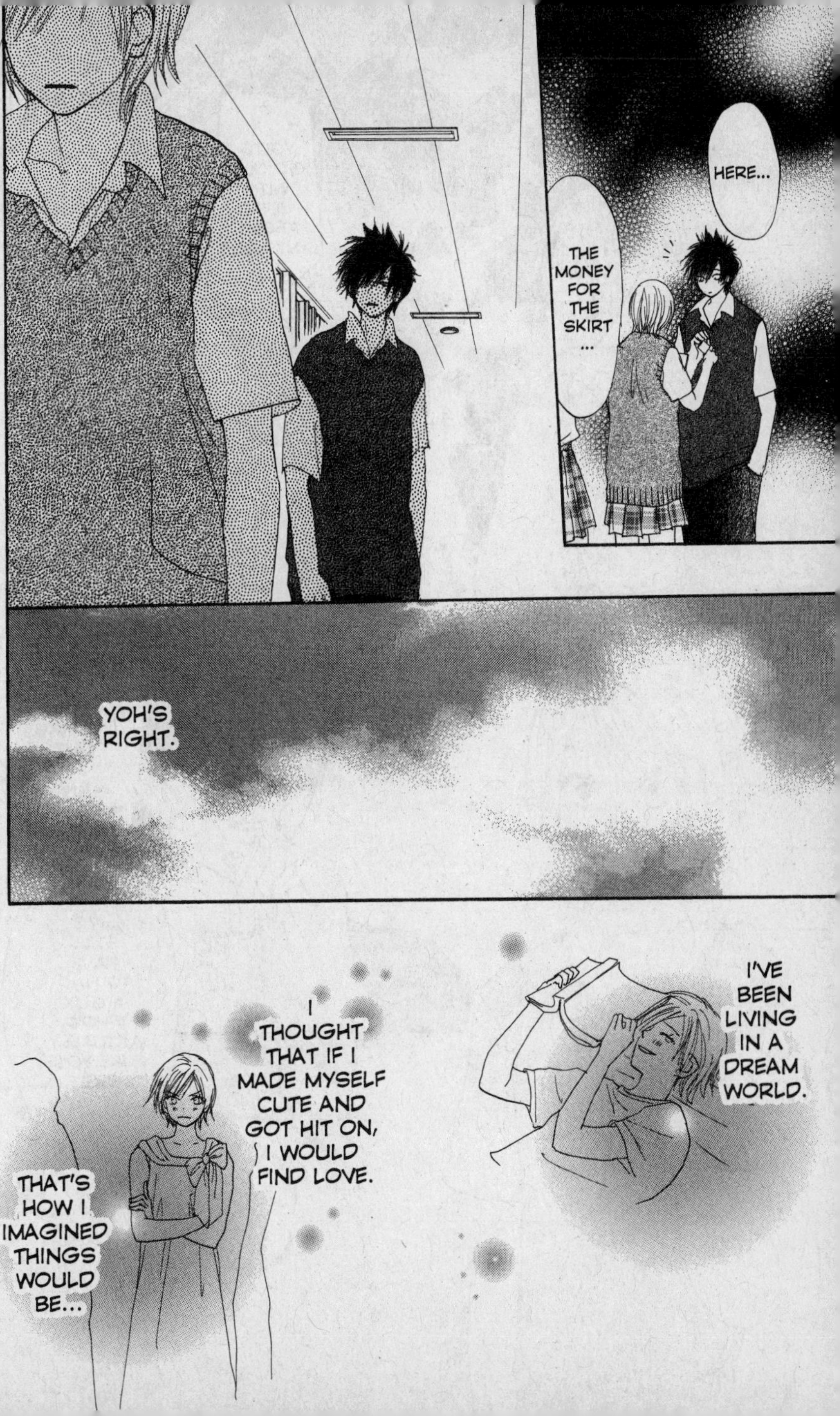
HERE...
THE MONEY FOR THE SKIRT...
YOH'S RIGHT.
I'VE BEEN LIVING IN A DREAM WORLD.
I THOUGHT THAT IF I MADE MYSELF CUTE AND GOT HIT ON, I WOULD FIND LOVE.
THAT'S HOW I IMAGINED THINGS WOULD BE...

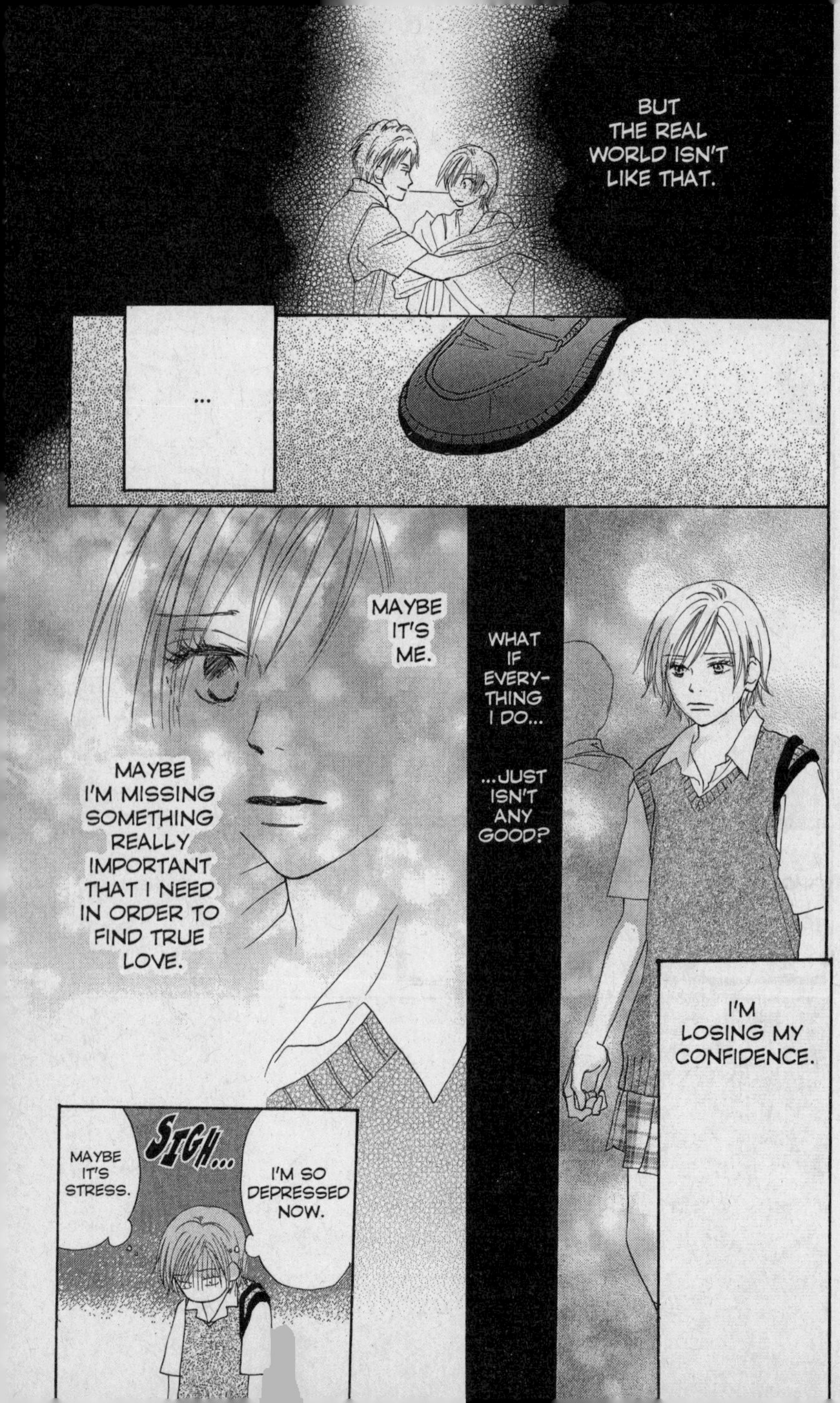

BUT THE REAL WORLD ISN'T LIKE THAT.
...
WHAT IF EVERYTHING I DO...
...JUST ISN'T ANY GOOD?
I'M LOSING MY CONFIDENCE.
MAYBE IT'S ME.
MAYBE I'M MISSING SOMETHING REALLY IMPORTANT THAT I NEED IN ORDER TO FIND TRUE LOVE.
I'M SO DEPRESSED NOW.
SIGH...
MAYBE IT'S STRESS.

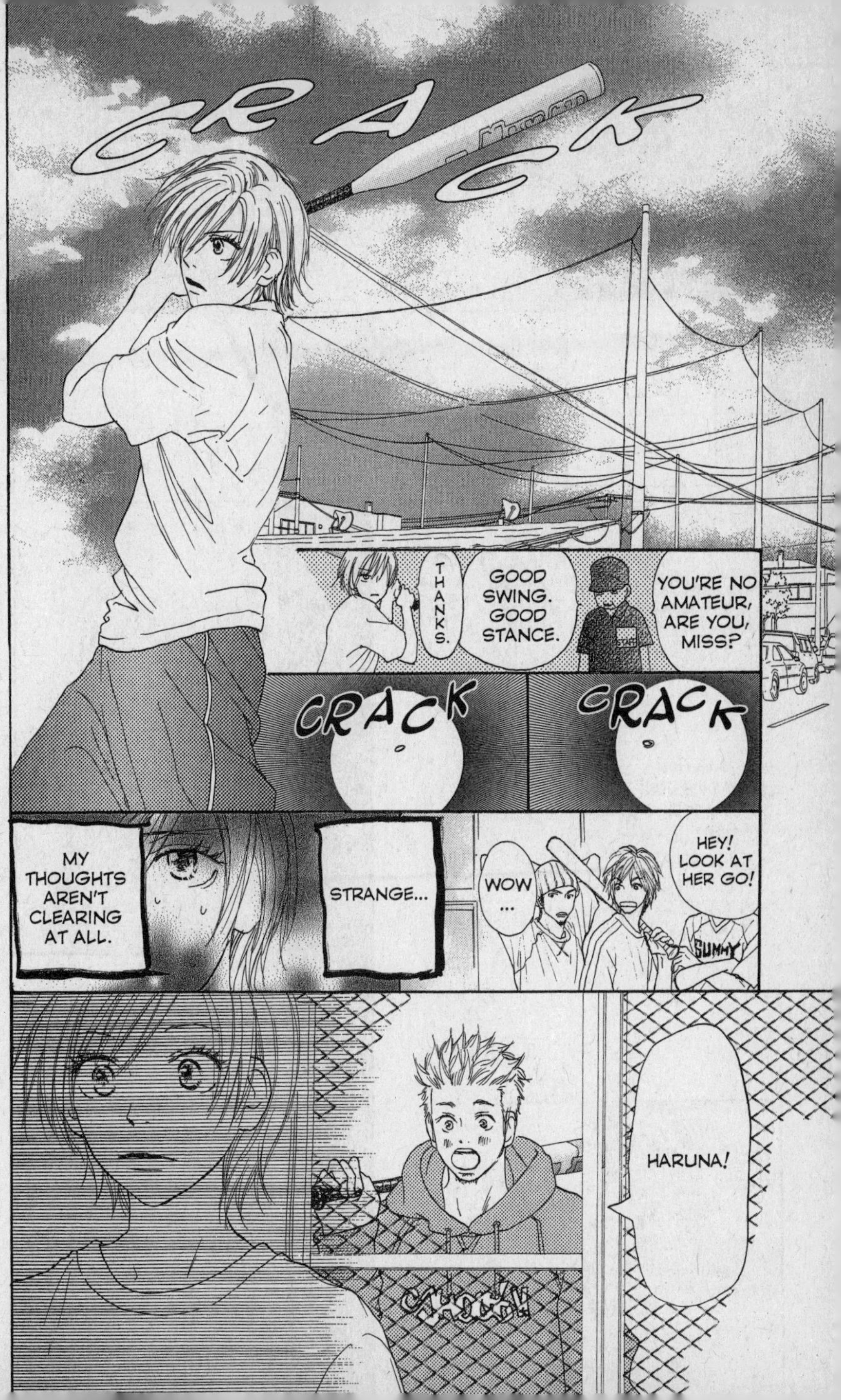
CRACK
YOU'RE NO AMATEUR, ARE YOU, MISS?
GOOD SWING. GOOD STANCE.
THANKS.
CRACK
CRACK
HEY! LOOK AT HER GO!
WOW...
STRANGE...
MY THOUGHTS AREN'T CLEARING AT ALL.
HARUNA!

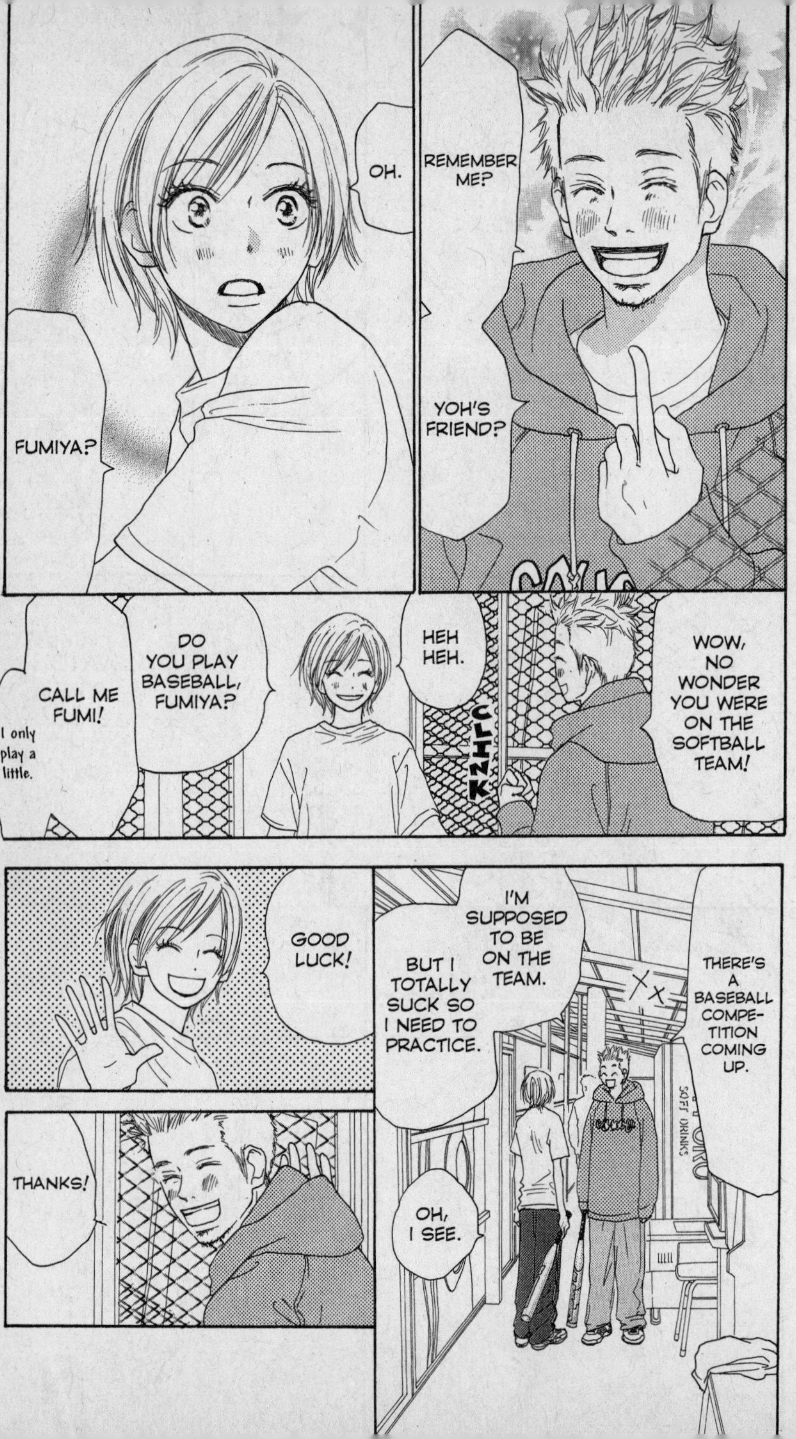
REMEMBER ME?
YOH'S FRIEND?
OH.
FUMIYA?
WOW, NO WONDER YOU WERE ON THE SOFTBALL TEAM!
CLINK
HEH HEH.
DO YOU PLAY BASEBALL, FUMIYA?
CALL ME FUMI!
I only play a little.
THERE'S A BASEBALL COMPE-TITION COMING UP.
I'M SUPPOSED TO BE ON THE TEAM.
BUT I TOTALLY SUCK SO I NEED TO PRACTICE.
SOFT DRINKS
OH, I SEE.
GOOD LUCK!
THANKS!

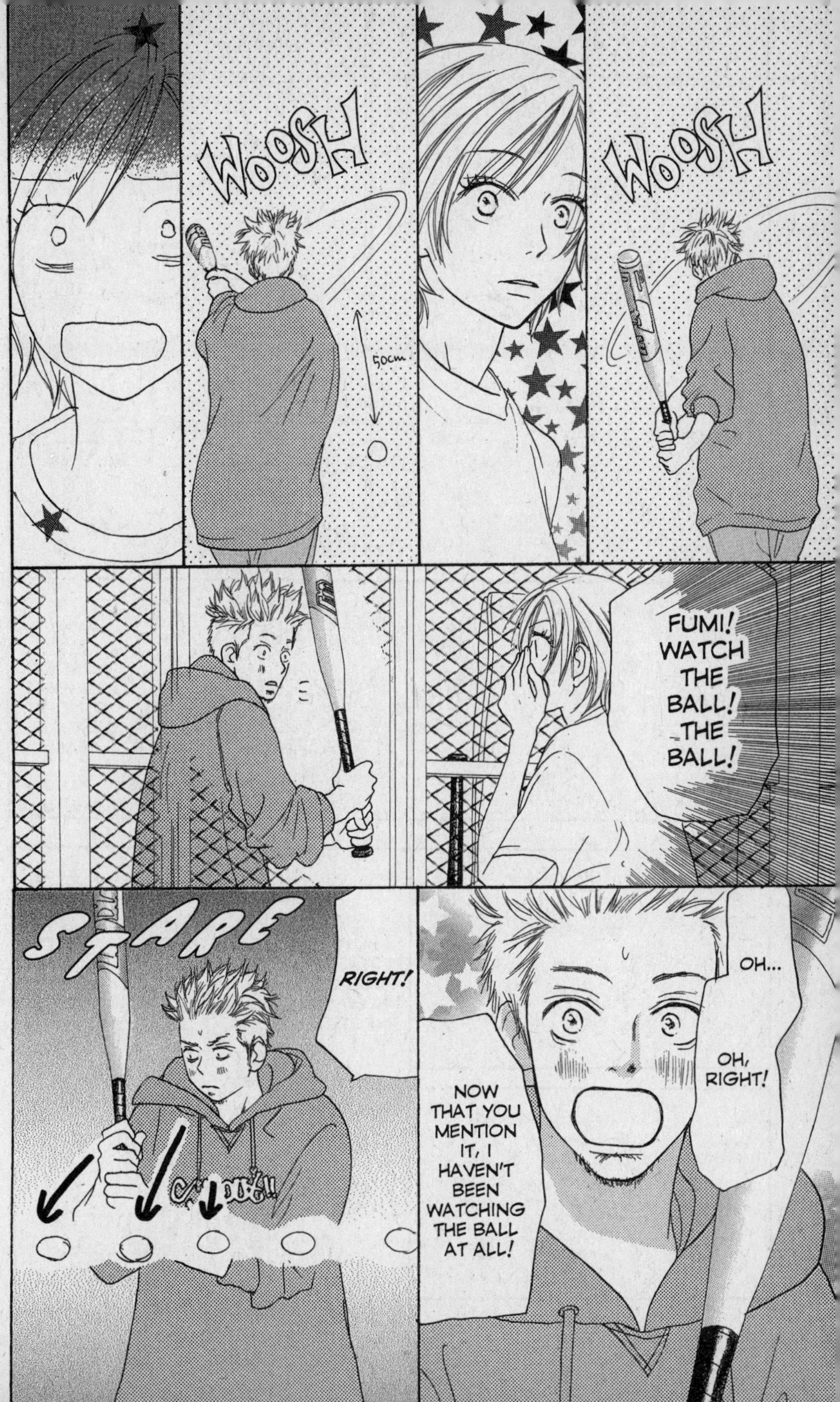
WOOSH
WOOSH
50cm
FUMI! WATCH THE BALL! THE BALL!
OH...
OH, RIGHT!
NOW THAT YOU MENTION IT, I HAVEN'T BEEN WATCHING THE BALL AT ALL!
RIGHT!
STARE

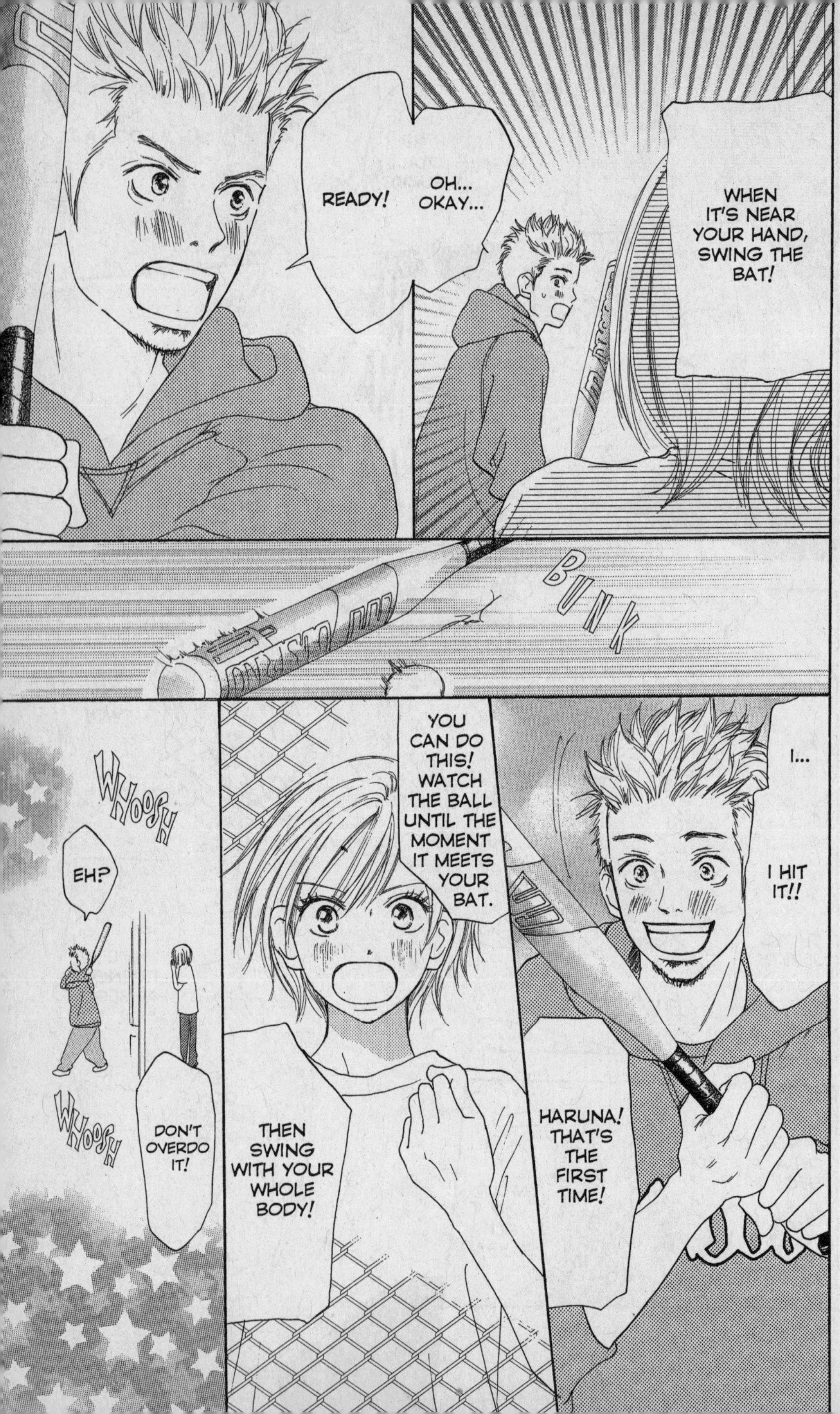
WHEN IT'S NEAR YOUR HAND, SWING THE BAT!
OH... OKAY...
READY!
BUNK
I...
I HIT IT!!
HARUNA! THAT'S THE FIRST TIME!
YOU CAN DO THIS! WATCH THE BALL UNTIL THE MOMENT IT MEETS YOUR BAT.
THEN SWING WITH YOUR WHOLE BODY!
WHOOSH
EH?
WHOOSH
DON'T OVERDO IT!

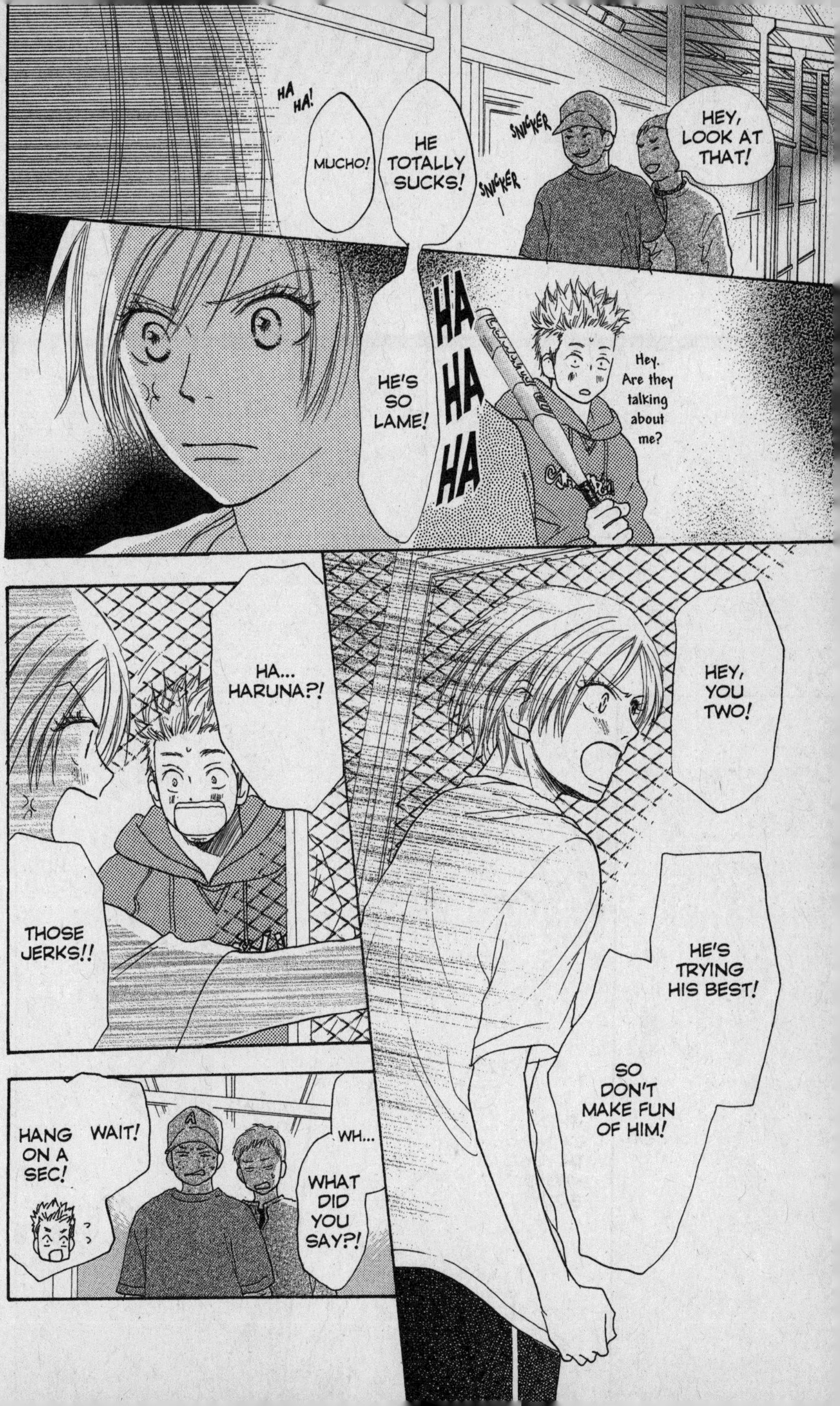
HEY, LOOK AT THAT!
SNICKER
SNICKER
HE TOTALLY SUCKS!
MUCHO!
HA HA!
Hey. Are they talking about me?
HA HA HA
HE'S SO LAME!
HEY, YOU TWO!
HE'S TRYING HIS BEST!
SO DON'T MAKE FUN OF HIM!
HA... HARUNA?!
THOSE JERKS!!
WH...
WHAT DID YOU SAY?!
WAIT!
HANG ON A SEC!

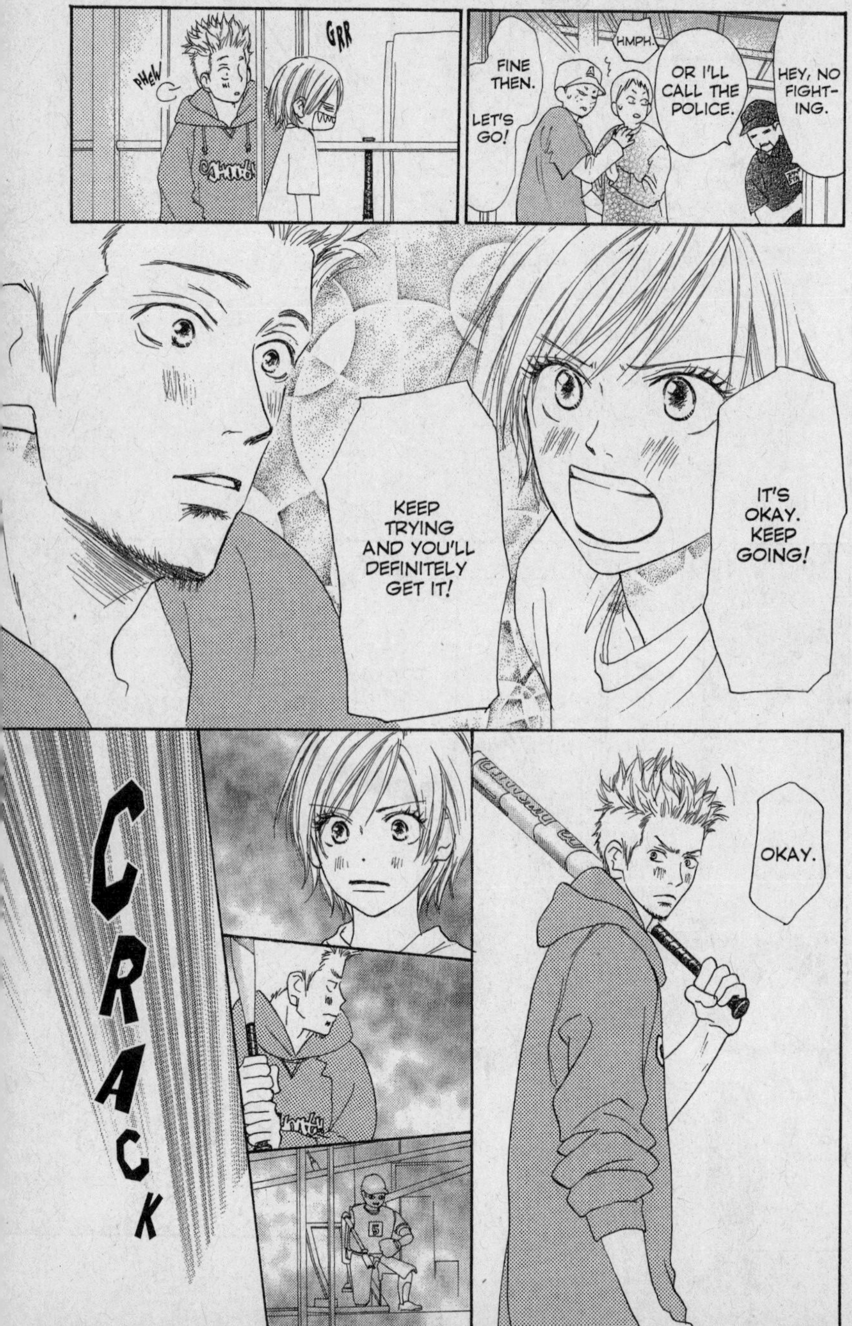
HEY, NO FIGHT-ING.
OR I'LL CALL THE POLICE.
HMPH.
FINE THEN.
LET'S GO!
GRR
PHEW
IT'S OKAY. KEEP GOING!
KEEP TRYING AND YOU'LL DEFINITELY GET IT!
OKAY.
CRACK

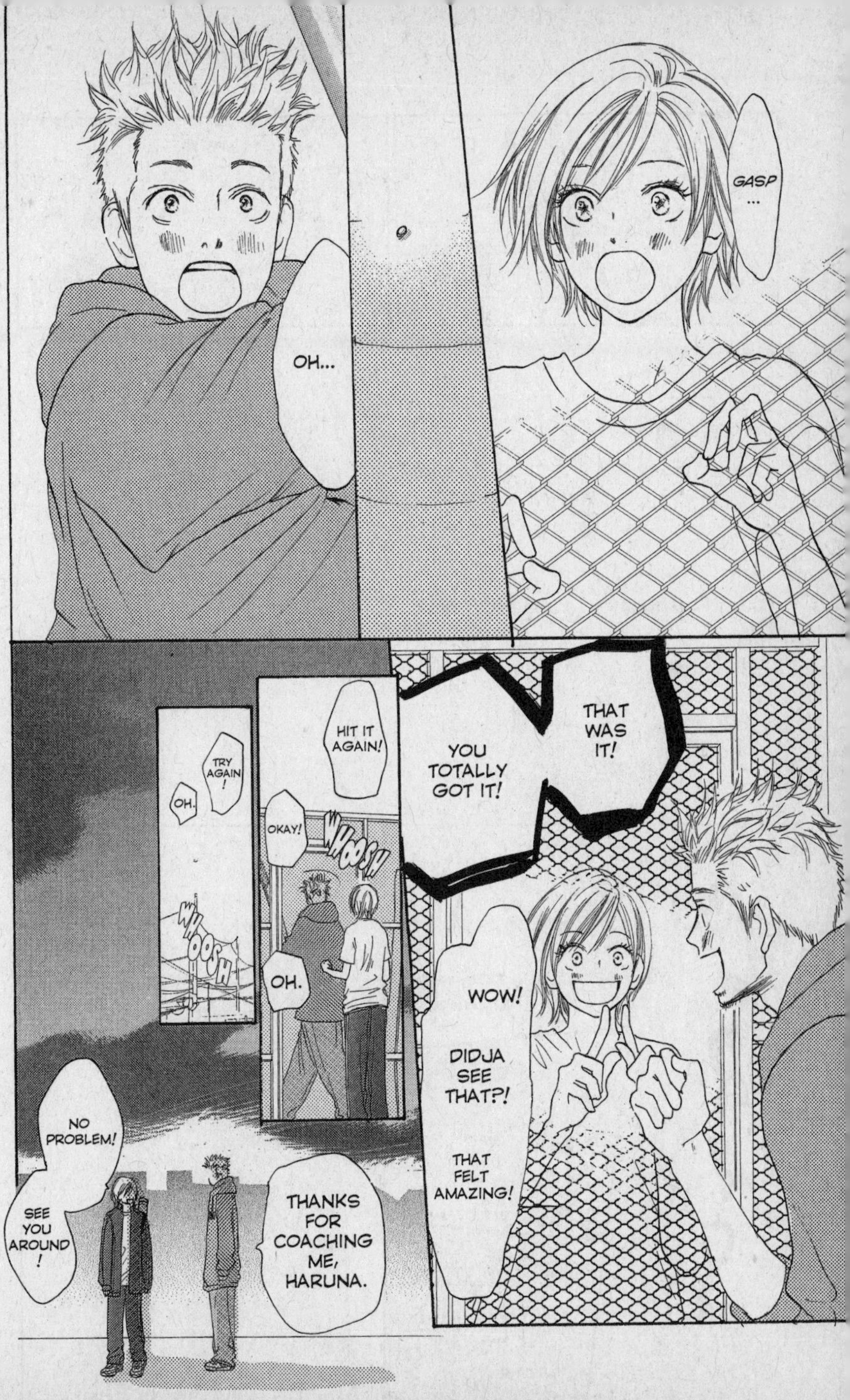
GASP ...
OH...
THAT WAS IT!
YOU TOTALLY GOT IT!
WOW!
DIDJA SEE THAT?!
THAT FELT AMAZING!
HIT IT AGAIN!
OKAY!
WHOOSH
OH.
TRY AGAIN!
OH.
WHOOSH
THANKS FOR COACHING ME, HARUNA.
NO PROBLEM!
SEE YOU AROUND!

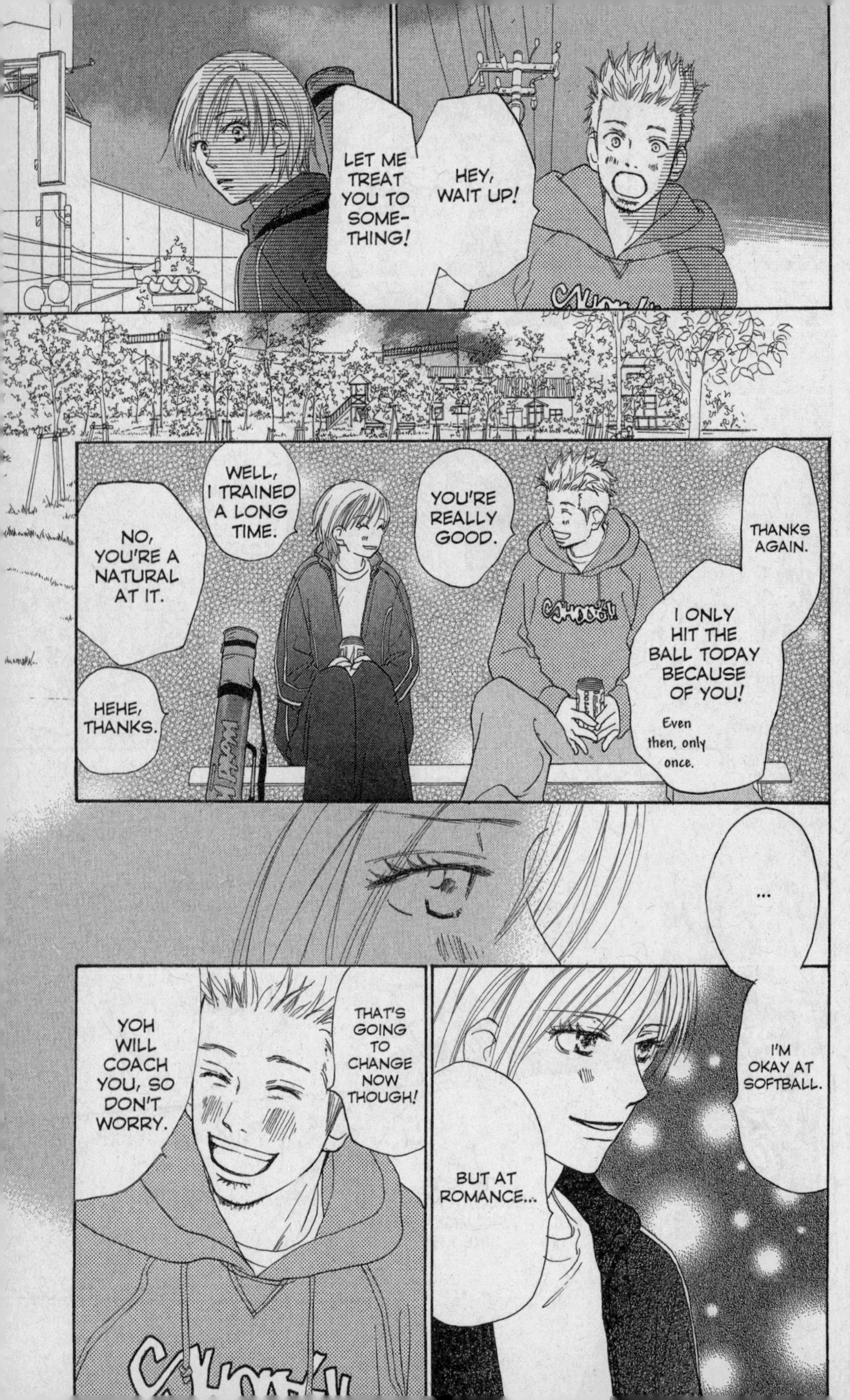
HEY, WAIT UP!
LET ME TREAT YOU TO SOME-THING!
THANKS AGAIN.
I ONLY HIT THE BALL TODAY BECAUSE OF YOU!
Even then, only once.
YOU'RE REALLY GOOD.
WELL, I TRAINED A LONG TIME.
NO, YOU'RE A NATURAL AT IT.
HEHE, THANKS.
...
I'M OKAY AT SOFTBALL.
BUT AT ROMANCE...
THAT'S GOING TO CHANGE NOW THOUGH!
YOH WILL COACH YOU, SO DON'T WORRY.

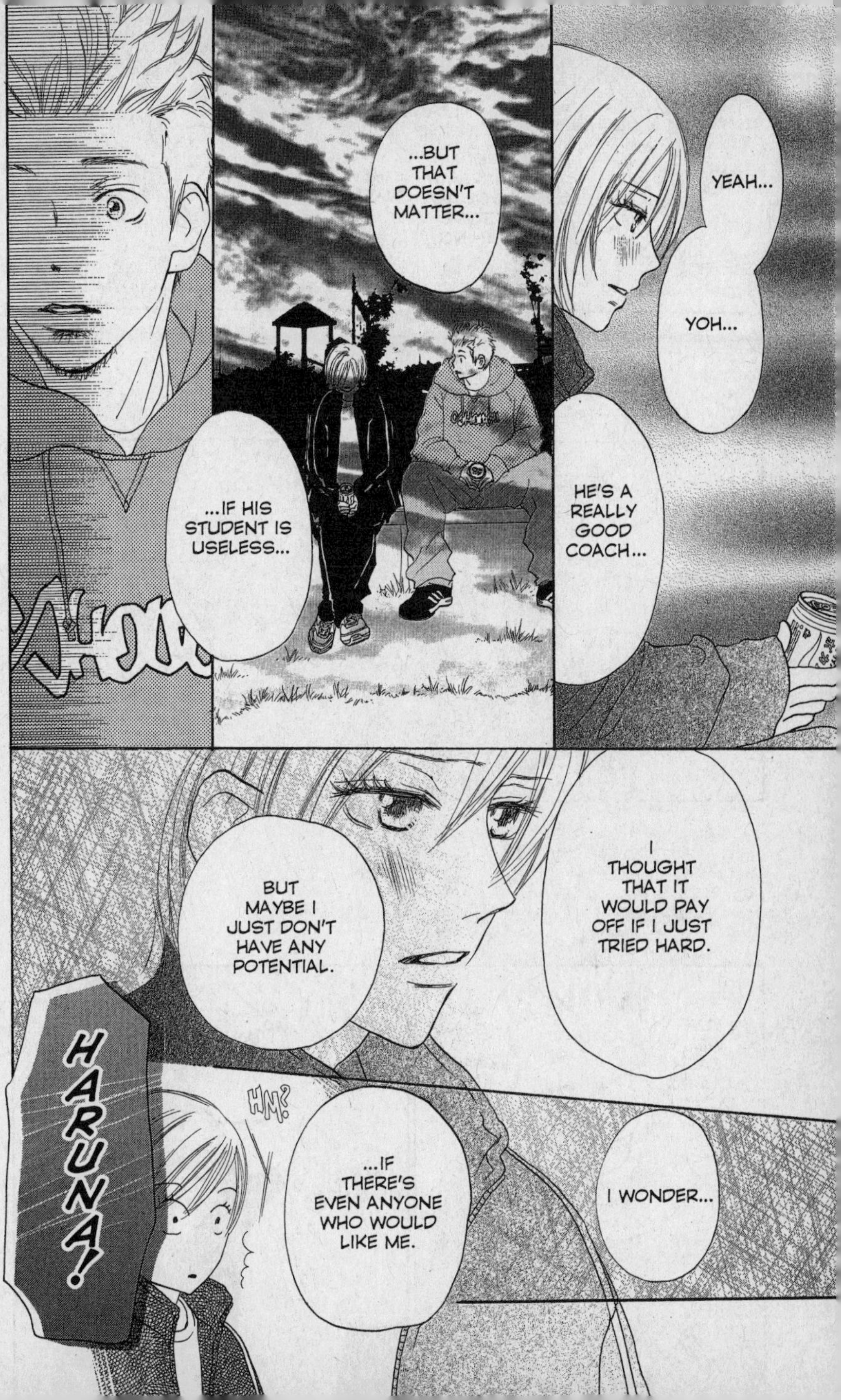
YEAH...
YOH...
HE'S A REALLY GOOD COACH...
...BUT THAT DOESN'T MATTER...
...IF HIS STUDENT IS USELESS...
I THOUGHT THAT IT WOULD PAY OFF IF I JUST TRIED HARD.
BUT MAYBE I JUST DON'T HAVE ANY POTENTIAL.
I WONDER...
...IF THERE'S EVEN ANYONE WHO WOULD LIKE ME.
HM?
HARUNA!

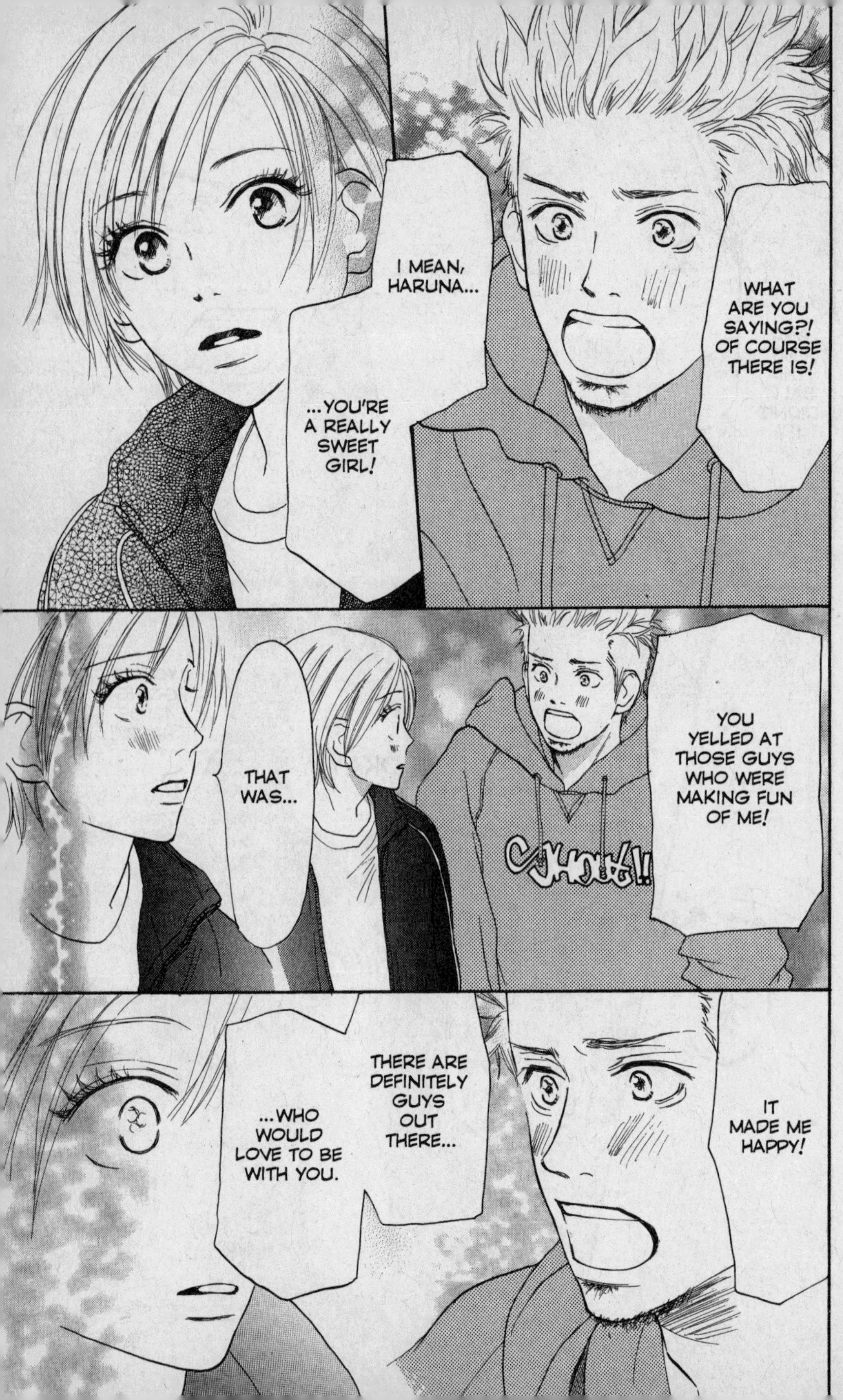
WHAT ARE YOU SAYING?! OF COURSE THERE IS!
I MEAN, HARUNA...
...YOU'RE A REALLY SWEET GIRL!
YOU YELLED AT THOSE GUYS WHO WERE MAKING FUN OF ME!
THAT WAS...
IT MADE ME HAPPY!
THERE ARE DEFINITELY GUYS OUT THERE...
...WHO WOULD LOVE TO BE WITH YOU.

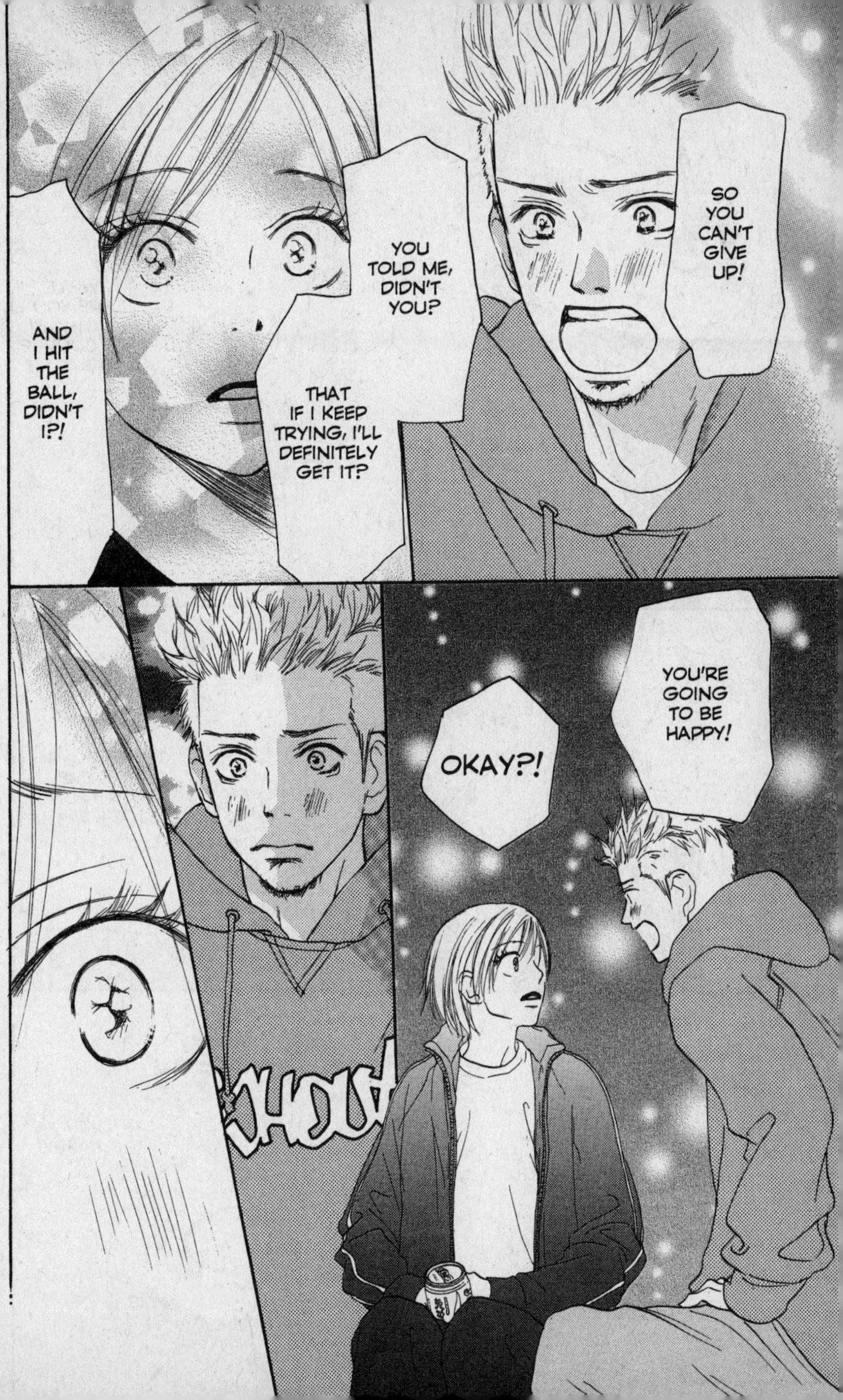
SO YOU CAN'T GIVE UP!
YOU TOLD ME, DIDN'T YOU?
THAT IF I KEEP TRYING, I'LL DEFINITELY GET IT?
AND I HIT THE BALL, DIDN'T I?!
YOU'RE GOING TO BE HAPPY!
OKAY?!

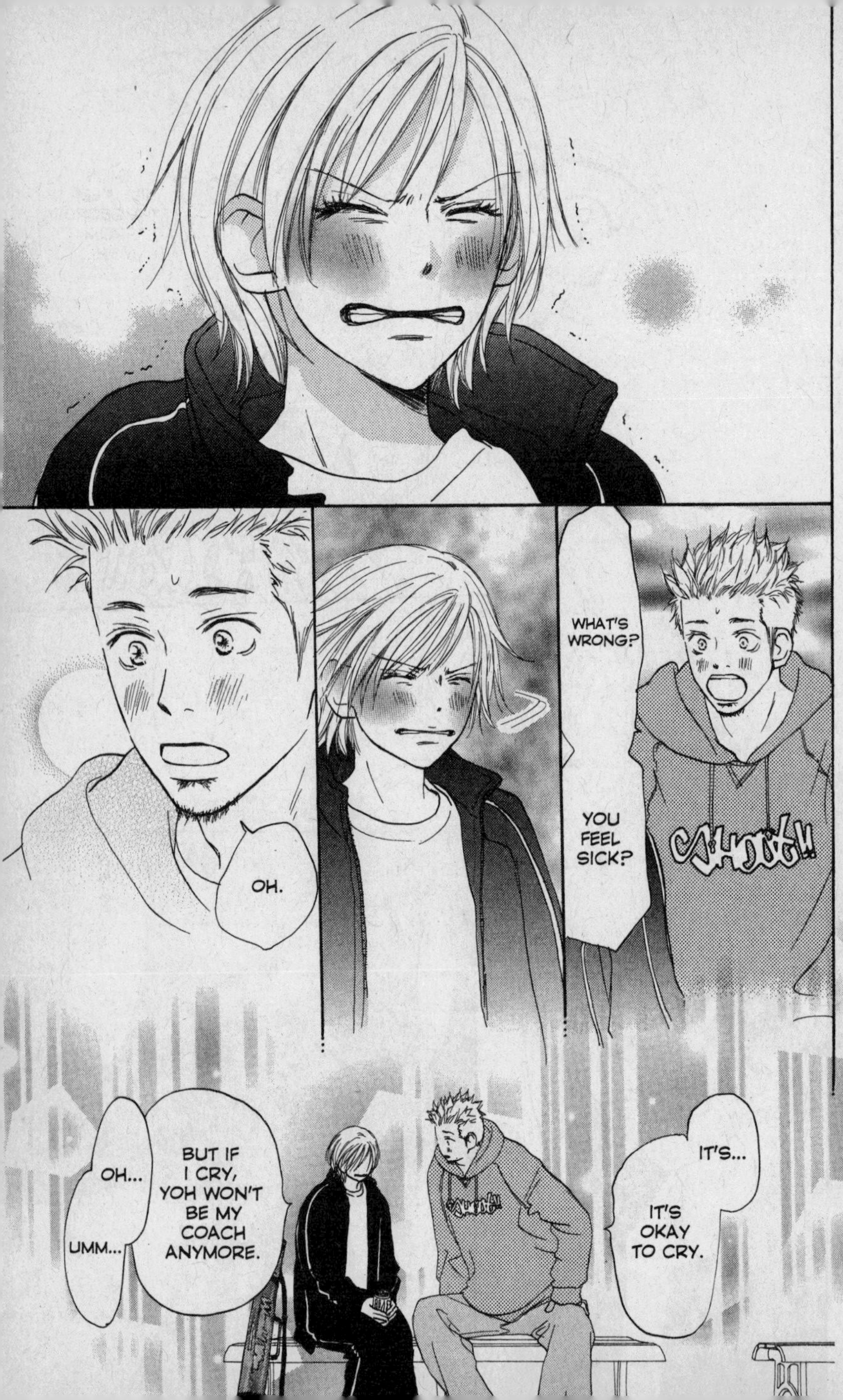

WHAT'S WRONG?
YOU FEEL SICK?
OH.
IT'S...
IT'S OKAY TO CRY.
BUT IF I CRY, YOH WON'T BE MY COACH ANYMORE.
OH...
UMM...

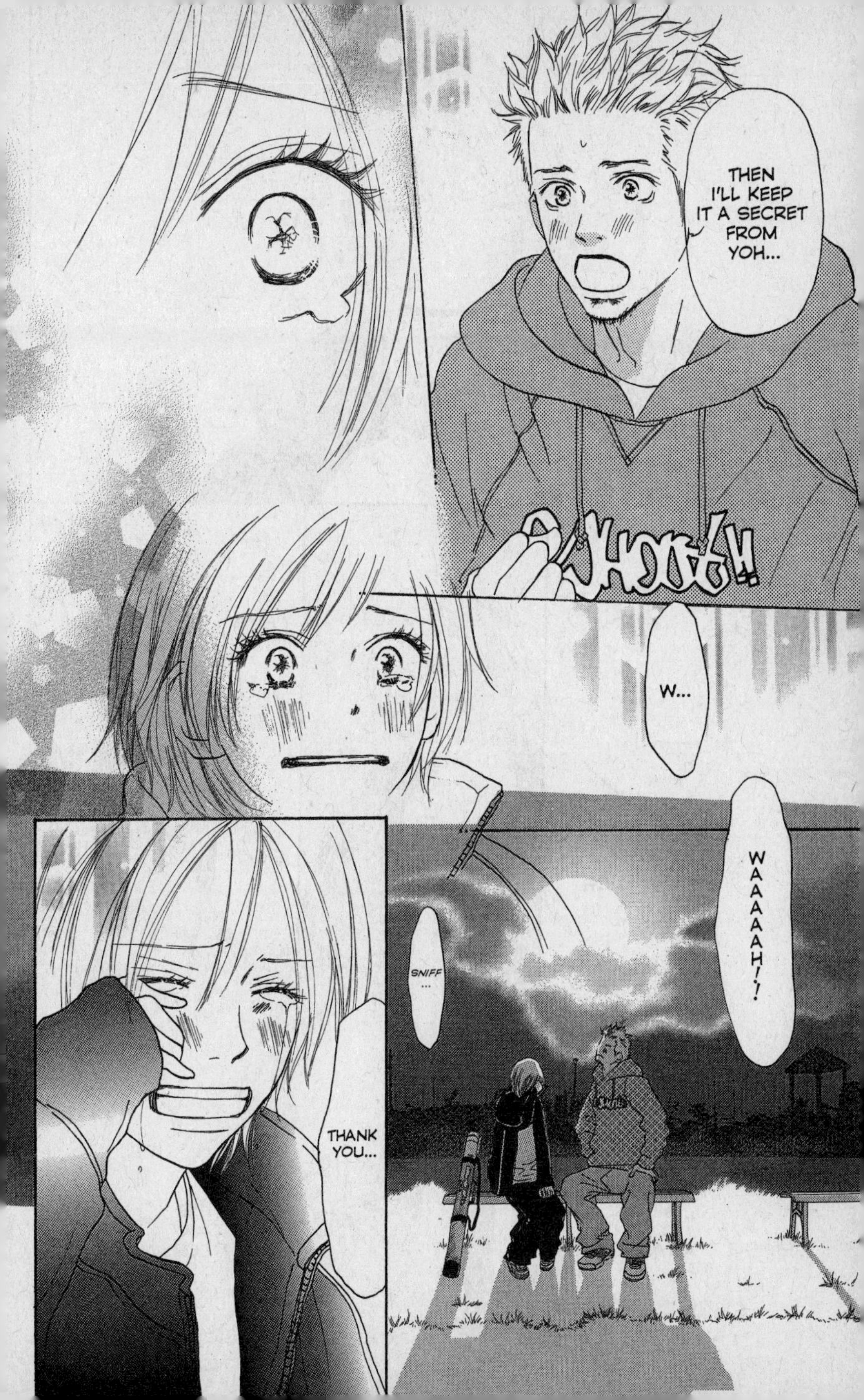
THEN I'LL KEEP IT A SECRET FROM YOH...
SHOOT!!
W...
WAAAAAAH!?!
SNIFF ...
THANK YOU...

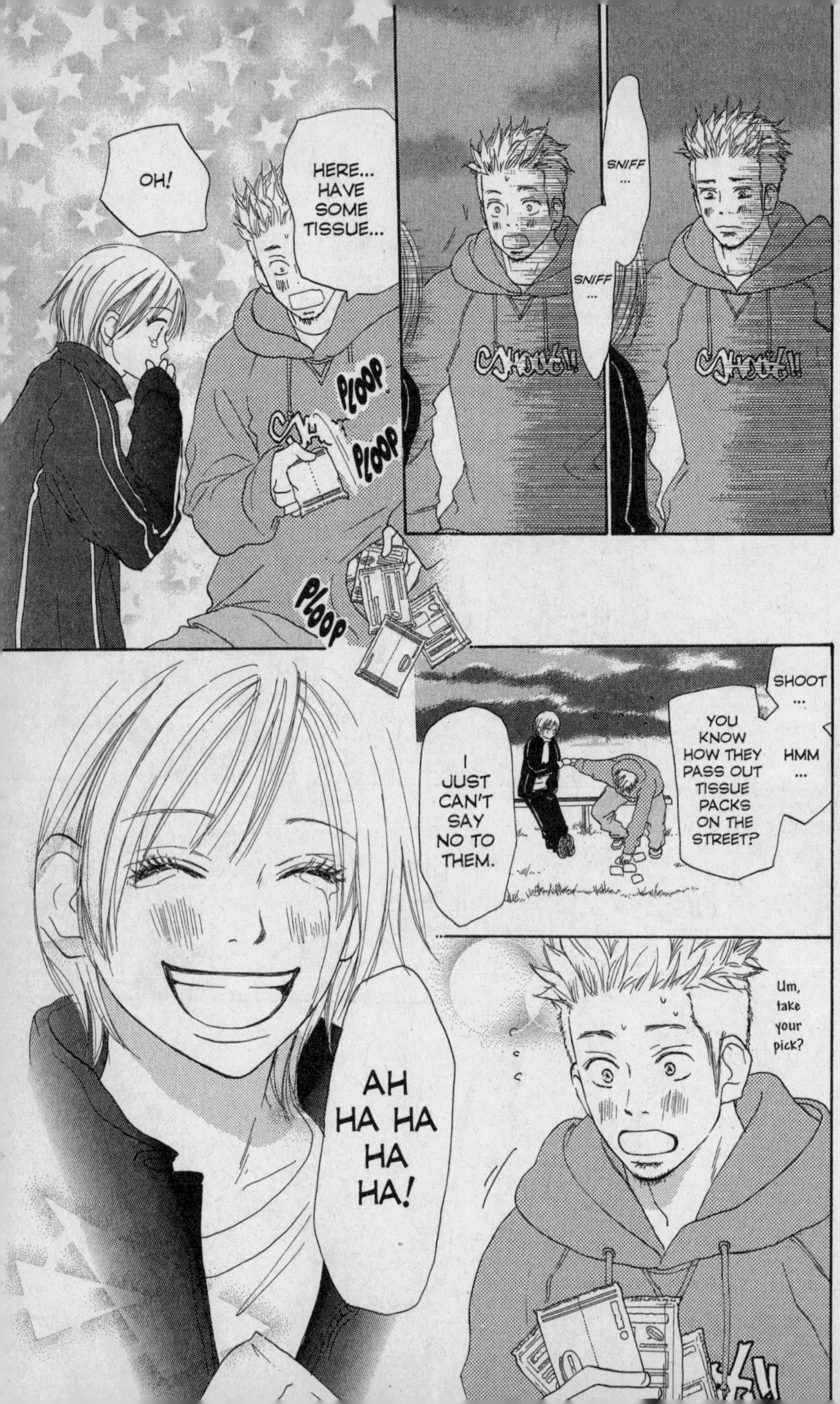
SNIFF ...
SNIFF ...
HERE... HAVE SOME TISSUE...
OH!
PLOOP
PLOOP
PLOOP
SHOOT ...
HMM ...
YOU KNOW HOW THEY PASS OUT TISSUE PACKS ON THE STREET?
I JUST CAN'T SAY NO TO THEM.
Um, take your pick?
AH HA HA HA HA!

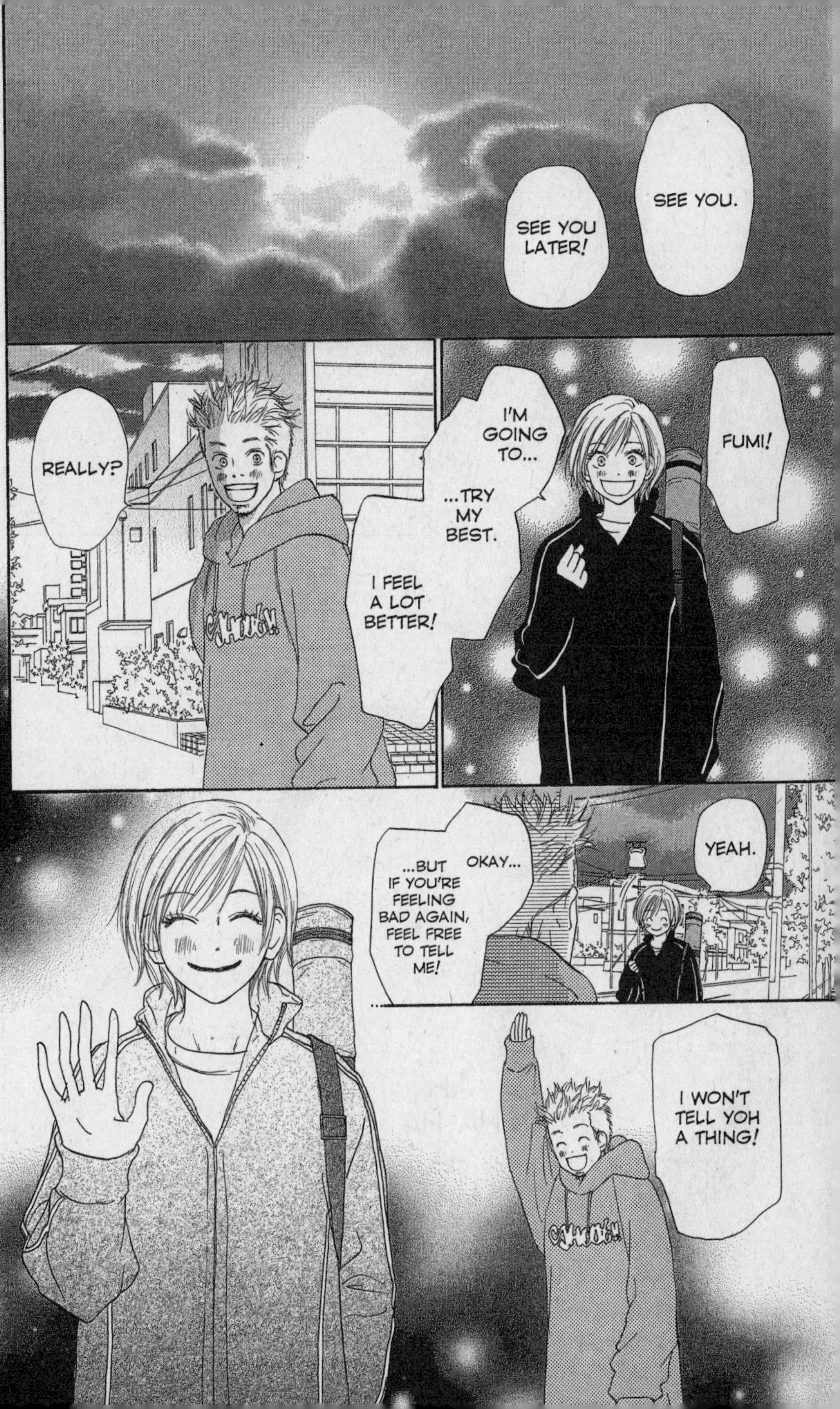
SEE YOU.
SEE YOU LATER!
FUMI!
I'M GOING TO...
...TRY MY BEST.
I FEEL A LOT BETTER!
REALLY?
YEAH.
OKAY...
...BUT IF YOU'RE FEELING BAD AGAIN, FEEL FREE TO TELL ME!
I WON'T TELL YOH A THING!

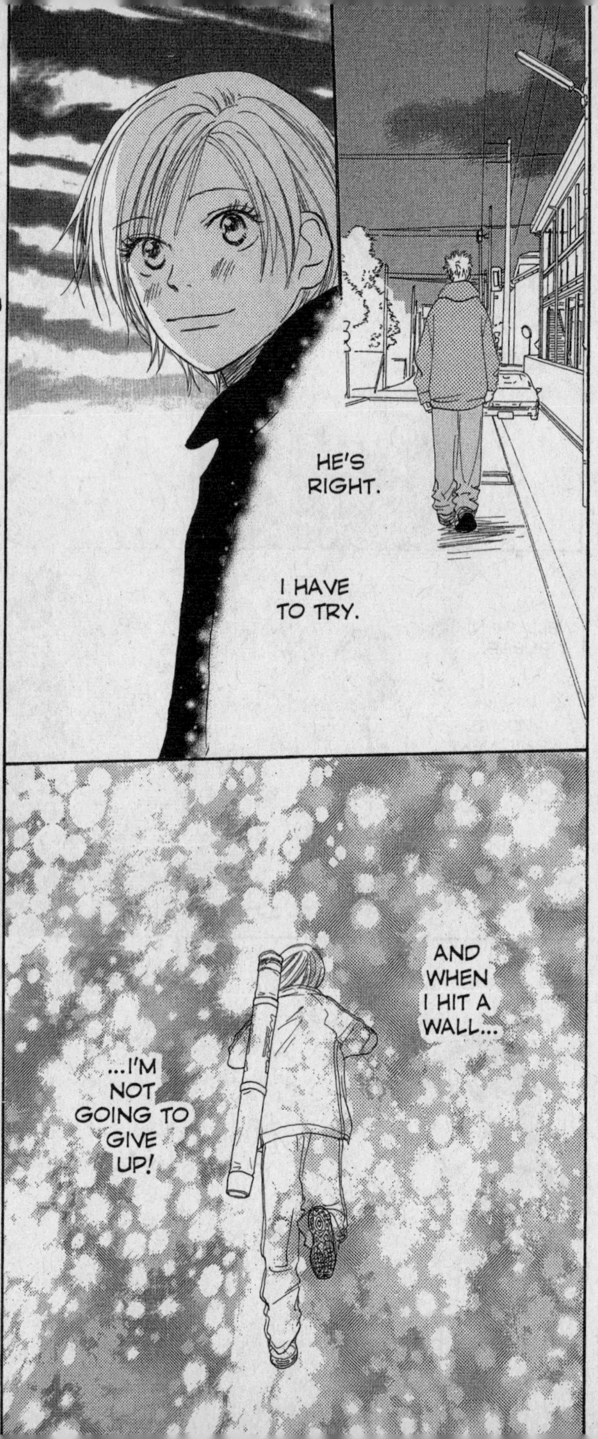
HE'S RIGHT.
I HAVE TO TRY.
AND WHEN I HIT A WALL...
...I'M NOT GOING TO GIVE UP!

3

I've been forgetful recently, so I've been writing down everything that I think of. But then I forget that I wrote it down. Or I forget what the note was about. So it hasn't really turned out to be much of a solution.

When I was a student, I must have had tests and stuff like that. But I can't remember how I managed to memorize everything. Maybe that's why I hate tests so much...because I'm so bad at them! I still dream that I've done badly on a test sometimes. Often right before a deadline. I wonder if my brain links the stress somehow. Or maybe not.

Because I'm so forgetful, people I work with often have to remind me of stuff.

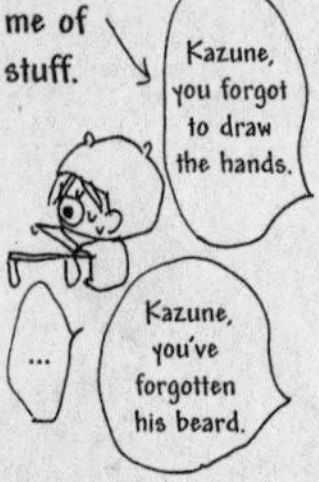
Kazune, you forgot to draw the hands.
...
Kazune, you've forgotten his beard.

Thank you so much, everyone!

See you in the next volume!

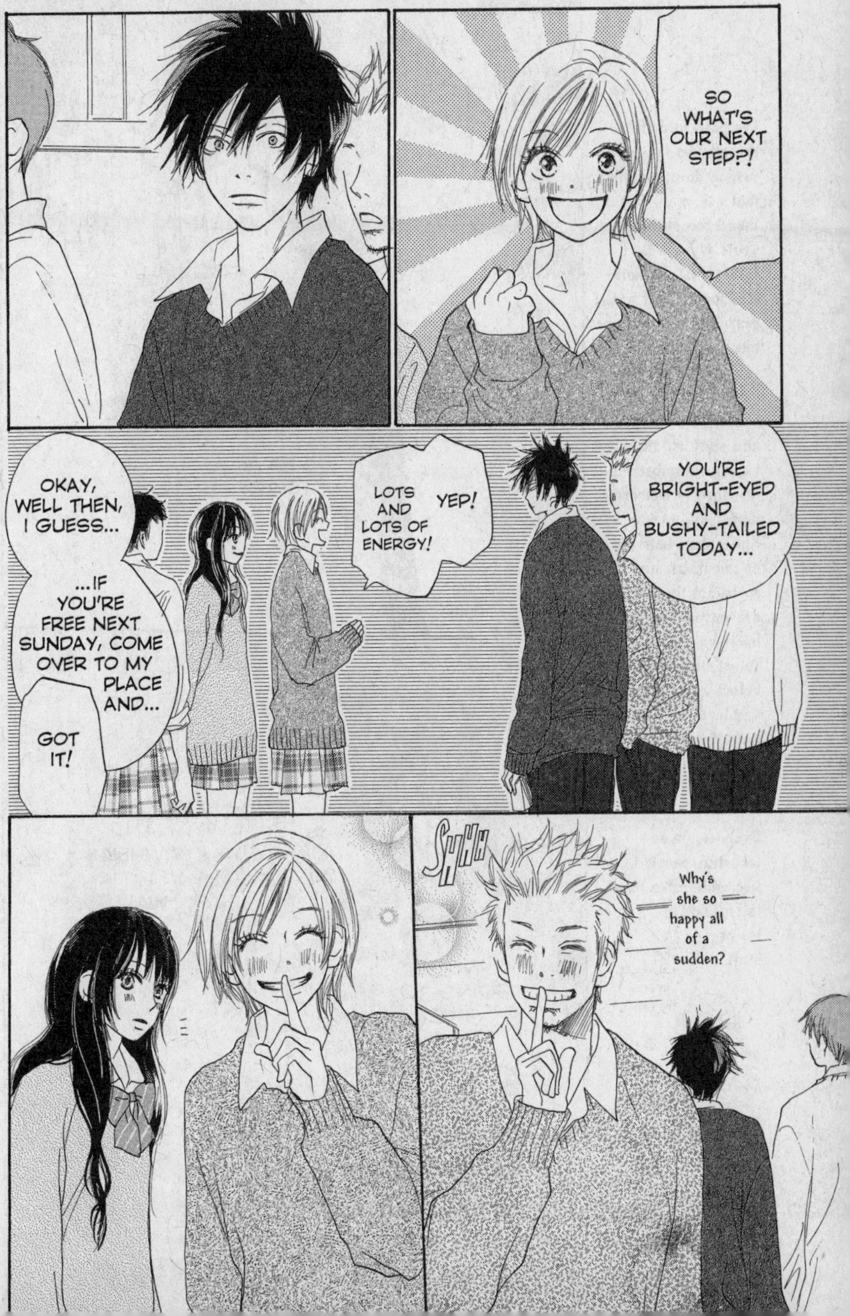
SO WHAT'S OUR NEXT STEP?!
YOU'RE BRIGHT-EYED AND BUSHY-TAILED TODAY...
YEP!
LOTS AND LOTS OF ENERGY!
OKAY, WELL THEN, I GUESS...
...IF YOU'RE FREE NEXT SUNDAY, COME OVER TO MY PLACE AND...
GOT IT!
SHHH
Why's she so happy all of a sudden?

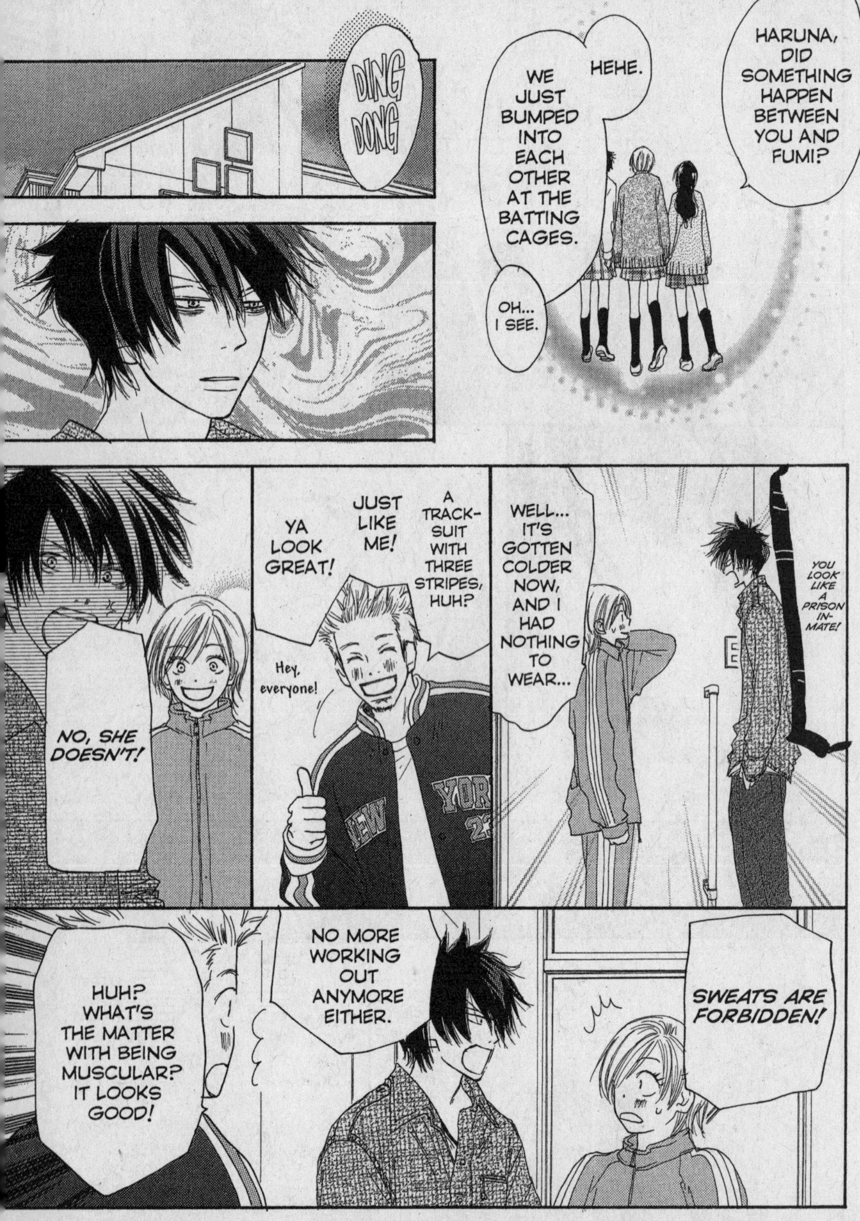
HARUNA, DID SOMETHING HAPPEN BETWEEN YOU AND FUMI?
HEHE.
WE JUST BUMPED INTO EACH OTHER AT THE BATTING CAGES.
OH... I SEE.
DING DONG
YOU LOOK LIKE A PRISON IN-MATE!
WELL... IT'S GOTTEN COLDER NOW, AND I HAD NOTHING TO WEAR...
A TRACK-SUIT WITH THREE STRIPES, HUH?
JUST LIKE ME!
YA LOOK GREAT!
Hey, everyone!
NO, SHE DOESN'T!
SWEATS ARE FORBIDDEN!
NO MORE WORKING OUT ANYMORE EITHER.
HUH? WHAT'S THE MATTER WITH BEING MUSCULAR? IT LOOKS GOOD!

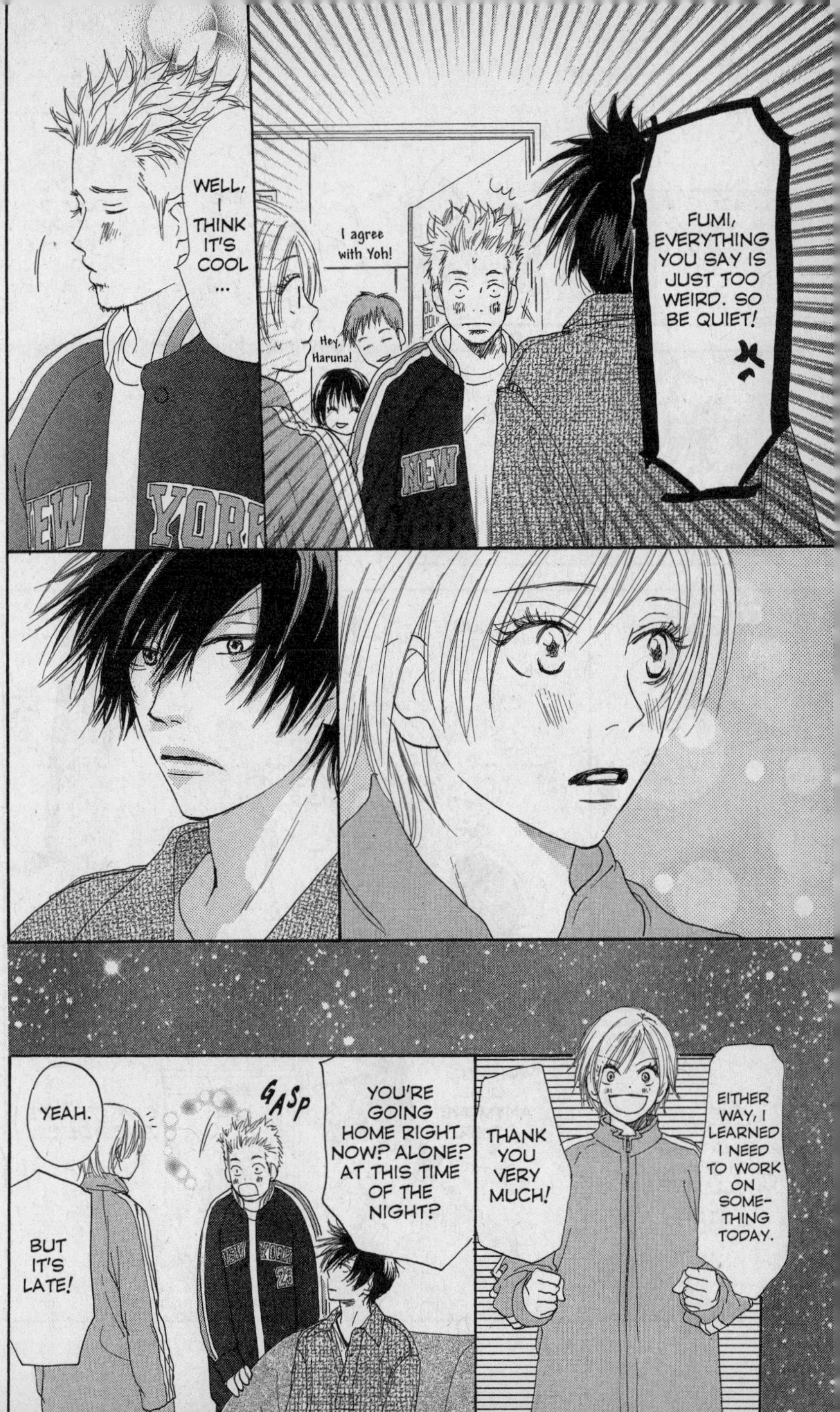
FUMI, EVERYTHING YOU SAY IS JUST TOO WEIRD. SO BE QUIET!
I agree with Yoh!
Hey, Haruna!
WELL, I THINK IT'S COOL ...
EITHER WAY, I LEARNED I NEED TO WORK ON SOME-THING TODAY.
THANK YOU VERY MUCH!
YOU'RE GOING HOME RIGHT NOW? ALONE? AT THIS TIME OF THE NIGHT?
GASP
YEAH.
BUT IT'S LATE!

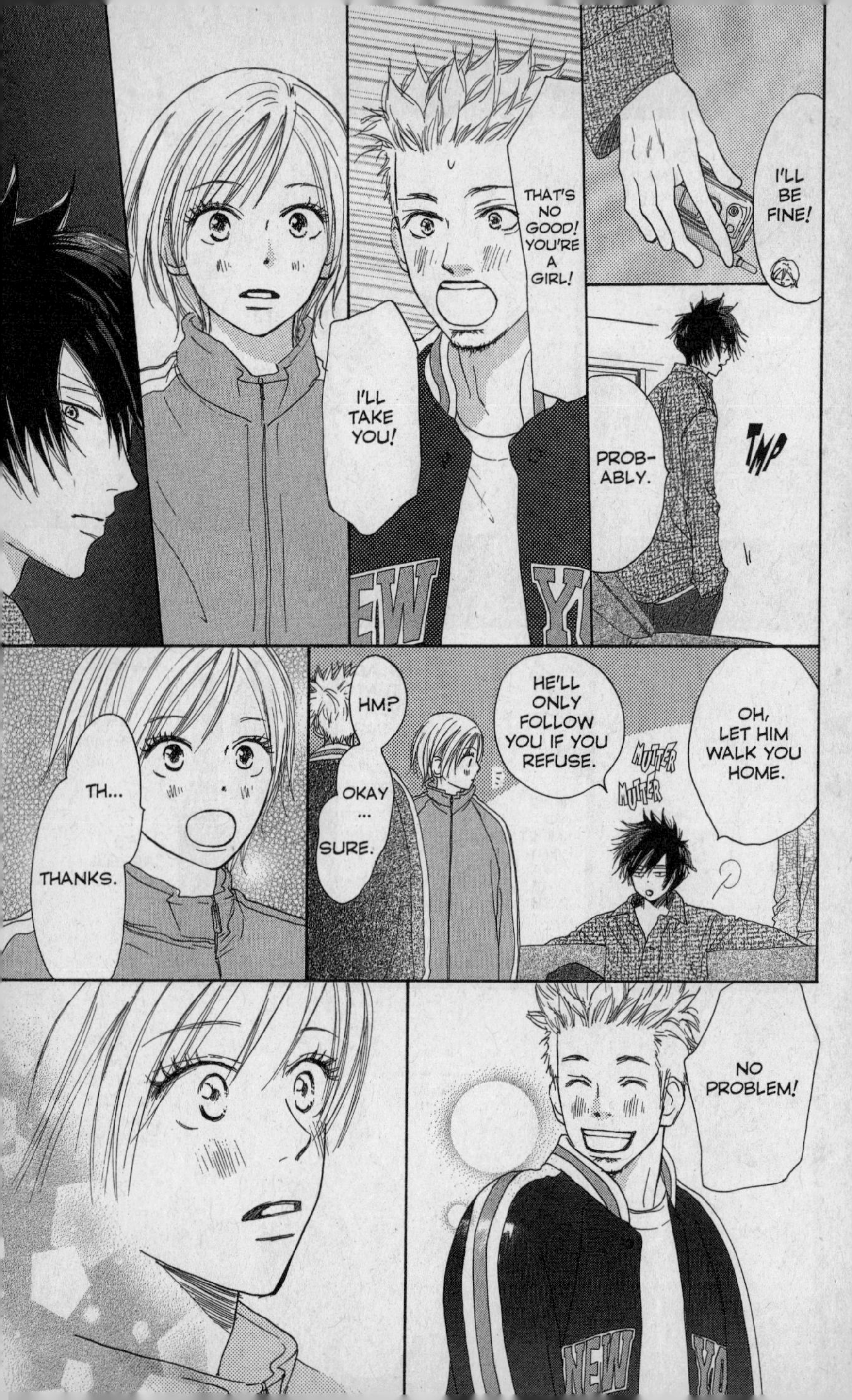
I'LL BE FINE!
PROBABLY.
TMP
THAT'S NO GOOD! YOU'RE A GIRL!
I'LL TAKE YOU!
OH, LET HIM WALK YOU HOME.
MUTTER MUTTER
HE'LL ONLY FOLLOW YOU IF YOU REFUSE.
HM?
OKAY ... SURE.
TH...
THANKS.
NO PROBLEM!

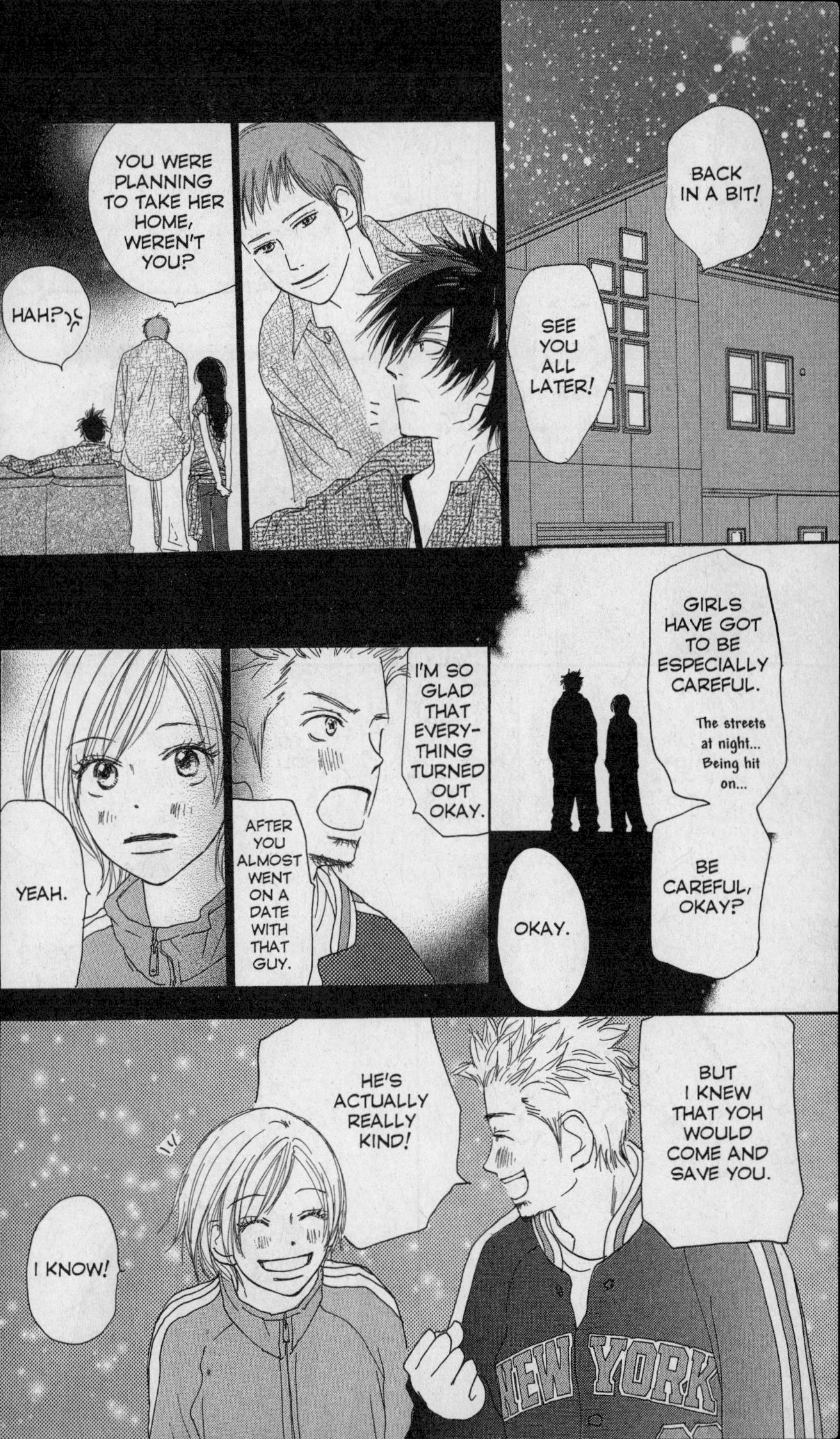
BACK IN A BIT!
SEE YOU ALL LATER!
YOU WERE PLANNING TO TAKE HER HOME, WEREN'T YOU?
HAH?
GIRLS HAVE GOT TO BE ESPECIALLY CAREFUL.
The streets at night... Being hit on...
BE CAREFUL, OKAY?
OKAY.
I'M SO GLAD THAT EVERY-THING TURNED OUT OKAY.
AFTER YOU ALMOST WENT ON A DATE WITH THAT GUY.
YEAH.
BUT I KNEW THAT YOH WOULD COME AND SAVE YOU.
HE'S ACTUALLY REALLY KIND!
I KNOW!
NEW YORK

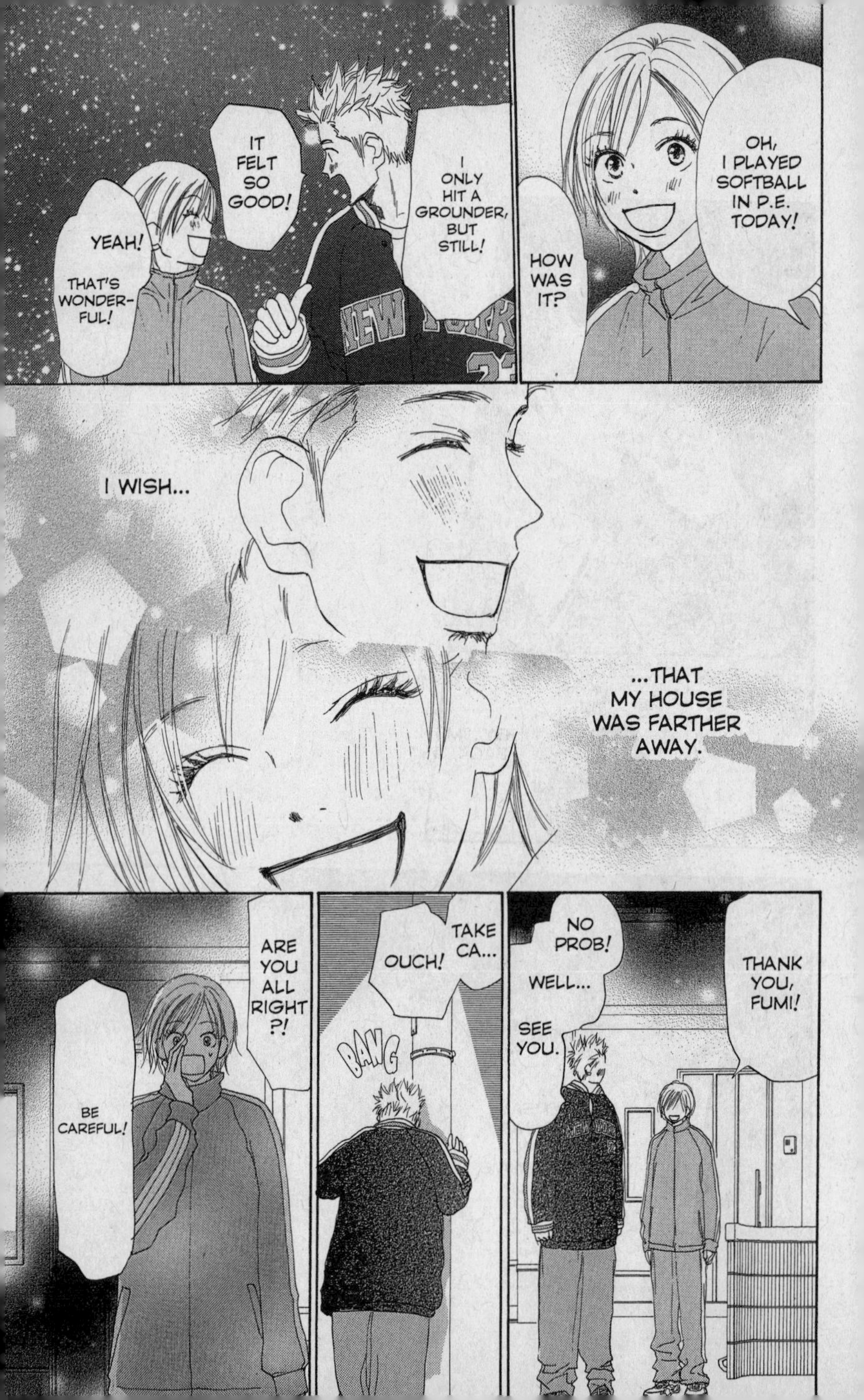
OH, I PLAYED SOFTBALL IN P.E. TODAY!
HOW WAS IT?
I ONLY HIT A GROUNDER, BUT STILL!
IT FELT SO GOOD!
YEAH!
THAT'S WONDERFUL!
I WISH...
...THAT MY HOUSE WAS FARTHER AWAY.
THANK YOU, FUMI!
NO PROB!
WELL...
SEE YOU.
TAKE CA...
OUCH!
BANG
ARE YOU ALL RIGHT?!
BE CAREFUL!

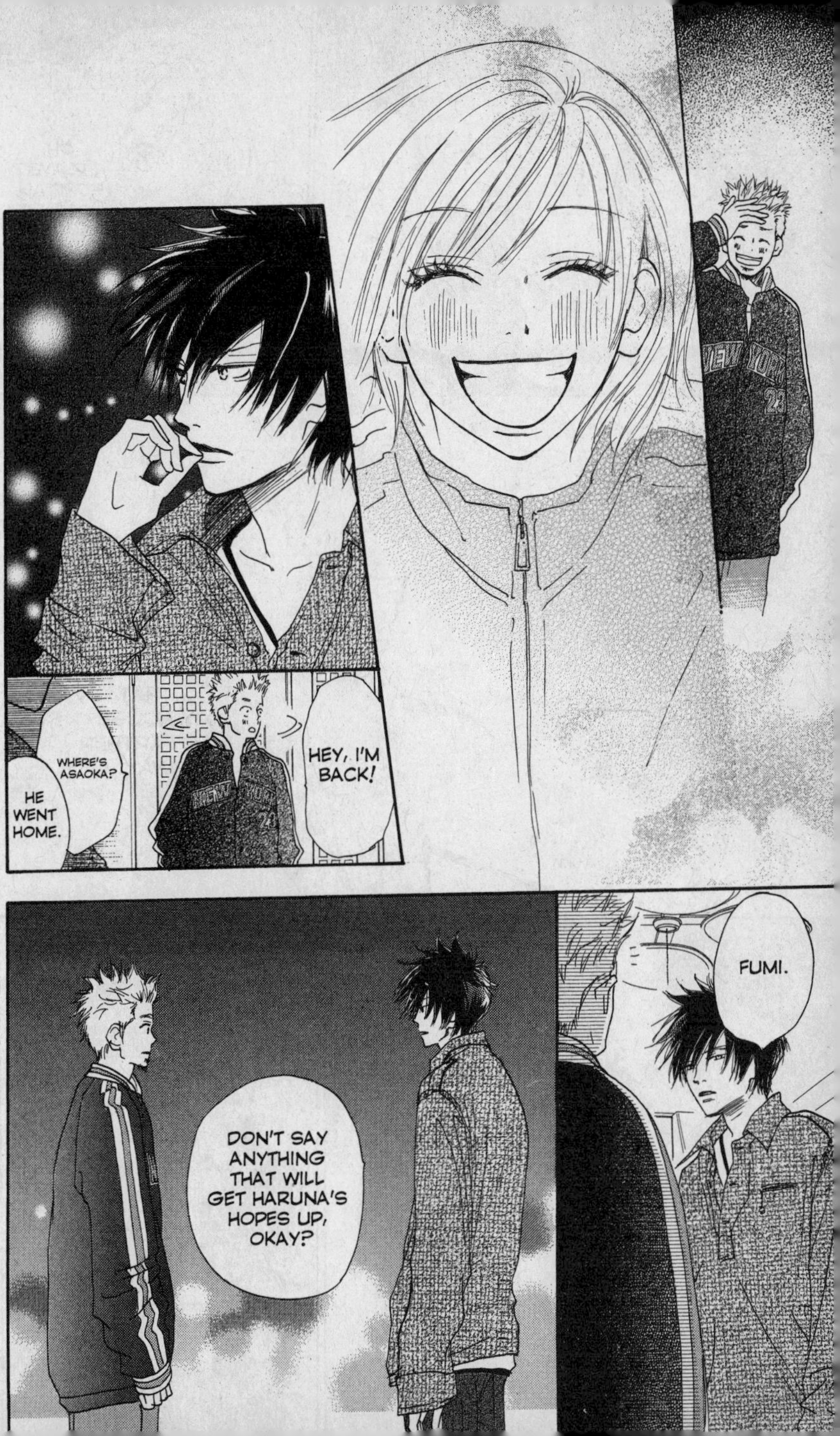
HEY, I'M BACK!
WHERE'S ASAOKA?
HE WENT HOME.
FUMI.
DON'T SAY ANYTHING THAT WILL GET HARUNA'S HOPES UP, OKAY?

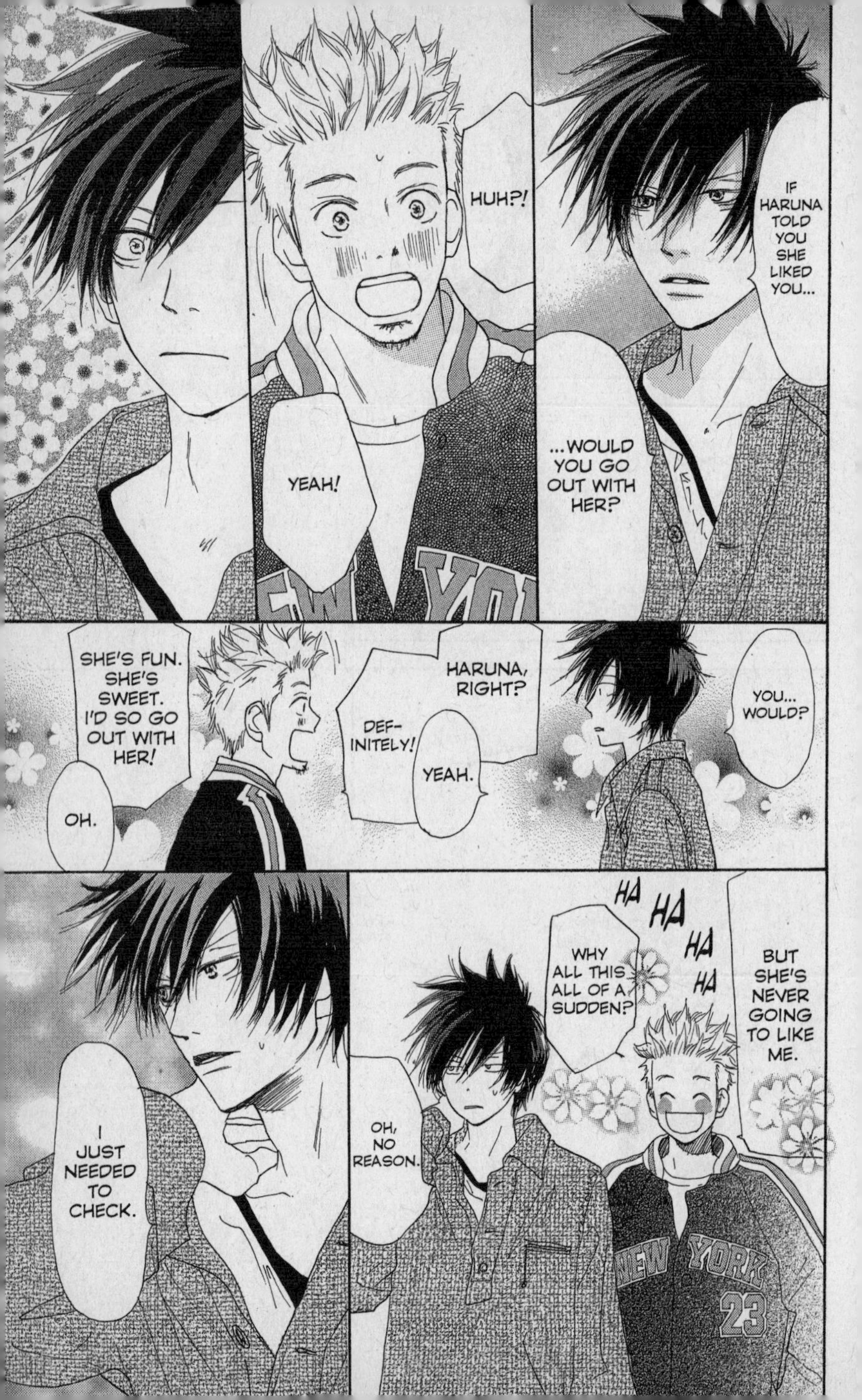
IF HARUNA TOLD YOU SHE LIKED YOU...
...WOULD YOU GO OUT WITH HER?
HUH?!
YEAH!
YOU... WOULD?
HARUNA, RIGHT?
DEF-INITELY!
YEAH.
SHE'S FUN. SHE'S SWEET. I'D SO GO OUT WITH HER!
OH.
BUT SHE'S NEVER GOING TO LIKE ME.
HA HA HA HA
WHY ALL THIS ALL OF A SUDDEN?
OH, NO REASON.
I JUST NEEDED TO CHECK.

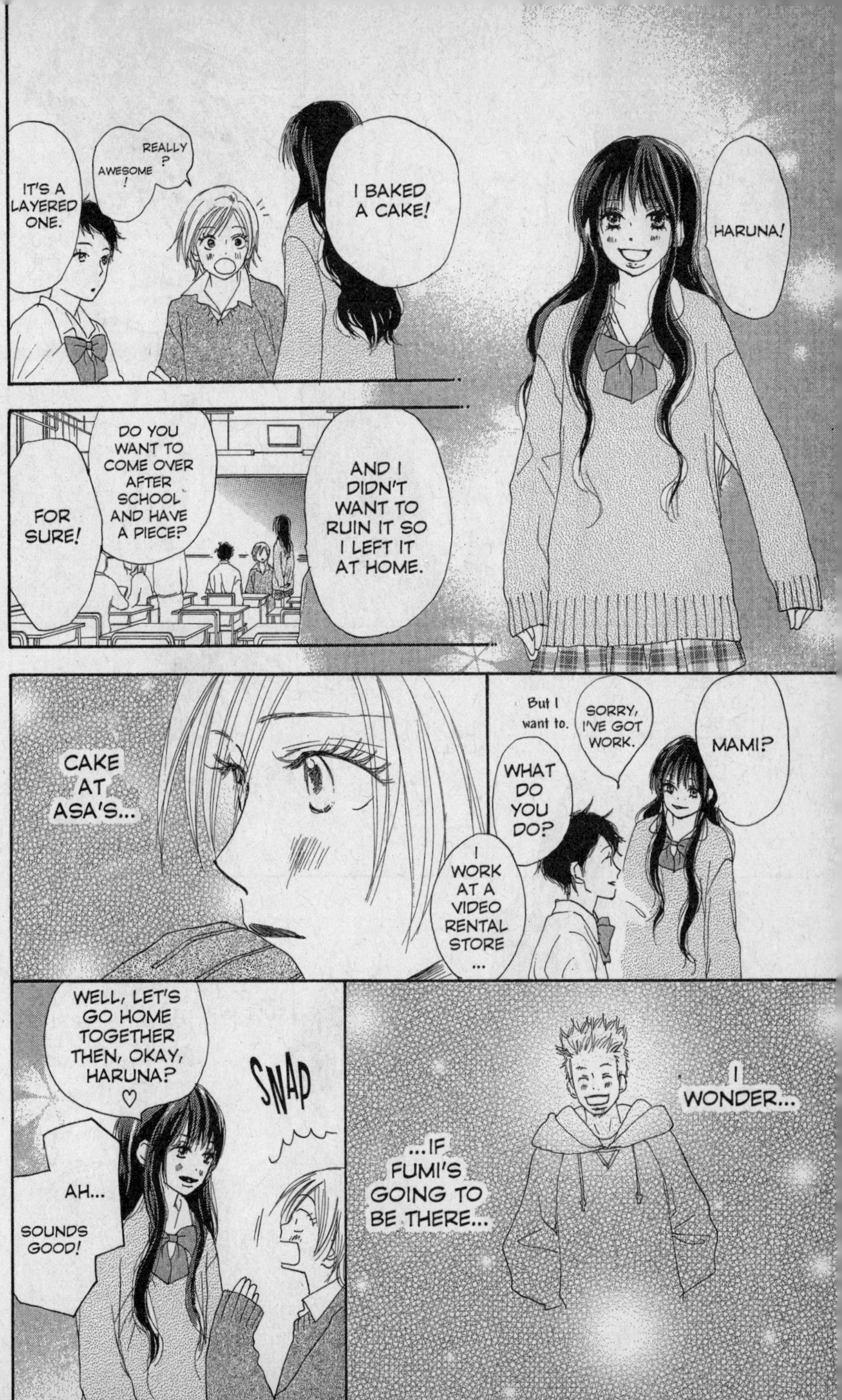
HARUNA!
I BAKED A CAKE!
REALLY?
AWESOME!
IT'S A LAYERED ONE.
AND I DIDN'T WANT TO RUIN IT SO I LEFT IT AT HOME.
DO YOU WANT TO COME OVER AFTER SCHOOL AND HAVE A PIECE?
FOR SURE!
MAMI?
SORRY, I'VE GOT WORK.
But I want to.
WHAT DO YOU DO?
I WORK AT A VIDEO RENTAL STORE...
CAKE AT ASA'S...
I WONDER...
...IF FUMI'S GOING TO BE THERE...
WELL, LET'S GO HOME TOGETHER THEN, OKAY, HARUNA? ♡
SNAP
AH...
SOUNDS GOOD!

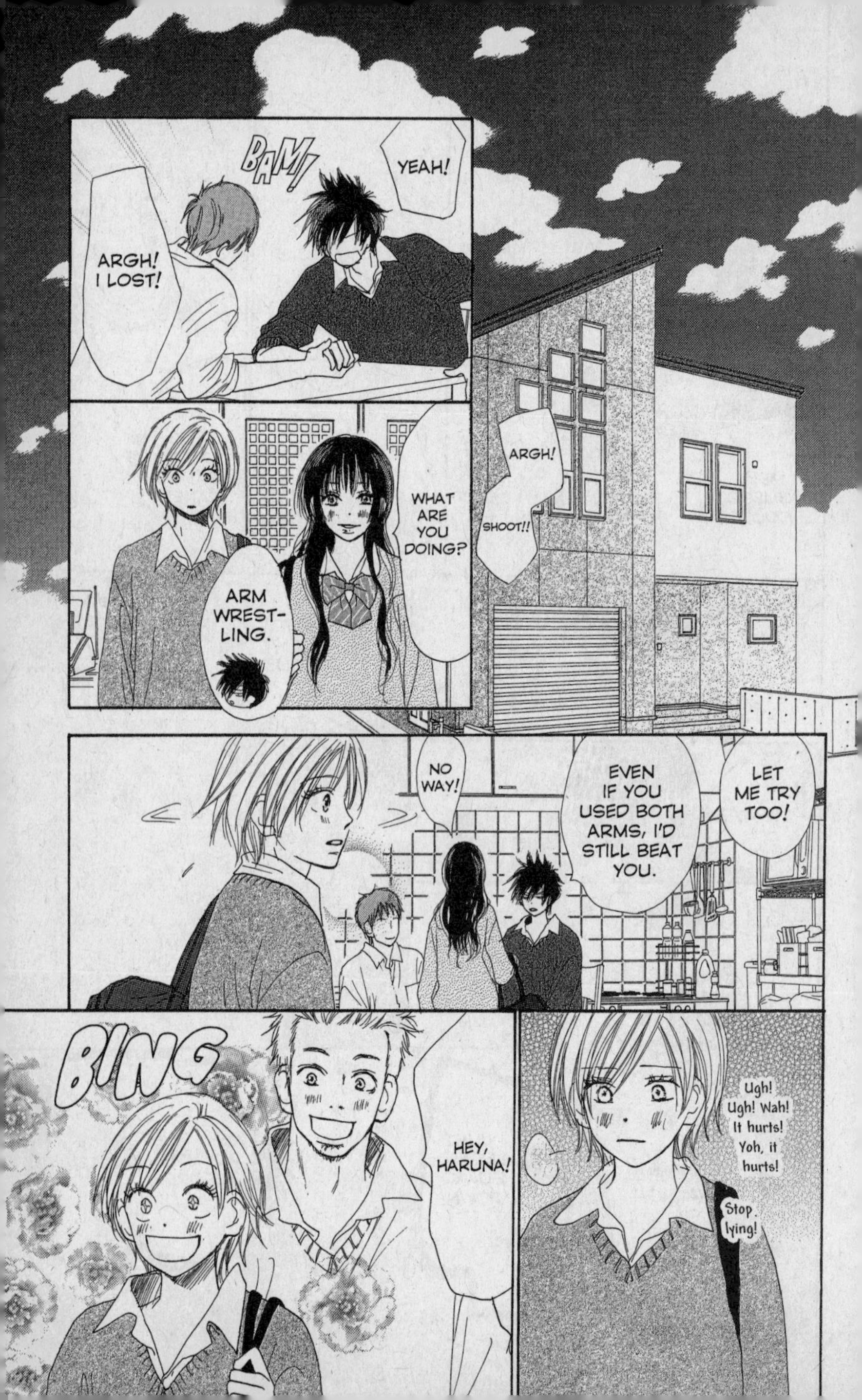
ARGH!
SHOOT!!
BAM!
YEAH!
ARGH! I LOST!
WHAT ARE YOU DOING?
ARM WRESTLING.
LET ME TRY TOO!
EVEN IF YOU USED BOTH ARMS, I'D STILL BEAT YOU.
NO WAY!
Ugh! Ugh! Wah! It hurts! Yoh, it hurts!
Stop lying!
BING
HEY, HARUNA!

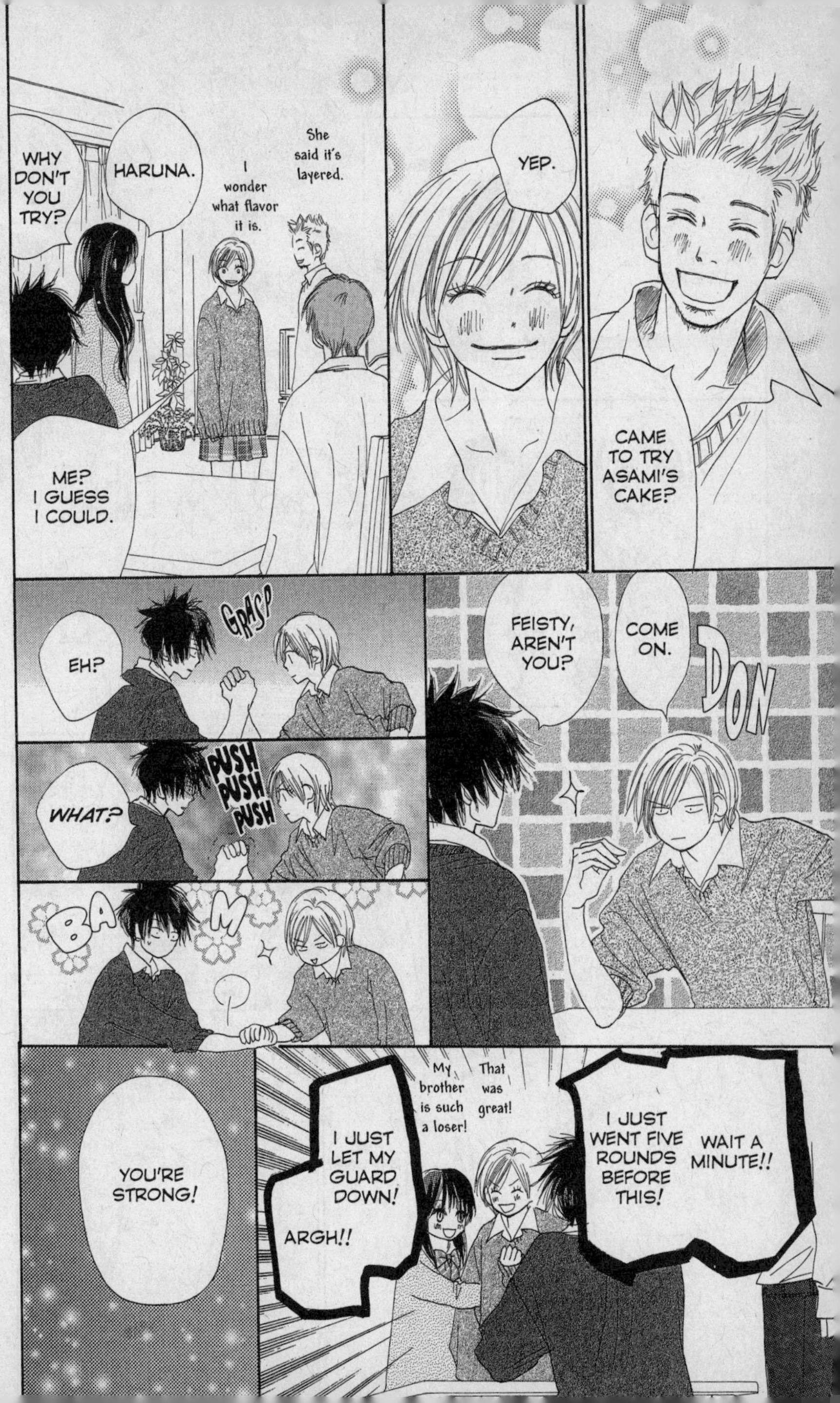

CAME TO TRY ASAMI'S CAKE?
YEP.
She said it's layered.
I wonder what flavor it is.
HARUNA.
WHY DON'T YOU TRY?
ME? I GUESS I COULD.
COME ON.
FEISTY, AREN'T YOU?
DON
GRASP
EH?
PUSH PUSH PUSH
WHAT?
BAM
WAIT A MINUTE!!
I JUST WENT FIVE ROUNDS BEFORE THIS!
That was great!
My brother is such a loser!
I JUST LET MY GUARD DOWN!
ARGH!!
YOU'RE STRONG!

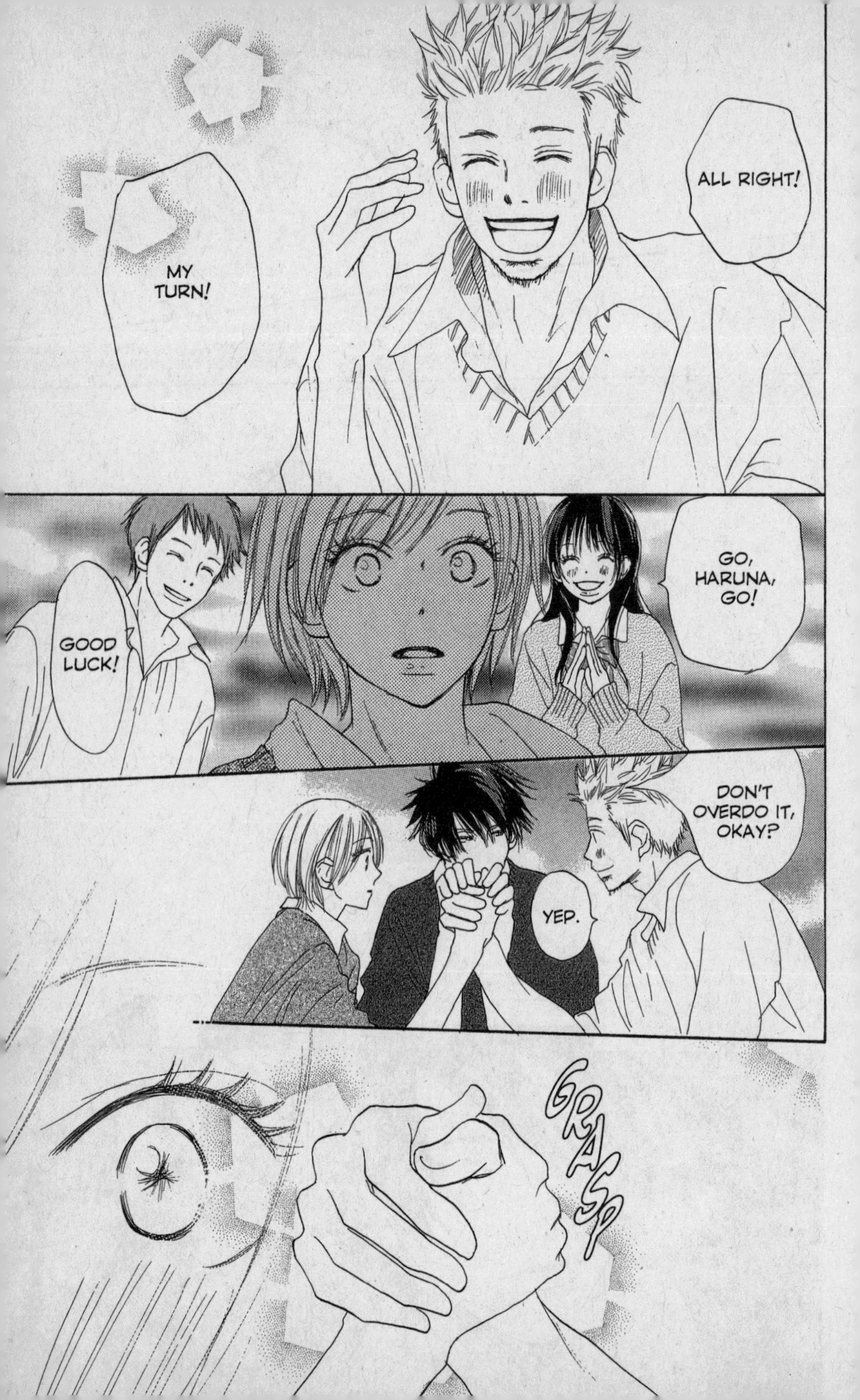
ALL RIGHT!
MY TURN!
GO, HARUNA, GO!
GOOD LUCK!
DON'T OVERDO IT, OKAY?
YEP.
GRASP

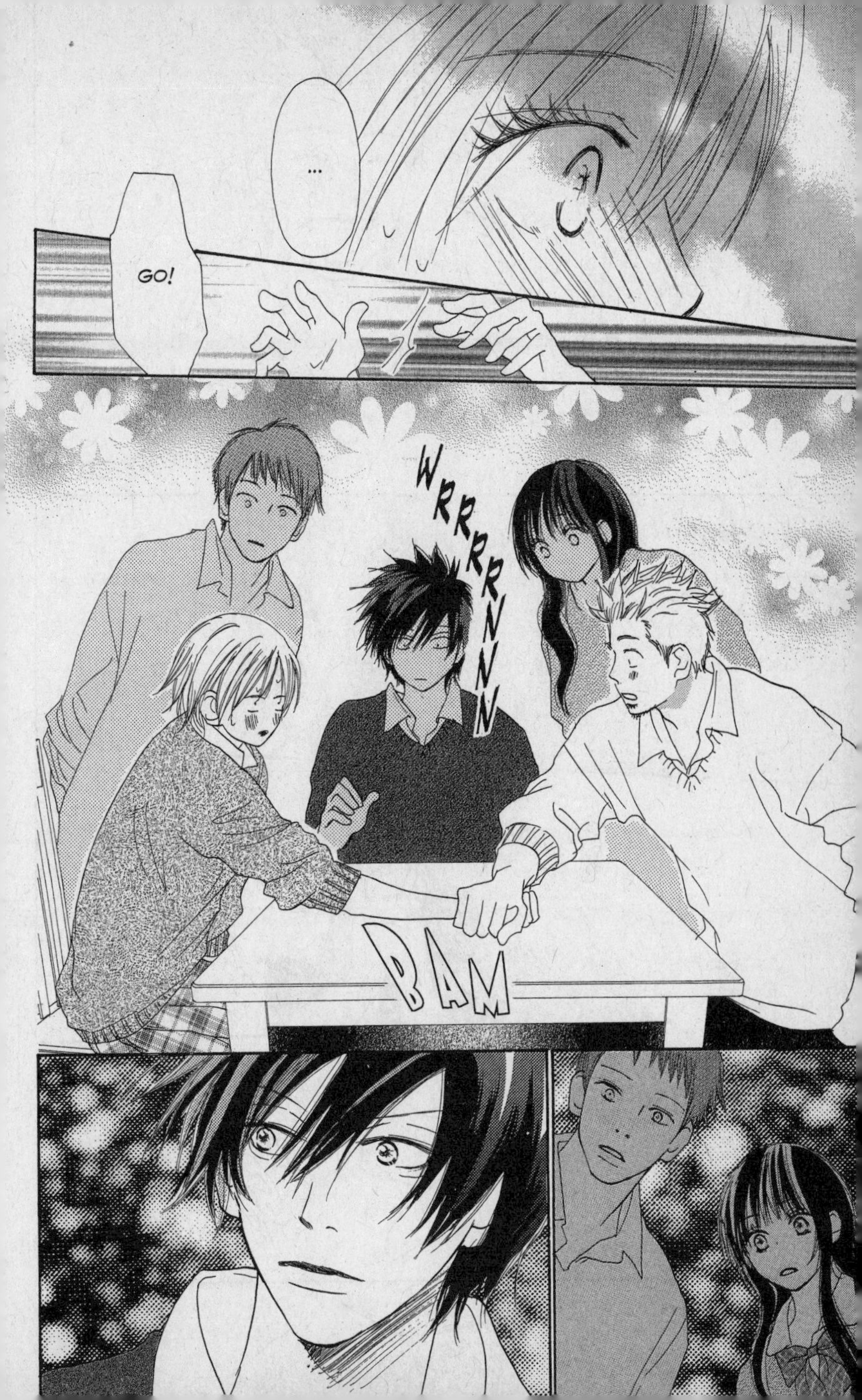
...
GO!
WRRRRNNNN
BAM

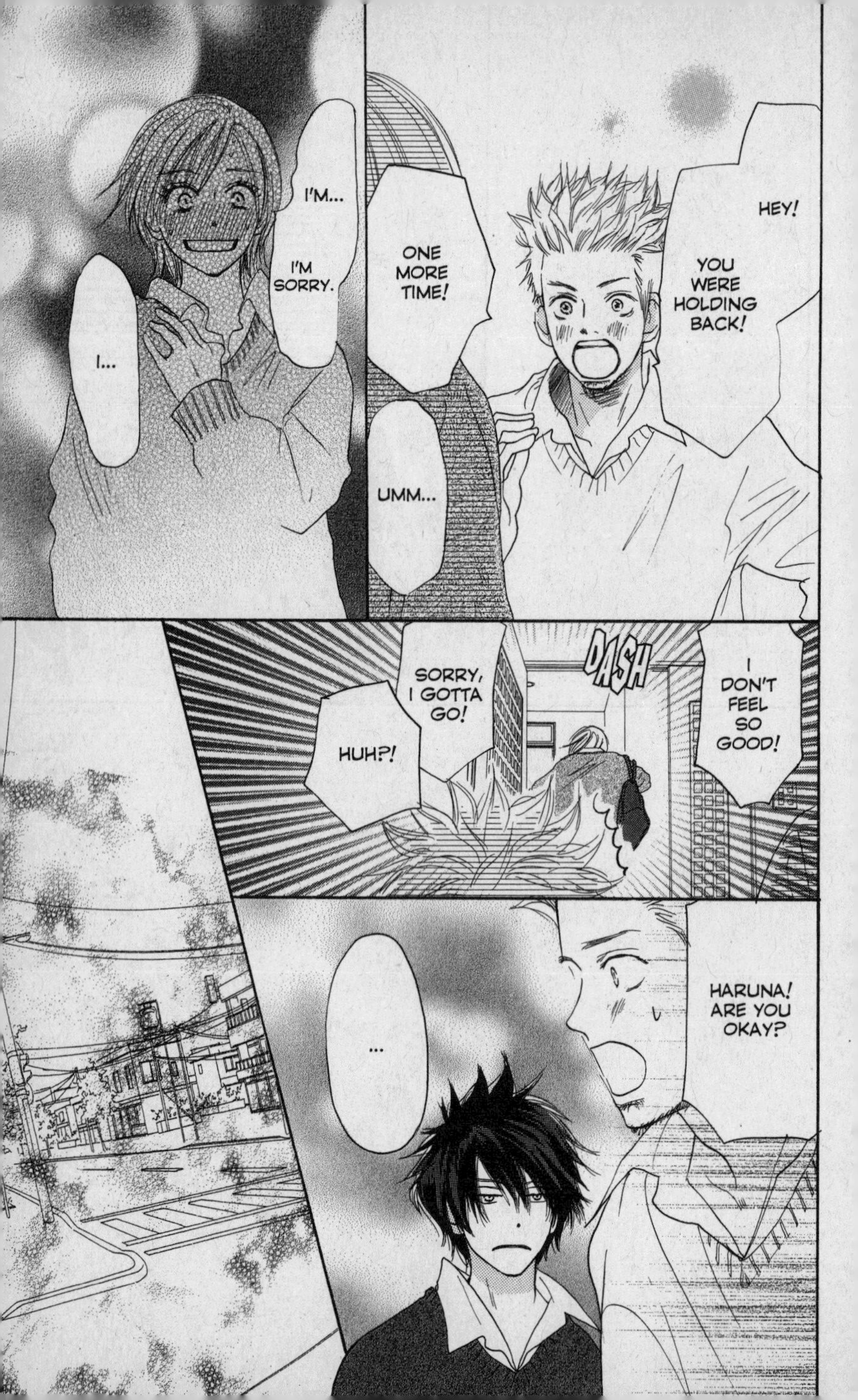
HEY!
YOU WERE HOLDING BACK!
ONE MORE TIME!
UMM...
I'M...
I'M SORRY.
I...
I DON'T FEEL SO GOOD!
DASH
SORRY, I GOTTA GO!
HUH?!
HARUNA! ARE YOU OKAY?
...

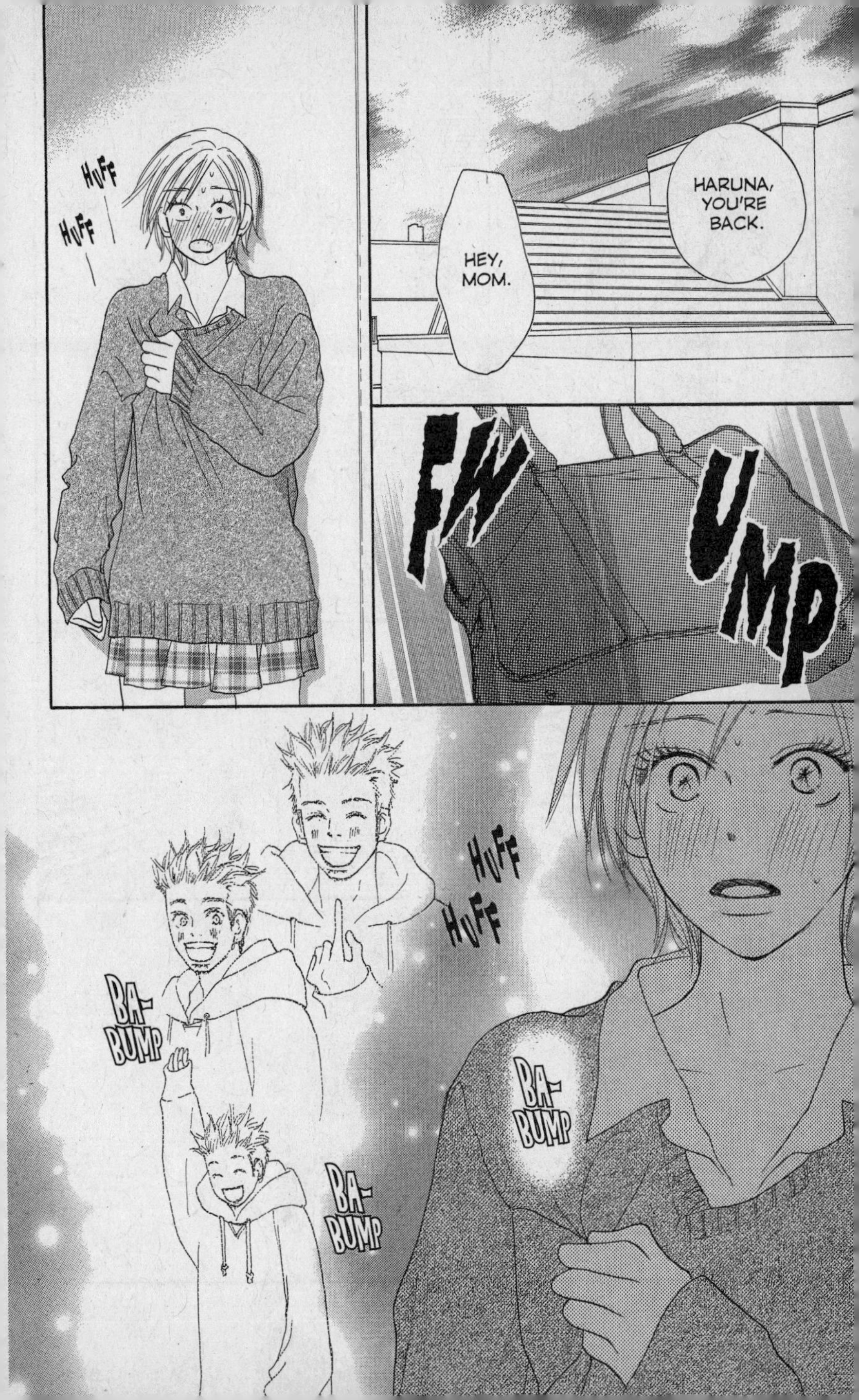
HARUNA, YOU'RE BACK.
HEY, MOM.
FWUMP
HUFF
HUFF
HUFF
HUFF
BA-BUMP
BA-BUMP
BA-BUMP

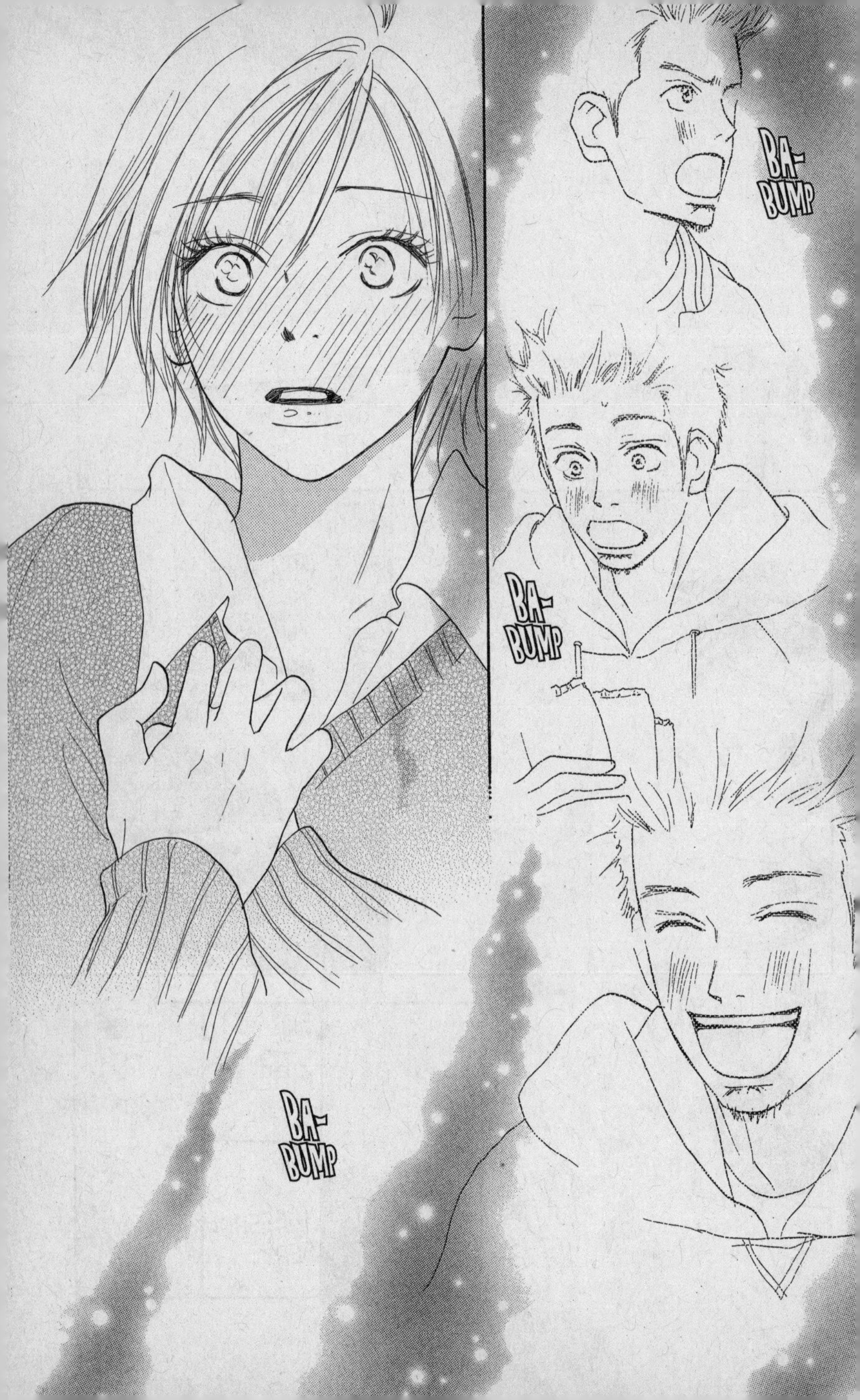
BA-BUMP
BA-BUMP
BA-BUMP

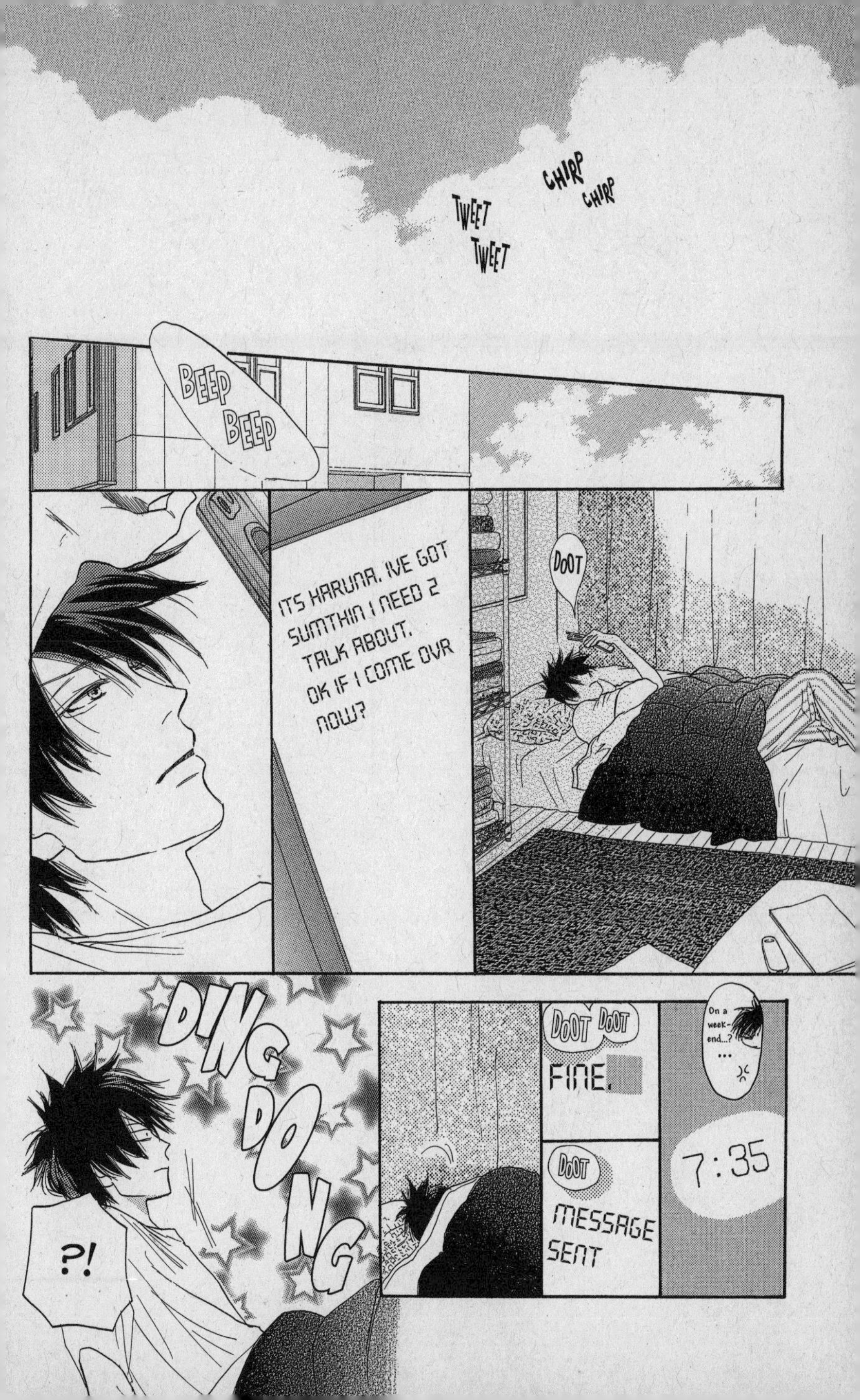
CHIRP CHIRP
TWEET TWEET
BEEP BEEP
DOOT
ITS HARUNA. IVE GOT SUMTHIN I NEED 2 TALK ABOUT. OK IF I COME OVR NOW?
On a week-end...?
...
7:35
DOOT DOOT
FINE.
DOOT
MESSAGE SENT
DING DONG
?!

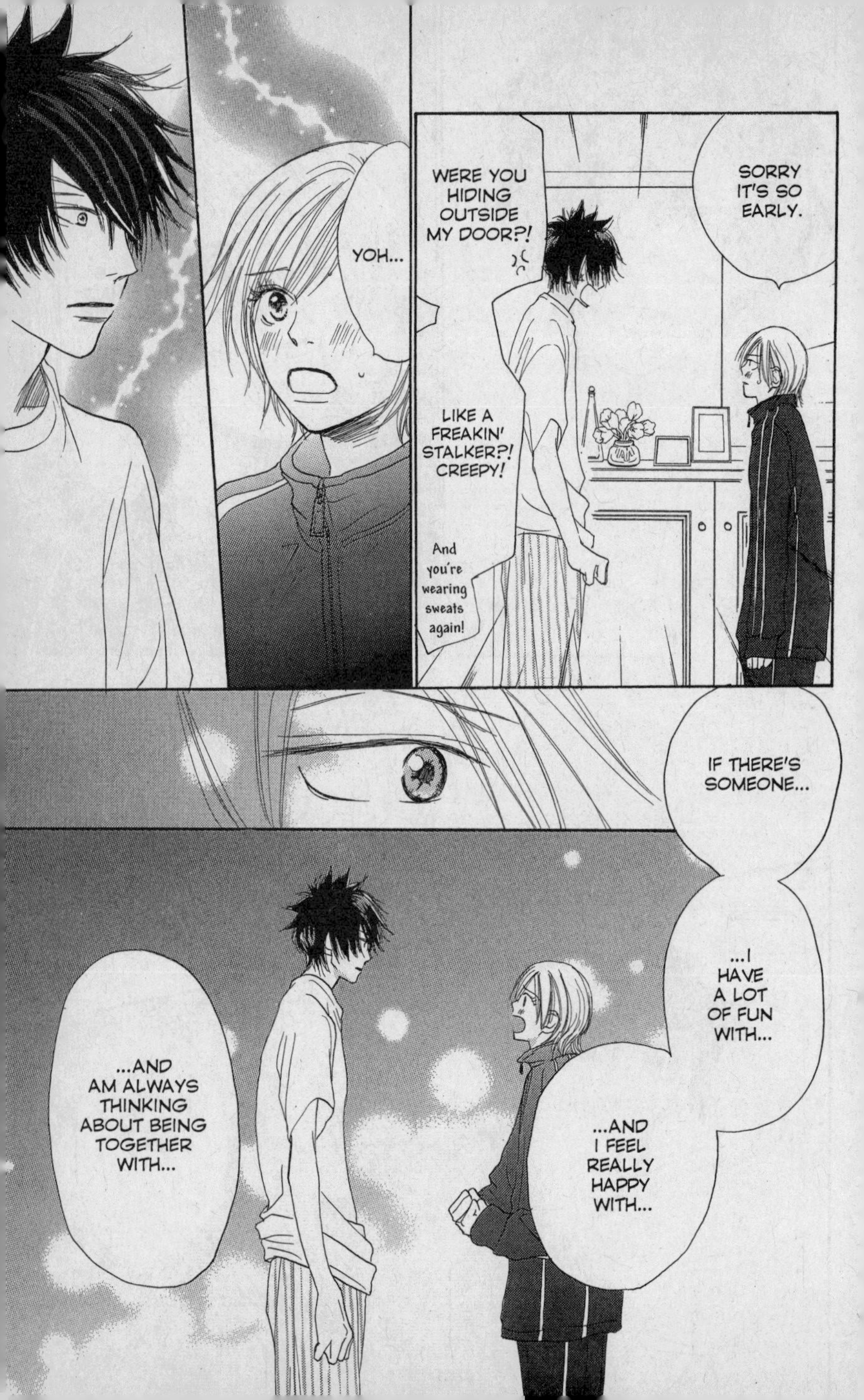
SORRY IT'S SO EARLY.
WERE YOU HIDING OUTSIDE MY DOOR?!
LIKE A FREAKIN' STALKER?! CREEPY!
And you're wearing sweats again!
YOH...
IF THERE'S SOMEONE...
...I HAVE A LOT OF FUN WITH...
...AND I FEEL REALLY HAPPY WITH...
...AND AM ALWAYS THINKING ABOUT BEING TOGETHER WITH...

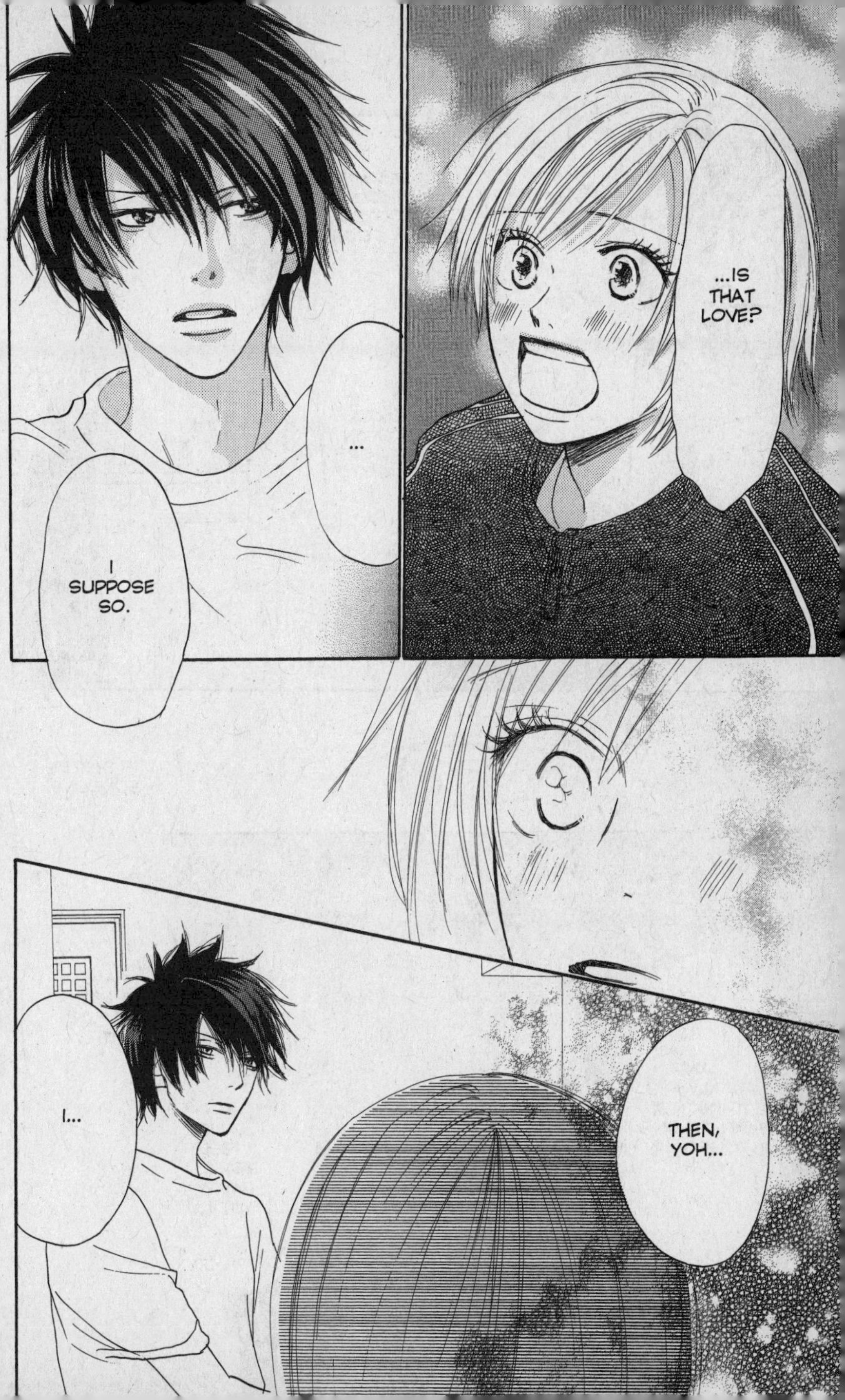
...IS THAT LOVE?
...
I SUPPOSE SO.
THEN, YOH...
I...

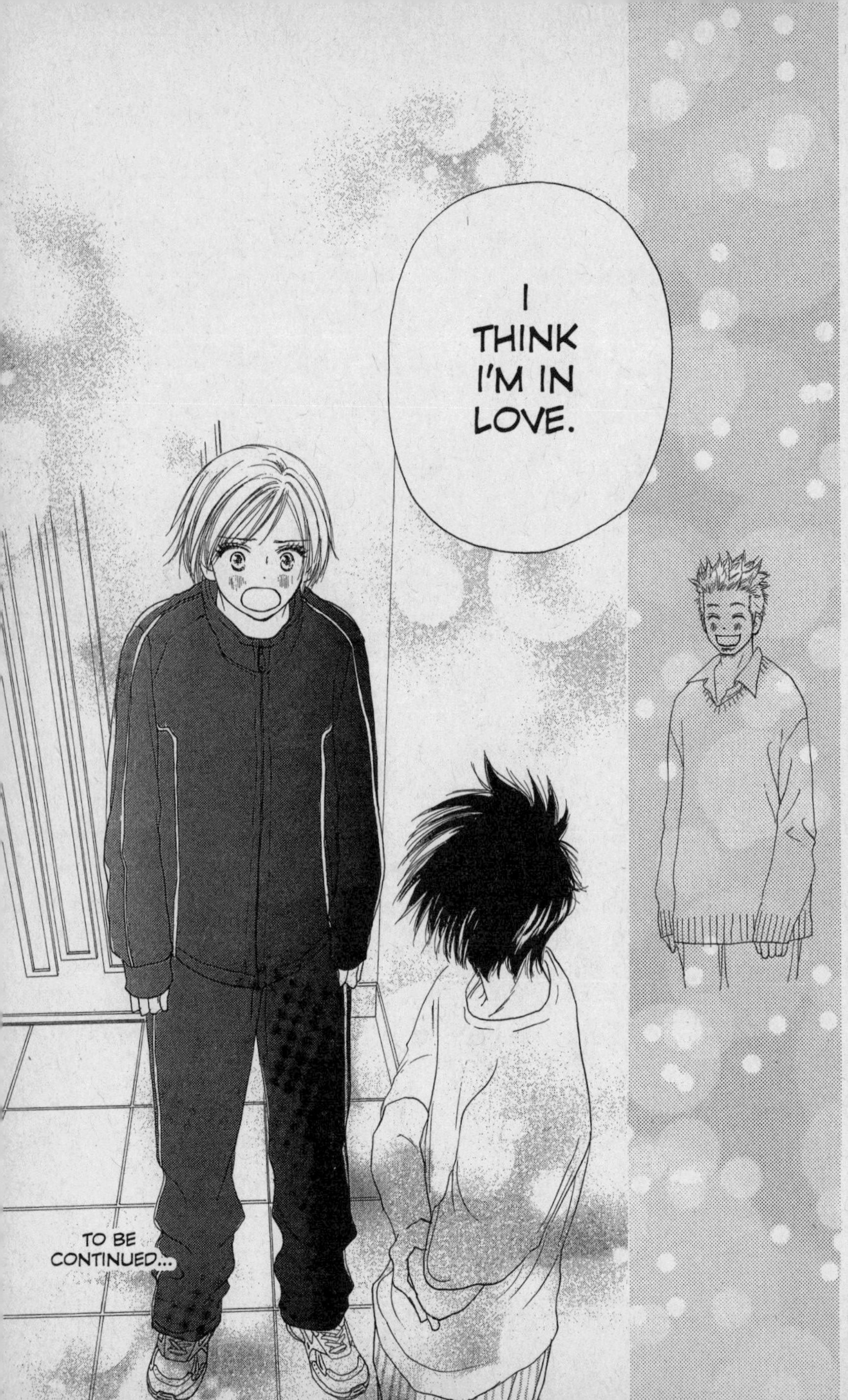
I THINK I'M IN LOVE.
TO BE CONTINUED...

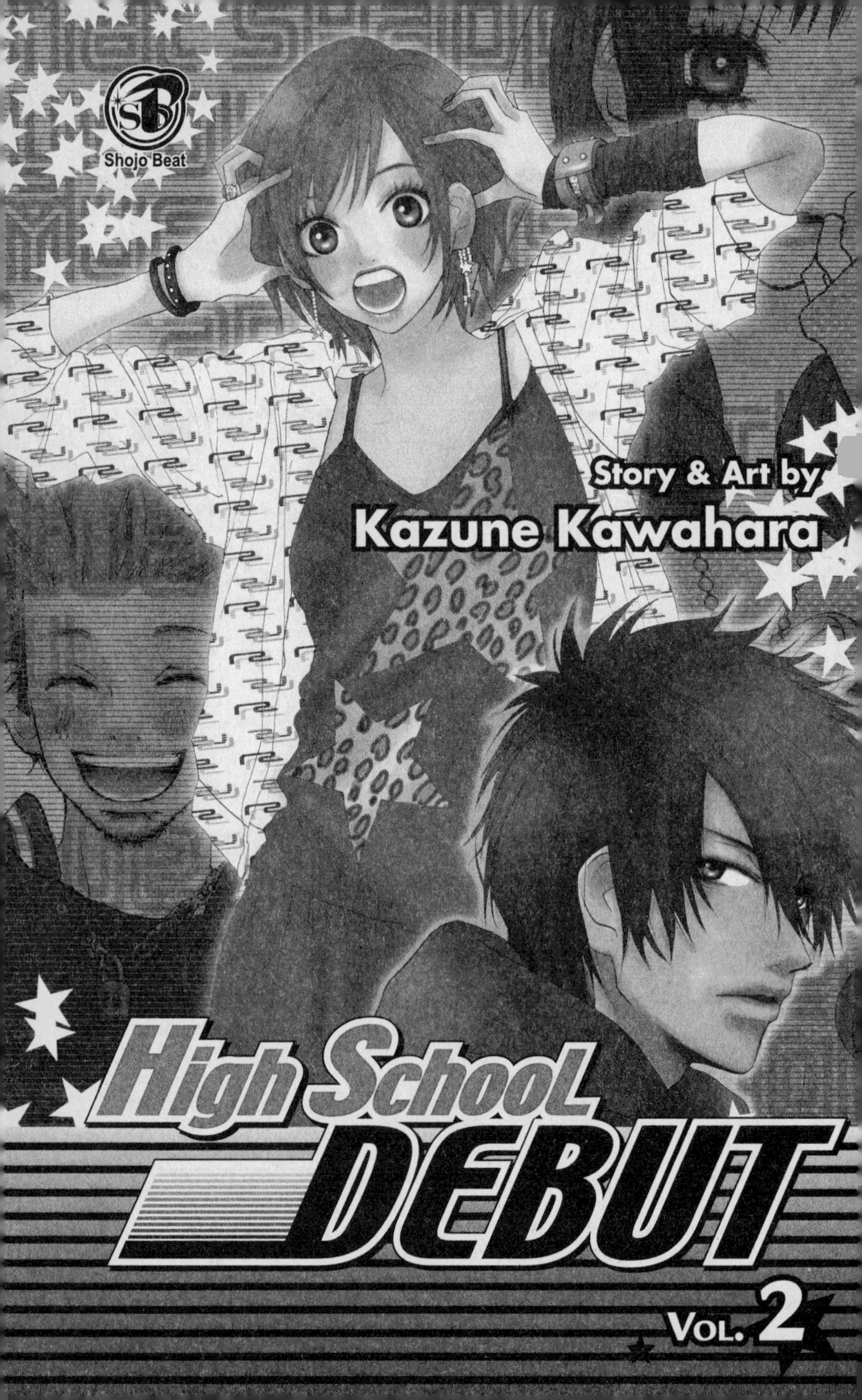
Shojo Beat
Story & Art by
Kazune Kawahara
High School
DEBUT
VOL. 2

High School DEBUT

★ ★ Contents

Story Thus Far...

High school freshman Haruna was a sporty girl and an ace player for her softball team back in junior high. Now that she's in high school, she wants to give her all to finding true love instead! Unfortunately, all her efforts are in vain as she can't even get a boy interested in her. Luckily, she bumps into Yoh, a guy who knows all about what makes girls popular with guys. At first he refuses to become Haruna's "love coach," partly because he had a bad experience with his ex-girlfriend and has become disillusioned with girls and being popular. When he sees Haruna's determination, however, Yoh changes his mind and decides to be her coach after all!

Haruna's delighted when she gets hit on for the first time in her life, but she becomes quite shocked when she realizes she's been deceived. Trying to take her mind off things at the batting center, she bumps into Yoh's friend Fumiya, who cheers her up. Haruna then starts to think of Fumiya as more than a friend...

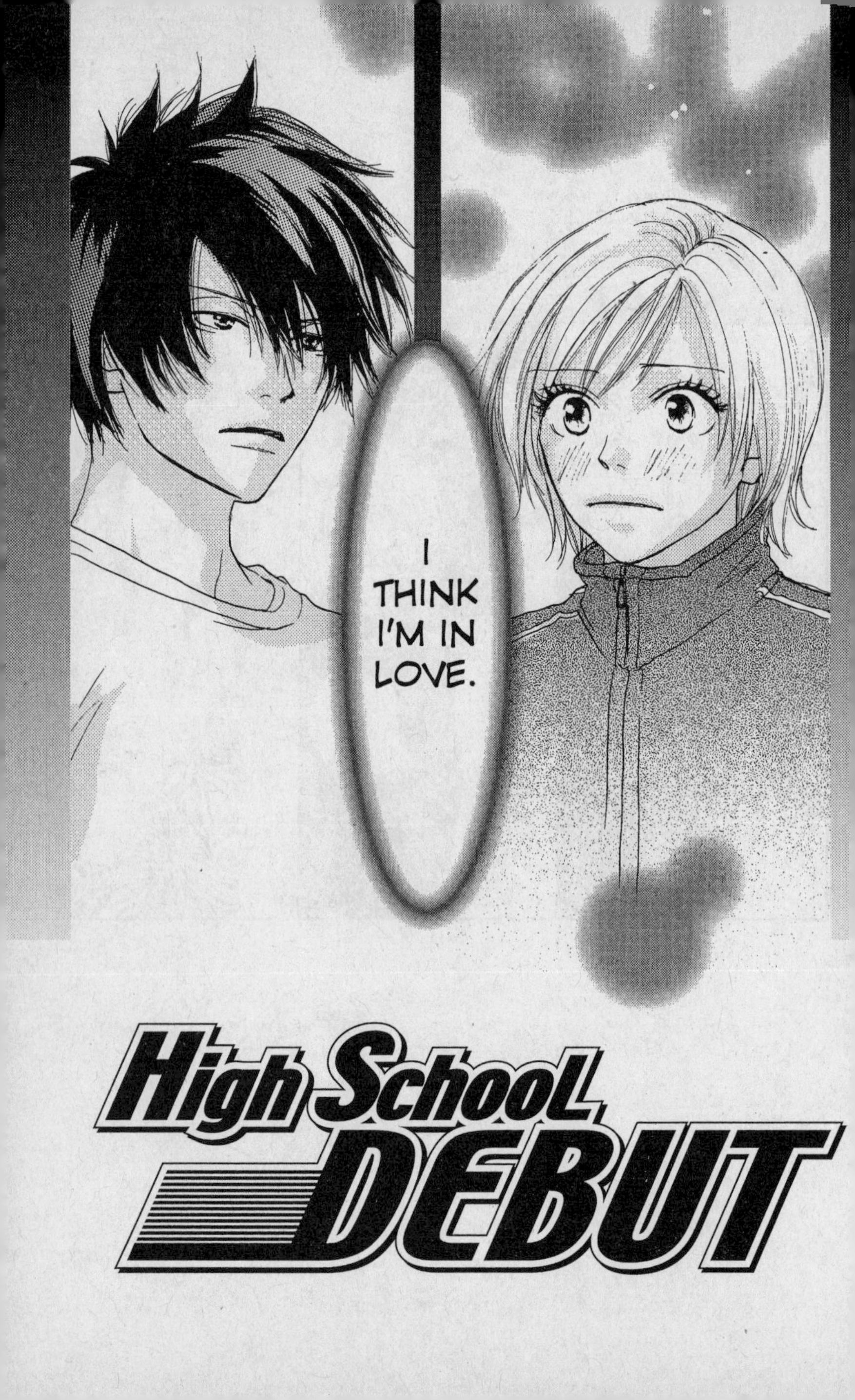
I THINK I'M IN LOVE.
High School DEBUT

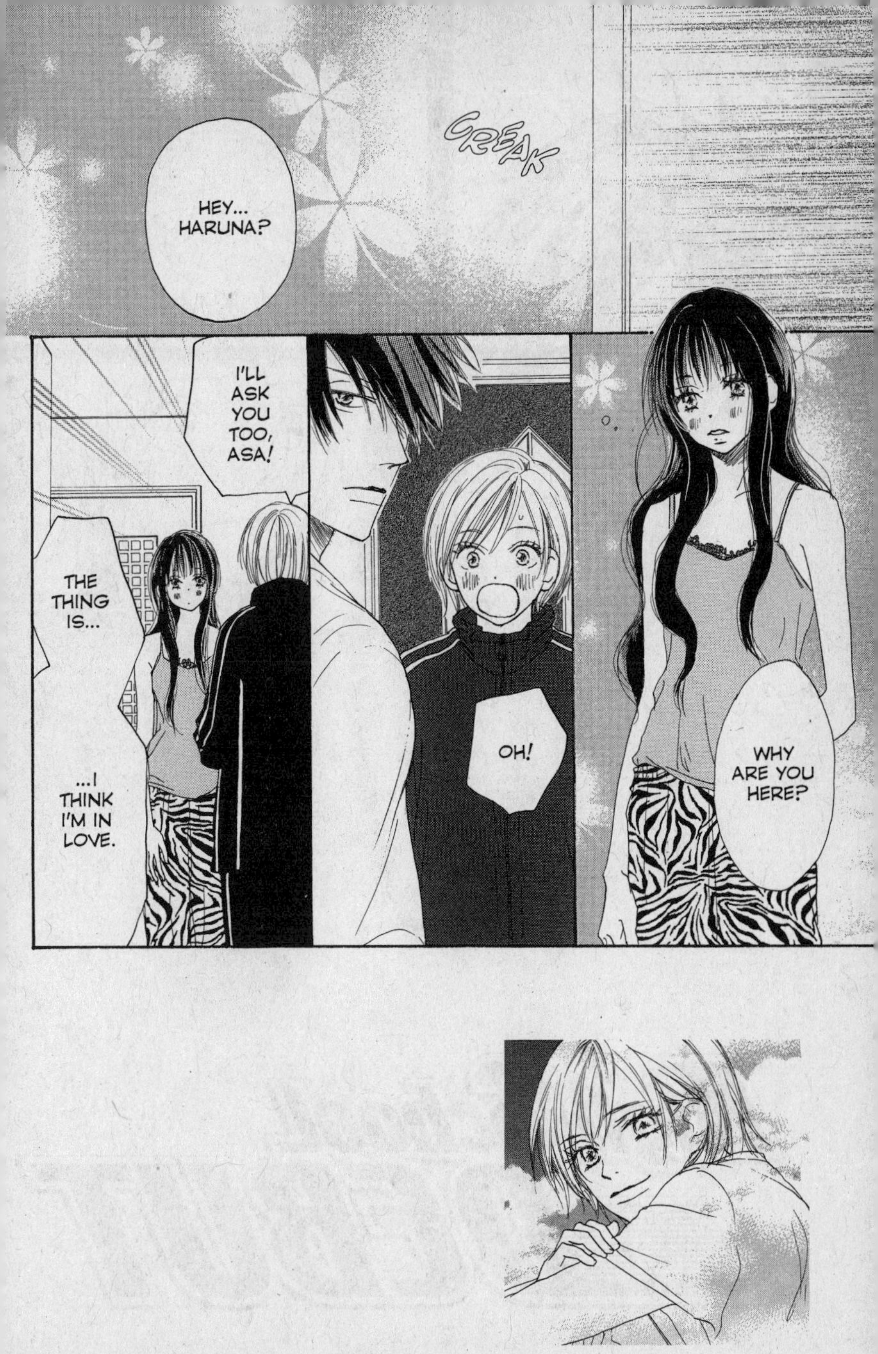
CREAK
HEY... HARUNA?
WHY ARE YOU HERE?
OH!
I'LL ASK YOU TOO, ASA!
THE THING IS...
...I THINK I'M IN LOVE.

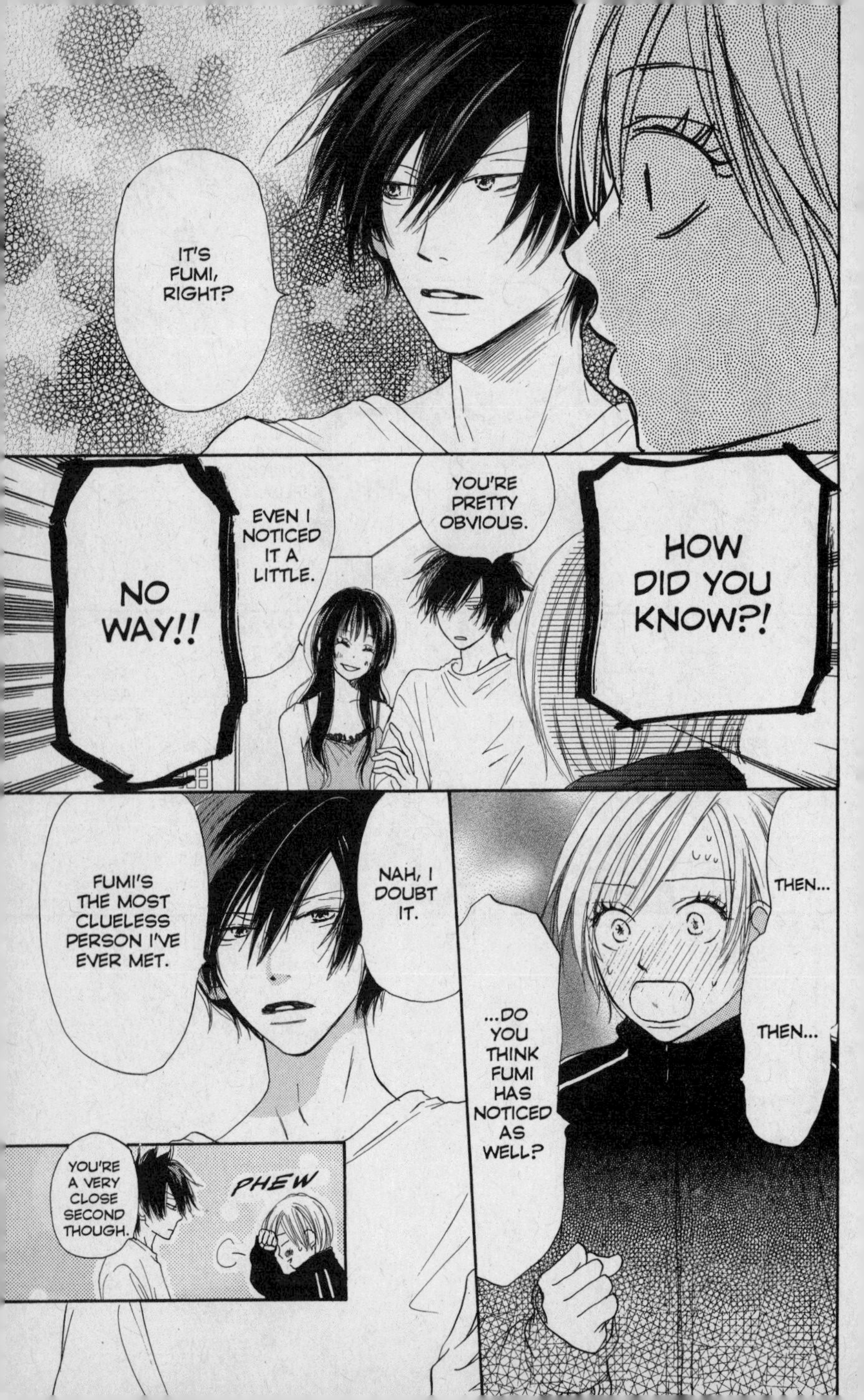
IT'S FUMI, RIGHT?
HOW DID YOU KNOW?!
YOU'RE PRETTY OBVIOUS.
EVEN I NOTICED IT A LITTLE.
NO WAY!!
THEN...
THEN...
...DO YOU THINK FUMI HAS NOTICED AS WELL?
NAH, I DOUBT IT.
FUMI'S THE MOST CLUELESS PERSON I'VE EVER MET.
PHEW
YOU'RE A VERY CLOSE SECOND THOUGH.

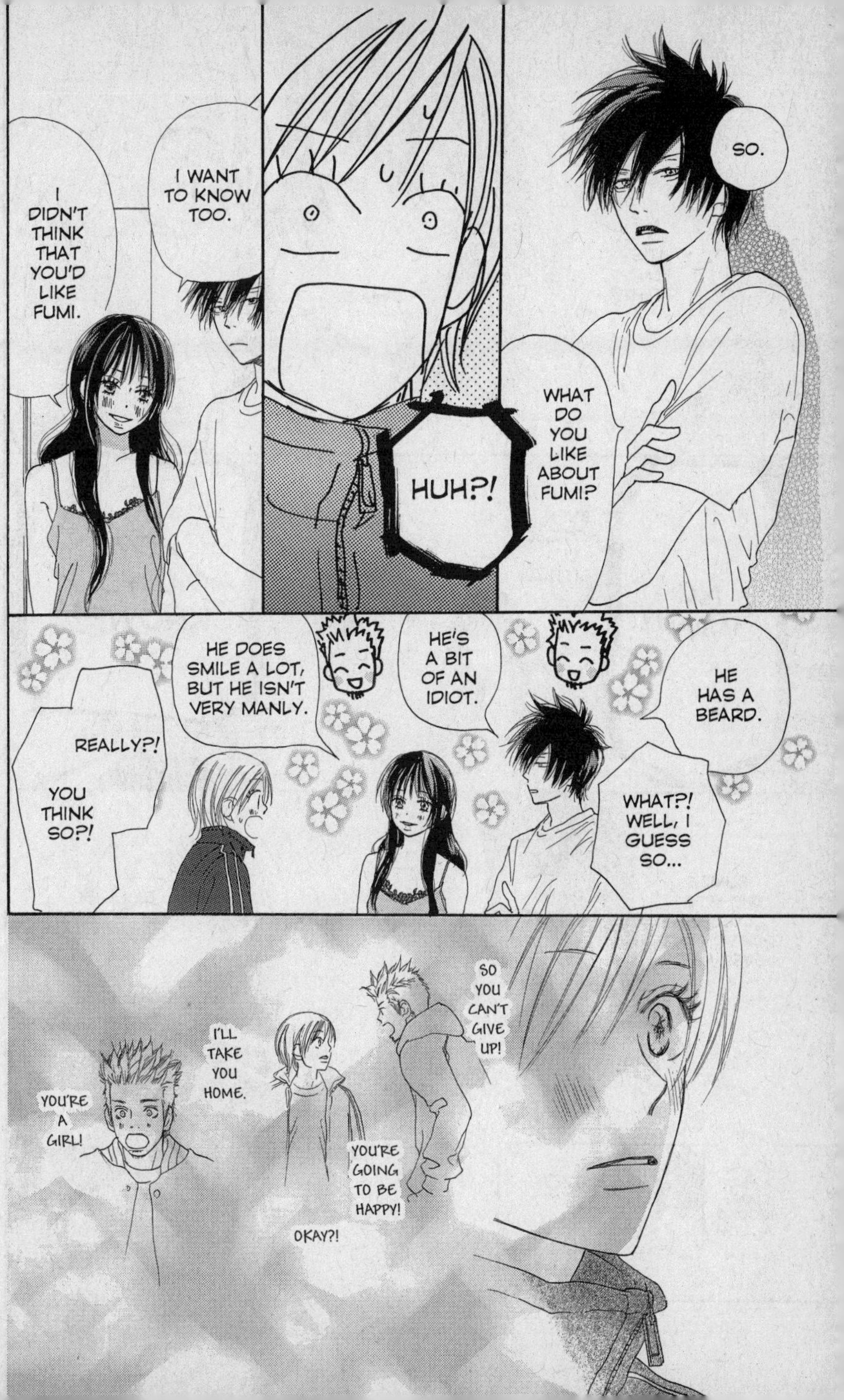
SO.
WHAT DO YOU LIKE ABOUT FUMI?
HUH?!
I WANT TO KNOW TOO.
I DIDN'T THINK THAT YOU'D LIKE FUMI.
HE HAS A BEARD.
WHAT?! WELL, I GUESS SO...
HE'S A BIT OF AN IDIOT.
HE DOES SMILE A LOT, BUT HE ISN'T VERY MANLY.
REALLY?!
YOU THINK SO?!
SO YOU CAN'T GIVE UP!
I'LL TAKE YOU HOME.
YOU'RE A GIRL!
YOU'RE GOING TO BE HAPPY!
OKAY?!

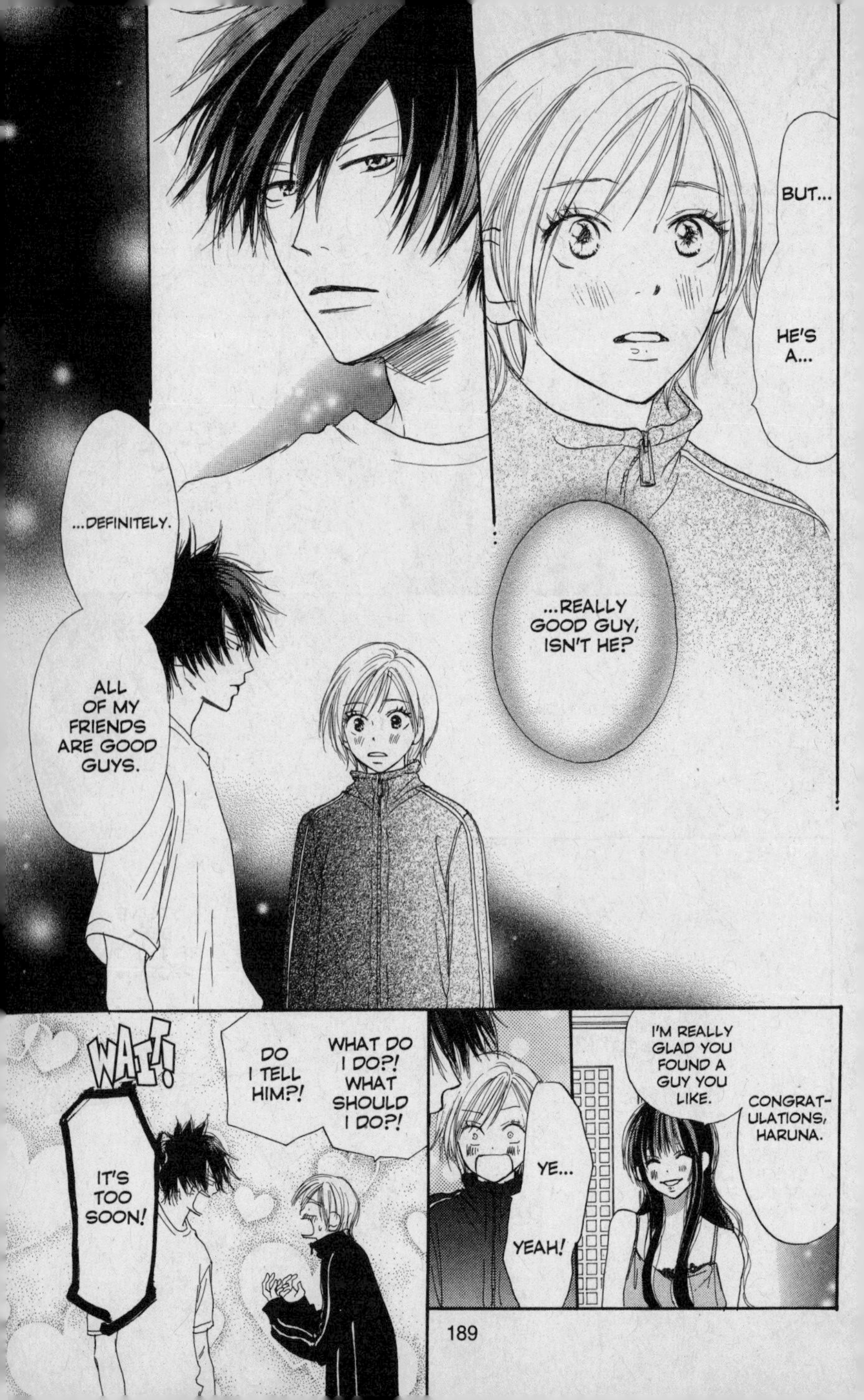
BUT...
HE'S A...
...REALLY GOOD GUY, ISN'T HE?
...DEFINITELY.
ALL OF MY FRIENDS ARE GOOD GUYS.
CONGRAT-ULATIONS, HARUNA.
I'M REALLY GLAD YOU FOUND A GUY YOU LIKE.
YE...
YEAH!
WHAT DO I DO?! WHAT SHOULD I DO?!
DO I TELL HIM?!
WAIT!
IT'S TOO SOON!

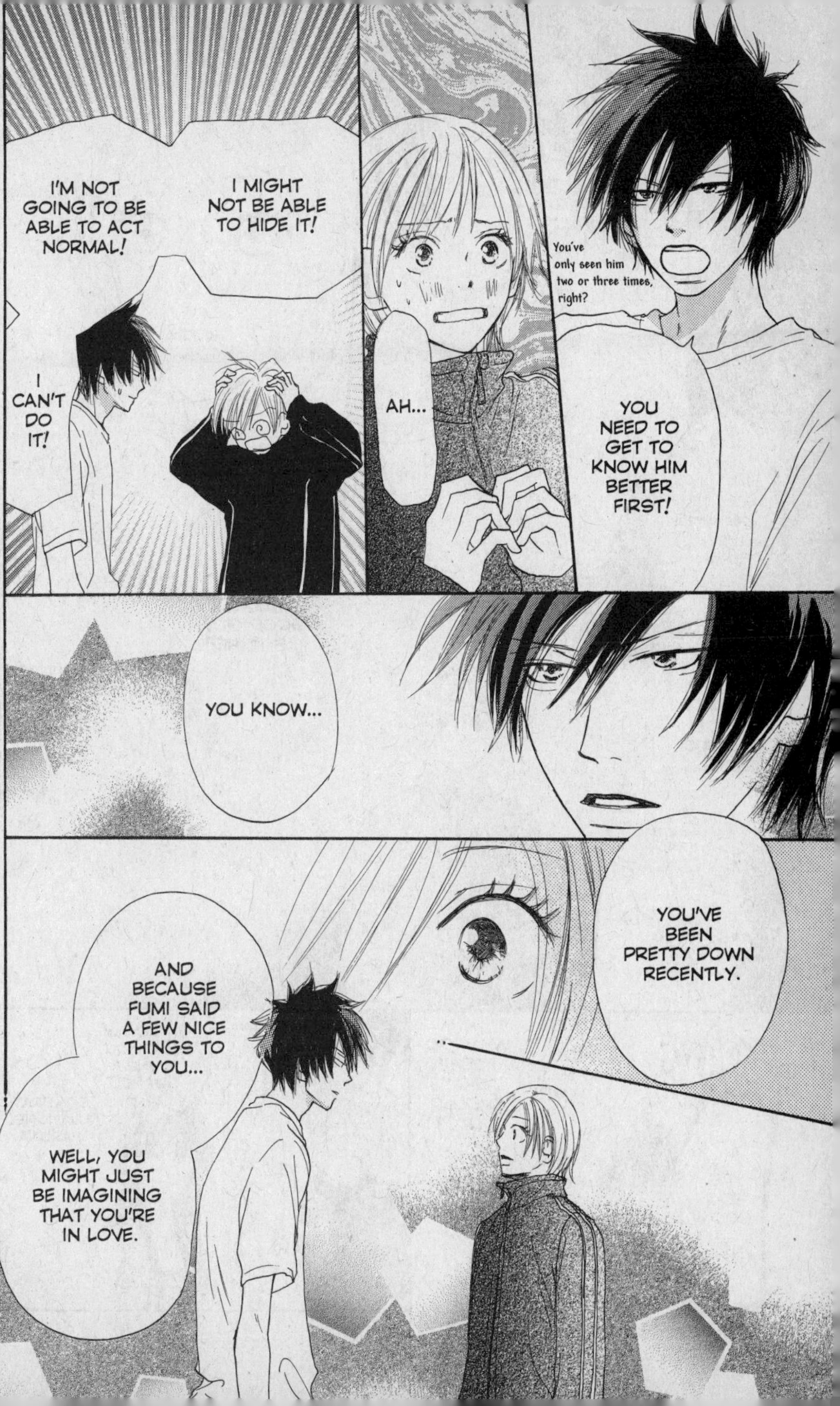
You've only seen him two or three times, right?
YOU NEED TO GET TO KNOW HIM BETTER FIRST!
AH...
I MIGHT NOT BE ABLE TO HIDE IT!
I'M NOT GOING TO BE ABLE TO ACT NORMAL!
I CAN'T DO IT!
YOU KNOW...
YOU'VE BEEN PRETTY DOWN RECENTLY.
AND BECAUSE FUMI SAID A FEW NICE THINGS TO YOU...
WELL, YOU MIGHT JUST BE IMAGINING THAT YOU'RE IN LOVE.

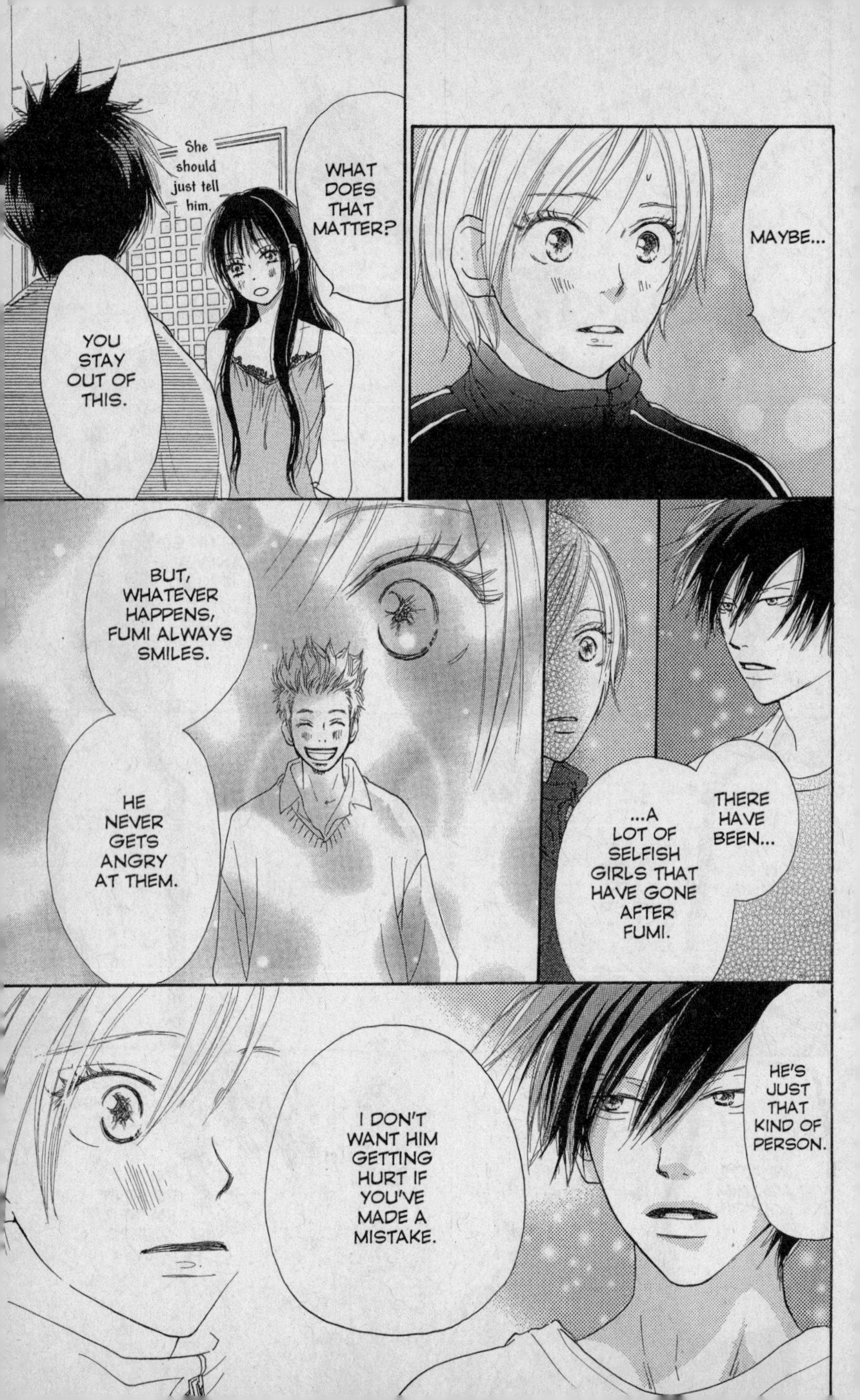
MAYBE...
WHAT DOES THAT MATTER?
She should just tell him.
YOU STAY OUT OF THIS.
THERE HAVE BEEN...
...A LOT OF SELFISH GIRLS THAT HAVE GONE AFTER FUMI.
BUT, WHATEVER HAPPENS, FUMI ALWAYS SMILES.
HE NEVER GETS ANGRY AT THEM.
HE'S JUST THAT KIND OF PERSON.
I DON'T WANT HIM GETTING HURT IF YOU'VE MADE A MISTAKE.

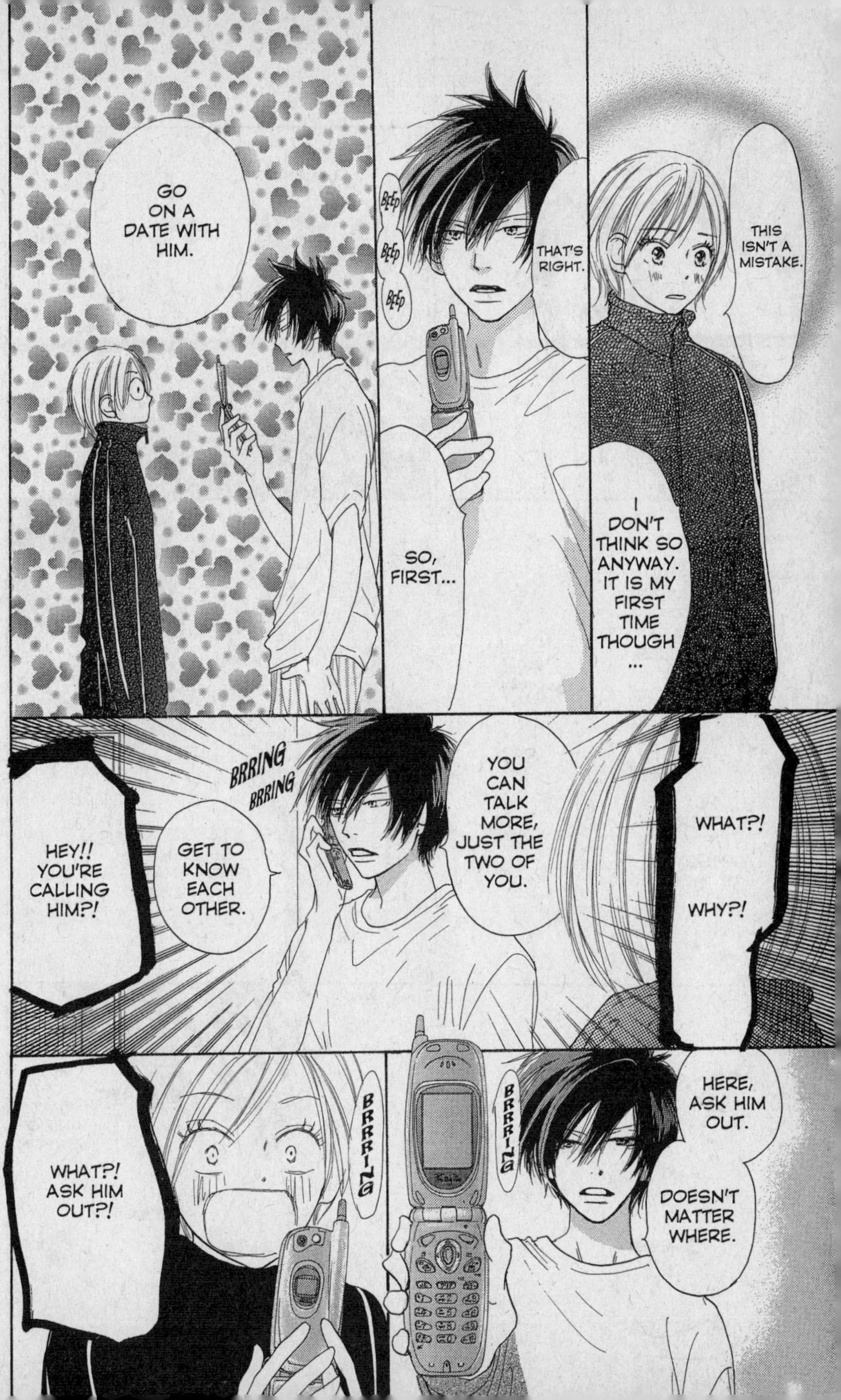
THIS ISN'T A MISTAKE.
I DON'T THINK SO ANYWAY. IT IS MY FIRST TIME THOUGH...
THAT'S RIGHT.
BEEP
BEEP
BEEP
SO, FIRST...
GO ON A DATE WITH HIM.
WHAT?!
WHY?!
YOU CAN TALK MORE, JUST THE TWO OF YOU.
BRRING
BRRING
GET TO KNOW EACH OTHER.
HEY!! YOU'RE CALLING HIM?!
HERE, ASK HIM OUT.
DOESN'T MATTER WHERE.
BRRRING
BRRRING
WHAT?! ASK HIM OUT?!

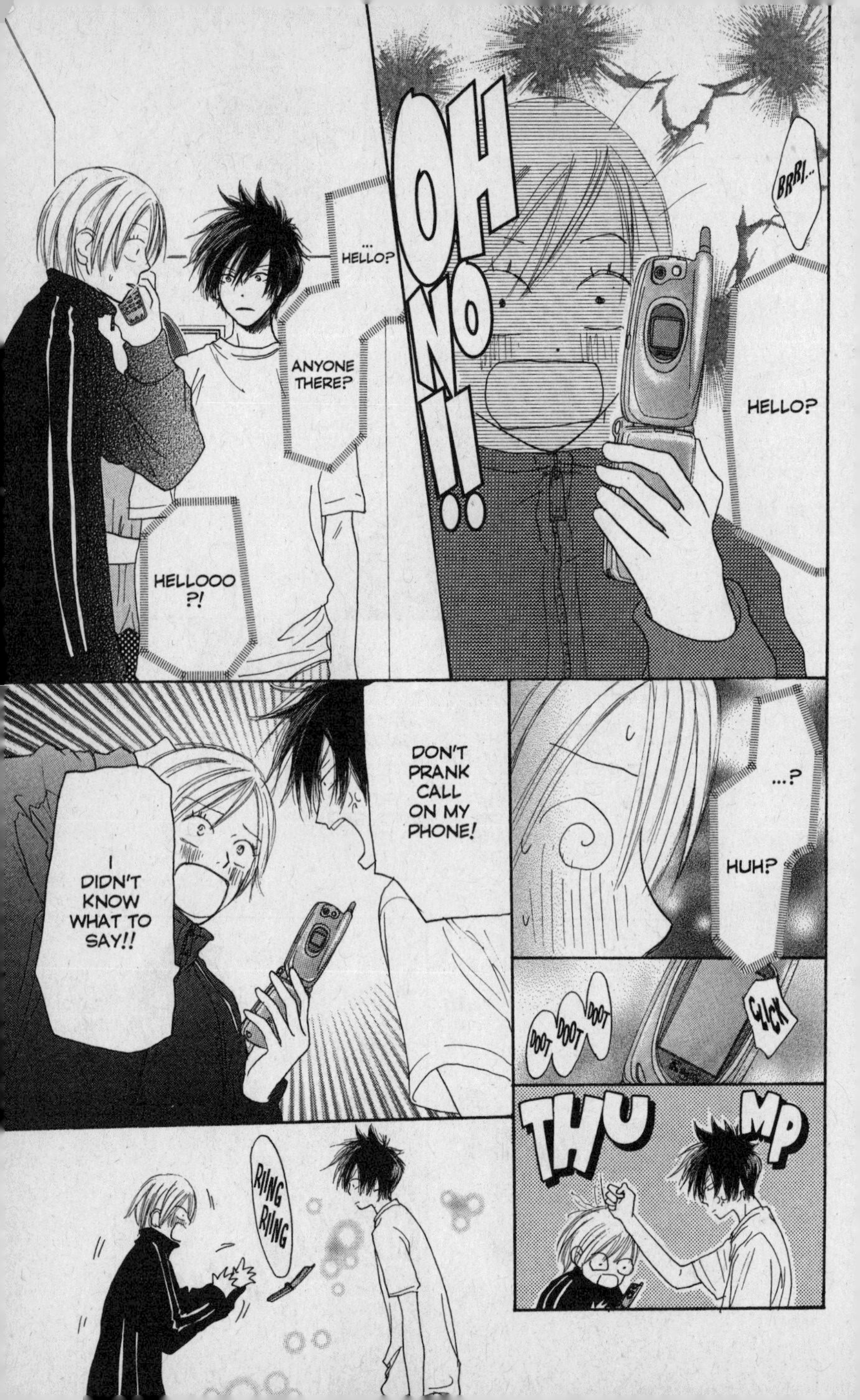
BRRI...
HELLO?
OH NO!!
... HELLO?
ANYONE THERE?
HELLOOO ?!
...?
HUH?
DOOT DOOT DOOT
CLICK
THU MP
DON'T PRANK CALL ON MY PHONE!
I DIDN'T KNOW WHAT TO SAY!!
RIING RIING

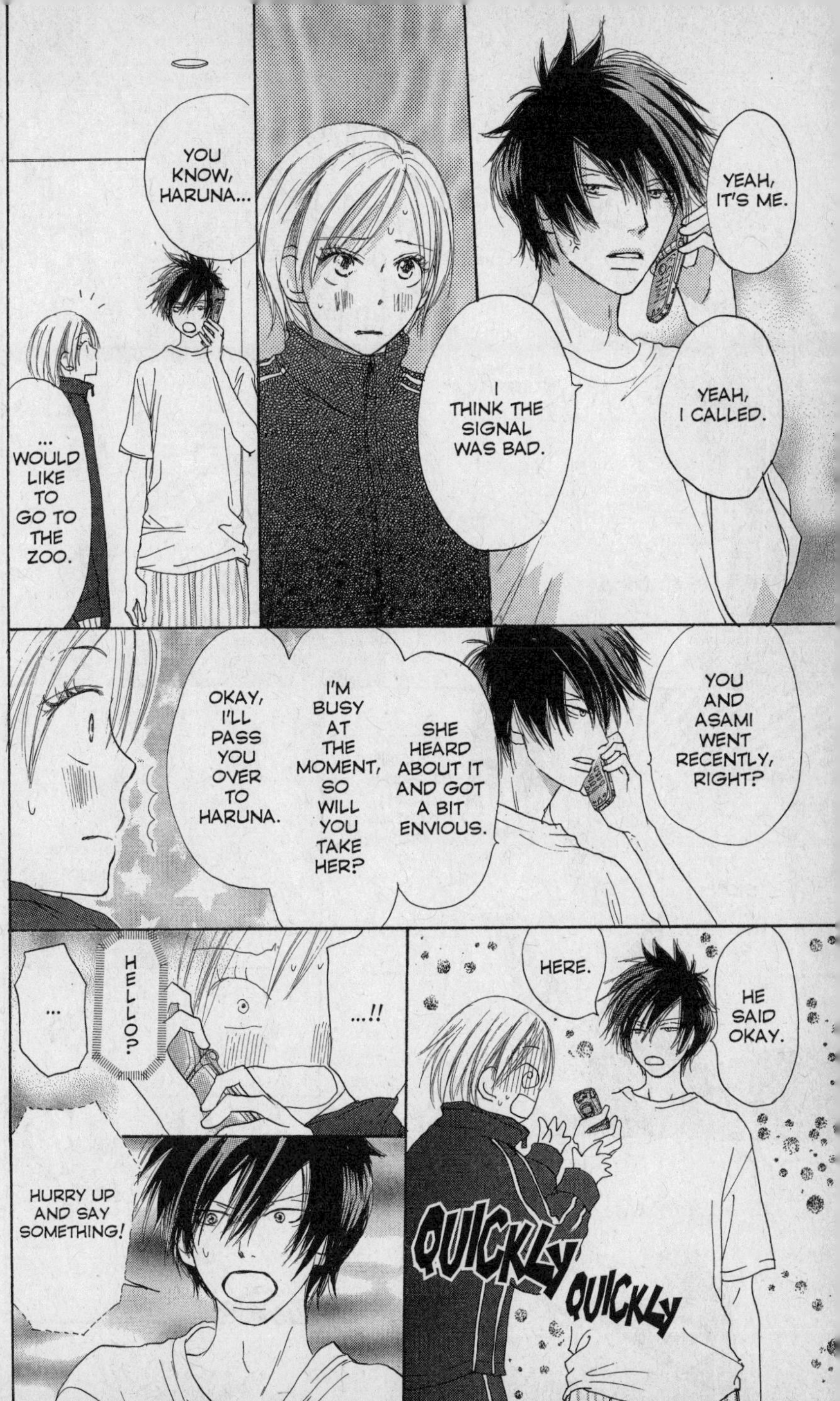

YEAH, IT'S ME.
YEAH, I CALLED.
I THINK THE SIGNAL WAS BAD.
YOU KNOW, HARUNA...
...WOULD LIKE TO GO TO THE ZOO.
YOU AND ASAMI WENT RECENTLY, RIGHT?
SHE HEARD ABOUT IT AND GOT A BIT ENVIOUS.
I'M BUSY AT THE MOMENT, SO WILL YOU TAKE HER?
OKAY, I'LL PASS YOU OVER TO HARUNA.
HE SAID OKAY.
HERE.
QUICKLY
QUICKLY
...!!
HELLO?
...
HURRY UP AND SAY SOMETHING!

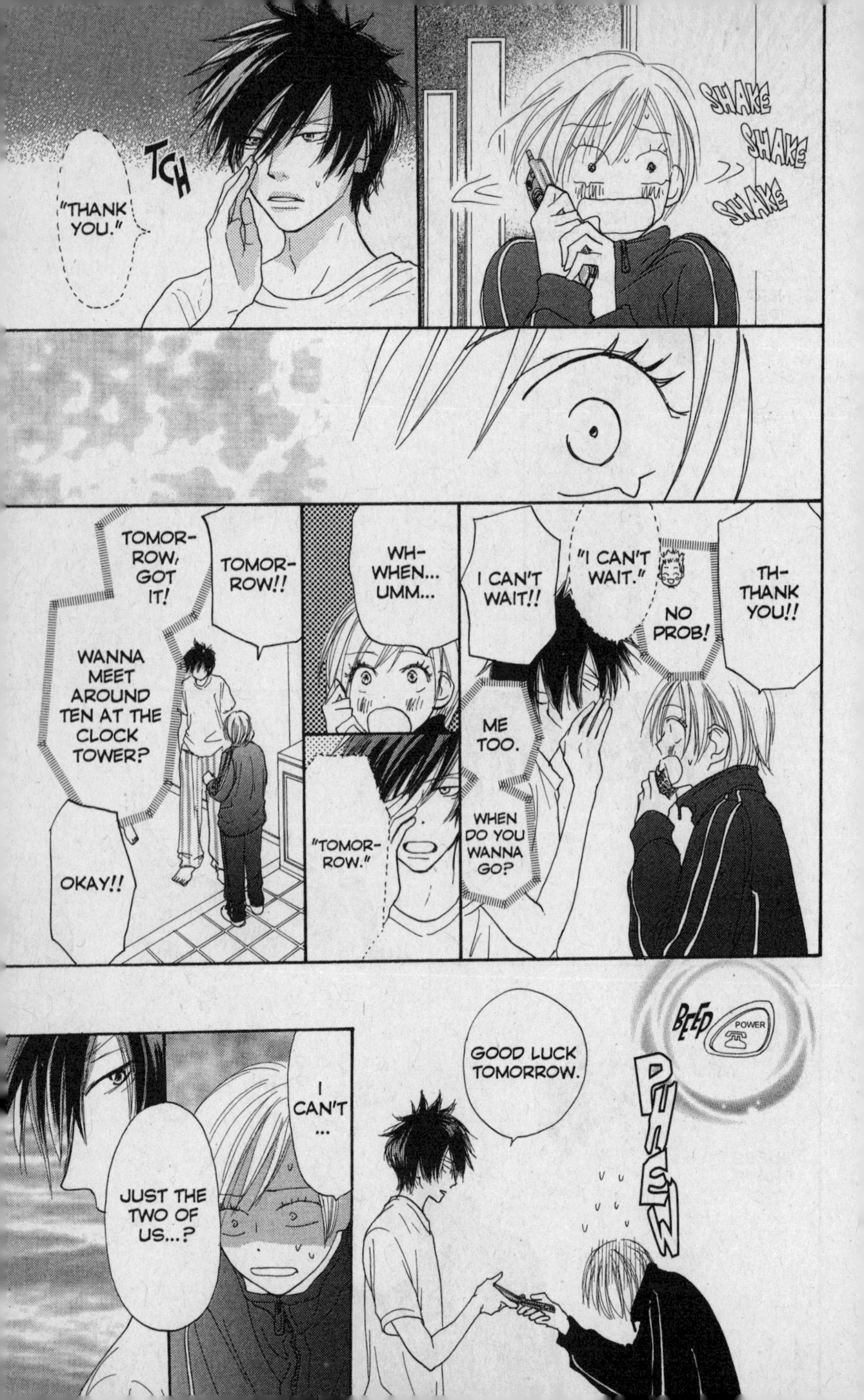
SHAKE
SHAKE
SHAKE
TCH
"THANK YOU."
TH-THANK YOU!!
NO PROB!
"I CAN'T WAIT."
I CAN'T WAIT!!
ME TOO.
WHEN DO YOU WANNA GO?
WH-WHEN... UMM...
"TOMORROW."
TOMORROW!!
TOMORROW, GOT IT!
WANNA MEET AROUND TEN AT THE CLOCK TOWER?
OKAY!!
BEEP
POWER
GOOD LUCK TOMORROW.
PHEW
I CAN'T...
JUST THE TWO OF US...?

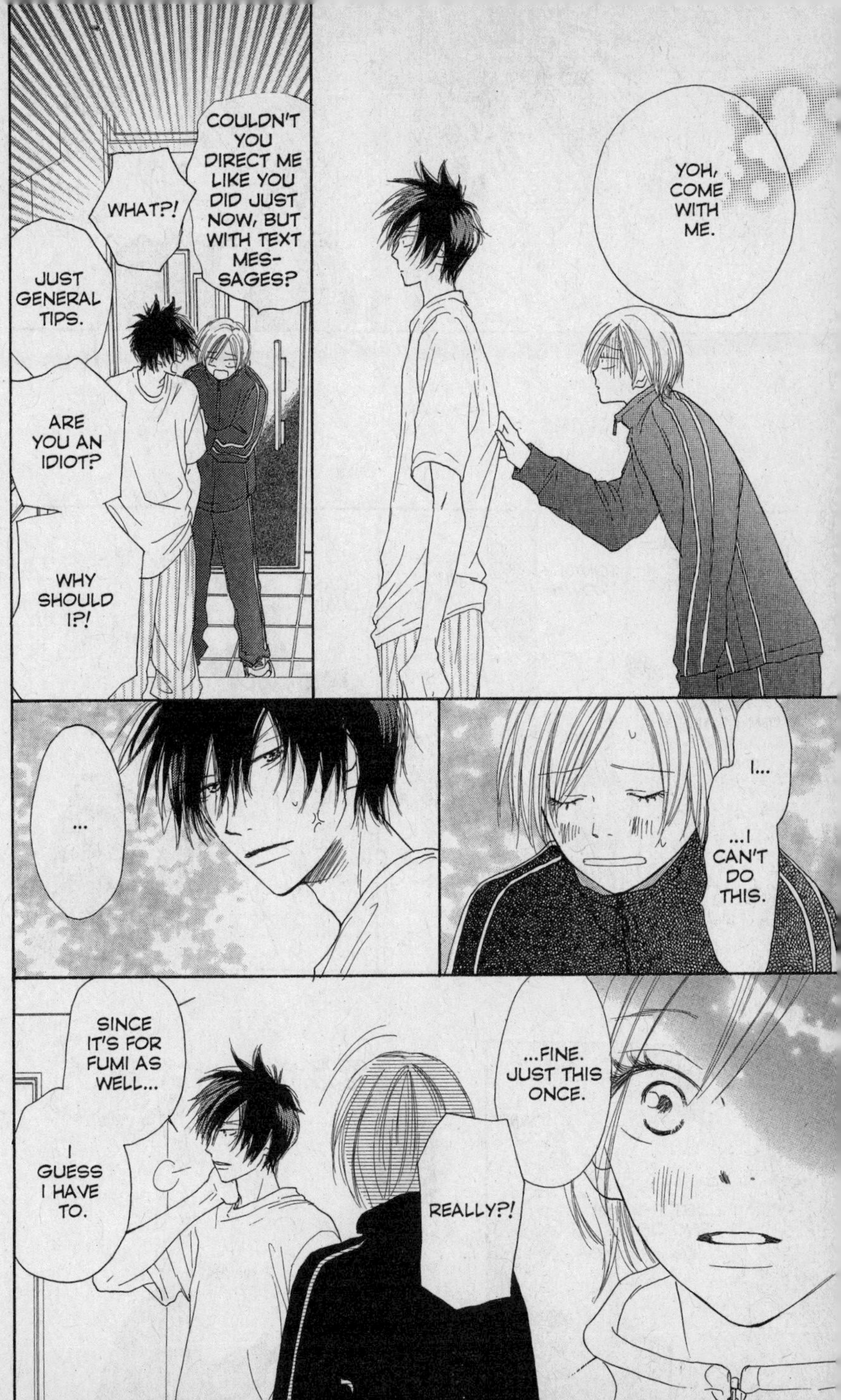
YOH, COME WITH ME.
COULDN'T YOU DIRECT ME LIKE YOU DID JUST NOW, BUT WITH TEXT MES-SAGES?
WHAT?!
JUST GENERAL TIPS.
ARE YOU AN IDIOT?
WHY SHOULD I?!
I...
...I CAN'T DO THIS.
...
...FINE. JUST THIS ONCE.
REALLY?!
SINCE IT'S FOR FUMI AS WELL...
I GUESS I HAVE TO.

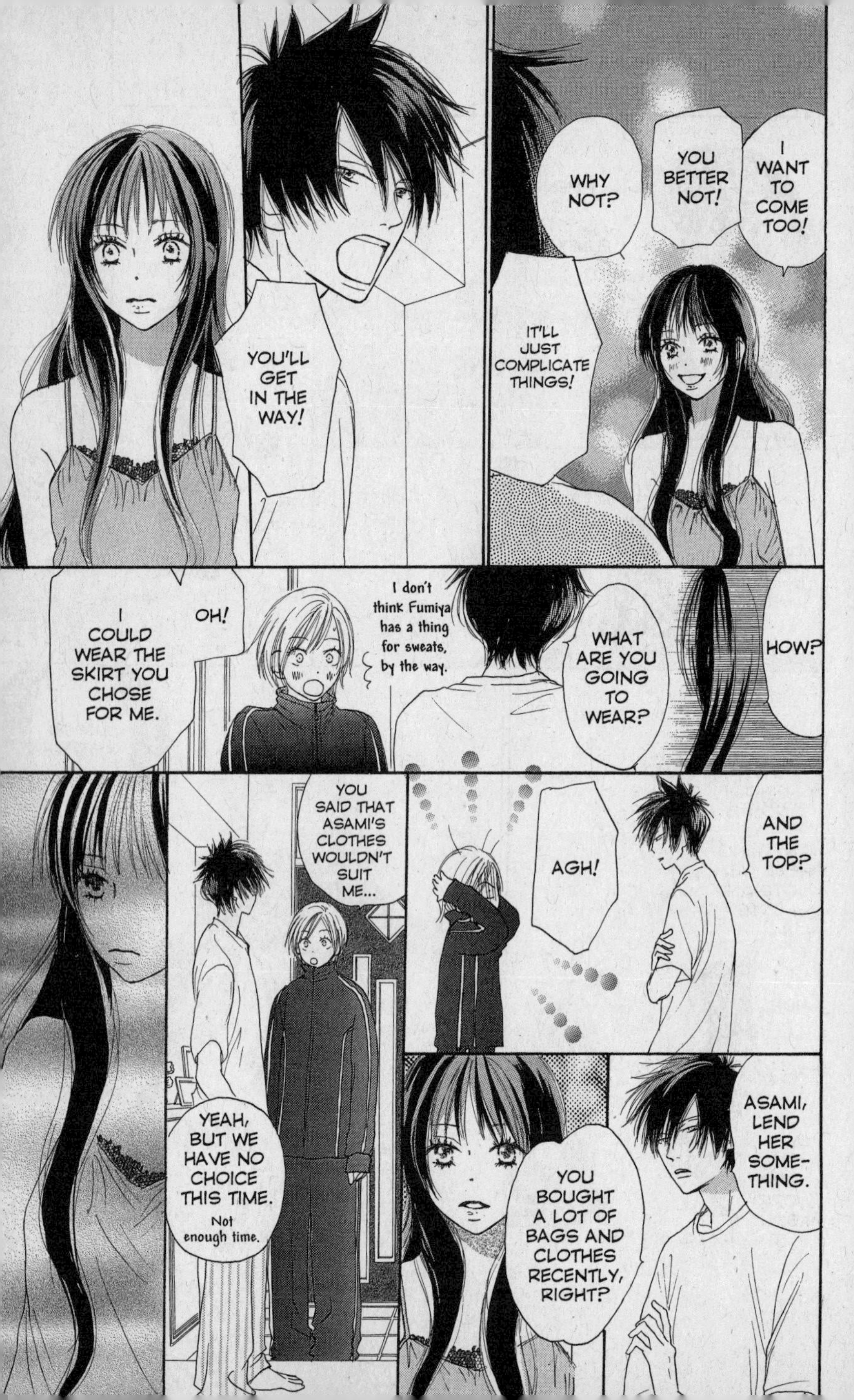
I WANT TO COME TOO!
YOU BETTER NOT!
WHY NOT?
IT'LL JUST COMPLICATE THINGS!
YOU'LL GET IN THE WAY!
HOW?
WHAT ARE YOU GOING TO WEAR?
I don't think Fumiya has a thing for sweats, by the way.
OH!
I COULD WEAR THE SKIRT YOU CHOSE FOR ME.
AND THE TOP?
AGH!
ASAMI, LEND HER SOME-THING.
YOU BOUGHT A LOT OF BAGS AND CLOTHES RECENTLY, RIGHT?
YOU SAID THAT ASAMI'S CLOTHES WOULDN'T SUIT ME...
YEAH, BUT WE HAVE NO CHOICE THIS TIME.
Not enough time.

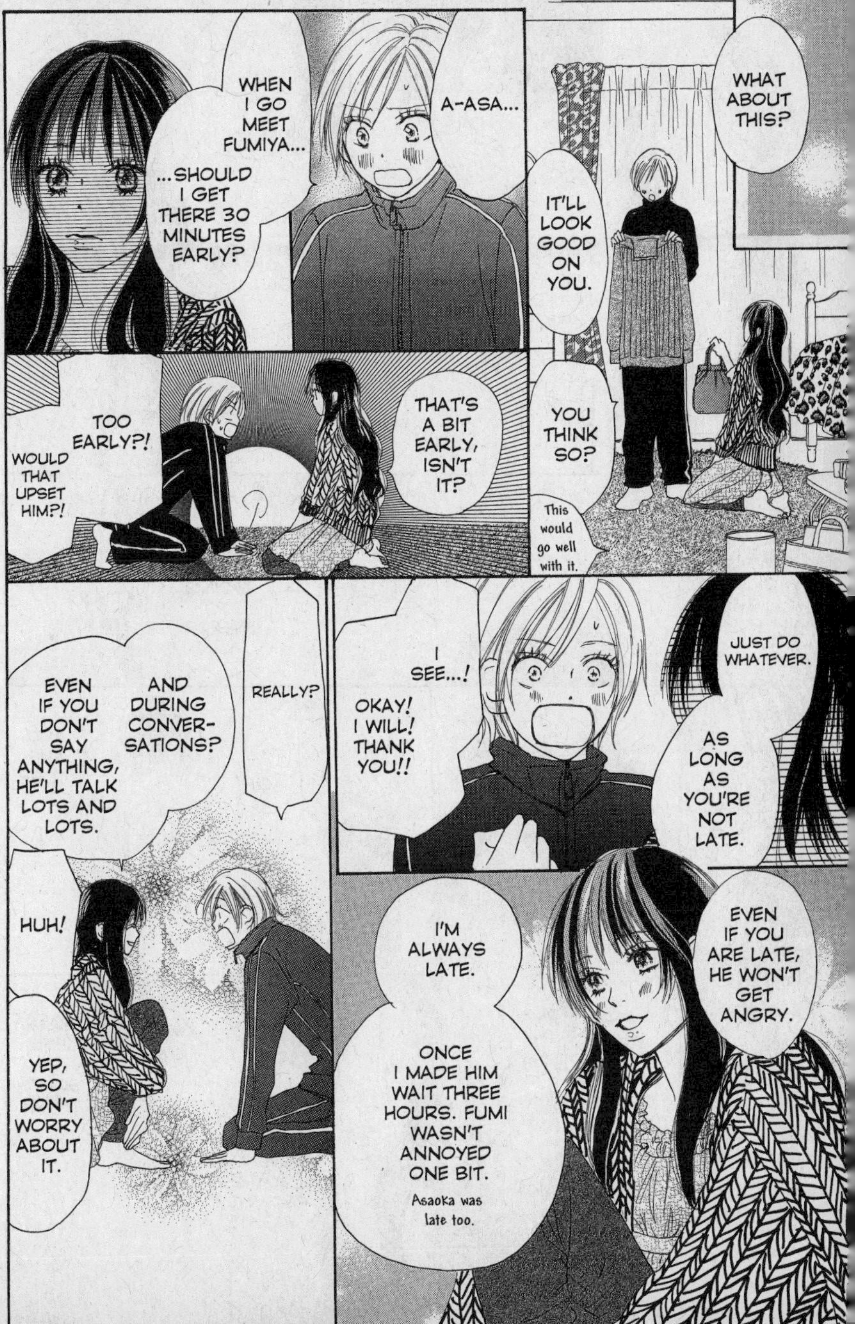
WHAT ABOUT THIS?
IT'LL LOOK GOOD ON YOU.
YOU THINK SO?
This would go well with it.
A-ASA...
WHEN I GO MEET FUMIYA...
...SHOULD I GET THERE 30 MINUTES EARLY?
THAT'S A BIT EARLY, ISN'T IT?
TOO EARLY?!
WOULD THAT UPSET HIM?!
JUST DO WHATEVER.
AS LONG AS YOU'RE NOT LATE.
I SEE...!
OKAY! I WILL! THANK YOU!!
REALLY?
AND DURING CONVERSATIONS?
EVEN IF YOU DON'T SAY ANYTHING, HE'LL TALK LOTS AND LOTS.
EVEN IF YOU ARE LATE, HE WON'T GET ANGRY.
I'M ALWAYS LATE.
ONCE I MADE HIM WAIT THREE HOURS. FUMI WASN'T ANNOYED ONE BIT.
Asaoka was late too.
HUH!
YEP, SO DON'T WORRY ABOUT IT.

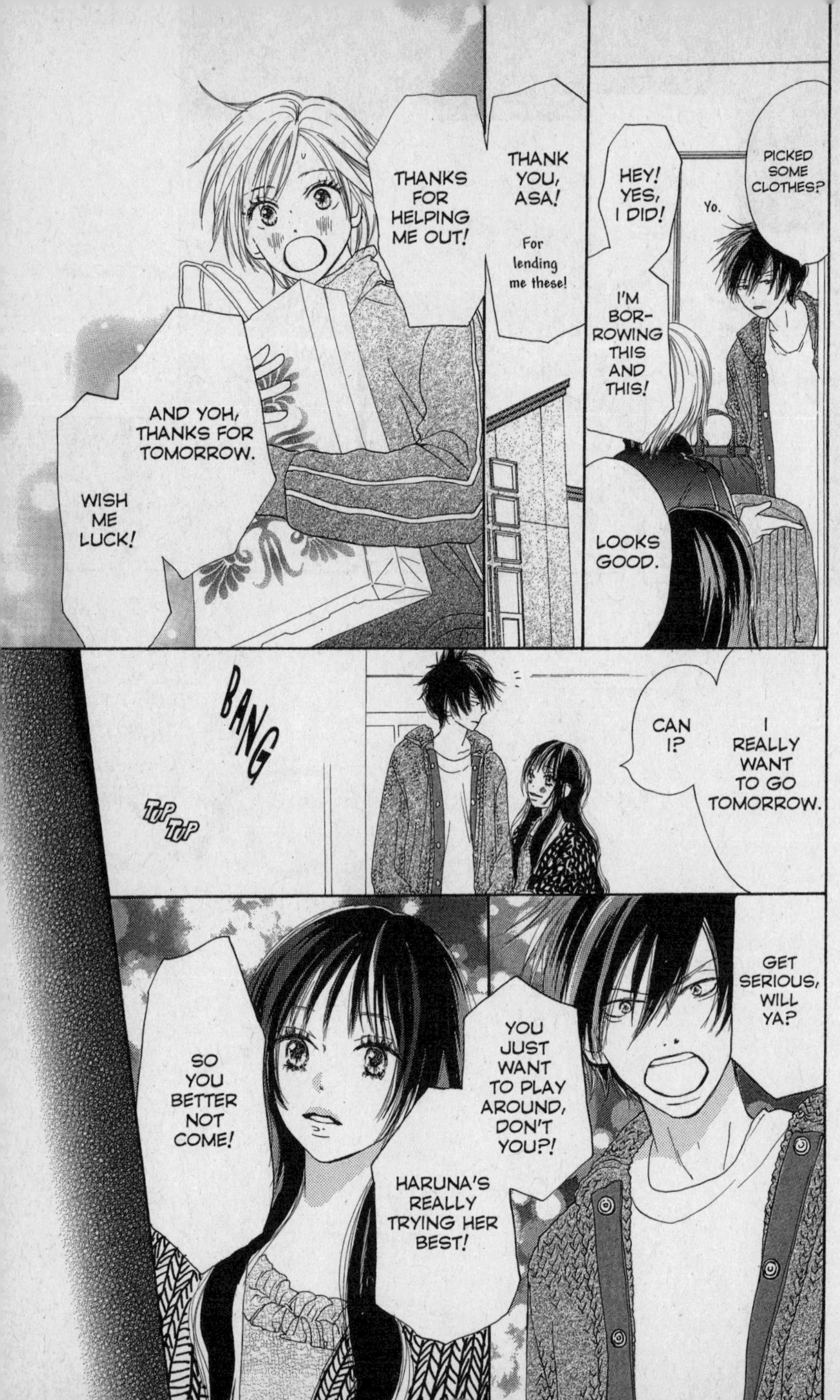
Yo.
PICKED SOME CLOTHES?
HEY! YES, I DID!
I'M BOR-ROWING THIS AND THIS!
LOOKS GOOD.
THANK YOU, ASA!
For lending me these!
THANKS FOR HELPING ME OUT!
AND YOH, THANKS FOR TOMORROW.
WISH ME LUCK!
I REALLY WANT TO GO TOMORROW.
CAN I?
BANG
TUP TUP
GET SERIOUS, WILL YA?
YOU JUST WANT TO PLAY AROUND, DON'T YOU?!
HARUNA'S REALLY TRYING HER BEST!
SO YOU BETTER NOT COME!

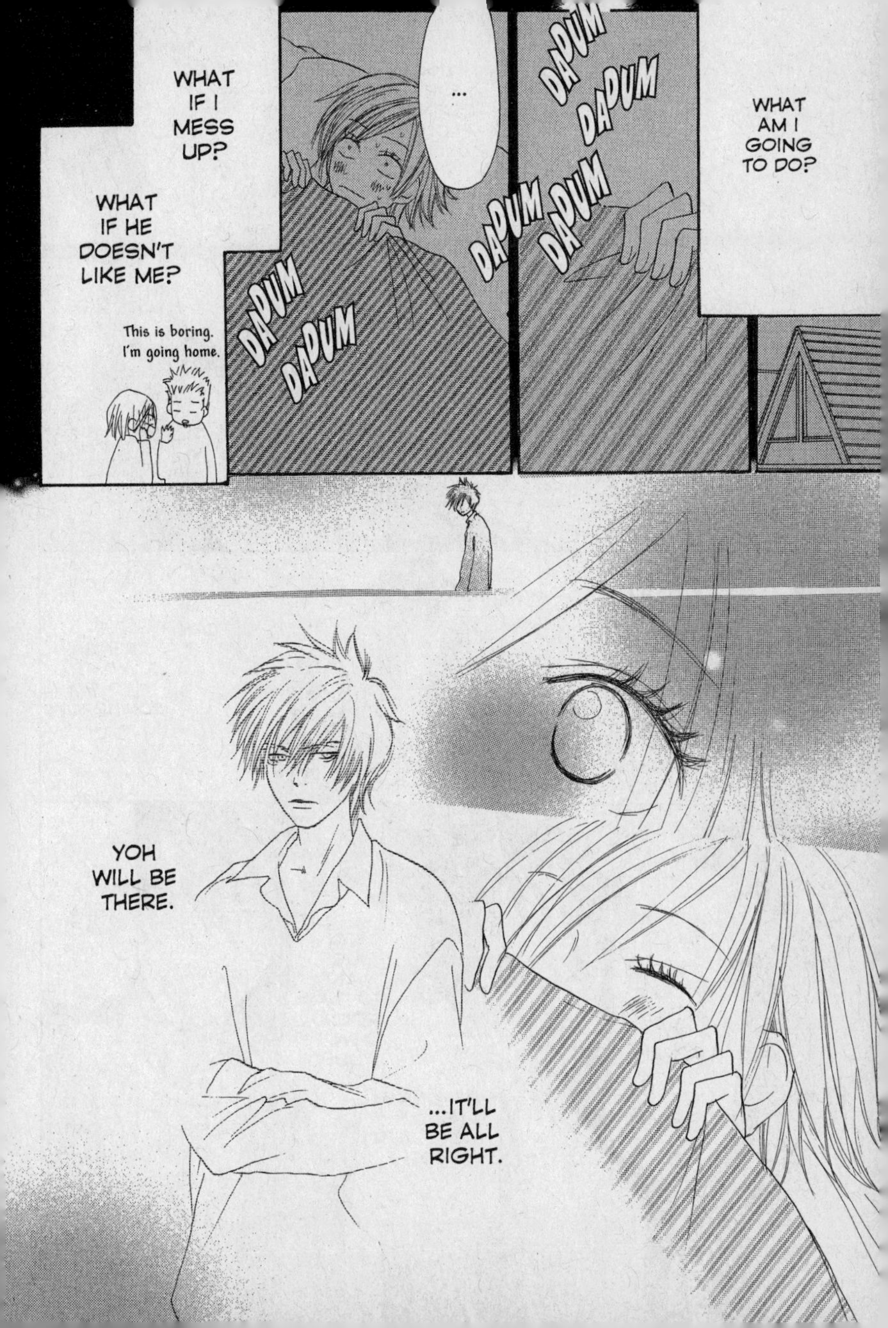
WHAT AM I GOING TO DO?
DADUM
DADUM
DADUM
DADUM
...
DADUM
DADUM
DADUM
WHAT IF I MESS UP?
WHAT IF HE DOESN'T LIKE ME?
This is boring. I'm going home.
YOH WILL BE THERE.
...IT'LL BE ALL RIGHT.

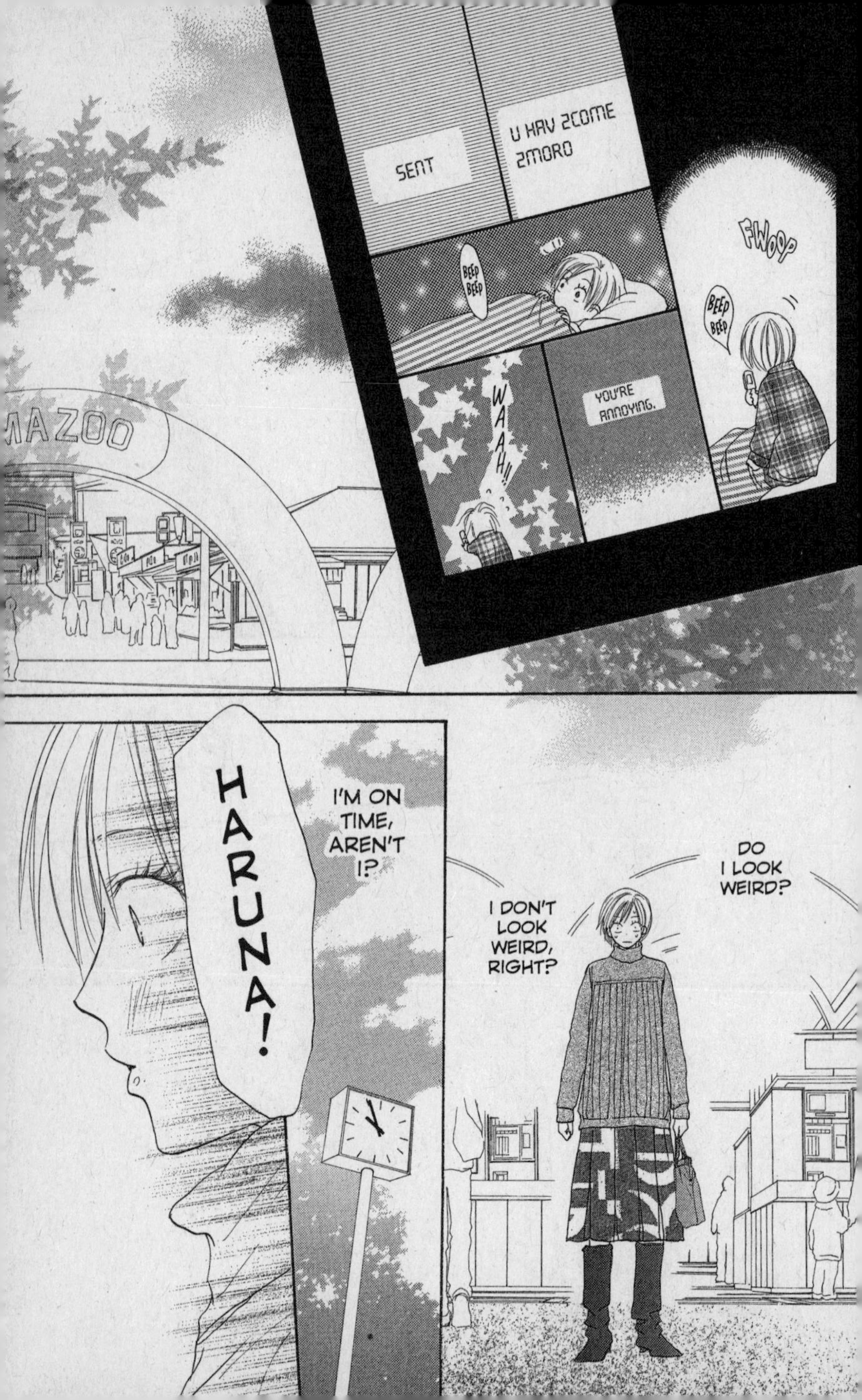
U HAV 2COME 2MORO
SENT
FWOOP
BEEP BEEP
BEEP BEEP
YOU'RE ANNOYING.
WAAAH!!
DO I LOOK WEIRD?
I DON'T LOOK WEIRD, RIGHT?
I'M ON TIME, AREN'T I!?
HARUNA!

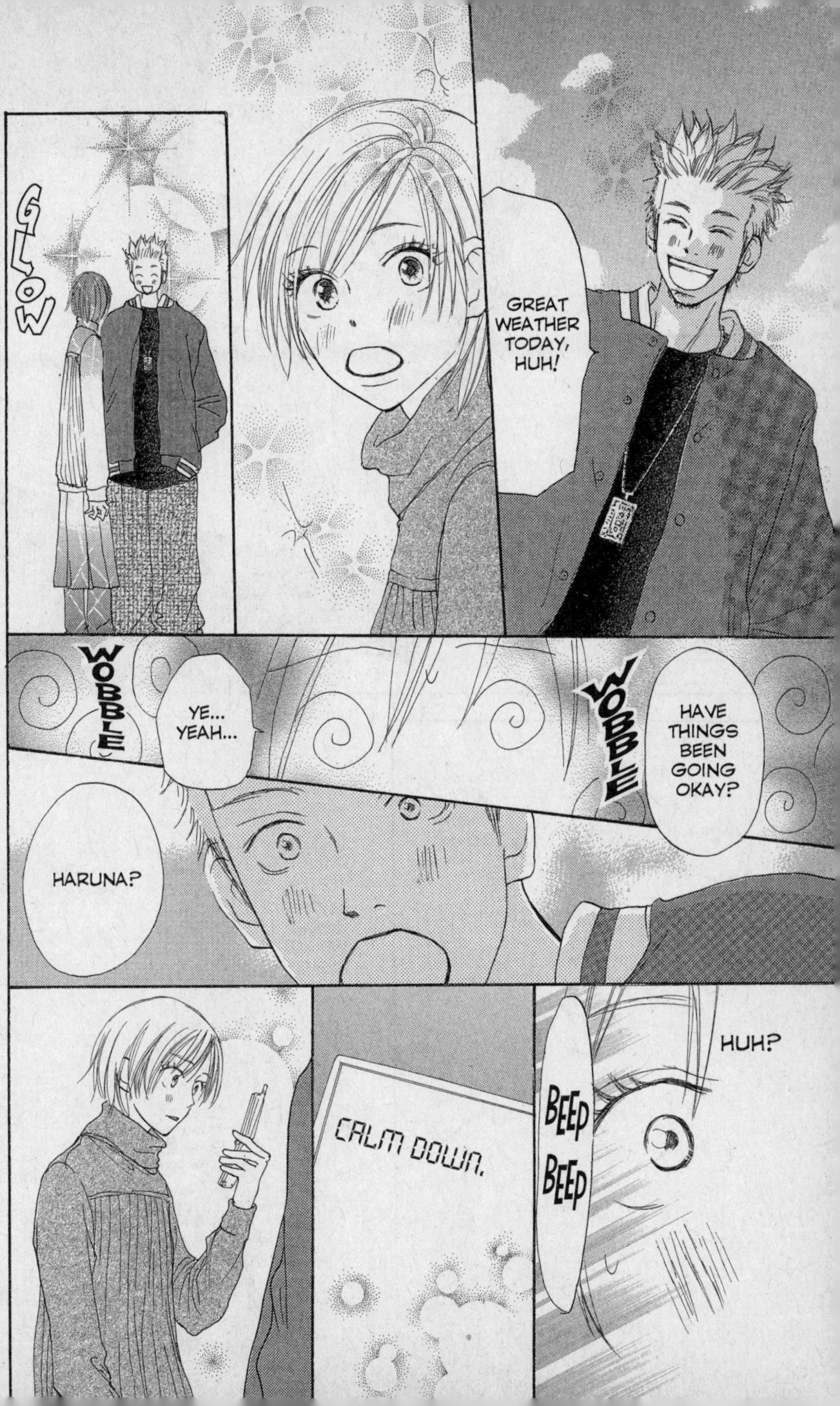
GREAT WEATHER TODAY, HUH!
GLOW
HAVE THINGS BEEN GOING OKAY?
WOBBLE
YE... YEAH...
WOBBLE
HARUNA?
HUH?
BEEP BEEP
CALM DOWN.

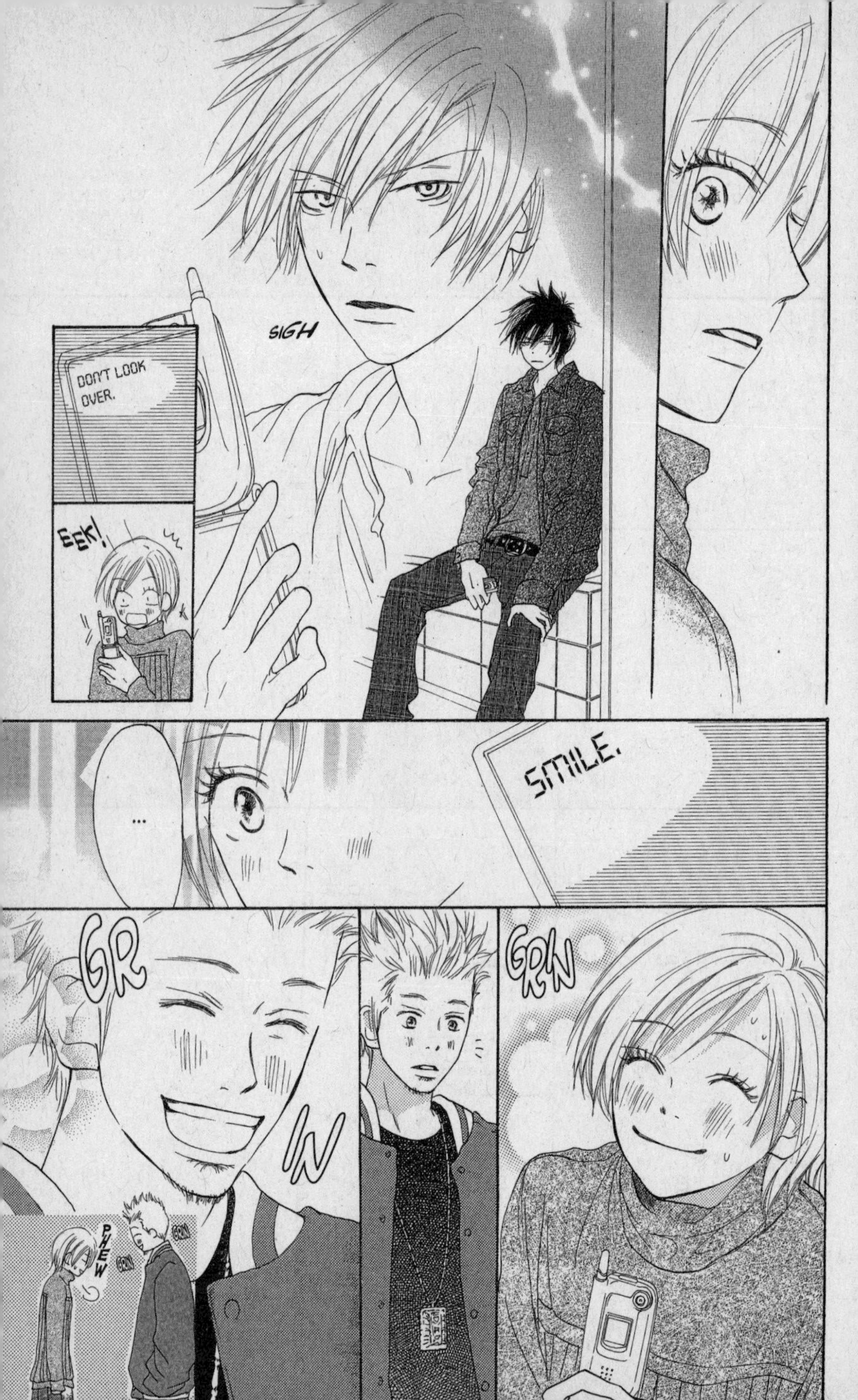
SIGH
DON'T LOOK OVER.
EEK!
SMILE.
...
GRIN
GR
IN
PHEW

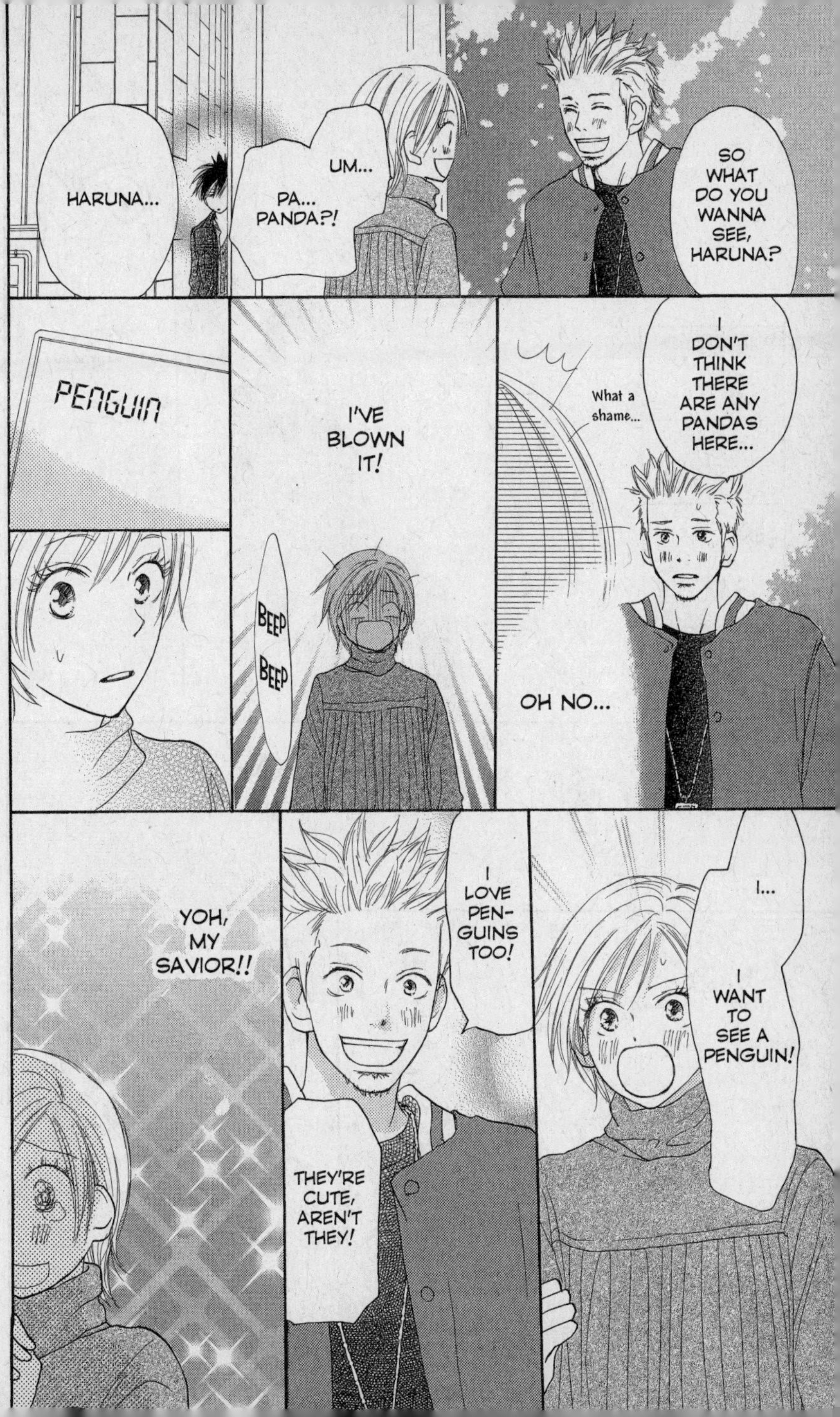
SO WHAT DO YOU WANNA SEE, HARUNA?
UM... PA... PANDA?!
HARUNA...
I DON'T THINK THERE ARE ANY PANDAS HERE...
What a shame...
OH NO...
I'VE BLOWN IT!
BEEP BEEP
PENGUIN
I... I WANT TO SEE A PENGUIN!
I LOVE PEN-GUINS TOO!
THEY'RE CUTE, AREN'T THEY!
YOH, MY SAVIOR!!

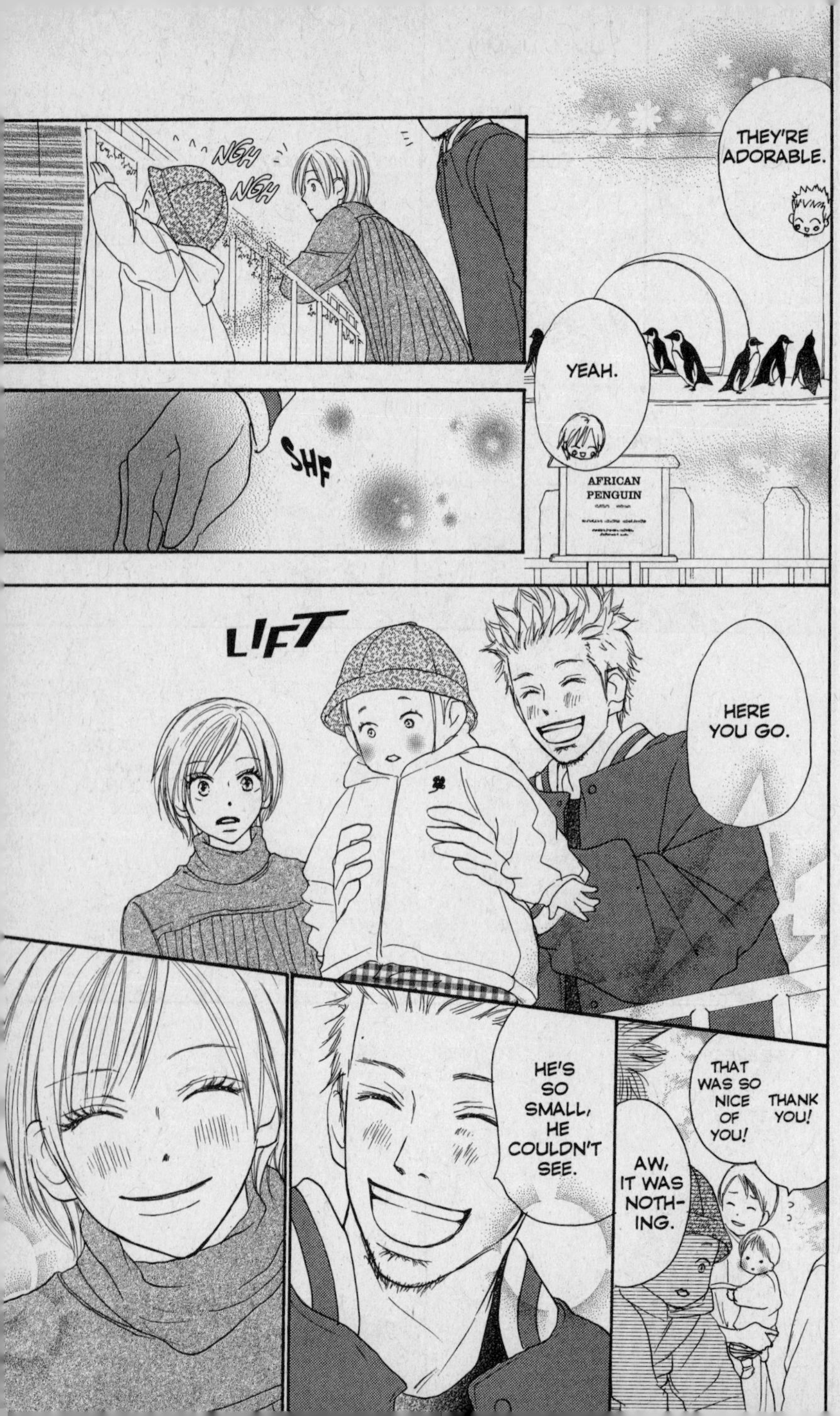
THEY'RE ADORABLE.
YEAH.
AFRICAN PENGUIN
NGH NGH
SHF
HERE YOU GO.
LIFT
THANK YOU!
THAT WAS SO NICE OF YOU!
AW, IT WAS NOTH-ING.
HE'S SO SMALL, HE COULDN'T SEE.

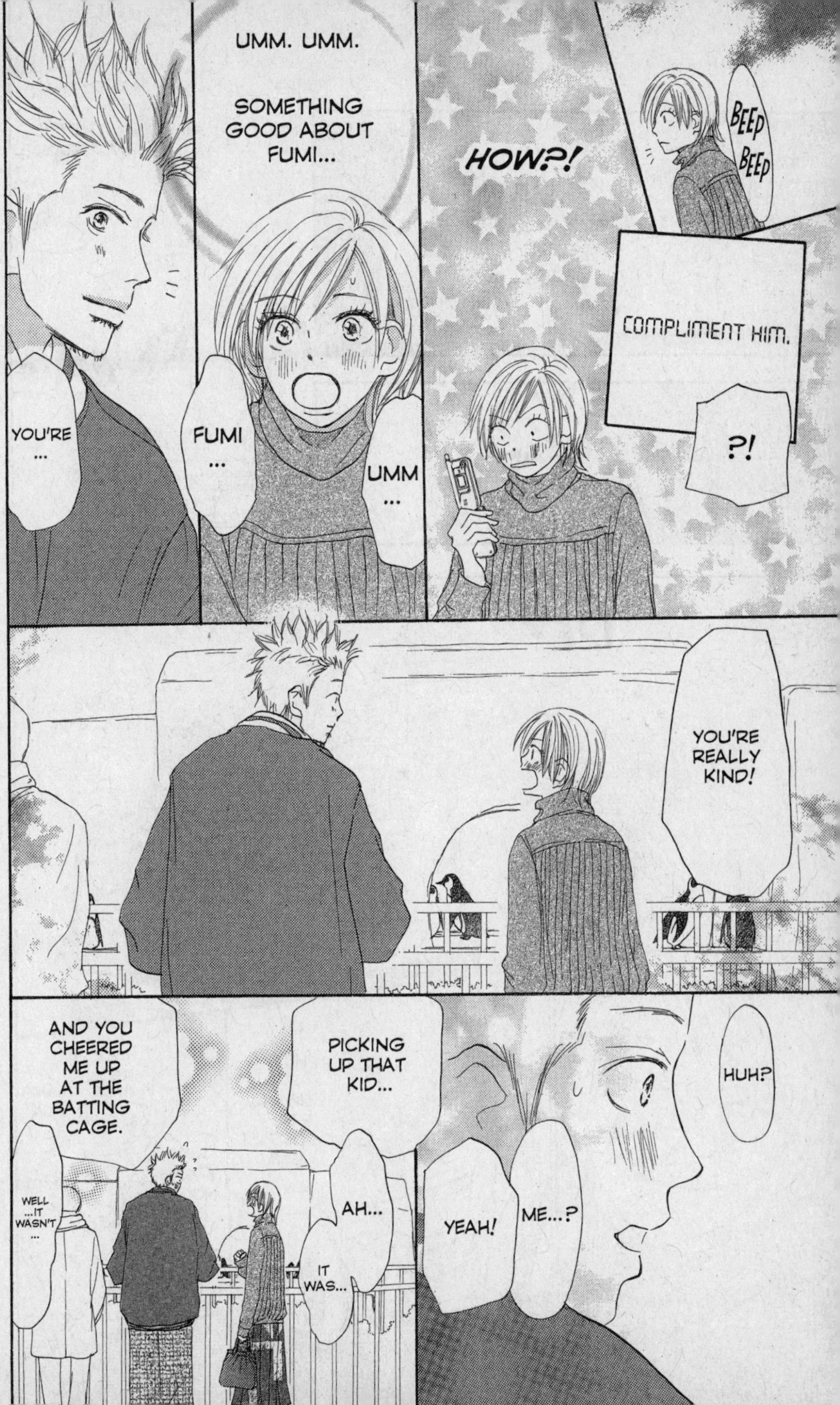
BEEP BEEP
COMPLIMENT HIM.
?!
HOW?!
UMM. UMM.
SOMETHING GOOD ABOUT FUMI...
UMM ...
FUMI ...
YOU'RE ...
YOU'RE REALLY KIND!
HUH?
ME...?
YEAH!
PICKING UP THAT KID...
AND YOU CHEERED ME UP AT THE BATTING CAGE.
AH...
IT WAS...
WELL ...IT WASN'T ...

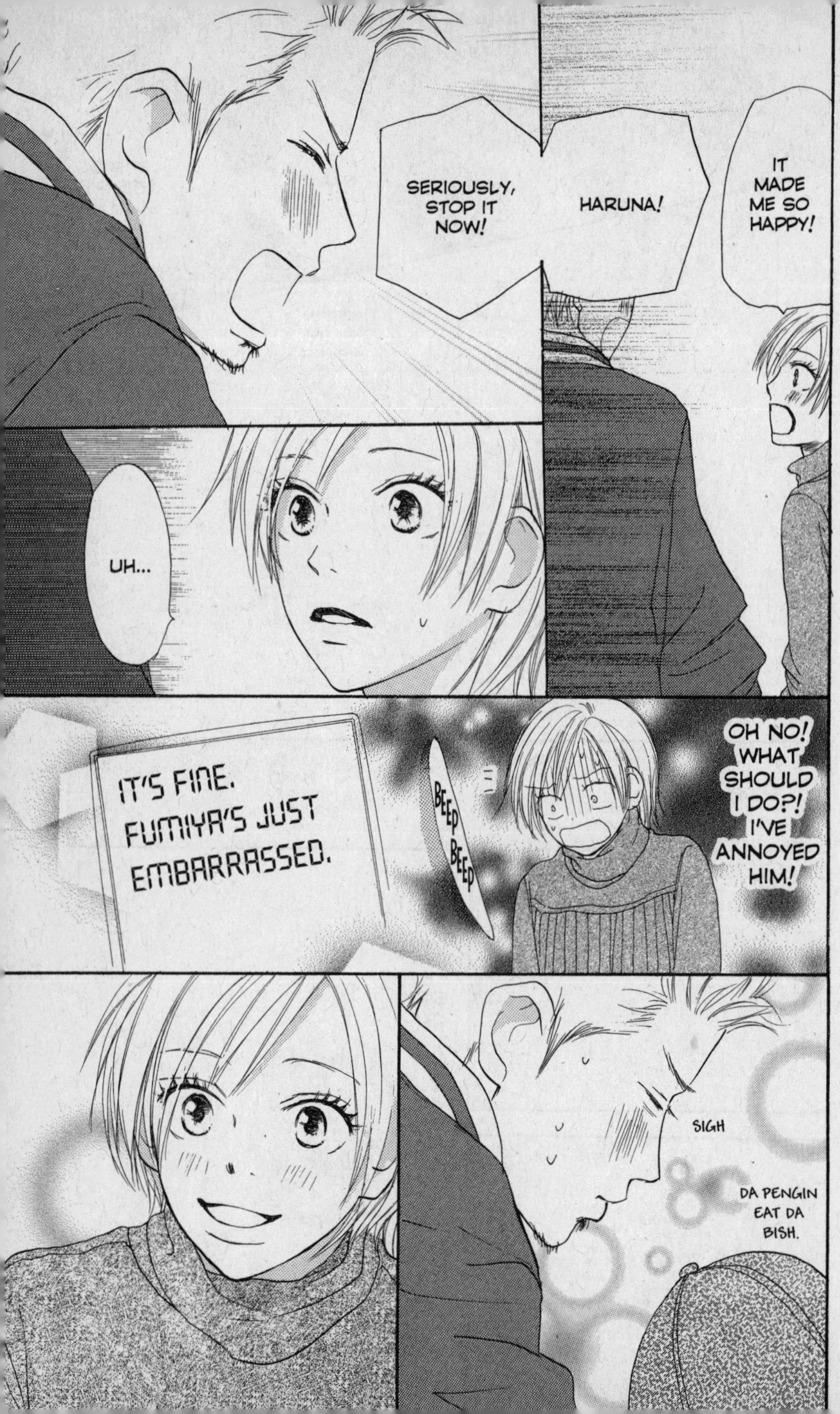
IT MADE ME SO HAPPY!
HARUNA!
SERIOUSLY, STOP IT NOW!
UH...
OH NO! WHAT SHOULD I DO?! I'VE ANNOYED HIM!
BEEP BEEP
IT'S FINE. FUMIYA'S JUST EMBARRASSED.
SIGH
DA PENGIN EAT DA BISH.

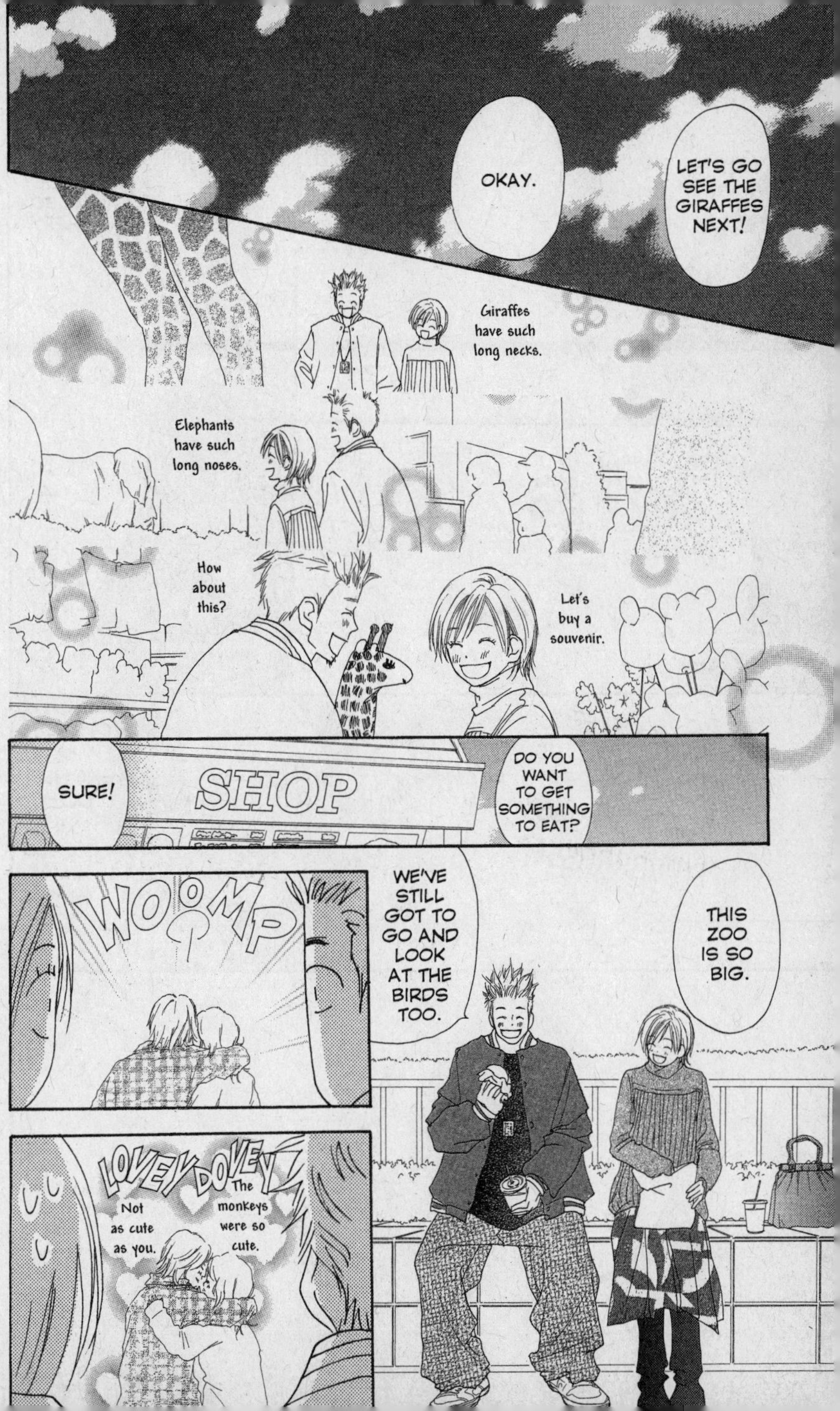
LET'S GO SEE THE GIRAFFES NEXT!
OKAY.
Giraffes have such long necks.
Elephants have such long noses.
Let's buy a souvenir.
How about this?
DO YOU WANT TO GET SOMETHING TO EAT?
SURE!
SHOP
THIS ZOO IS SO BIG.
WE'VE STILL GOT TO GO AND LOOK AT THE BIRDS TOO.
WOOMP
LOVEY DOVEY
The monkeys were so cute.
Not as cute as you.

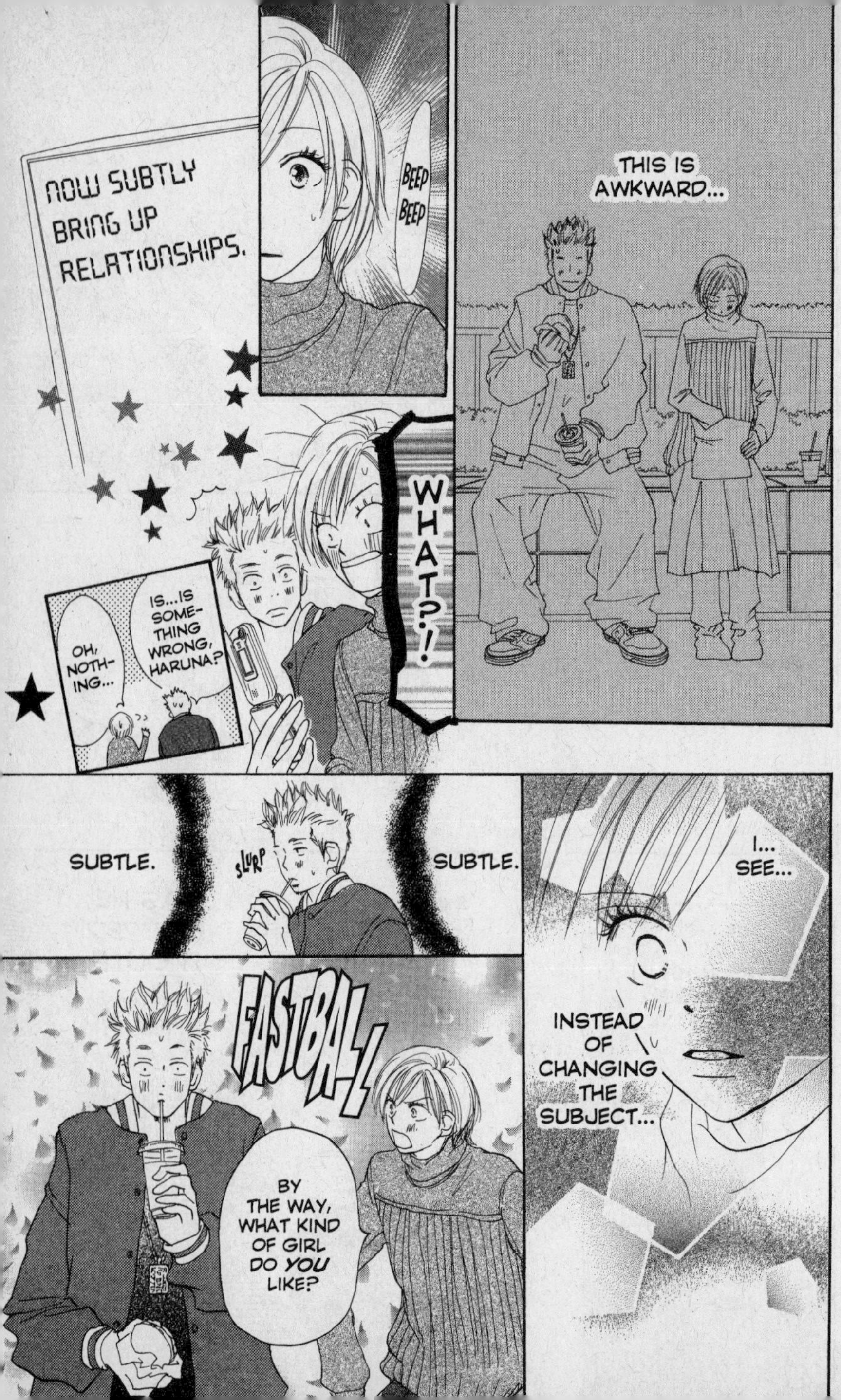
THIS IS AWKWARD...
BEEP BEEP
NOW SUBTLY BRING UP RELATIONSHIPS.
WHAT?!
IS...IS SOMETHING WRONG, HARUNA?
OH, NOTHING...
I... SEE...
INSTEAD OF CHANGING THE SUBJECT...
SUBTLE.
SLURP
SUBTLE.
FASTBALL
BY THE WAY, WHAT KIND OF GIRL DO YOU LIKE?

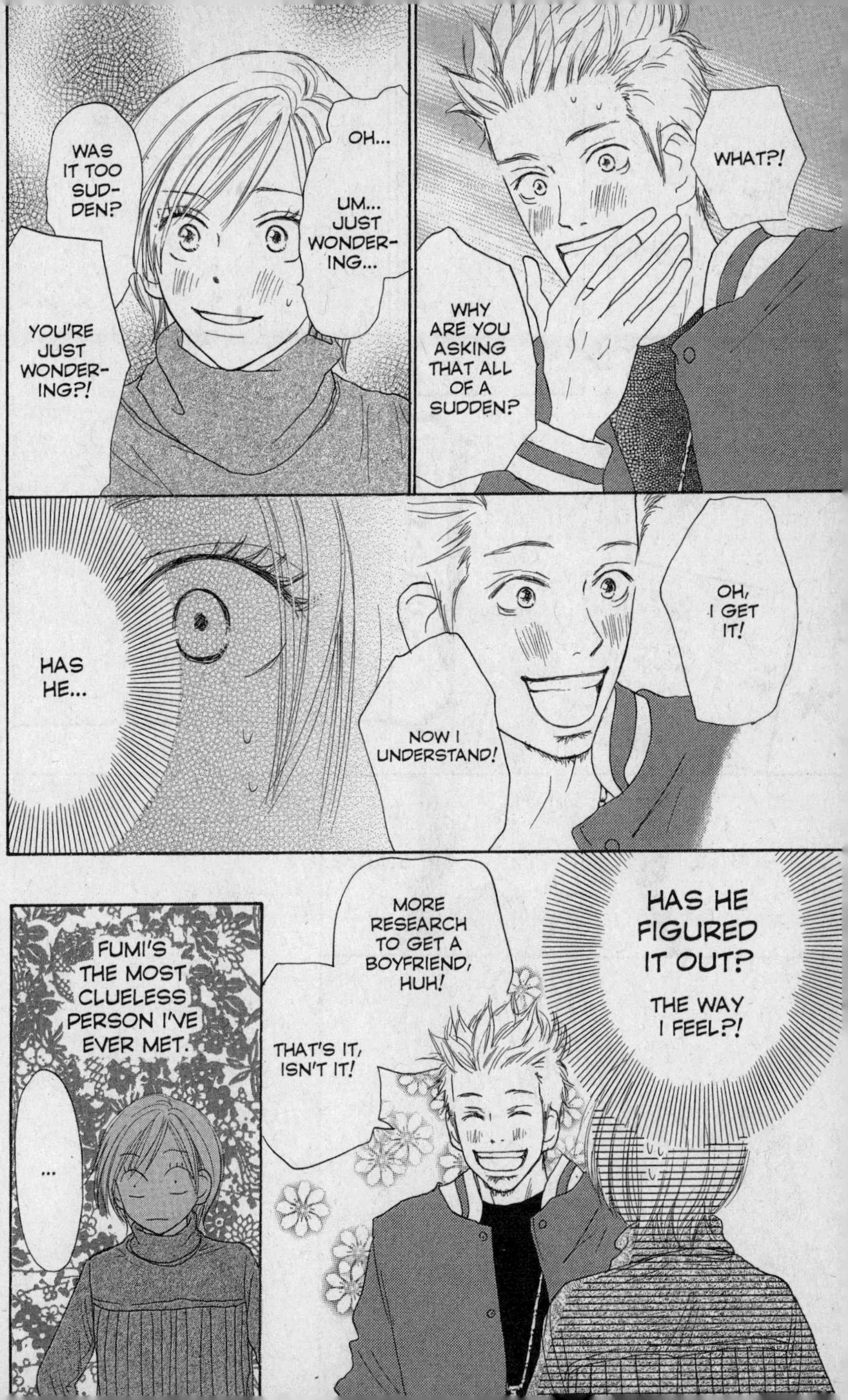
WHAT?!
WHY ARE YOU ASKING THAT ALL OF A SUDDEN?
OH...
UM... JUST WONDERING...
WAS IT TOO SUD-DEN?
YOU'RE JUST WONDER-ING?!
OH, I GET IT!
NOW I UNDERSTAND!
HAS HE...
HAS HE FIGURED IT OUT?
THE WAY I FEEL?!
MORE RESEARCH TO GET A BOYFRIEND, HUH!
THAT'S IT, ISN'T IT!
FUMI'S THE MOST CLUELESS PERSON I'VE EVER MET.
...

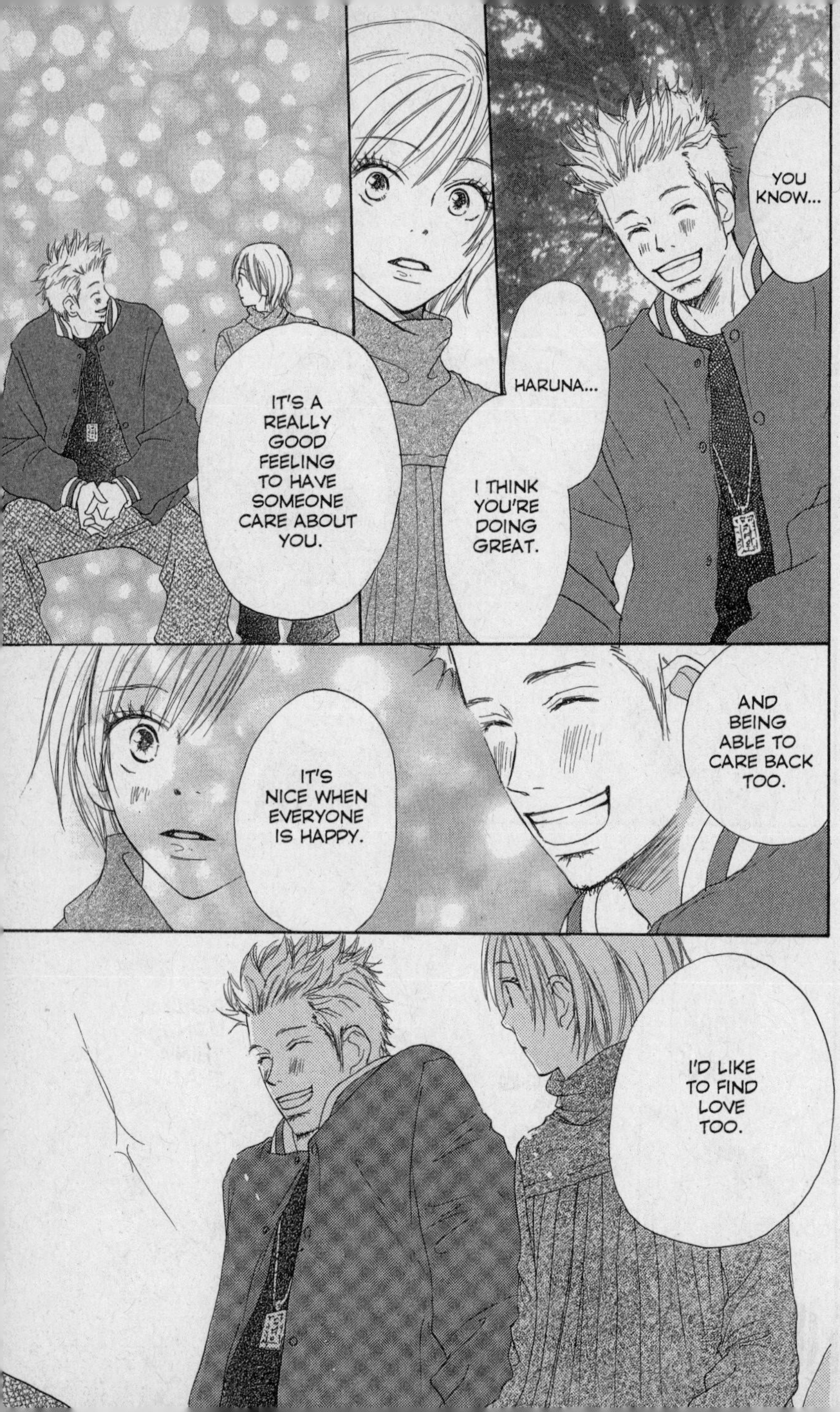
YOU KNOW...
HARUNA...
I THINK YOU'RE DOING GREAT.
IT'S A REALLY GOOD FEELING TO HAVE SOMEONE CARE ABOUT YOU.
AND BEING ABLE TO CARE BACK TOO.
IT'S NICE WHEN EVERYONE IS HAPPY.
I'D LIKE TO FIND LOVE TOO.

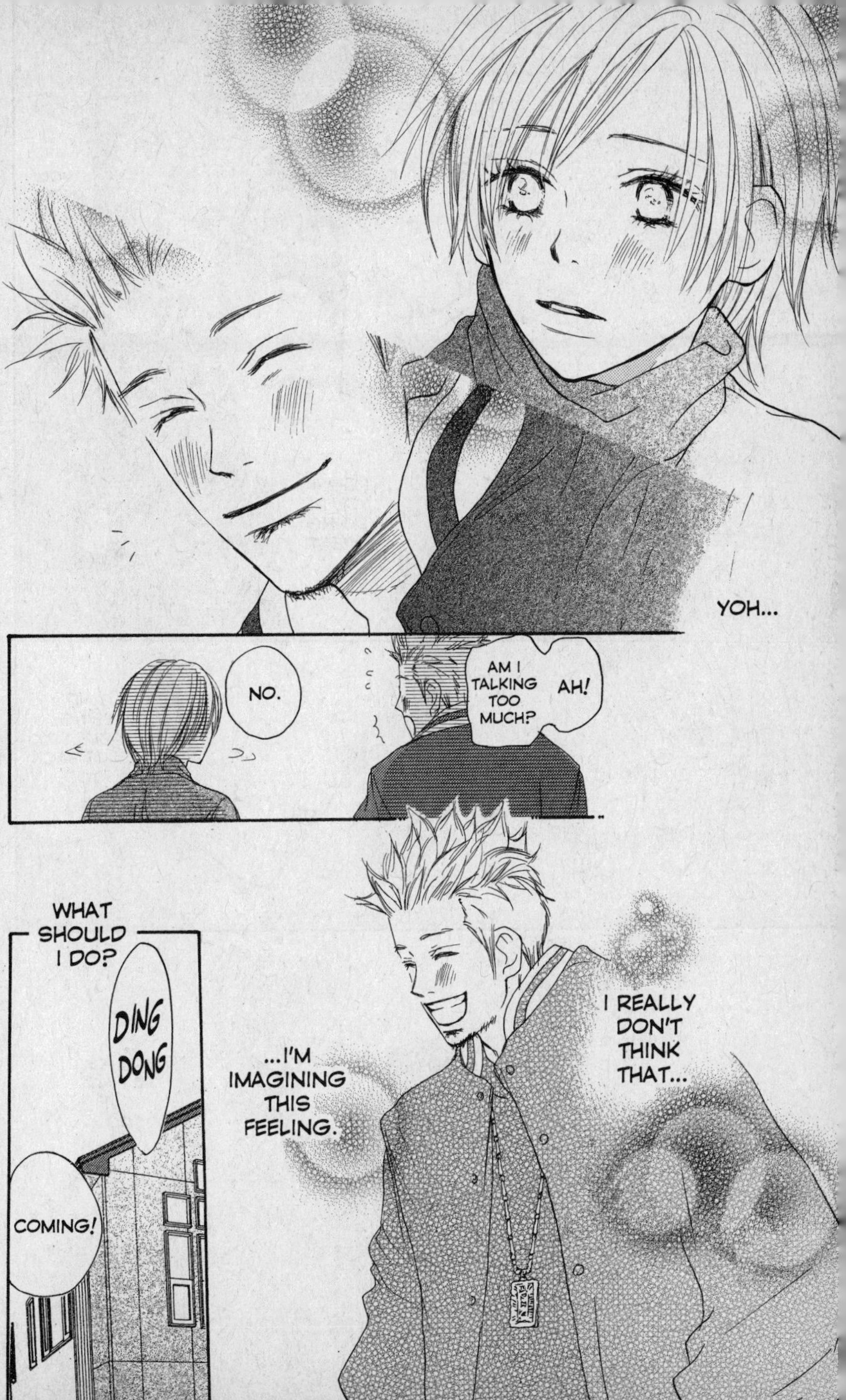
YOH...
AH!
AM I TALKING TOO MUCH?
NO.
I REALLY DON'T THINK THAT...
...I'M IMAGINING THIS FEELING.
WHAT SHOULD I DO?
DING DONG
COMING!

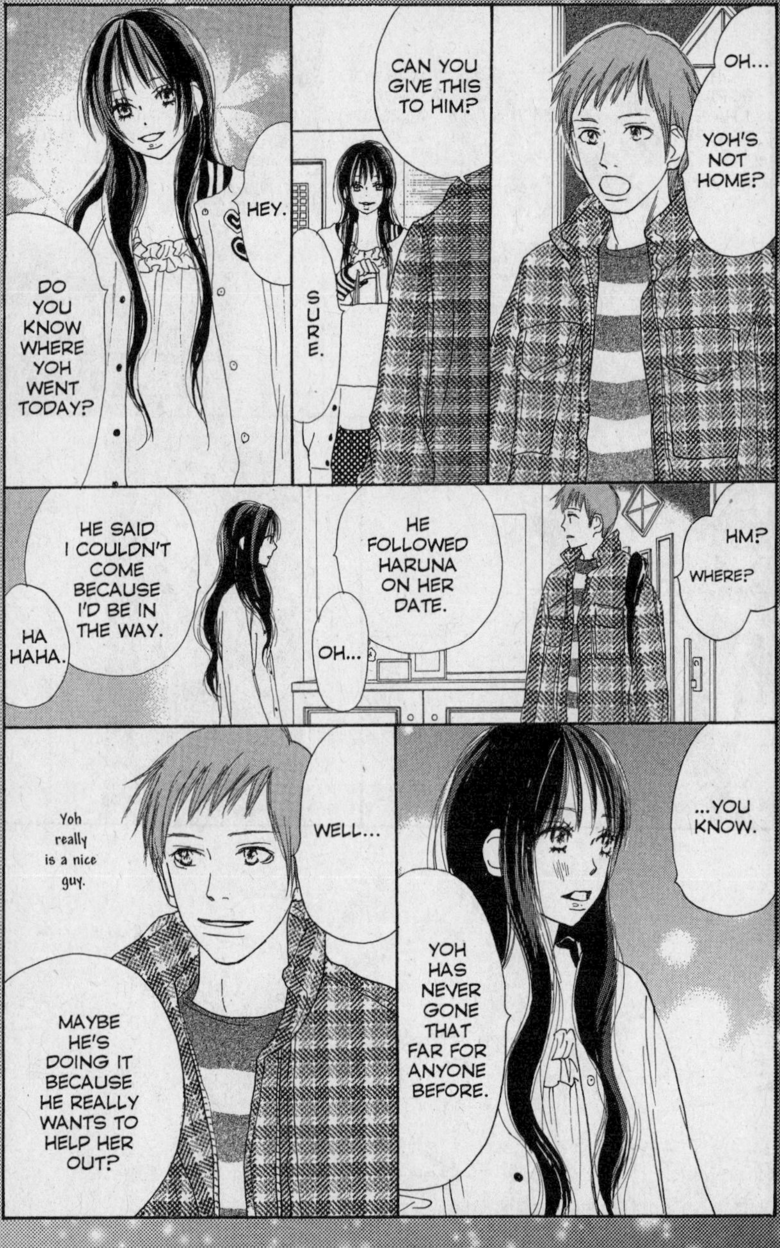
OH...
YOH'S NOT HOME?
CAN YOU GIVE THIS TO HIM?
SURE.
HEY.
DO YOU KNOW WHERE YOH WENT TODAY?
HM?
WHERE?
HE FOLLOWED HARUNA ON HER DATE.
OH...
HE SAID I COULDN'T COME BECAUSE I'D BE IN THE WAY.
HA HAHA.
...YOU KNOW.
YOH HAS NEVER GONE THAT FAR FOR ANYONE BEFORE.
WELL...
Yoh really is a nice guy.
MAYBE HE'S DOING IT BECAUSE HE REALLY WANTS TO HELP HER OUT?

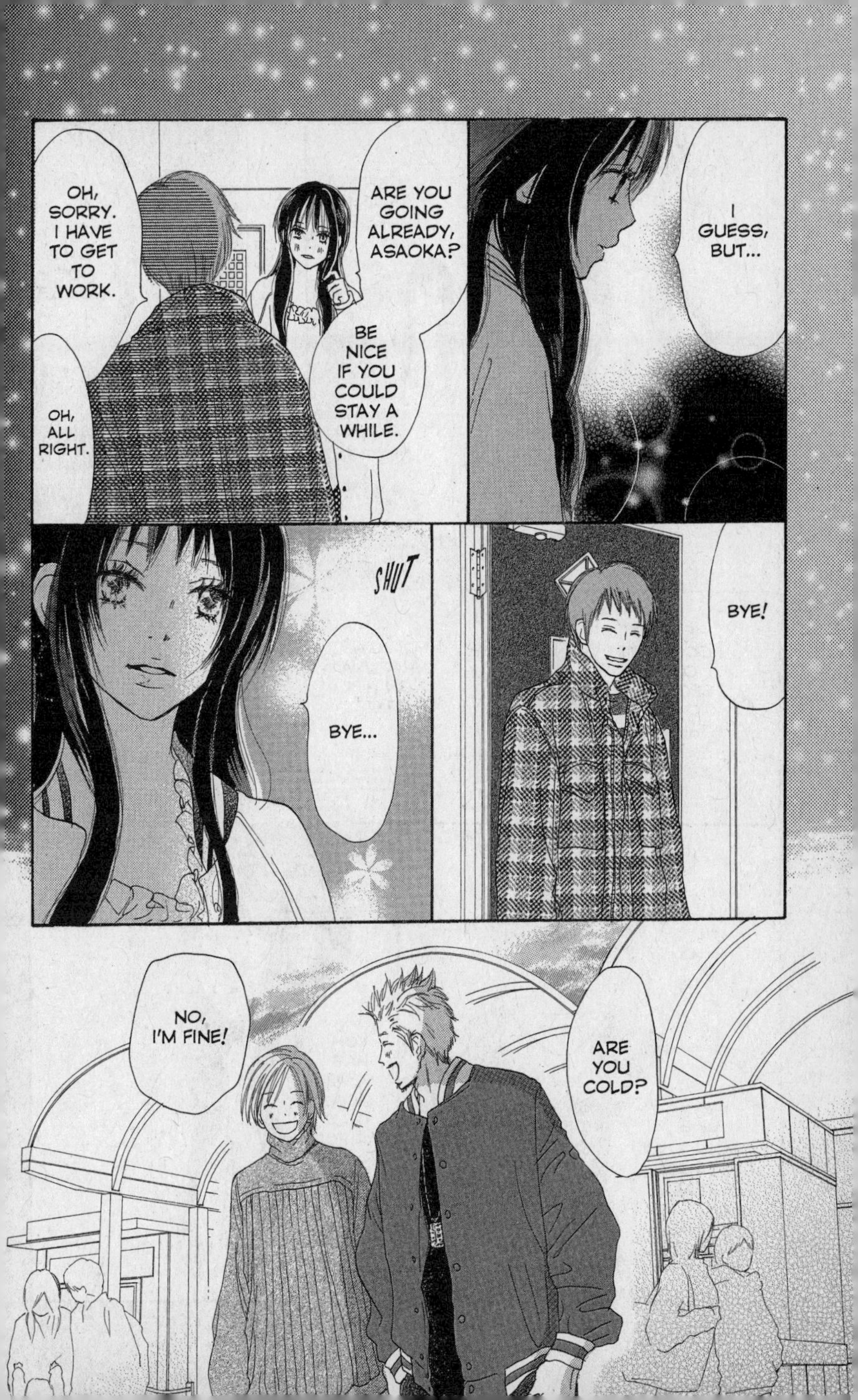
I GUESS, BUT...
ARE YOU GOING ALREADY, ASAOKA?
OH, SORRY. I HAVE TO GET TO WORK.
BE NICE IF YOU COULD STAY A WHILE.
OH, ALL RIGHT.
BYE!
SHUT
BYE...
ARE YOU COLD?
NO, I'M FINE!

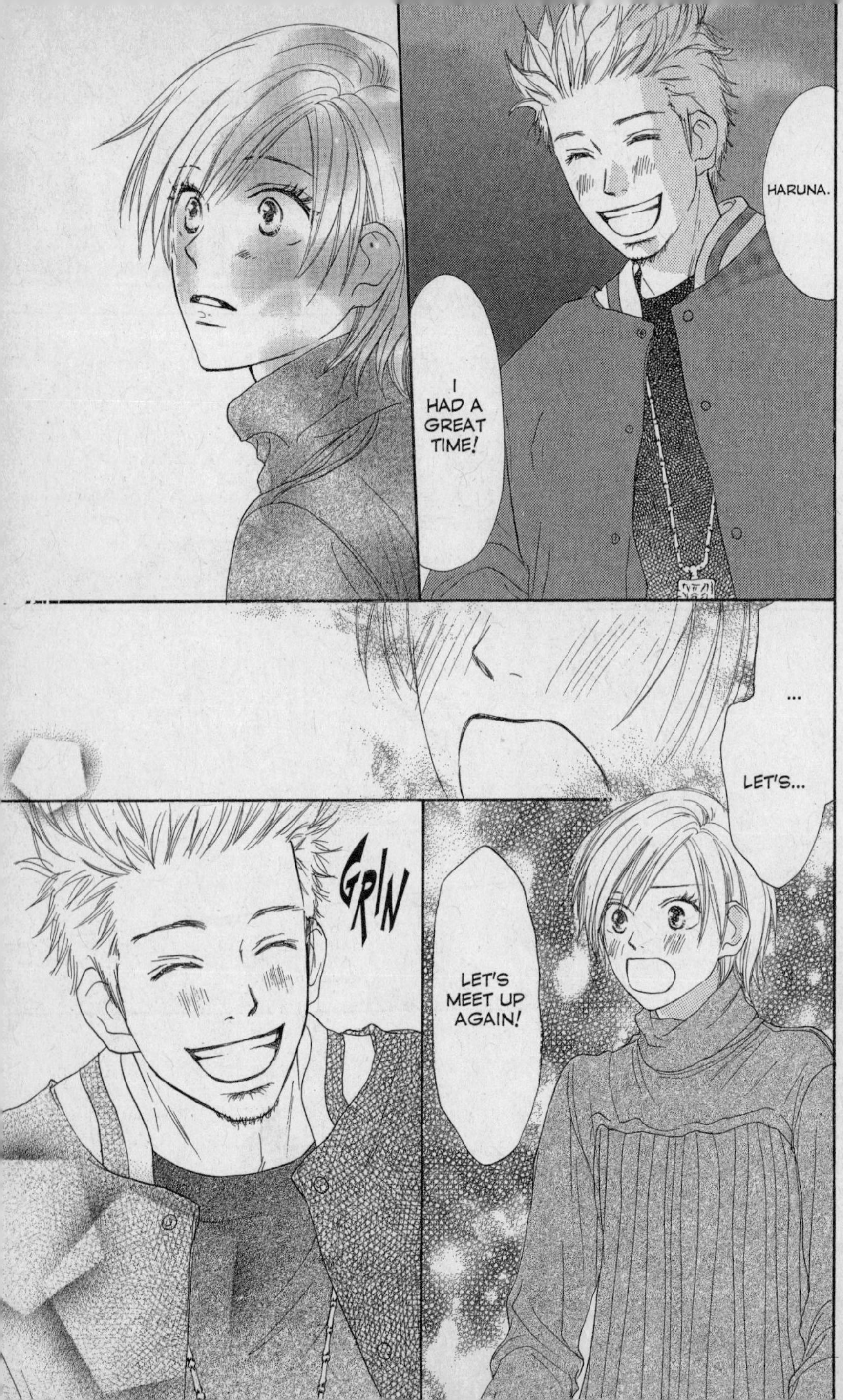
HARUNA.
I HAD A GREAT TIME!
...
LET'S...
LET'S MEET UP AGAIN!
GRIN

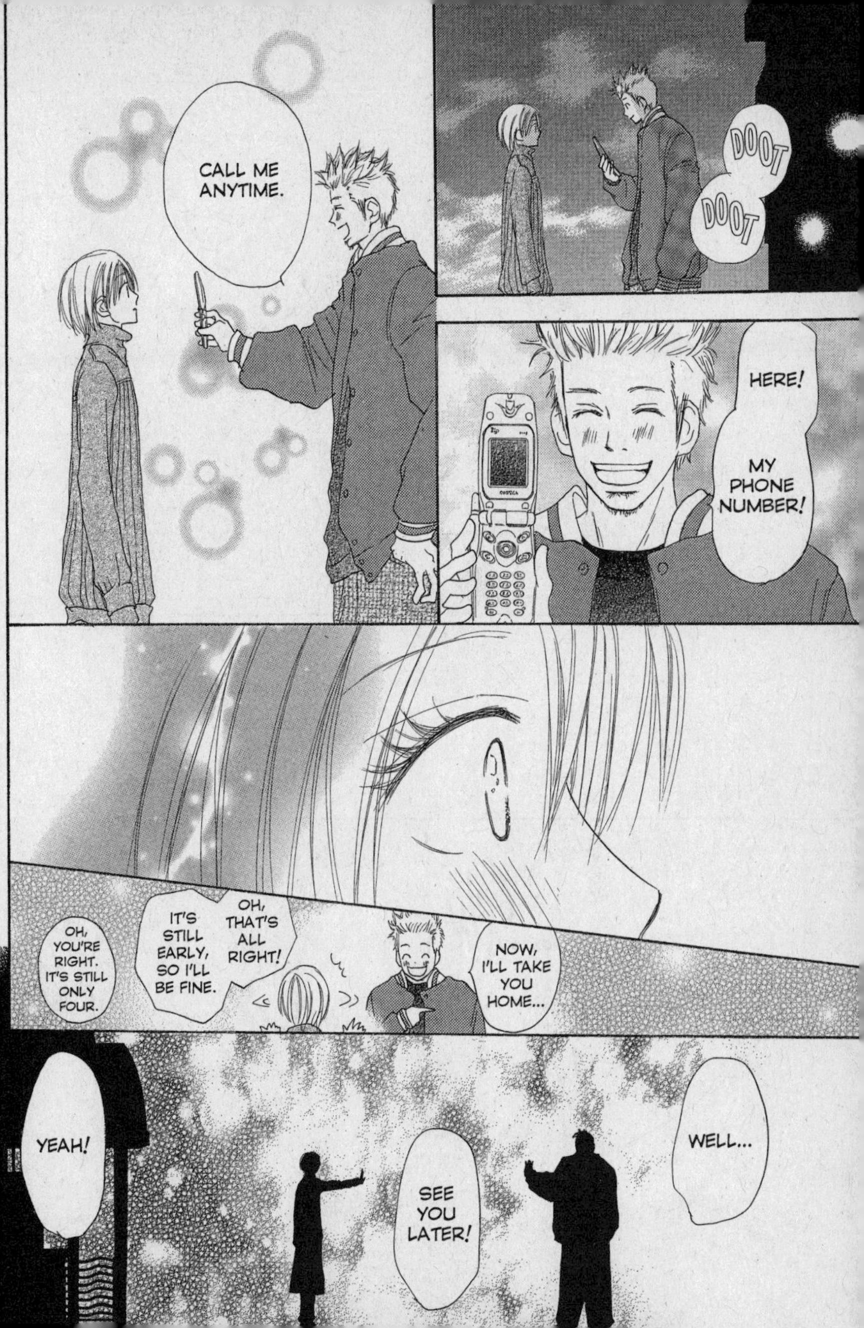
DOOT
DOOT
HERE!
MY PHONE NUMBER!
CALL ME ANYTIME.
NOW, I'LL TAKE YOU HOME...
OH, THAT'S ALL RIGHT!
IT'S STILL EARLY, SO I'LL BE FINE.
OH, YOU'RE RIGHT. IT'S STILL ONLY FOUR.
WELL...
SEE YOU LATER!
YEAH!

1

Hello. It's the terribly forgetful Kawahara here. I was watching T.V. today. They said that the reason for early forgetfulness was bad kidneys and that I should drink sword bean tea. I'll go get some tomorrow. What if it makes me come up with some great ideas for manga? Something that would make me really concentrate every day. Or allow me to finish something in one day! I would drink anything... I would eat anything...

This is unrelated, but when I was small, I was really picky. Spinach was the only vegetable I'd really eat. I had lots of likes and dislikes, but I really loved to eat spinach and drink milk.

The milk I got for lunch was never enough.

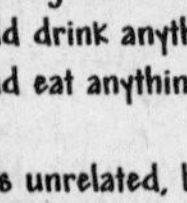

At home, they'll always give me milk instead of water unless I say something.

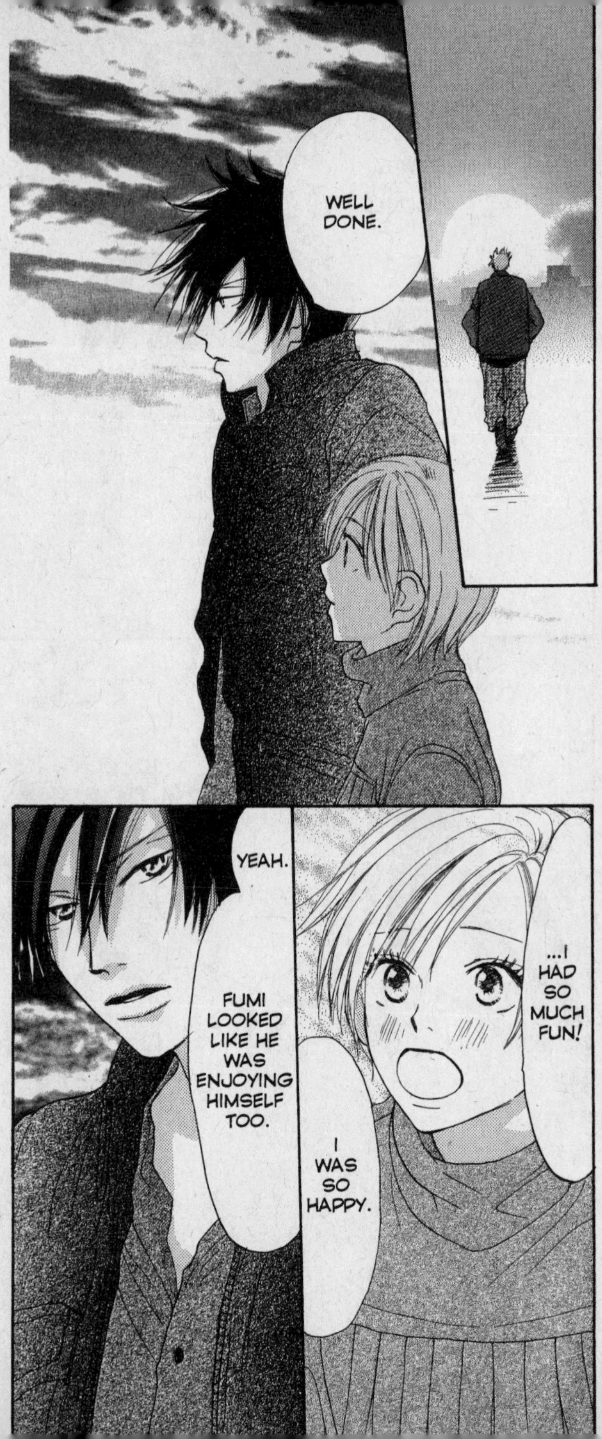
WELL DONE.
...I HAD SO MUCH FUN!
I WAS SO HAPPY.
FUMI LOOKED LIKE HE WAS ENJOYING HIMSELF TOO.
YEAH.

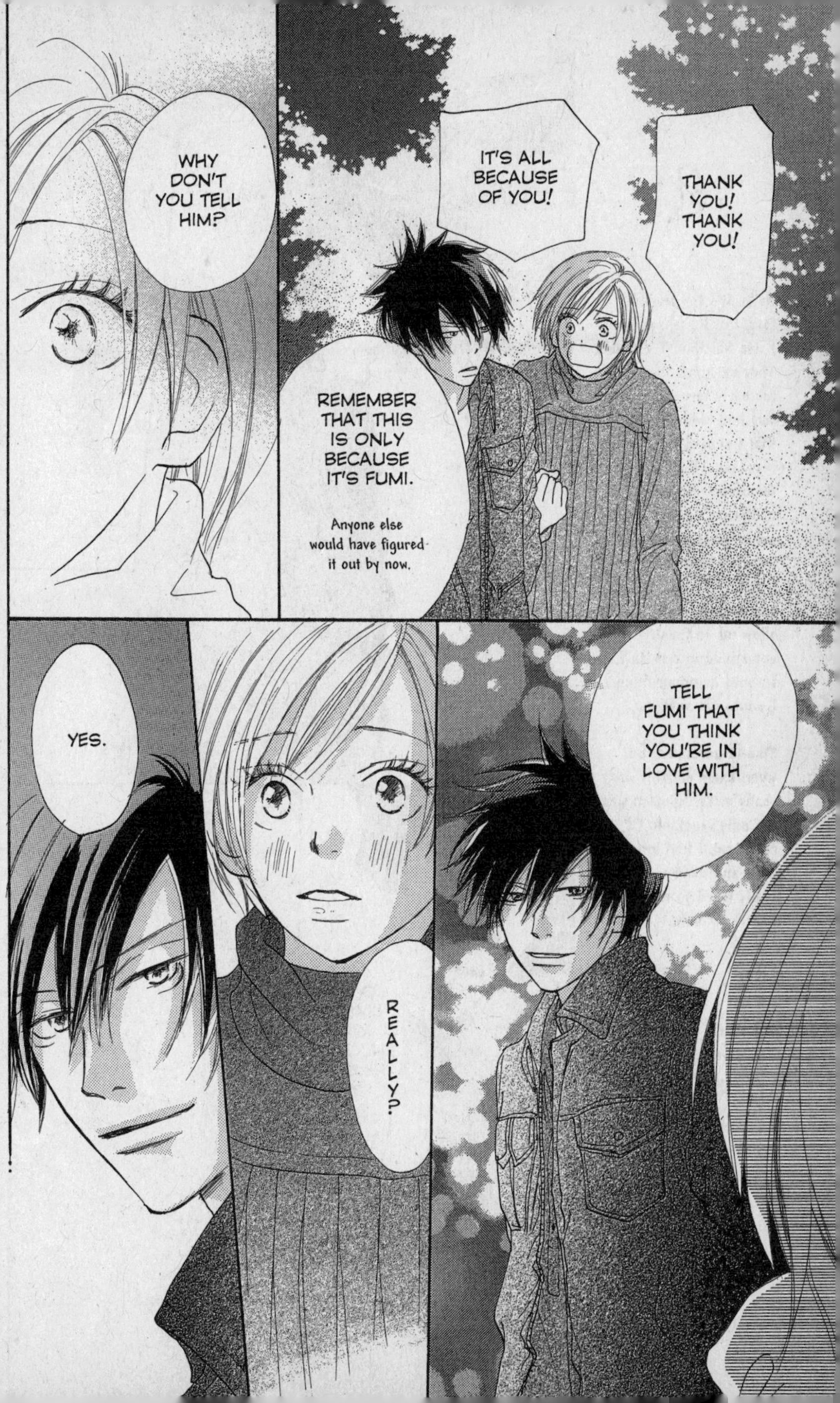
THANK YOU! THANK YOU!
IT'S ALL BECAUSE OF YOU!
REMEMBER THAT THIS IS ONLY BECAUSE IT'S FUMI.
Anyone else would have figured it out by now.
WHY DON'T YOU TELL HIM?
TELL FUMI THAT YOU THINK YOU'RE IN LOVE WITH HIM.
REALLY?
YES.

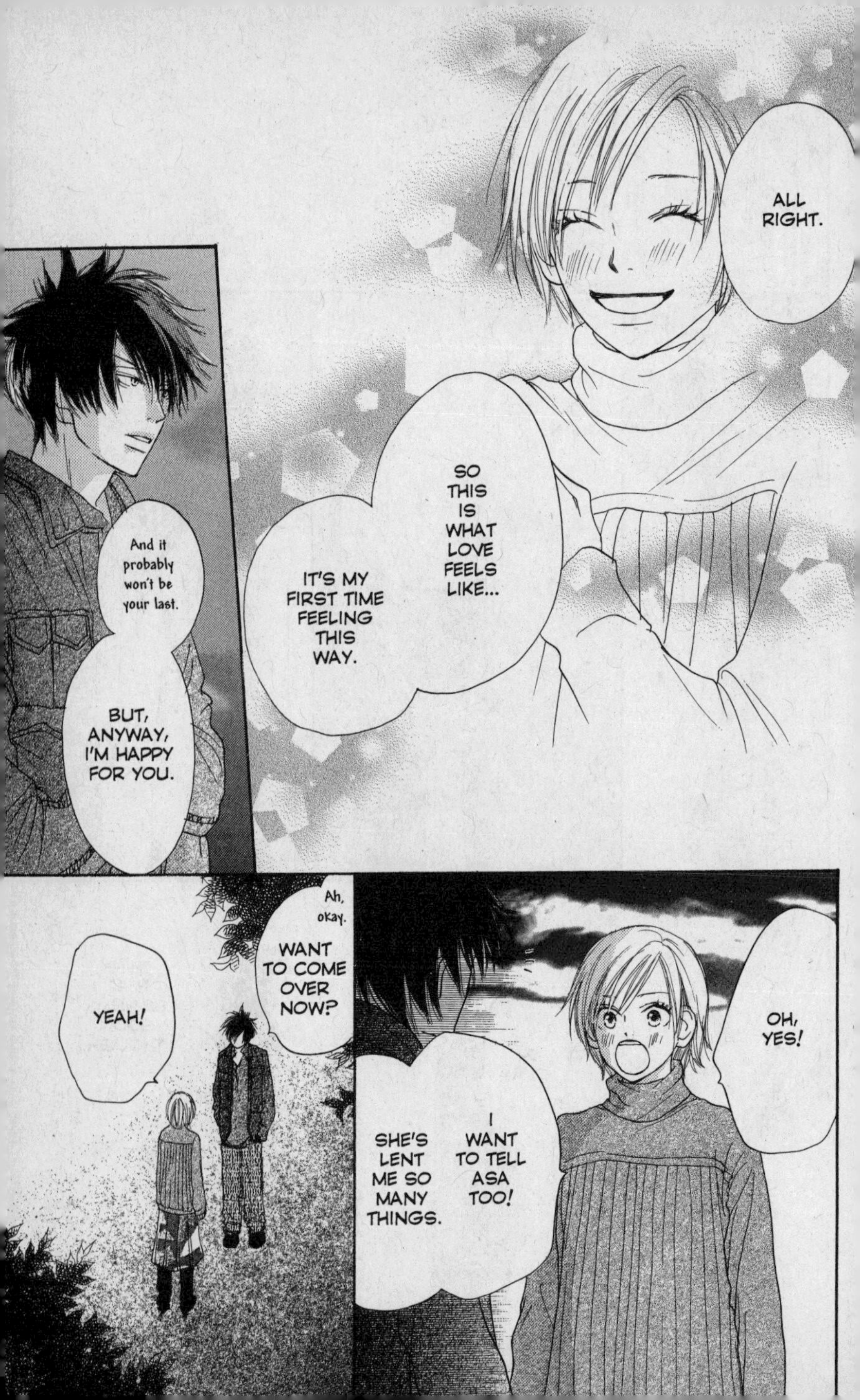
ALL RIGHT.
SO THIS IS WHAT LOVE FEELS LIKE...
IT'S MY FIRST TIME FEELING THIS WAY.
And it probably won't be your last.
BUT, ANYWAY, I'M HAPPY FOR YOU.
OH, YES!
I WANT TO TELL ASA TOO!
SHE'S LENT ME SO MANY THINGS.
Ah, okay.
WANT TO COME OVER NOW?
YEAH!

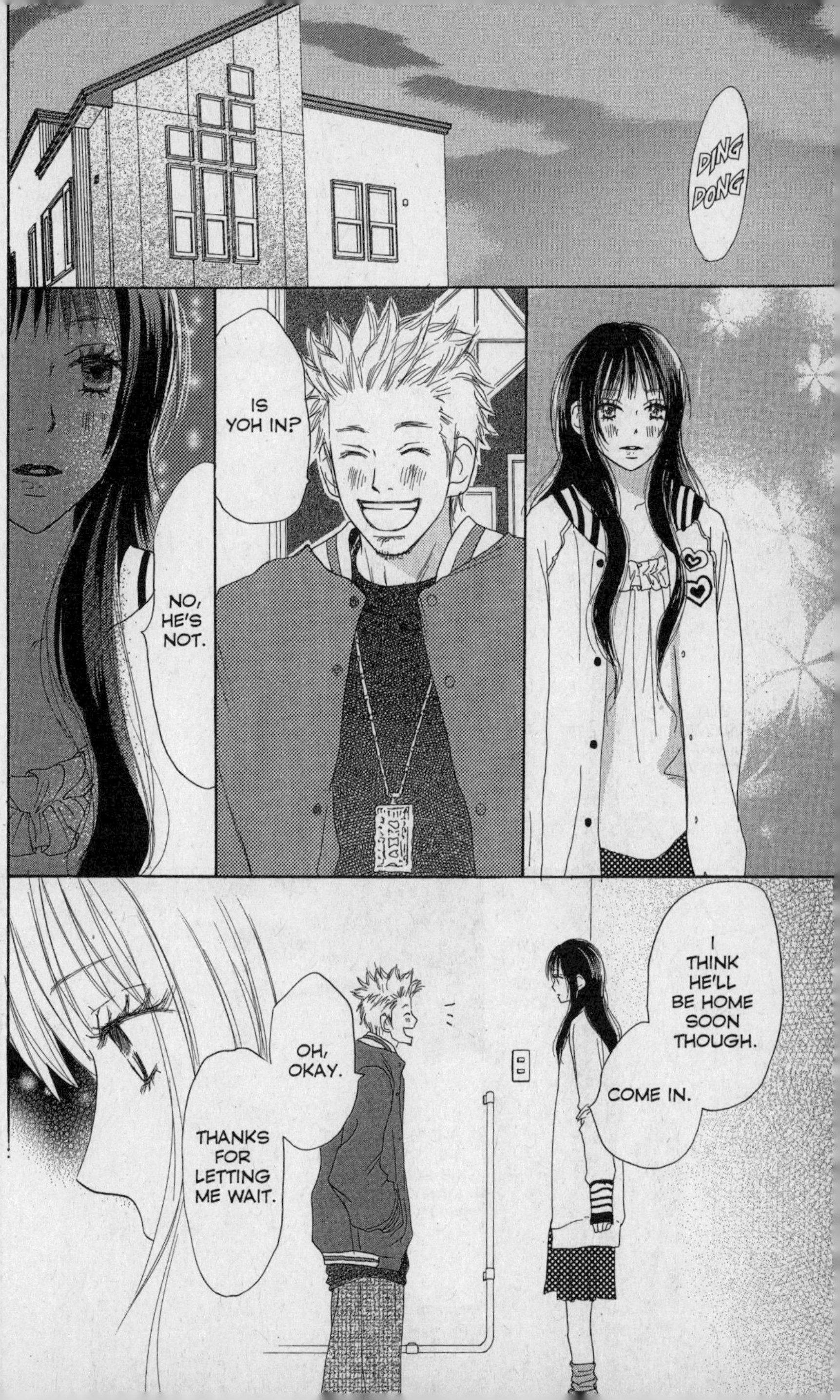
DING DONG
IS YOH IN?
NO, HE'S NOT.
I THINK HE'LL BE HOME SOON THOUGH.
COME IN.
OH, OKAY.
THANKS FOR LETTING ME WAIT.

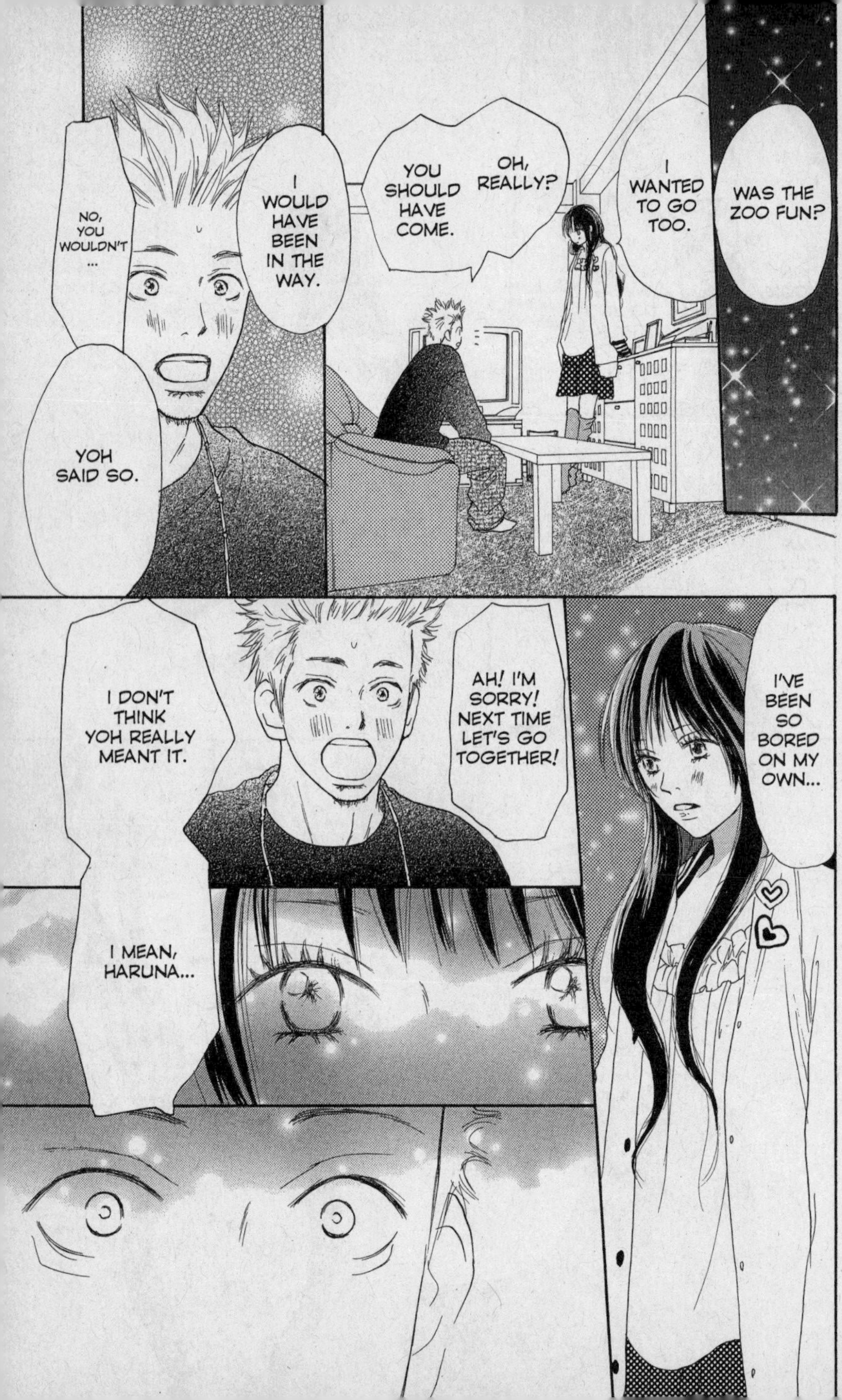

WAS THE ZOO FUN?
I WANTED TO GO TOO.
OH, REALLY?
YOU SHOULD HAVE COME.
I WOULD HAVE BEEN IN THE WAY.
NO, YOU WOULDN'T ...
YOH SAID SO.
I'VE BEEN SO BORED ON MY OWN...
AH! I'M SORRY! NEXT TIME LET'S GO TOGETHER!
I DON'T THINK YOH REALLY MEANT IT.
I MEAN, HARUNA...

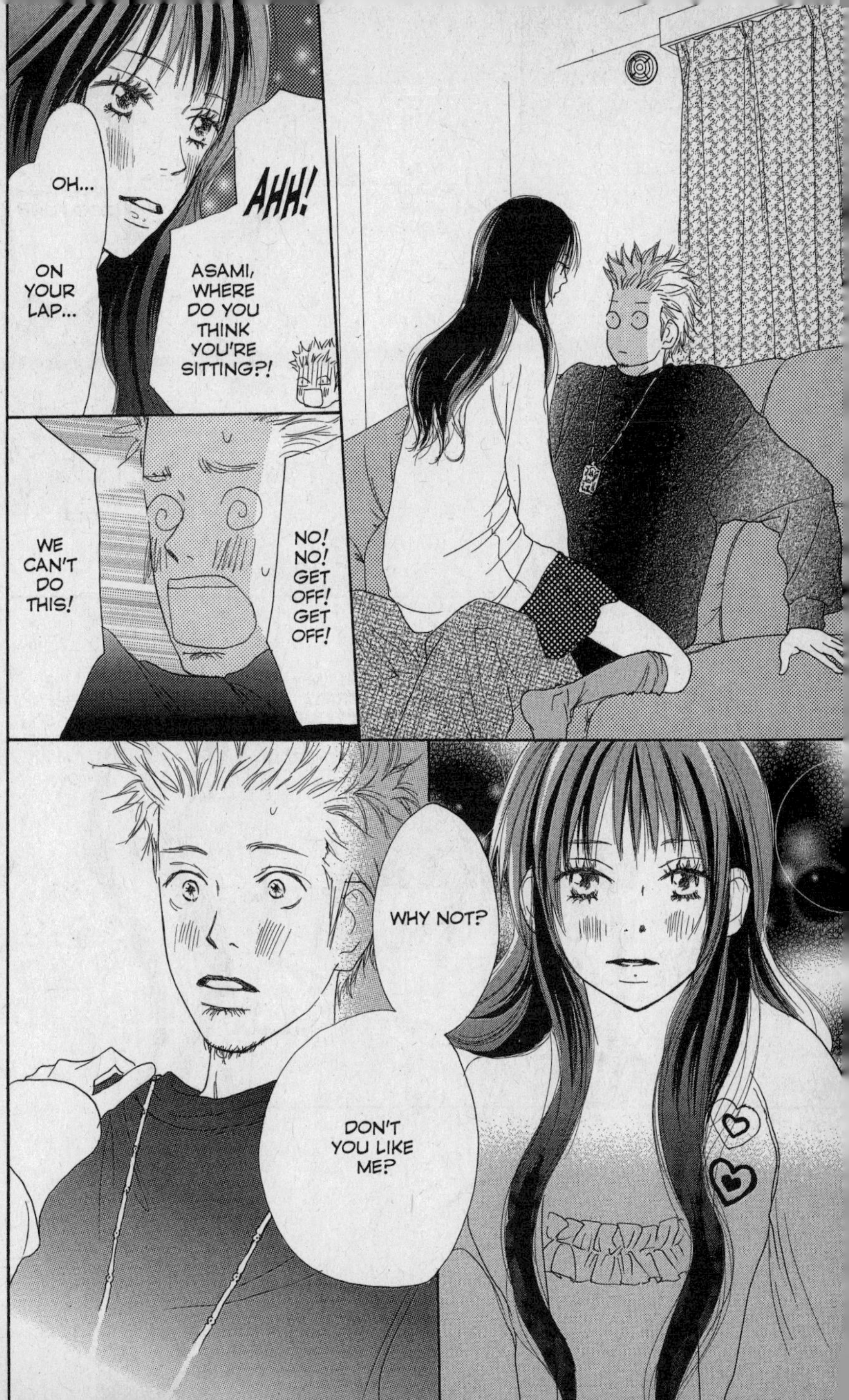
AHH!
ASAMI, WHERE DO YOU THINK YOU'RE SITTING?!
OH...
ON YOUR LAP...
NO! NO! GET OFF! GET OFF!
WE CAN'T DO THIS!
WHY NOT?
DON'T YOU LIKE ME?

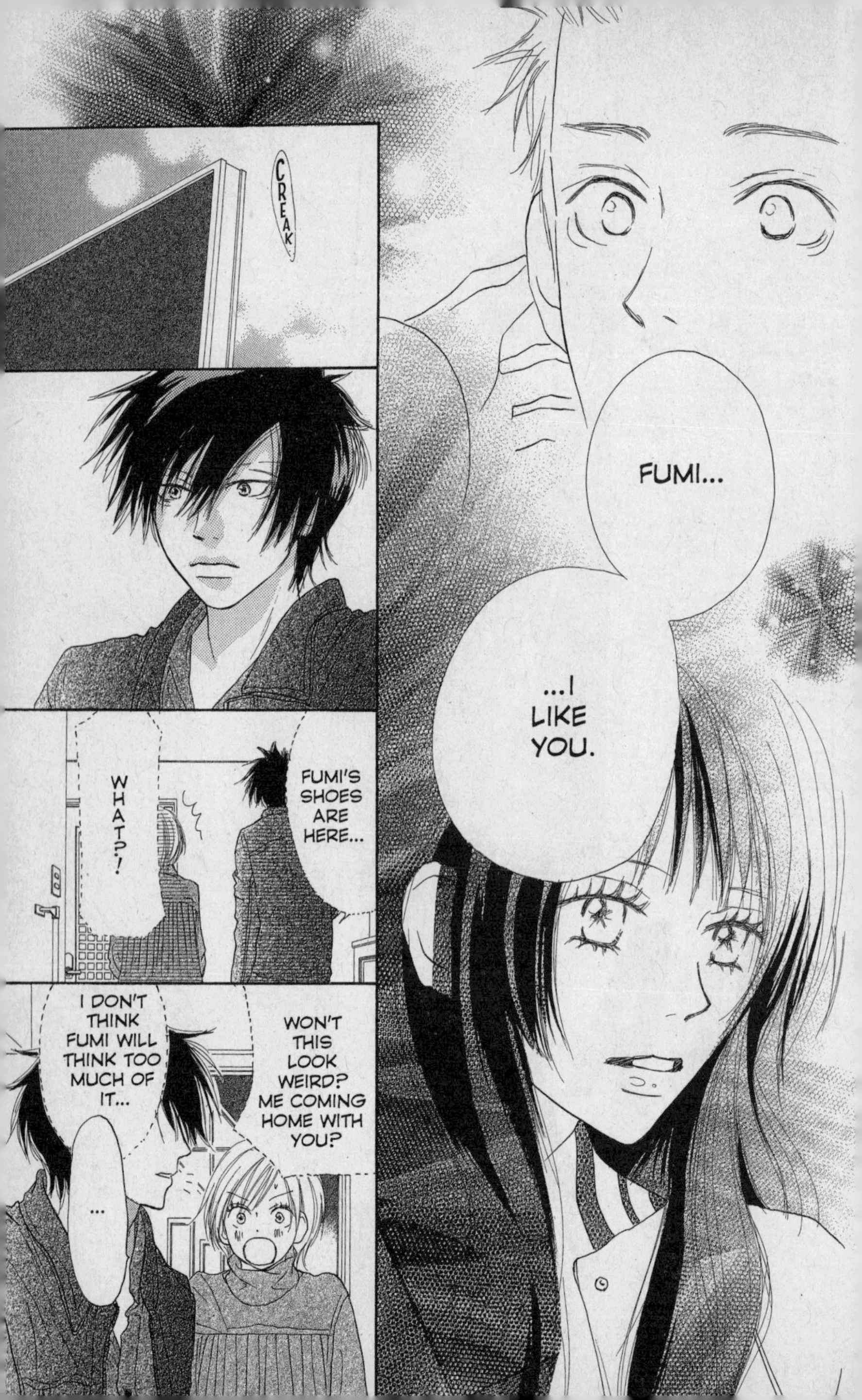
FUMI...
...I LIKE YOU.
CREAK
FUMI'S SHOES ARE HERE...
WHAT?!
WON'T THIS LOOK WEIRD? ME COMING HOME WITH YOU?
I DON'T THINK FUMI WILL THINK TOO MUCH OF IT...
...

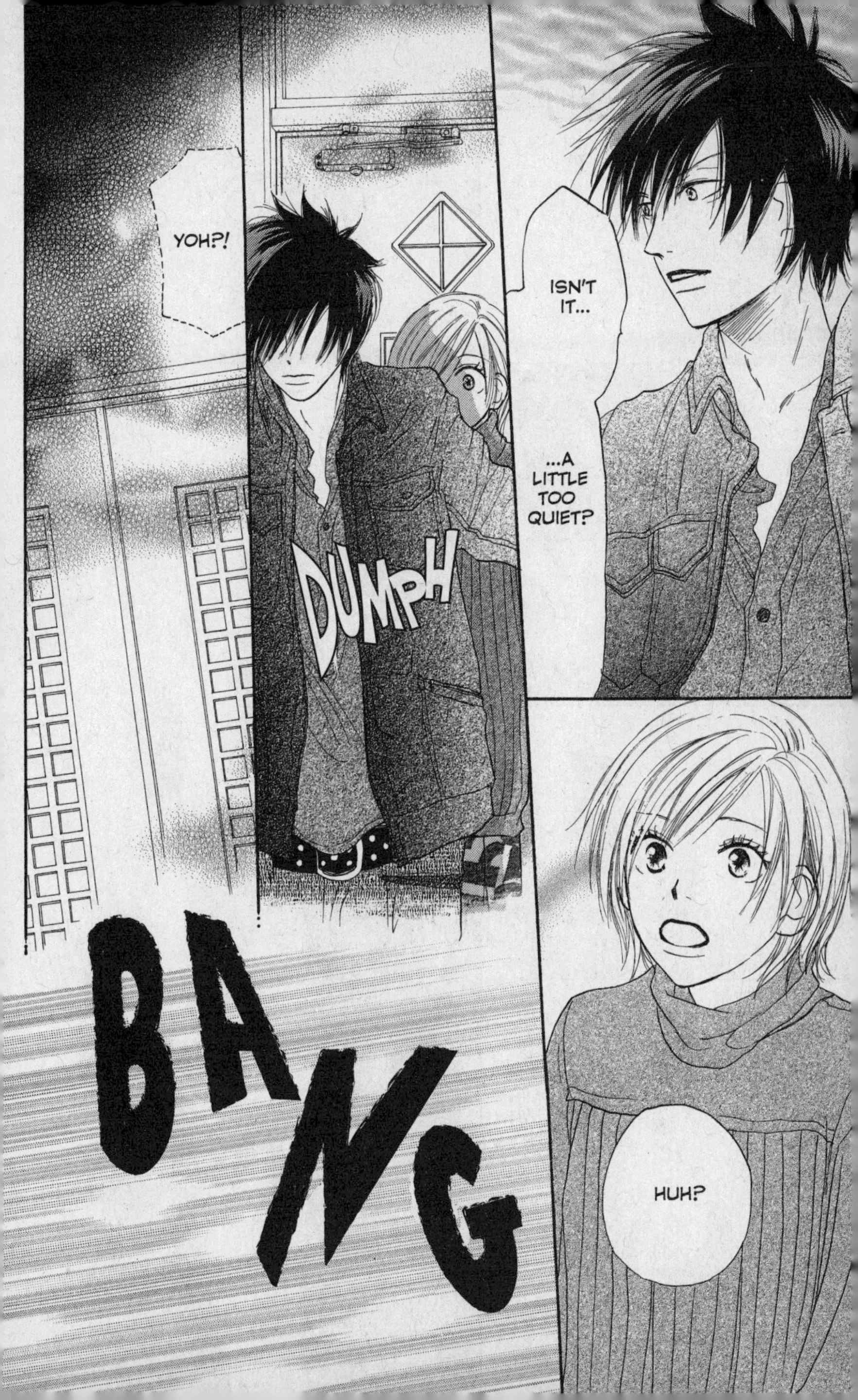
ISN'T IT...
...A LITTLE TOO QUIET?
HUH?
BANG
DUMPH
YOH?!

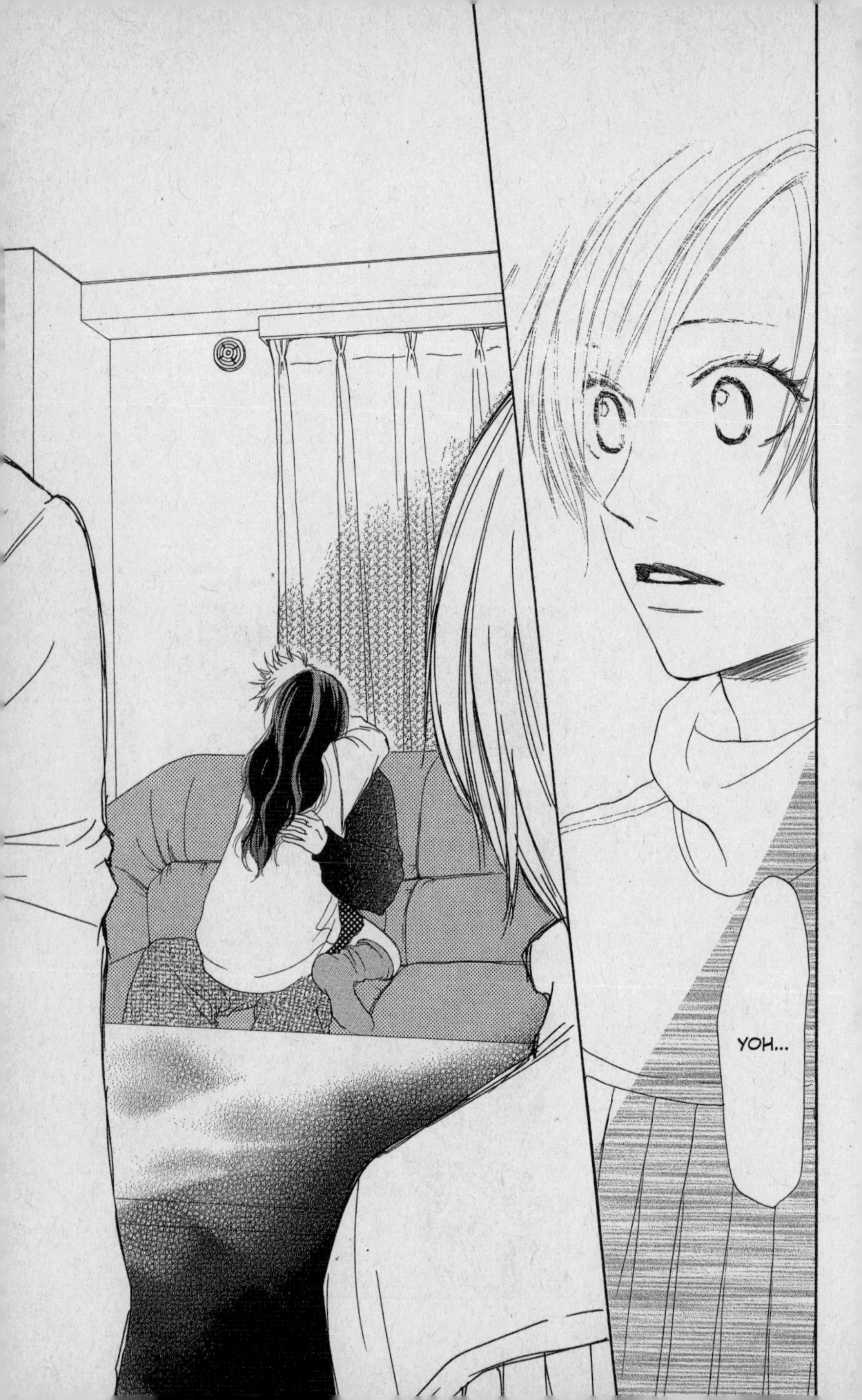
YOH...

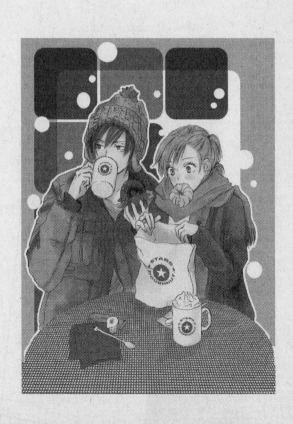

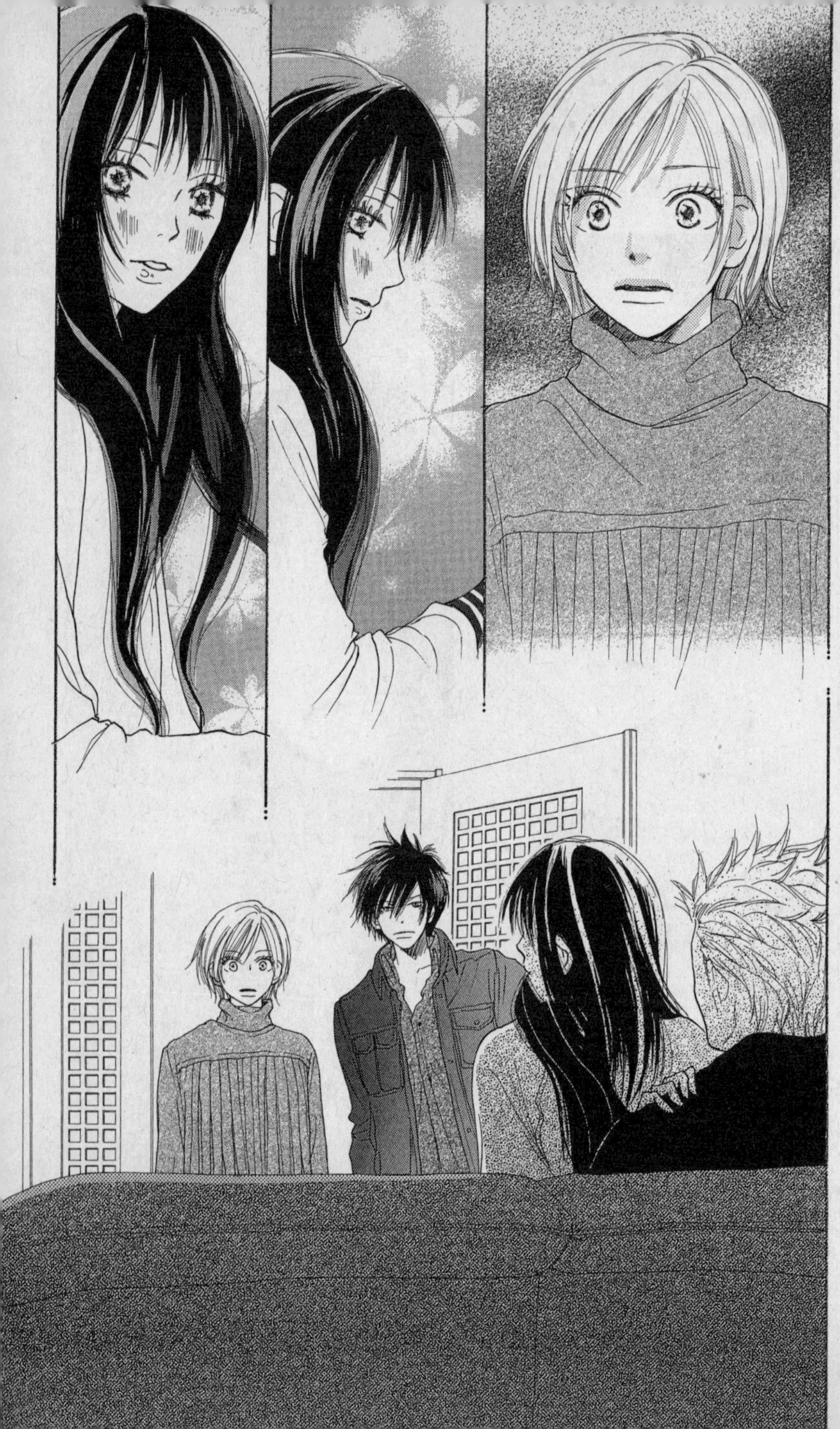

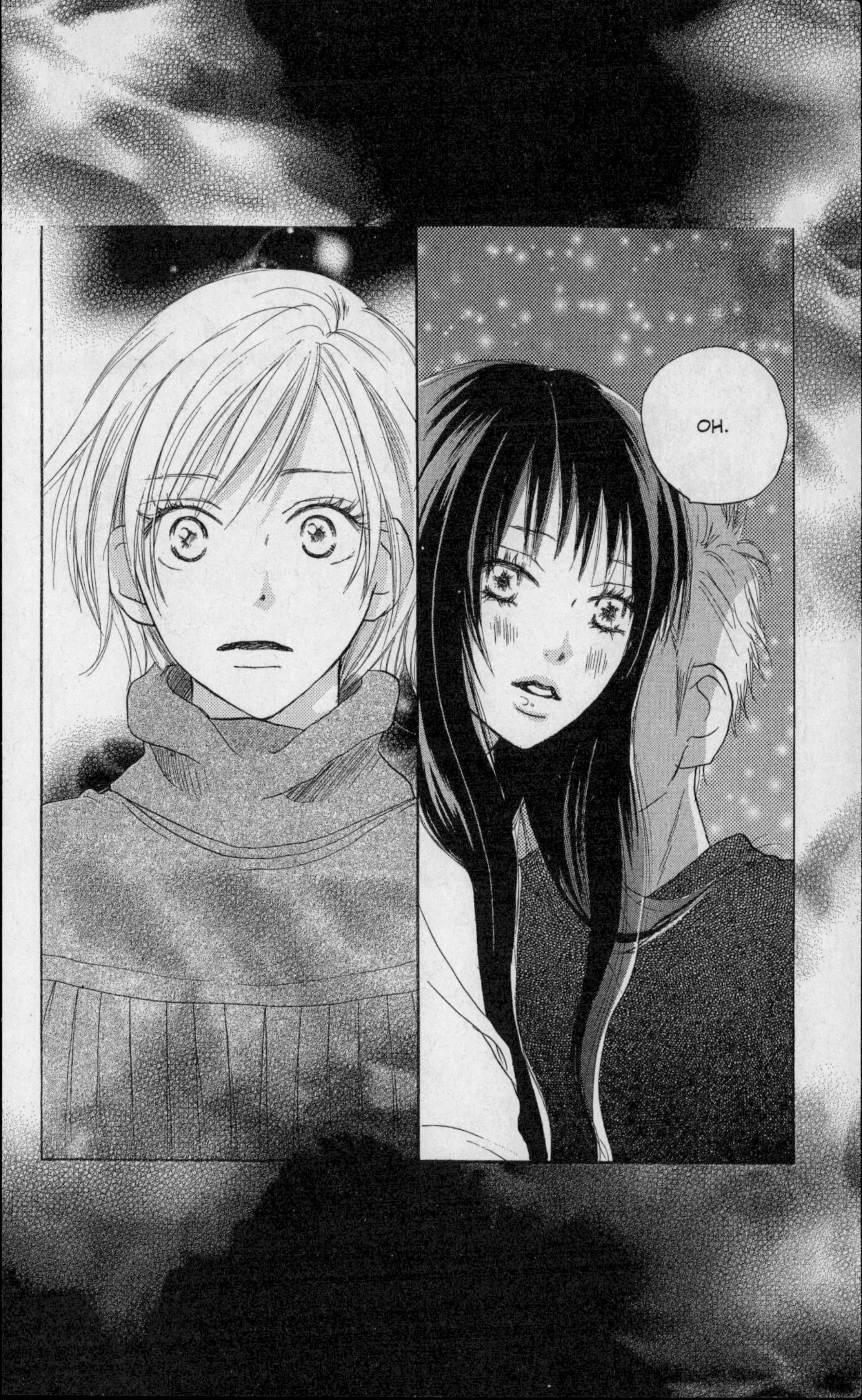
OH.

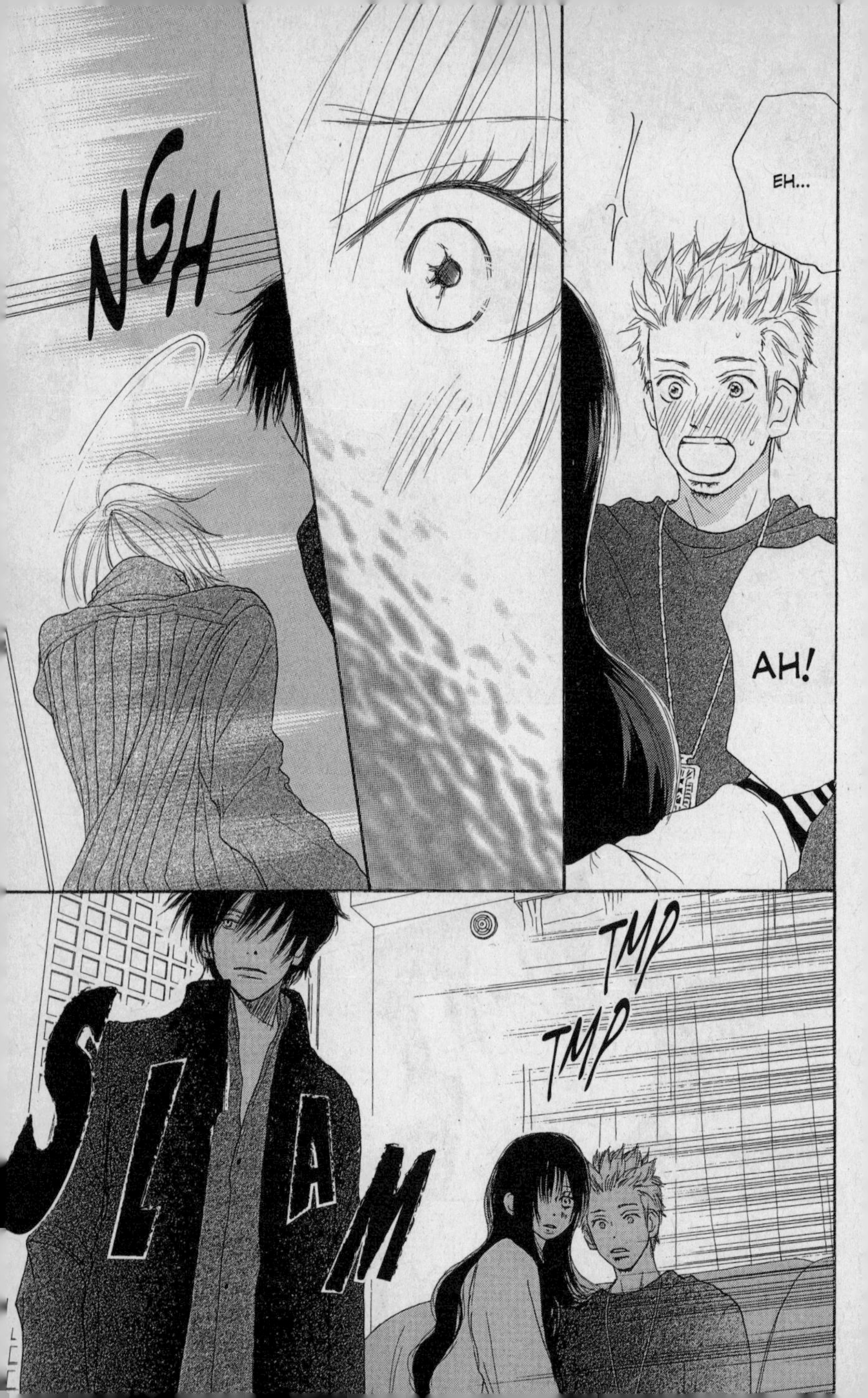
EH...
AH!
NGH
TMP
TMP
SLAM

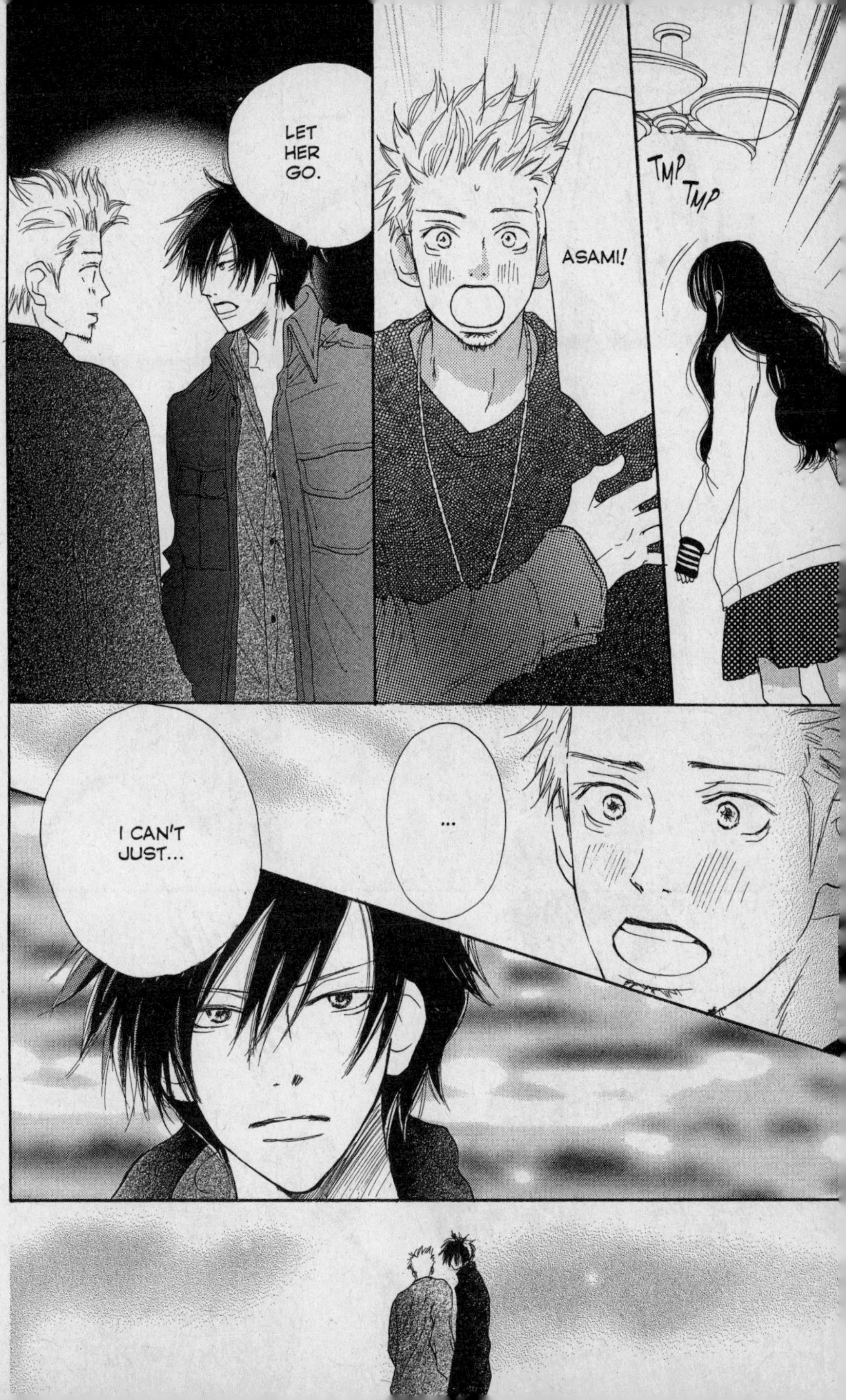
TMP TMP
ASAMI!
LET HER GO.
...
I CAN'T JUST...

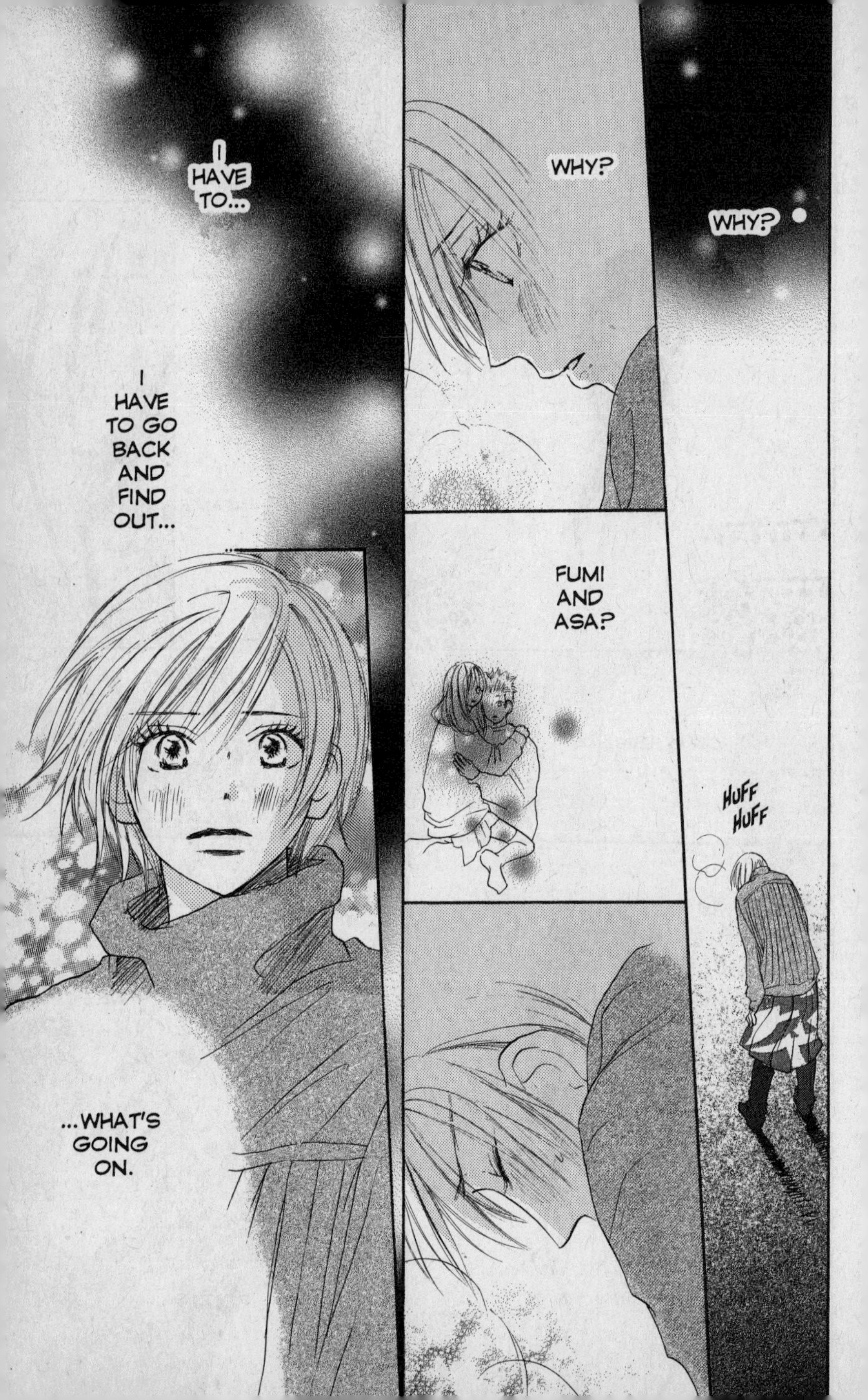
WHY?
HUFF HUFF
WHY?
FUMI AND ASA?
I HAVE TO...
I HAVE TO GO BACK AND FIND OUT...
...WHAT'S GOING ON.

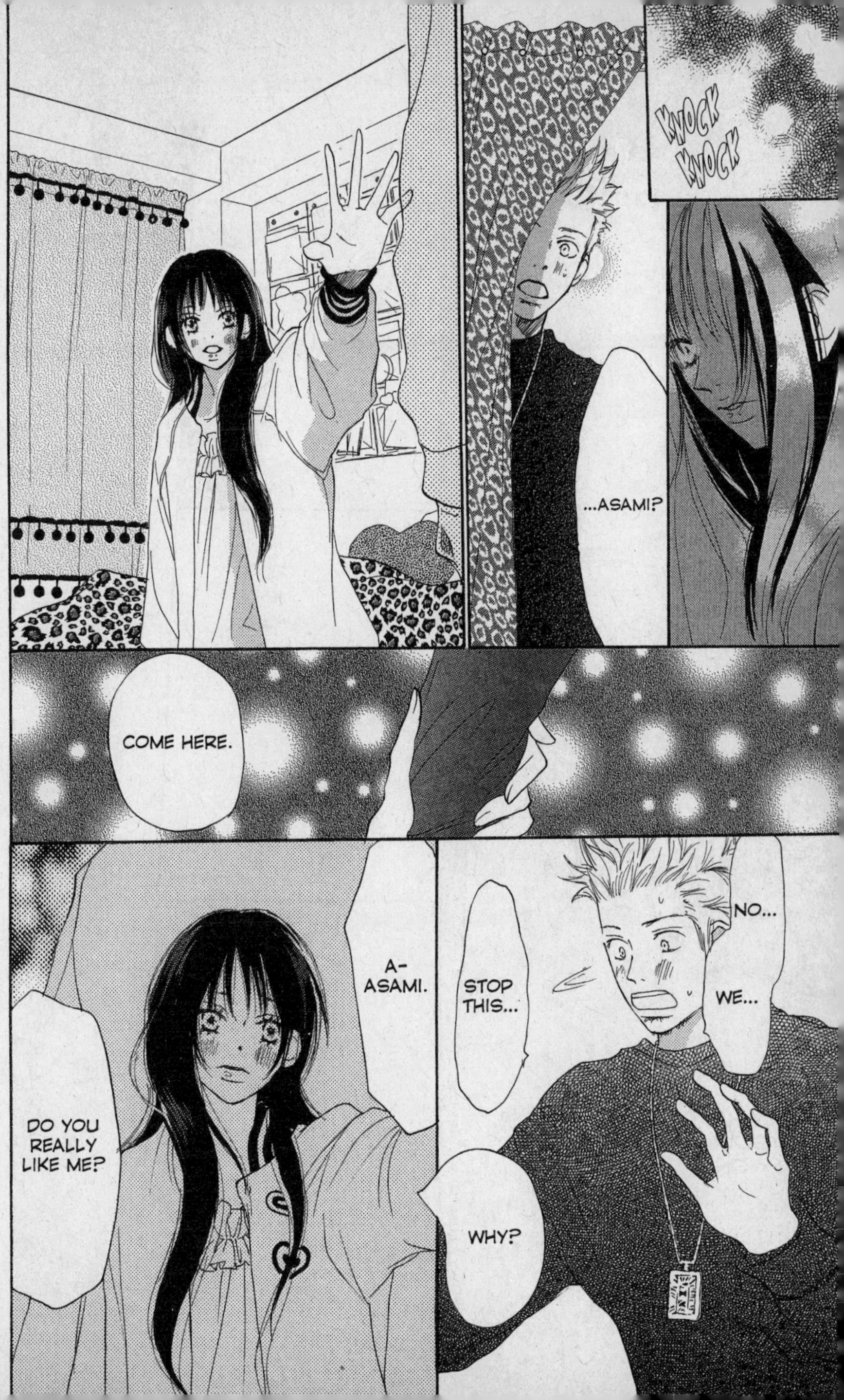
KNOCK KNOCK
...ASAMI?
COME HERE.
NO...
WE...
STOP THIS...
WHY?
A-ASAMI.
DO YOU REALLY LIKE ME?

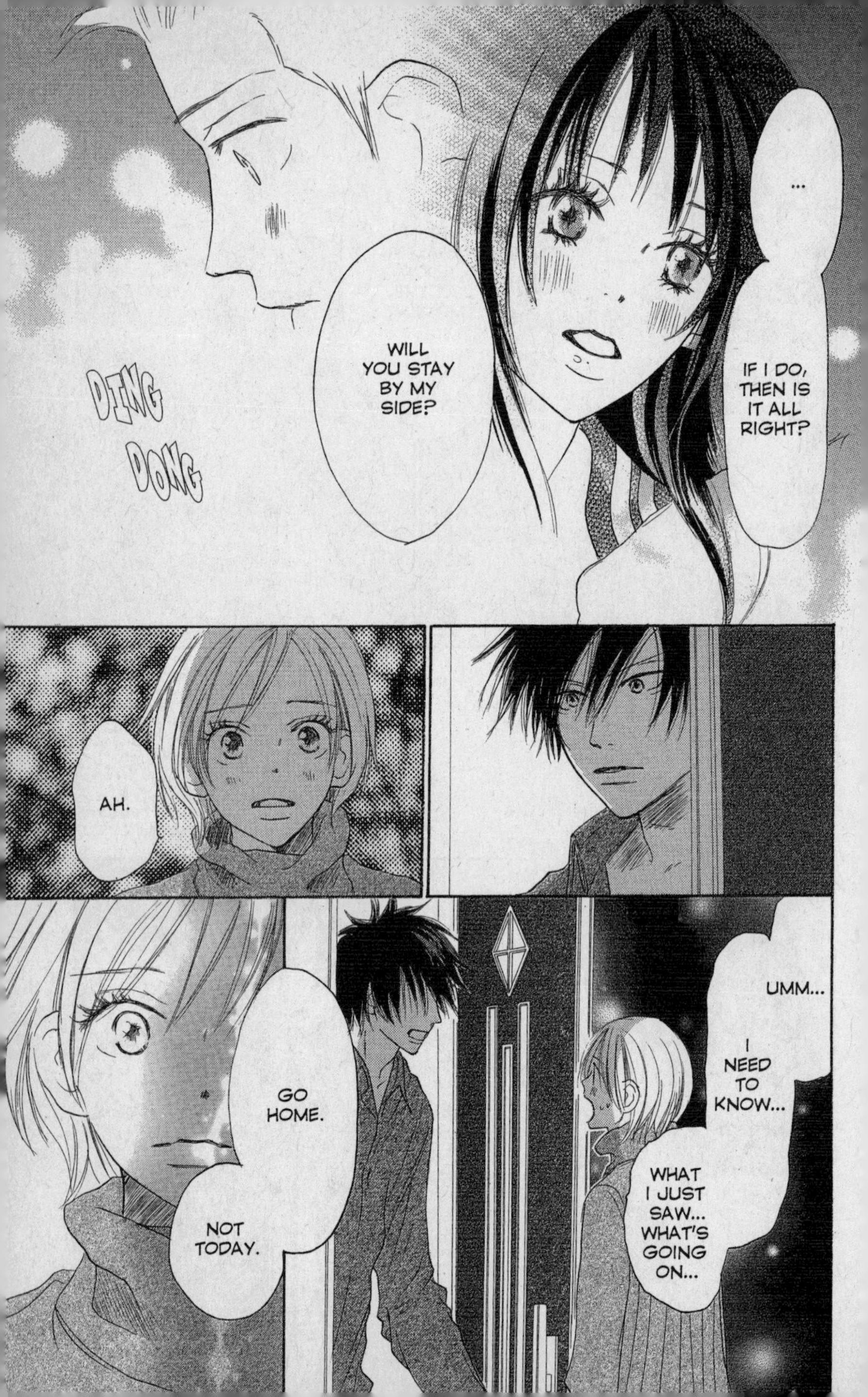
...
IF I DO, THEN IS IT ALL RIGHT?
WILL YOU STAY BY MY SIDE?
DING DONG
AH.
UMM...
I NEED TO KNOW...
WHAT I JUST SAW... WHAT'S GOING ON...
GO HOME.
NOT TODAY.

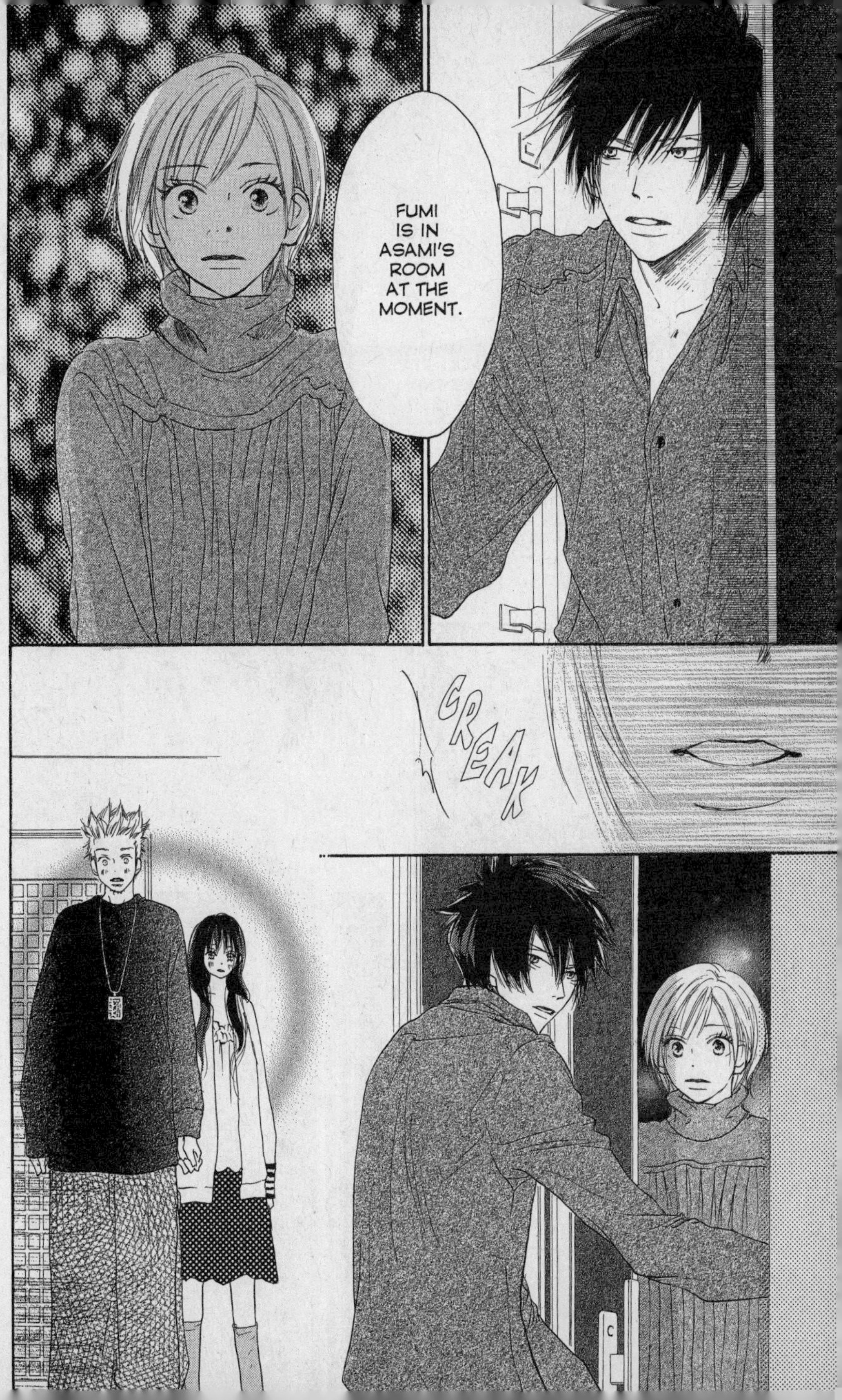
FUMI IS IN ASAMI'S ROOM AT THE MOMENT.
CREAK

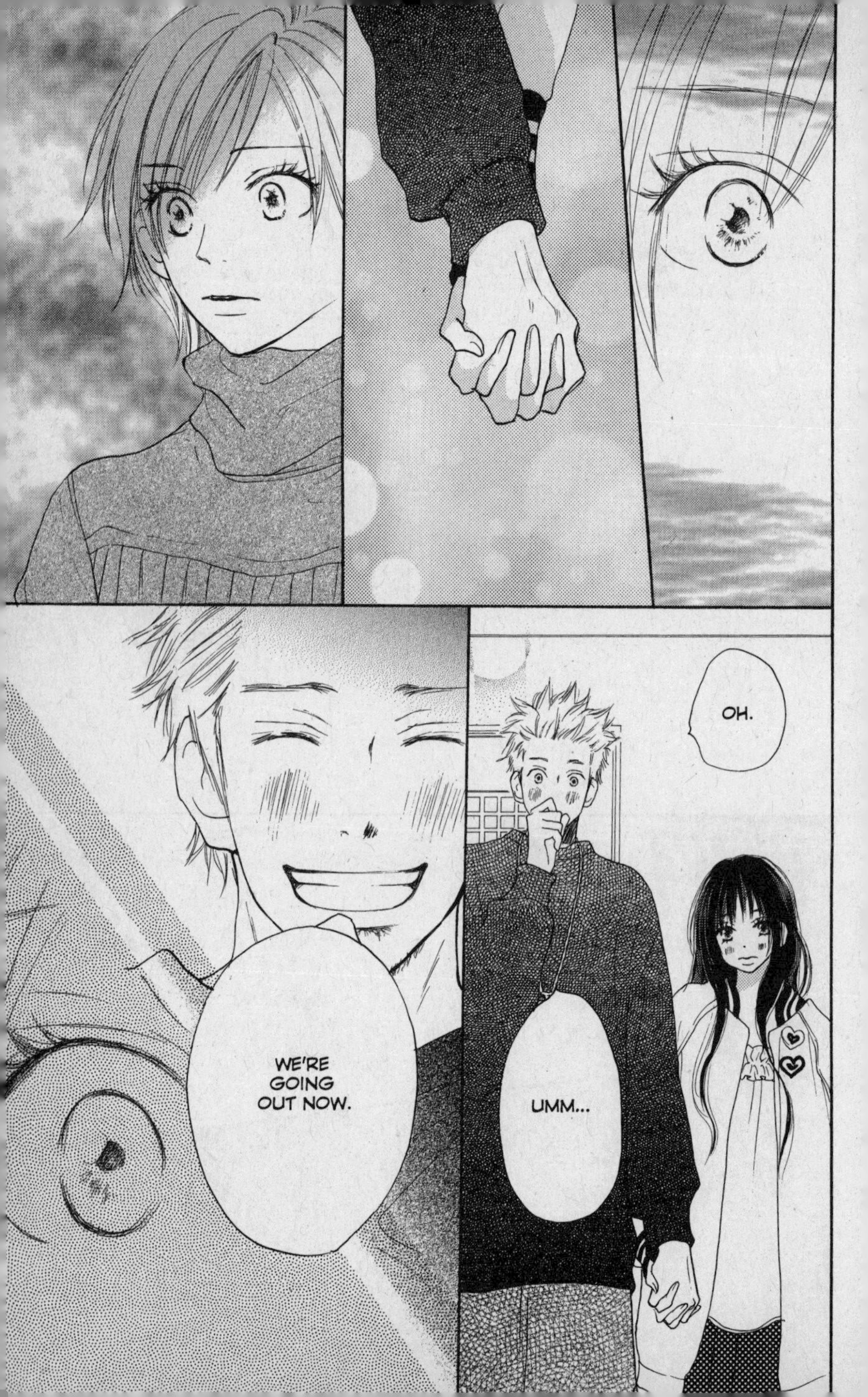
OH.
UMM...
WE'RE GOING OUT NOW.

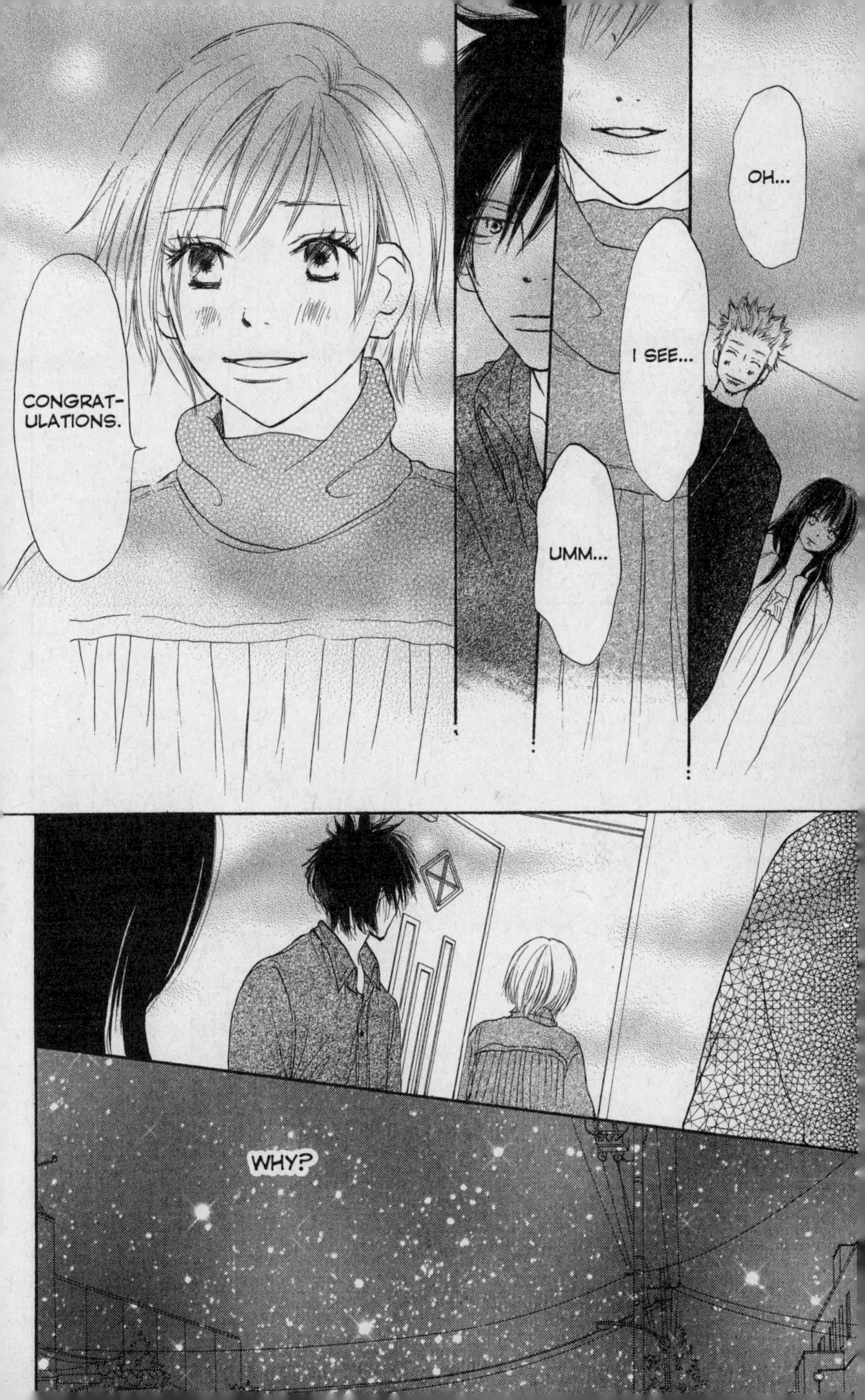

OH...
I SEE...
UMM...
CONGRAT-ULATIONS.
WHY?

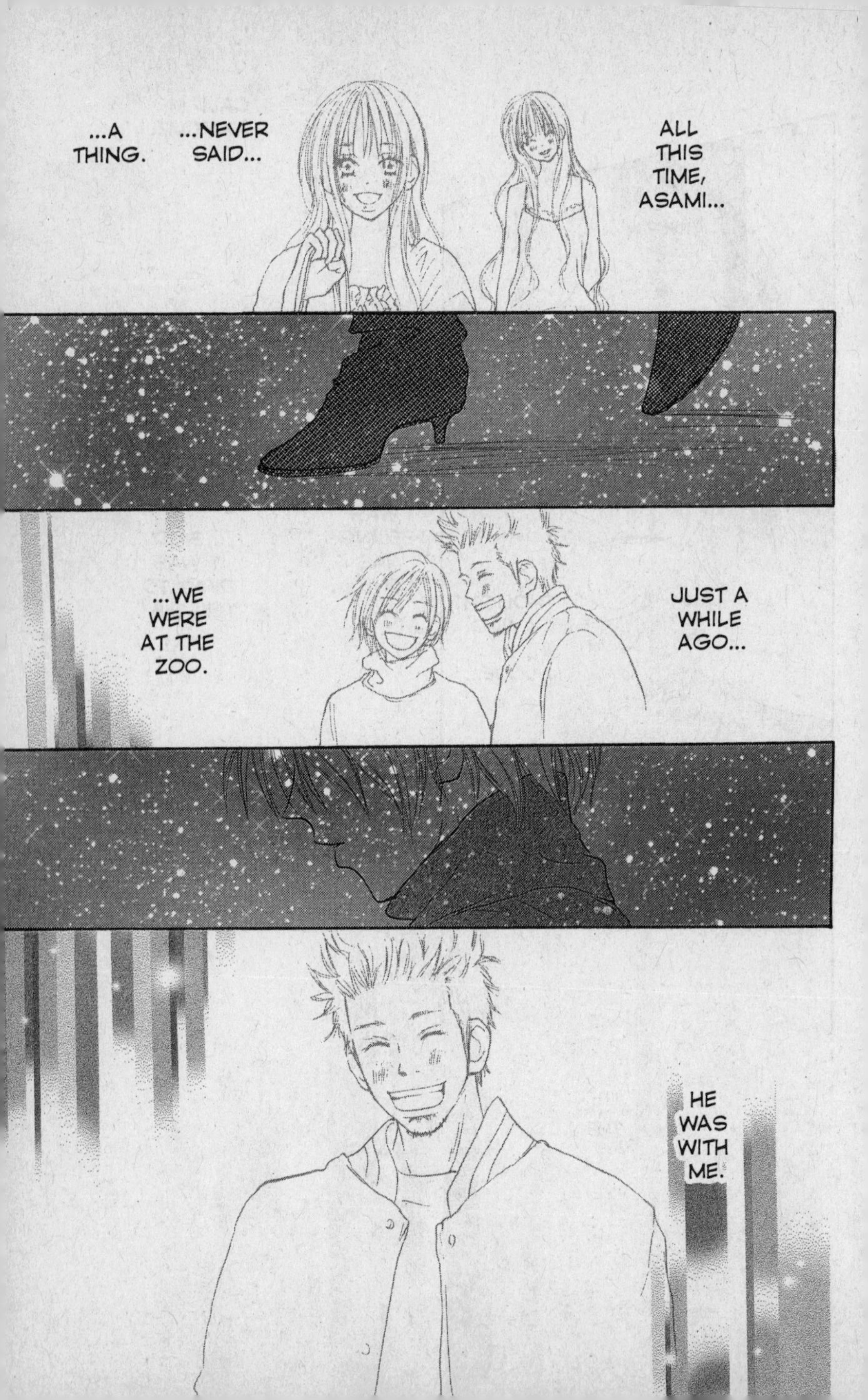
ALL THIS TIME, ASAMI...
...NEVER SAID...
...A THING.
JUST A WHILE AGO...
...WE WERE AT THE ZOO.
HE WAS WITH ME.

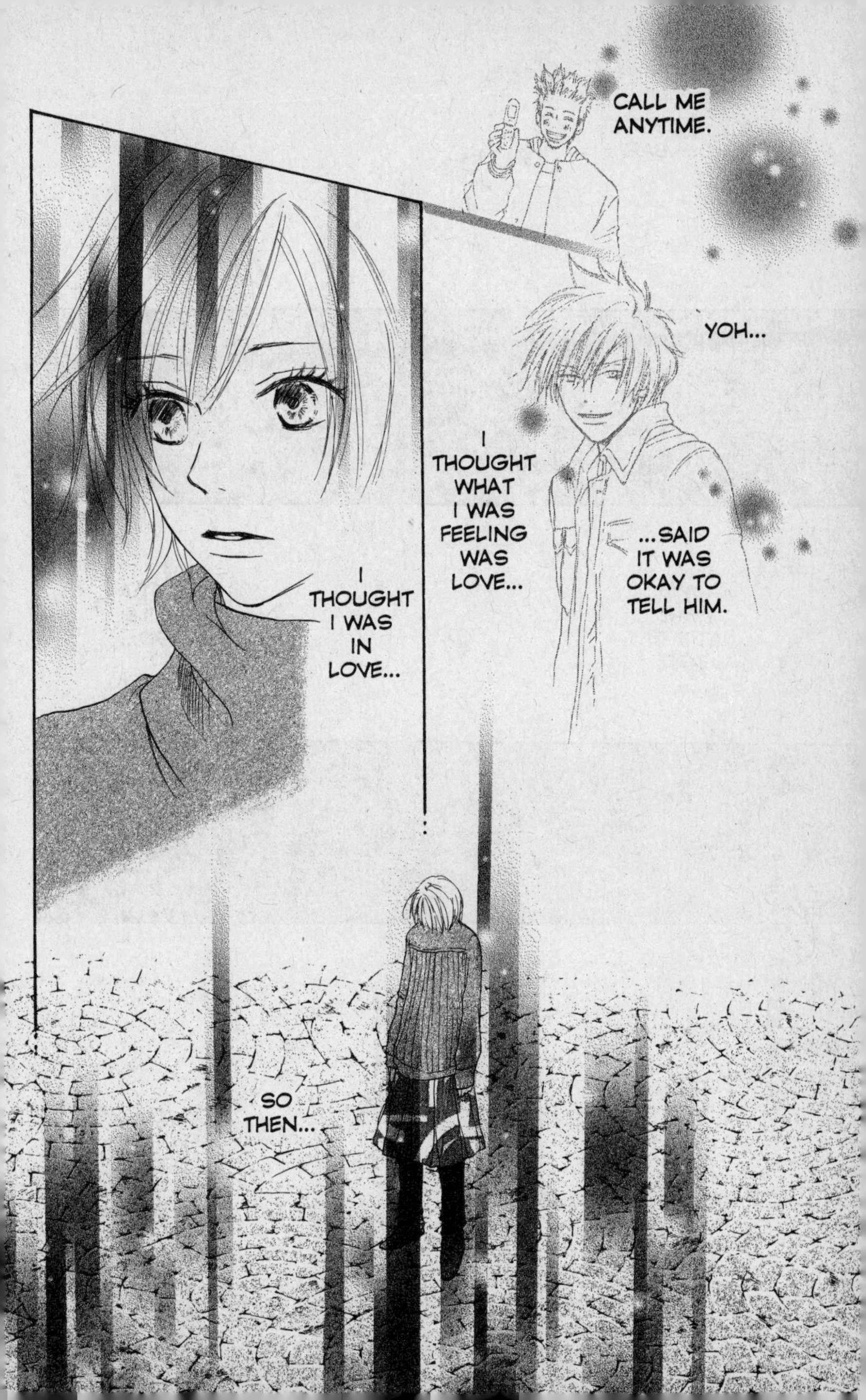
CALL ME ANYTIME.
YOH...
...SAID IT WAS OKAY TO TELL HIM.
I THOUGHT WHAT I WAS FEELING WAS LOVE...
I THOUGHT I WAS IN LOVE...
SO THEN...

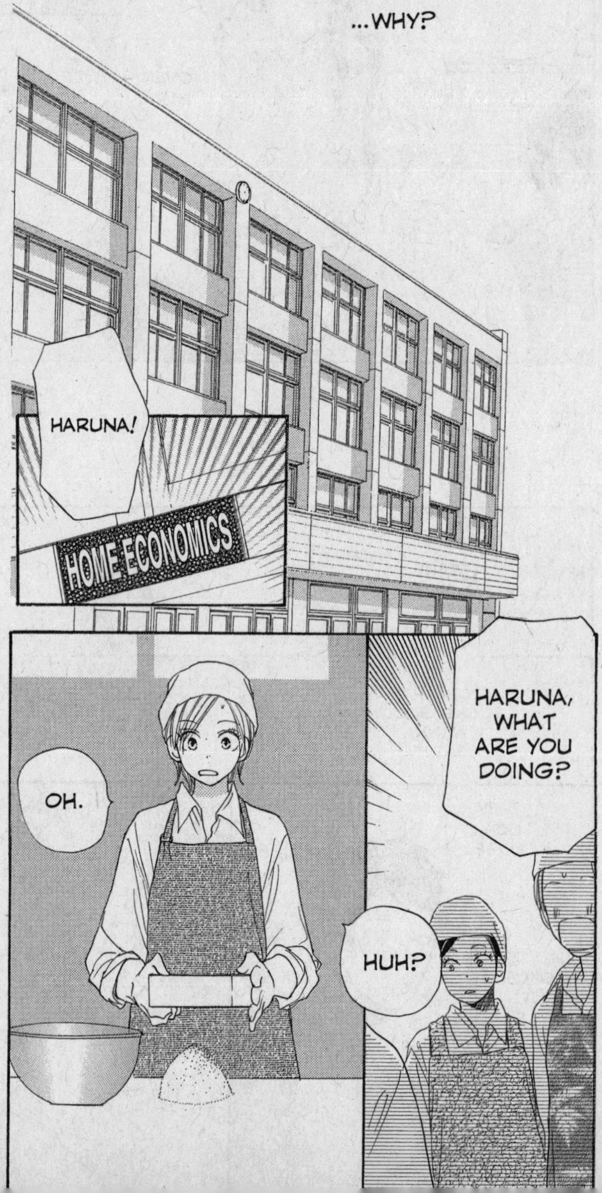
...WHY?
HARUNA!
HOME ECONOMICS
HARUNA, WHAT ARE YOU DOING?
HUH?
OH.

2

It's not an exciting story, but I lose a lot of things and get stuff stolen all the time. My bike often gets stolen. It's happened four times now. Last time, a neighbor downstairs told me.

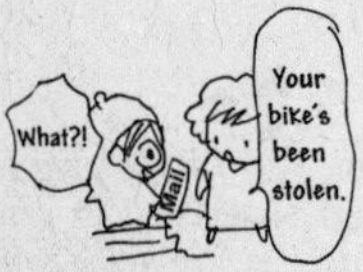
Your bike's been stolen.
What?!
Mail

When I went to look at where I'd left my bike, I saw that it was true.

So I've decided to give up now. I walk. No one has stolen my car yet though...

Also, I often lose my train pass.

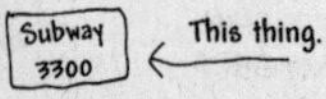
Subway 3300
This thing.

I've lost five cards in all. I lose it when I put it in my pocket, go to town, and come home. Argh...I wonder why...I wonder if drinking that tea will stop this from happening?

That's it for today. I'll keep working hard! Hope to see you again soon!

Kazune Kawahara
2004

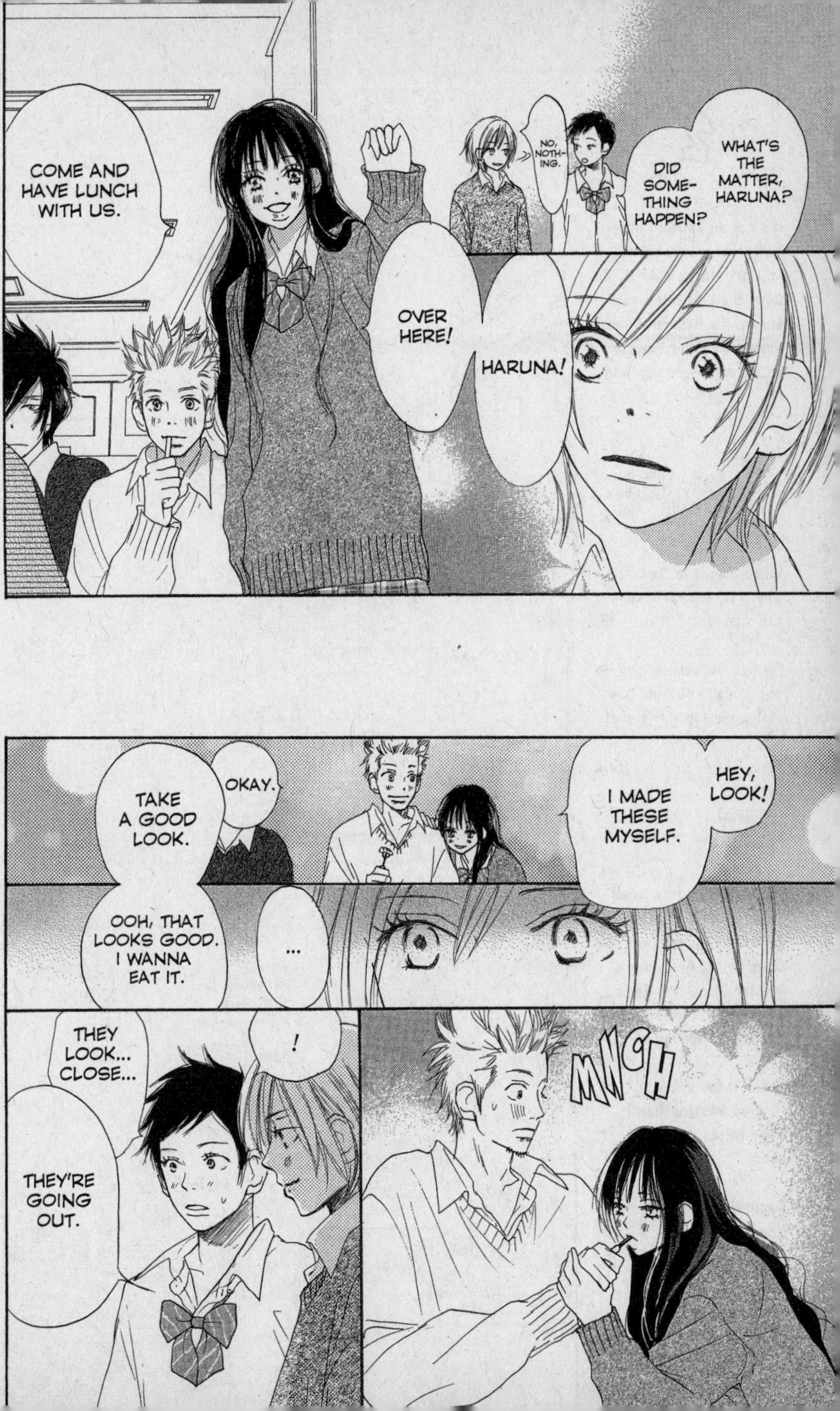
WHAT'S THE MATTER, HARUNA?
DID SOMETHING HAPPEN?
NO, NOTHING.
HARUNA!
OVER HERE!
COME AND HAVE LUNCH WITH US.
HEY, LOOK!
I MADE THESE MYSELF.
OKAY.
TAKE A GOOD LOOK.
...
OOH, THAT LOOKS GOOD. I WANNA EAT IT.
MNCH
!
THEY LOOK... CLOSE...
THEY'RE GOING OUT.

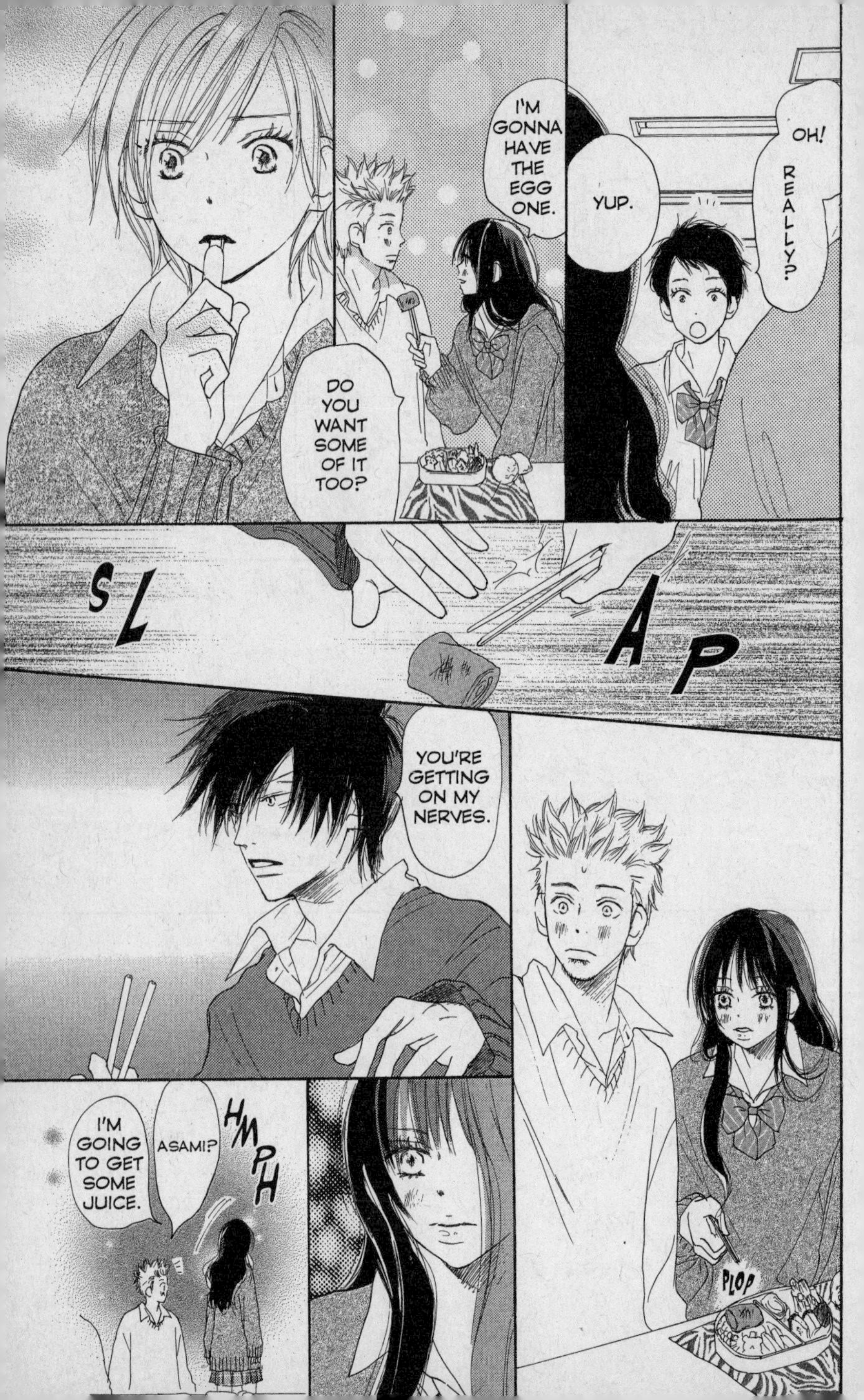
OH! REALLY?
YUP.
I'M GONNA HAVE THE EGG ONE.
DO YOU WANT SOME OF IT TOO?
SLAP
PLOP
YOU'RE GETTING ON MY NERVES.
HMPH
ASAMI?
I'M GOING TO GET SOME JUICE.

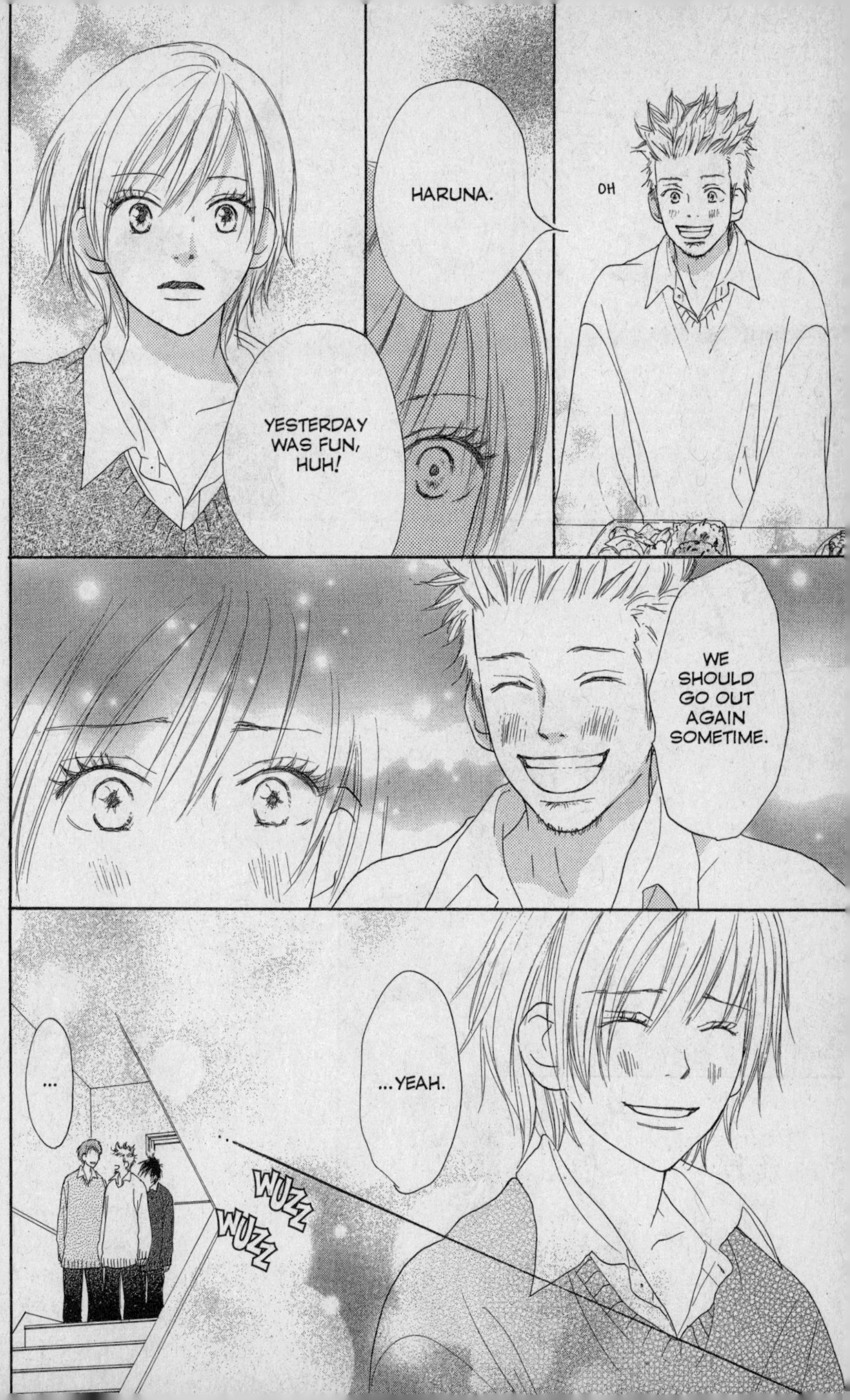
OH
HARUNA.
YESTERDAY WAS FUN, HUH!
WE SHOULD GO OUT AGAIN SOMETIME.
...YEAH.
...
WUZZ
WUZZ

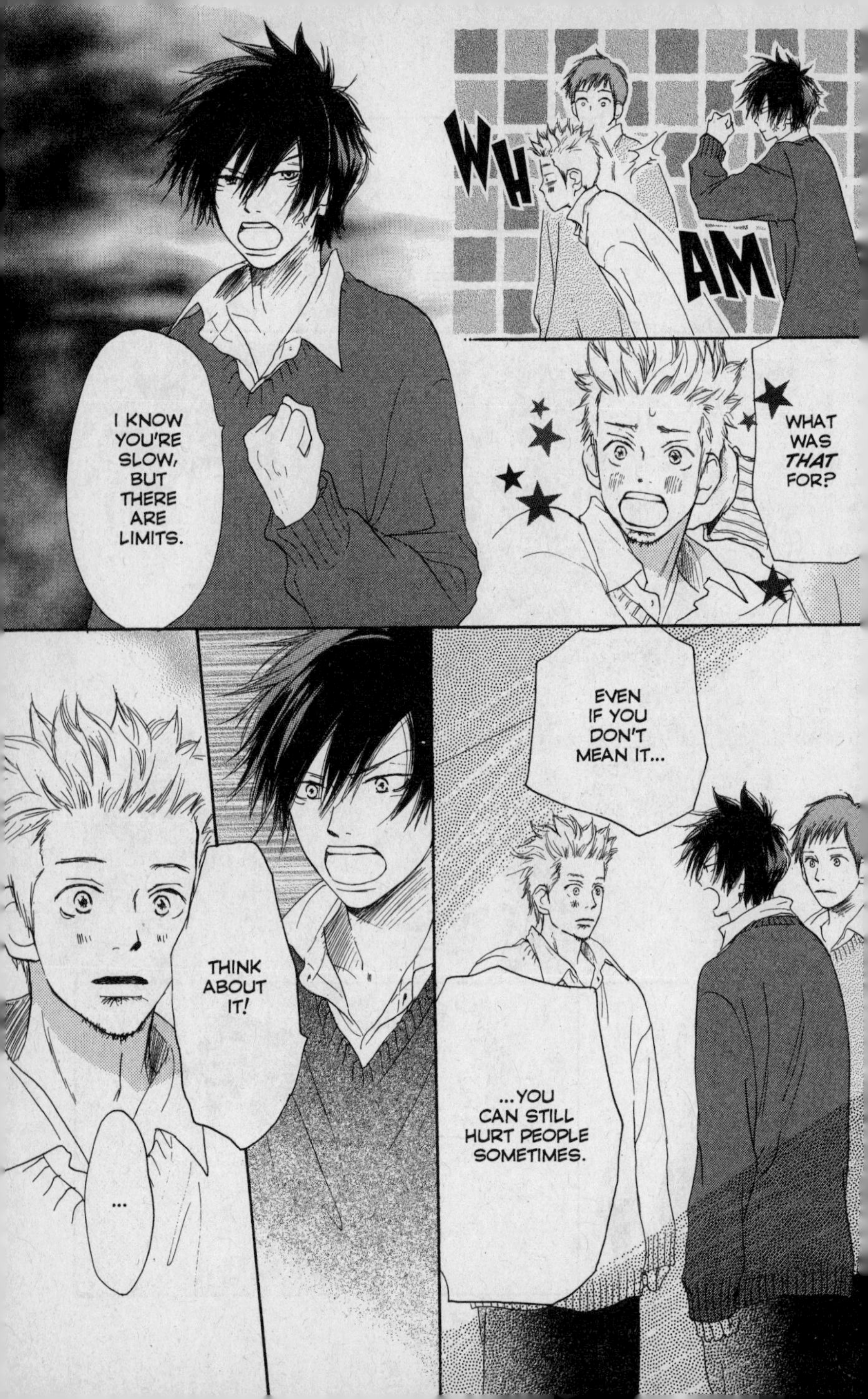
WHAM
WHAT WAS *THAT* FOR?
I KNOW YOU'RE SLOW, BUT THERE ARE LIMITS.
EVEN IF YOU DON'T MEAN IT...
...YOU CAN STILL HURT PEOPLE SOMETIMES.
THINK ABOUT IT!
...

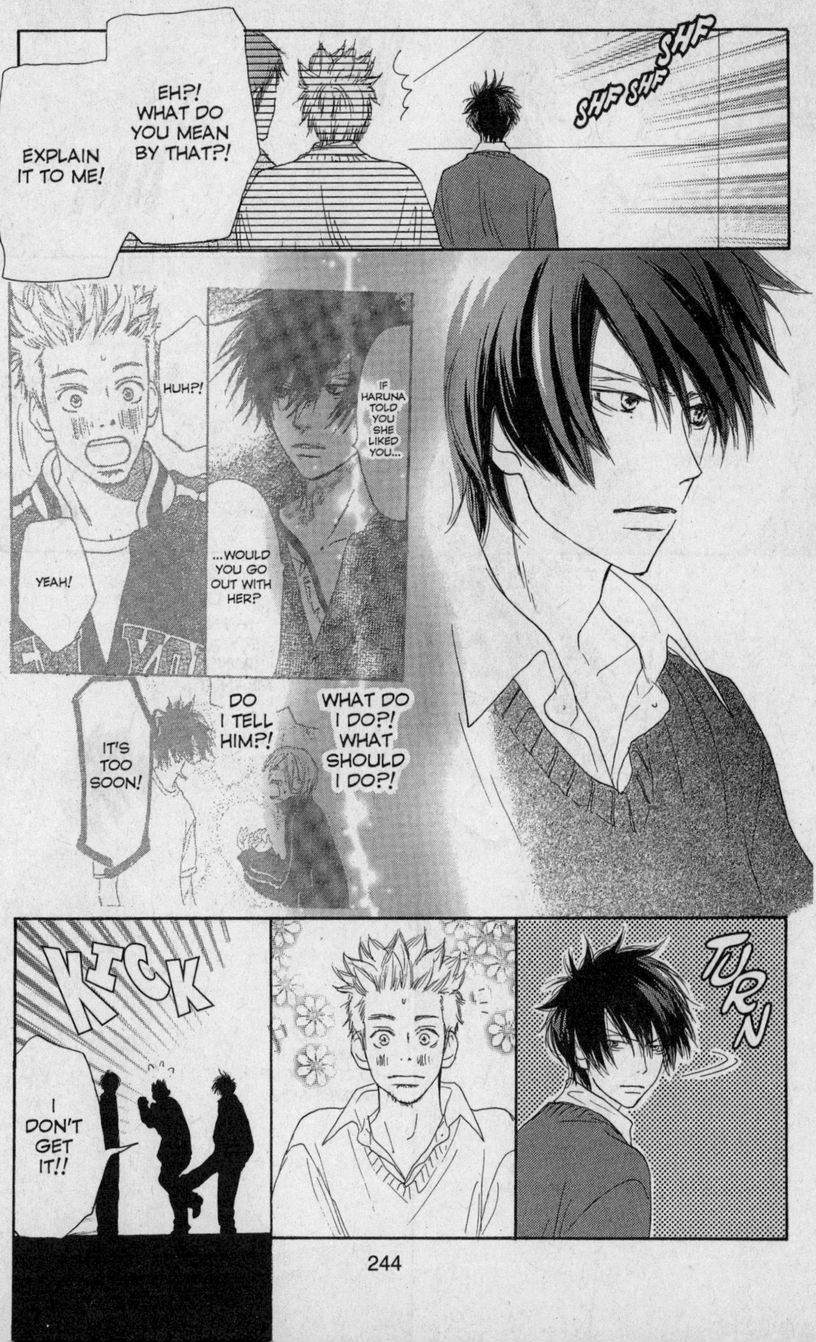
SHF SHF SHF
EH?! WHAT DO YOU MEAN BY THAT?!
EXPLAIN IT TO ME!
IF HARUNA TOLD YOU SHE LIKED YOU...
...WOULD YOU GO OUT WITH HER?
HUH?!
YEAH!
WHAT DO I DO?! WHAT SHOULD I DO?!
DO I TELL HIM?!
IT'S TOO SOON!
TURN
KICK
I DON'T GET IT!!

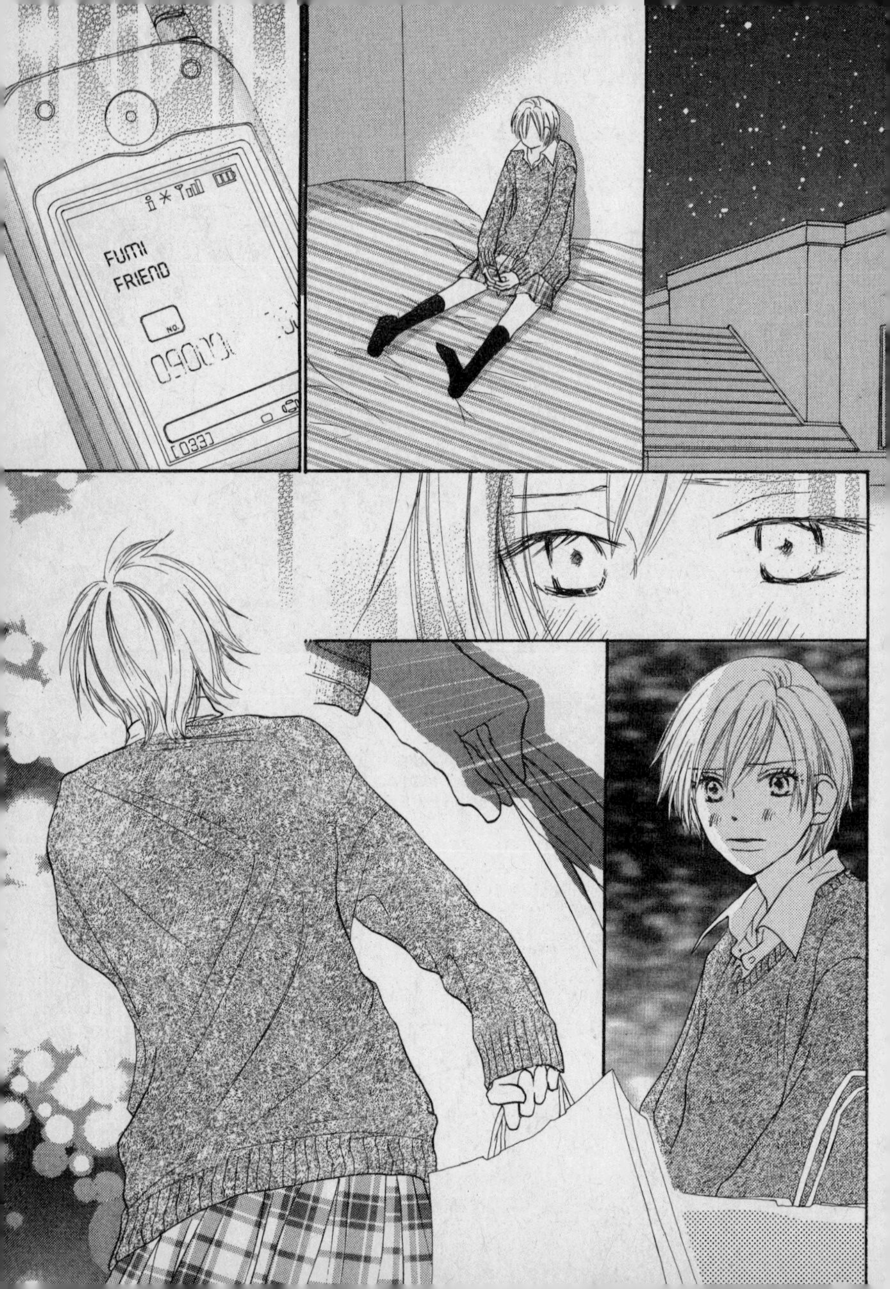
FUMI
FRIEND

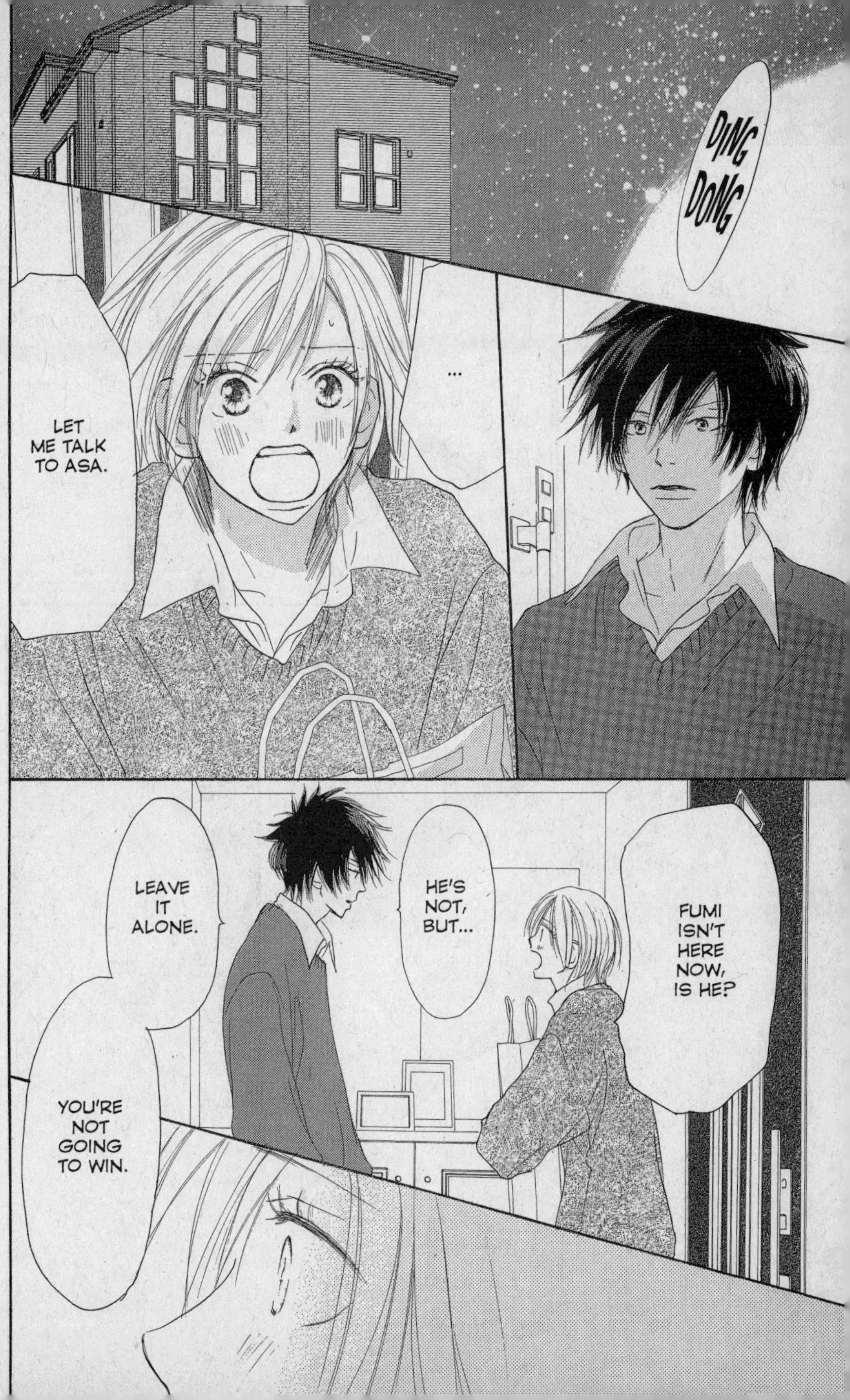
DING DONG
...
LET ME TALK TO ASA.
FUMI ISN'T HERE NOW, IS HE?
HE'S NOT, BUT...
LEAVE IT ALONE.
YOU'RE NOT GOING TO WIN.

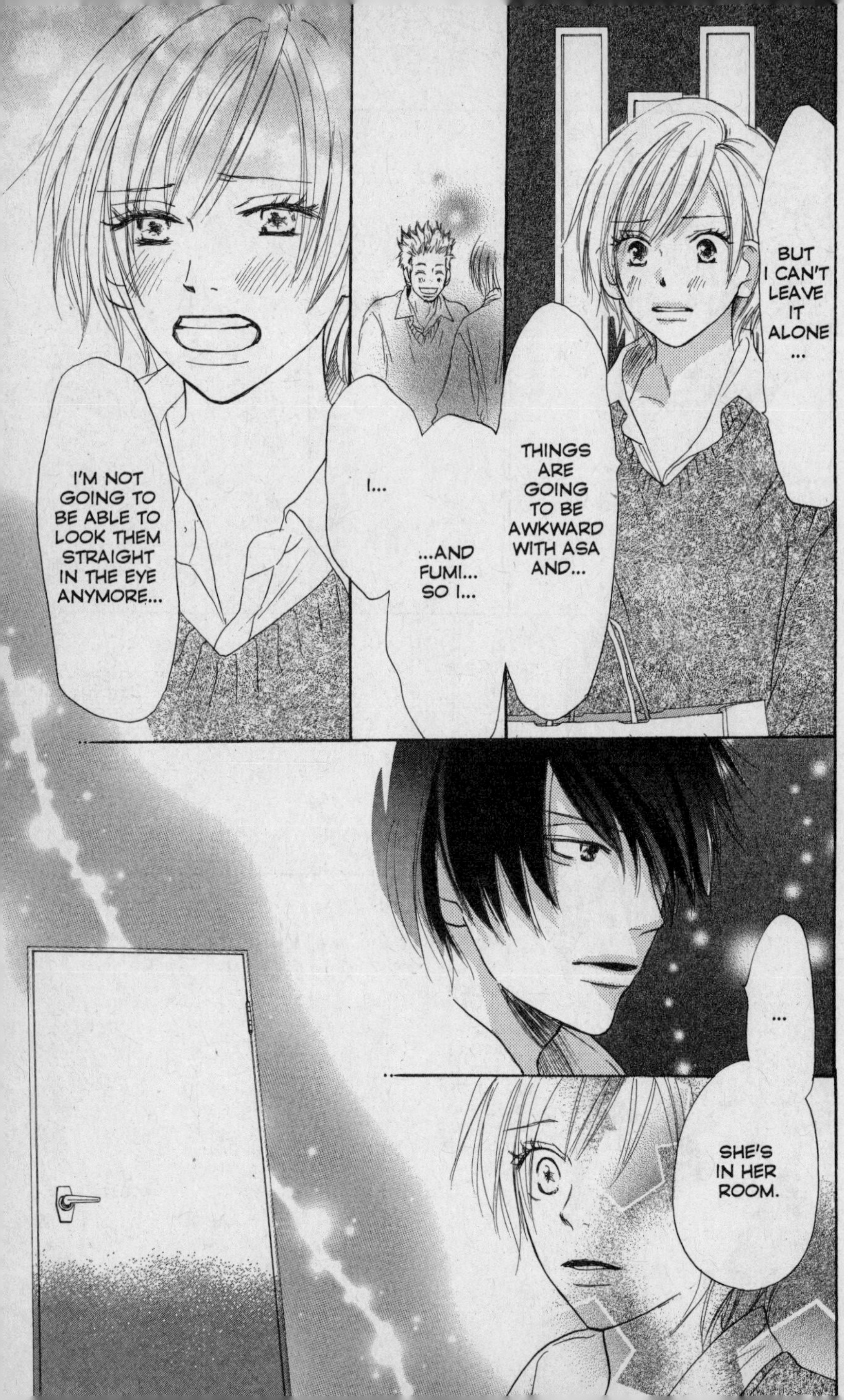
BUT I CAN'T LEAVE IT ALONE ...
THINGS ARE GOING TO BE AWKWARD WITH ASA AND...
I...
...AND FUMI... SO I...
I'M NOT GOING TO BE ABLE TO LOOK THEM STRAIGHT IN THE EYE ANYMORE...
...
SHE'S IN HER ROOM.

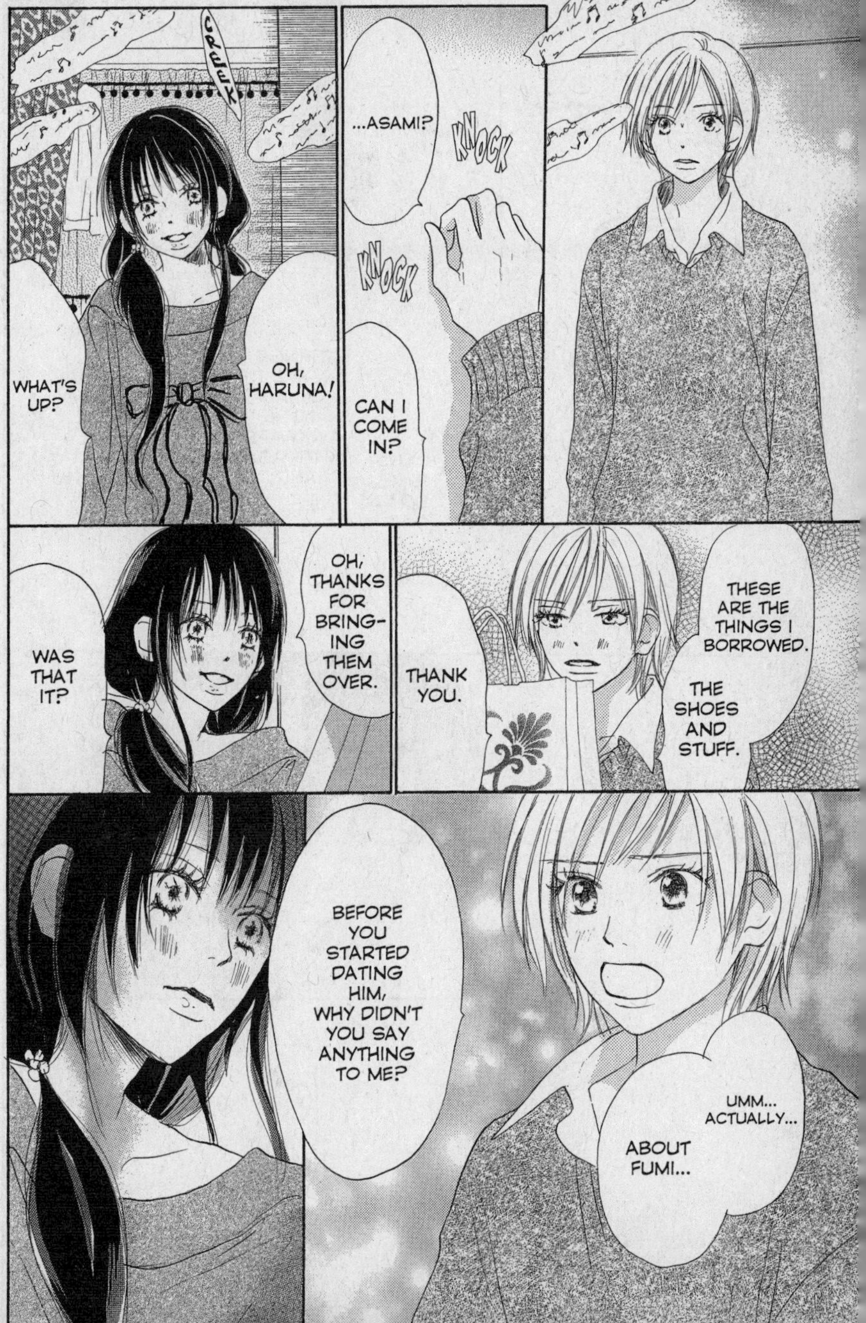
...ASAMI?
KNOCK
KNOCK
CAN I COME IN?
CREEK
OH, HARUNA!
WHAT'S UP?
THESE ARE THE THINGS I BORROWED.
THE SHOES AND STUFF.
THANK YOU.
OH, THANKS FOR BRING-ING THEM OVER.
WAS THAT IT?
UMM... ACTUALLY...
ABOUT FUMI...
BEFORE YOU STARTED DATING HIM, WHY DIDN'T YOU SAY ANYTHING TO ME?

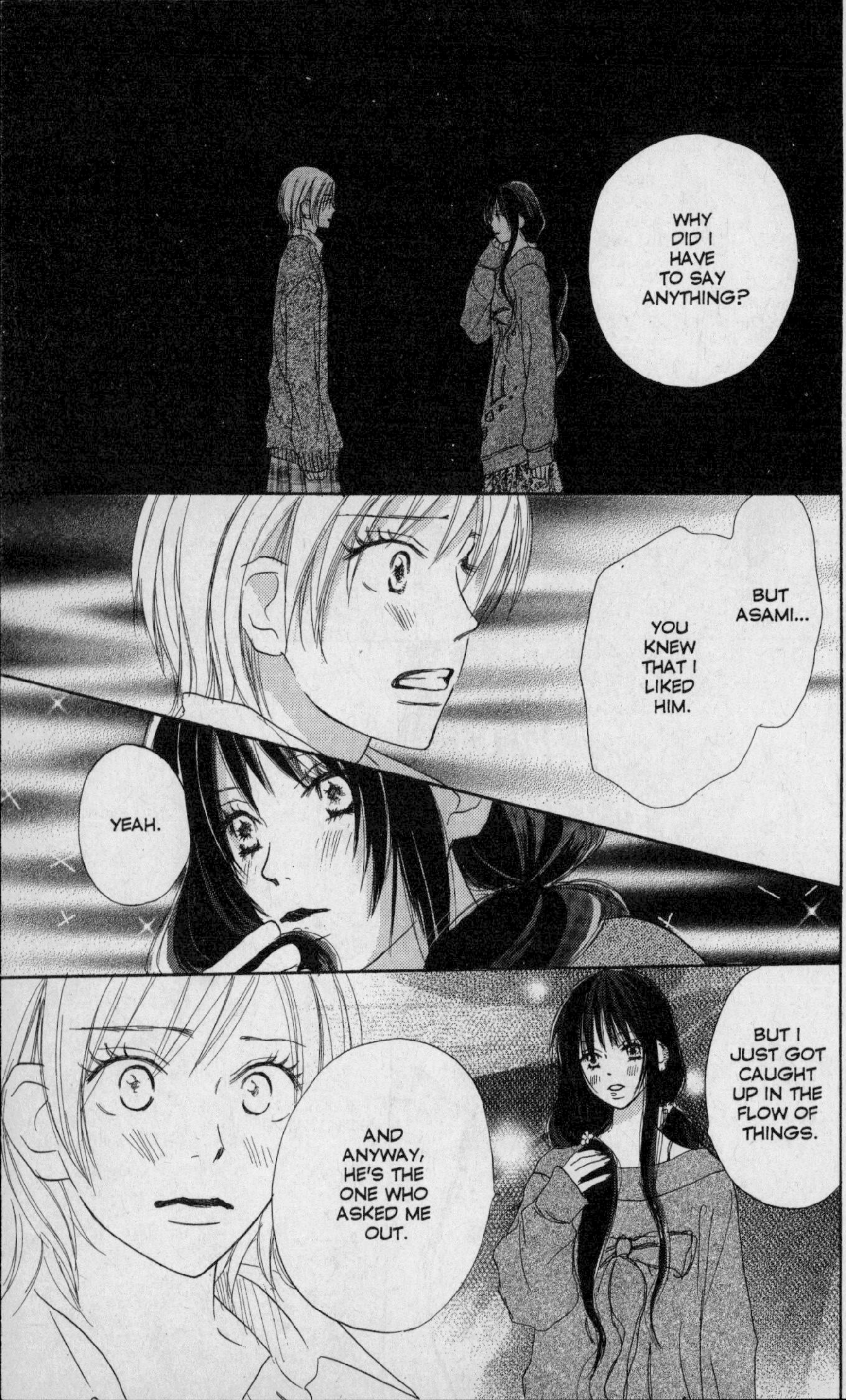
WHY DID I HAVE TO SAY ANYTHING?
BUT ASAMI...
YOU KNEW THAT I LIKED HIM.
YEAH.
BUT I JUST GOT CAUGHT UP IN THE FLOW OF THINGS.
AND ANYWAY, HE'S THE ONE WHO ASKED ME OUT.

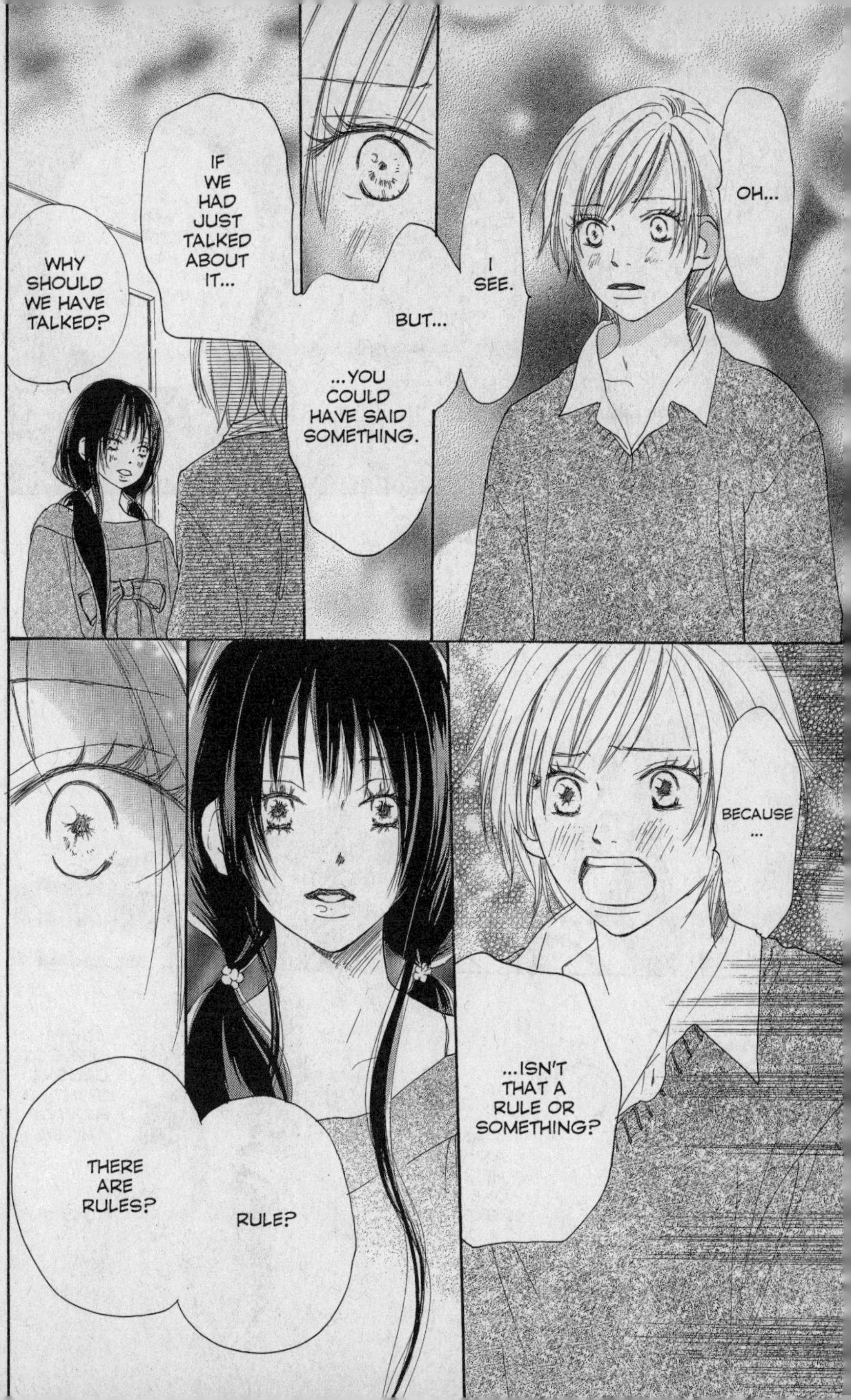
OH...
I SEE.
BUT...
...YOU COULD HAVE SAID SOMETHING.
IF WE HAD JUST TALKED ABOUT IT...
WHY SHOULD WE HAVE TALKED?
BECAUSE ...
...ISN'T THAT A RULE OR SOMETHING?
RULE?
THERE ARE RULES?

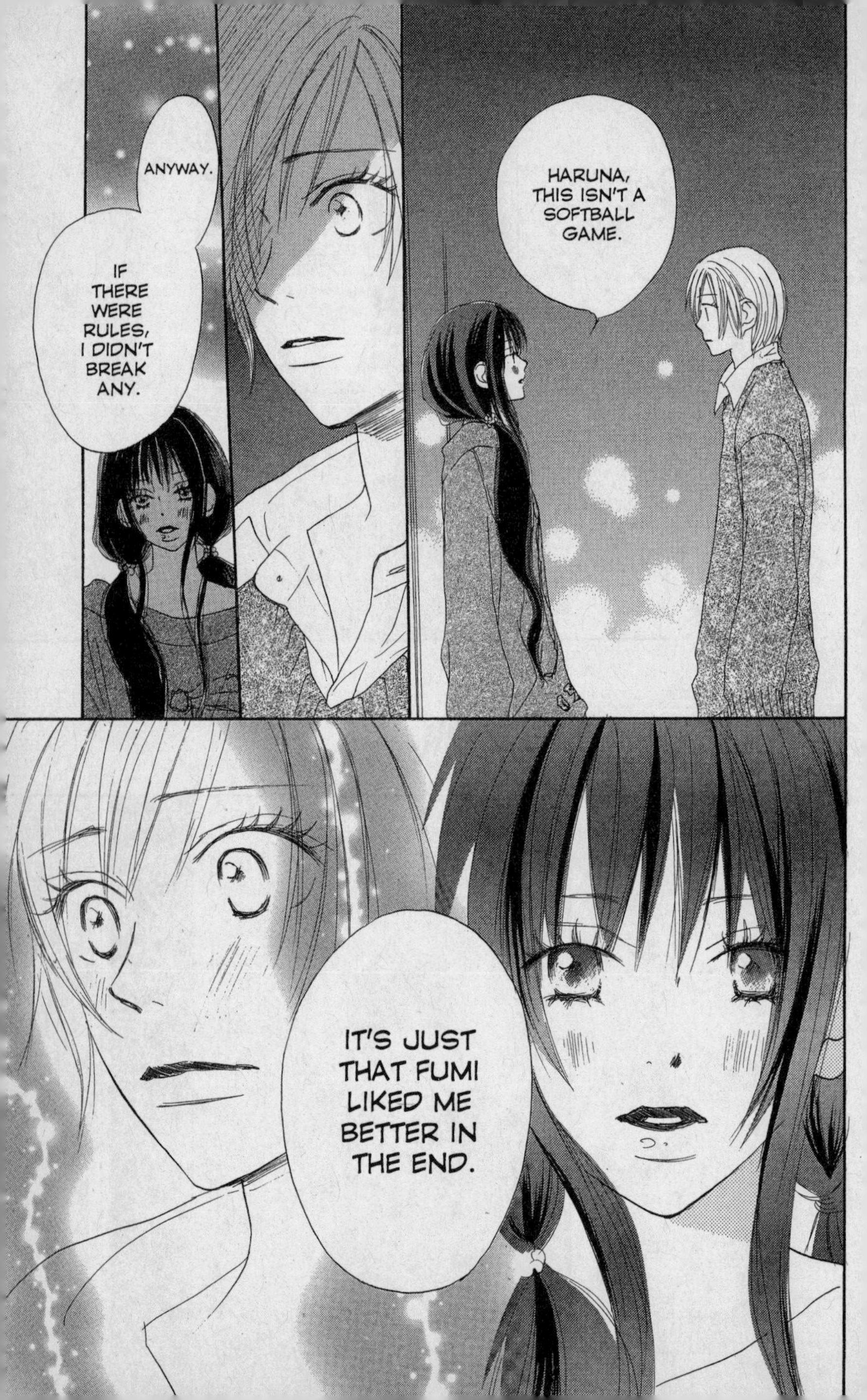
HARUNA, THIS ISN'T A SOFTBALL GAME.
ANYWAY.
IF THERE WERE RULES, I DIDN'T BREAK ANY.
IT'S JUST THAT FUMI LIKED ME BETTER IN THE END.

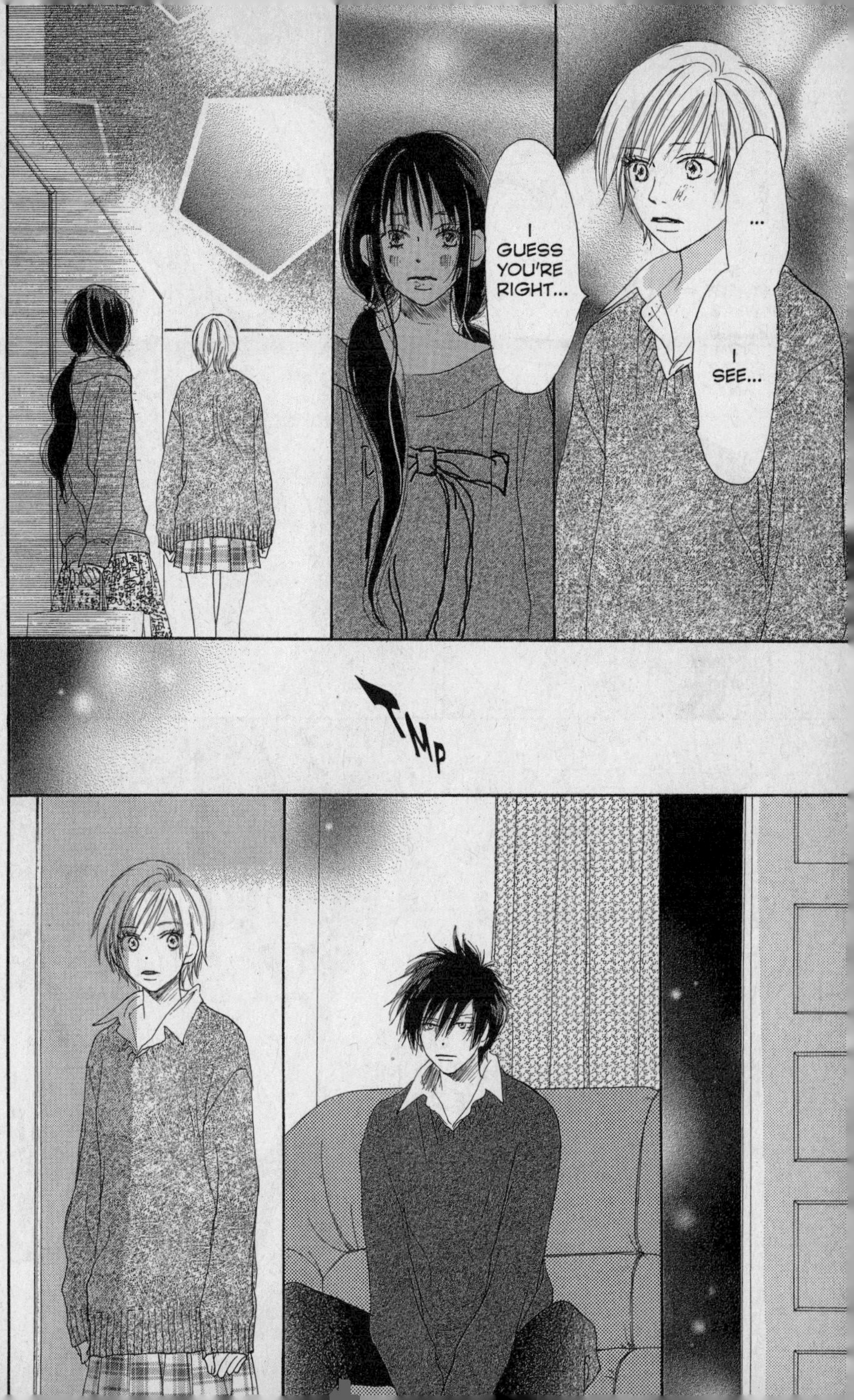
...
I SEE...
I GUESS YOU'RE RIGHT...
TMP

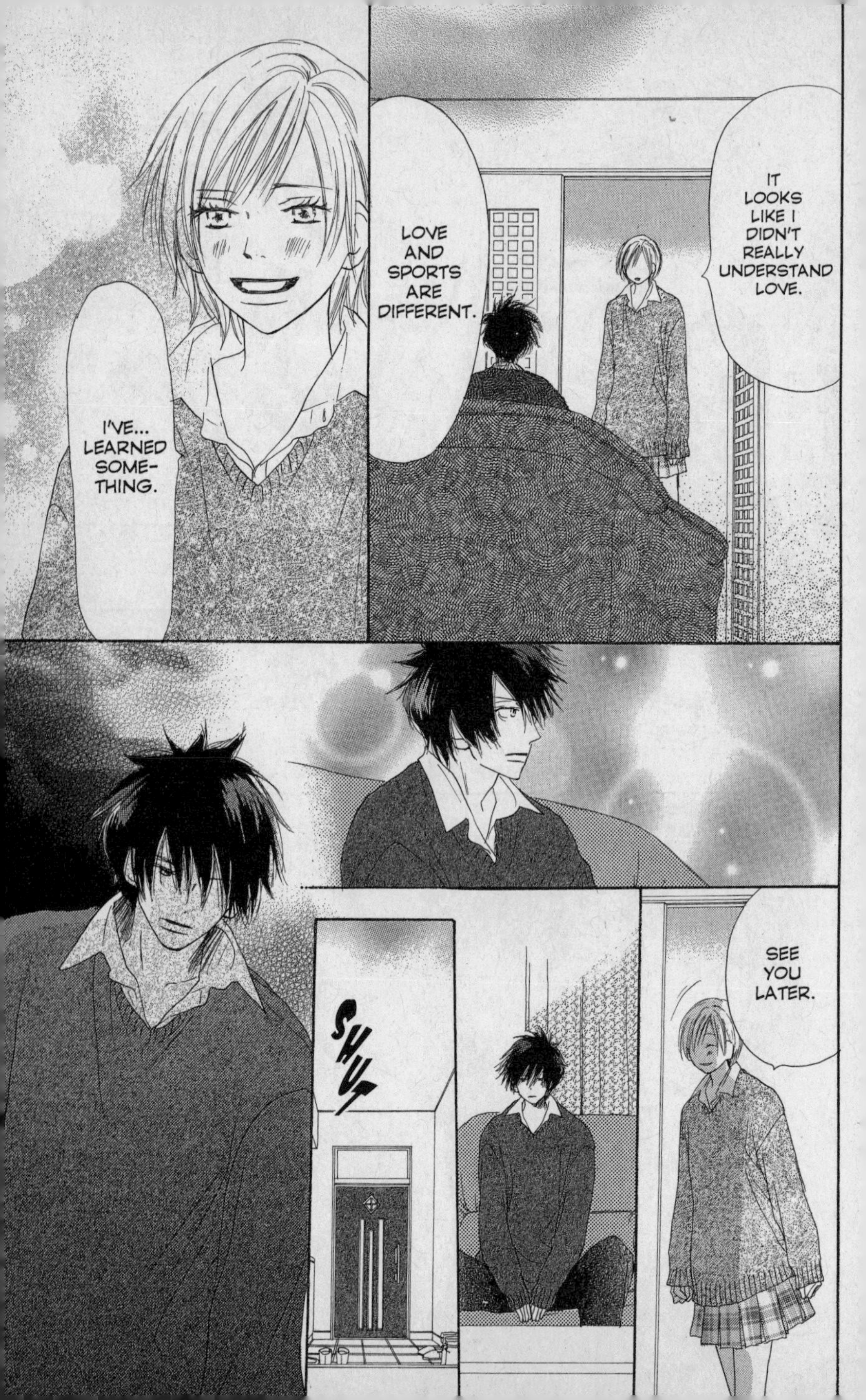
IT LOOKS LIKE I DIDN'T REALLY UNDERSTAND LOVE.
LOVE AND SPORTS ARE DIFFERENT.
I'VE... LEARNED SOME-THING.
SEE YOU LATER.
SHUT

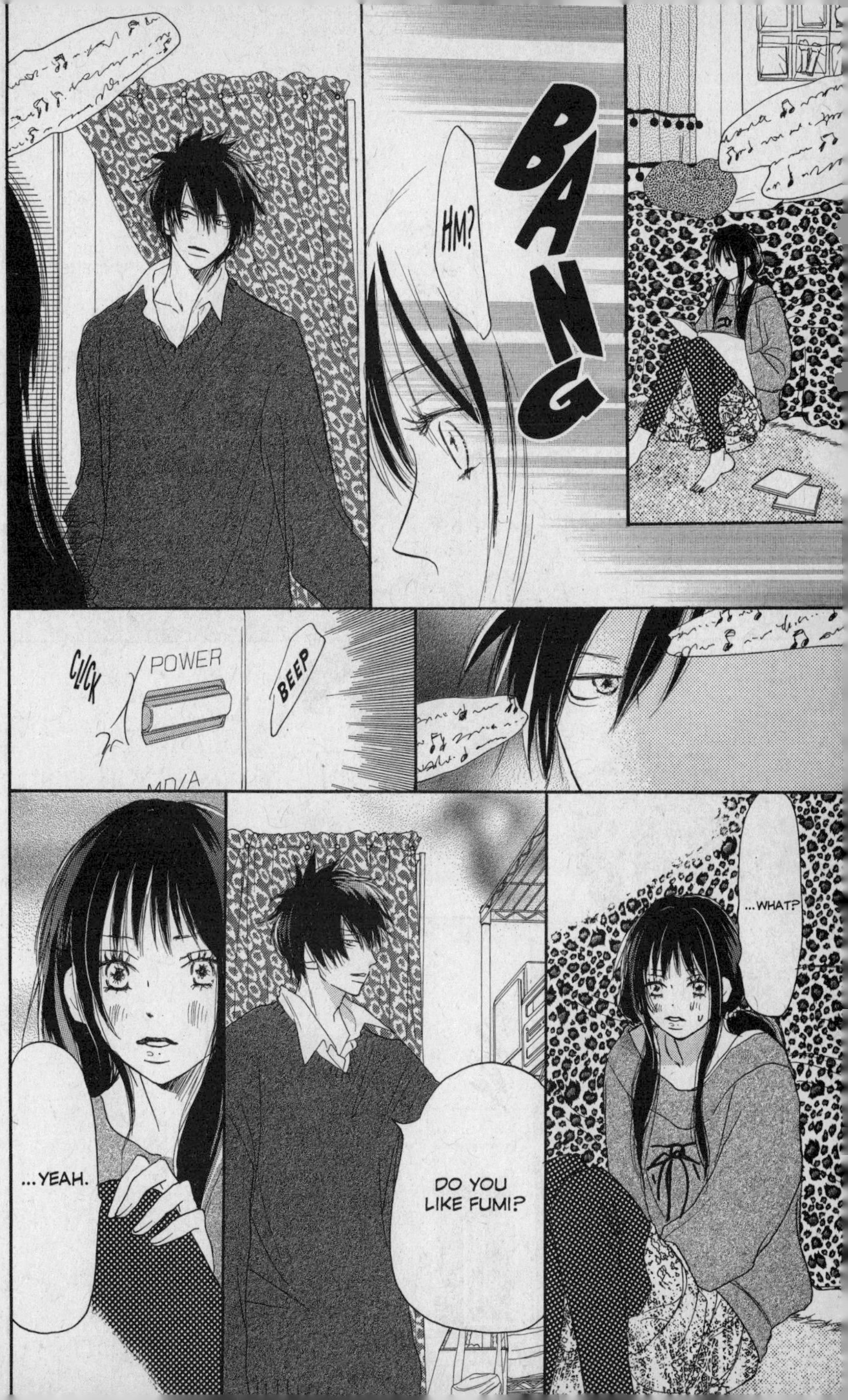
BANG
HM?
BEEP
POWER
CLICK
...WHAT?
DO YOU LIKE FUMI?
...YEAH.

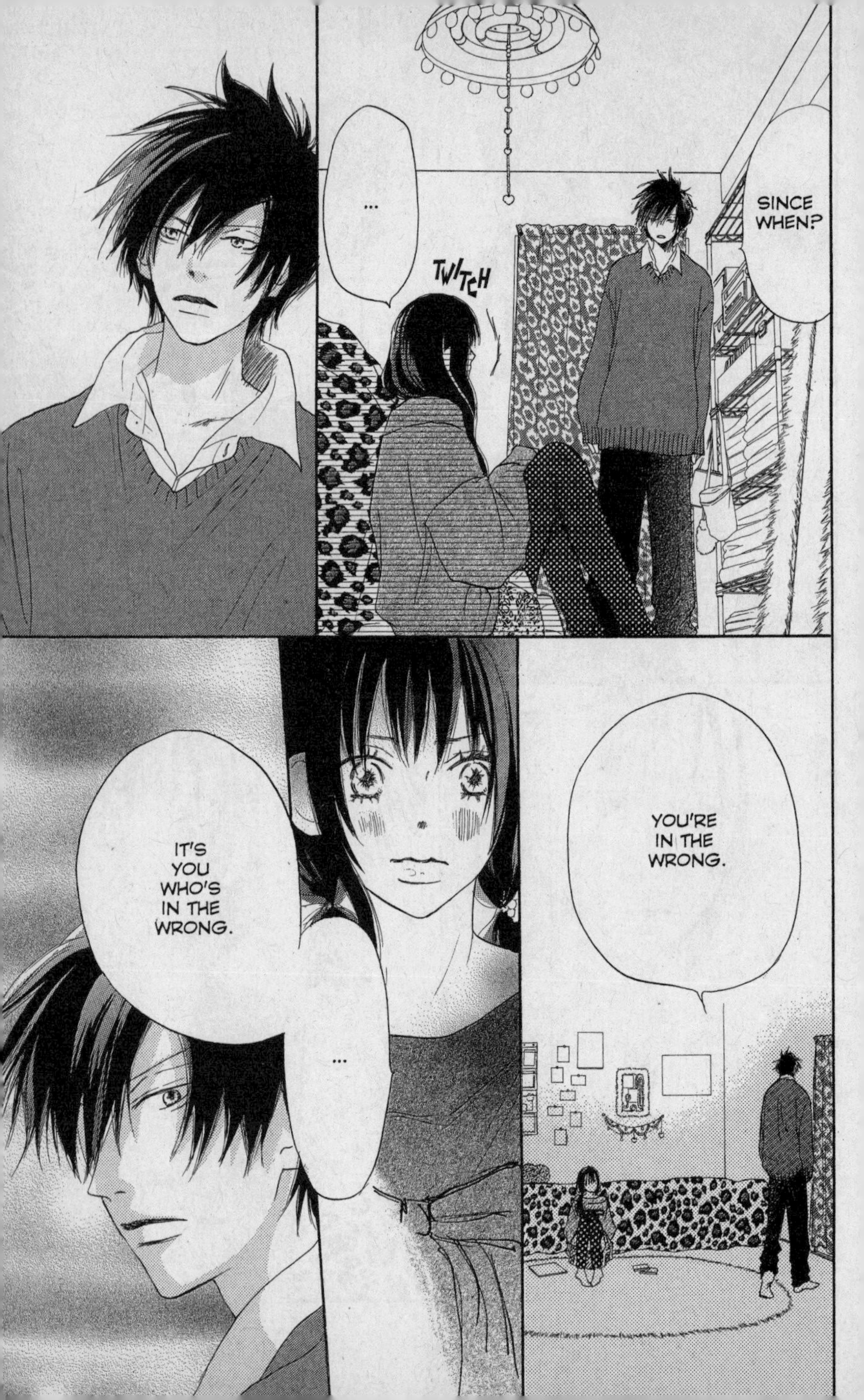
SINCE WHEN?
...
TWITCH
YOU'RE IN THE WRONG.
IT'S YOU WHO'S IN THE WRONG.
...

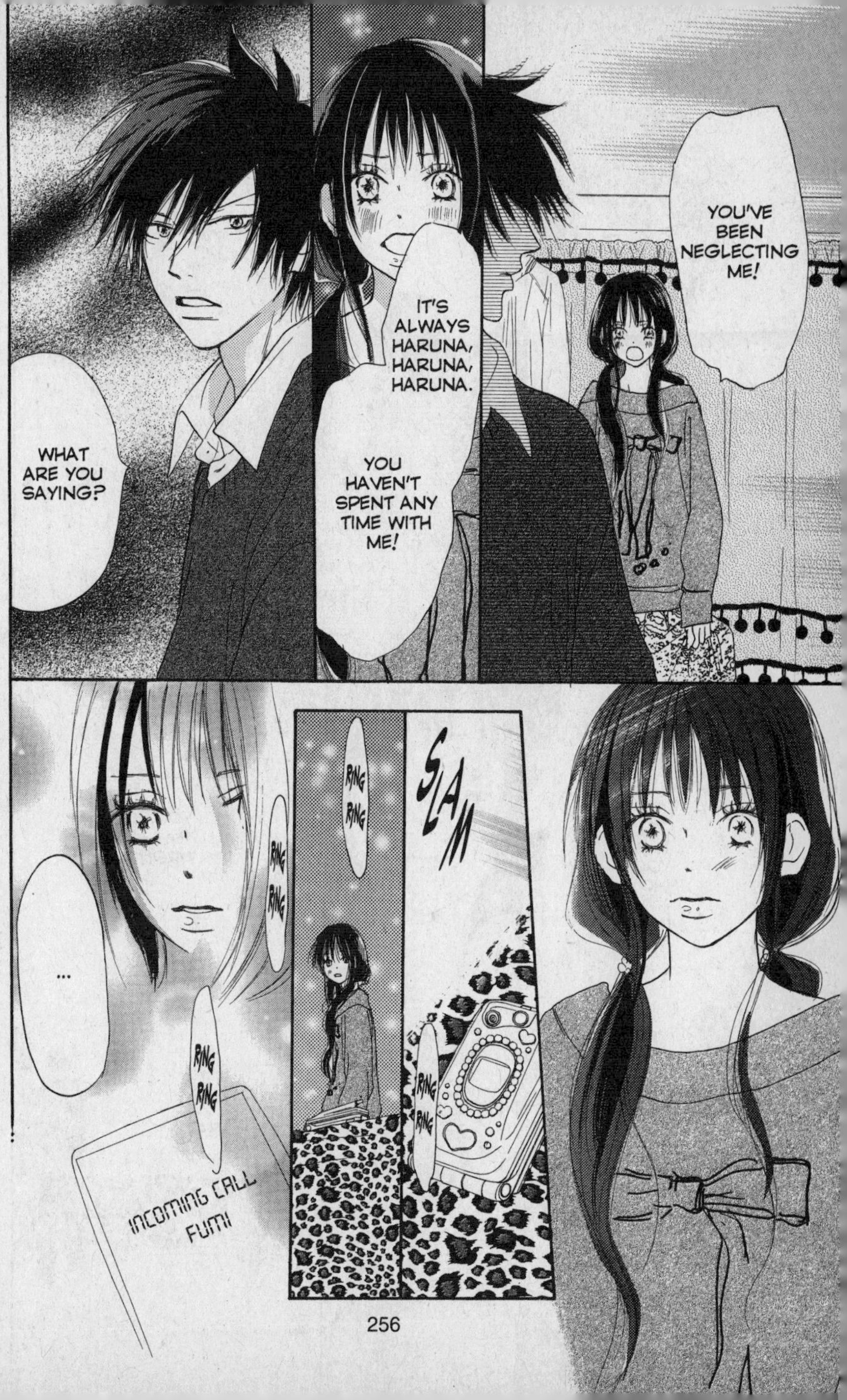
YOU'VE BEEN NEGLECTING ME!
IT'S ALWAYS HARUNA, HARUNA, HARUNA.
YOU HAVEN'T SPENT ANY TIME WITH ME!
WHAT ARE YOU SAYING?
SLAM
RING RING
RING RING
RING RING
...
RING RING
INCOMING CALL
FUMI

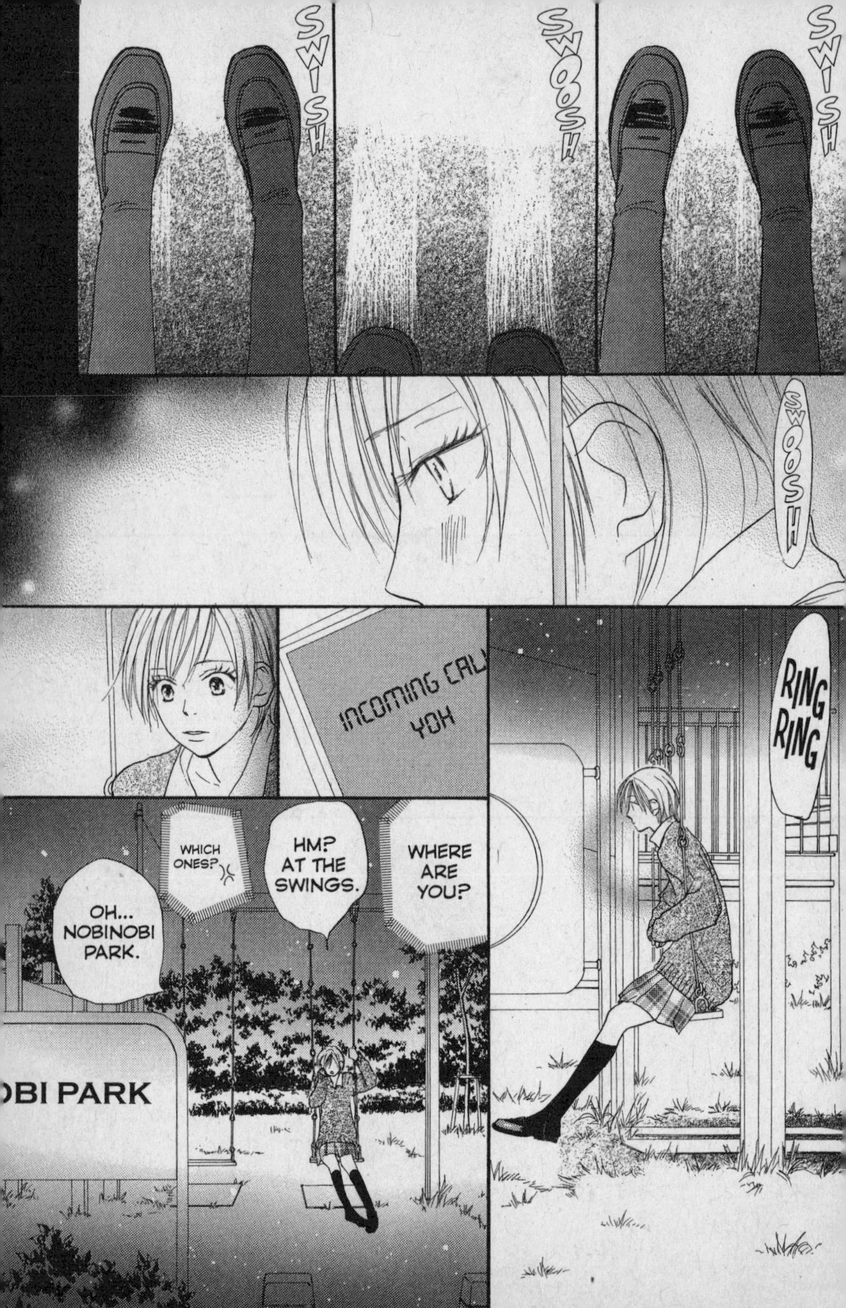
SWISH
SWOOSH
SWISH
SWOOSH
RING RING
INCOMING CAL
YOH
WHERE ARE YOU?
HM? AT THE SWINGS.
WHICH ONES?
OH... NOBINOBI PARK.
OBI PARK

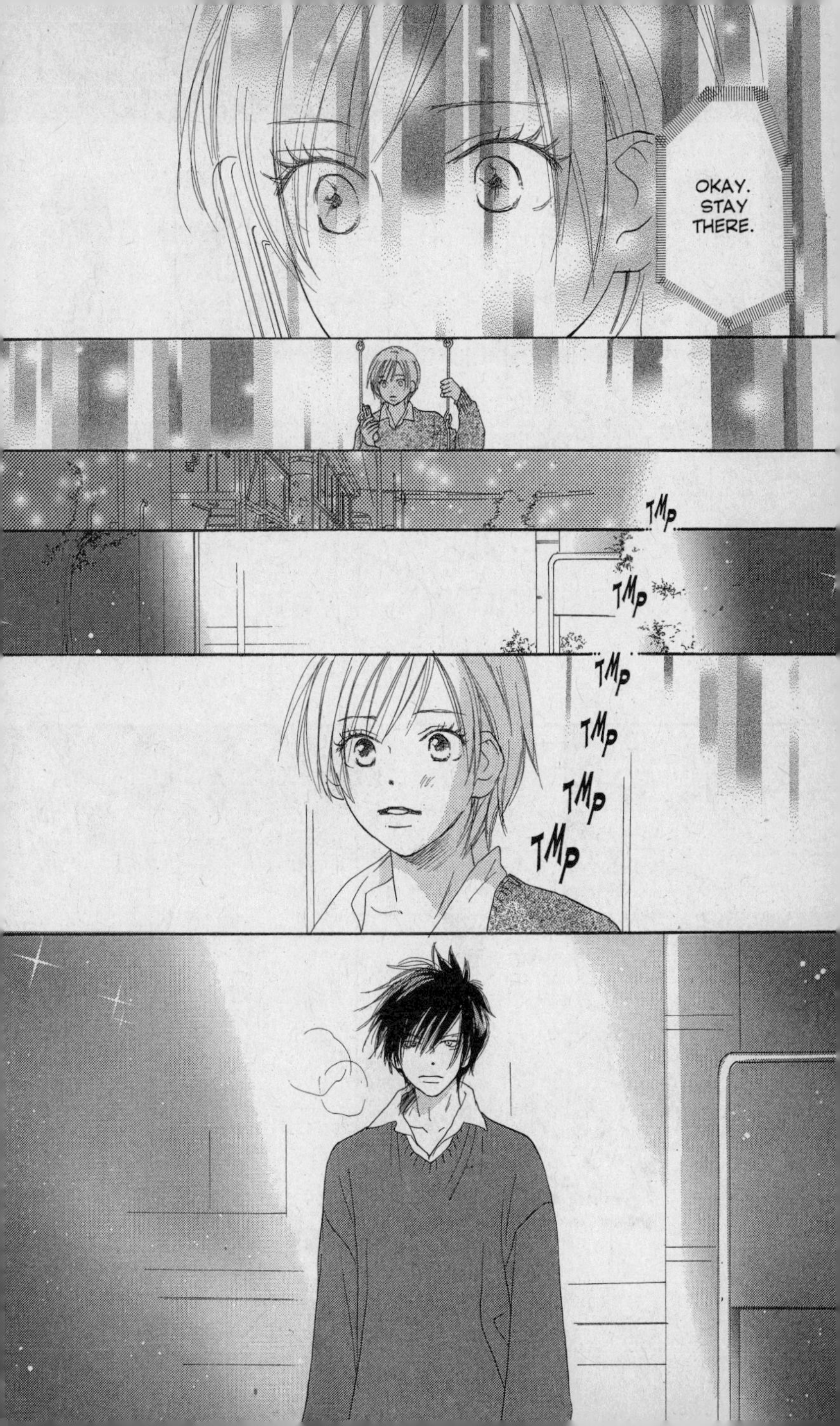
OKAY. STAY THERE.
TMP
TMP
TMP
TMP
TMP
TMP

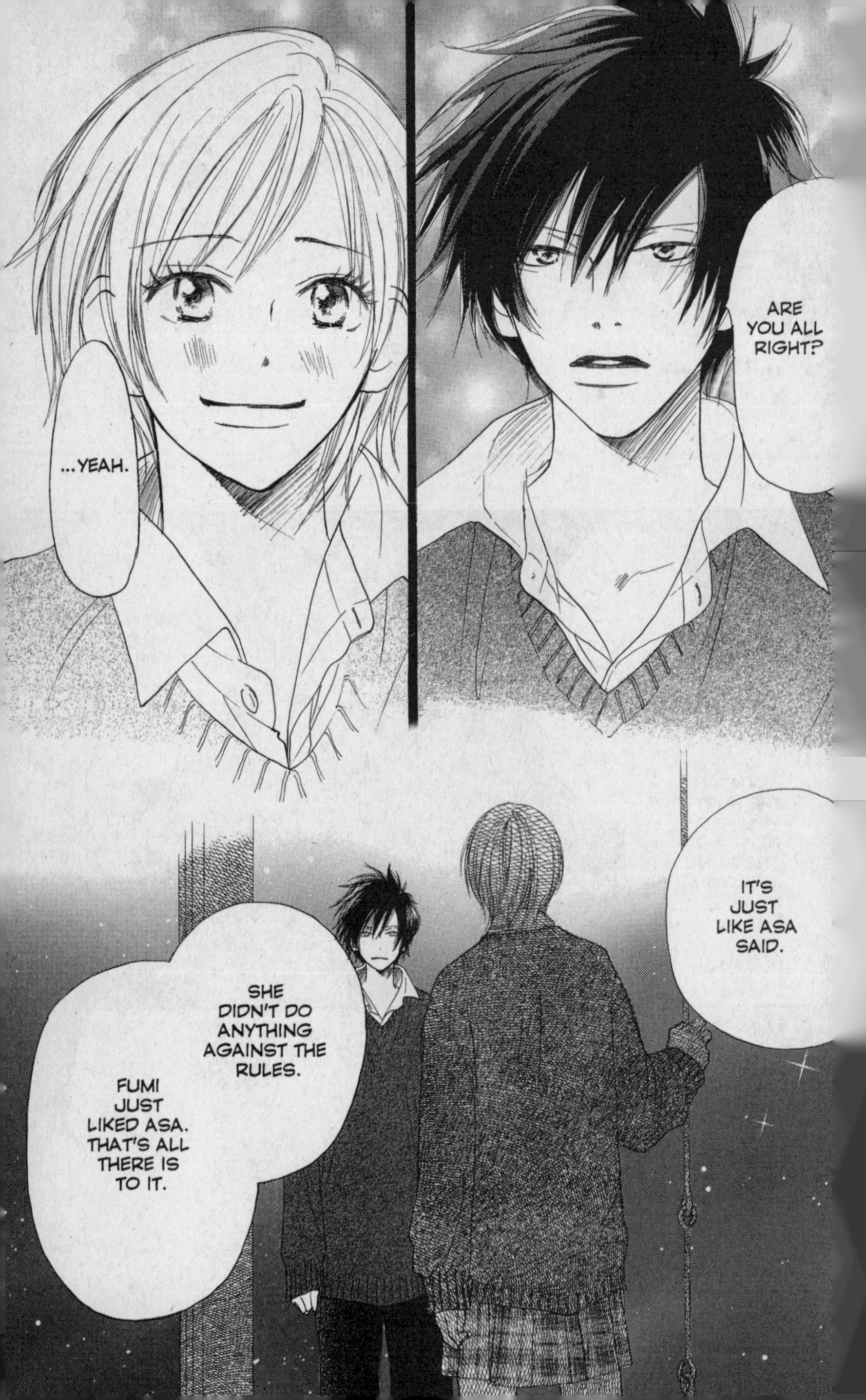
ARE YOU ALL RIGHT?
...YEAH.
IT'S JUST LIKE ASA SAID.
SHE DIDN'T DO ANYTHING AGAINST THE RULES.
FUMI JUST LIKED ASA. THAT'S ALL THERE IS TO IT.

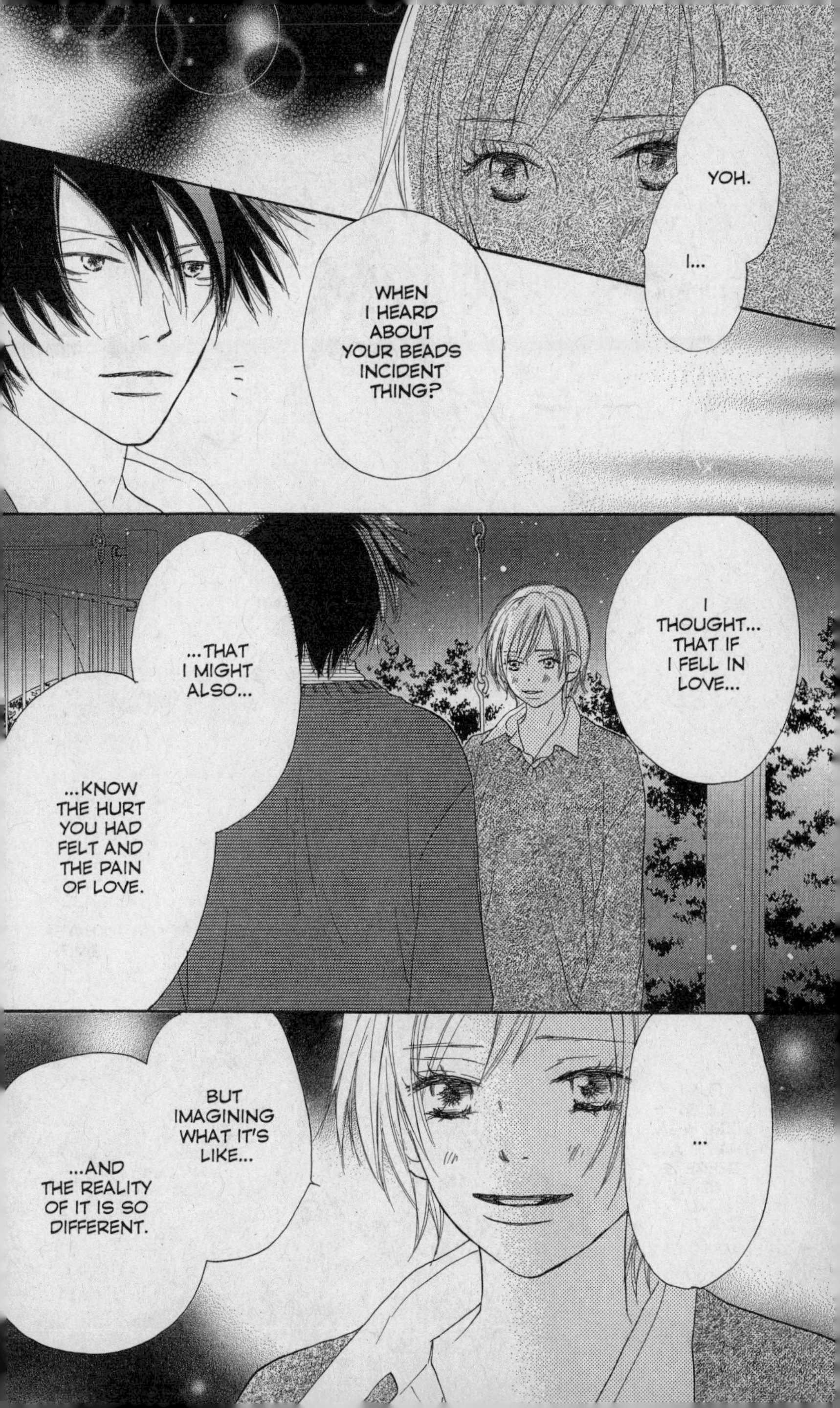
YOH.
I...
WHEN I HEARD ABOUT YOUR BEADS INCIDENT THING?
I THOUGHT... THAT IF I FELL IN LOVE...
...THAT I MIGHT ALSO...
...KNOW THE HURT YOU HAD FELT AND THE PAIN OF LOVE.
...
BUT IMAGINING WHAT IT'S LIKE...
...AND THE REALITY OF IT IS SO DIFFERENT.

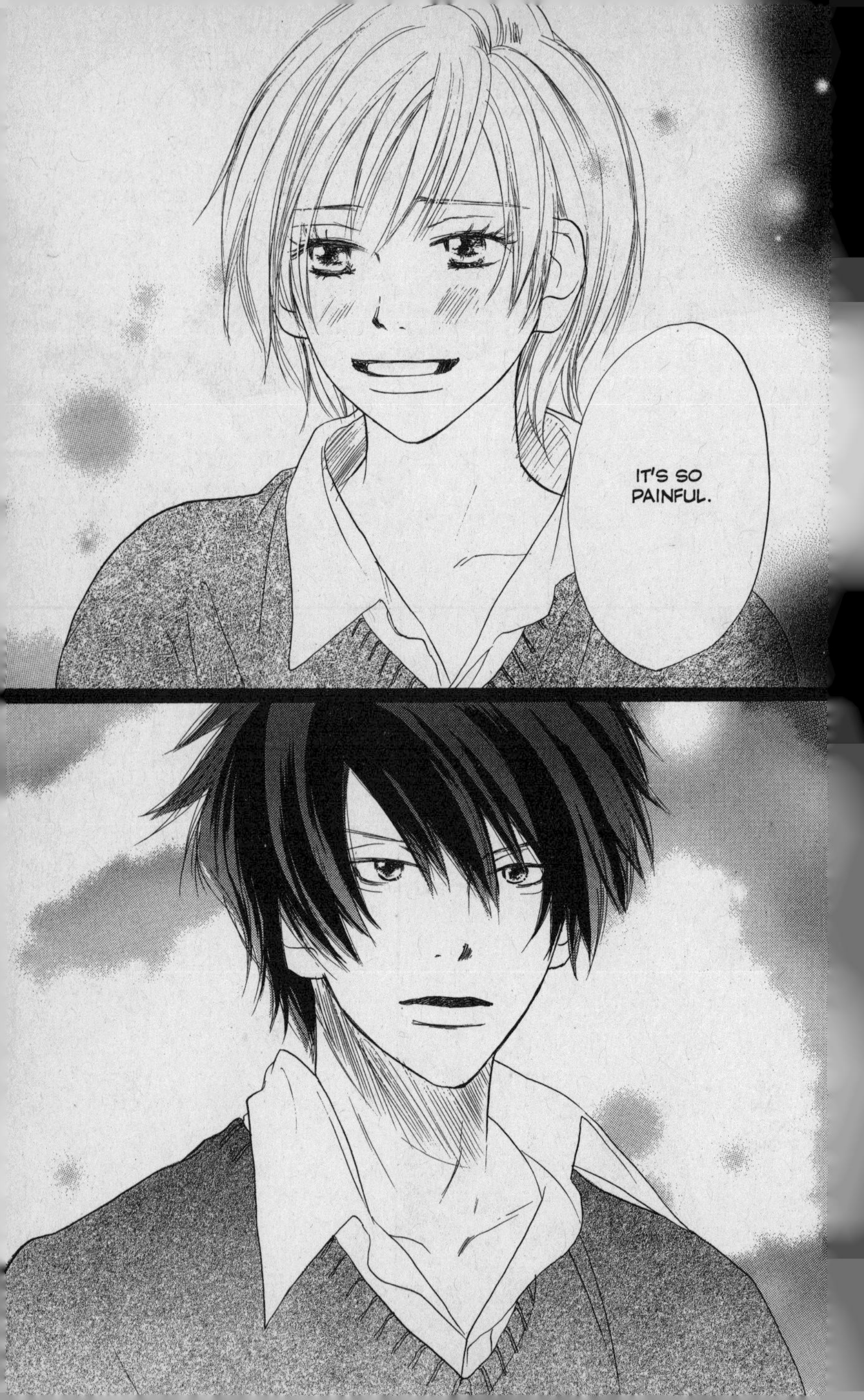
IT'S SO PAINFUL.

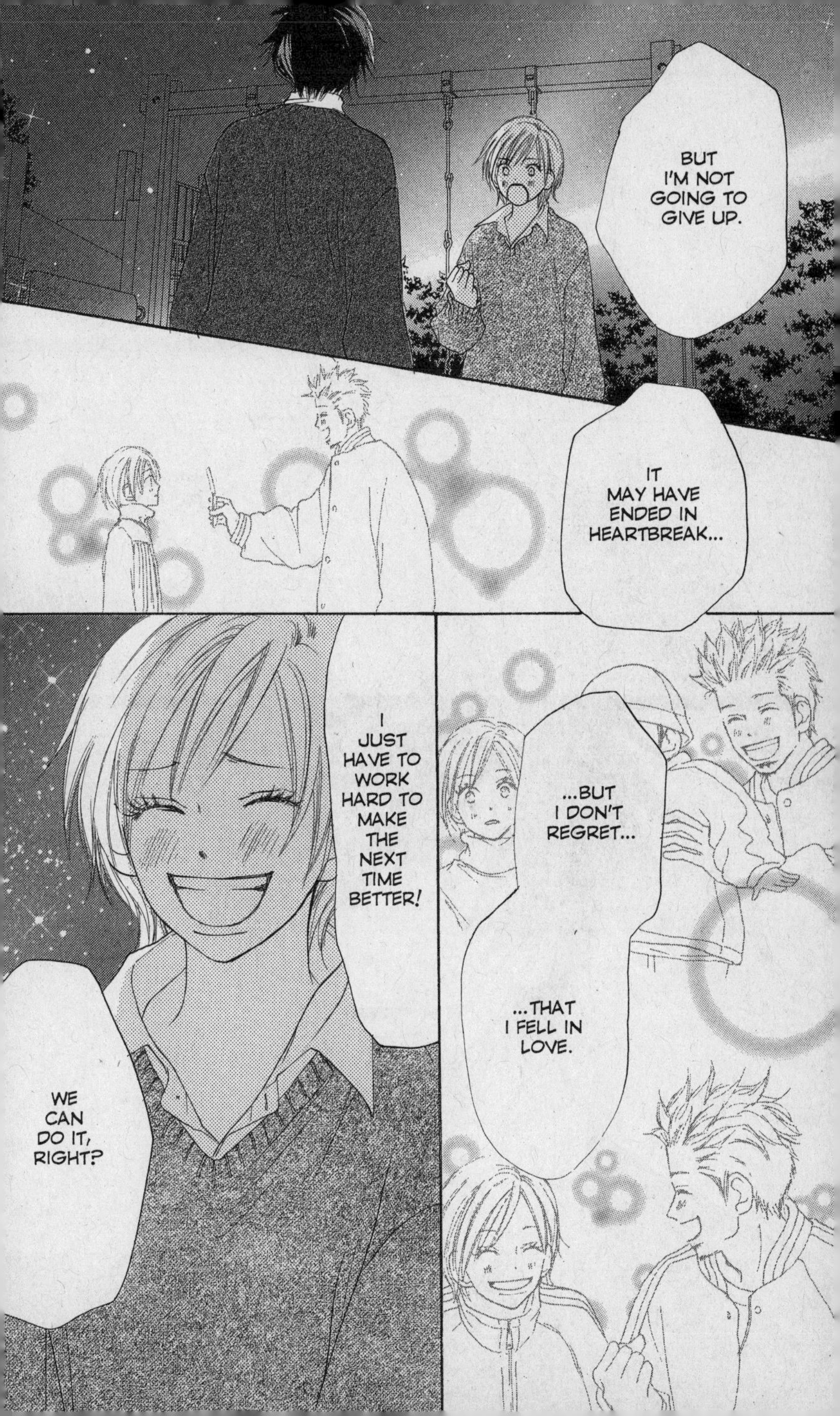
BUT I'M NOT GOING TO GIVE UP.
IT MAY HAVE ENDED IN HEARTBREAK...
...BUT I DON'T REGRET...
...THAT I FELL IN LOVE.
I JUST HAVE TO WORK HARD TO MAKE THE NEXT TIME BETTER!
WE CAN DO IT, RIGHT?

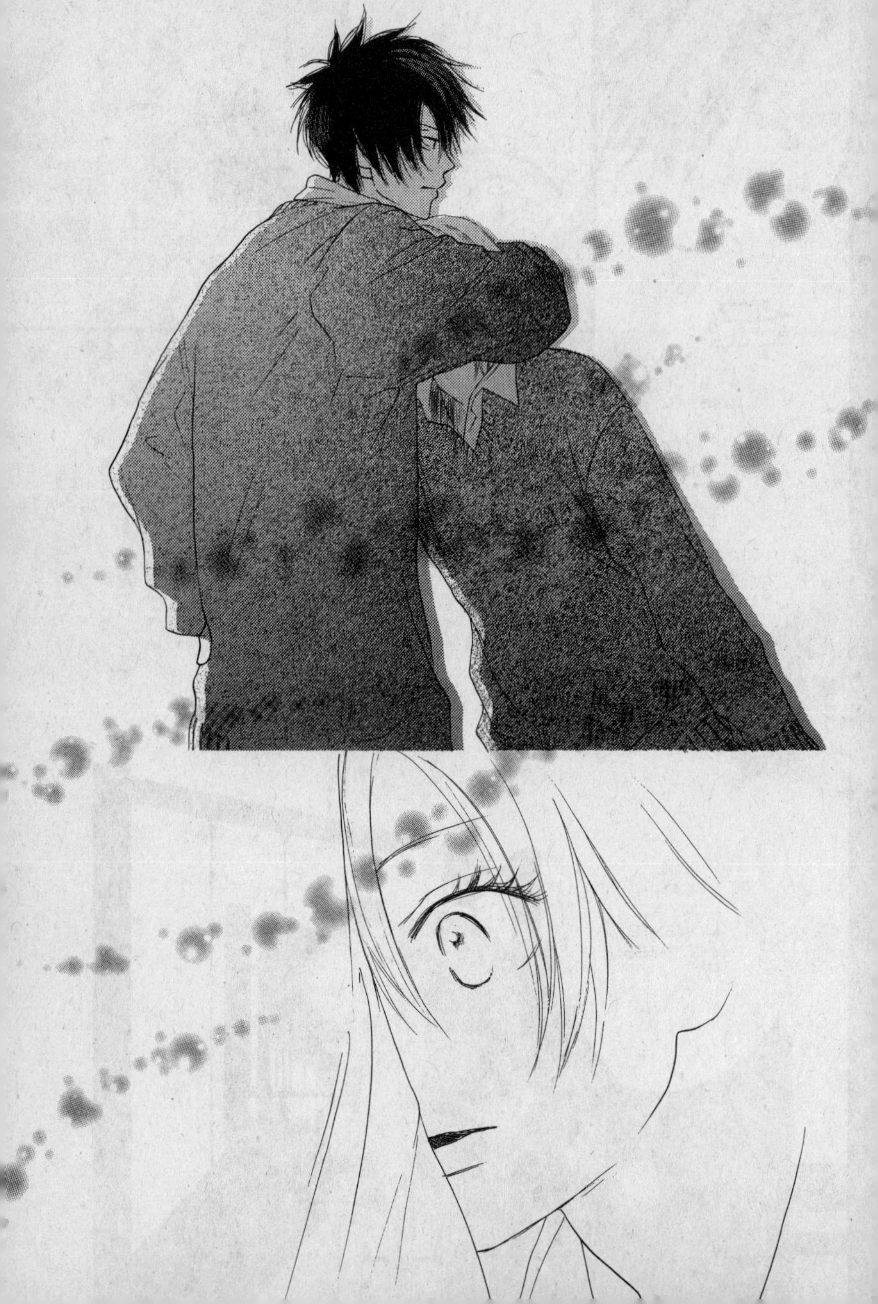

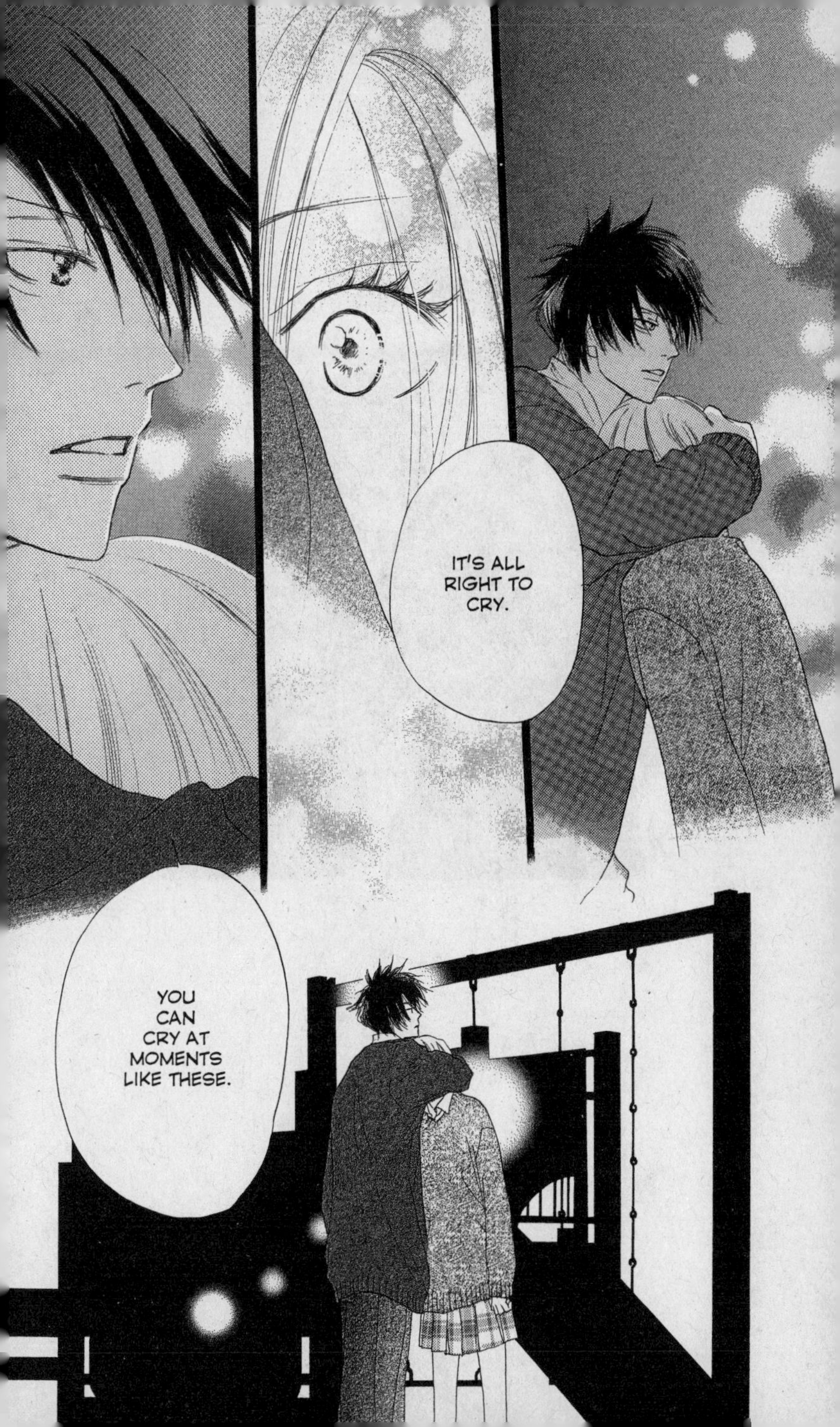
IT'S ALL RIGHT TO CRY.
YOU CAN CRY AT MOMENTS LIKE THESE.

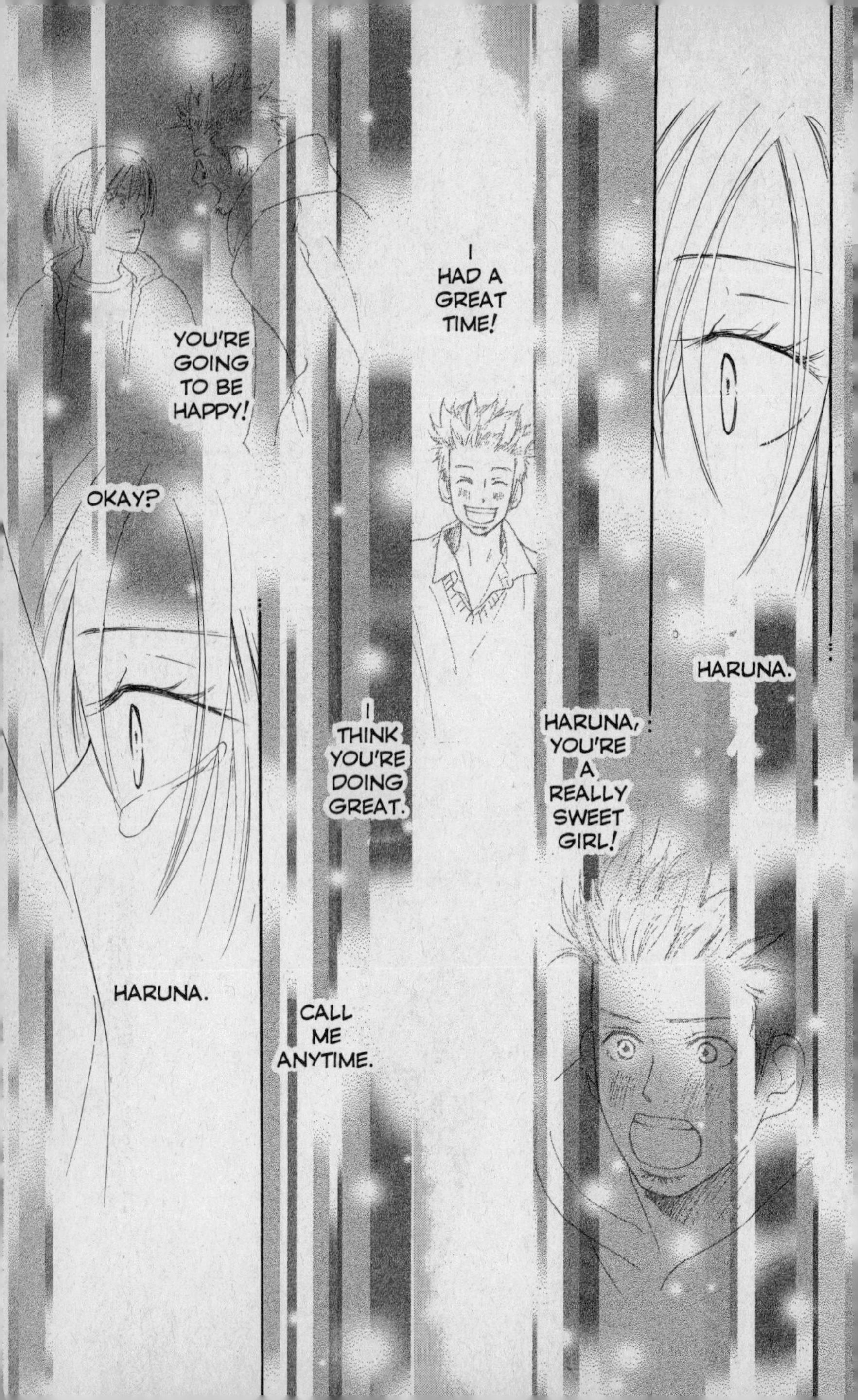
HARUNA.
HARUNA, YOU'RE A REALLY SWEET GIRL!
I HAD A GREAT TIME!
I THINK YOU'RE DOING GREAT.
CALL ME ANYTIME.
YOU'RE GOING TO BE HAPPY!
OKAY?
HARUNA.

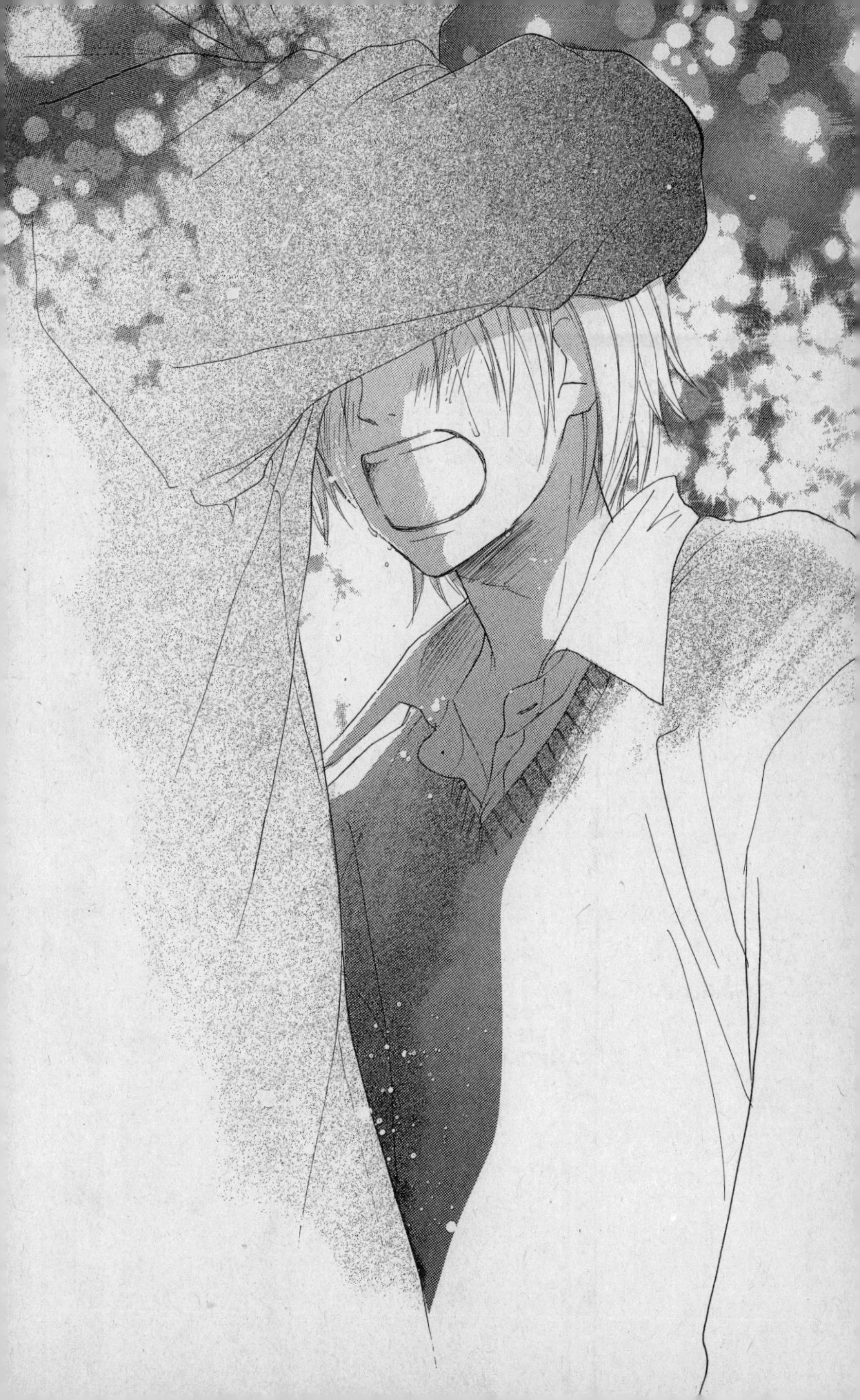

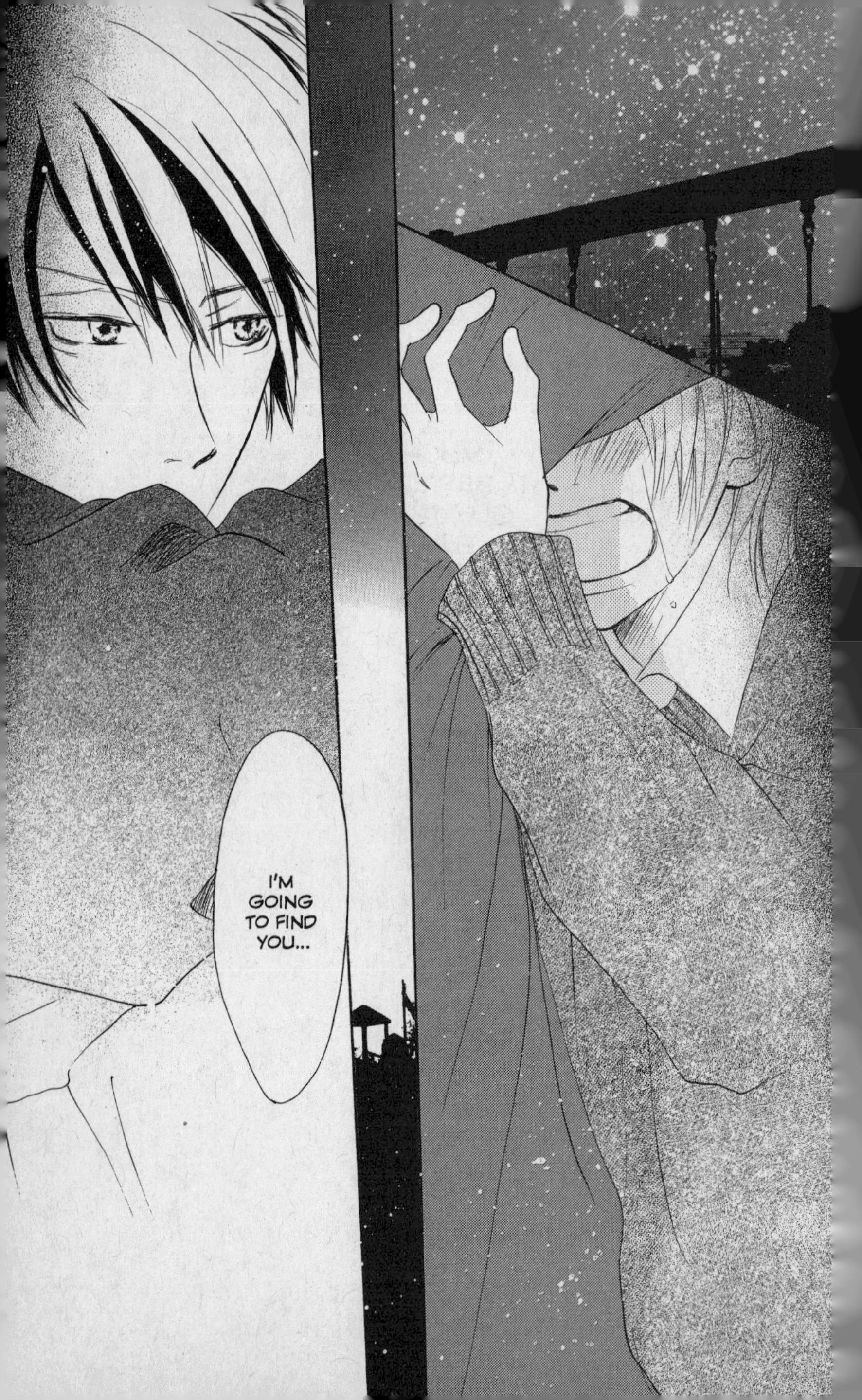
I'M GOING TO FIND YOU...

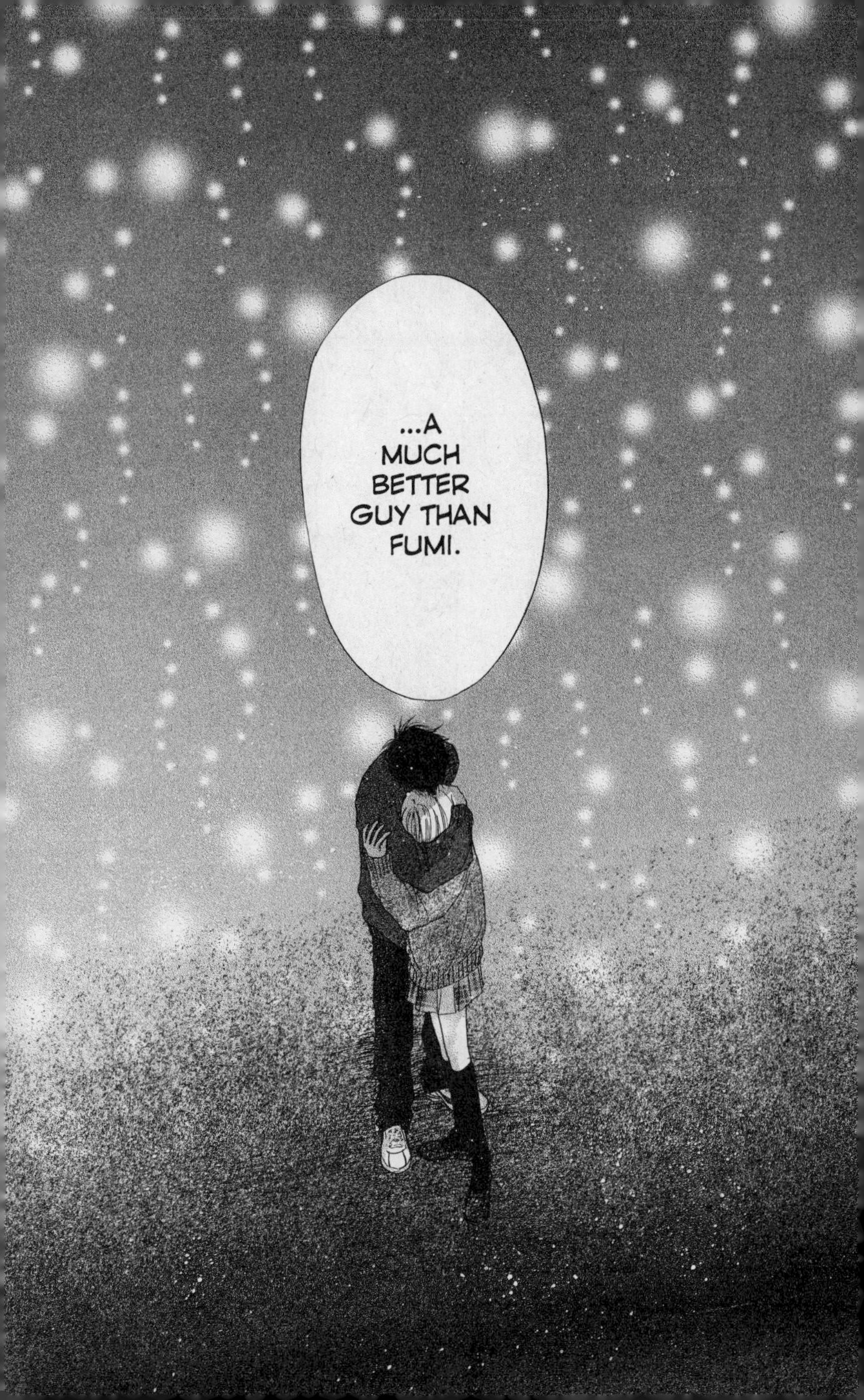
...A MUCH BETTER GUY THAN FUMI.

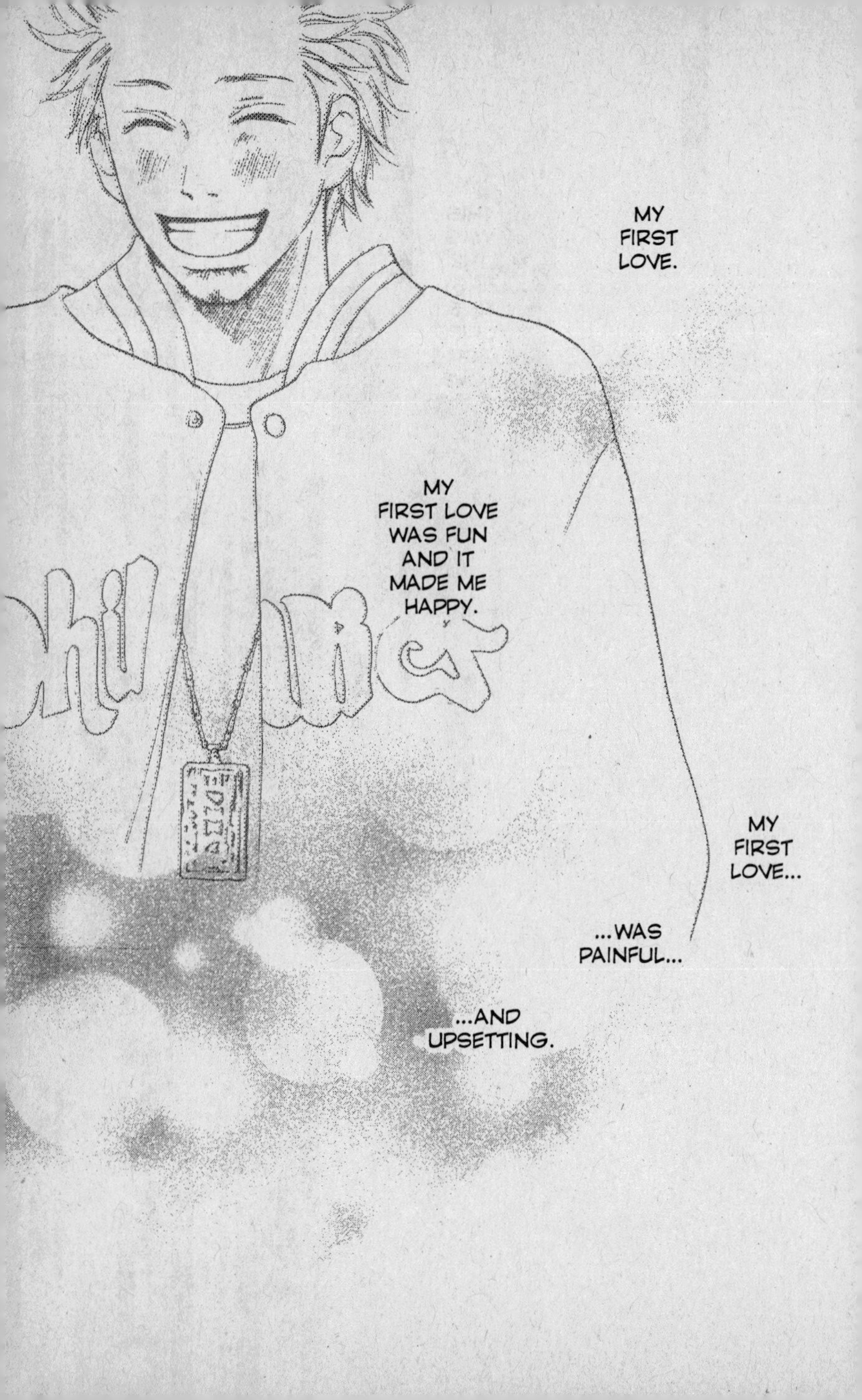
MY FIRST LOVE.
MY FIRST LOVE WAS FUN AND IT MADE ME HAPPY.
MY FIRST LOVE...
...WAS PAINFUL...
...AND UPSETTING.

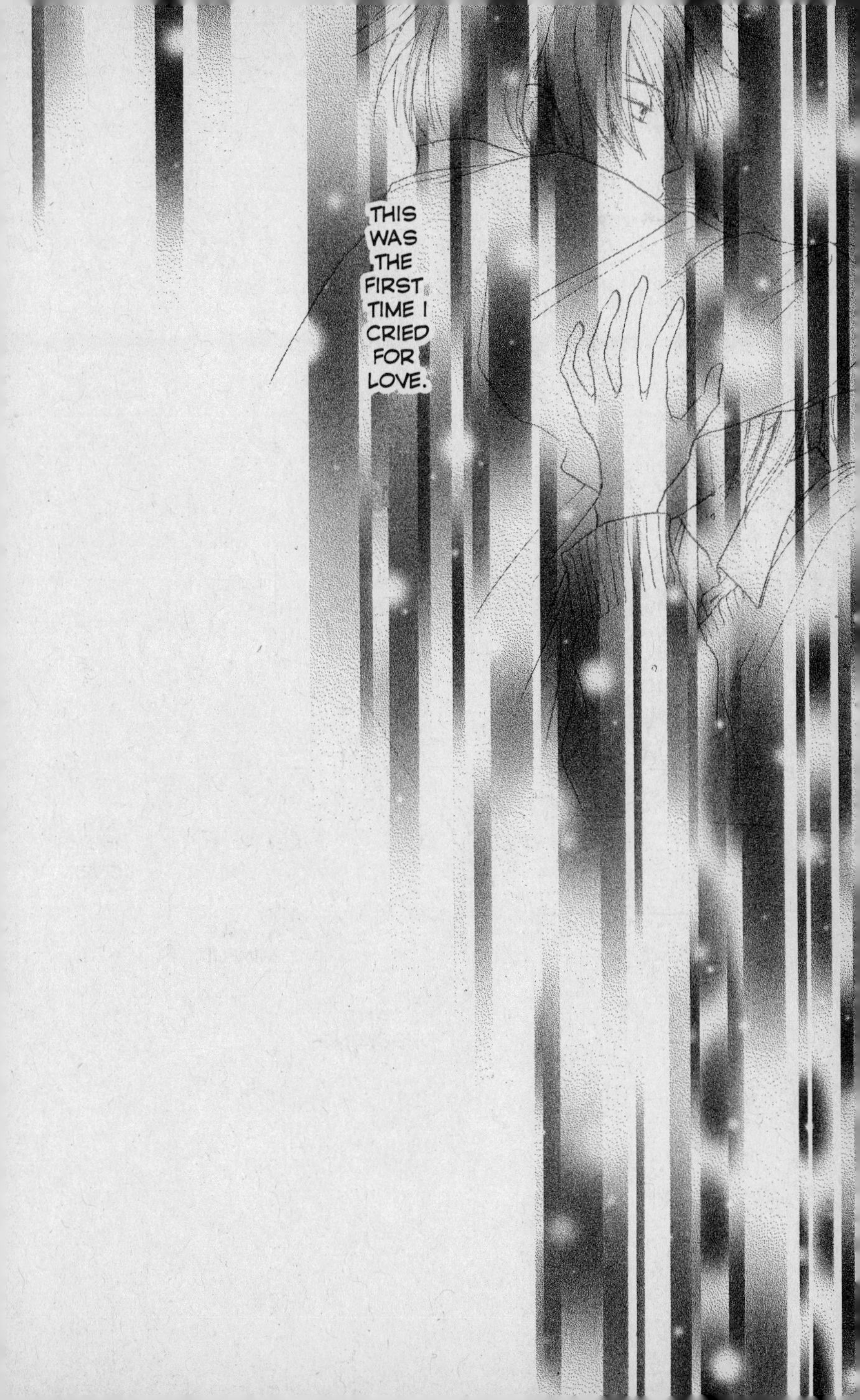
THIS WAS THE FIRST TIME I CRIED FOR LOVE.

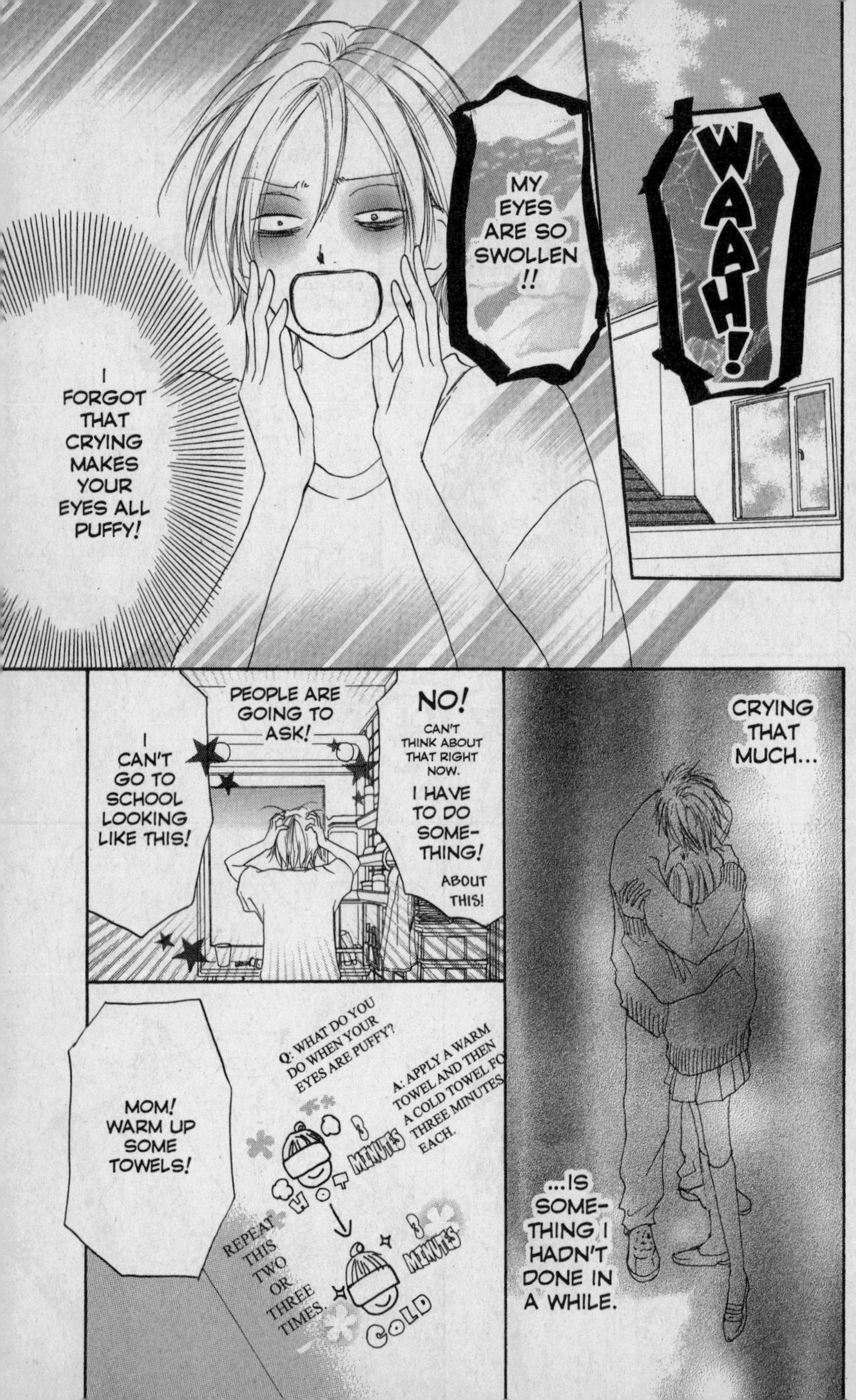
WAAH!
MY EYES ARE SO SWOLLEN!!
I FORGOT THAT CRYING MAKES YOUR EYES ALL PUFFY!
CRYING THAT MUCH...
...IS SOMETHING I HADN'T DONE IN A WHILE.
NO!
CAN'T THINK ABOUT THAT RIGHT NOW.
I HAVE TO DO SOME-THING!
ABOUT THIS!
PEOPLE ARE GOING TO ASK!
I CAN'T GO TO SCHOOL LOOKING LIKE THIS!
Q: WHAT DO YOU DO WHEN YOUR EYES ARE PUFFY?
A: APPLY A WARM TOWEL AND THEN A COLD TOWEL FOR THREE MINUTES EACH.
3 MINUTES
HOT
3 MINUTES
COLD
REPEAT THIS TWO OR THREE TIMES.
MOM! WARM UP SOME TOWELS!

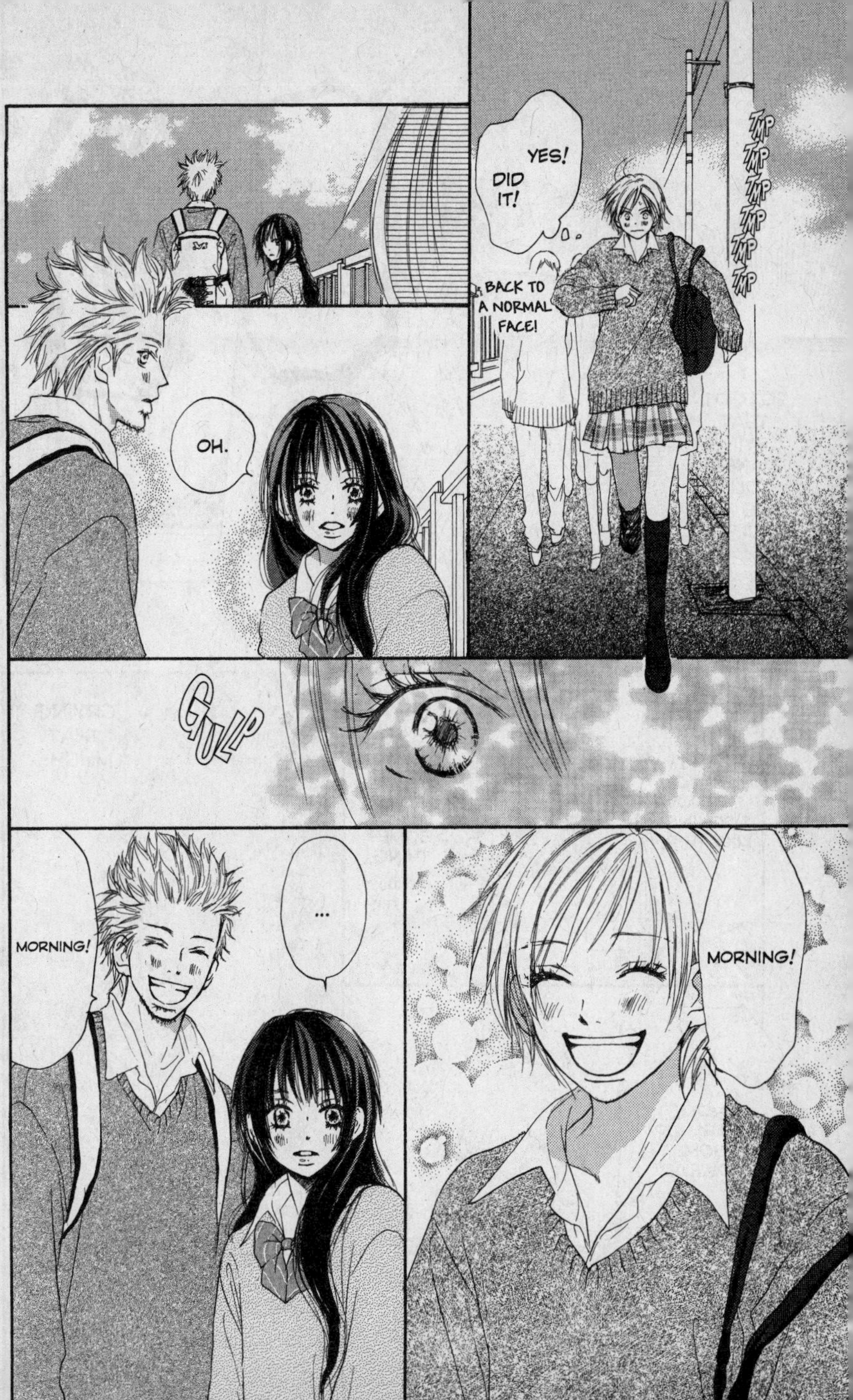
YES! DID IT!
BACK TO A NORMAL FACE!
TMP TMP TMP TMP TMP TMP
OH.
GULP
MORNING!
...
MORNING!

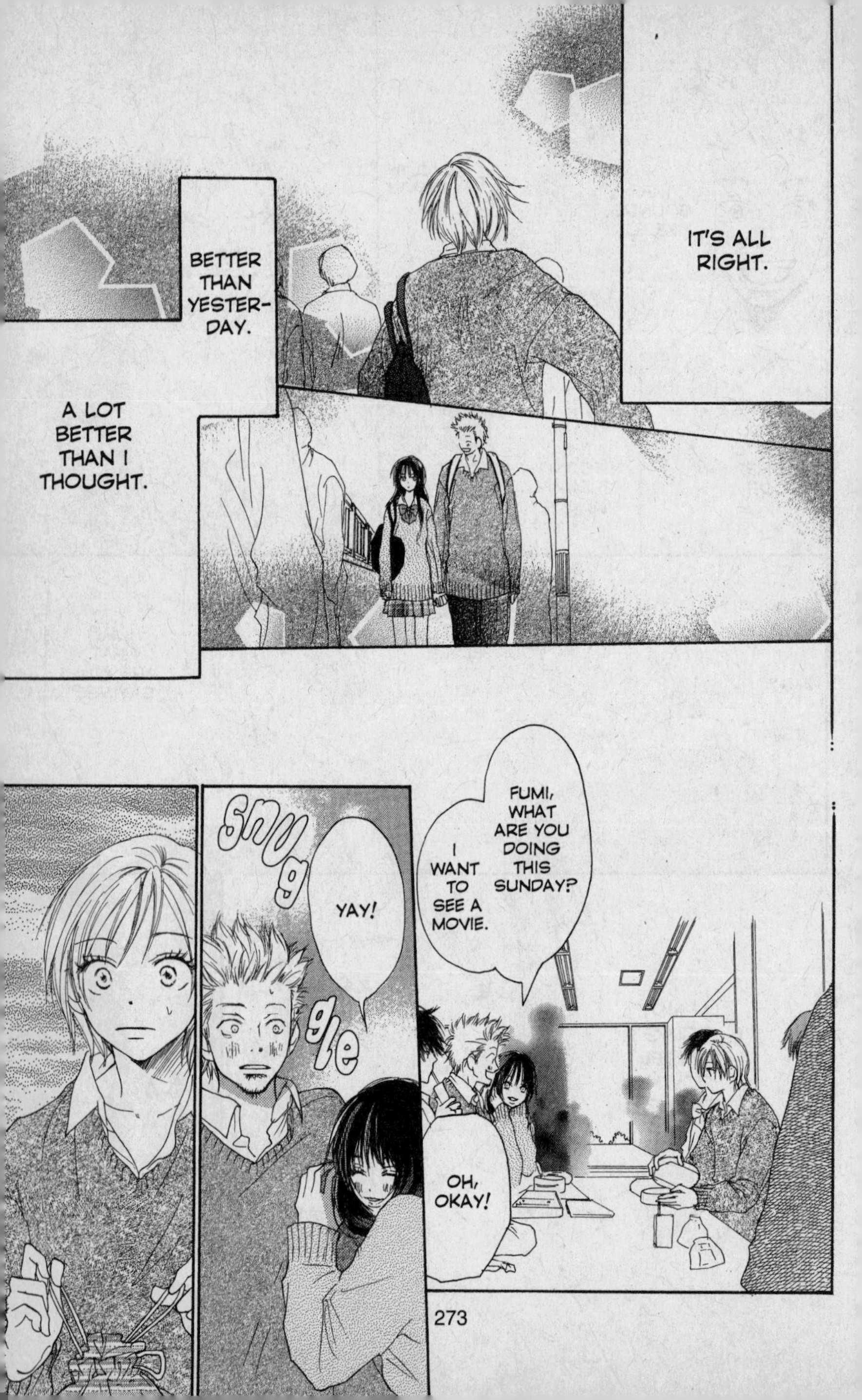
IT'S ALL RIGHT.
BETTER THAN YESTER-DAY.
A LOT BETTER THAN I THOUGHT.
FUMI, WHAT ARE YOU DOING THIS SUNDAY?
I WANT TO SEE A MOVIE.
OH, OKAY!
YAY!
snuggle

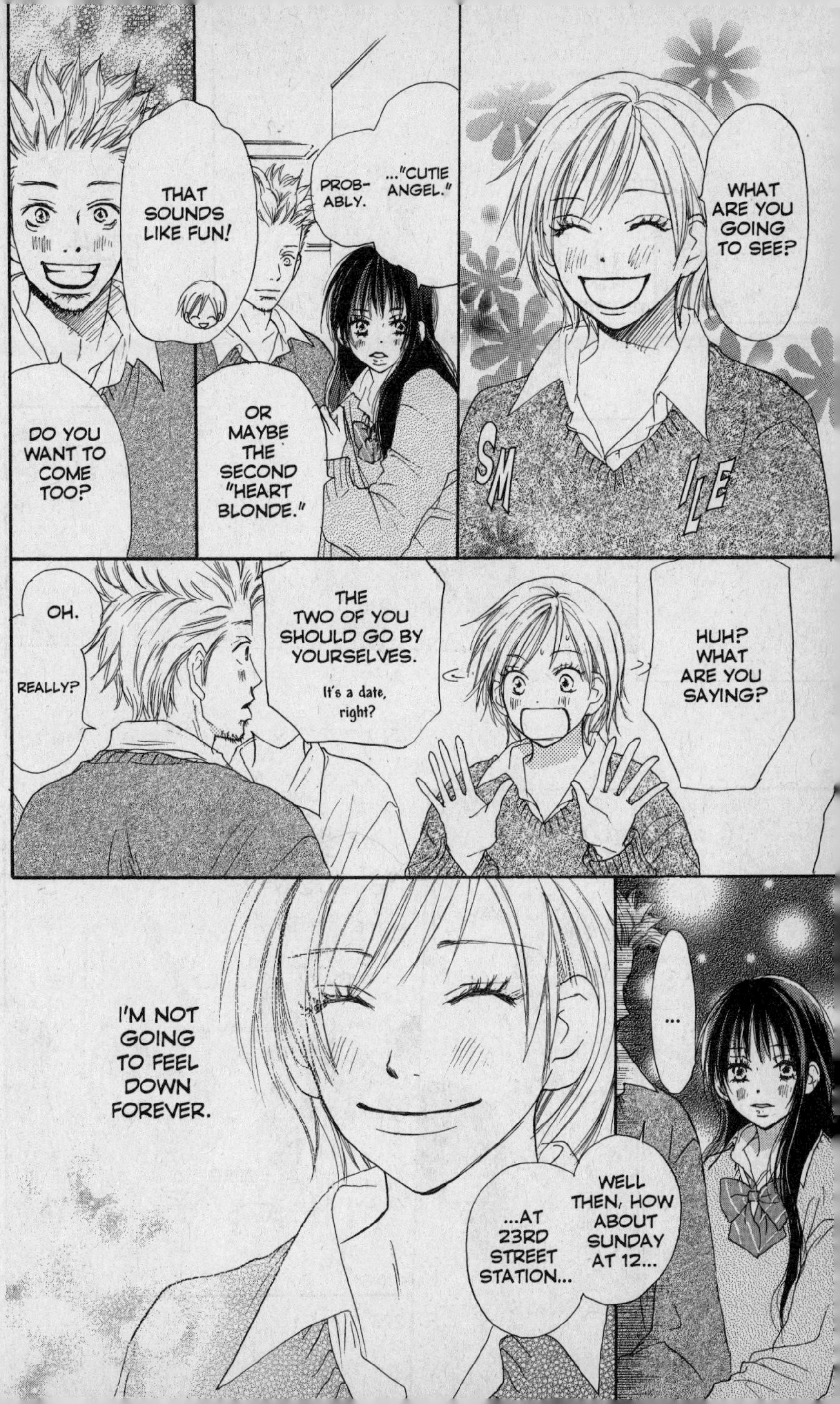
WHAT ARE YOU GOING TO SEE?
SMILE
..."CUTIE ANGEL."
PROB-ABLY.
OR MAYBE THE SECOND "HEART BLONDE."
THAT SOUNDS LIKE FUN!
DO YOU WANT TO COME TOO?
HUH? WHAT ARE YOU SAYING?
THE TWO OF YOU SHOULD GO BY YOURSELVES.
It's a date, right?
OH.
REALLY?
...
I'M NOT GOING TO FEEL DOWN FOREVER.
WELL THEN, HOW ABOUT SUNDAY AT 12...
...AT 23RD STREET STATION...

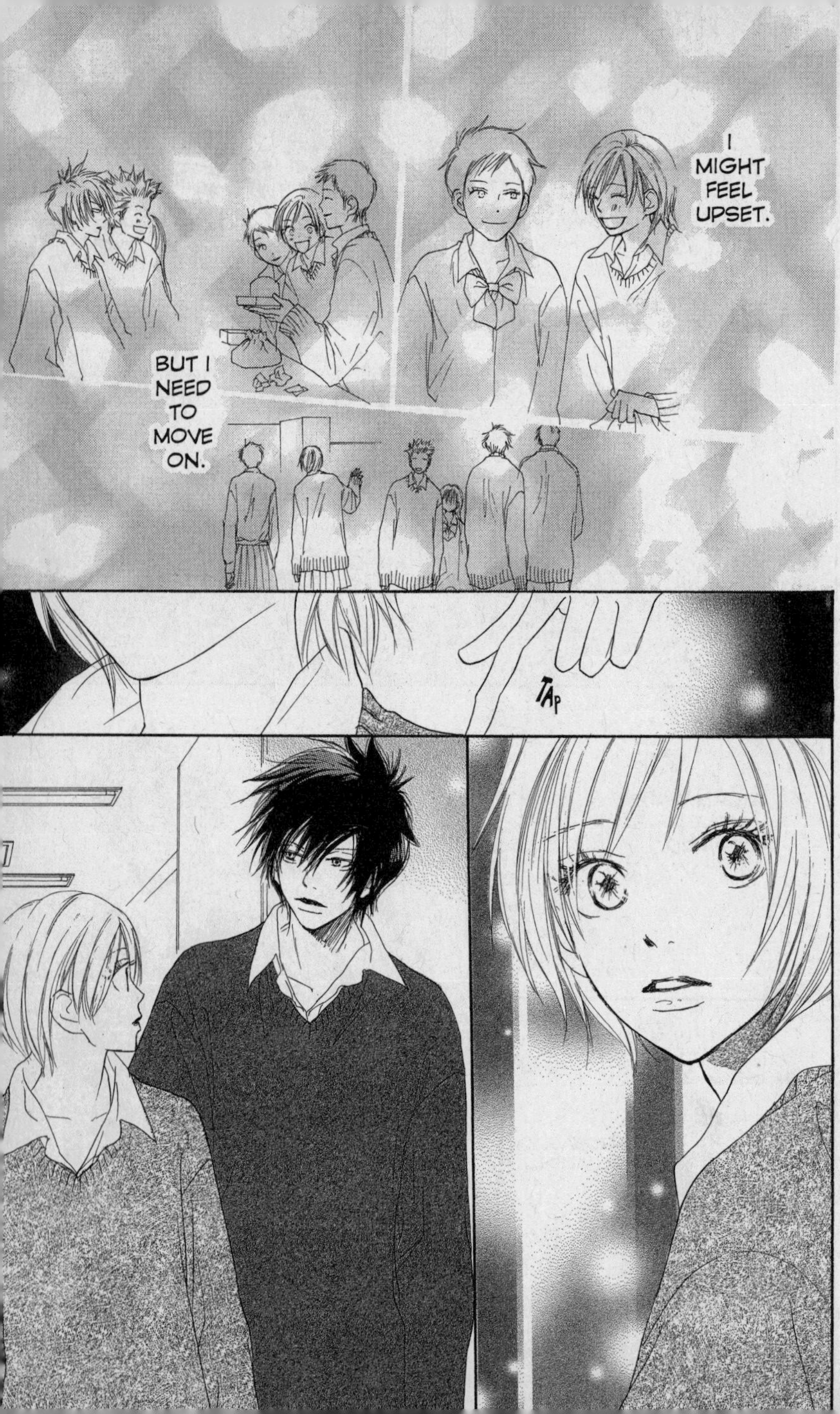
I MIGHT FEEL UPSET.
BUT I NEED TO MOVE ON.
TAP

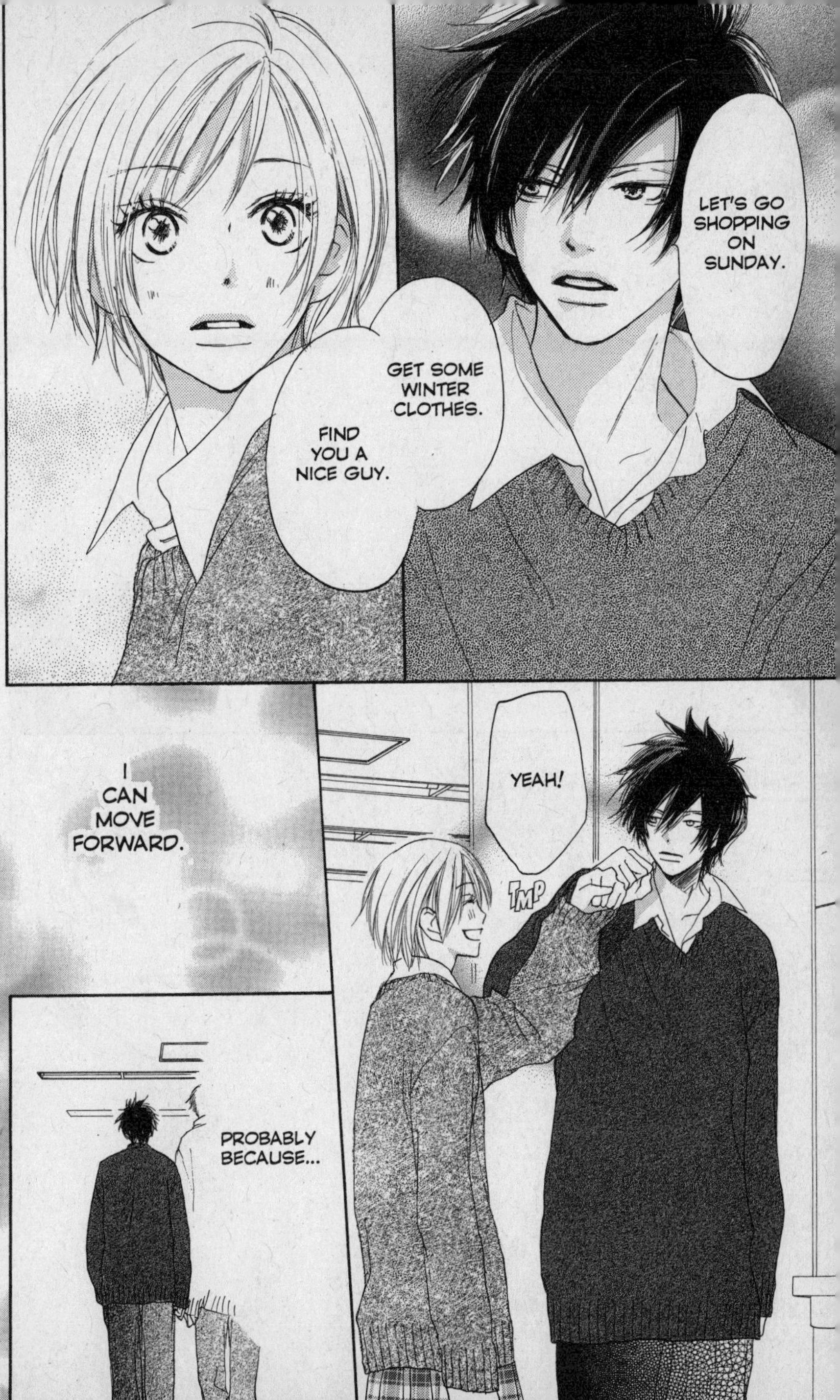
LET'S GO SHOPPING ON SUNDAY.
GET SOME WINTER CLOTHES.
FIND YOU A NICE GUY.
YEAH!
TMP
I CAN MOVE FORWARD.
PROBABLY BECAUSE...

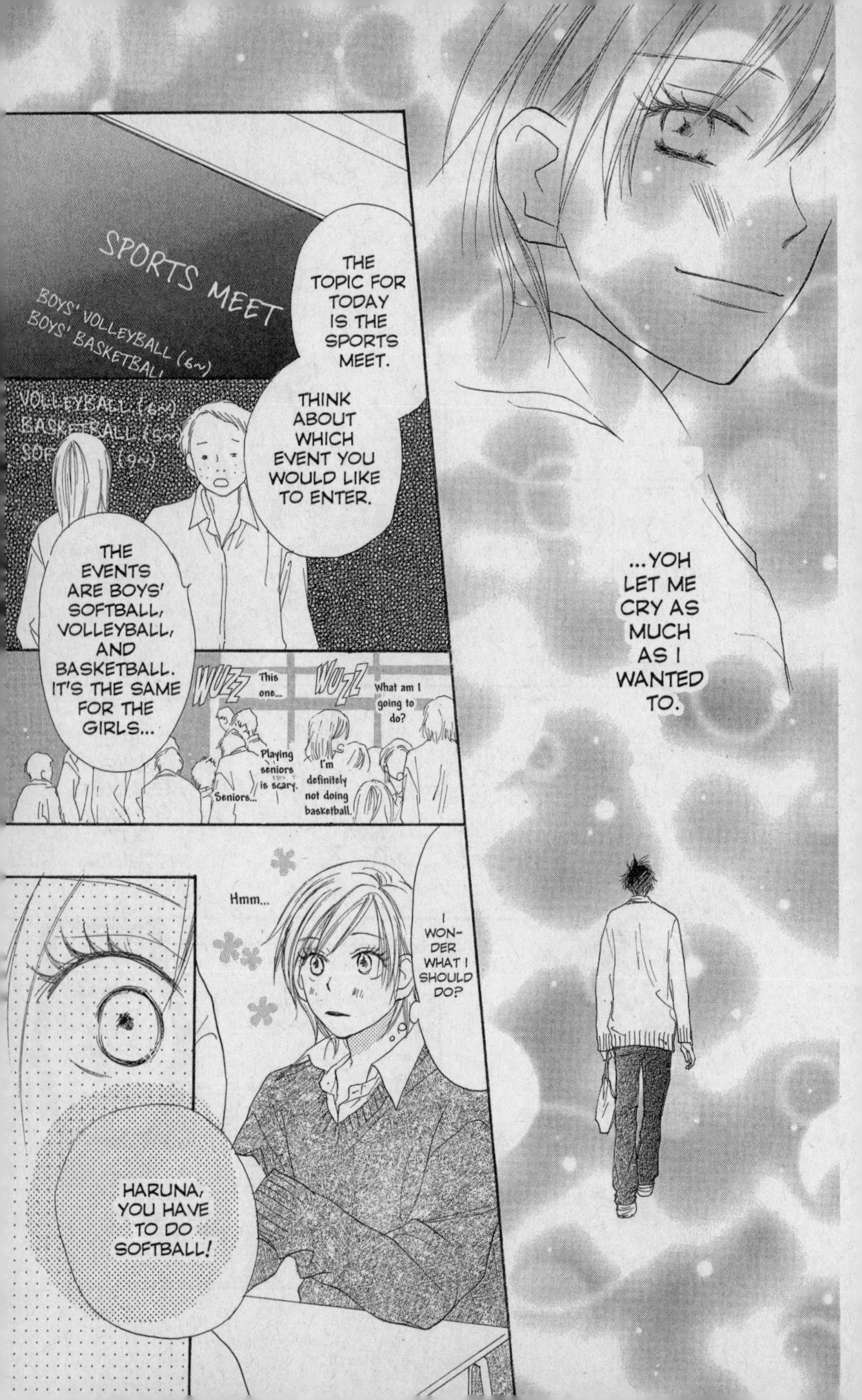
...YOH LET ME CRY AS MUCH AS I WANTED TO.
SPORTS MEET
BOYS' VOLLEYBALL (6~)
BOYS' BASKETBALL
THE TOPIC FOR TODAY IS THE SPORTS MEET.
THINK ABOUT WHICH EVENT YOU WOULD LIKE TO ENTER.
THE EVENTS ARE BOYS' SOFTBALL, VOLLEYBALL, AND BASKETBALL. IT'S THE SAME FOR THE GIRLS...
WUZZ
WUZZ
What am I going to do?
This one...
I'm definitely not doing basketball.
Playing seniors is scary.
Seniors...
I WONDER WHAT I SHOULD DO?
Hmm...
HARUNA, YOU HAVE TO DO SOFTBALL!

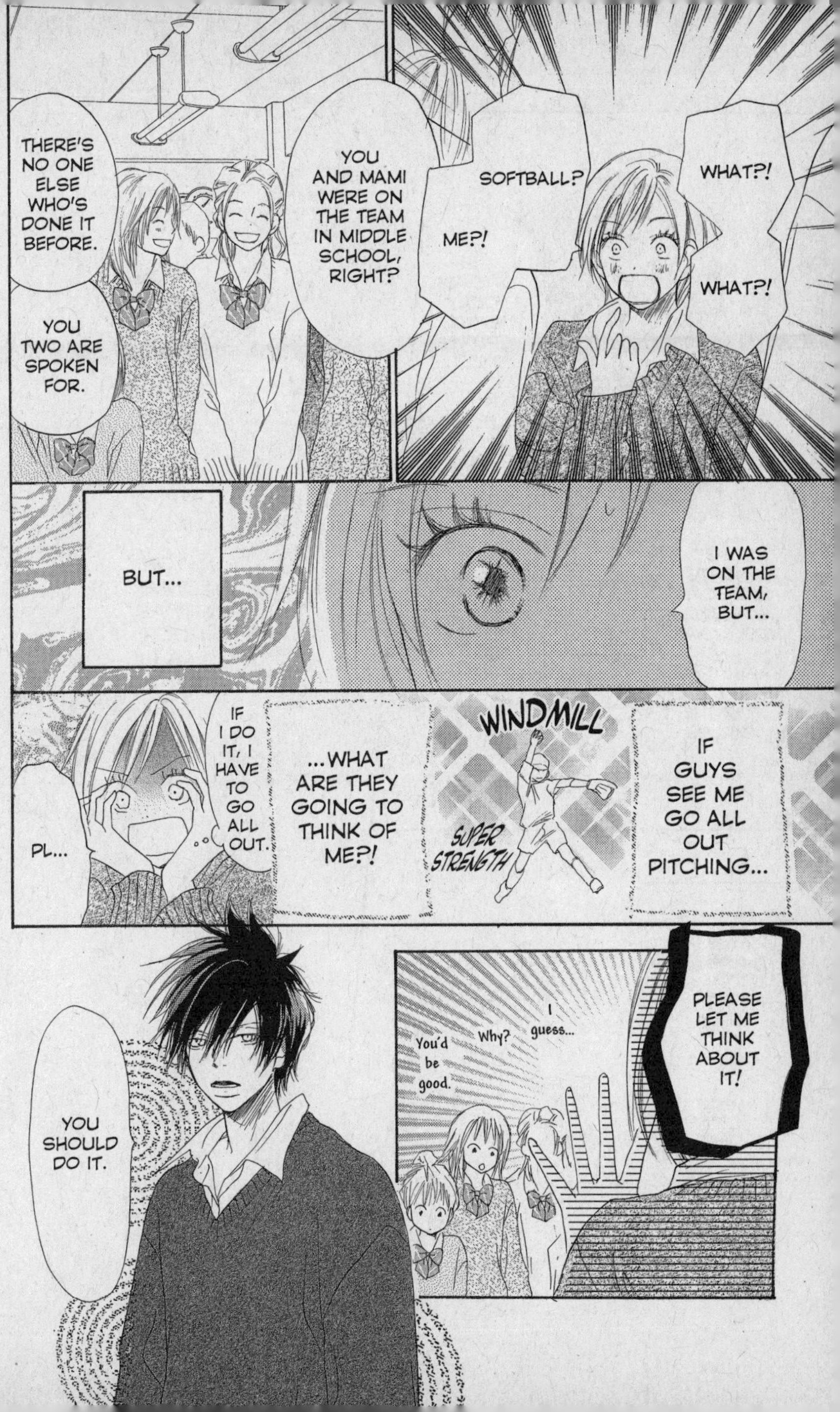
WHAT?!
WHAT?!
SOFTBALL?
ME?!
YOU AND MAMI WERE ON THE TEAM IN MIDDLE SCHOOL, RIGHT?
THERE'S NO ONE ELSE WHO'S DONE IT BEFORE.
YOU TWO ARE SPOKEN FOR.
I WAS ON THE TEAM, BUT...
BUT...
IF GUYS SEE ME GO ALL OUT PITCHING...
WINDMILL
SUPER STRENGTH
...WHAT ARE THEY GOING TO THINK OF ME?!
IF I DO IT, I HAVE TO GO ALL OUT.
PL...
PLEASE LET ME THINK ABOUT IT!
I guess...
Why?
You'd be good.
YOU SHOULD DO IT.

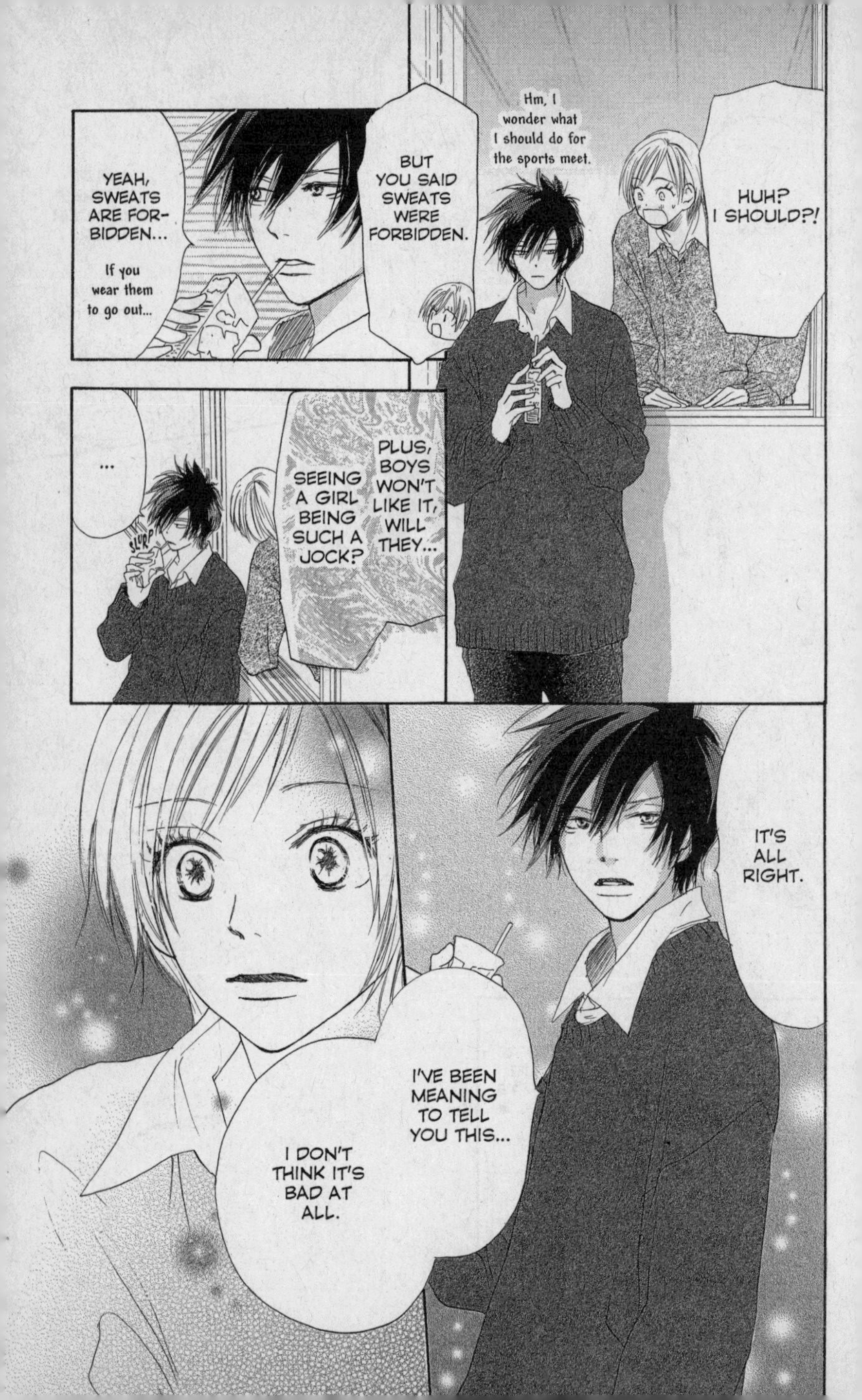
Hm, I wonder what I should do for the sports meet.
HUH? I SHOULD?!
BUT YOU SAID SWEATS WERE FORBIDDEN.
YEAH, SWEATS ARE FOR-BIDDEN...
If you wear them to go out...
PLUS, BOYS WON'T LIKE IT, WILL THEY...
SEEING A GIRL BEING SUCH A JOCK?
...
SLURP
IT'S ALL RIGHT.
I'VE BEEN MEANING TO TELL YOU THIS...
I DON'T THINK IT'S BAD AT ALL.

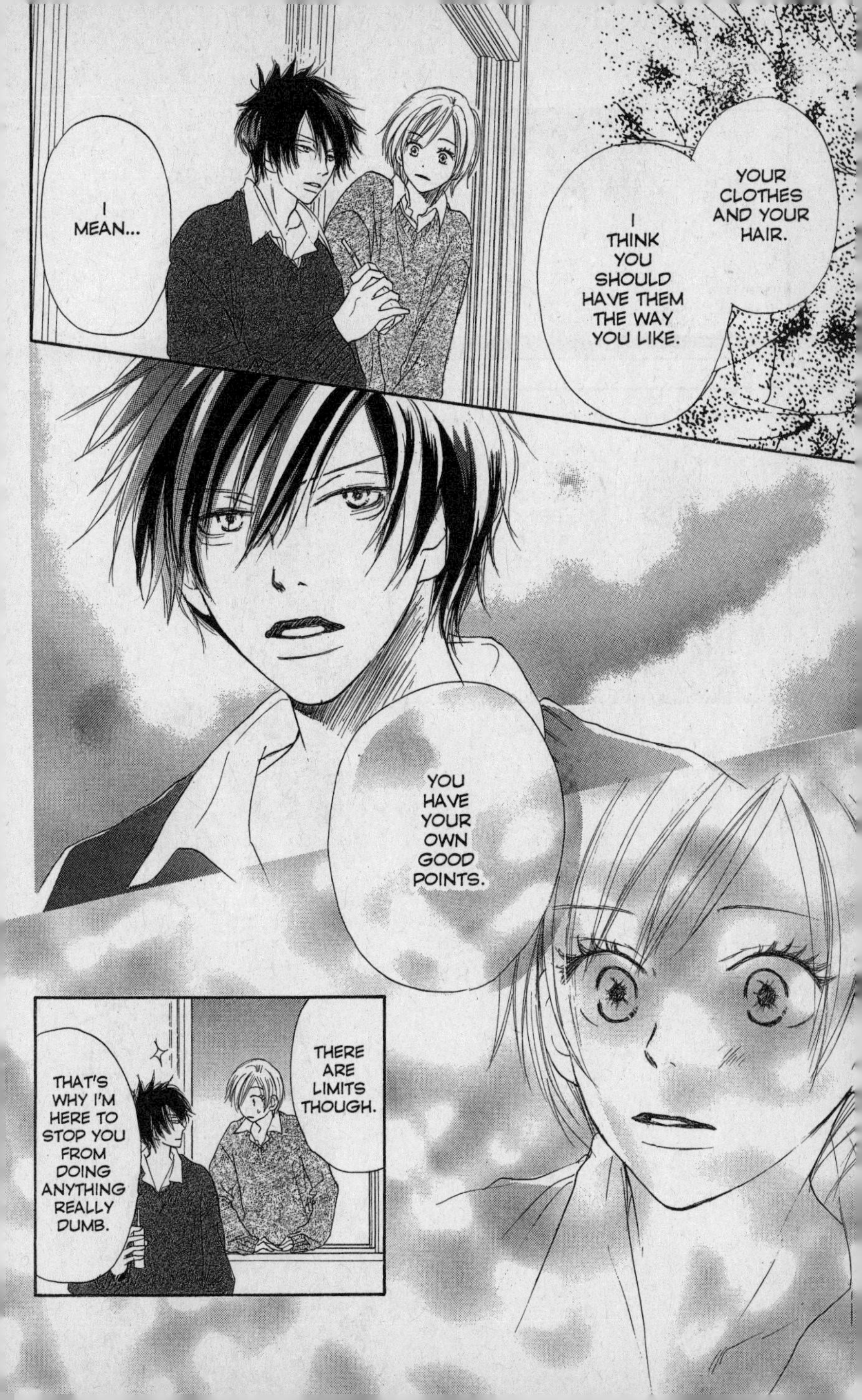
YOUR CLOTHES AND YOUR HAIR.
I THINK YOU SHOULD HAVE THEM THE WAY YOU LIKE.
I MEAN...
YOU HAVE YOUR OWN GOOD POINTS.
THERE ARE LIMITS THOUGH.
THAT'S WHY I'M HERE TO STOP YOU FROM DOING ANYTHING REALLY DUMB.

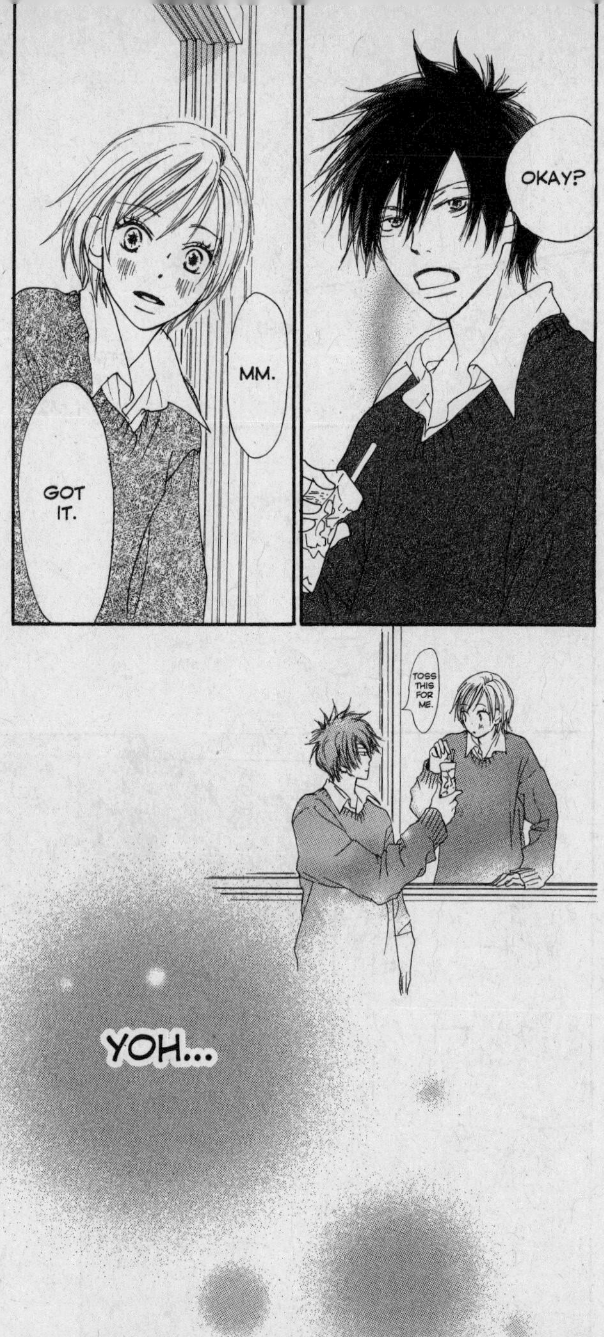
OKAY?
MM.
GOT IT.
TOSS THIS FOR ME.
YOH...

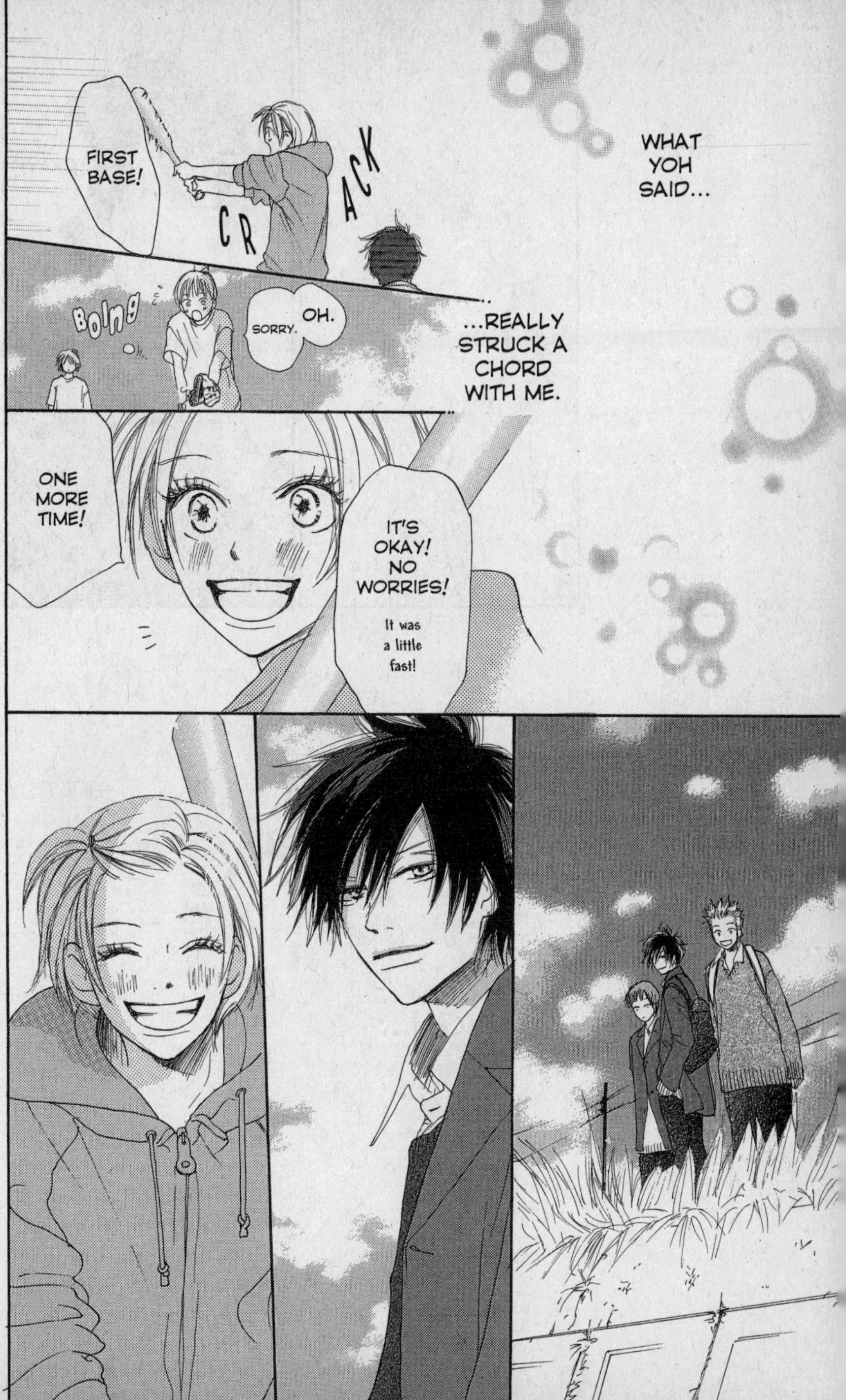
WHAT YOH SAID...
FIRST BASE!
CRACK
...REALLY STRUCK A CHORD WITH ME.
OH.
SORRY.
Boing
IT'S OKAY! NO WORRIES!
It was a little fast!
ONE MORE TIME!

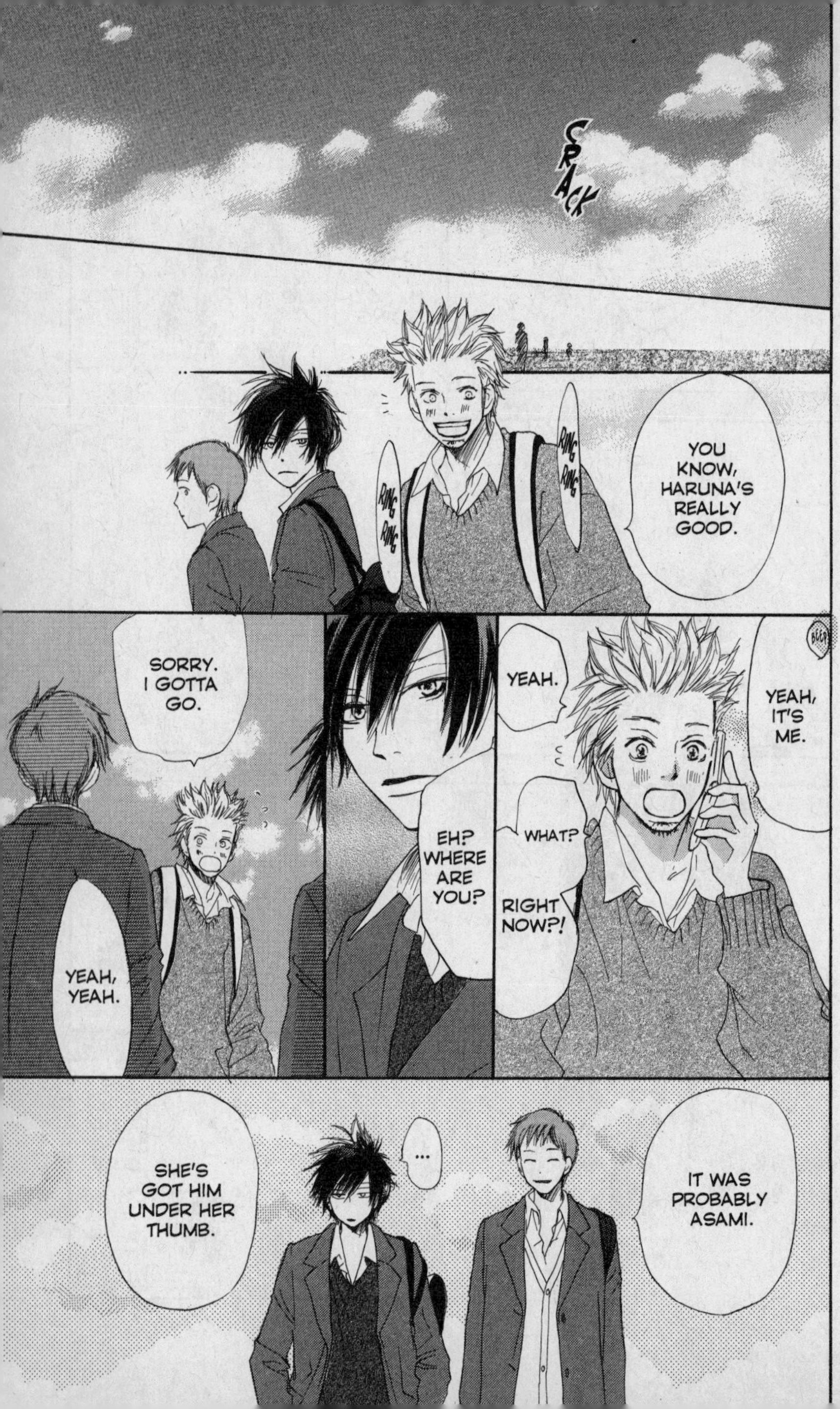
CRACK
YOU KNOW, HARUNA'S REALLY GOOD.
RING RING
RING RING
YEAH, IT'S ME.
BEEP
YEAH.
WHAT?
RIGHT NOW?!
EH? WHERE ARE YOU?
SORRY. I GOTTA GO.
YEAH, YEAH.
IT WAS PROBABLY ASAMI.
...
SHE'S GOT HIM UNDER HER THUMB.

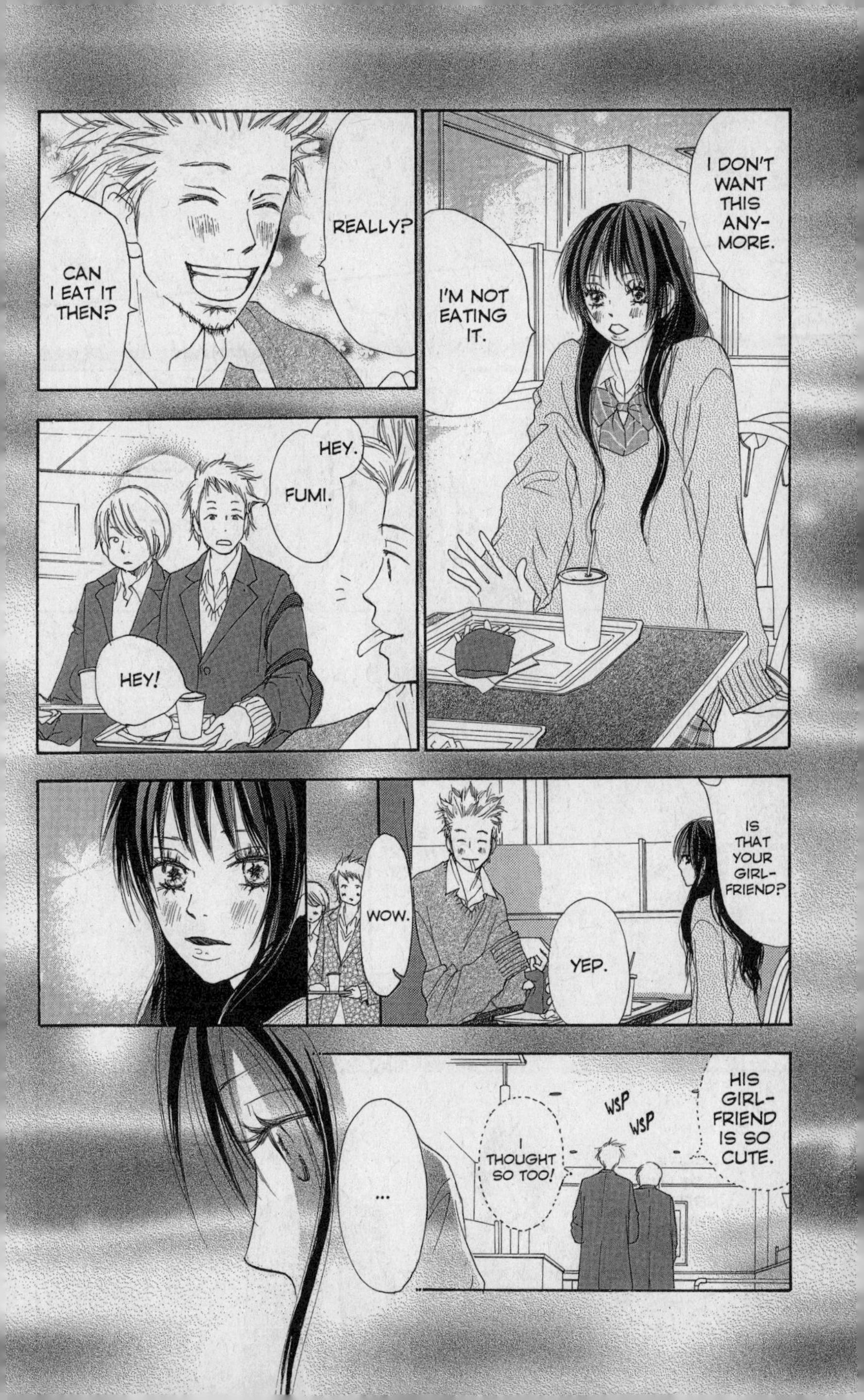
I DON'T WANT THIS ANYMORE.
I'M NOT EATING IT.
REALLY?
CAN I EAT IT THEN?
HEY.
FUMI.
HEY!
IS THAT YOUR GIRLFRIEND?
YEP.
WOW.
HIS GIRLFRIEND IS SO CUTE.
WSP
WSP
I THOUGHT SO TOO!
...

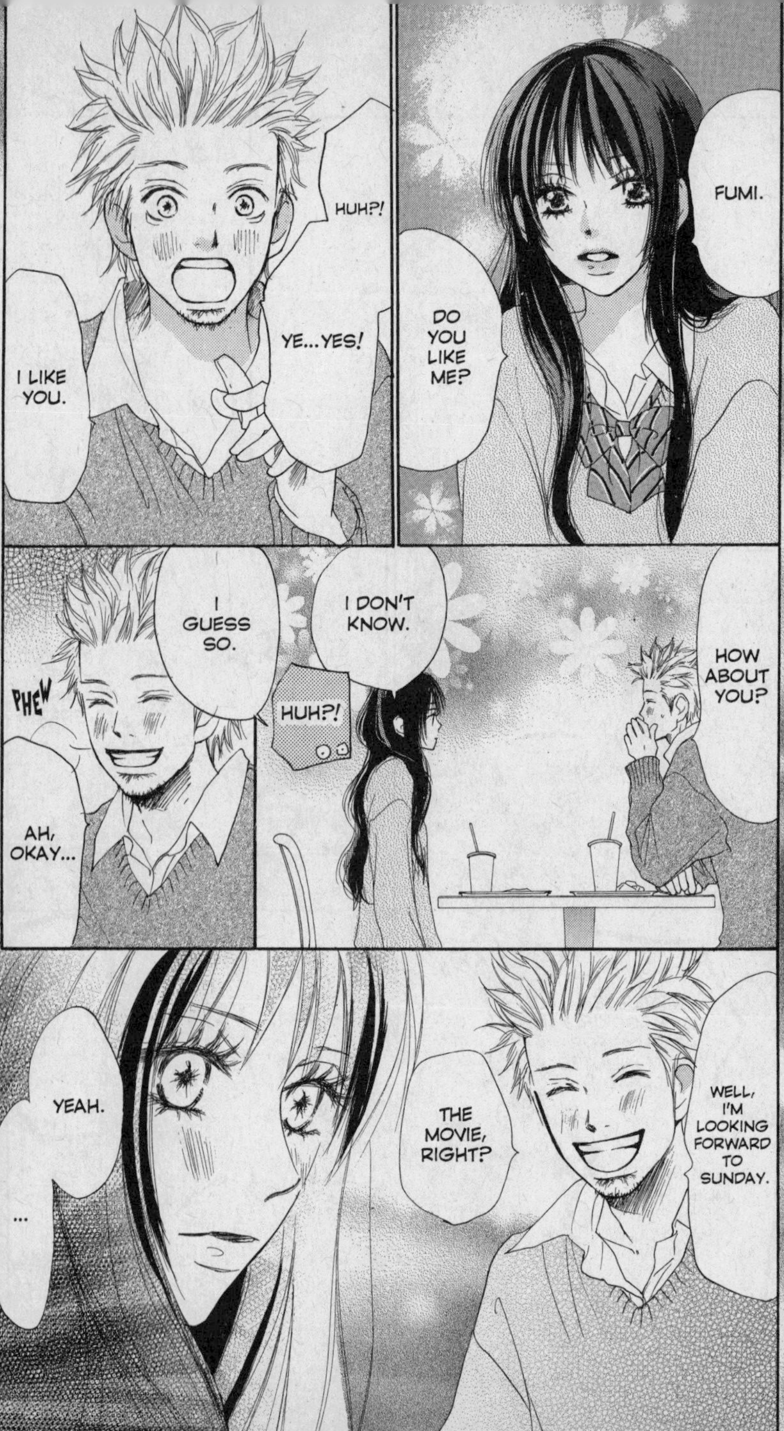
FUMI.
DO YOU LIKE ME?
HUH?!
YE...YES!
I LIKE YOU.
HOW ABOUT YOU?
I DON'T KNOW.
HUH?!
I GUESS SO.
PHEW
AH, OKAY...
WELL, I'M LOOKING FORWARD TO SUNDAY.
THE MOVIE, RIGHT?
YEAH.
...

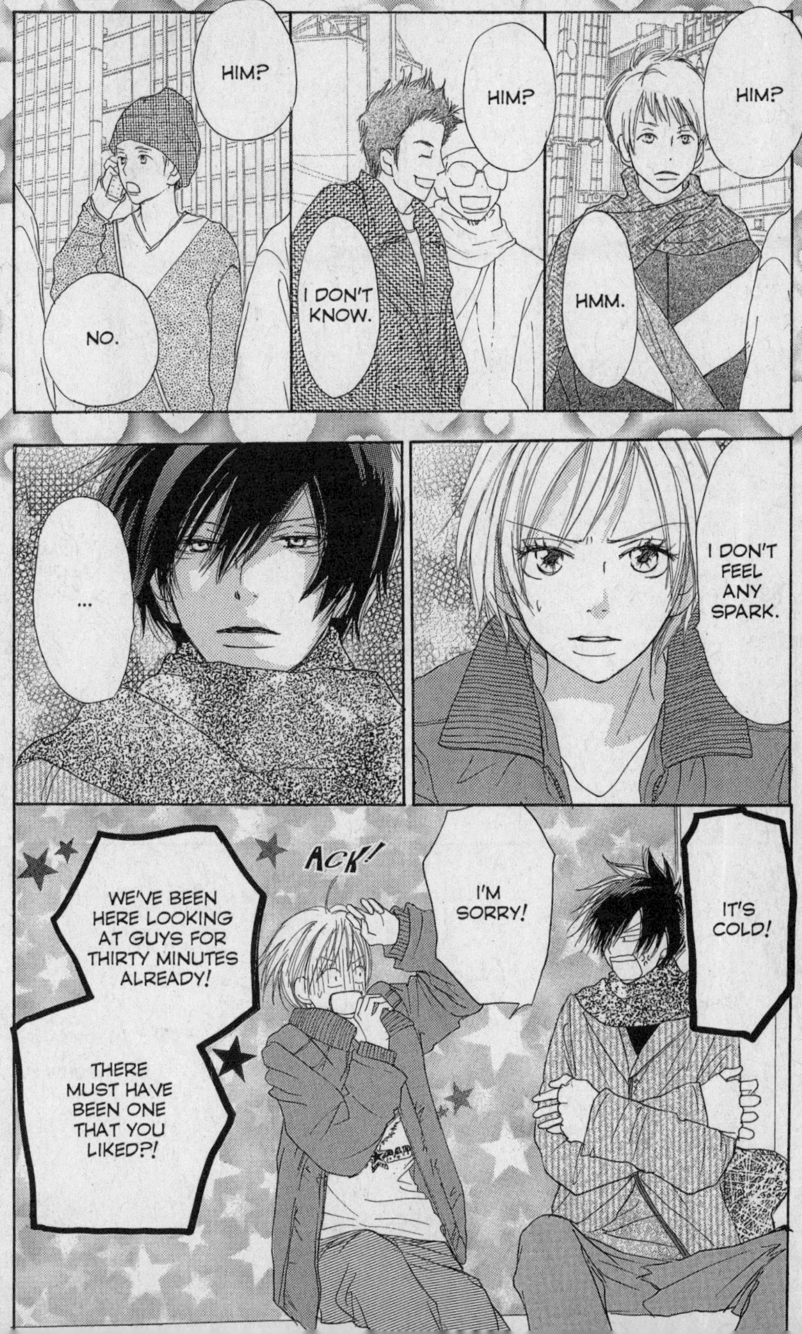
HIM?
HMM.
HIM?
I DON'T KNOW.
HIM?
NO.
I DON'T FEEL ANY SPARK.
...
IT'S COLD!
I'M SORRY!
ACK!
WE'VE BEEN HERE LOOKING AT GUYS FOR THIRTY MINUTES ALREADY!
THERE MUST HAVE BEEN ONE THAT YOU LIKED?!

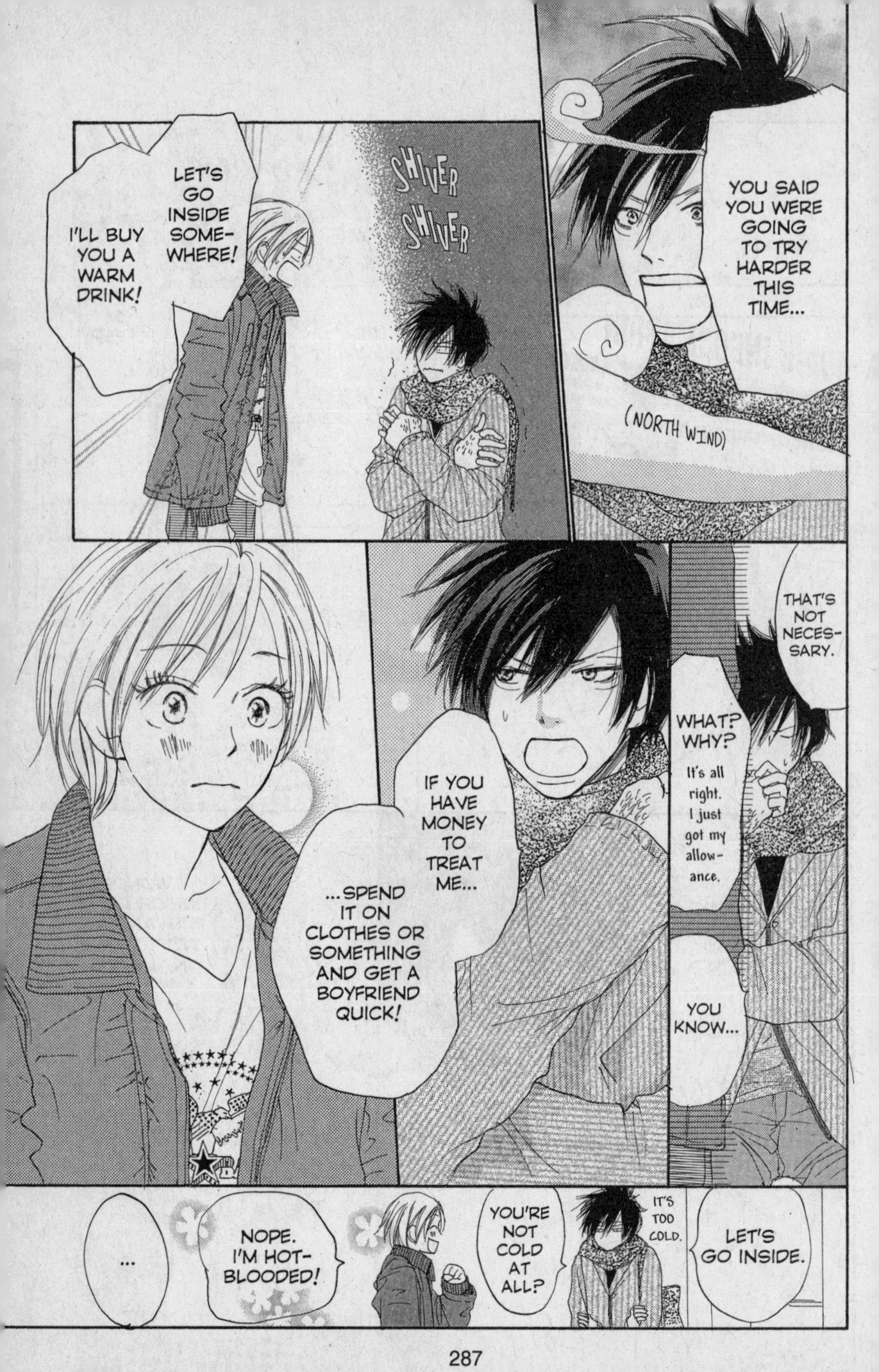
YOU SAID YOU WERE GOING TO TRY HARDER THIS TIME...
(NORTH WIND)
SHIVER SHIVER
LET'S GO INSIDE SOME-WHERE!
I'LL BUY YOU A WARM DRINK!
THAT'S NOT NECES-SARY.
WHAT? WHY?
It's all right. I just got my allow-ance.
YOU KNOW...
IF YOU HAVE MONEY TO TREAT ME...
...SPEND IT ON CLOTHES OR SOMETHING AND GET A BOYFRIEND QUICK!
LET'S GO INSIDE.
IT'S TOO COLD.
YOU'RE NOT COLD AT ALL?
NOPE. I'M HOT-BLOODED!
...

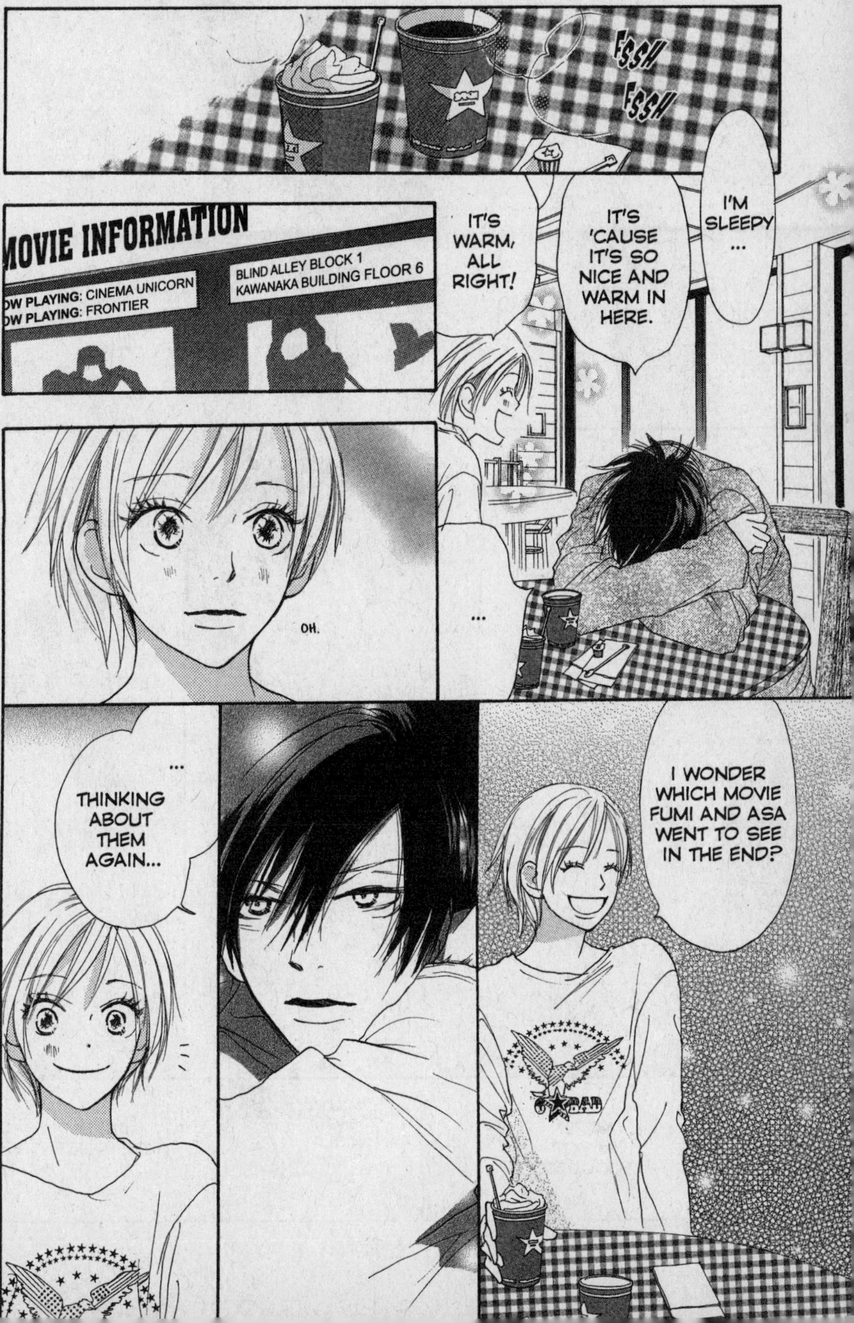
FSSH
FSSH
I'M SLEEPY...
IT'S 'CAUSE IT'S SO NICE AND WARM IN HERE.
IT'S WARM, ALL RIGHT!
...
MOVIE INFORMATION
BLIND ALLEY BLOCK 1
KAWANAKA BUILDING FLOOR 6
OW PLAYING: CINEMA UNICORN
OW PLAYING: FRONTIER
OH.
I WONDER WHICH MOVIE FUMI AND ASA WENT TO SEE IN THE END?
... THINKING ABOUT THEM AGAIN...

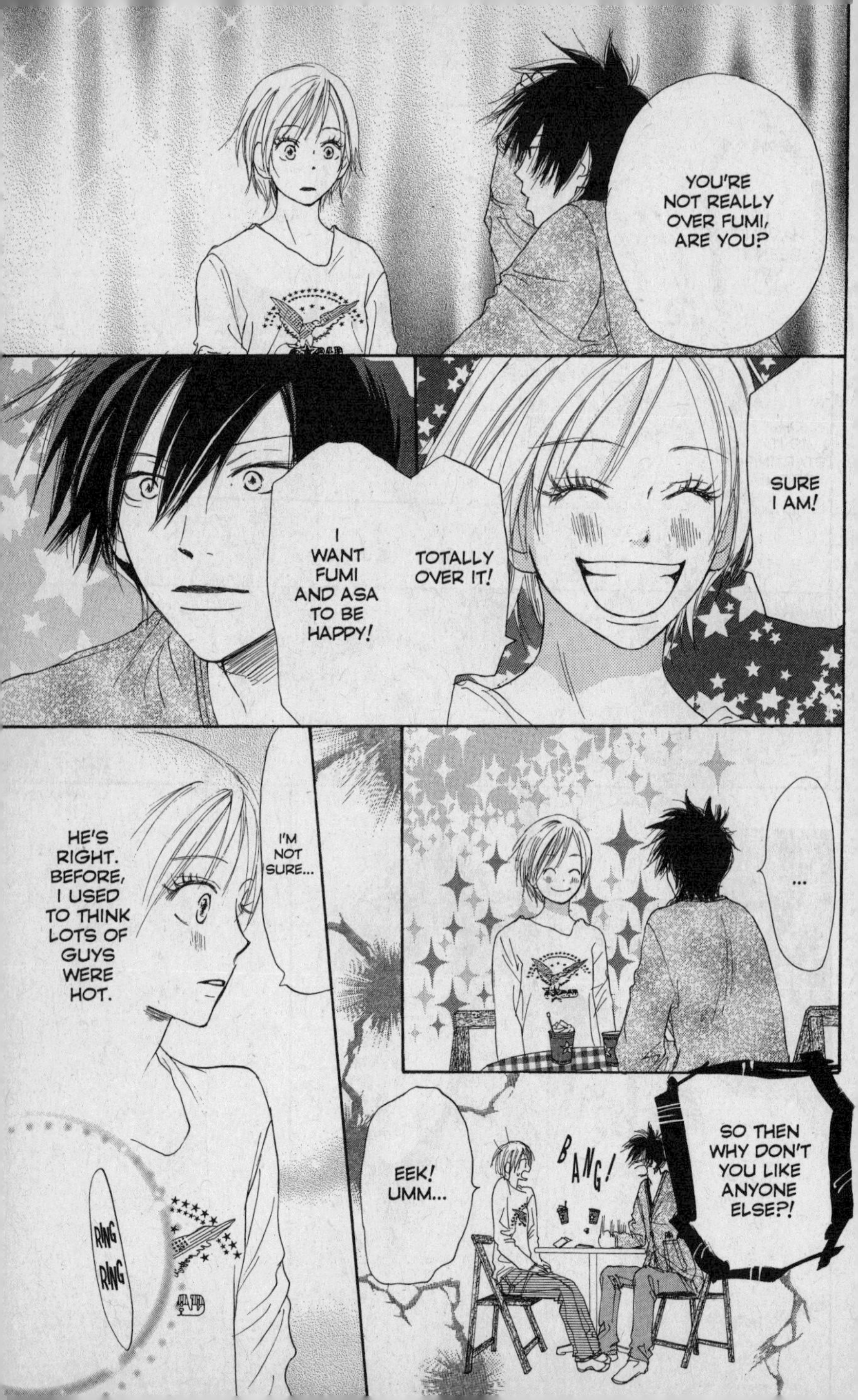
YOU'RE NOT REALLY OVER FUMI, ARE YOU?
SURE I AM!
TOTALLY OVER IT!
I WANT FUMI AND ASA TO BE HAPPY!
...
SO THEN WHY DON'T YOU LIKE ANYONE ELSE?!
BANG!
EEK! UMM...
I'M NOT SURE...
HE'S RIGHT. BEFORE, I USED TO THINK LOTS OF GUYS WERE HOT.
RING RING

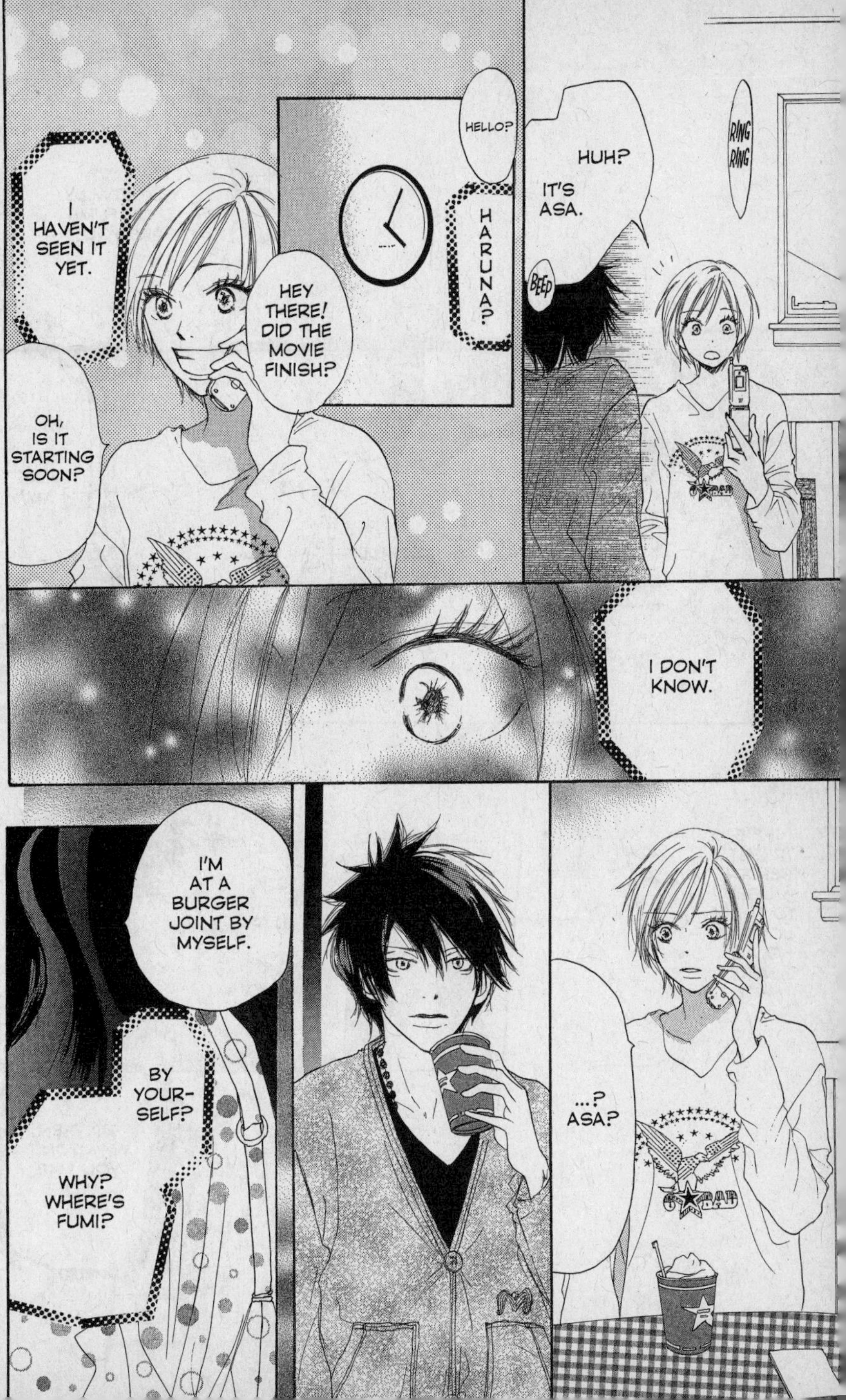
RING RING
HUH? IT'S ASA.
BEEP
HELLO?
HARUNA?
HEY THERE! DID THE MOVIE FINISH?
I HAVEN'T SEEN IT YET.
OH, IS IT STARTING SOON?
I DON'T KNOW.
...? ASA?
I'M AT A BURGER JOINT BY MYSELF.
BY YOURSELF?
WHY? WHERE'S FUMI?

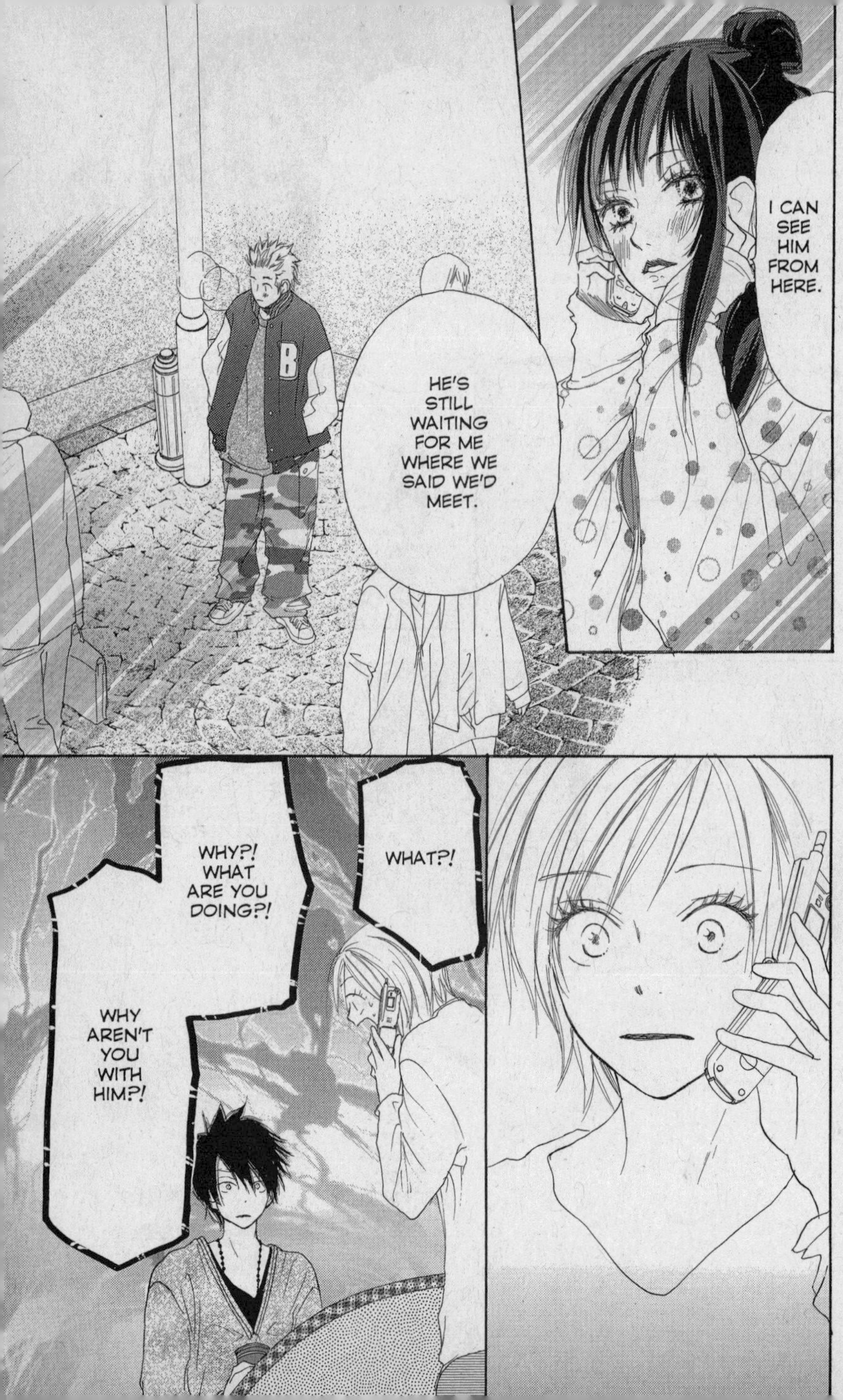
I CAN SEE HIM FROM HERE.
HE'S STILL WAITING FOR ME WHERE WE SAID WE'D MEET.
WHAT?!
WHY?! WHAT ARE YOU DOING?!
WHY AREN'T YOU WITH HIM?!

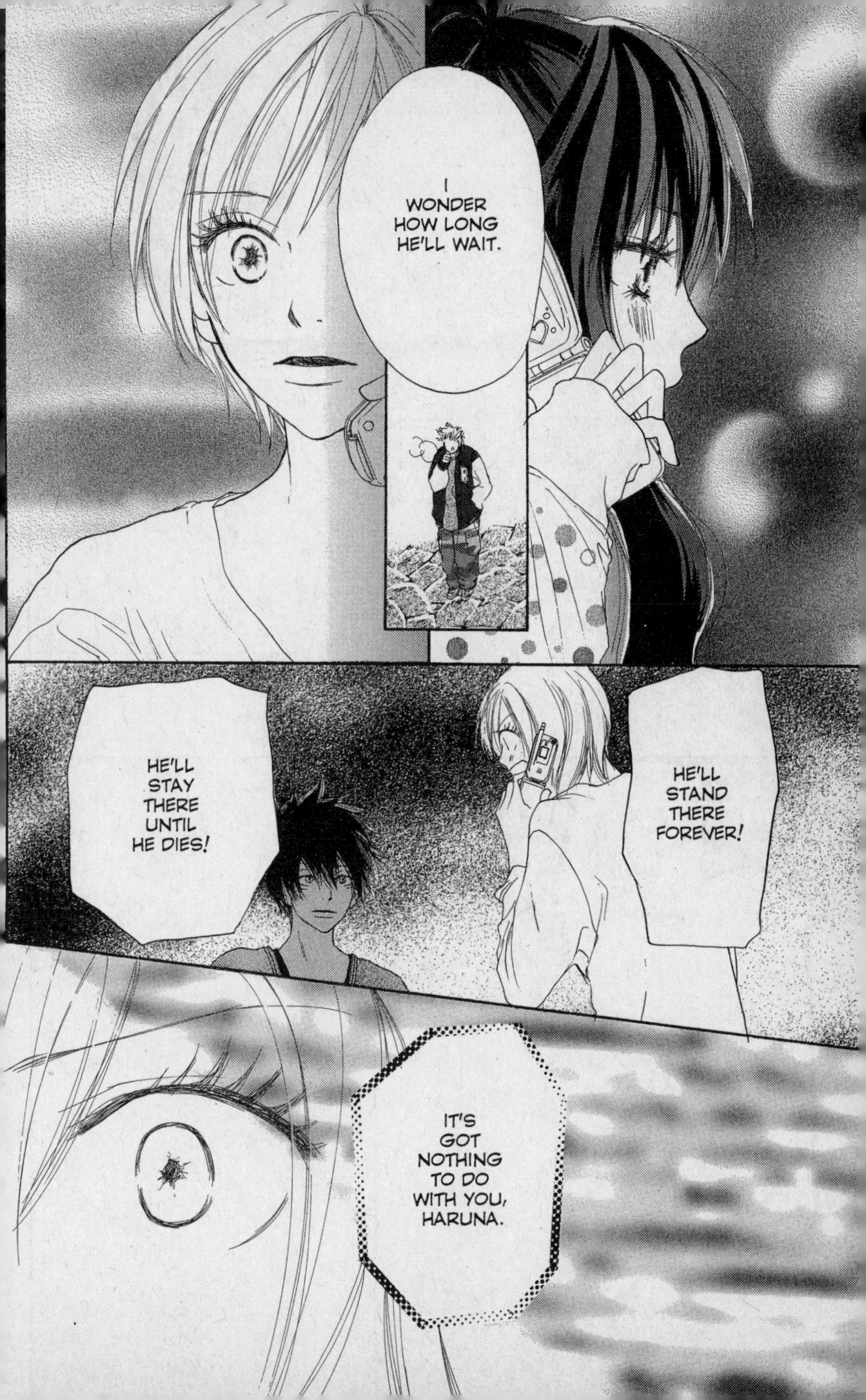
I WONDER HOW LONG HE'LL WAIT.
HE'LL STAND THERE FOREVER!
HE'LL STAY THERE UNTIL HE DIES!
IT'S GOT NOTHING TO DO WITH YOU, HARUNA.

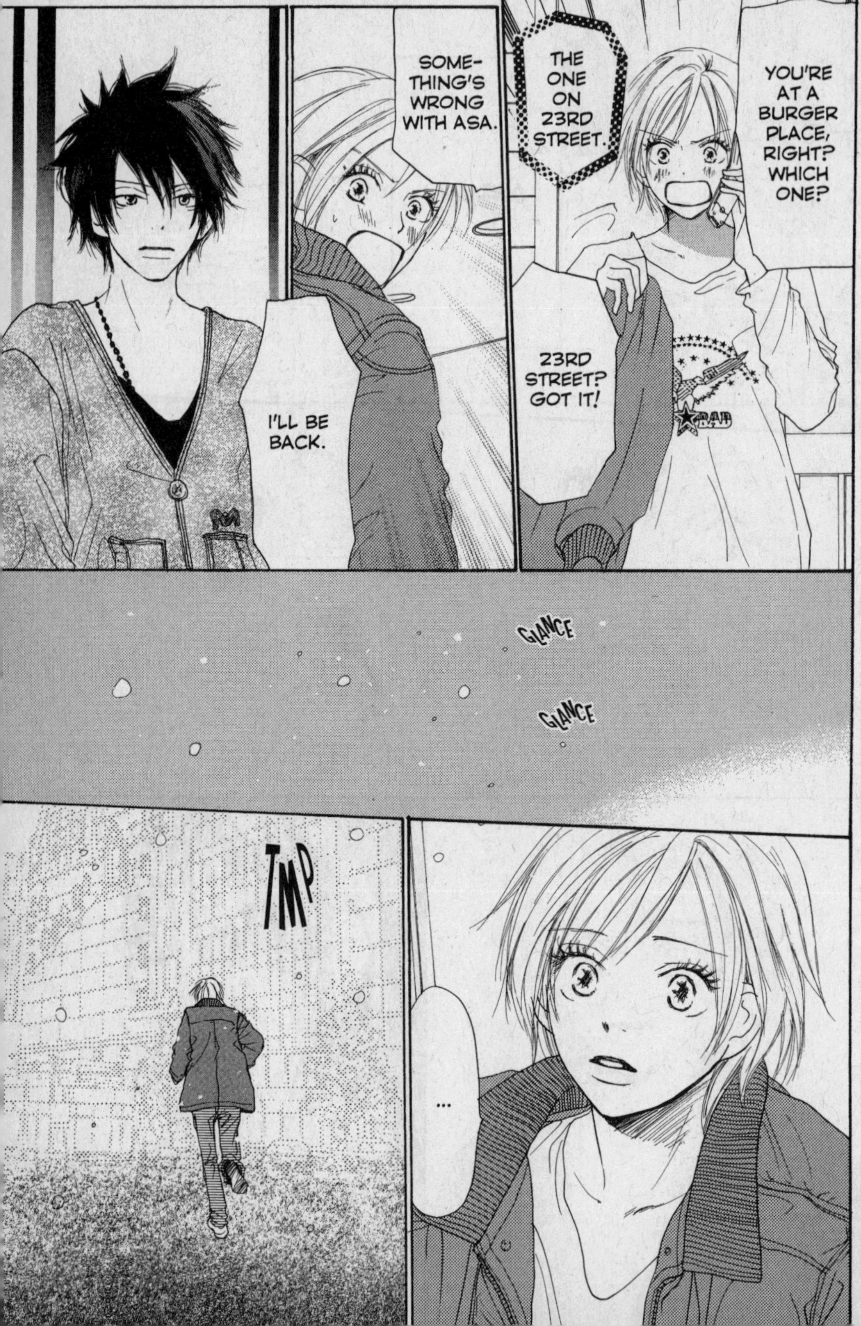
YOU'RE AT A BURGER PLACE, RIGHT? WHICH ONE?
THE ONE ON 23RD STREET.
23RD STREET? GOT IT!
SOME-THING'S WRONG WITH ASA.
I'LL BE BACK.
GLANCE
GLANCE
...
TMP

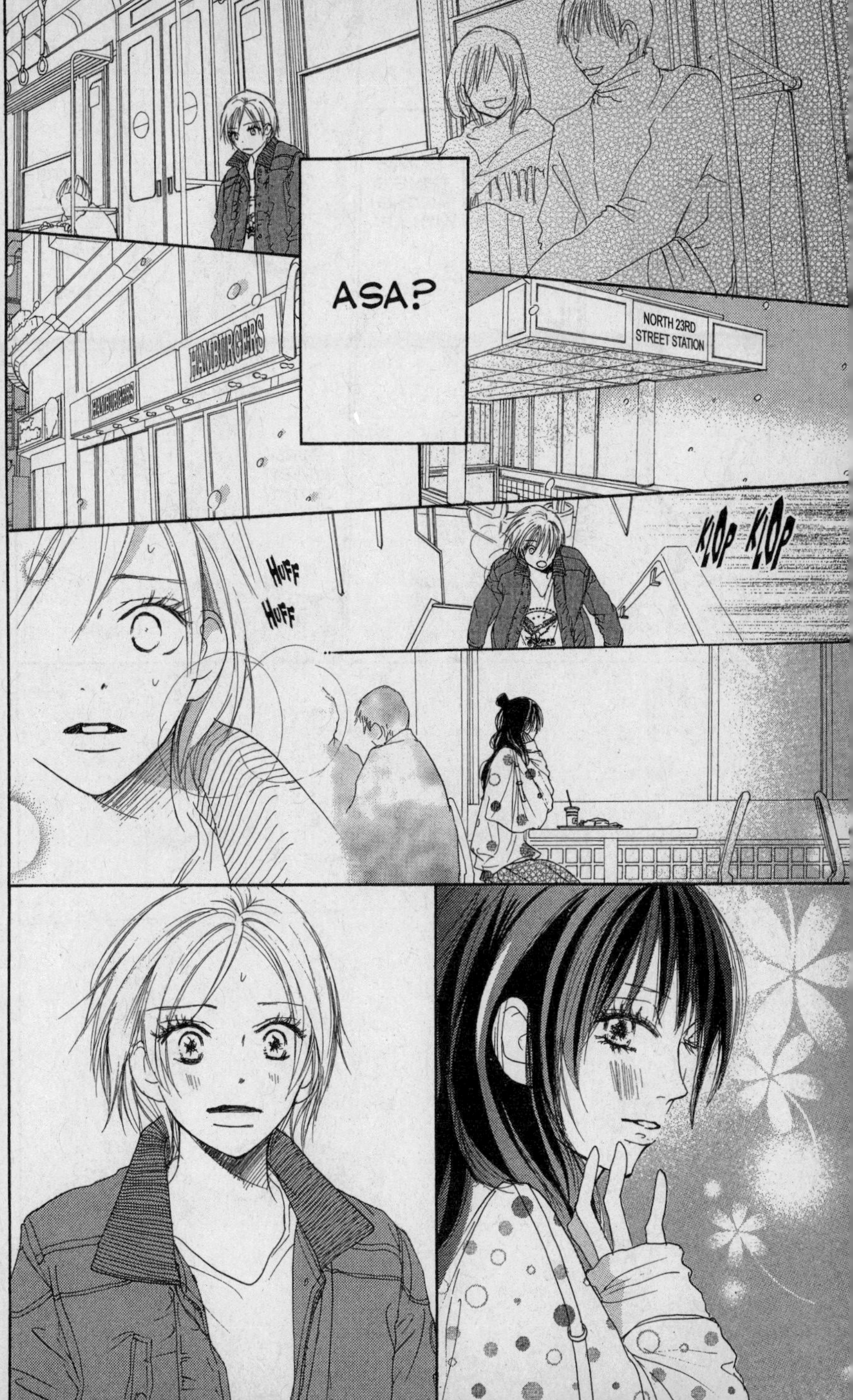
ASA?
NORTH 23RD STREET STATION
HAMBURGERS
HAMBURGERS
KLOP KLOP
HUFF HUFF

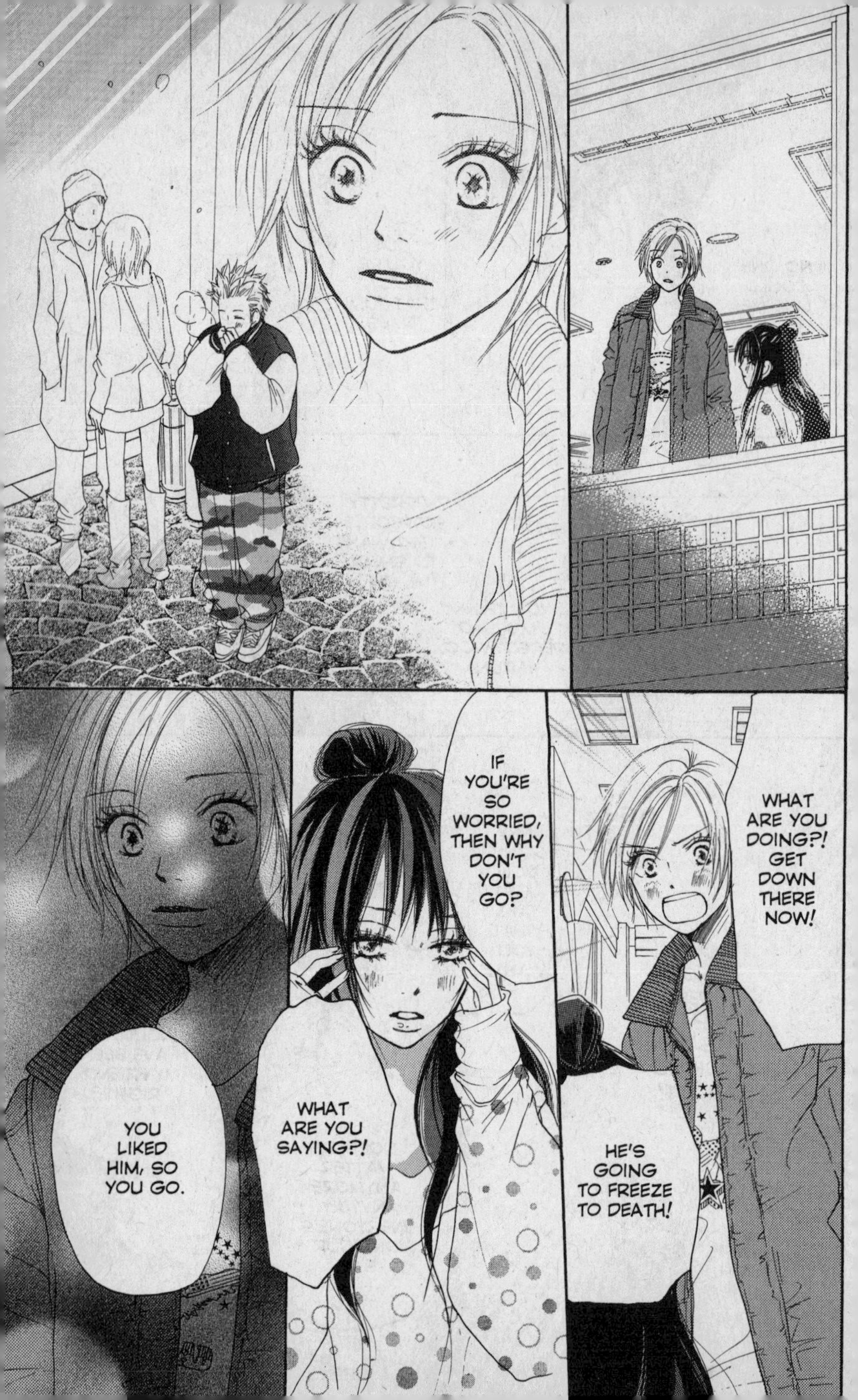
WHAT ARE YOU DOING?! GET DOWN THERE NOW!
HE'S GOING TO FREEZE TO DEATH!
IF YOU'RE SO WORRIED, THEN WHY DON'T YOU GO?
WHAT ARE YOU SAYING?!
YOU LIKED HIM, SO YOU GO.

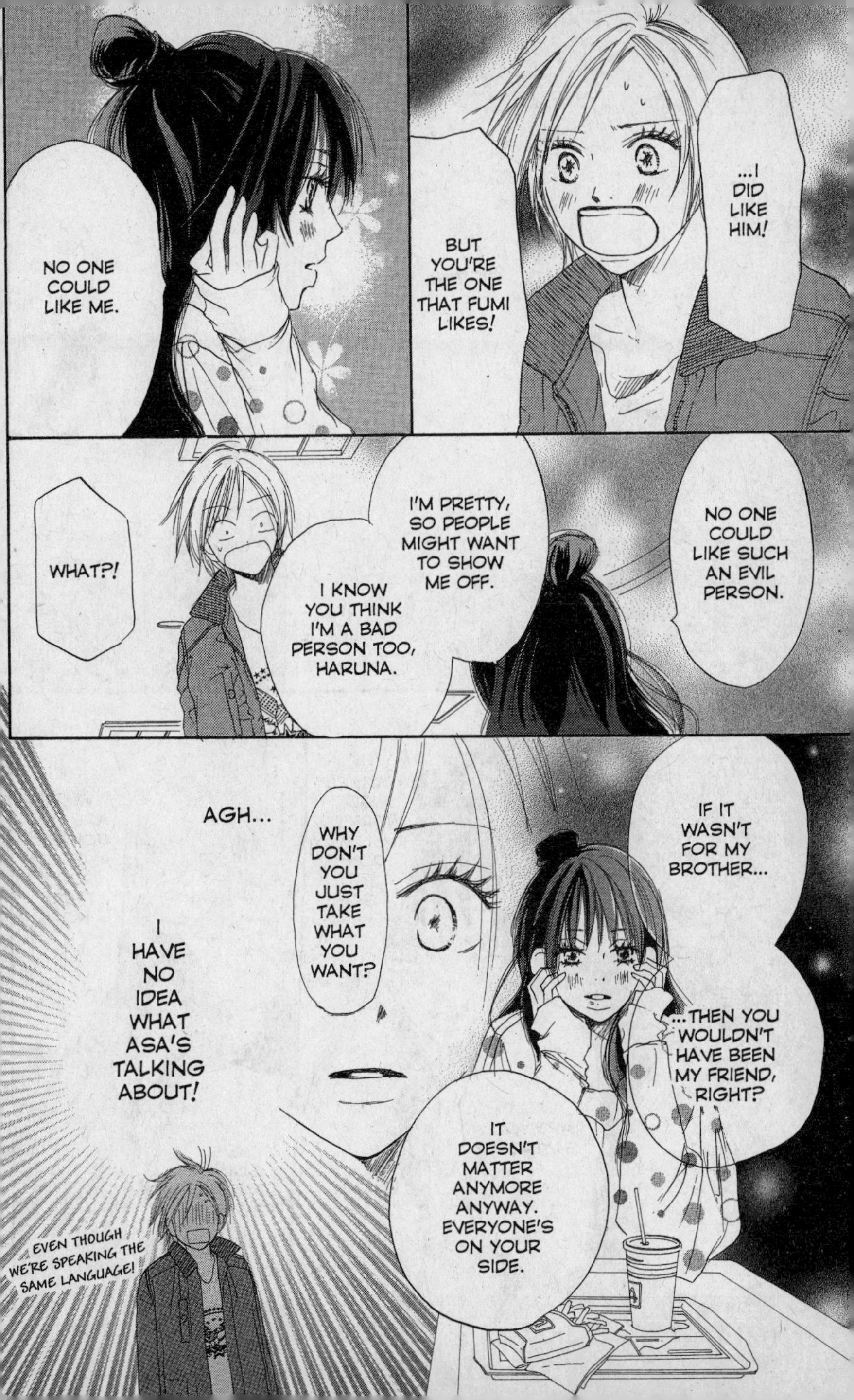
...I DID LIKE HIM!
BUT YOU'RE THE ONE THAT FUMI LIKES!
NO ONE COULD LIKE ME.
NO ONE COULD LIKE SUCH AN EVIL PERSON.
I'M PRETTY, SO PEOPLE MIGHT WANT TO SHOW ME OFF.
I KNOW YOU THINK I'M A BAD PERSON TOO, HARUNA.
WHAT?!
IF IT WASN'T FOR MY BROTHER...
...THEN YOU WOULDN'T HAVE BEEN MY FRIEND, RIGHT?
IT DOESN'T MATTER ANYMORE ANYWAY. EVERYONE'S ON YOUR SIDE.
WHY DON'T YOU JUST TAKE WHAT YOU WANT?
AGH...
I HAVE NO IDEA WHAT ASA'S TALKING ABOUT!
EVEN THOUGH WE'RE SPEAKING THE SAME LANGUAGE!

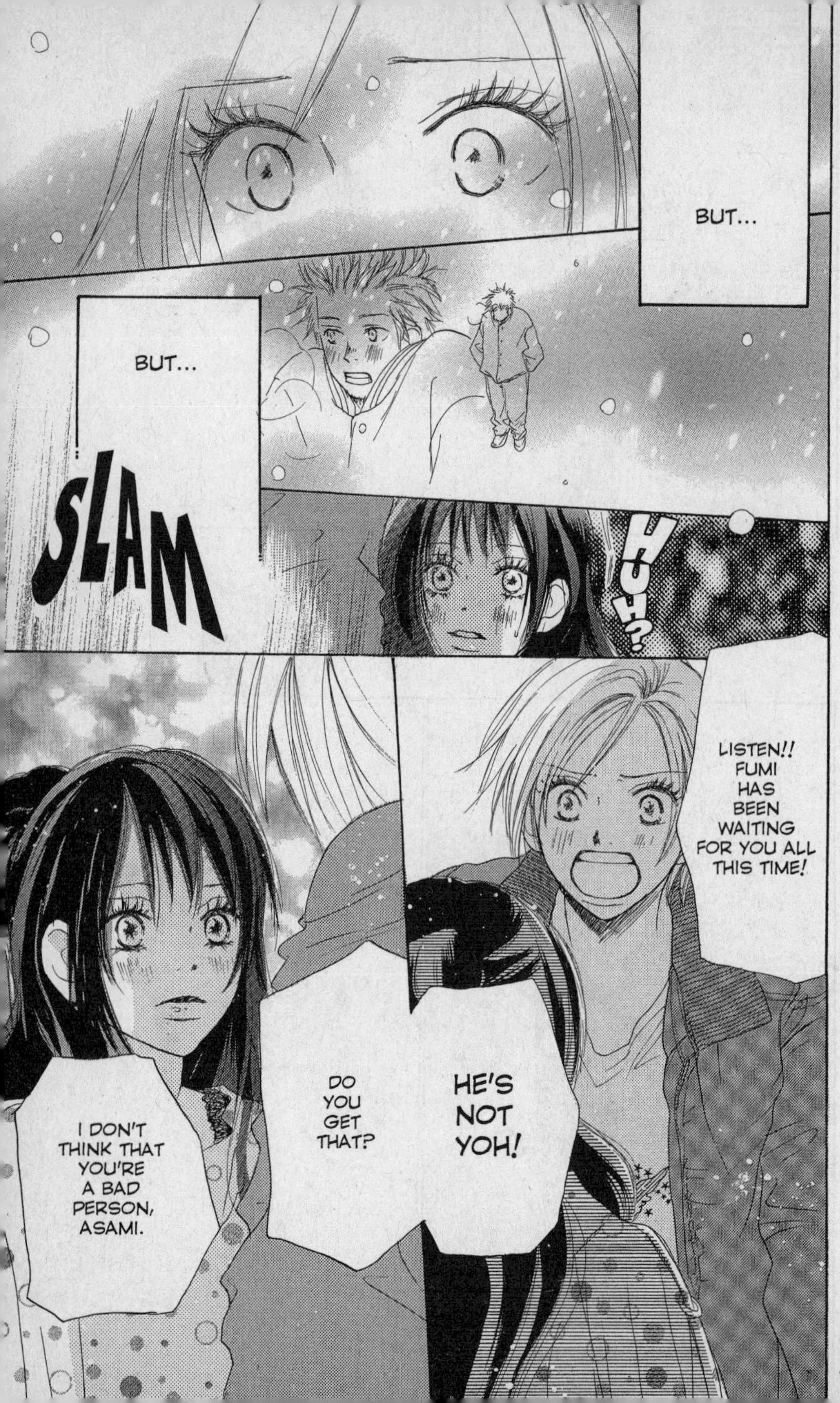
BUT...
BUT...
HUH?
SLAM
LISTEN!! FUMI HAS BEEN WAITING FOR YOU ALL THIS TIME!
HE'S NOT YOH!
DO YOU GET THAT?
I DON'T THINK THAT YOU'RE A BAD PERSON, ASAMI.

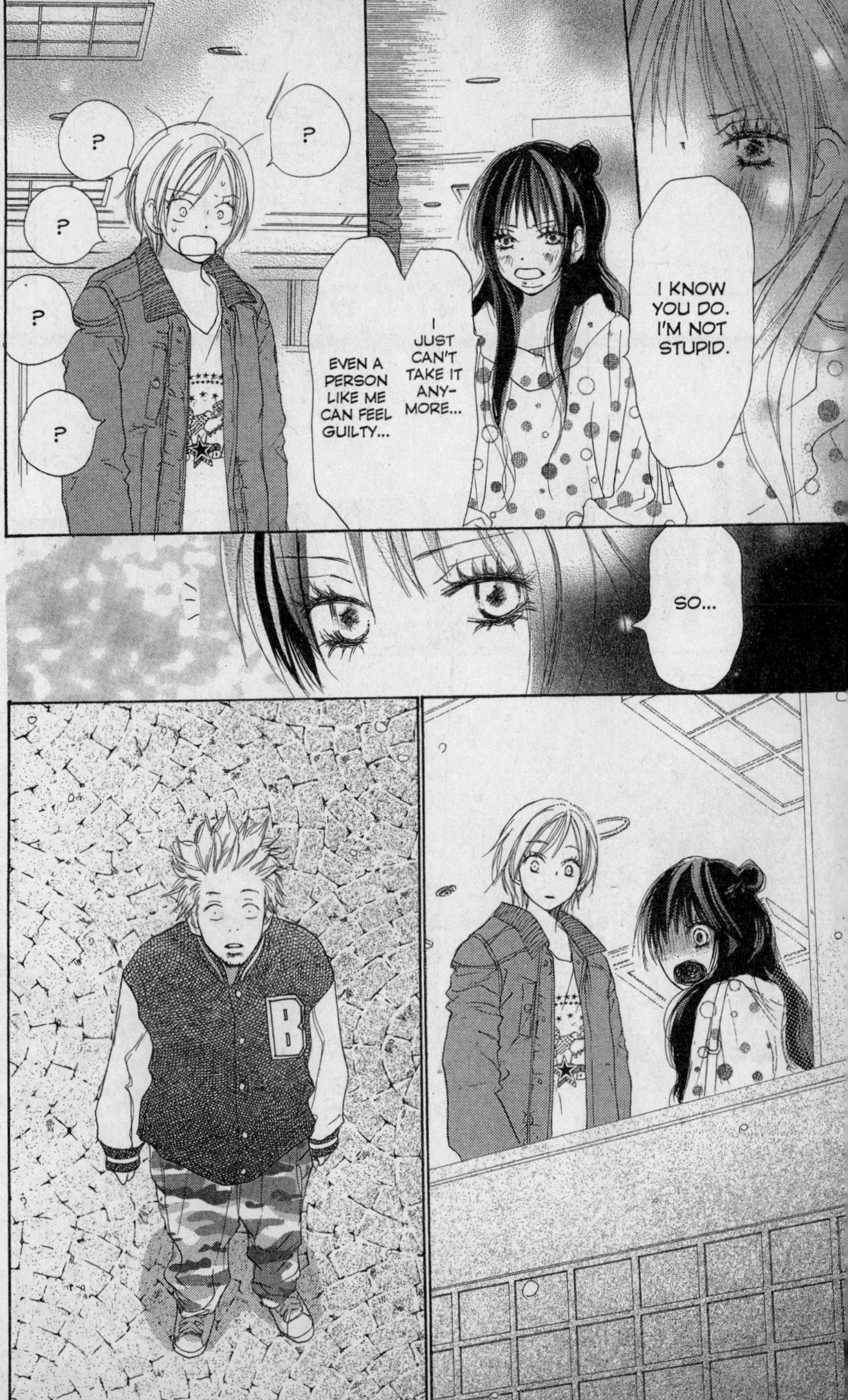
I KNOW YOU DO. I'M NOT STUPID.
I JUST CAN'T TAKE IT ANY-MORE...
EVEN A PERSON LIKE ME CAN FEEL GUILTY...
?
?
?
?
?
SO...

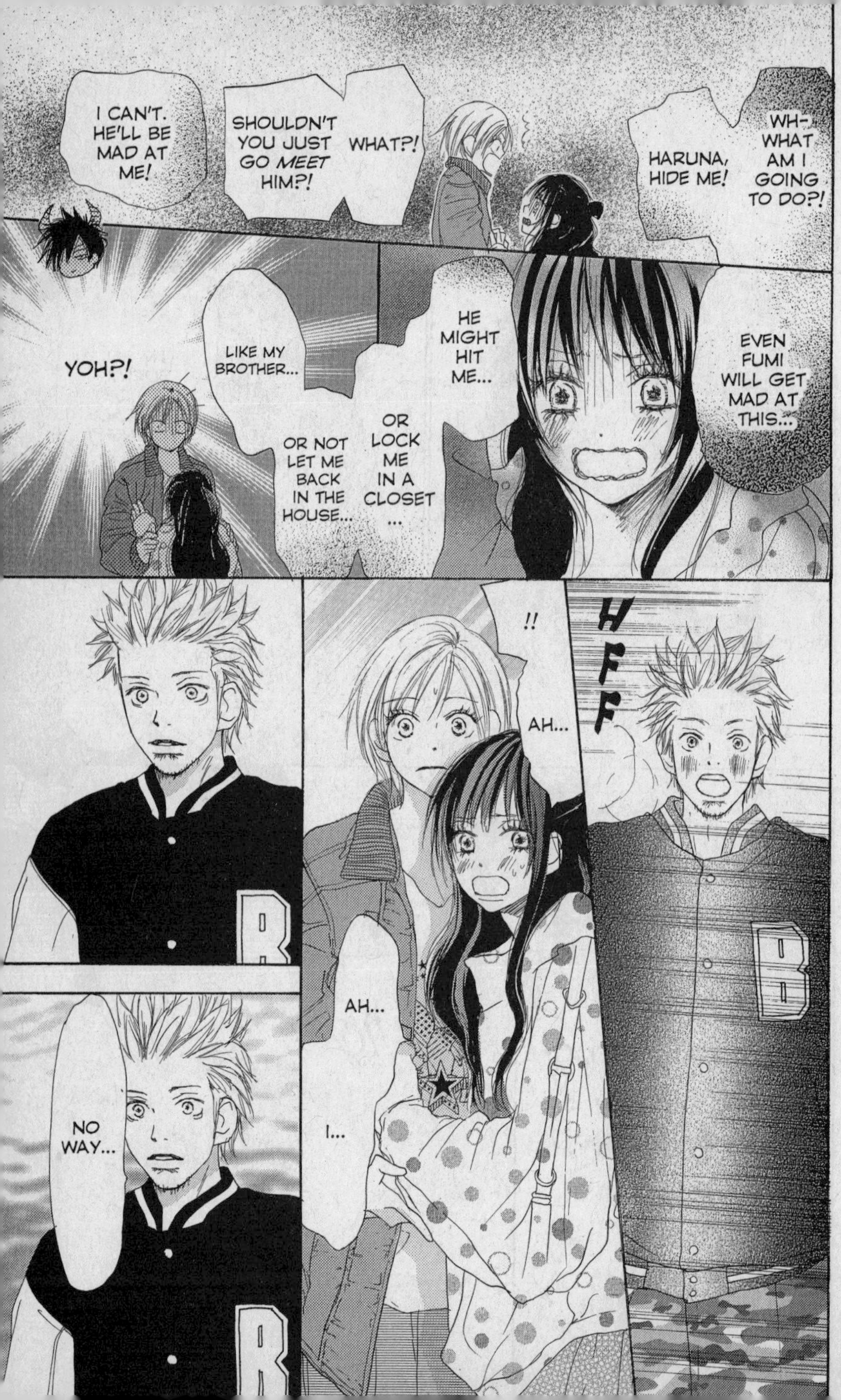
WH- WHAT AM I GOING TO DO?!
HARUNA, HIDE ME!
WHAT?!
SHOULDN'T YOU JUST GO *MEET* HIM?!
I CAN'T. HE'LL BE MAD AT ME!
EVEN FUMI WILL GET MAD AT THIS...
HE MIGHT HIT ME...
OR LOCK ME IN A CLOSET ...
LIKE MY BROTHER...
OR NOT LET ME BACK IN THE HOUSE...
YOH?!
HFF
AH...
!!
AH...
I...
NO WAY...

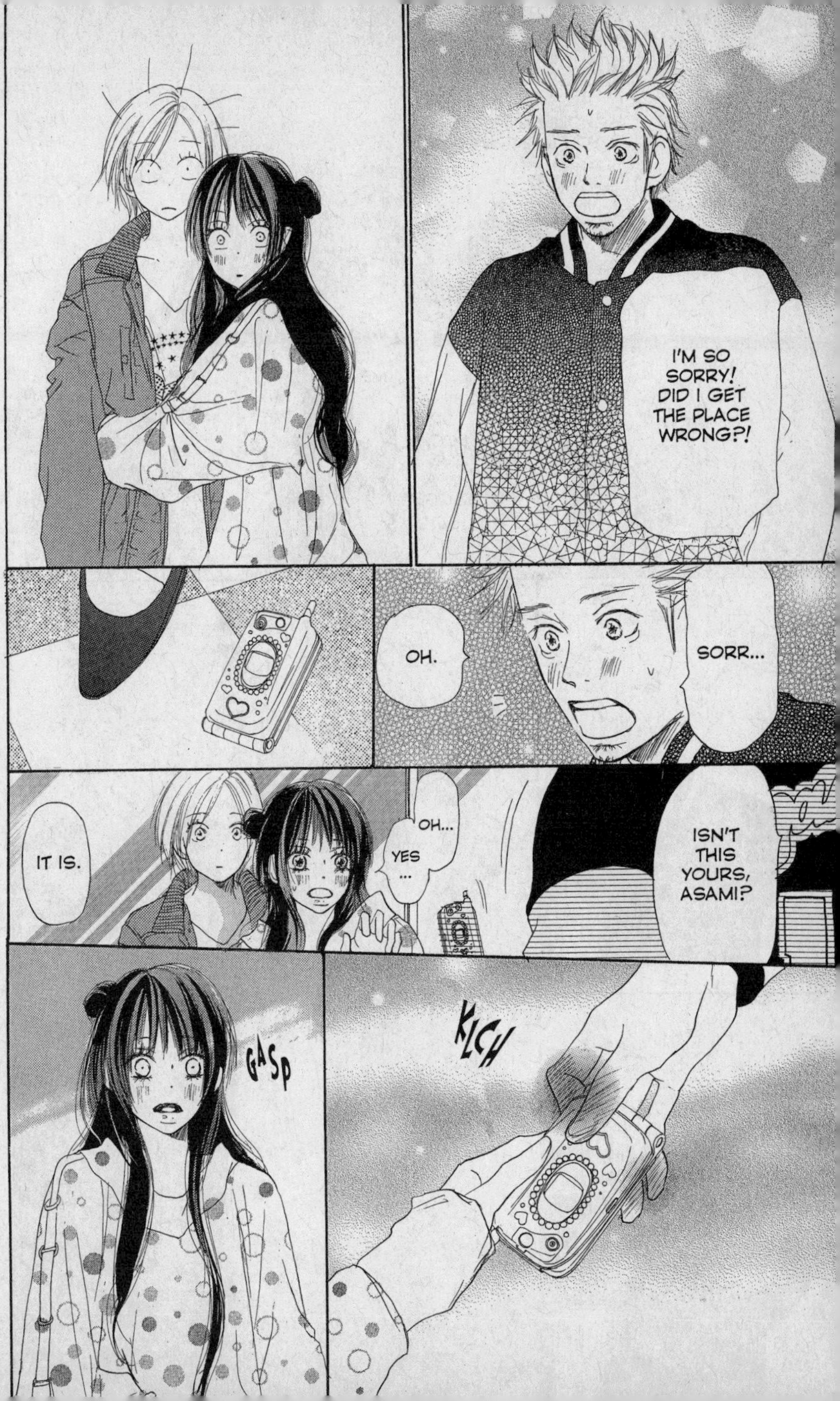
I'M SO SORRY! DID I GET THE PLACE WRONG?!
SORR...
OH.
ISN'T THIS YOURS, ASAMI?
OH... YES ...
IT IS.
KLCH
GASP

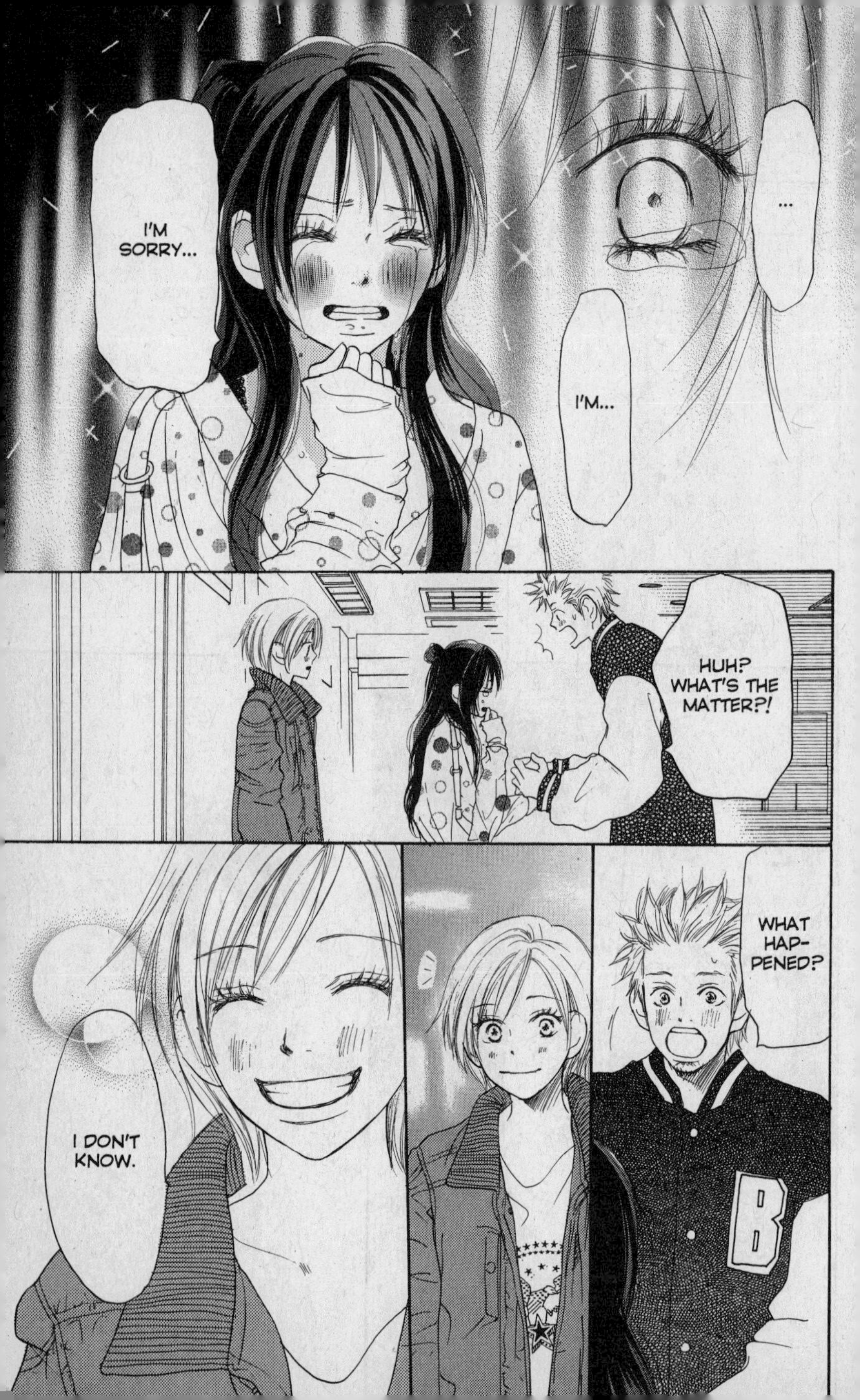
...
I'M...
I'M SORRY...
HUH? WHAT'S THE MATTER?!
WHAT HAP-PENED?
I DON'T KNOW.

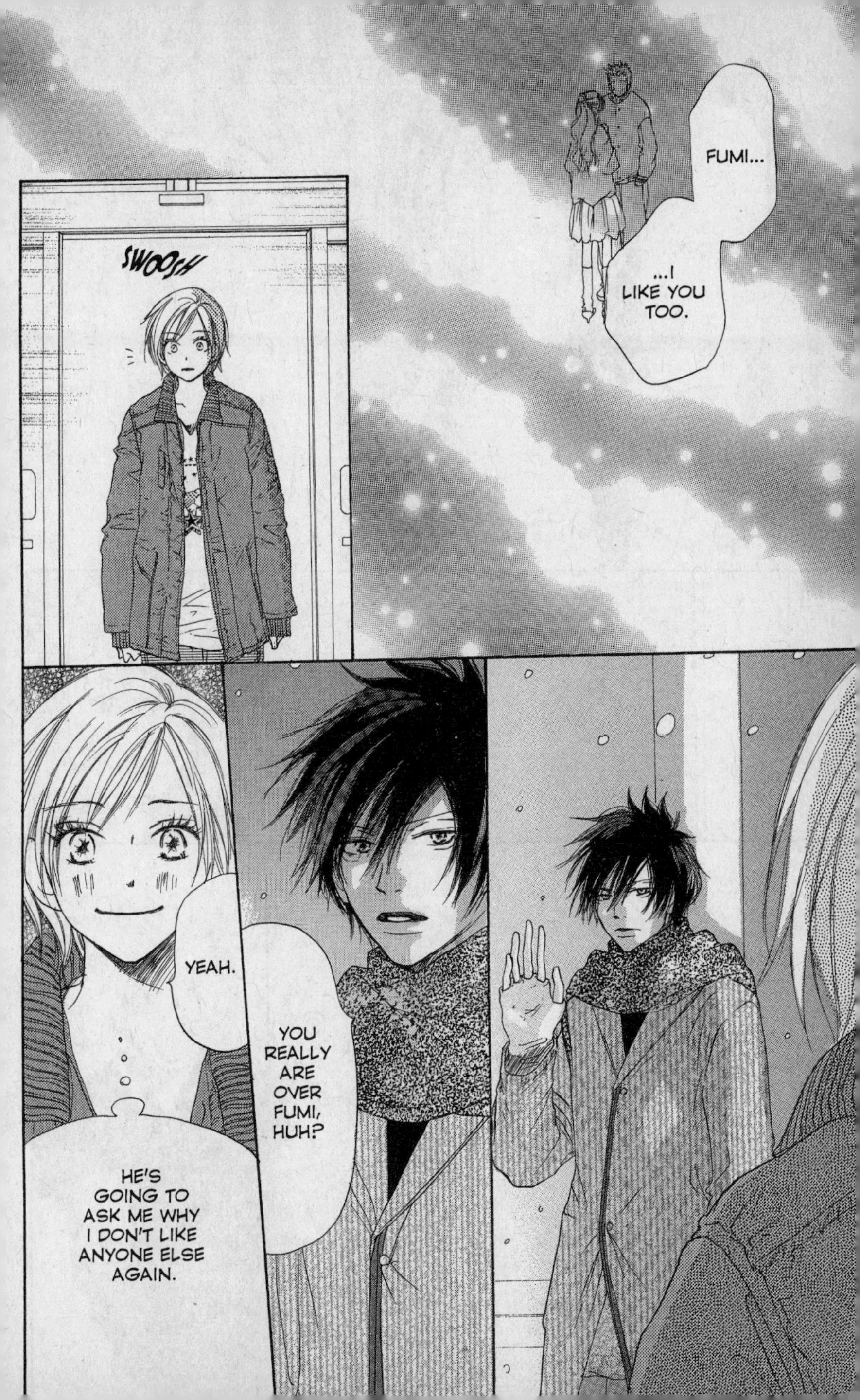
FUMI...
...I LIKE YOU TOO.
SWOOSH
YOU REALLY ARE OVER FUMI, HUH?
YEAH.
HE'S GOING TO ASK ME WHY I DON'T LIKE ANYONE ELSE AGAIN.

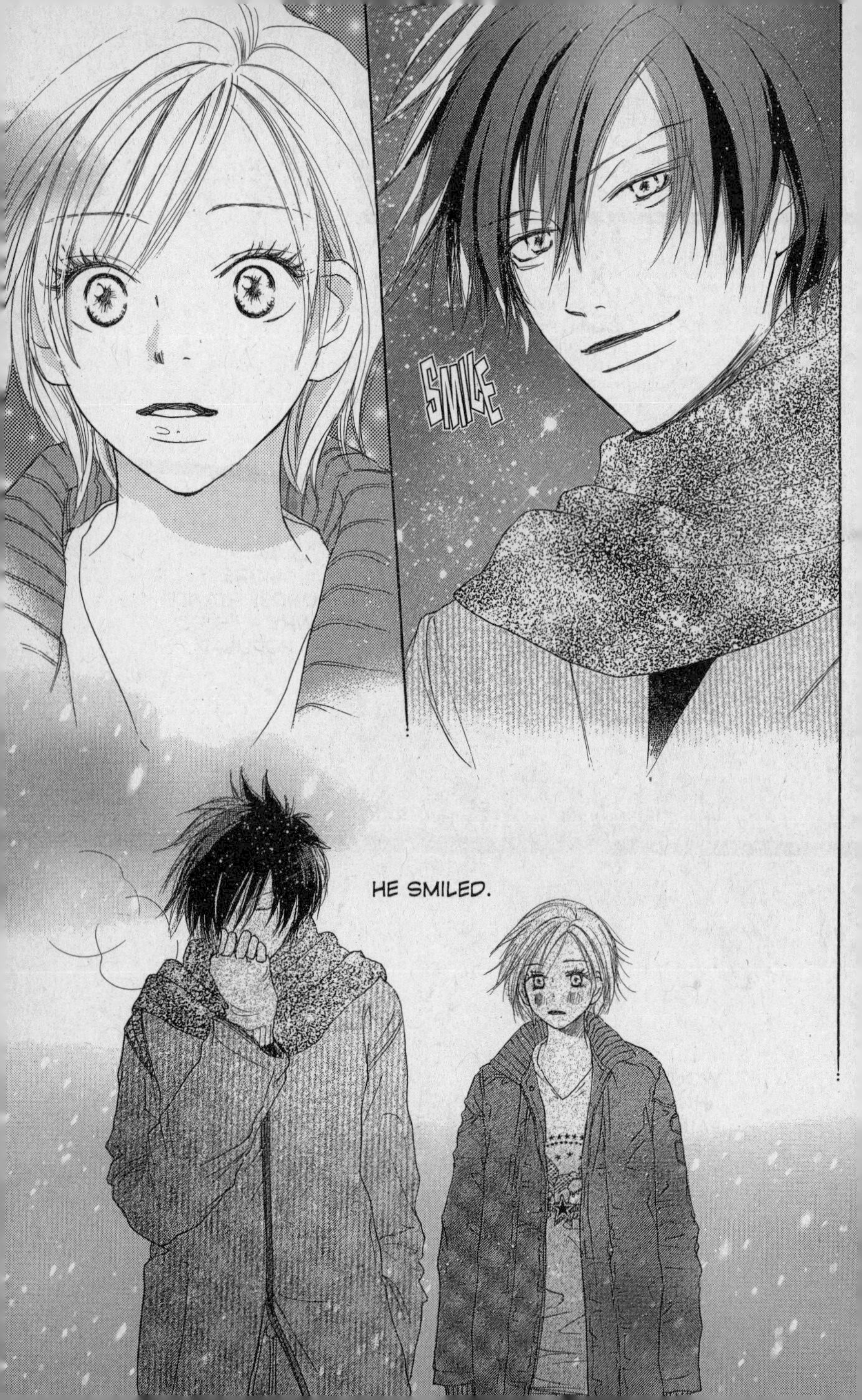
SMILE
HE SMILED.

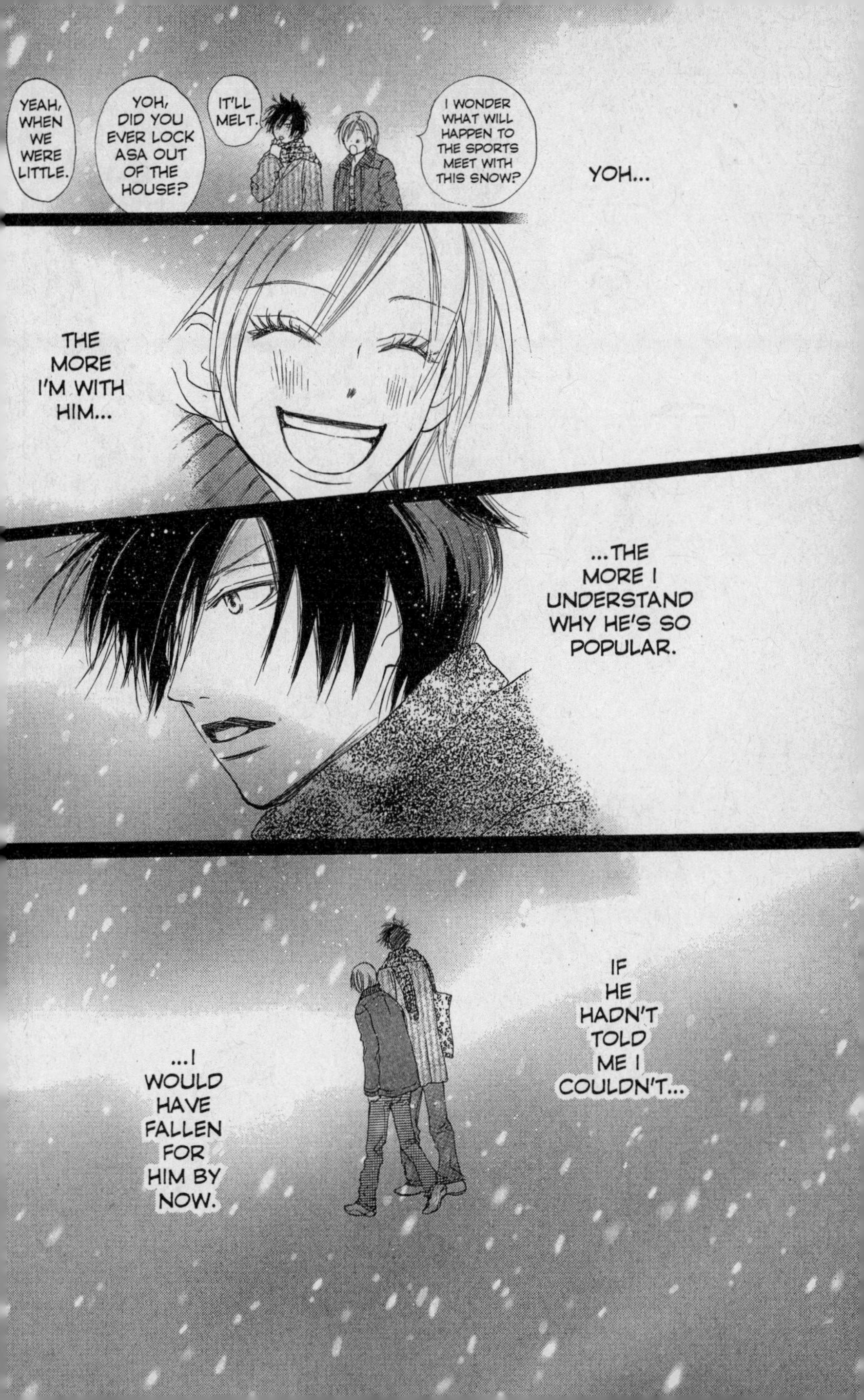
YOH...
I WONDER WHAT WILL HAPPEN TO THE SPORTS MEET WITH THIS SNOW?
IT'LL MELT.
YOH, DID YOU EVER LOCK ASA OUT OF THE HOUSE?
YEAH, WHEN WE WERE LITTLE.
THE MORE I'M WITH HIM...
...THE MORE I UNDERSTAND WHY HE'S SO POPULAR.
IF HE HADN'T TOLD ME I COULDN'T...
...I WOULD HAVE FALLEN FOR HIM BY NOW.

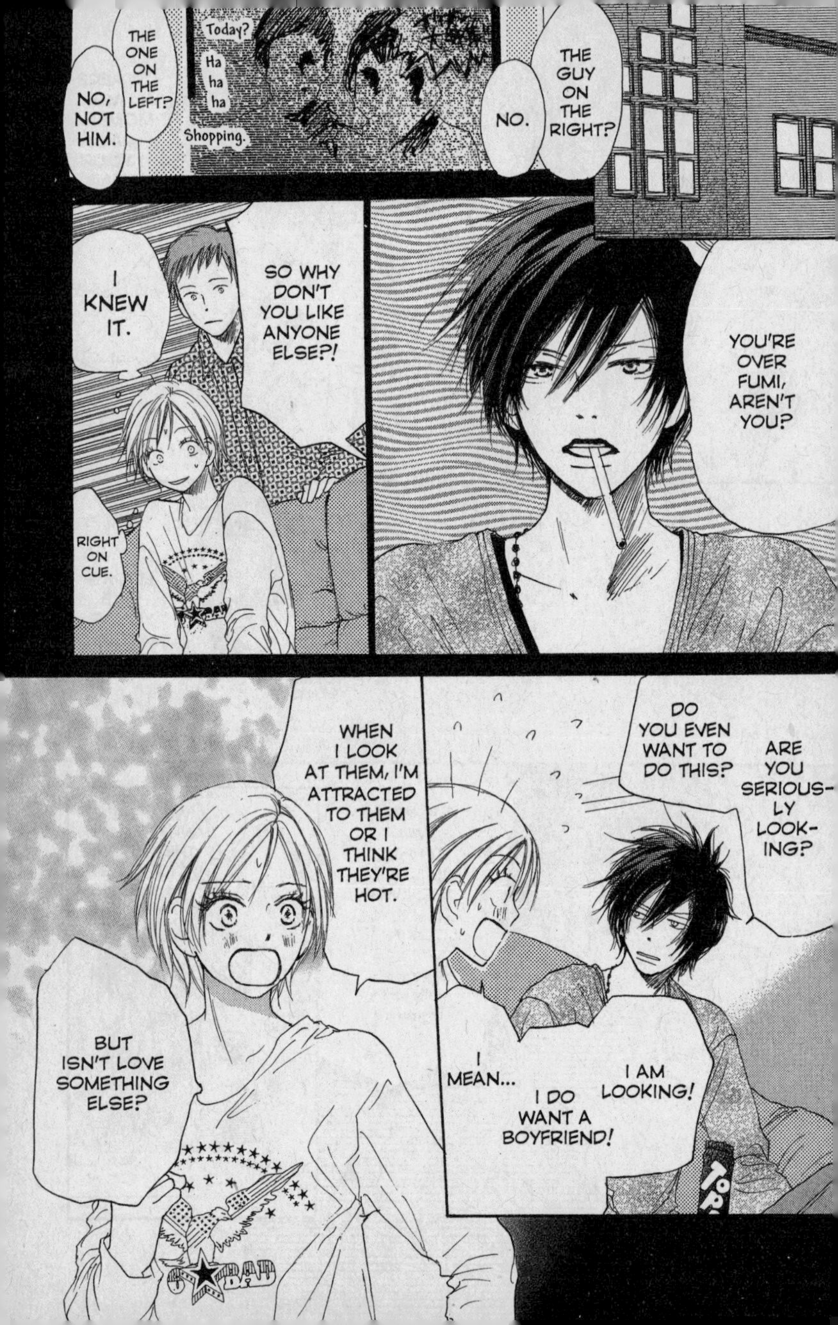
THE GUY ON THE RIGHT?
NO.
Today?
Ha ha ha
Shopping.
THE ONE ON THE LEFT?
NO, NOT HIM.
YOU'RE OVER FUMI, AREN'T YOU?
SO WHY DON'T YOU LIKE ANYONE ELSE?!
I KNEW IT.
RIGHT ON CUE.
ARE YOU SERIOUSLY LOOKING?
DO YOU EVEN WANT TO DO THIS?
I AM LOOKING!
I DO WANT A BOYFRIEND!
I MEAN...
WHEN I LOOK AT THEM, I'M ATTRACTED TO THEM OR I THINK THEY'RE HOT.
BUT ISN'T LOVE SOMETHING ELSE?

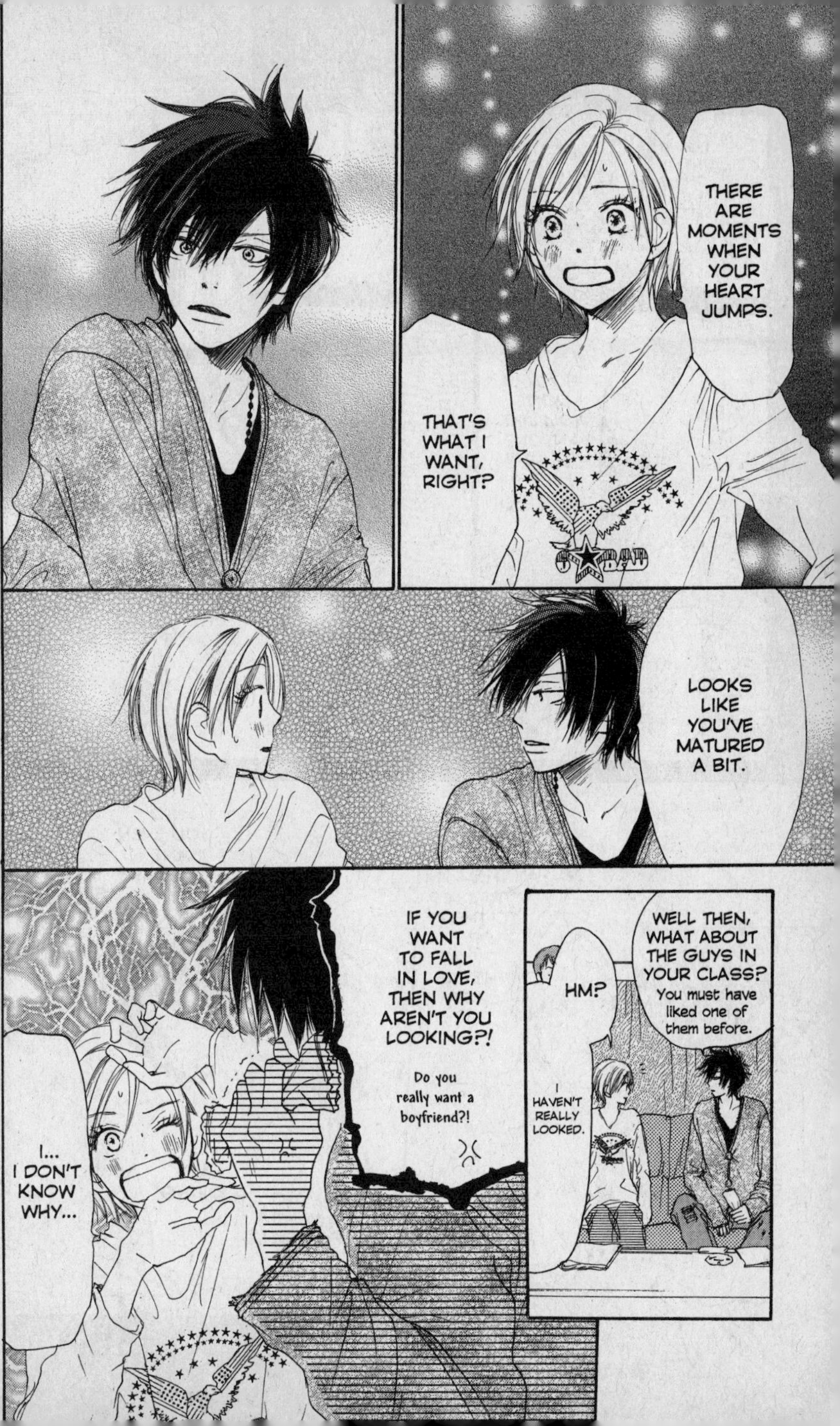
THERE ARE MOMENTS WHEN YOUR HEART JUMPS.
THAT'S WHAT I WANT, RIGHT?
LOOKS LIKE YOU'VE MATURED A BIT.
WELL THEN, WHAT ABOUT THE GUYS IN YOUR CLASS? You must have liked one of them before.
HM?
I HAVEN'T REALLY LOOKED.
IF YOU WANT TO FALL IN LOVE, THEN WHY AREN'T YOU LOOKING?!
Do you really want a boyfriend?!
I... I DON'T KNOW WHY...

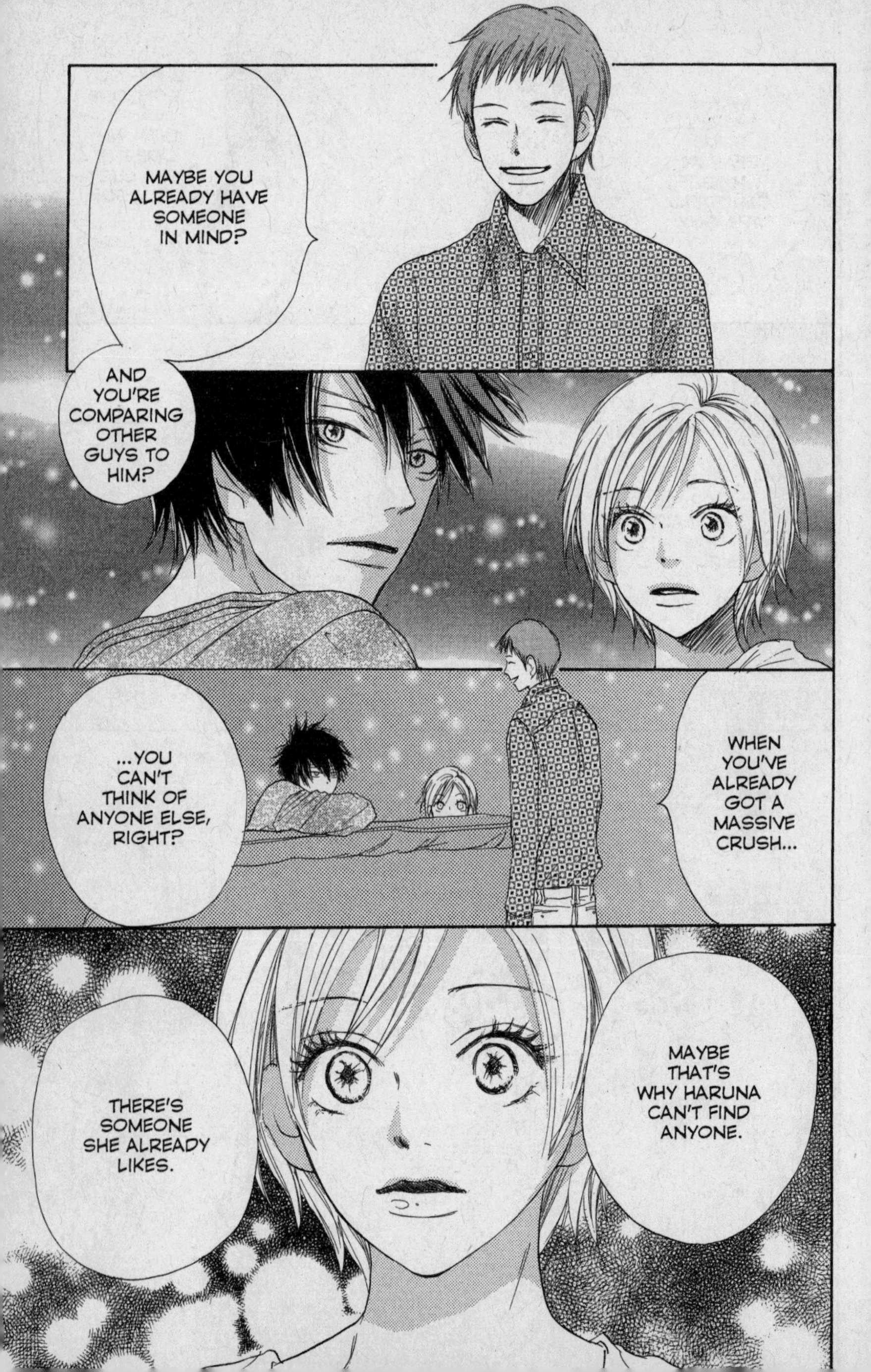
MAYBE YOU ALREADY HAVE SOMEONE IN MIND?
AND YOU'RE COMPARING OTHER GUYS TO HIM?
WHEN YOU'VE ALREADY GOT A MASSIVE CRUSH...
...YOU CAN'T THINK OF ANYONE ELSE, RIGHT?
MAYBE THAT'S WHY HARUNA CAN'T FIND ANYONE.
THERE'S SOMEONE SHE ALREADY LIKES.

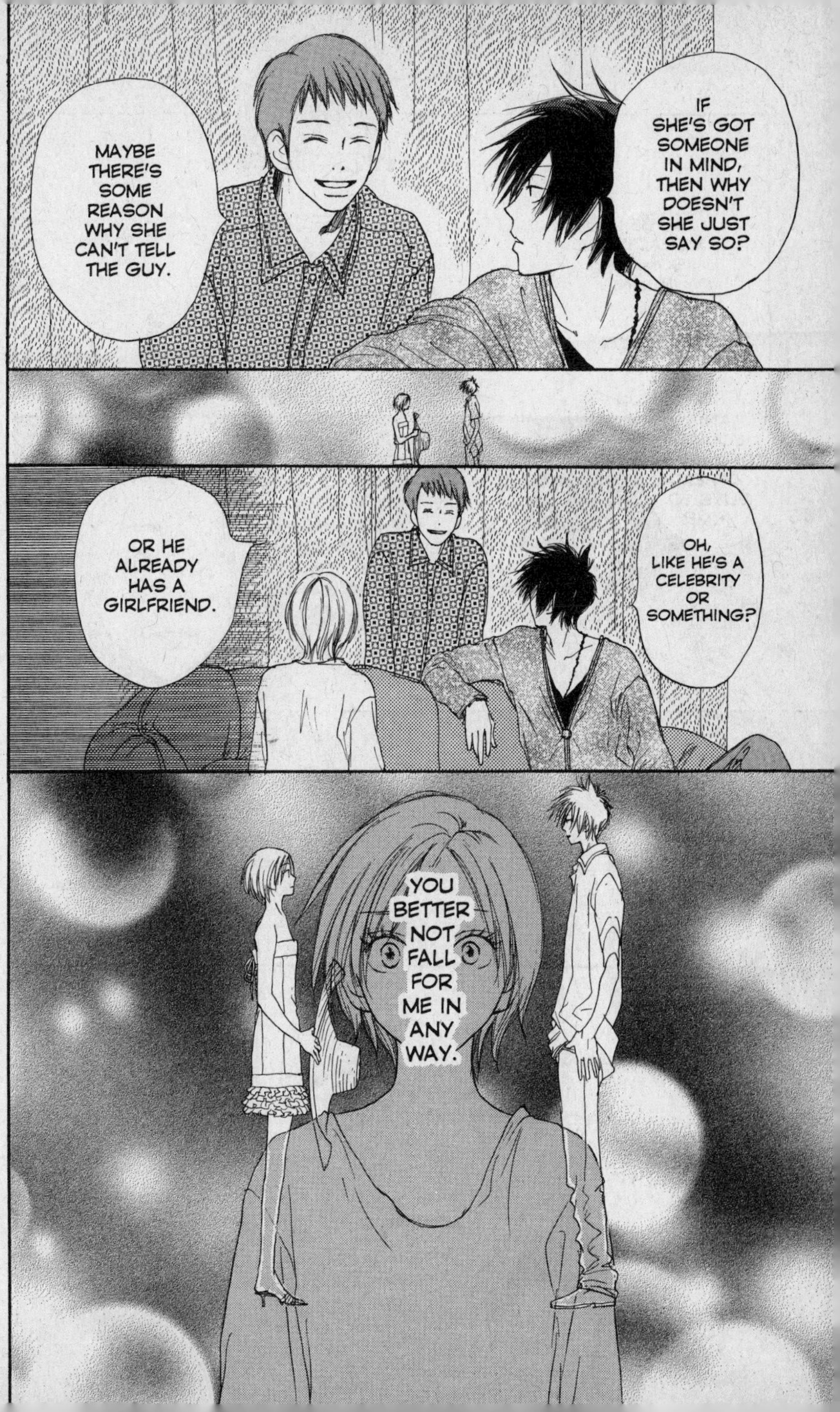
IF SHE'S GOT SOMEONE IN MIND, THEN WHY DOESN'T SHE JUST SAY SO?
MAYBE THERE'S SOME REASON WHY SHE CAN'T TELL THE GUY.
OH, LIKE HE'S A CELEBRITY OR SOMETHING?
OR HE ALREADY HAS A GIRLFRIEND.
YOU BETTER NOT FALL FOR ME IN ANY WAY.

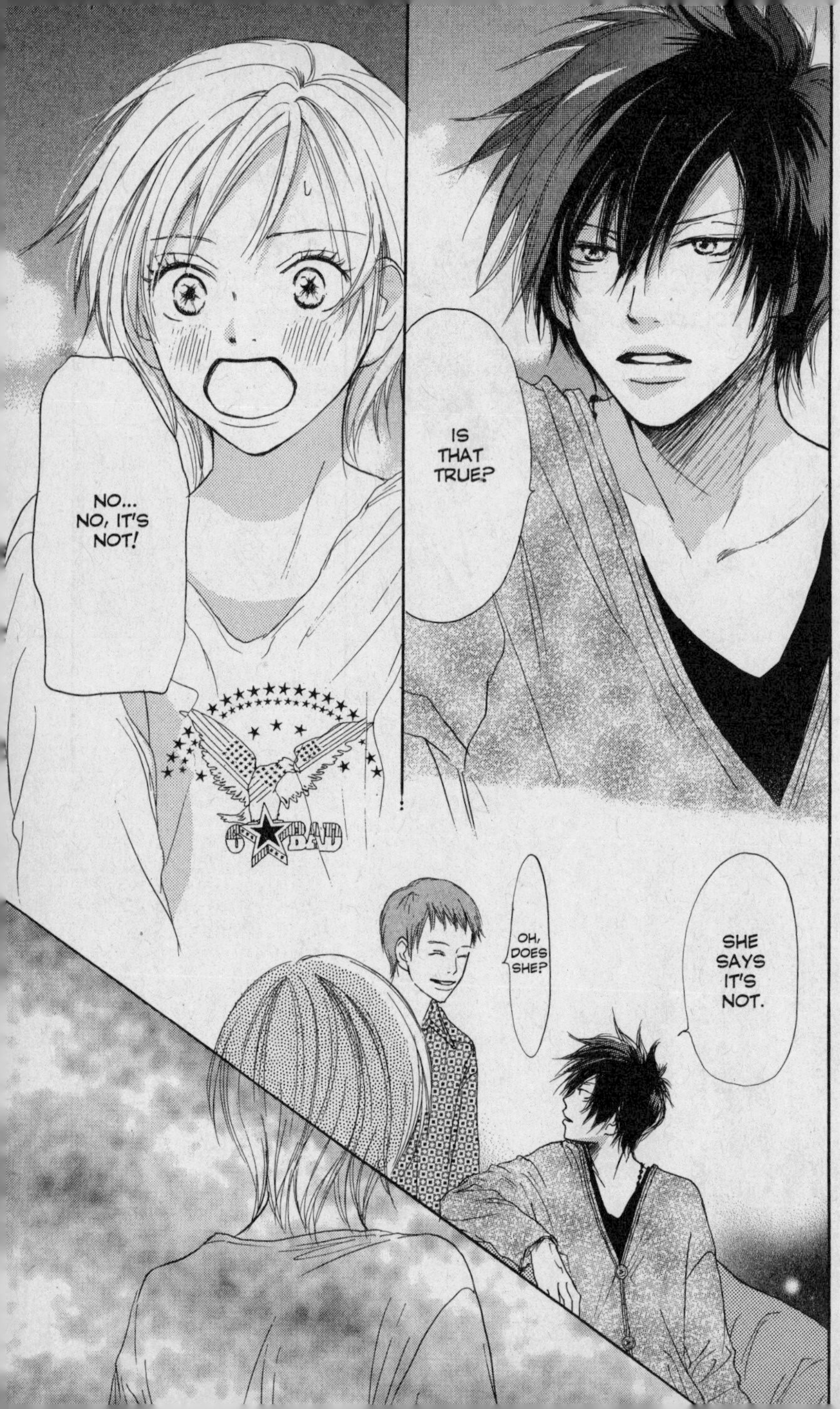
IS THAT TRUE?
NO... NO, IT'S NOT!
SHE SAYS IT'S NOT.
OH, DOES SHE?

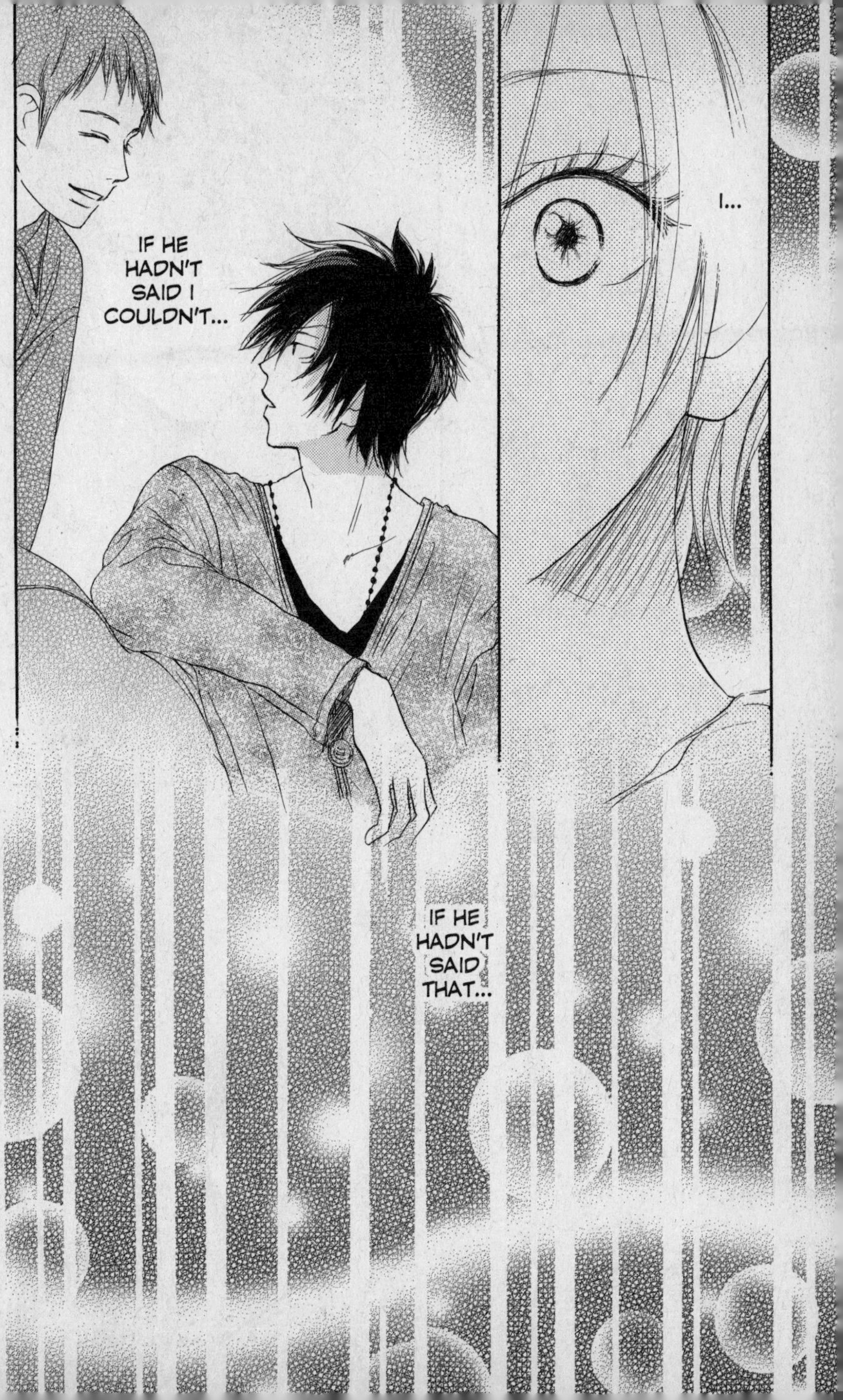
I...
IF HE HADN'T SAID I COULDN'T...
IF HE HADN'T SAID THAT...

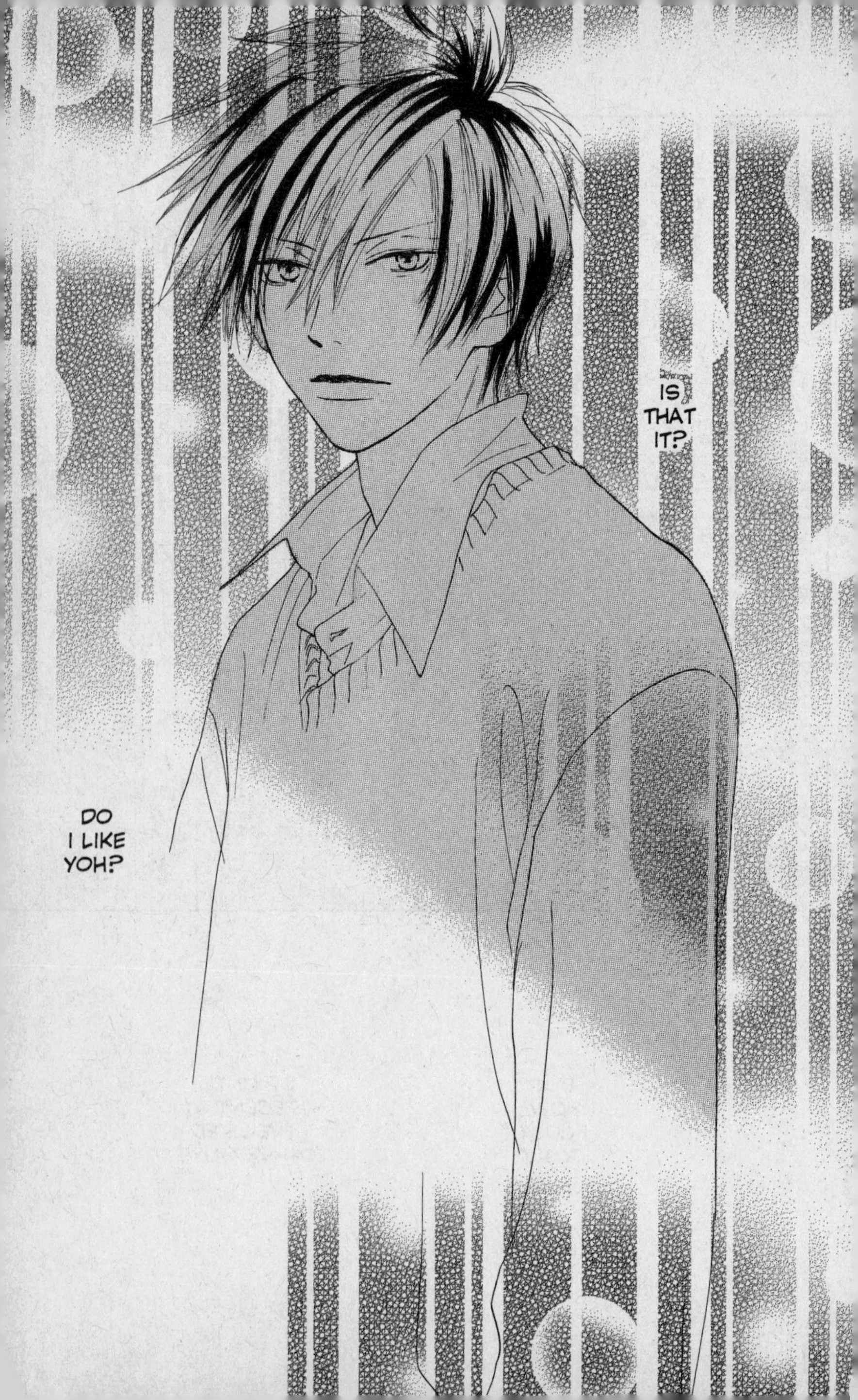
IS THAT IT?
DO I LIKE YOH?

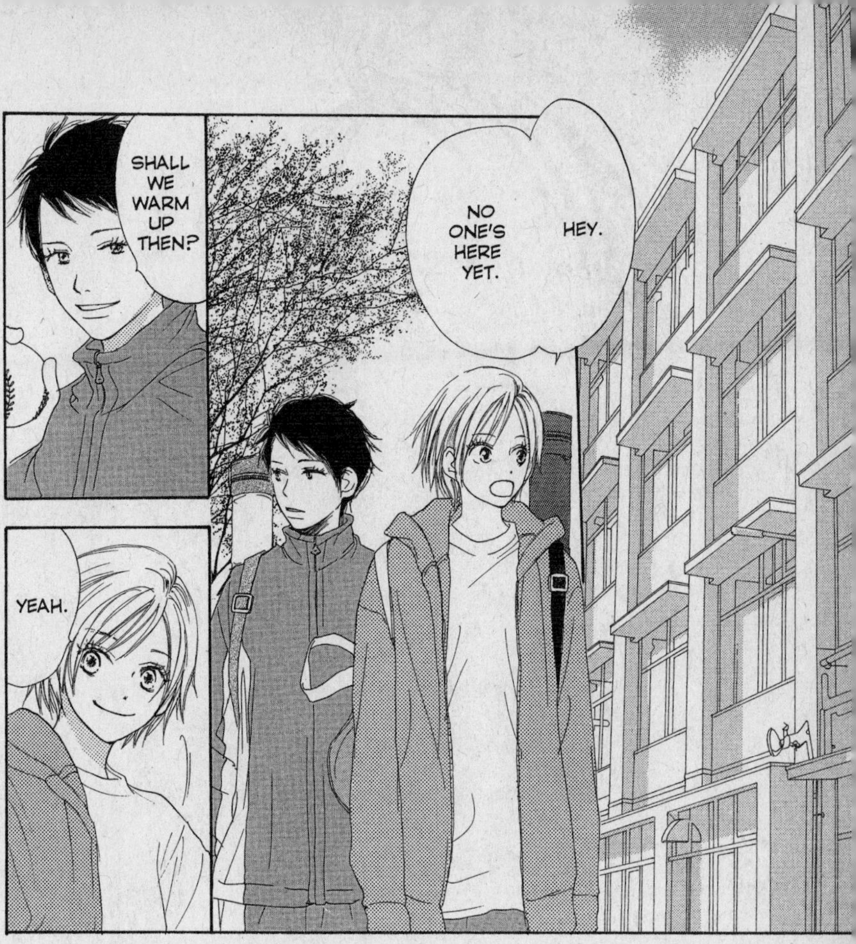
HEY.
NO ONE'S HERE YET.
SHALL WE WARM UP THEN?
YEAH.

UP UNTIL RECENTLY, I'VE LIKED OTHER GUYS.

BUT NOW, I JUST DON'T.

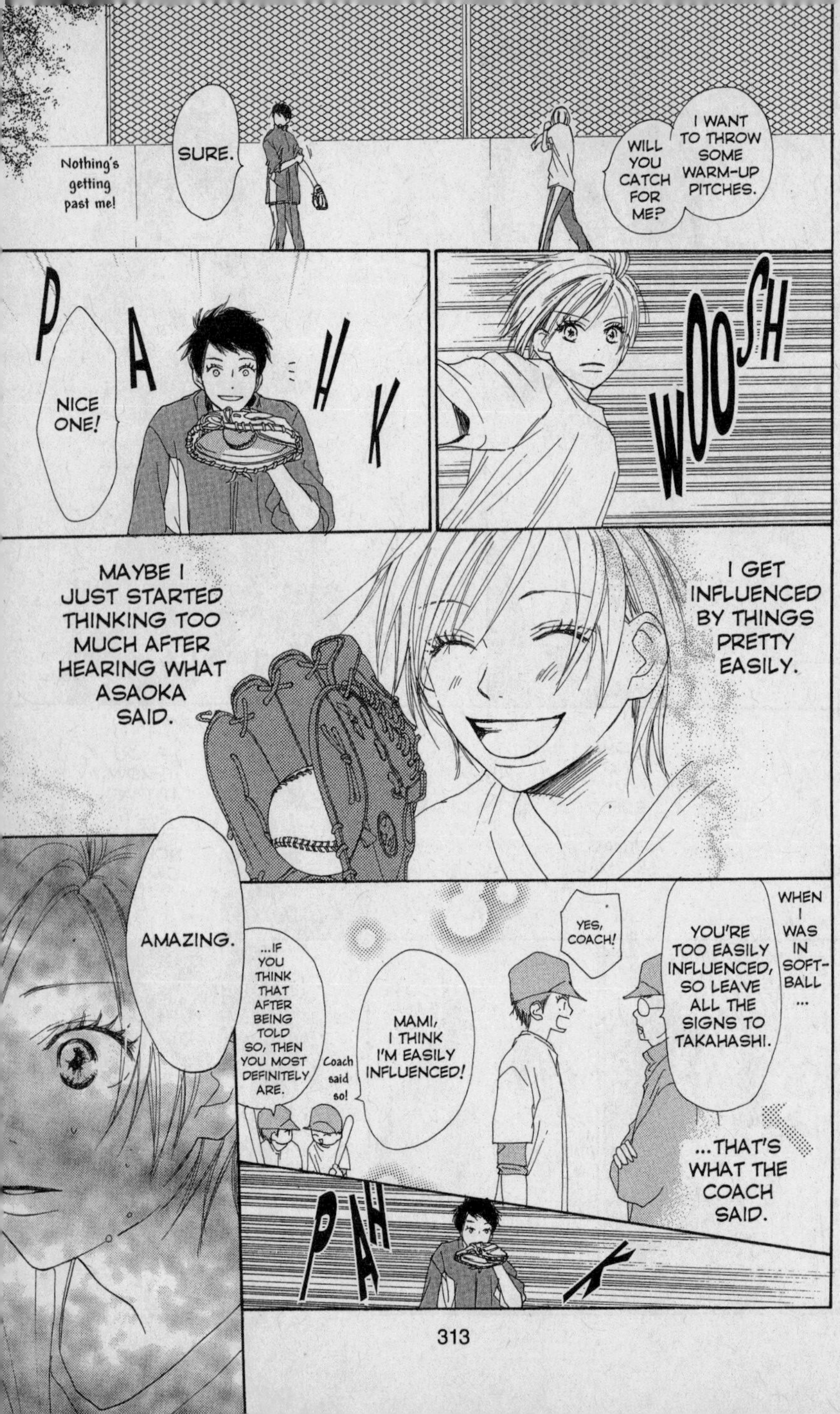
I WANT TO THROW SOME WARM-UP PITCHES. WILL YOU CATCH FOR ME?
SURE.
Nothing's getting past me!
WOOSH
PAHK
NICE ONE!
I GET INFLUENCED BY THINGS PRETTY EASILY.
MAYBE I JUST STARTED THINKING TOO MUCH AFTER HEARING WHAT ASAOKA SAID.
WHEN I WAS IN SOFT-BALL ...
YOU'RE TOO EASILY INFLUENCED, SO LEAVE ALL THE SIGNS TO TAKAHASHI.
YES, COACH!
MAMI, I THINK I'M EASILY INFLUENCED!
Coach said so!
...IF YOU THINK THAT AFTER BEING TOLD SO, THEN YOU MOST DEFINITELY ARE.
...THAT'S WHAT THE COACH SAID.
PAHK
AMAZING.

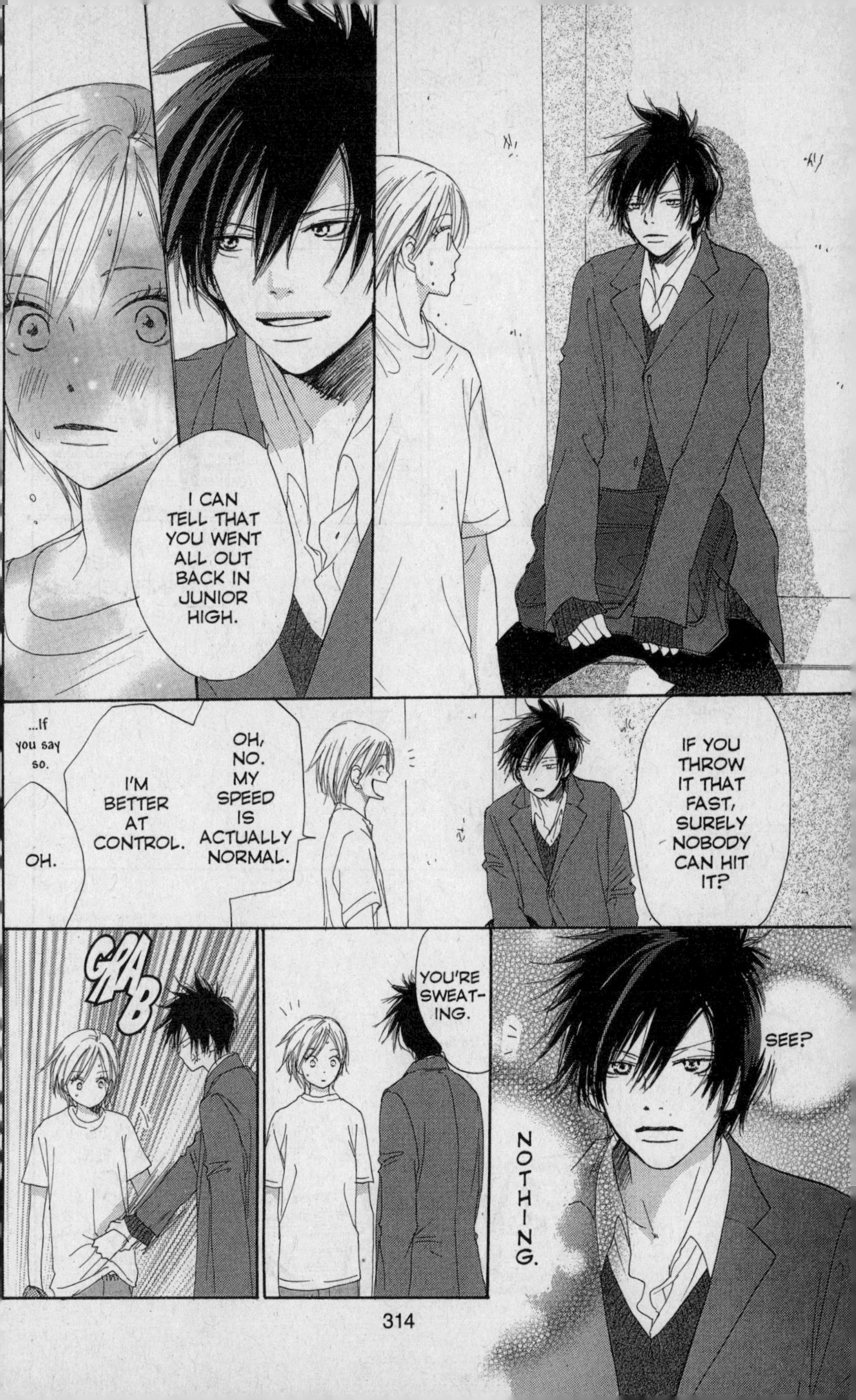
I CAN TELL THAT YOU WENT ALL OUT BACK IN JUNIOR HIGH.
IF YOU THROW IT THAT FAST, SURELY NOBODY CAN HIT IT?
OH, NO. MY SPEED IS ACTUALLY NORMAL.
I'M BETTER AT CONTROL.
OH.
...If you say so.
SEE?
NOTHING.
YOU'RE SWEAT-ING.
GRAB

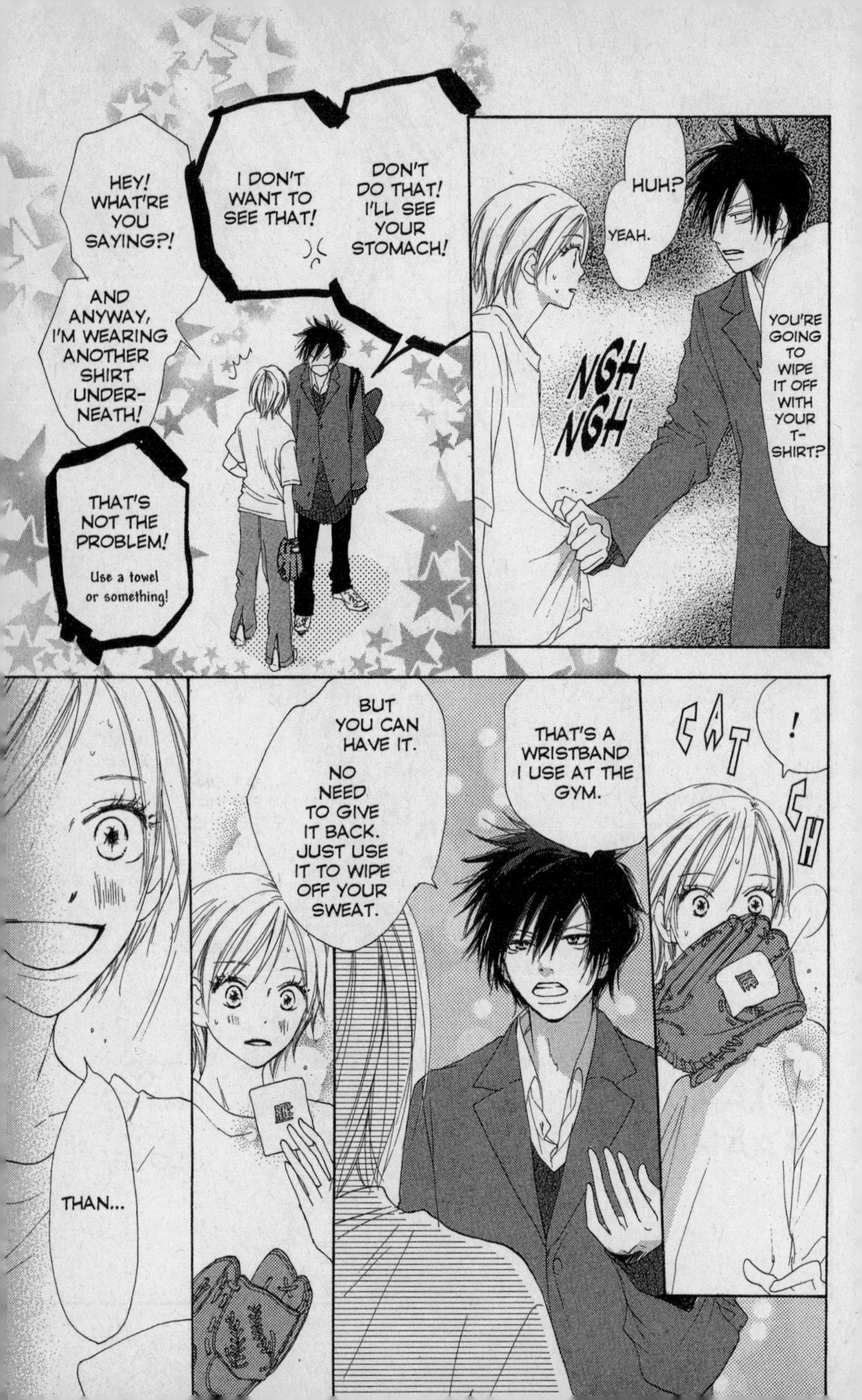

HUH?
YEAH.
YOU'RE GOING TO WIPE IT OFF WITH YOUR T-SHIRT?
NGH NGH
DON'T DO THAT! I'LL SEE YOUR STOMACH!
I DON'T WANT TO SEE THAT!
HEY! WHAT'RE YOU SAYING?!
AND ANYWAY, I'M WEARING ANOTHER SHIRT UNDER-NEATH!
THAT'S NOT THE PROBLEM!
Use a towel or something!
!
CATCH
THAT'S A WRISTBAND I USE AT THE GYM.
BUT YOU CAN HAVE IT.
NO NEED TO GIVE IT BACK. JUST USE IT TO WIPE OFF YOUR SWEAT.
THAN...

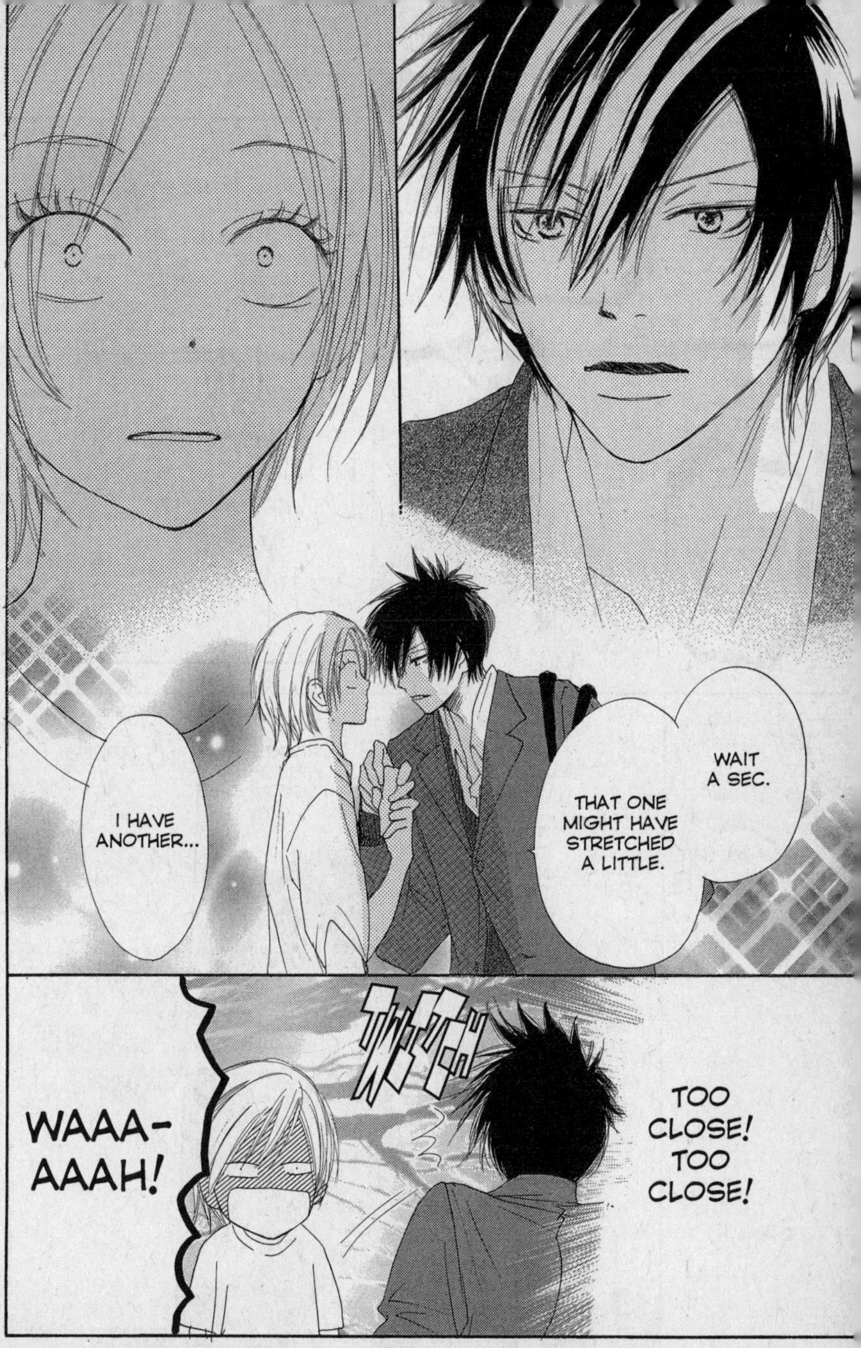
WAIT A SEC.
THAT ONE MIGHT HAVE STRETCHED A LITTLE.
I HAVE ANOTHER...
TOO CLOSE! TOO CLOSE!
WAAAA-AAAH!

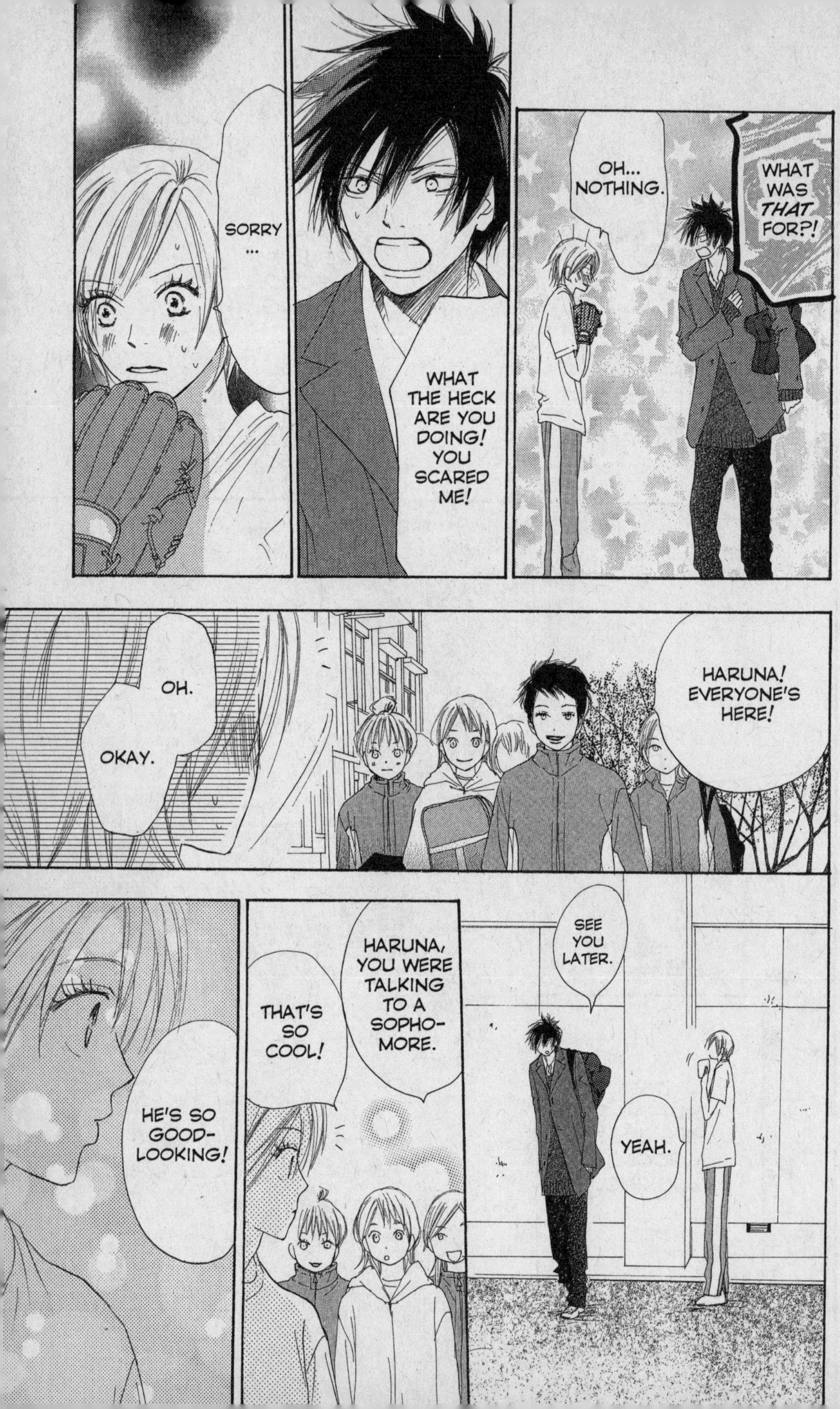
WHAT WAS *THAT* FOR?!
OH... NOTHING.
WHAT THE HECK ARE YOU DOING! YOU SCARED ME!
SORRY ...
HARUNA! EVERYONE'S HERE!
OH.
OKAY.
SEE YOU LATER.
YEAH.
HARUNA, YOU WERE TALKING TO A SOPHO-MORE.
THAT'S SO COOL!
HE'S SO GOOD-LOOKING!

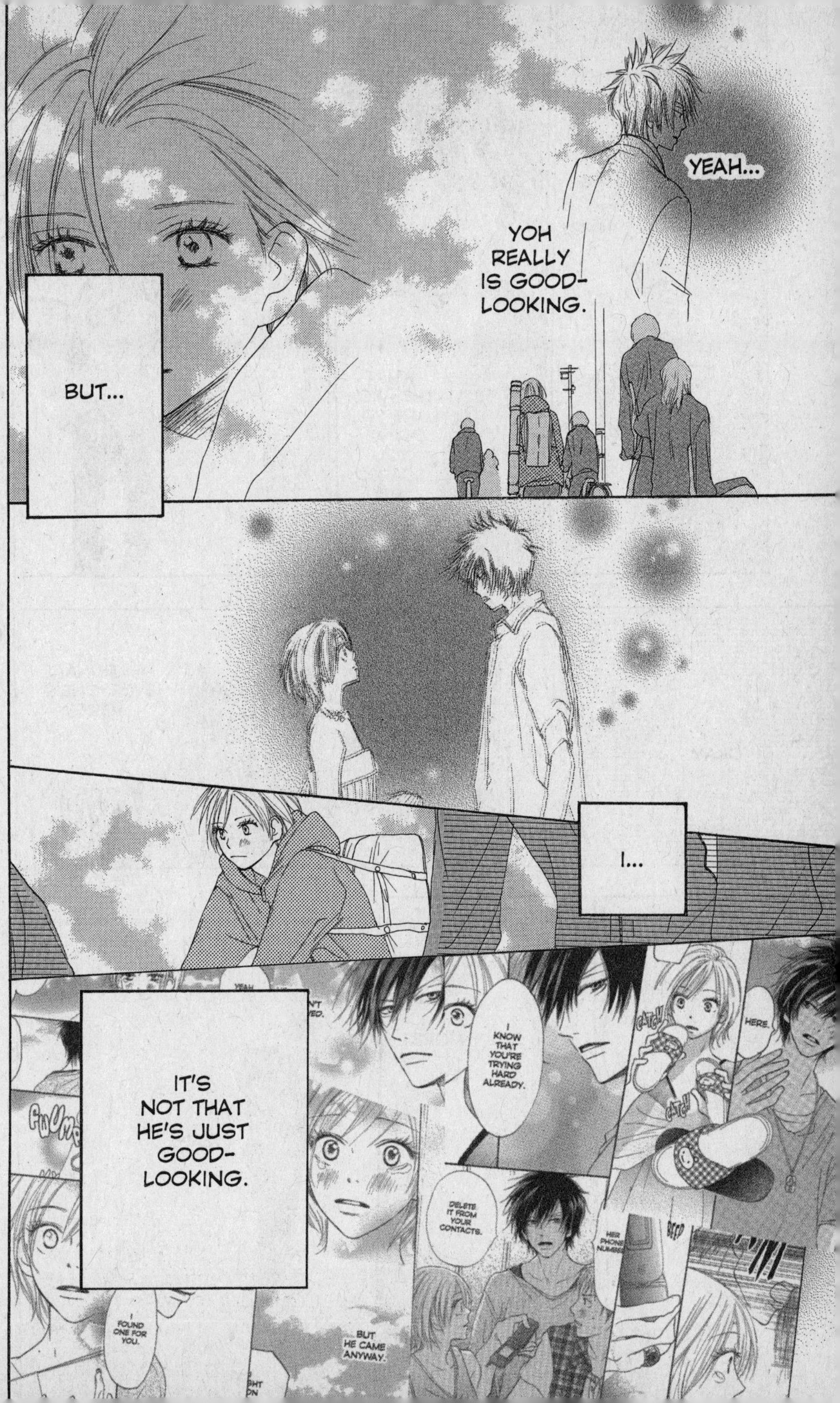
YEAH...
YOH REALLY IS GOOD-LOOKING.
BUT...
I...
HERE.
I KNOW THAT YOU'RE TRYING HARD ALREADY.
IT'S NOT THAT HE'S JUST GOOD-LOOKING.
DELETE IT FROM YOUR CONTACTS.
BUT HE CAME ANYWAY.
I FOUND ONE FOR YOU.

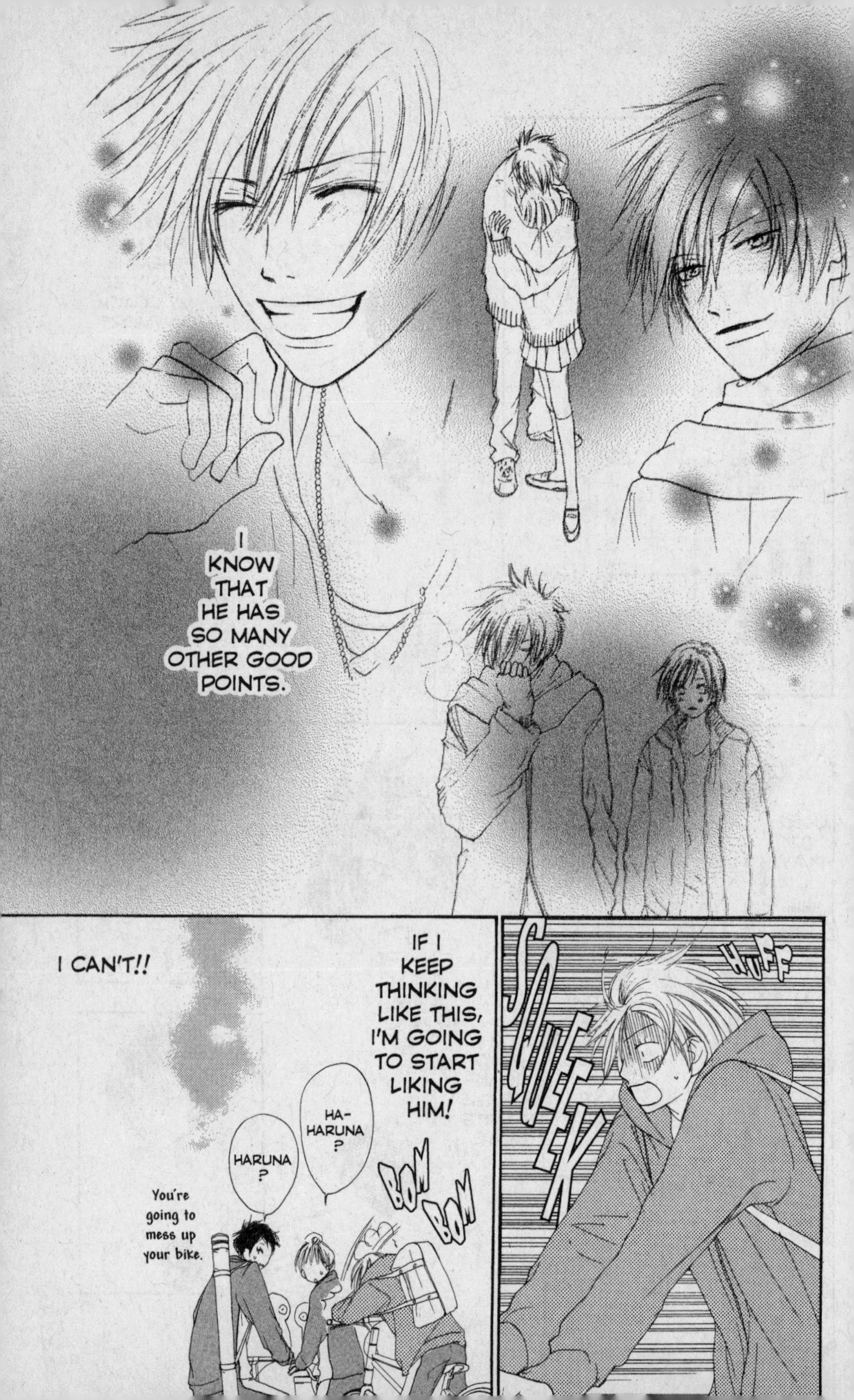
I KNOW THAT HE HAS SO MANY OTHER GOOD POINTS.
SQUEEK
HUFF
IF I KEEP THINKING LIKE THIS, I'M GOING TO START LIKING HIM!
I CAN'T!!
BOM BOM
HA-HARUNA?
HARUNA?
You're going to mess up your bike.

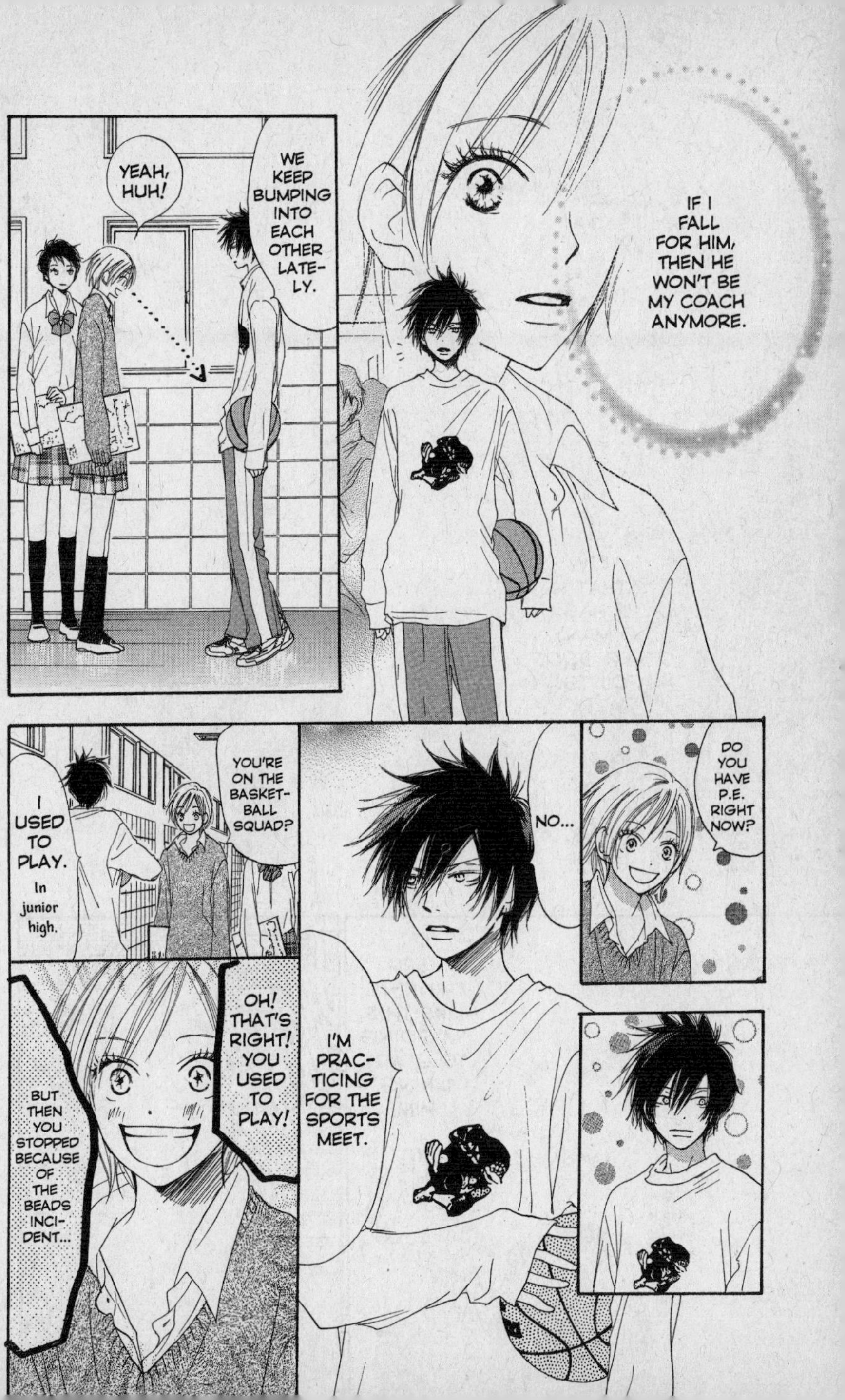

IF I FALL FOR HIM, THEN HE WON'T BE MY COACH ANYMORE.
WE KEEP BUMPING INTO EACH OTHER LATELY.
YEAH, HUH!
DO YOU HAVE P.E. RIGHT NOW?
NO...
I'M PRACTICING FOR THE SPORTS MEET.
YOU'RE ON THE BASKETBALL SQUAD?
I USED TO PLAY.
In junior high.
OH! THAT'S RIGHT! YOU USED TO PLAY!
BUT THEN YOU STOPPED BECAUSE OF THE BEADS INCIDENT...

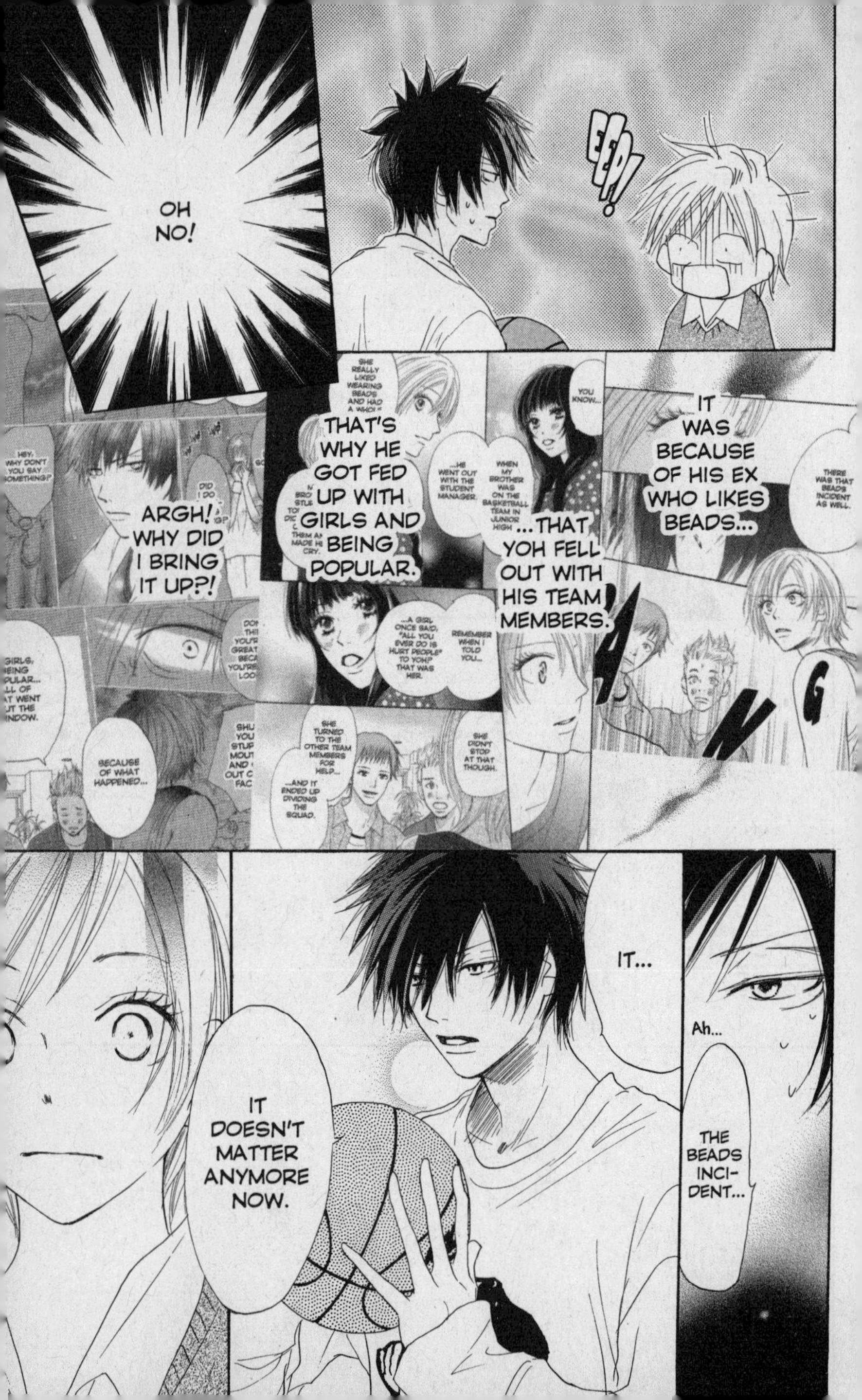
EEP!
OH NO!
IT WAS BECAUSE OF HIS EX WHO LIKES BEADS...
THERE WAS THAT BEADS INCIDENT AS WELL.
BANG
...THAT YOH FELL OUT WITH HIS TEAM MEMBERS.
YOU KNOW...
WHEN MY BROTHER WAS ON THE BASKETBALL TEAM IN JUNIOR HIGH
...HE WENT OUT WITH THE STUDENT MANAGER.
THAT'S WHY HE GOT FED UP WITH GIRLS AND BEING POPULAR.
REMEMBER WHEN I TOLD YOU...
...A GIRL ONCE SAID, "ALL YOU EVER DO IS HURT PEOPLE" TO YOH? THAT WAS HER.
SHE DIDN'T STOP AT THAT THOUGH.
SHE TURNED TO THE OTHER TEAM MEMBERS FOR HELP...
...AND IT ENDED UP DIVIDING THE SQUAD.
ARGH! WHY DID I BRING IT UP?!
HEY, WHY DON'T YOU SAY SOMETHING?
BECAUSE OF WHAT HAPPENED...
Ah...
THE BEADS INCI-DENT...
IT...
IT DOESN'T MATTER ANYMORE NOW.

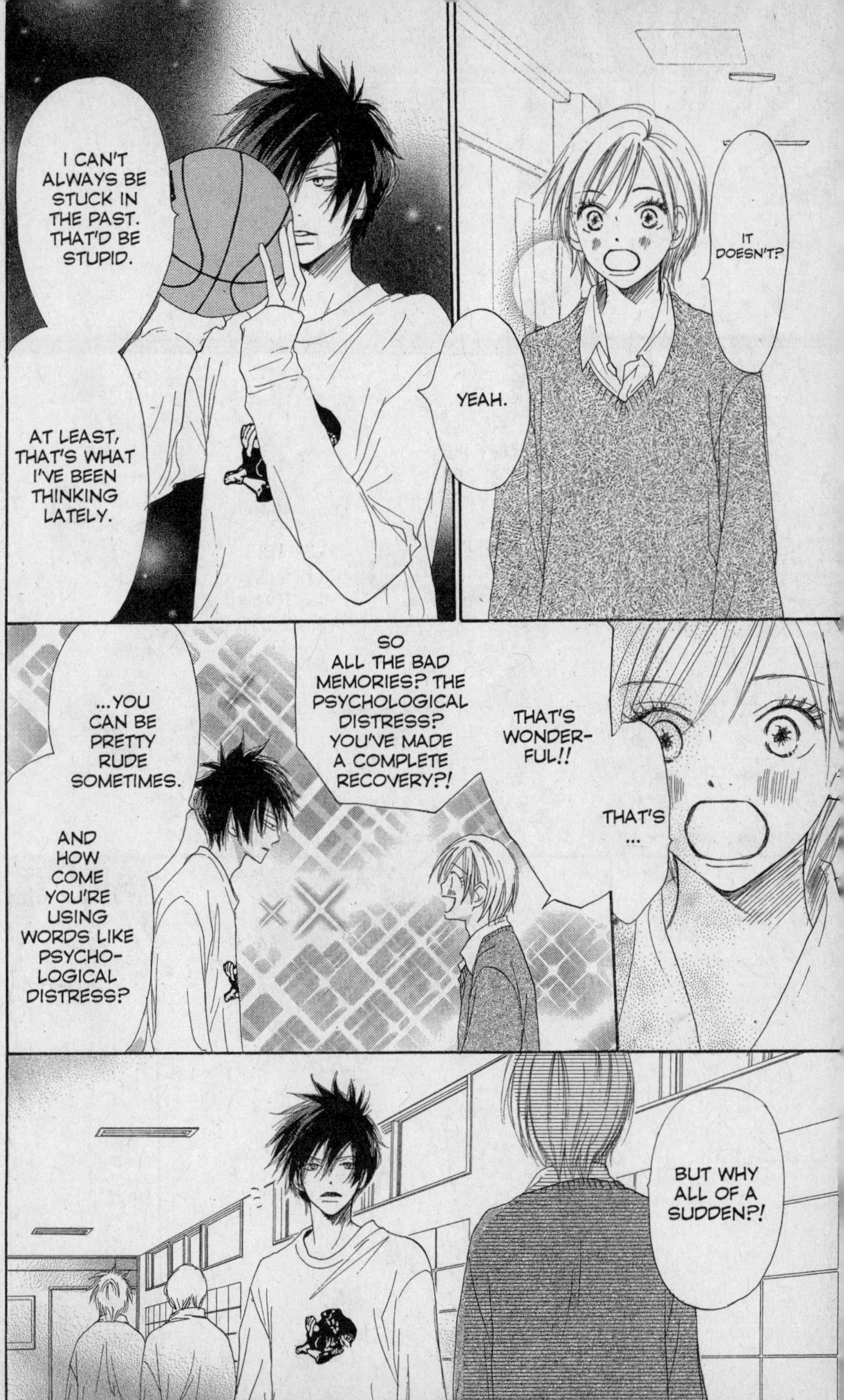
IT DOESN'T?
YEAH.
I CAN'T ALWAYS BE STUCK IN THE PAST. THAT'D BE STUPID.
AT LEAST, THAT'S WHAT I'VE BEEN THINKING LATELY.
THAT'S...
THAT'S WONDERFUL!!
SO ALL THE BAD MEMORIES? THE PSYCHOLOGICAL DISTRESS? YOU'VE MADE A COMPLETE RECOVERY?!
...YOU CAN BE PRETTY RUDE SOMETIMES.
AND HOW COME YOU'RE USING WORDS LIKE PSYCHOLOGICAL DISTRESS?
BUT WHY ALL OF A SUDDEN?!

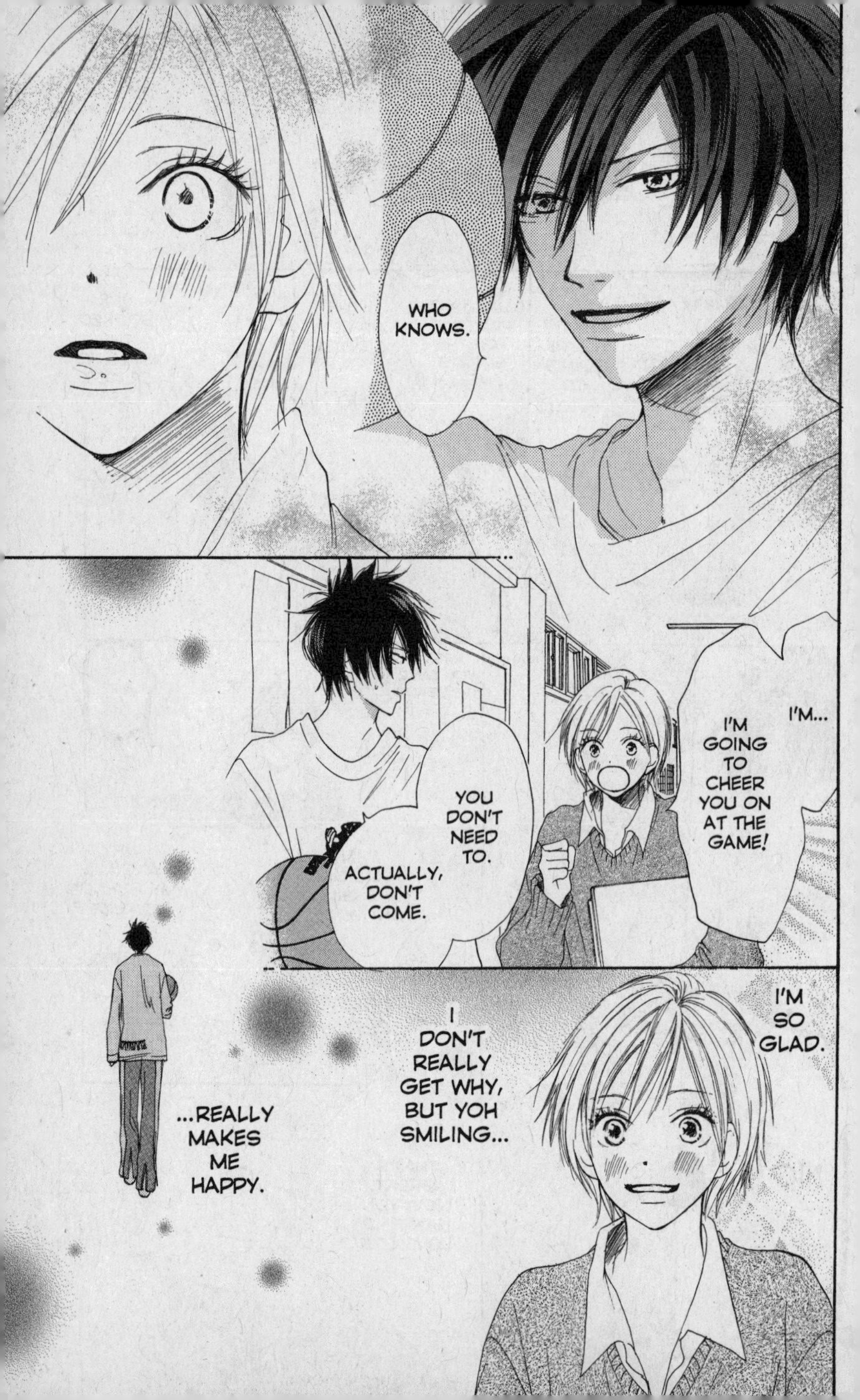
WHO KNOWS.
I'M...
I'M GOING TO CHEER YOU ON AT THE GAME!
YOU DON'T NEED TO.
ACTUALLY, DON'T COME.
I'M SO GLAD.
I DON'T REALLY GET WHY, BUT YOH SMILING...
...REALLY MAKES ME HAPPY.

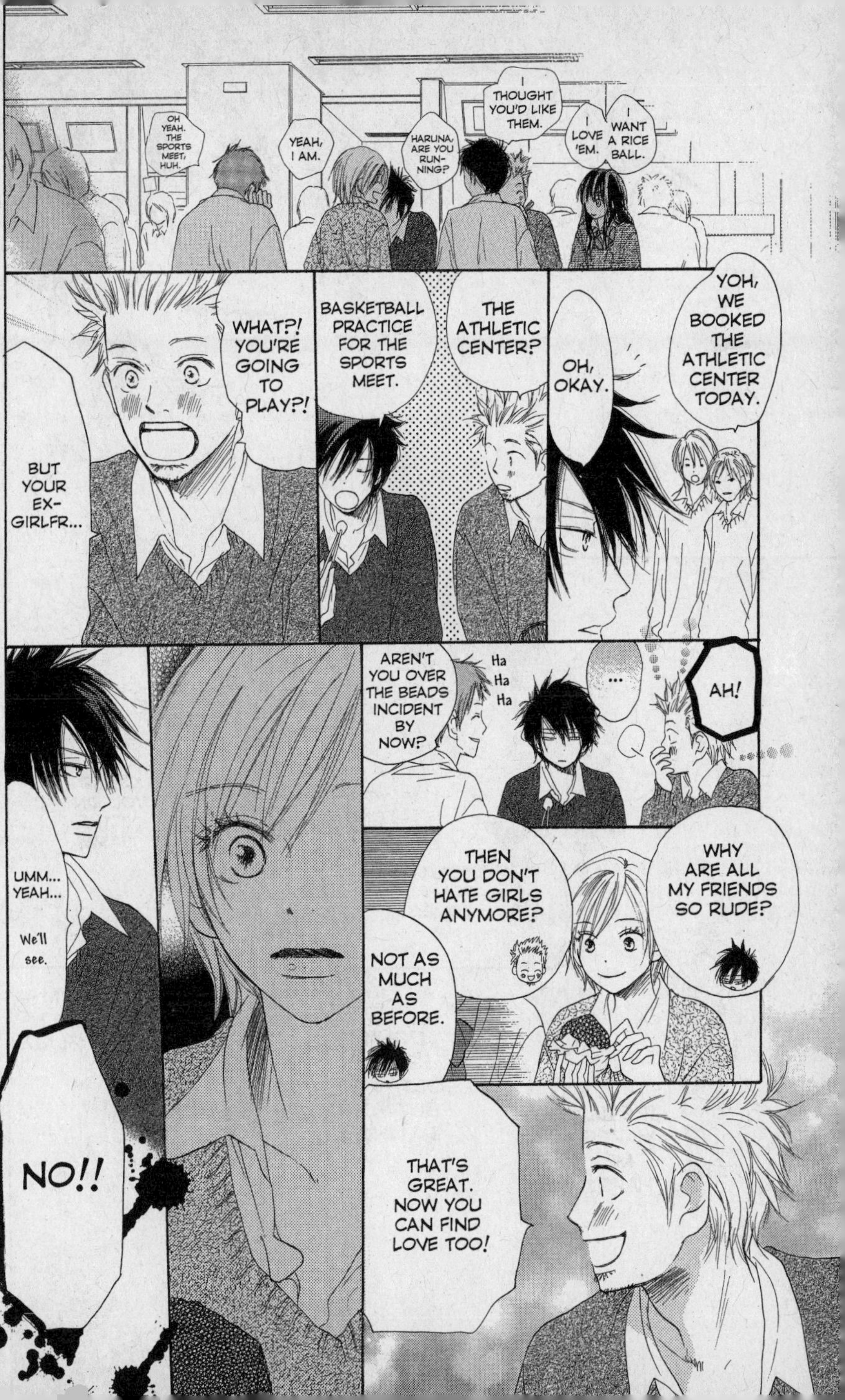
I WANT A RICE BALL.
I LOVE 'EM.
I THOUGHT YOU'D LIKE THEM.
HARUNA, ARE YOU RUN-NING?
YEAH, I AM.
OH YEAH. THE SPORTS MEET, HUH.
YOH, WE BOOKED THE ATHLETIC CENTER TODAY.
OH, OKAY.
THE ATHLETIC CENTER?
BASKETBALL PRACTICE FOR THE SPORTS MEET.
WHAT?! YOU'RE GOING TO PLAY?!
BUT YOUR EX-GIRLFR...
AH!
...
Ha Ha Ha
AREN'T YOU OVER THE BEADS INCIDENT BY NOW?
WHY ARE ALL MY FRIENDS SO RUDE?
THEN YOU DON'T HATE GIRLS ANYMORE?
NOT AS MUCH AS BEFORE.
THAT'S GREAT. NOW YOU CAN FIND LOVE TOO!
UMM... YEAH...
We'll see.
NO!!

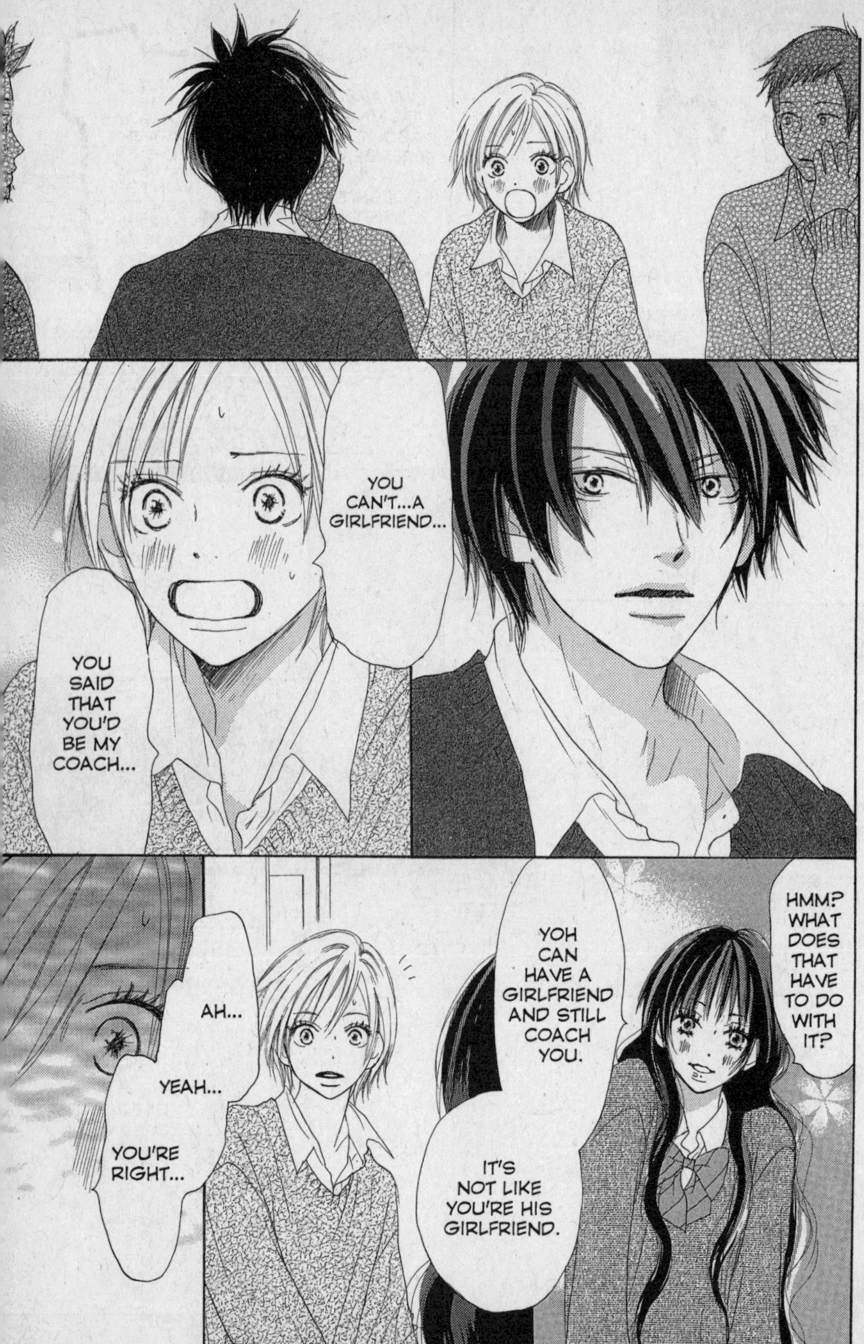
YOU CAN'T...A GIRLFRIEND...
YOU SAID THAT YOU'D BE MY COACH...
HMM? WHAT DOES THAT HAVE TO DO WITH IT?
YOH CAN HAVE A GIRLFRIEND AND STILL COACH YOU.
IT'S NOT LIKE YOU'RE HIS GIRLFRIEND.
AH...
YEAH...
YOU'RE RIGHT...

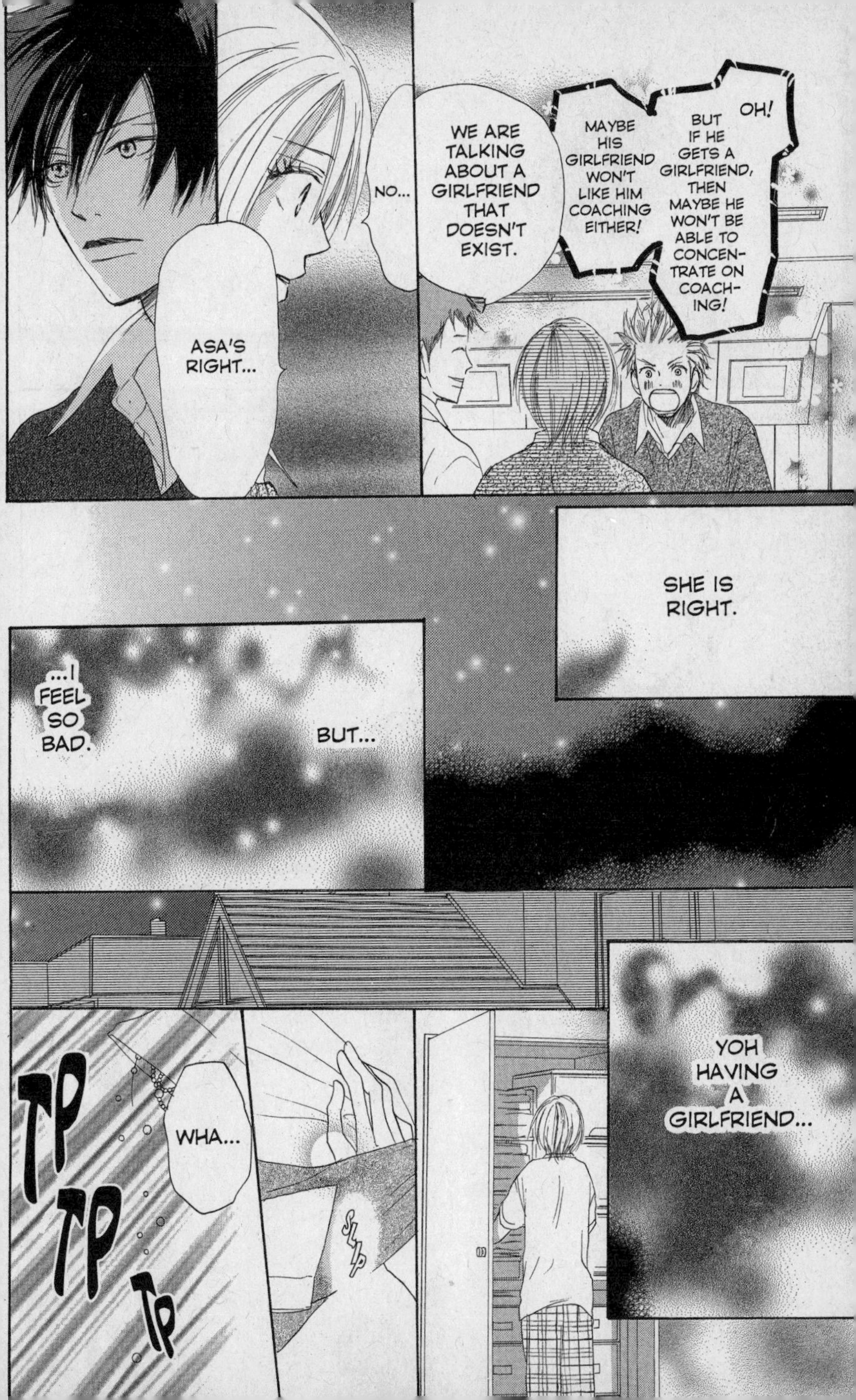
OH!
BUT IF HE GETS A GIRLFRIEND, THEN MAYBE HE WON'T BE ABLE TO CONCENTRATE ON COACHING!
MAYBE HIS GIRLFRIEND WON'T LIKE HIM COACHING EITHER!
WE ARE TALKING ABOUT A GIRLFRIEND THAT DOESN'T EXIST.
NO...
ASA'S RIGHT...
SHE IS RIGHT.
BUT...
...I FEEL SO BAD.
YOH HAVING A GIRLFRIEND...
SLIP
WHA...
TP TP TP

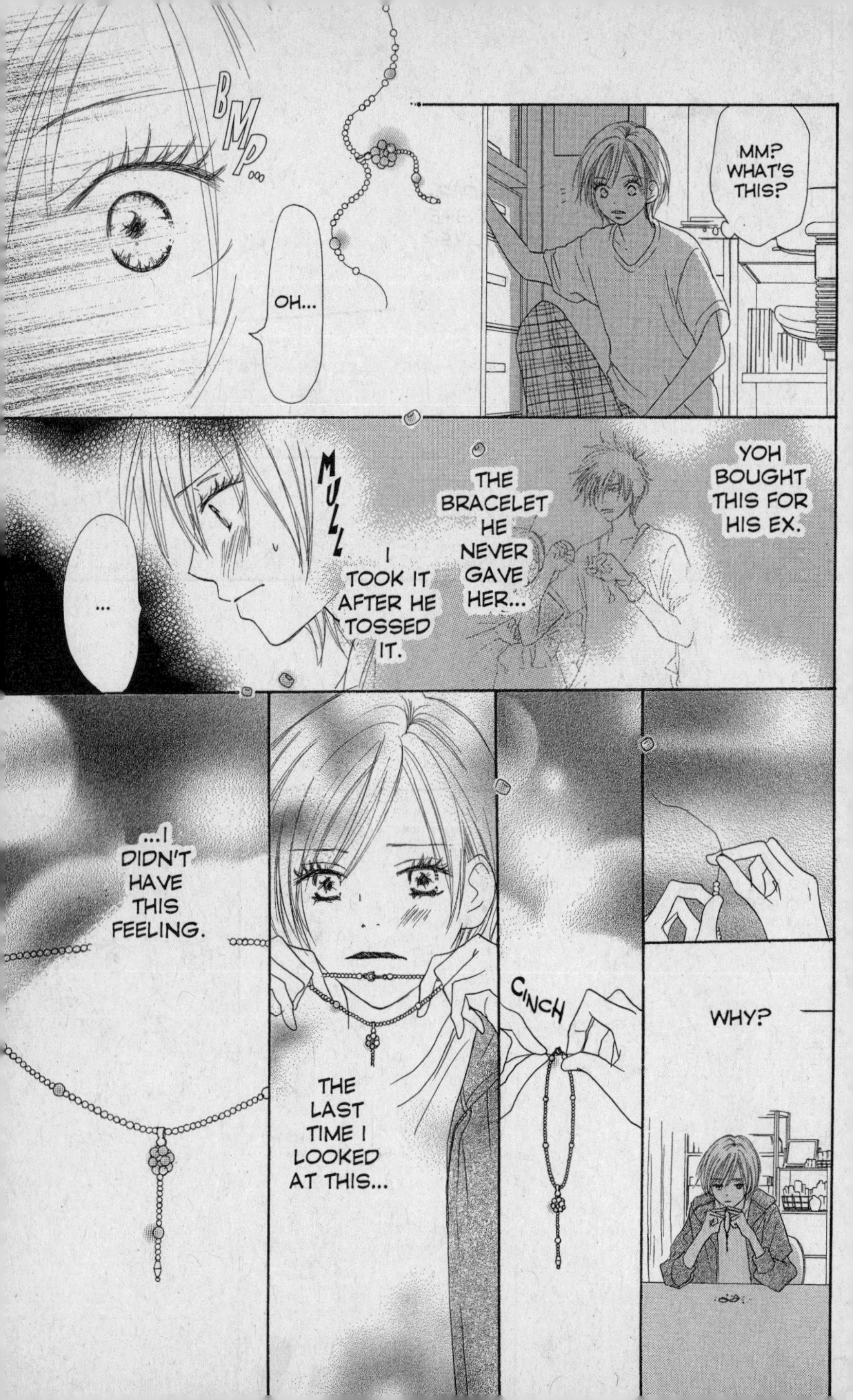
MM? WHAT'S THIS?
BMP...
OH...
YOH BOUGHT THIS FOR HIS EX.
THE BRACELET HE NEVER GAVE HER...
I TOOK IT AFTER HE TOSSED IT.
MULL
...
WHY?
CINCH
THE LAST TIME I LOOKED AT THIS...
...I DIDN'T HAVE THIS FEELING.

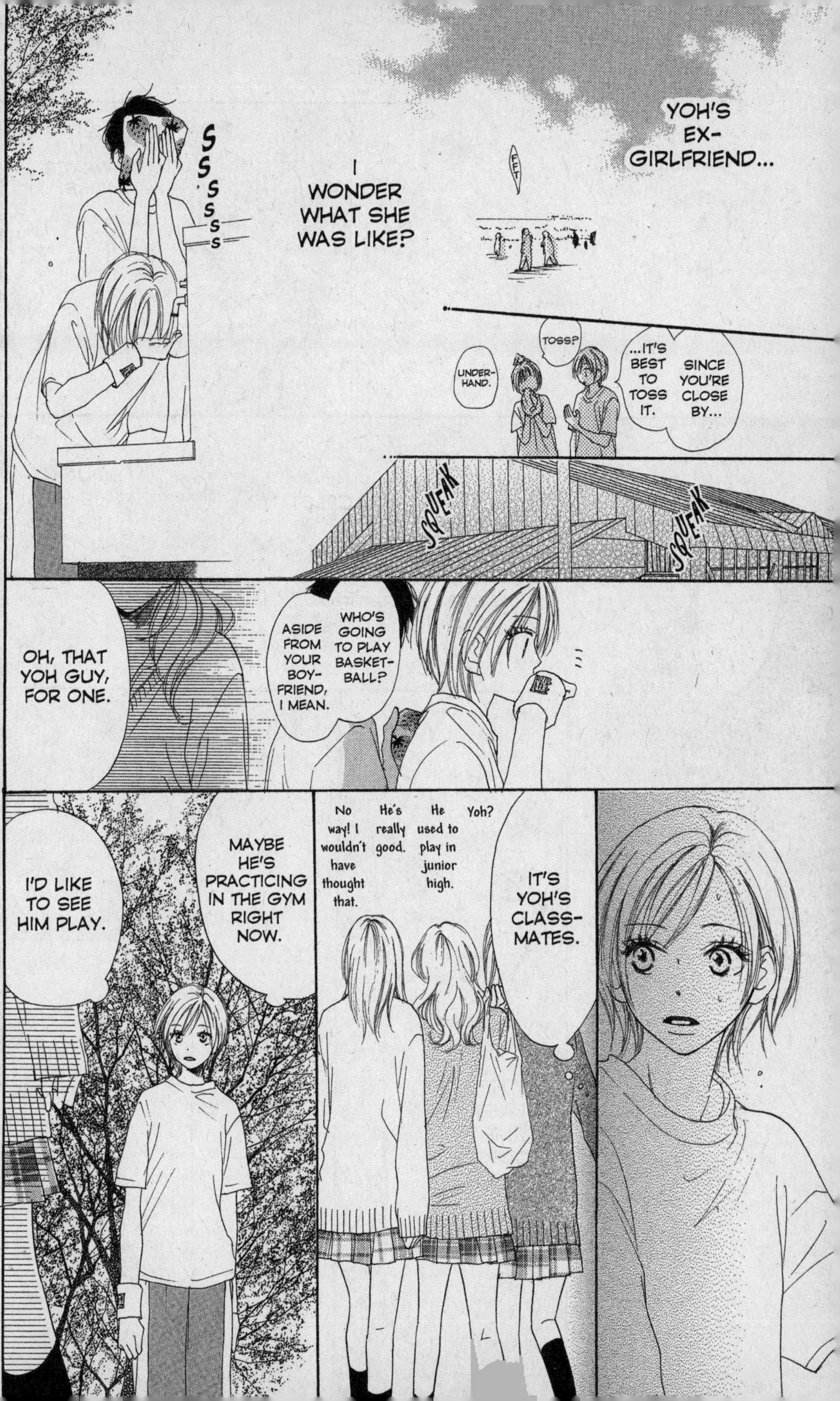
YOH'S EX-GIRLFRIEND...
FFT
SINCE YOU'RE CLOSE BY...
...IT'S BEST TO TOSS IT.
TOSS?
UNDER-HAND.
SQUEAK
SQUEAK
I WONDER WHAT SHE WAS LIKE?
SSSSS
WHO'S GOING TO PLAY BASKET-BALL?
ASIDE FROM YOUR BOY-FRIEND, I MEAN.
OH, THAT YOH GUY, FOR ONE.
IT'S YOH'S CLASS-MATES.
Yoh?
He used to play in junior high.
He's really good.
No way! I wouldn't have thought that.
MAYBE HE'S PRACTICING IN THE GYM RIGHT NOW.
I'D LIKE TO SEE HIM PLAY.

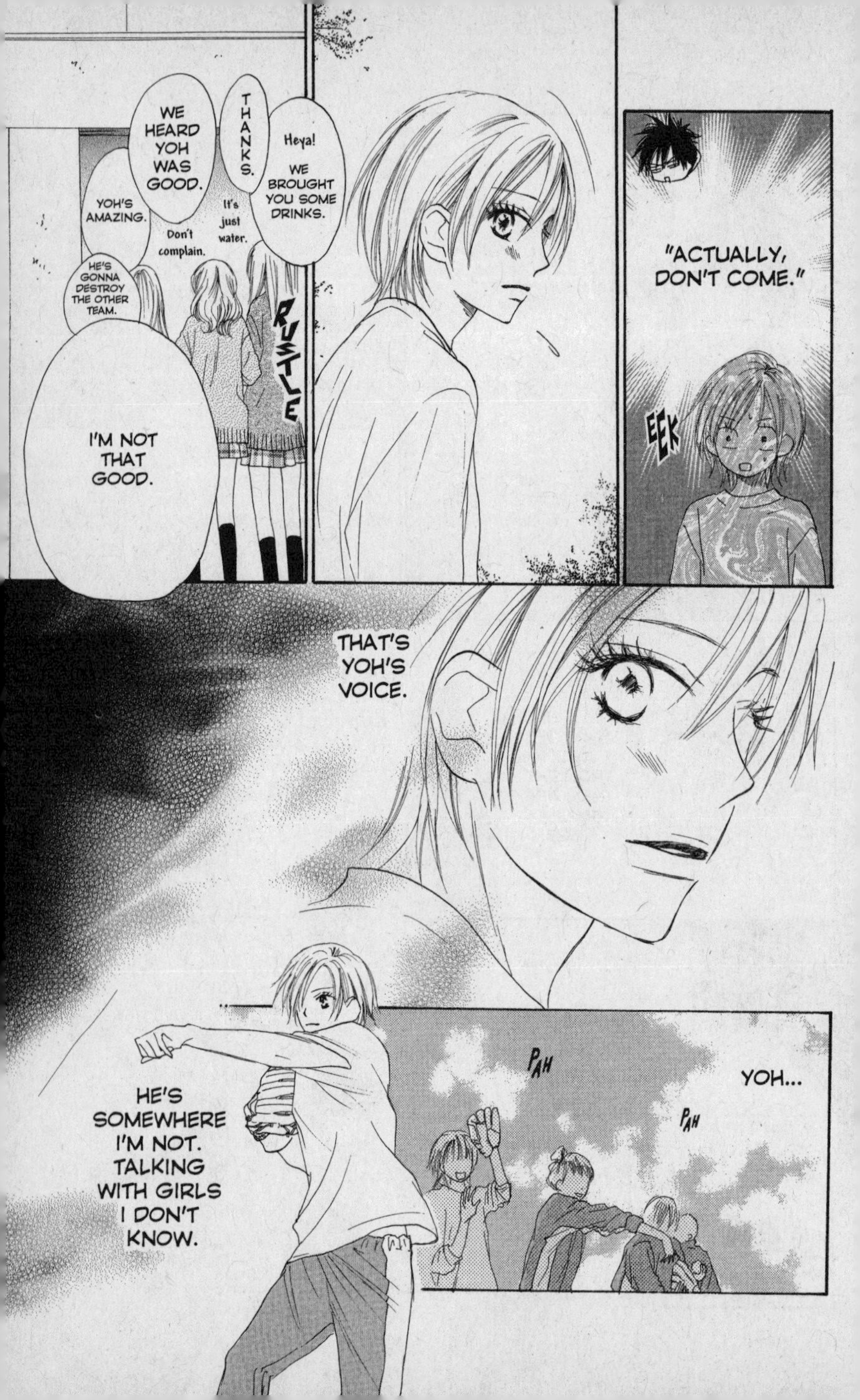
"ACTUALLY, DON'T COME."
EEK
Heya! WE BROUGHT YOU SOME DRINKS.
THANKS.
It's just water.
WE HEARD YOH WAS GOOD.
Don't complain.
YOH'S AMAZING.
HE'S GONNA DESTROY THE OTHER TEAM.
RUSTLE
I'M NOT THAT GOOD.
THAT'S YOH'S VOICE.
YOH...
PAH
PAH
HE'S SOMEWHERE I'M NOT. TALKING WITH GIRLS I DON'T KNOW.

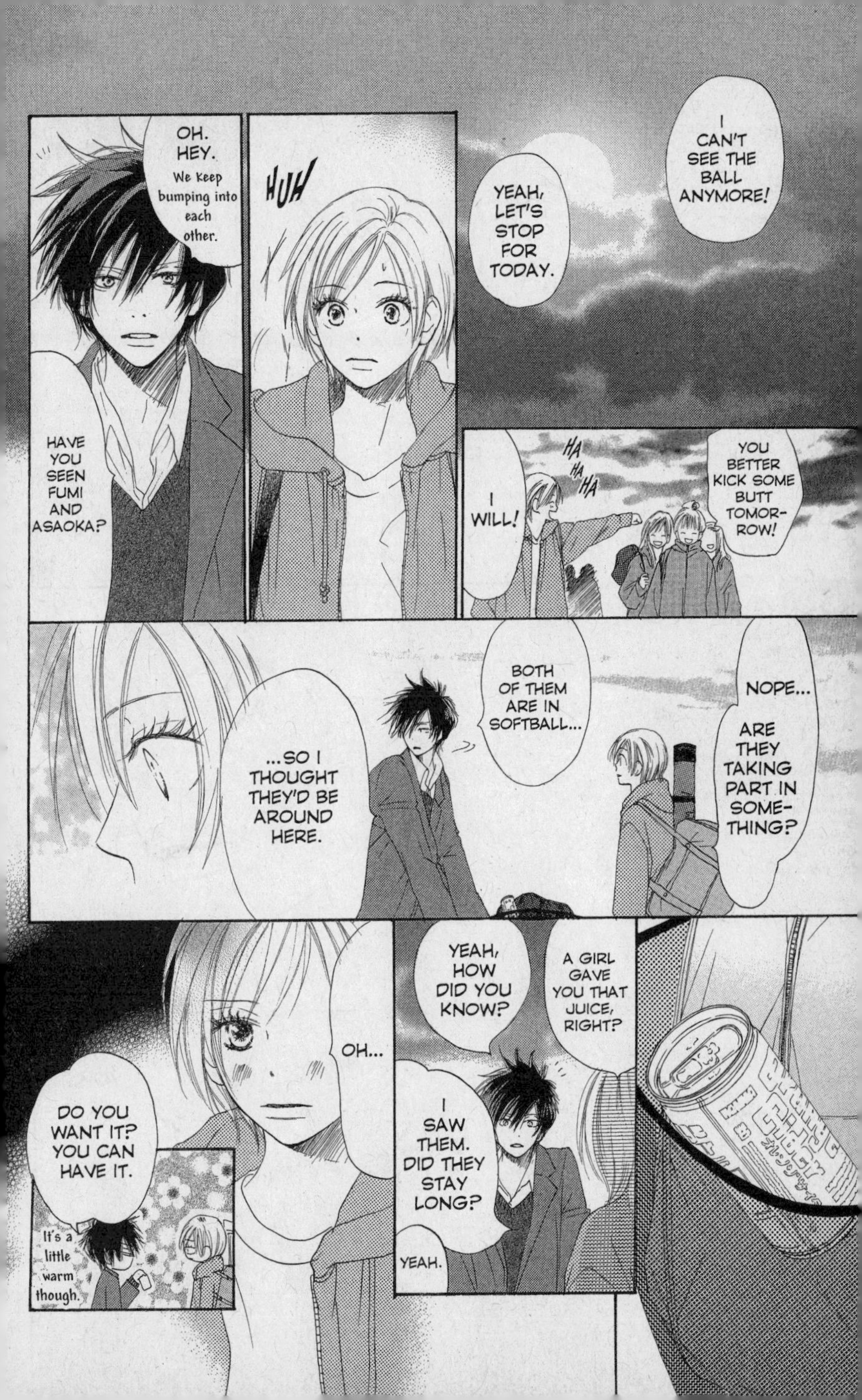
I CAN'T SEE THE BALL ANYMORE!
YEAH, LET'S STOP FOR TODAY.
YOU BETTER KICK SOME BUTT TOMORROW!
HA HA HA
I WILL!
HUH
OH. HEY.
We keep bumping into each other.
HAVE YOU SEEN FUMI AND ASAOKA?
NOPE...
ARE THEY TAKING PART IN SOMETHING?
BOTH OF THEM ARE IN SOFTBALL...
...SO I THOUGHT THEY'D BE AROUND HERE.
A GIRL GAVE YOU THAT JUICE, RIGHT?
YEAH, HOW DID YOU KNOW?
I SAW THEM. DID THEY STAY LONG?
YEAH.
OH...
DO YOU WANT IT? YOU CAN HAVE IT.
It's a little warm though.

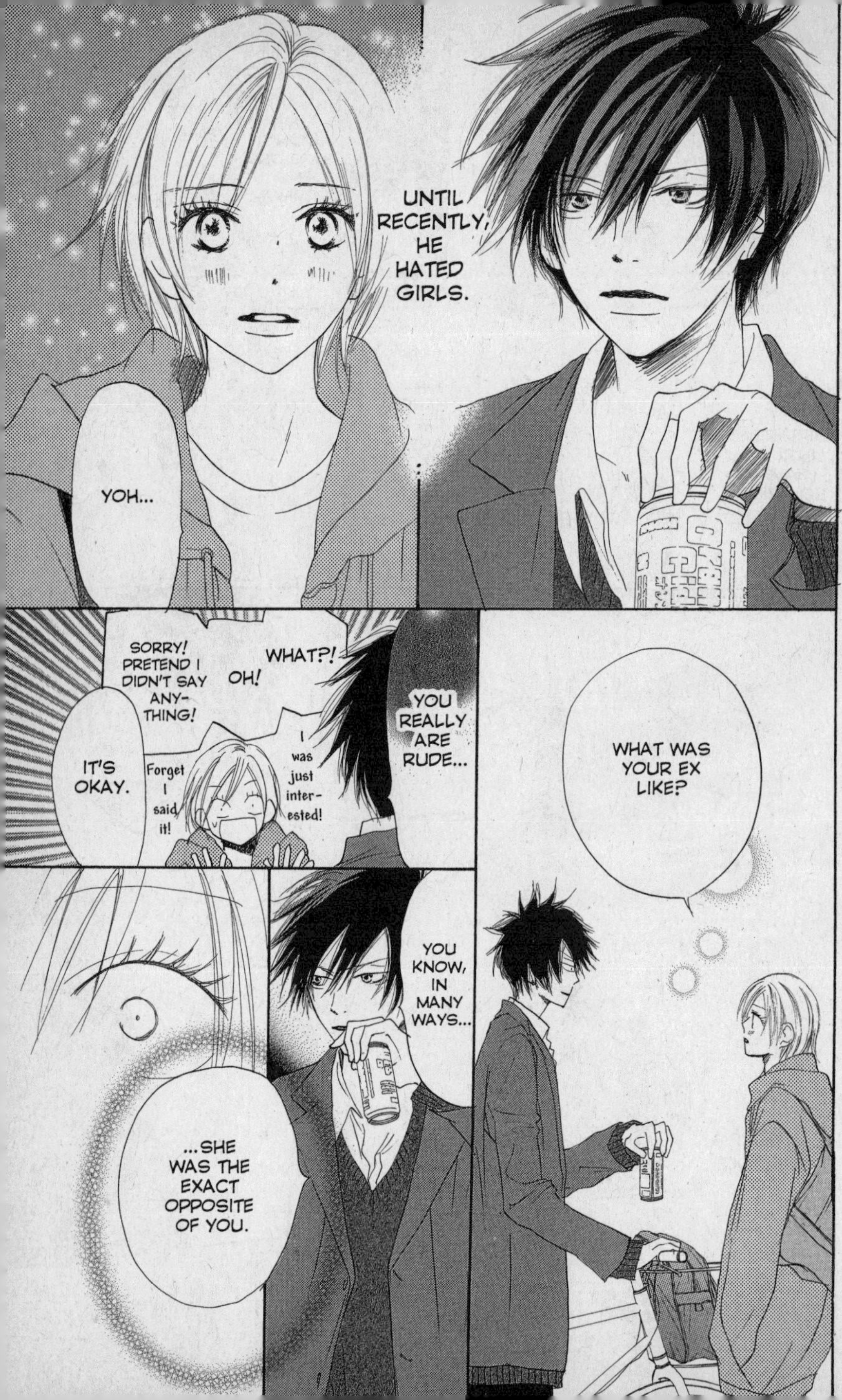
UNTIL RECENTLY, HE HATED GIRLS.
YOH...
WHAT WAS YOUR EX LIKE?
YOU REALLY ARE RUDE...
I was just inter-ested!
WHAT?!
OH!
SORRY! PRETEND I DIDN'T SAY ANY-THING!
Forget I said it!
IT'S OKAY.
YOU KNOW, IN MANY WAYS...
...SHE WAS THE EXACT OPPOSITE OF YOU.

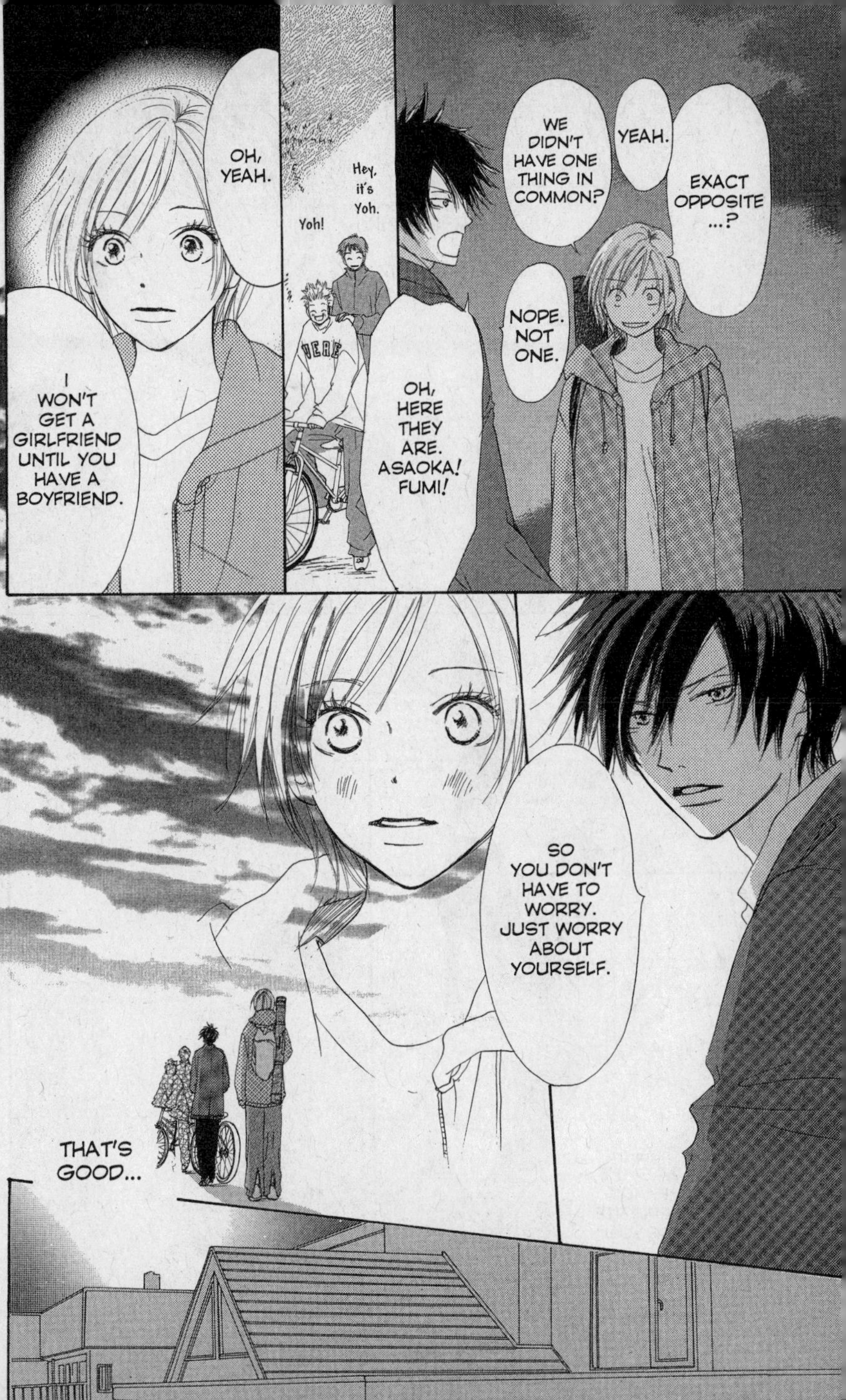
EXACT OPPOSITE ...?
YEAH.
WE DIDN'T HAVE ONE THING IN COMMON?
NOPE. NOT ONE.
Hey, it's Yoh.
Yoh!
OH, HERE THEY ARE. ASAOKA! FUMI!
OH, YEAH.
I WON'T GET A GIRLFRIEND UNTIL YOU HAVE A BOYFRIEND.
SO YOU DON'T HAVE TO WORRY. JUST WORRY ABOUT YOURSELF.
THAT'S GOOD...

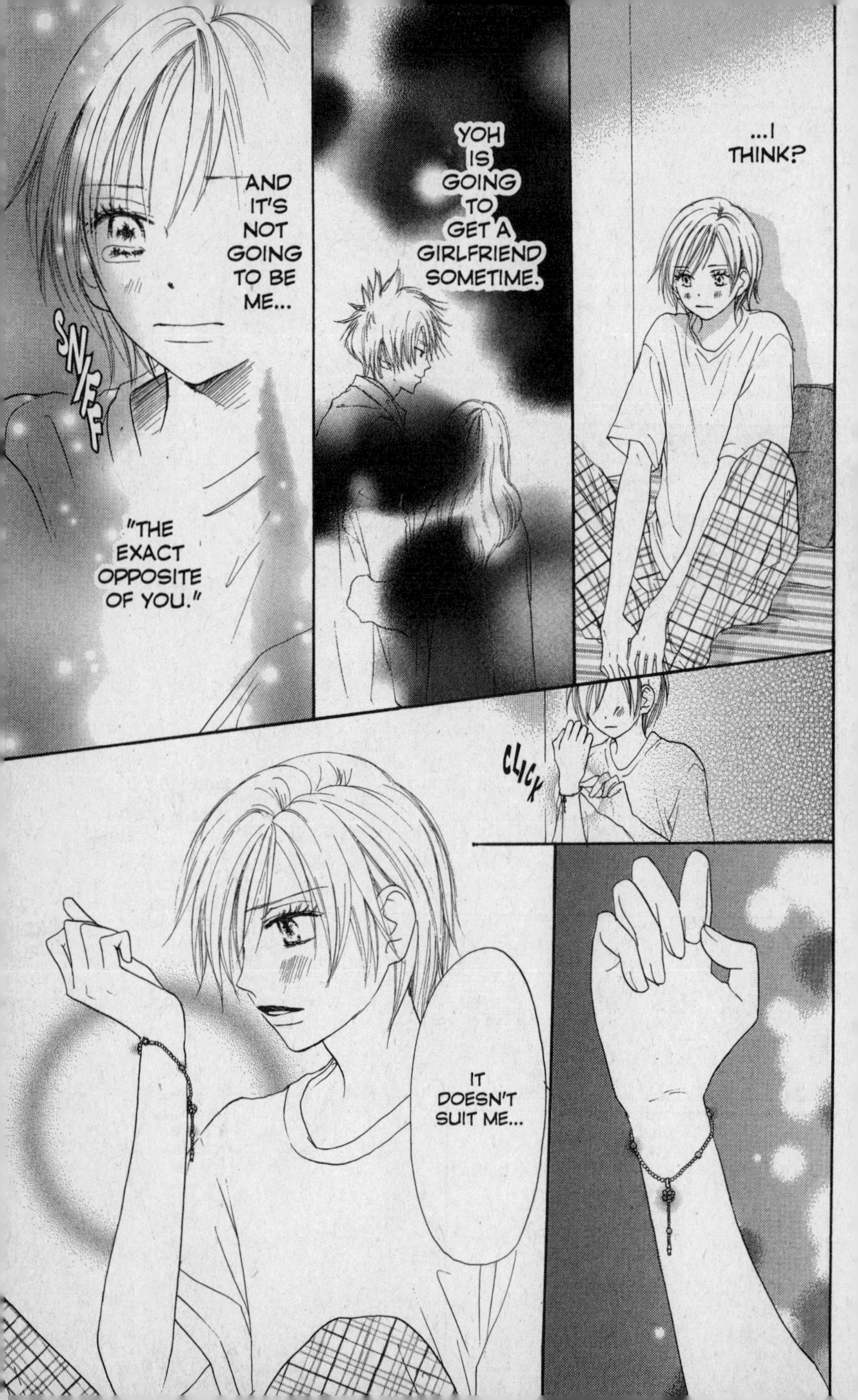
...I THINK?
YOH IS GOING TO GET A GIRLFRIEND SOMETIME.
AND IT'S NOT GOING TO BE ME...
SNIFF
"THE EXACT OPPOSITE OF YOU."
CLICK
IT DOESN'T SUIT ME...

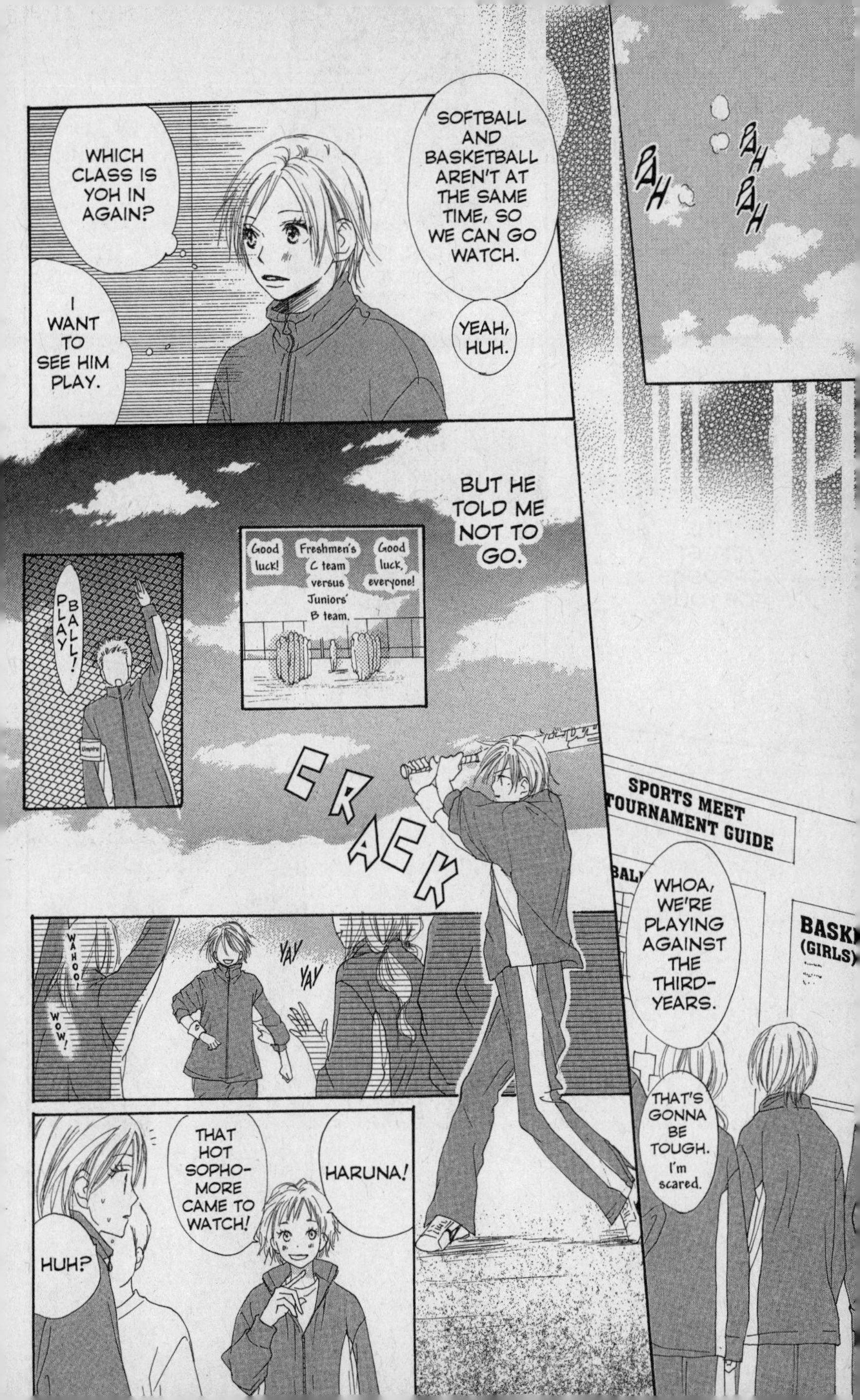

PAH
PAH
PAH
SOFTBALL AND BASKETBALL AREN'T AT THE SAME TIME, SO WE CAN GO WATCH.
YEAH, HUH.
WHICH CLASS IS YOH IN AGAIN?
I WANT TO SEE HIM PLAY.
SPORTS MEET TOURNAMENT GUIDE
BASK
(GIRLS)
WHOA, WE'RE PLAYING AGAINST THE THIRD-YEARS.
THAT'S GONNA BE TOUGH. I'm scared.
BUT HE TOLD ME NOT TO GO.
Good luck!
Freshmen's C team versus Juniors' B team.
Good luck, everyone!
PLAY BALL!
Umpire
CRACK
YAY YAY
WAHOO!
WOW!
HARUNA!
THAT HOT SOPHOMORE CAME TO WATCH!
HUH?

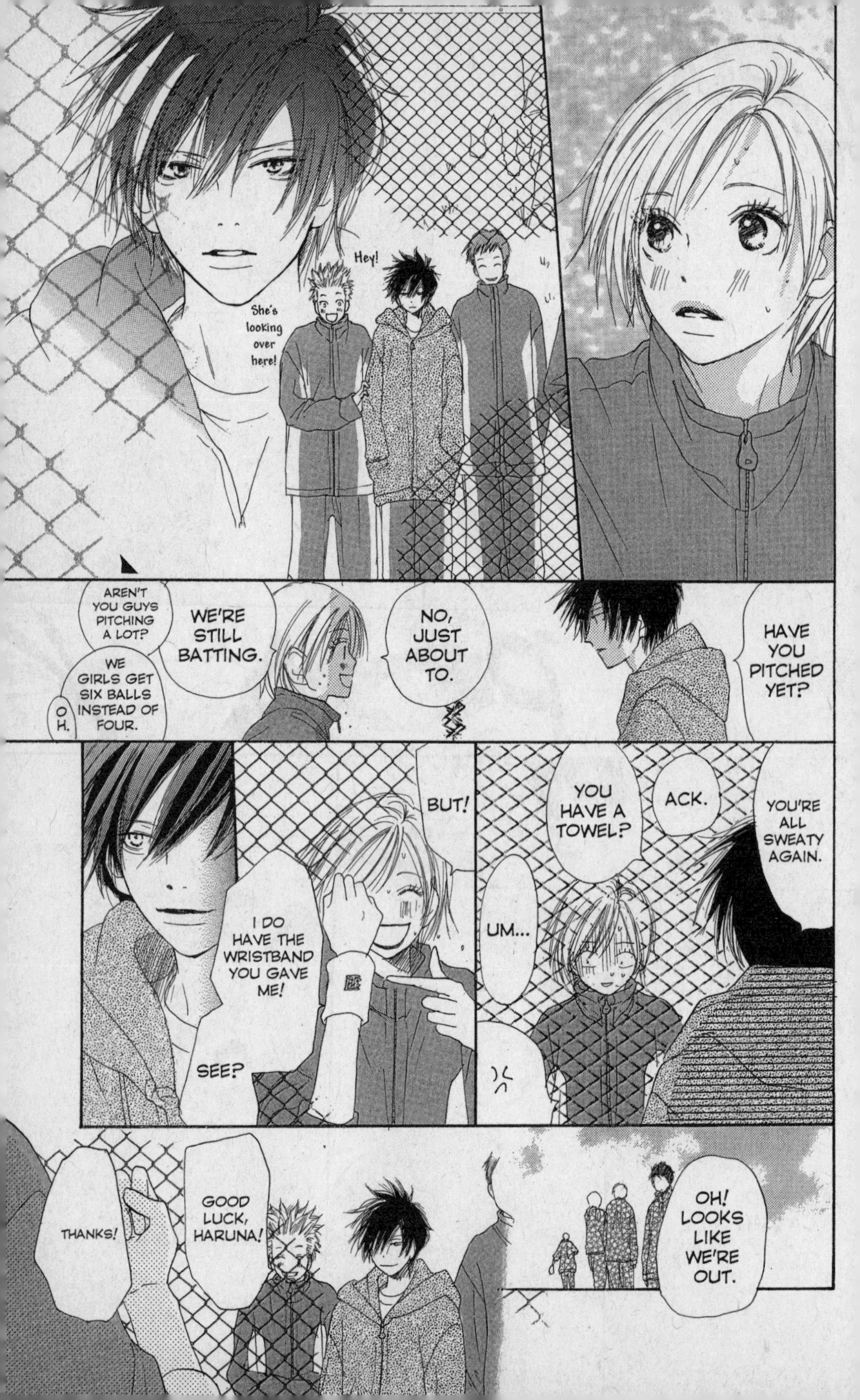
Hey!
She's looking over here!
HAVE YOU PITCHED YET?
NO, JUST ABOUT TO.
WE'RE STILL BATTING.
AREN'T YOU GUYS PITCHING A LOT?
WE GIRLS GET SIX BALLS INSTEAD OF FOUR.
OH.
YOU'RE ALL SWEATY AGAIN.
ACK.
YOU HAVE A TOWEL?
UM...
BUT!
I DO HAVE THE WRISTBAND YOU GAVE ME!
SEE?
OH! LOOKS LIKE WE'RE OUT.
GOOD LUCK, HARUNA!
THANKS!

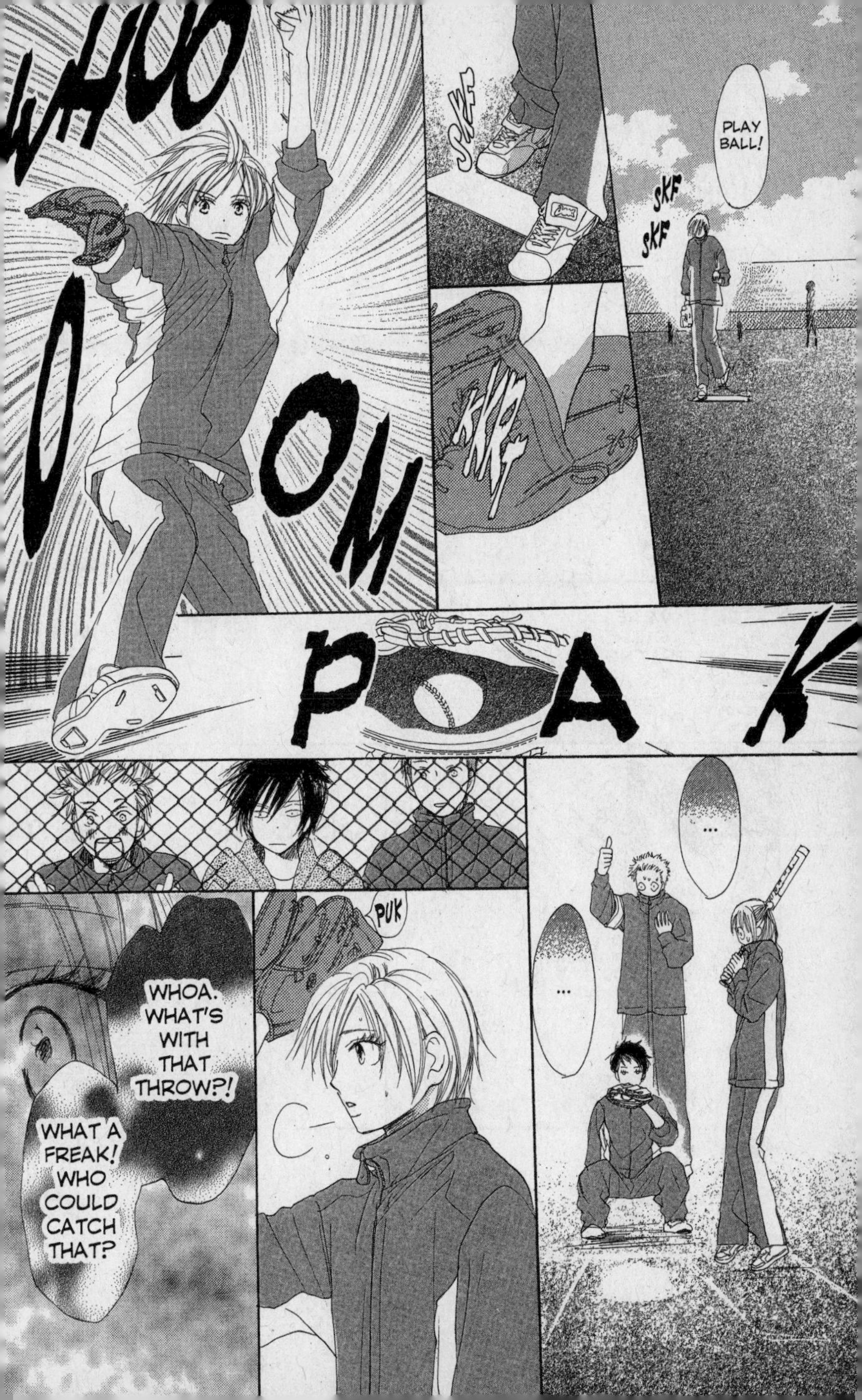
PLAY BALL!
SKF SKF
SKF
KKR
WHOOOOOM
POAK
...
...
PUK
WHOA. WHAT'S WITH THAT THROW?!
WHAT A FREAK! WHO COULD CATCH THAT?

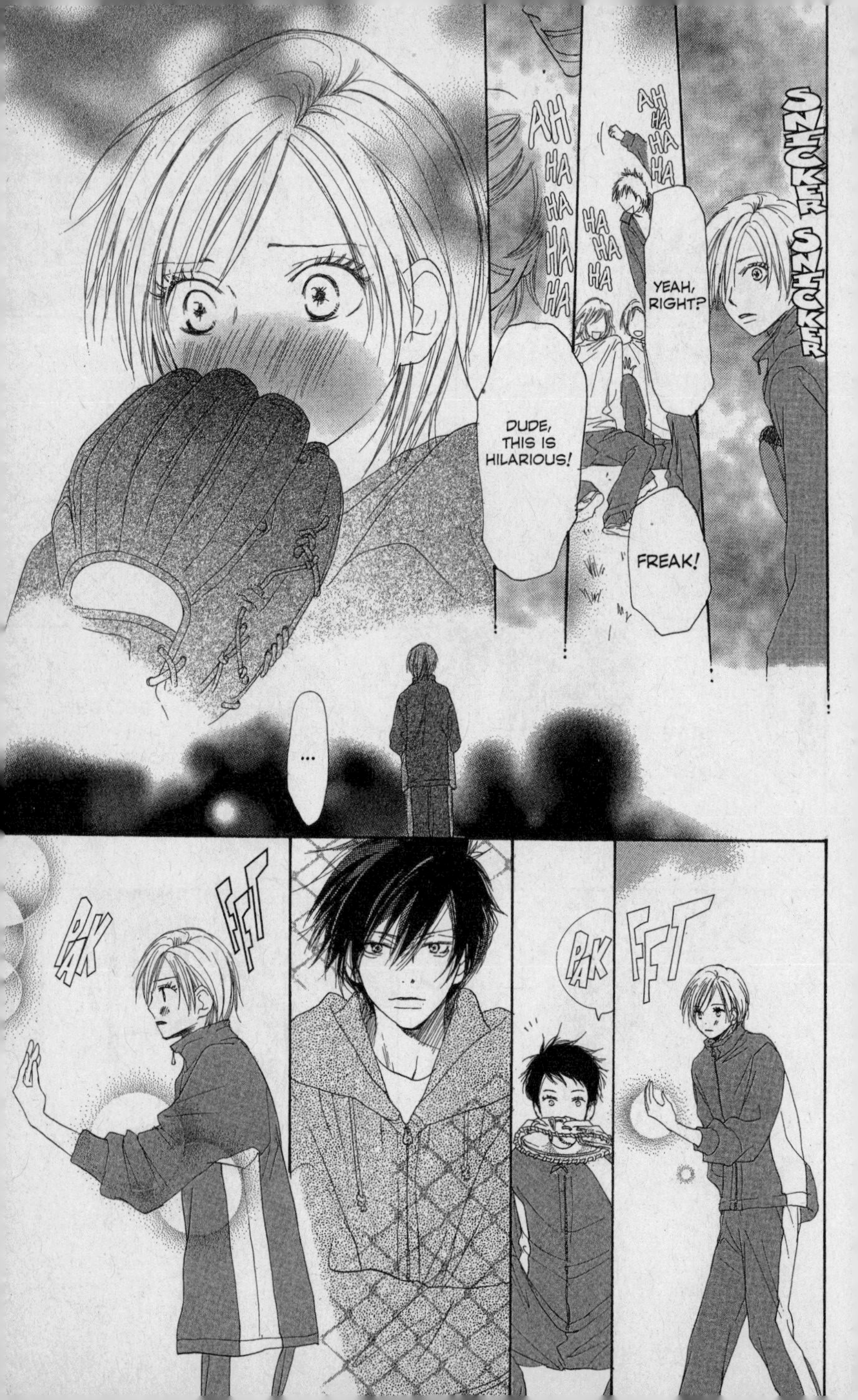

SNICKER SNICKER
AH HA HA HA
YEAH, RIGHT?
HA HA HA HA
FREAK!
AH HA HA HA HA HA
DUDE, THIS IS HILARIOUS!
...
FFT
PAK
FFT
PAK

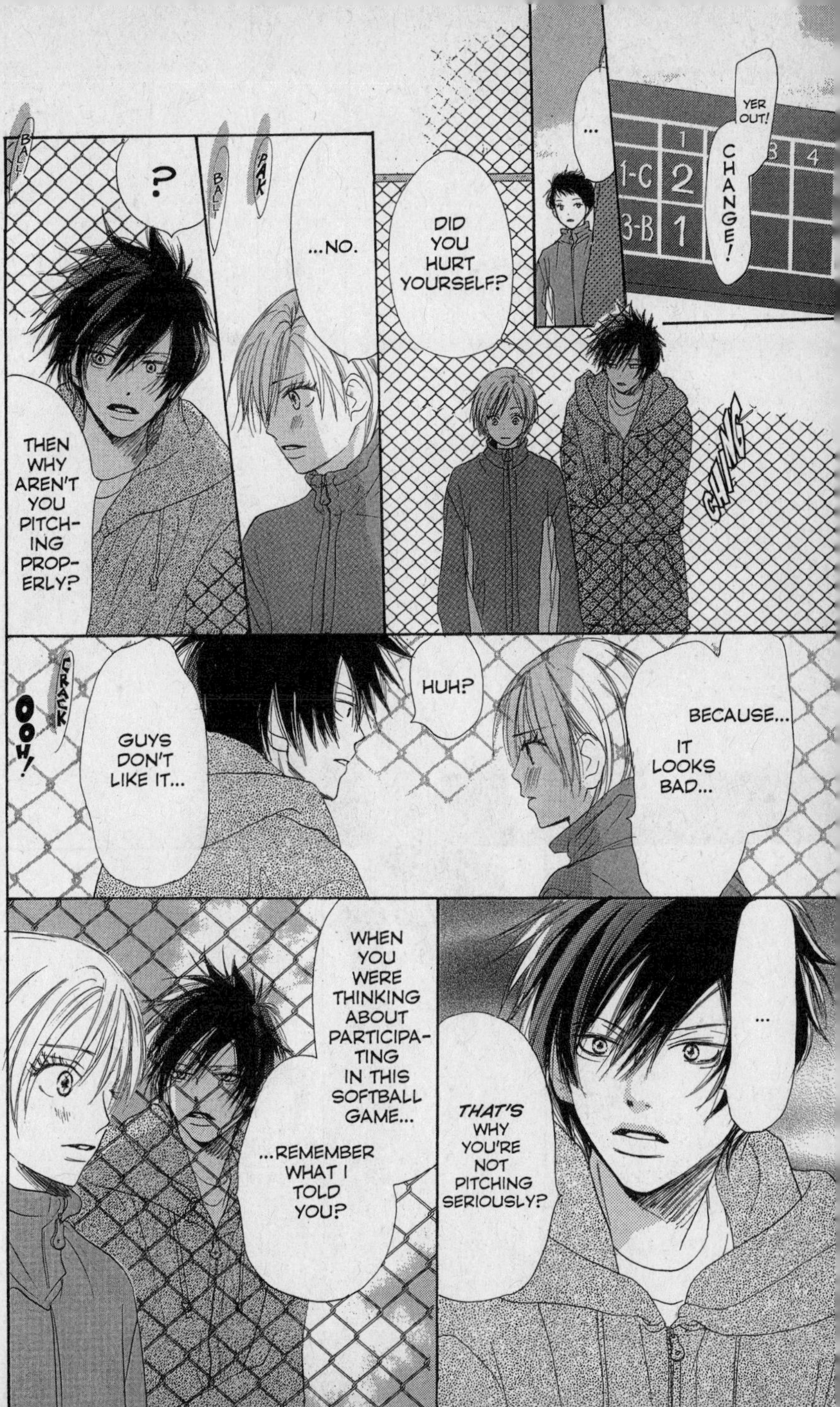

YER OUT!
CHANGE!
1
3
4
1-C 2
3-B 1
...
DID YOU HURT YOURSELF?
CHING
...NO.
PAK
BALL
?
BALL
THEN WHY AREN'T YOU PITCH-ING PROP-ERLY?
BECAUSE...
IT LOOKS BAD...
HUH?
GUYS DON'T LIKE IT...
CRACK
OOOH!
...
THAT'S WHY YOU'RE NOT PITCHING SERIOUSLY?
WHEN YOU WERE THINKING ABOUT PARTICIPA-TING IN THIS SOFTBALL GAME...
...REMEMBER WHAT I TOLD YOU?

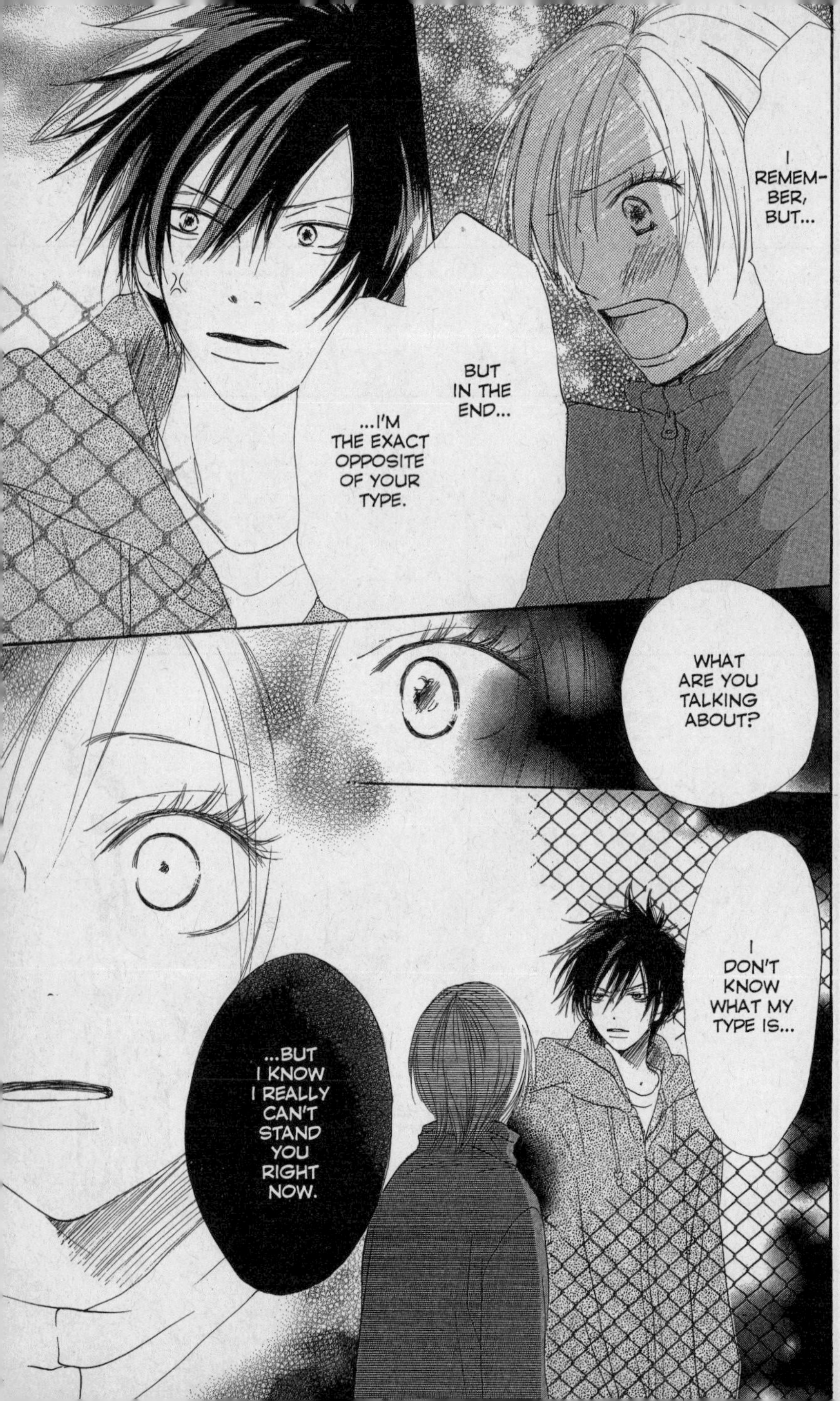
I REMEMBER, BUT...
BUT IN THE END...
...I'M THE EXACT OPPOSITE OF YOUR TYPE.
WHAT ARE YOU TALKING ABOUT?
I DON'T KNOW WHAT MY TYPE IS...
...BUT I KNOW I REALLY CAN'T STAND YOU RIGHT NOW.

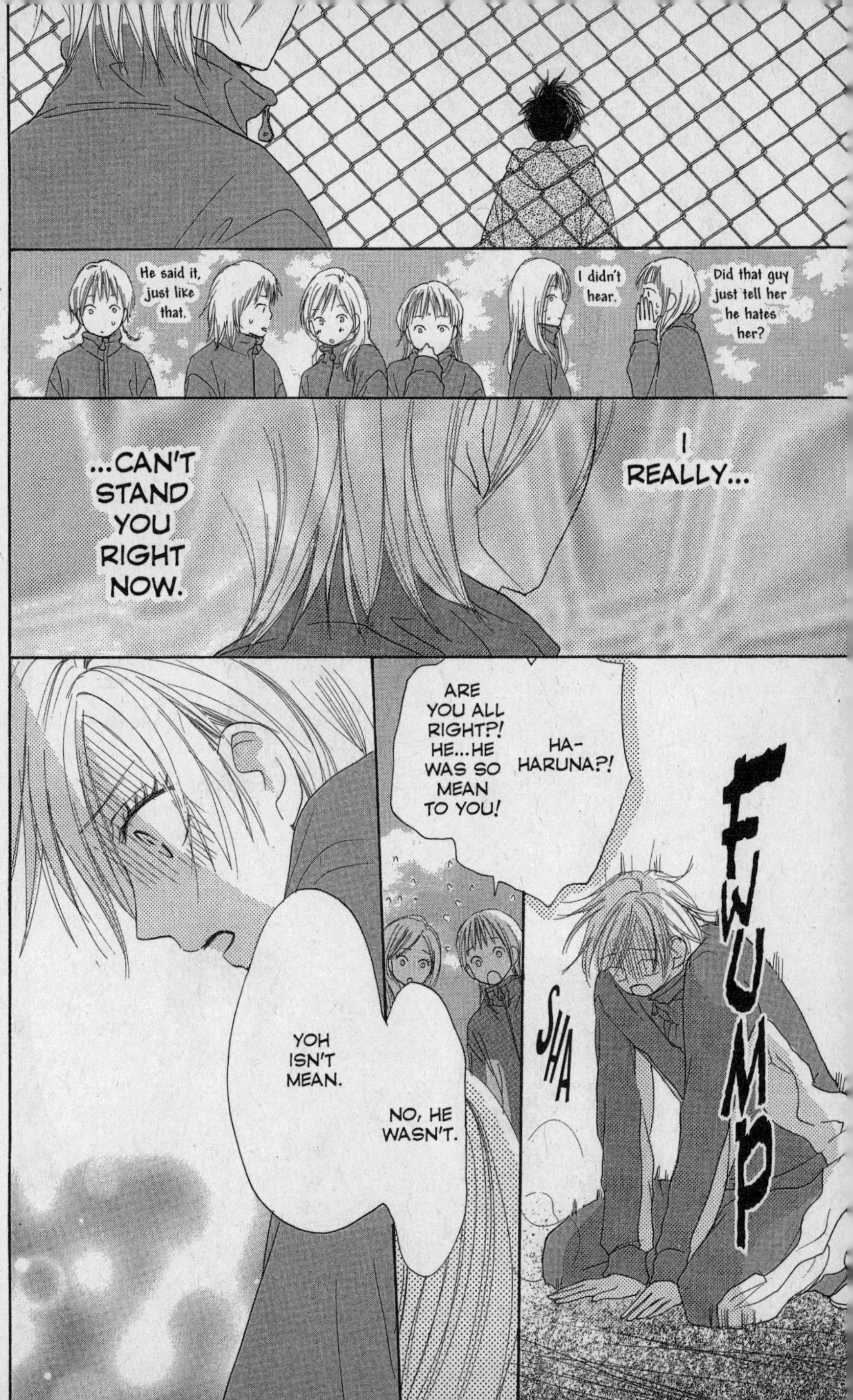
Did that guy just tell her he hates her?
I didn't hear.
He said it, just like that.
I REALLY...
...CAN'T STAND YOU RIGHT NOW.
FWUMP
SHA
HA-HARUNA?!
ARE YOU ALL RIGHT?! HE...HE WAS SO MEAN TO YOU!
YOH ISN'T MEAN.
NO, HE WASN'T.

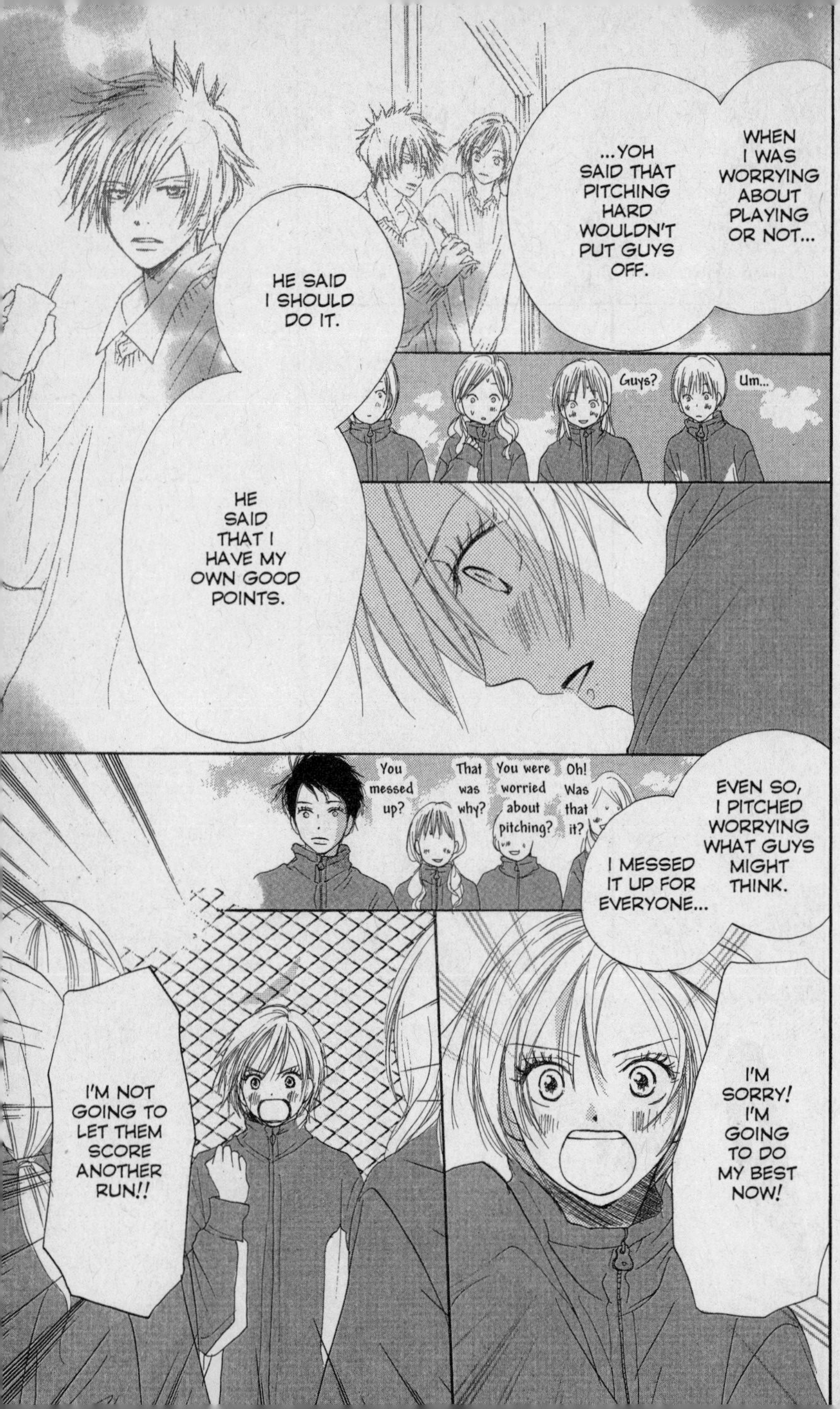
WHEN I WAS WORRYING ABOUT PLAYING OR NOT...
...YOH SAID THAT PITCHING HARD WOULDN'T PUT GUYS OFF.
HE SAID I SHOULD DO IT.
Um...
Guys?
HE SAID THAT I HAVE MY OWN GOOD POINTS.
EVEN SO, I PITCHED WORRYING WHAT GUYS MIGHT THINK.
I MESSED IT UP FOR EVERYONE...
Oh! Was that it?
You were worried about pitching?
That was why?
You messed up?
I'M SORRY! I'M GOING TO DO MY BEST NOW!
I'M NOT GOING TO LET THEM SCORE ANOTHER RUN!!

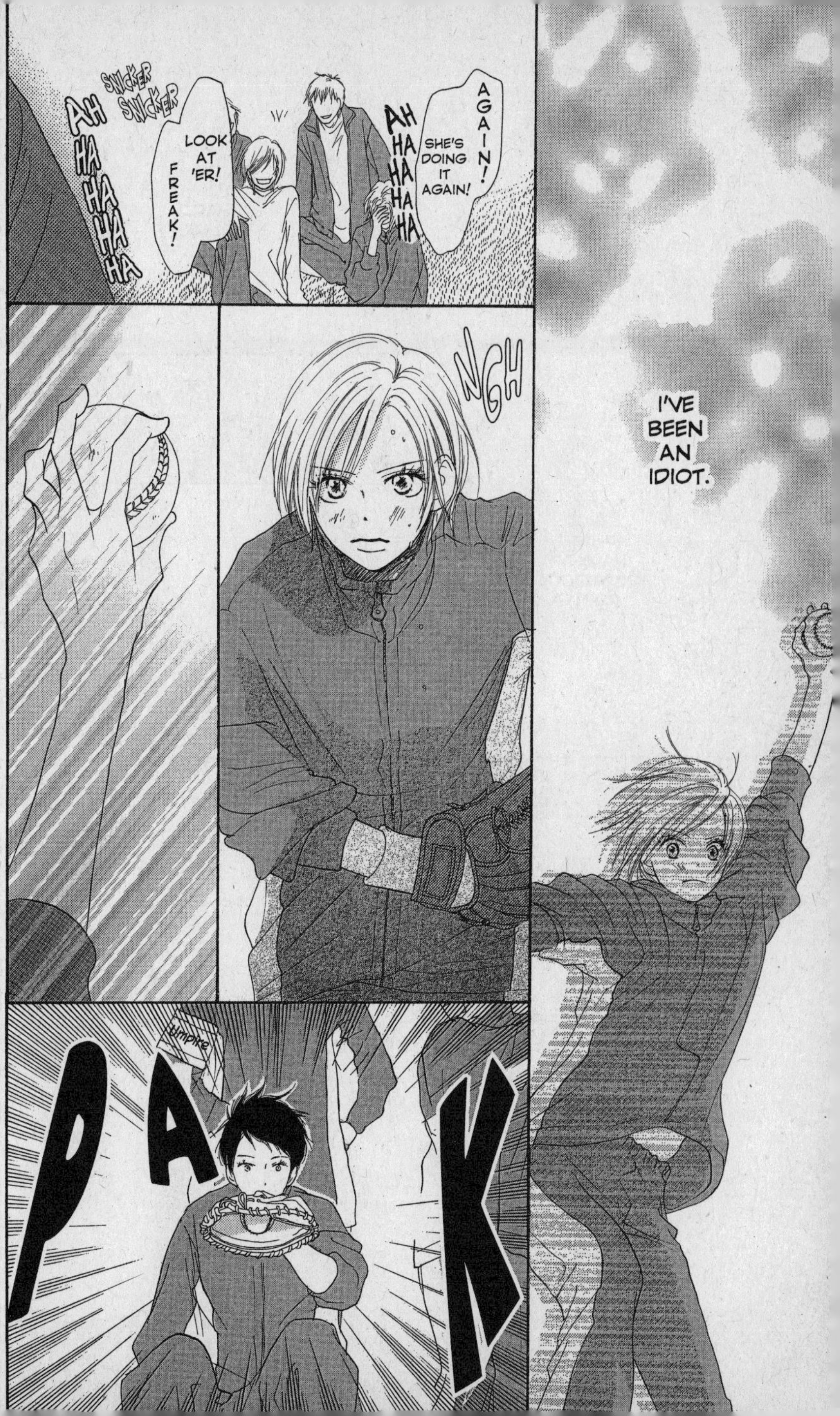
I'VE BEEN AN IDIOT.
AGAIN!
SHE'S DOING IT AGAIN!
AH HA HA HA HA HA
SNICKER SNICKER
LOOK AT 'ER!
FREAK!
AH HA HA HA HA HA
NGH
PAK
umpire

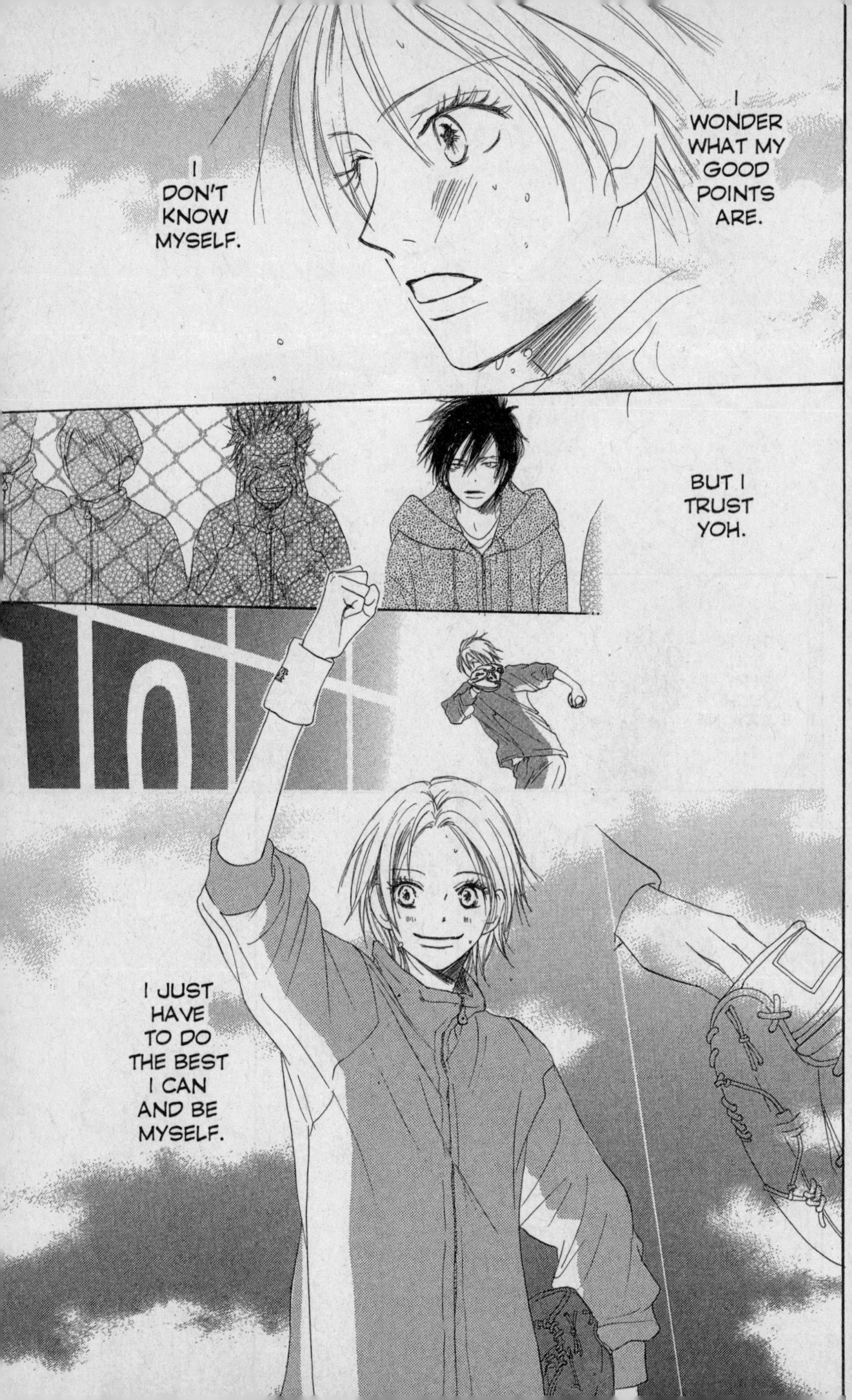
I WONDER WHAT MY GOOD POINTS ARE.
I DON'T KNOW MYSELF.
BUT I TRUST YOH.
I JUST HAVE TO DO THE BEST I CAN AND BE MYSELF.

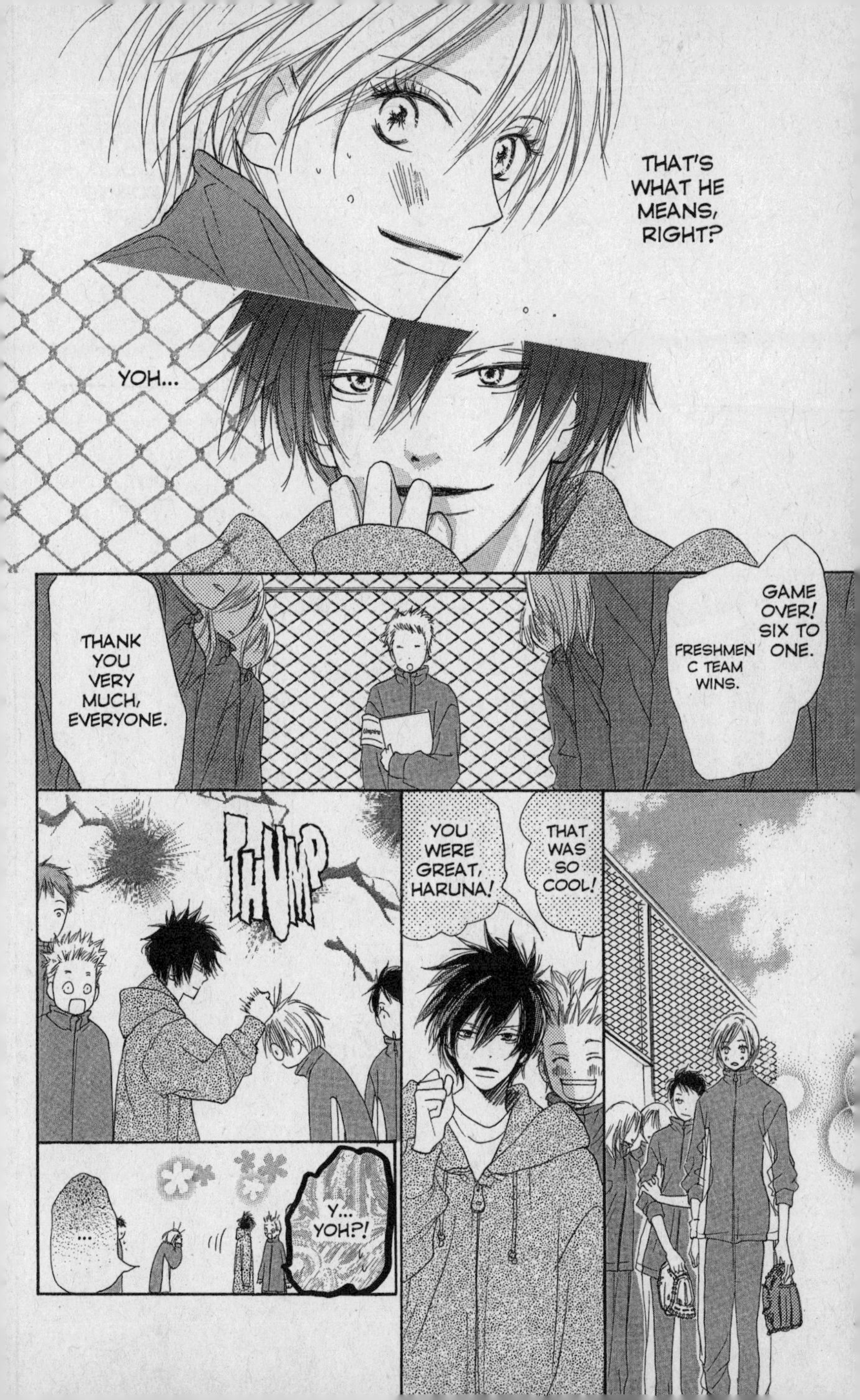
THAT'S WHAT HE MEANS, RIGHT?
YOH...
GAME OVER! SIX TO ONE.
FRESHMEN C TEAM WINS.
THANK YOU VERY MUCH, EVERYONE.
THAT WAS SO COOL!
YOU WERE GREAT, HARUNA!
THUMP
Y... YOH?!
...

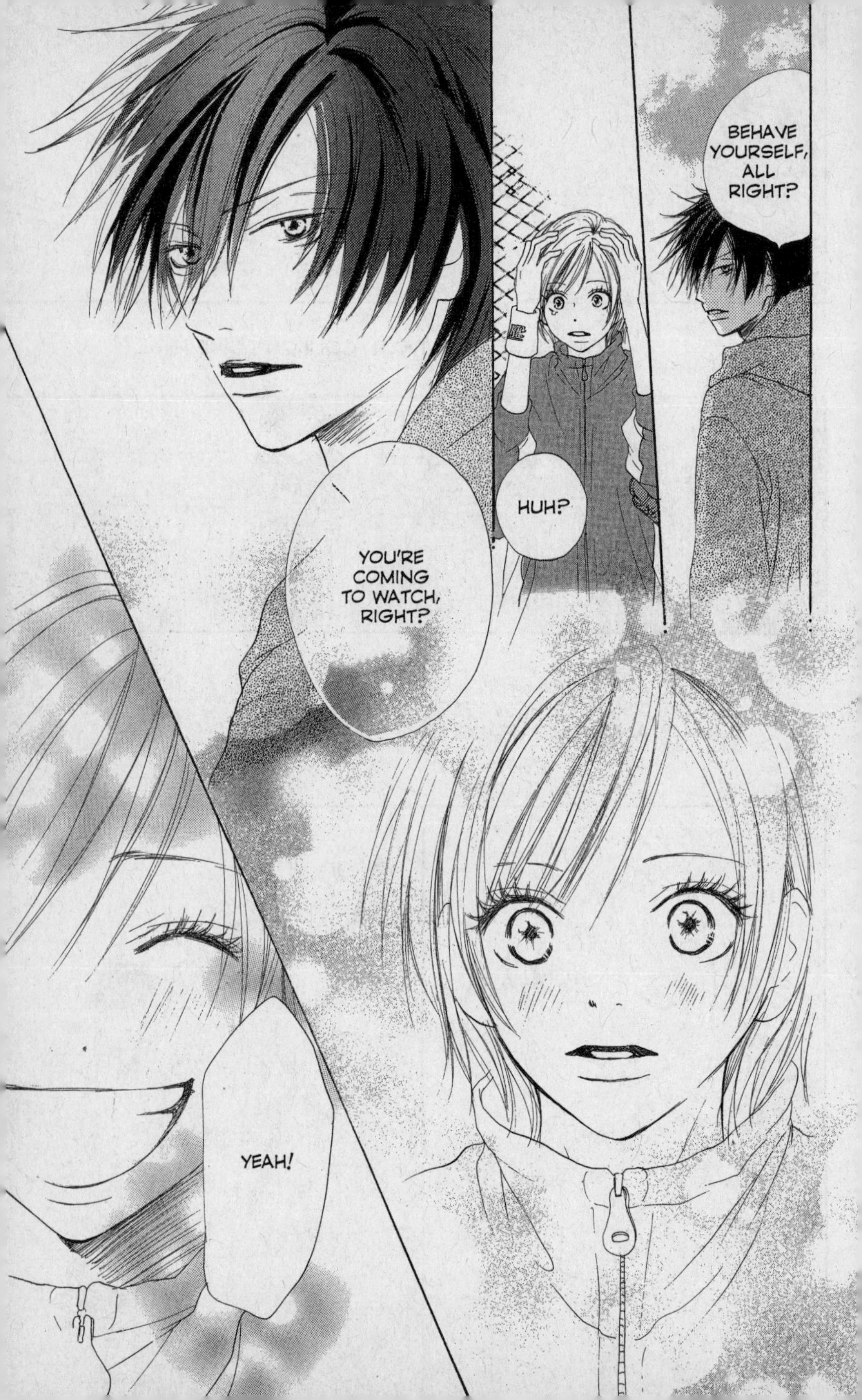
BEHAVE YOURSELF, ALL RIGHT?
HUH?
YOU'RE COMING TO WATCH, RIGHT?
YEAH!

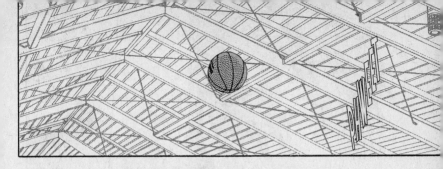

BECAUSE HE SAID THAT I COULDN'T LIKE HIM...

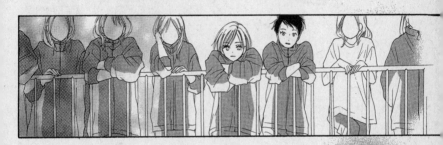

...I'VE BEEN DENYING HOW I FEEL. AND I GOT JEALOUS.

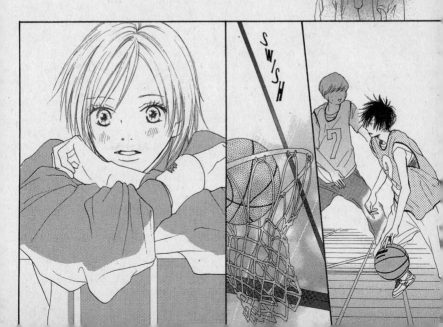

SWISH

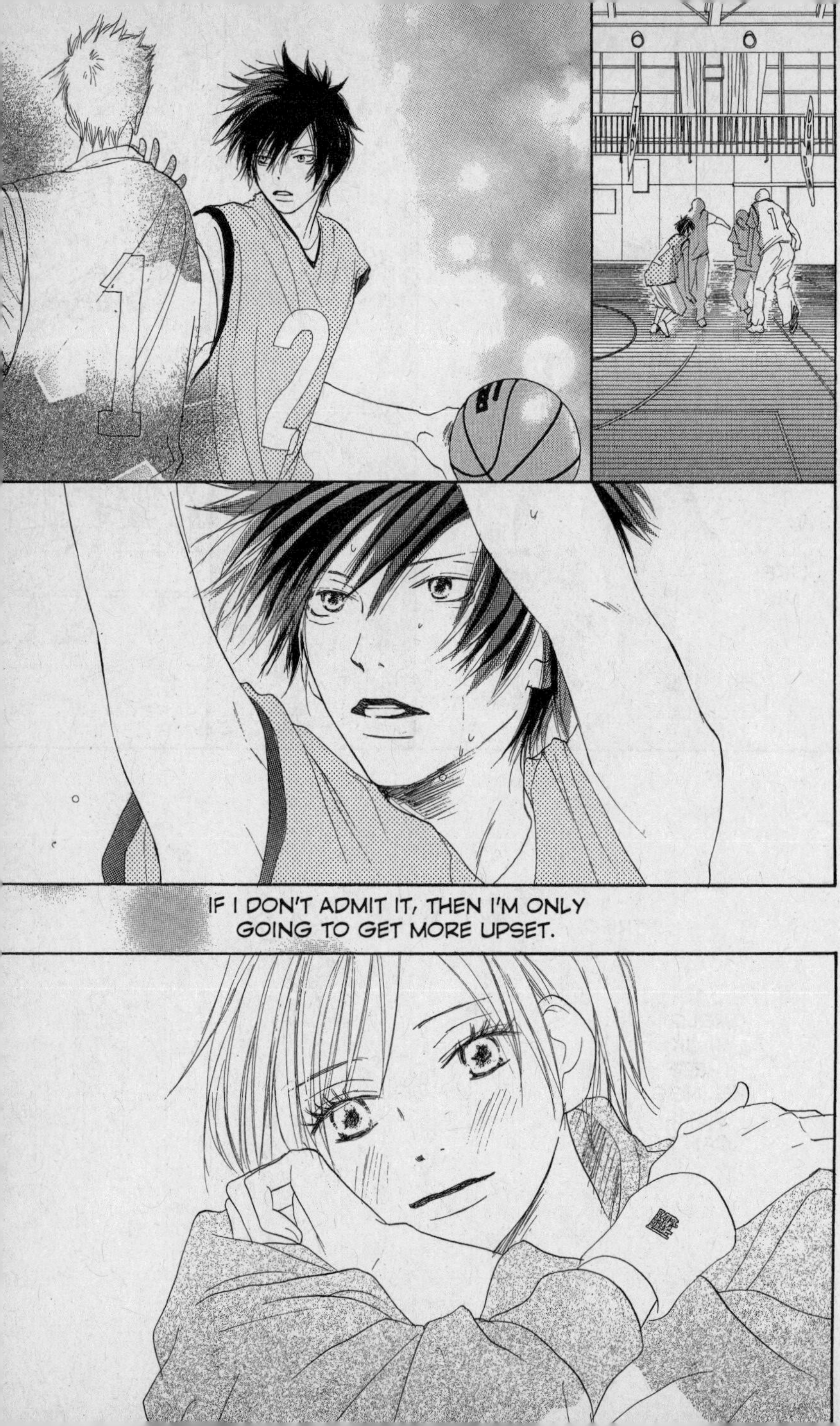
DUMDUM
THMP
IF I DON'T ADMIT IT, THEN I'M ONLY GOING TO GET MORE UPSET.

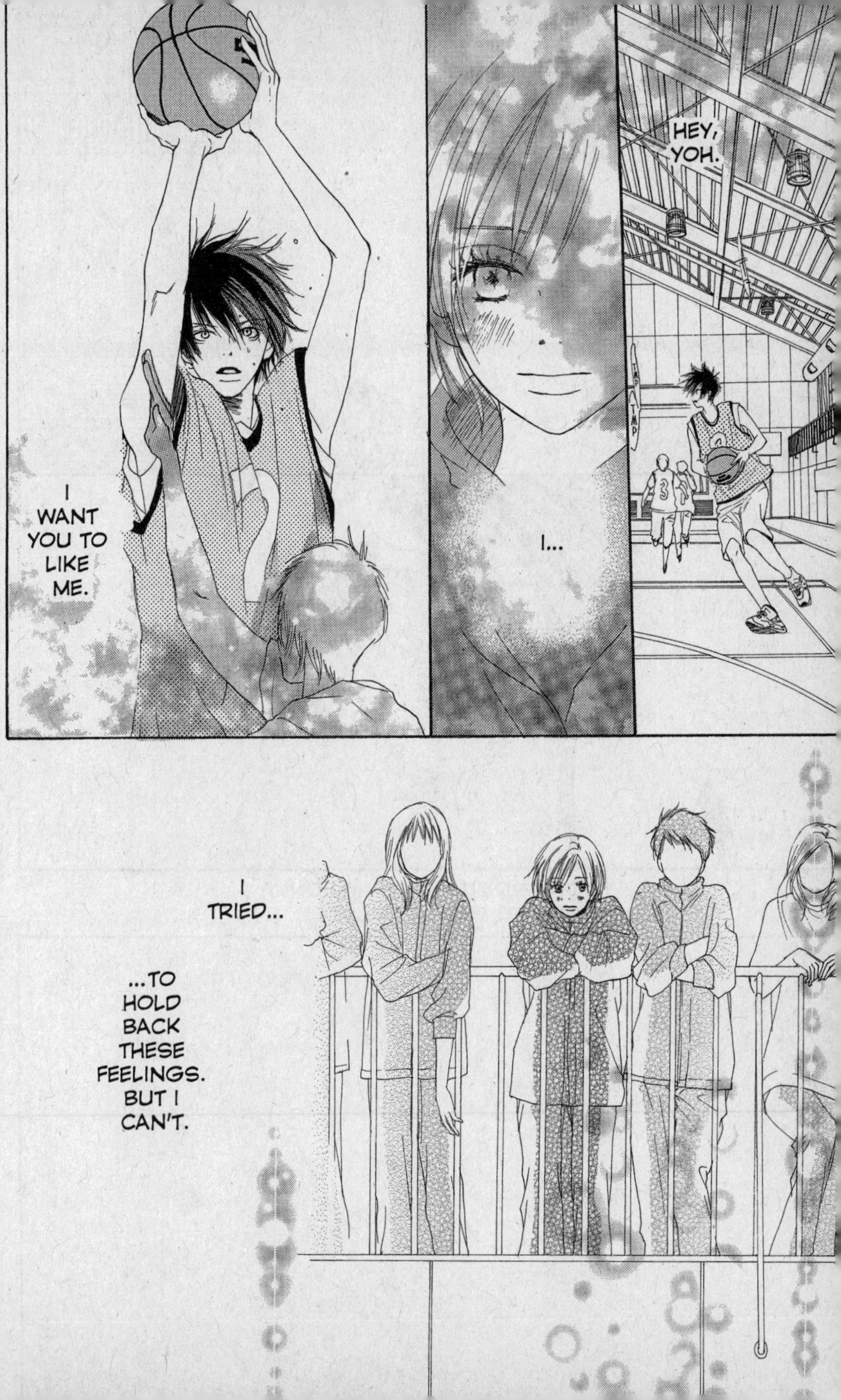
HEY, YOH.
I...
I WANT YOU TO LIKE ME.
I TRIED...
...TO HOLD BACK THESE FEELINGS. BUT I CAN'T.

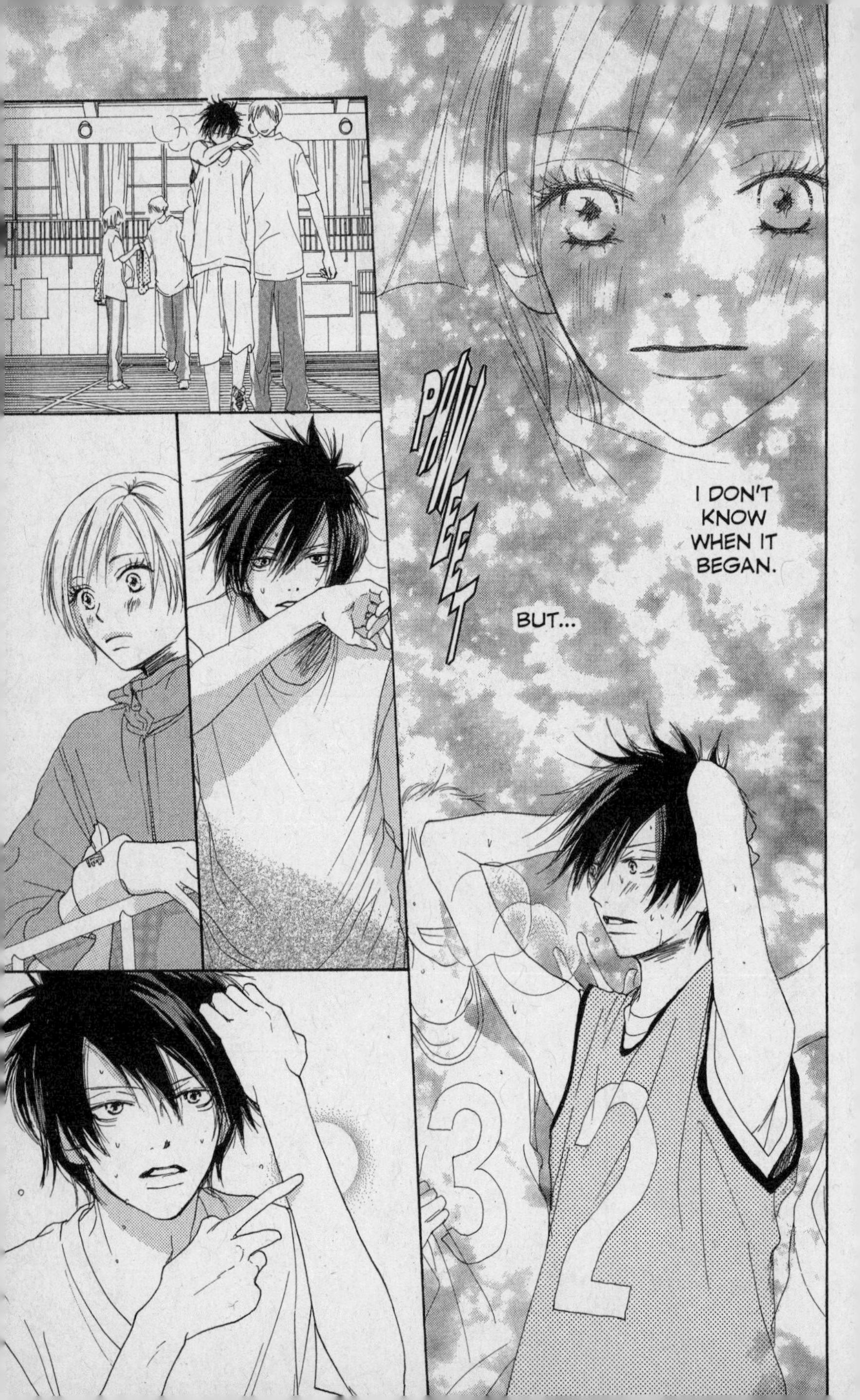
I DON'T KNOW WHEN IT BEGAN.
BUT...
PHWEET

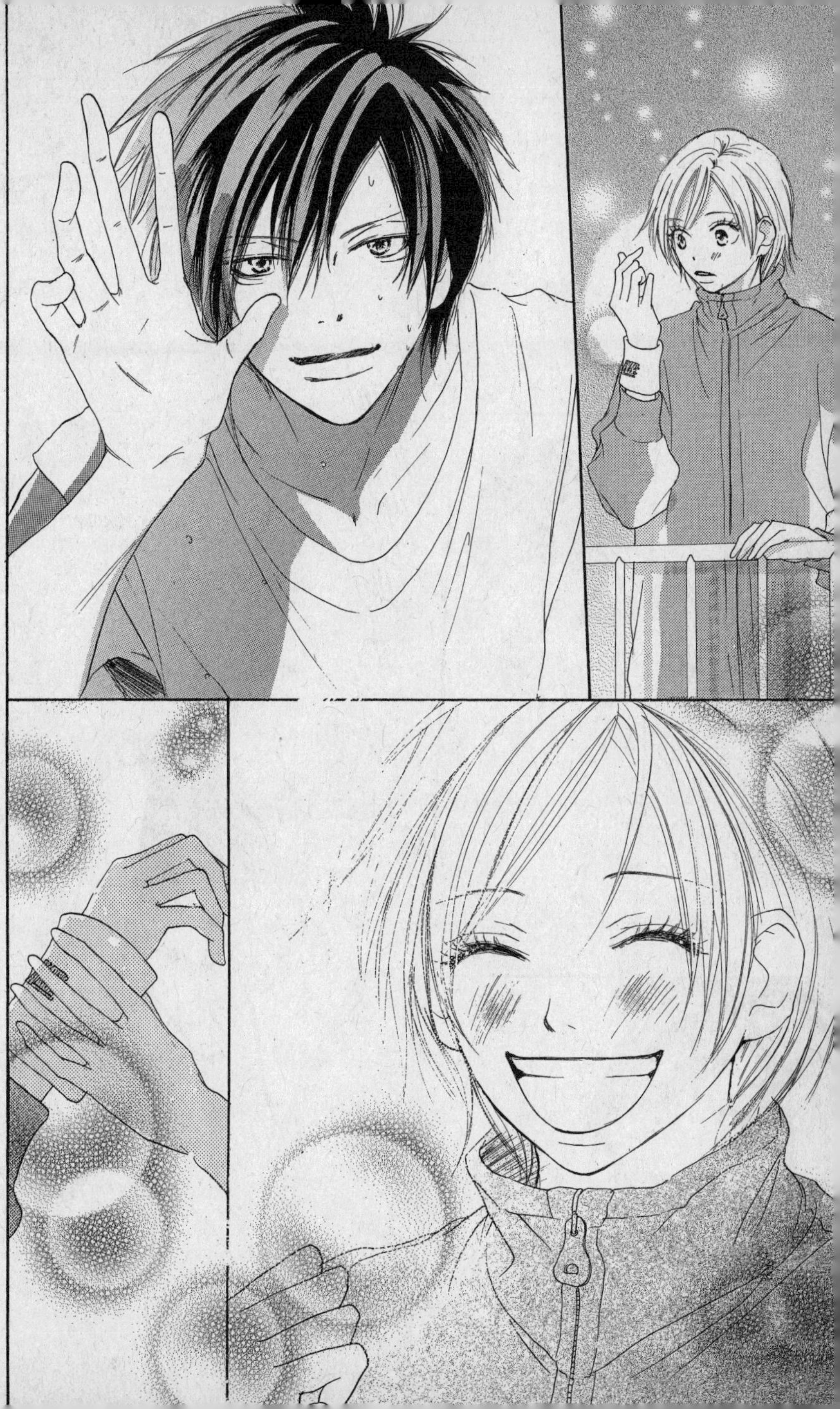

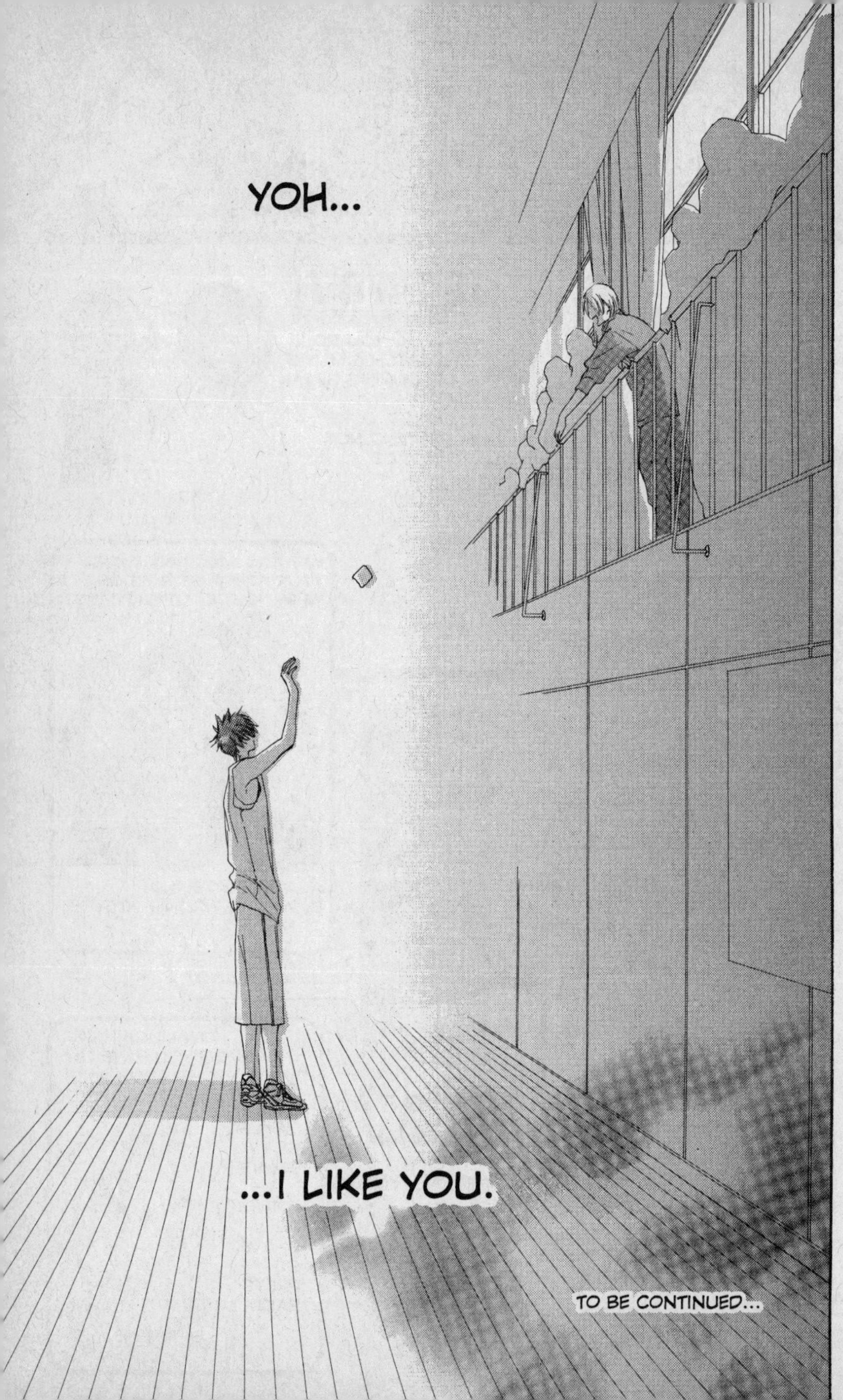
YOH...
...I LIKE YOU.
TO BE CONTINUED...

LESSON ON HOW TO BE HOT

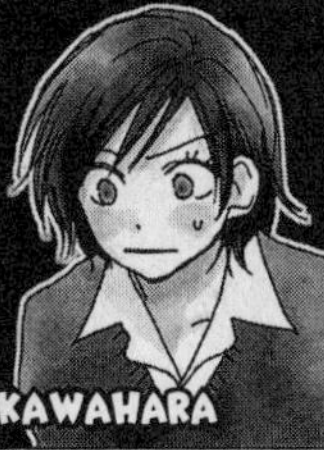

ILLUSTRATED BY: KAZUNE KAWAHARA

START

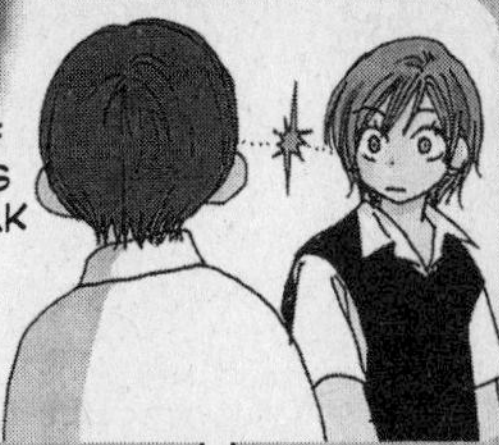

WHAT DO YOU DO IF YOU CATCH A GUY'S GAZE DURING BREAK TIME?
A: MAKE A JOKE
B: PRETEND NOT TO NOTICE

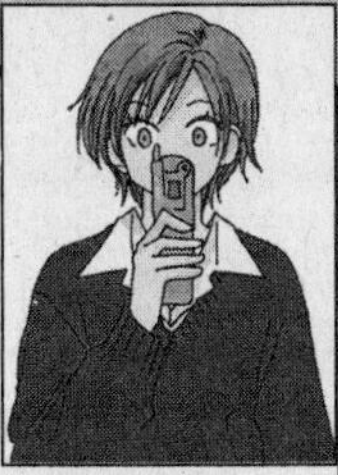

YOU GET A TEXT MESSAGE FROM YOUR FRIEND; HOW DO YOU REPLY?

A: TYPE EVERY LETTER IN PROPERLY
B: TYPE IT QUICKLY USING TXT SPK

A

B

WHAT DO YOU THINK IF ONLY YOUR FRIEND GETS HIT ON WHEN YOU'RE OUT SHOPPING?

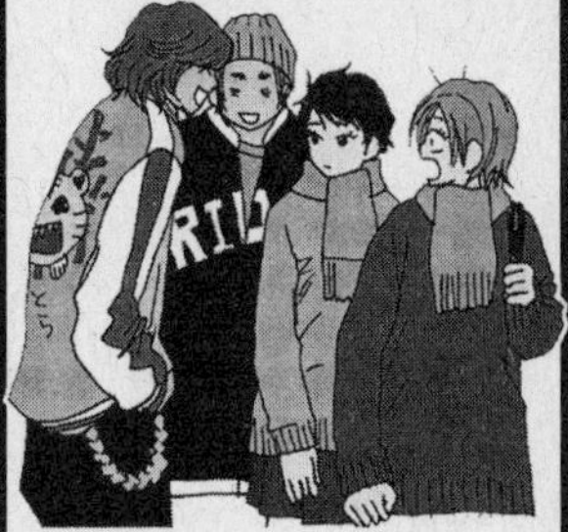
RI

A: ARE THEY BLIND?!
B: WHAT'S WRONG WITH ME...

DO YOU ACT DIFFERENTLY IN FRONT OF YOUR GUY FRIENDS AND GIRL FRIENDS?

A: I DON'T ACT ANY DIFFERENTLY.
B: I'M A DIFFERENT PERSON!

YOU LIKE A GUY. WHAT DO YOU DO WHEN YOU FIND OUT THE TYPE OF GIRL HE LIKES?

A: USE IT AS REFERENCE
B: I TOTALLY CHANGE MYSELF TO BE THAT TYPE!

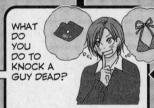

WHAT DO YOU DO TO KNOCK A GUY DEAD?

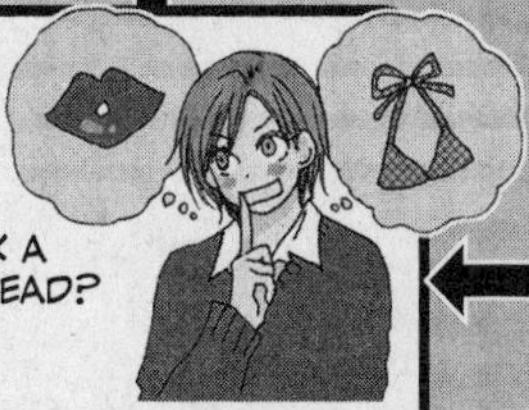

A: BEAUTIFUL LIPS
B: SHOW SOME CLEAVAGE

HOW MUCH HAIR DO YOU HAVE ON YOUR ARMS AND LEGS?

A: I SHAVE EVERY DAY, SO SILKY SMOOTH.
B: I FORGET TO SHAVE, SO PRETTY HAIRY.

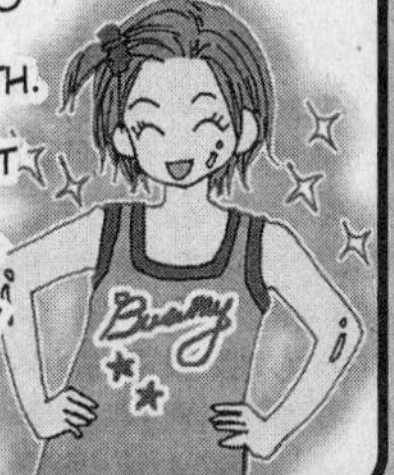

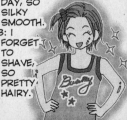

YOUR DATE CANCELS ON YOU; WHAT DO YOU DO?

A: MESSAGE A FRIEND
B: READ MANGA

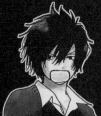

DEMON COACH YOH'S TEST AND

YOH'S DIAGNOSIS AND ADVICE

EXPERT

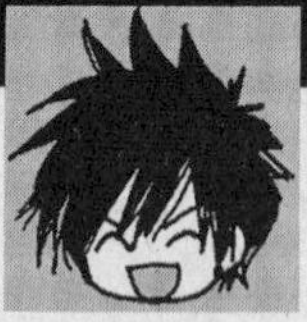

YOU'RE FUN AND POPULAR, SO LOTS OF GUYS FALL FOR YOU. YOU'RE ALSO GOOD AT GIVING ALL THE RIGHT SIGNS TO THE GUY YOU LIKE. YOU'RE PERFECT AS YOU ARE, SO DON'T CHANGE!

MASTER

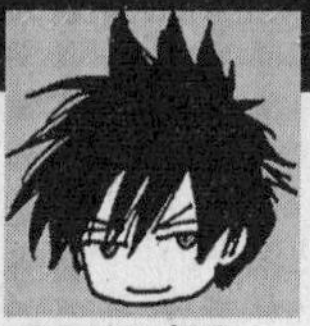

YOU'RE A GIRL THAT'S GOOD AT GETTING PEOPLE TO LIKE YOU. YOU KNOW WHEN TO LAUGH AND YOU EASILY MAKE FRIENDS, SO YOU'RE POPULAR WITH THE GUYS. JUST MAKE SURE YOU DON'T END UP "JUST A FRIEND." GO FOR IT!

AVERAGE

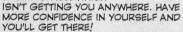

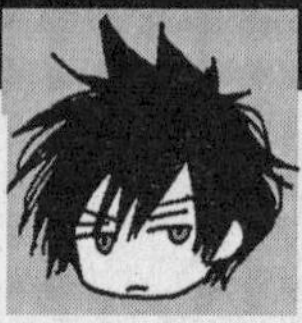

YOU HAVE YOUR OWN SPECIAL CHARMS, AND GUYS WHO NOTICE LIKE YOU. BUT YOU HOLD BACK A LITTLE, WHICH ISN'T GETTING YOU ANYWHERE. HAVE MORE CONFIDENCE IN YOURSELF AND YOU'LL GET THERE!

AMATEUR

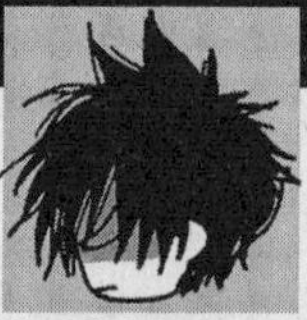

HEY, HEY! YOU'RE AS BAD AS HARUNA! YOU'RE TOTALLY CLUELESS. YOU DON'T KNOW YOUR OWN GOOD POINTS OR WHAT A GUY WANTS. IT'S GOOD TO BE INNOCENT, BUT YOU NEED TO STUDY ALONG WITH HARUNA!

HOW DO YOU WRAP UP A PRESENT FOR A GUY?

A: SIMPLE AND PLAIN
B: PRETTY WITH BOWS

THE CLASS CLOWN MAKES FUN OF YOU!

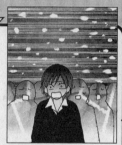

A: LAUGH ALONG ANYWAY
B: SULK...

HOW MANY FUN THINGS DO YOU KNOW THAT YOU COULD SHARE WITH SOMEONE ELSE?

A: MORE THAN ONE
B: NOTHING...

YOU GET WITH THE GUY YOU LIKE. WHAT DO YOU DO FIRST?

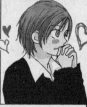

A: ASK FRIENDS FOR ADVICE.
B: WORRY ABOUT IT ON YOUR OWN.

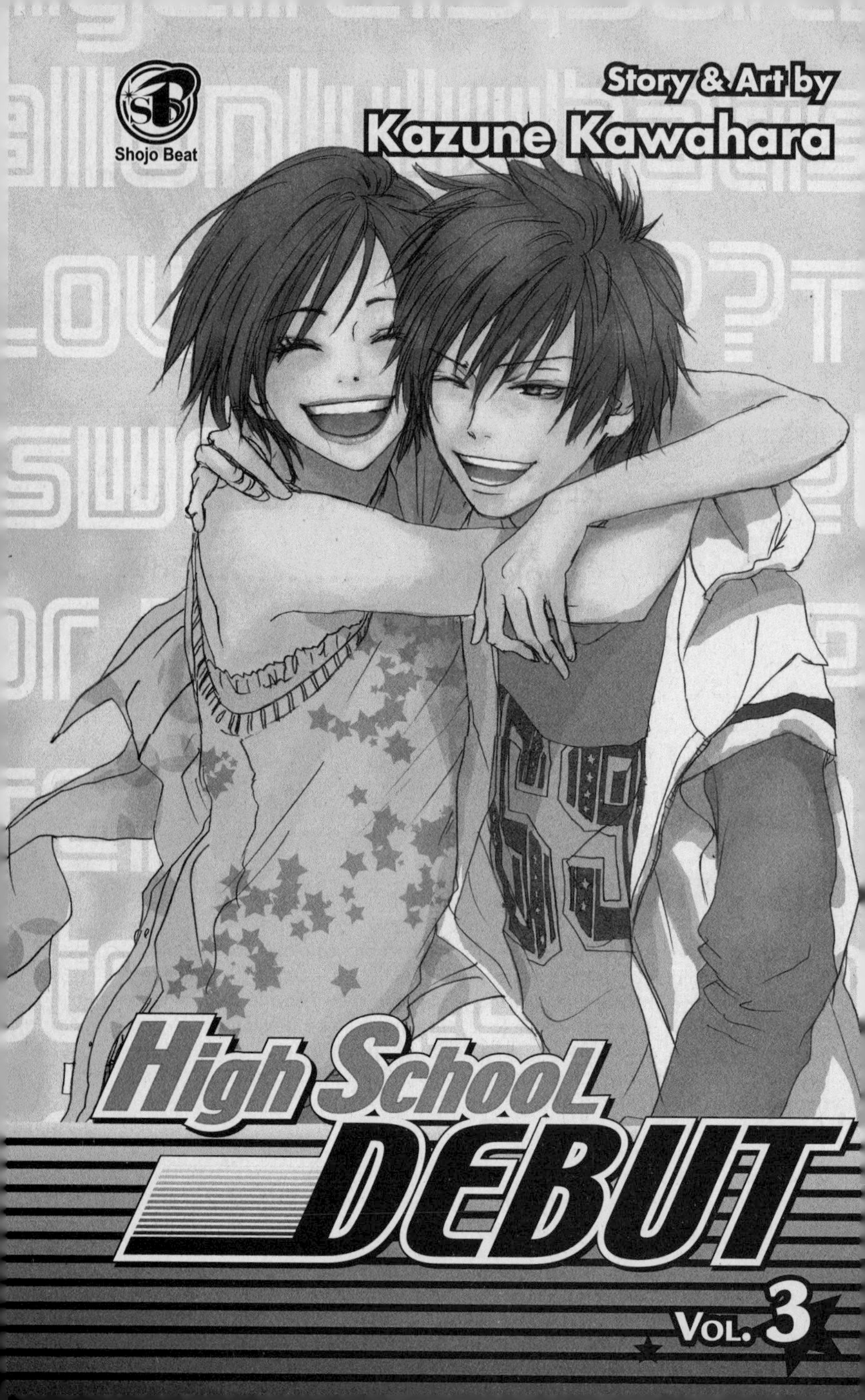
Shojo Beat
Story & Art by
Kazune Kawahara
High School
DEBUT
VOL. 3

High School DEBUT

★★ Contents

Story Thus Far...

High school freshman Haruna was a sporty girl and an ace player for her softball team back in junior high. Now that she's in high school, she wants to give her all to finding true love instead! She gets Yoh, a guy who knows how to be popular, to be her "love coach" and falls in love for the first time with his friend Fumi. When her heart is broken, she's able to pick herself back up with Yoh's support and an optimistic attitude. However, she doesn't find herself drawn to other guys as she starts to notice Yoh more and more.

At a school sports competition, Haruna is chosen to be the pitcher for the softball team. However, worried that Yoh's ex-girlfriend is the complete opposite of her, she refrains from using her true althletic abilities. Yoh, who came to cheer her on, becomes upset at her reasoning and tells her, "I really can't stand you right now." Awakened by these harsh words, Haruna decides to give her all to the game and helps her team win the championship. At the same time, she now fully realizes that she likes Yoh...

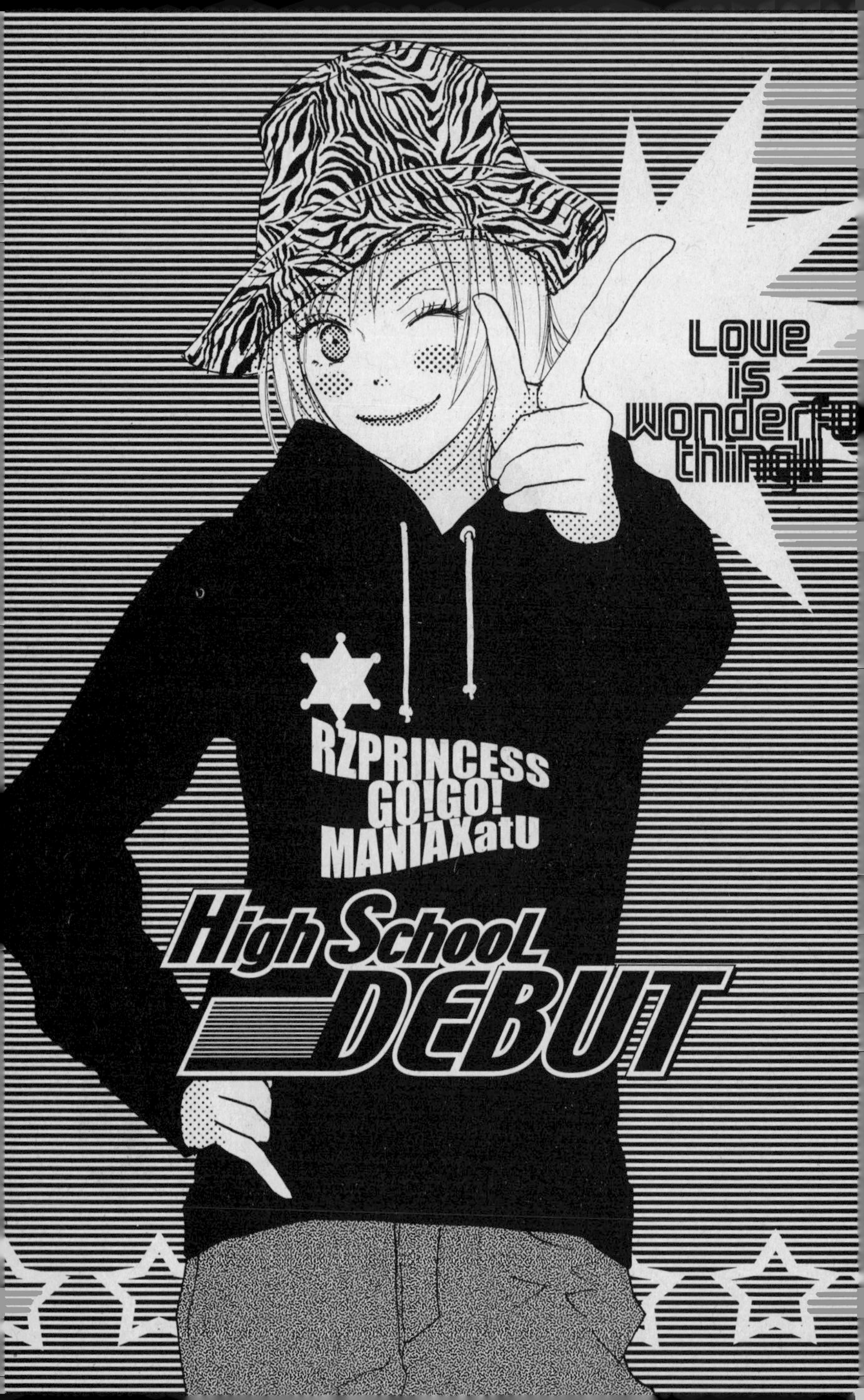
Love is wonderfu thing!!
RZPRINCESS GO!GO! MANIAXatu
High School DEBUT

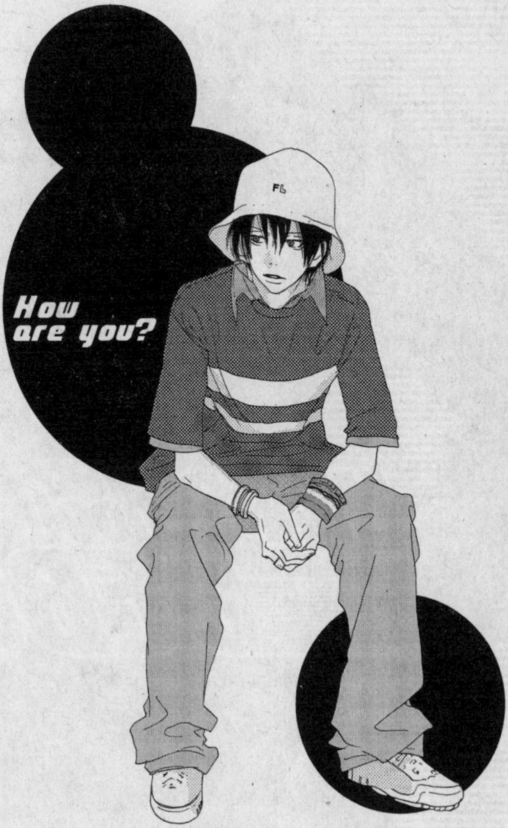
How
are you?
FL

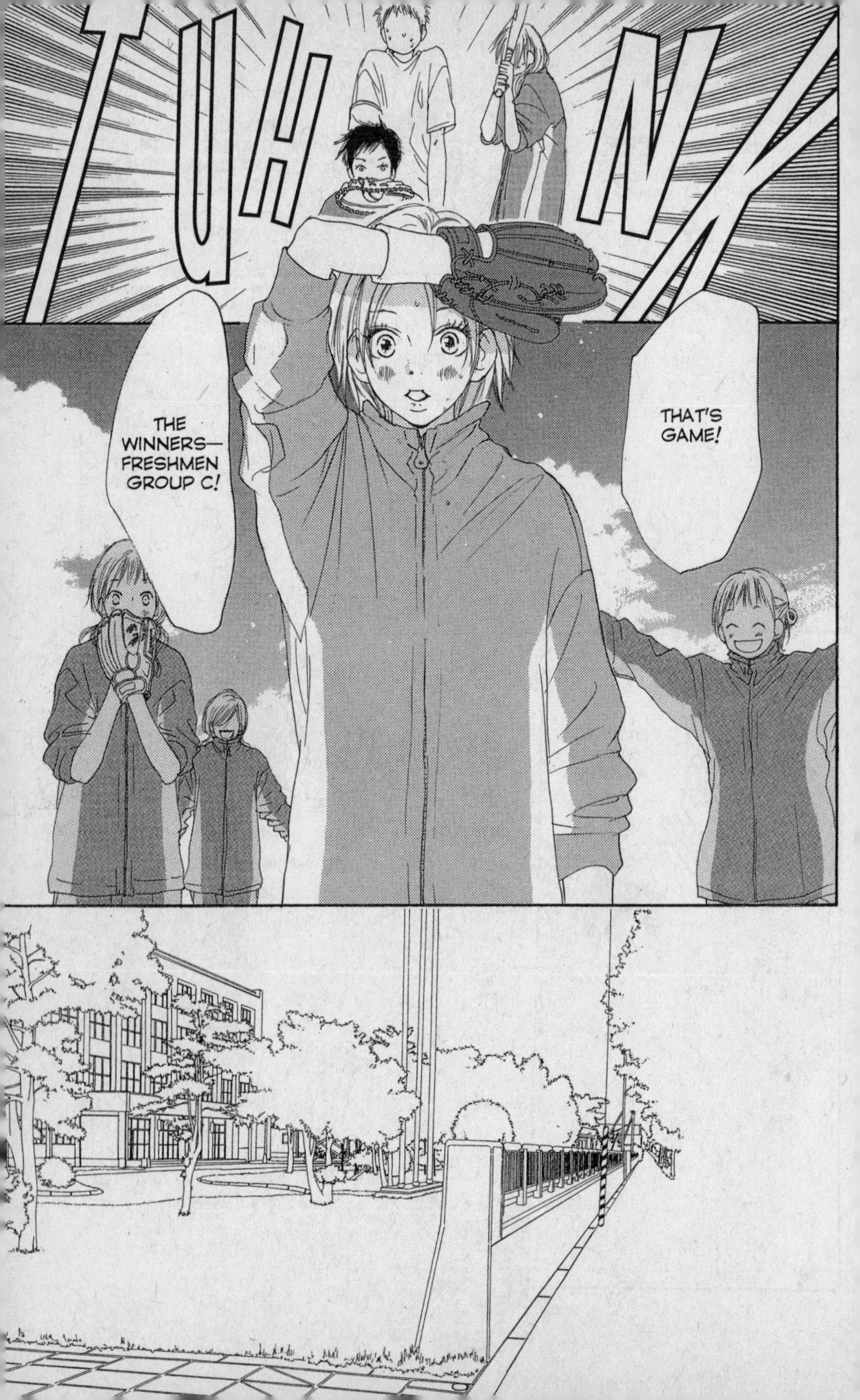
TUHNK
THAT'S GAME!
THE WINNERS—FRESHMEN GROUP C!

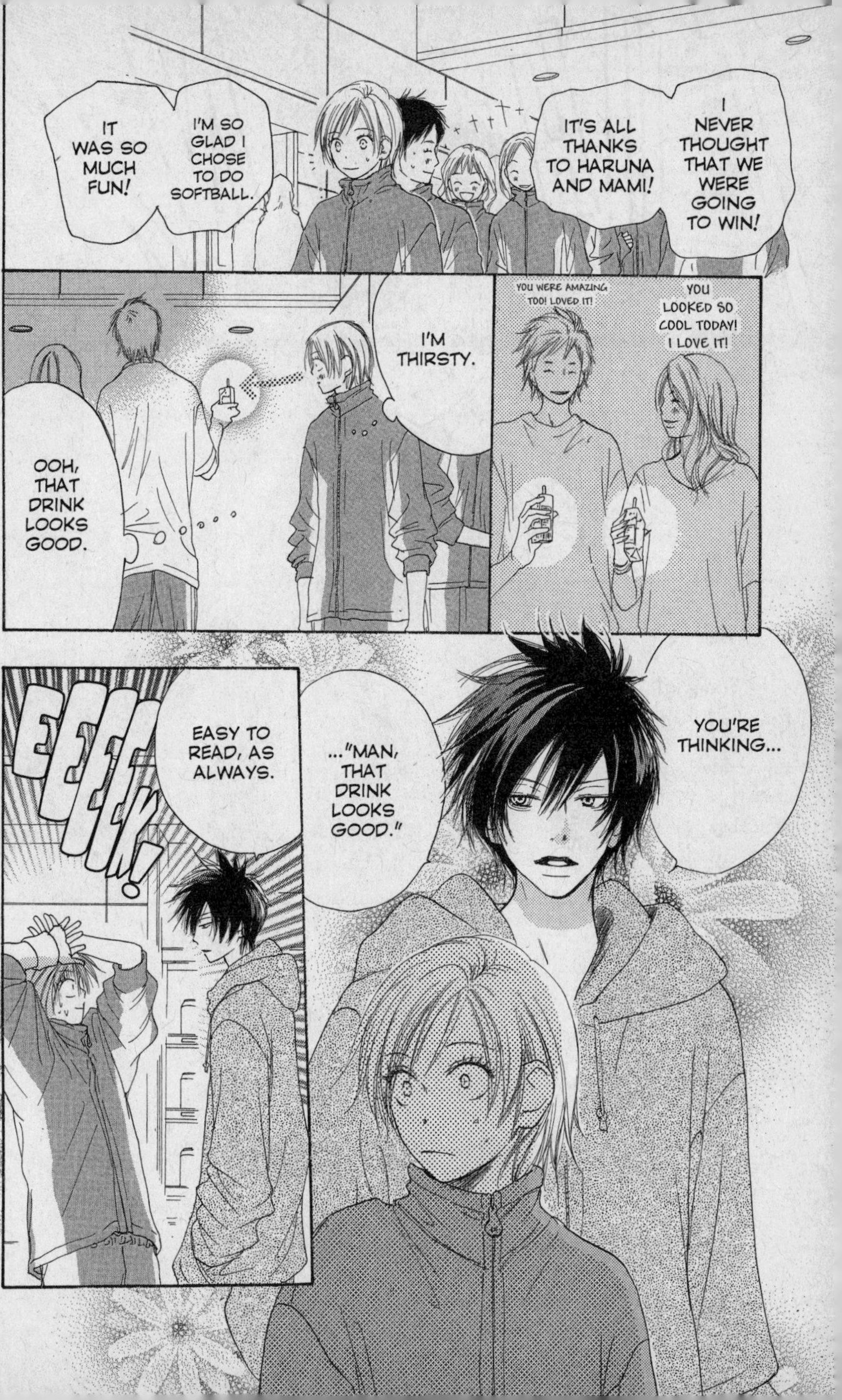
I NEVER THOUGHT THAT WE WERE GOING TO WIN!
IT'S ALL THANKS TO HARUNA AND MAMI!
I'M SO GLAD I CHOSE TO DO SOFTBALL.
IT WAS SO MUCH FUN!
YOU LOOKED SO COOL TODAY! I LOVE IT!
YOU WERE AMAZING TOO! LOVED IT!
I'M THIRSTY.
OOH, THAT DRINK LOOKS GOOD.
YOU'RE THINKING...
..."MAN, THAT DRINK LOOKS GOOD."
EASY TO READ, AS ALWAYS.
EEEEEK!

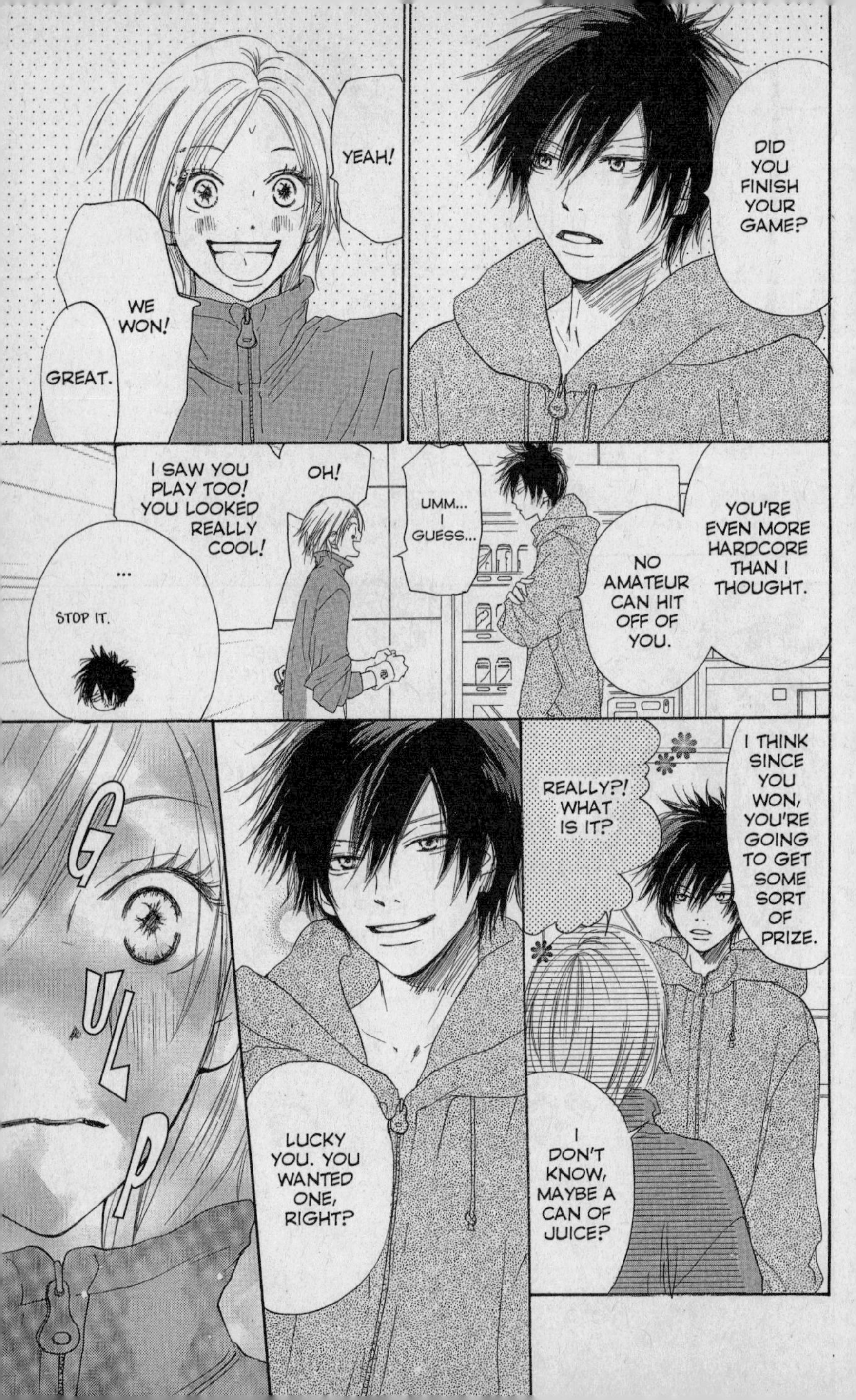
DID YOU FINISH YOUR GAME?
YEAH!
WE WON!
GREAT.
YOU'RE EVEN MORE HARDCORE THAN I THOUGHT.
NO AMATEUR CAN HIT OFF OF YOU.
UMM... I GUESS...
OH!
I SAW YOU PLAY TOO! YOU LOOKED REALLY COOL!
...
STOP IT.
I THINK SINCE YOU WON, YOU'RE GOING TO GET SOME SORT OF PRIZE.
REALLY?! WHAT IS IT?
I DON'T KNOW, MAYBE A CAN OF JUICE?
LUCKY YOU. YOU WANTED ONE, RIGHT?
GULP

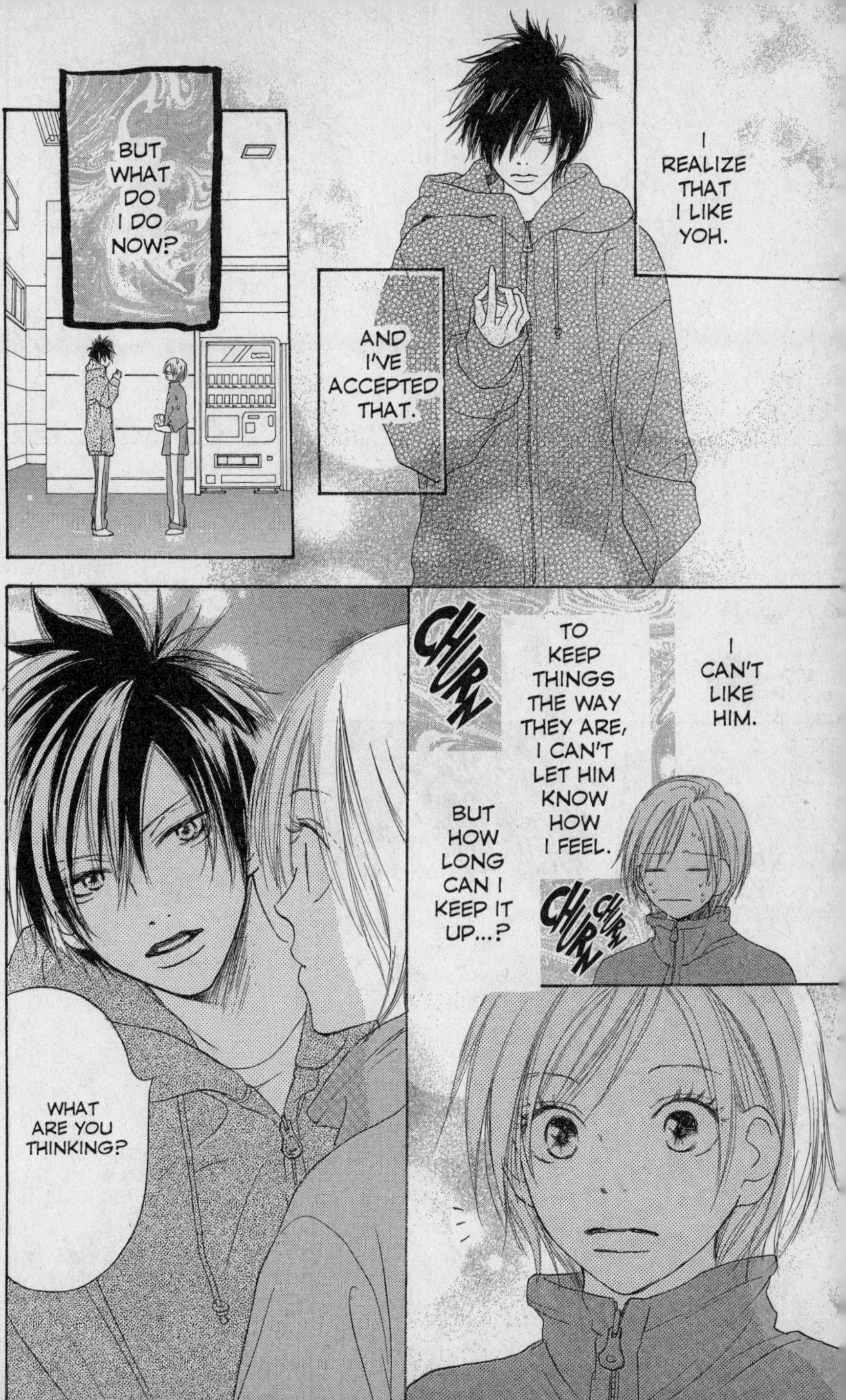
I REALIZE THAT I LIKE YOH.
AND I'VE ACCEPTED THAT.
BUT WHAT DO I DO NOW?
I CAN'T LIKE HIM.
TO KEEP THINGS THE WAY THEY ARE, I CAN'T LET HIM KNOW HOW I FEEL.
CHURN
BUT HOW LONG CAN I KEEP IT UP...?
CHURN CHURN
WHAT ARE YOU THINKING?

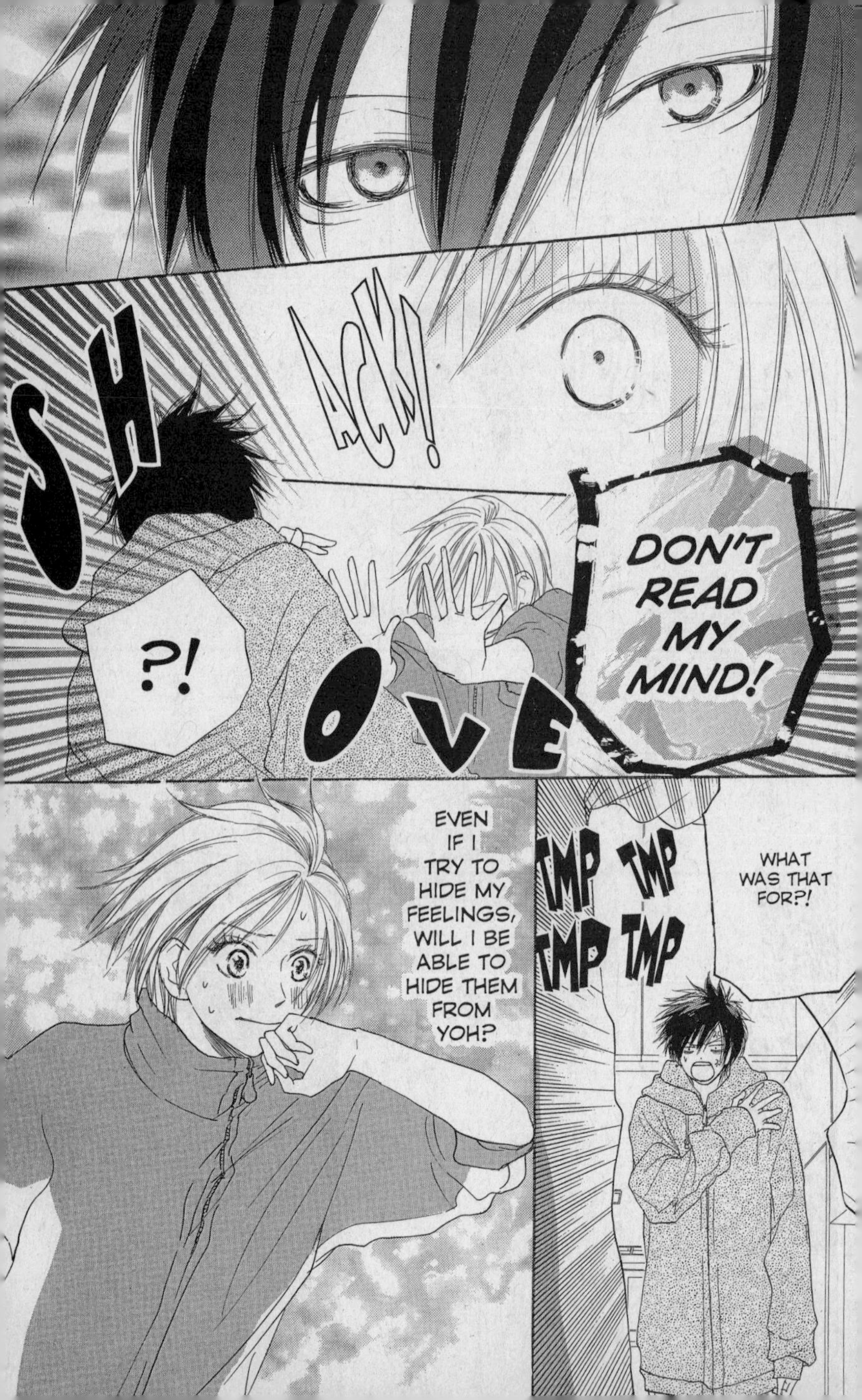
ACK!
DON'T READ MY MIND!
SHOVE
?!
WHAT WAS THAT FOR?!
TMP TMP TMP TMP
EVEN IF I TRY TO HIDE MY FEELINGS, WILL I BE ABLE TO HIDE THEM FROM YOH?

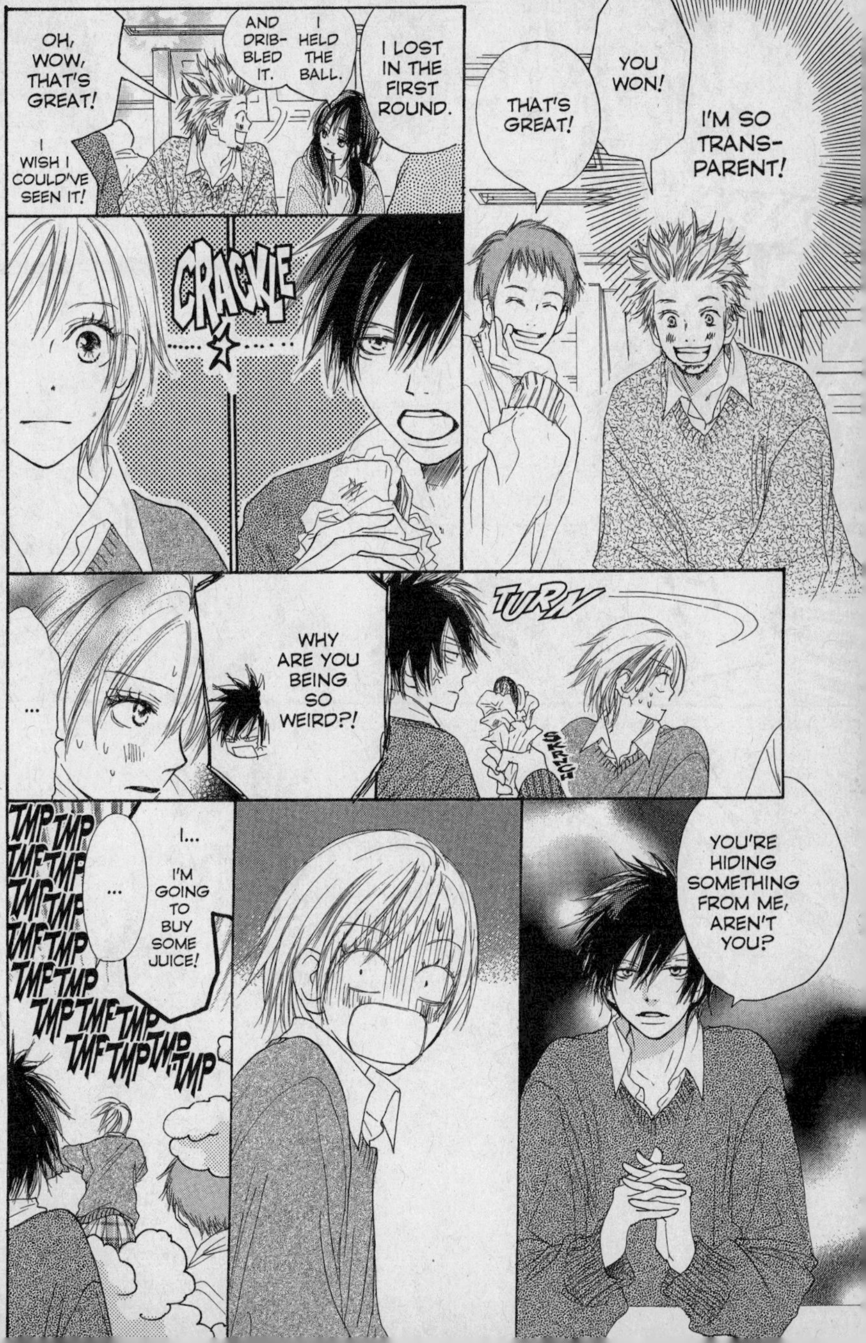
YOU WON!
THAT'S GREAT!
I'M SO TRANS-PARENT!
I LOST IN THE FIRST ROUND.
I HELD THE BALL.
AND DRIB-BLED IT.
OH, WOW, THAT'S GREAT!
I WISH I COULD'VE SEEN IT!
CRACKLE
TURN
SKRNCH
WHY ARE YOU BEING SO WEIRD?!
...
YOU'RE HIDING SOMETHING FROM ME, AREN'T YOU?
I...
I'M GOING TO BUY SOME JUICE!
...
TMP TMP TMP TMP TMP TMP TMP TMP TMP TMP TMP TMP TMP TMP TMP TMP TMP TMP TMP

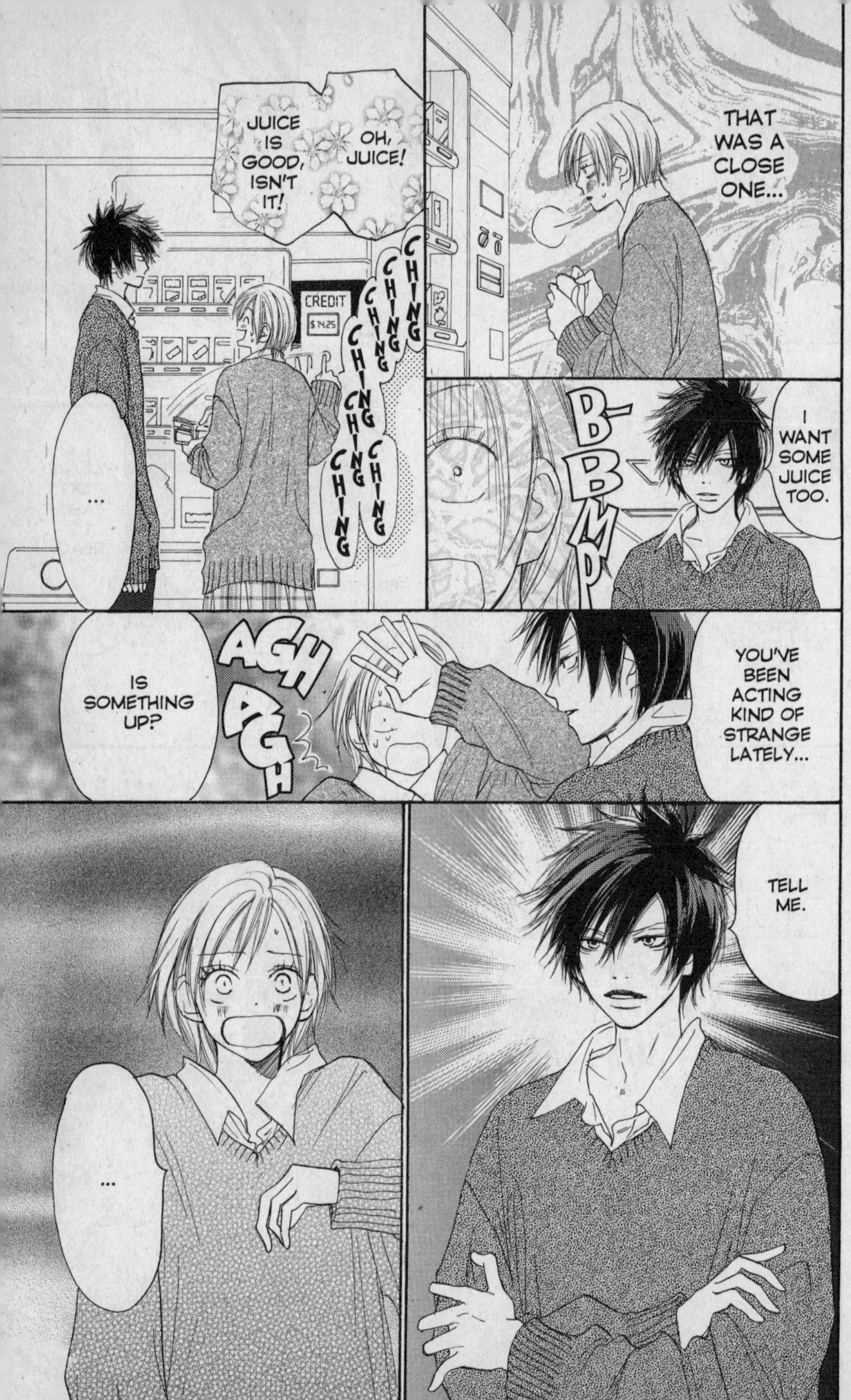
THAT WAS A CLOSE ONE...
B-BUMP
I WANT SOME JUICE TOO.
OH, JUICE!
JUICE IS GOOD, ISN'T IT!
CREDIT
$14.25
CHING CHING CHING CHING CHING CHING CHING CHING
...
YOU'VE BEEN ACTING KIND OF STRANGE LATELY...
AGH AGH
IS SOMETHING UP?
TELL ME.
...

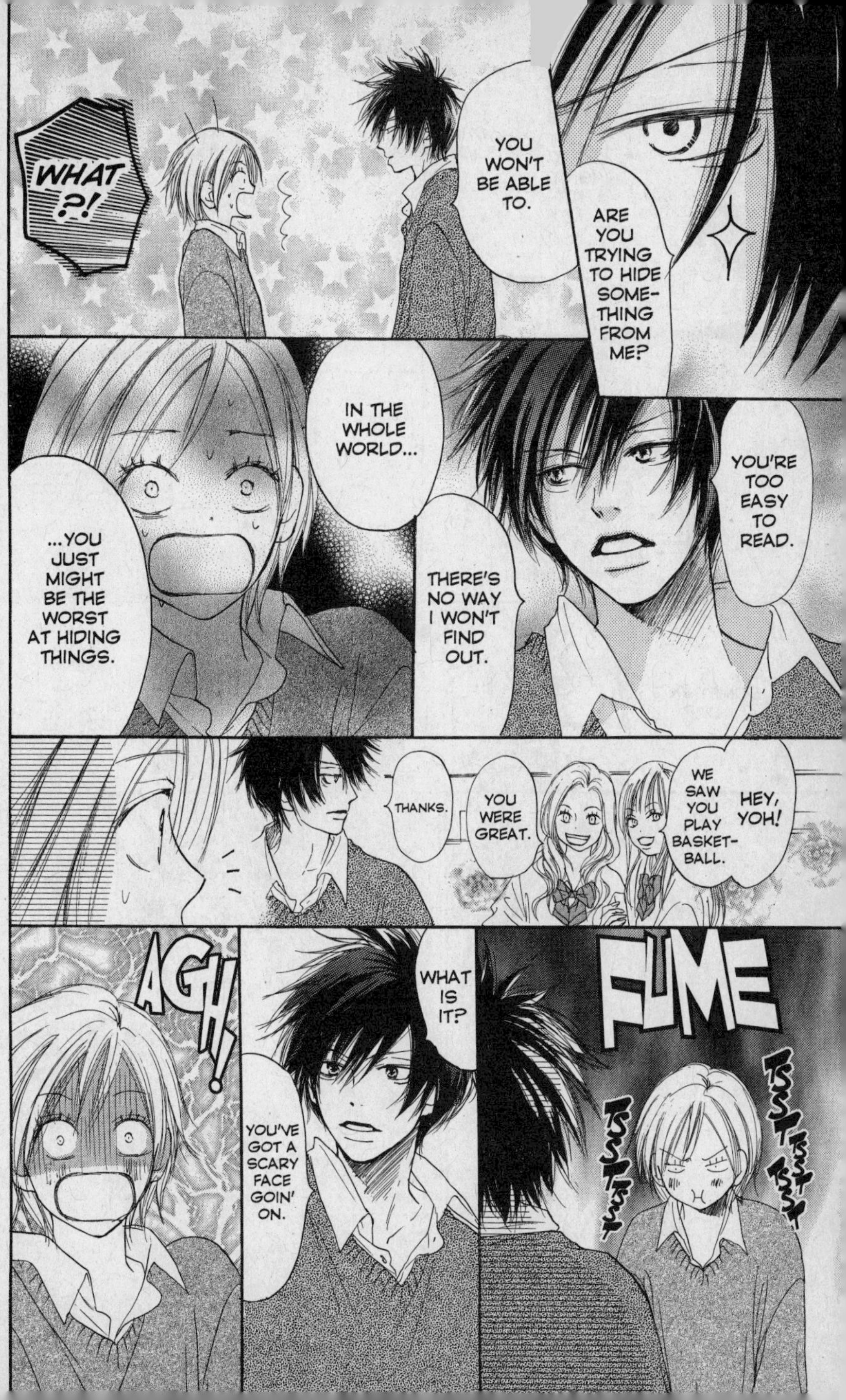
ARE YOU TRYING TO HIDE SOME-THING FROM ME?
YOU WON'T BE ABLE TO.
WHAT ?!
YOU'RE TOO EASY TO READ.
THERE'S NO WAY I WON'T FIND OUT.
IN THE WHOLE WORLD...
...YOU JUST MIGHT BE THE WORST AT HIDING THINGS.
HEY, YOH!
WE SAW YOU PLAY BASKET-BALL.
YOU WERE GREAT.
THANKS.
FUME
TSST TSST TSST
TSST TSST
WHAT IS IT?
YOU'VE GOT A SCARY FACE GOIN' ON.
AGH!

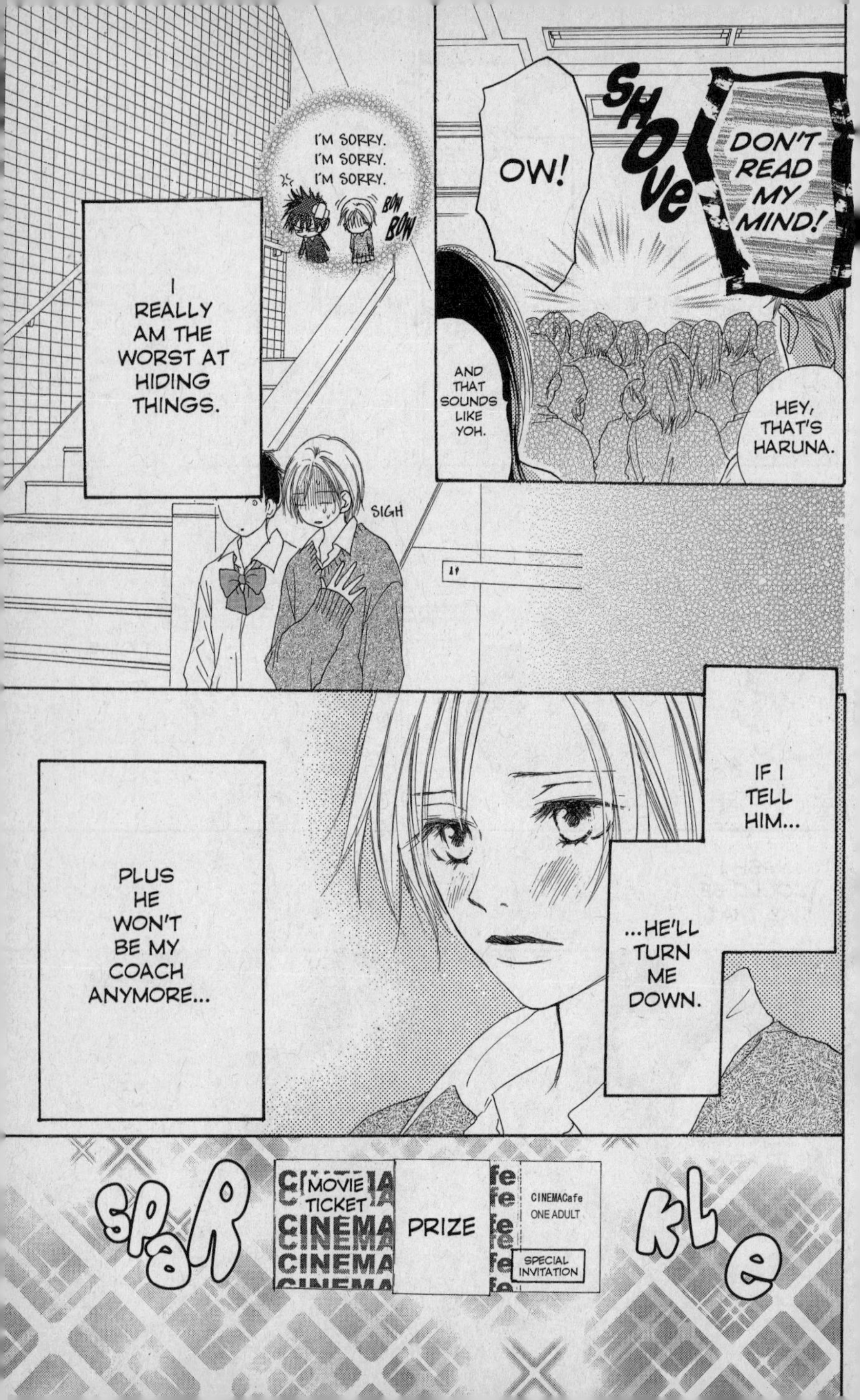
HEY, THAT'S HARUNA.
AND THAT SOUNDS LIKE YOH.
OW!
SHOVE
DON'T READ MY MIND!
I'M SORRY. I'M SORRY. I'M SORRY.
BOW BOW
I REALLY AM THE WORST AT HIDING THINGS.
SIGH
IF I TELL HIM...
...HE'LL TURN ME DOWN.
PLUS HE WON'T BE MY COACH ANYMORE...
SPARKLE
MOVIE TICKET
CINEMA
PRIZE
CINEMACafe
ONE ADULT
SPECIAL INVITATION

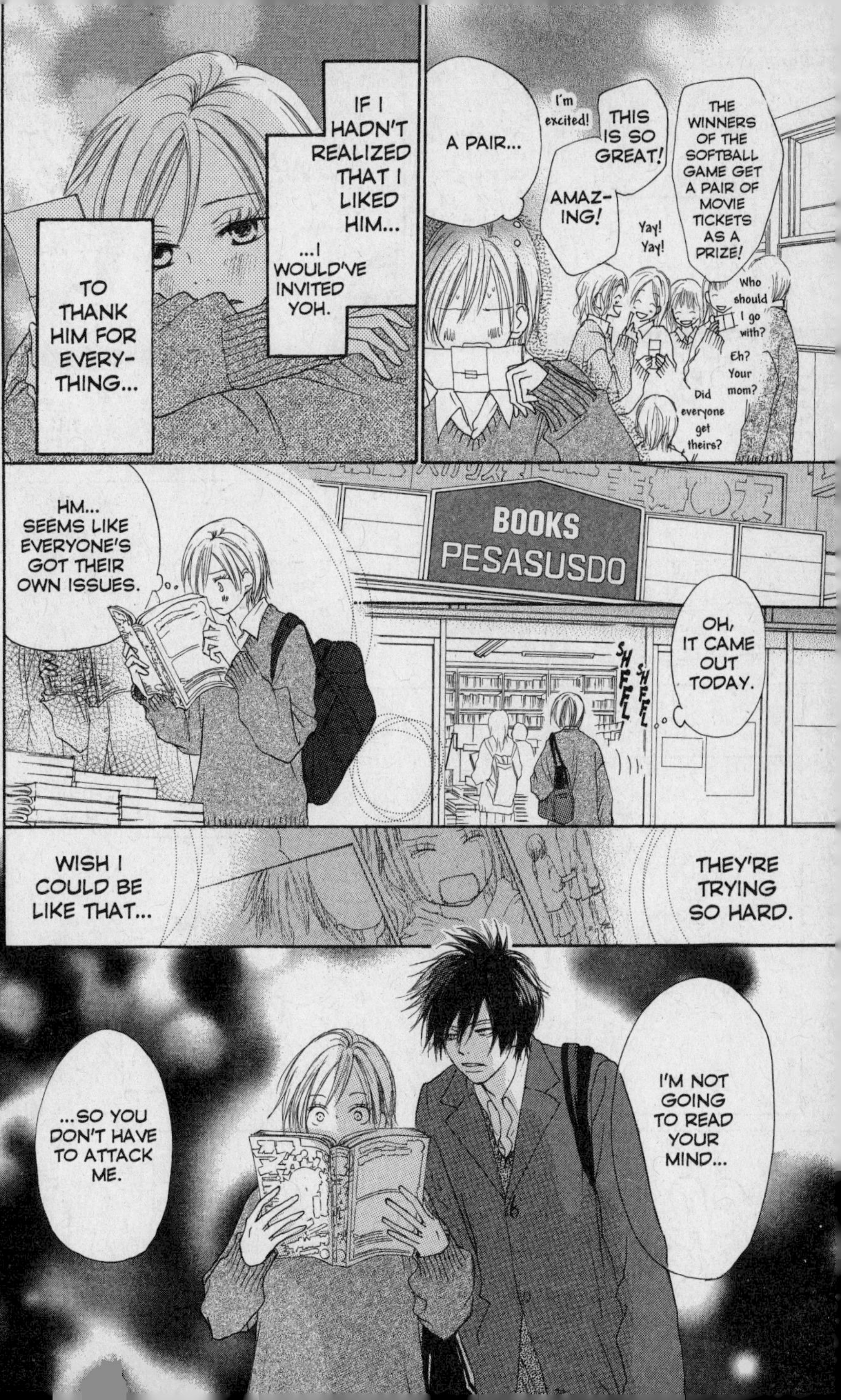
THE WINNERS OF THE SOFTBALL GAME GET A PAIR OF MOVIE TICKETS AS A PRIZE!
Who should I go with?
Eh? Your mom?
THIS IS SO GREAT!
I'm excited!
Yay! Yay!
AMAZ-ING!
Did everyone get theirs?
A PAIR...
IF I HADN'T REALIZED THAT I LIKED HIM...
...I WOULD'VE INVITED YOH.
TO THANK HIM FOR EVERY-THING...
OH, IT CAME OUT TODAY.
SHFFL
SHFFL
BOOKS
PESASUSDO
HM... SEEMS LIKE EVERYONE'S GOT THEIR OWN ISSUES.
THEY'RE TRYING SO HARD.
WISH I COULD BE LIKE THAT...
I'M NOT GOING TO READ YOUR MIND...
...SO YOU DON'T HAVE TO ATTACK ME.

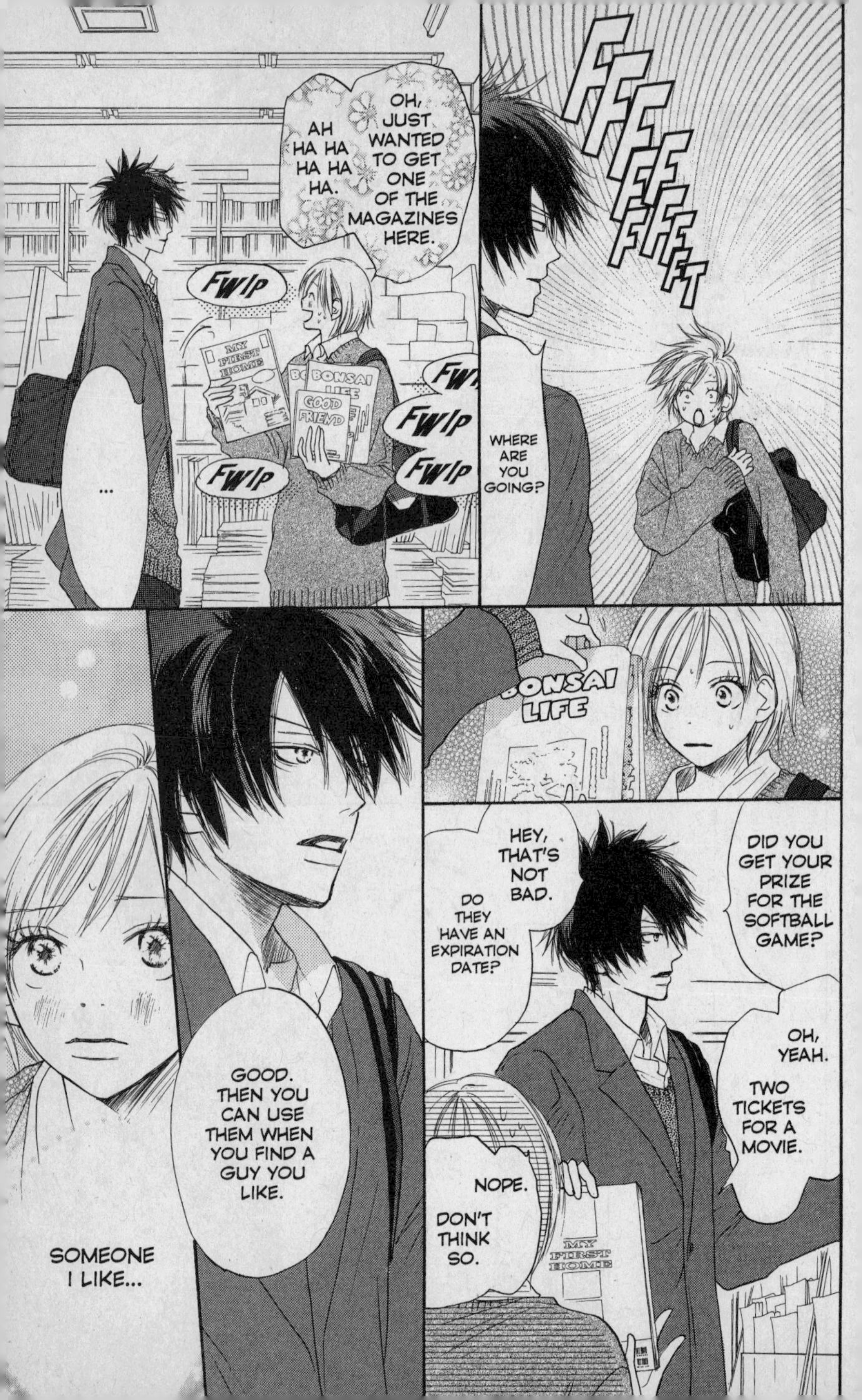
FFFFFFFFFFFT
WHERE ARE YOU GOING?
OH, JUST WANTED TO GET ONE OF THE MAGAZINES HERE.
AH HA HA HA HA HA.
FWIP
MY FIRST HOME
BONSAI LIFE
GOOD FRIEND
FWIP
FWIP
FWIP
FWIP
...
BONSAI LIFE
DID YOU GET YOUR PRIZE FOR THE SOFTBALL GAME?
HEY, THAT'S NOT BAD.
DO THEY HAVE AN EXPIRATION DATE?
OH, YEAH.
TWO TICKETS FOR A MOVIE.
NOPE.
DON'T THINK SO.
MY FIRST HOME
GOOD. THEN YOU CAN USE THEM WHEN YOU FIND A GUY YOU LIKE.
SOMEONE I LIKE...

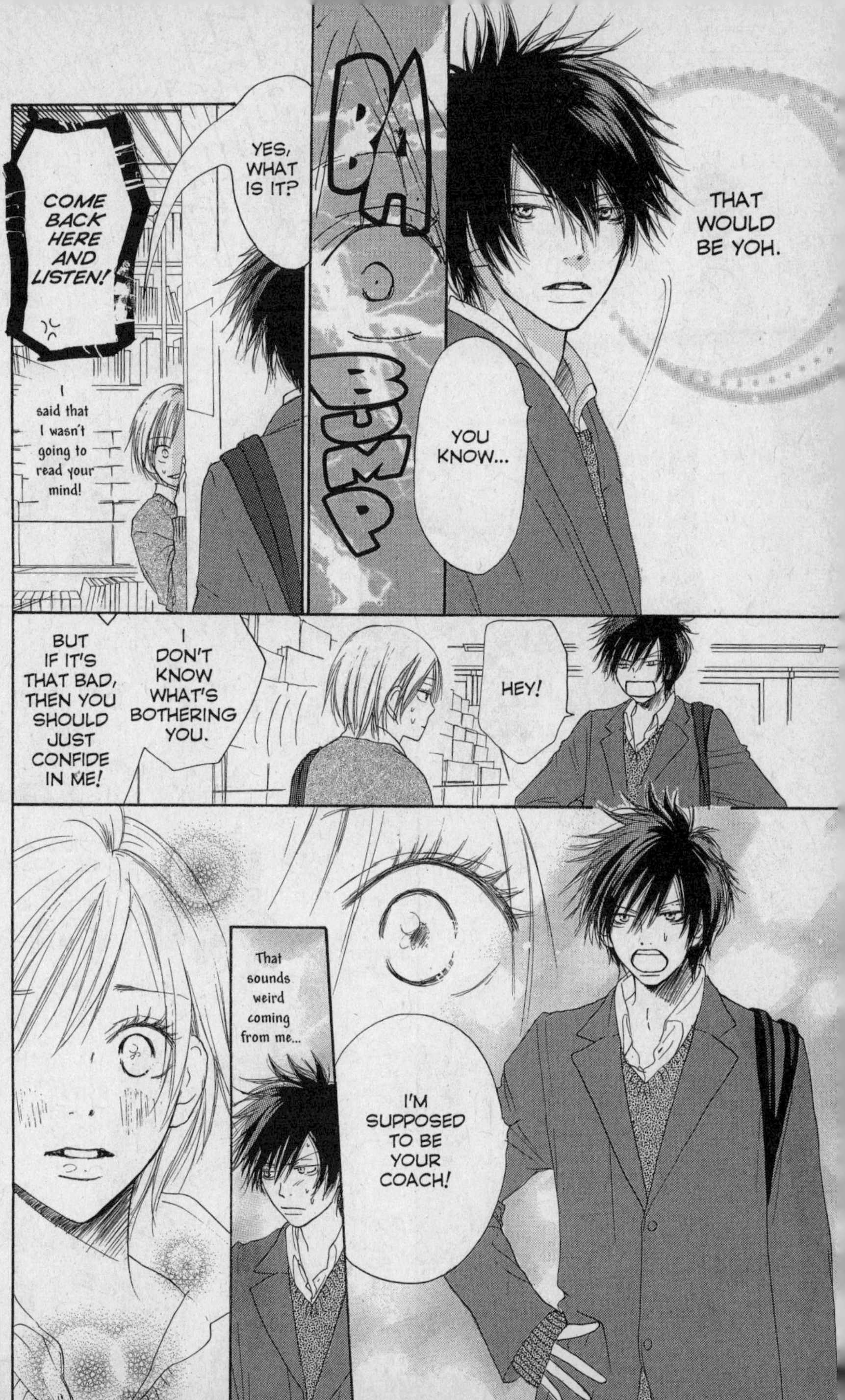
THAT WOULD BE YOH.
YOU KNOW...
BA
BUMP
YES, WHAT IS IT?
COME BACK HERE AND LISTEN!
I said that I wasn't going to read your mind!
HEY!
I DON'T KNOW WHAT'S BOTHERING YOU.
BUT IF IT'S THAT BAD, THEN YOU SHOULD JUST CONFIDE IN ME!
I'M SUPPOSED TO BE YOUR COACH!
That sounds weird coming from me...

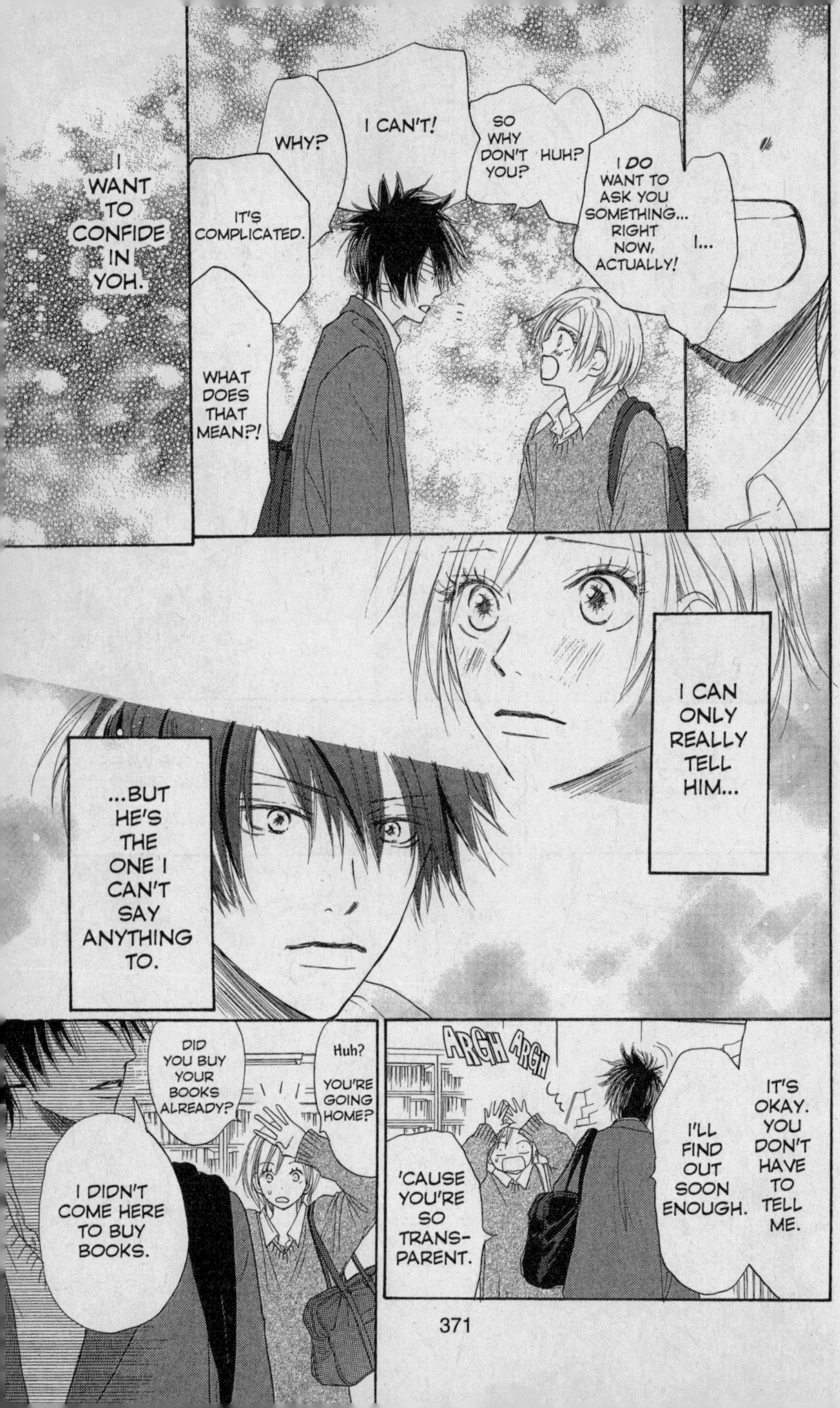
I...
I DO WANT TO ASK YOU SOMETHING... RIGHT NOW, ACTUALLY!
HUH?
SO WHY DON'T YOU?
I CAN'T!
WHY?
IT'S COMPLICATED.
WHAT DOES THAT MEAN?!
I WANT TO CONFIDE IN YOH.
I CAN ONLY REALLY TELL HIM...
...BUT HE'S THE ONE I CAN'T SAY ANYTHING TO.
IT'S OKAY. YOU DON'T HAVE TO TELL ME.
I'LL FIND OUT SOON ENOUGH.
'CAUSE YOU'RE SO TRANS-PARENT.
ARGH ARGH
Huh?
YOU'RE GOING HOME?
DID YOU BUY YOUR BOOKS ALREADY?
I DIDN'T COME HERE TO BUY BOOKS.

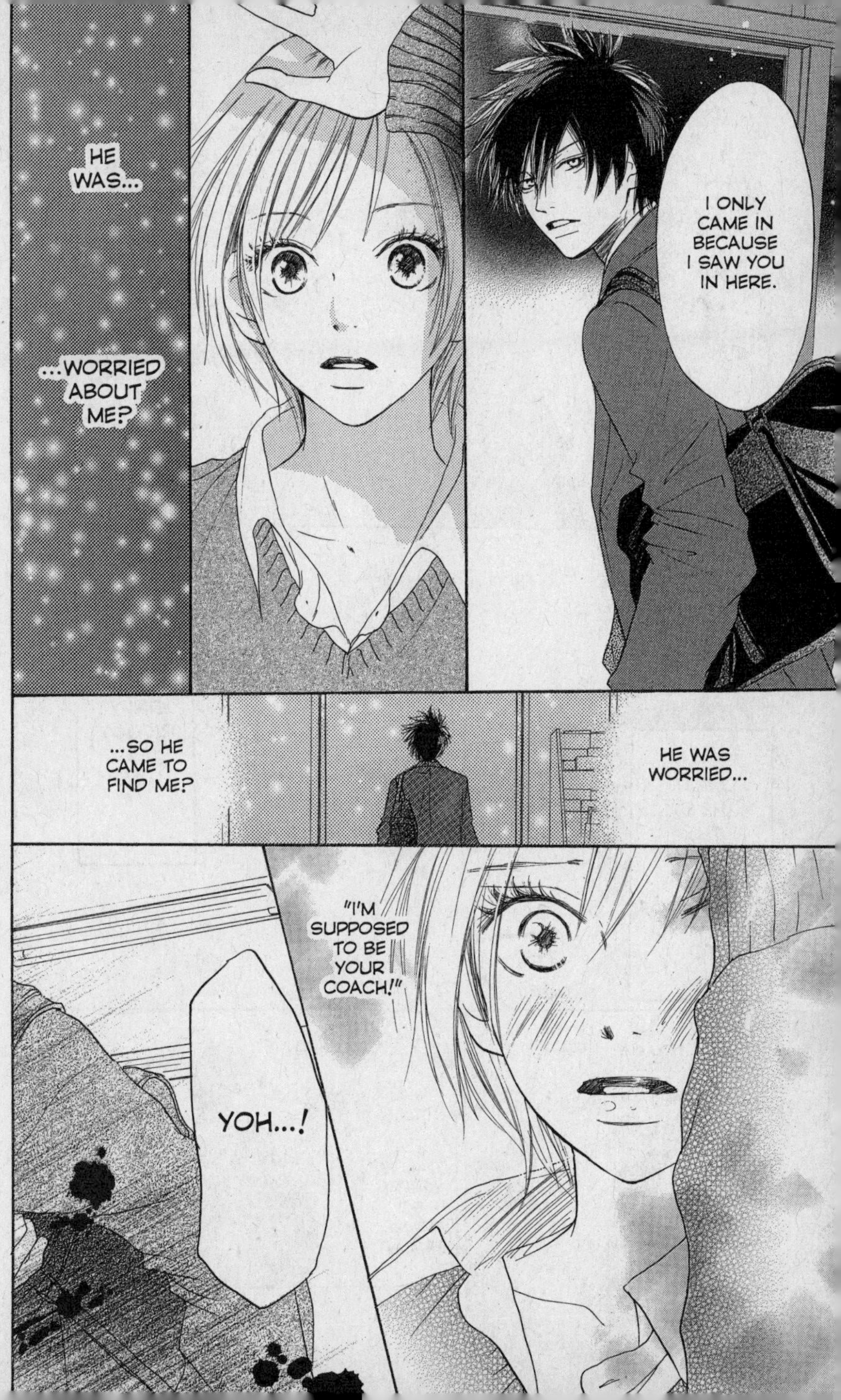
I ONLY CAME IN BECAUSE I SAW YOU IN HERE.
HE WAS...
...WORRIED ABOUT ME?
HE WAS WORRIED...
...SO HE CAME TO FIND ME?
"I'M SUPPOSED TO BE YOUR COACH!"
YOH...!

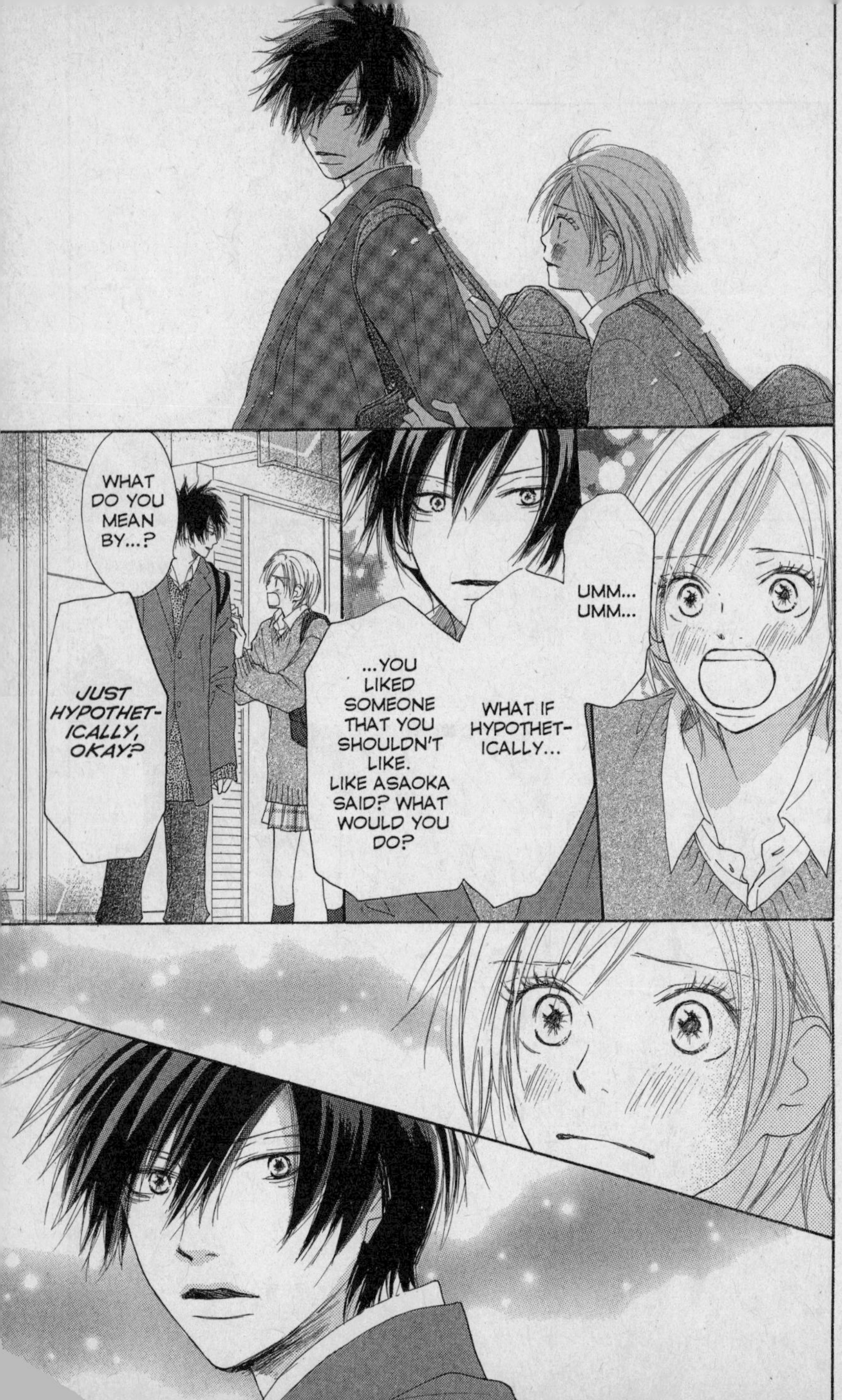
UMM... UMM...
WHAT IF HYPOTHETICALLY...
...YOU LIKED SOMEONE THAT YOU SHOULDN'T LIKE. LIKE ASAOKA SAID? WHAT WOULD YOU DO?
WHAT DO YOU MEAN BY...?
JUST HYPOTHETICALLY, OKAY?

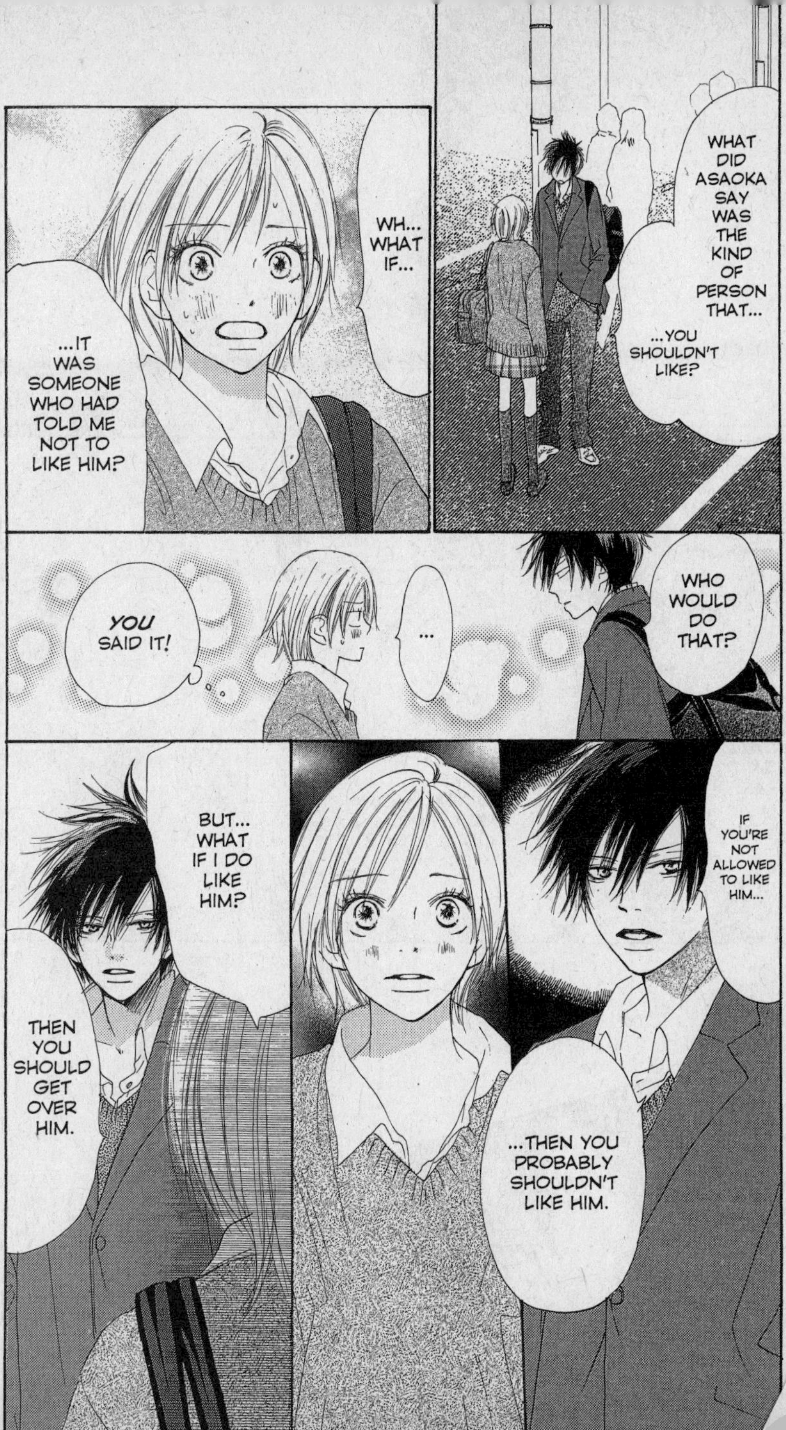
WHAT DID ASAOKA SAY WAS THE KIND OF PERSON THAT...
...YOU SHOULDN'T LIKE?
WH... WHAT IF...
...IT WAS SOMEONE WHO HAD TOLD ME NOT TO LIKE HIM?
WHO WOULD DO THAT?
...
YOU SAID IT!
IF YOU'RE NOT ALLOWED TO LIKE HIM...
...THEN YOU PROBABLY SHOULDN'T LIKE HIM.
BUT... WHAT IF I DO LIKE HIM?
THEN YOU SHOULD GET OVER HIM.

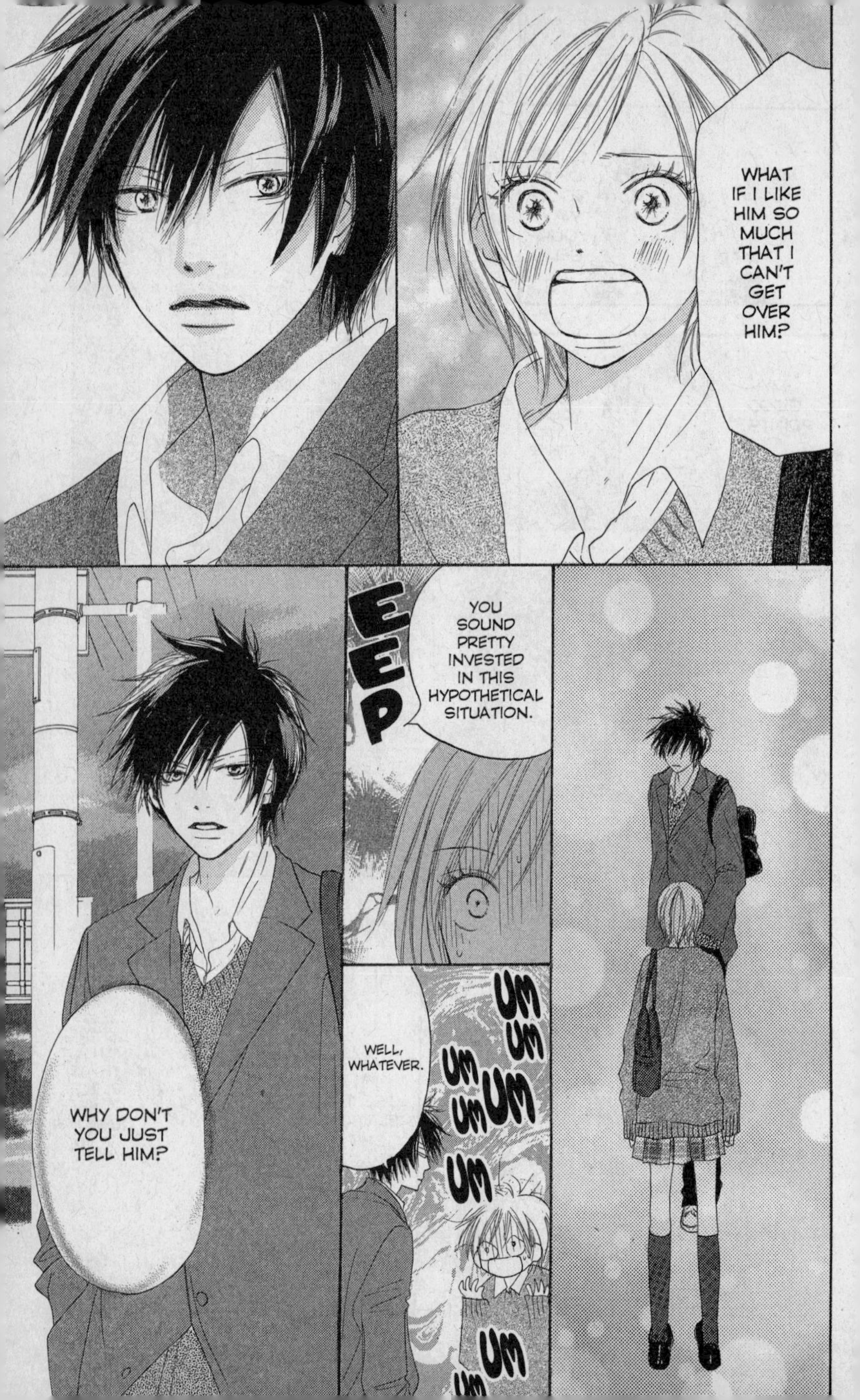
WHAT IF I LIKE HIM SO MUCH THAT I CAN'T GET OVER HIM?
EEP
YOU SOUND PRETTY INVESTED IN THIS HYPOTHETICAL SITUATION.
UM UM UM UM UM UM UM
WELL, WHATEVER.
UM UM UM
WHY DON'T YOU JUST TELL HIM?

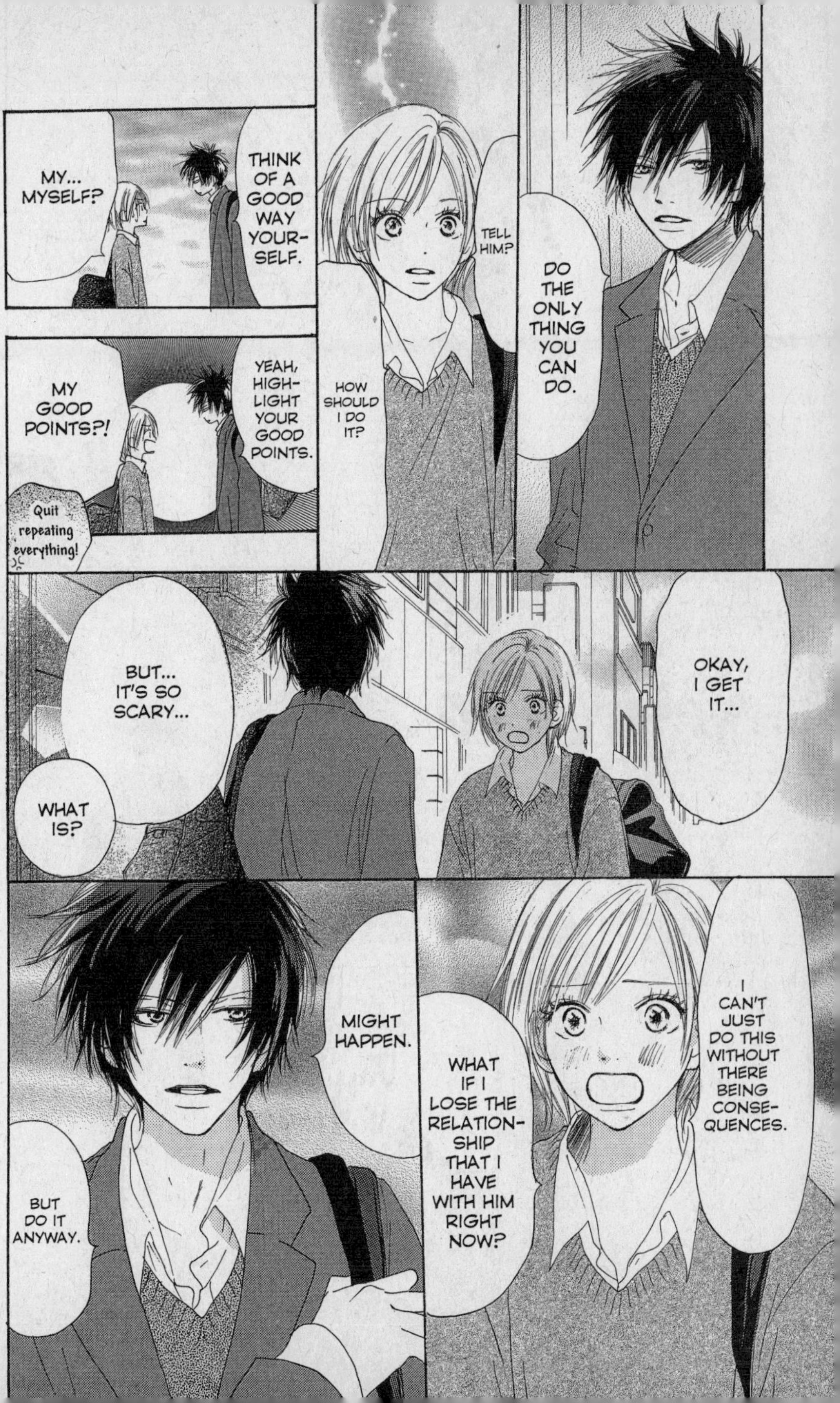
DO THE ONLY THING YOU CAN DO.
TELL HIM?
HOW SHOULD I DO IT?
THINK OF A GOOD WAY YOUR-SELF.
MY... MYSELF?
YEAH, HIGH-LIGHT YOUR GOOD POINTS.
MY GOOD POINTS?!
Quit repeating everything!
OKAY, I GET IT...
BUT... IT'S SO SCARY...
WHAT IS?
I CAN'T JUST DO THIS WITHOUT THERE BEING CONSE-QUENCES.
WHAT IF I LOSE THE RELATION-SHIP THAT I HAVE WITH HIM RIGHT NOW?
MIGHT HAPPEN.
BUT DO IT ANYWAY.

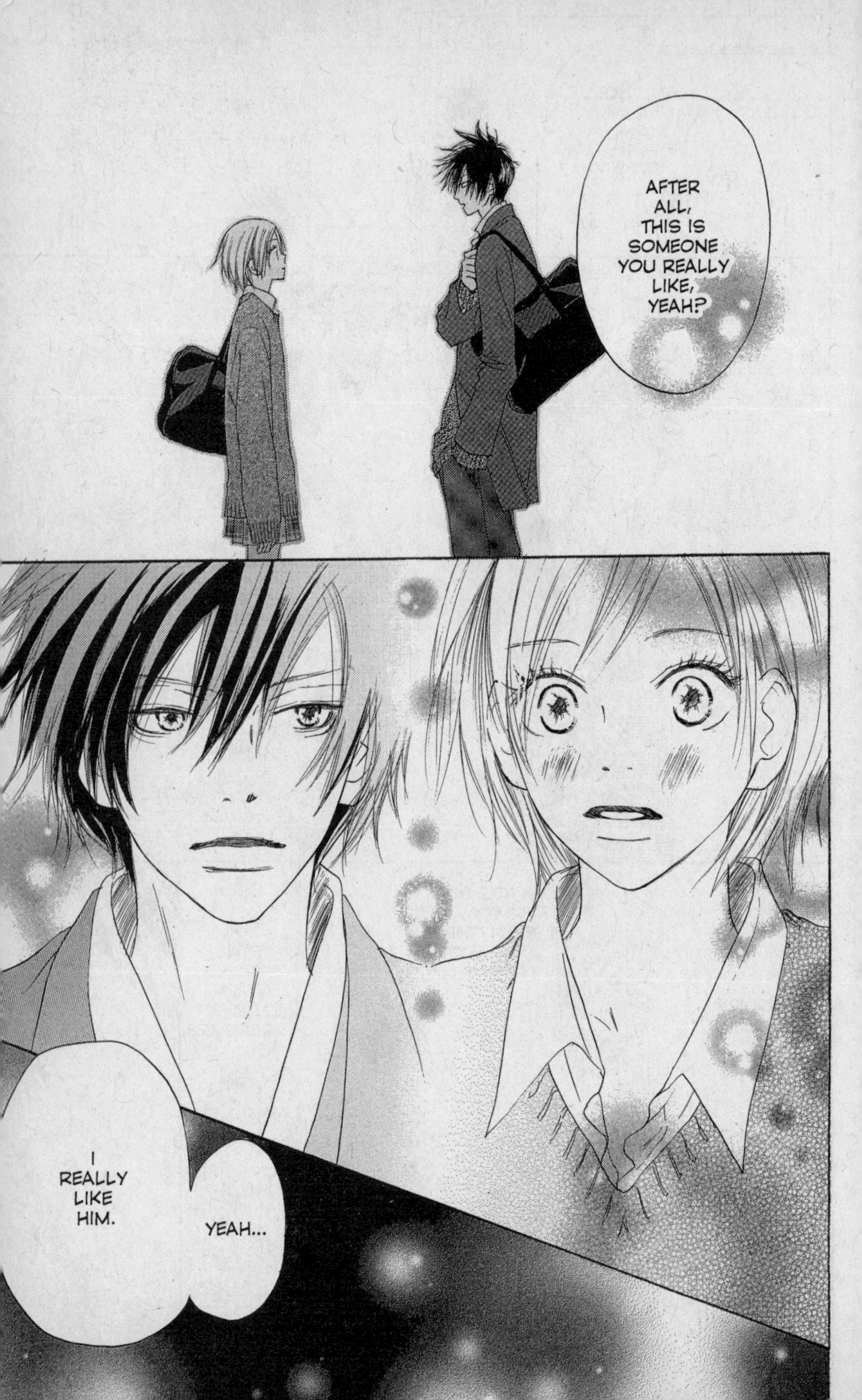
AFTER ALL, THIS IS SOMEONE YOU REALLY LIKE, YEAH?
YEAH...
I REALLY LIKE HIM.

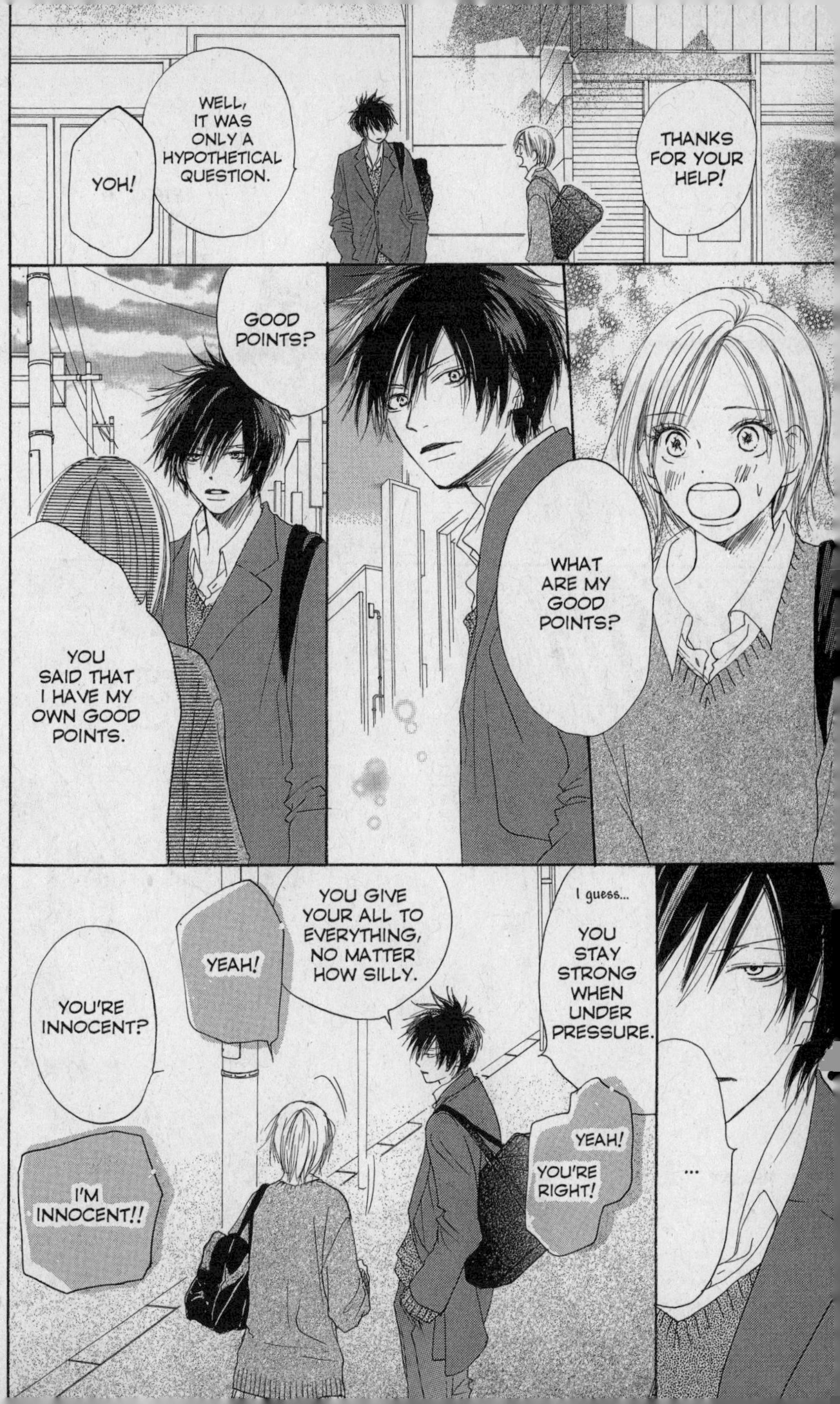
THANKS FOR YOUR HELP!
WELL, IT WAS ONLY A HYPOTHETICAL QUESTION.
YOH!
WHAT ARE MY GOOD POINTS?
GOOD POINTS?
YOU SAID THAT I HAVE MY OWN GOOD POINTS.
...
I guess...
YOU STAY STRONG WHEN UNDER PRESSURE.
YEAH!
YOU'RE RIGHT!
YOU GIVE YOUR ALL TO EVERYTHING, NO MATTER HOW SILLY.
YEAH!
YOU'RE INNOCENT?
I'M INNOCENT!!

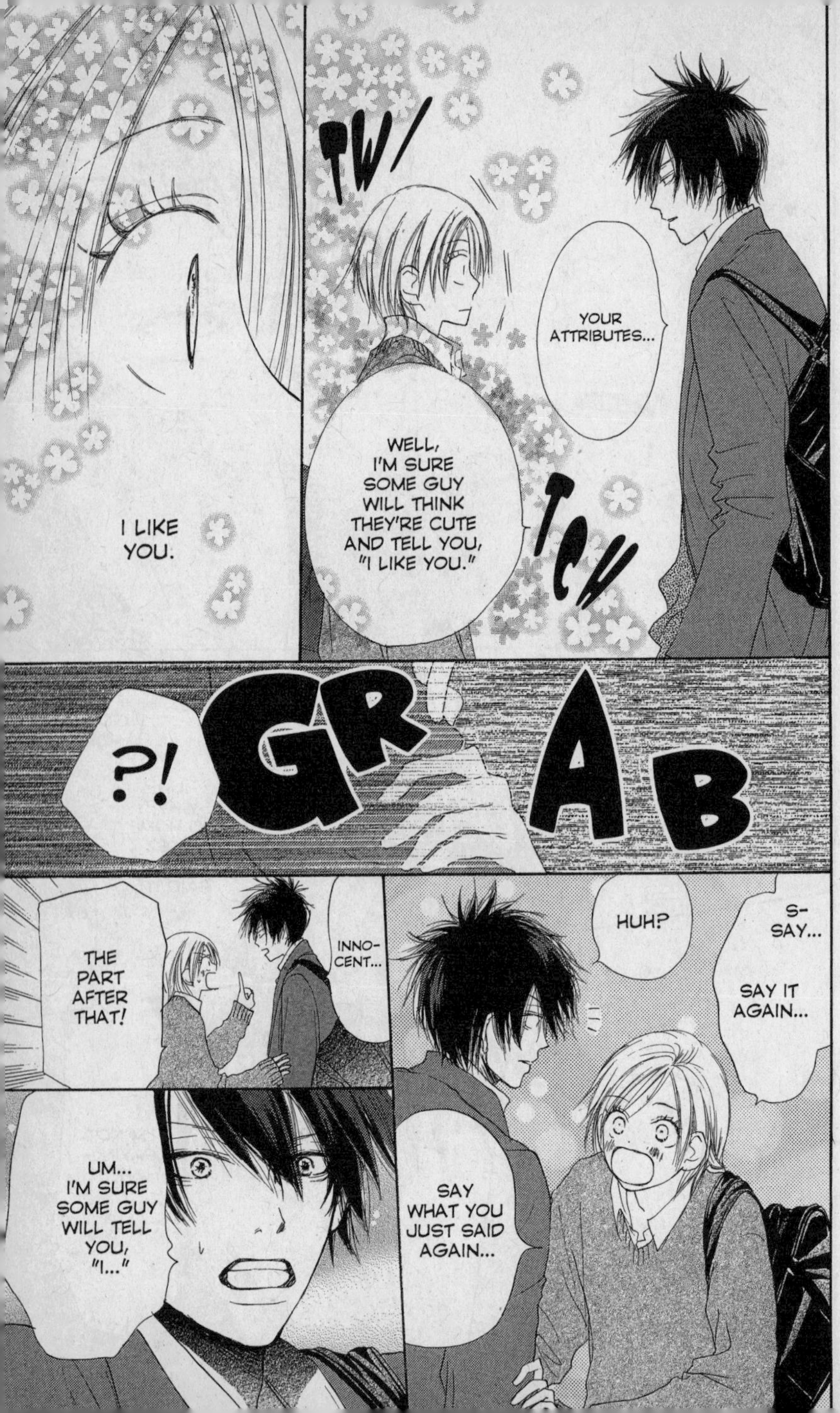
YOUR ATTRIBUTES...
TW
WELL, I'M SURE SOME GUY WILL THINK THEY'RE CUTE AND TELL YOU, "I LIKE YOU."
TCH
I LIKE YOU.
GRAB
?!
S- SAY...
SAY IT AGAIN...
HUH?
SAY WHAT YOU JUST SAID AGAIN...
INNO- CENT...
THE PART AFTER THAT!
UM... I'M SURE SOME GUY WILL TELL YOU, "I..."

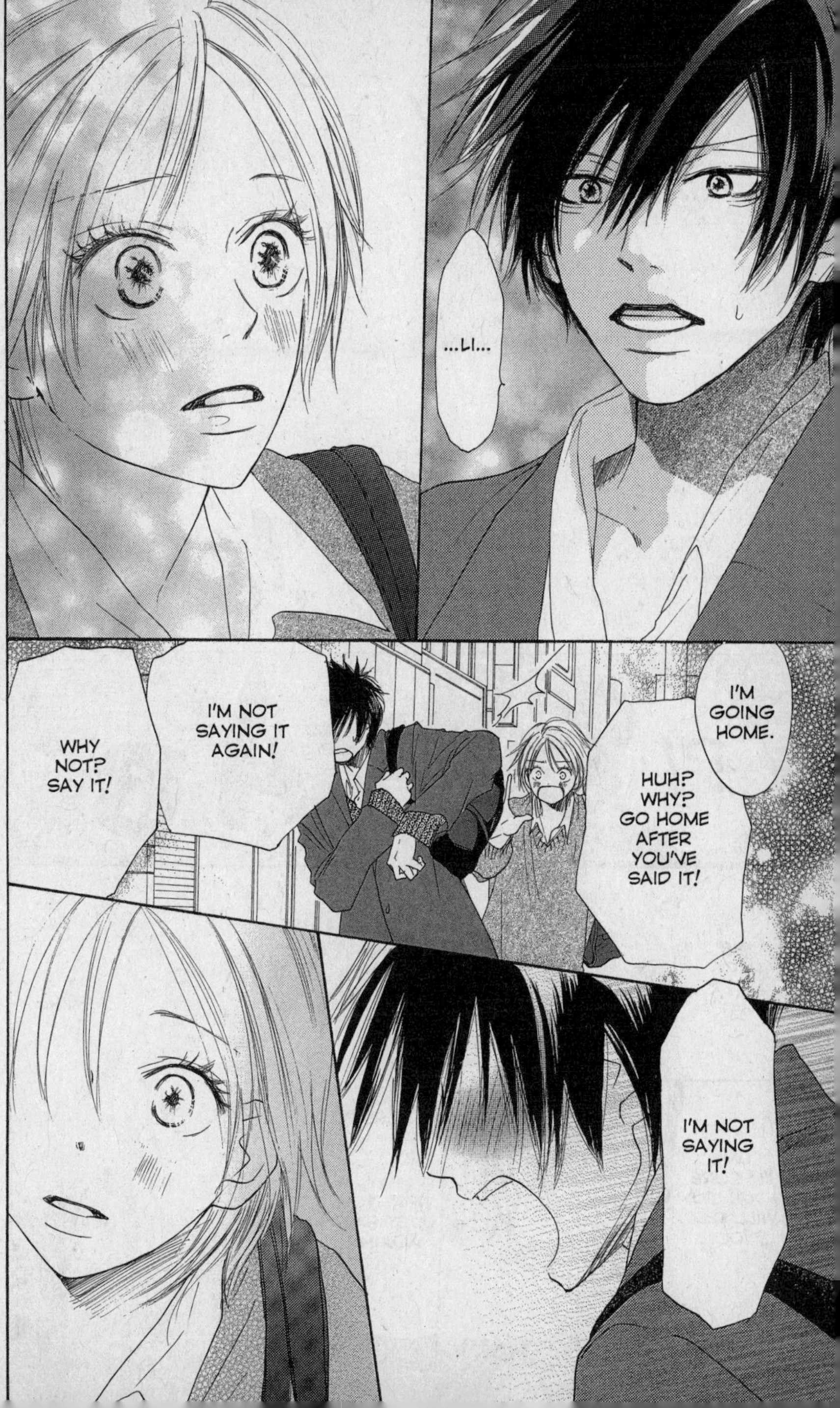
...LI...
I'M GOING HOME.
HUH? WHY? GO HOME AFTER YOU'VE SAID IT!
I'M NOT SAYING IT AGAIN!
WHY NOT? SAY IT!
I'M NOT SAYING IT!

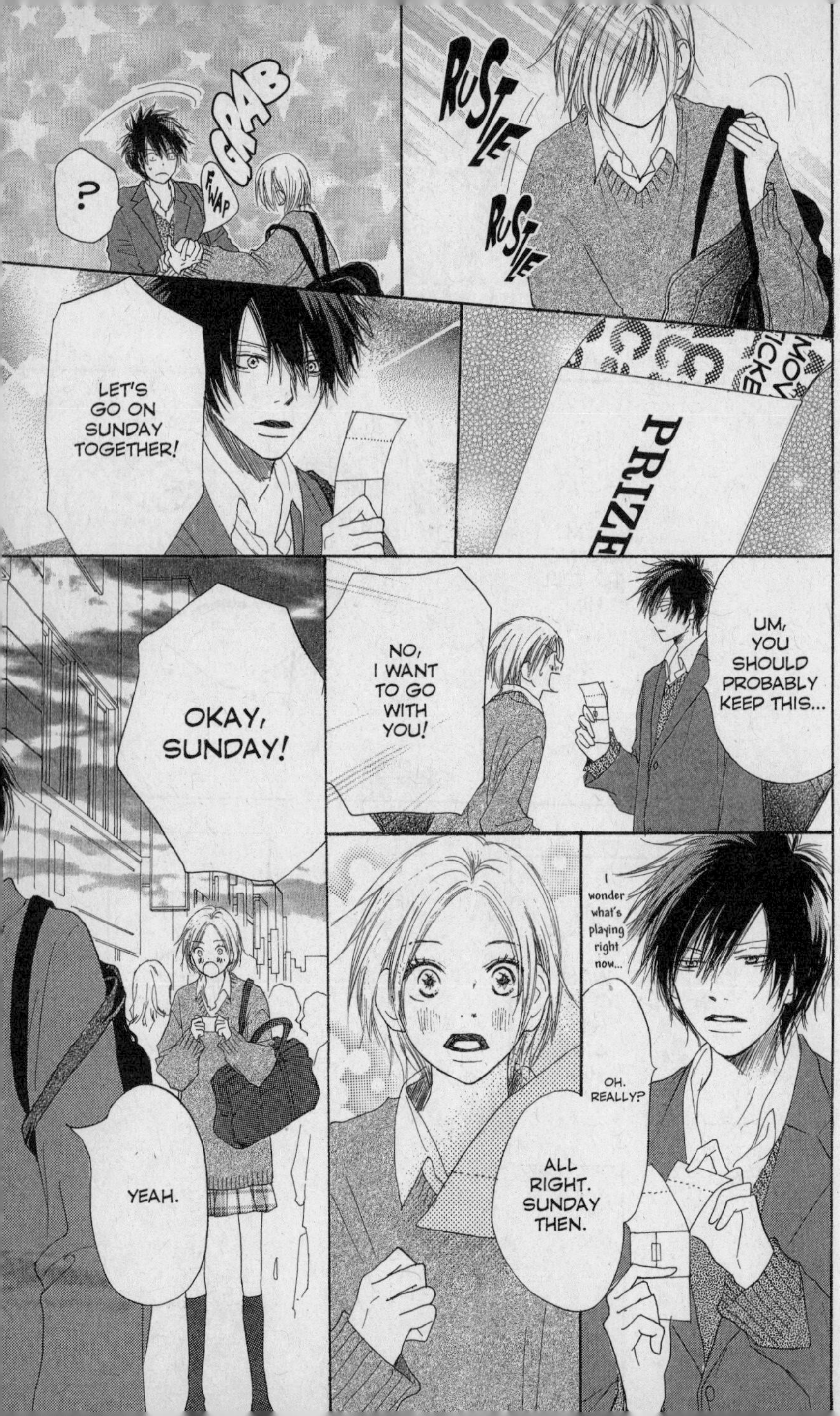
RUSTLE
RUSTLE
GRAB
FWAP
?
PRIZE
LET'S GO ON SUNDAY TOGETHER!
UM, YOU SHOULD PROBABLY KEEP THIS...
NO, I WANT TO GO WITH YOU!
I wonder what's playing right now...
OH. REALLY?
ALL RIGHT. SUNDAY THEN.
OKAY, SUNDAY!
YEAH.

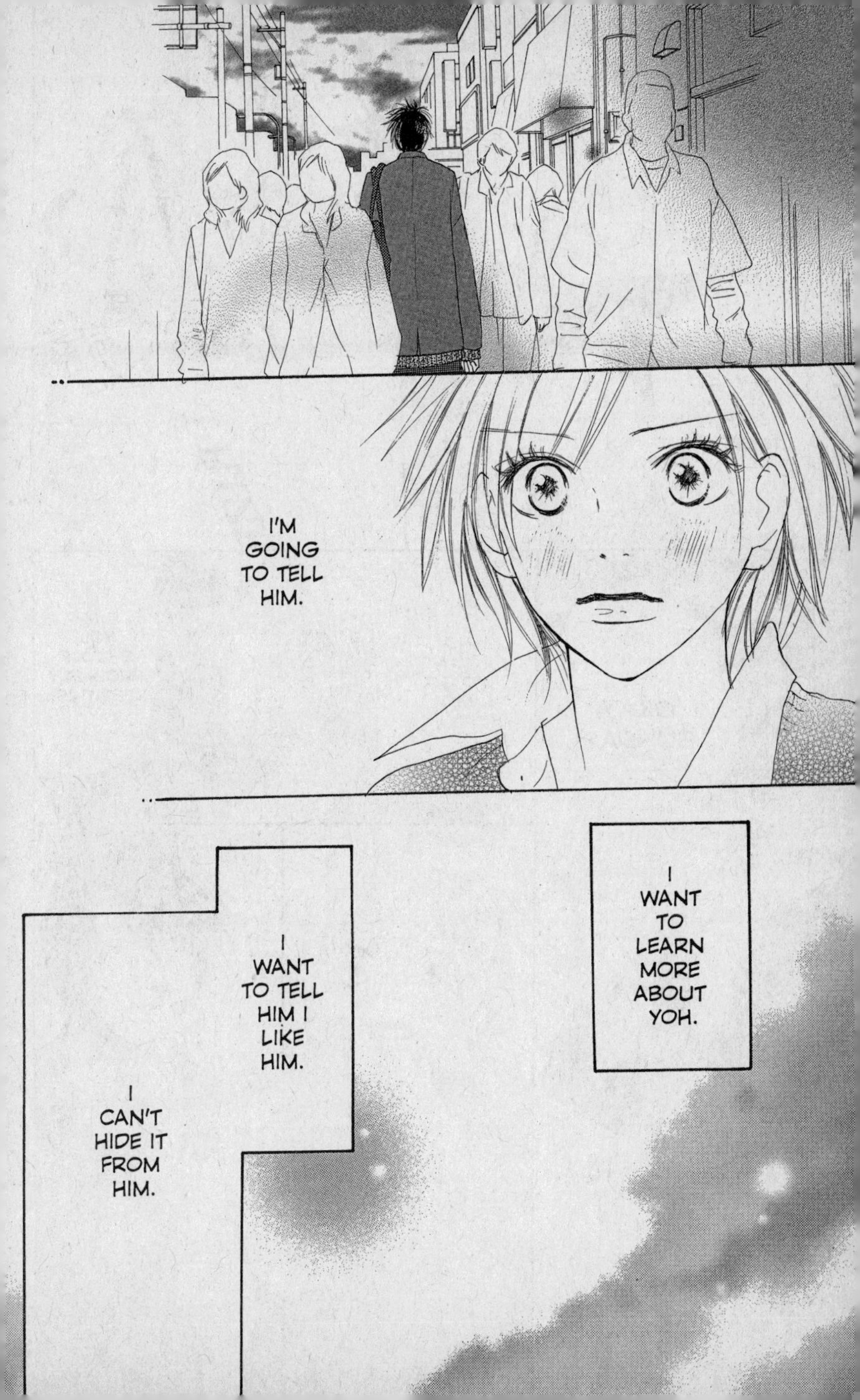
I'M GOING TO TELL HIM.
I WANT TO LEARN MORE ABOUT YOH.
I WANT TO TELL HIM I LIKE HIM.
I CAN'T HIDE IT FROM HIM.

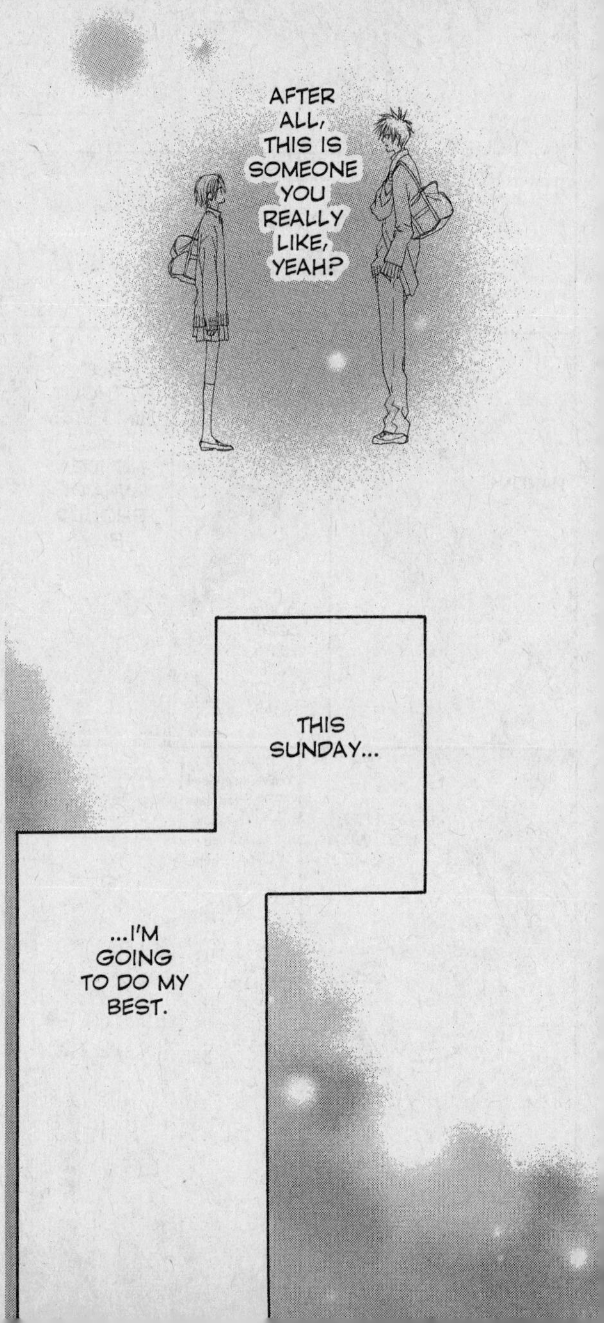
AFTER ALL, THIS IS SOMEONE YOU REALLY LIKE, YEAH?
THIS SUNDAY...
...I'M GOING TO DO MY BEST.

1

Hello. Are you all doing well? I'm doing just fine. Recently, the windshield wipers on my car broke. It was a big hassle.

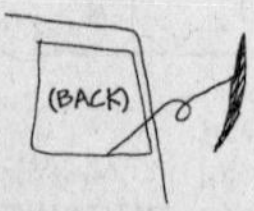
(BACK)

"What a piece of junk!" I got mad for a second, but then when I calmed down, I thought it looked kind of funny and was kind of glad it happened. So I regained my senses and proceeded to back up, but I hit a Harley that was parked behind me. (I guess I hadn't fully regained my senses after all). The Harley was without a scratch, but there was a round dent on my car. I guess if you put something that's 660cc against something that's 1000cc, the 1000cc is just that much stronger. Since the dent didn't affect my car's performance, I left it alone. However, I'm starting to think I should get it fixed because other people keep asking me, "What happened?"

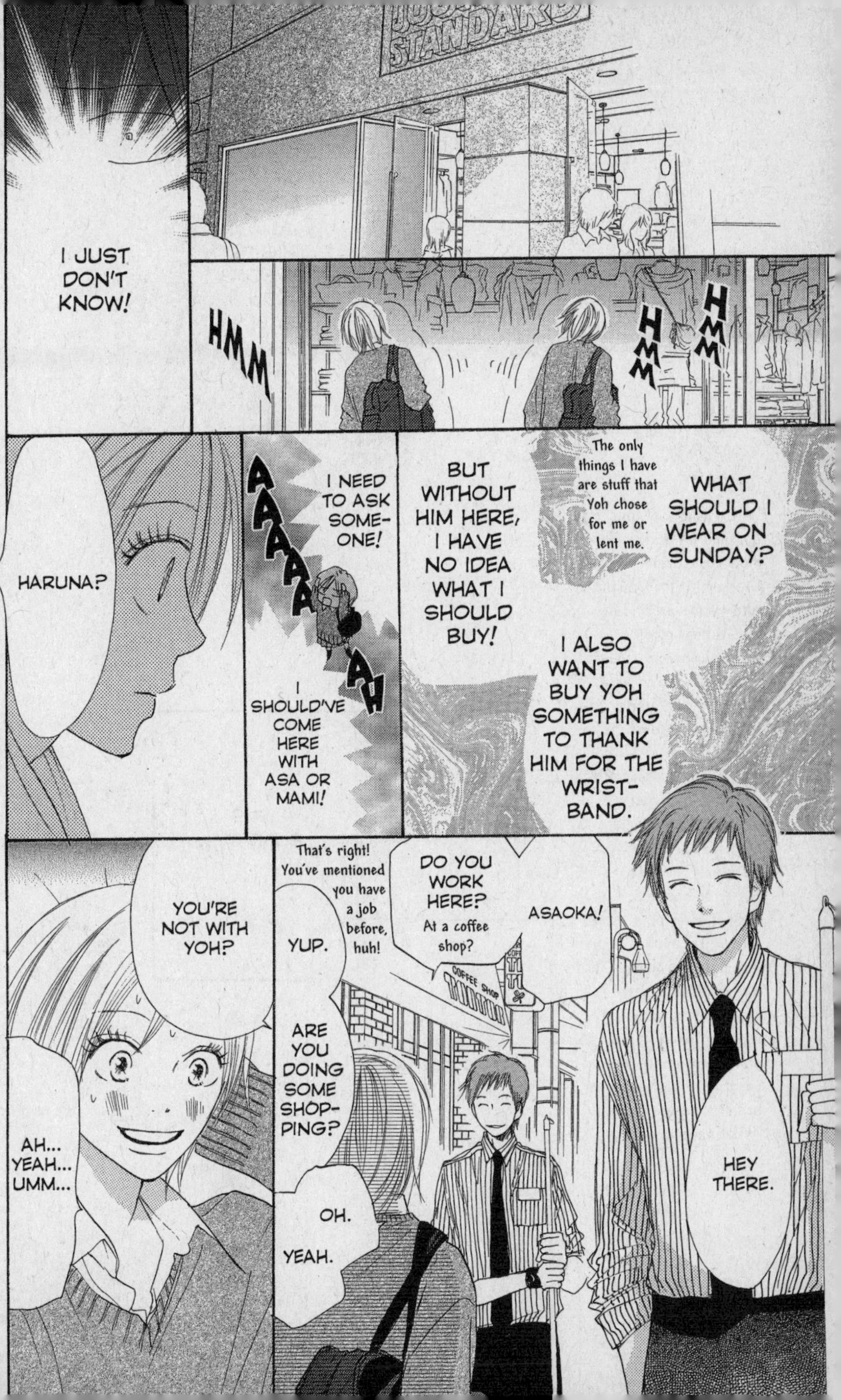
STANDARD
HMM
HMM
HMM
I JUST DON'T KNOW!
WHAT SHOULD I WEAR ON SUNDAY?
The only things I have are stuff that Yoh chose for me or lent me.
BUT WITHOUT HIM HERE, I HAVE NO IDEA WHAT I SHOULD BUY!
I ALSO WANT TO BUY YOH SOMETHING TO THANK HIM FOR THE WRIST-BAND.
I NEED TO ASK SOME-ONE!
AAAAAAH
I SHOULD'VE COME HERE WITH ASA OR MAMI!
HARUNA?
HEY THERE.
ASAOKA!
DO YOU WORK HERE? At a coffee shop?
That's right! You've mentioned you have a job before, huh!
YUP.
COFFEE SHOP
ARE YOU DOING SOME SHOP-PING?
OH.
YEAH.
YOU'RE NOT WITH YOH?
AH... YEAH... UMM...

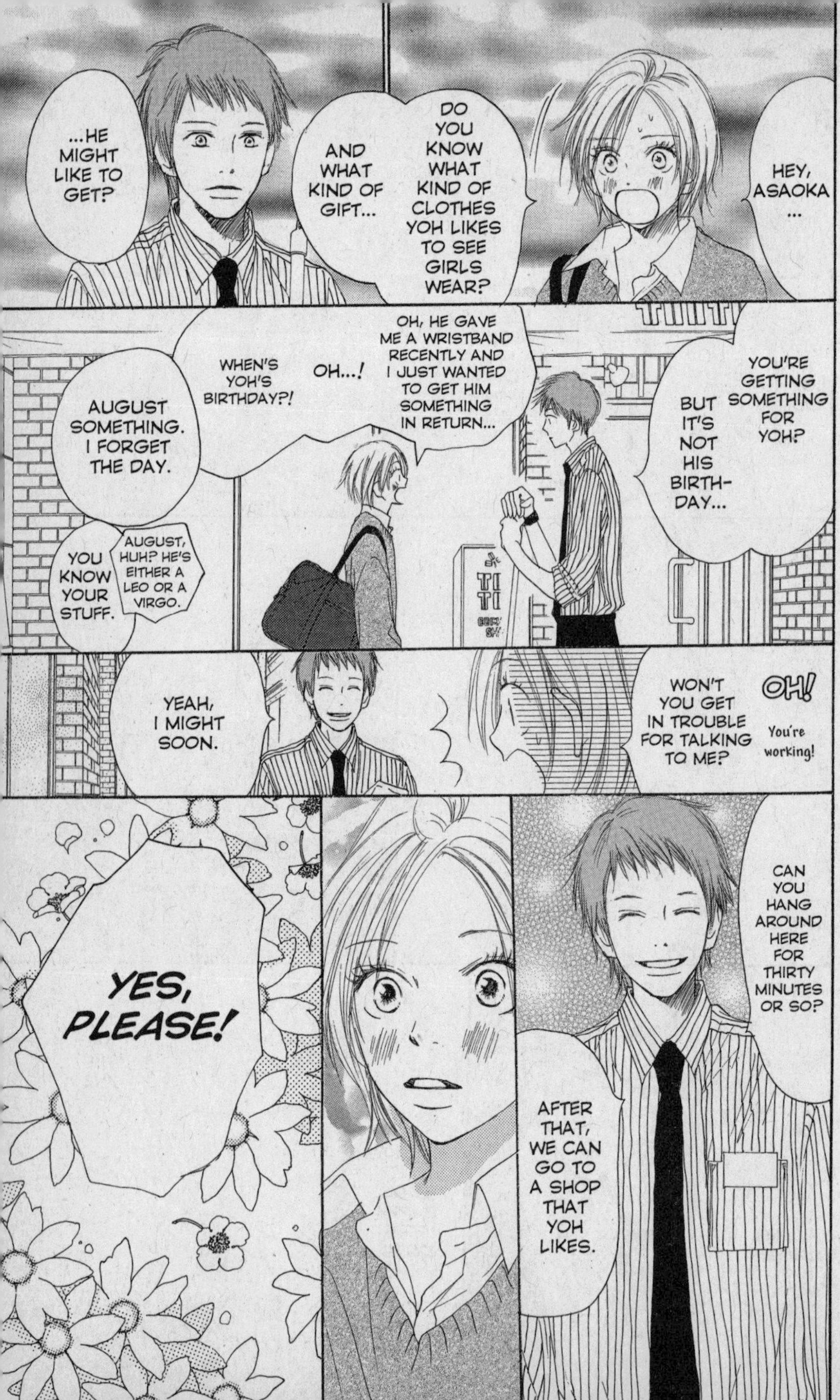
HEY, ASAOKA...
DO YOU KNOW WHAT KIND OF CLOTHES YOH LIKES TO SEE GIRLS WEAR?
AND WHAT KIND OF GIFT...
...HE MIGHT LIKE TO GET?
YOU'RE GETTING SOMETHING FOR YOH?
BUT IT'S NOT HIS BIRTHDAY...
OH, HE GAVE ME A WRISTBAND RECENTLY AND I JUST WANTED TO GET HIM SOMETHING IN RETURN...
OH...!
WHEN'S YOH'S BIRTHDAY?!
AUGUST SOMETHING. I FORGET THE DAY.
AUGUST, HUH? HE'S EITHER A LEO OR A VIRGO.
YOU KNOW YOUR STUFF.
OH!
You're working!
WON'T YOU GET IN TROUBLE FOR TALKING TO ME?
YEAH, I MIGHT SOON.
CAN YOU HANG AROUND HERE FOR THIRTY MINUTES OR SO?
AFTER THAT, WE CAN GO TO A SHOP THAT YOH LIKES.
YES, PLEASE!

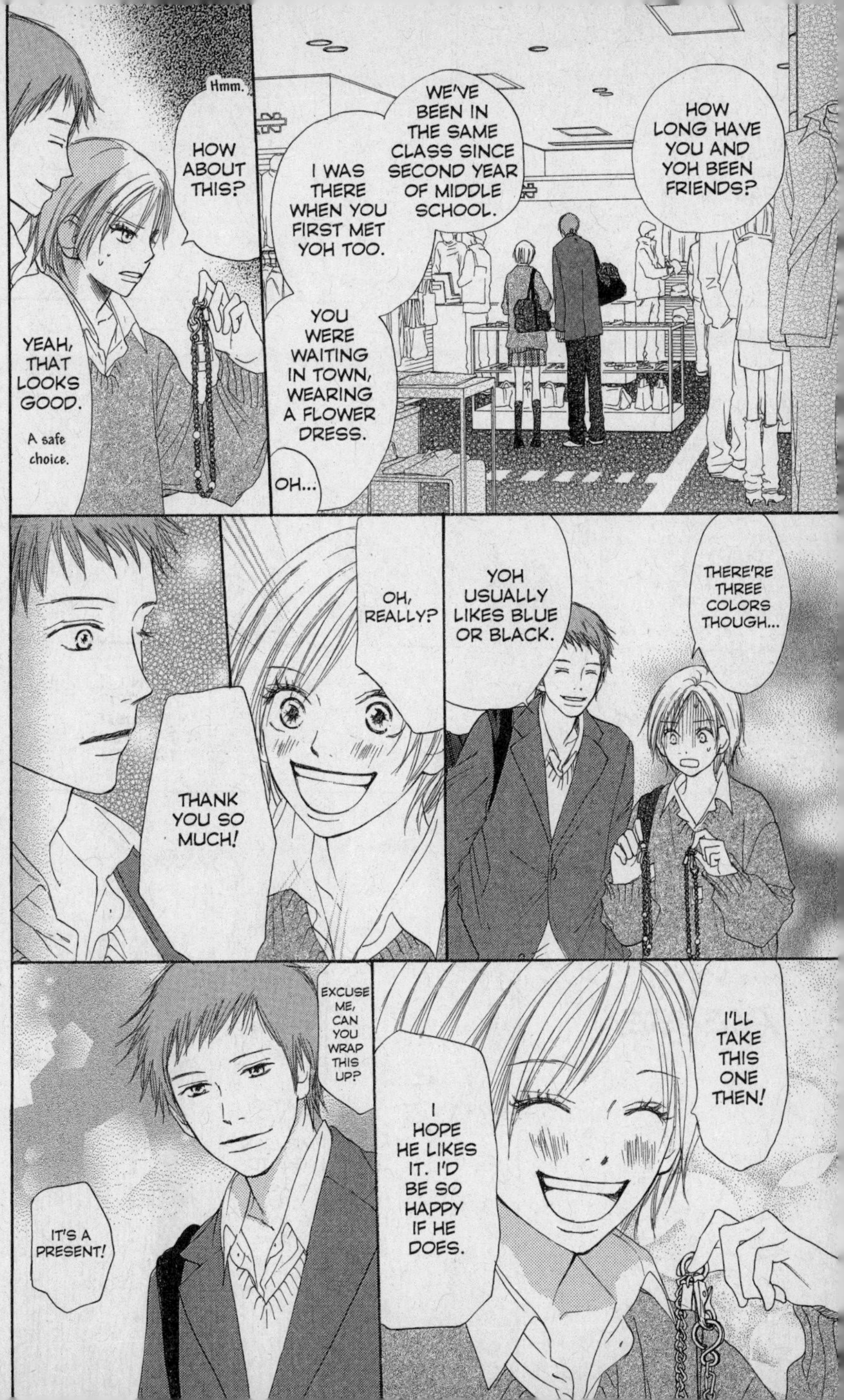
HOW LONG HAVE YOU AND YOH BEEN FRIENDS?
WE'VE BEEN IN THE SAME CLASS SINCE SECOND YEAR OF MIDDLE SCHOOL.
I WAS THERE WHEN YOU FIRST MET YOH TOO.
YOU WERE WAITING IN TOWN, WEARING A FLOWER DRESS.
OH...
Hmm.
HOW ABOUT THIS?
YEAH, THAT LOOKS GOOD.
A safe choice.
THERE'RE THREE COLORS THOUGH...
YOH USUALLY LIKES BLUE OR BLACK.
OH, REALLY?
THANK YOU SO MUCH!
I'LL TAKE THIS ONE THEN!
I HOPE HE LIKES IT. I'D BE SO HAPPY IF HE DOES.
EXCUSE ME, CAN YOU WRAP THIS UP?
IT'S A PRESENT!

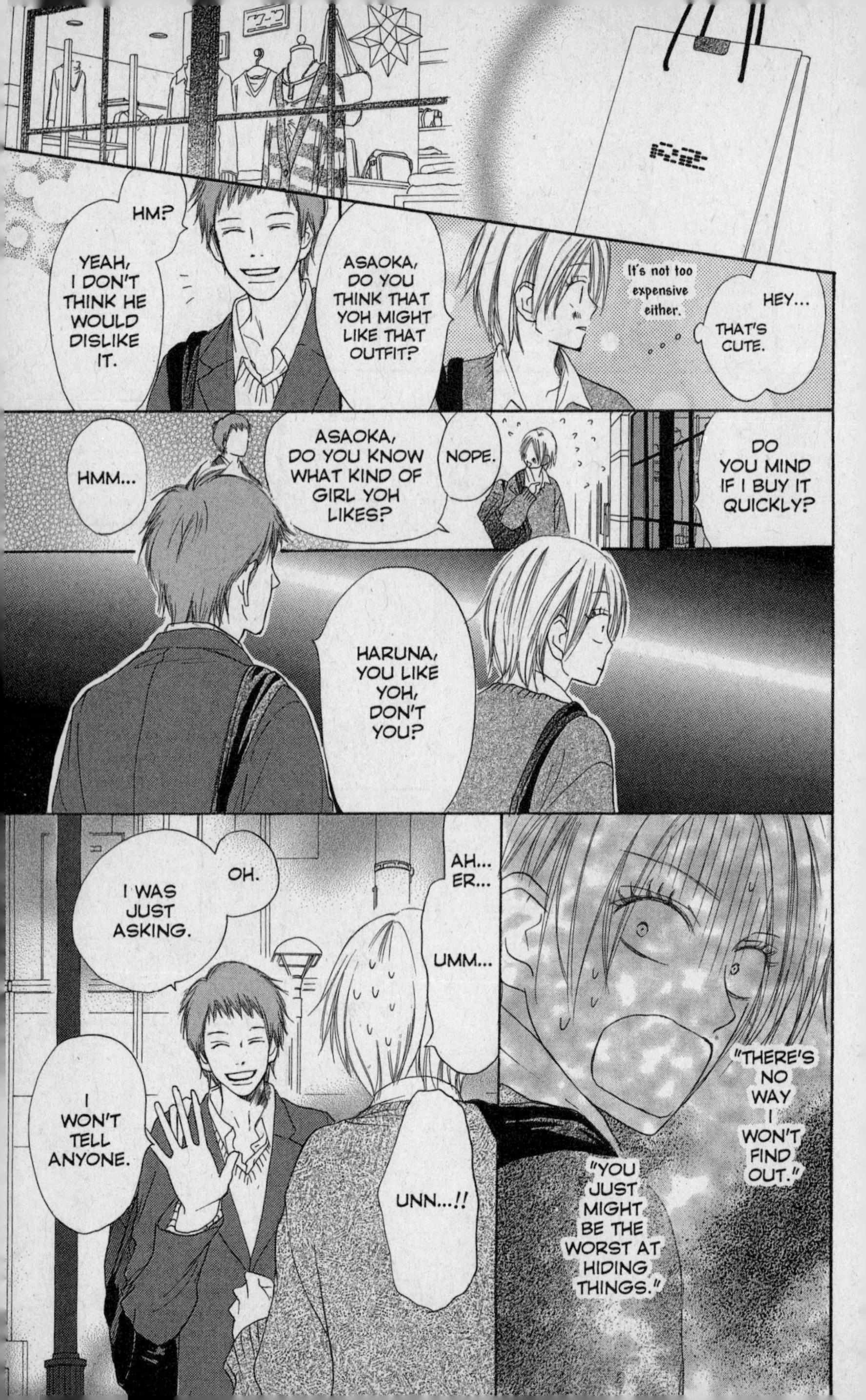
HEY... THAT'S CUTE.
It's not too expensive either.
ASAOKA, DO YOU THINK THAT YOH MIGHT LIKE THAT OUTFIT?
HM?
YEAH, I DON'T THINK HE WOULD DISLIKE IT.
DO YOU MIND IF I BUY IT QUICKLY?
NOPE.
ASAOKA, DO YOU KNOW WHAT KIND OF GIRL YOH LIKES?
HMM...
HARUNA, YOU LIKE YOH, DON'T YOU?
"THERE'S NO WAY I WON'T FIND OUT."
"YOU JUST MIGHT BE THE WORST AT HIDING THINGS."
AH... ER...
OH.
I WAS JUST ASKING.
UMM...
I WON'T TELL ANYONE.
UNN...!!

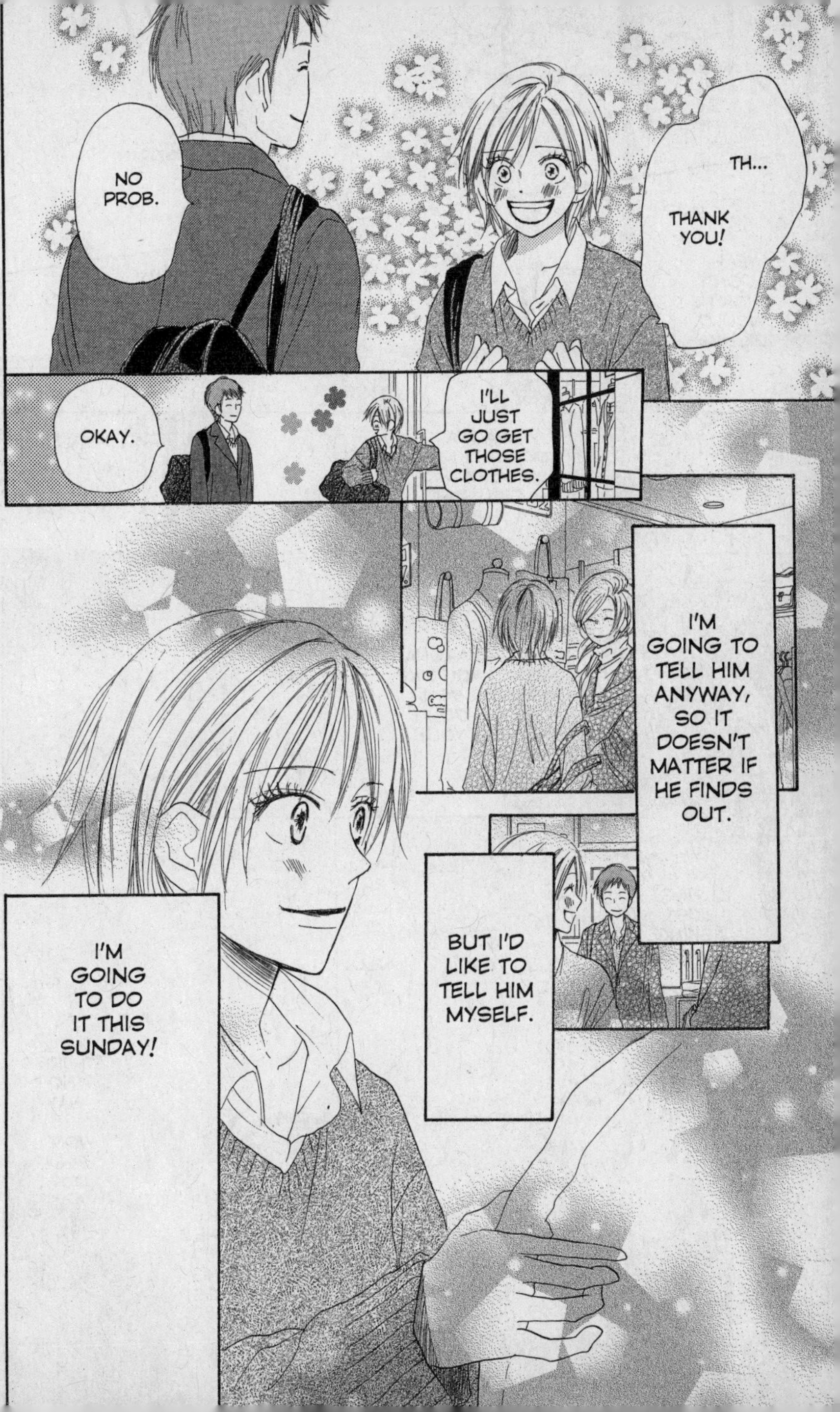
TH...
THANK YOU!
NO PROB.
I'LL JUST GO GET THOSE CLOTHES.
OKAY.
I'M GOING TO TELL HIM ANYWAY, SO IT DOESN'T MATTER IF HE FINDS OUT.
BUT I'D LIKE TO TELL HIM MYSELF.
I'M GOING TO DO IT THIS SUNDAY!

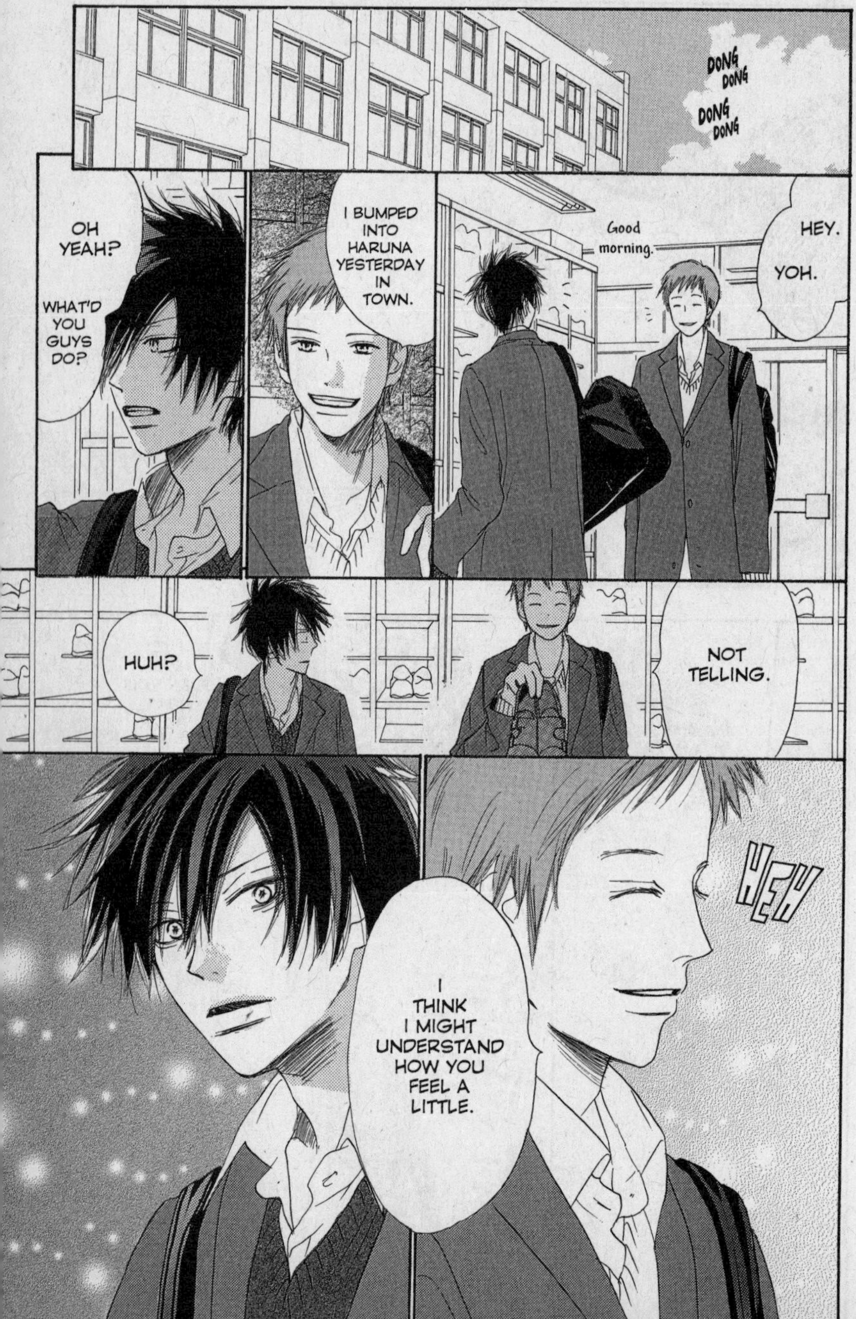
DONG DONG
DONG DONG
HEY.
Good morning.
YOH.
I BUMPED INTO HARUNA YESTERDAY IN TOWN.
OH YEAH?
WHAT'D YOU GUYS DO?
NOT TELLING.
HUH?
HEH
I THINK I MIGHT UNDERSTAND HOW YOU FEEL A LITTLE.

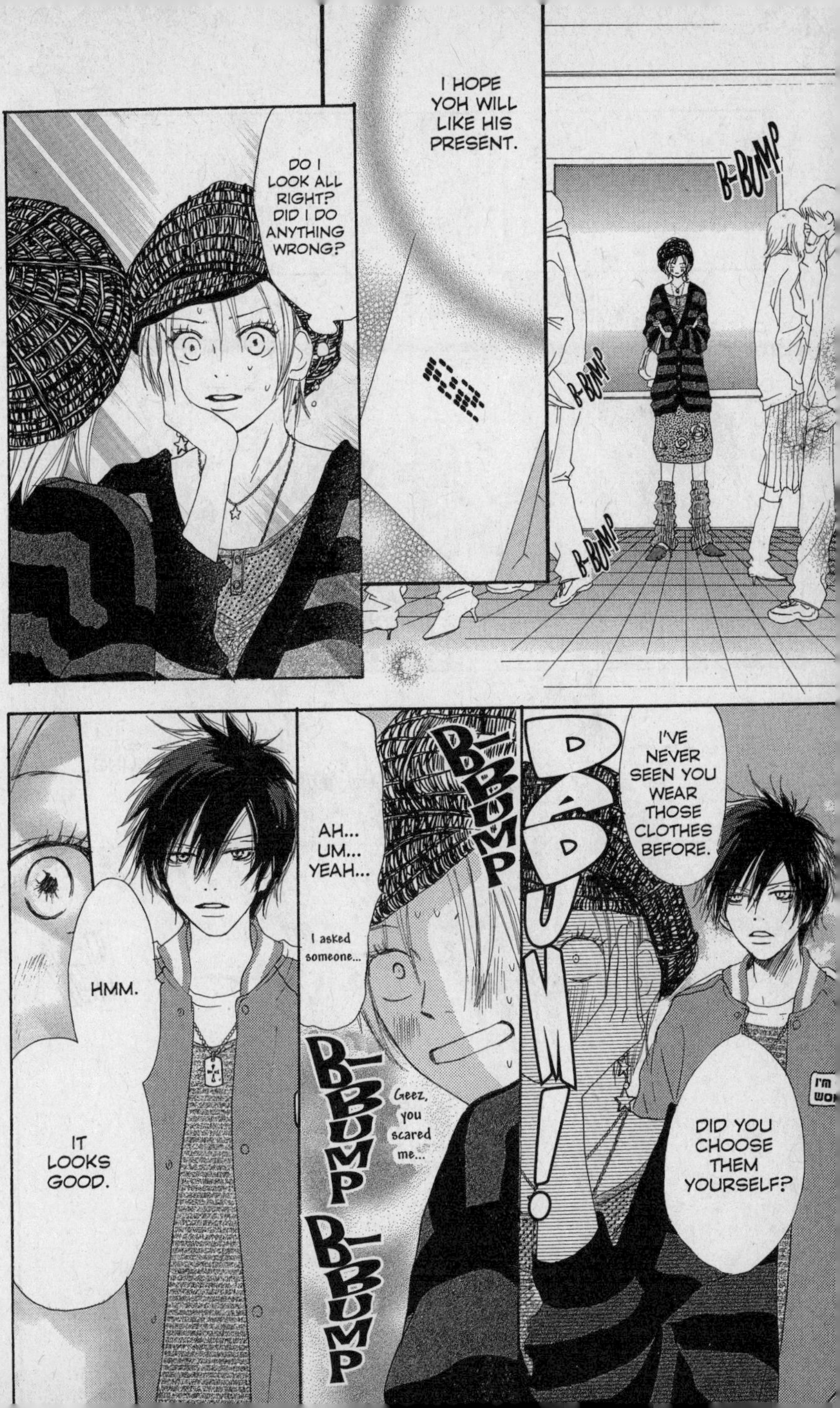
B-BUMP
B-BUMP
B-BUMP
I HOPE YOH WILL LIKE HIS PRESENT.
DO I LOOK ALL RIGHT? DID I DO ANYTHING WRONG?
I'VE NEVER SEEN YOU WEAR THOSE CLOTHES BEFORE.
DADUN!
DID YOU CHOOSE THEM YOURSELF?
B-BUMP
AH... UM... YEAH...
I asked someone...
B-BUMP
Geez, you scared me...
B-BUMP
HMM.
IT LOOKS GOOD.

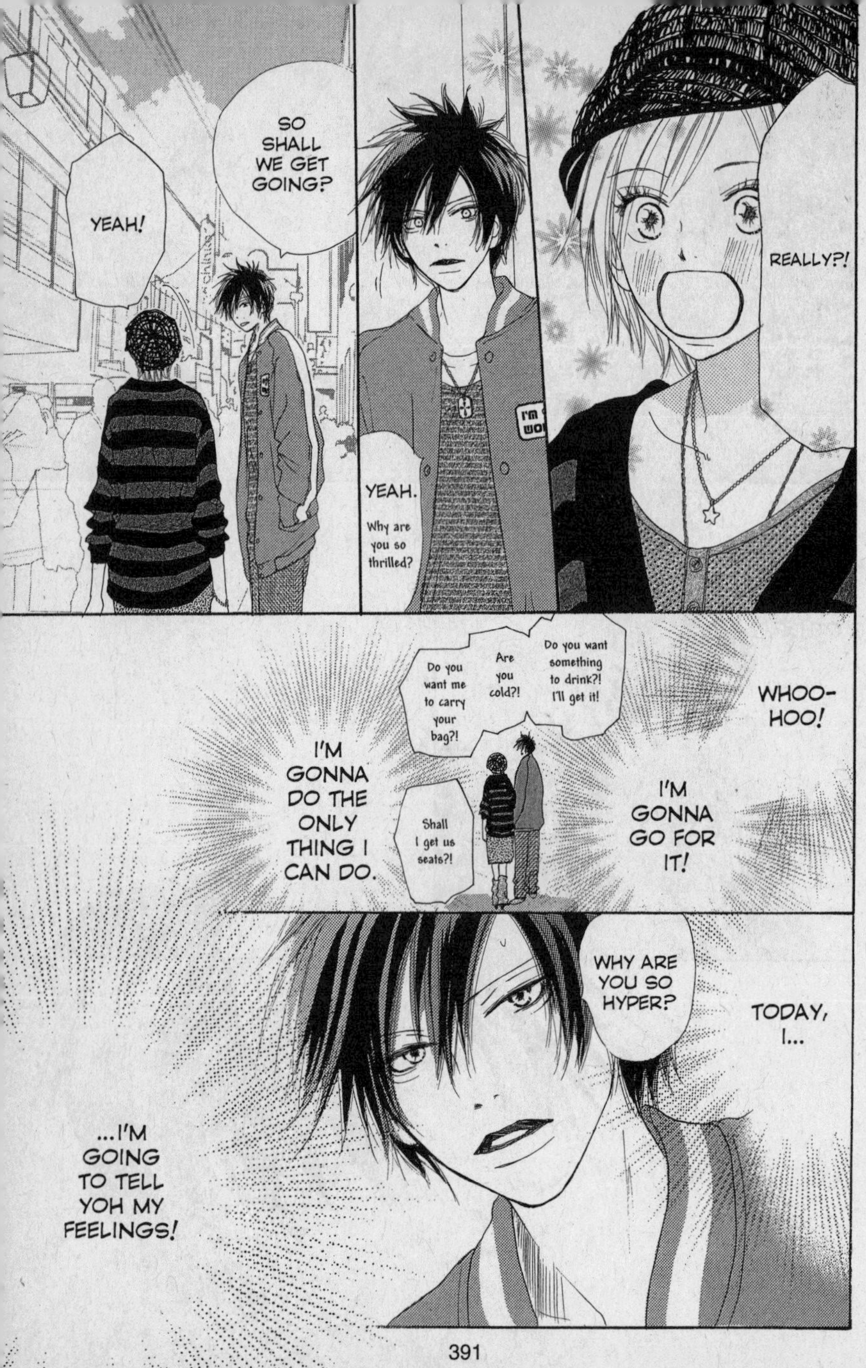
REALLY?!
YEAH.
Why are you so thrilled?
SO SHALL WE GET GOING?
YEAH!
WHOO-HOO!
Do you want something to drink?! I'll get it!
Are you cold?!
Do you want me to carry your bag?!
I'M GONNA GO FOR IT!
Shall I get us seats?!
I'M GONNA DO THE ONLY THING I CAN DO.
TODAY, I...
WHY ARE YOU SO HYPER?
...I'M GOING TO TELL YOH MY FEELINGS!

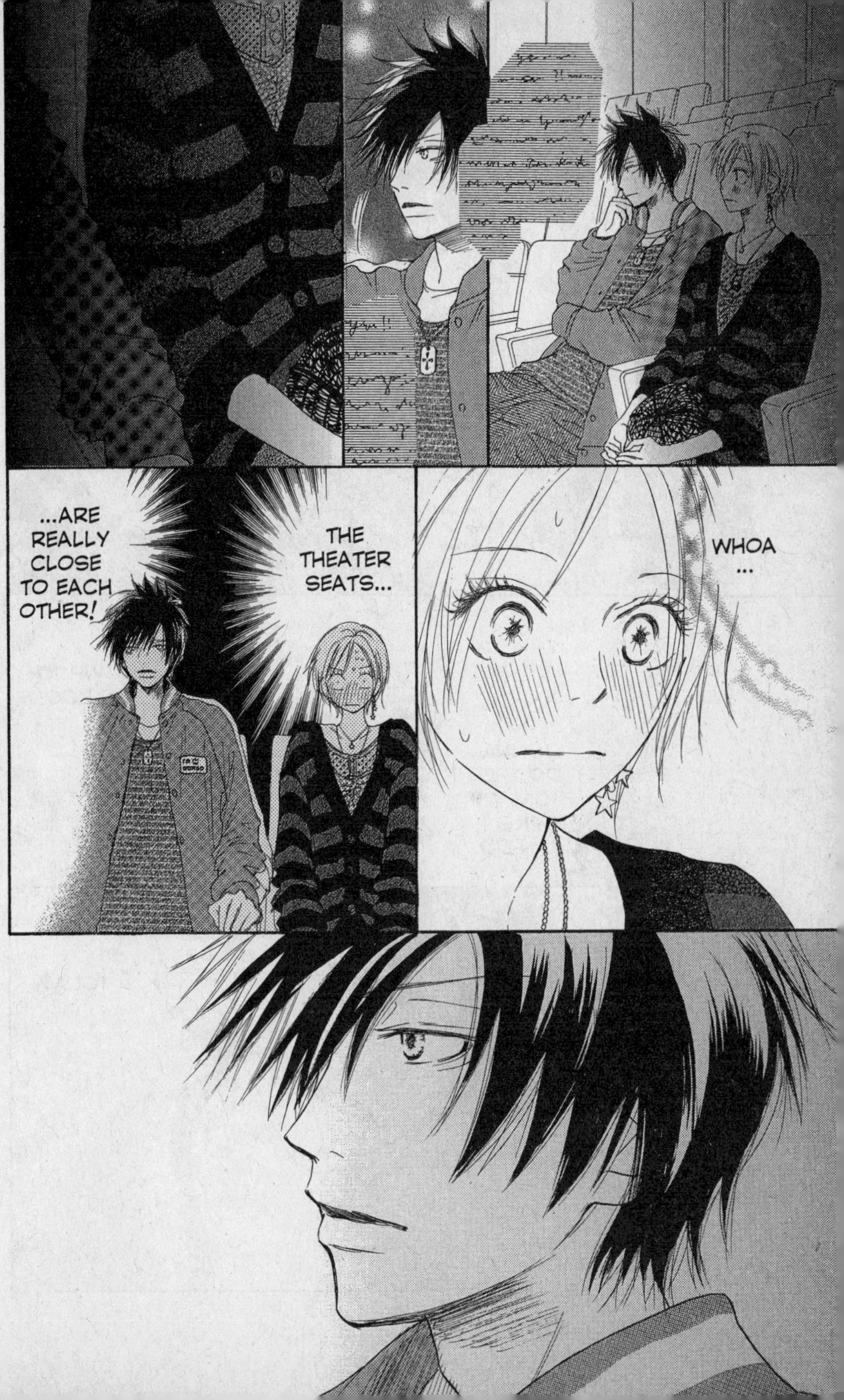
WHOA ...
THE THEATER SEATS...
...ARE REALLY CLOSE TO EACH OTHER!

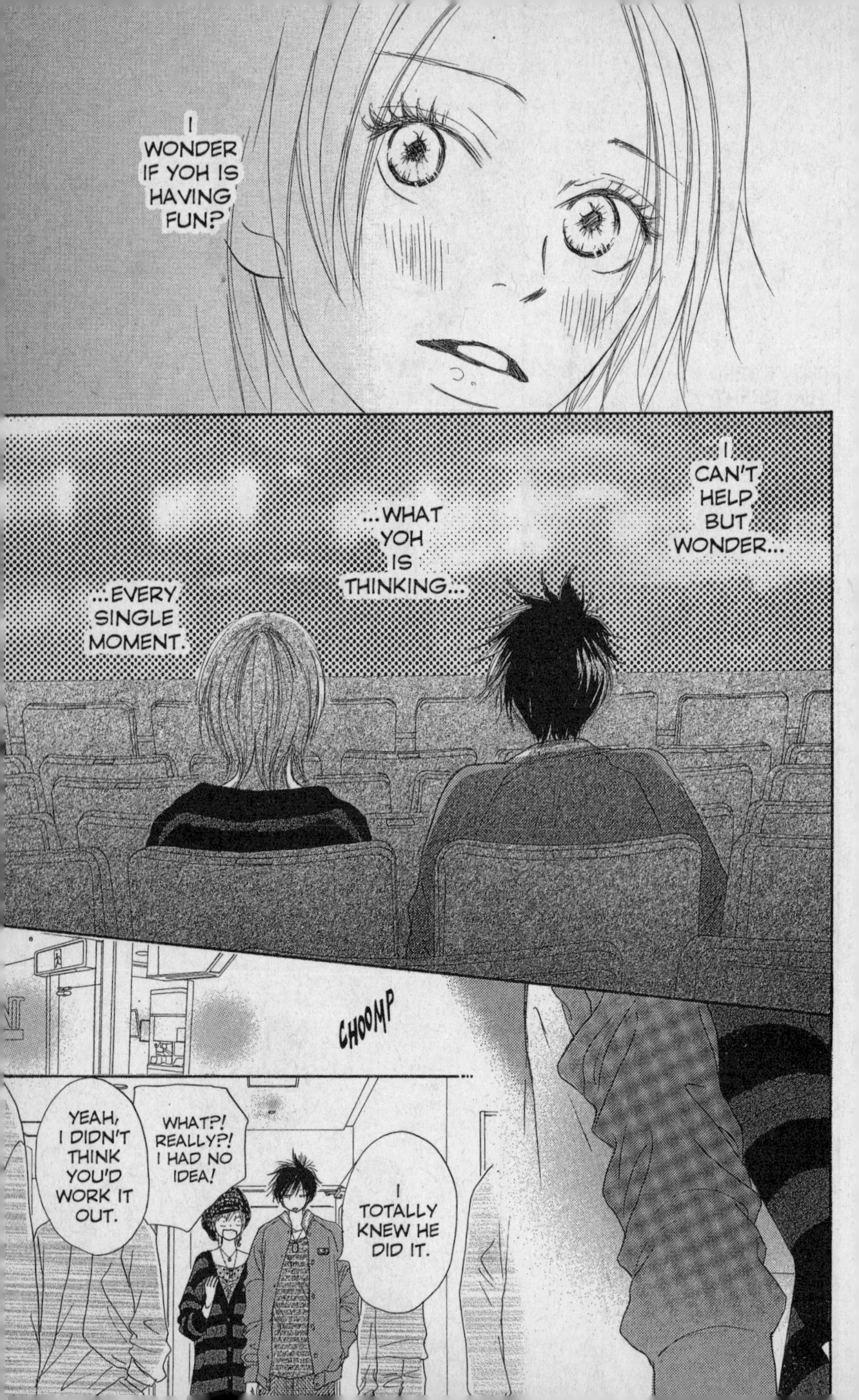
I WONDER IF YOH IS HAVING FUN?
I CAN'T HELP BUT WONDER...
...WHAT YOH IS THINKING...
...EVERY SINGLE MOMENT.
CHOOMP
I TOTALLY KNEW HE DID IT.
WHAT?! REALLY?! I HAD NO IDEA!
YEAH, I DIDN'T THINK YOU'D WORK IT OUT.

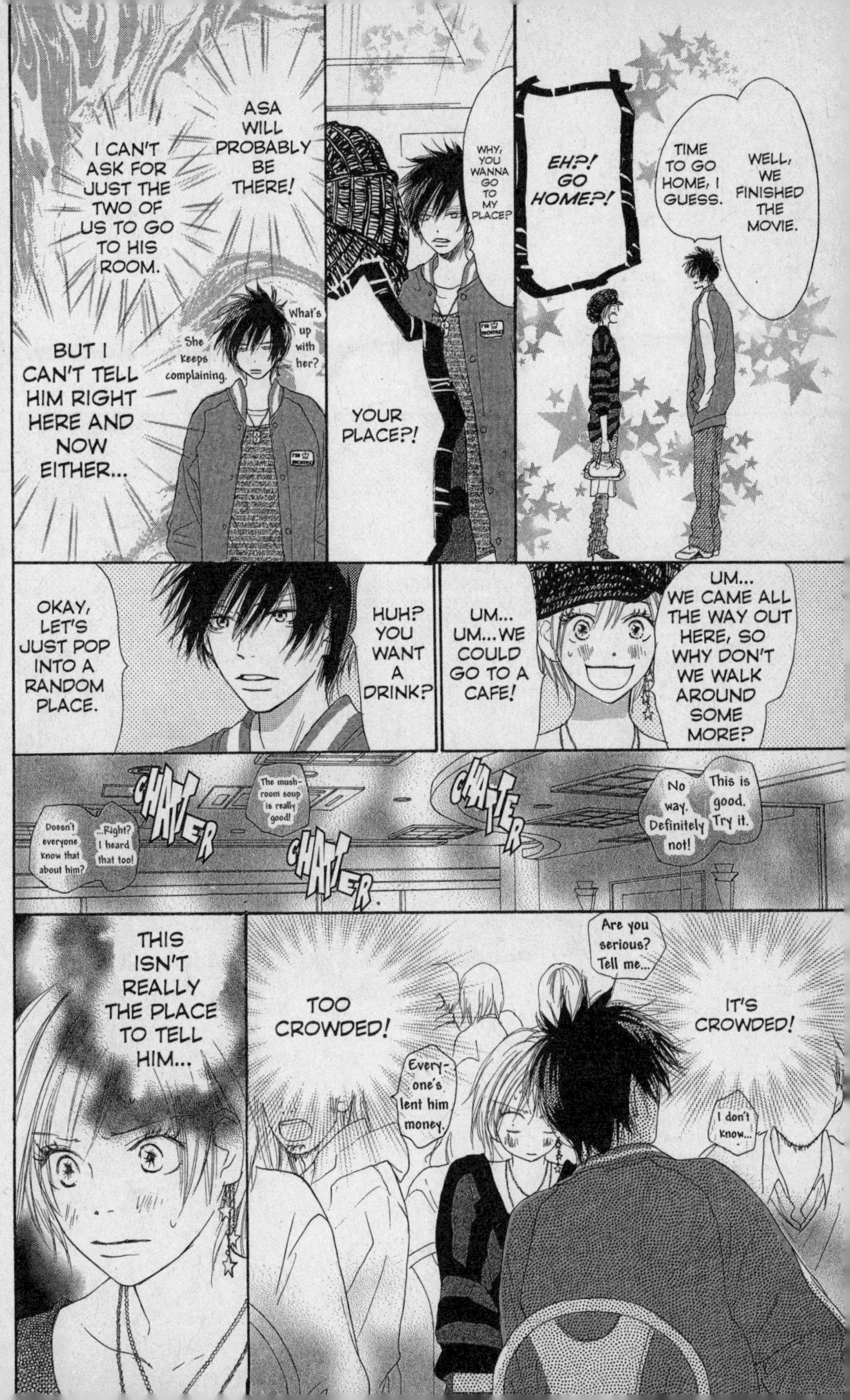
WELL, WE FINISHED THE MOVIE.
TIME TO GO HOME, I GUESS.
EH?! GO HOME?!
WHY, YOU WANNA GO TO MY PLACE?
YOUR PLACE?!
ASA WILL PROBABLY BE THERE!
I CAN'T ASK FOR JUST THE TWO OF US TO GO TO HIS ROOM.
What's up with her?
She keeps complaining.
BUT I CAN'T TELL HIM RIGHT HERE AND NOW EITHER...
UM... WE CAME ALL THE WAY OUT HERE, SO WHY DON'T WE WALK AROUND SOME MORE?
UM... UM...WE COULD GO TO A CAFE!
HUH? YOU WANT A DRINK?
OKAY, LET'S JUST POP INTO A RANDOM PLACE.
This is good. Try it.
No way. Definitely not!
CHATTER
The mush-room soup is really good!
CHATTER
...Right? I heard that too!
Doesn't everyone know that about him?
CHATTER
IT'S CROWDED!
Are you serious? Tell me...
I don't know...
Every-one's lent him money.
TOO CROWDED!
THIS ISN'T REALLY THE PLACE TO TELL HIM...

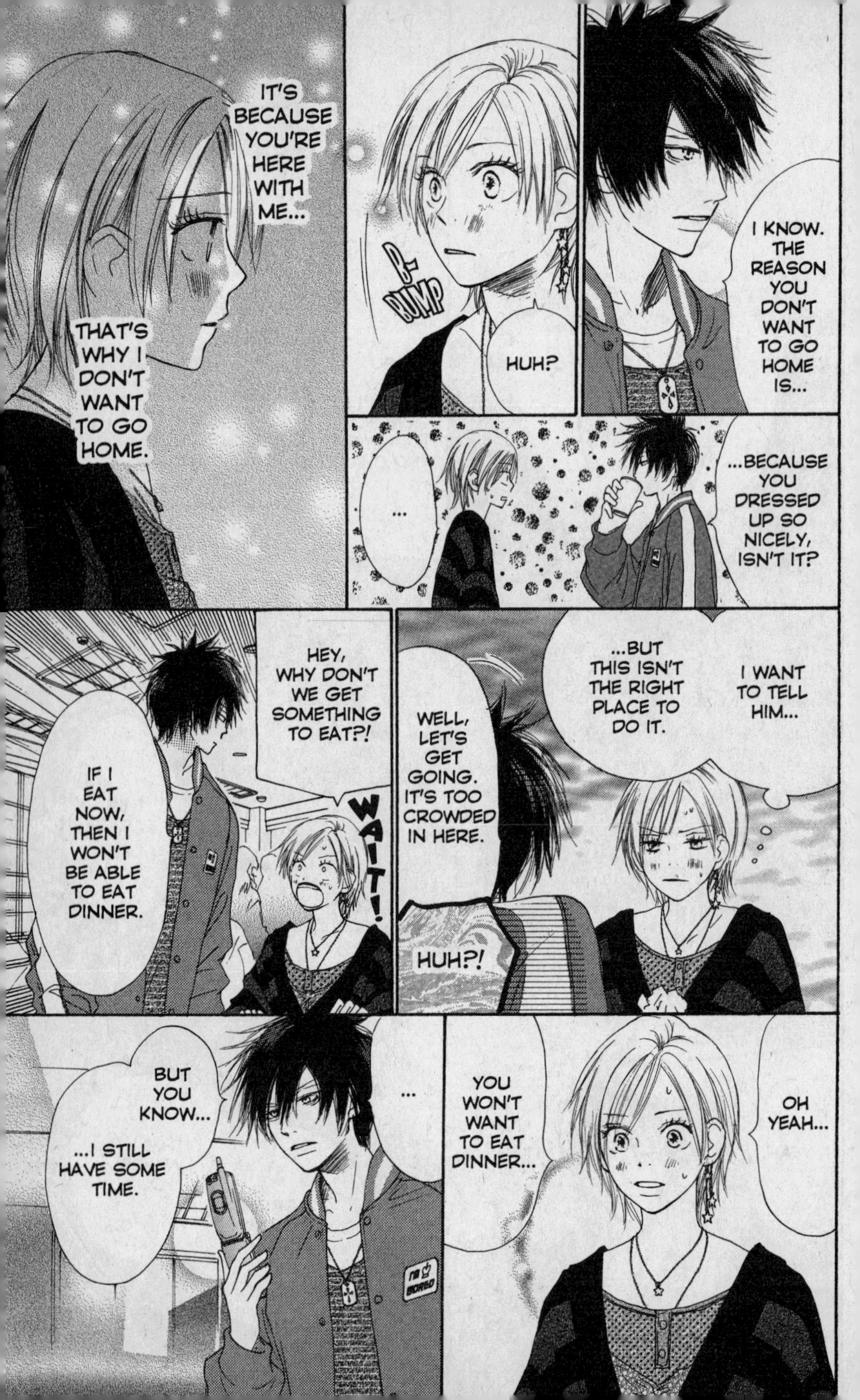
I KNOW. THE REASON YOU DON'T WANT TO GO HOME IS...
B-BUMP
HUH?
...BECAUSE YOU DRESSED UP SO NICELY, ISN'T IT?
...
IT'S BECAUSE YOU'RE HERE WITH ME...
THAT'S WHY I DON'T WANT TO GO HOME.
I WANT TO TELL HIM...
...BUT THIS ISN'T THE RIGHT PLACE TO DO IT.
WELL, LET'S GET GOING. IT'S TOO CROWDED IN HERE.
HUH?!
HEY, WHY DON'T WE GET SOMETHING TO EAT?!
WAIT!
IF I EAT NOW, THEN I WON'T BE ABLE TO EAT DINNER.
OH YEAH...
YOU WON'T WANT TO EAT DINNER...
...
BUT YOU KNOW...
...I STILL HAVE SOME TIME.

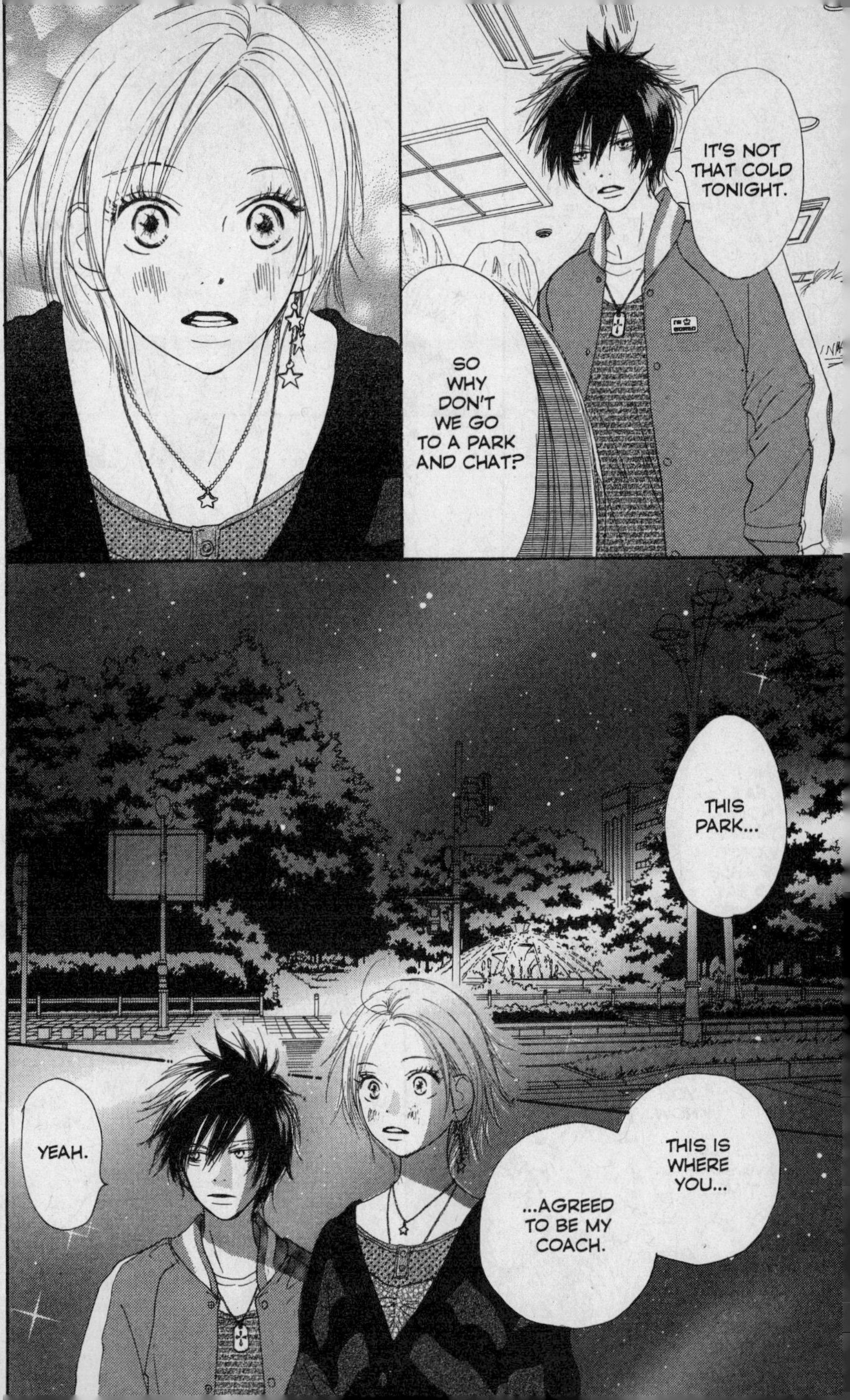
IT'S NOT THAT COLD TONIGHT.
SO WHY DON'T WE GO TO A PARK AND CHAT?
THIS PARK...
THIS IS WHERE YOU...
...AGREED TO BE MY COACH.
YEAH.

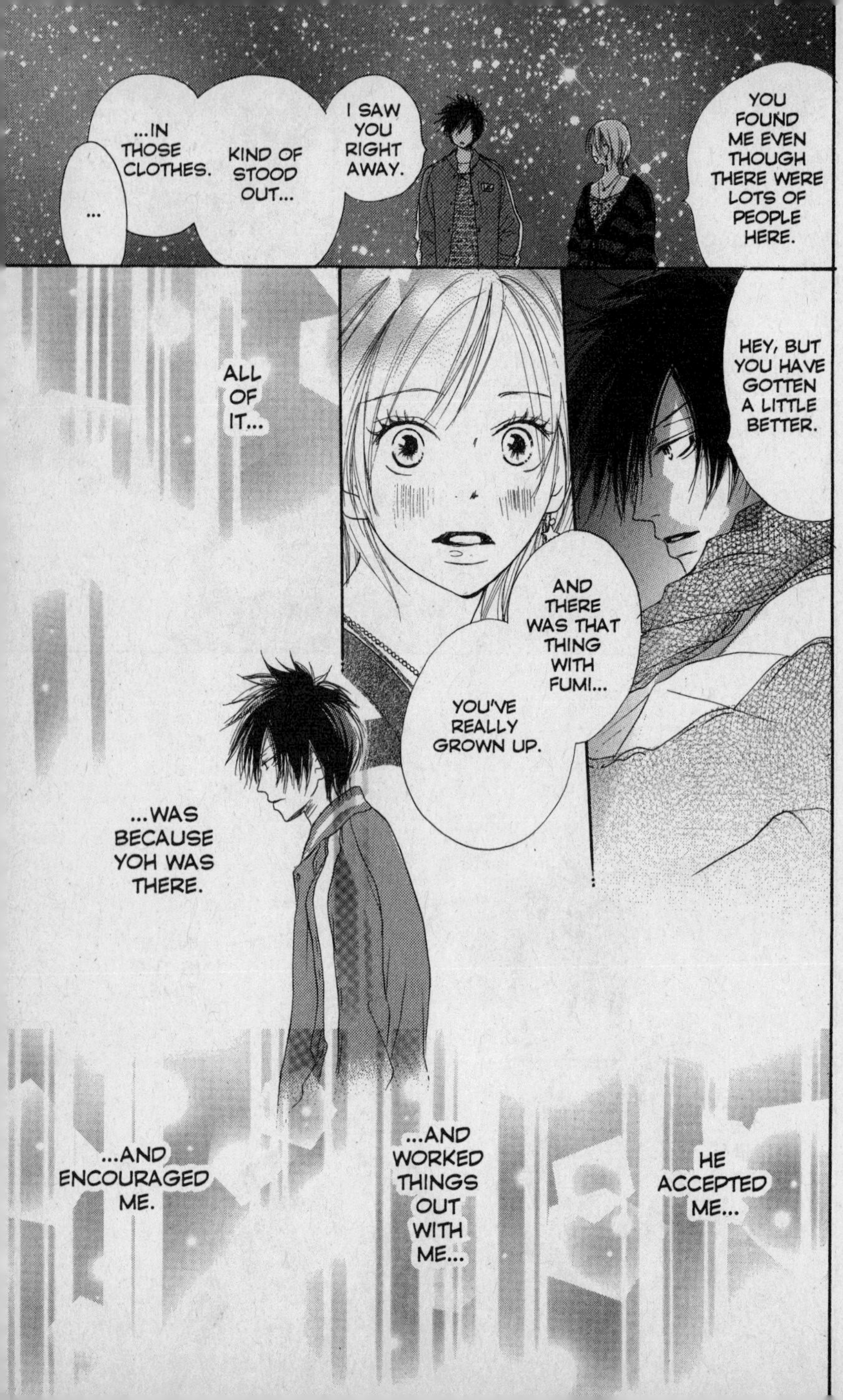
YOU FOUND ME EVEN THOUGH THERE WERE LOTS OF PEOPLE HERE.
I SAW YOU RIGHT AWAY.
KIND OF STOOD OUT...
...IN THOSE CLOTHES.
...
HEY, BUT YOU HAVE GOTTEN A LITTLE BETTER.
AND THERE WAS THAT THING WITH FUMI...
YOU'VE REALLY GROWN UP.
ALL OF IT...
...WAS BECAUSE YOH WAS THERE.
HE ACCEPTED ME...
...AND WORKED THINGS OUT WITH ME...
...AND ENCOURAGED ME.

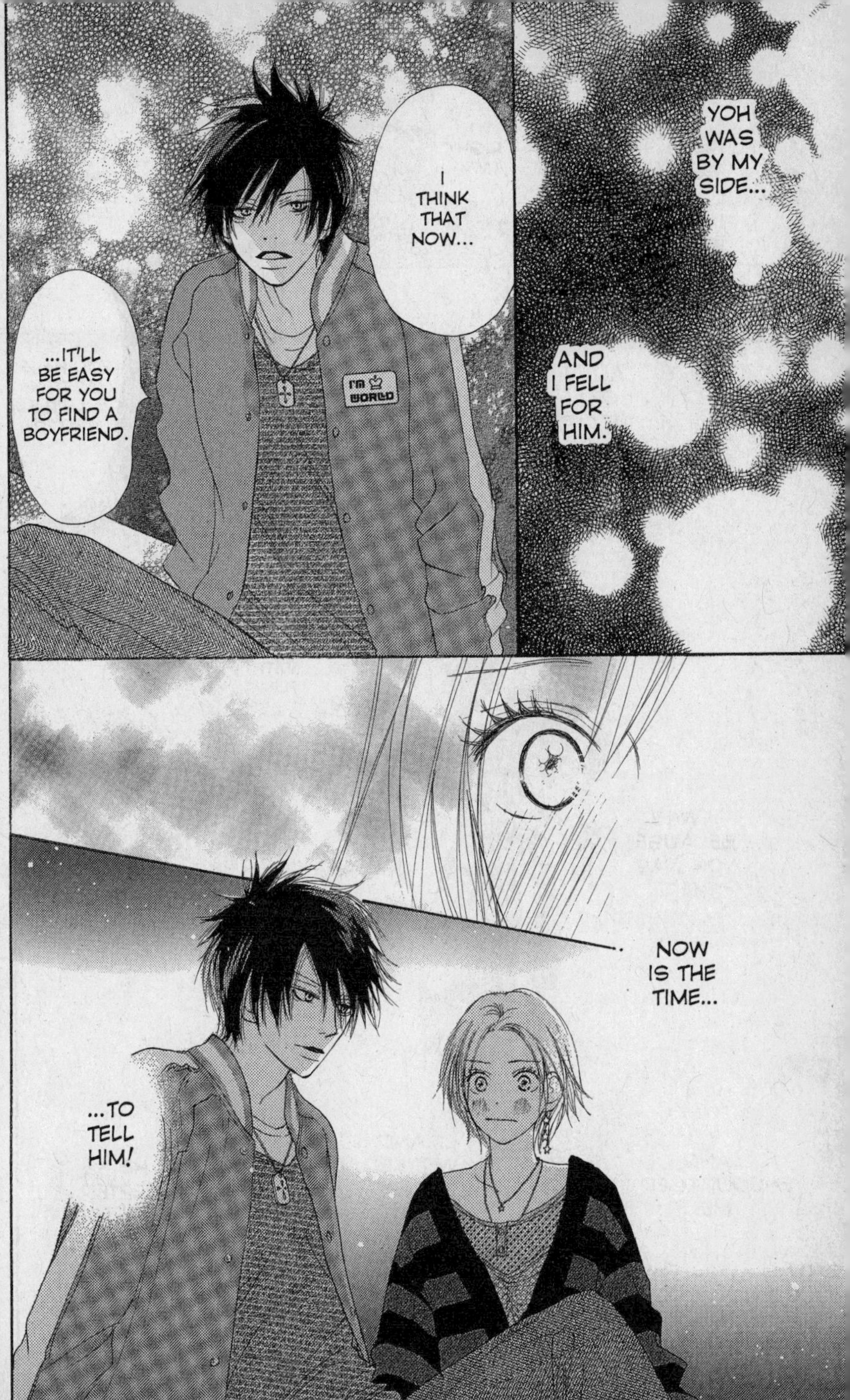
YOH WAS BY MY SIDE...
AND I FELL FOR HIM.
I THINK THAT NOW...
...IT'LL BE EASY FOR YOU TO FIND A BOYFRIEND.
NOW IS THE TIME...
...TO TELL HIM!

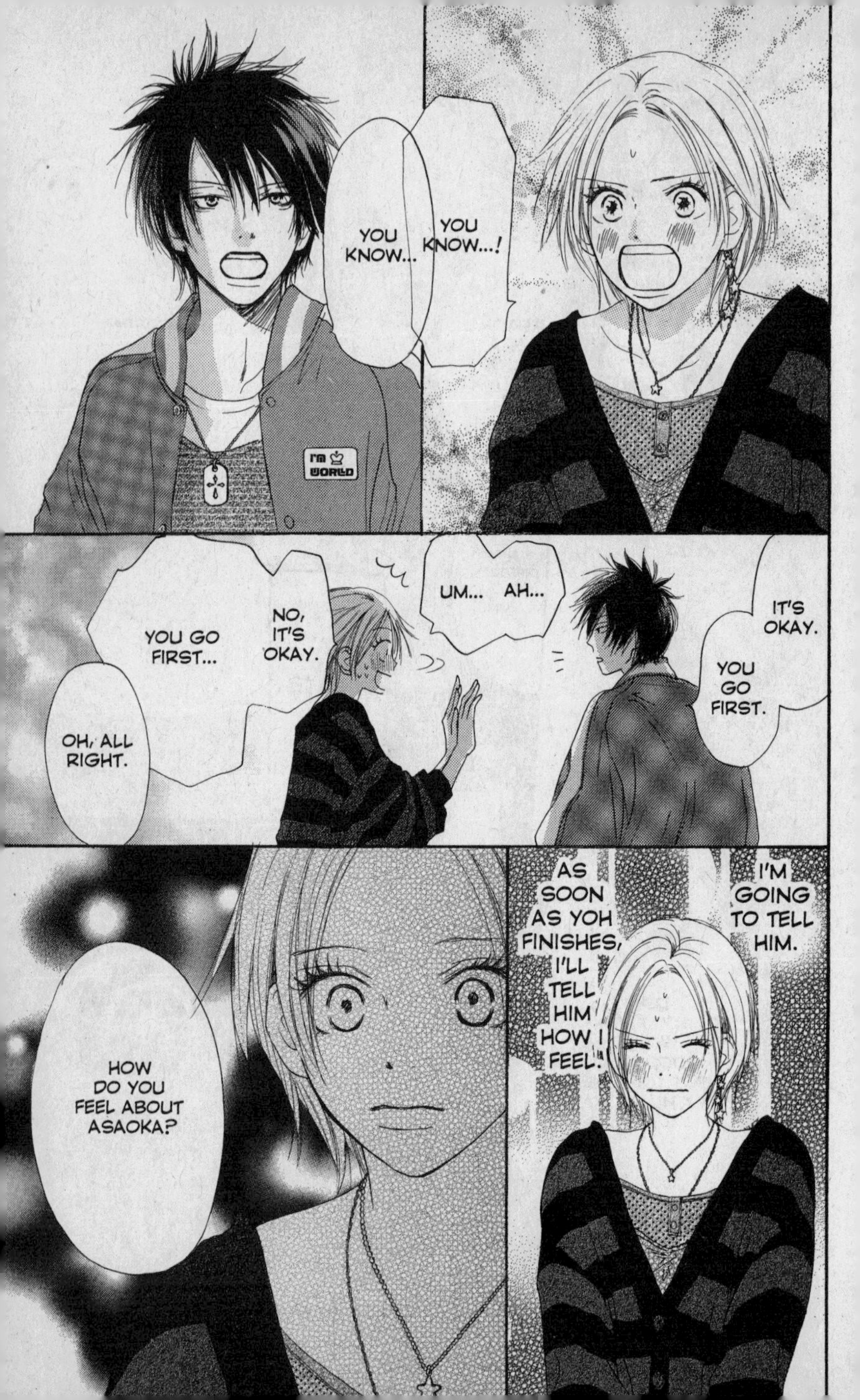
YOU KNOW...!
YOU KNOW...
IT'S OKAY. YOU GO FIRST.
UM... AH...
NO, IT'S OKAY. YOU GO FIRST...
OH, ALL RIGHT.
I'M GOING TO TELL HIM.
AS SOON AS YOH FINISHES, I'LL TELL HIM HOW I FEEL.
HOW DO YOU FEEL ABOUT ASAOKA?

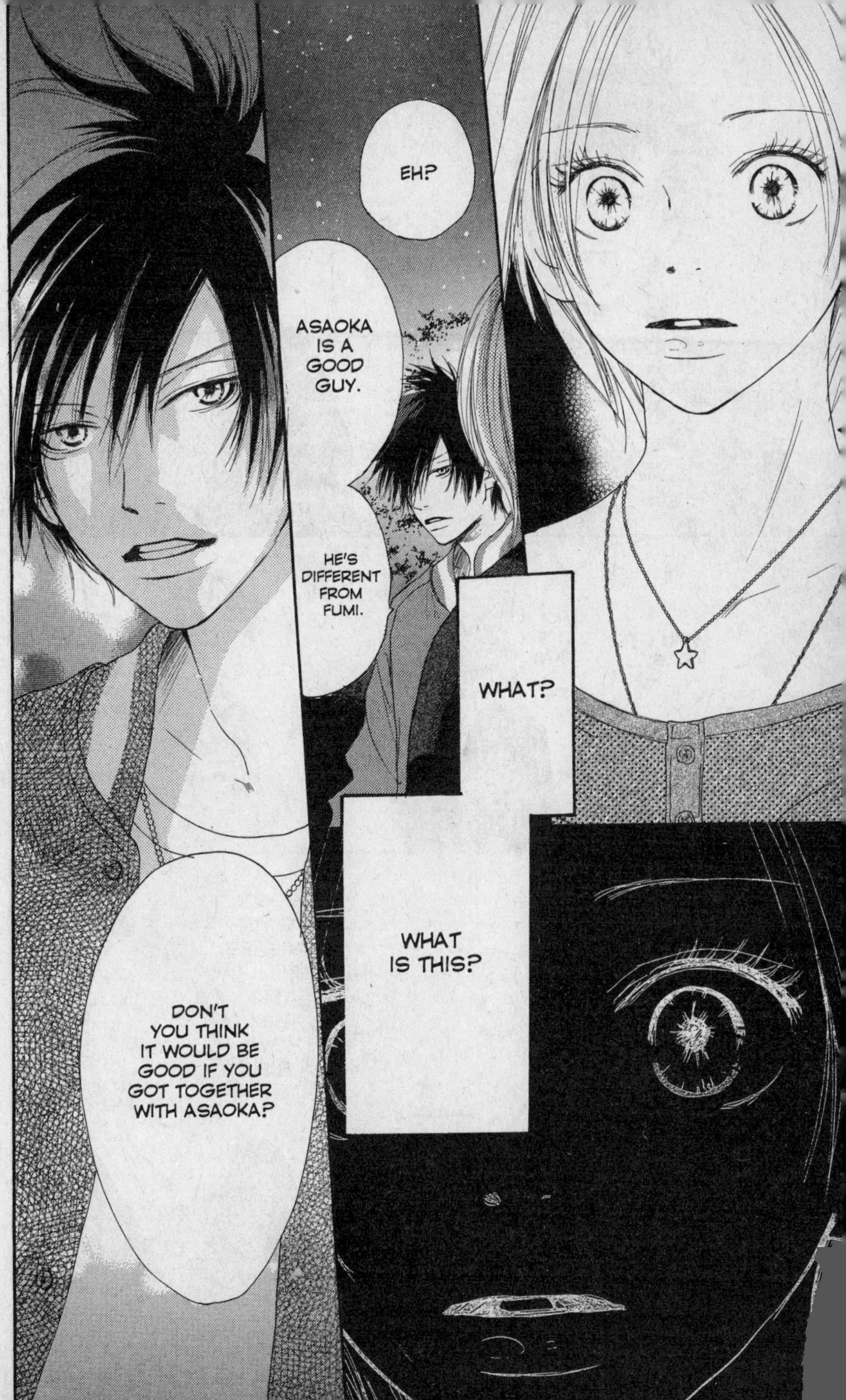
EH?
ASAOKA IS A GOOD GUY.
HE'S DIFFERENT FROM FUMI.
DON'T YOU THINK IT WOULD BE GOOD IF YOU GOT TOGETHER WITH ASAOKA?
WHAT?
WHAT IS THIS?

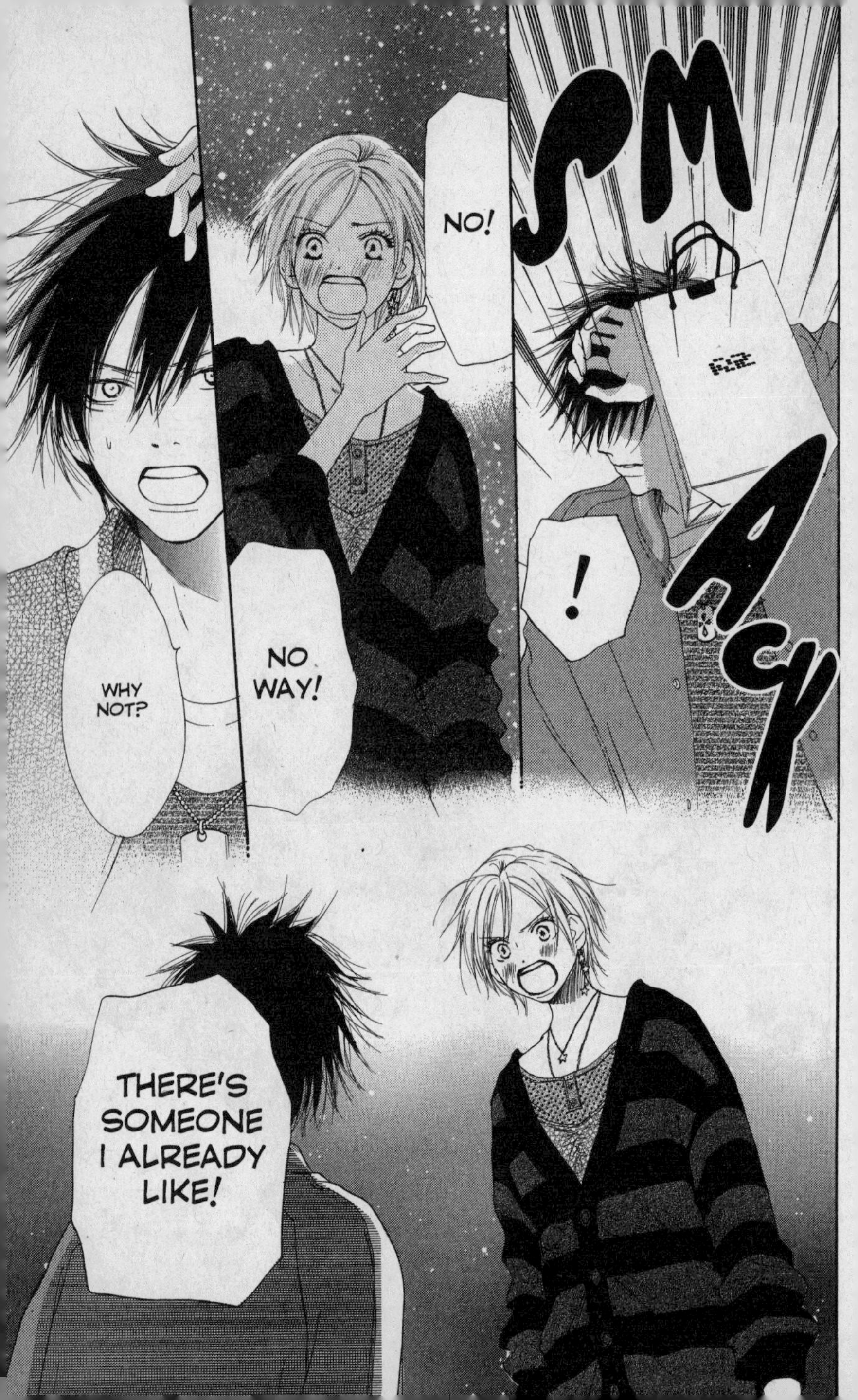
SMACK
!
NO!
NO WAY!
WHY NOT?
THERE'S SOMEONE I ALREADY LIKE!

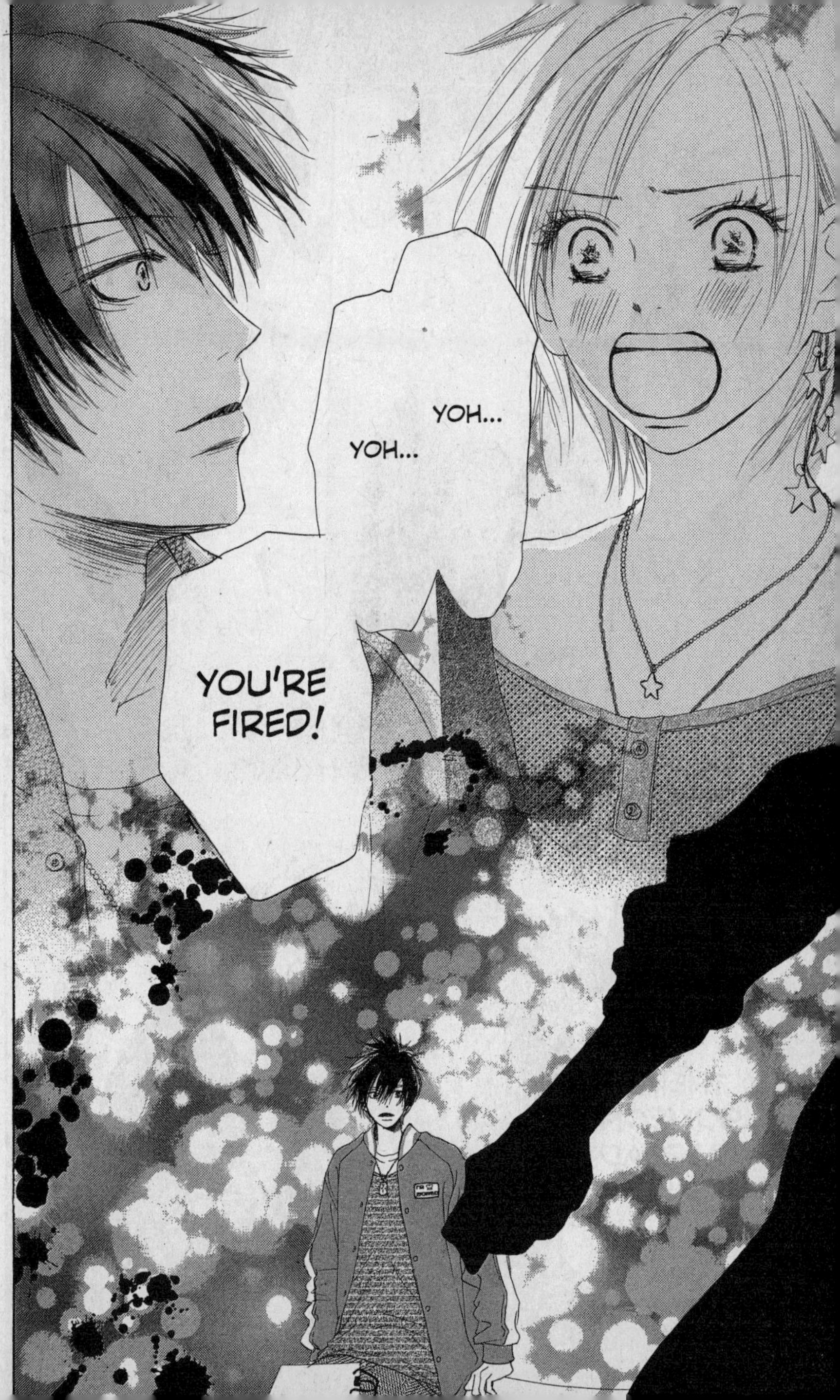
YOH... YOH...
YOU'RE FIRED!

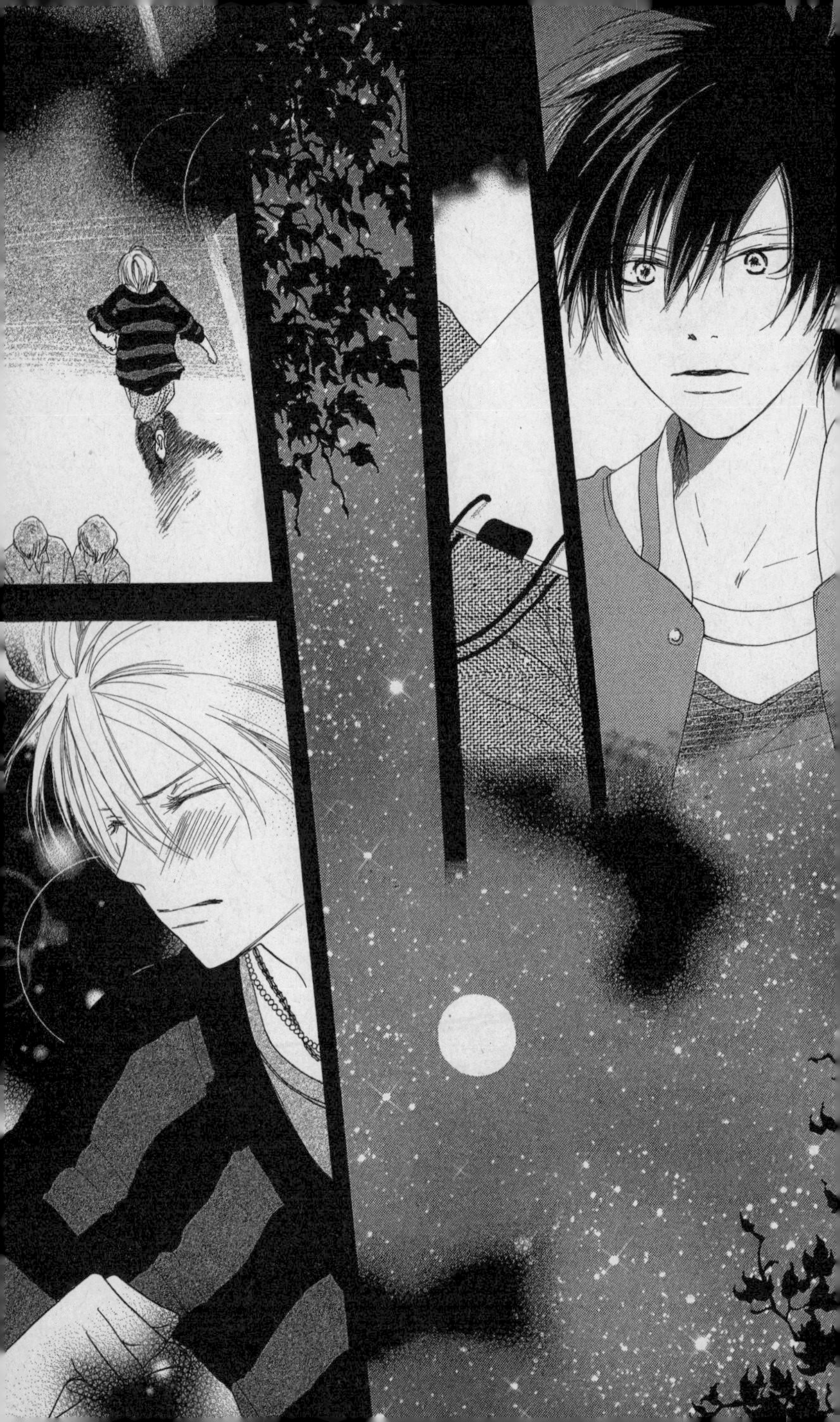

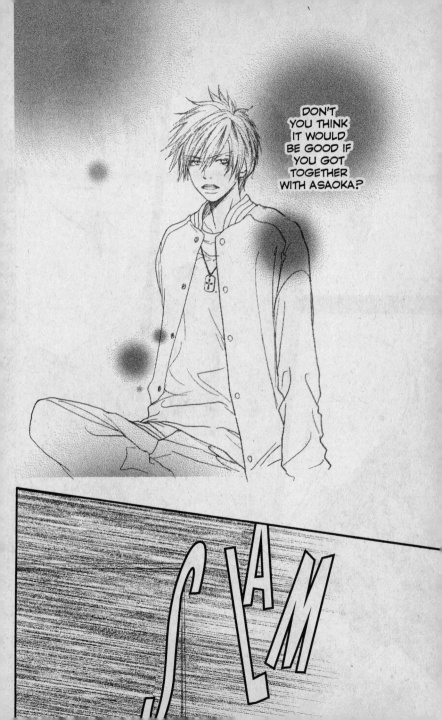

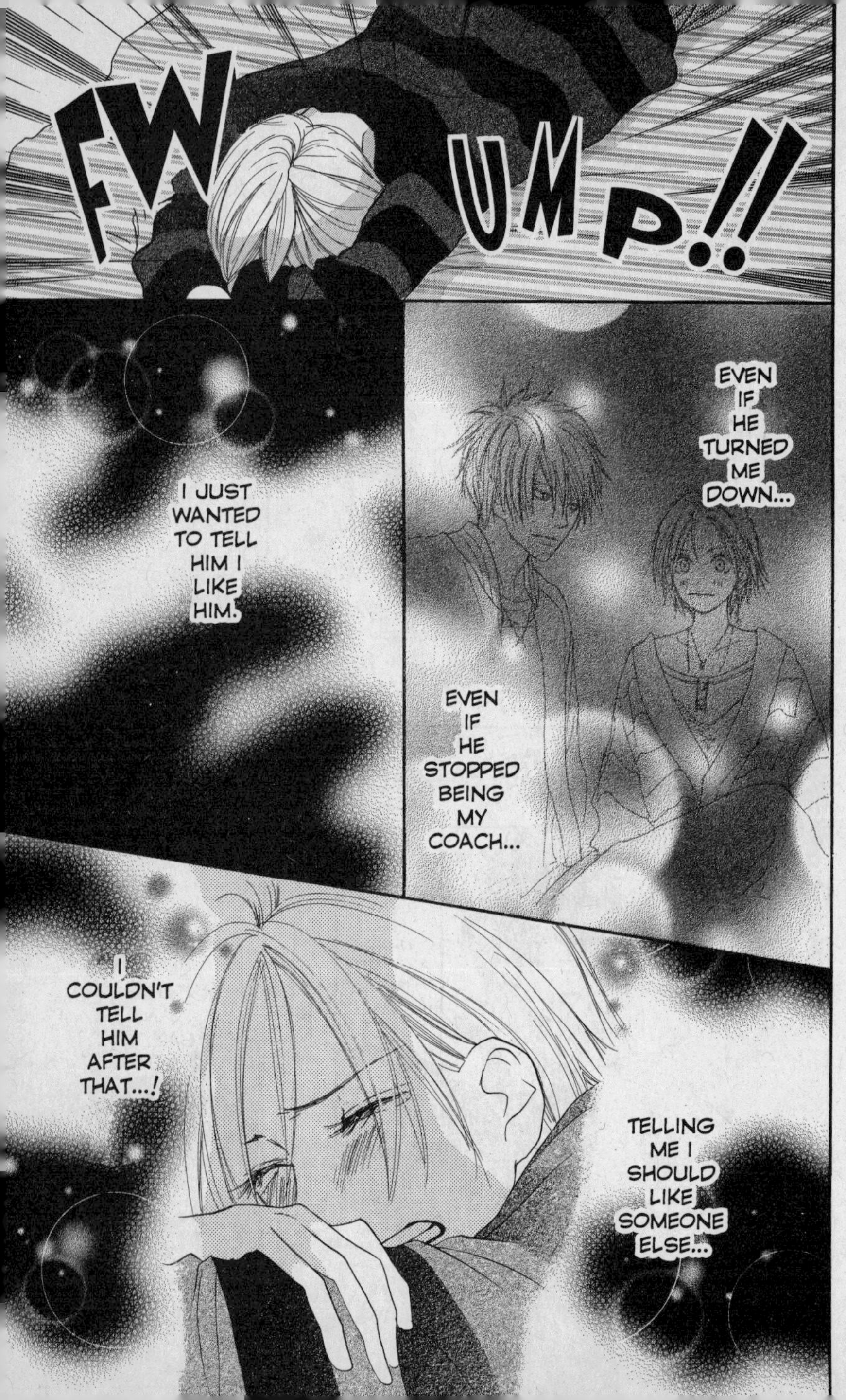
FWUMP!!
EVEN IF HE TURNED ME DOWN...
EVEN IF HE STOPPED BEING MY COACH...
I JUST WANTED TO TELL HIM I LIKE HIM.
TELLING ME I SHOULD LIKE SOMEONE ELSE...
I COULDN'T TELL HIM AFTER THAT...!

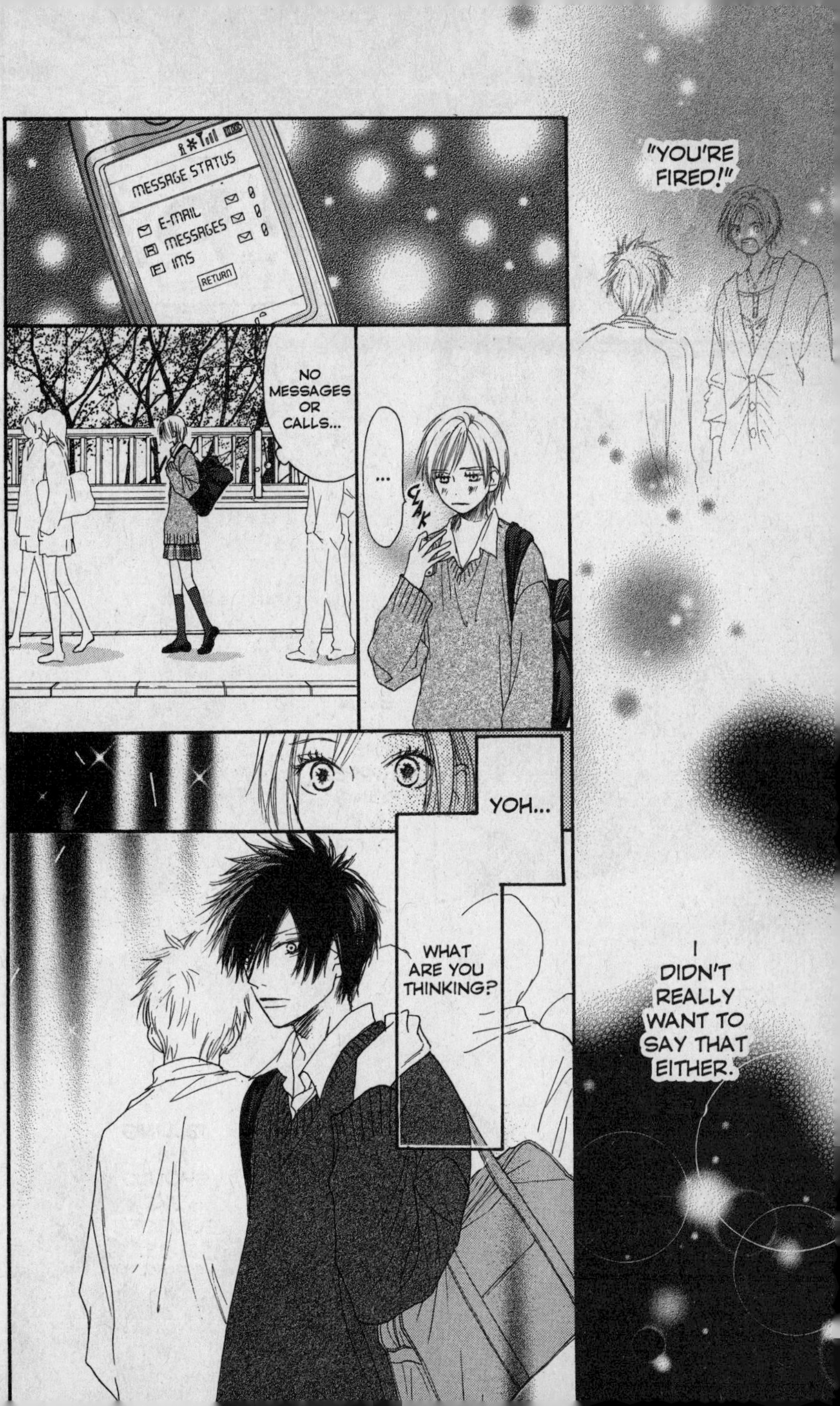
"YOU'RE FIRED!"
I DIDN'T REALLY WANT TO SAY THAT EITHER.
MESSAGE STATUS
E-MAIL 0
MESSAGES 0
IMS 0
RETURN
...
CLAK
NO MESSAGES OR CALLS...
YOH...
WHAT ARE YOU THINKING?

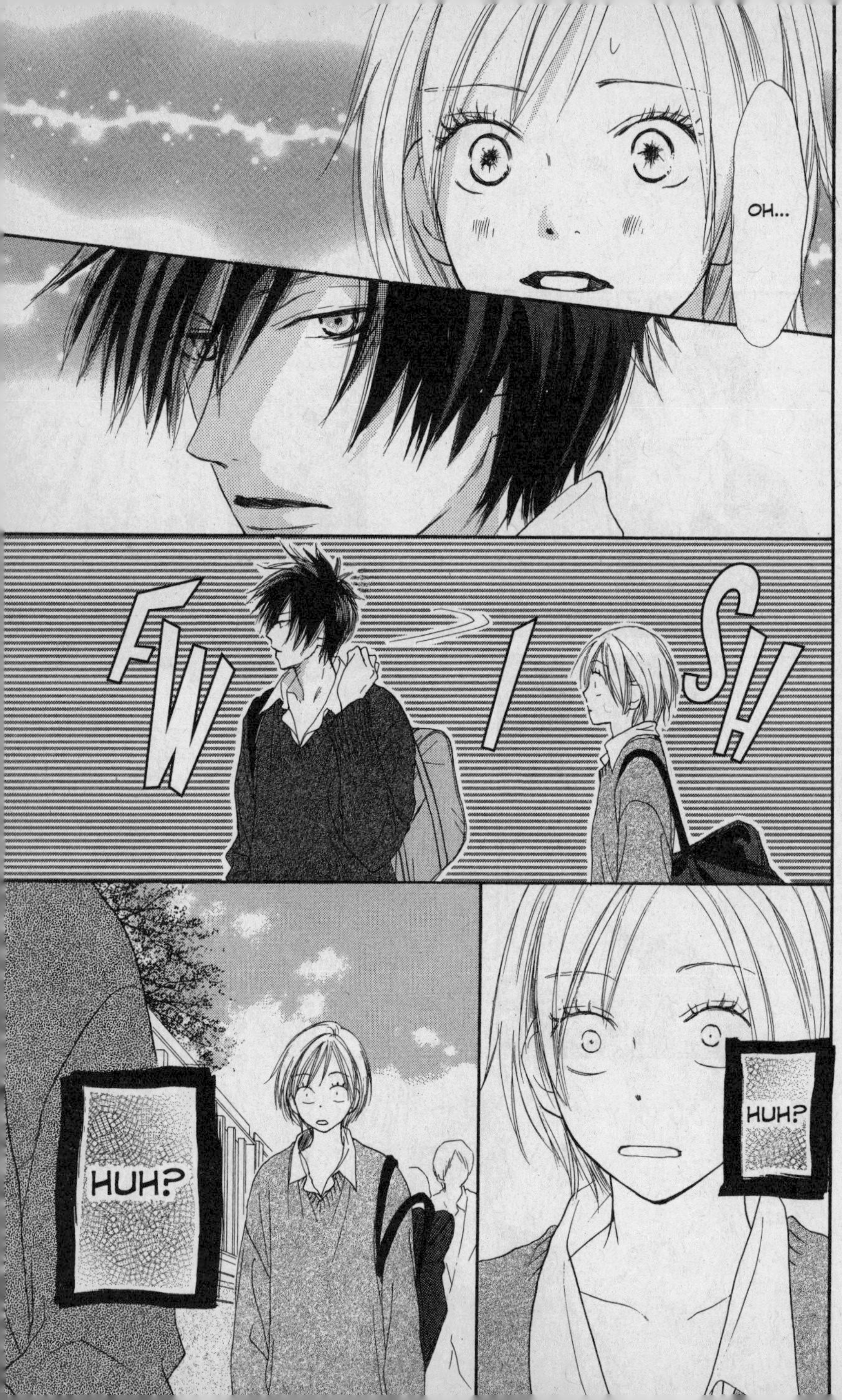
OH...
FWISH
HUH?
HUH?

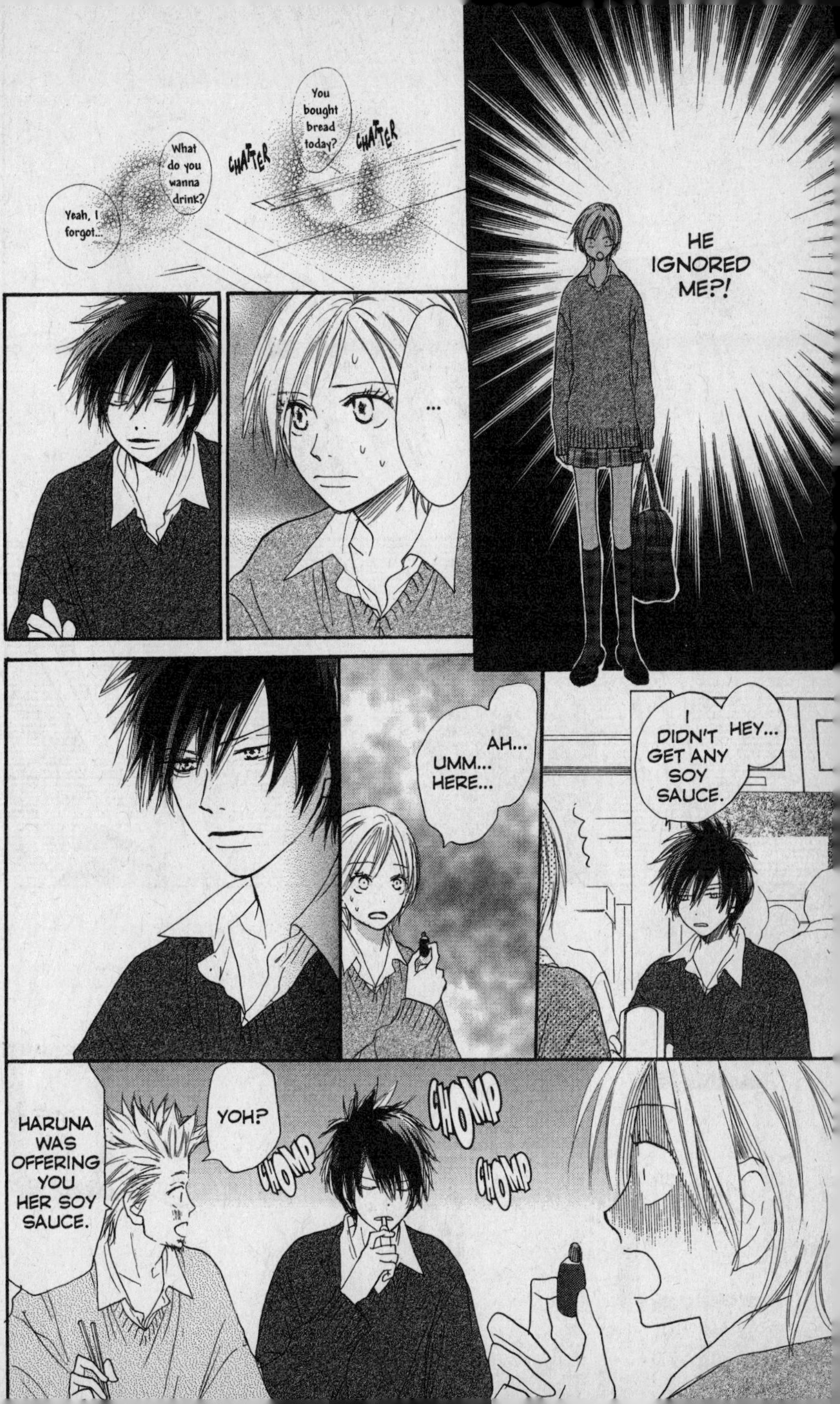
HE IGNORED ME?!
CHATTER
You bought bread today?
CHATTER
What do you wanna drink?
Yeah, I forgot...
...
HEY...
I DIDN'T GET ANY SOY SAUCE.
AH... UMM... HERE...
CHOMP
CHOMP
CHOMP
YOH?
HARUNA WAS OFFERING YOU HER SOY SAUCE.

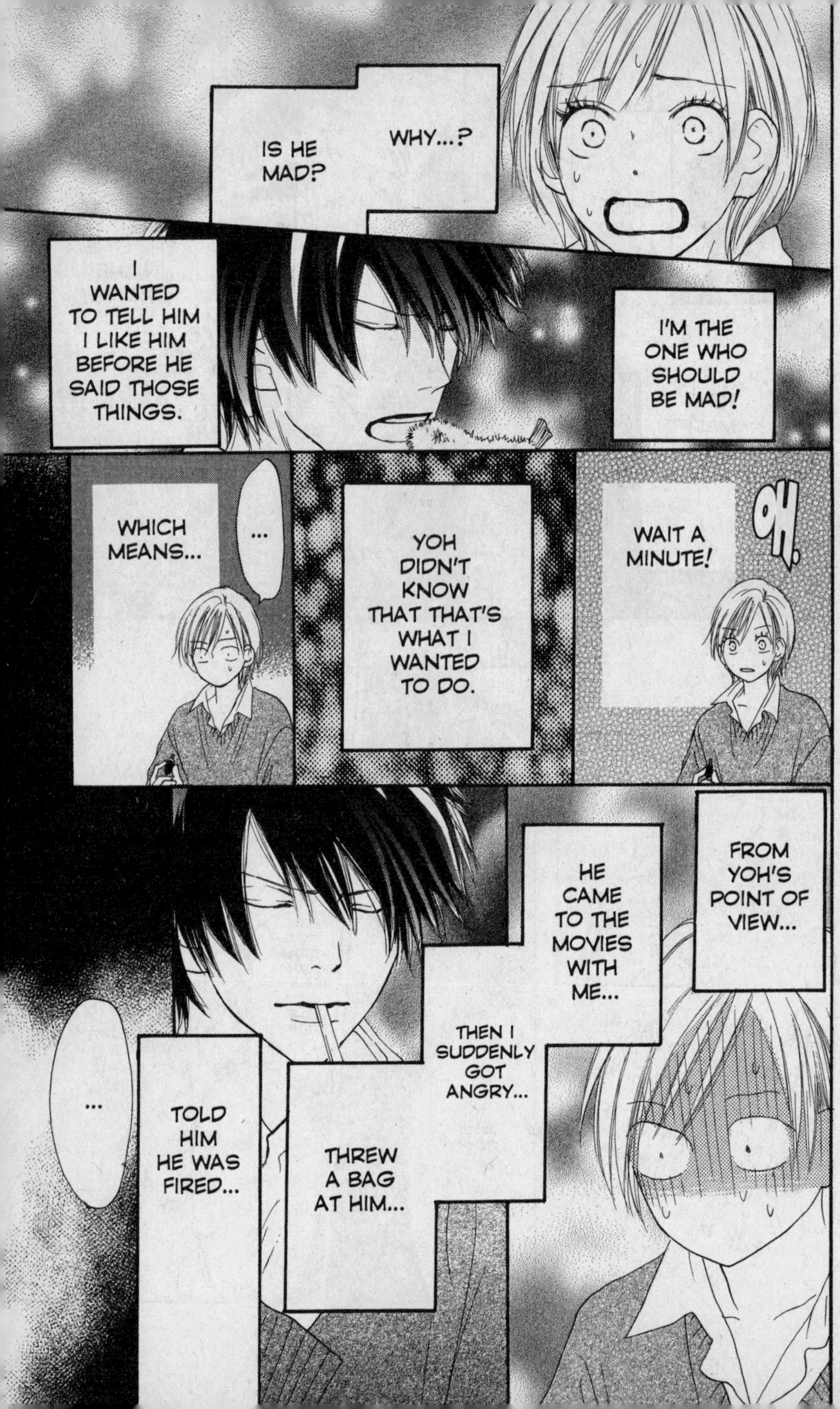
WHY...?
IS HE MAD?
I'M THE ONE WHO SHOULD BE MAD!
I WANTED TO TELL HIM I LIKE HIM BEFORE HE SAID THOSE THINGS.
OH.
WAIT A MINUTE!
YOH DIDN'T KNOW THAT THAT'S WHAT I WANTED TO DO.
...
WHICH MEANS...
FROM YOH'S POINT OF VIEW...
HE CAME TO THE MOVIES WITH ME...
THEN I SUDDENLY GOT ANGRY...
THREW A BAG AT HIM...
TOLD HIM HE WAS FIRED...
...

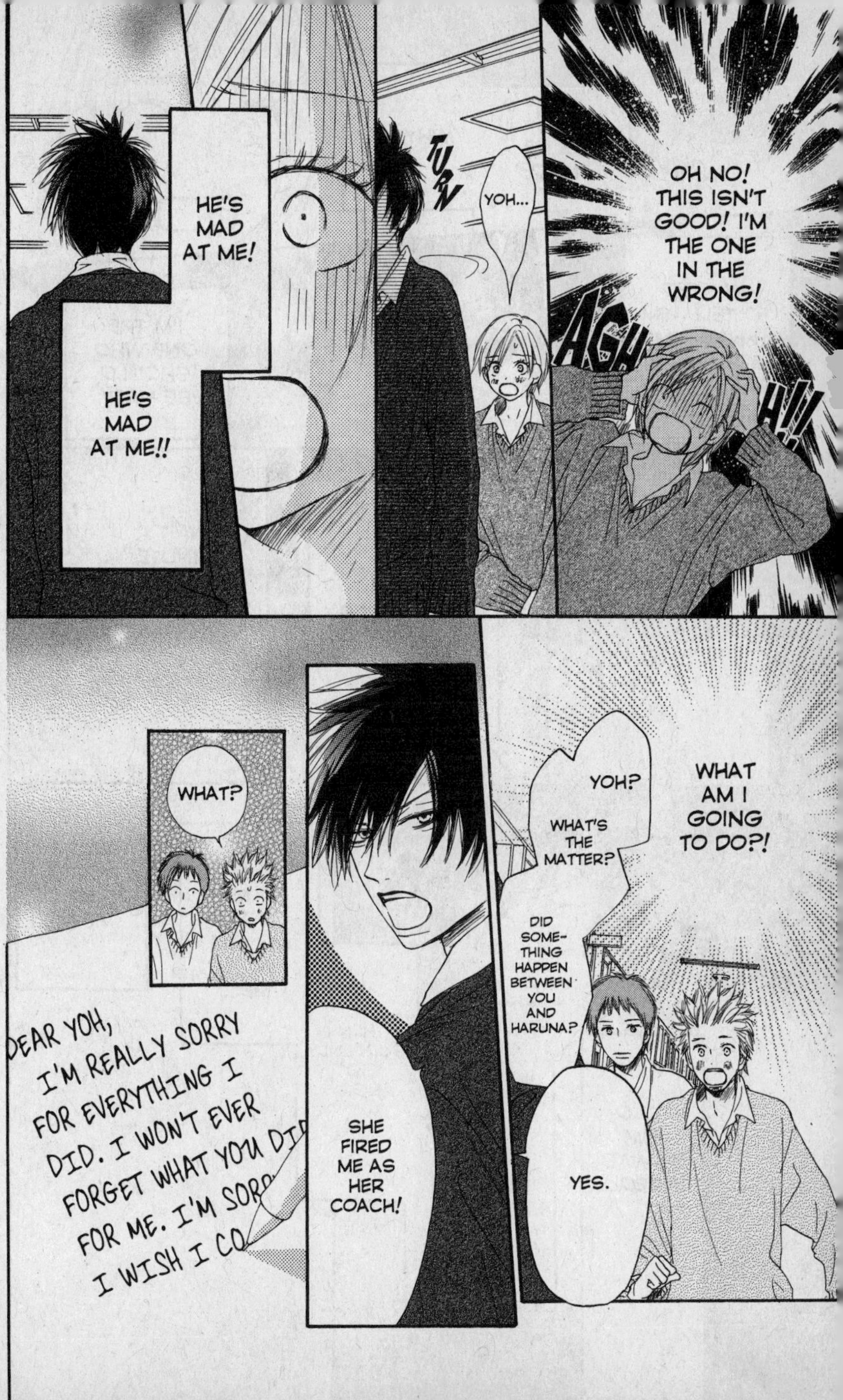
OH NO! THIS ISN'T GOOD! I'M THE ONE IN THE WRONG!
AGH
H!!
TURN
YOH...
HE'S MAD AT ME!
HE'S MAD AT ME!!
WHAT AM I GOING TO DO?!
YOH? WHAT'S THE MATTER?
DID SOMETHING HAPPEN BETWEEN YOU AND HARUNA?
YES.
SHE FIRED ME AS HER COACH!
WHAT?
DEAR YOH, I'M REALLY SORRY FOR EVERYTHING I DID. I WON'T EVER FORGET WHAT YOU DI
FOR ME. I'M SORR
I WISH I CO

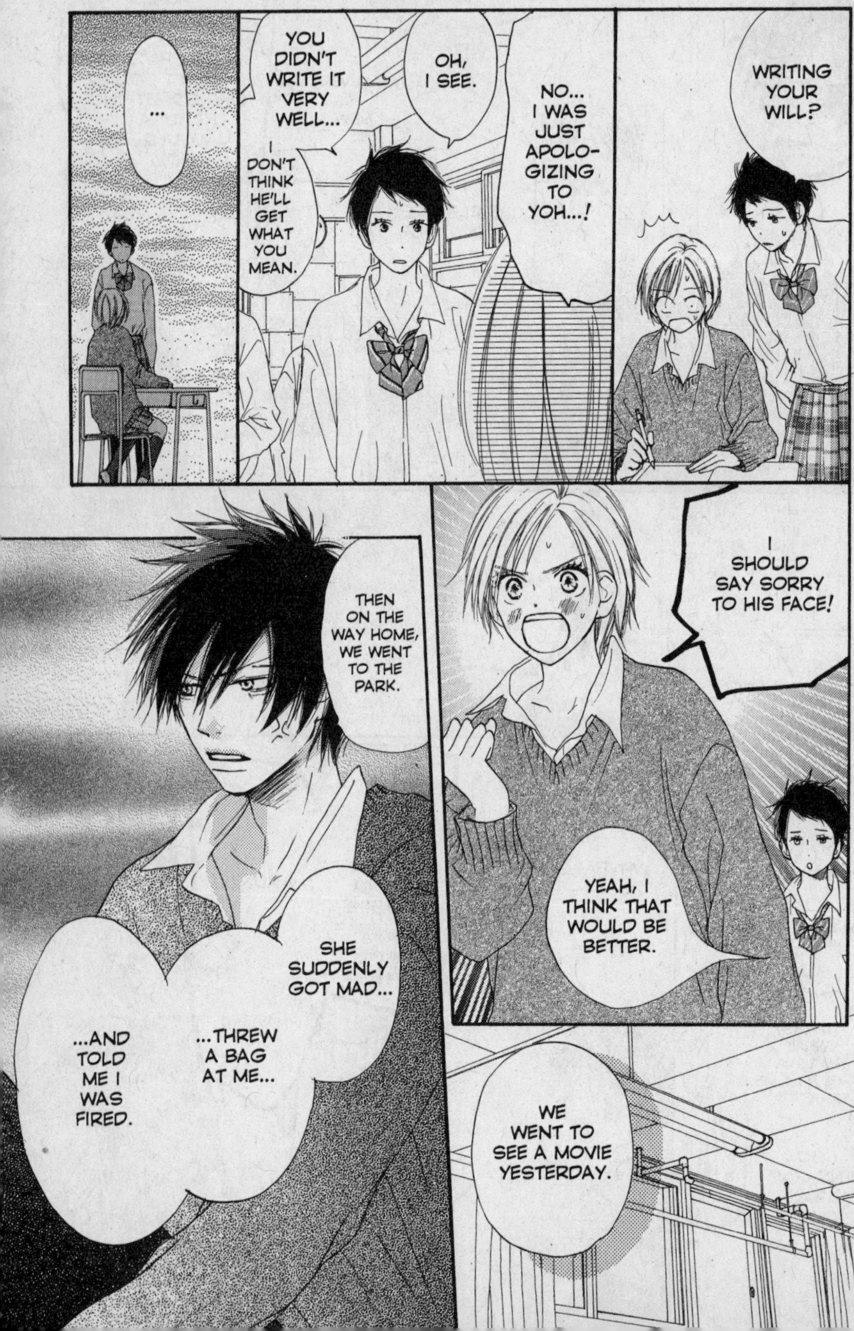
WRITING YOUR WILL?
NO... I WAS JUST APOLOGIZING TO YOH...!
OH, I SEE.
YOU DIDN'T WRITE IT VERY WELL...
I DON'T THINK HE'LL GET WHAT YOU MEAN.
...
I SHOULD SAY SORRY TO HIS FACE!
YEAH, I THINK THAT WOULD BE BETTER.
WE WENT TO SEE A MOVIE YESTERDAY.
THEN ON THE WAY HOME, WE WENT TO THE PARK.
SHE SUDDENLY GOT MAD...
...THREW A BAG AT ME...
...AND TOLD ME I WAS FIRED.

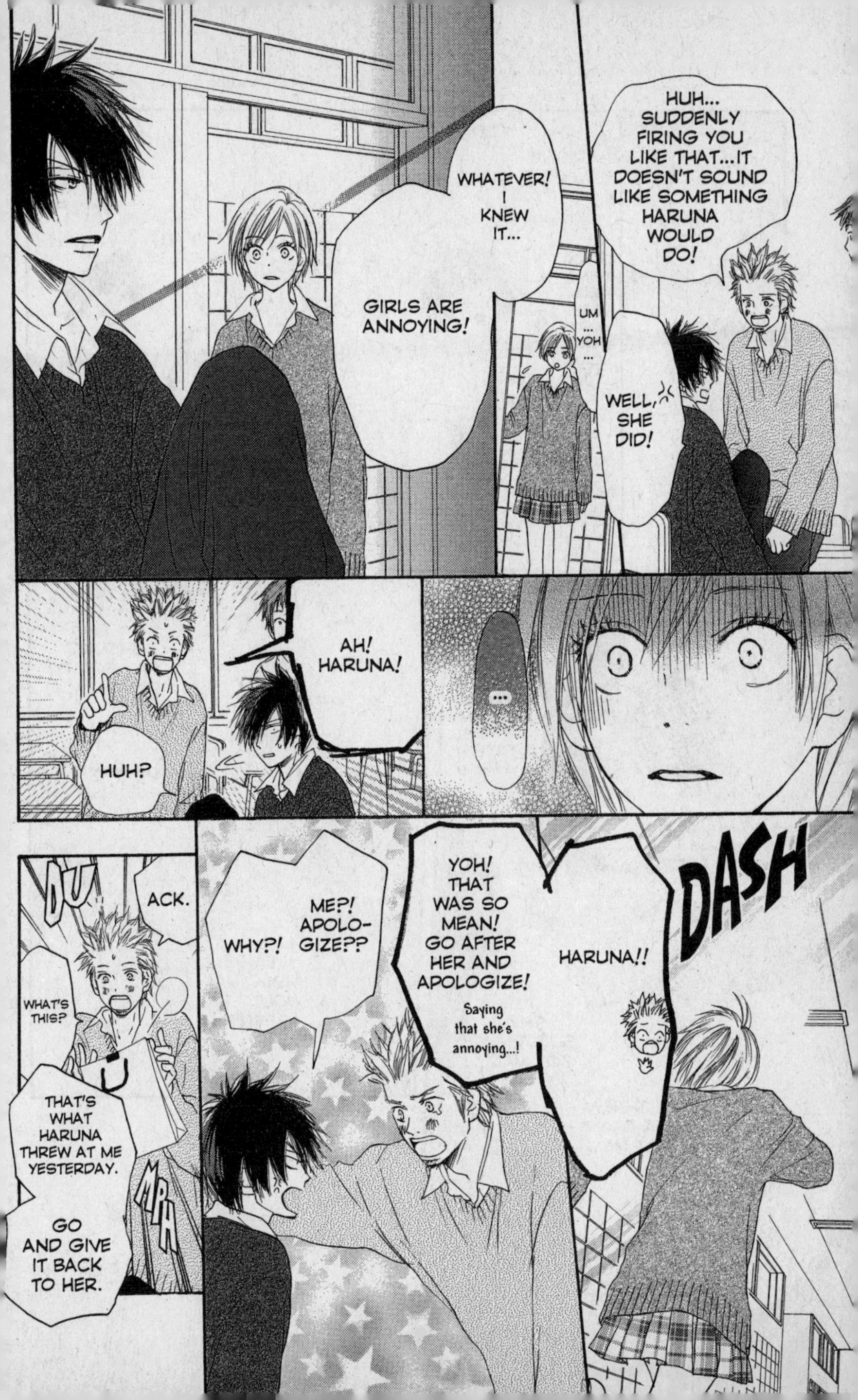
HUH... SUDDENLY FIRING YOU LIKE THAT...IT DOESN'T SOUND LIKE SOMETHING HARUNA WOULD DO!
WELL, SHE DID!
UM ... YOH ...
WHATEVER! I KNEW IT...
GIRLS ARE ANNOYING!
...
AH! HARUNA!
HUH?
DASH
HARUNA!!
YOH! THAT WAS SO MEAN! GO AFTER HER AND APOLOGIZE!
Saying that she's annoying...!
ME?! APOLOGIZE??
WHY?!
DU
ACK.
WHAT'S THIS?
THAT'S WHAT HARUNA THREW AT ME YESTERDAY.
MPH
GO AND GIVE IT BACK TO HER.

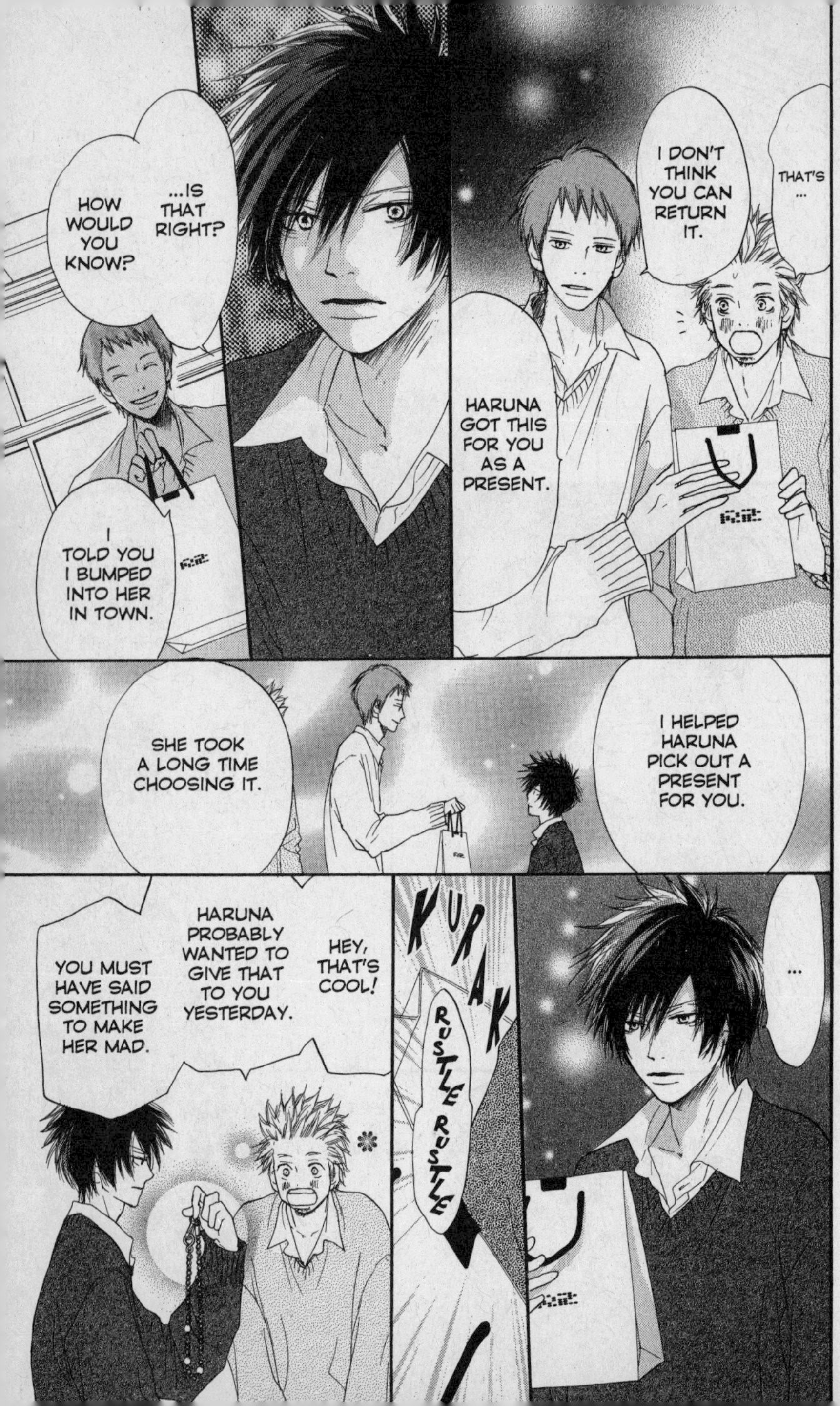
THAT'S ...
I DON'T THINK YOU CAN RETURN IT.
HARUNA GOT THIS FOR YOU AS A PRESENT.
...IS THAT RIGHT?
HOW WOULD YOU KNOW?
I TOLD YOU I BUMPED INTO HER IN TOWN.
I HELPED HARUNA PICK OUT A PRESENT FOR YOU.
SHE TOOK A LONG TIME CHOOSING IT.
...
KURAK
RUSTLE RUSTLE
HEY, THAT'S COOL!
HARUNA PROBABLY WANTED TO GIVE THAT TO YOU YESTERDAY.
YOU MUST HAVE SAID SOMETHING TO MAKE HER MAD.

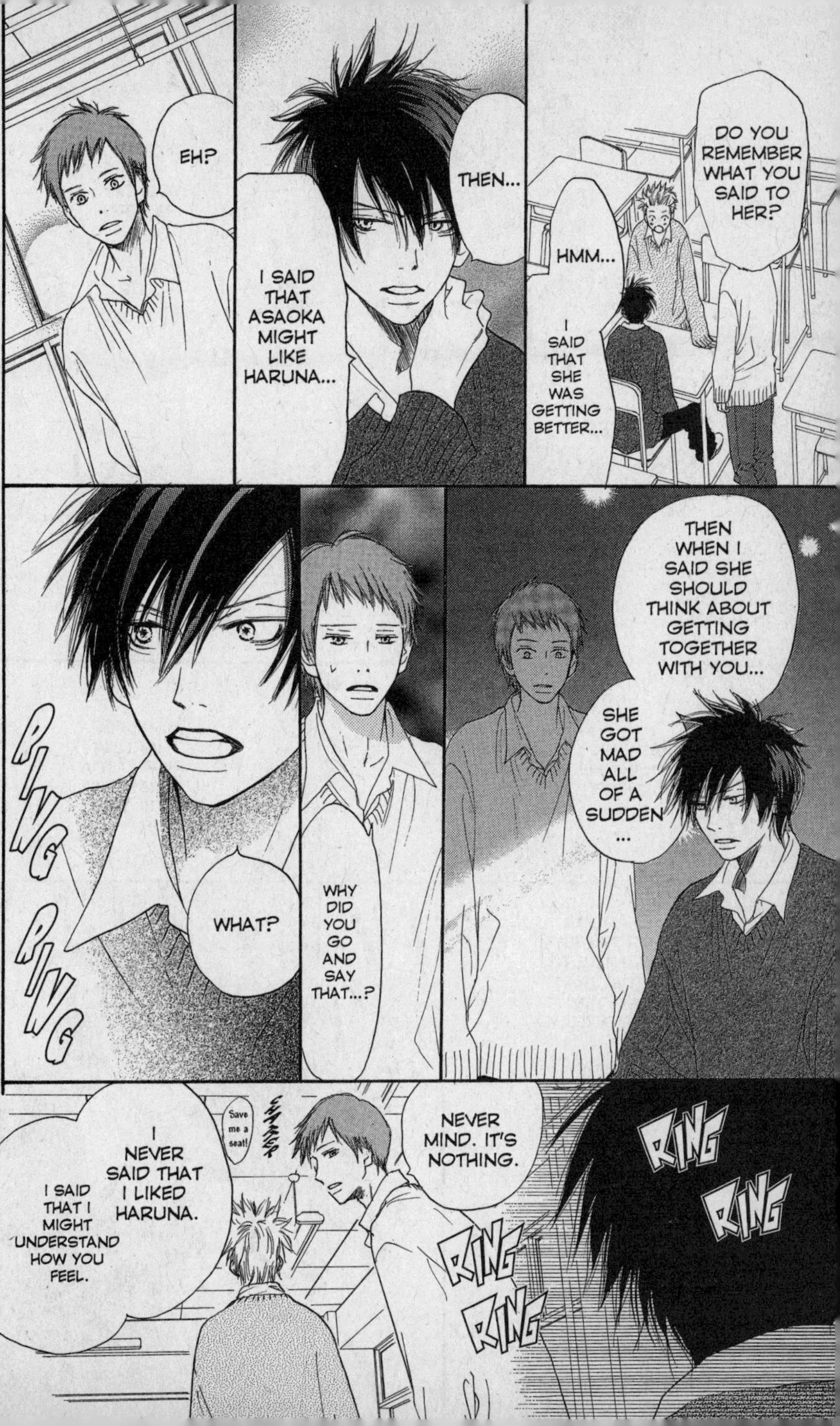
DO YOU REMEMBER WHAT YOU SAID TO HER?
HMM...
I SAID THAT SHE WAS GETTING BETTER...
THEN...
I SAID THAT ASAOKA MIGHT LIKE HARUNA...
EH?
THEN WHEN I SAID SHE SHOULD THINK ABOUT GETTING TOGETHER WITH YOU...
SHE GOT MAD ALL OF A SUDDEN ...
WHY DID YOU GO AND SAY THAT...?
WHAT?
RING RING
RING RING
RING RING
NEVER MIND. IT'S NOTHING.
Save me a seat!
I NEVER SAID THAT I LIKED HARUNA.
I SAID THAT I MIGHT UNDERSTAND HOW YOU FEEL.

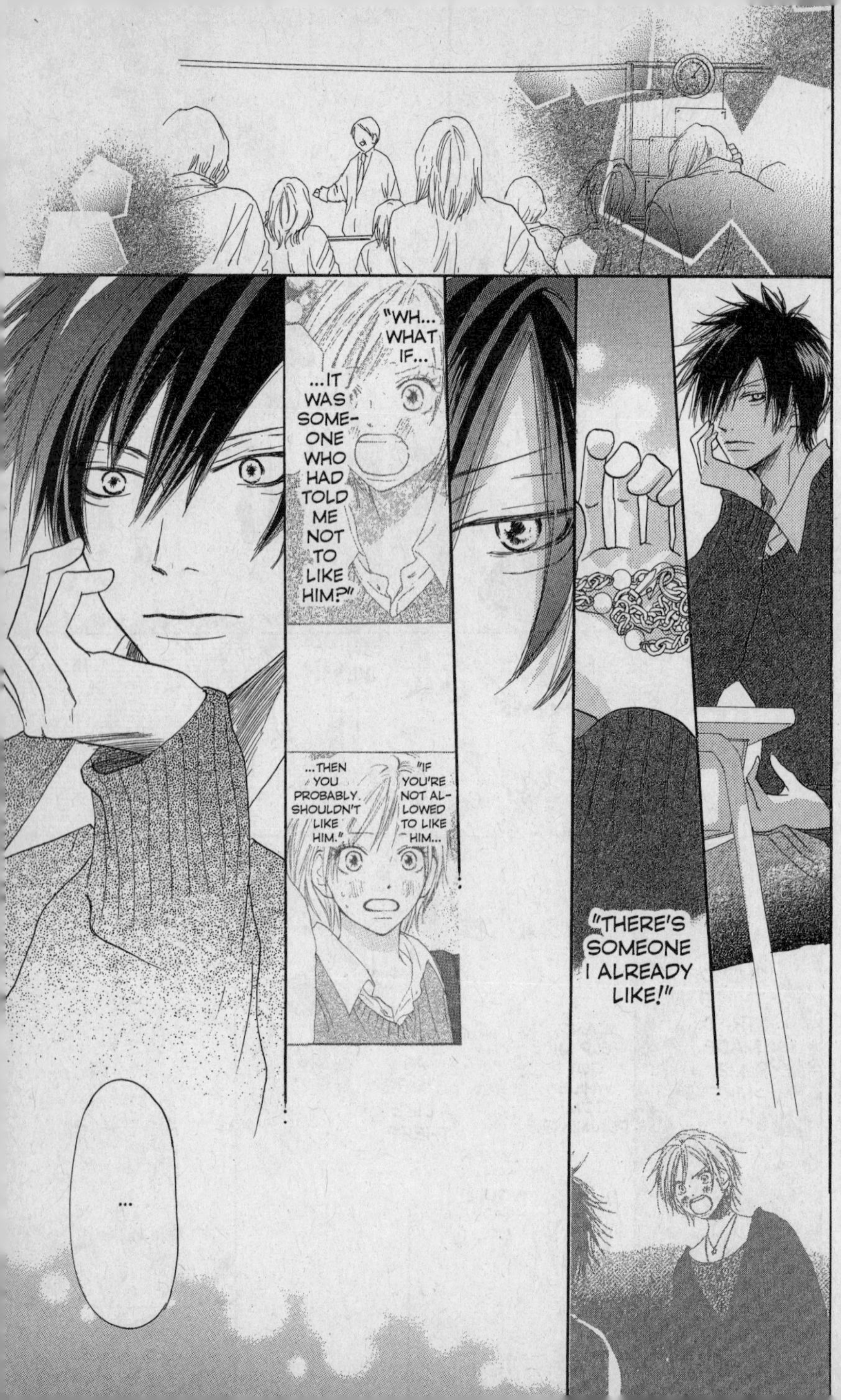
"THERE'S SOMEONE I ALREADY LIKE!"
"WH... WHAT IF...
...IT WAS SOMEONE WHO HAD TOLD ME NOT TO LIKE HIM?"
"IF YOU'RE NOT ALLOWED TO LIKE HIM...
...THEN YOU PROBABLY SHOULDN'T LIKE HIM."
...

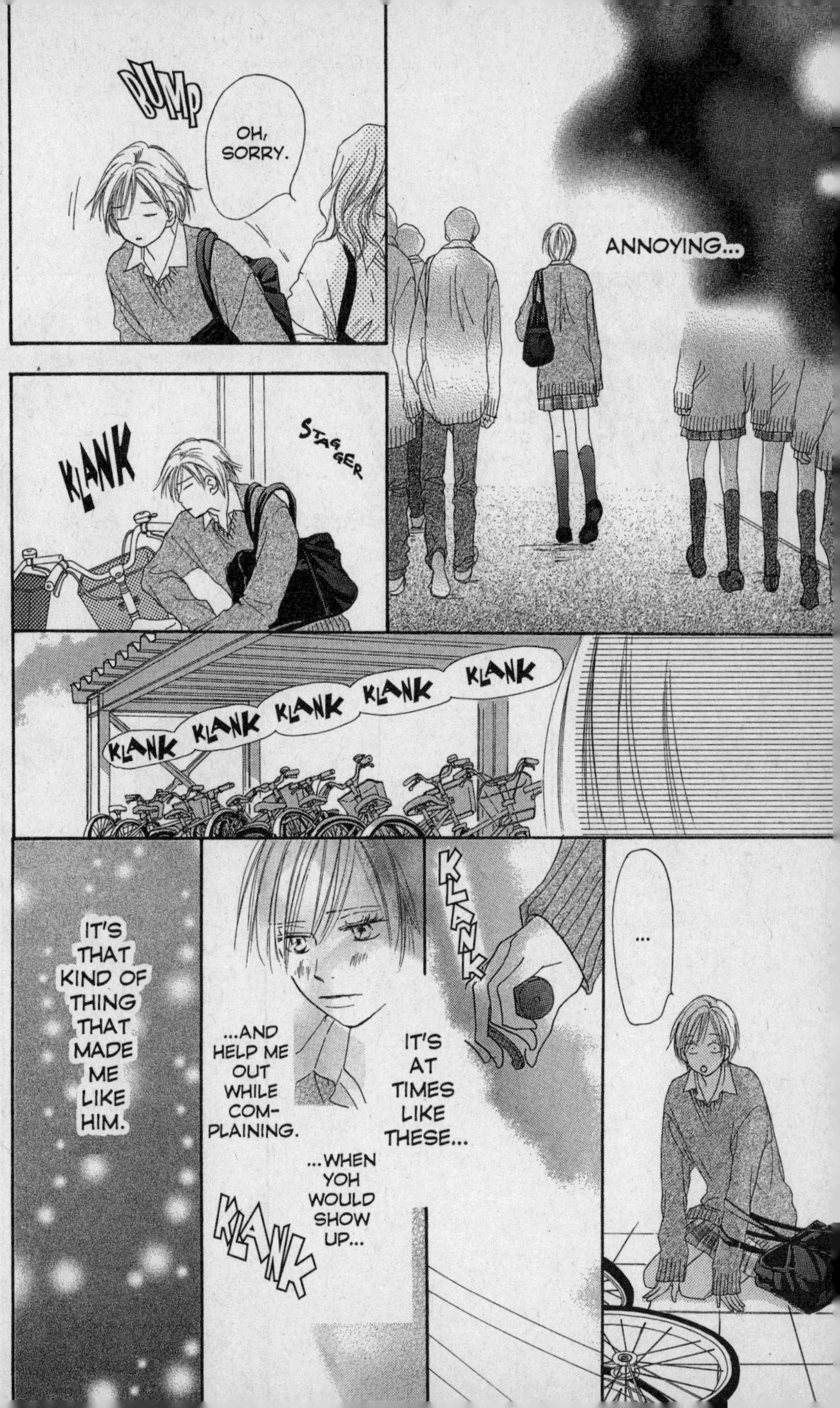
ANNOYING...
BUMP
OH, SORRY.
KLANK
STAGGER
KLANK
KLANK
KLANK
KLANK
KLANK
...
KLANK
IT'S AT TIMES LIKE THESE...
...WHEN YOH WOULD SHOW UP...
...AND HELP ME OUT WHILE COM-PLAINING.
KLANK
IT'S THAT KIND OF THING THAT MADE ME LIKE HIM.

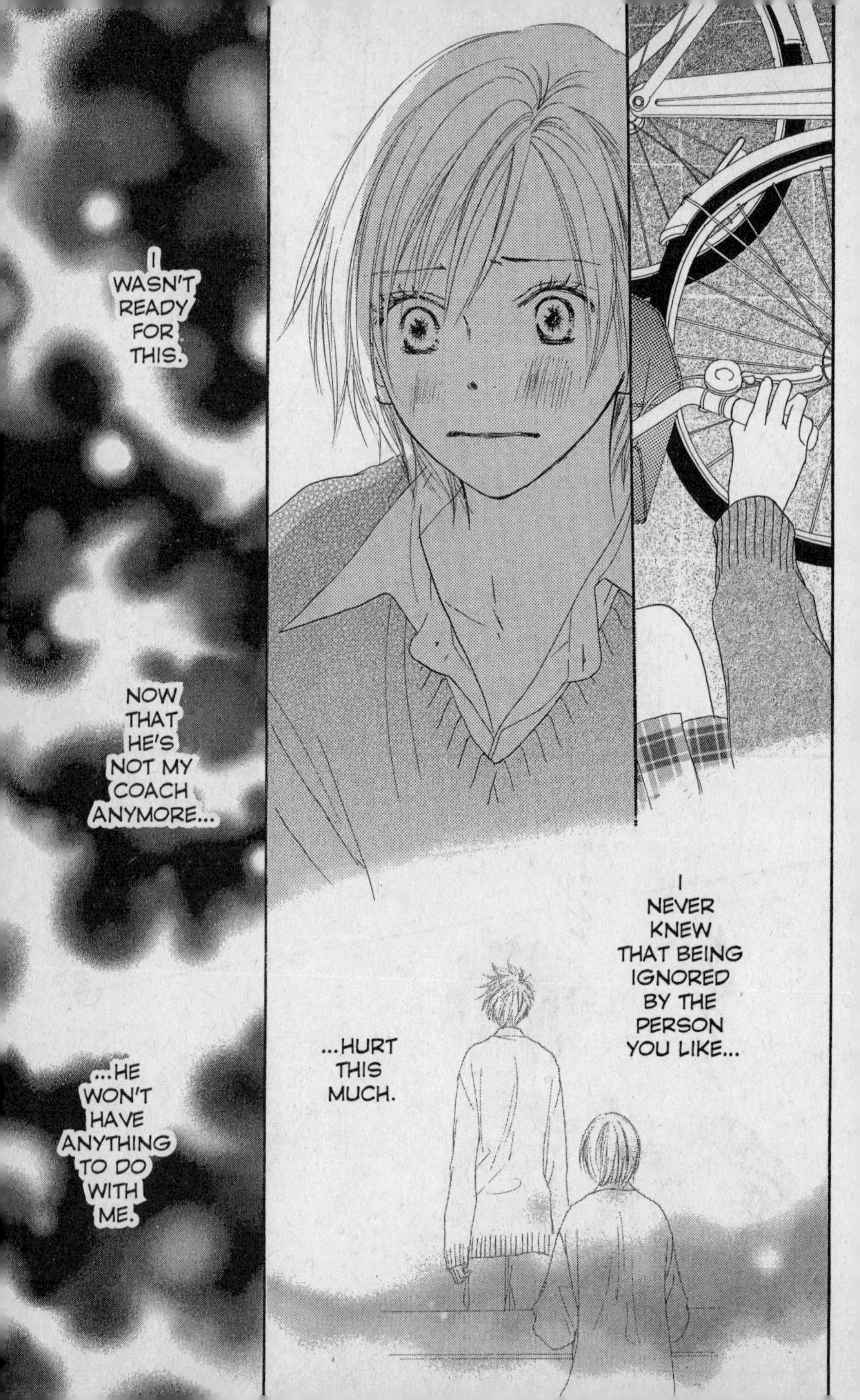
I NEVER KNEW THAT BEING IGNORED BY THE PERSON YOU LIKE...
...HURT THIS MUCH.
I WASN'T READY FOR THIS.
NOW THAT HE'S NOT MY COACH ANYMORE...
...HE WON'T HAVE ANYTHING TO DO WITH ME.

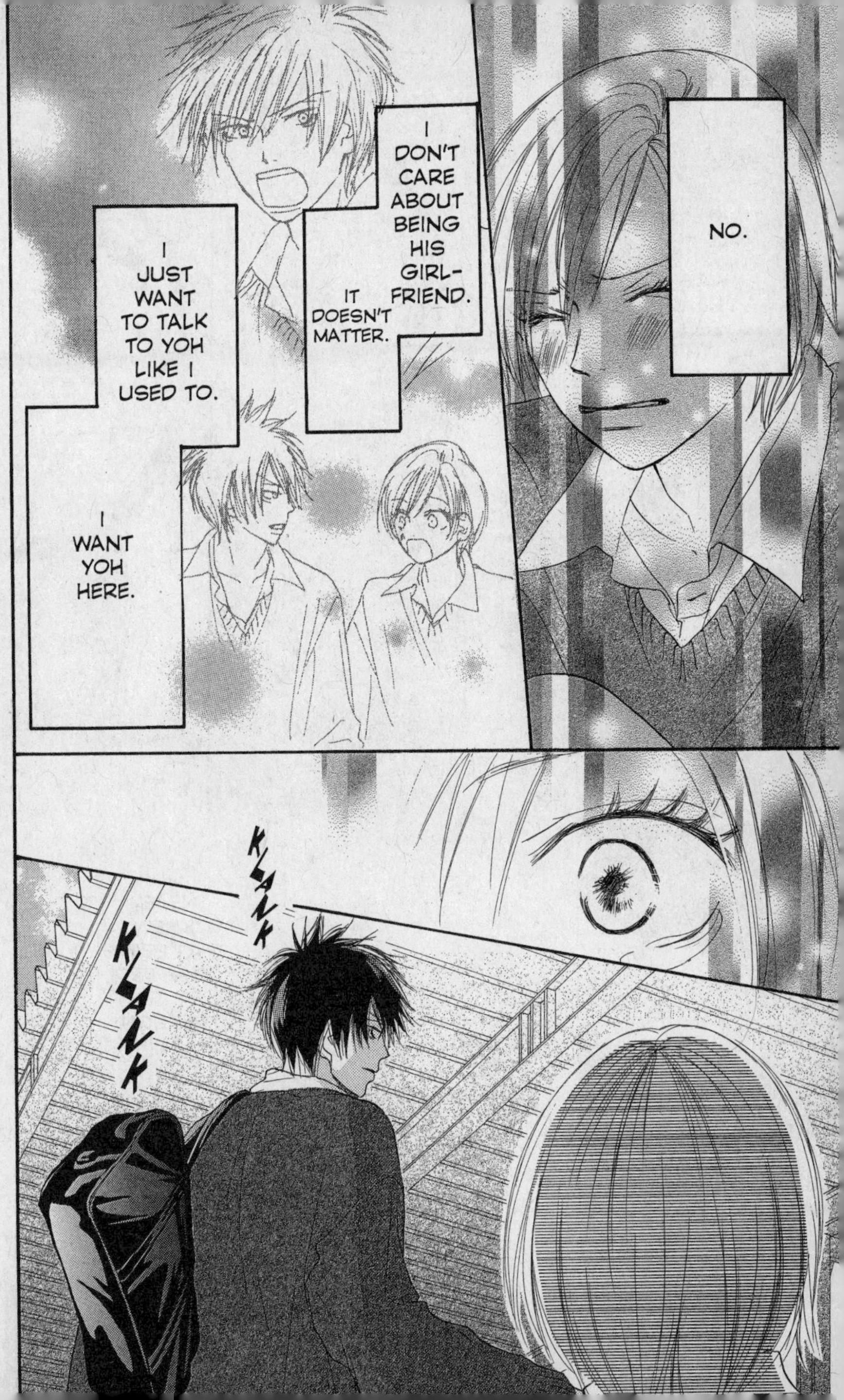
NO.
I DON'T CARE ABOUT BEING HIS GIRL-FRIEND.
IT DOESN'T MATTER.
I JUST WANT TO TALK TO YOH LIKE I USED TO.
I WANT YOH HERE.
KLANK
KLANK KLANK

2

I'm sorry, but I'm going to write about my relatives again. My nieces are pretty cute now that they've turned three and one. The younger ones cries like this:

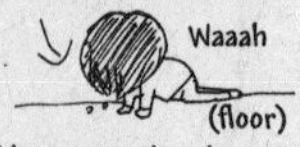
Waaah
(floor)

Also, recently, she surprised me by saying this...

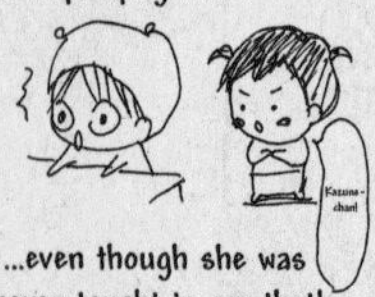
Kazune-chan!

...even though she was never taught to say that!

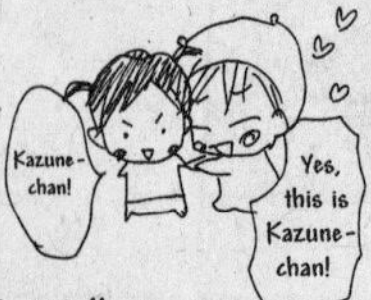
Kazune-chan!
Yes, this is Kazune-chan!

Cuuute!!

As for the older niece, when she tried to put something into a backpack and found that it was full of her little sister's toys, she said:

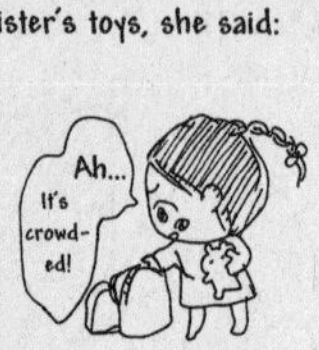
Ah...
It's crowd-ed!

"It's crowded..." Sooo cute! I think I'll try saying that too. I wonder if someone will tell me I'm cute for saying it. Probably not.

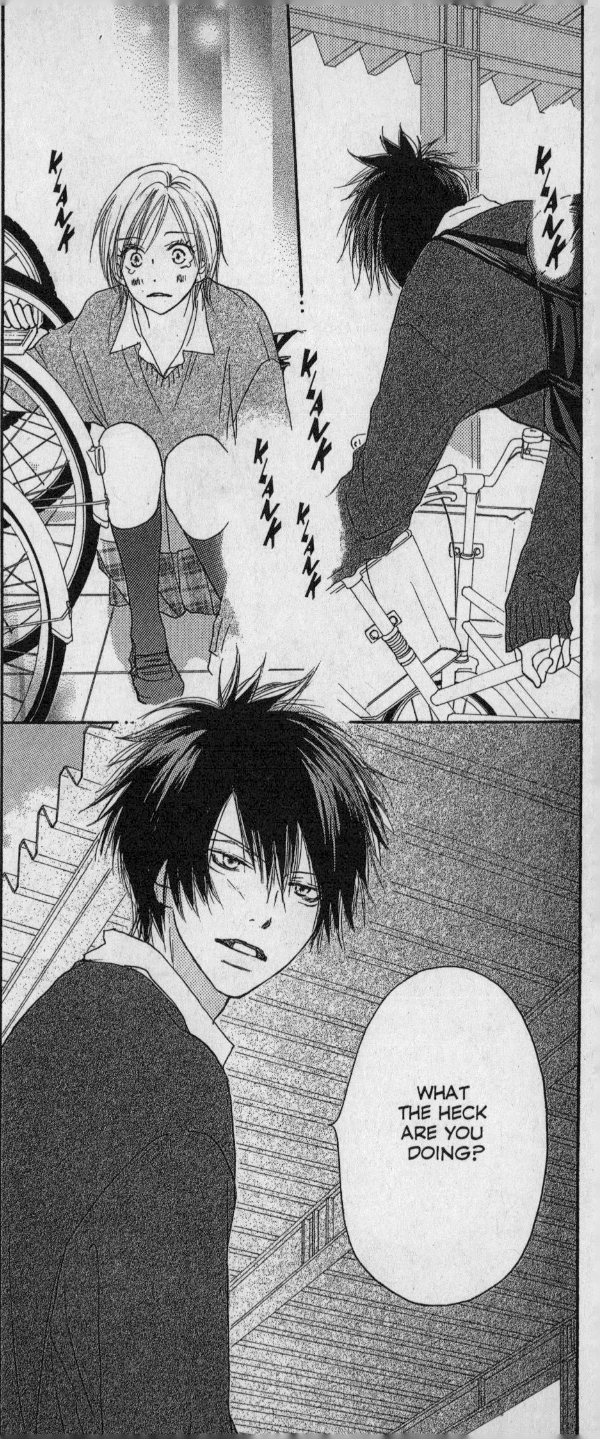
KLANK
KLANK
KLANK
KLANK
KLANK
WHAT THE HECK ARE YOU DOING?

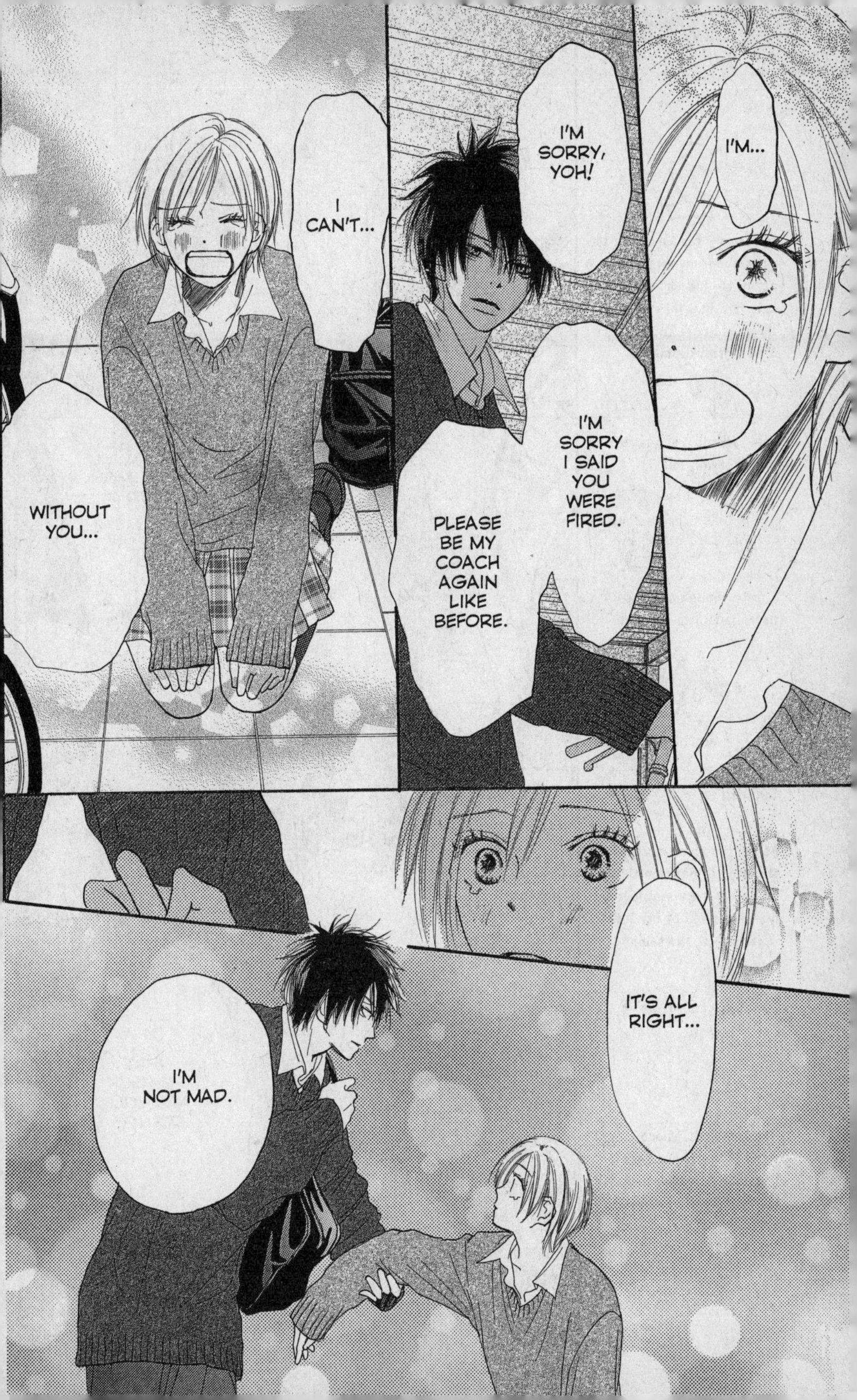
I'M...
I'M SORRY, YOH!
I'M SORRY I SAID YOU WERE FIRED.
PLEASE BE MY COACH AGAIN LIKE BEFORE.
I CAN'T...
WITHOUT YOU...
IT'S ALL RIGHT...
I'M NOT MAD.

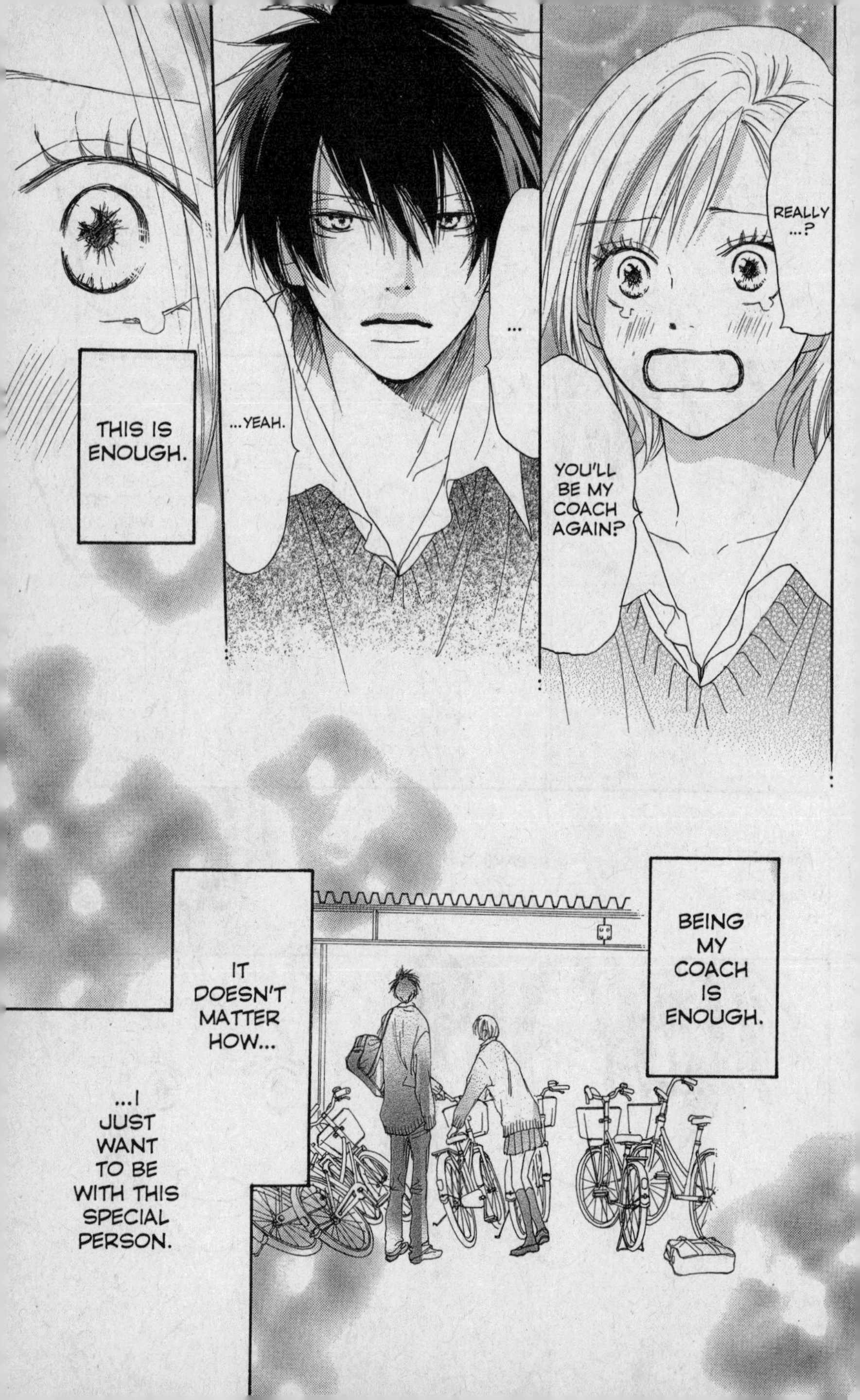
REALLY ...?
YOU'LL BE MY COACH AGAIN?
...
...YEAH.
THIS IS ENOUGH.
BEING MY COACH IS ENOUGH.
IT DOESN'T MATTER HOW...
...I JUST WANT TO BE WITH THIS SPECIAL PERSON.

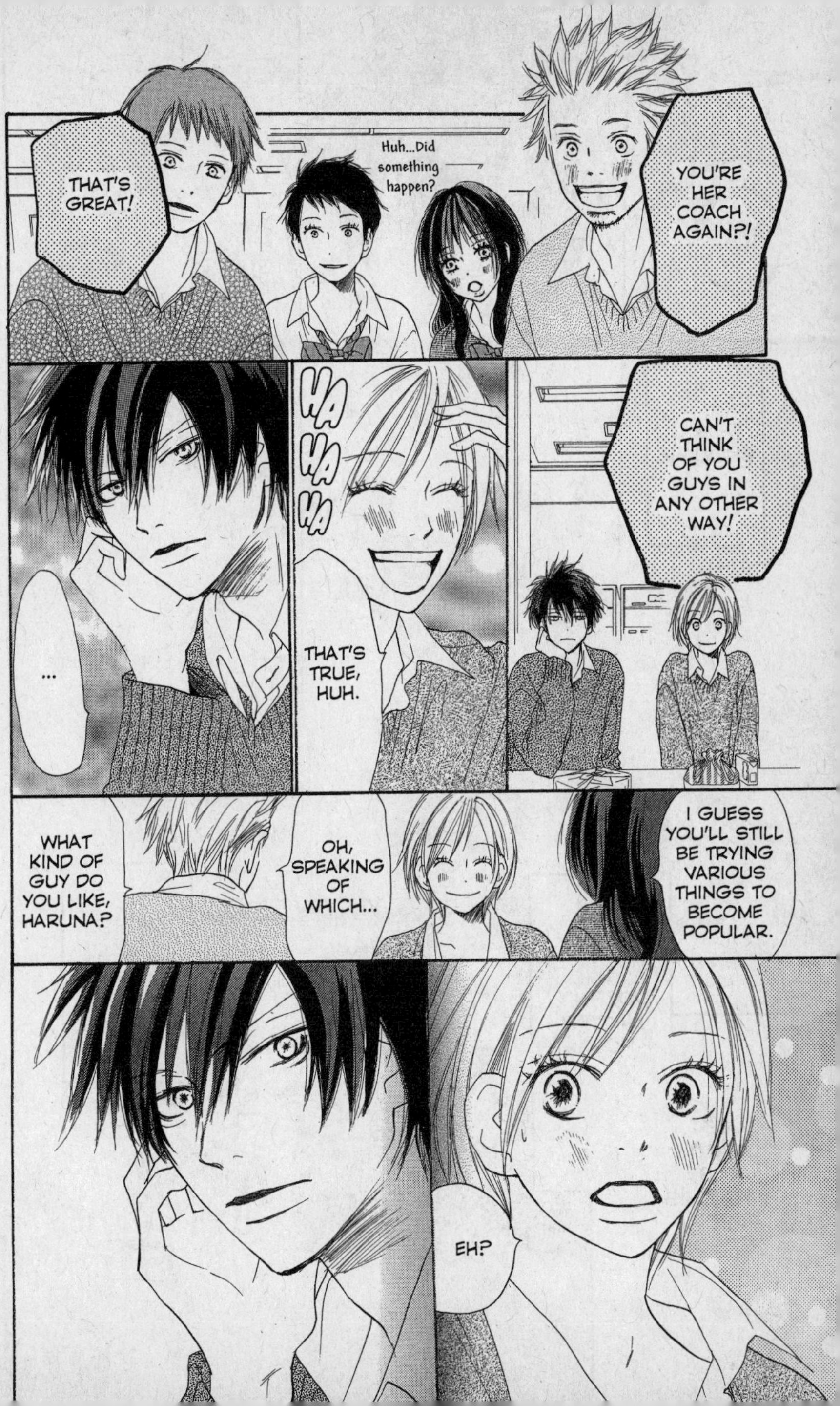
YOU'RE HER COACH AGAIN?!
Huh...Did something happen?
THAT'S GREAT!
CAN'T THINK OF YOU GUYS IN ANY OTHER WAY!
HA HA HA HA
THAT'S TRUE, HUH.
...
I GUESS YOU'LL STILL BE TRYING VARIOUS THINGS TO BECOME POPULAR.
OH, SPEAKING OF WHICH...
WHAT KIND OF GUY DO YOU LIKE, HARUNA?
EH?

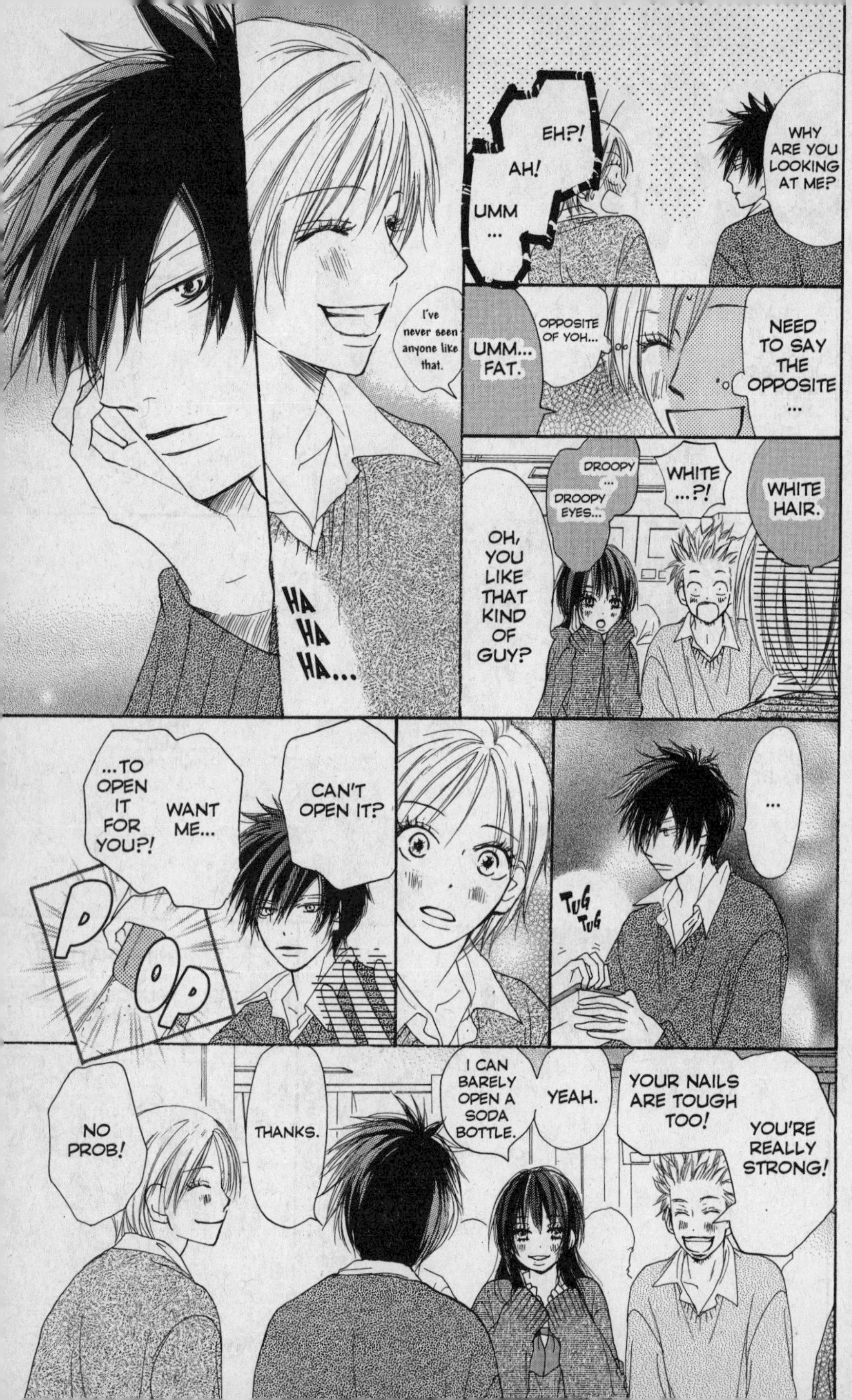
WHY ARE YOU LOOKING AT ME?
EH?! AH! UMM...
NEED TO SAY THE OPPOSITE...
OPPOSITE OF YOH...
UMM... FAT.
WHITE HAIR.
WHITE...?!
DROOPY... DROOPY EYES...
OH, YOU LIKE THAT KIND OF GUY?
I've never seen anyone like that.
HA HA HA...
...
TUG TUG
CAN'T OPEN IT?
WANT ME...
...TO OPEN IT FOR YOU?!
POP
YOU'RE REALLY STRONG!
YOUR NAILS ARE TOUGH TOO!
YEAH.
I CAN BARELY OPEN A SODA BOTTLE.
THANKS.
NO PROB!

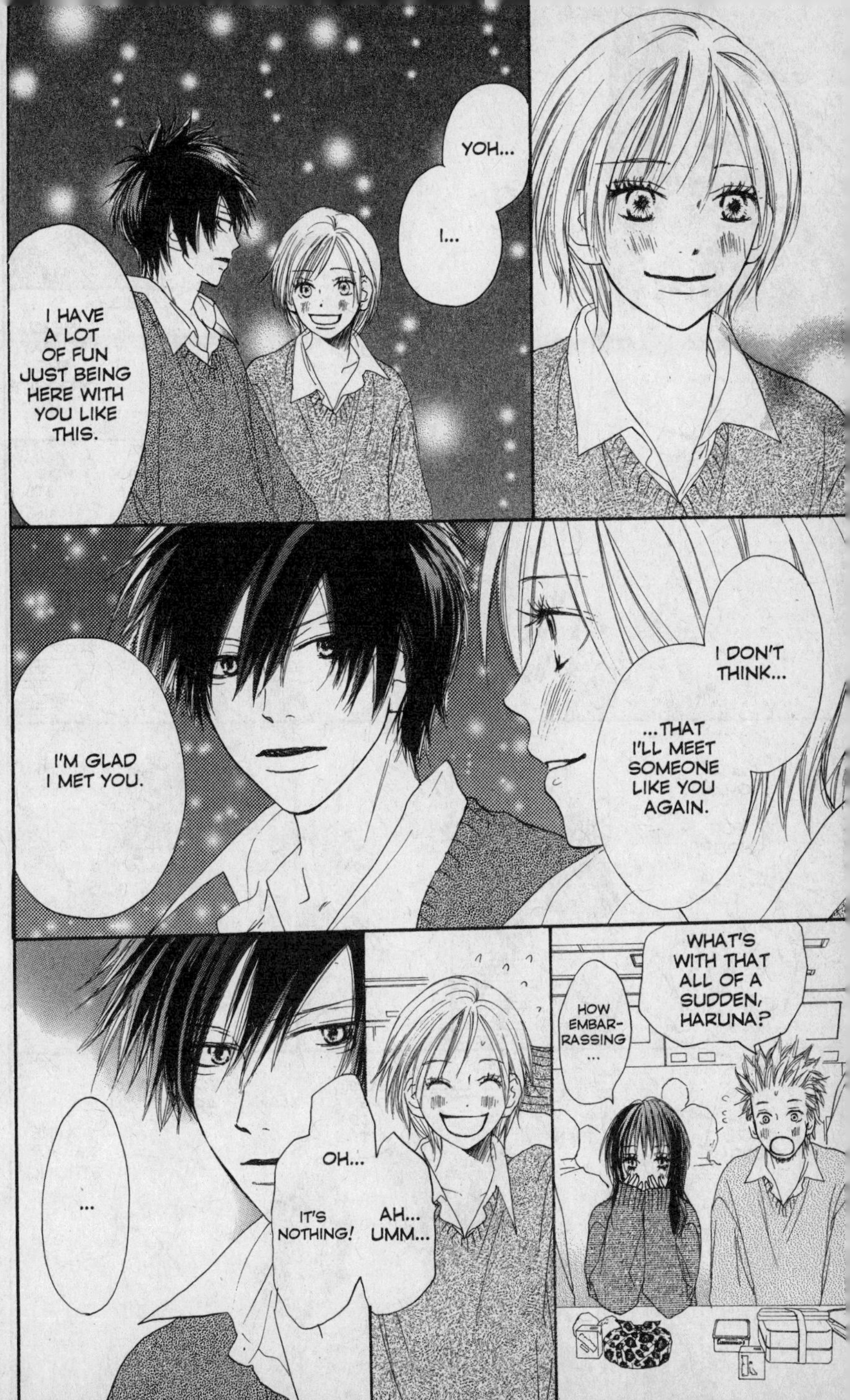
YOH...
I...
I HAVE A LOT OF FUN JUST BEING HERE WITH YOU LIKE THIS.
I DON'T THINK...
...THAT I'LL MEET SOMEONE LIKE YOU AGAIN.
I'M GLAD I MET YOU.
WHAT'S WITH THAT ALL OF A SUDDEN, HARUNA?
HOW EMBAR-RASSING...
OH...
AH... UMM...
IT'S NOTHING!
...

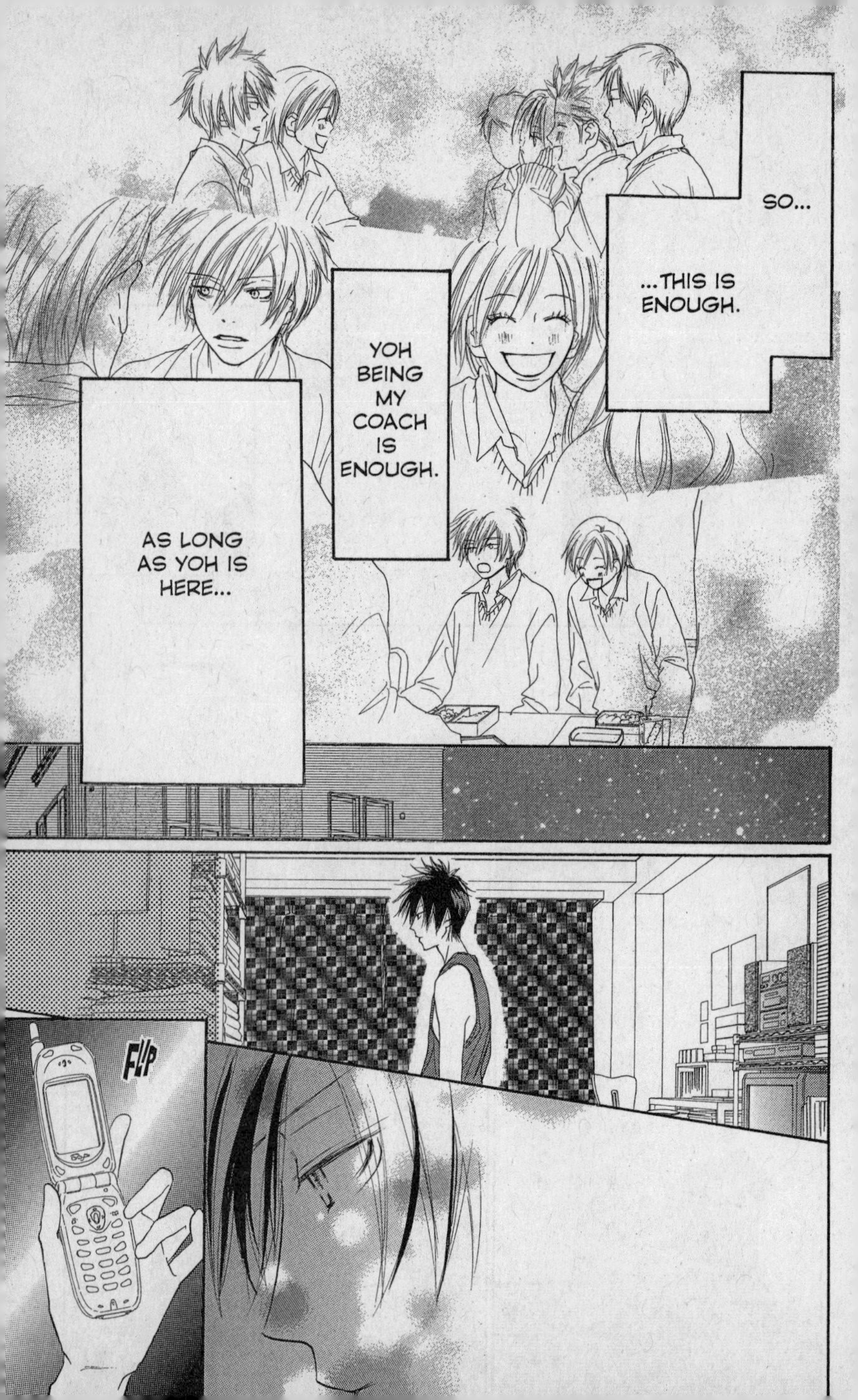
SO...
...THIS IS ENOUGH.
YOH BEING MY COACH IS ENOUGH.
AS LONG AS YOH IS HERE...
FLIP

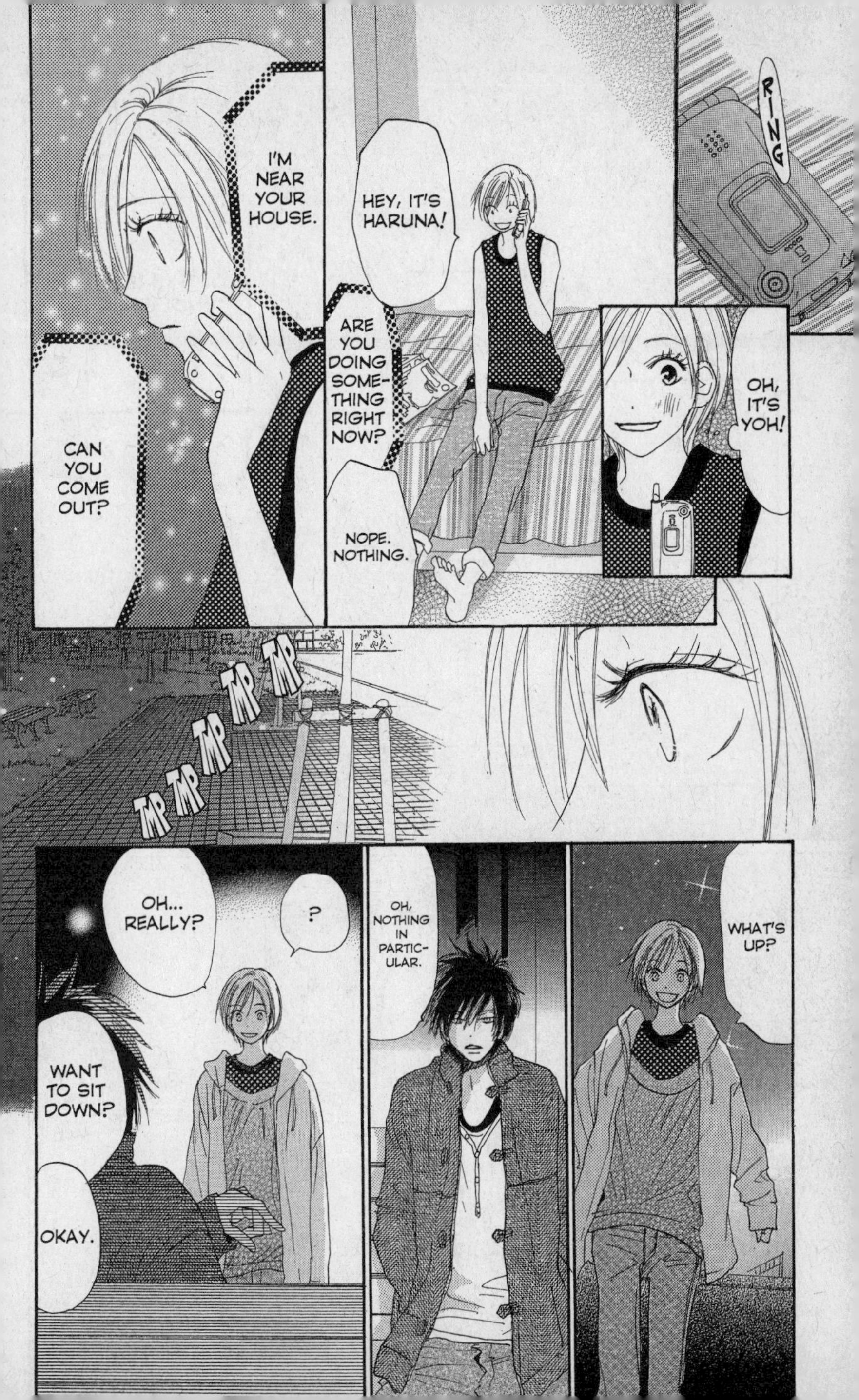
RING
OH, IT'S YOH!
HEY, IT'S HARUNA!
ARE YOU DOING SOME-THING RIGHT NOW?
NOPE. NOTHING.
I'M NEAR YOUR HOUSE.
CAN YOU COME OUT?
TMP TMP TMP TMP TMP
WHAT'S UP?
OH, NOTHING IN PARTIC-ULAR.
OH... REALLY?
?
WANT TO SIT DOWN?
OKAY.

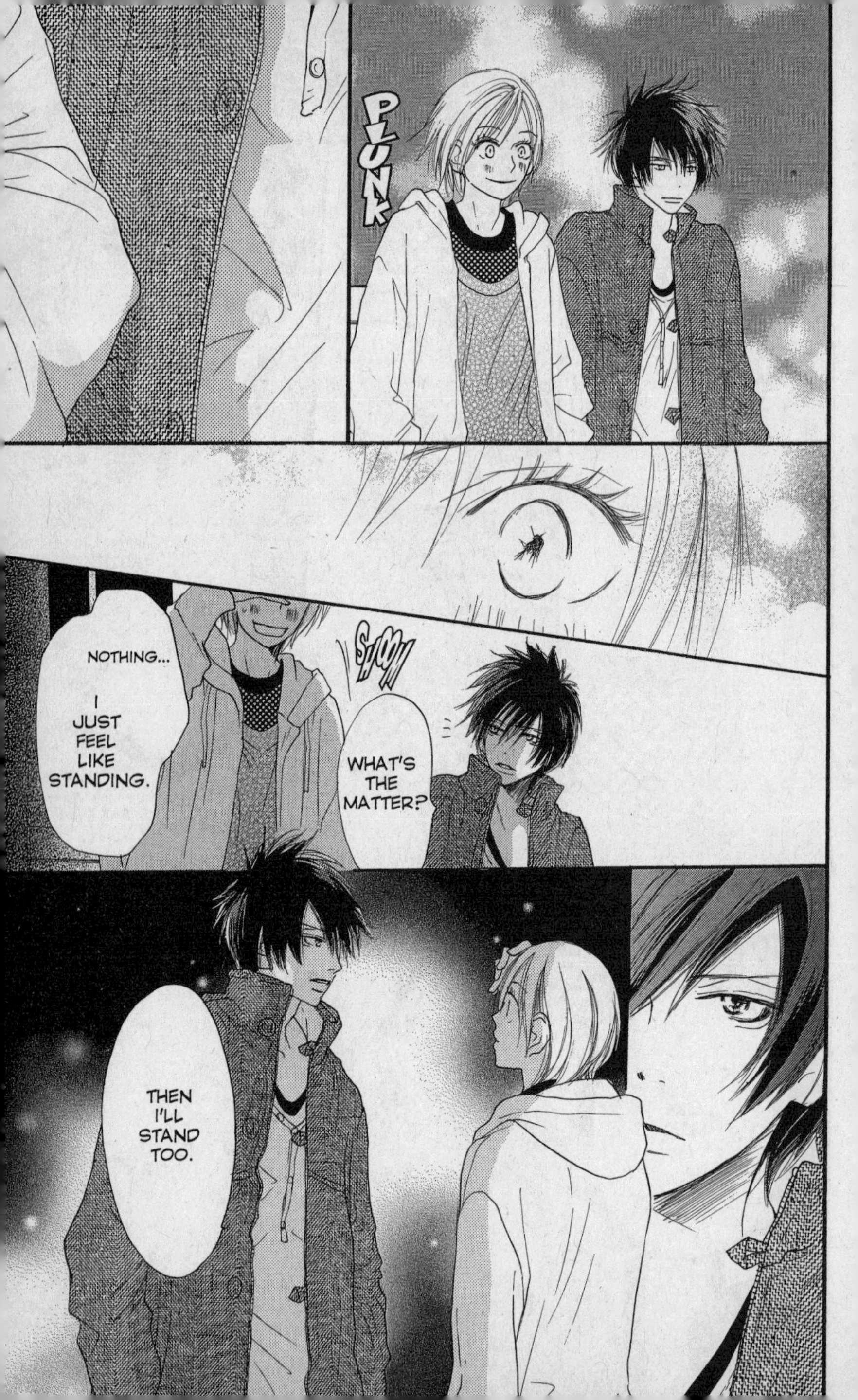
PLUNK
SHOOM
WHAT'S THE MATTER?
NOTHING...
I JUST FEEL LIKE STANDING.
THEN I'LL STAND TOO.

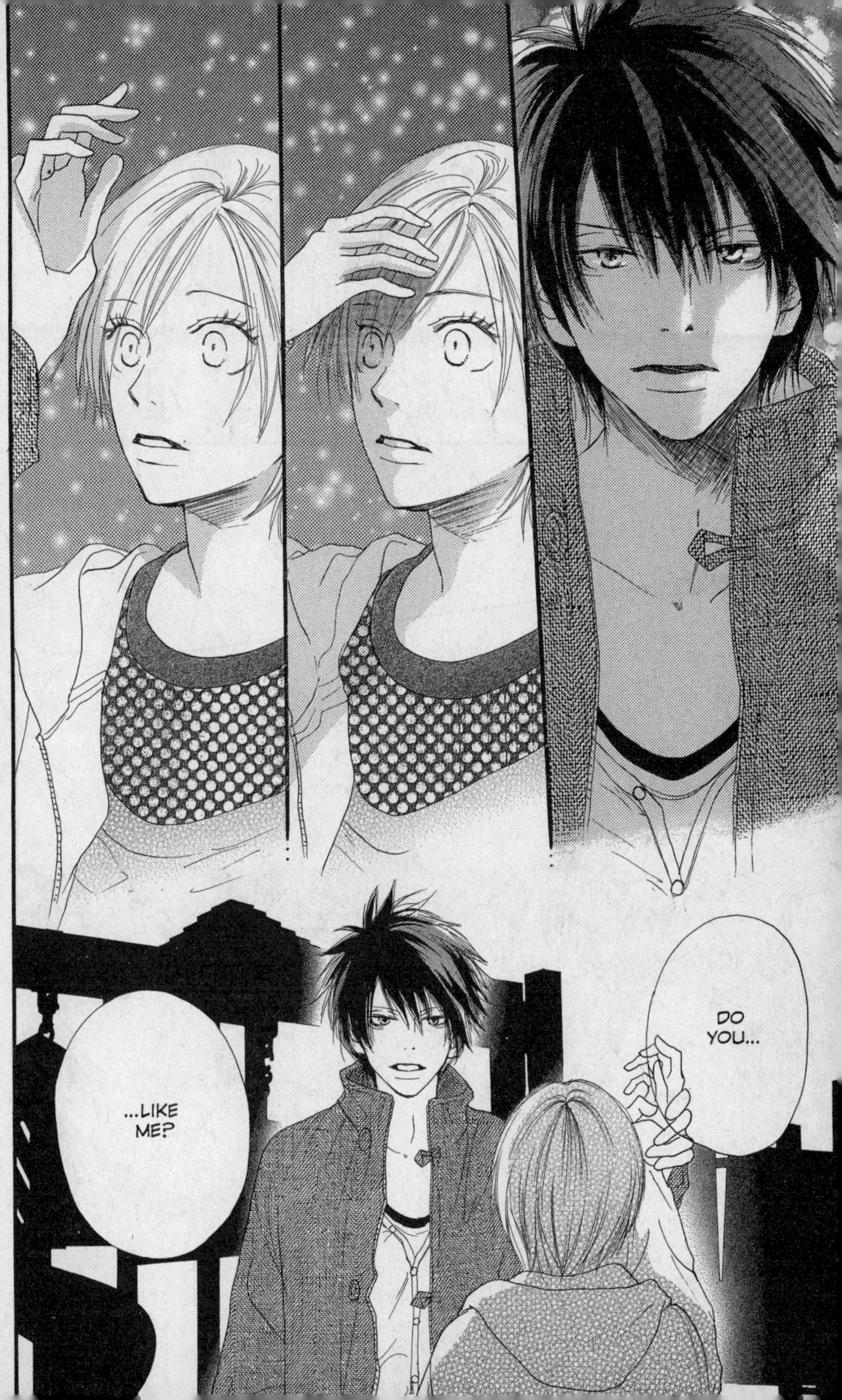
DO YOU...
...LIKE ME?

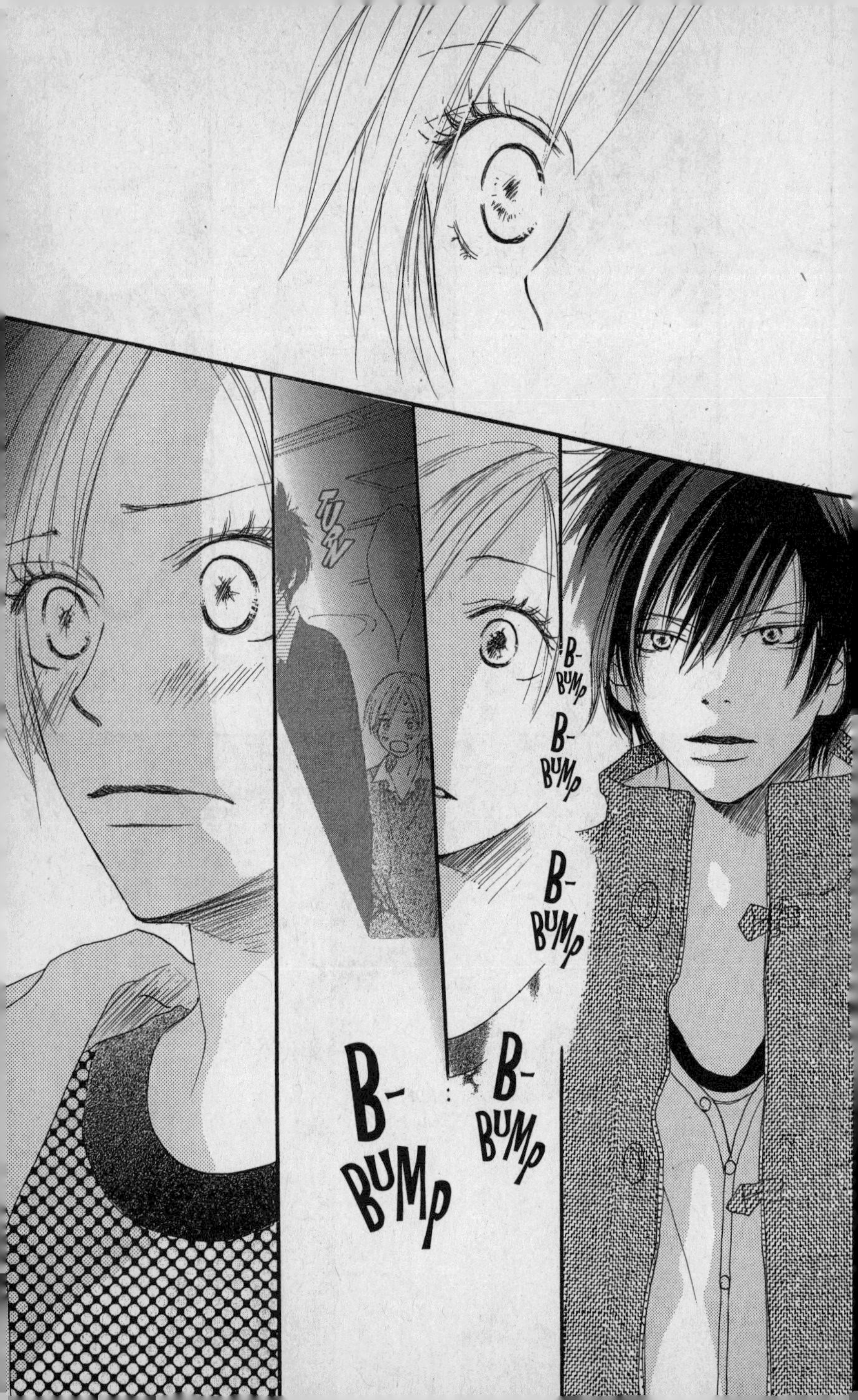
B-BUMP
B-BUMP
B-BUMP
B-BUMP
B-BUMP
TURN

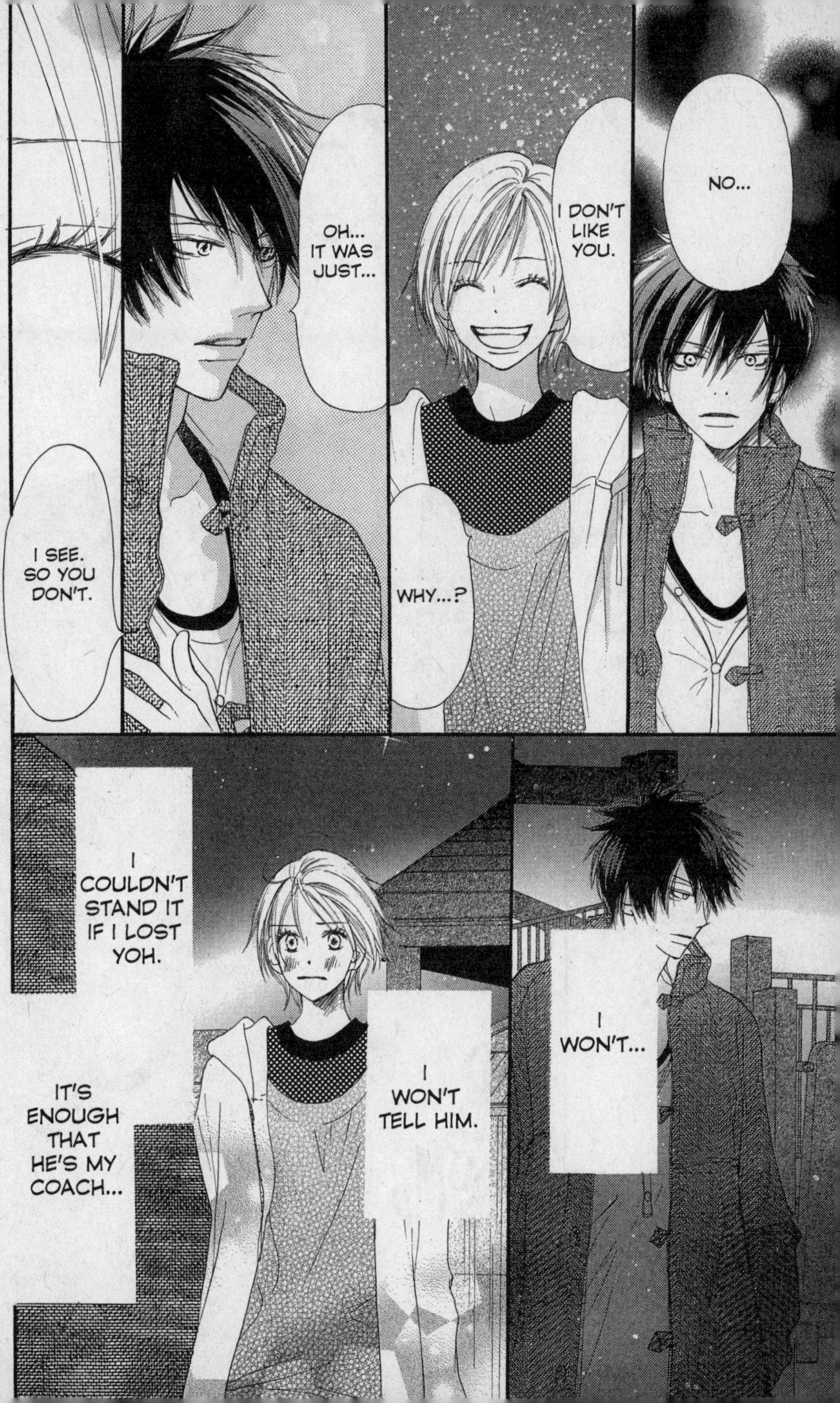
NO...
I DON'T LIKE YOU.
WHY...?
OH... IT WAS JUST...
I SEE. SO YOU DON'T.
I WON'T...
I WON'T TELL HIM.
I COULDN'T STAND IT IF I LOST YOH.
IT'S ENOUGH THAT HE'S MY COACH...

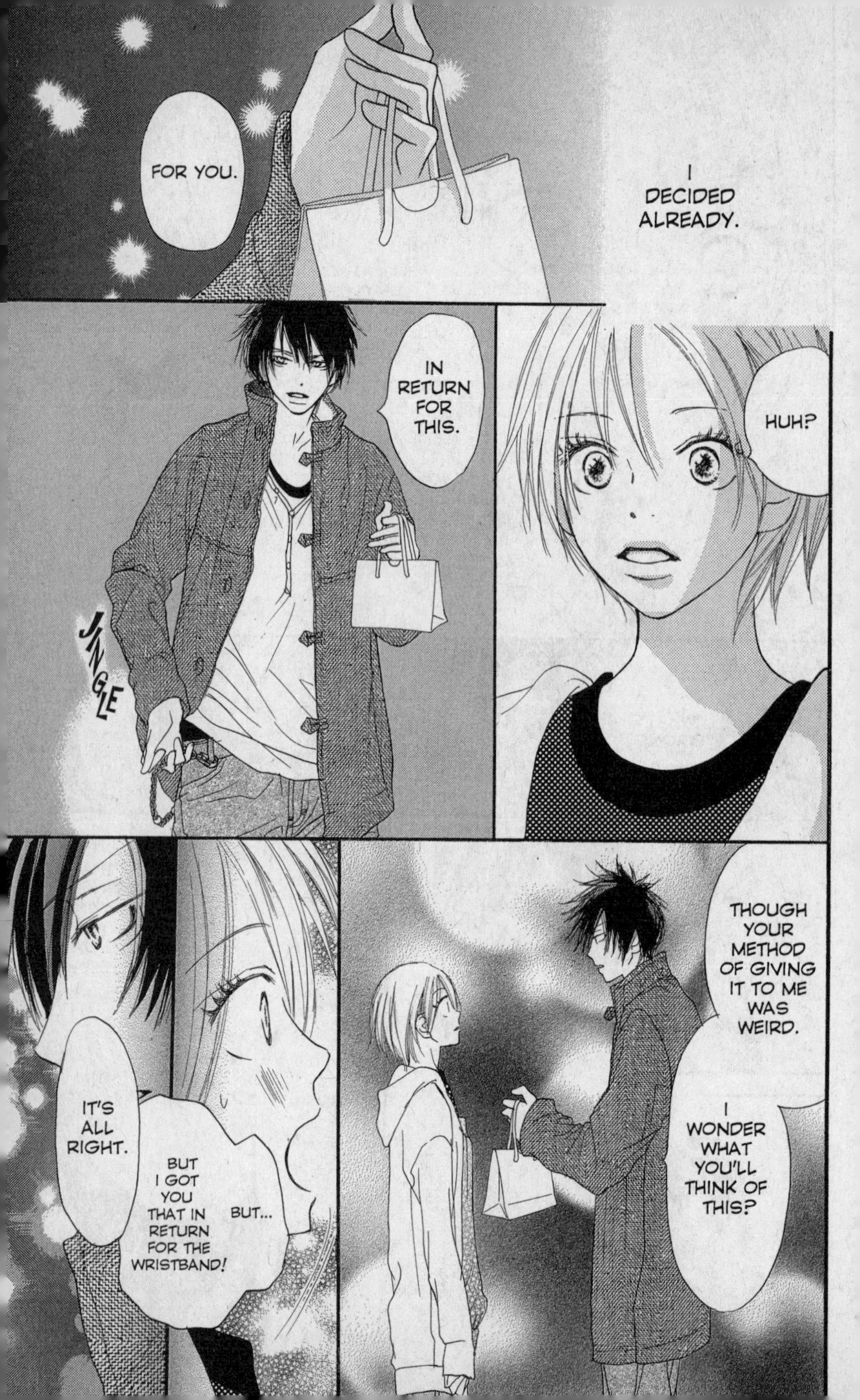
I DECIDED ALREADY.
FOR YOU.
HUH?
IN RETURN FOR THIS.
JINGLE
THOUGH YOUR METHOD OF GIVING IT TO ME WAS WEIRD.
I WONDER WHAT YOU'LL THINK OF THIS?
BUT I GOT YOU THAT IN RETURN FOR THE WRISTBAND!
BUT...
IT'S ALL RIGHT.

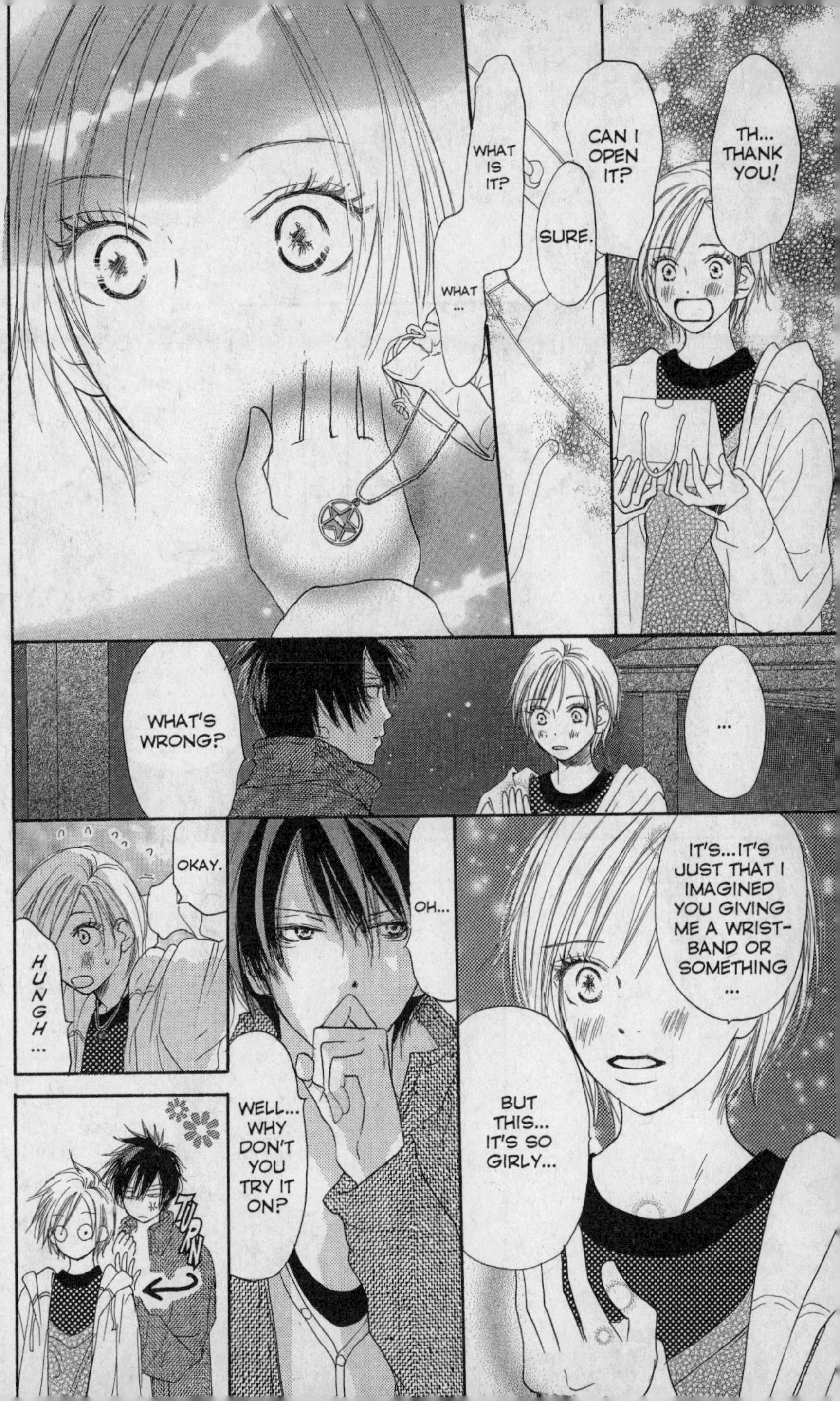
TH... THANK YOU!
CAN I OPEN IT?
SURE.
WHAT IS IT?
WHAT ...
...
WHAT'S WRONG?
IT'S...IT'S JUST THAT I IMAGINED YOU GIVING ME A WRIST-BAND OR SOMETHING ...
BUT THIS... IT'S SO GIRLY...
OH...
WELL... WHY DON'T YOU TRY IT ON?
OKAY.
HUNGH ...
TURN

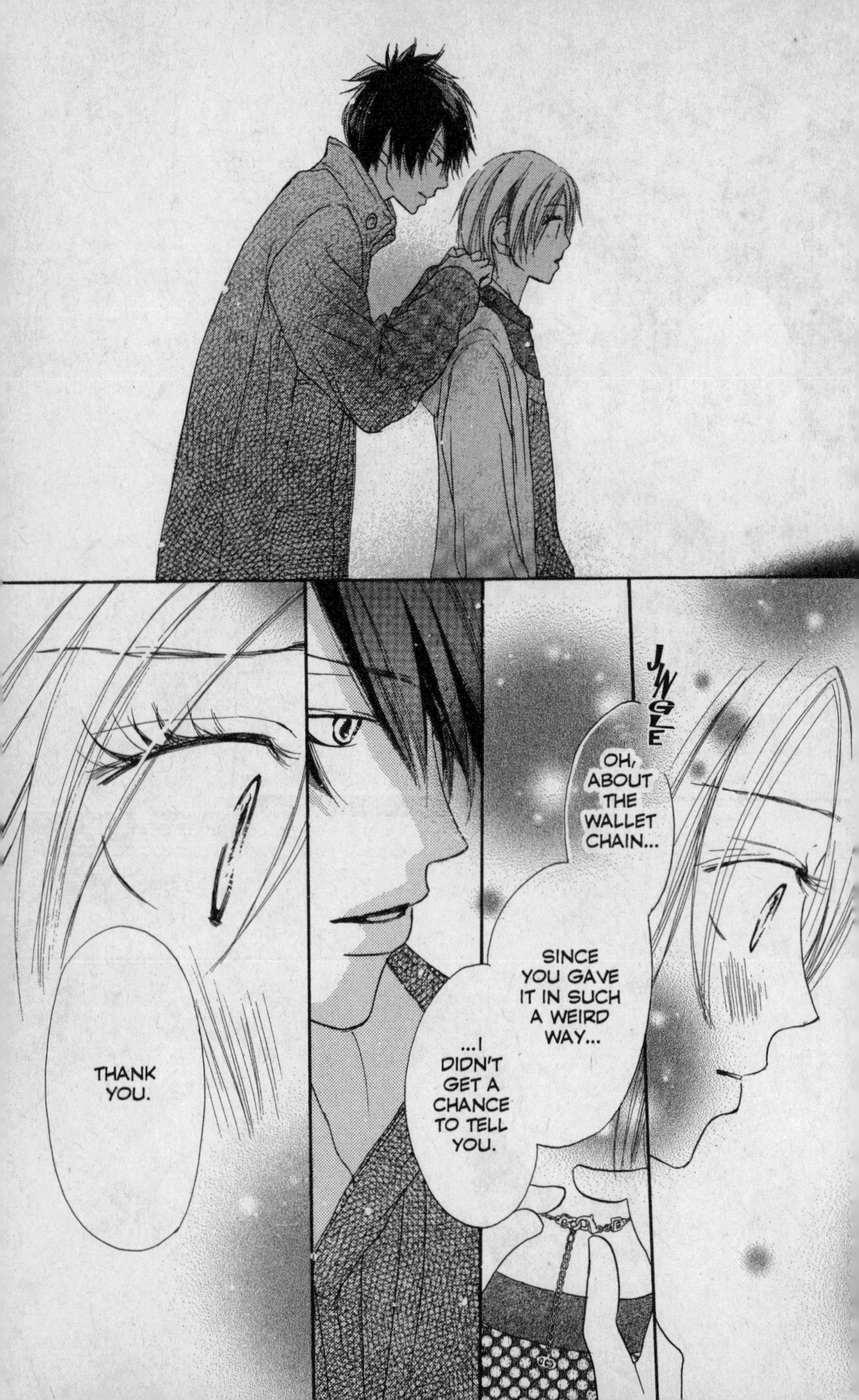
JINGLE
OH, ABOUT THE WALLET CHAIN...
SINCE YOU GAVE IT IN SUCH A WEIRD WAY...
...I DIDN'T GET A CHANCE TO TELL YOU.
THANK YOU.

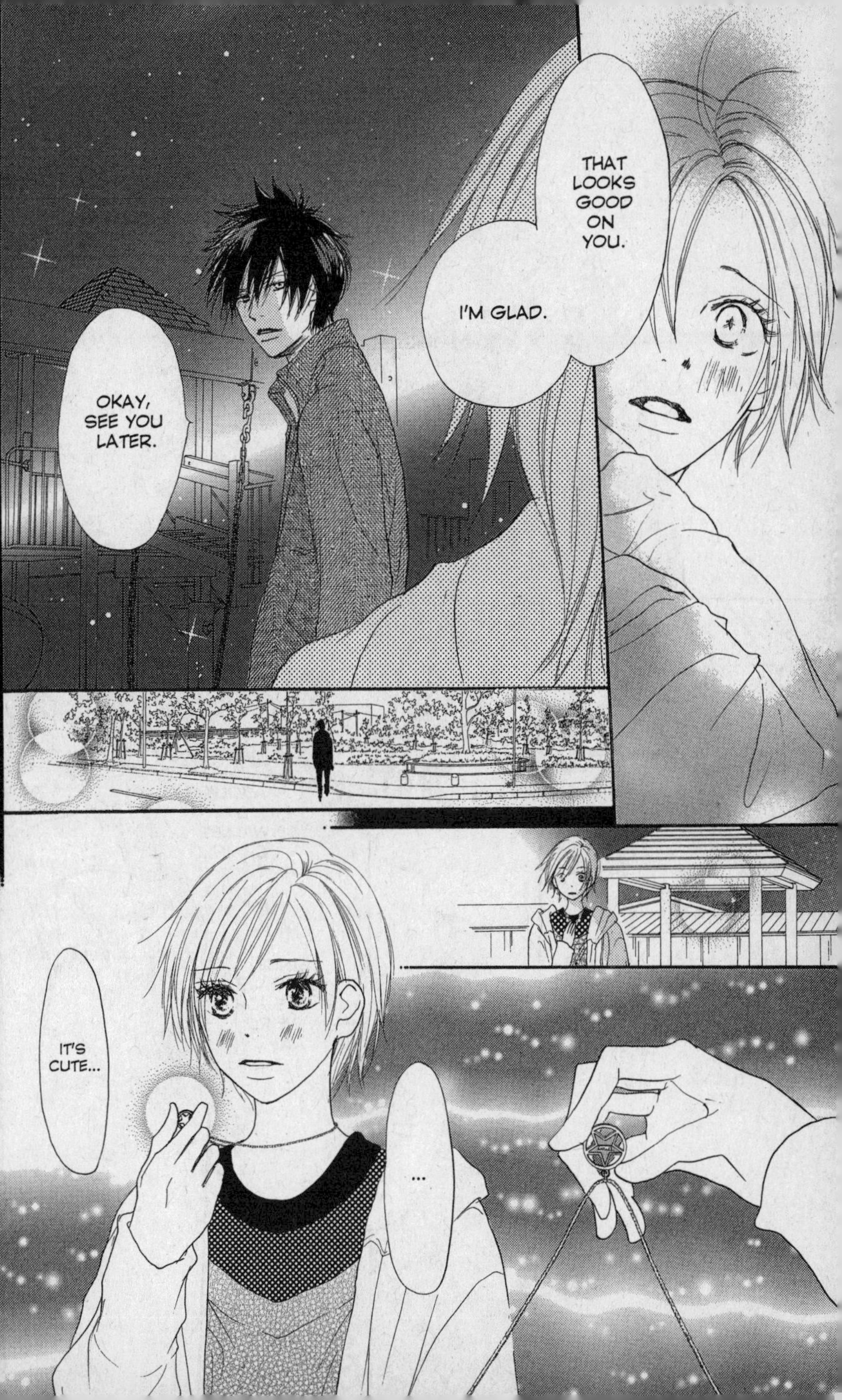
THAT LOOKS GOOD ON YOU.
I'M GLAD.
OKAY, SEE YOU LATER.
...
IT'S CUTE...

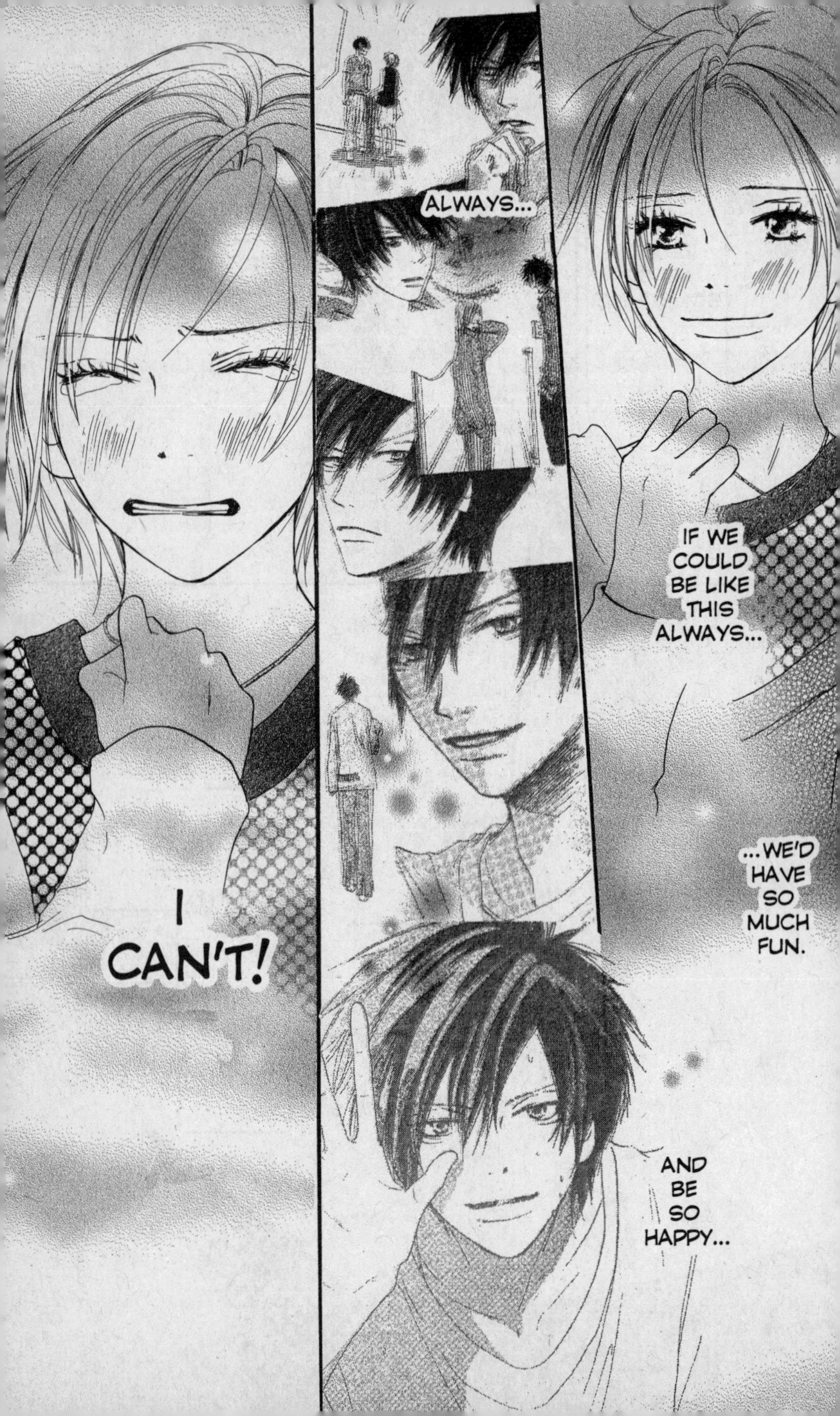
IF WE COULD BE LIKE THIS ALWAYS...
...WE'D HAVE SO MUCH FUN.
ALWAYS...
AND BE SO HAPPY...
I CAN'T!

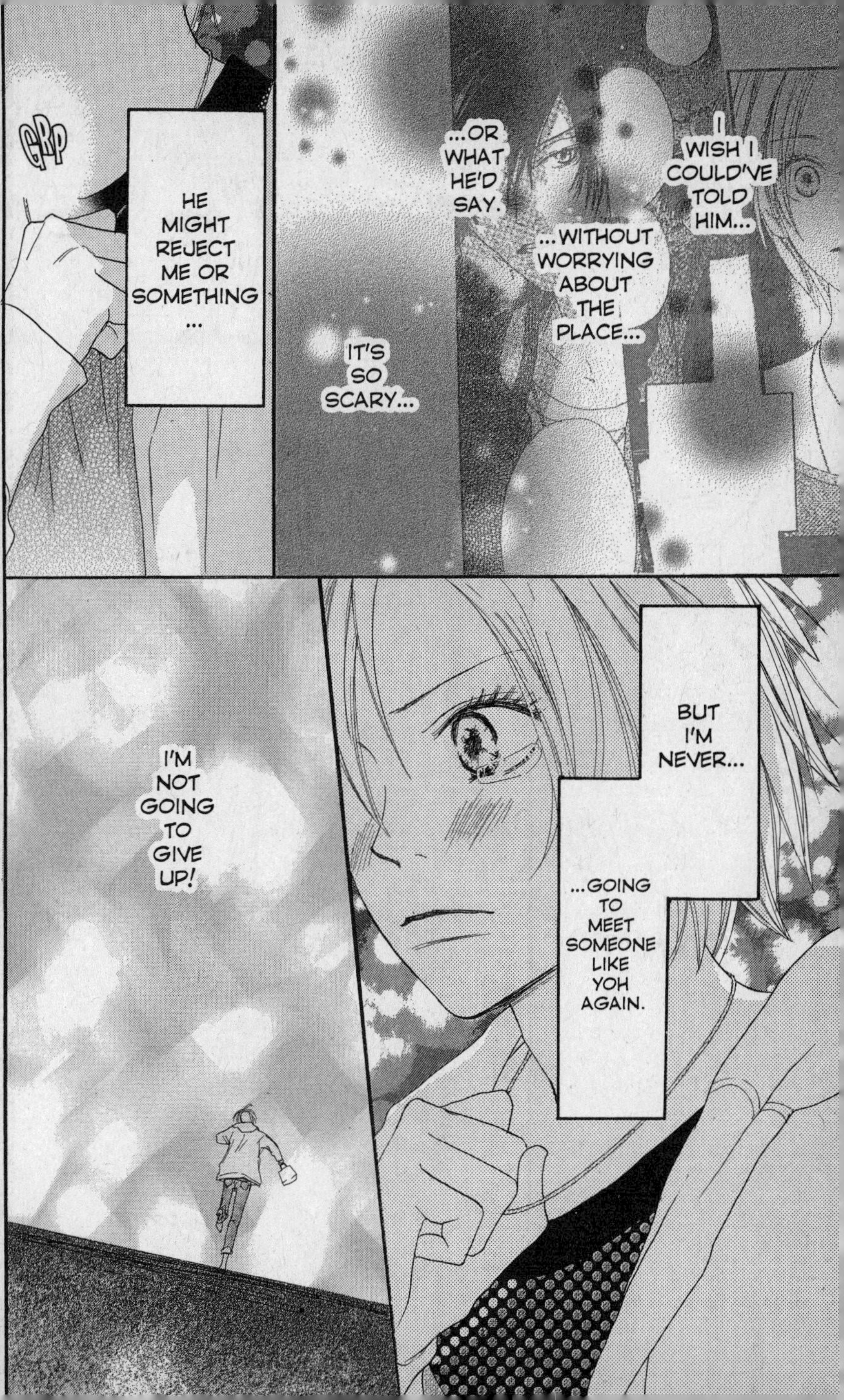
I WISH I COULD'VE TOLD HIM...
...WITHOUT WORRYING ABOUT THE PLACE...
...OR WHAT HE'D SAY.
IT'S SO SCARY...
HE MIGHT REJECT ME OR SOMETHING...
GRP
BUT I'M NEVER...
...GOING TO MEET SOMEONE LIKE YOH AGAIN.
I'M NOT GOING TO GIVE UP!

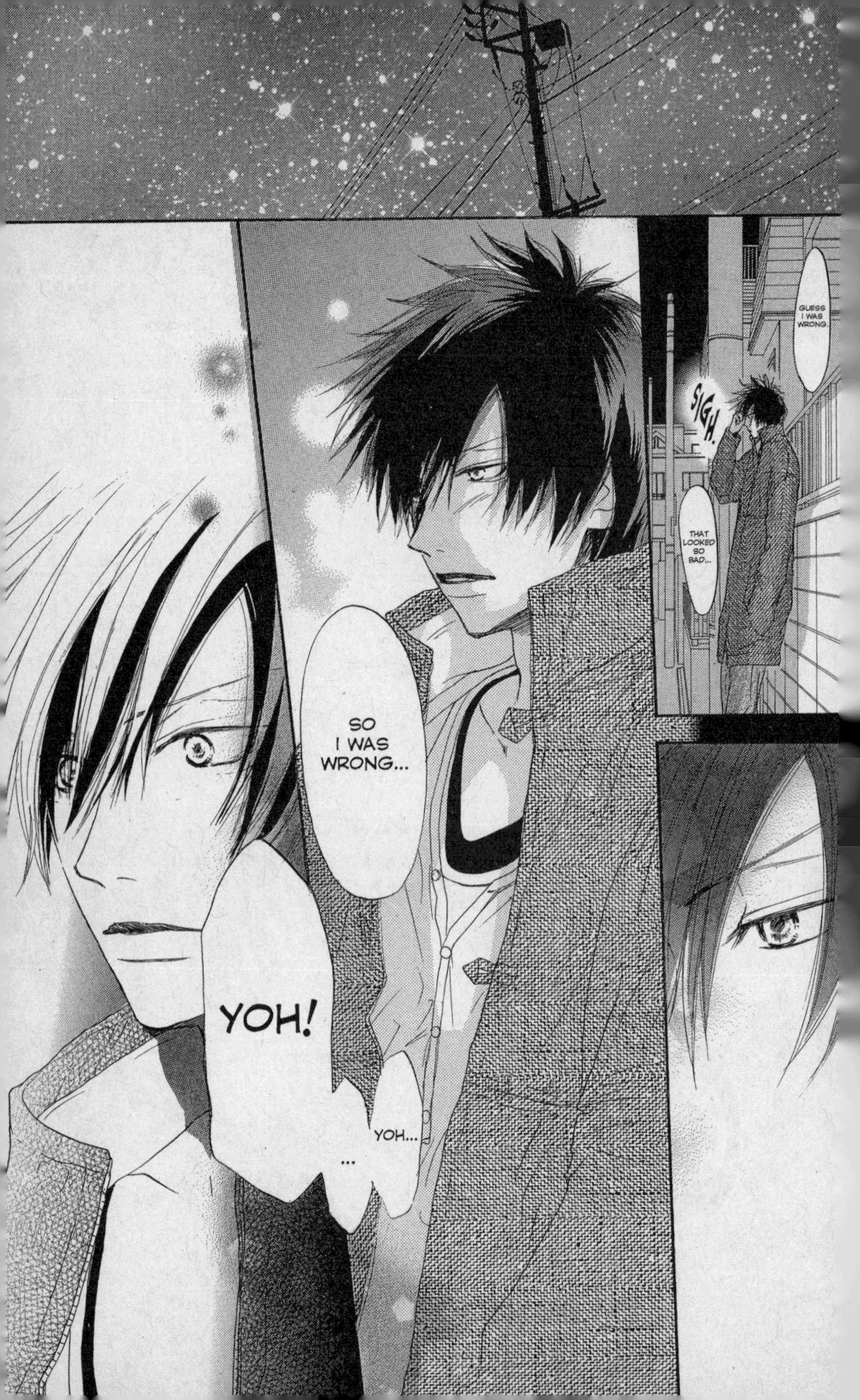
GUESS I WAS WRONG.
SIGH.
THAT LOOKED SO BAD...
SO I WAS WRONG...
YOH!
YOH...
...

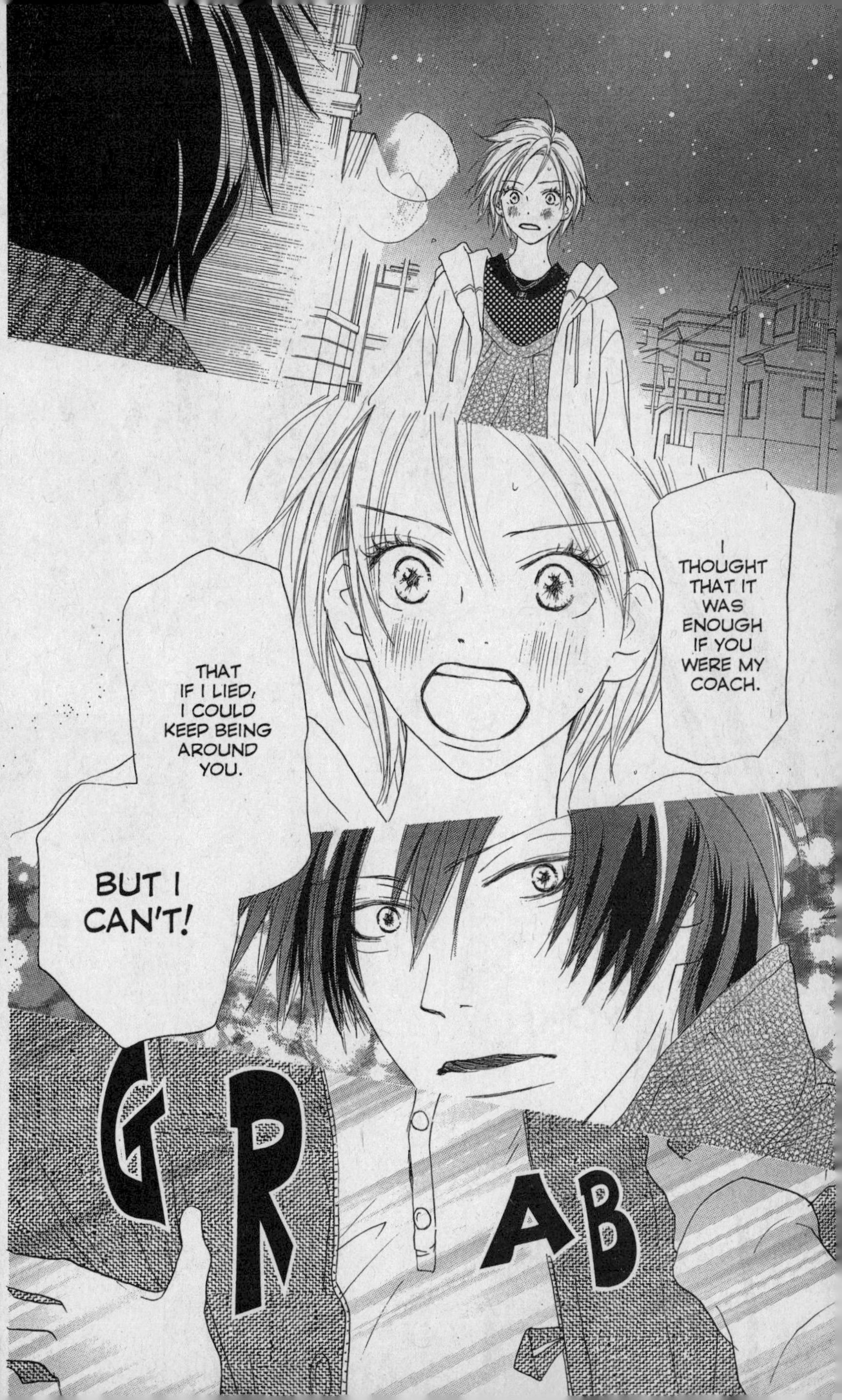
I THOUGHT THAT IT WAS ENOUGH IF YOU WERE MY COACH.
THAT IF I LIED, I COULD KEEP BEING AROUND YOU.
BUT I CAN'T!
GRAB

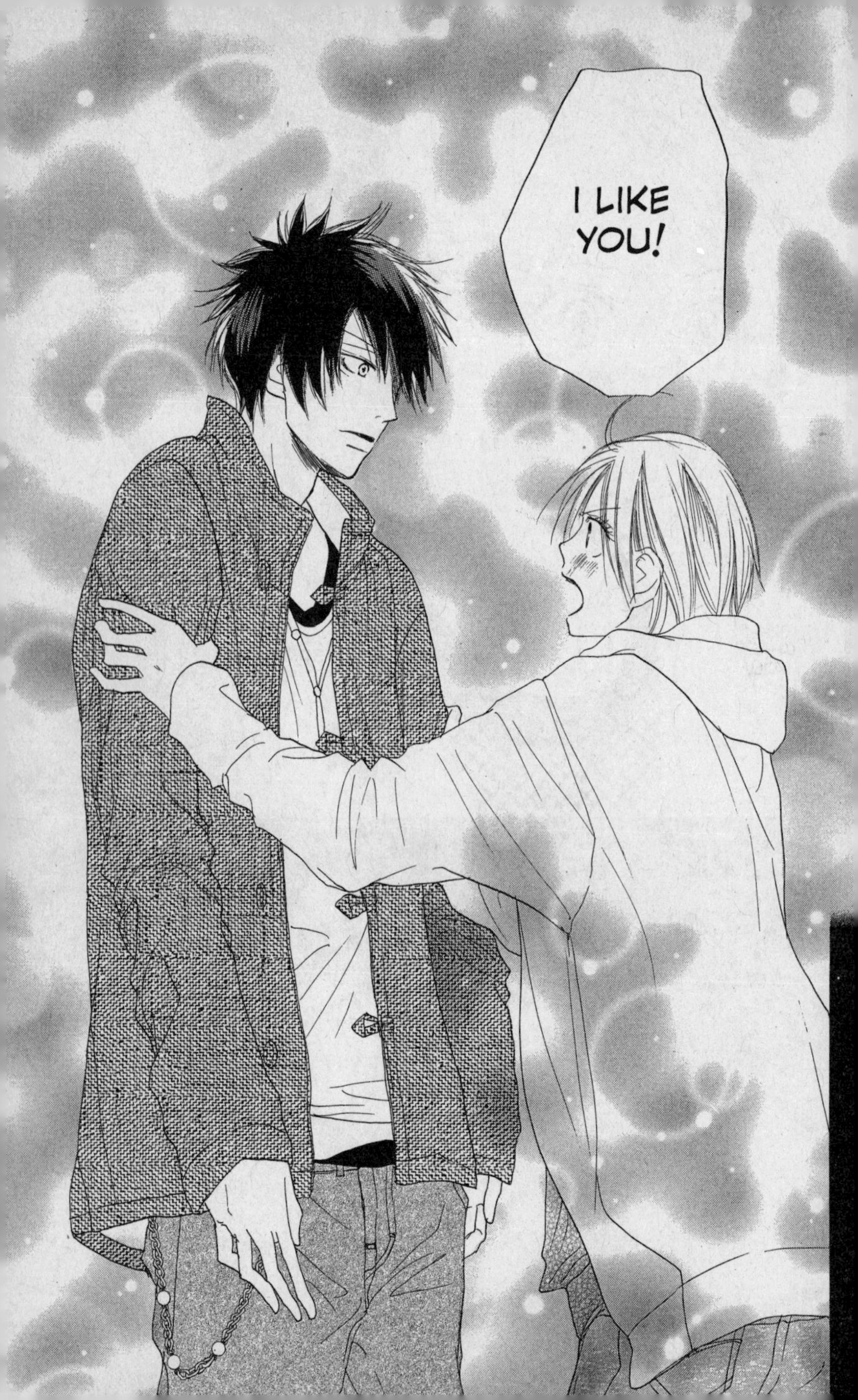
I LIKE YOU!

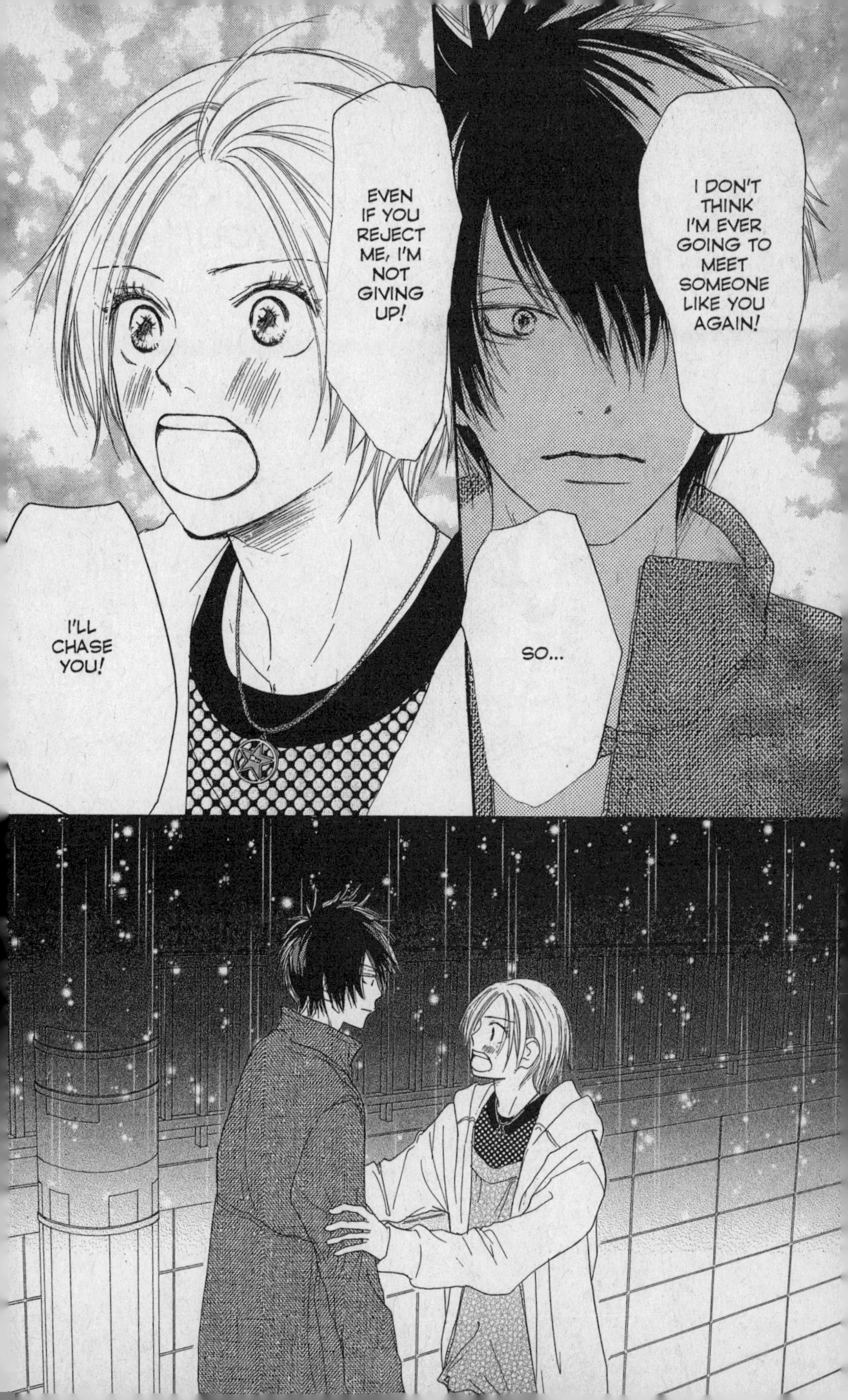
I DON'T THINK I'M EVER GOING TO MEET SOMEONE LIKE YOU AGAIN!
EVEN IF YOU REJECT ME, I'M NOT GIVING UP!
SO...
I'LL CHASE YOU!

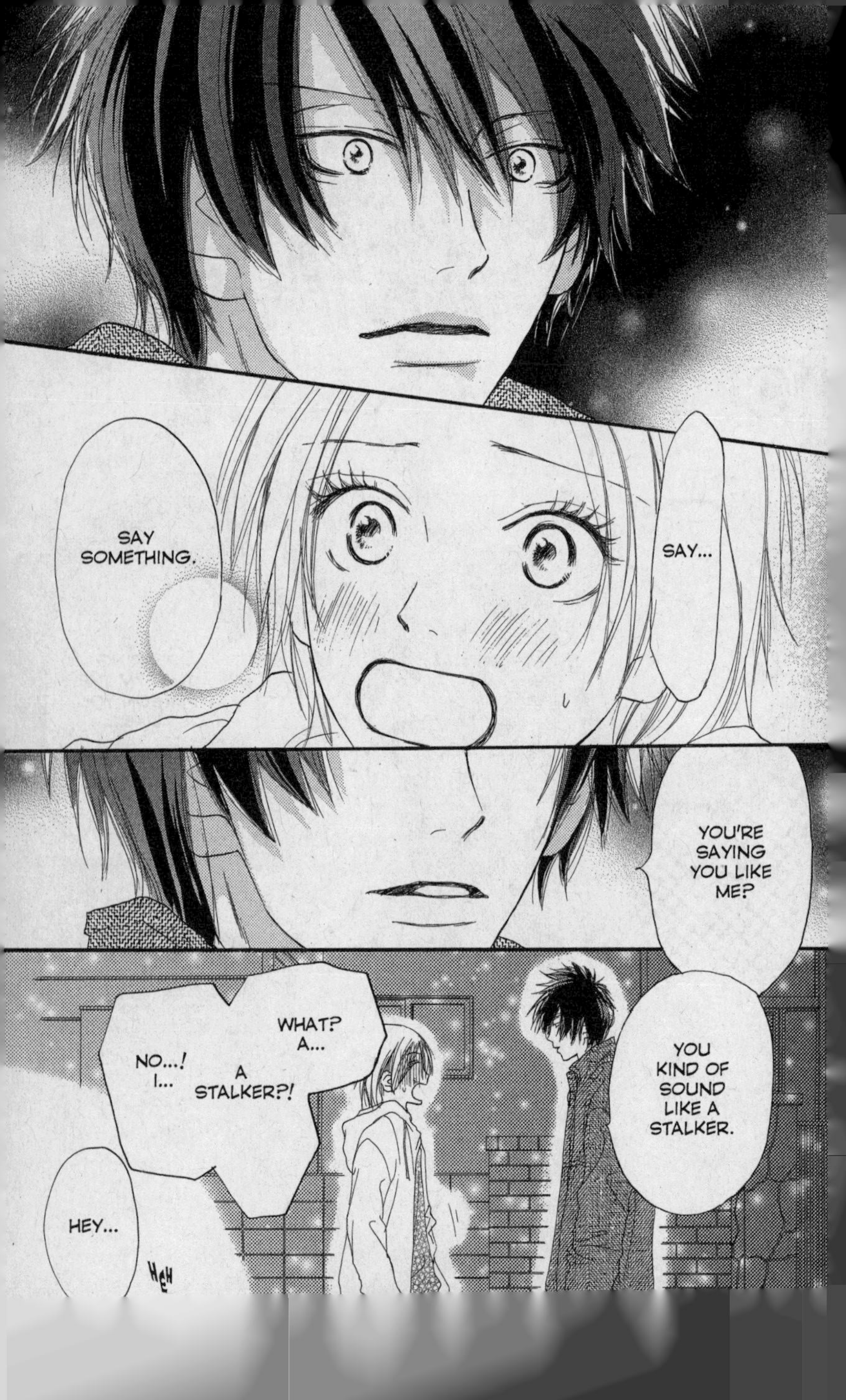
SAY...
SAY SOMETHING.
YOU'RE SAYING YOU LIKE ME?
YOU KIND OF SOUND LIKE A STALKER.
WHAT? A...
A STALKER?!
NO...! I...
HEH
HEY...

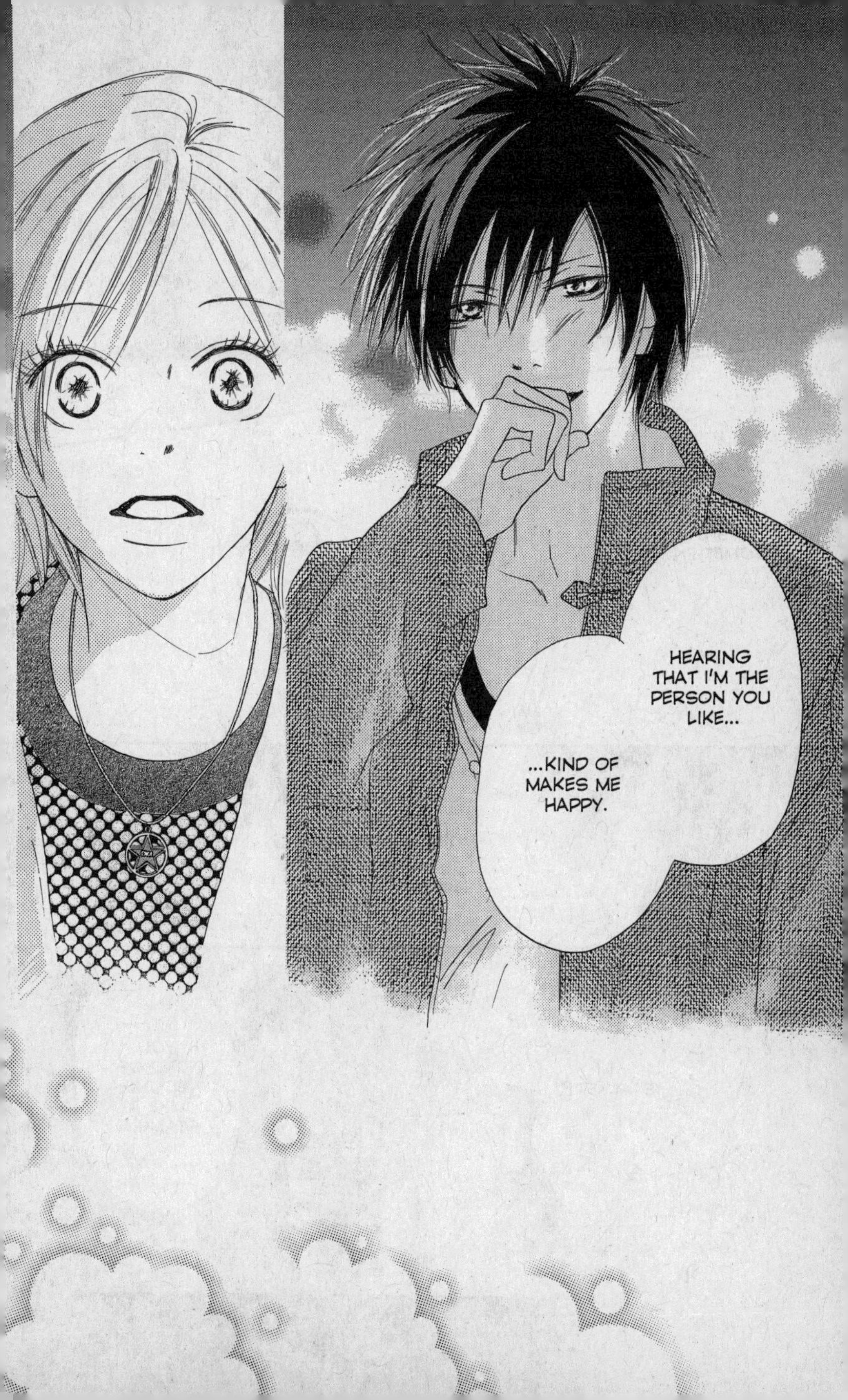
HEARING THAT I'M THE PERSON YOU LIKE...
...KIND OF MAKES ME HAPPY.

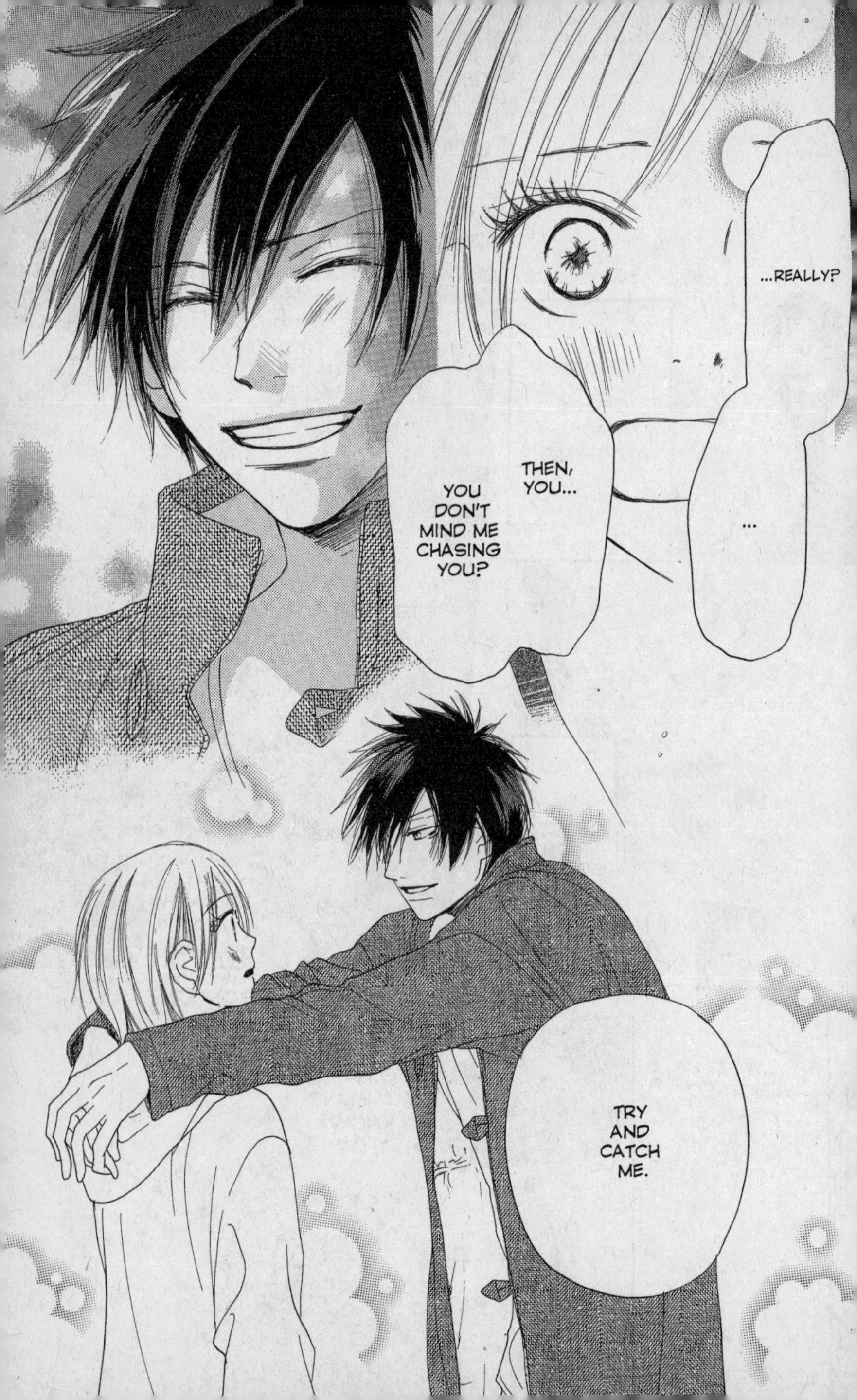
...REALLY?
...
THEN, YOU...
YOU DON'T MIND ME CHASING YOU?
TRY AND CATCH ME.

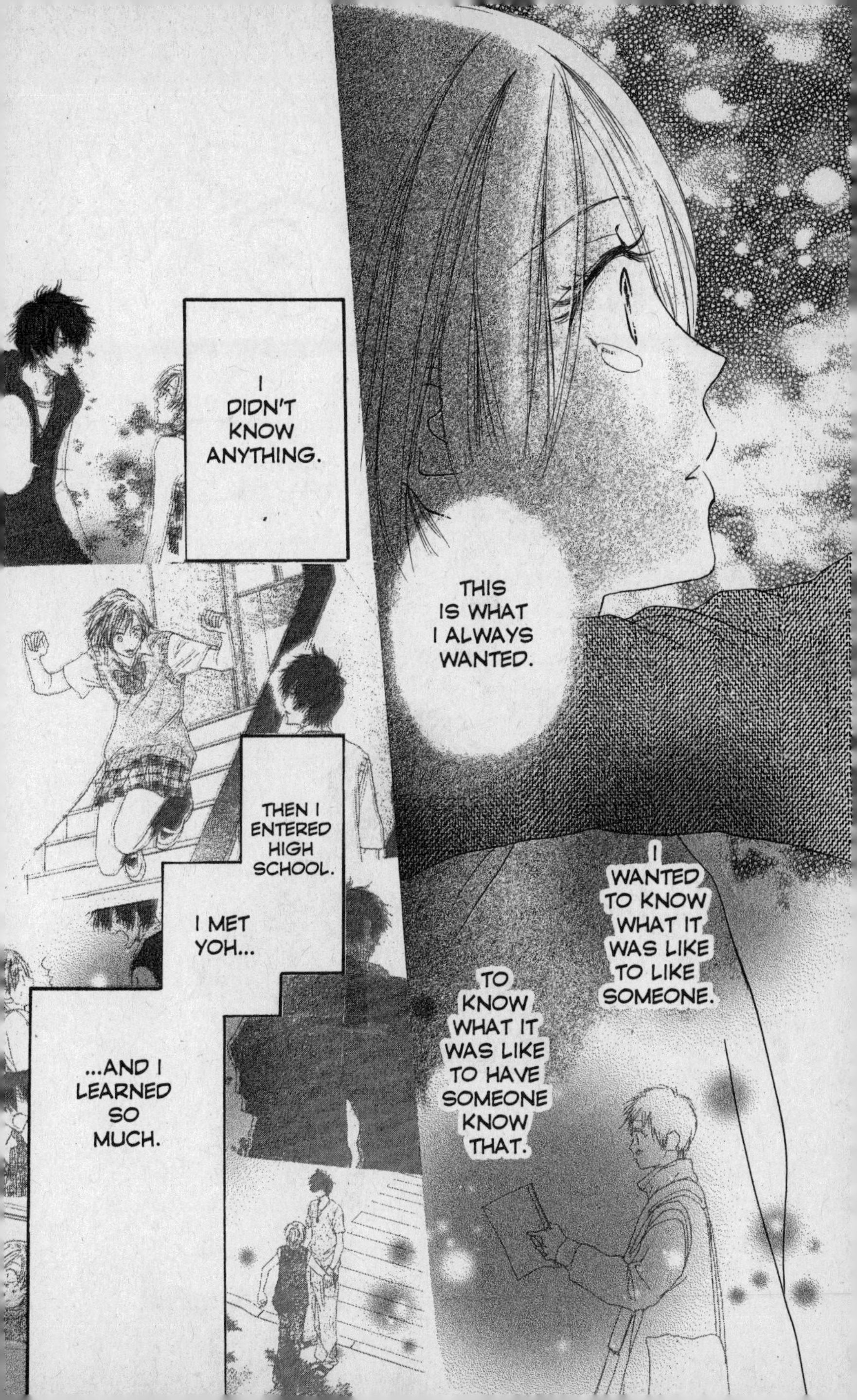
THIS IS WHAT I ALWAYS WANTED.
I WANTED TO KNOW WHAT IT WAS LIKE TO LIKE SOMEONE.
TO KNOW WHAT IT WAS LIKE TO HAVE SOMEONE KNOW THAT.
I DIDN'T KNOW ANYTHING.
THEN I ENTERED HIGH SCHOOL.
I MET YOH...
...AND I LEARNED SO MUCH.

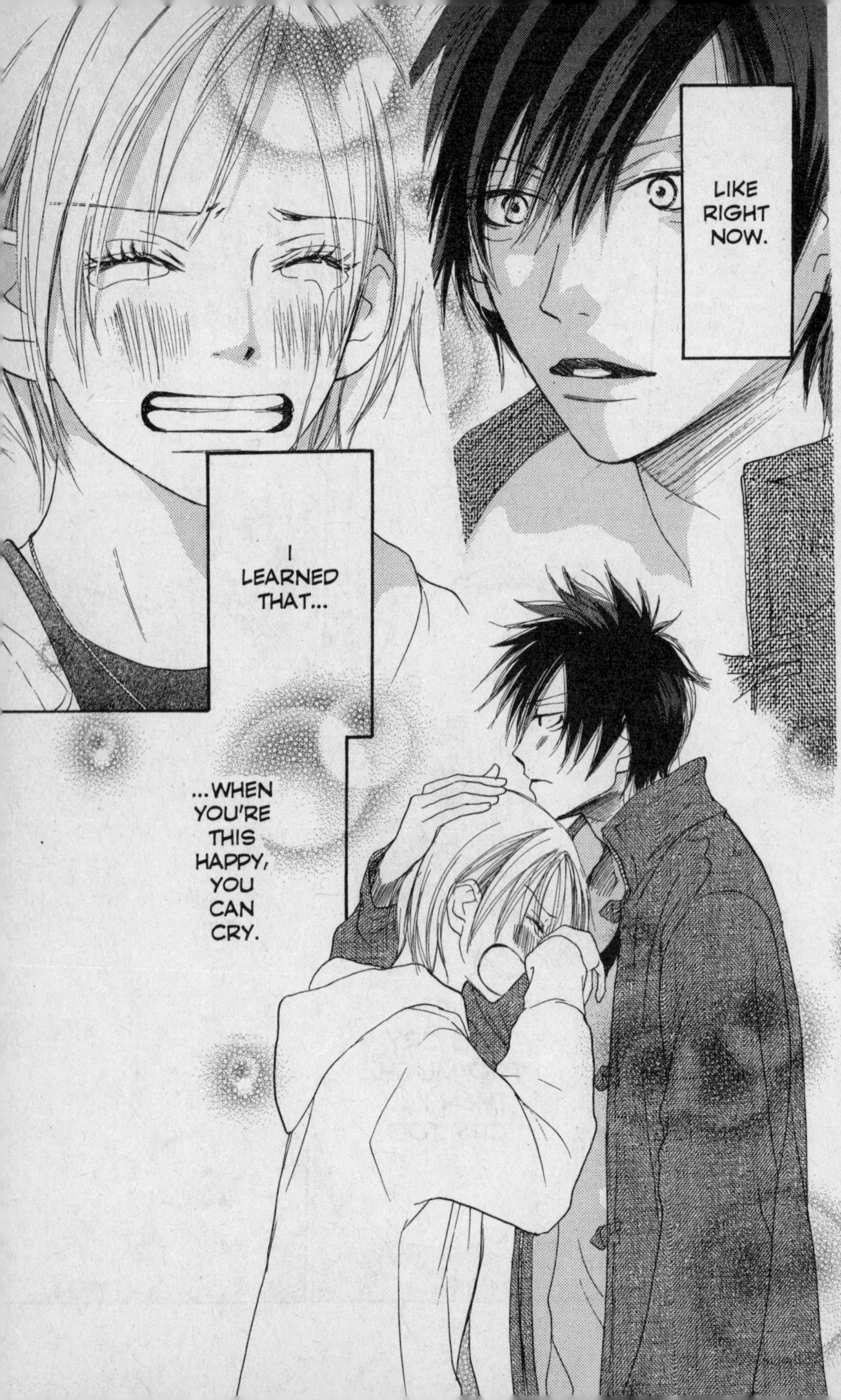
LIKE RIGHT NOW.
I LEARNED THAT...
...WHEN YOU'RE THIS HAPPY, YOU CAN CRY.

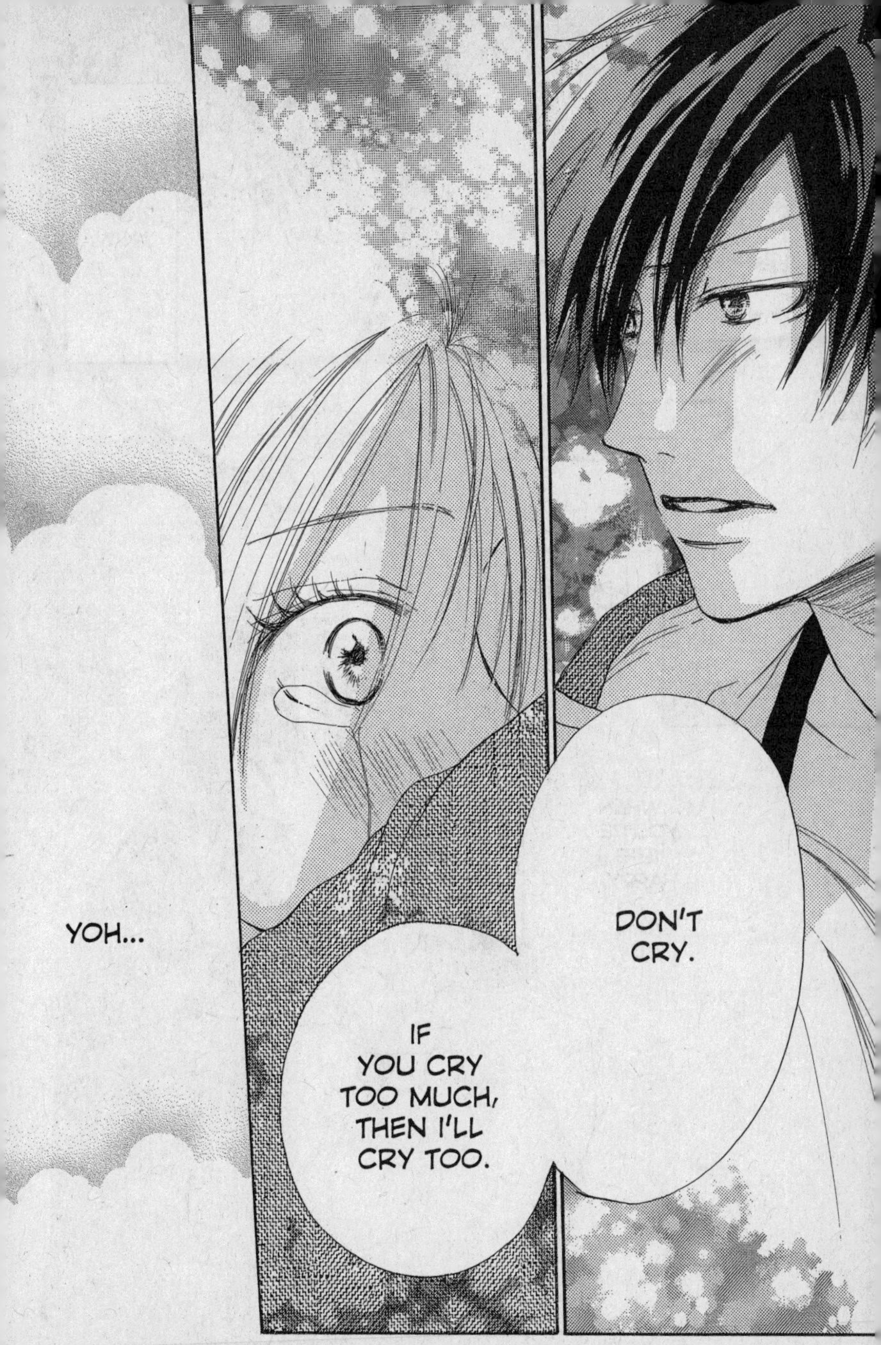
DON'T CRY.
IF YOU CRY TOO MUCH, THEN I'LL CRY TOO.
YOH...

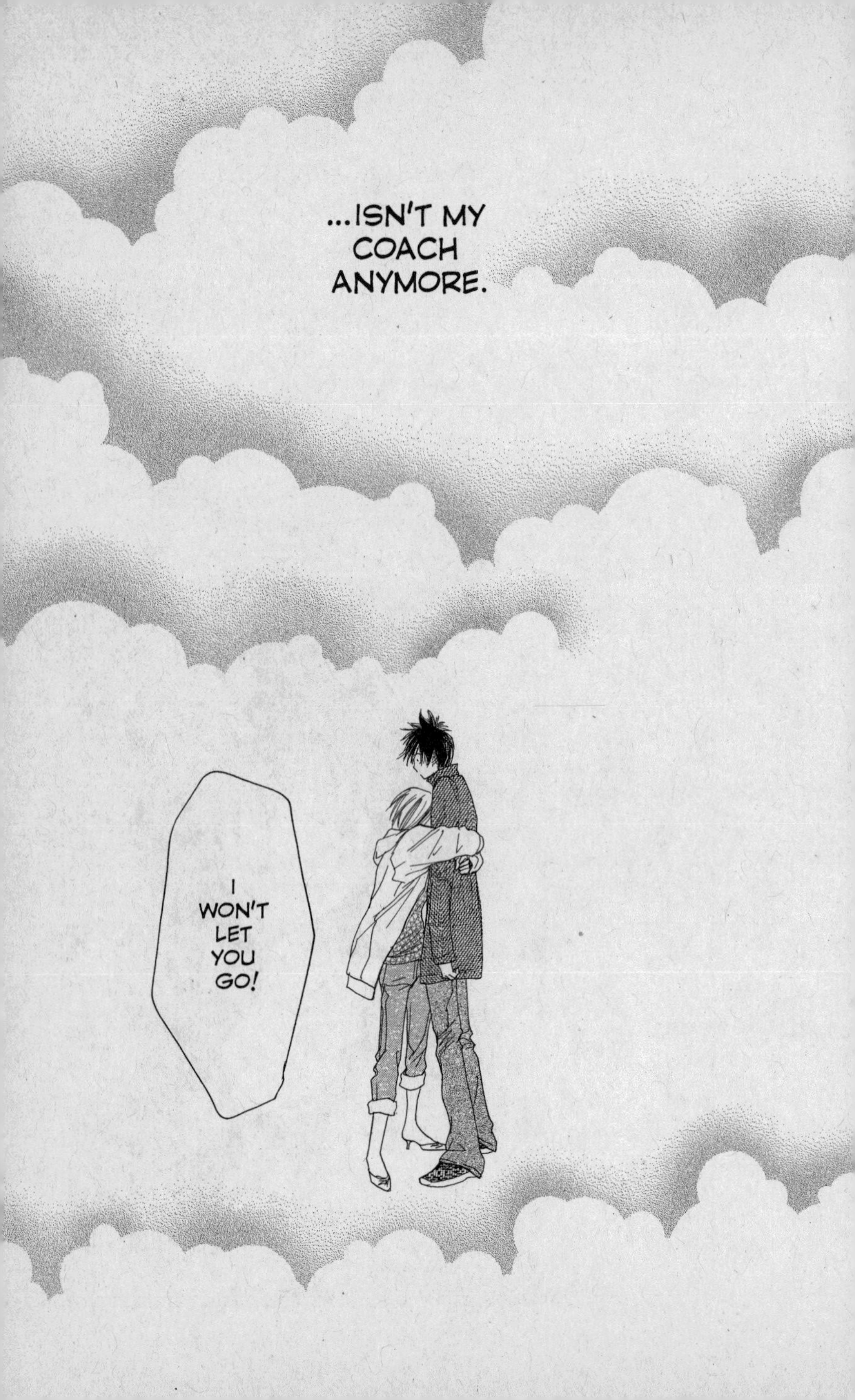
...ISN'T MY COACH ANYMORE.
I WON'T LET YOU GO!

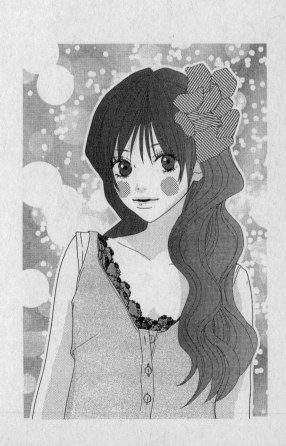

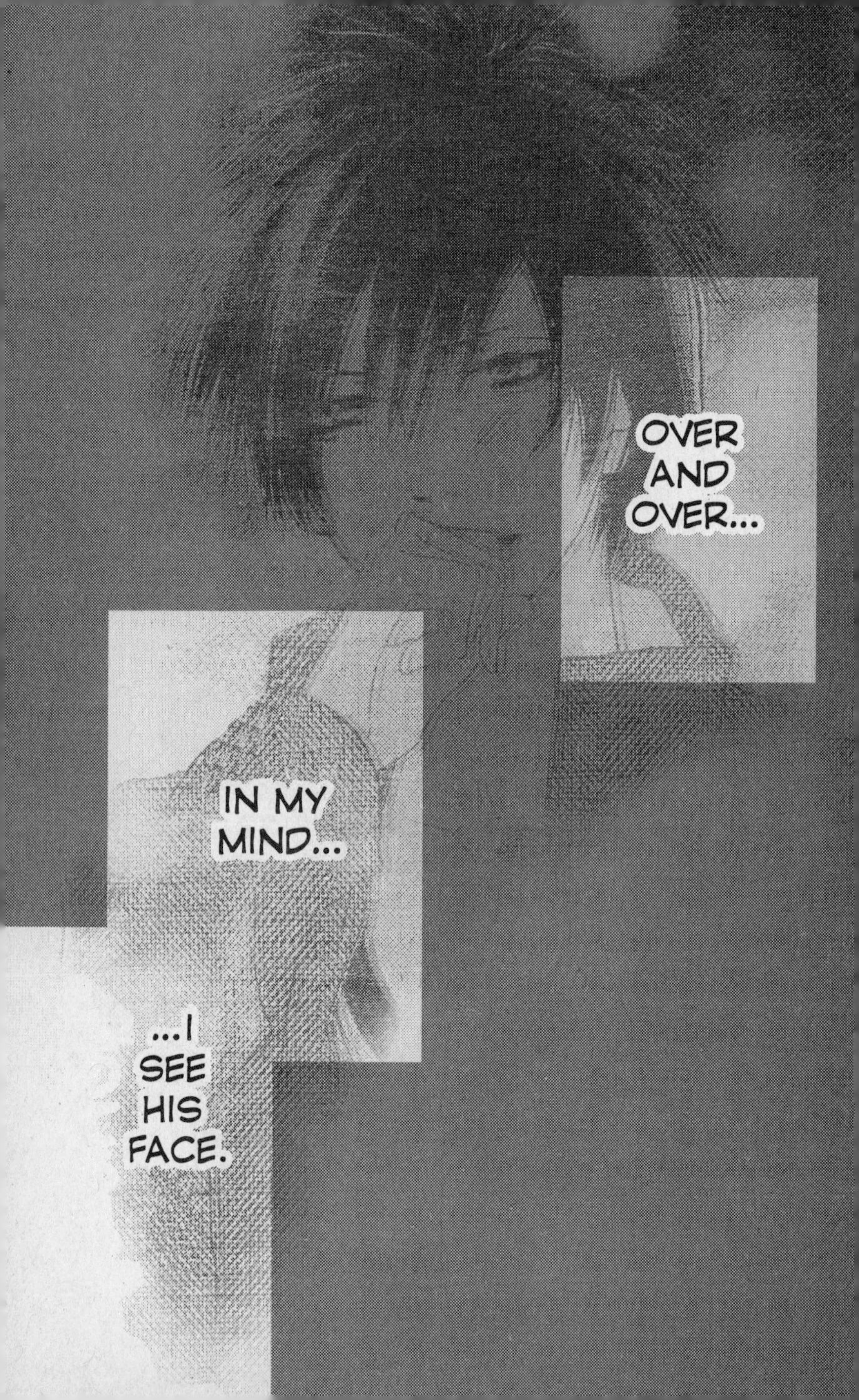
OVER AND OVER...
IN MY MIND...
...I SEE HIS FACE.

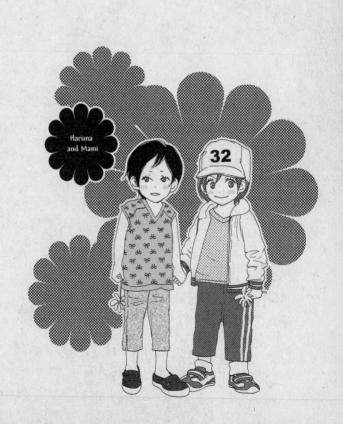

Haruna
and Mami

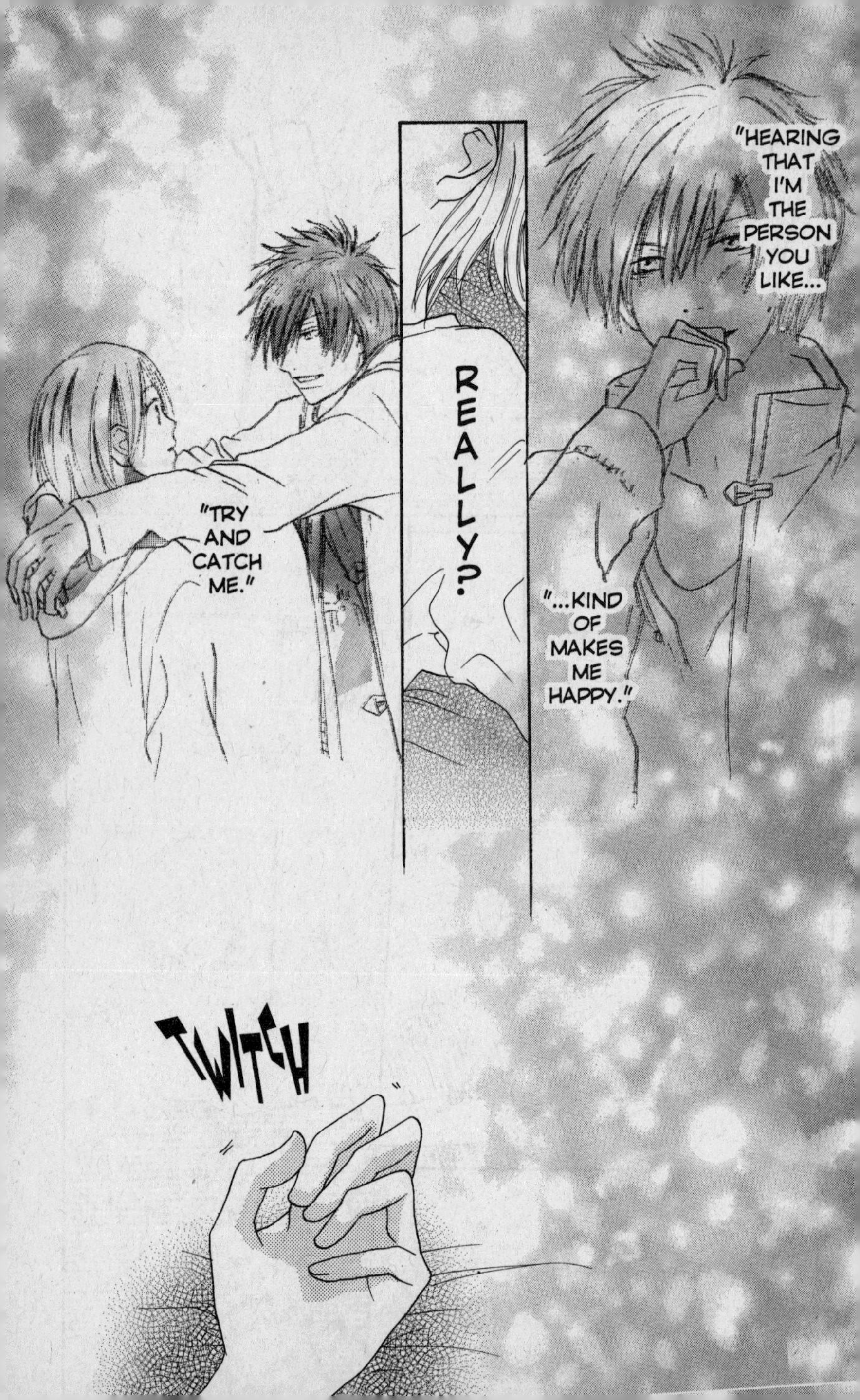
"HEARING THAT I'M THE PERSON YOU LIKE...
"...KIND OF MAKES ME HAPPY."
REALLY?
"TRY AND CATCH ME."
TWITCH

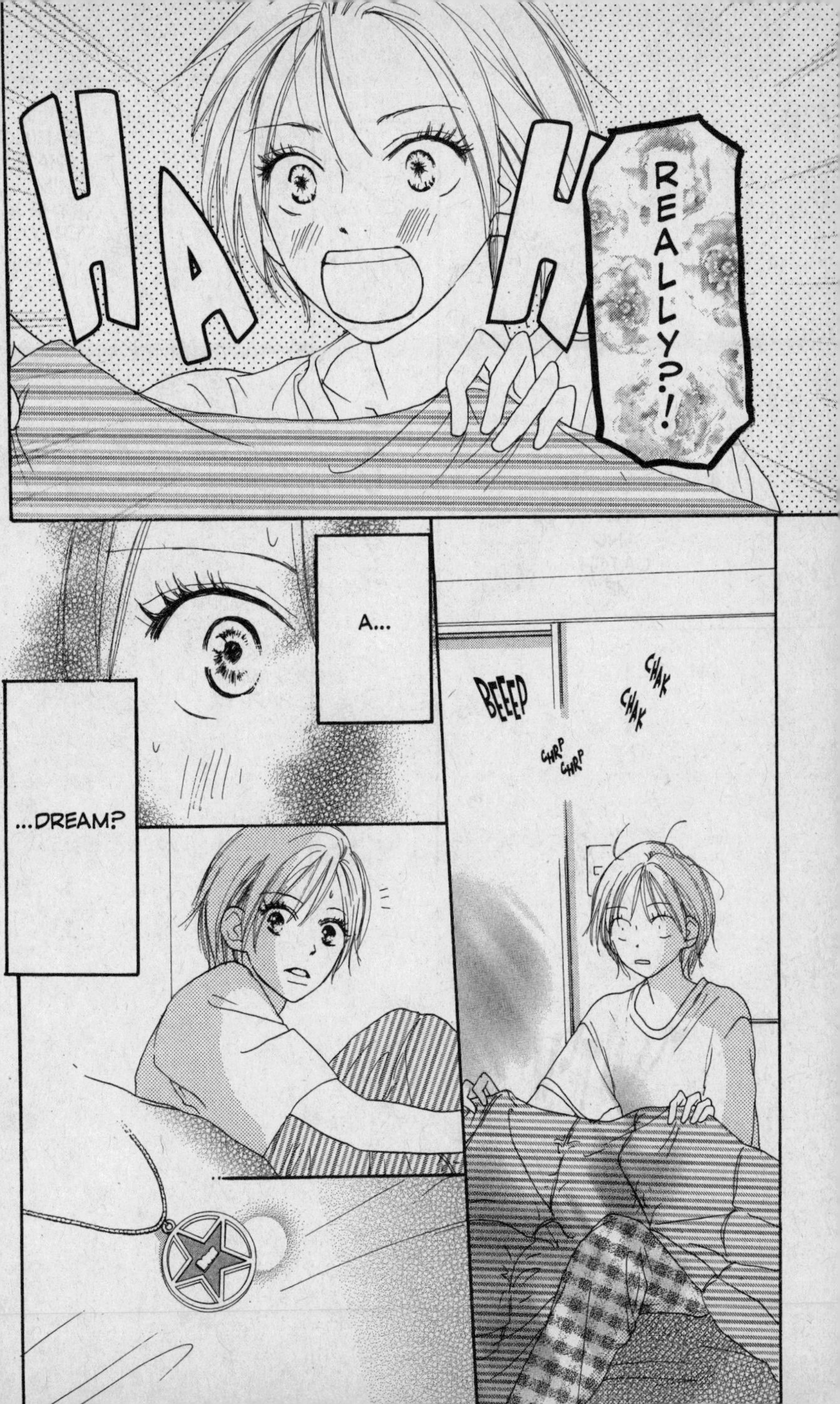
REALLY?!
HAH
CHAK CHAK
BEEEP
CHRP CHRP
A...
...DREAM?

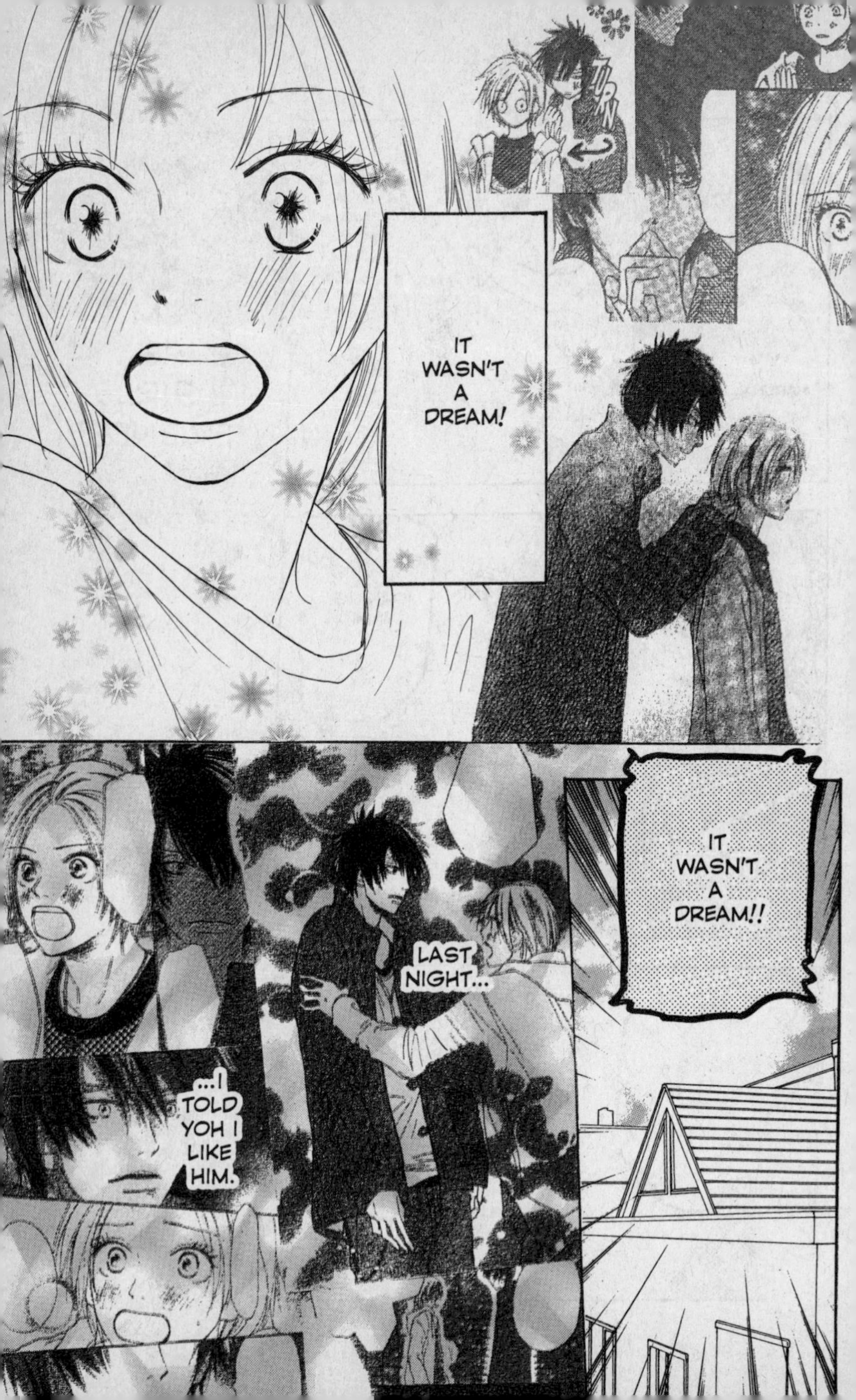
TURN
IT WASN'T A DREAM!
IT WASN'T A DREAM!!
LAST NIGHT...
...I TOLD YOH I LIKE HIM.

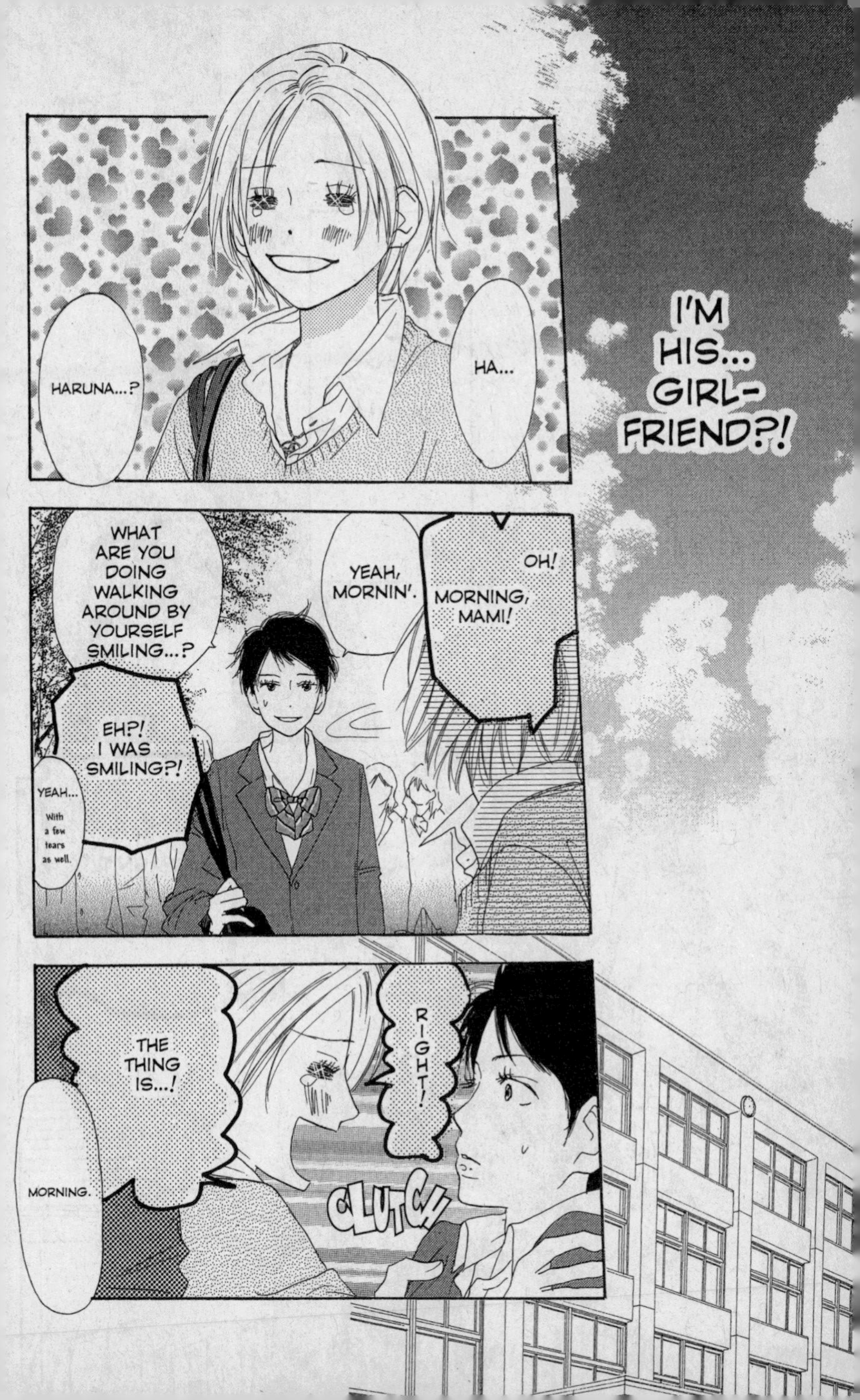
I'M HIS... GIRL-FRIEND?!
HA...
HARUNA...?
OH!
MORNING, MAMI!
YEAH, MORNIN'.
WHAT ARE YOU DOING WALKING AROUND BY YOURSELF SMILING...?
EH?! I WAS SMILING?!
YEAH...
With a few tears as well.
RIGHT!
THE THING IS...!
CLUTCH
MORNING.

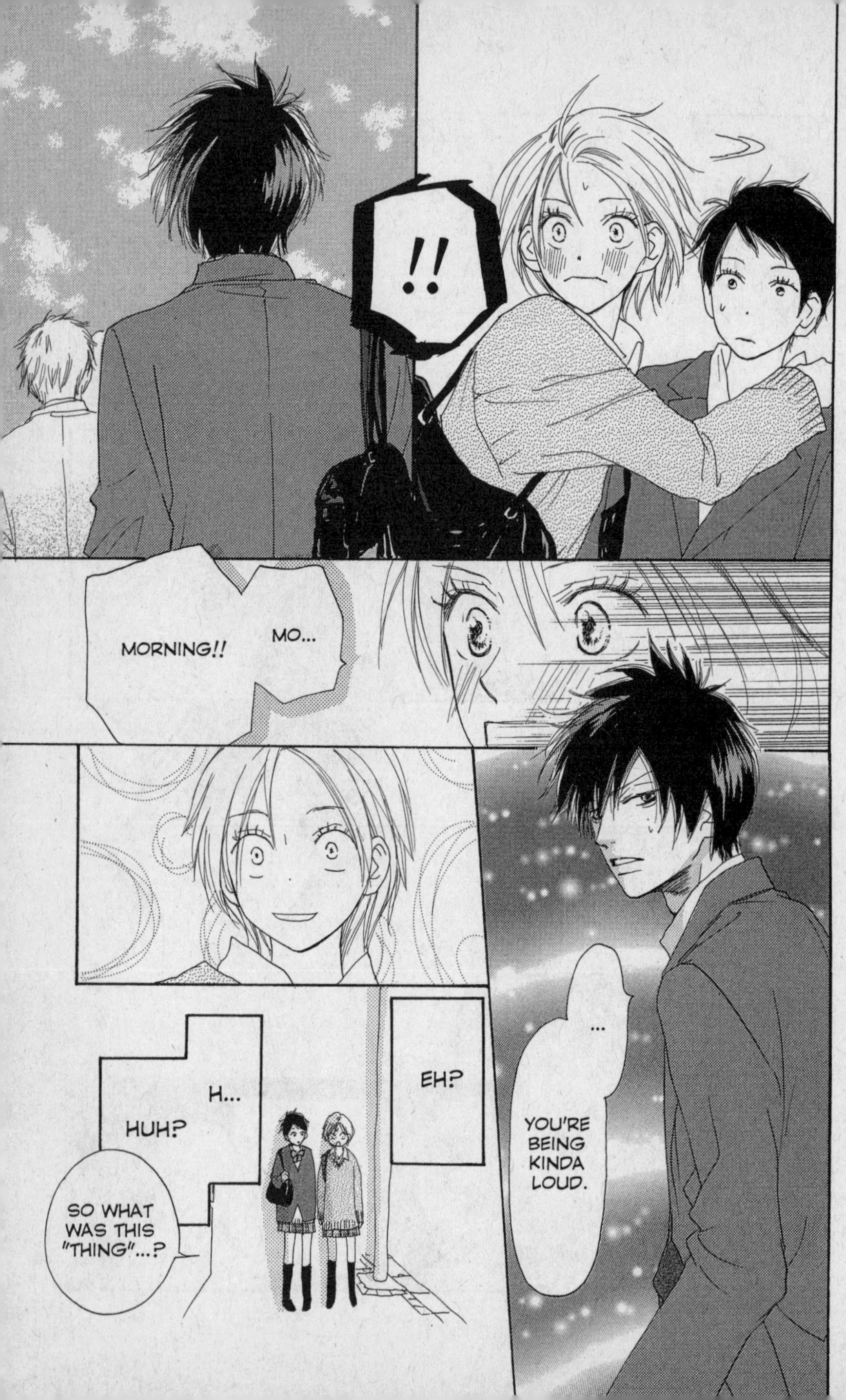
!!
MO... MORNING!!
... YOU'RE BEING KINDA LOUD.
EH?
H... HUH?
SO WHAT WAS THIS "THING"...?

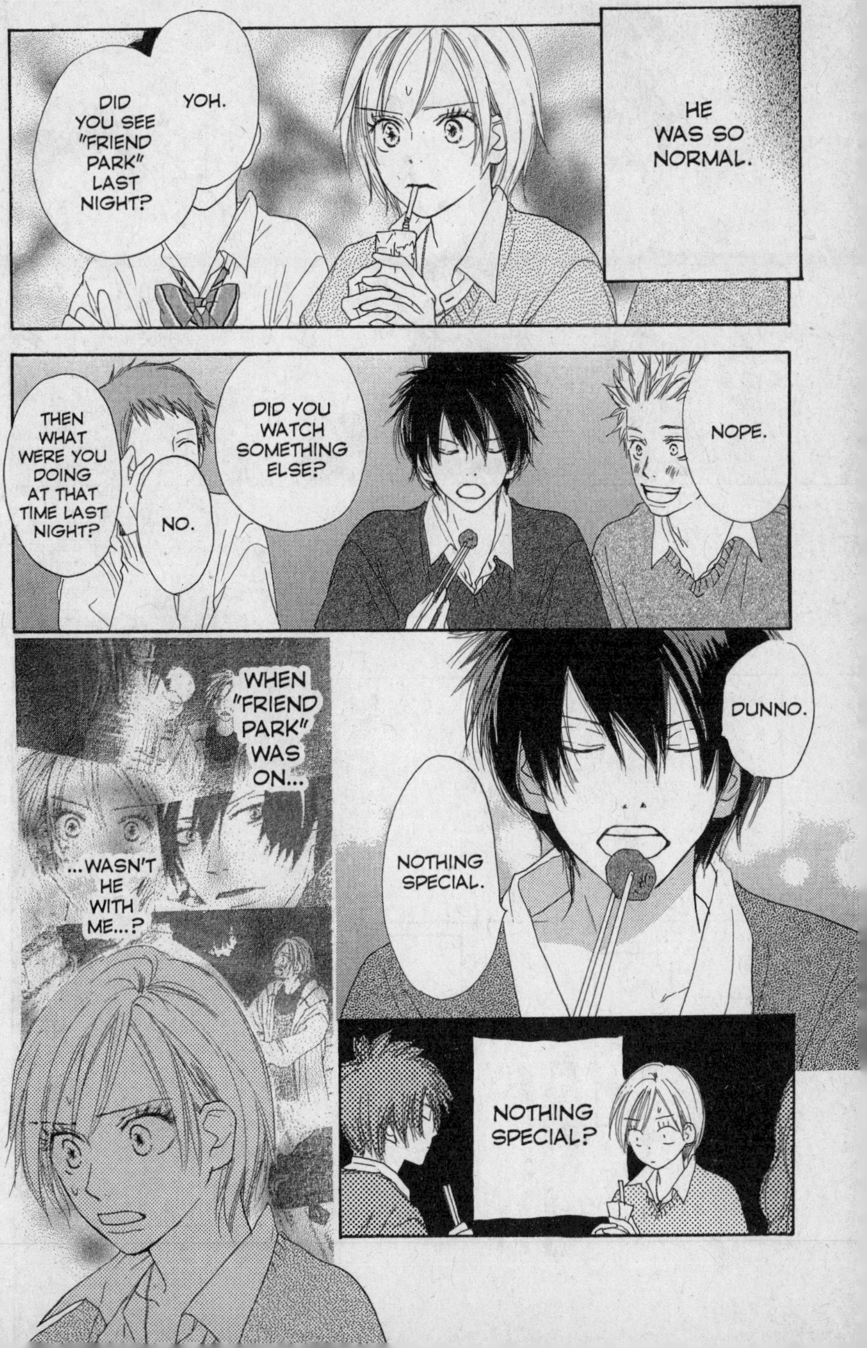

HE WAS SO NORMAL.
YOH.
DID YOU SEE "FRIEND PARK" LAST NIGHT?
NOPE.
DID YOU WATCH SOMETHING ELSE?
NO.
THEN WHAT WERE YOU DOING AT THAT TIME LAST NIGHT?
DUNNO.
NOTHING SPECIAL.
NOTHING SPECIAL?
WHEN "FRIEND PARK" WAS ON...
...WASN'T HE WITH ME...?

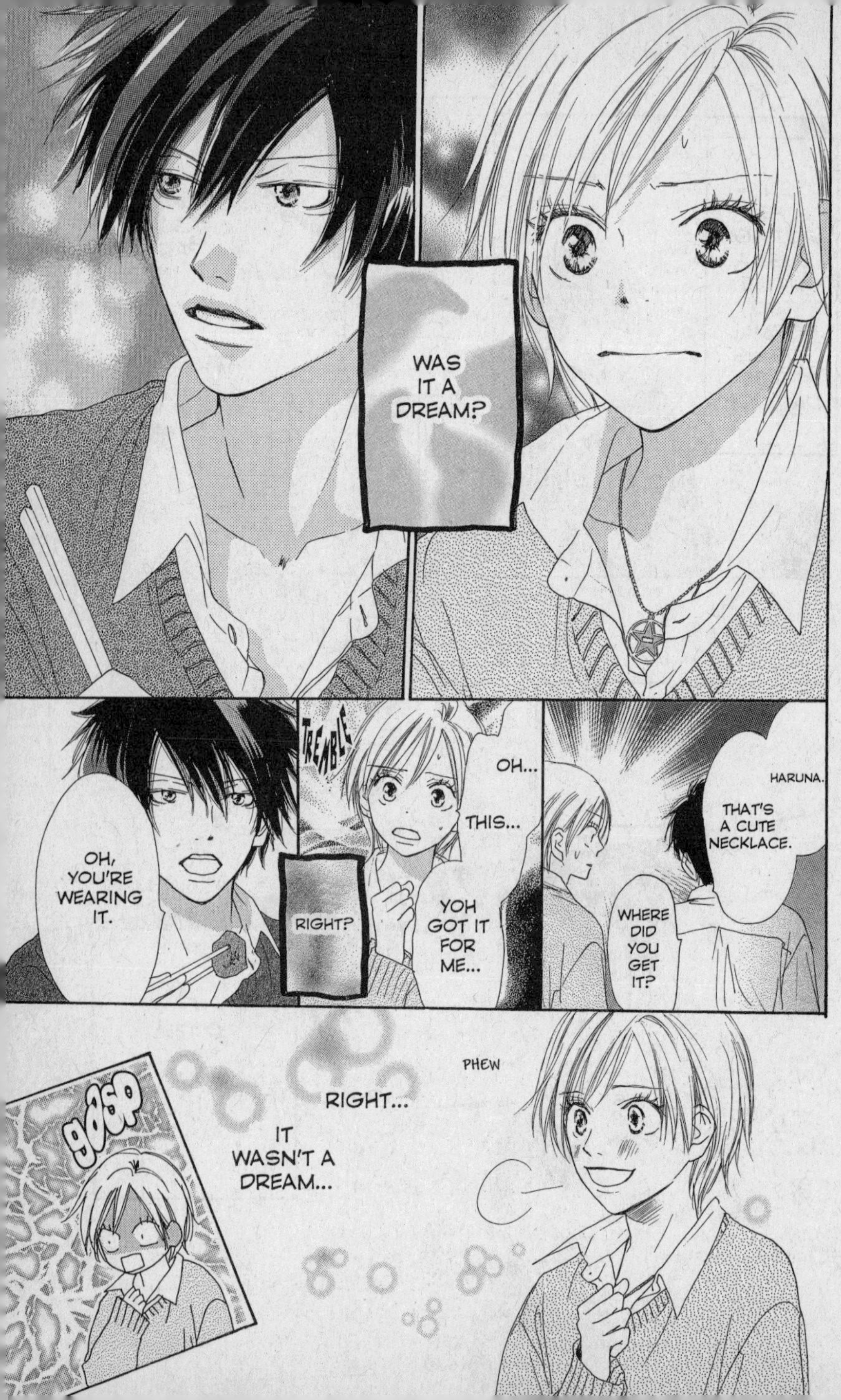
WAS IT A DREAM?
HARUNA.
THAT'S A CUTE NECKLACE.
WHERE DID YOU GET IT?
TREMBLE
OH...
THIS...
YOH GOT IT FOR ME...
RIGHT?
OH, YOU'RE WEARING IT.
PHEW
RIGHT...
IT WASN'T A DREAM...
GASP

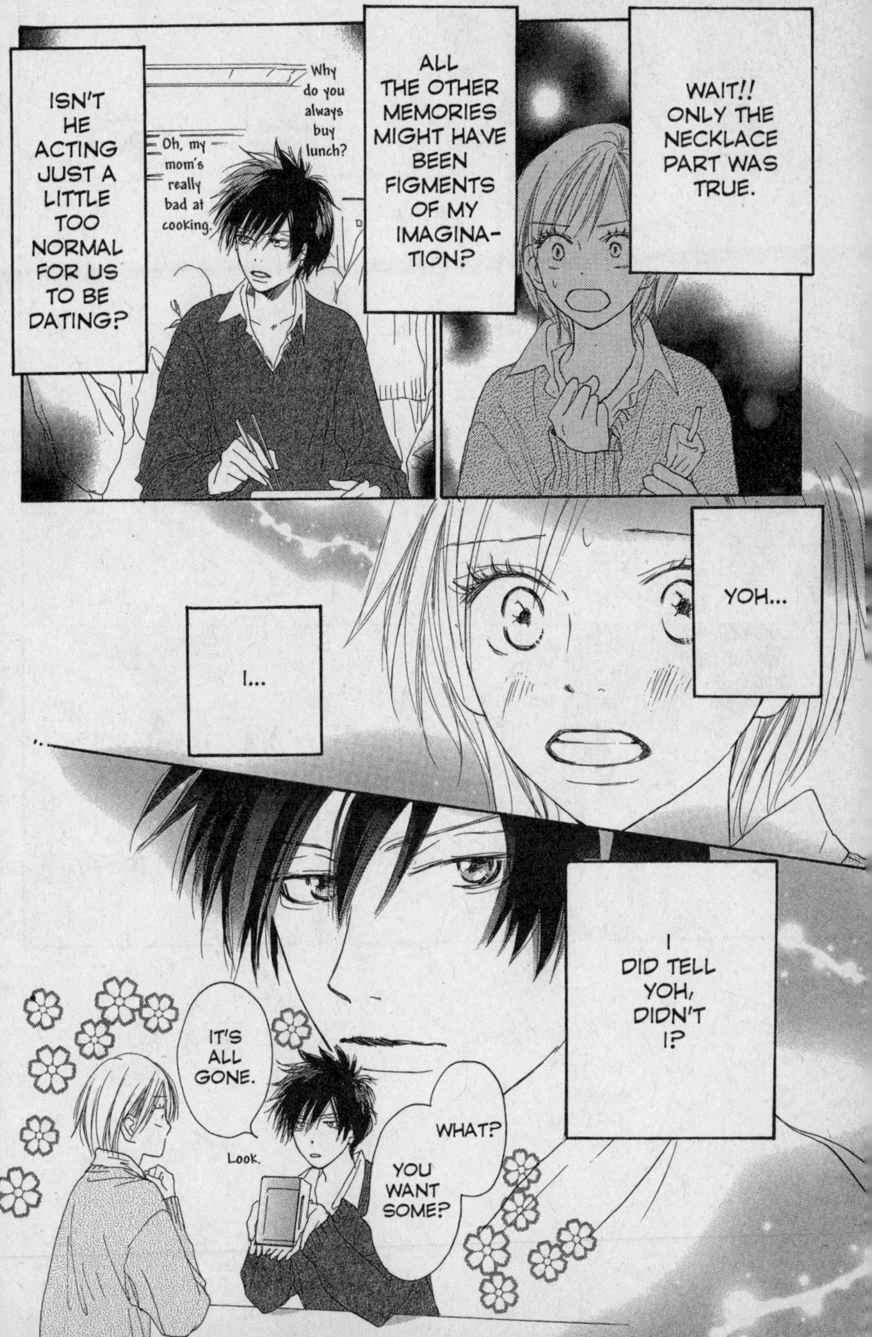
WAIT!! ONLY THE NECKLACE PART WAS TRUE.
ALL THE OTHER MEMORIES MIGHT HAVE BEEN FIGMENTS OF MY IMAGINATION?
Why do you always buy lunch?
Oh, my mom's really bad at cooking.
ISN'T HE ACTING JUST A LITTLE TOO NORMAL FOR US TO BE DATING?
YOH...
I...
I DID TELL YOH, DIDN'T I?
WHAT? YOU WANT SOME?
Look.
IT'S ALL GONE.

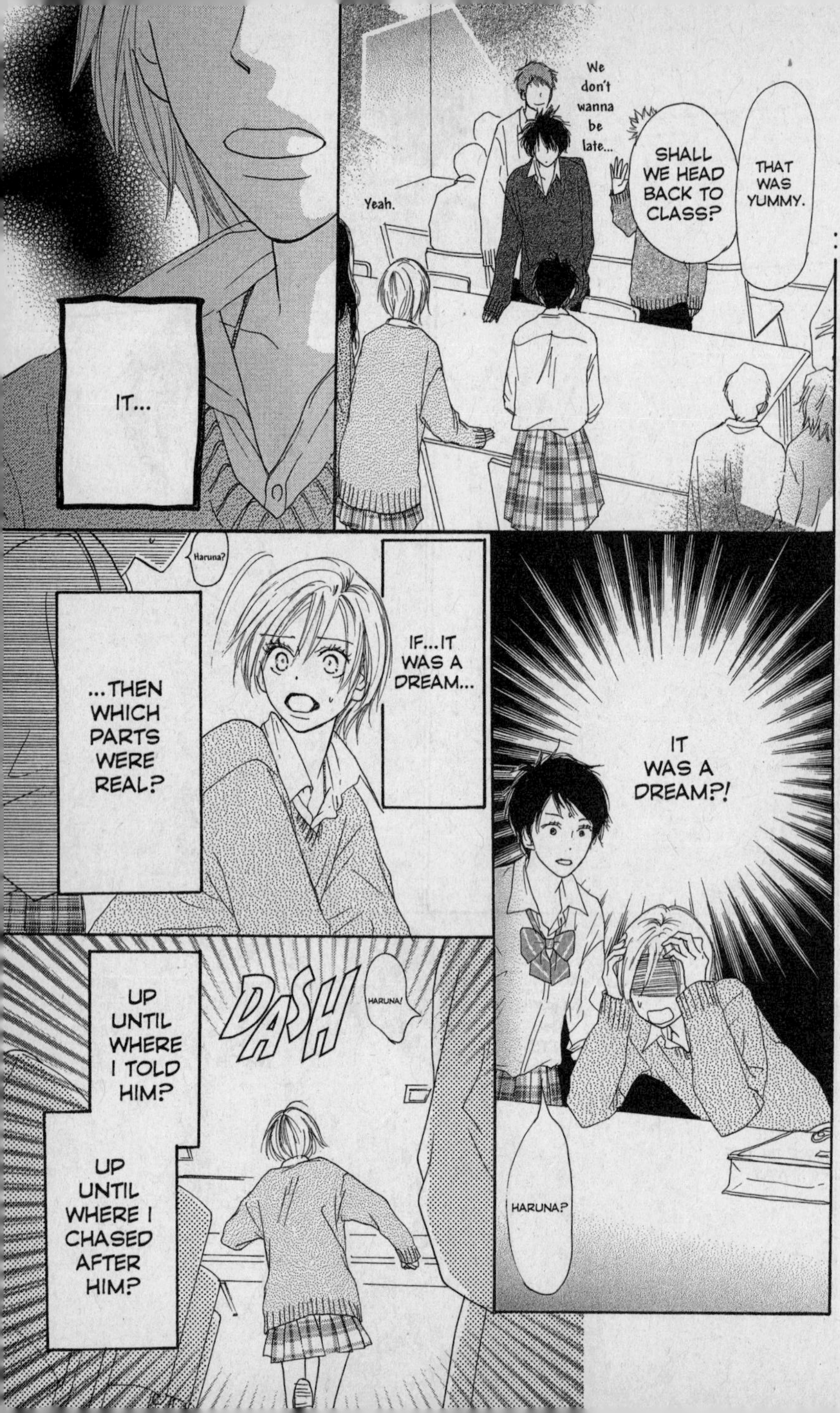
THAT WAS YUMMY.
SHALL WE HEAD BACK TO CLASS?
We don't wanna be late...
Yeah.
IT...
IT WAS A DREAM?!
HARUNA?
IF...IT WAS A DREAM...
Haruna?
...THEN WHICH PARTS WERE REAL?
HARUNA!
DASH
UP UNTIL WHERE I TOLD HIM?
UP UNTIL WHERE I CHASED AFTER HIM?

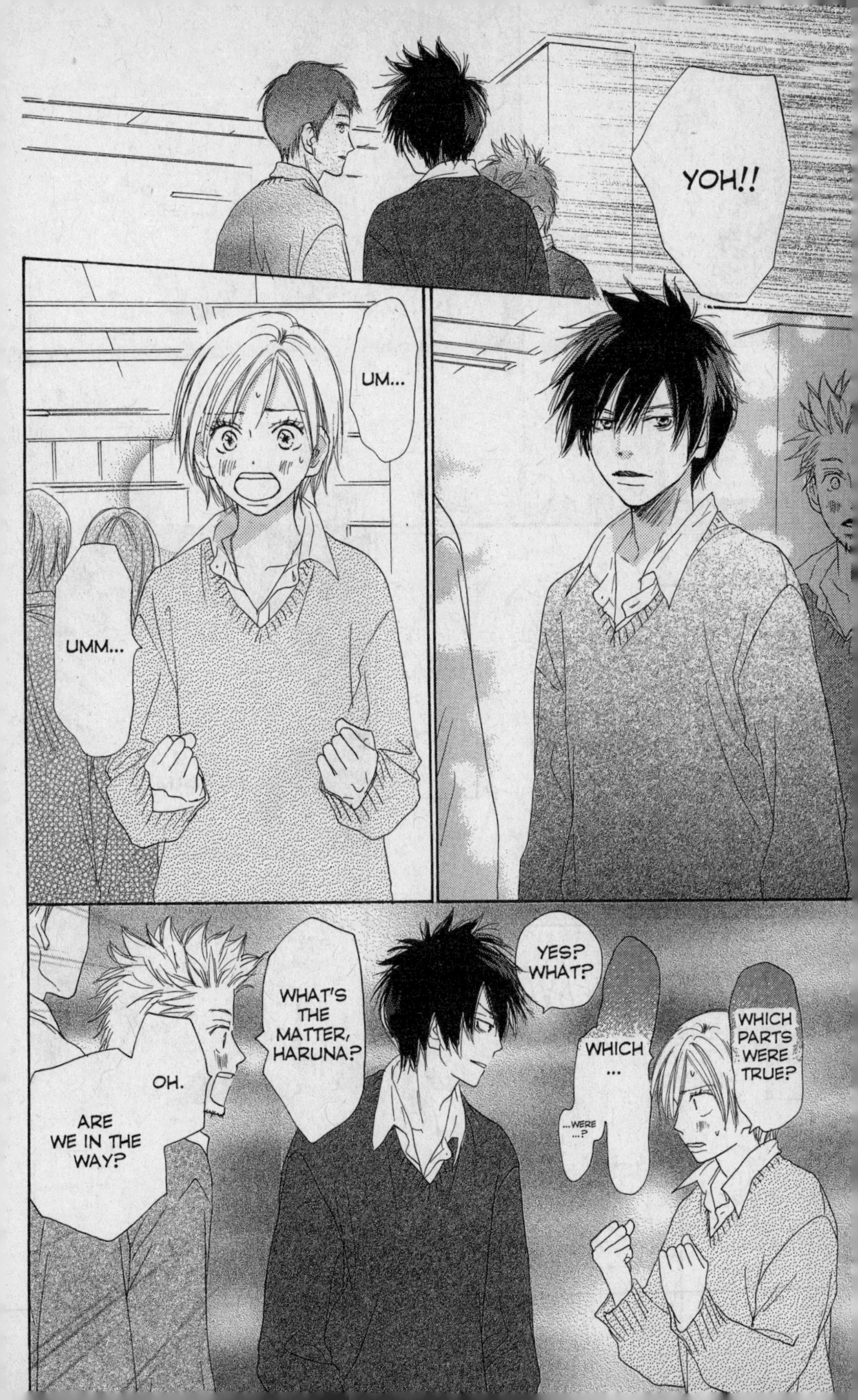
YOH!!
UM...
UMM...
WHICH PARTS WERE TRUE?
WHICH ...
...WERE ...?
YES? WHAT?
WHAT'S THE MATTER, HARUNA?
OH.
ARE WE IN THE WAY?

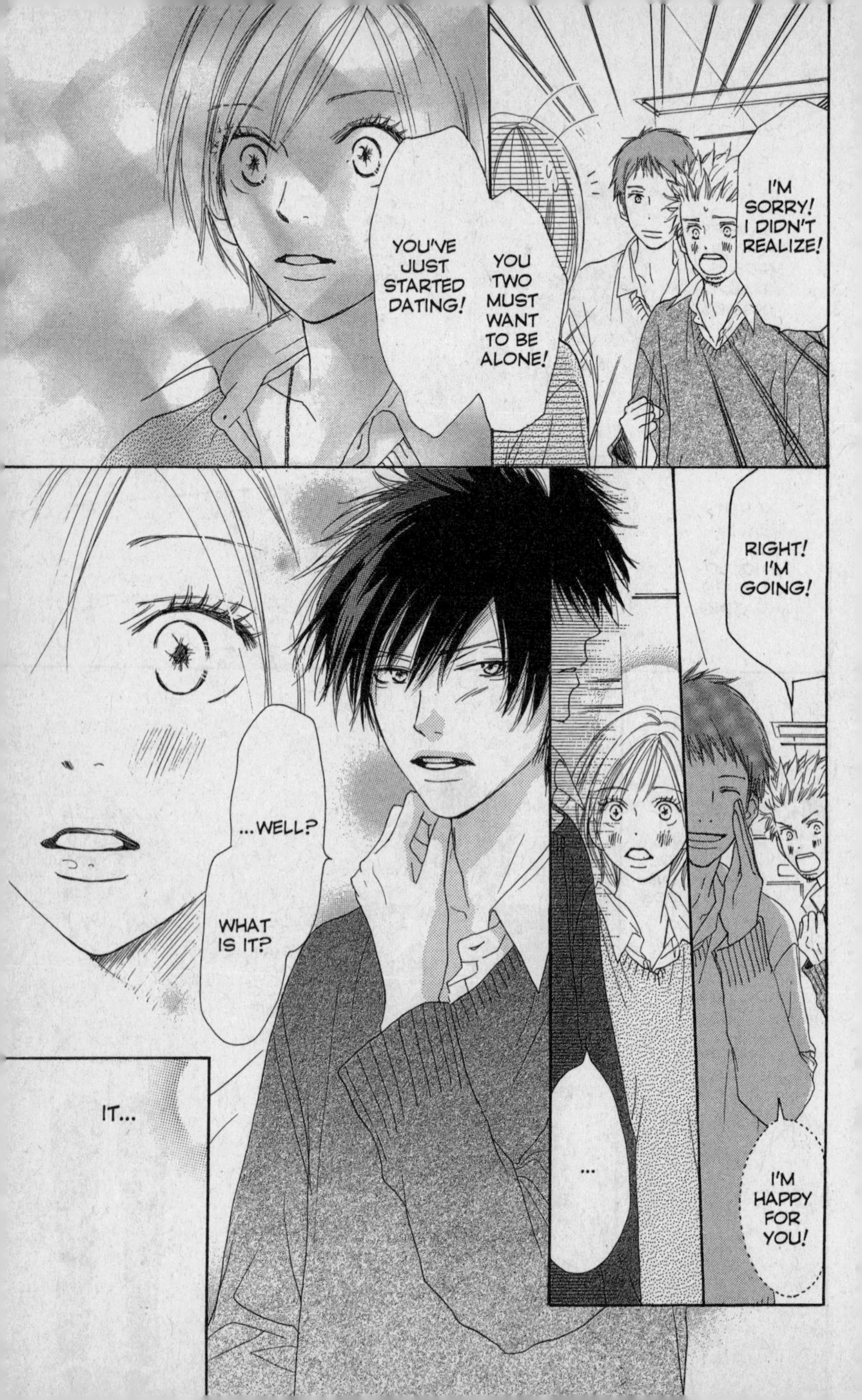
I'M SORRY! I DIDN'T REALIZE!
YOU TWO MUST WANT TO BE ALONE!
YOU'VE JUST STARTED DATING!
RIGHT! I'M GOING!
I'M HAPPY FOR YOU!
...
...WELL?
WHAT IS IT?
IT...

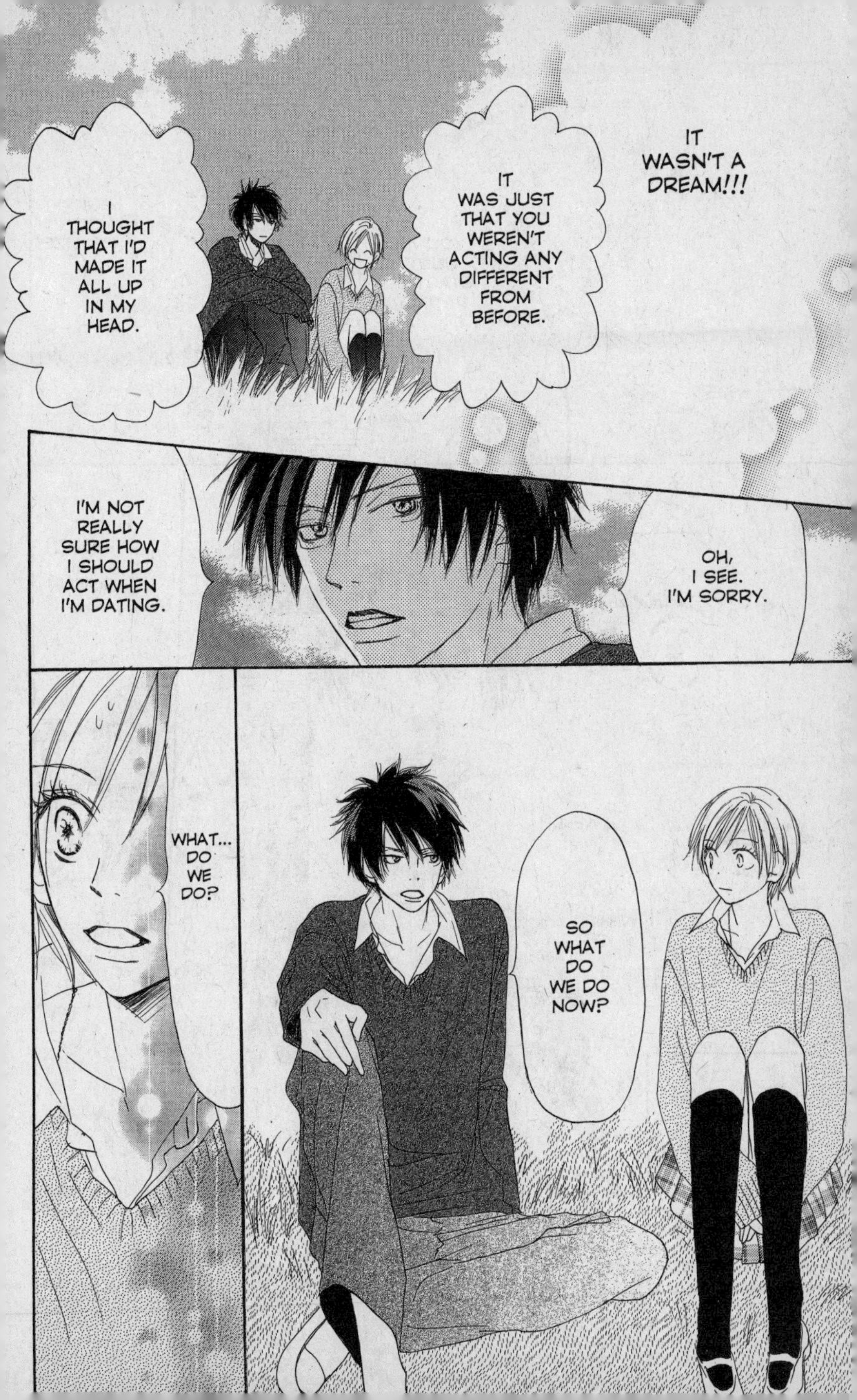
IT WASN'T A DREAM!!!
IT WAS JUST THAT YOU WEREN'T ACTING ANY DIFFERENT FROM BEFORE.
I THOUGHT THAT I'D MADE IT ALL UP IN MY HEAD.
OH, I SEE. I'M SORRY.
I'M NOT REALLY SURE HOW I SHOULD ACT WHEN I'M DATING.
SO WHAT DO WE DO NOW?
WHAT... DO WE DO?

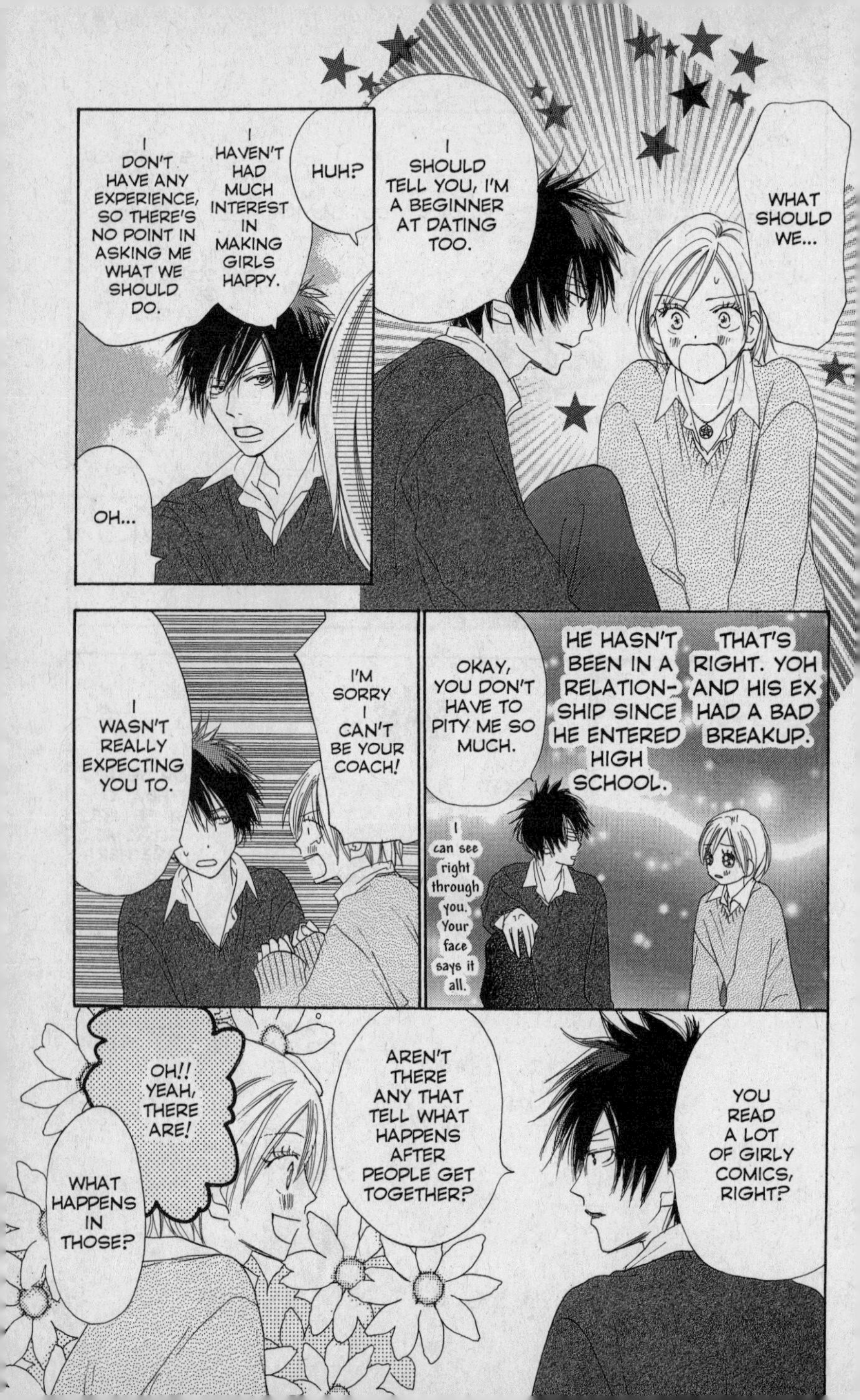
WHAT SHOULD WE...
I SHOULD TELL YOU, I'M A BEGINNER AT DATING TOO.
HUH?
I HAVEN'T HAD MUCH INTEREST IN MAKING GIRLS HAPPY.
I DON'T HAVE ANY EXPERIENCE, SO THERE'S NO POINT IN ASKING ME WHAT WE SHOULD DO.
OH...
THAT'S RIGHT. YOH AND HIS EX HAD A BAD BREAKUP.
HE HASN'T BEEN IN A RELATION-SHIP SINCE HE ENTERED HIGH SCHOOL.
OKAY, YOU DON'T HAVE TO PITY ME SO MUCH.
I can see right through you. Your face says it all.
I'M SORRY I CAN'T BE YOUR COACH!
I WASN'T REALLY EXPECTING YOU TO.
YOU READ A LOT OF GIRLY COMICS, RIGHT?
AREN'T THERE ANY THAT TELL WHAT HAPPENS AFTER PEOPLE GET TOGETHER?
OH!! YEAH, THERE ARE!
WHAT HAPPENS IN THOSE?

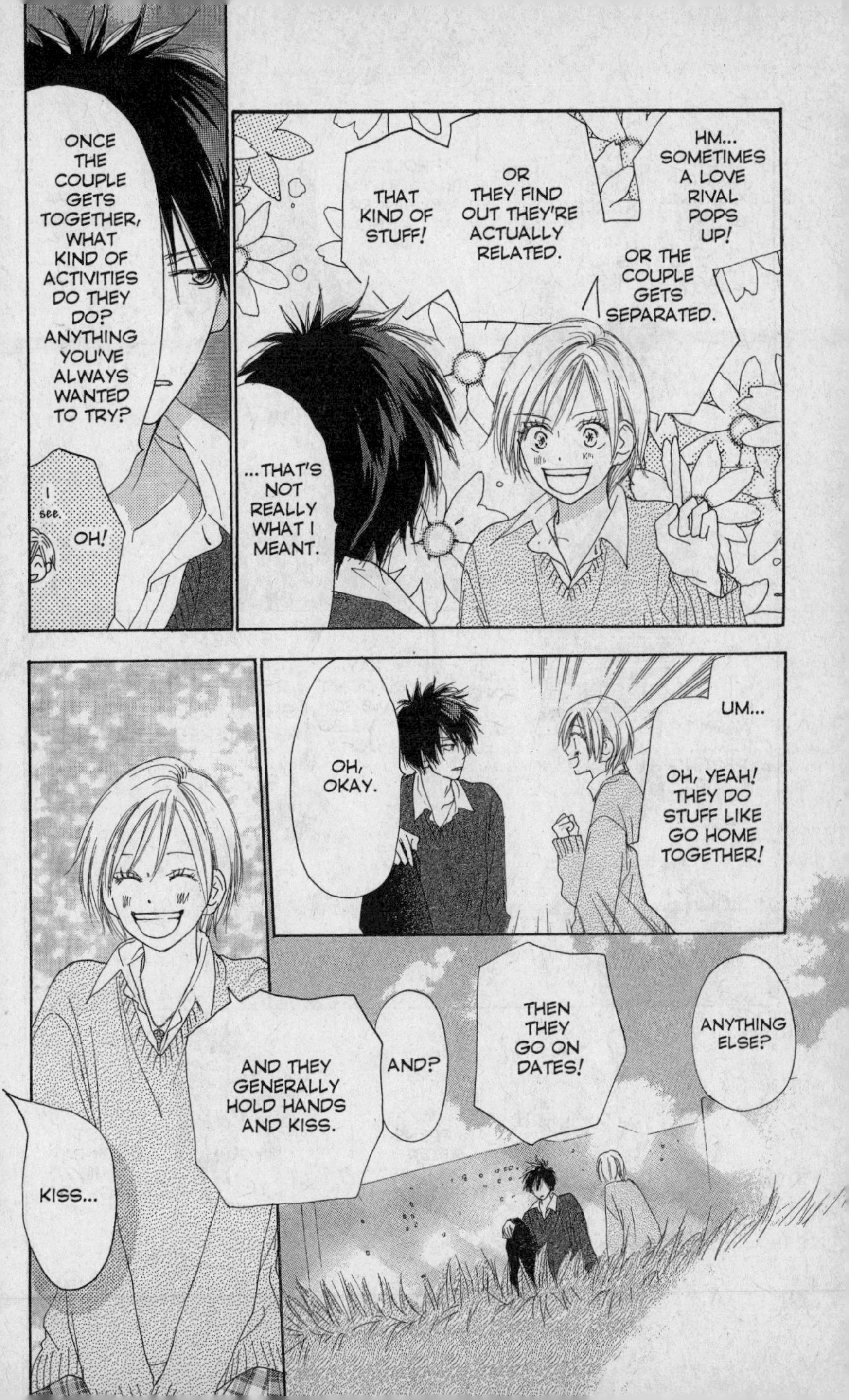
HM... SOMETIMES A LOVE RIVAL POPS UP!
OR THE COUPLE GETS SEPARATED.
OR THEY FIND OUT THEY'RE ACTUALLY RELATED.
THAT KIND OF STUFF!
...THAT'S NOT REALLY WHAT I MEANT.
ONCE THE COUPLE GETS TOGETHER, WHAT KIND OF ACTIVITIES DO THEY DO? ANYTHING YOU'VE ALWAYS WANTED TO TRY?
OH!
I see.
UM...
OH, YEAH! THEY DO STUFF LIKE GO HOME TOGETHER!
OH, OKAY.
ANYTHING ELSE?
THEN THEY GO ON DATES!
AND?
AND THEY GENERALLY HOLD HANDS AND KISS.
KISS...

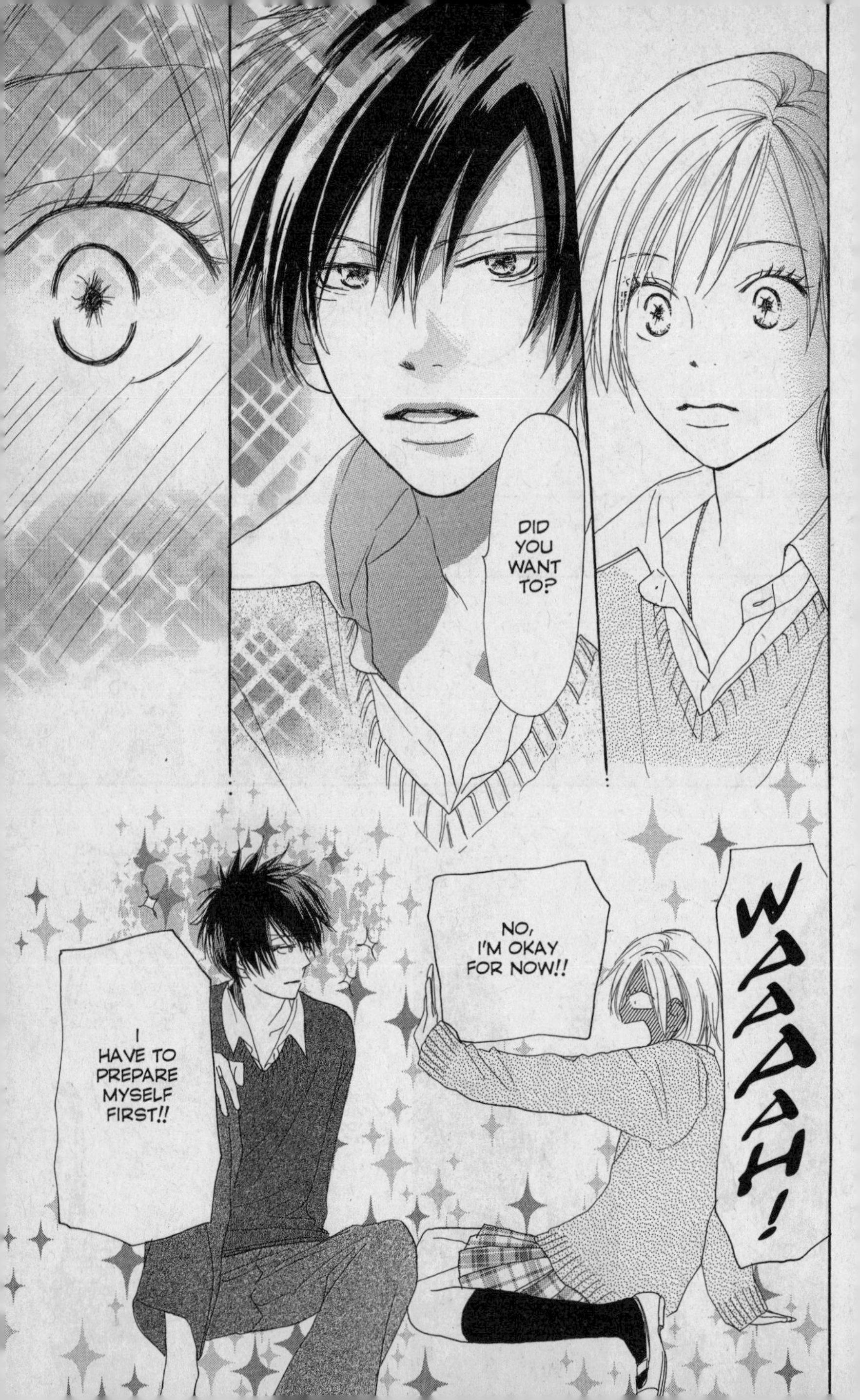
DID YOU WANT TO?
WAAAAH!
NO, I'M OKAY FOR NOW!!
I HAVE TO PREPARE MYSELF FIRST!!

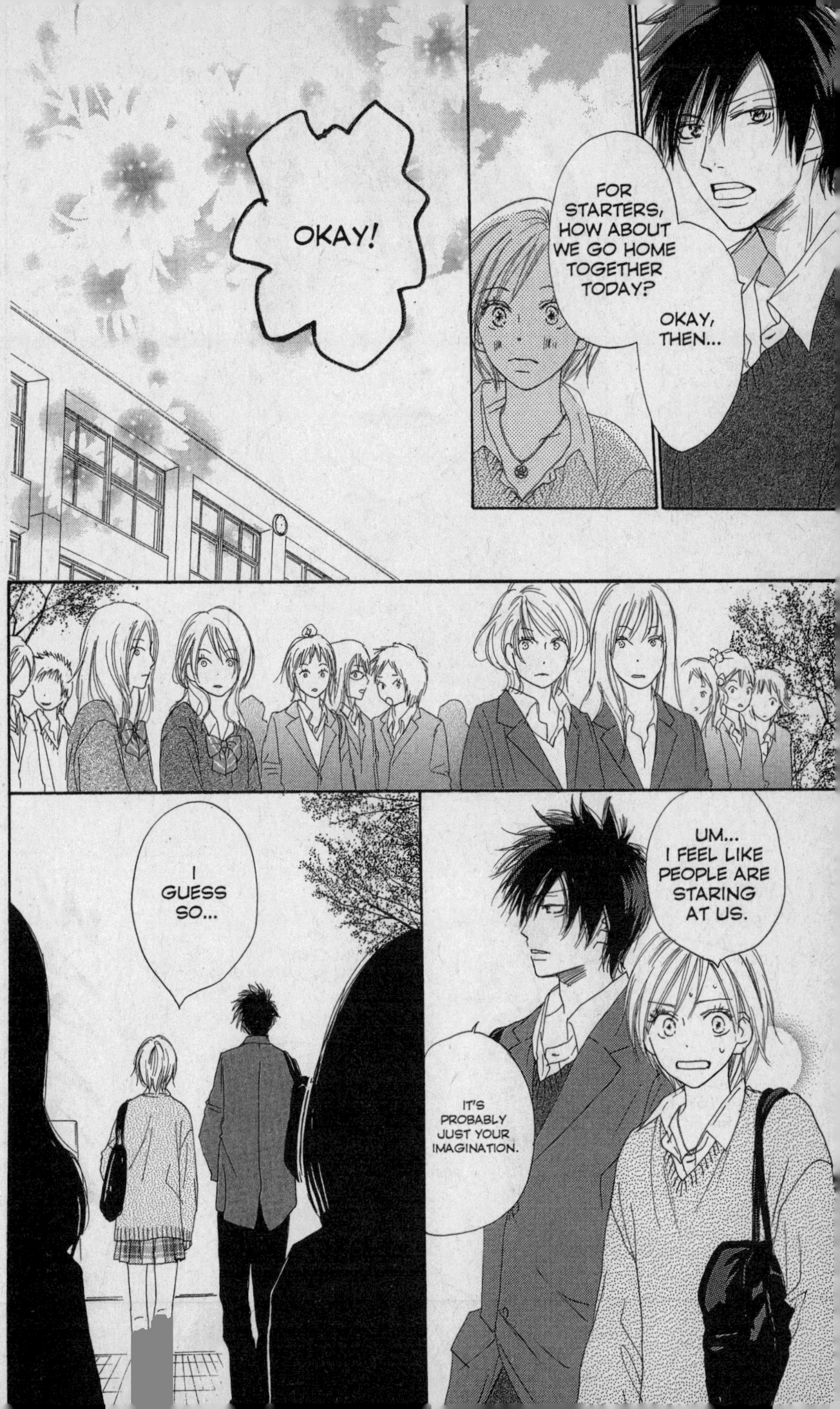
OKAY, THEN...
FOR STARTERS, HOW ABOUT WE GO HOME TOGETHER TODAY?
OKAY!
UM... I FEEL LIKE PEOPLE ARE STARING AT US.
IT'S PROBABLY JUST YOUR IMAGINATION.
I GUESS SO...

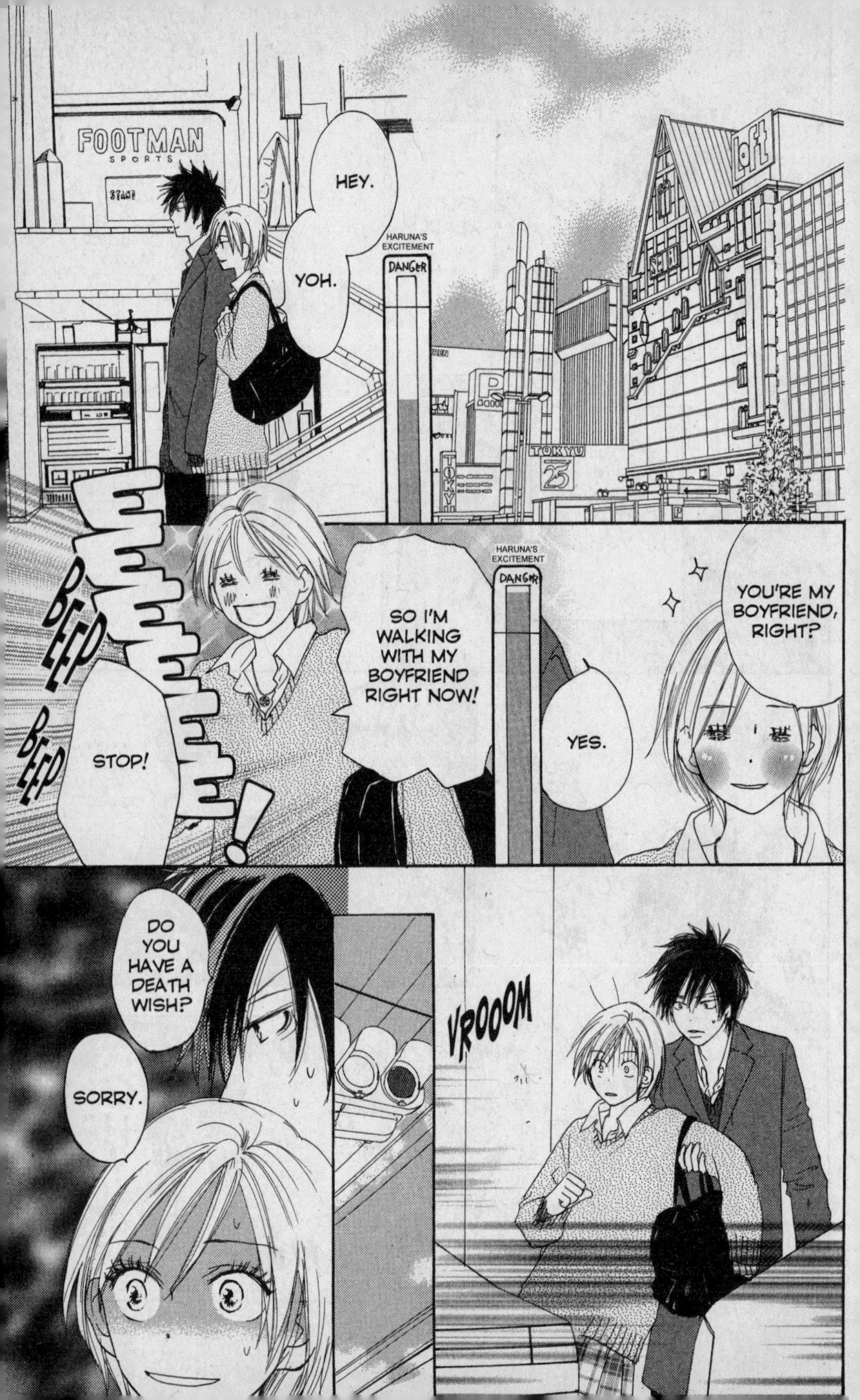
loft
HEY.
HARUNA'S EXCITEMENT
DANGER
YOH.
FOOTMAN SPORTS
TOKYU
YOU'RE MY BOYFRIEND, RIGHT?
HARUNA'S EXCITEMENT
DANGER
YES.
SO I'M WALKING WITH MY BOYFRIEND RIGHT NOW!
BEEP
BEEP
BEEP
STOP!
VROOOM
DO YOU HAVE A DEATH WISH?
SORRY.

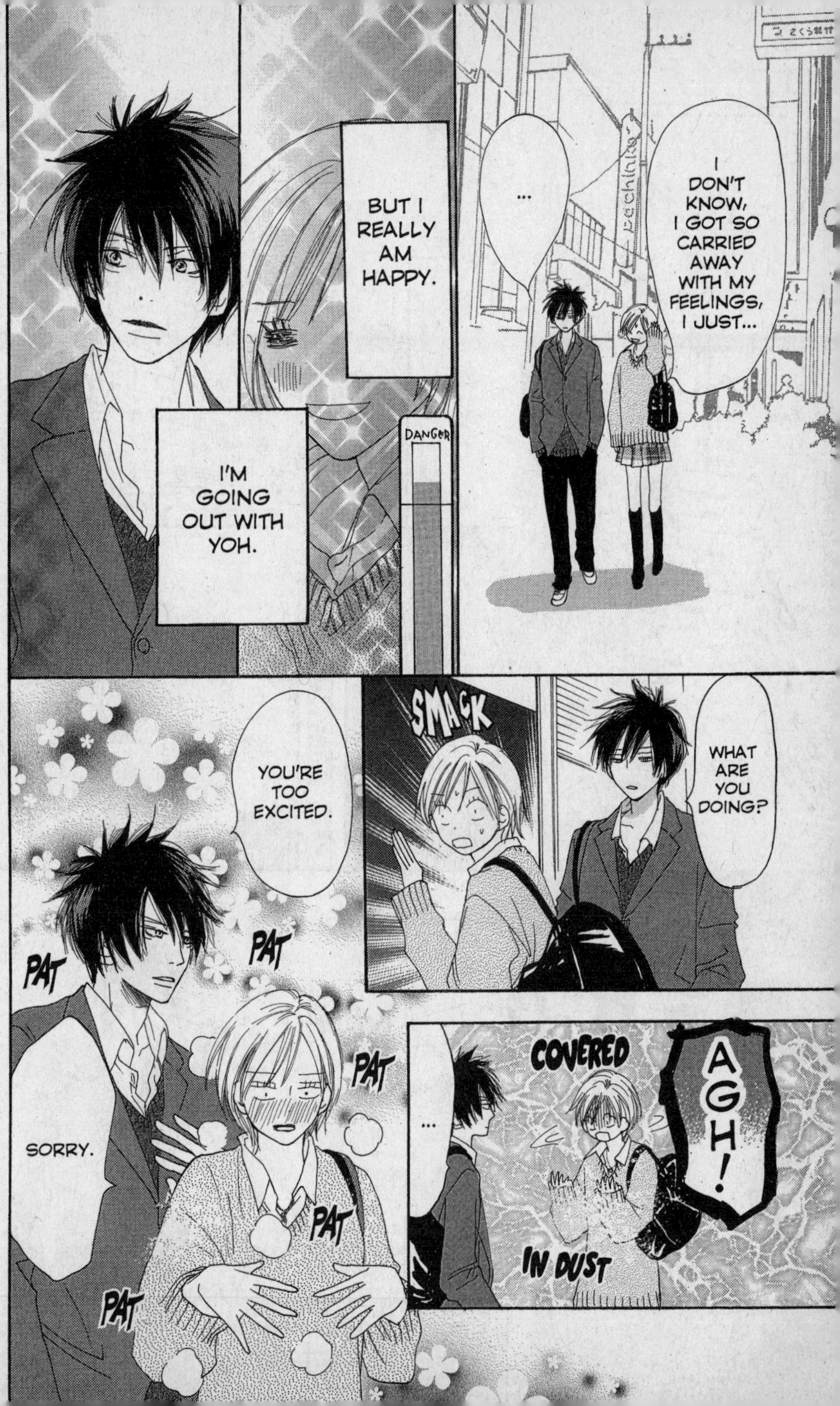
I DON'T KNOW, I GOT SO CARRIED AWAY WITH MY FEELINGS, I JUST...
...
BUT I REALLY AM HAPPY.
DANGER
I'M GOING OUT WITH YOH.
SMACK
WHAT ARE YOU DOING?
AGH!
COVERED IN DUST
...
YOU'RE TOO EXCITED.
PAT
PAT
PAT
SORRY.
PAT
PAT

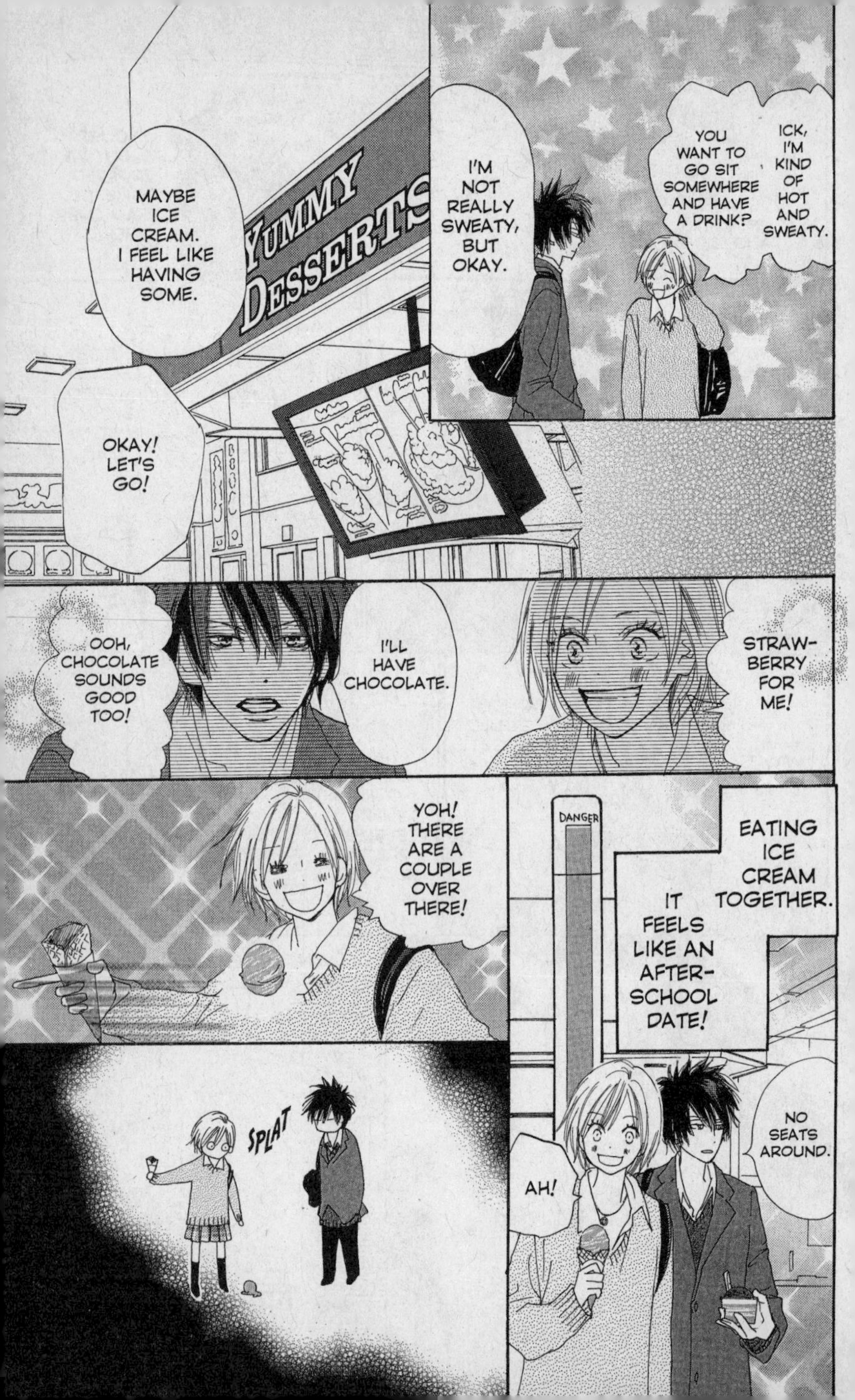
ICK, I'M KIND OF HOT AND SWEATY.
YOU WANT TO GO SIT SOMEWHERE AND HAVE A DRINK?
I'M NOT REALLY SWEATY, BUT OKAY.
YUMMY DESSERTS
MAYBE ICE CREAM. I FEEL LIKE HAVING SOME.
OKAY! LET'S GO!
STRAW-BERRY FOR ME!
I'LL HAVE CHOCOLATE.
OOH, CHOCOLATE SOUNDS GOOD TOO!
EATING ICE CREAM TOGETHER.
IT FEELS LIKE AN AFTER-SCHOOL DATE!
DANGER
NO SEATS AROUND.
AH!
YOH! THERE ARE A COUPLE OVER THERE!
SPLAT

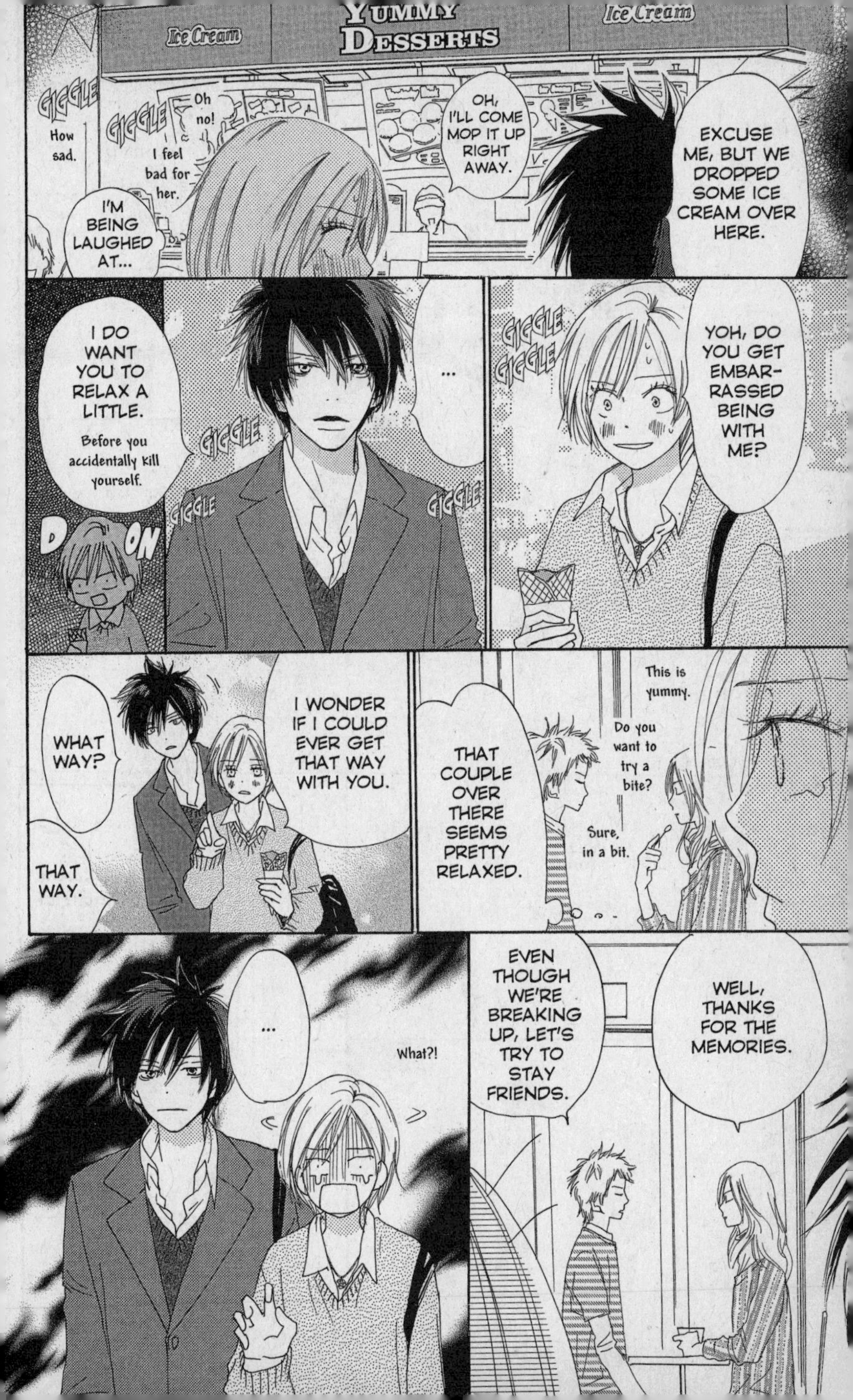
YUMMY DESSERTS
Ice Cream
Ice Cream
EXCUSE ME, BUT WE DROPPED SOME ICE CREAM OVER HERE.
OH, I'LL COME MOP IT UP RIGHT AWAY.
Oh no!
I feel bad for her.
GIGGLE
GIGGLE
How sad.
I'M BEING LAUGHED AT...
GIGGLE GIGGLE
YOH, DO YOU GET EMBARRASSED BEING WITH ME?
...
GIGGLE
GIGGLE
GIGGLE
I DO WANT YOU TO RELAX A LITTLE.
Before you accidentally kill yourself.
DON
This is yummy.
Do you want to try a bite?
Sure, in a bit.
THAT COUPLE OVER THERE SEEMS PRETTY RELAXED.
I WONDER IF I COULD EVER GET THAT WAY WITH YOU.
WHAT WAY?
THAT WAY.
WELL, THANKS FOR THE MEMORIES.
EVEN THOUGH WE'RE BREAKING UP, LET'S TRY TO STAY FRIENDS.
What?!
...

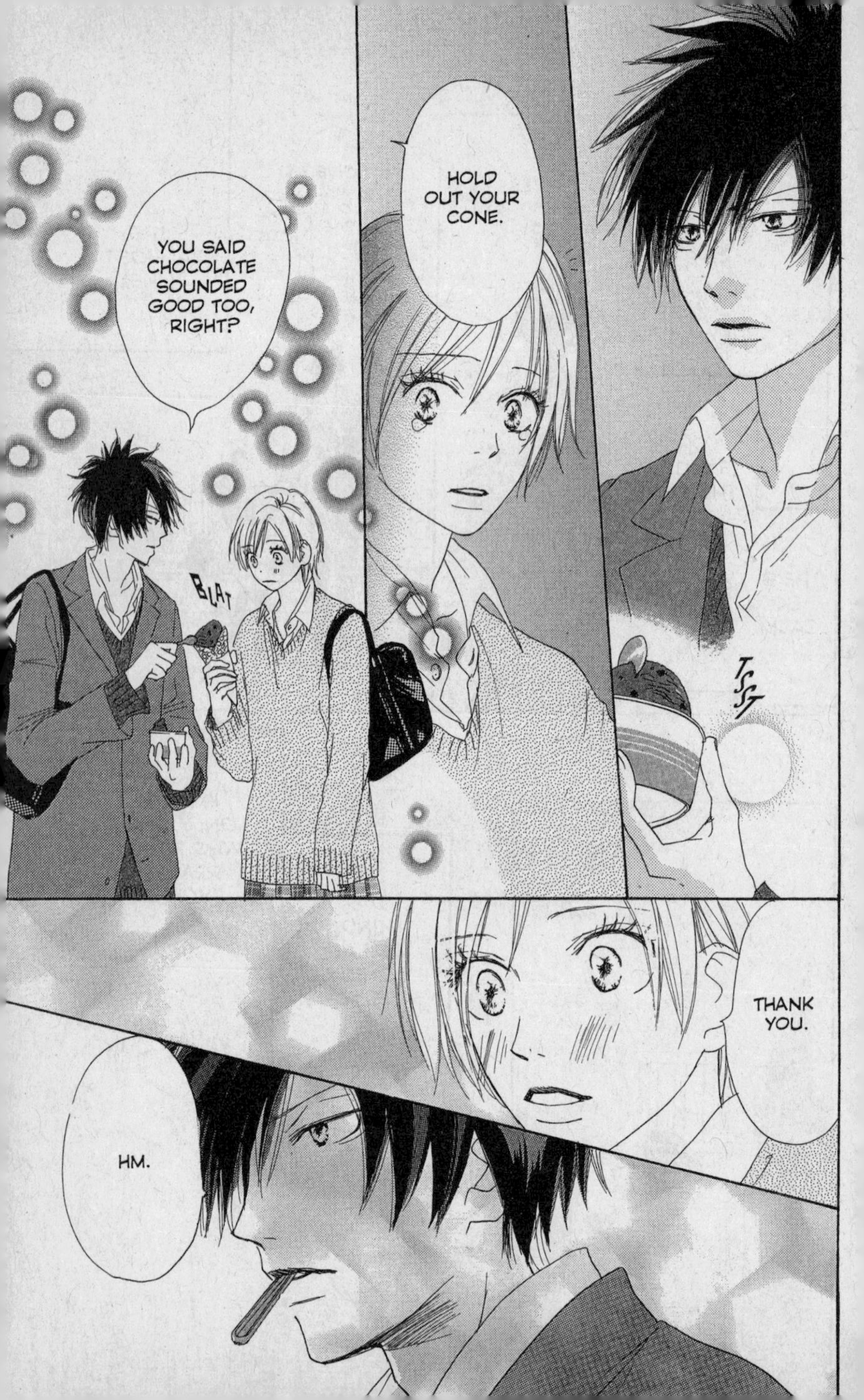
TSST
HOLD OUT YOUR CONE.
YOU SAID CHOCOLATE SOUNDED GOOD TOO, RIGHT?
BLAT
THANK YOU.
HM.

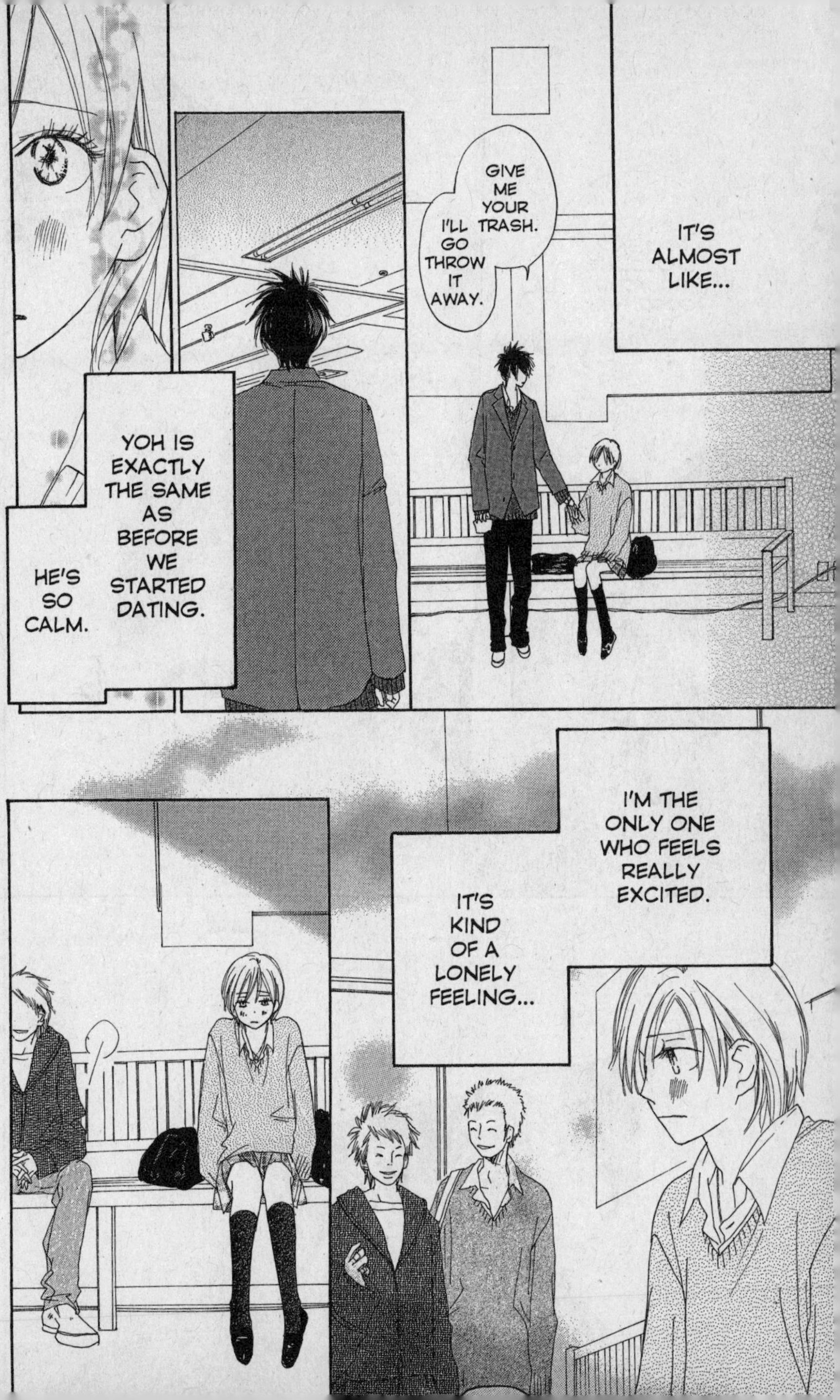
IT'S ALMOST LIKE...
GIVE ME YOUR TRASH. I'LL GO THROW IT AWAY.
YOH IS EXACTLY THE SAME AS BEFORE WE STARTED DATING.
HE'S SO CALM.
I'M THE ONLY ONE WHO FEELS REALLY EXCITED.
IT'S KIND OF A LONELY FEELING...

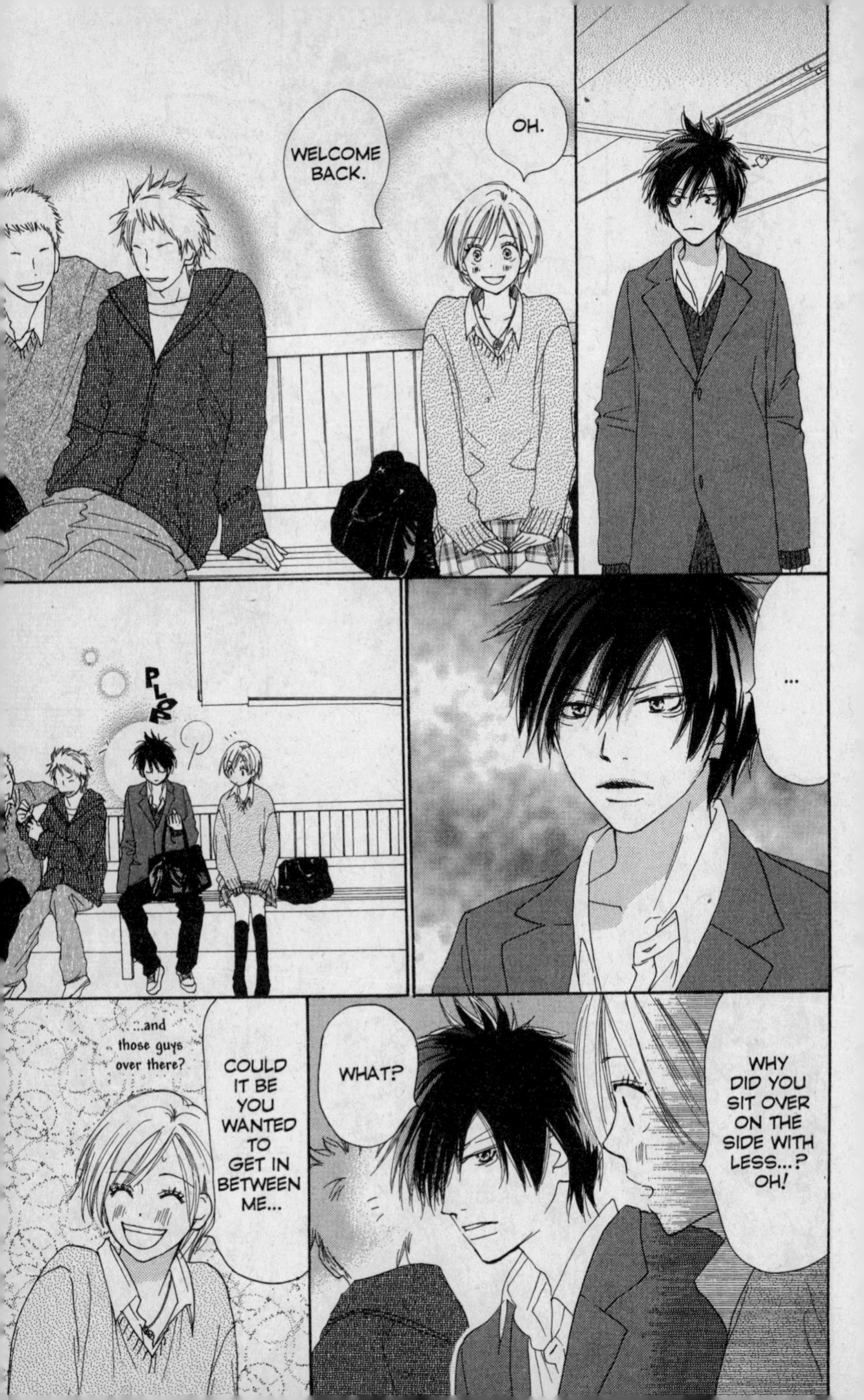
OH.
WELCOME BACK.
...
PLOP
WHY DID YOU SIT OVER ON THE SIDE WITH LESS...? OH!
WHAT?
COULD IT BE YOU WANTED TO GET IN BETWEEN ME...
...and those guys over there?

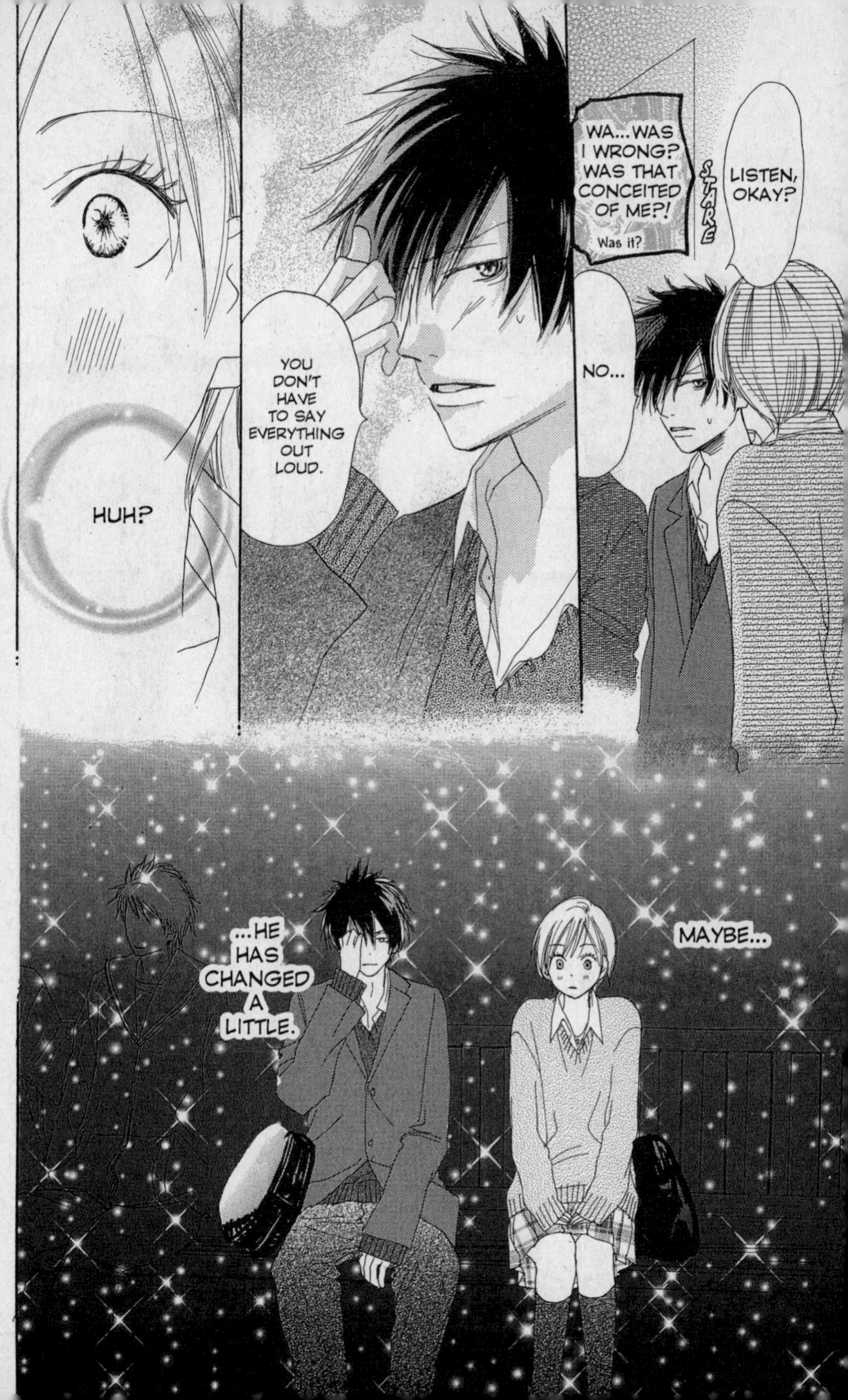
LISTEN, OKAY?
STARE
WA...WAS I WRONG? WAS THAT CONCEITED OF ME?!
Was it?
NO...
YOU DON'T HAVE TO SAY EVERYTHING OUT LOUD.
HUH?
MAYBE...
...HE HAS CHANGED A LITTLE.

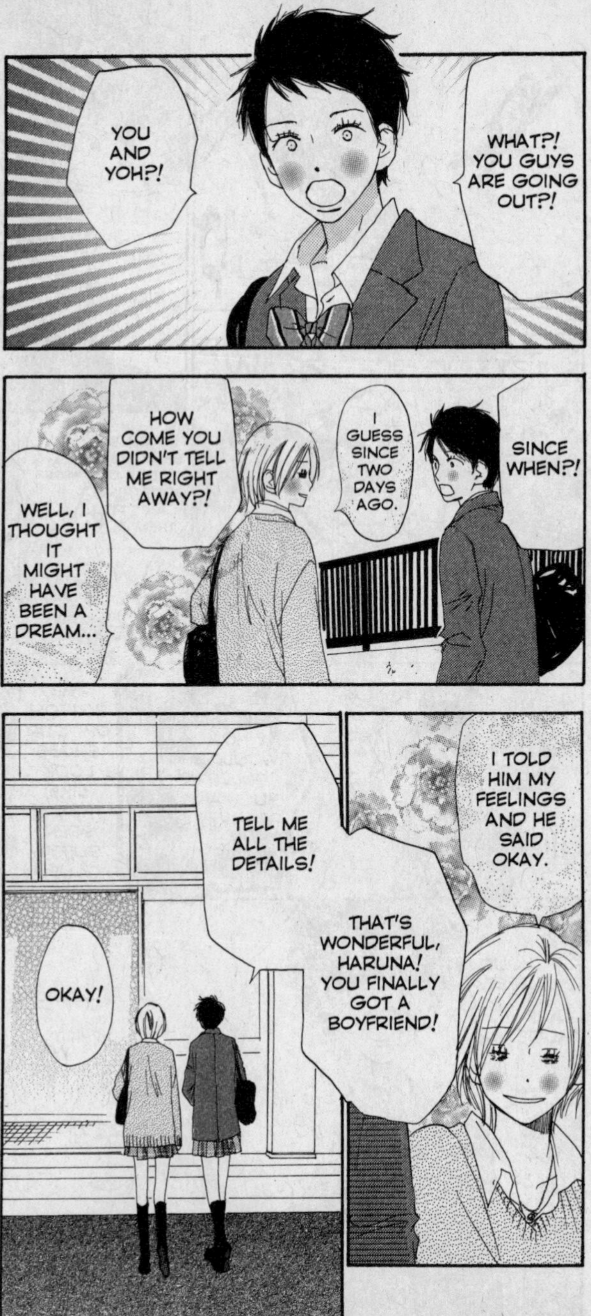
WHAT?! YOU GUYS ARE GOING OUT?!
YOU AND YOH?!
SINCE WHEN?!
I GUESS SINCE TWO DAYS AGO.
HOW COME YOU DIDN'T TELL ME RIGHT AWAY?!
WELL, I THOUGHT IT MIGHT HAVE BEEN A DREAM...
I TOLD HIM MY FEELINGS AND HE SAID OKAY.
THAT'S WONDERFUL, HARUNA! YOU FINALLY GOT A BOYFRIEND!
TELL ME ALL THE DETAILS!
OKAY!

3

Recently, I've been getting into children's books and end up crying when I read them. I mean, I've always liked children's literature... They're just right. They're not very difficult... But unlike when I was a child, now that I'm an adult, I tend to go...

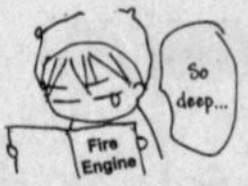
So deep...
Fire Engine

Or I read some sort of meaning into them even though I'm not sure whether the writer originally intended to have that meaning or not.

When I rent children's videos and watch them with my nieces, I usually end up crying.

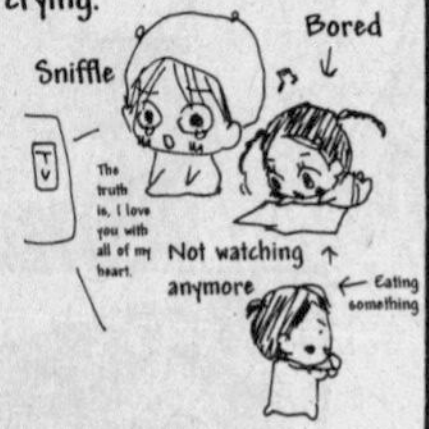
Bored
Sniffle
TV
The truth is, I love you with all of my heart.
Not watching anymore
Eating something

I think you're meant to cry during those times. Little things are very moving. Children's stuff is jam-packed with emotion.

Well anyway, I'd be happy if you join us for the next volume. This has been the very adult Kazune.

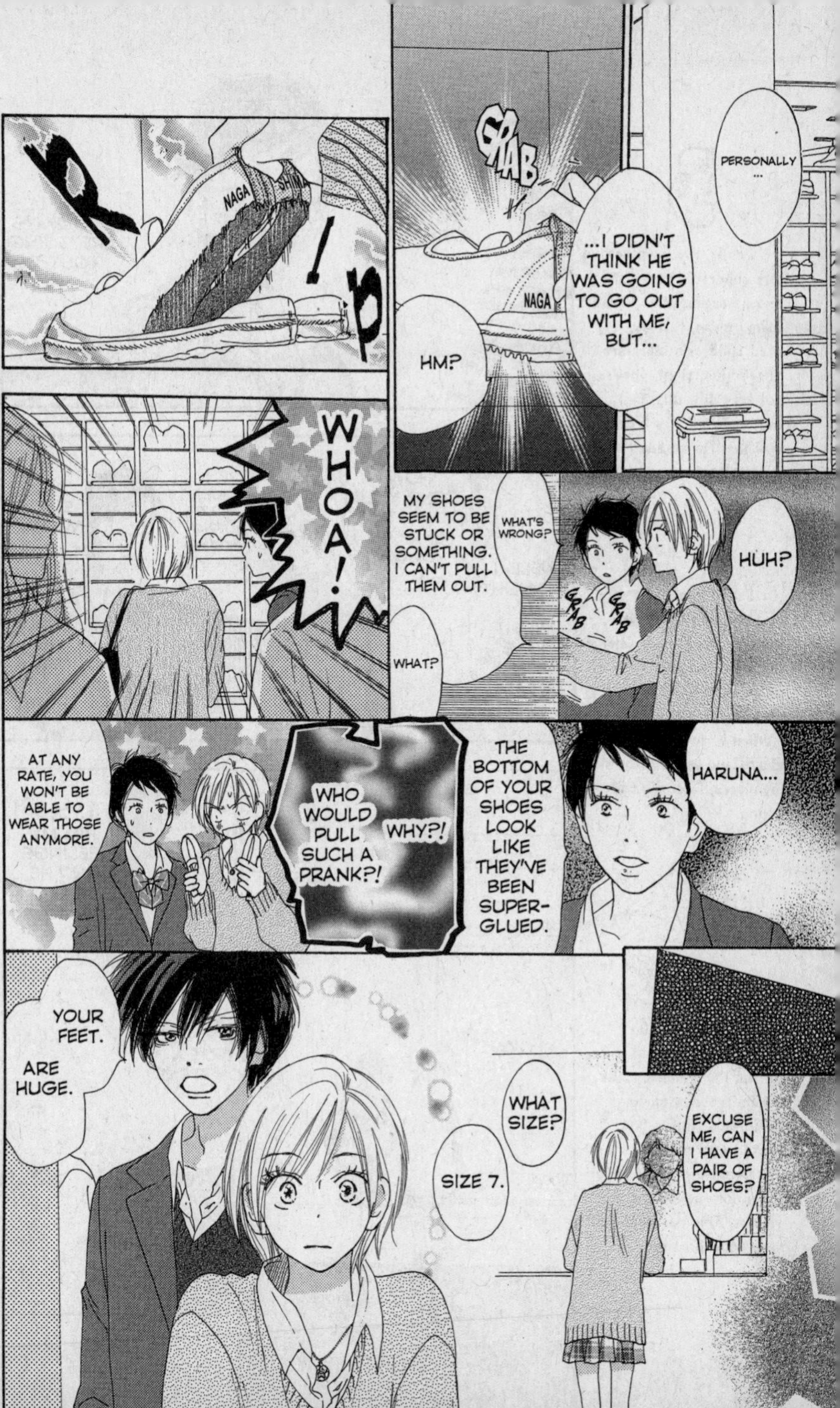
PERSONALLY...
...I DIDN'T THINK HE WAS GOING TO GO OUT WITH ME, BUT...
HM?
GRAB
NAGA
NAGA SHIMA
HUH?
WHAT'S WRONG?
MY SHOES SEEM TO BE STUCK OR SOMETHING. I CAN'T PULL THEM OUT.
WHAT?
GRAB GRAB
WHOA!!
HARUNA...
THE BOTTOM OF YOUR SHOES LOOK LIKE THEY'VE BEEN SUPER-GLUED.
WHY?!
WHO WOULD PULL SUCH A PRANK?!
AT ANY RATE, YOU WON'T BE ABLE TO WEAR THOSE ANYMORE.
EXCUSE ME, CAN I HAVE A PAIR OF SHOES?
WHAT SIZE?
SIZE 7.
YOUR FEET.
ARE HUGE.

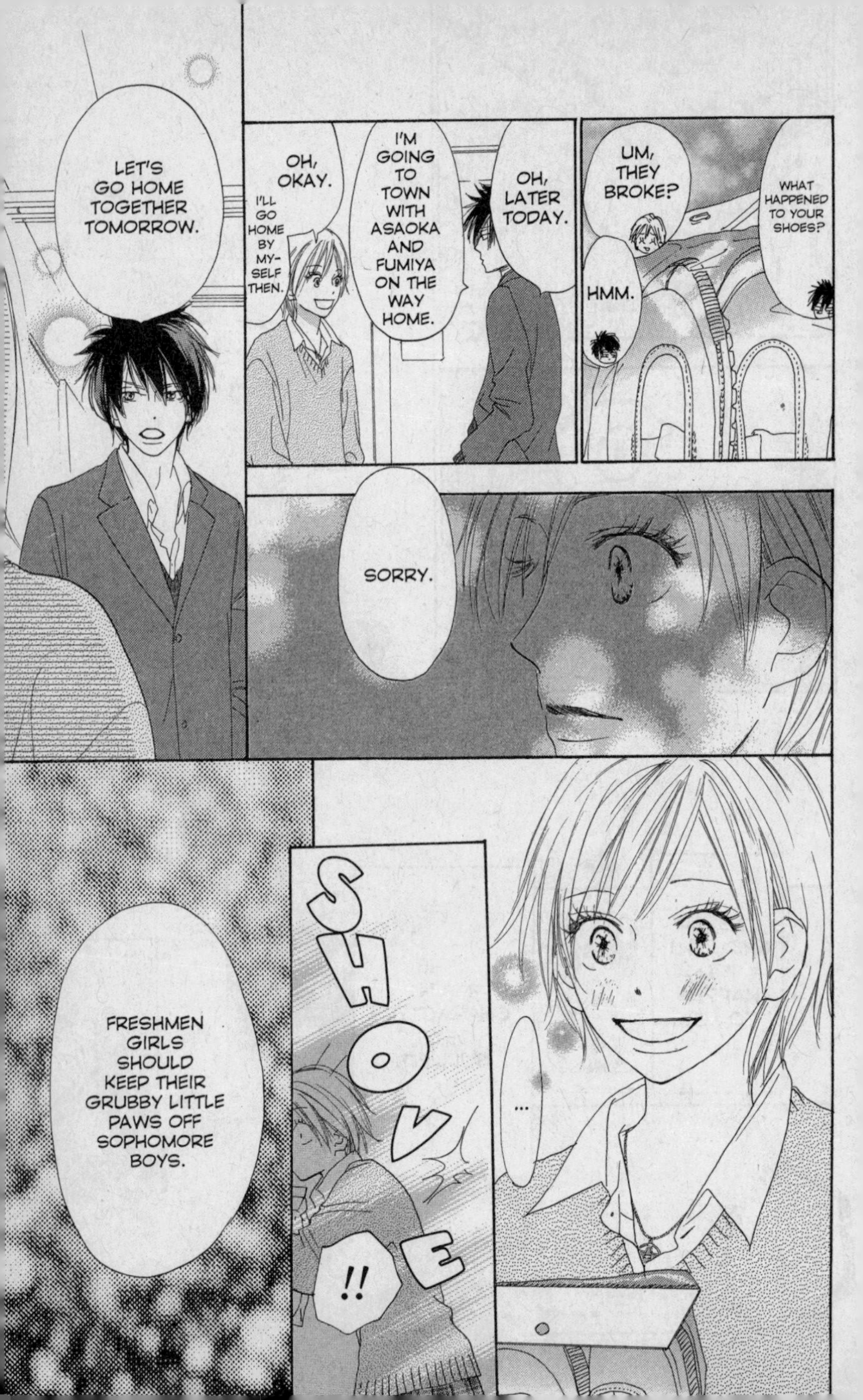
WHAT HAPPENED TO YOUR SHOES?
UM, THEY BROKE?
HMM.
OH, LATER TODAY.
I'M GOING TO TOWN WITH ASAOKA AND FUMIYA ON THE WAY HOME.
OH, OKAY.
I'LL GO HOME BY MY-SELF THEN.
SORRY.
LET'S GO HOME TOGETHER TOMORROW.
...
SHOVE
!!
FRESHMEN GIRLS SHOULD KEEP THEIR GRUBBY LITTLE PAWS OFF SOPHOMORE BOYS.

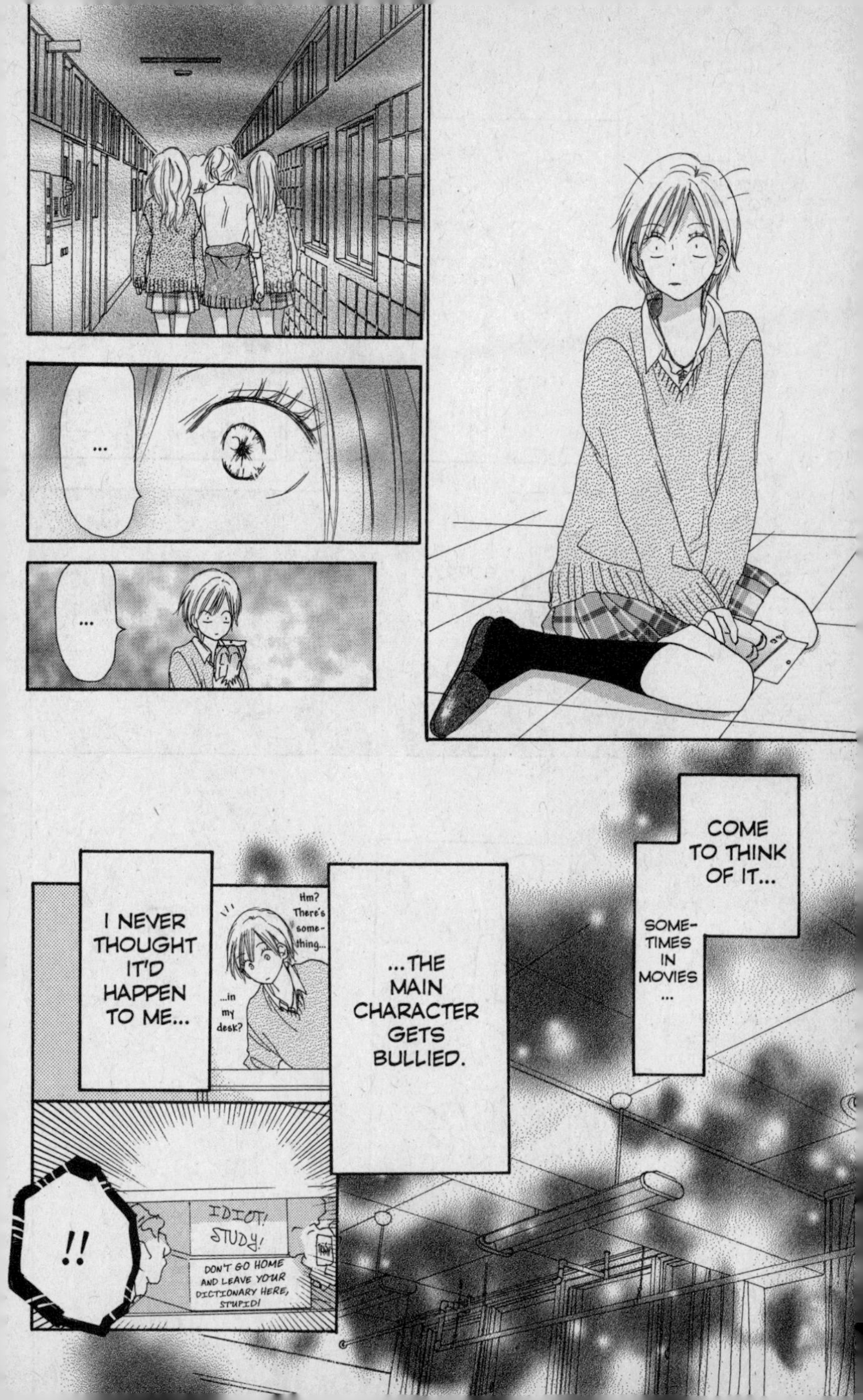
...
...
COME TO THINK OF IT...
SOMETIMES IN MOVIES...
...THE MAIN CHARACTER GETS BULLIED.
I NEVER THOUGHT IT'D HAPPEN TO ME...
Hm? There's something...
...in my desk?
!!
IDIOT! STUDY!
DON'T GO HOME AND LEAVE YOUR DICTIONARY HERE, STUPID!

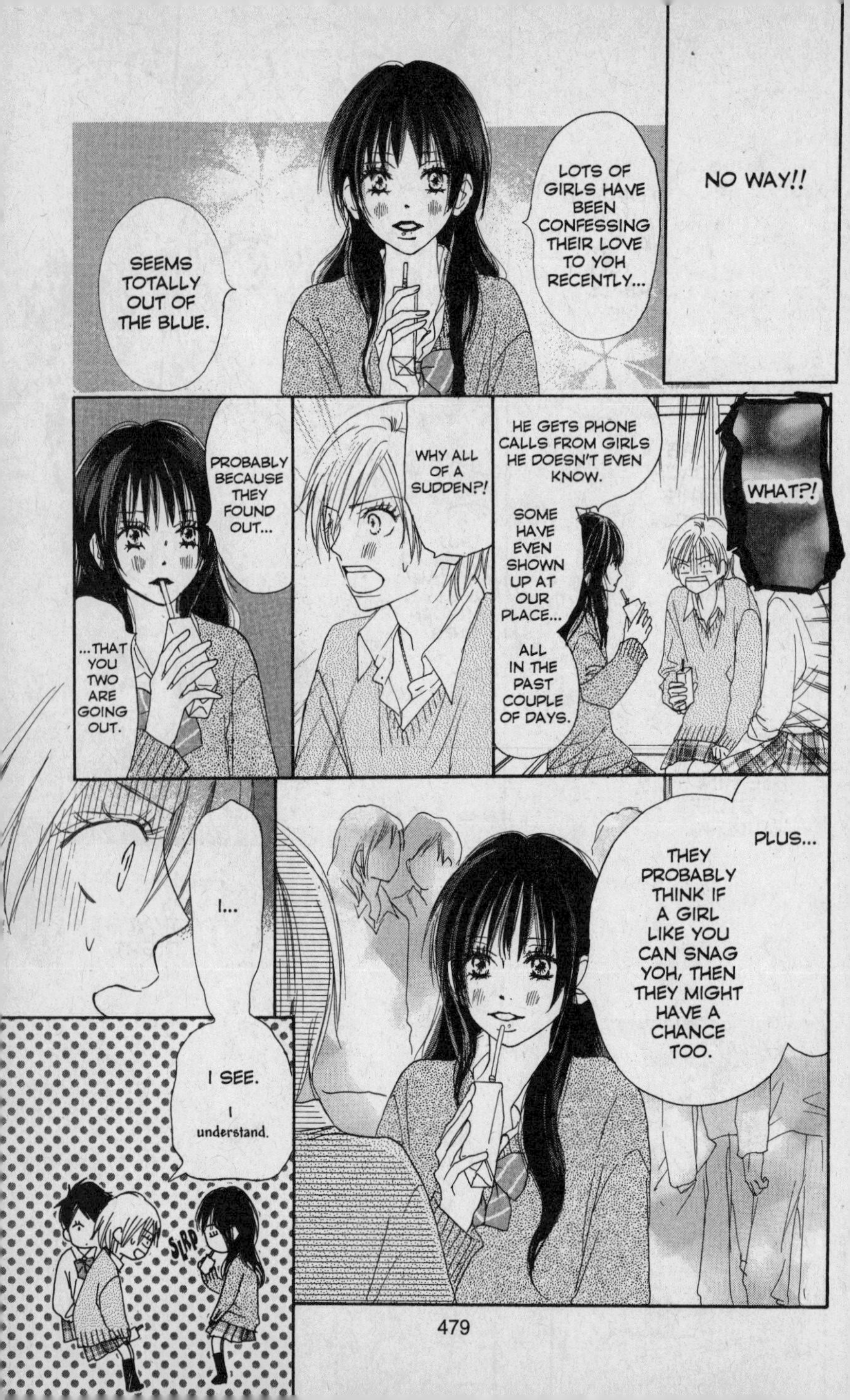
NO WAY!!
LOTS OF GIRLS HAVE BEEN CONFESSING THEIR LOVE TO YOH RECENTLY...
SEEMS TOTALLY OUT OF THE BLUE.
WHAT?!
HE GETS PHONE CALLS FROM GIRLS HE DOESN'T EVEN KNOW.
SOME HAVE EVEN SHOWN UP AT OUR PLACE...
ALL IN THE PAST COUPLE OF DAYS.
WHY ALL OF A SUDDEN?!
PROBABLY BECAUSE THEY FOUND OUT...
...THAT YOU TWO ARE GOING OUT.
PLUS...
THEY PROBABLY THINK IF A GIRL LIKE YOU CAN SNAG YOH, THEN THEY MIGHT HAVE A CHANCE TOO.
I...
I SEE.
I understand.
SLRP

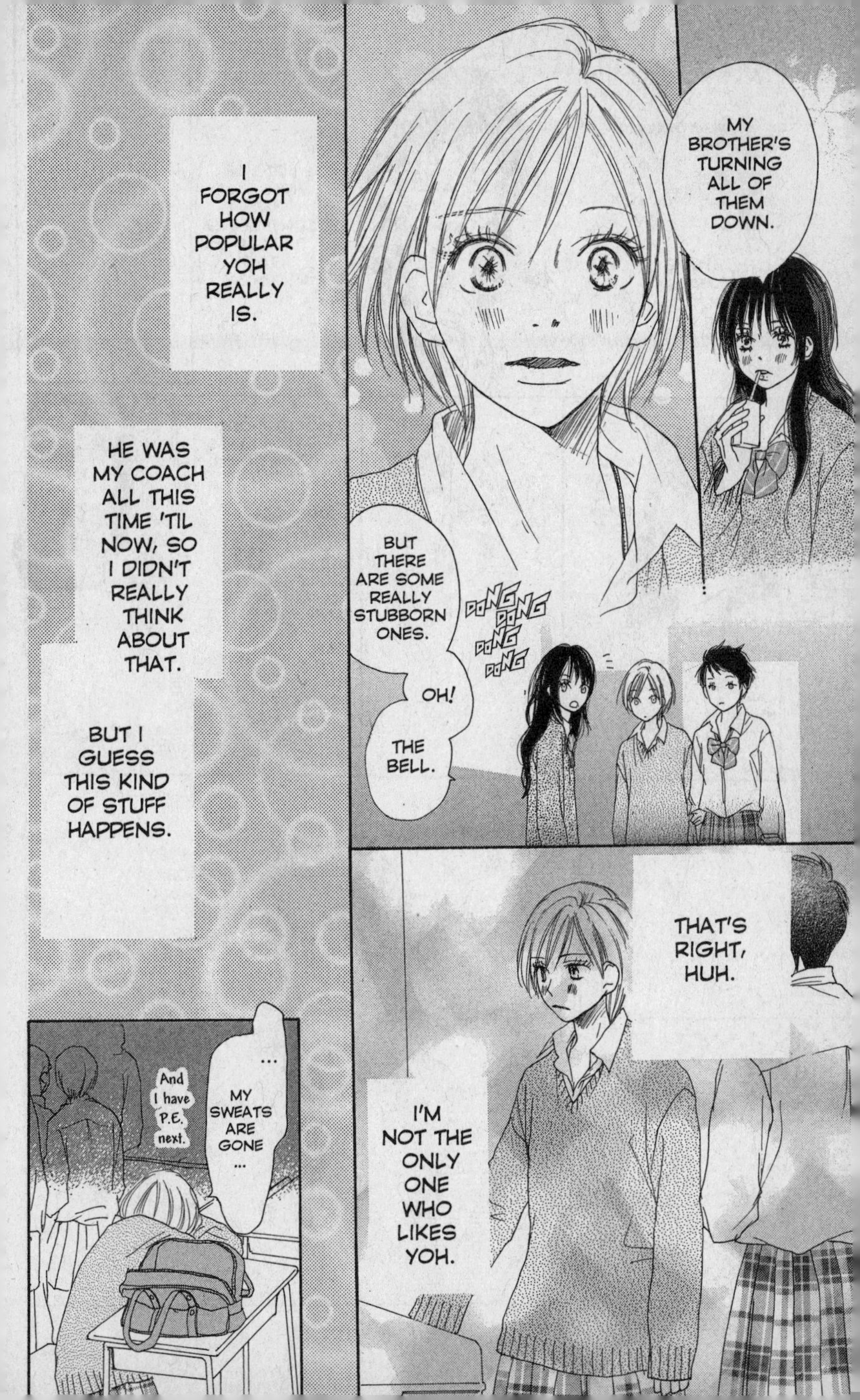

MY BROTHER'S TURNING ALL OF THEM DOWN.
BUT THERE ARE SOME REALLY STUBBORN ONES.
DONG DONG DONG DONG
OH!
THE BELL.
I FORGOT HOW POPULAR YOH REALLY IS.
HE WAS MY COACH ALL THIS TIME 'TIL NOW, SO I DIDN'T REALLY THINK ABOUT THAT.
BUT I GUESS THIS KIND OF STUFF HAPPENS.
THAT'S RIGHT, HUH.
I'M NOT THE ONLY ONE WHO LIKES YOH.
...
MY SWEATS ARE GONE ...
And I have P.E. next.

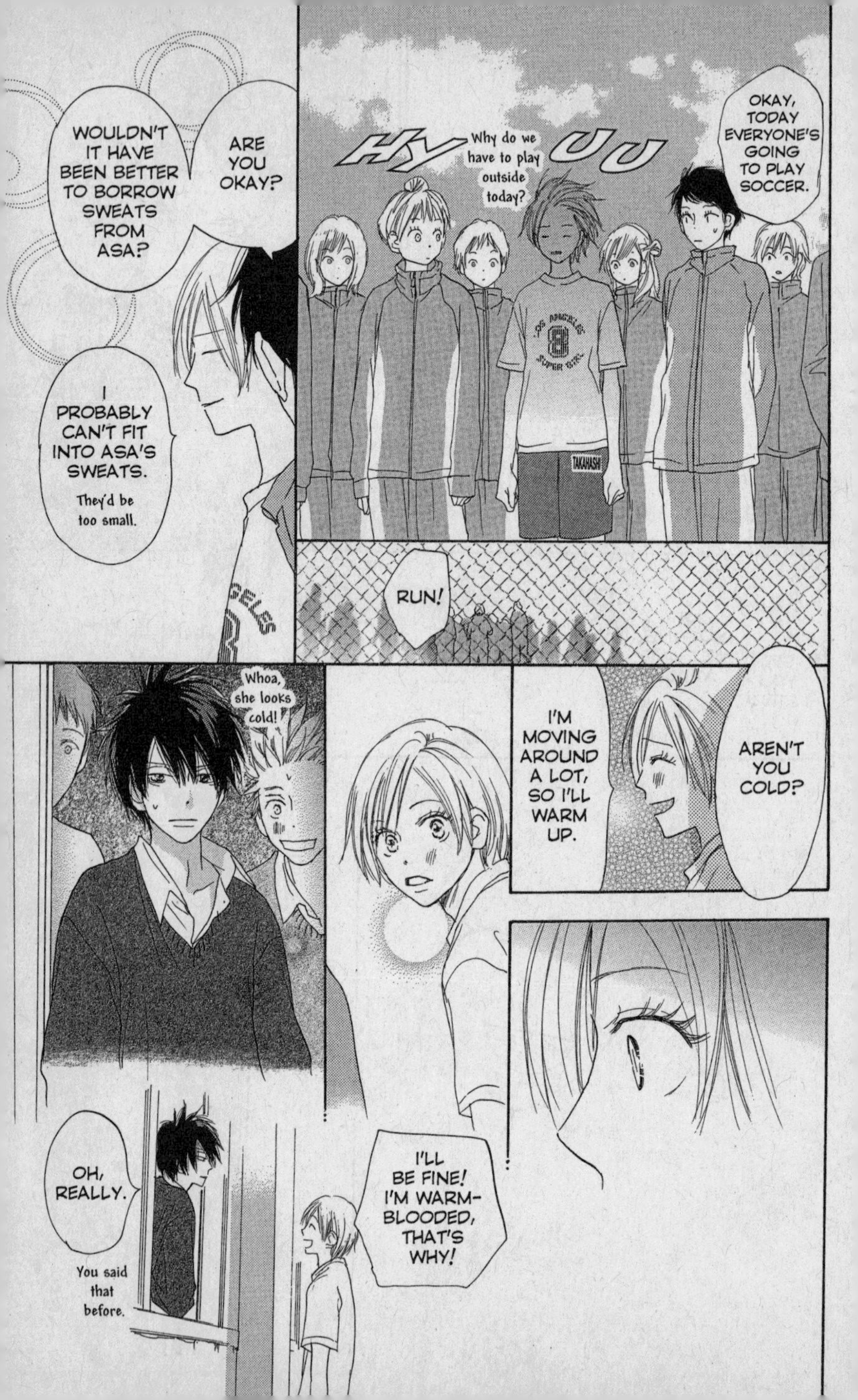
OKAY, TODAY EVERYONE'S GOING TO PLAY SOCCER.
HYUU
Why do we have to play outside today?
TAKAHASHI
RUN!
ARE YOU OKAY?
WOULDN'T IT HAVE BEEN BETTER TO BORROW SWEATS FROM ASA?
I PROBABLY CAN'T FIT INTO ASA'S SWEATS.
They'd be too small.
AREN'T YOU COLD?
I'M MOVING AROUND A LOT, SO I'LL WARM UP.
I'LL BE FINE! I'M WARM-BLOODED, THAT'S WHY!
Whoa, she looks cold!
OH, REALLY.
You said that before.

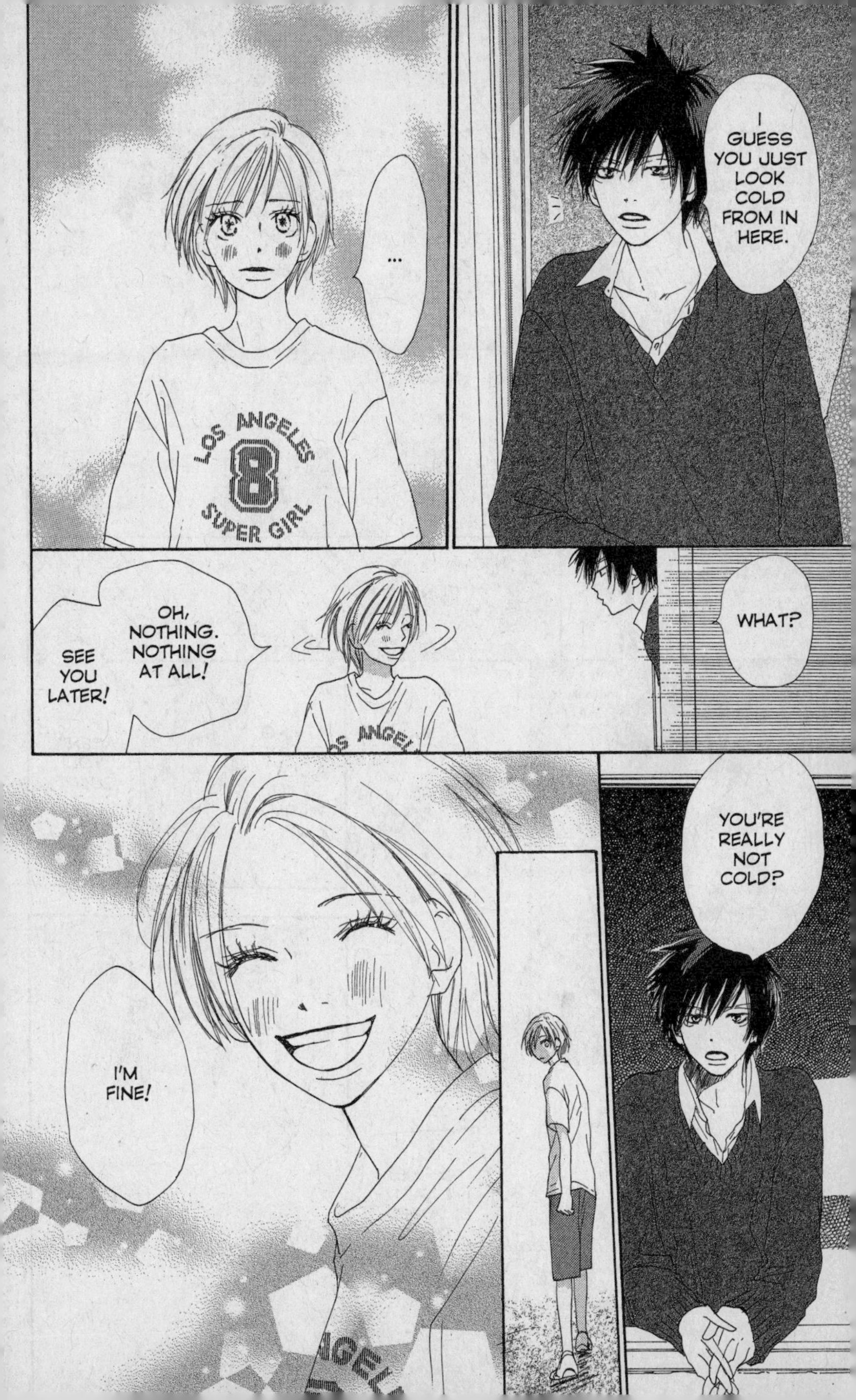
I GUESS YOU JUST LOOK COLD FROM IN HERE.
...
LOS ANGELES 8 SUPER GIRL
WHAT?
OH, NOTHING. NOTHING AT ALL!
SEE YOU LATER!
YOU'RE REALLY NOT COLD?
I'M FINE!

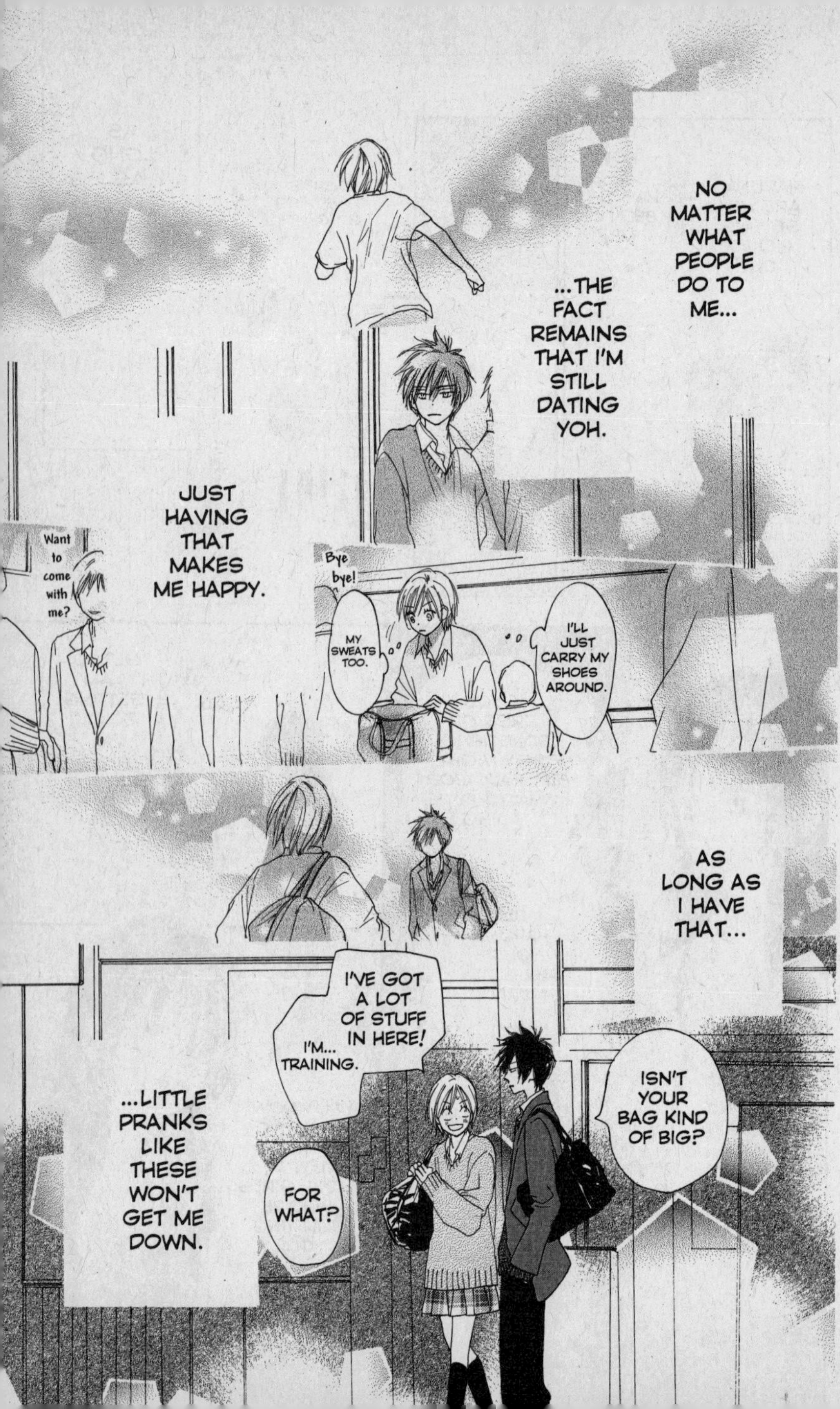
NO MATTER WHAT PEOPLE DO TO ME...
...THE FACT REMAINS THAT I'M STILL DATING YOH.
JUST HAVING THAT MAKES ME HAPPY.
I'LL JUST CARRY MY SHOES AROUND.
Bye bye!
MY SWEATS TOO.
Want to come with me?
AS LONG AS I HAVE THAT...
...LITTLE PRANKS LIKE THESE WON'T GET ME DOWN.
ISN'T YOUR BAG KIND OF BIG?
I'VE GOT A LOT OF STUFF IN HERE!
I'M... TRAINING.
FOR WHAT?

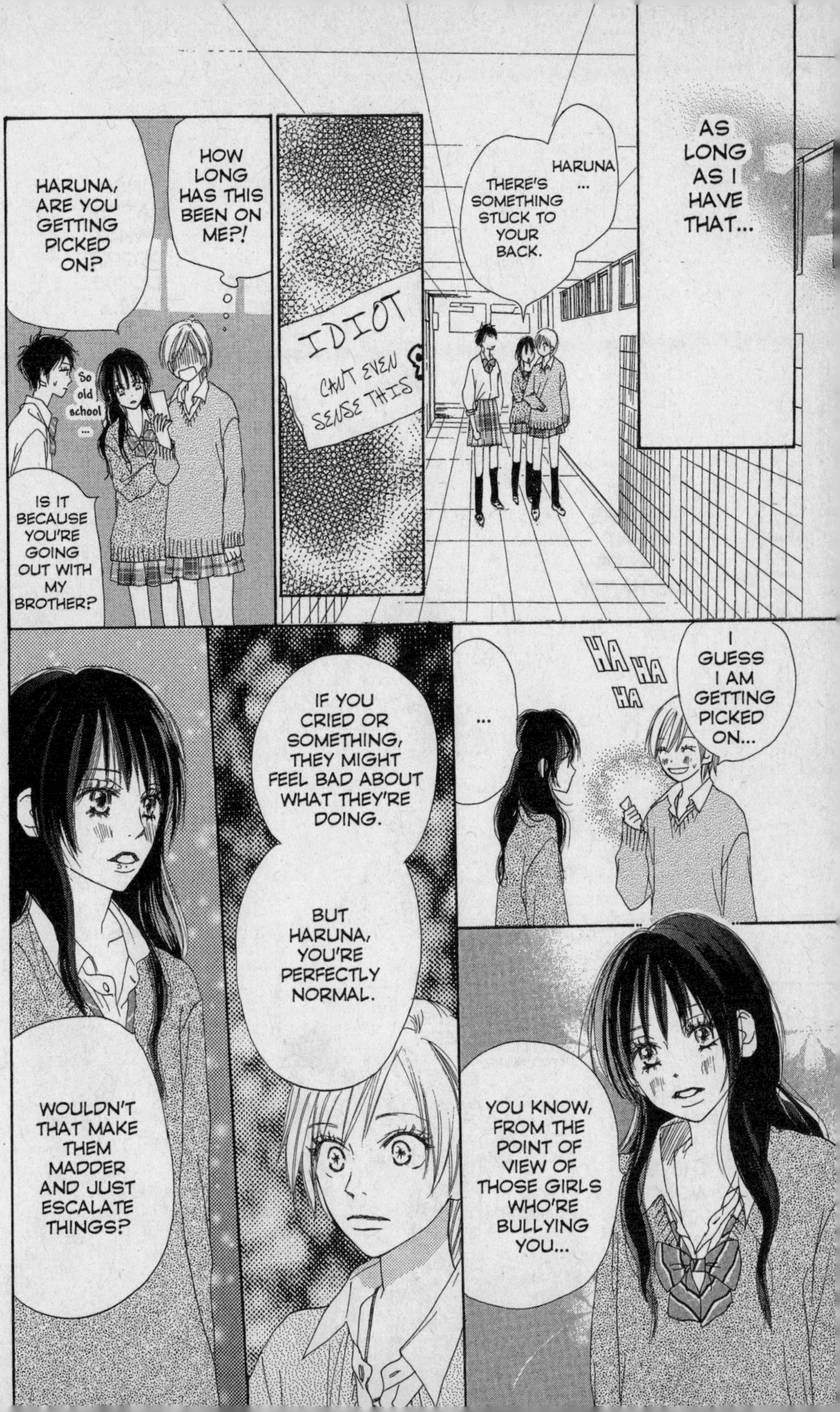
AS LONG AS I HAVE THAT...
HARUNA... THERE'S SOMETHING STUCK TO YOUR BACK.
IDIOT
CAN'T EVEN SENSE THIS
HOW LONG HAS THIS BEEN ON ME?!
HARUNA, ARE YOU GETTING PICKED ON?
So old school...
IS IT BECAUSE YOU'RE GOING OUT WITH MY BROTHER?
I GUESS I AM GETTING PICKED ON...
HA HA HA
...
YOU KNOW, FROM THE POINT OF VIEW OF THOSE GIRLS WHO'RE BULLYING YOU...
IF YOU CRIED OR SOMETHING, THEY MIGHT FEEL BAD ABOUT WHAT THEY'RE DOING.
BUT HARUNA, YOU'RE PERFECTLY NORMAL.
WOULDN'T THAT MAKE THEM MADDER AND JUST ESCALATE THINGS?

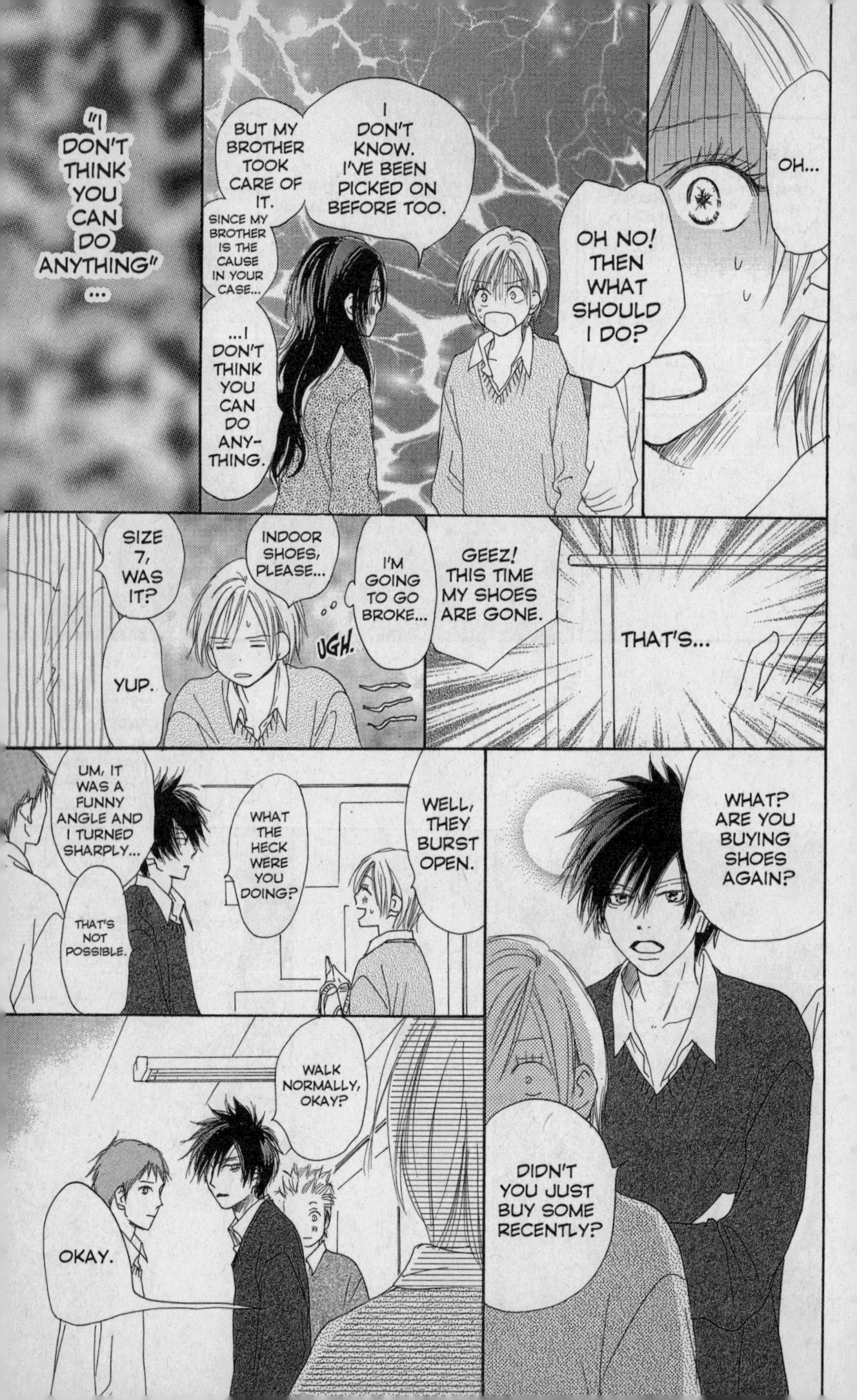
OH...
OH NO! THEN WHAT SHOULD I DO?
I DON'T KNOW. I'VE BEEN PICKED ON BEFORE TOO.
BUT MY BROTHER TOOK CARE OF IT.
SINCE MY BROTHER IS THE CAUSE IN YOUR CASE...
...I DON'T THINK YOU CAN DO ANY-THING.
"I DON'T THINK YOU CAN DO ANYTHING"...
THAT'S...
GEEZ! THIS TIME MY SHOES ARE GONE.
I'M GOING TO GO BROKE...
UGH.
INDOOR SHOES, PLEASE...
SIZE 7, WAS IT?
YUP.
WHAT? ARE YOU BUYING SHOES AGAIN?
DIDN'T YOU JUST BUY SOME RECENTLY?
WELL, THEY BURST OPEN.
WHAT THE HECK WERE YOU DOING?
UM, IT WAS A FUNNY ANGLE AND I TURNED SHARPLY...
THAT'S NOT POSSIBLE.
WALK NORMALLY, OKAY?
OKAY.

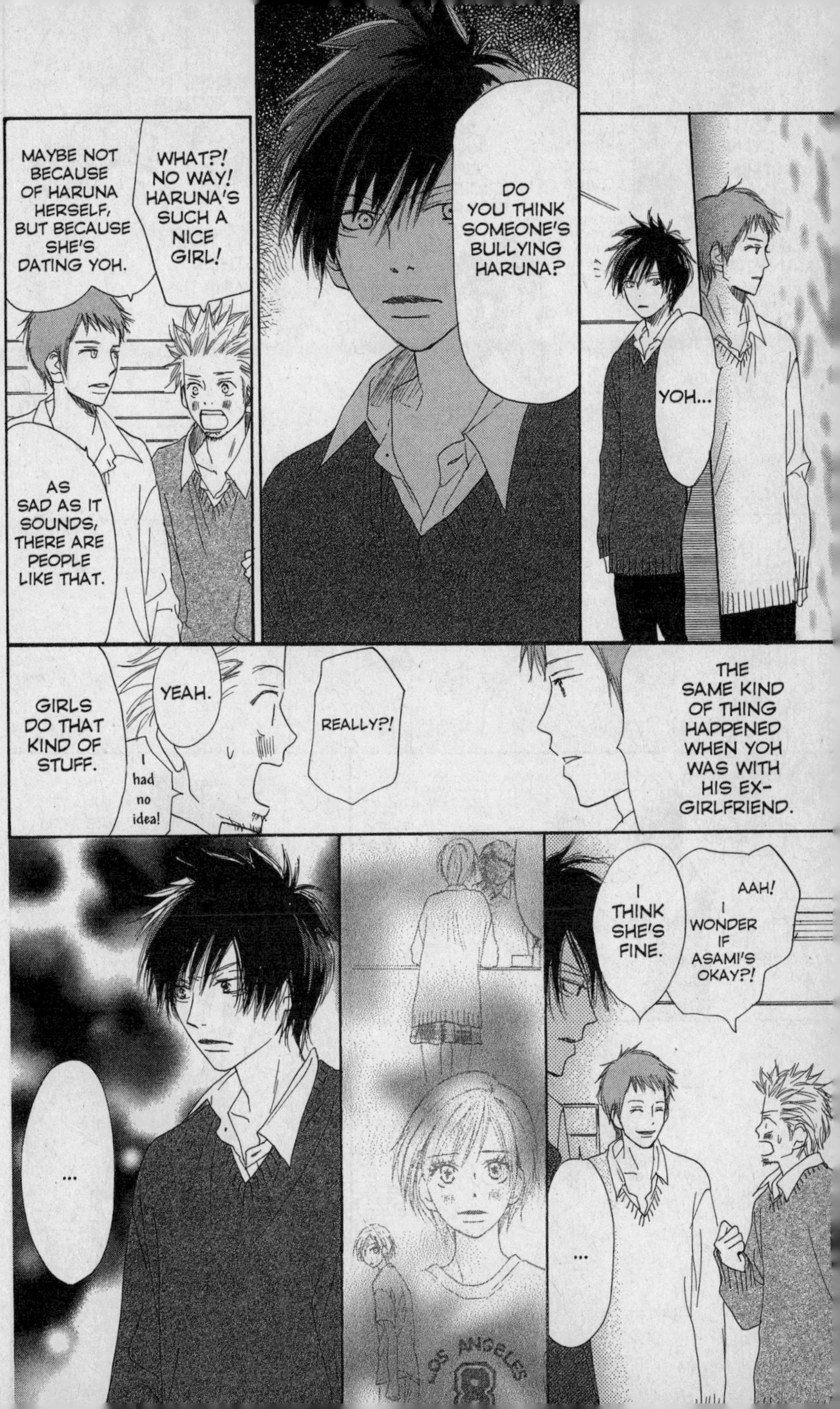
YOH...
DO YOU THINK SOMEONE'S BULLYING HARUNA?
WHAT?! NO WAY! HARUNA'S SUCH A NICE GIRL!
MAYBE NOT BECAUSE OF HARUNA HERSELF, BUT BECAUSE SHE'S DATING YOH.
AS SAD AS IT SOUNDS, THERE ARE PEOPLE LIKE THAT.
THE SAME KIND OF THING HAPPENED WHEN YOH WAS WITH HIS EX-GIRLFRIEND.
REALLY?!
YEAH.
GIRLS DO THAT KIND OF STUFF.
I had no idea!
AAH! I WONDER IF ASAMI'S OKAY?!
I THINK SHE'S FINE.
...
LOS ANGELES
...

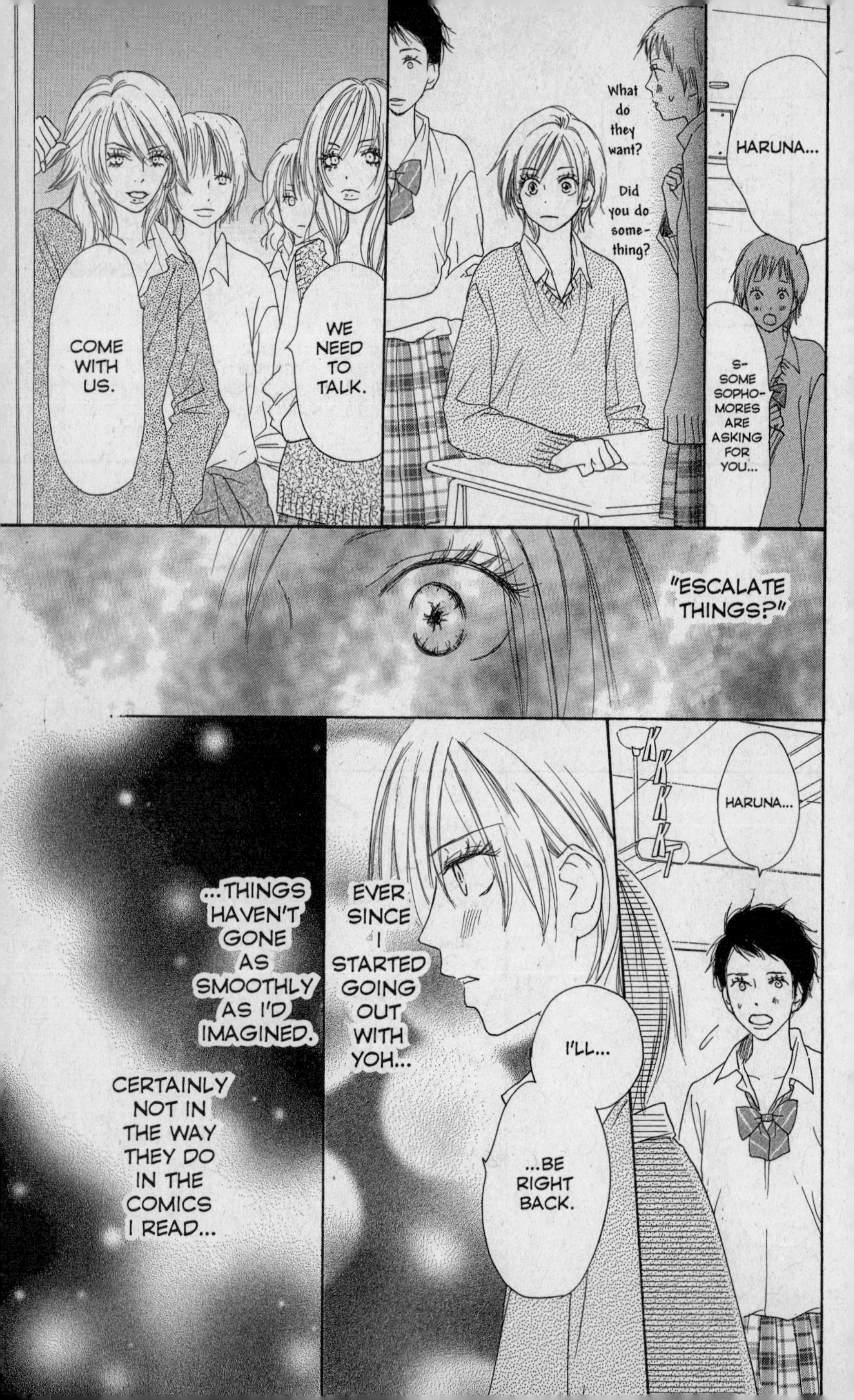
HARUNA...
S-SOME SOPHOMORES ARE ASKING FOR YOU...
What do they want?
Did you do some-thing?
WE NEED TO TALK.
COME WITH US.
"ESCALATE THINGS?"
KKKKT
HARUNA...
I'LL...
...BE RIGHT BACK.
EVER SINCE I STARTED GOING OUT WITH YOH...
...THINGS HAVEN'T GONE AS SMOOTHLY AS I'D IMAGINED.
CERTAINLY NOT IN THE WAY THEY DO IN THE COMICS I READ...

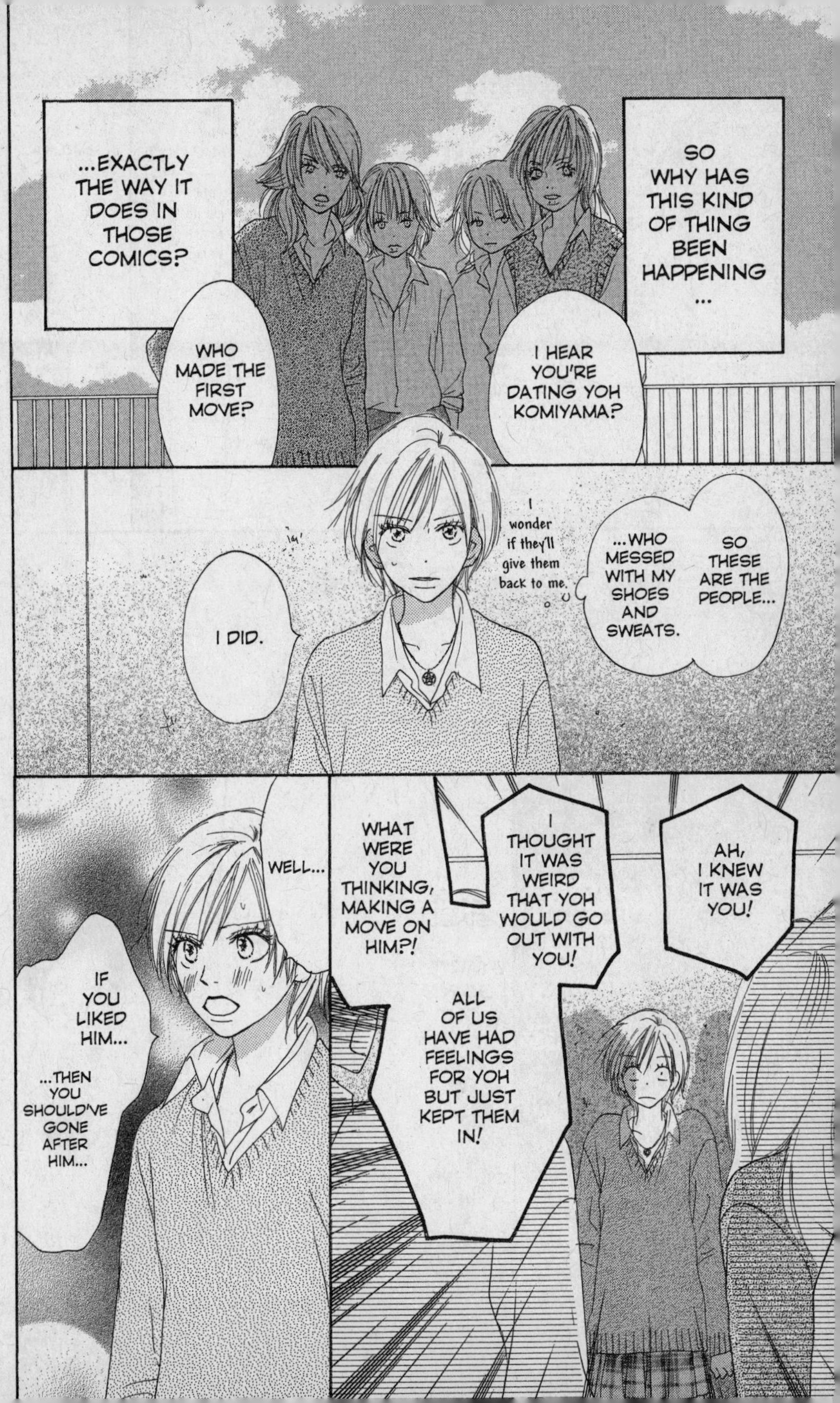
SO WHY HAS THIS KIND OF THING BEEN HAPPENING...
...EXACTLY THE WAY IT DOES IN THOSE COMICS?
I HEAR YOU'RE DATING YOH KOMIYAMA?
WHO MADE THE FIRST MOVE?
SO THESE ARE THE PEOPLE...
...WHO MESSED WITH MY SHOES AND SWEATS.
I wonder if they'll give them back to me.
I DID.
AH, I KNEW IT WAS YOU!
I THOUGHT IT WAS WEIRD THAT YOH WOULD GO OUT WITH YOU!
WHAT WERE YOU THINKING, MAKING A MOVE ON HIM?!
ALL OF US HAVE HAD FEELINGS FOR YOH BUT JUST KEPT THEM IN!
WELL...
IF YOU LIKED HIM...
...THEN YOU SHOULD'VE GONE AFTER HIM...

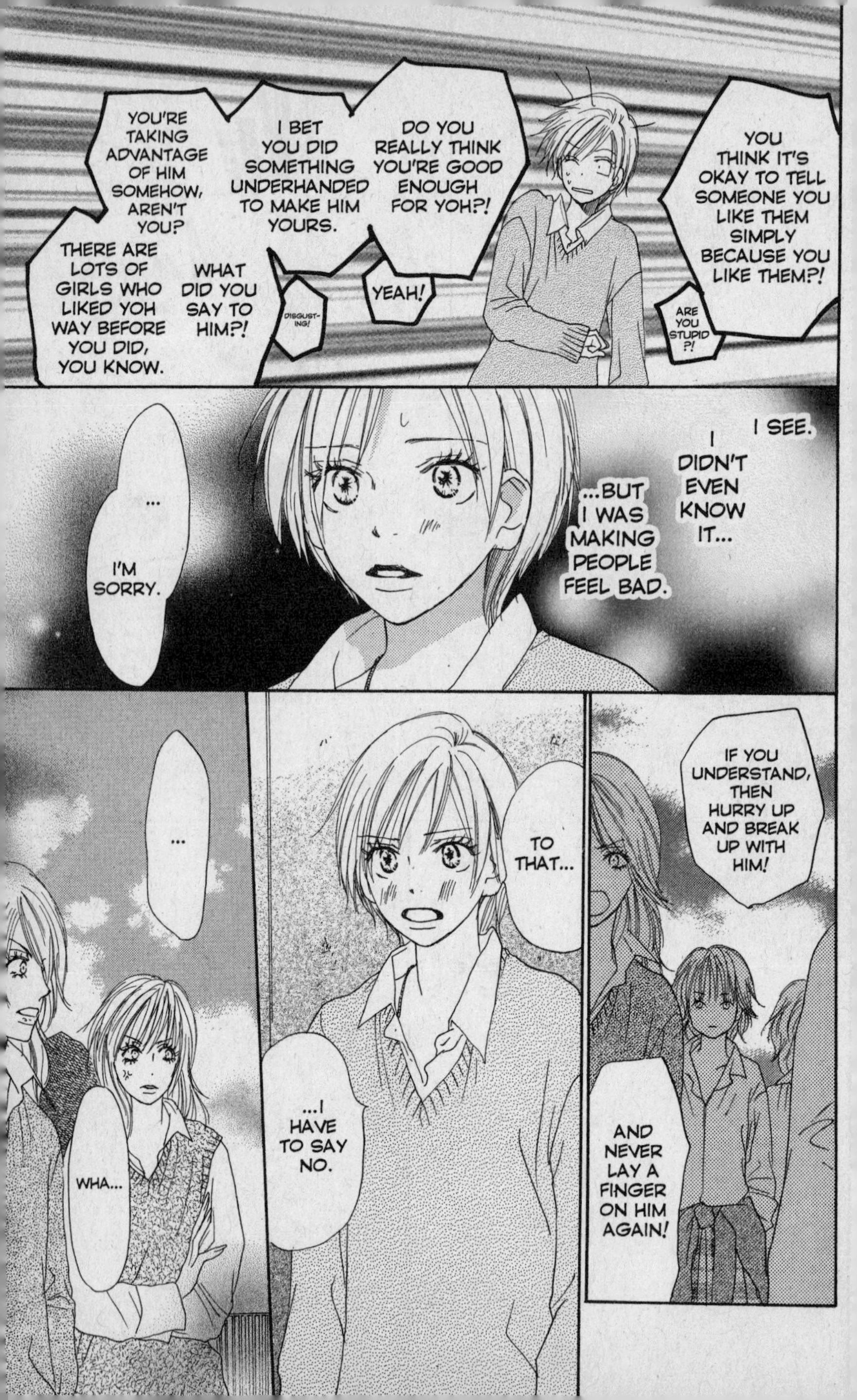
YOU THINK IT'S OKAY TO TELL SOMEONE YOU LIKE THEM SIMPLY BECAUSE YOU LIKE THEM?!
ARE YOU STUPID?!
DO YOU REALLY THINK YOU'RE GOOD ENOUGH FOR YOH?!
YEAH!
I BET YOU DID SOMETHING UNDERHANDED TO MAKE HIM YOURS.
DISGUSTING!
YOU'RE TAKING ADVANTAGE OF HIM SOMEHOW, AREN'T YOU?
WHAT DID YOU SAY TO HIM?!
THERE ARE LOTS OF GIRLS WHO LIKED YOH WAY BEFORE YOU DID, YOU KNOW.
I SEE.
I DIDN'T EVEN KNOW IT...
...BUT I WAS MAKING PEOPLE FEEL BAD.
...
I'M SORRY.
IF YOU UNDERSTAND, THEN HURRY UP AND BREAK UP WITH HIM!
AND NEVER LAY A FINGER ON HIM AGAIN!
TO THAT...
...I HAVE TO SAY NO.
...
WHA...

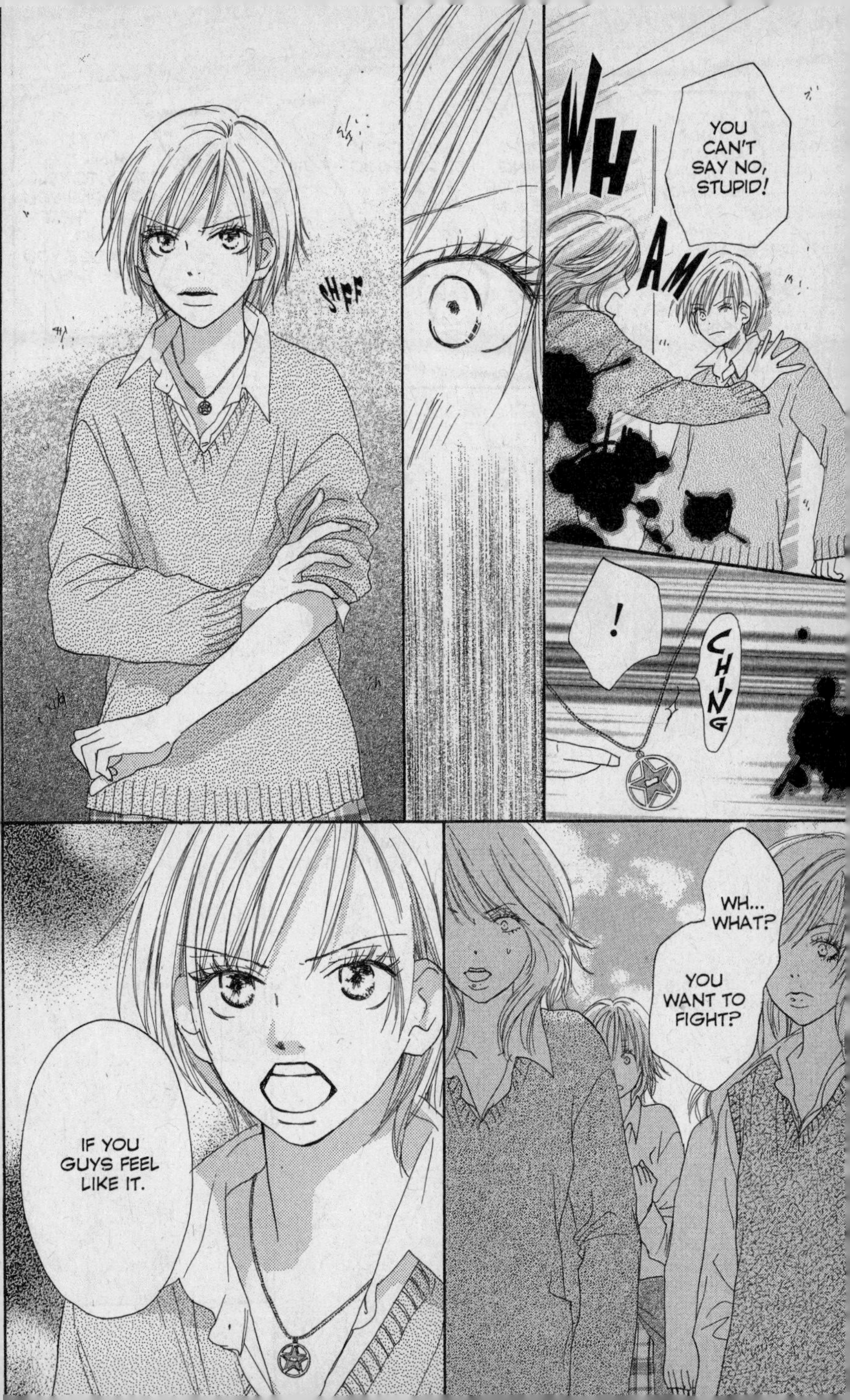
YOU CAN'T SAY NO, STUPID!
WHAM
!
CHING
SHFF
WH... WHAT?
YOU WANT TO FIGHT?
IF YOU GUYS FEEL LIKE IT.

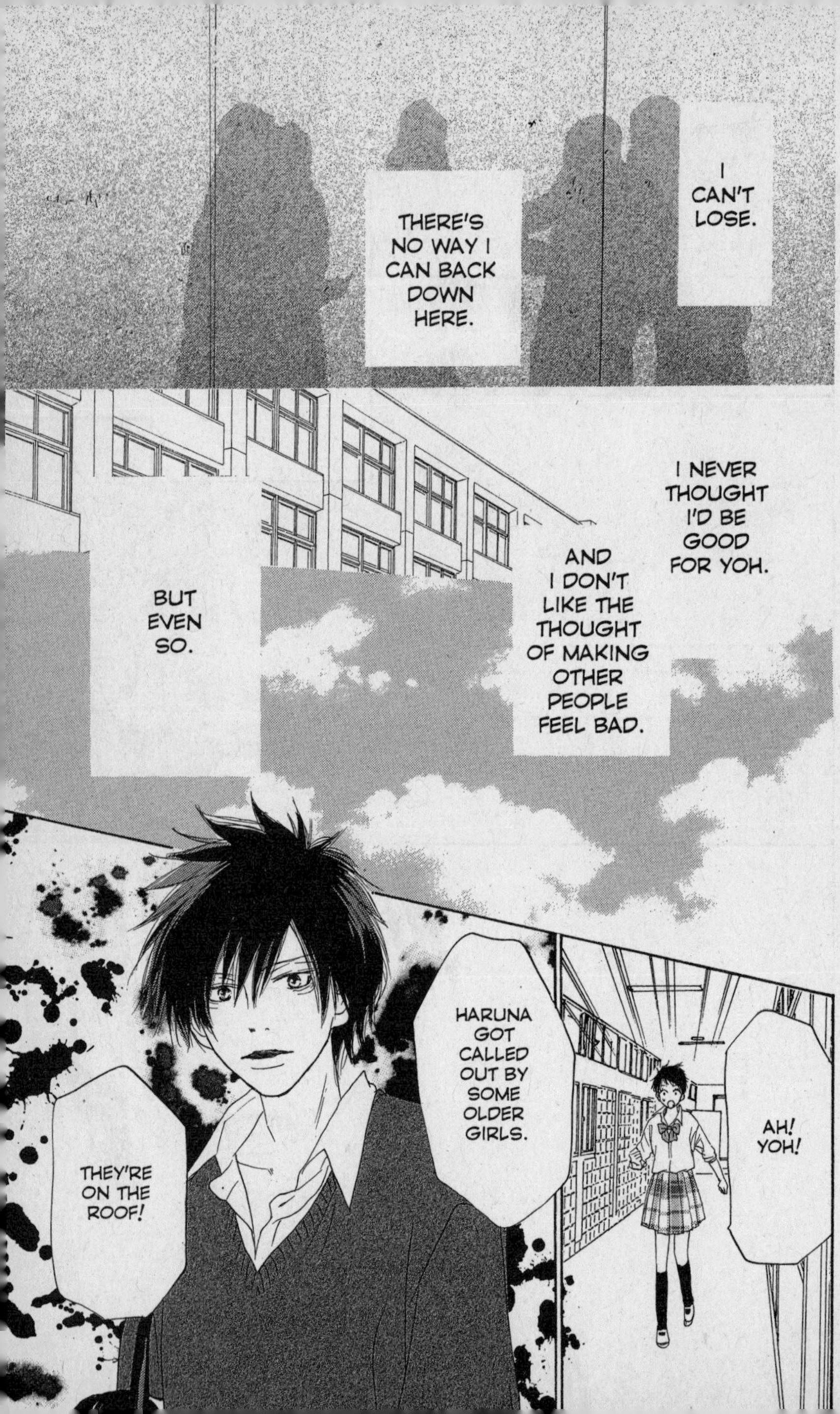
I CAN'T LOSE.
THERE'S NO WAY I CAN BACK DOWN HERE.
I NEVER THOUGHT I'D BE GOOD FOR YOH.
AND I DON'T LIKE THE THOUGHT OF MAKING OTHER PEOPLE FEEL BAD.
BUT EVEN SO.
AH! YOH!
HARUNA GOT CALLED OUT BY SOME OLDER GIRLS.
THEY'RE ON THE ROOF!

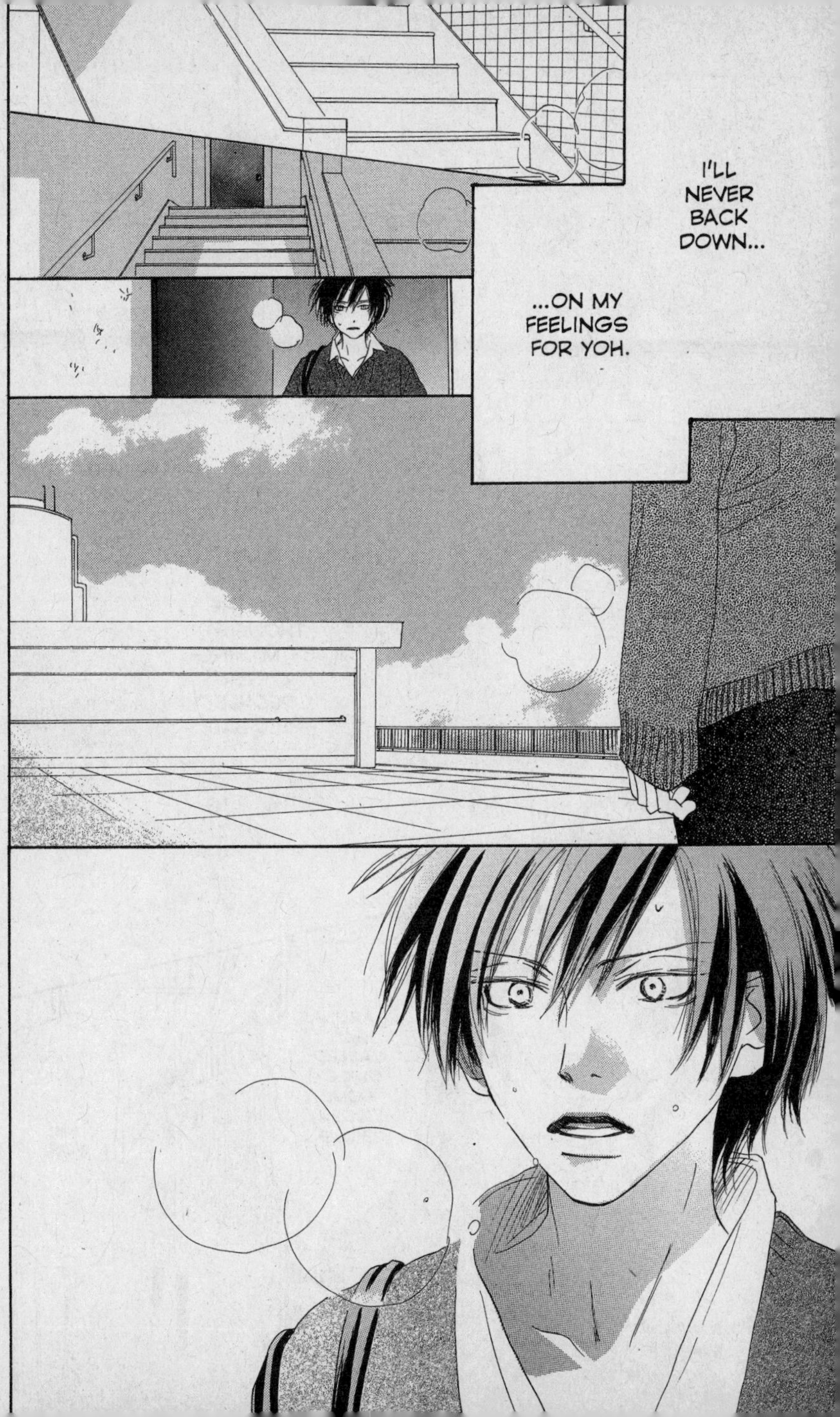
I'LL NEVER BACK DOWN...
...ON MY FEELINGS FOR YOH.

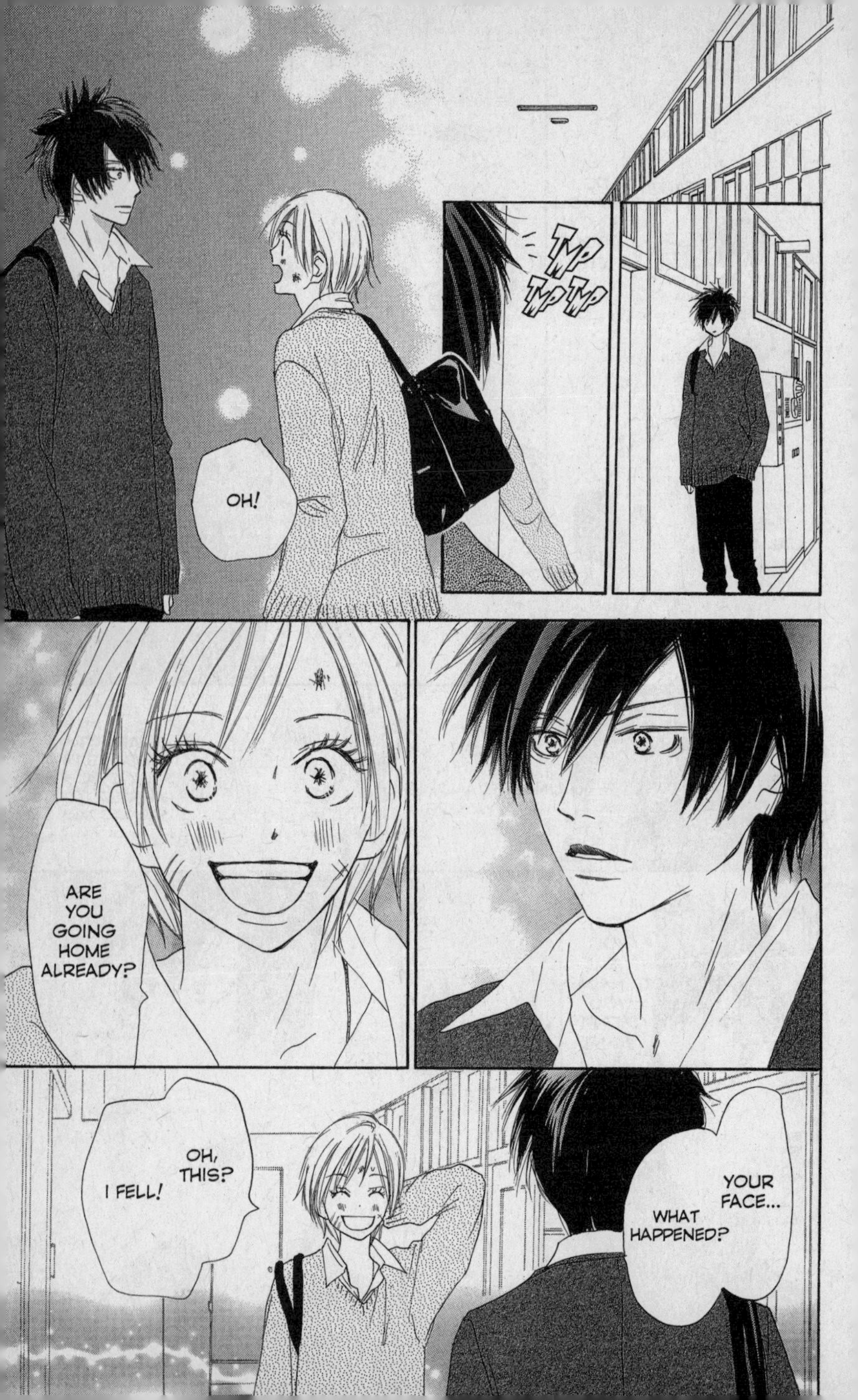

TMP TMP TMP TMP
OH!
ARE YOU GOING HOME ALREADY?
YOUR FACE... WHAT HAPPENED?
OH, THIS? I FELL!

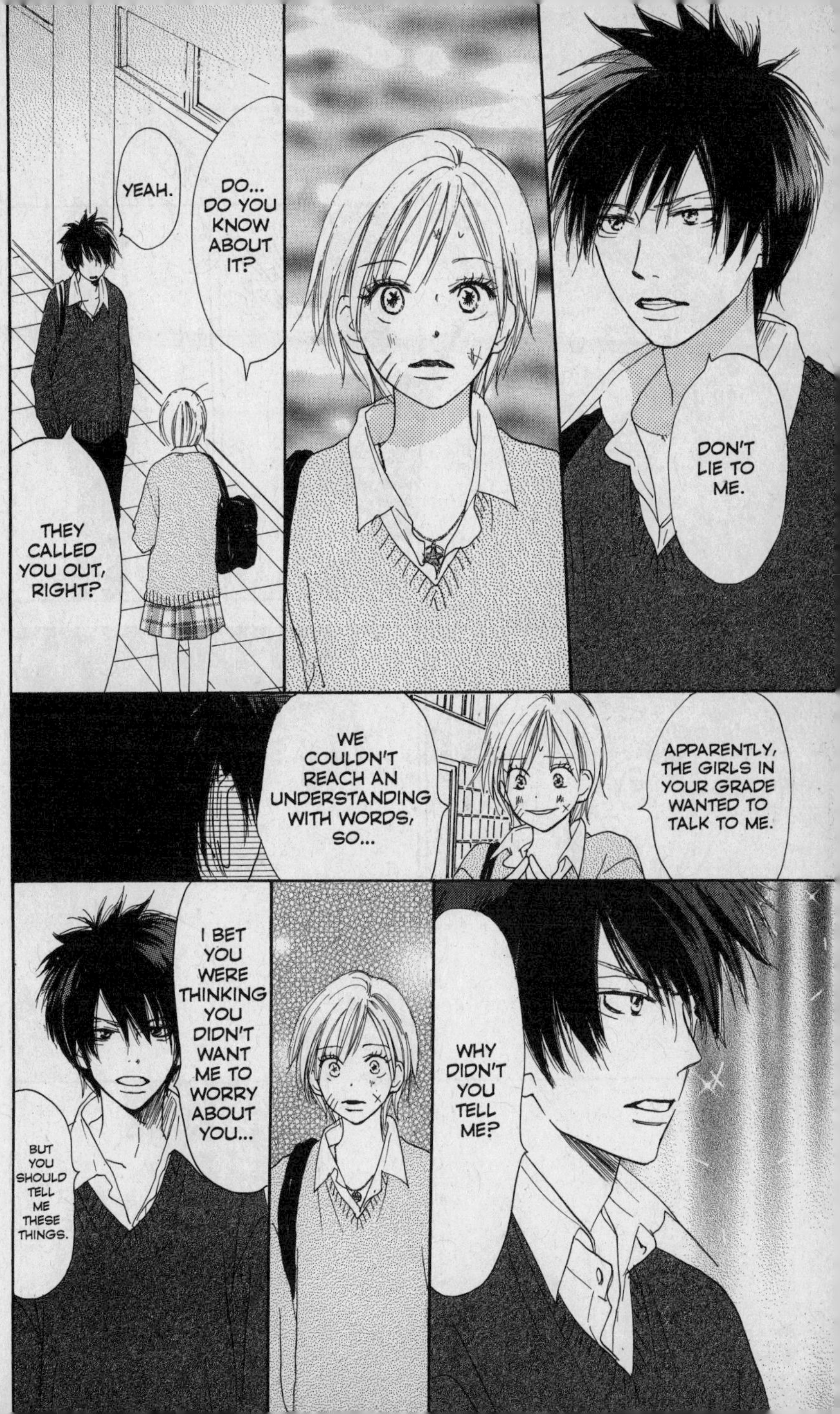
DON'T LIE TO ME.
DO... DO YOU KNOW ABOUT IT?
YEAH.
THEY CALLED YOU OUT, RIGHT?
APPARENTLY, THE GIRLS IN YOUR GRADE WANTED TO TALK TO ME.
WE COULDN'T REACH AN UNDERSTANDING WITH WORDS, SO...
WHY DIDN'T YOU TELL ME?
I BET YOU WERE THINKING YOU DIDN'T WANT ME TO WORRY ABOUT YOU...
BUT YOU SHOULD TELL ME THESE THINGS.

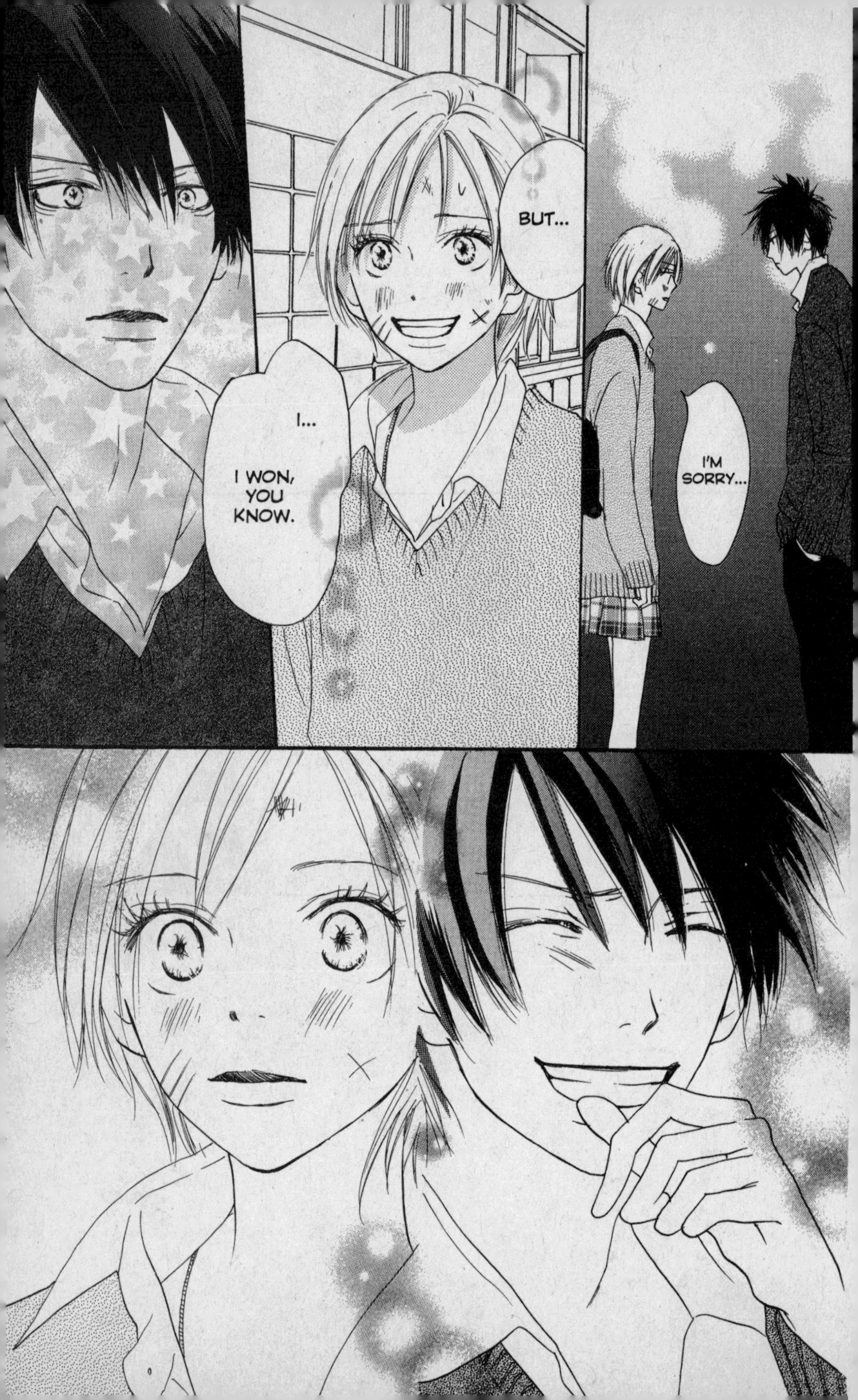
I'M SORRY...
BUT...
I...
I WON, YOU KNOW.

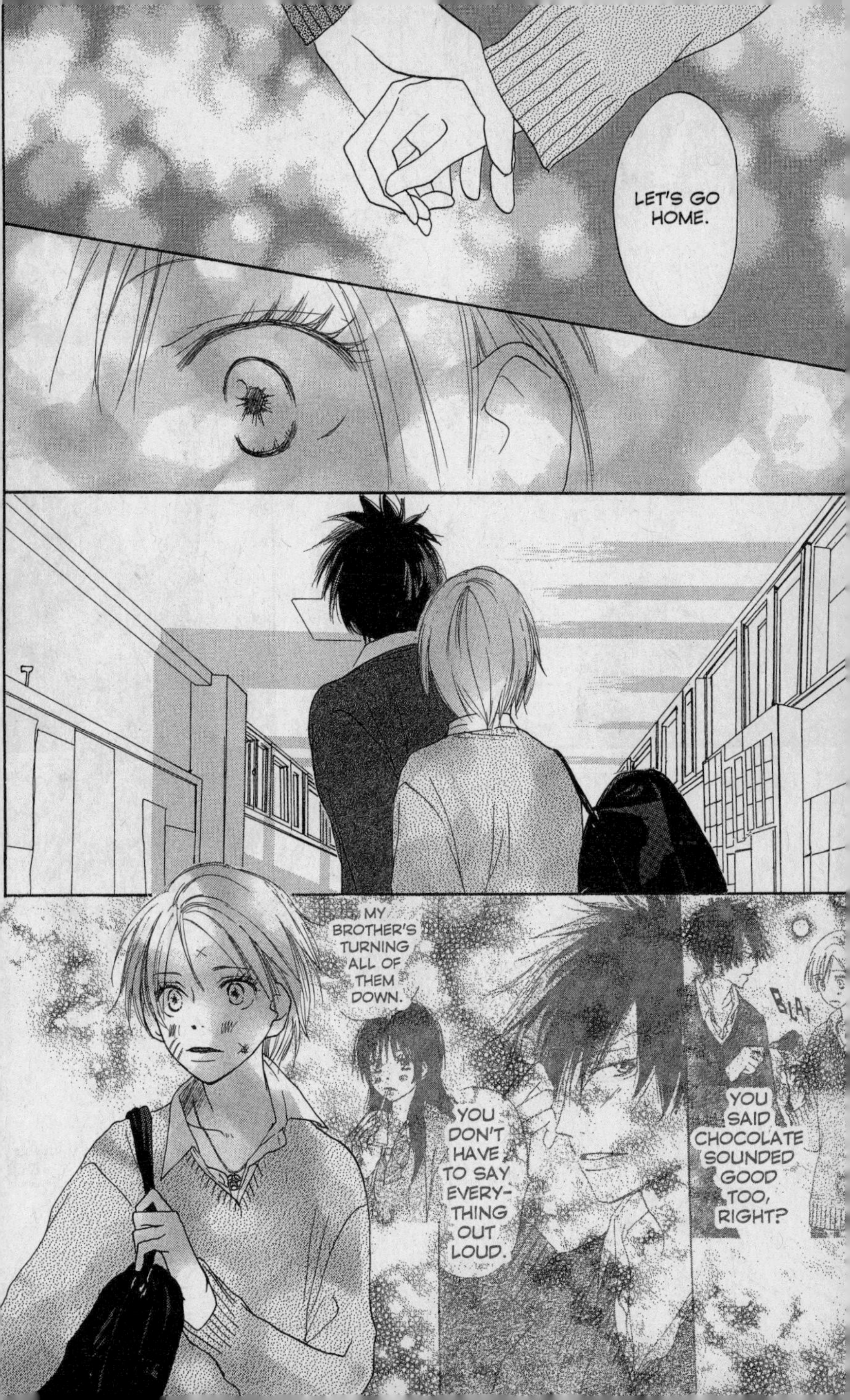
LET'S GO HOME.
BLAT
YOU SAID CHOCOLATE SOUNDED GOOD TOO, RIGHT?
YOU DON'T HAVE TO SAY EVERYTHING OUT LOUD.
MY BROTHER'S TURNING ALL OF THEM DOWN.

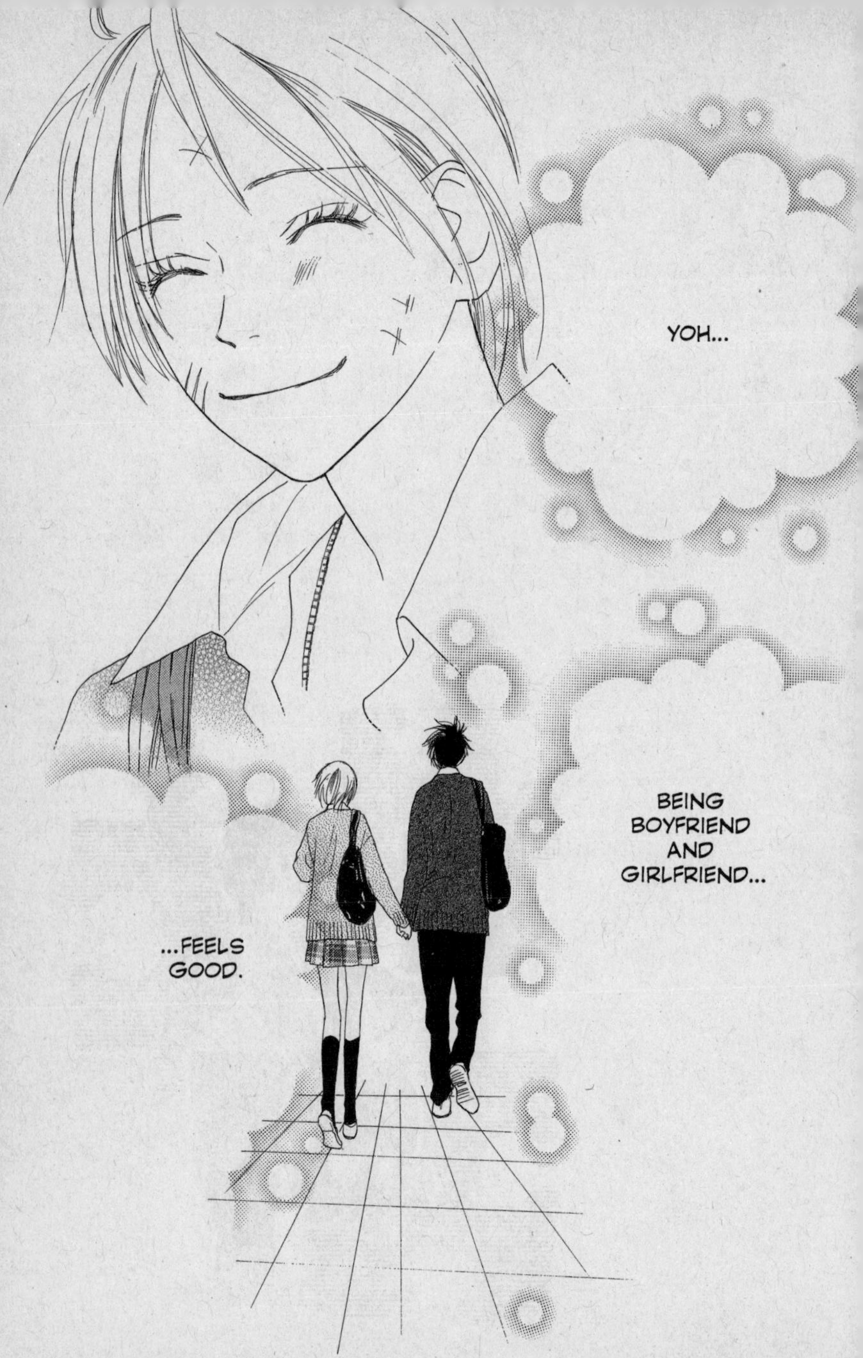
YOH...
BEING BOYFRIEND AND GIRLFRIEND...
...FEELS GOOD.

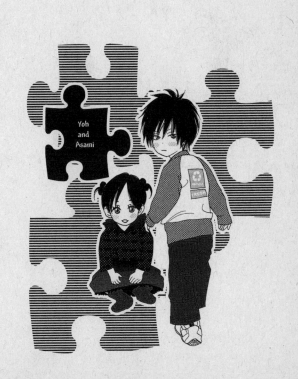

Yoh
and
Asami

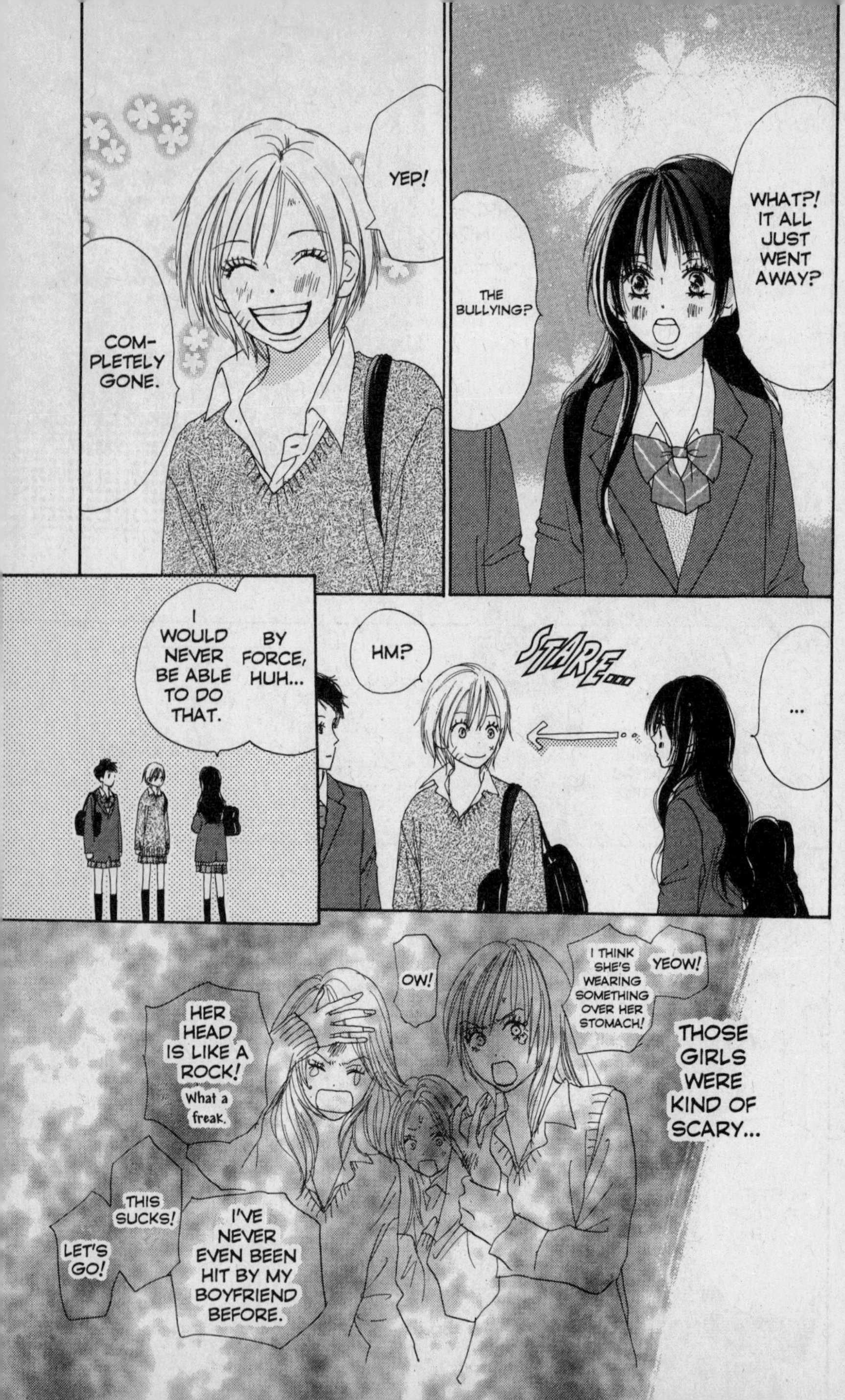
WHAT?! IT ALL JUST WENT AWAY?
THE BULLYING?
YEP!
COMPLETELY GONE.
...
STARE...
HM?
BY FORCE, HUH...
I WOULD NEVER BE ABLE TO DO THAT.
THOSE GIRLS WERE KIND OF SCARY...
YEOW!
I THINK SHE'S WEARING SOMETHING OVER HER STOMACH!
OW!
HER HEAD IS LIKE A ROCK!
What a freak.
I'VE NEVER EVEN BEEN HIT BY MY BOYFRIEND BEFORE.
THIS SUCKS!
LET'S GO!

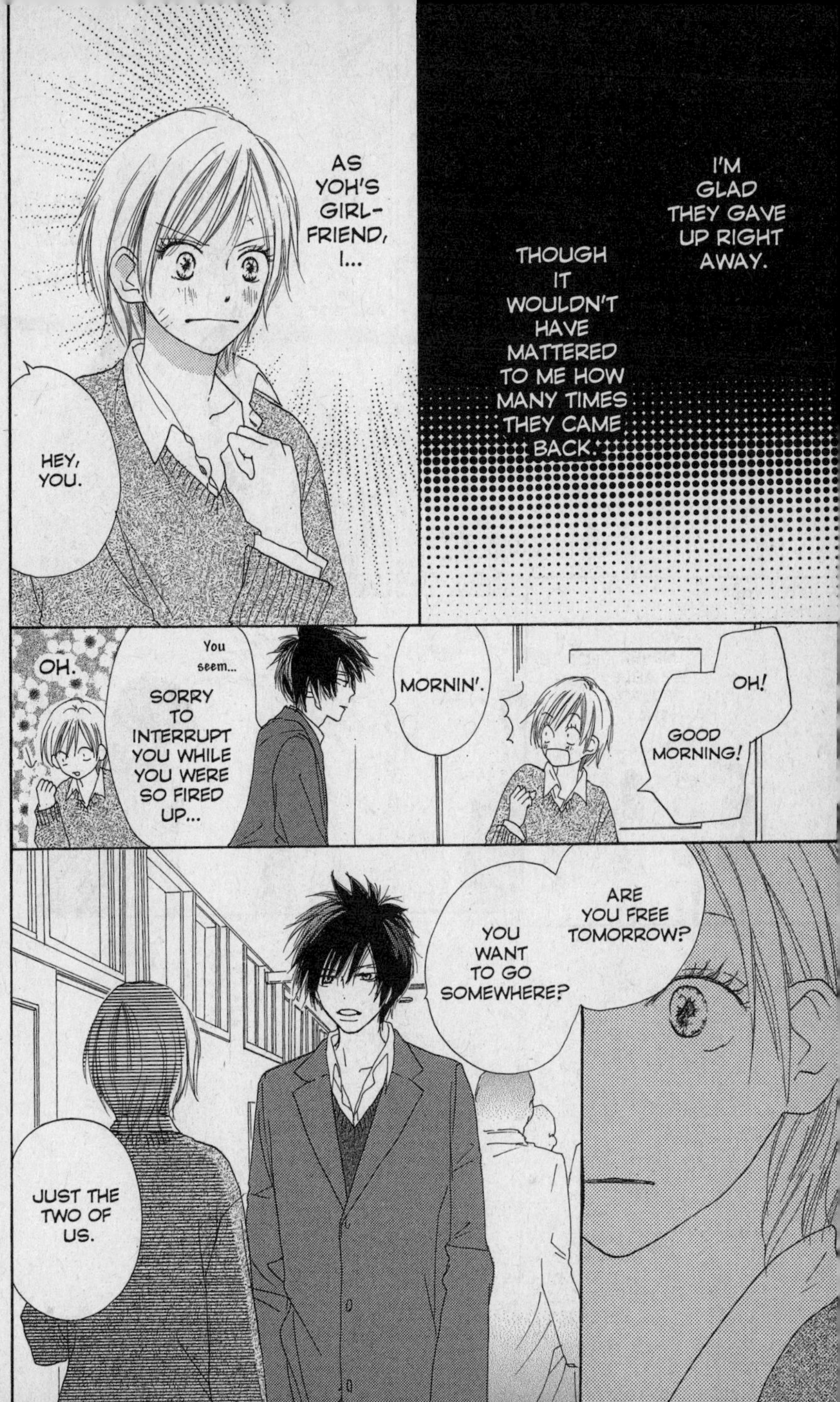
I'M GLAD THEY GAVE UP RIGHT AWAY.
THOUGH IT WOULDN'T HAVE MATTERED TO ME HOW MANY TIMES THEY CAME BACK.
AS YOH'S GIRL-FRIEND, I...
HEY, YOU.
OH! GOOD MORNING!
MORNIN'.
You seem...
SORRY TO INTERRUPT YOU WHILE YOU WERE SO FIRED UP...
OH.
ARE YOU FREE TOMORROW?
YOU WANT TO GO SOMEWHERE?
JUST THE TWO OF US.

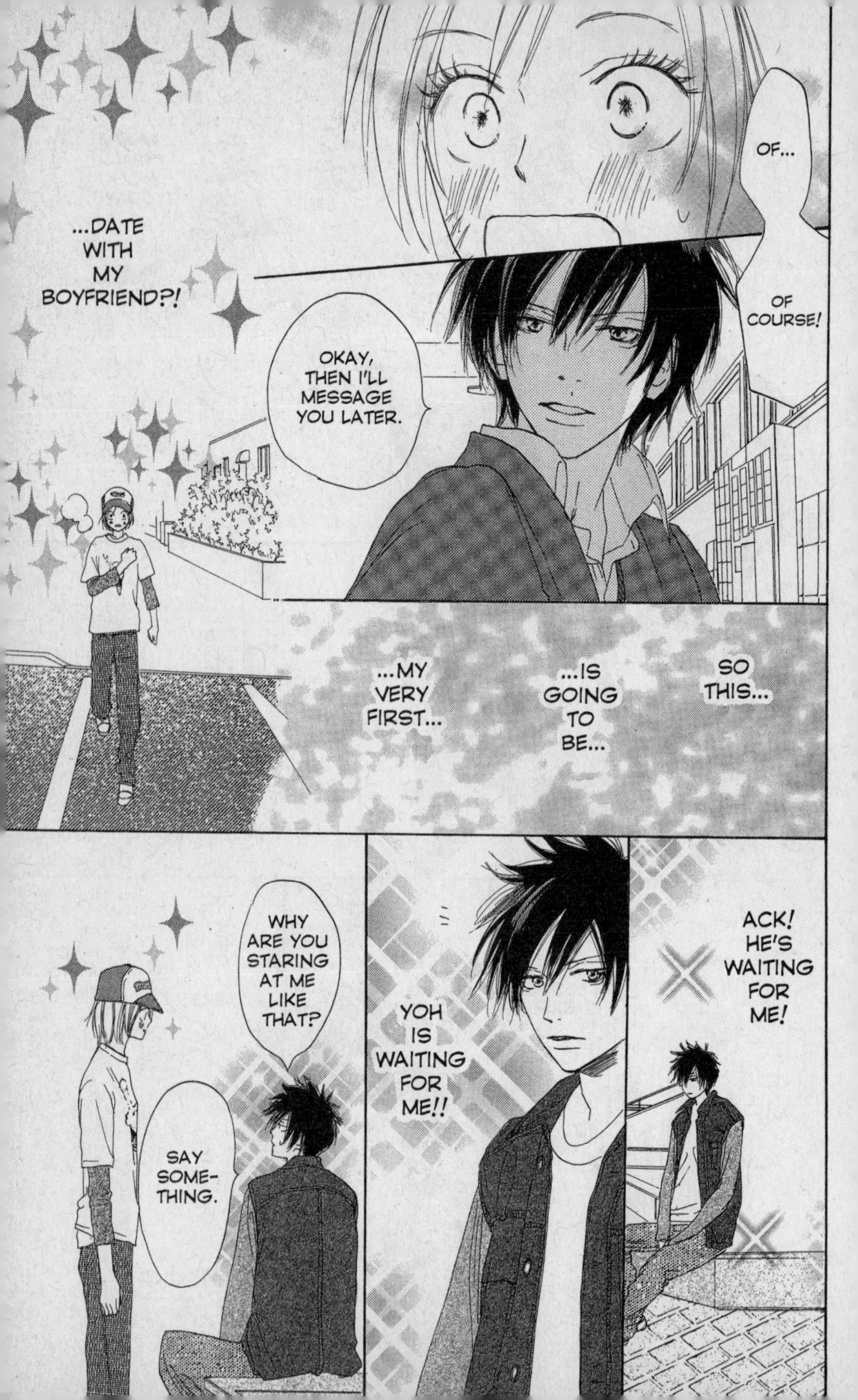
OF...
OF COURSE!
OKAY, THEN I'LL MESSAGE YOU LATER.
SO THIS...
...IS GOING TO BE...
...MY VERY FIRST...
...DATE WITH MY BOYFRIEND?!
ACK! HE'S WAITING FOR ME!
YOH IS WAITING FOR ME!!
WHY ARE YOU STARING AT ME LIKE THAT?
SAY SOME-THING.

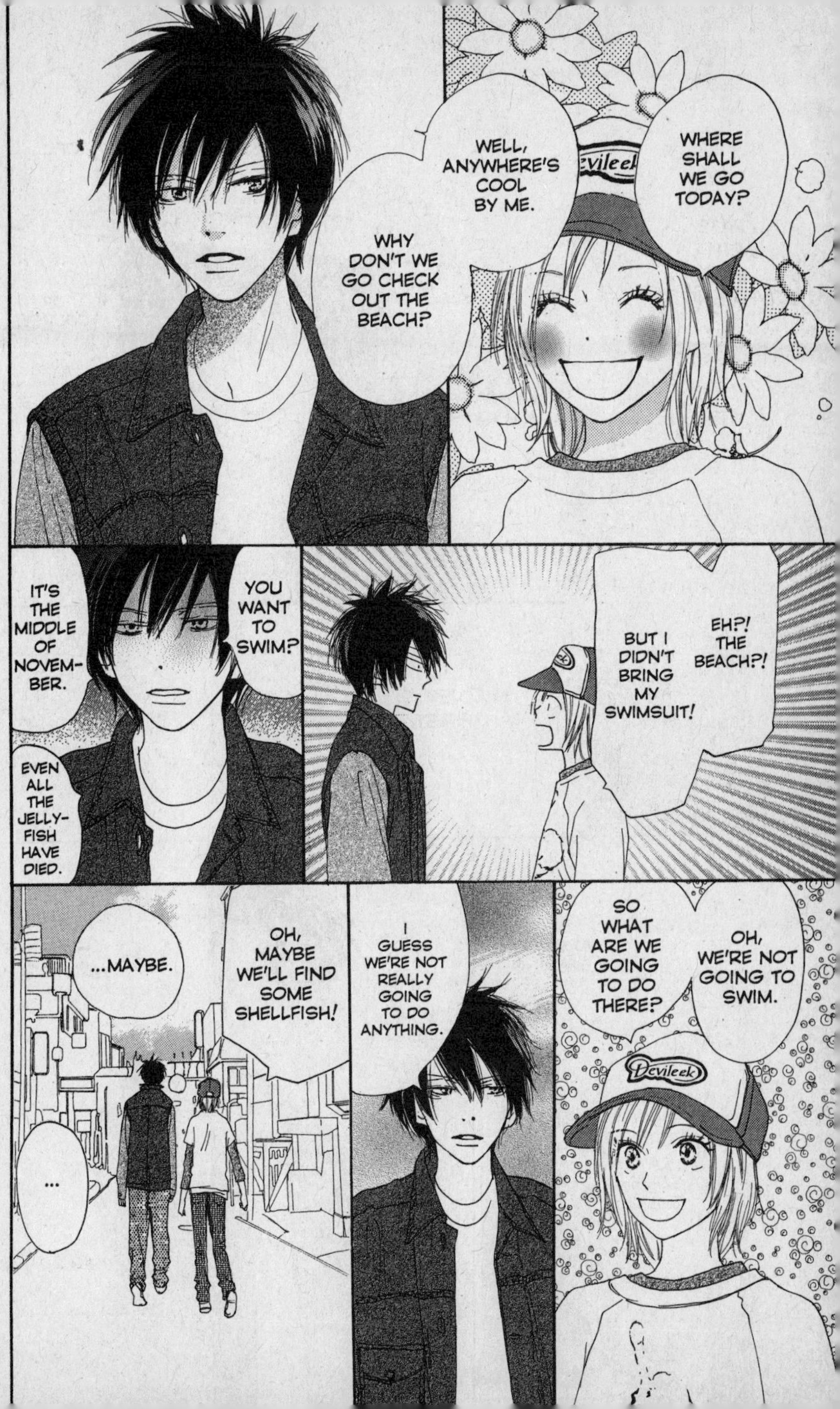
WHERE SHALL WE GO TODAY?
WELL, ANYWHERE'S COOL BY ME.
WHY DON'T WE GO CHECK OUT THE BEACH?
EH?! THE BEACH?!
BUT I DIDN'T BRING MY SWIMSUIT!
YOU WANT TO SWIM?
IT'S THE MIDDLE OF NOVEMBER.
EVEN ALL THE JELLYFISH HAVE DIED.
OH, WE'RE NOT GOING TO SWIM.
SO WHAT ARE WE GOING TO DO THERE?
I GUESS WE'RE NOT REALLY GOING TO DO ANYTHING.
OH, MAYBE WE'LL FIND SOME SHELLFISH!
...MAYBE.
...

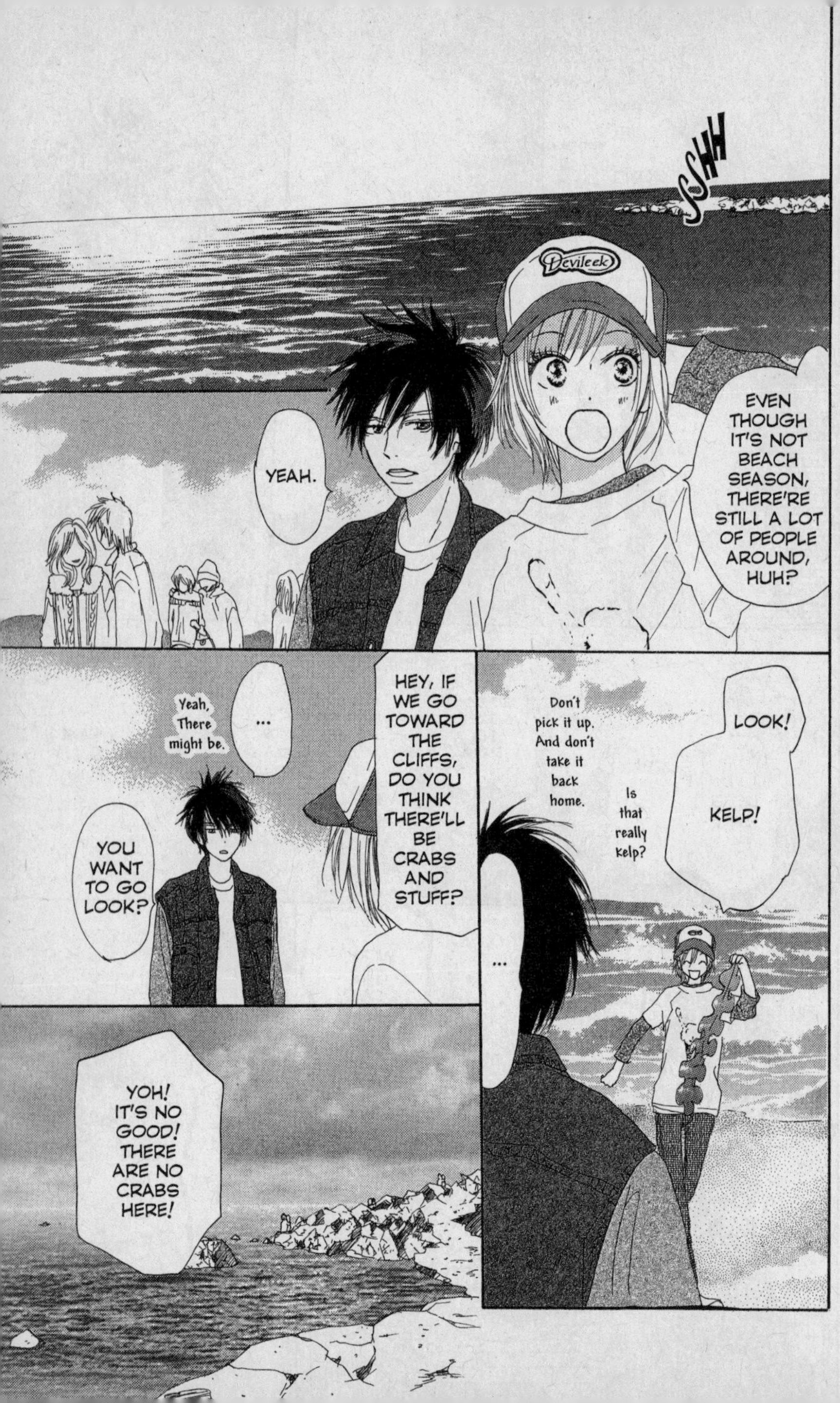
SHHH
EVEN THOUGH IT'S NOT BEACH SEASON, THERE'RE STILL A LOT OF PEOPLE AROUND, HUH?
YEAH.
LOOK! KELP!
Is that really kelp?
Don't pick it up. And don't take it back home.
...
HEY, IF WE GO TOWARD THE CLIFFS, DO YOU THINK THERE'LL BE CRABS AND STUFF?
...
Yeah, There might be.
YOU WANT TO GO LOOK?
YOH! IT'S NO GOOD! THERE ARE NO CRABS HERE!

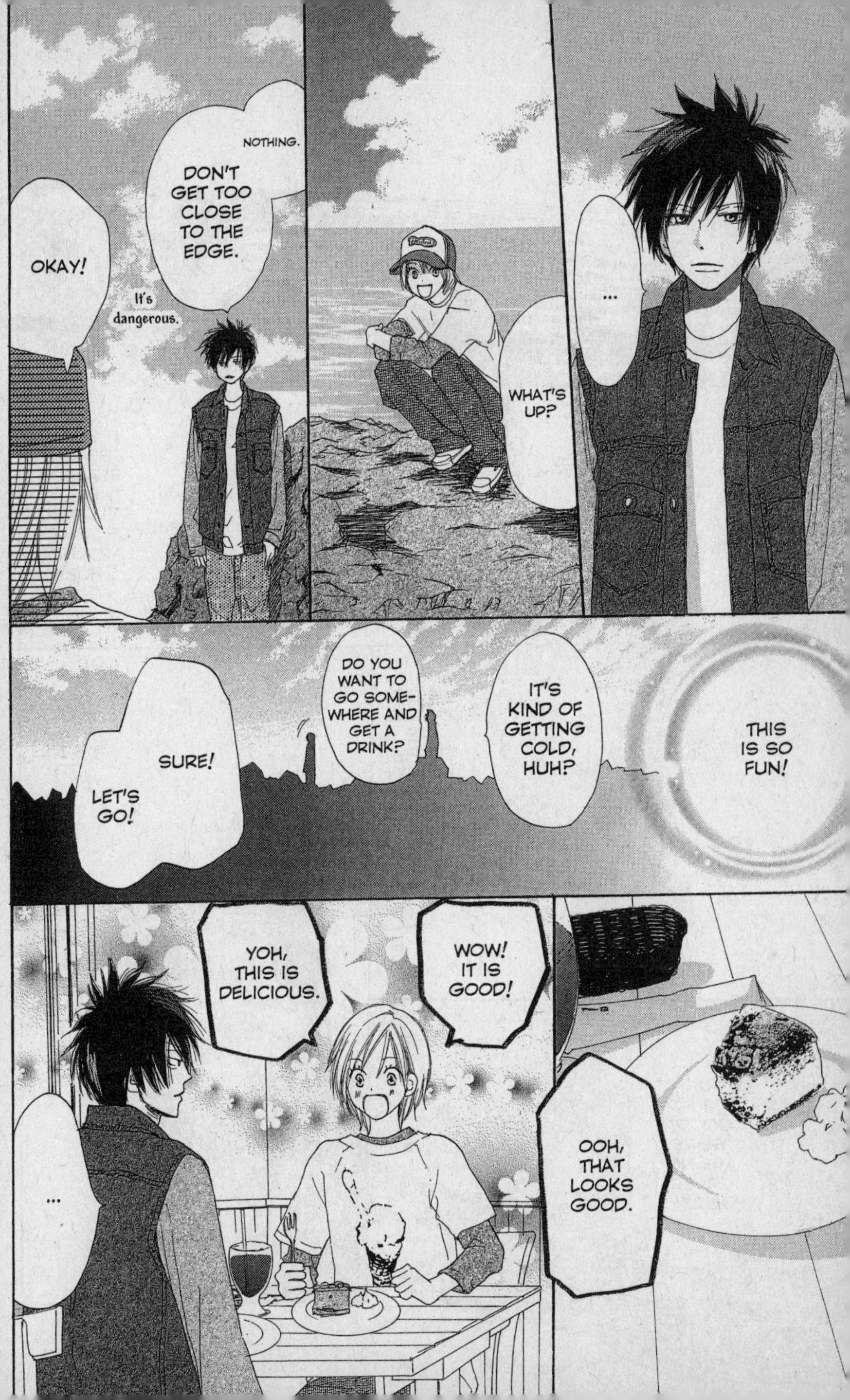
...
WHAT'S UP?
NOTHING.
DON'T GET TOO CLOSE TO THE EDGE.
It's dangerous.
OKAY!
THIS IS SO FUN!
IT'S KIND OF GETTING COLD, HUH?
DO YOU WANT TO GO SOMEWHERE AND GET A DRINK?
SURE!
LET'S GO!
OOH, THAT LOOKS GOOD.
WOW! IT IS GOOD!
YOH, THIS IS DELICIOUS.
...

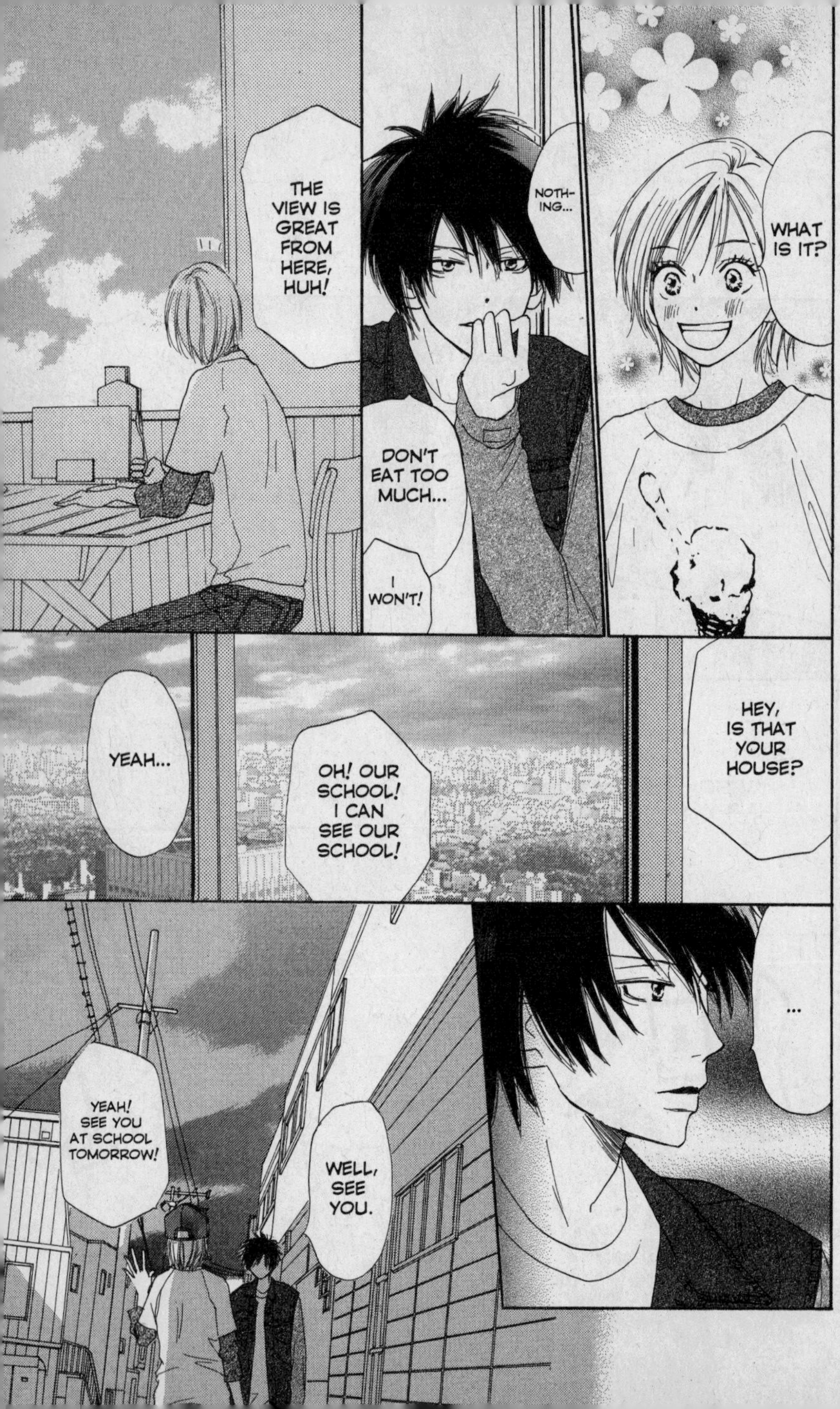
WHAT IS IT?
NOTH-ING...
DON'T EAT TOO MUCH...
I WON'T!
THE VIEW IS GREAT FROM HERE, HUH!
HEY, IS THAT YOUR HOUSE?
OH! OUR SCHOOL! I CAN SEE OUR SCHOOL!
YEAH...
...
WELL, SEE YOU.
YEAH! SEE YOU AT SCHOOL TOMORROW!

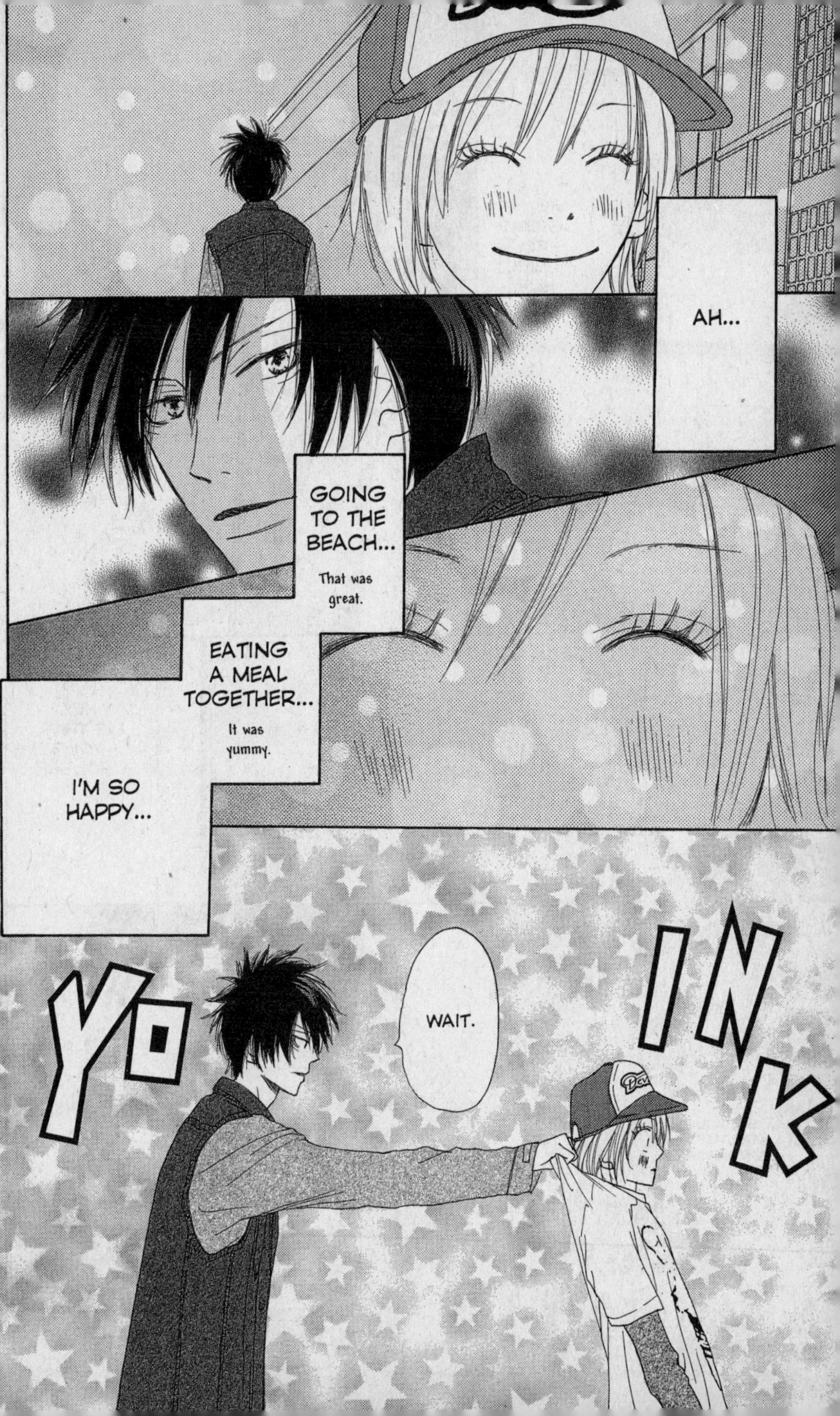
AH...
GOING TO THE BEACH...
That was great.
EATING A MEAL TOGETHER...
It was yummy.
I'M SO HAPPY...
YOINK
WAIT.

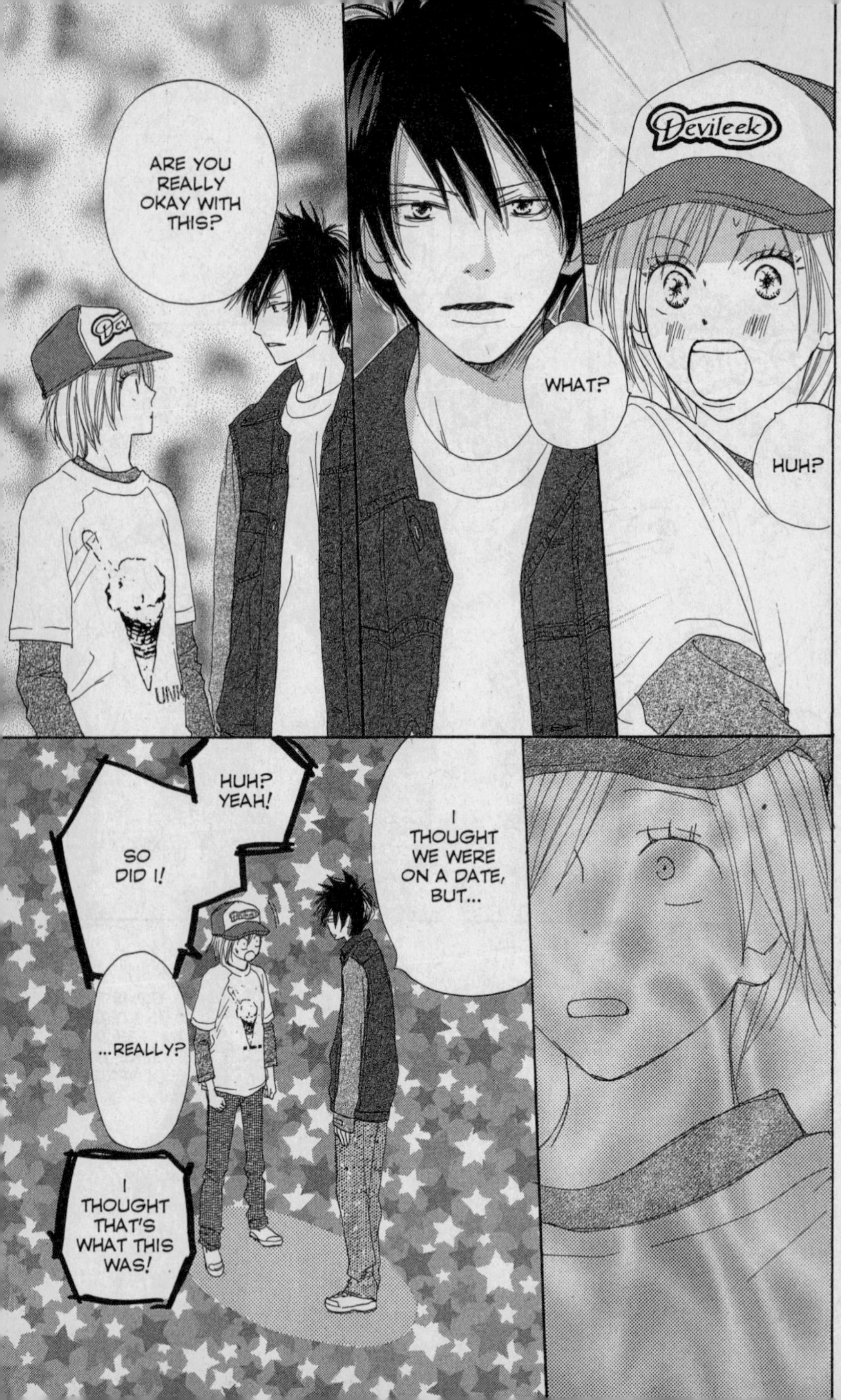
Devileek
WHAT?
HUH?
ARE YOU REALLY OKAY WITH THIS?
I THOUGHT WE WERE ON A DATE, BUT...
HUH? YEAH!
SO DID I!
...REALLY?
I THOUGHT THAT'S WHAT THIS WAS!

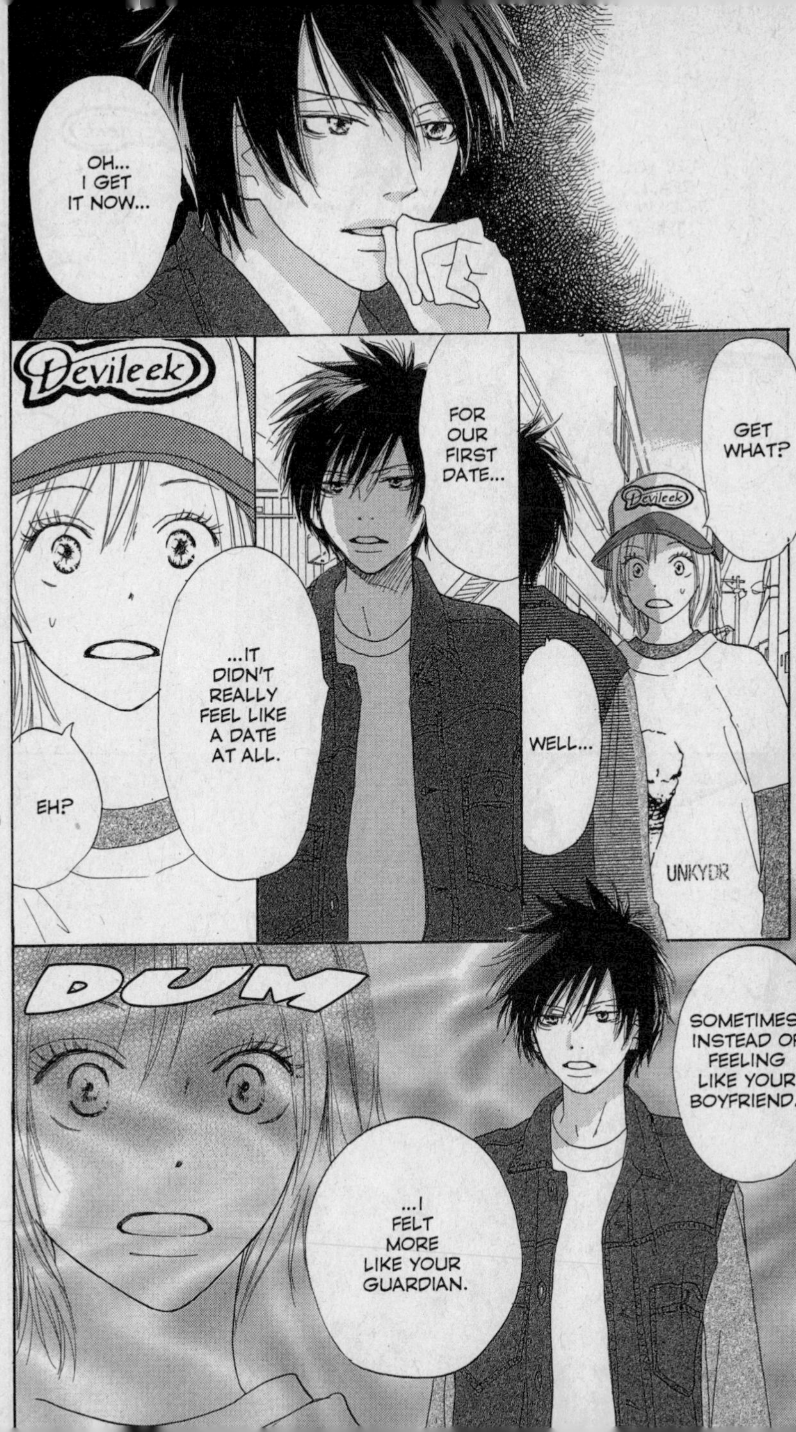
OH... I GET IT NOW...
GET WHAT?
Devileek
WELL...
UNKYDR
FOR OUR FIRST DATE...
...IT DIDN'T REALLY FEEL LIKE A DATE AT ALL.
Devileek
EH?
SOMETIMES, INSTEAD OF FEELING LIKE YOUR BOYFRIEND...
DUM
...I FELT MORE LIKE YOUR GUARDIAN.

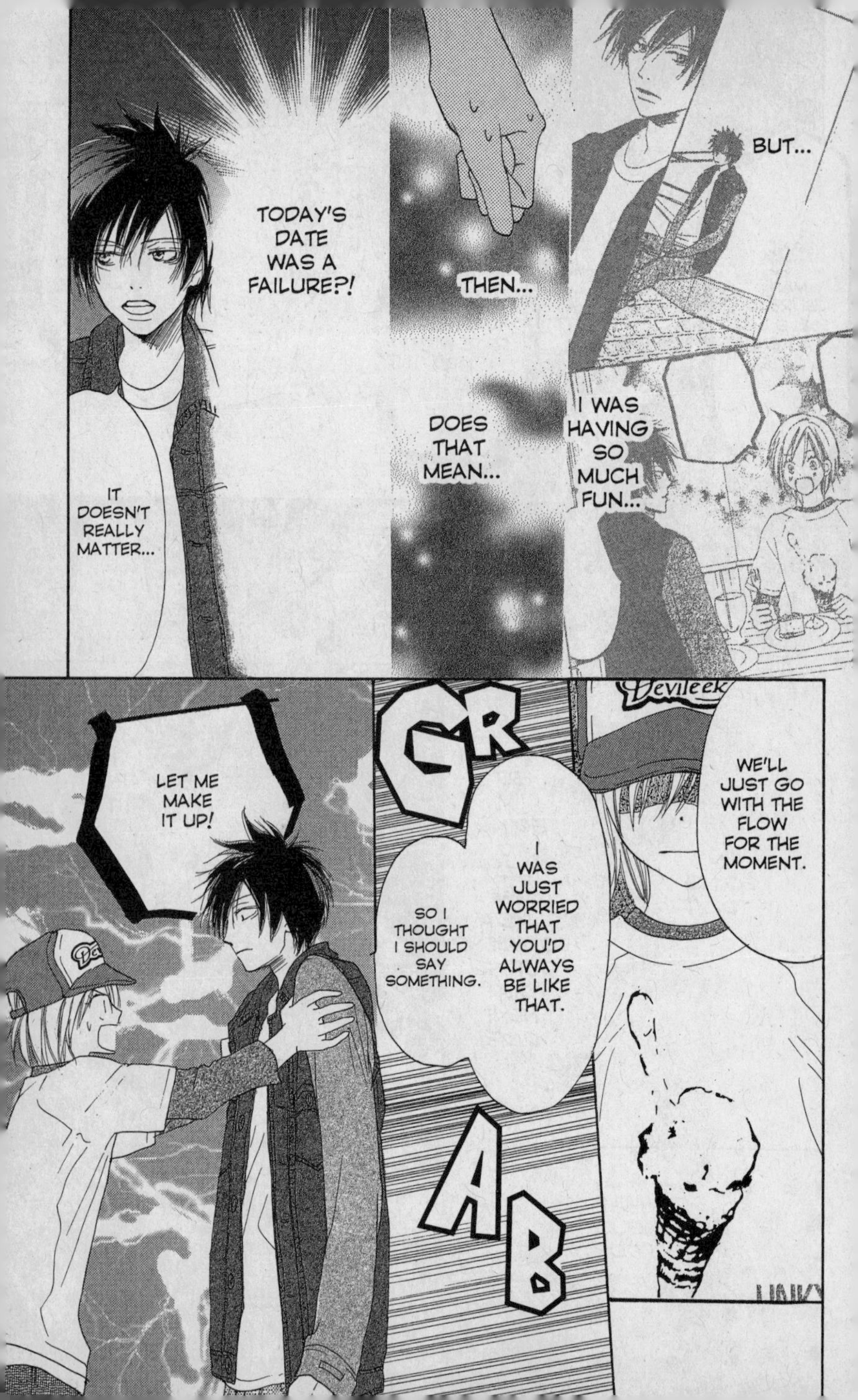
BUT...
I WAS HAVING SO MUCH FUN...
THEN...
DOES THAT MEAN...
TODAY'S DATE WAS A FAILURE?!
IT DOESN'T REALLY MATTER...
Devileek
WE'LL JUST GO WITH THE FLOW FOR THE MOMENT.
GR
I WAS JUST WORRIED THAT YOU'D ALWAYS BE LIKE THAT.
SO I THOUGHT I SHOULD SAY SOMETHING.
AB
LET ME MAKE IT UP!

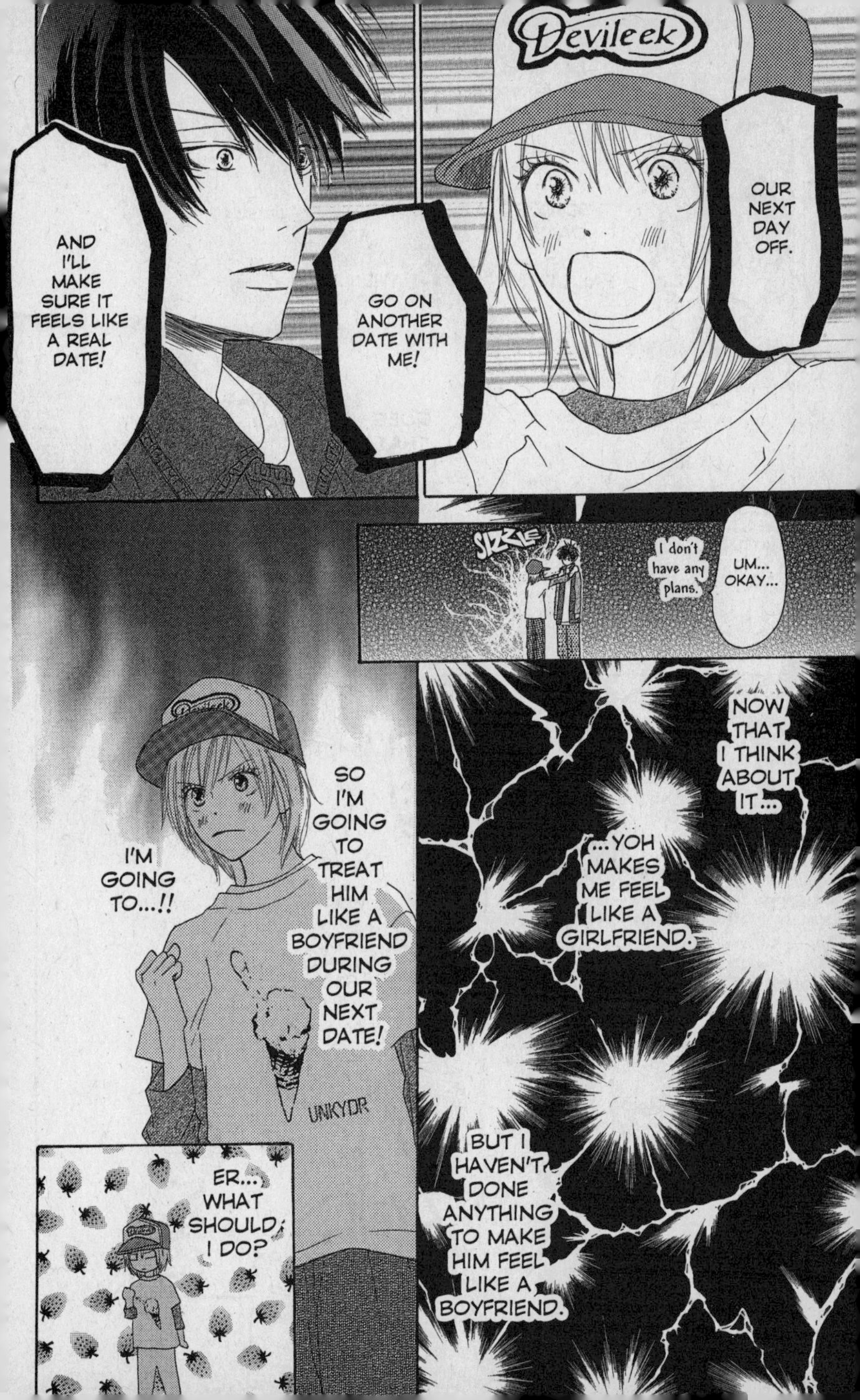
OUR NEXT DAY OFF.
GO ON ANOTHER DATE WITH ME!
AND I'LL MAKE SURE IT FEELS LIKE A REAL DATE!
UM... OKAY...
I don't have any plans.
SIZZLE
NOW THAT I THINK ABOUT IT...
...YOH MAKES ME FEEL LIKE A GIRLFRIEND.
BUT I HAVEN'T DONE ANYTHING TO MAKE HIM FEEL LIKE A BOYFRIEND.
SO I'M GOING TO TREAT HIM LIKE A BOYFRIEND DURING OUR NEXT DATE!
I'M GOING TO...!!
ER... WHAT SHOULD I DO?

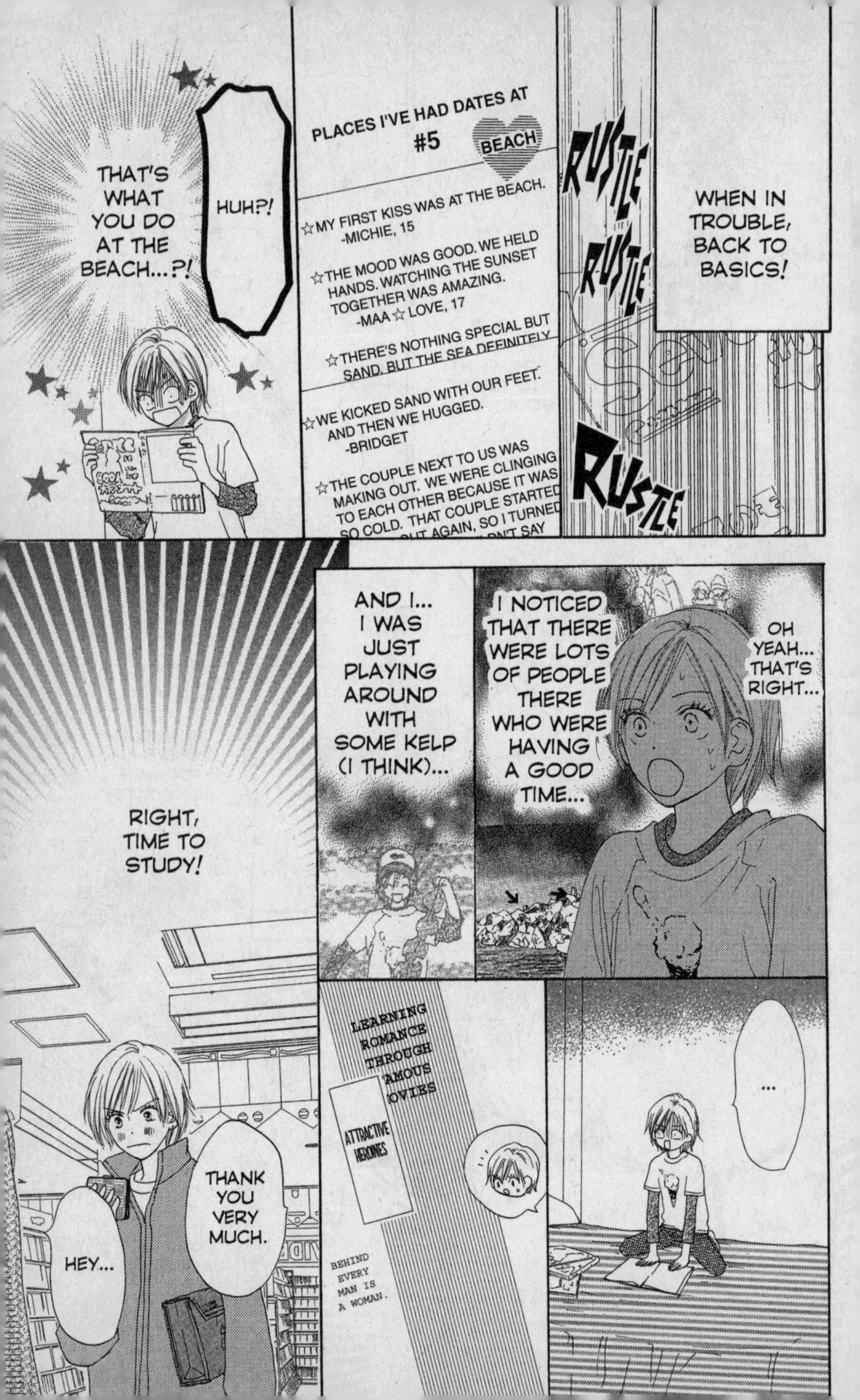
WHEN IN TROUBLE, BACK TO BASICS!
RUSTLE RUSTLE
RUSTLE
PLACES I'VE HAD DATES AT
#5
BEACH
☆MY FIRST KISS WAS AT THE BEACH. -MICHIE, 15
☆THE MOOD WAS GOOD. WE HELD HANDS. WATCHING THE SUNSET TOGETHER WAS AMAZING. -MAA☆LOVE, 17
☆THERE'S NOTHING SPECIAL BUT SAND. BUT THE SEA DEFINITELY
☆WE KICKED SAND WITH OUR FEET. AND THEN WE HUGGED. -BRIDGET
☆THE COUPLE NEXT TO US WAS MAKING OUT. WE WERE CLINGING TO EACH OTHER BECAUSE IT WAS SO COLD. THAT COUPLE STARTED
HUH?!
THAT'S WHAT YOU DO AT THE BEACH...?!
OH YEAH... THAT'S RIGHT...
I NOTICED THAT THERE WERE LOTS OF PEOPLE THERE WHO WERE HAVING A GOOD TIME...
AND I... I WAS JUST PLAYING AROUND WITH SOME KELP (I THINK)...
...
LEARNING ROMANCE THROUGH AMOUS OVIES
ATTRACTIVE HEROINES
BEHIND EVERY MAN IS A WOMAN.
RIGHT, TIME TO STUDY!
THANK YOU VERY MUCH.
HEY...

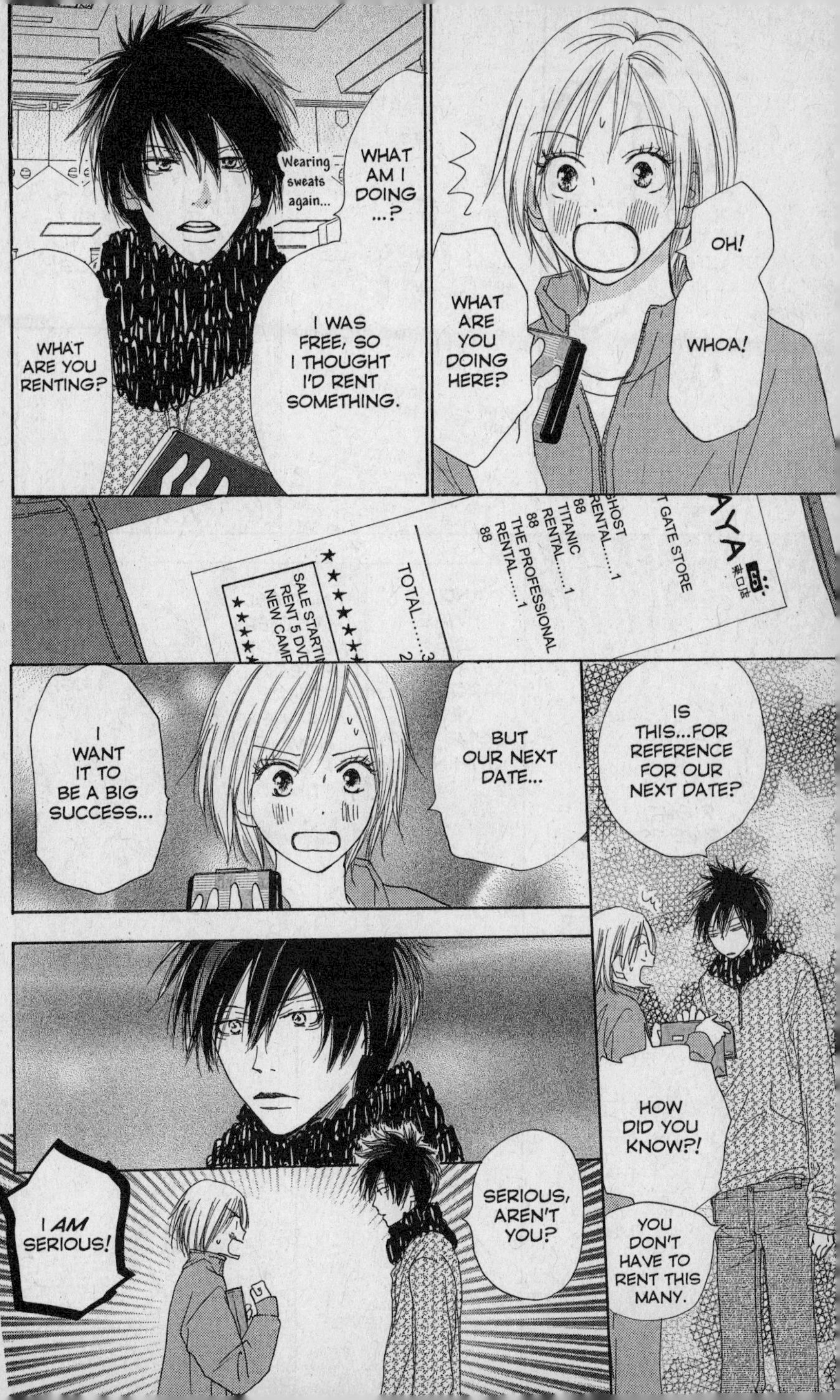
OH!
WHOA!
WHAT ARE YOU DOING HERE?
WHAT AM I DOING ...?
Wearing sweats again...
I WAS FREE, SO I THOUGHT I'D RENT SOMETHING.
WHAT ARE YOU RENTING?
AYA
T GATE STORE
GHOST
RENTAL.....1
88
TITANIC
RENTAL.....1
88
THE PROFESSIONAL
RENTAL.....1
88
TOTAL.....3
IS THIS...FOR REFERENCE FOR OUR NEXT DATE?
HOW DID YOU KNOW?!
YOU DON'T HAVE TO RENT THIS MANY.
BUT OUR NEXT DATE...
I WANT IT TO BE A BIG SUCCESS...
SERIOUS, AREN'T YOU?
I *AM* SERIOUS!

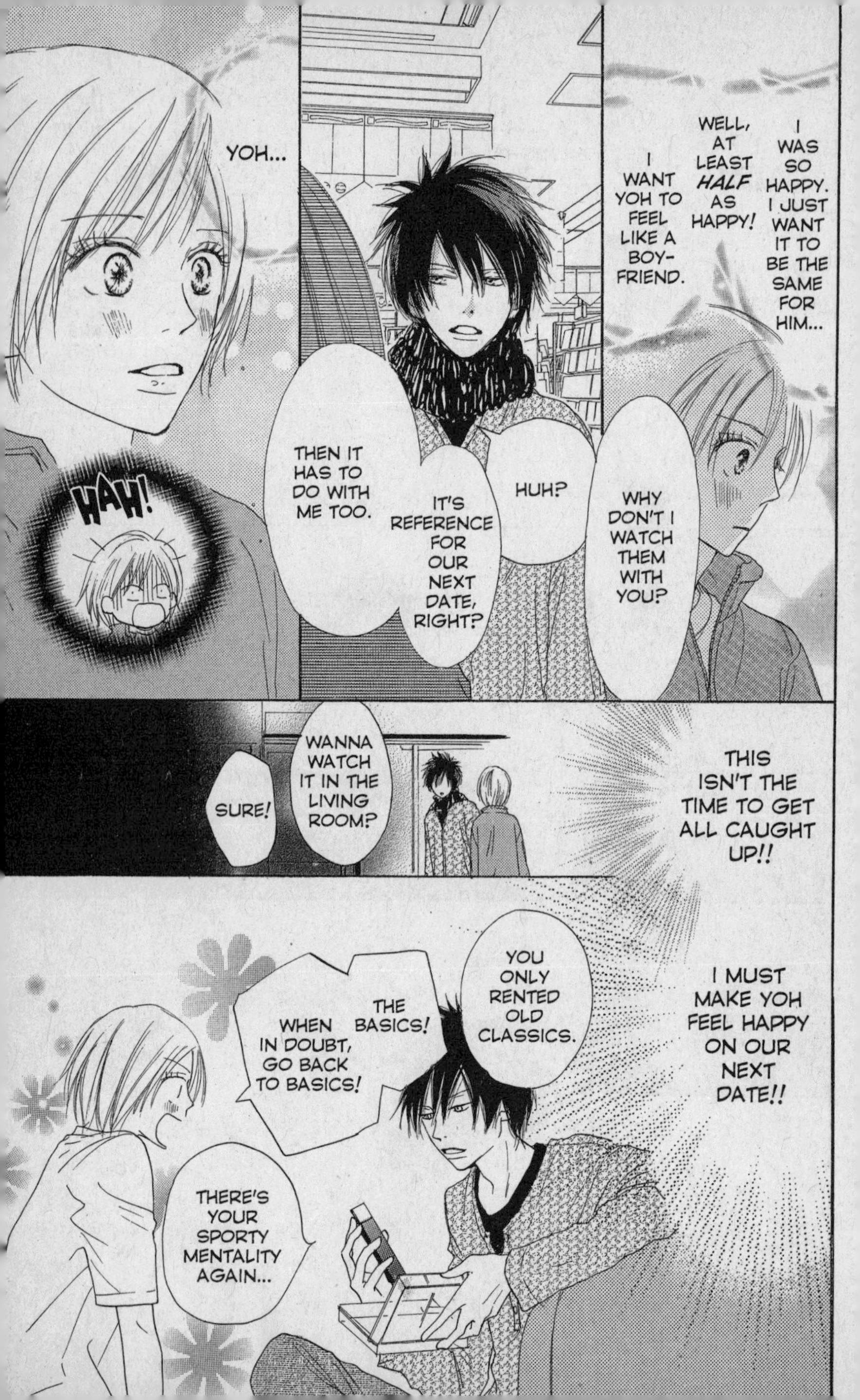
I WAS SO HAPPY. I JUST WANT IT TO BE THE SAME FOR HIM...
WELL, AT LEAST HALF AS HAPPY!
I WANT YOH TO FEEL LIKE A BOY-FRIEND.
WHY DON'T I WATCH THEM WITH YOU?
HUH?
IT'S REFERENCE FOR OUR NEXT DATE, RIGHT?
THEN IT HAS TO DO WITH ME TOO.
YOH...
HAH!
THIS ISN'T THE TIME TO GET ALL CAUGHT UP!!
WANNA WATCH IT IN THE LIVING ROOM?
SURE!
I MUST MAKE YOH FEEL HAPPY ON OUR NEXT DATE!!
YOU ONLY RENTED OLD CLASSICS.
THE BASICS!
WHEN IN DOUBT, GO BACK TO BASICS!
THERE'S YOUR SPORTY MENTALITY AGAIN...

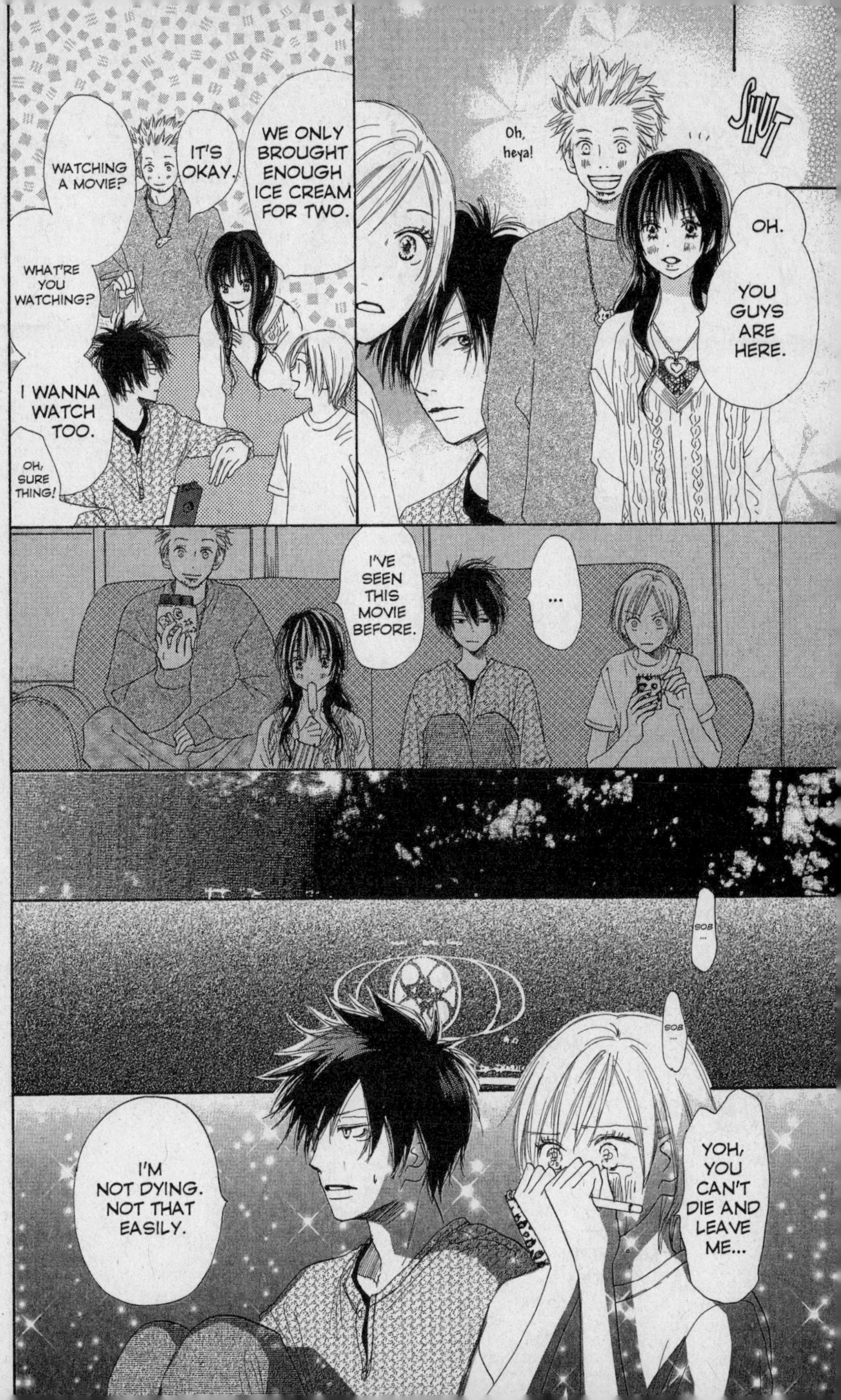
SHUT
OH. YOU GUYS ARE HERE.
Oh, heya!
WE ONLY BROUGHT ENOUGH ICE CREAM FOR TWO.
IT'S OKAY.
WATCHING A MOVIE?
WHAT'RE YOU WATCHING?
I WANNA WATCH TOO.
OH, SURE THING!
...
I'VE SEEN THIS MOVIE BEFORE.
SOB...
SOB...
YOH, YOU CAN'T DIE AND LEAVE ME...
I'M NOT DYING. NOT THAT EASILY.

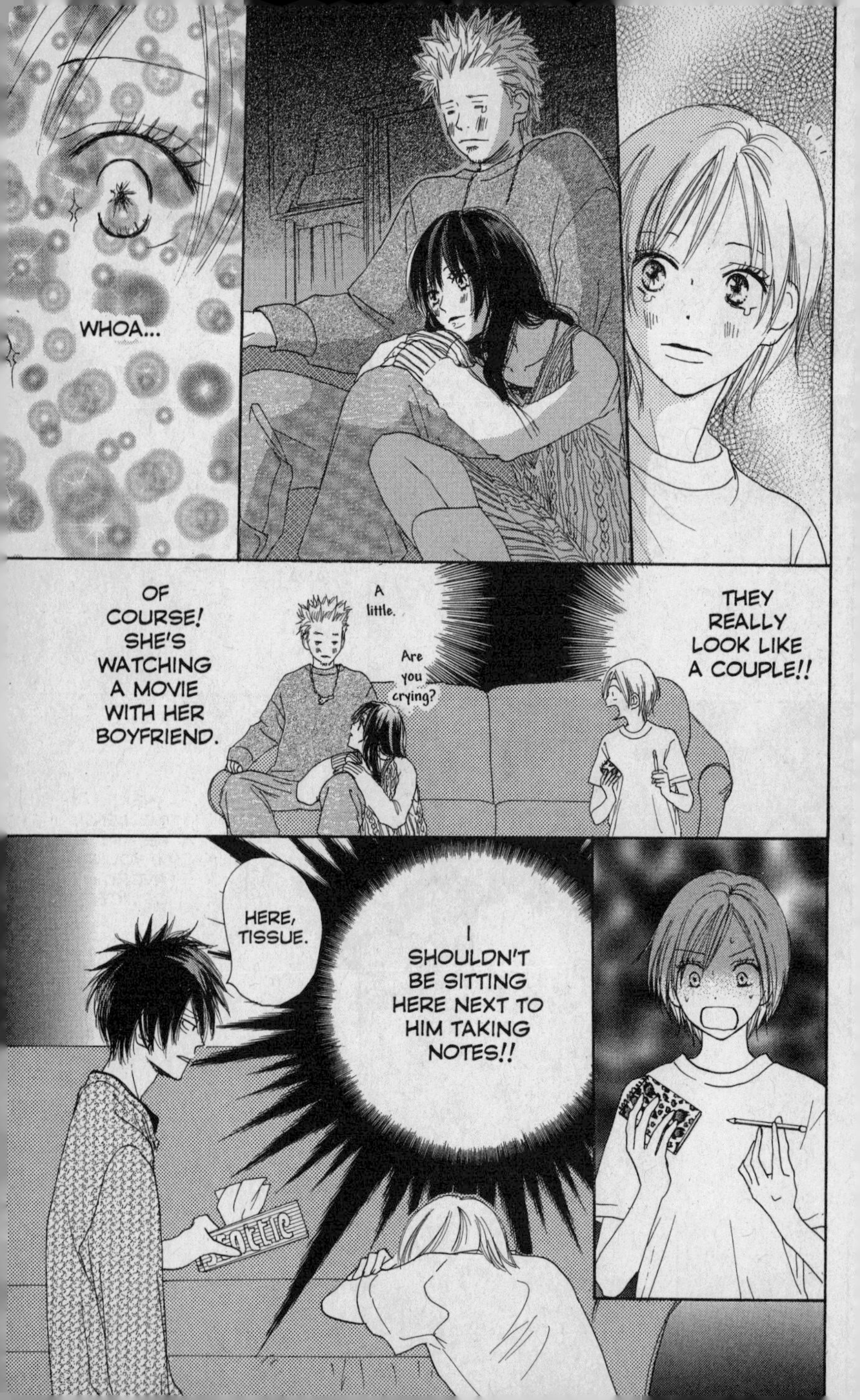
WHOA...
THEY REALLY LOOK LIKE A COUPLE!!
Are you crying?
A little.
OF COURSE! SHE'S WATCHING A MOVIE WITH HER BOYFRIEND.
I SHOULDN'T BE SITTING HERE NEXT TO HIM TAKING NOTES!!
HERE, TISSUE.

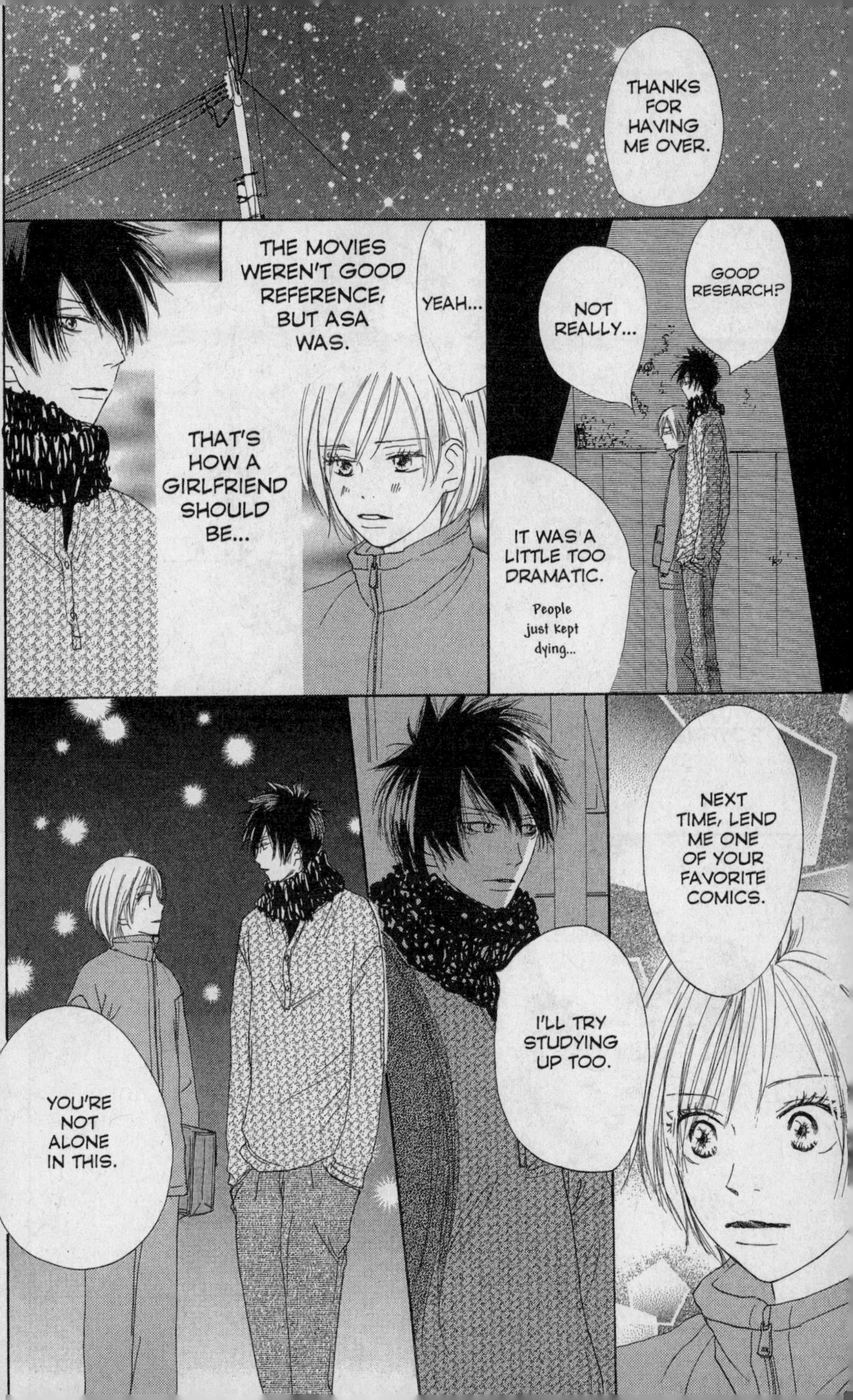
THANKS FOR HAVING ME OVER.
GOOD RESEARCH?
NOT REALLY...
IT WAS A LITTLE TOO DRAMATIC.
People just kept dying...
YEAH...
THE MOVIES WEREN'T GOOD REFERENCE, BUT ASA WAS.
THAT'S HOW A GIRLFRIEND SHOULD BE...
NEXT TIME, LEND ME ONE OF YOUR FAVORITE COMICS.
I'LL TRY STUDYING UP TOO.
YOU'RE NOT ALONE IN THIS.

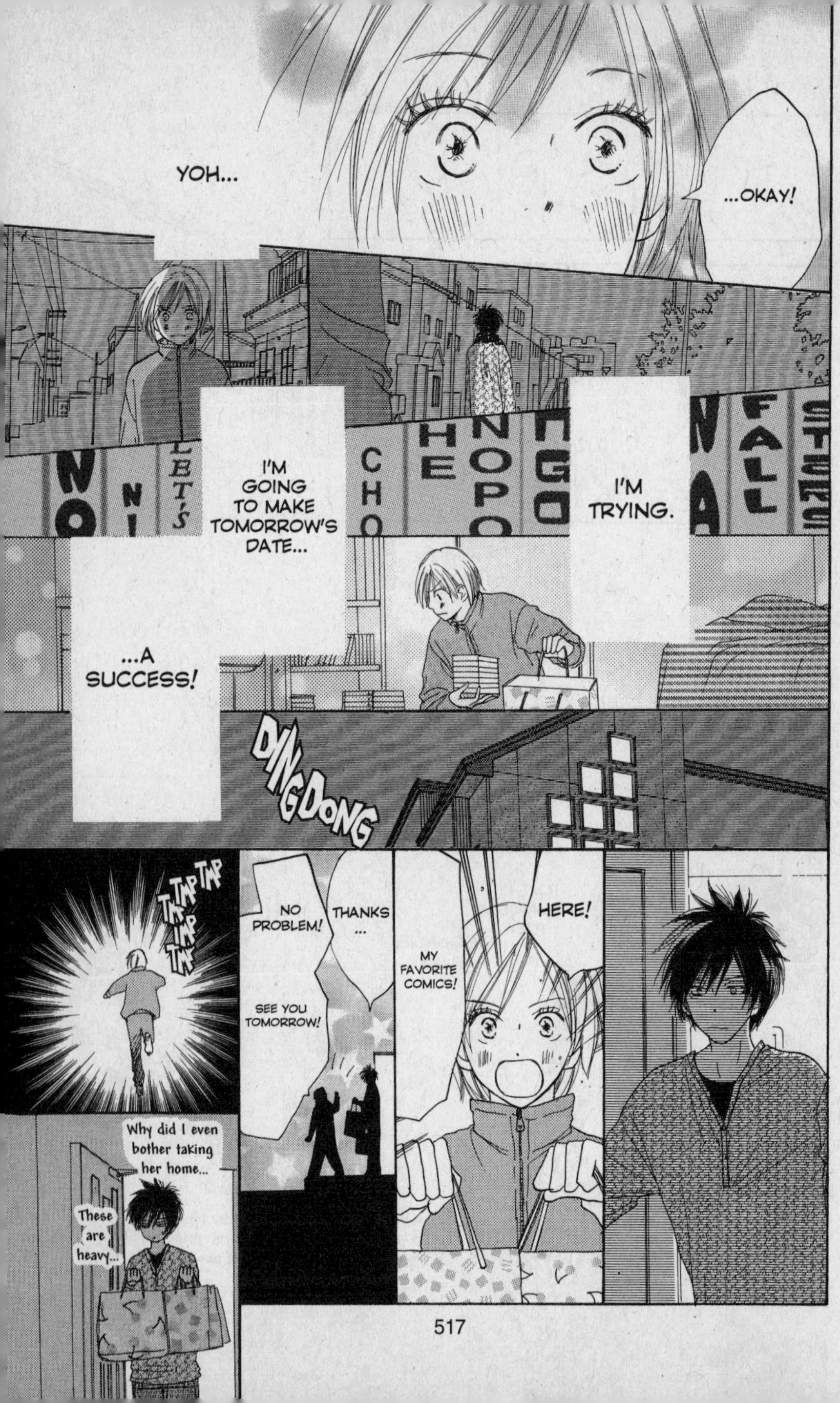
...OKAY!
YOH...
I'M TRYING.
I'M GOING TO MAKE TOMORROW'S DATE...
...A SUCCESS!
DING DONG
HERE!
MY FAVORITE COMICS!
THANKS...
NO PROBLEM!
SEE YOU TOMORROW!
TMP TMP TMP TMP TMP
Why did I even bother taking her home...
These are heavy...

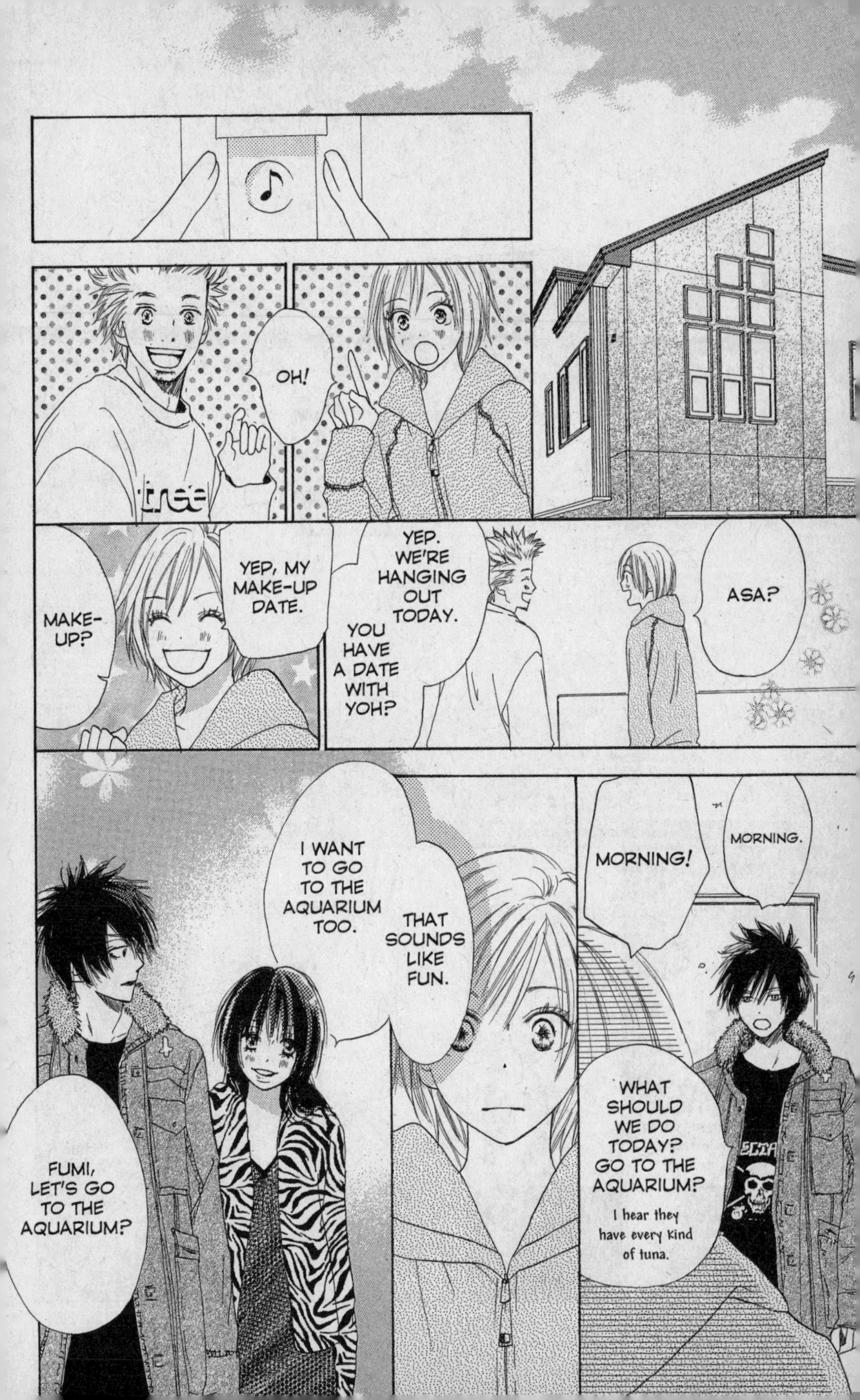
OH!
ASA?
YEP. WE'RE HANGING OUT TODAY.
YOU HAVE A DATE WITH YOH?
YEP, MY MAKE-UP DATE.
MAKE-UP?
MORNING.
MORNING!
WHAT SHOULD WE DO TODAY? GO TO THE AQUARIUM?
I hear they have every kind of tuna.
I WANT TO GO TO THE AQUARIUM TOO.
THAT SOUNDS LIKE FUN.
FUMI, LET'S GO TO THE AQUARIUM?

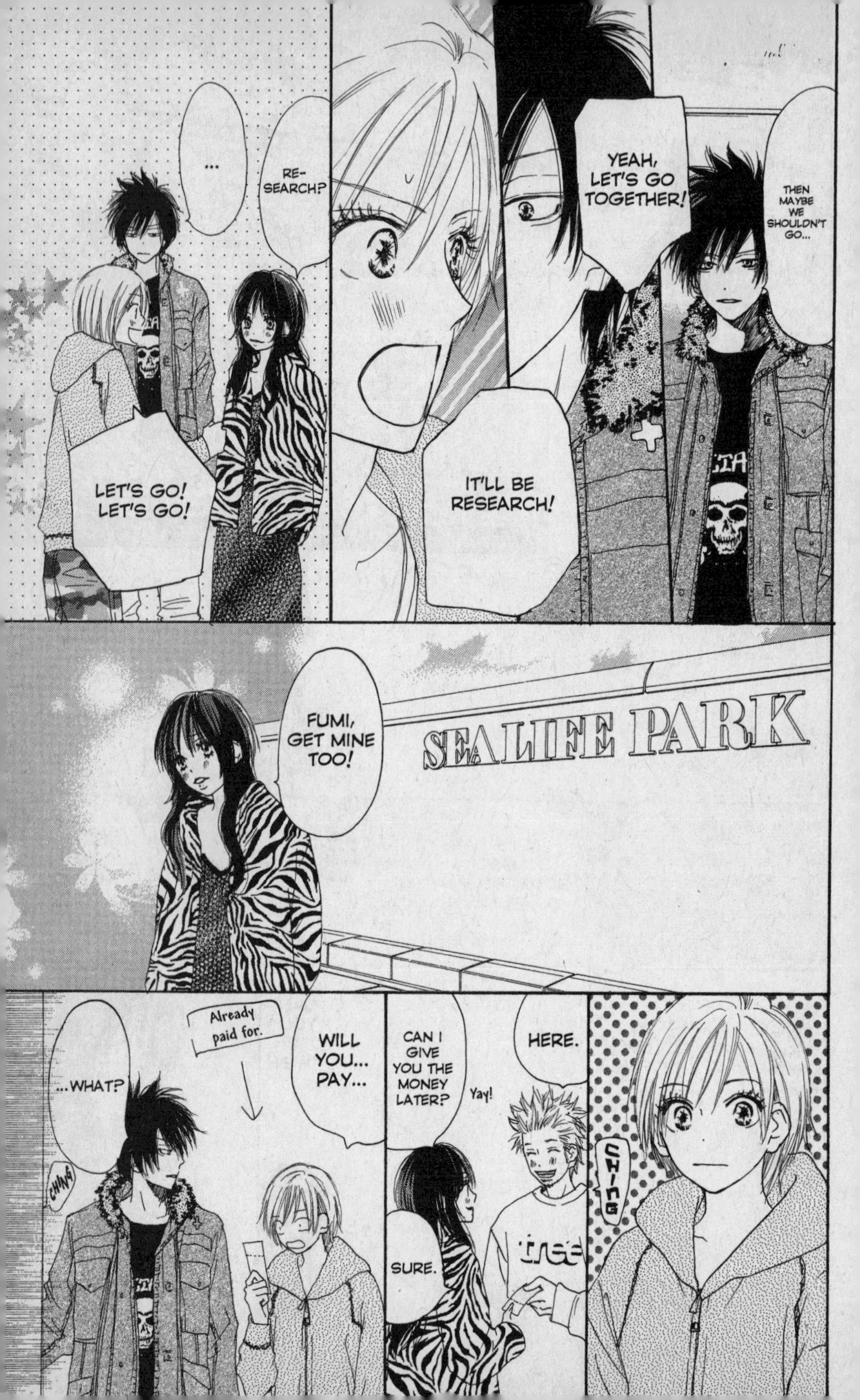

THEN MAYBE WE SHOULDN'T GO...
YEAH, LET'S GO TOGETHER!
IT'LL BE RESEARCH!
RE-SEARCH?
...
LET'S GO! LET'S GO!
SEALIFE PARK
FUMI, GET MINE TOO!
CHING
HERE.
Yay!
CAN I GIVE YOU THE MONEY LATER?
SURE.
WILL YOU... PAY...
Already paid for.
...WHAT?
CHING

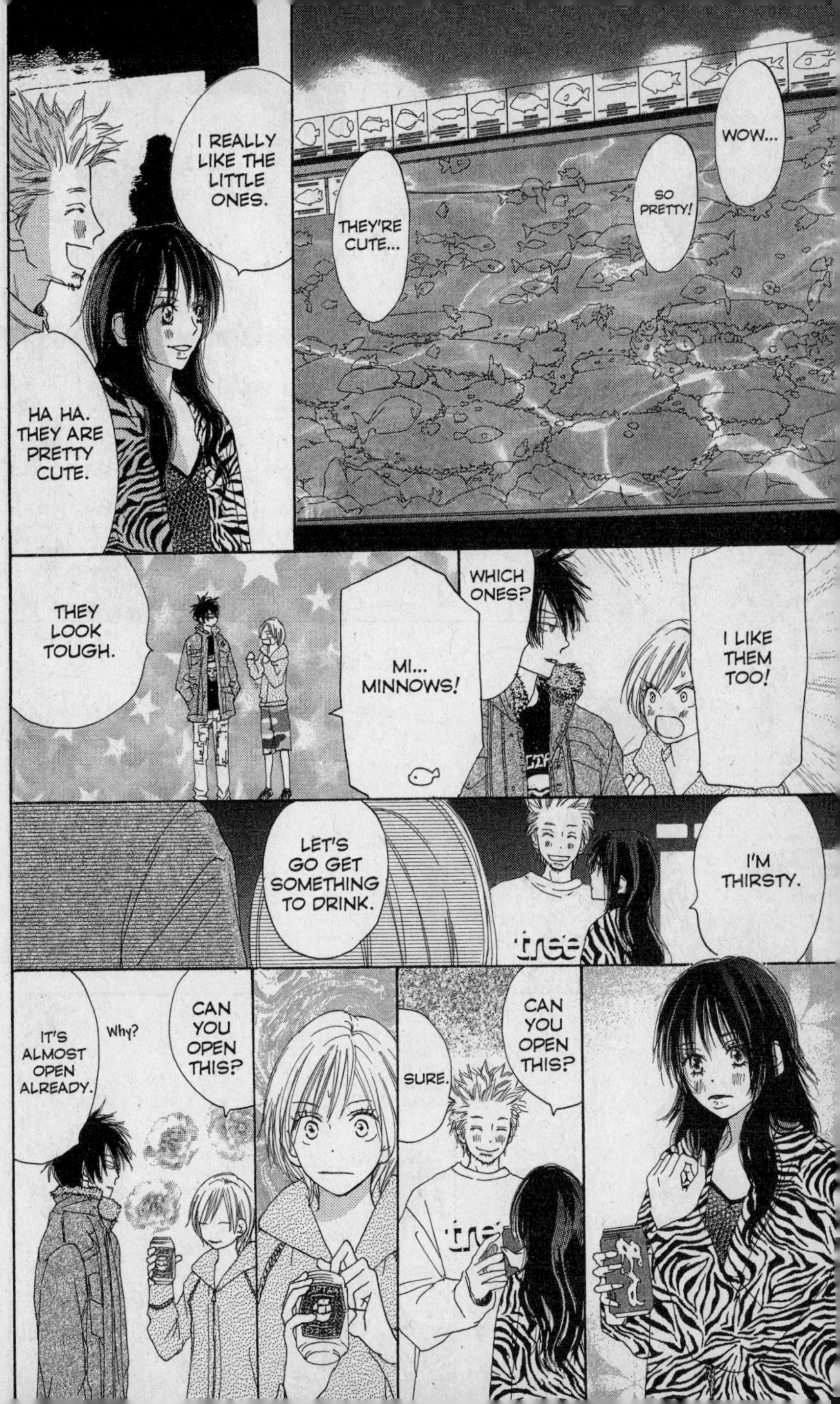
WOW...
SO PRETTY!
THEY'RE CUTE...
I REALLY LIKE THE LITTLE ONES.
HA HA. THEY ARE PRETTY CUTE.
I LIKE THEM TOO!
WHICH ONES?
MI... MINNOWS!
THEY LOOK TOUGH.
I'M THIRSTY.
LET'S GO GET SOMETHING TO DRINK.
CAN YOU OPEN THIS?
SURE.
CAN YOU OPEN THIS?
Why?
IT'S ALMOST OPEN ALREADY.

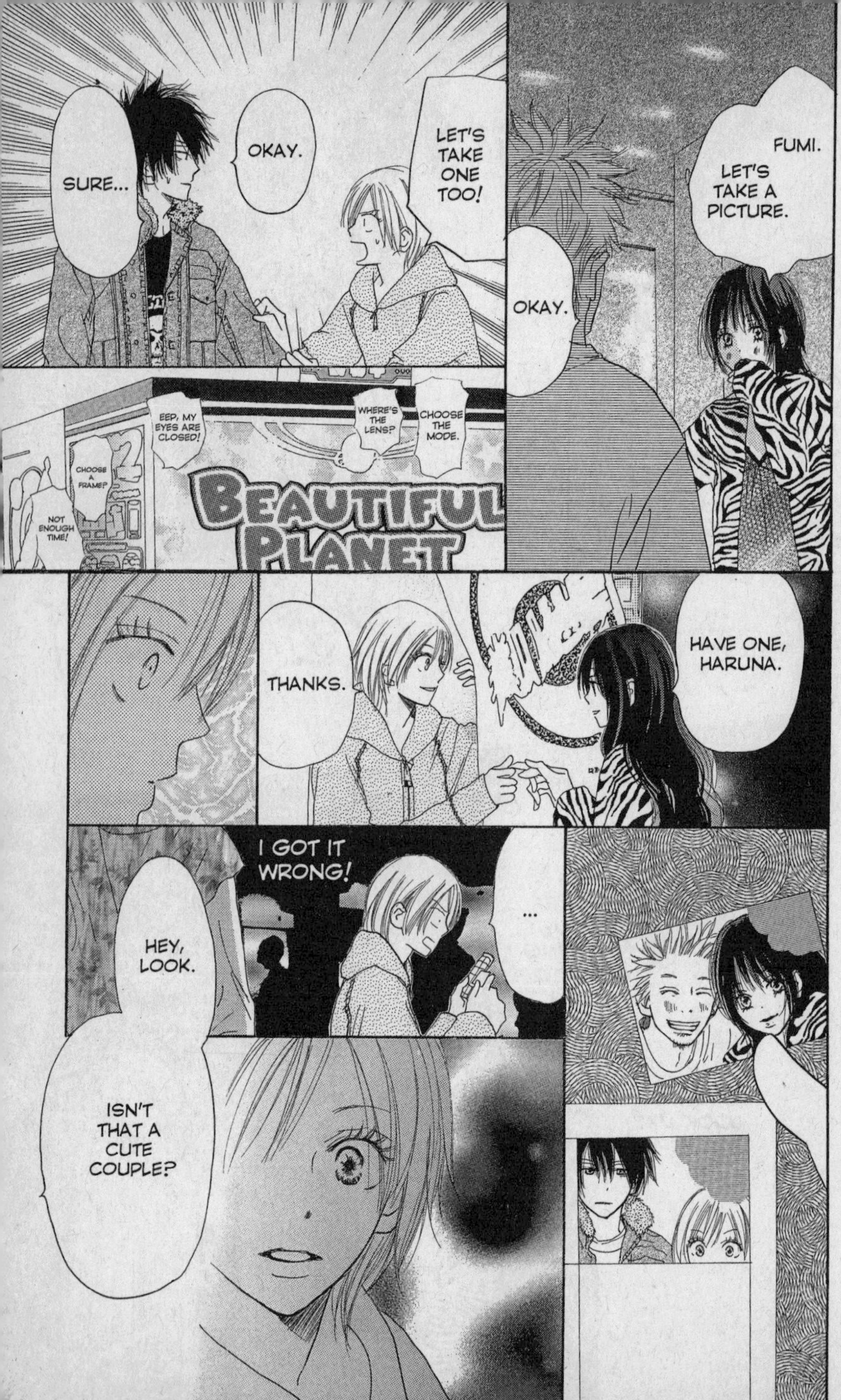
FUMI.
LET'S TAKE A PICTURE.
OKAY.
LET'S TAKE ONE TOO!
OKAY.
SURE...
CHOOSE THE MODE.
WHERE'S THE LENS?
EEP, MY EYES ARE CLOSED!
CHOOSE A FRAME?
NOT ENOUGH TIME!
BEAUTIFUL PLANET
HAVE ONE, HARUNA.
THANKS.
...
I GOT IT WRONG!
HEY, LOOK.
ISN'T THAT A CUTE COUPLE?

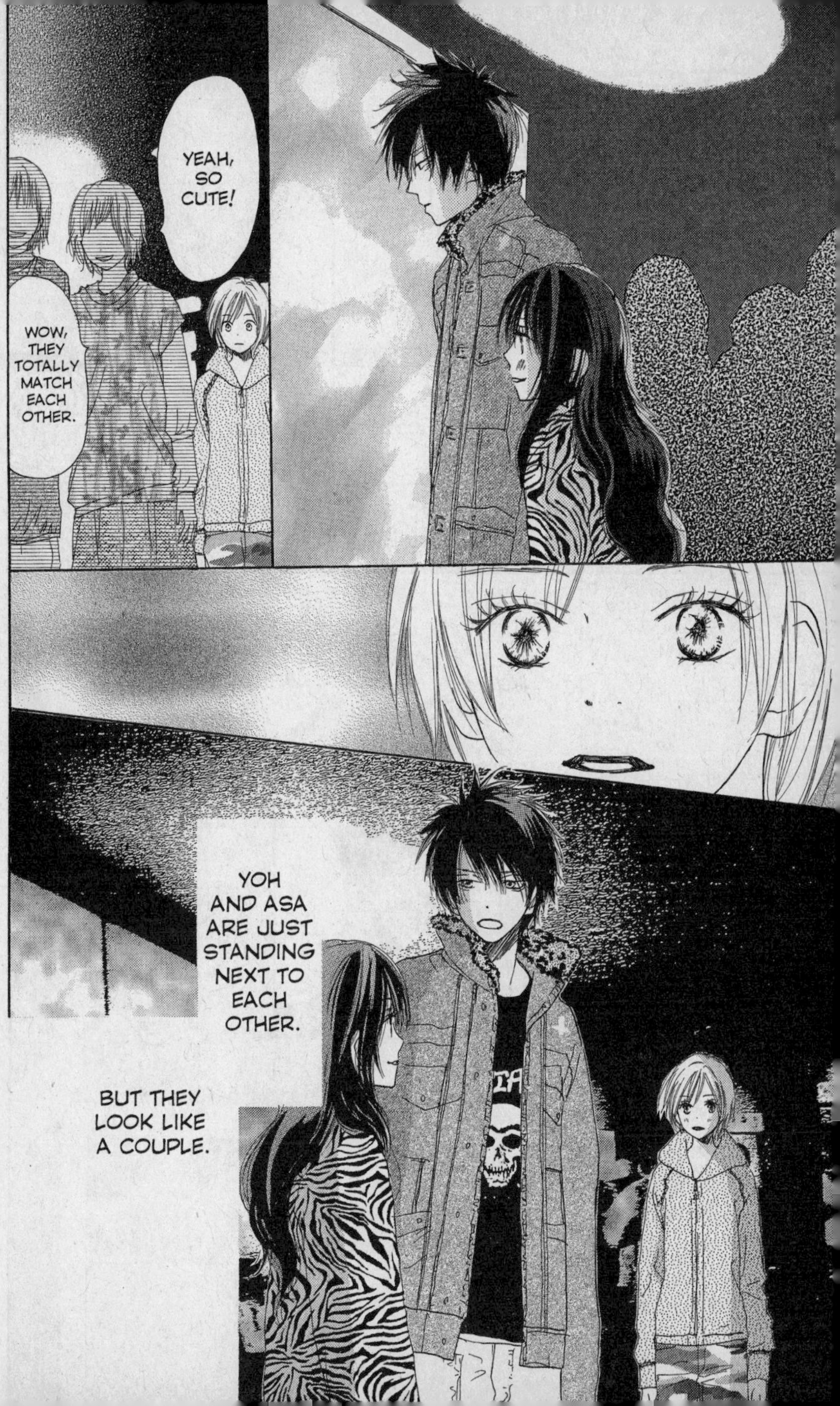
YEAH, SO CUTE!
WOW, THEY TOTALLY MATCH EACH OTHER.
YOH AND ASA ARE JUST STANDING NEXT TO EACH OTHER.
BUT THEY LOOK LIKE A COUPLE.

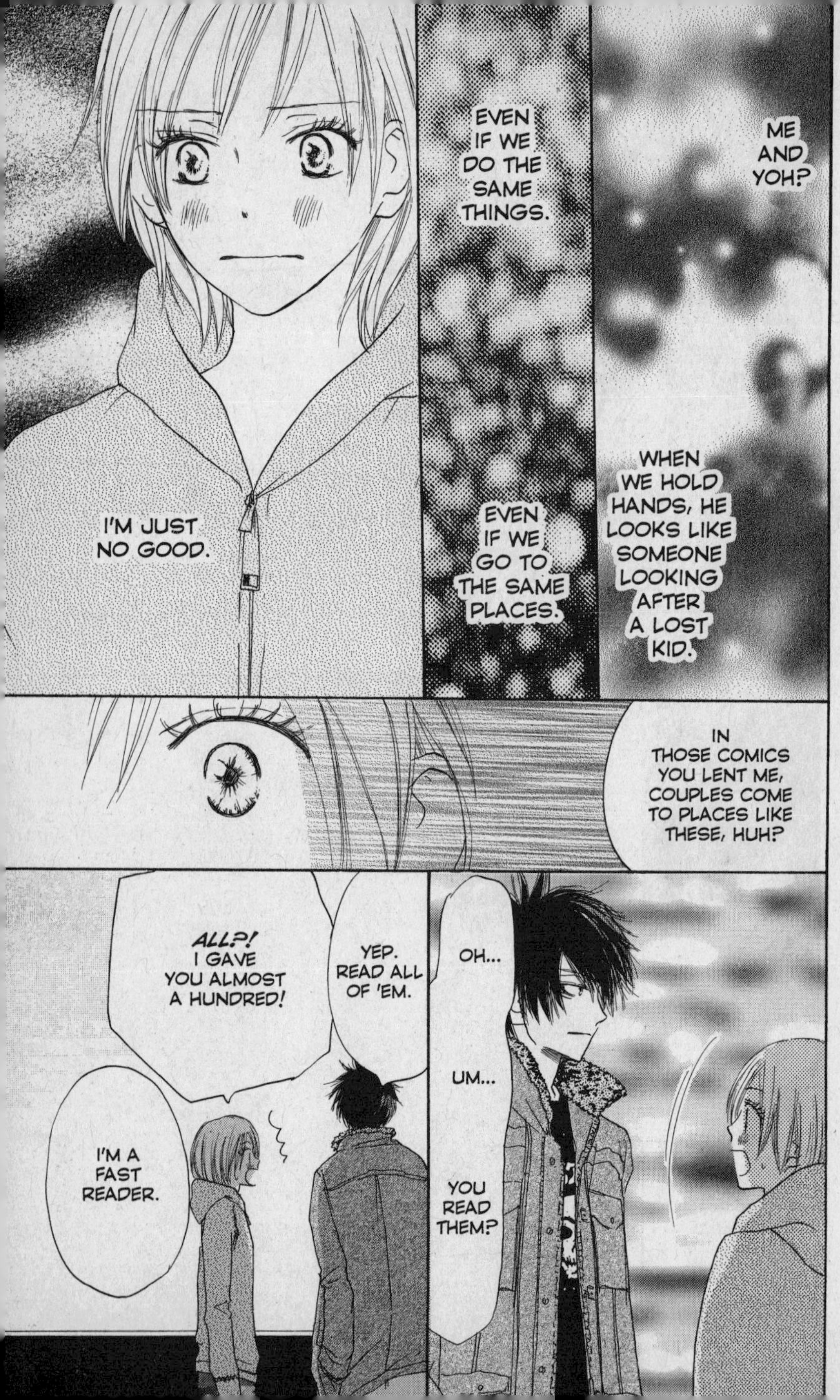
ME AND YOH?
WHEN WE HOLD HANDS, HE LOOKS LIKE SOMEONE LOOKING AFTER A LOST KID.
EVEN IF WE DO THE SAME THINGS.
EVEN IF WE GO TO THE SAME PLACES.
I'M JUST NO GOOD.
IN THOSE COMICS YOU LENT ME, COUPLES COME TO PLACES LIKE THESE, HUH?
OH...
UM...
YOU READ THEM?
YEP. READ ALL OF 'EM.
ALL?! I GAVE YOU ALMOST A HUNDRED!
I'M A FAST READER.

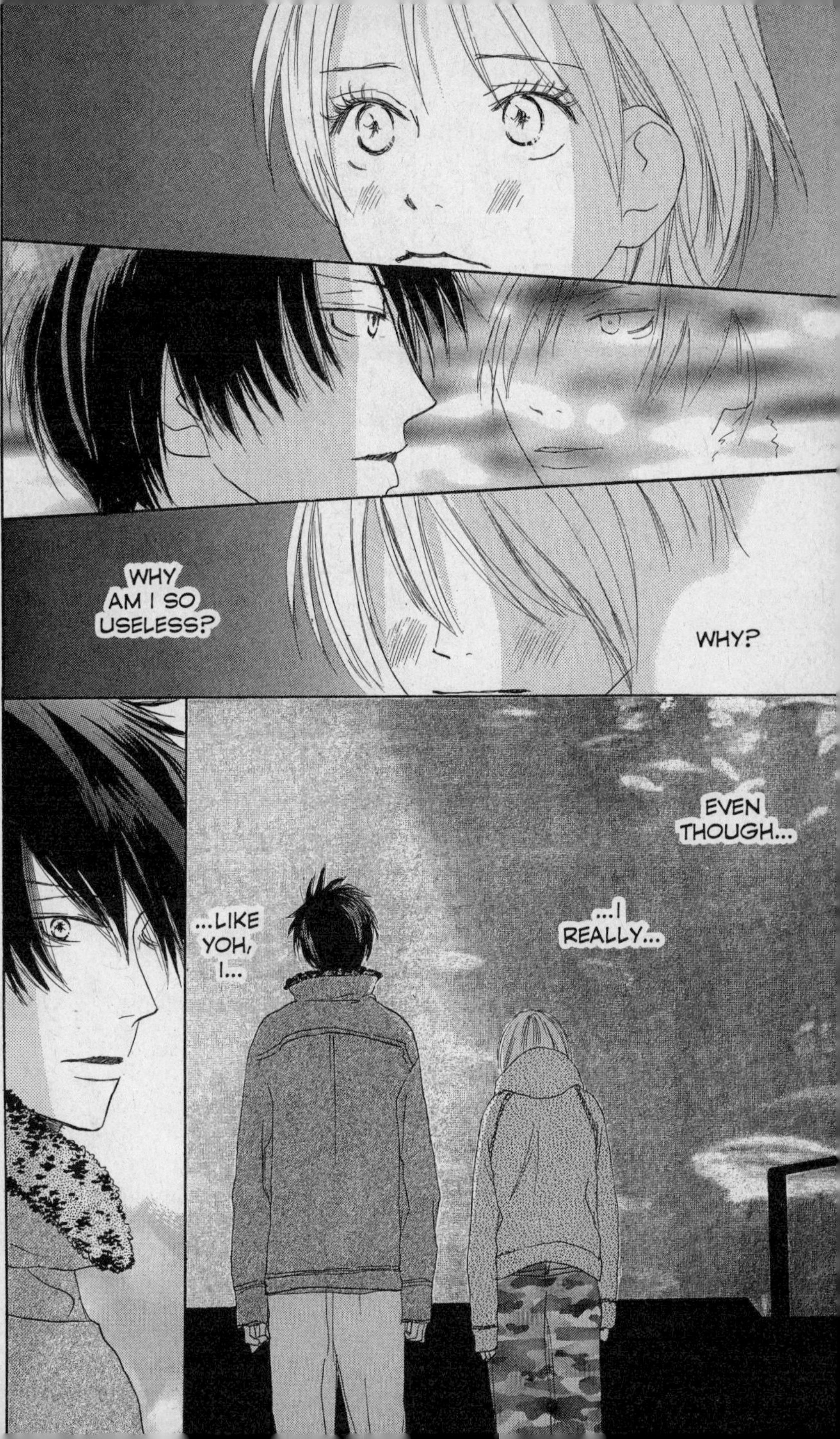
WHY?
WHY AM I SO USELESS?
EVEN THOUGH...
...I REALLY...
...LIKE YOH, I...

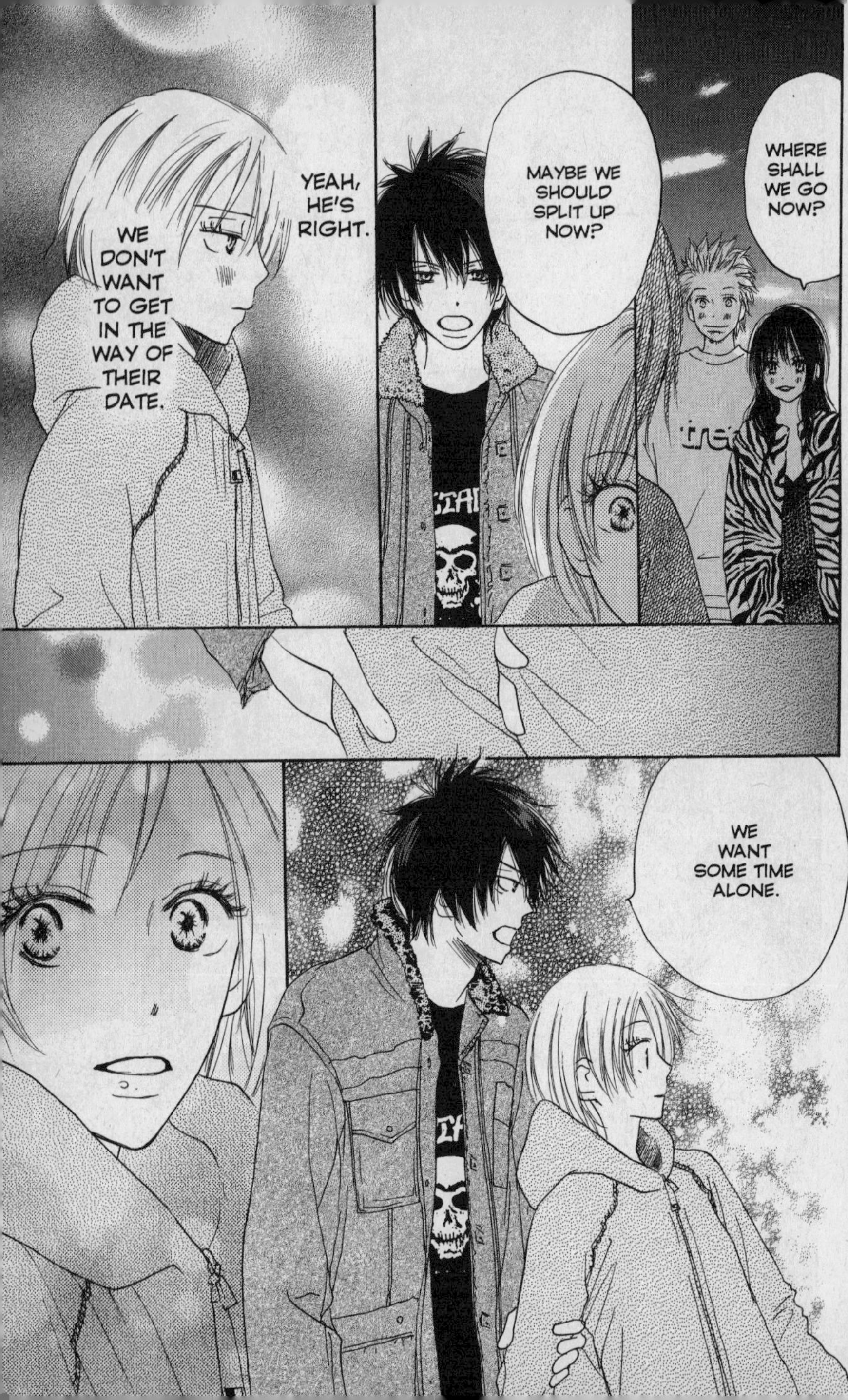
WHERE SHALL WE GO NOW?
MAYBE WE SHOULD SPLIT UP NOW?
YEAH, HE'S RIGHT.
WE DON'T WANT TO GET IN THE WAY OF THEIR DATE.
WE WANT SOME TIME ALONE.

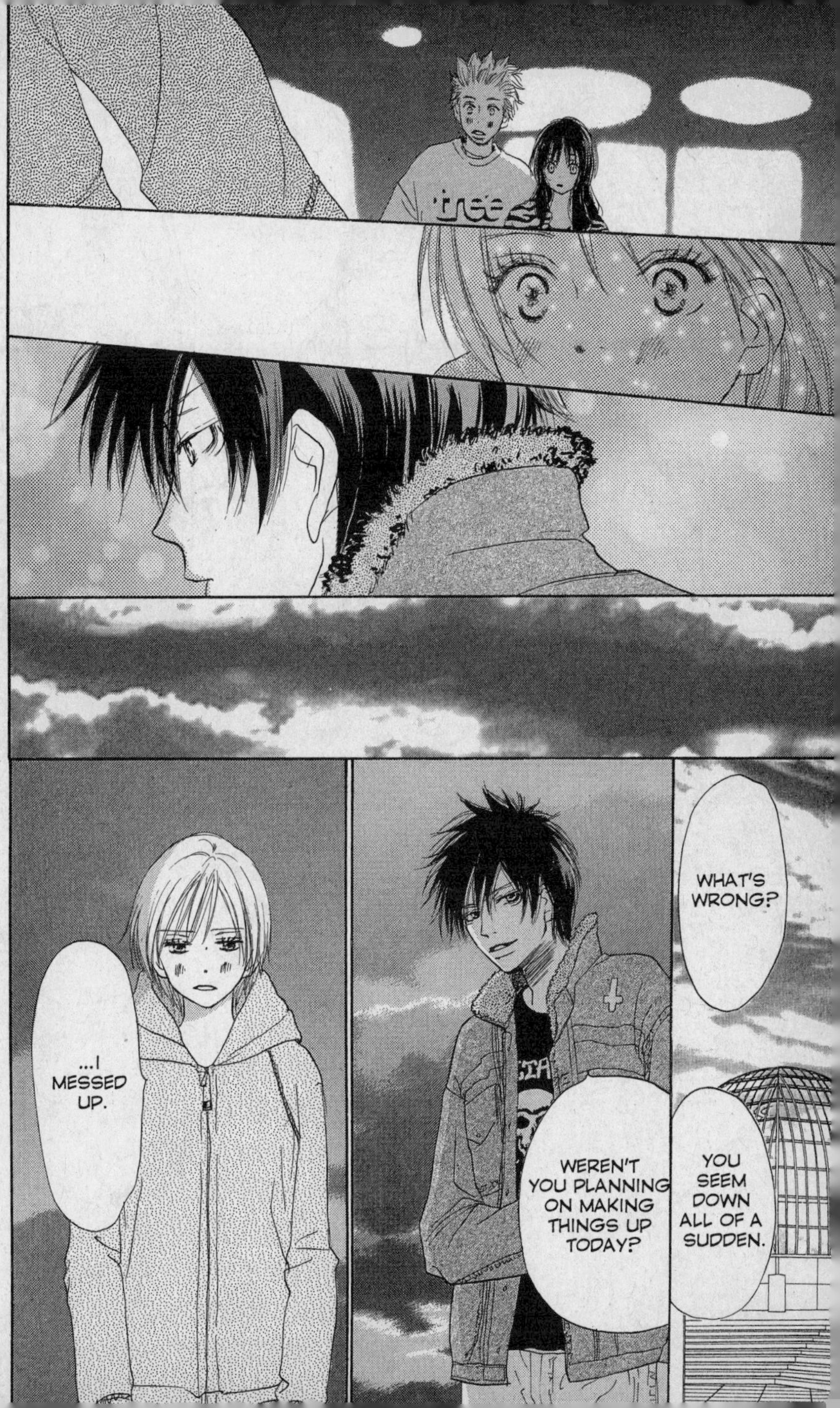
WHAT'S WRONG?
YOU SEEM DOWN ALL OF A SUDDEN.
WEREN'T YOU PLANNING ON MAKING THINGS UP TODAY?
...I MESSED UP.

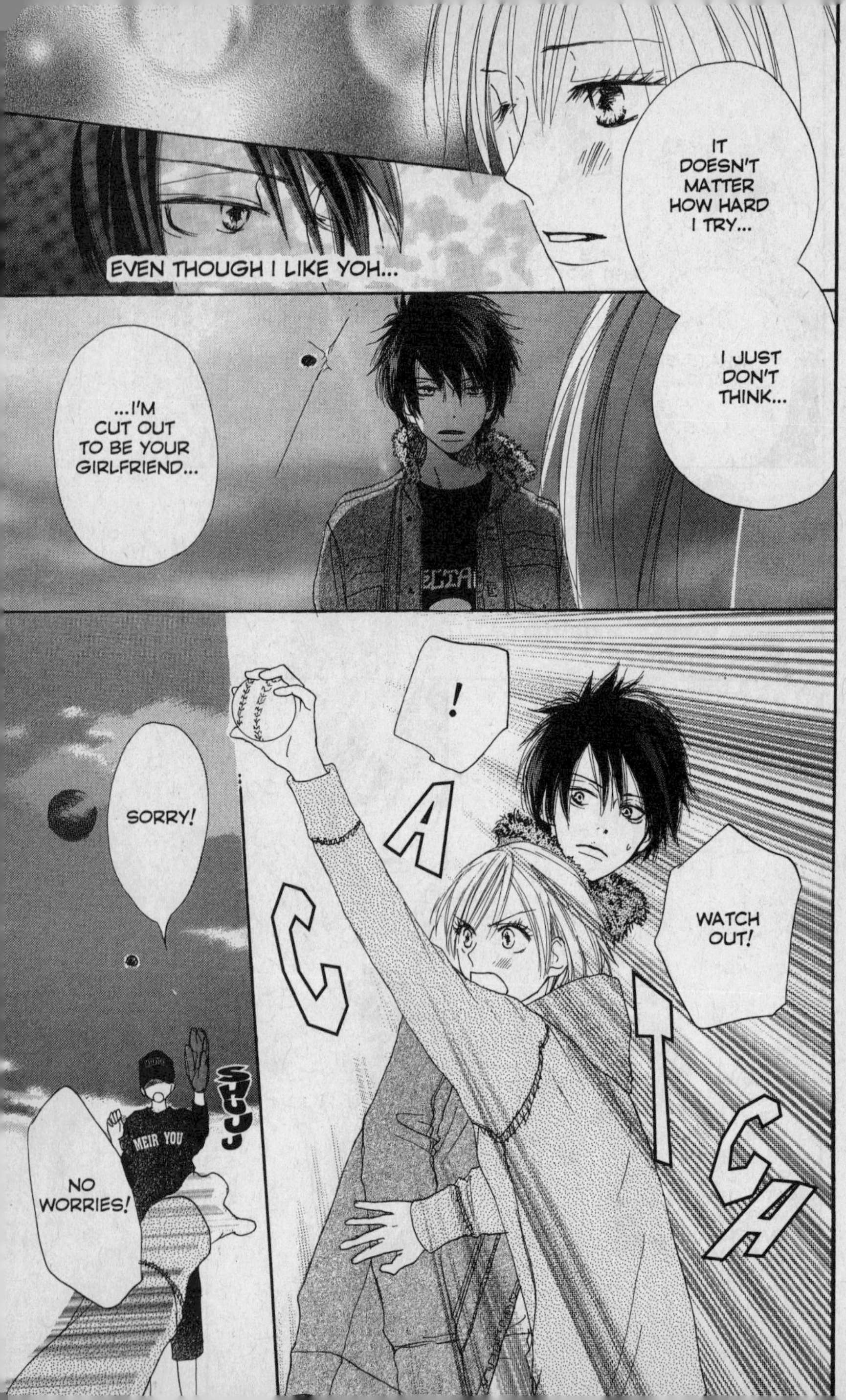
IT DOESN'T MATTER HOW HARD I TRY...
EVEN THOUGH I LIKE YOH...
I JUST DON'T THINK...
...I'M CUT OUT TO BE YOUR GIRLFRIEND...
!
WATCH OUT!
CATCH
SORRY!
SHUU
NO WORRIES!

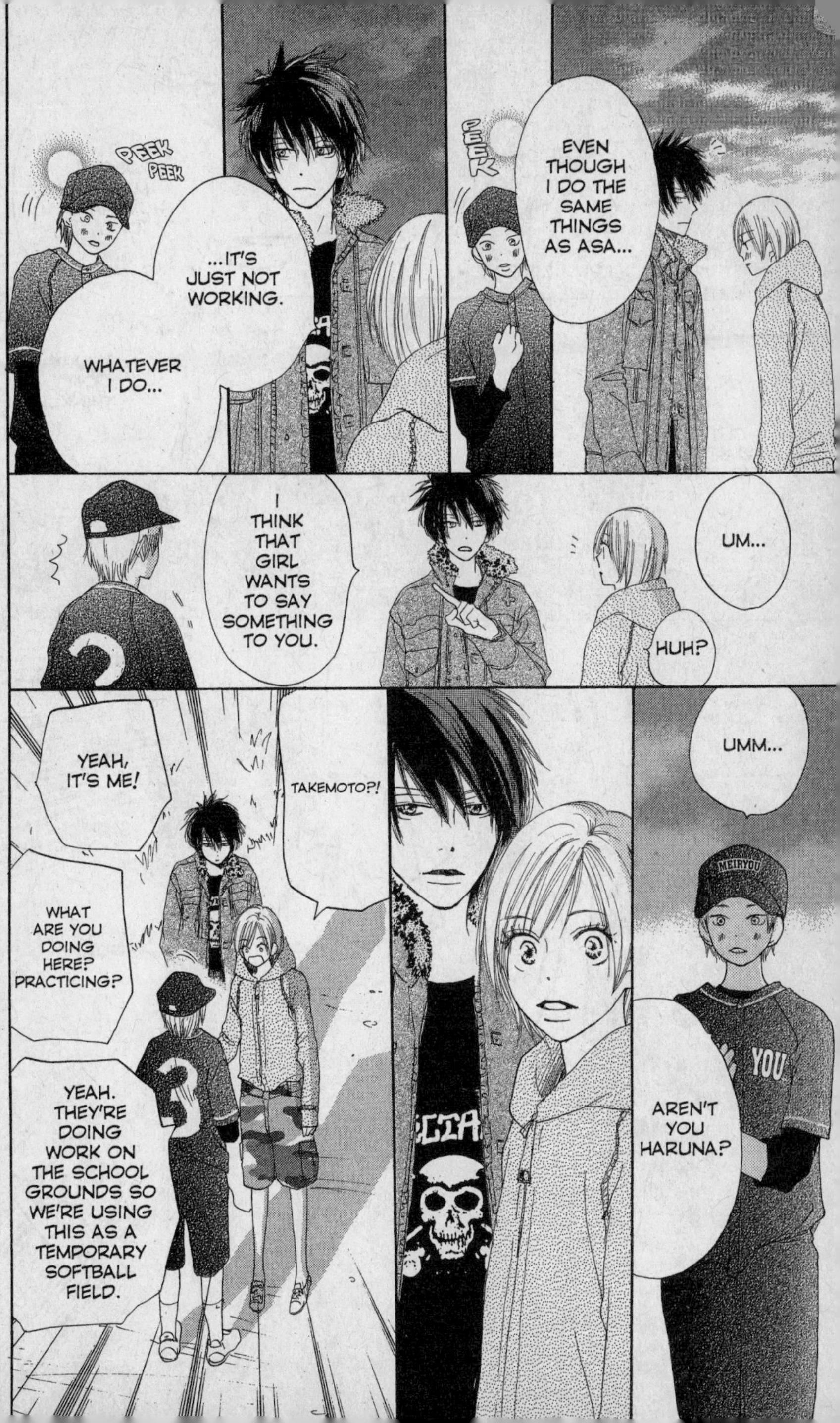
PEEK
EVEN THOUGH I DO THE SAME THINGS AS ASA...
PEEK PEEK
...IT'S JUST NOT WORKING.
WHATEVER I DO...
UM...
HUH?
I THINK THAT GIRL WANTS TO SAY SOMETHING TO YOU.
UMM...
MEIRYOU
YOU
AREN'T YOU HARUNA?
TAKEMOTO?!
YEAH, IT'S ME!
WHAT ARE YOU DOING HERE? PRACTICING?
YEAH. THEY'RE DOING WORK ON THE SCHOOL GROUNDS SO WE'RE USING THIS AS A TEMPORARY SOFTBALL FIELD.

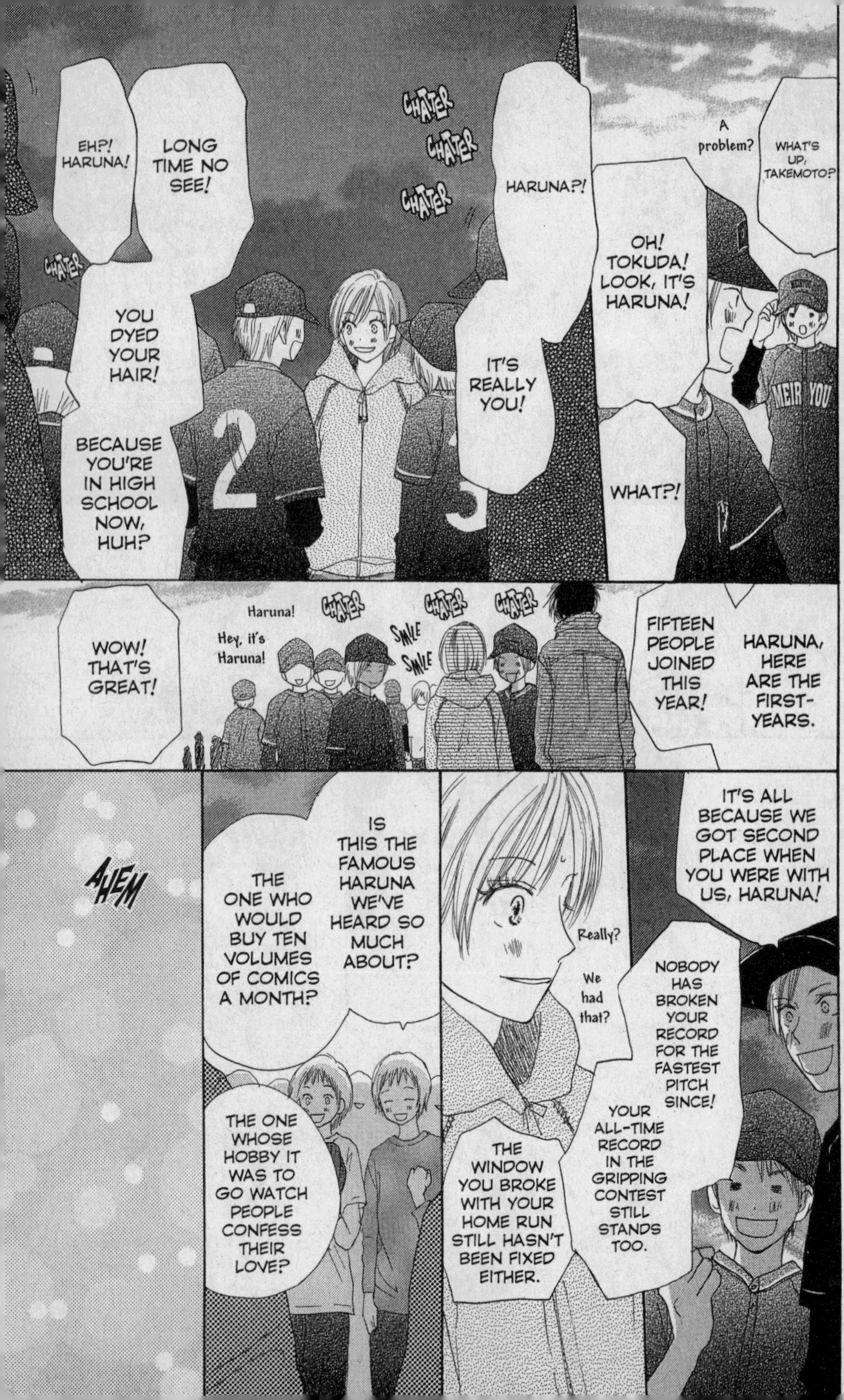
WHAT'S UP, TAKEMOTO?
A problem?
OH! TOKUDA! LOOK, IT'S HARUNA!
WHAT?!
HARUNA?!
IT'S REALLY YOU!
CHATTER
CHATTER
CHATTER
LONG TIME NO SEE!
EH?! HARUNA!
CHATTER
YOU DYED YOUR HAIR!
BECAUSE YOU'RE IN HIGH SCHOOL NOW, HUH?
HARUNA, HERE ARE THE FIRST-YEARS.
FIFTEEN PEOPLE JOINED THIS YEAR!
CHATTER
CHATTER
SMILE
SMILE
CHATTER
Haruna!
Hey, it's Haruna!
WOW! THAT'S GREAT!
IT'S ALL BECAUSE WE GOT SECOND PLACE WHEN YOU WERE WITH US, HARUNA!
NOBODY HAS BROKEN YOUR RECORD FOR THE FASTEST PITCH SINCE!
YOUR ALL-TIME RECORD IN THE GRIPPING CONTEST STILL STANDS TOO.
THE WINDOW YOU BROKE WITH YOUR HOME RUN STILL HASN'T BEEN FIXED EITHER.
Really?
We had that?
IS THIS THE FAMOUS HARUNA WE'VE HEARD SO MUCH ABOUT?
THE ONE WHO WOULD BUY TEN VOLUMES OF COMICS A MONTH?
THE ONE WHOSE HOBBY IT WAS TO GO WATCH PEOPLE CONFESS THEIR LOVE?
AHEM

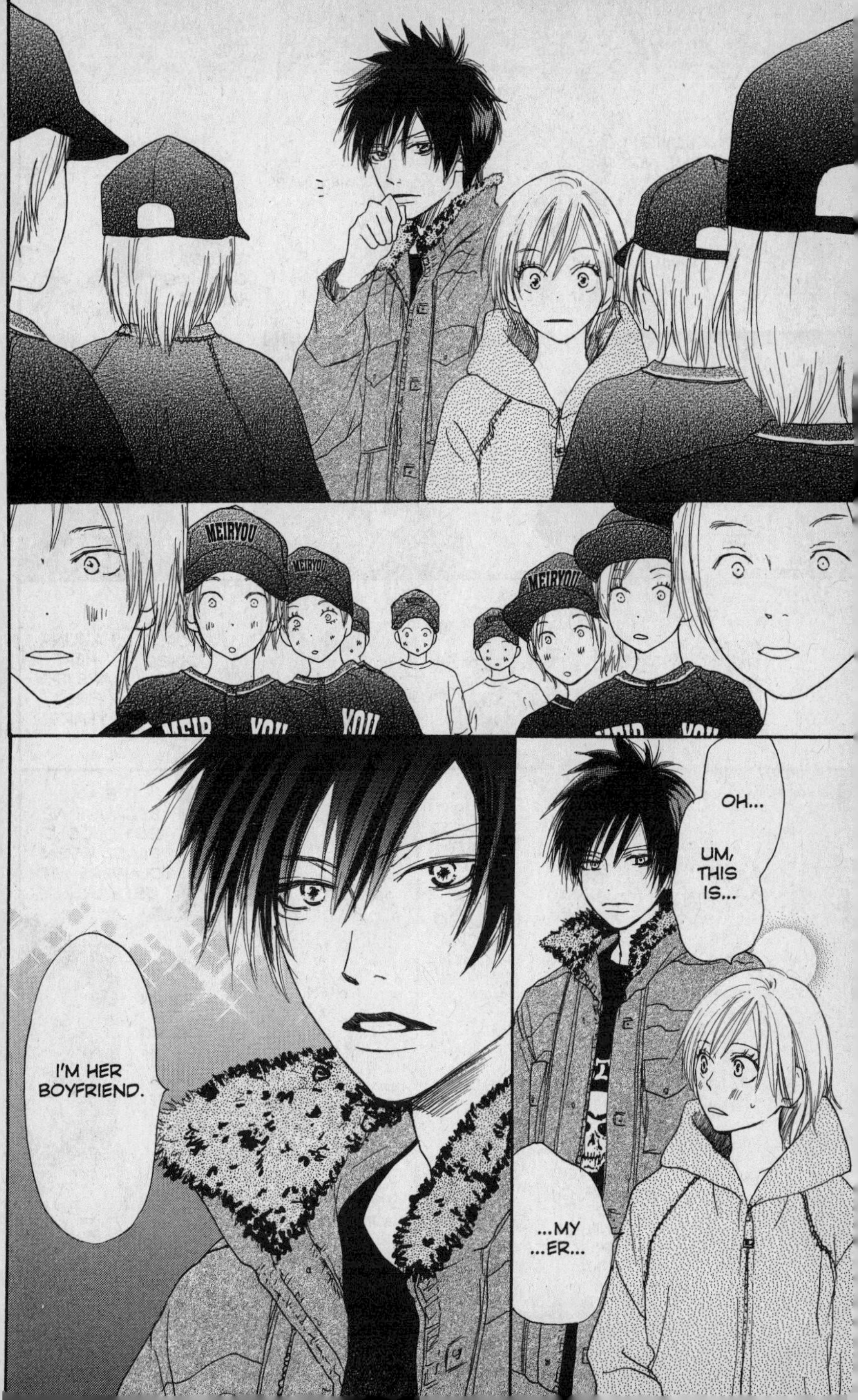
MEIRYOU
OH...
UM, THIS IS...
...MY ...ER...
I'M HER BOYFRIEND.

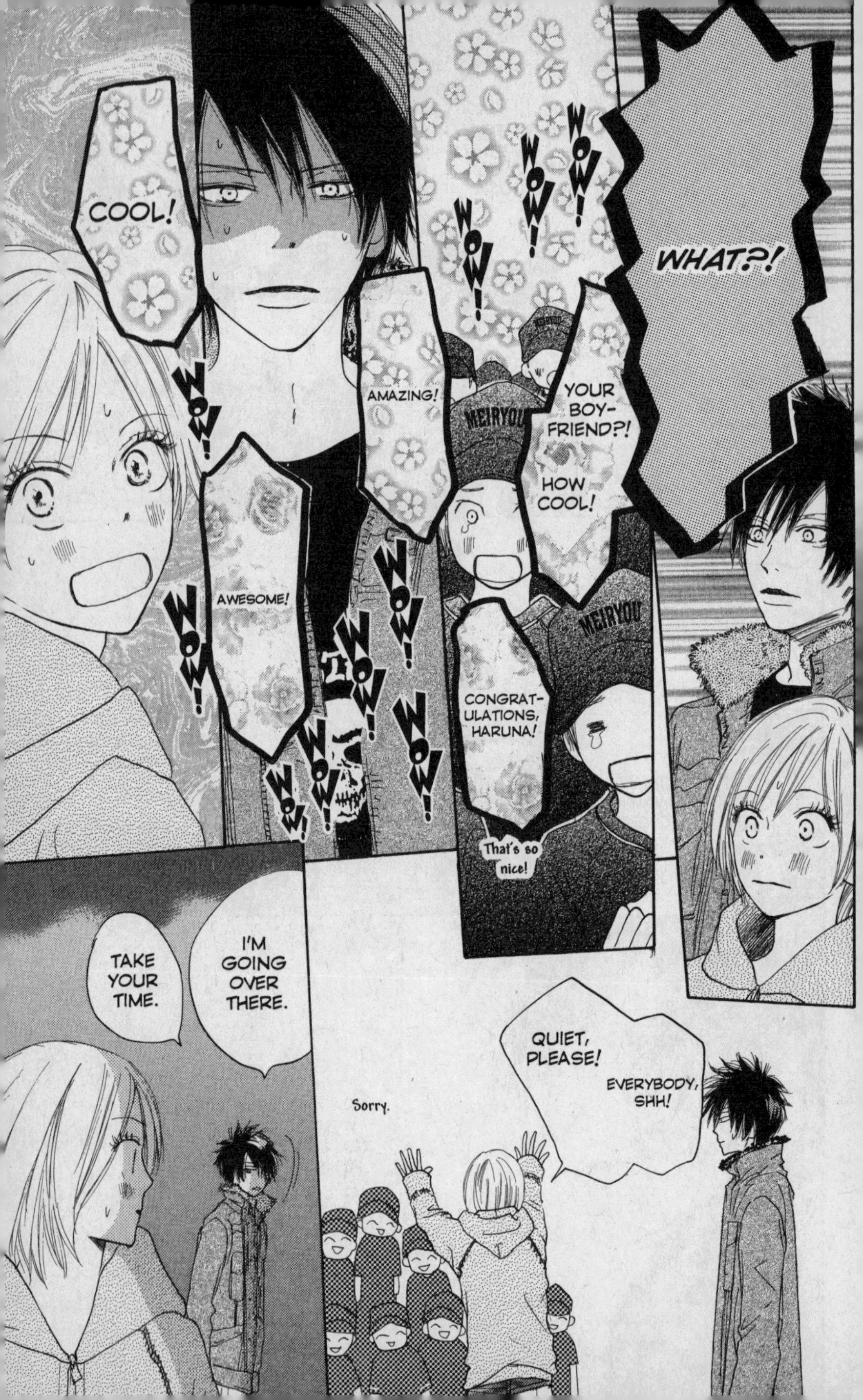
WHAT?!
WOW!
WOW!
WOW!
YOUR BOY-FRIEND?!
HOW COOL!
CONGRAT-ULATIONS, HARUNA!
That's so nice!
AMAZING!
WOW!
WOW!
WOW!
COOL!
WOW!
AWESOME!
WOW!
WOW!
WOW!
QUIET, PLEASE!
EVERYBODY, SHH!
Sorry.
I'M GOING OVER THERE.
TAKE YOUR TIME.

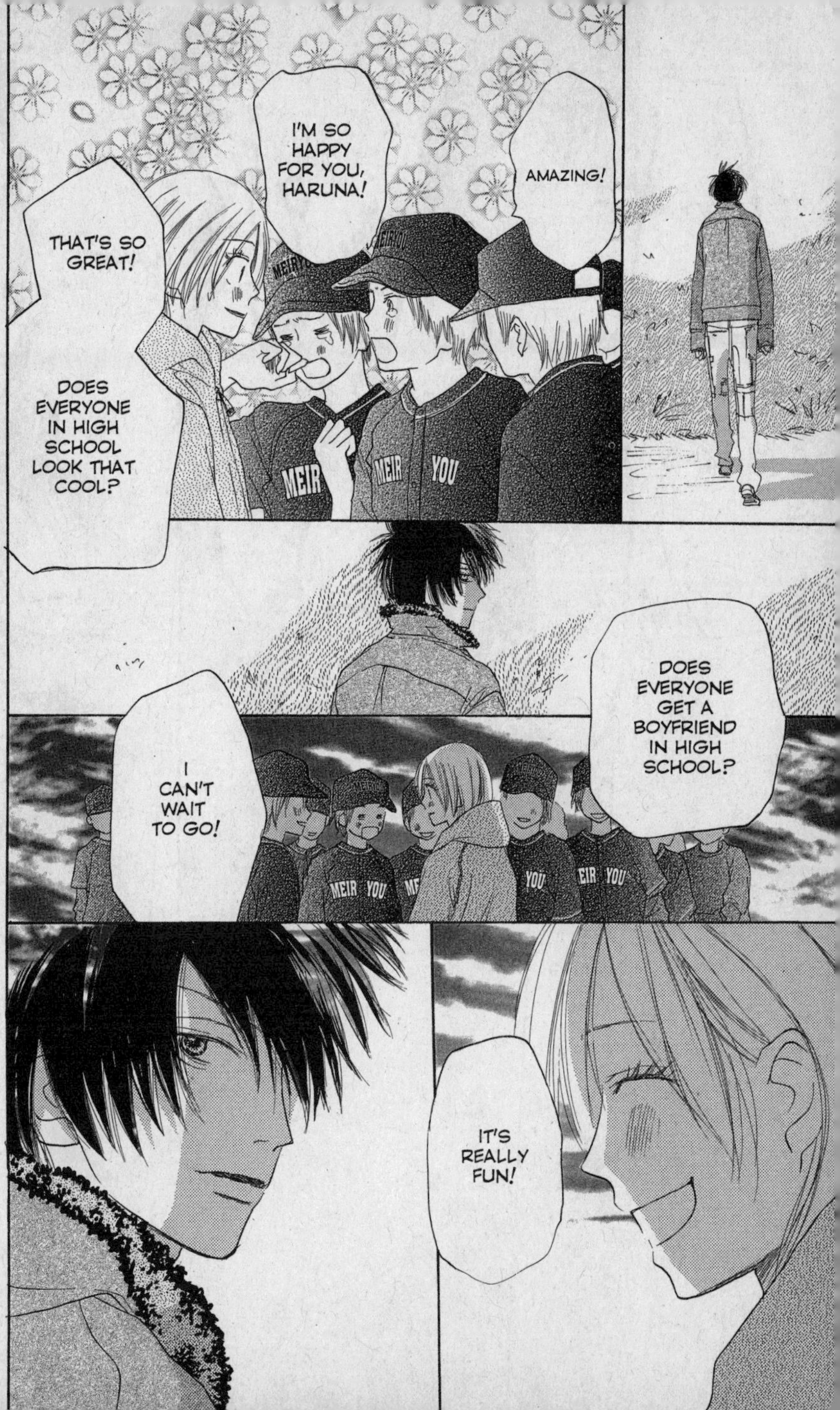
AMAZING!
I'M SO HAPPY FOR YOU, HARUNA!
THAT'S SO GREAT!
DOES EVERYONE IN HIGH SCHOOL LOOK THAT COOL?
DOES EVERYONE GET A BOYFRIEND IN HIGH SCHOOL?
I CAN'T WAIT TO GO!
IT'S REALLY FUN!

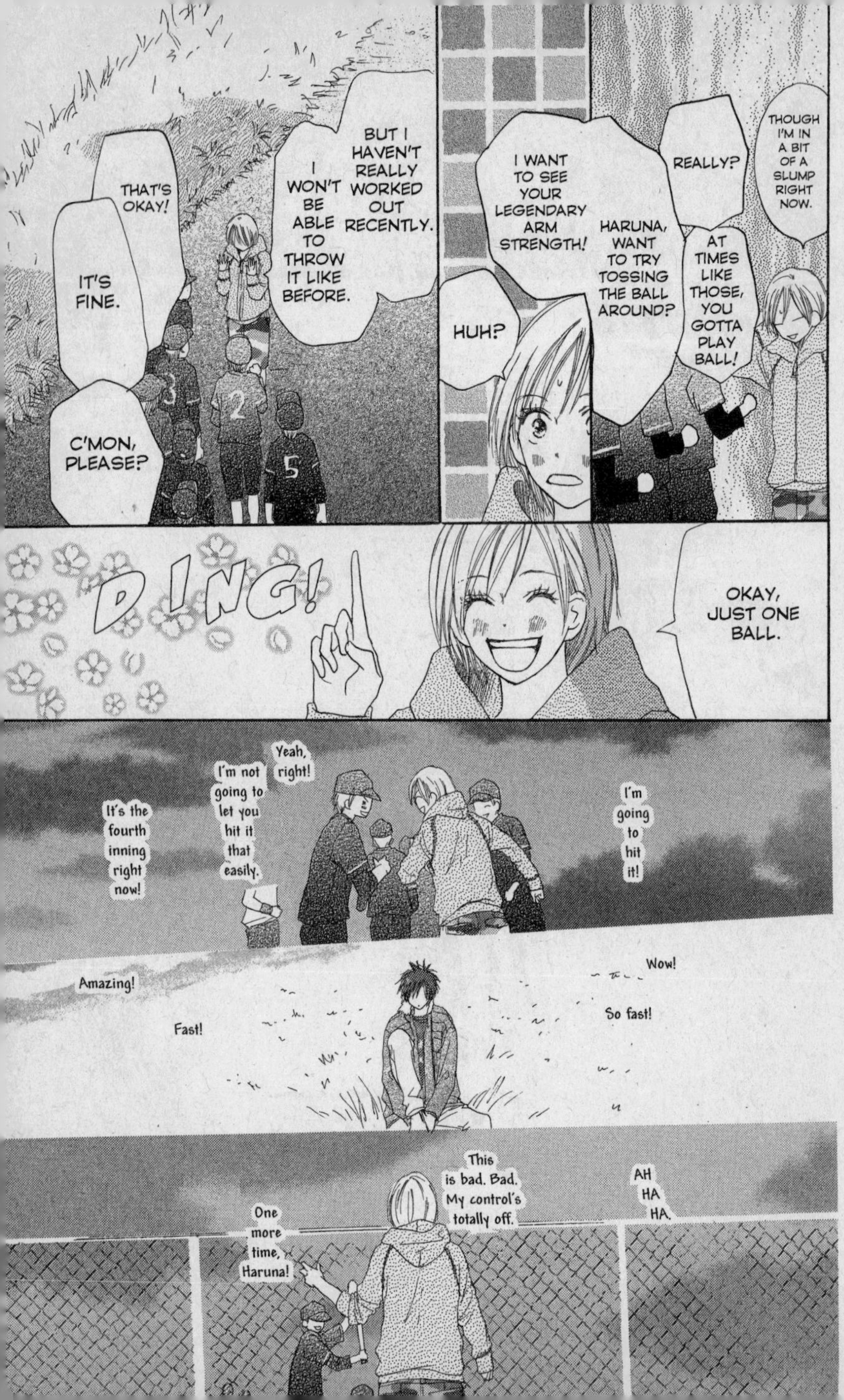
THOUGH I'M IN A BIT OF A SLUMP RIGHT NOW.
REALLY?
AT TIMES LIKE THOSE, YOU GOTTA PLAY BALL!
HARUNA, WANT TO TRY TOSSING THE BALL AROUND?
I WANT TO SEE YOUR LEGENDARY ARM STRENGTH!
HUH?
BUT I HAVEN'T REALLY WORKED OUT RECENTLY.
I WON'T BE ABLE TO THROW IT LIKE BEFORE.
THAT'S OKAY!
IT'S FINE.
C'MON, PLEASE?
OKAY, JUST ONE BALL.
DING!
I'm going to hit it!
Yeah, right!
I'm not going to let you hit it that easily.
It's the fourth inning right now!
Wow!
So fast!
Amazing!
Fast!
AH HA HA.
This is bad. Bad. My control's totally off.
One more time, Haruna!

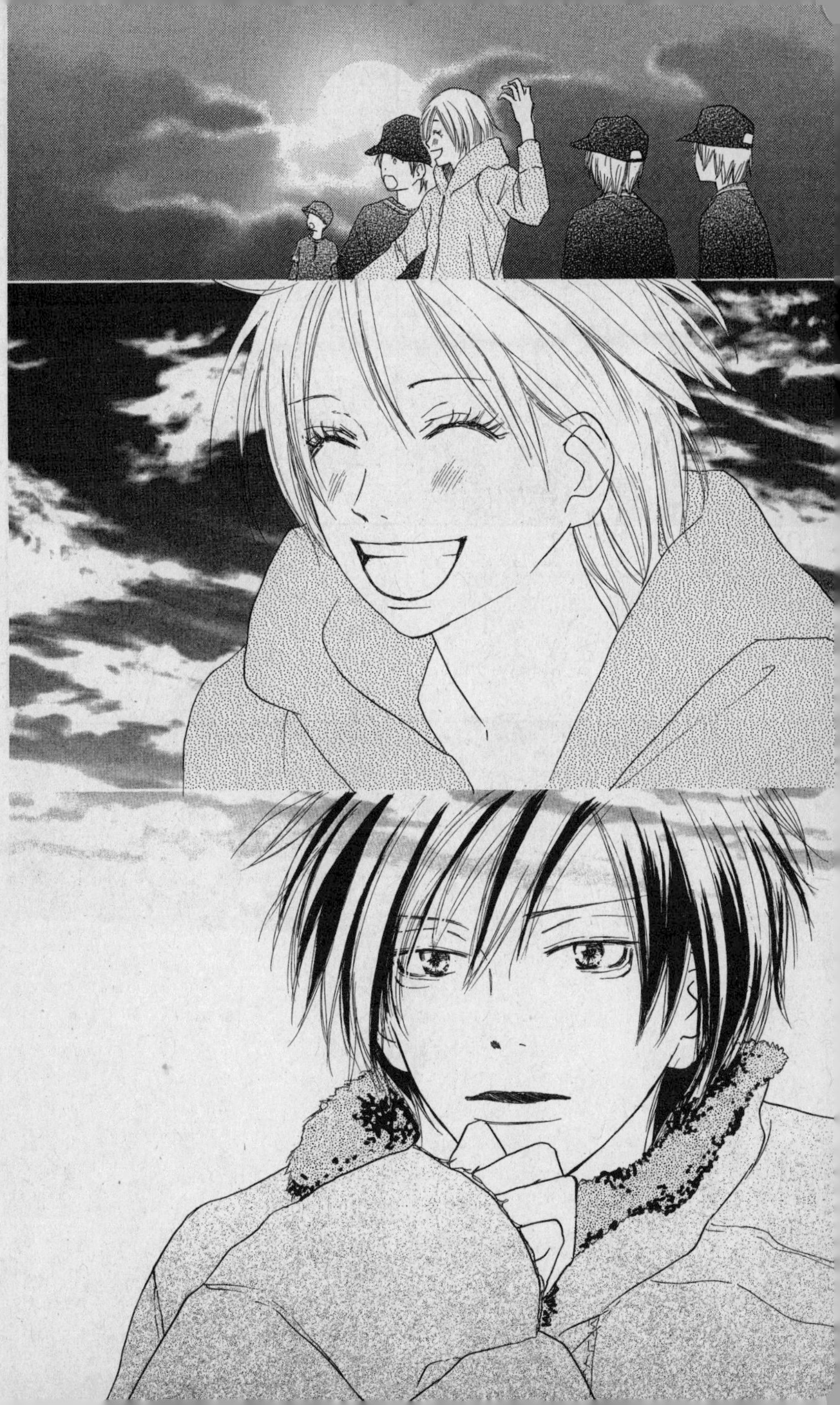

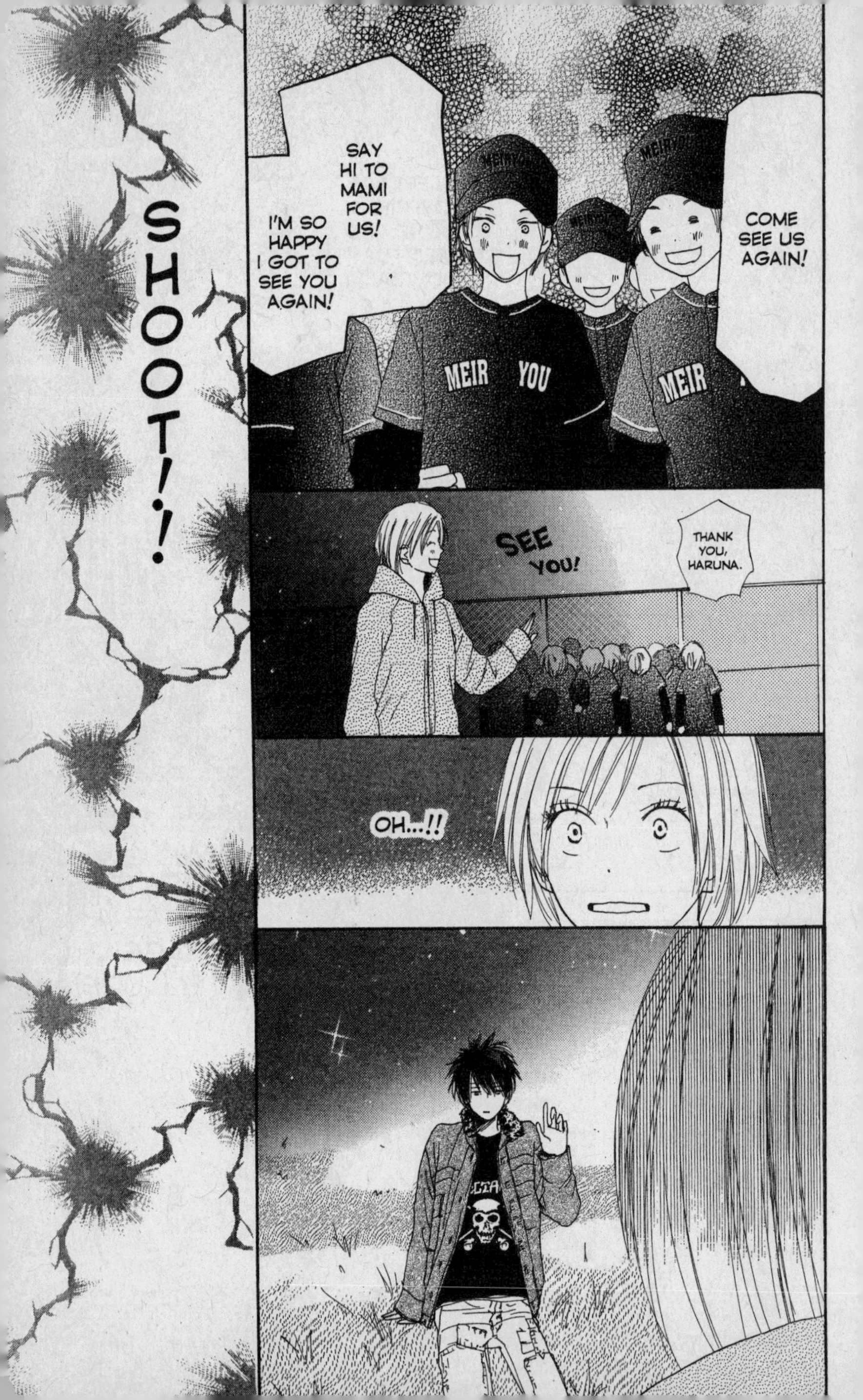
COME SEE US AGAIN!
SAY HI TO MAMI FOR US!
I'M SO HAPPY I GOT TO SEE YOU AGAIN!
THANK YOU, HARUNA.
SEE YOU!
OH...!!
SHOOT!!

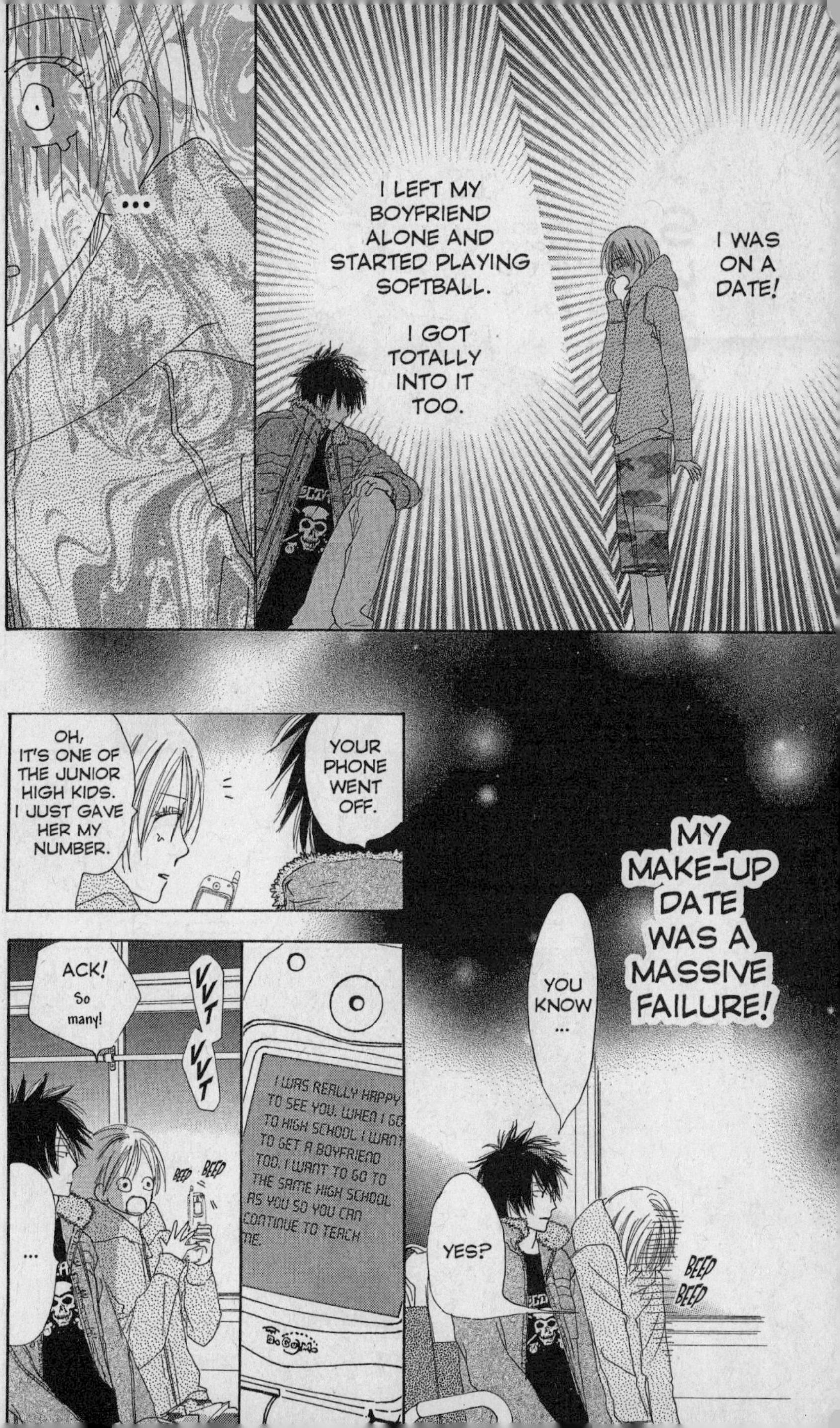
I WAS ON A DATE!
I LEFT MY BOYFRIEND ALONE AND STARTED PLAYING SOFTBALL.
I GOT TOTALLY INTO IT TOO.
...
MY MAKE-UP DATE WAS A MASSIVE FAILURE!
YOU KNOW...
YES?
BEEP BEEP
YOUR PHONE WENT OFF.
OH, IT'S ONE OF THE JUNIOR HIGH KIDS. I JUST GAVE HER MY NUMBER.
I WAS REALLY HAPPY TO SEE YOU. WHEN I GO TO HIGH SCHOOL I WANT TO GET A BOYFRIEND TOO. I WANT TO GO TO THE SAME HIGH SCHOOL AS YOU SO YOU CAN CONTINUE TO TEACH ME.
ACK! So many!
VVT VVT
BEEP BEEP
...

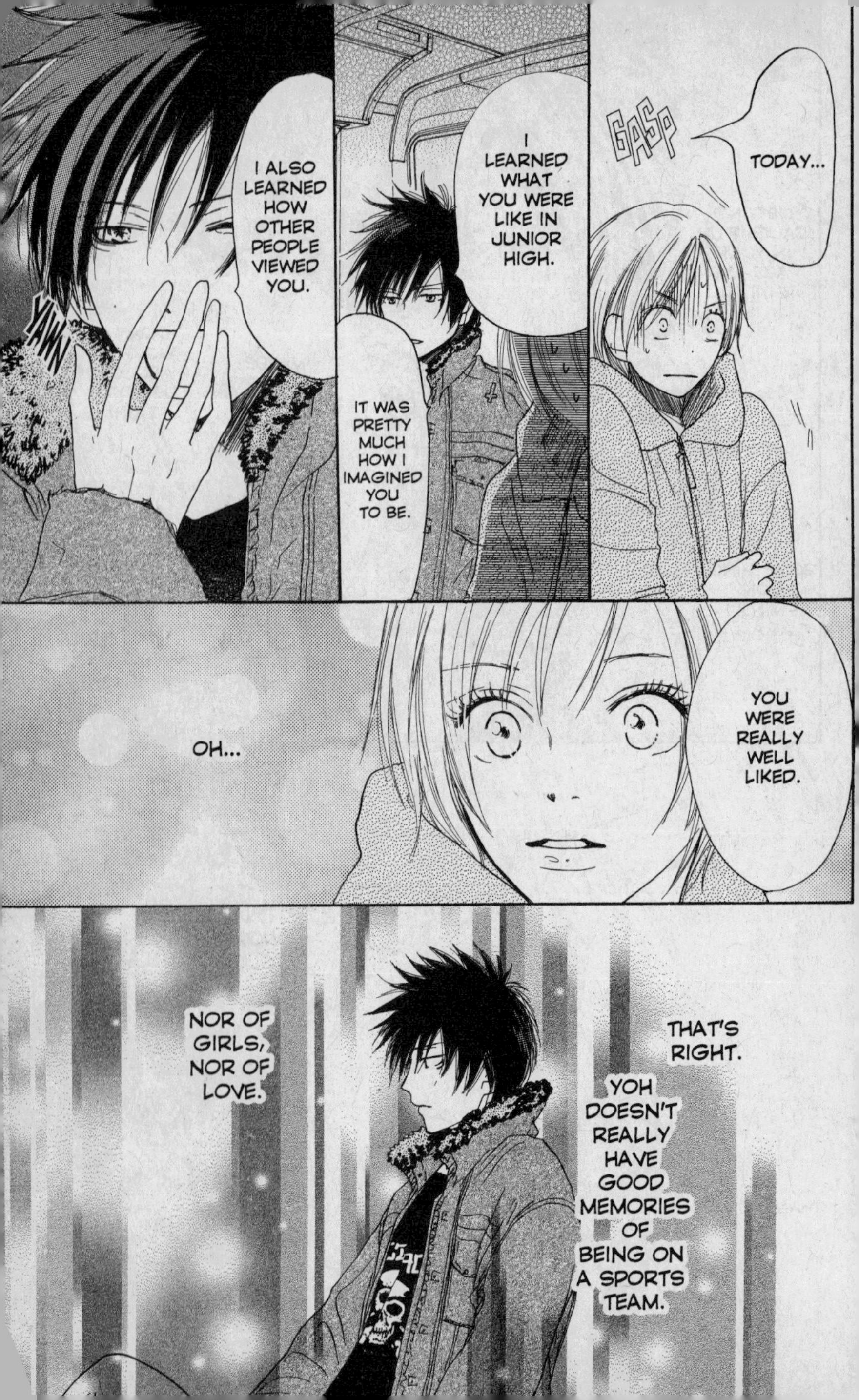
TODAY...
GASP
I LEARNED WHAT YOU WERE LIKE IN JUNIOR HIGH.
IT WAS PRETTY MUCH HOW I IMAGINED YOU TO BE.
I ALSO LEARNED HOW OTHER PEOPLE VIEWED YOU.
YAWN
YOU WERE REALLY WELL LIKED.
OH...
THAT'S RIGHT.
YOH DOESN'T REALLY HAVE GOOD MEMORIES OF BEING ON A SPORTS TEAM.
NOR OF GIRLS, NOR OF LOVE.

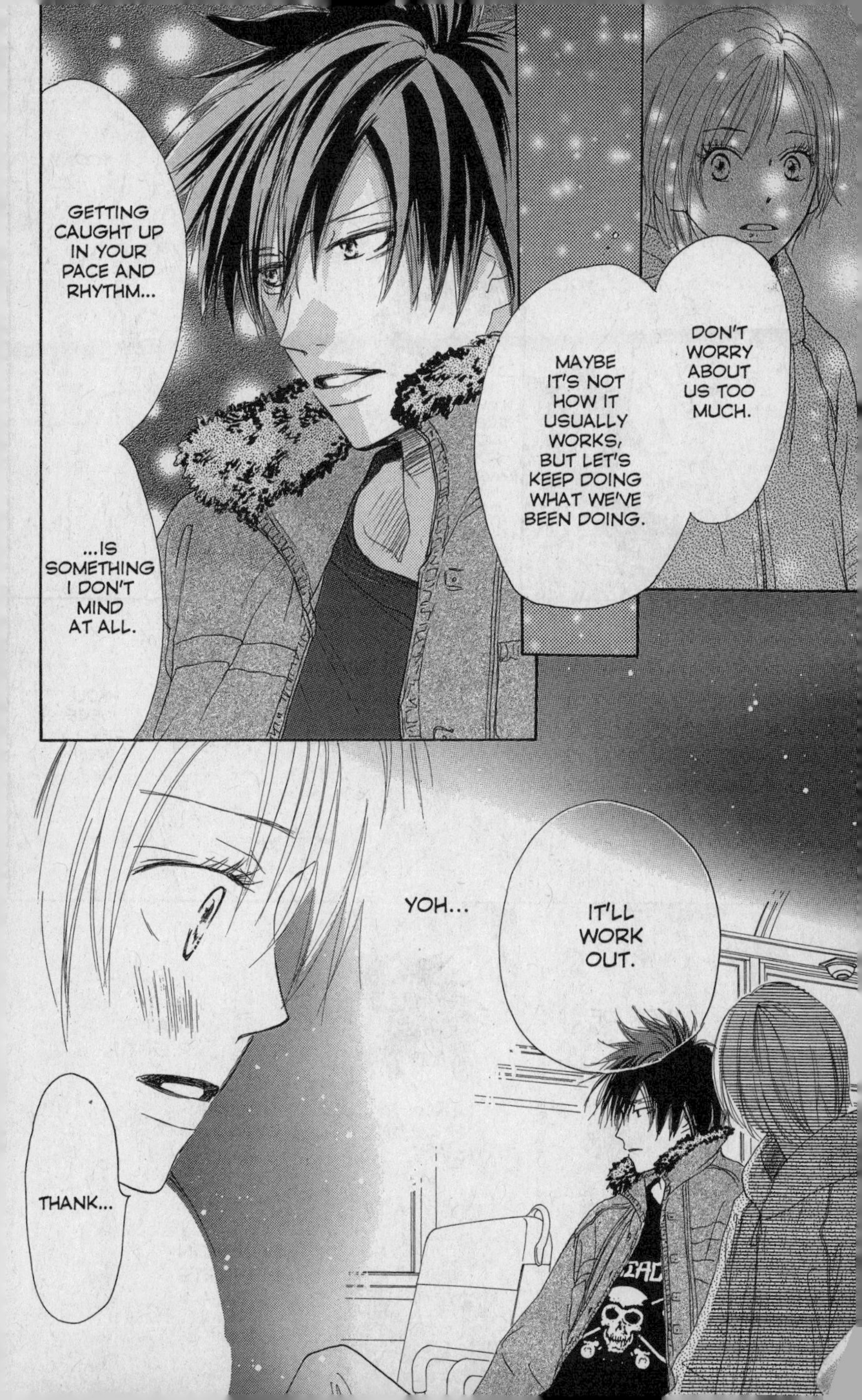
DON'T WORRY ABOUT US TOO MUCH.
MAYBE IT'S NOT HOW IT USUALLY WORKS, BUT LET'S KEEP DOING WHAT WE'VE BEEN DOING.
GETTING CAUGHT UP IN YOUR PACE AND RHYTHM...
...IS SOMETHING I DON'T MIND AT ALL.
IT'LL WORK OUT.
YOH...
THANK...

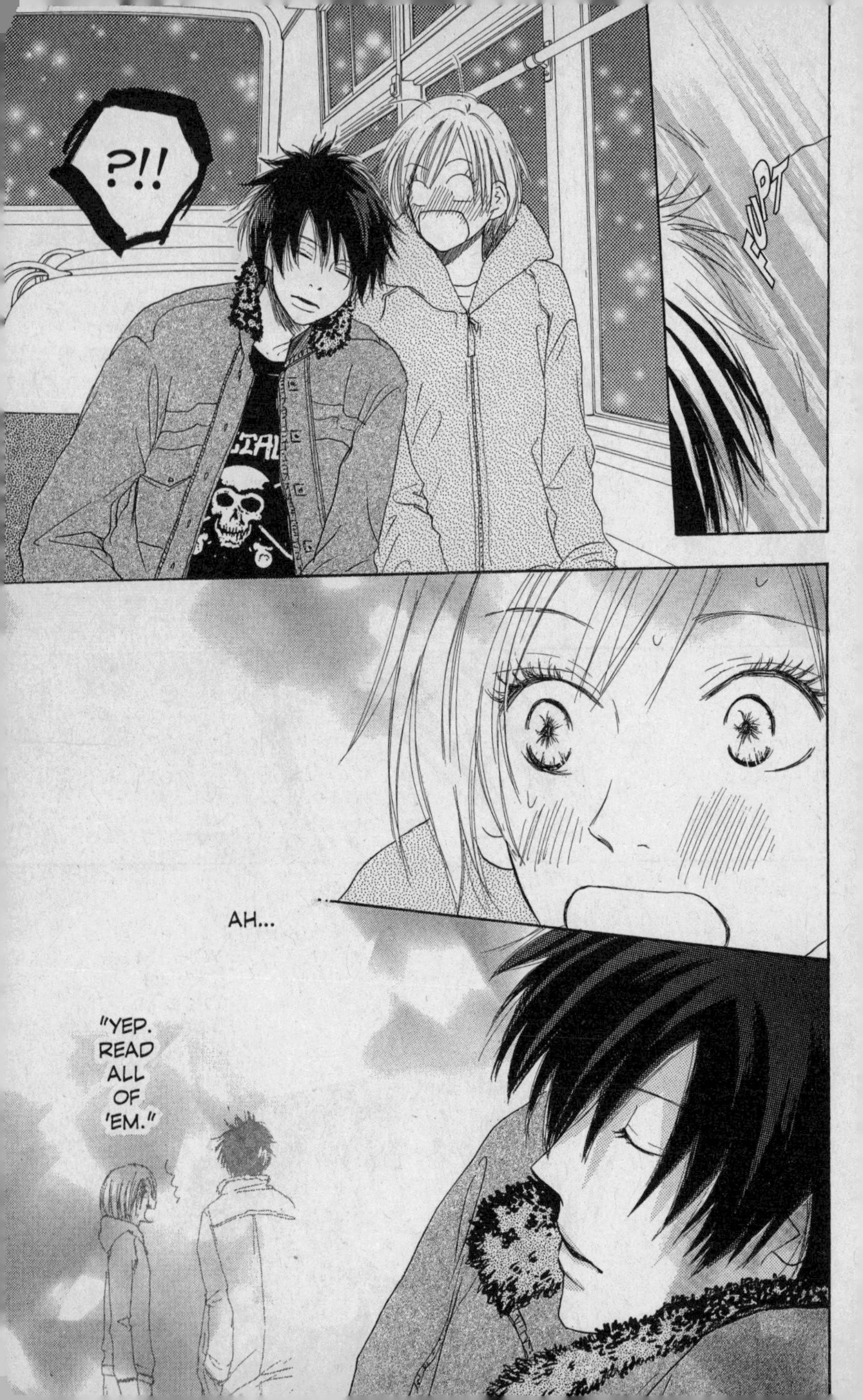
FUPT
?!!
AH...
"YEP. READ ALL OF 'EM."

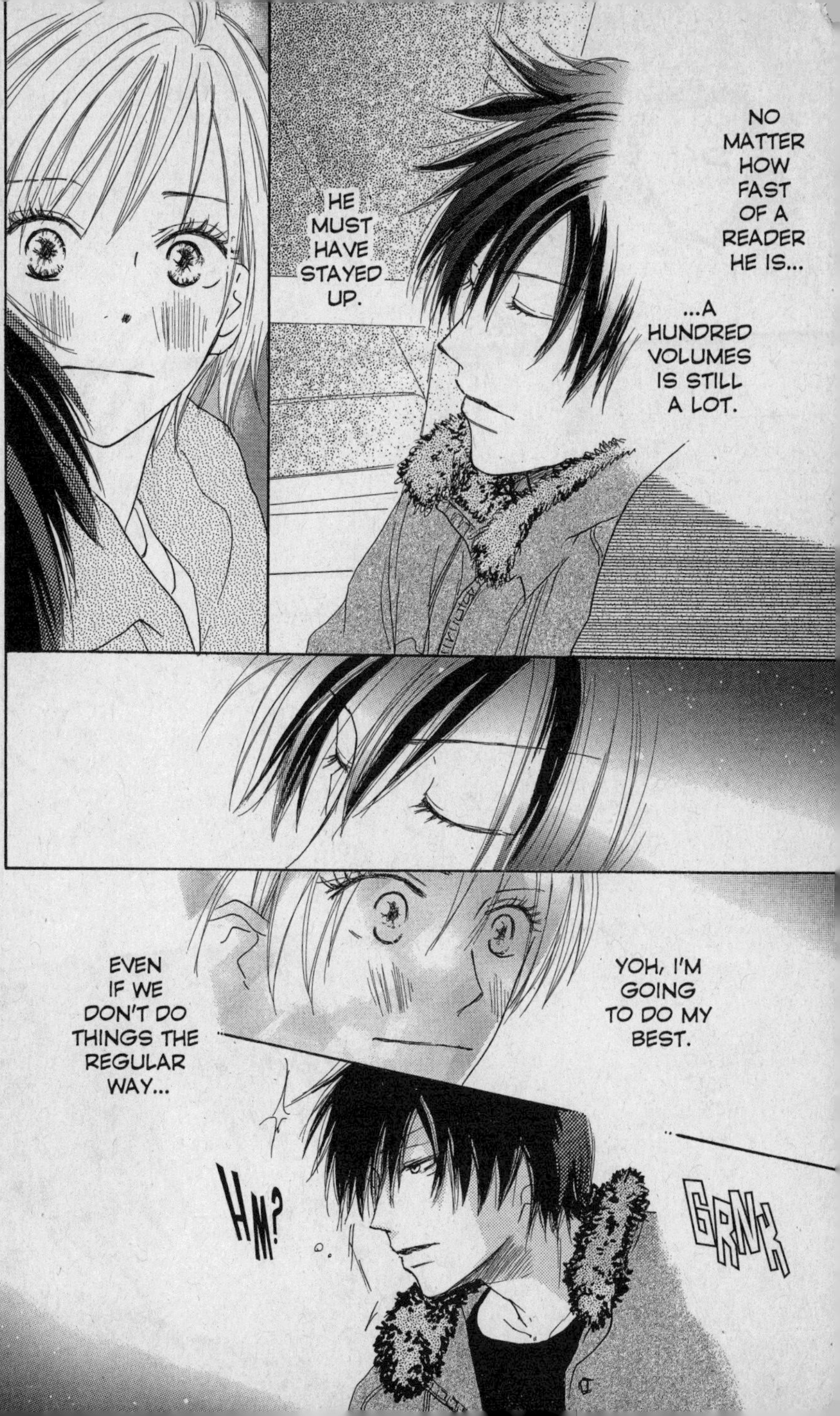
NO MATTER HOW FAST OF A READER HE IS...
...A HUNDRED VOLUMES IS STILL A LOT.
HE MUST HAVE STAYED UP.
YOH, I'M GOING TO DO MY BEST.
EVEN IF WE DON'T DO THINGS THE REGULAR WAY...
GRNK
HM?

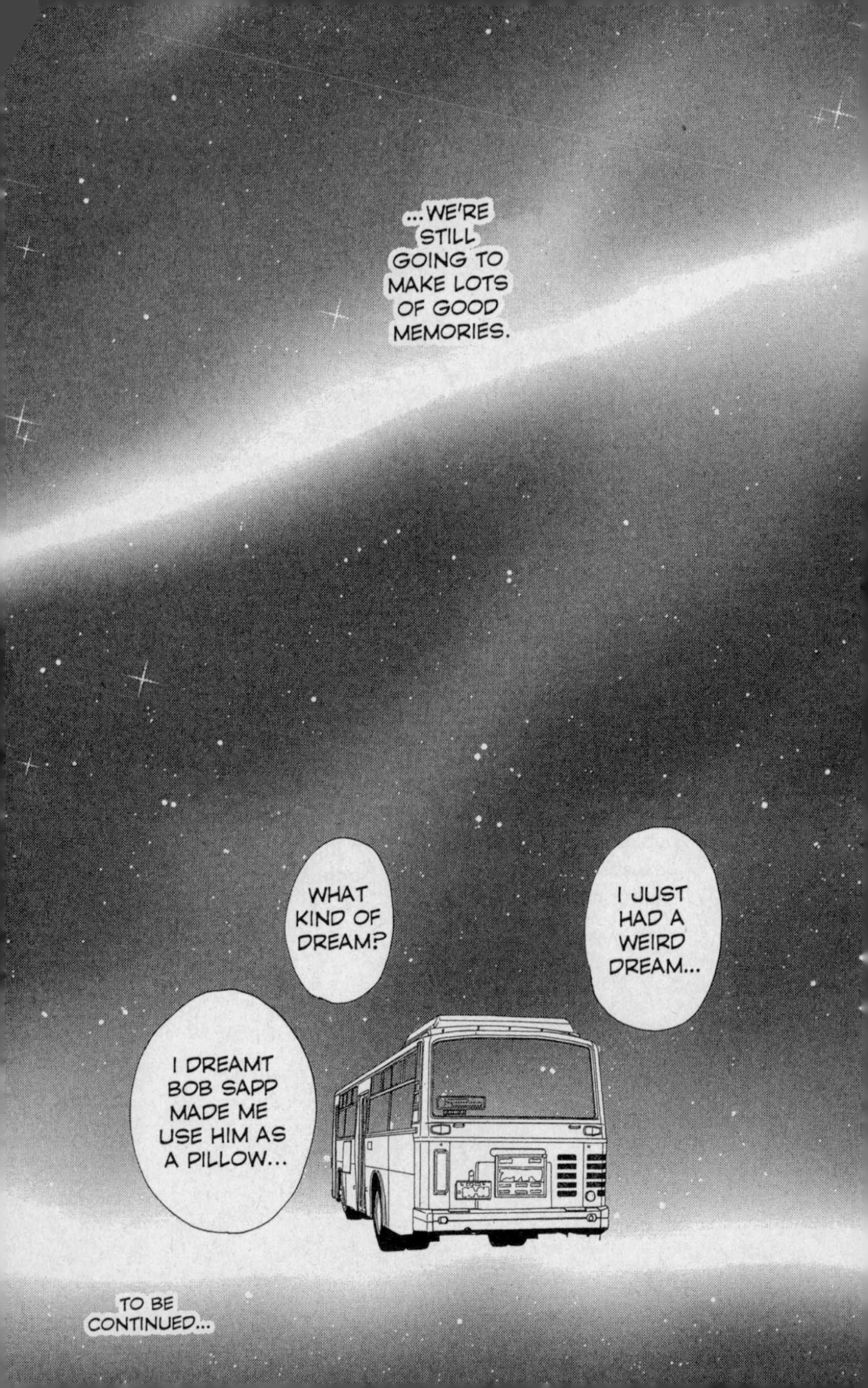
...WE'RE STILL GOING TO MAKE LOTS OF GOOD MEMORIES.
I JUST HAD A WEIRD DREAM...
WHAT KIND OF DREAM?
I DREAMT BOB SAPP MADE ME USE HIM AS A PILLOW...
TO BE CONTINUED...

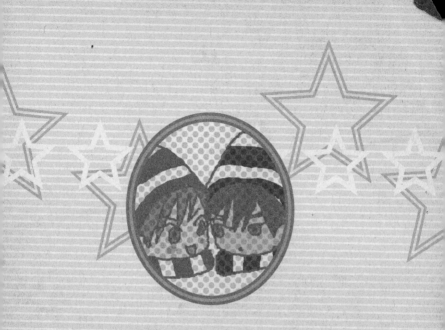

Kazune Kawahara is from Hokkaido Prefecture and was born on March 11 (a Pisces!). She made her manga debut at age 18 with *Kare no Ichiban Sukina Hito* (His Most Favorite Person). She is the author of *My Love Story!!* (originally published as *Ore Monogatari!!* in Japan's *Bessatsu Margaret* magazine). Her hobby is interior redecorating.

HIGH SCHOOL DEBUT
3-IN-1 EDITION
VOLUME 1
A compilation of graphic novel volumes 1-3

STORY & ART BY
KAZUNE KAWAHARA

Translation & Adaptation/Gemma Collinge
Touch-up Art & Lettering/Mark Griffin
Design/Izumi Hirayama (Graphic Novel Edition)
Design/Yukiko Whitley (3-in-1 Edition)
Editor/Amy Yu

KOKO DEBUT © 2003 by Kazune Kawahara
All rights reserved.
First published in Japan in 2003 by SHUEISHA Inc., Tokyo.
English translation rights arranged by SHUEISHA Inc.

Printed in the U.S.A.

Published by VIZ Media, LLC
P.O. Box 77010
San Francisco, CA 94107

10 9 8 7 6 5 4 3 2 1
First printing, February 2014

www.viz.com

www.shojobeat.com

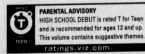
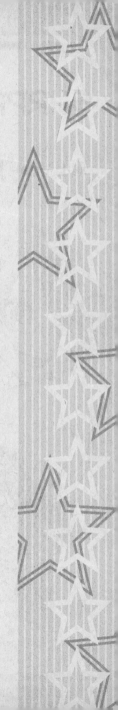

SURPRISE!

You may be reading the wrong way!

It's true: In keeping with the original Japanese comic format, this book reads from right to left—so action, sound effects and word balloons are completely reversed. This preserves the orientation of the original artwork—plus, it's fun! Check out the diagram shown here to get the hang of things, and then turn to the other side of the book to get started!

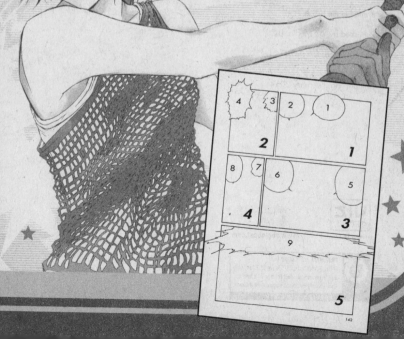